THE
BOOK
OF THE
STATES

1988-89 EDITION

Volume 27

The Council of State Governments
Lexington, Kentucky

Copyright 1988
The Council of State Governments
Iron Works Pike
P.O. Box 11910
Lexington, Kentucky 40578

Manufactured in the United States

ISBN 0-87292-076-3
Price: $42.50

CONTENTS

TABLES

Chapter Ten
STATE PAGES

FOREWORD

Through the biennial series, *The Book of the States*, The Council of State Governments continues to demonstrate its role as the source of information for and about the states. For over a half a century, *The Book of the States* has chronicled the structure, functions, finances and personnel of each state, documenting significant trends and changes. This book is about the state of the states. It contains a wealth of facts, figures, insights and information pertaining to all aspects of state government. The Council of State Governments is committed to providing in-depth, timely information about state government in all aspects of its work.

May 1988

Carl W. Stenberg
Executive Director

STAFF

William Carlton Currens
Editor-in-Chief
Research and Information Development

Katherine T. Tyson
Assistant to the Editor-in-Chief

Joy Hart Seibert
Researcher

Typographers
A. Turner Williams
Connie D. Pfeffer

Nancy C. Pickens
Indexer

Proofreaders
Shirley Hadley
Susan Muntz

With the assistance of: Dag Ryen, *Deputy Director of Information Services*; Doug Dill, *Manager of Publications*; Jo Ann Ewalt, *Marketing Manager*; Elaine S. Knapp, *Senior Editor*; Janice Penkalski, *Editorial Assistant*; and Linda Wagar, *Editorial Assistant*.

ACKNOWLEDGEMENTS

Many thanks to the hundreds of individuals in the states who provided data and information; to the authors who graciously shared their expertise; to Professor Albert L. Sturm (1911-1988) who wrote about state constitutions in this publication for nearly twenty years; and to the thousands of state officials who, through their daily work, contributed to the story of state government presented in this volume.

CHAPTER ONE

STATE CONSTITUTIONS

STATE CONSTITUTIONS AND CONSTIUTIONAL REVISION: 1986-87

By Albert L. Sturm and Janice C. May

GENERAL OVERVIEW: USE OF AUTHORIZED METHODS

State constitutional change proceeded at a modest pace in 1986-87. As table A indicates 275 constitutional propositions were submitted to the voters in 47 states; 204 were approved, including two adopted in Delaware by legislative action only. These totals represent an increase over the preceding biennium, but fall short of those proposed or adopted during the first half of the 1980s. However, as Table B shows, the number of statewide propositions proposed or adopted in 1986-87 was second only to the 1980-81 figures. Also, the approval rate for propositions in 1986-87 was the highest.

No new state constitutions were adopted or became effective during the biennium, but Rhode Island's 12th constitutional convention, which was in session throughout 1986, submitted an editorial revision without substantive change as well as 13 other ballot questions that called for substantial revision. The "rewrite" and seven of the other questions were approved.

Tables 1.2, 1.3 and 1.4 summarize the procedures associated with three methods used in 1986-87 to initiate constitutional change: proposal by the state legislature, available in all states; the constitutional initiative, authorized in 17 state constitutions; and the constitutional convention, available in all states (although not expressly authorized in nine state constitutions). A fourth method to initiate and submit proposed constitutional changes to the electorate, the constitutional commission (expressly authorized only in the Florida constitution) was not used in 1986-87, nor in any of the bienniums shown in Table A.

Legislative proposal, constitutional initiative

Legislative proposal, the most commonly used procedure for initiating constitutional change, accounted for 88 percent of the 275 proposed changes submitted to the voters in 1986-87. The adoption rate of legislative proposals, which historically has been much higher than that of other methods, reached the highest rate of the decade 77.7 percent.

As Table 1.3 indicates, 17 states adopted the constitutional initiative, appropriate only for making limited constitutional change. During 1986-87, the method accounted for 18 proposed constitutional amendments in nine states. Two other proposals, including one which would have allowed capital punishment, were removed from the ballot by the Michigan Supreme Court. Five of the constitutional initiatives were adopted, for a modest approval rate of 27.7 percent, well below half that for legislative submissions. The number of constitutional initiatives proposed and adopted in the nine states during the biennium were as follows: Arizona (1-0), Arkansas (3-1), California (2-1), Colorado (1-0), Florida (2-1), Montana (2-1), North Dakota (1-0), Ohio (1-0) and Oregon (5-1).

Constitutions conventions

The constitutional convention is the oldest, best known, and most traditional method to revise extensively an old constitution or write a new one. Through 1987, more than 230 state constitutional assemblies have convened. This method is usually initiated by the state legislature after the voters approve a convention call. An increasing number of state constitu-

Albert L. Sturm was professor emeritus, Center for Public Administration and Policy, Virginia Polytechnic Institute and State University, Blacksburg, Virginia, and Janice C. May is associate professor of Government, the University of Texas at Austin.

tions require asking voters periodically if a constitutional convention should be called. As Table 1.4 shows, 14 state constitutions contain such a provision: eight states provide for submission of the convention question to the voters every 20 years; one state, every 16 years; four states, every 10 years; and one, every nine years. During the biennium, mandatory periodic convention calls were placed on the ballot in November 1986 in Connecticut and Hawaii. Both were defeated, by a vote of 207,704 for and 379,812 against in Connecticut and 139,236 for and 173,977 against in Hawaii.

Only one state constitutional convention was operative during 1986-87 — Rhode Island's 12th constitutional convention. As reported in the last volume of *The Book of the States*, Rhode Island voters approved the convention call on Nov. 6, 1984 by a vote of 155,337 to 131,648. The enabling act, which was approved by the Rhode Island General Assembly on June 19, 1985, provided for an unlimited constitutional convention with 100 delegates to be elected on a non-partisan basis, one from each lower house district, on Nov. 5, 1985. The Rhode Island General Assembly appropriated initially $50,000 and later added $335,965 to provide for convention expenses. Actual convention expenditures totaled $333,622. Delegates served without compensation except for expenses.

The convention convened at the State House in Providence on Jan. 6, 1986, and adjourned Dec. 4, 1986, after having held 14 plenary sessions. Principal officers elected by the convention were a president, Keven A. McKenna, three vice presidents, a secretary and a treasurer. The convention rules provided for nine standing committees which handled 288 resolutions for constitutional change introduced by convention delegates. A total of 25 proposed amendments received at least 51 votes on second passage, the minimum required to be placed on the ballot. These 25 proposals were combined by common category into 14 ballot questions for submission to the electorate with the result that some ballot questions contained more than one amendment.

At the referendum on Nov. 4, 1986, the voters approved eight of the 14 propositions. The following questions identified by their ballot titles were adopted: 1- Rewrite of the Present Constitution, 6- Ethics in Government, 7- Budget Powers and Executive Succession, 8- Rights of the People, 9- Shore Use and Environmental Protection, 10- Felon Office Holding and Voting, 11- Libraries and 12- Bail. Rejected were 2- Judicial Selection and Discipline, 3- Legislative Pay and Mileage, 4- Four-year Term and Recall, 5- Voter Initiative, 13- Home Rule and 14- Paramount Right to Life/Abortion.

Summaries in the last two volumes of *The Book of the States* contained brief accounts of constitutional developments in the District of Columbia where a proposed Constitution of the State of New Columbia, drafted by a constitutional convention and approved by the voters in 1982, was transmitted to the U.S. Congress in the fall of 1983. On Sept. 12, 1983, D.C. Delegate Walter C. Fauntroy introduced H.R. 3861, the New Columbia Admissions Act, on which hearings were held. In response to criticisms of the proposed constitution, revisions were proposed. Finally, on May 6, 1987 the Council of the District of Columbia approved a revised document, which was transmitted to the Congress. Among the highlights of the document are the following: 11 sections instead of 18; a short 10-section Bill of Rights that parallels the U.S. Bill of Rights with the exception that an equality clause has replaced the 10th Amendment; a unicameral legislature elected by a combination of single-member districts and at-large elections; provision for amendment by legislative submission and voter approval; a relatively strong governor, no lieutenant governor, an attorney general, and

Table A

State Constitutional Changes by Method of Initiation
1980–81, 1982–83, 1984–85 and 1986–87

Method of Initiation	Number of states involved				Total proposals				Total adopted				Percentage adopted			
	1980 −81	1982 −83	1984 −85	1986 −87	1980 −81	1982 −83	1984 −85	1986 −87	1980 −81	1982 −83	1984 −85	1986 −87	1980 −81	1982 −83	1984 −85	1986 −87
All methods	46	45	45	47	388	345	238	275	272	258	158	204	70.1	73.0	65.5*	74.3*
Legislative proposal	46	45	45	46	362	330	211	243	265	255	144	191	73.2	75.5*	67.3*	77.7*
Constitutional initiative	11	9	10	9	18	15	17	18	5	3	8	5	27.8	20.0	47.1	27.7
Constitutional convention	2	-	1	1	8	-	10	14	2	-	6	8	25.0	-	60.0	57.1
Constitutional commission	−	−	−	−	−	−	−	−	−	−	−	−	−	−	−	−

*In calculating these percentages, the amendments adopted in Delaware (where proposals are not submitted to the voters) are excluded.

several constitutional boards; a two-tiered court system with merit selection of judges and 15-year terms; two fiscal articles (Budget and Financial Management, Borrowing) that together constitute about one-third of the 53-page charter; initiative, referendum, recall; and advisory neighborhood commissions. Deleted were several articles on policy, among them Land and the Environment, Public Services, Health, Housing and Social Services, and Labor. H.R. 51, the D.C. statehood bill in the 100th Congress (1987-88), was reported out favorably from committee, and House floor action was anticipated in 1988.

Constitutional commissions

Constitutional commissions generally serve two major purposes: to study the constitution and propose needed changes and to prepare for a constitutional convention. Commissions in Mississippi and Utah were the only ones operative during the biennium.

As reported in the last volume of *The Book of the States*, William A. Allain, of Mississippi, created the Governor's Constitutional Study Commission in mid-November 1985. With more than 350 members widely representative of the state's social, economic, political and professional structure, both official and unofficial, this body drafted a proposed constitution. In January 1987, Gov. Allain recommended to the legislature that it place on the ballot the question of calling a constitutional convention. The Senate approved a bill providing for the referendum, but it failed in the House committee.

By late 1987, two distinct approaches to state constitutional revision in Mississippi had developed. Newly elected Gov. Ray Mabus, like his predecessor, strongly advocated calling a constitutional convention, preferably in 1988. Under new leadership in the House of Representatives, prospects for success of this approach improved. The other proposal for substantive revision came primarily from those who opposed a convention. On request of leaders of this group, the Mississippi Economic Council (the statewide Chamber of Commerce) prepared a series of approximately 60 amendments to the existing constitution for introduction in the legislature early in 1988. Although these amendments would strengthen the governor's authority to organize the executive branch, they are designed primarily to delete surplusage and outmoded provisions and to improve the language of the present document.

The Utah Constitutional Revision Commission, a permanent body since 1977, is required by statute to submit recommendations for constitutional revision to the legislature at least 60 days before each regular session. Action on the commission's recommendations through 1987 included voter approval of revised articles on the executive branch, revenue and taxation, the judicial branch, the legislative branch and education. Proposed revisions of the articles on local government and public debt were submitted to the legislature in 1988. For more information on the Utah and Mississippi commissions, see Table 1.5.

In Oregon, an unsuccessful attempt was made in the legislature in 1987 to establish a constitutional revision commission. A proposed joint resolution (H.J.R. 28) provided for a 17-member bipartisan commission to be appointed by the president of the senate (six members), the speaker of the house (seven members), the governor (two members), and the chief justice of the state Supreme Court (two members). The commission was to report on proposals for revision of the Oregon constitution to the next legislative assembly. Although sponsored by 25 representatives and 10 senators, the resolution died.

In summary, during 1986-87, a total of 47 states took some official action to amend or revise their constitutions. All 47 states used the method of legislative proposal to initiate one or more changes, nine states used the constitutional initiative and only one convened a constitutional convention. The three states that took no action during this period were Minnesota, Pennsylvania and Tennessee.

SUBSTANTIVE CHANGES

With some exceptions, state constitutional proposals during the 1986-87 biennium accomplished relatively minor changes in state and local government. The Rhode Island constitutional convention's general revision propositions were, overall, the most substantial and the most comprehensive in scope. In four states, the legislature submitted revisions of entire articles — Utah and Kansas on education, North Dakota on the executive and Wisconsin on elections, but only the Utah and Wisconsin revisions passed.

Table B offers an overview of the general subject matter of state constitutional change by two-year periods during the 1980s. All proposals are grouped into two major categories:

those of general statewide application, which are by far the most numerous and involved 47 states in 1986-87 and proposed local amendments initiated by five states (Alabama, Delaware, Louisiana, Maryland and Texas) during the biennium. (Local amendments apply to only one or a few local areas or political subdivisions.) Of the 251 statewide proposals, 183 (exclusive of Delaware) or 73 percent were ratified by the electorate, a higher adoption rate than the preceding six years. Of the 24 local amendments, 20 were adopted. The number of local amendments declined substantially following their elimination under the new Georgia Constitution of 1982.

In Table B, statewide amendments are further classified under the principal subject matter areas of state constitutions, identified for convenience by the titles of articles found in virtually all state constitutions. Articles on the legislature and on finance typically draw the most propositions. During the biennium, 49 legislative proposals and 45 finance and taxation measures were recorded. The highest approval rates were registered by the articles on suffrage and elections (90.9 percent), the judicial article (83.3 percent) and the executive (82.6 percent). Aside from the general revision proposals (57 percent approval), the lowest rates were received by finance and taxation (64.4 percent), local government (64.7 percent) and state and local debt (66.6 percent).

The Bill of Rights, suffrage and elections.

In four states, Delaware, Maine, New Mexico and West Virginia, amendments protecting the right to keep and bear arms were approved. The New Mexico proposal prohibited local governmental regulation of the right. A declaration making English the official language was adopted in California; legislative authorization to reform tort law and to regulate the drinking age was approved in Montana. An equal rights amendment was defeated by Vermont voters, but the Rhode Island electorate approved a provision prohibiting discrimination on the grounds of gender, race or handicap. On the same ballot the Rhode Island electorate also approved free speech, due process and equal protection clauses and a statement that individual rights protected by the Rhode Island Constitution "stand independent of the U.S. Constitution." In addition, voters ratified a third ballot question that expanded environmental rights, primarily the rights of fishery and privileges of the shore.

Four proposals to state bills of rights concerned criminal justice, fewer than during the last biennium. Three of the proposed changes, all of which passed, authorized judges to deny bail for certain offenses. The Illinois bail amendment applies to persons accused of crimes that carry mandatory prison terms; the Mississippi law, to offenses punishable by imprisonment for life or a maximum of 20 years or more; and the Rhode Island provision (one of the general revision questions), to offenses for the unlawful sale or distribution of controlled substances punishable by a sentence of 10 or more years. The fourth change guaranteed certain rights to victims of crime, including restitution and

Table B

Substantive Changes in State Constitutions:
Proposed and Adopted, 1980–81, 1982–83, 1984–85, and 1986-87

Subject Matter	Total Proposed				Total Adopted				Percentage Adopted			
	1980 –81	1982 –83	1984 –85	1986 –87	1980 –81	1982 –83	1984 –85	1986 –87	1980 –81	1982 –83	1984 –85	1986 –87
Proposals of statewide applicability	254	226	228	251	160	149	154	184	63.0	65.9*	67.1*	72.9**
Bill of rights	13	13	9	12*	10	13	7	10*	76.9	100.0	77.7	81.8**
Suffrage and elections	5	5	5	11	5	4	5	10	100.0	80.0	100.0	90.9
Legislative branch	43	32	37	49	21	18	19	35	48.8	56.3	51.5	71.4
Executive branch	21	19	30	23	10	9	20	19	47.6	47.4	66.7	82.6
Judicial branch	23	26	19	18	17	21	16	15	73.9	80.8	78.9*	83.3
Local government	11	13	16	17	4	9	13	11	36.4	69.2	75.0*	64.7
Finance and taxation	77	48	67	45	52	28	43	29	67.5	58.3*	64.2	64.4
State and local debt	20	26	21	12	13	19	16	8	65.0	73.1	76.2	66.6
State functions	23	31	17	29	16	18	9	22	69.6	58.1	52.9	75.8
Amendment and revision	9	2	2	0	7	1	2	0	77.8	50.0	100.0	0
General revision proposals	1	1	0	14	0	1	0	8	0	100.0	0	57.1
Miscellaneous proposals	8	10	5	22	5	8	4	17	62.5	80.0	80.0	77.2
Local amendments	134	123	10	24***	112	107	4	20*	83.6	87.0	40.0	79.1**

*One Delaware proposal was included.
**In calculating these percentages the changes adopted in Delaware (where proposals are not submitted to the voters) are excluded.
***One Delaware proposal was excluded.

the right to speak in court. Adopted by the voters of Rhode Island, it was one of the rights in a ballot question called, "Rights of the People."

Another Rhode Island proposal, one well publicized, would have created a "paramount right to life without regard to age, health, function or condition of dependency." It also expressly banned abortions and their public funding within the limits of federal law. The proposition failed together with three other anti-abortion measures in Arkansas, Massachusetts and Oregon, all of which were concerned mainly with funding of abortions. Of interest also was the amendment adopted in Mississippi that deleted an anti-miscegenation section of the General Provisions Article.

All but one of the 11 proposals to change the suffrage and elections articles passed including three Wisconsin amendments that cleaned up the language of the elections article. In Rhode Island, voters approved changes in the rights of felons and certain misdemeanants to hold office and to vote. Under the provisions, holding public office would be automatically restored upon completion of the entire sentence, including suspended portions, probation and parole. Another successful Rhode Island ballot question, Ethics in Government, proposed a voluntary system of public financing of political campaigns and a limit on private contributions.

The only elections measure to fail was one of two North Carolina propositions to change elections in that state. Moving the election of all statewide officers to the fall of odd-numbered years was killed, but a requirement for midterm elections to fill certain vacancies was approved. A Georgia amendment concerning procedures for suspending certain public officials upon their indictment also passed.

The three branches of government

Collectively, the proposals to change the legislative, executive and judicial articles constituted over one-third of the statewide propositions, exclusive of the Rhode Island general revision. Relative to the other articles the legislative article drew by far the most proposals, as was true during the entire decade, but the adoption rate lagged behind as usual. Amendments to the judicial article enjoyed high approval rates throughout the decade, but not until the current biennium did adoptions to the executive article reach the 80 percent mark.

A total of 24 of the 49 legislative proposals concerned legislative powers, organization, procedure and membership. Of eight amendments affecting legislative-executive relations, measures rejected at the polls in Alaska and Michigan would have authorized the legislative veto of administrative rules and regulations. Also rejected was a Texas proposal allowing the speaker to serve on executive committees and agencies. Measures that passed were a prohibition of the pocket veto in election years (Missouri), changes in impeachment (Nebraska and Rhode Island), authorization to the legislature to give the governor removal power (Wyoming), and authorization for interim hearings on confirmation of gubernatorial appointments (New Mexico).

Revisions of constitutional provisions on apportionment were approved in Idaho, Maine, Oregon and Vermont. The Idaho amendment authorized changes in the size of the two houses (30 to 35 senators and a House no larger than twice the number of senators). The Vermont proposition synchronized that state's apportionment cycle with the 10-year federal census.

Only one proposition concerned legislative pay. An unsuccessful attempt was made in Rhode Island to increase the compensation of state legislators from $5.00 a day for 60 days, which had been set in 1900, to a pay scale based on the average weekly earnings of Rhode Island manufacturing workers. In Texas, voters rejected a proposal to allow legislators to serve in offices where the compensation had been increased during their term, but they agreed to a change in rules governing captions. Mississippi voters rejected a change in conflict of interest provisions.

Seven proposals involved legislative terms, qualifications and vacancies. Washington voters turned down six-year terms for senators and four year terms for representatives, while the Rhode Island electorate rejected a change from two to four-year terms for legislators and other statewide elective offices as well as a recall procedure. Residence in the district as a qualification for House members was adopted in Maine and in Mississippi. The Maryland electorate approved a provision that requires persons filling a vacancy in either legislative chamber to be of the same political party, if any, of the replaced person. In Washington a provision on vacancies was defeated as was a Nebraska amendment that would have changed the date on which legislative terms begin and when the legislature would convene in regular session.

Three propositions concerned the initiative and referendum. The voters of Rhode Island turned down a convention ballot proposal that would have established the initiative and referendum. Under a successful Oregon measure the legislature was authorized to provide by law for the settlement of certain disputes over the proper number of signatures on petitions. In Wyoming, a measure changing the election base for the enactment or rejection of propositions was adopted.

The remaining proposals for change of the legislative article were primarily concerned with policy, and will be reviewed under fiscal and other policy articles.

Few major changes were proposed in executive articles during the biennium. A North Dakota amendment that revised the entire article was rejected at the polls as was a comprehensive revision of the Colorado state personnel system. The most numerous proposals concerned terms of and succession to executive office; all but one passed. Two of these were Mississippi amendments that allowed the governor to serve an additional term and allowed the state treasurer to succeed himself. New Mexico voters approved a measure limiting state executive offices to two consecutive four-year terms beginning in 1991. Proposals for changing the beginning of terms of certain officers passed in Louisiana and North Dakota, as did a clarification of succession to the Rhode Island governorship, but the Rhode Island proposal for four-year terms for statewide elective officers failed.

The governor's power was trimmed in two states. In Texas an amendment passed that allowed the legislature to limit the appointment power of lame duck governors, and in Oklahoma the electorate approved a proposition that removed power from the governor and other members of the Board of Pardons and Paroles to grant paroles to convicts sentenced to death or to life without parole. Editorial revision of the provision on the Idaho Board of Pardons and Paroles was approved.

An attempt to take away the power of the lieutenant governor to preside over the senate was defeated in South Dakota. In Utah, the office of superintendent of public instruction was abolished; in Oklahoma, all mention of the chief mine inspector was deleted from the constitution, but in Kentucky, the voters rejected the proposition to replace the elective public school superintendent with an appointed one. The creation of a state department of public education and a state board of education was adopted in New Mexico. In Florida, the voters approved a statewide special prosecutor in the attorney general's office. A Rhode Island item in the approved Ethics in Government ballot question required the legislature to establish a nonpartisan ethics commission.

In addition to the Colorado proposal revising the personnel system, several other propositions concerned civil service and personnel policies such as retirement. A California constitutional initiative that would have substantially limited compensation of public officers and employees, including specification of the annual salary of the governor and other constitutional officers, was defeated at the polls. In New York, an amendment to allow certain aliens to earn civil service credits was adopted. Montana voters approved the abolition of a salary commission that set pay for public officers, whereas the Washington electorate approved such a body. Certain changes in the Michigan salary commission's authority were rejected.

The proposed amendments to the article on the judiciary dealt mainly with judicial selection, tenure and discipline; judicial powers; and court organization. In Rhode Island, Ohio and Connecticut, merit selection of judges or some component thereof was proposed to the voters, but only in Connecticut was it approved. The rejected Rhode Island measure also had incorporated a mandatory retirement age (72 years) and abolished the state Supreme Court's advisory opinion function. In Washington, an amendment that established a commission on judicial conduct was adopted.

In Hawaii, the voters ratified an amendment that gives the Supreme Court authority to appoint retired judges to serve temporarily on certain courts. In Louisiana, the voters turned down one proposal to allow the high court power to appoint temporary judges in certain courts but approved a similar amendment on the second try. A measure adopted in Virginia authorizes the Supreme Court to answer questions of Virginia law certified to it by federal courts and courts of other states.

Amendments authorizing the right of the state to appeal in criminal cases were adopted in Texas, where a flat ban on the right of appeal had been in force for more than 100 years, and in Virginia where a provision concerned only appeals from preliminary rulings of circuit courts. Among other proposals that passed were increase in the civil jurisdiction of municipal courts in Arkansas, legislative authority to make uniform terms of office of all magistrates in South Carolina, state funding of clerks of courts in Maryland, and denial of compensation to a judge suspended from office after initial conviction in Georgia. A measure making compensation increases uniform by categories of judges failed in Wyoming.

Local government, finance

During the biennium, approximately two-thirds of proposed changes to the local government articles were approved. The Rhode Island constitutional convention submitted a comprehensive home rule ballot proposal that was rejected at the polls. It provided for expansion of legislative powers, including taxing power of cities and counties with charters, local initiative procedures, the requirement that local voters approve new or increased local tax exemptions, and a requirement that the state reimburse municipalities for state-mandated expenditures. The largest category of local article changes concerned terms and tenure of local officers, but only three of seven amendments were adopted: four-year terms for sheriffs in two Delaware counties (a local amendment), four-year terms for Idaho coroners and additional successive terms for Kentucky mayors. The four proposals that failed all concerned county offices: a limit of four consecutive terms for all county offices (New Mexico), four-year terms for county elective offices and justices of the peace (Arkansas), repeal of the limit on sheriff succession (West Virginia) and five year terms for sheriffs (New Jersey).

Colorado voters refused to approve an amendment that authorized boards of county commissioners to set compensation for county officers, and Missouri voters approved an amendment to keep county officials' compensation from exceeding limits set by the legislature or other proper authority. Among other amendments that passed were a Texas measure that allowed the legislature to set municipal liability limits by defining proprietary and governmental functions, a California proposition that all counties have an office of elective district attorney, a Colorado proposal that eliminated a requirement that franchises in home rule cities must receive majority approval, and a Maryland proposition that repealed the requirement that county commissioners be elected on the general ticket of each county. Texas voters turned down an amendment that would have allowed counties to perform unpaid work for other governments.

During the first six years of the 1980s, proposed changes in the fiscal articles were relatively numerous and outnumbered those submitted to the other articles. This pattern did not hold during 1986-87. Not only was the finance and taxation article second to the legislative article, but the number of propositions submitted was the lowest of the decade although close to the 1982-83 figure. The fact there were fewer propositions may suggest less popular enthusiasm for a battery of highly restrictive measures. And, in fact, the voters rejected major tax and expenditures limitations during the biennium, while approving a relatively large number of bond proposals for such purposes as supporting public education and promoting economic development.

A highlight of the biennium was the defeat of three major tax limitation measures, all of which were constitutional initiatives. Montana voters rejected a proposal to abolish the property tax, to make the sales tax contingent upon voter approval by initiative or referendum, and to require voter approval of any new or increase in taxes. The Colorado electorate turned down a proposition that required any new or increase in state or local taxes to be approved at a biennial election. And Oregonians refused to adopt a property tax change that would have replaced existing limitations with maximum property tax rates, would have limited assessed property value increases and would have allowed new or increased rates only on approval of a majority of the people voting on the issue at two annual elections. The only tax that was abolished during the biennium was the Oklahoma poll tax. Oregon voters approved a measure to remove retirement income (social security and railroad pensions) from the Oregon income tax. On the other hand, adding new or increasing existing taxes met with mixed results. Oklahoma voters approved two new tax amendments, one authorizing county voters to levy a tax for solid waste management services and another authorizing a state tax on certain federal property. Also, Washington voters approved additional taxes for school construction and, in Texas, property taxes were allowed for special districts providing emergency services. But the perennial quest in Oregon for a state sales tax was rejected again. Louisiana voters rejected an increase in the car license tax and additional levee district taxes; the West Virginia electorate voted down a 1 percent sales tax for state highways and bridges; and in Texas a property tax increase for rural fire prevention districts failed.

A few measures granting relief from existing state and local tax limitations were adopted. In California, four measures passed. One authorized a waiver for municipalities (for the purpose of retiring general obligation bonds) of the 1 percent property tax rate increase limitation. The other California measures liberalized assessment values for certain properties. A Washington measure authorizing relief from a 1 percent limit failed, however.

With respect to spending policies, Alaska voters decided to retain a limit on state appropriations first imposed in 1982, but in Arizona the voters approved an increase in school district spending limits although rejecting another measure to allow two year adjustments to spending limits. Several new funds were created, among them the Louisiana Wildlife and Fisheries Conservation Fund, the Georgia Children's Trust Fund, and a trust fund for education in Mississippi. Another electorally successful Louisiana amendment authorized funds to finance quality education and academic research. Measures to set up funds to finance economic development were passed in Texas and Wyoming, although Texas voters rejected a related proposal to provide state financing of new Texas products and businesses.

As usual, many amendments proposed exemptions from the property tax. During the biennium six passed and six failed. Among those adopted was a Kansas measure that permitted the exemption to promote economic development.

Another fiscal highlight of the biennium was the willingness of voters to approve new bond and spending proposals many of which were designed to improve the state and local infrastructure and to promote economic development. Of 14 proposals in nine states to issue bonds, nine passed in six states. Among those approved were proposals in Texas to authorize bonds for the federal Supercollider project if won by the state, for state corrections, mental hospital facilities and for water development; North Carolina proposals authorizing revenue bonds for education and local development of seaport and airports; and an Ohio proposition to finance local infrastructure. Among those that failed were an Oregon measure to finance state-county prisons and one in Ohio to build schools.

Among other approved fiscal propositions were a California amendment to transfer all proceeds from the motor fuels tax to local governments, a Kansas proposition establishing a classified property tax system, and a Mississippi measure revising property tax assessment ratios and authorizing legislative limitation of taxation of nuclear power plants.

State functions, constitutional revision, miscellaneous

Most contemporary state constitutions contain separate articles on major policy or functional areas, primarily education, corporations, health and welfare, and conservation. Policy provisions are also incorporated in the legislative and several other articles. This means that amendments to change policy articles do not represent all the policy proposals in any given biennium.

The total number of propositions concerning policy articles during 1986-87 was almost double that of the past biennium but comparable to the 1982-83 period. Of the 29 proposals, well over half (19) concerned education and most of the remainder pertained to corporations (18). The large number of education amendments is reflective of growing concern about state responsibility to improve public education. The fact that 79 percent (15) were approved is an indication of public support for these efforts. In this regard, highly significant proposals were adopted in Mississippi and West Virginia. In Mississippi, the constitution was changed to require that the legislature provide for the support of free public schools and to set up a trust fund for education. In West Virginia, state funding of a minimum foundation program was adopted. In two other states, revised education articles were submitted to the voters. The Utah proposal, a substantive revision, was adopted, but the editorial changes to the Kansas document were rejected.

Other important provisions concerned state aid to private schools. A South Dakota proposal authorizing the loan of state-owned nonsectarian textbooks was adopted, but the Massachusetts amendment to allow state and local governments to "extend aid to nonpublic schools and nonpublic students within the limits of the U.S. Constitution" failed. Indiana voters rejected a related proposition that gave permissive authority to use the common school fund for any purpose.

Eight proposals, of which six were adopted, were amendments to articles on corporations. Mississippi measures, with a purpose to delete outmoded provisions, accounted for four of these. A similar purpose was served by an Oklahoma amendment that relieved railroads of the requirement to charge no more than 2 cents a mile for first class passengers. Both the Mississippi and Oklahoma amendments found favor with the voters. In Arizona, an amendment that authorized the corporation commission to reduce regulation of some telecommunication services and to assure available and affordable telephone service statewide was rejected.

The remaining proposals were an electorally unsuccessful tort reform amendment to the Arizona Constitution and an amendment which was adopted to the conservation article of the New York Constitution permitting changes in ski trails in the "forever wild" section.

Articles on amendment and revision in state constitutions have never attracted many proposals, but the 1986-87 biennium was the first of the decade in which none was submitted to the voters. Proposals for change in articles entitled Miscellaneous or, in some states, General Provisions were at an all-time high for the decade. Inasmuch as 12 of the 22 measures dealt with social and moral issues, such as lotteries and casino gambling, the increase was probably the result of increased popular concern about such matters and also of the desire to raise needed revenues without raising taxes.

Adding two propositions in other articles to the four in the miscellaneous article, six propositions concerned lotteries. New state lotteries were authorized in Florida, Kansas, South Dakota and Wisconsin, but rejected in North Dakota. The Ohio proposal earmarked proceeds from the lottery for education. An Oregon proposal to legalize raffles for charitable groups passed, casino gambling on a local option basis failed in Florida, but pari-mutuel betting proposals passed in Kansas and Wisconsin. In Missouri, voters approved horse racing by local option. Kansas voters approved sale of liquor by the drink, and Oklahomans adopted a measure requiring winemakers to sell to all licensed wholesale distributors in the state. Proposals on abortions and on miscegenation have already been reviewed. The remaining propositions were truly miscellaneous, including two on salary commissions, already reviewed; an Oklahoma provision deleting

regulations prohibiting employment of women and girls in underground mines, which passed; and changes in wills in Mississippi and community property in Texas, both of which passed.

STATE CONSTITUTIONAL SOURCES AND RESOURCES

Literature on state constitutions continued to grow during the biennium, encouraged in part by the bicentennial celebration of the drafting of the U.S. Constitution. Two collections of papers were an outgrowth of a national conference, "State Constitutional Law in the Third Century of American Federalism: New Developments and Possibilities," held in Philadelphia March 15-17, 1987. Sponsored by the Center for the Study of Federalism at Temple University in cooperation with the American Bar Association, the Philadelphia Bar Association and the U.S. Commission on Intergovernmental Relations, and supported by the National Endowment of the Humanities, it drew more than 100 judges, attorneys, law professors, public officials, social scientists and other scholars and citizens. Conference papers as well as other articles were published in *The Annals of the American Academy of Political and Social Sciences*, 496 (March 1988) under the title "State Constitutions in a Federal System." John Kincaid was special editor of the issue. Conference papers in condensed form also appeared in Intergovernmental Perspective, 13, 2 (Spring 1987), a publication of the U.S. Advisory Commission on Intergovernmental Relations.

An entire issue of *Publius, The Journal of Federalism*, 17, 1 (Winter 1987), edited by G. Alan Tarr and Mary Cornelia Porter, was devoted to state constitutions. Entitled "New Developments in State Constitutional Law," it consisted of nine articles written by law professors and political scientists. *The National Law Journal*, Sept. 29, 1986, published a new bibliography on state constitutions in a special section compiled by Ronald K.L. Collins and Peter J. Galie.

Constitutional revision developments in Mississippi generated new publications in that state during the biennium. The Policy Research Center of the University of Mississippi released a 219 page volume in 1986 entitled, *A Contemporary Analysis of Mississippi's Constitutional Government: Proceedings of a Forum May 2-3, 1986*. Dana B. Brammer and John Winkle III served as editors. "Symposium on

Constitution Revision in Mississippi," consisting of five articles, appeared in the *Mississippi Law Journal*, 56, 1 (April 1986).

Other publications were underway but not released during the biennium. To continue with its bibliographical collection of state constitutional materials for the years 1959 through 1978, the Congressional Information Service plans to publish in 1989, a new microfiche collection covering the period from 1979 through Dec. 31, 1988. The new work will include official proceedings, debates and reports of state constitutional conventions and commissions, the most current versions of constitutions as well as publications relating to the amendment process in all 50 states. A second major enterprise in progress is a constitutional history and a provision-by-provision analysis of each of the constitutions of the 50 states. Entitled *State Constitutions of the American States*, the first volume, which will be published by the Greenwood Press, is expected in 1989. G. Alan Tarr is the editor of the series.

The selected list of references at the end of this summary analysis includes several works of particular significance: *Sources and Documents of United States Constitutions* (edited and annotated by William J. Swindler with Donald Musch), designed to integrate national and state constitutional documents into a reference collection on American constitutional developments; *Model State Constitution*, first published in 1923 by the National Municipal League and since revised six times; and *Index Digest of State Constitutions* prepared by the Legislative Drafting Research Fund at Columbia University. The selected list necessarily excludes many specific items on constitutional reform efforts in particular states and numerous special studies. Students, planners and participants in constitutional revision should consult the official documents and the special studies prepared for constitutional-making in given states, as well as publications of The Council of State Governments, the U.S. Advisory Commission on Intergovernmental Relations, the National Civic League and the League of Women Voters. Particularly useful are the complete, annotated and comparative analyses of the Illinois and Texas constitutions prepared for the delegates to the constitutional conventions in those states. In addition, a vast quantity of ephemeral material is stored in the archives and libraries of states where major constitutional reform efforts have occurred. Excepting the holdings of the Library of Congress, probably the most extensive collections of fugitive and published materials on state constitutions are those of the National Civic League and the Council of State Governments.

Sources of periodic reviews and updates of state constitutional developments include the biennial summary of official activities in *The Book of the States*. The 1982-83 volume featured a 50-year review of state constitutional history and bibliography. Since 1982, Ronald K.L. Collins has authored articles on state constitutional law that have appeared periodically in *The National Law Journal*. From 1970 through 1985, Albert L.Sturm contributed an annual survey of state constitutional developments to the *National Civic Review*.

Selected References

Bamberger, Phylis Skloot, ed. *Recent Developments in State Constitutional Law*. New York, N.Y.: Practising Law Institute, 1985.

Brammer, Dana B. and John Winkle III, eds. *A Contemporary Analysis of Mississippi's Constitutional Government: Proceedings of a Forum May 2-3, 1986*. Oxford, Miss.: The Public Policy Research Center, University of Mississippi, October 1986.

Brown, Cynthia E., comp. *State Constitutional Conventions: From Independence to the Completion of the Present Union, A Bibliography*. Westport, Conn.: Greenwood Press, 1973.

Clem, Alan L., ed. *Contemporary Approaches to State Constitutional Revision*. Vermillion, S.D.: Governmental Research Bureau, University of South Dakota, 1970.

Collins, Ronald K.L., comp. and ed. "Bills and Declarations of Rights Digest." *The American Bench, Judges of the Nation*. 3rd ed. Minneapolis, Minn.: Reginald Bishop Forster and Associates, Inc., 1985, 2483-2655.

Constitutions of the United States: National and State. 2nd ed. 2 vols. Dobbs Ferry, N.Y.: Oceana Publications, 1974. Loose leaf. Updated periodically.

Cornwell, Elmer E., Jr., et al. *Constitutional Conventions: The Politics of Revision*. New York, N.Y.: National Municipal League, 1974. (In second series of the National Municipal League's *State Constitution Studies*.)

Dishman, Robert B., *State Constitutions: The Shape of the Document*. Rev. ed. New York, N.Y.: National Municipal League, 1968. (In first series of the National Municipal League's State Constitution Studies.)

Edwards, William A., ed. *Index Digest of State Constitutions*. 2nd ed. Dobbs Ferry, N.Y.: Oceana Publications, 1959. Prepared by the Legislative Drafting Research Fund, Columbia University.

Elazar, Daniel J., ed. Series of articles on American state constitutions and the constitutions of selected foreign states. *Publius: The Journal of Federalism* 12, 2 (Winter 1982): entire issue.

Grad, Frank P., *The State Constitution: Its Function and Form for Our Time*. New York, N.Y.: National Municipal League, 1968. Reprinted from *Virginia Law Review* 54, 5 (June 1968). (In first series of the National Municipal League's *State Constitution Studies*.)

Graves, W. Brooke. "State Constitutional Law: A Twenty-five Year Summary." *William and Mary Law Review* 8,1 (Fall 1966): 1-48.

_____, ed. *Major Problems in State Constitutional Revision*. Chicago: Public Administration Service, 1960.

Kincaid, John, special ed. "State Constitutions in a Federal System." *The Annals of the American Academy of Political and Social Sciences* 496 (March 1988): entire issue.

Leach, Richard H., ed. *Compacts of Antiquity: State Constitutions*. Atlanta, Ga.: Southern Newspaper Publishers Association Foundation, 1969.

May, Janice C. "Constitutional Amendment and Revision Revisited." *Publius: The Journal of Federalism* 17, 1 (Winter 1987): 153-179.

_____. "Texas Constitutional Revision: Lessons and Laments." *National Civic Review* 66, 2 (February 1977): 64-69.

_____, *The Texas Constitutional Revision Experience in the Seventies*. Austin, TX.: Sterling Swift Publishing Company, 1975.

McGraw, Bradley D., ed. *Developments in State Constitutional Law*, The Williamsburg Conference. St. Paul, Minn.: West Publishing Co., 1985.

Model State Constitution. 6th ed. New York, N.Y.: National Municipal League, 1963. Revised 1968.

Pisciotte, Joseph P., ed. *Studies in Illinois Constitution Making*. 10 vols. Urbana, Ill.: University of Illinois Press, 1972-1980.

Sachs, Barbara Faith, ed. *Index to Constitutions of the United States: National and State*. London, Rome and New York: Oceana

Publications, 1980. Prepared by the Legislative Drafting Research Fund, Columbia University. The first two in the series are: *Fundamental Liberties and Rights: A Fifty-State Index* (1980), and Laws, *Legislatures and Legislative Procedures: A Fifty-State Index* (1982).

Schrag, Philip G. *Behind the Scenes: The Politics of a Constitutional Convention*. Washington, D.C.: Georgetown University Press, 1985.

Southwick, Leslie H. "State Constitutional Revision: Mississippi and the South." *The Mississippi Lawyer* 32, 3 (November - December 1985): 21-25.

State Constitutional Convention Studies. 11 vols. New York, N.Y.: National Municipal League, 1969-1978.

State Constitution Studies. 10 vols. in two series. New York, N.Y.: National Municipal League, 1960-1965.

State Constitutional Conventions, Commissions, and Amendments, 1959-1978: An Annotated Bibliography. 2 vols. Washington, D.C.: Congressional Information Service, 1981. This bibliography incorporates the contents of the following two supplements to the Browne bibliography:

    Yarger, Susan Rice, comp. *State Constitutional Conventions, 1959-1975: A Bibliography*. Westport, Conn.: Greenwood Press, 1976.

    Canning, Bonnie, comp. *State Constitutional Conventions, Revisions, and Amendments, 1959-1976: A Bibliography*. Westport, Conn.: Greenwood Press, 1977.

State Constitutional Conventions, Commissions, and Amendments on Microfiche. 4 pts. [Microform]. Westport, Conn.: Greenwood Press, 1972-1976; Washington, D.C.: Congressional Information Service, 1977-1981.

Sturm, Albert L., *A Bibliography on State Constitutions and Constitutional Revision*, 1945-1975. Englewood, Colo.: The Citizens Conference on State Legislatures, August 1975.

_____. Annual summary analyses of state constitutional developments. Published in the January or February issues of the *National Civic Review* 1970-1985.

_____. "The Development of American State Constitutions." *Publius: The Journal of Federalism* 12,2 (Winter 1982): 57-98.

CONSTITUTIONS

_____. *Thirty Years of State Constitution Making*, 1938-1968. New York, N.Y.: National Municipal League, 1970.

Swindler, William J., ed. *Sources of Documents of United States Constitutions*. 10 vols. Dobbs Ferry, N.Y.: Oceana Publications, Inc. 1973-1979.

_____ ed. (vol. 1), with Donald Musch (vols. 2-4). *Sources and Documents of U.S. Constitutions, Second Series: 1492-1800*. 4 vols. Dobbs Ferry, N.Y.: Oceana Publications, Inc. 1982-1986.

"Symposium on Constitutional Revision in Mississippi," *Mississippi Law Journal*, 56, 1 (April 1986): 1-163.

"Symposium: The Emergence of State Constitutional Law." *Texas Law Review* 63, 6 and 7 (March/April 1985): 959-1375.

Tarr, G. Alan and Mary Cornelia Porter, eds. "New Developments in State Constitutional Law." *Publius: The Journal of Federalism* 17, 1 (Winter 1987): entire issue.

Wheeler, John P., Jr. *The Constitutional Convention: A Manual on Its Planning, Organization and Operation*. New York, N.Y.: National Municipal League, 1961.

_____. ed. *Salient Issues of Constitutional Revision*. New York, N.Y.: National Municipal League, 1961.

Table 1.1
GENERAL INFORMATION ON STATE CONSTITUTIONS
(As of December 31, 1987)

State or other jurisdiction	Number of constitutions*	Dates of adoption	Effective date of present constitution	Estimated length (number of words)	Number of amendments Submitted to voters	Adopted
Alabama	6	1819, 1861, 1865, 1868, 1875, 1901	Nov. 28, 1901	174,000	679	471
Alaska	1	1956	Jan. 3, 1959	13,000	30	21
Arizona	1	1911	Feb. 14, 1912	28,876(a)	191	105
Arkansas	5	1836, 1861, 1864, 1868, 1874	Oct. 30, 1874	40,720(a)	160	73(b)
California	2	1849, 1879	July 4, 1879	33,350	768	460
Colorado	1	1876	Aug. 1, 1876	45,679	231	109
Connecticut	4	1818(c), 1965	Dec. 30, 1965	9,564	26	25
Delaware	4	1776, 1792, 1831, 1897	June 10, 1897	19,000	(d)	117
Florida	6	1839, 1861, 1865, 1868, 1886, 1968	Jan. 7, 1969	25,100	68	44
Georgia	10	1777, 1789, 1798, 1861, 1865, 1868, 1877, 1945, 1976, 1982	July 1, 1983	25,000	20(e)	18
Hawaii	1(f)	1950	Aug. 21, 1959	17,453(a)	86	78
Idaho	1	1889	July 3, 1890	21,500	186	106
Illinois	4	1818, 1848, 1870, 1970	July 1, 1971	13,200	9	4
Indiana	2	1816, 1851	Nov. 1, 1851	9,377(a)	67	36
Iowa	2	1846, 1857	Sept. 3, 1857	12,500	49	46(g)
Kansas	1	1859	Jan. 29, 1861	11,865	114	86(g)
Kentucky	4	1792, 1799, 1850, 1891	Sept. 28, 1891	23,500	56	27
Louisiana	11	1812, 1845, 1852, 1861, 1864, 1868, 1879, 1898, 1913, 1921, 1974	Jan. 1, 1975	51,448(a)	36	22
Maine	1	1819	March 15, 1820	13,500	184	156(h)
Maryland	4	1776, 1851, 1864, 1867	Oct. 5, 1867	41,349(a)	231	199
Massachusetts	1	1780	Oct. 25, 1780	36,690(a,i)	143	116
Michigan	4	1835, 1850, 1908, 1963	Jan. 1, 1964	20,000	44	15
Minnesota	1	1857	May 11, 1858	9,500	203	109
Mississippi	4	1817, 1832, 1869, 1890	Nov. 1, 1890	24,000	141	70
Missouri	4	1820, 1865, 1875, 1945	March 30, 1945	42,000	107	68
Montana	2	1889, 1972	July 1, 1973	11,866(a)	21	13
Nebraska	2	1866, 1875	Oct. 12, 1875	20,048(a)	278	184
Nevada	1	1864	Oct. 31, 1864	20,770	168	103(g)
New Hampshire	2	1776, 1784	June 2, 1784	9,200	272(j)	141(j)
New Jersey	3	1776, 1844, 1947	Jan. 1, 1948	17,086	49	36
New Mexico	1	1911	Jan. 6, 1912	27,200	224	114
New York	4	1777, 1822, 1846, 1894	Jan. 1, 1895	80,000	272	205
North Carolina	3	1776, 1868, 1970	July 1, 1971	11,000	34	27
North Dakota	1	1889	Nov. 2, 1889	20,564	215(k)	124(k)
Ohio	2	1802, 1851	Sept. 1, 1851	36,900	244	144
Oklahoma	1	1907	Nov. 16, 1907	68,800	264(l)	124(l)
Oregon	1	1857	Feb. 14, 1859	26,090	361	183
Pennsylvania	5	1776, 1790, 1838, 1873, 1968(m)	1968(m)	21,675	24(m)	19(m)
Rhode Island	2	1842(c)	May 2, 1843	19,026(a,i)	98	52
South Carolina	7	1776, 1778, 1790, 1861, 1865, 1868, 1895	Jan. 1, 1896	22,500(n)	639(o)	455(o)
South Dakota	1	1889	Nov. 2, 1889	23,300	181	94
Tennessee	3	1796, 1835, 1870	Feb. 23, 1870	15,300	55	32
Texas	5	1845, 1861, 1866, 1869, 1876	Feb. 15, 1876	62,000	459	304
Utah	1	1895	Jan. 4, 1896	11,000	124	75
Vermont	3	1777, 1786, 1793	July 9, 1793	6,600	208	50
Virginia	6	1776, 1830, 1851, 1869, 1902, 1970	July 1, 1971	18,500	23	20
Washington	1	1889	Nov. 11, 1889	29,400	147	80
West Virginia	2	1863, 1872	April 9, 1872	25,600	102	62
Wisconsin	1	1848	May 29, 1848	13,500	167	124(g)
Wyoming	1	1889	July 10, 1890	31,800	96	56
American Samoa	2	1960, 1967	July 1, 1967	6,000	13	7
No. Mariana Is.	1	1977	Oct. 24, 1977	. . . .	. . .	. . .
Puerto Rico	1	1952	July 25, 1952	9,281(a)	6	6

GENERAL INFORMATION ON STATE CONSTITUTIONS—Continued

*The constitutions referred to in this table include those Civil War documents customarily listed by the individual states.

(a) Actual word count.

(b) Eight of the approved amendments have been superseded and are not printed in the current edition of the constitution. The total adopted does not include five amendments that were invalidated.

(c) Colonial charters with some alterations served as the first constitutions in Connecticut (1638, 1662) and in Rhode Island (1663).

(d) Proposed amendments are not submitted to the voters in Delaware.

(e) The new Georgia constitution eliminates the need for local amendments, which have been a long-term problem for state constitution makers.

(f) As a kingdom and a republic, Hawaii had five constitutions.

(g) The figure given includes amendments approved by the voters and later nullified by the state supreme court in Iowa (three), Kansas (one), Nevada (six) and Wisconsin (two).

(h) The figure does not include one amendment approved by the voters in 1967 that is inoperative until implemented by legislation.

(i) The printed constitution includes many provisions that have been annulled. The length of effective provisions is an estimated 24,122 words (12,400 annulled) in Massachusetts and, in Rhode Island before the "rewrite" of the constitution in 1986, it was 11,399 words (7,627 annulled).

(j) The constitution of 1784 was extensively revised in 1792. Figures show proposals and adoptions since the constitution was adopted in 1784.

(k) The figures do not include submission and approval of the constitution of 1889 itself and of Article XX; these are constitutional questions included in some counts of constitutional amendments and would add two to the figure in each column.

(l) The figures include five amendments submitted to, and approved by the voters which were, by decisions of the Oklahoma or U.S. Supreme Courts, rendered inoperative or ruled invalid, unconstitutional, or illegally submitted.

(m) Certain sections of the constitution were revised by the limited constitutional convention of 1967-68. Amendments proposed and adopted are since 1968.

(n) Of the estimated length, approximately two-thirds is of general statewide effect; the remainder is local amendments.

(o) As of 1981, of the 626 proposed amendments submitted to the voters, 130 were of general statewide effect and 496 were local; the voters rejected 83 (12 statewide, 71 local). Of the remaining 543, the General Assembly refused to approve 100 (22 statewide, 78 local), and 443 (96 statewide, 347 local) were finally added to the constitution.

Table 1.2
CONSTITUTIONAL AMENDMENT PROCEDURE: BY THE LEGISLATURE
Constitutional Provisions

State or other jurisdiction	Legislative vote required for proposal(a)	Consideration by two sessions required	Vote required for ratification	Limitation on the number of amendments submitted at one election
Alabama	3/5	No	Majority vote on amendment	None
Alaska	2/3	No	Majority vote on amendment	None
Arizona	Majority	No	Majority vote on amendment	None
Arkansas	Majority	No	Majority vote on amendment	3
California	2/3	No	Majority vote on amendment	None
Colorado	2/3	No	Majority vote on amendment	None(b)
Connecticut	(c)	(c)	Majority vote on amendment	None
Delaware	2/3	Yes	Not required	No referendum
Florida	3/5	No	Majority vote on amendment	None
Georgia	2/3	No	Majority vote on amendment	None
Hawaii	(d)	(d)	Majority vote on amendment(e)	None
Idaho	2/3	No	Majority vote on amendment	None
Illinois	3/5	No	(f)	3 articles
Indiana	Majority	Yes	Majority vote on amendment	None
Iowa	Majority	Yes	Majority vote on amendment	None
Kansas	2/3	No	Majority vote on amendment	5
Kentucky	3/5	No	Majority vote on amendment	4
Louisiana	2/3	No	Majority vote on amendment(g)	None
Maine	2/3(h)	No	Majority vote on amendment	None
Maryland	3/5	No	Majority vote on amendment	None
Massachusetts	Majority(i)	Yes	Majority vote on amendment	None
Michigan	2/3	No	Majority vote on amendment	None
Minnesota	Majority	No	Majority vote in election	None
Mississippi	2/3(j)	No	Majority vote on amendment	None
Missouri	Majority	No	Majority vote on amendment	None
Montana	2/3(h)	No	Majority vote on amendment	None
Nebraska	3/5	No	Majority vote on amendment(e)	None
Nevada	Majority	Yes	Majority vote on amendment	None
New Hampshire	3/5	No	2/3 vote on amendment	None
New Jersey	(k)	(k)	Majority vote on amendment	None(l)
New Mexico	Majority(m)	No	Majority vote on amendment(m)	None
New York	Majority	Yes	Majority vote on amendment	None
North Carolina	3/5	No	Majority vote on amendment	None
North Dakota	Majority	No	Majority vote on amendment	None
Ohio	3/5	No	Majority vote on amendment	None
Oklahoma	Majority	No	Majority vote on amendment	None
Oregon	(n)	No	Majority vote on amendment	None
Pennsylvania	Majority(o)	Yes(o)	Majority vote on amendment	None
Rhode Island	Majority	No	Majority vote on amendment	None
South Carolina	2/3(p)	Yes(p)	Majority vote on amendment	None
South Dakota	Majority	No	Majority vote on amendment	None
Tennessee	(q)	Yes(q)	Majority vote in election(r)	None
Texas	2/3	No	Majority vote on amendment	None
Utah	2/3	No	Majority vote on amendment	None
Vermont	(s)	Yes	Majority vote on amendment	None
Virginia	Majority	Yes	Majority vote on amendment	None
Washington	2/3	No	Majority vote on amendment	None
West Virginia	2/3	No	Majority vote on amendment	None
Wisconsin	Majority	Yes	Majority vote on amendment	None
Wyoming	2/3	No	Majority vote in election	None
American Samoa	3/5	No	Majority vote on amendment(t)	None
Puerto Rico	2/3(u)	No	Majority vote on amendment	3

CONSTITUTIONAL AMENDMENT PROCEDURE: BY THE LEGISLATURE—
Continued

(a) In all states not otherwise noted, the figure shown in the column refers to the proportion of elected members in each house required for approval of proposed constitutional amendments.

(b) Legislature may not propose amendments to more than six articles of the constitution in the same legislative session.

(c) Three-fourths vote in each house at one session, or majority vote in each house in two sessions between which an election has intervened.

(d) Two-thirds vote in each house at one session, or majority vote in each house in two sessions.

(e) Majority vote on amendment must be at least 50 percent of the total votes cast at the election; or, at a special election, a majority of the votes tallied which must be at least 30 percent of the total number of registered voters.

(f) Majority voting in election or three-fifths voting on amendment.

(g) If five or fewer political subdivisions of the state are affected, majority in state as a whole and also in affected subdivision(s) is required.

(h) Two-thirds of both houses.

(i) Majority of members elected sitting in joint session.

(j) The two-thirds must include not less than a majority elected to each house.

(k) Three-fifths of all members of each house at one session, or majority of all members of each house for two successive sessions.

(l) If a proposed amendment is not approved at the election when submitted, neither the same amendment nor one which would make substantially the same change for the constitution may be again submitted to the people before the third general election thereafter.

(m) Amendments concerning certain elective franchise and education matters require three-fourths vote of members elected and approval by three-fourths of electors voting in state and two-thirds of those voting in each county.

(n) Majority vote to amend constitution, two-thirds to revise ("revise" includes all or a part of the constitution).

(o) Emergency amendments may be passed by two-thirds vote of each house, followed by ratification by majority vote of electors in election held at least one month after legislative approval.

(p) Two-thirds of members of each house, first passage; majority of members of each house after popular ratification.

(q) Majority of members elected to both houses, first passage; two-thirds of members elected to both houses, second passage.

(r) Majority of all citizens voting for governor.

(s) Two-thirds vote senate, majority vote house, first passage; majority both houses, second passage. As of 1974, amendments may be submitted only every four years.

(t) Within 30 days after voter approval, governor must submit amendment(s) to U.S. Secretary of the Interior for approval.

(u) If approved by two-thirds of members of each house, amendment(s) submitted to voters at special referendum; if approved by not less than three-fourths of total members of each house, referendum may be held at next general election.

CONSTITUTIONS

Table 1.3
CONSTITUTIONAL AMENDMENT PROCEDURE: BY INITIATIVE
Constitutional Provisions

State	Number of signatures required on initiative petition	Distribution of signatures	Referendum vote
Arizona	15% of total votes cast for all candidates for governor at last election.	None specified.	Majority vote on amendment.
Arkansas	10% of voters for governor at last election.	Must include 5% of voters for governor in each of 15 counties.	Majority vote on amendment.
California	8% of total voters for all candidates for governor at last election.	None specified.	Majority vote on amendment.
Colorado	5% of total legal votes for all candidates for secretary of state at last general election.	None specified.	Majority vote on amendment.
Florida	8% of total votes cast in the state in the last election for presidential electors.	8% of total votes cast in each of 1/2 of the congressional districts.	Majority vote on amendment.
Illinois(a)	8% of total votes cast for candidates for governor at last election.	None specified.	Majority voting in election or 3/5 voting on amendment.
Massachusetts(b)	3% of total votes cast for governor at preceding biennial state election (not less than 25,000 qualified voters).	No more than 1/4 from any one county.	Majority vote on amendment which must be 30% of total ballots cast at election.
Michigan	10% of total voters for all candidates at last gubernatorial election.	None specified.	Majority vote on amendment.
Missouri	8% of legal voters for all candidates for governor at last election.	The 8% must be in each of 2/3 of the congressional districts in the state.	Majority vote on amendment.
Montana	10% of qualified electors, the number of qualified electors to be determined by number of votes cast for governor in preceding general election.	The 10% to include at least 10% of qualified electors in each of 2/5 of the legislative districts.	Majority vote on amendment.
Nebraska	10% of total votes for governor at last election.	The 10% must include 5% in each of 2/5 of the counties.	Majority vote on amendment which must be at least 35% of total vote at the election.
Nevada	10% of voters who voted in entire state in last general election.	10% of total voters who voted in each of 75% of the counties.	Majority vote on amendment in two consecutive general elections.
North Dakota	4% of population of the state.	None specified.	Majority vote on amendment.
Ohio	10% of total number of electors who voted for governor in last election.	At least 5% of qualified electors in each of 1/2 of counties in the state.	Majority vote on amendment.
Oklahoma	15% of legal voters for state office receiving highest number of voters at last general state election.	None specified.	Majority vote on amendment.
Oregon	8% of total votes for all candidates for governor at last election at which governor was elected for four-year term.	None specified.	Majority vote on amendment.
South Dakota	10% of total votes for governor in last election.	None specified.	Majority vote on amendment.

(a) Only Article IV, The Legislature, may be amended by initiative petition.

(b) Before being submitted to the electorate for ratification, initiative measures must be approved at two sessions of a successively elected legislature by not less than one-fourth of all members elected, sitting in joint session.

Table 1.4
PROCEDURES FOR CALLING CONSTITUTIONAL CONVENTIONS
Constitutional Provisions

State or other jurisdiction	Provision for convention	Legislative vote for submission of convention question(a)	Popular vote to authorize convention	Periodic submission of convention question required(b)	Popular vote required for ratification of convention proposals
Alabama	Yes	Majority	ME	No	Not specified
Alaska	Yes	No provision(c,d)	(c)	10 years(c)	Not specified(c)
Arizona	Yes	Majority	(e)	No	MP
Arkansas	No		No		
California	Yes	2/3	MP	No	MP
Colorado	Yes	2/3	MP	No	ME
Connecticut	Yes	2/3	MP	20 years(f)	MP
Delaware	Yes	2/3	MP	No	No provision
Florida	Yes	(g)	MP	No	Not specified
Georgia	Yes	(d)	No	No	MP
Hawaii	Yes	Not specified	MP	9 years	MP(h)
Idaho	Yes	2/3	MP	No	Not specified
Illinois	Yes	3/5	(i)	20 years	MP
Indiana	No		No		
Iowa	Yes	Majority	MP	10 years; 1970	MP
Kansas	Yes	2/3	MP	No	MP
Kentucky	Yes	Majority(j)	MP(k)	No	No provision
Louisiana	Yes	(d)	No	No	MP
Maine	Yes	(d)	No	No	No provision
Maryland	Yes	Majority	ME	20 years; 1970	MP
Massachusetts	No			No	Not specified
Michigan	Yes	Majority	MP	16 years; 1978	MP
Minnesota	Yes	2/3	ME	No	3/5 voting on proposal
Mississippi	No		No		
Missouri	Yes	Majority	MP	20 years; 1962	Not specified(l)
Montana	Yes(m)	2/3(n)	MP	20 years	MP
Nebraska	Yes	3/5	MP(o)	No	MP
Nevada	Yes	2/3	ME	No	No provision
New Hampshire	Yes	Majority	MP	10 years	2/3 voting on proposal
New Jersey	No		No		
New Mexico	Yes	2/3	MP	No	Not specified
New York	Yes	Majority	MP	20 years; 1957	MP
North Carolina	Yes	2/3	MP	No	MP
North Dakota	No		No		
Ohio	Yes	2/3	MP	20 years; 1932	MP
Oklahoma	Yes	Majority	(e)	20 years	MP
Oregon	Yes	Majority	(e)	No	No provision
Pennsylvania	No		No		
Rhode Island	Yes	Majority	MP	10 years	MP
South Carolina	Yes	(d)	ME	No	No provision
South Dakota	Yes	(d)	(d)	No	(p)
Tennessee	Yes(q)	Majority	MP	No	MP
Texas	No		No		
Utah	Yes	2/3	ME	No	MP
Vermont	No		No		
Virginia	Yes	(d)	No	No	MP
Washington	Yes	2/3	ME	No	Not specified
West Virginia	Yes	Majority	MP	No	Not specified
Wisconsin	Yes	Majority	MP	No	No provision
Wyoming	Yes	2/3	ME	No	Not specified
American Samoa	Yes	(r)	No	No	ME(s)
Puerto Rico	Yes	2/3	MP	No	MP

PROCEDURES FOR CALLING CONSTITUTIONAL CONVENTIONS—Continued

Key:

MP—Majority voting on the proposal.

ME—Majority voting in the election.

(a) In all states not otherwise noted, the entries in this column refer to the proportion of members elected to each house required to submit to the electorate the question of calling a constitutional convention.

(b) The number listed is the interval between required submissions on the question of calling a constitutional convention; where given, the date is that of the first required submission of the convention question.

(c) Unless provided otherwise by law, convention calls are to conform as nearly as possible to the act calling the 1955 convention, which provided for a legislative vote of a majority of members elected to each house and ratification by a majority vote on the proposals. The legislature may call a constitutional convention at any time.

(d) In these states, the legislature may call a convention without submitting the question to the people. The legislative vote required is two-thirds of the members elected to each house in Georgia, Louisiana, South Carolina and Virginia; two-thirds concurrent vote of both branches in Maine; three-fourths of all members of each house in South Dakota; and not specified in Alaska, but bills require majority vote of membership of each house. In South Dakota, the question of calling a convention may be initiated by the people in the same manner as an amendment to the constitution (see Table 1.3) and requires a majority vote on the question for approval.

(e) The law calling a convention must be approved by the people.

(f) The legislature shall submit the question 20 years after the last convention, or 20 years after the last vote on the question of calling a convention, whichever date is last.

(g) The power to call a convention is reserved to the people by petition.

(h) The majority must be 50 percent of the total votes cast at a general election or at a special election, a majority of the votes tallied which must be at least 30 percent of the total number of registered voters.

(i) Majority voting in the election, or three-fifths voting on the question.

(j) Must be approved during two legislative sessions.

(k) Majority must equal one-fourth of qualified voters at last general election.

(l) Majority of those voting on the proposal is assumed.

(m) The question of calling a constitutional convention may be submitted either by the legislature or by initiative petition to the secretary of state in the same manner as provided for initiated amendments (see Table 1.3).

(n) Two-thirds of all members of the legislature.

(o) Majority must be 35 percent of total votes cast at the election.

(p) Convention proposals are submitted to the electorate at a special election in a manner to be determined by the convention. Ratification by a majority of votes cast.

(q) Conventions may not be held more often than once in six years.

(r) Five years after effective date of constitutions, governor shall call a constitutional convention to consider changes proposed by a constitutional committee appointed by the governor. Delegates to the convention are to be elected by their county councils.

(s) If proposed amendments are approved by the voters, they must be submitted to the U.S. Secretary of the Interior for approval.

Table 1.5
STATE CONSTITUTIONAL COMMISSIONS
(Operative during January 1, 1986-December 31, 1987)

State	Name of commission	Method and date of creation and period of operation	Membership: number and type	Funding	Purpose of commission	Proposals and action
Mississippi	Governor's Constitutional Study Commission	Executive; appointed by a letter of invitation from Governor in mid-November 1985; completed work in late 1986.	More than 350 members widely representative of all branches of government, state and local, and of social, economic, professional, and political organizations in the state.	No appropriation. Members receive no compensation or per diem. Expenses are paid from resources of Governor's office.	To study the constitution and submit recommendations for revision to Governor by mid-October 1986.	The commission drafted a proposed new constitution and approved it in late 1986; in January 1987, Governor William B. Allain recommended that the legislature provide for a popular referendum on the question of calling a constitutional convention. This proposal failed in the House of Representatives.
Utah	Utah Constitutional Revision Commission	Statutory; Ch. 89, *Laws of Utah*, 1969; amended by Ch. 107, *Laws*, 1975; amended by Ch. 159, *Laws*, 1977, which made the commission permanent as of July 1, 1977. (Codified at Ch. 54, Title 63, *Utah Code Annotated*, 1953).	16; 1 ex officio, 9 appointed: by the Speaker of the House (3), President of the Senate (3), and Governor (3)—no more than 2 of each group to be from same party; and 6 additional members appointed by the 9 previously appointed members.	Appropriations through 1987 totaled $593,000 (The 1987 appropriation was $55,000, the same as for 1986).	Study constitution and recommend desirable changes, including proposed drafts.	Mandated to report recommendations at least 60 days before legislature convenes. Voter action on the commission's recommendations through 1987 included: approval of revised articles on the executive branch, revenue and taxation, the judicial branch, the legislative branch, and education. Proposed revisions of the articles on local government and public debt will be submitted to the legislature in 1988.

Table 1.6
CONSTITUTIONAL CONVENTIONS
1986-1987

State	Convention dates	Type of convention	Referendum on convention question	Preparatory bodies	Appropriations	Convention delegates	Convention proposals	Referendum on convention proposals
Rhode Island	January 6-December 4, 1986 (14 plenary sessions)	Unlimited	Nov. 6, 1984 Vote: 155,337 131,648	None (A bipartisan preparatory commission was created to assemble information on constitutional questions before the 1984 referendum on the convention question).	Original appropriation: $50,000. Later appropriation: $335,000. Expended: $333,622.	100 (elected November 5, 1985 from lower house districts; nonpartisan).	25 proposals approved by the convention were combined by common category into 14 ballot questions.	November 4, 1986: eight of the 14 proposed ballot questions for constitutional revision were approved.

CHAPTER TWO

STATE EXECUTIVE BRANCH

THE GOVERNORS, 1986-87

By Thad L. Beyle

Considerable interest in gubernatorial elections was expressed during 1986-87, a period between presidential campaigns. First, there was considerable political activity in the form of campaigning as 39 governorships were contested. Second, as the problems associated with the federal deficit and the ideological stance of the Reagan administration continued, governors and other state leaders made difficult decisions on the extent of their states' commitment to a range of policy concerns. Third was the continuing role of the governorship in producing serious presidential candidates after a period in which it was believed that governors could no longer be considered as potential candidates for president.[1] Fourth was the negative publicity fostered by the questionable actions of several governors, which in one case lead to an impeachment and in two others contributed to the incumbent's inability to win another term.

Gubernatorial Elections

Thirty-nine governorships were up for election in 1986-87. In nineteen of these contests the incumbent stood for an additional term, with 15 winning re-election. Of the four defeated incumbents, Bill Sheffield of Alaska lost in the Democratic party primary in 1986 and Democrat Edwin Edwards lost in Louisiana's primary in 1987. Two other Democratic incumbents, Mark White of Texas and Anthony Earl of Wisconsin, lost in the 1986 general elections in their states.

Of the 39 governorships up for election, 15 of the 19 incumbents were re-elected: Bill Clinton (D-Arkansas), George Deukmejian (R-California), William O'Neill (D-Connecticut), Joe Frank Harris (D-Georgia), James Thompson (R-Illinois), Terry Branstad (R-Iowa), Michael Dukakis (D-Massachusetts), James Blanchard (D-Michigan), Rudy Perpich (DFL-Minnesota), John Sununu (R-New Hampshire), Richard Bryan (D-Nevada), Mario Cuomo (D-New York), Richard Celeste (D-Ohio), Edward DiPrete (R-

Rhode Island), and Madeleine Kunin (D-Vermont).

Thirteen incumbent governors were constitutionally ineligible to seek another term: Bob Graham (D-Florida), George Ariyoshi (D-Hawaii), John Carlin (D-Kansas), Martha Layne Collins (D-Kentucky), Joseph Brennan (D-Maine), Harry Hughes (D-Maryland), Toney Anaya (D-New Mexico), George Nigh (D-Oklahoma), Victor Atiyeh (R-Oregon), Dick Thornburgh (R-Pennsylvania), Richard Riley (D-South Carolina), William Janklow (R-South Dakota), and Lamar Alexander (R-Tennessee). Seven incumbents opted to retire: George Wallace (D-Alabama), Bruce Babbitt (D-Arizona), Richard Lamm (D-Colorado), John Evans (D-Idaho), William Allain (D-Mississippi), Robert Kerry (D-Nebraska), and Ed Hershler (D-Wyoming).

These 20 outgoing governors, 16 Democrats and four Republicans, had served a combined total of 165 years. Most had been in office for two four-year terms, with only Allain, Anaya, Collins and Kerry serving four years. Four had served more than eight years: Wallace (16 nonconsecutive years), Ariyoshi (13 years), Hershler and Lamm (12 years each).

There has been a general trend in the 1980s for fewer gubernatorial incumbents to seek re-election. In the 1980-83 cycle of elections, 38 of the 46 eligible incumbents ran for re-election (83 percent), while in 1984-87, 26 of the 36 eligible incumbents ran (72 percent). In 1986-87, 19 of the 26 eligible incumbents ran (73 percent). Those incumbents seeking re-election in the 1980s generally have fared well, with 46 of 64 (72 percent) winning. These figures mirror the success rate for incumbents seeking re-election to other political offices, indicating an electoral bias for the incumbent.[1]

Excluding the successful incumbents, a large proportion of the governors elected in 1986-87

Thad L. Beyle is Professor of Political Science at the University of North Carolina at Chapel Hill.

Table A
COSTS OF GUBERNATORIAL CAMPAIGNS, 1986-87

Total campaign expenditures (1)

State	Year	W	All candidates	Winner	%	Winner's vote percent	Cost (2) per total vote
Alabama	1986	R*	$ 9,990,777	$ 960,866	10	56	$ 8.10
Alaska	1986	D**	6,311,219	1,380,146	22	47	114.26
Arizona	1986	R#	6,922,216	1,168,193	17	40	7.98
Arkansas	1986	D*	2,252,907	1,597,163	71	64	3.27
California	1986	R*	22,464,928	13,714,233	61	61	3.18
Colorado	1986	D#	6,204,938	1,797,709	29	58	5.91
Connecticut	1986	D*	3,878,640	2,550,437	66	58	3.94
Florida	1986	R#	23,990,965	4,279,212	18	55	7.09
Georgia	1986	D*	807,906	702,314	87	71	.69
Hawaii	1986	D#	6,711,865	1,830,720	27	52	20.09
Idaho	1986	D#	1,834,373	994,207	54	50	4.78
Illinois	1986	D*	8,916,247	6,634,929	74	53	2.82
Iowa	1986	R*	2,990,628	1,792,324	60	52	3.29
Kansas	1986	R#	6,390,771	1,575,269	25	52	7.60
Kentucky	1987	D#	(a)	(a)	(a)	65	
Louisiana	1987	D**	13,142,072	2,640,637	20	33	8.43
Maine	1986	R#	5,362,179	1,302,763	24	40	12.56
Maryland	1986	D#	4,949,183	3,689,563	75	82	4.49
Massachusetts	1986	D*	4,054,859	3,503,635	86	69	2.41
Michigan	1986	D*	9,362,420	2,988,839	32	68	3.98
Minnesota	1986	D*	4,744,363	2,032,523	43	56	3.41
Mississippi	1987	D#	8,702,199	2,952,105	34	54	12.08
Nebraska	1986	R#	3,992,790	1,486,116	37	53	7.09
Nevada	1986	D*	1,833,735	1,478,553	81	72	7.06
New Hampshire	1986	R*	1,369,823	823,616	60	54	5.46
New Mexico+	1986	R#	2,572,787	1,630,000	63	53	6.52
New York	1986	D*	6,998,540	5,458,457	78	65	1.64
Ohio	1986	D*	7,917,191	4,797,278	61	61	7.58
Oklahoma	1986	R*	3,856,218	1,234,944	32	47	5.12
Oregon	1986	D#	5,049,211	2,880,230	57	52	5.54
Pennsylvania	1986	D#	16,168,820	7,291,155	45	51	4.85
Rhode Island	1986	R*	2,445,198	1,034,498	42	65	7.79
South Carolina	1986	R#	6,865,817	3,018,144	44	51	9.20
South Dakota	1986	R#	2,482,094	1,172,662	47	52	8.43
Tennesee	1986	D#	14,635,833	4,113,698	28	54	12.10
Texas	1986	R***	33,515,785	10,910,104	33	53	9.98
Vermont	1986	D*	961,693	478,294	50	47	4.46
Wisconsin	1986	R***	2,900,140	1,188,406	41	53	1.93
Wyoming	1986	D#	2,428,892	312,877	13	54	14.75
1986 election totals			254,135,951	103,724,077	41	(36 states)	
1987 election totals			21,844,271	5,592,742	26	(2 states)	
1986-87 totals			$275,980,222	109,316,819	40	(38 states)	

Sources: State campaign finance filing offices; The Council of State Governments; Scott Mouw of the Department of Political Science, University of North Carolina at Chapel Hill; and Public Affairs Research Council, Louisiana.
Key:
(1) Includes primaries and general elections.
(2) Determined by dividing total campaign expenditures by total general election votes for the office.
* Incumbent ran and won.
** Incumbent ran and lost in party primary.
*** Incumbent ran and lost in general election.
# Open seat.
+ Incomplete data, only the two general election candidates included.
(a) Data not available.

had previously held a state level office. Six had formerly held a statewide office with two moving up from the treasurer's office (Roy Romer in Colorado and Kay Orr in Nebraska) and four former governors returning home (John Waihsee of Hawaii, acting governor in 1973-74; Cecil Andrus of Idaho, 1971-77; Henry Bellmon of Oklahoma, 1962-66; and Bill Clements of Texas, 1979-83). Other stepping-off positions for these new governors were the state legislature (Mike Hayden of Kansas, George Mickelson of South Dakota, Ned McWherter of Tennessee, Tommy Thompson of Wisconsin); the U.S. Congress (Buddy Roemer of Louisiana, John McKernan of Maine, Carroll Campbell of South Carolina); mayor of major city (Donald Shaefer from Baltimore and Bob Martinez from Tampa); a federal office (Guy Hunt of Alabama in the U.S. Department of Agriculture, former Assistant Secretary of Interior Garrey Carruthers of New Mexico, former Secretary of Transportation Neil Goldschmidt of Oregon, former U.S. Attorney Robert Casey of Pennsylvania). Evan Mecham of Arizona had served in the state legislature, but three of the new governors had no previous experience in elected office.

The 1986 race in Texas, in which former Gov. Clements unseated incumbent Gov. Mark White, was the most expensive gubernatorial race ever recorded at $33.5 million. The least expensive race of the biennium was the 1986 successful re-election bid by Georgia Gov. Harris at $807,000.

Four years earlier, in the 1982-83 elections for governor in these 39 states, the total expenditures reported were about $222 million; $182 million in 1982 and $40 million in 1983.

There were at least 287 separate candidates in these 39 governors races in 1986-87 as measured by those who filed campaign expenditure reports. Many candidates spent little or no money campaigning. Florida with 19 and Alaska with 17 topped the states with crowded fields of candidates. The most expensive individual campaigns were conducted by incumbent governors. White's unsuccessful bid in Texas cost $15.8 million; Deukmejian spent $13.7 million to win the California governor's race; and Clement in Texas spent $10.9 million in his successful bid for office.

Spending the most money in a campaign did not necessarily correlate with winning because in 13 of the 35 races, the winner spent less money than other candidates and only one of the 13 was the incumbent.[1] In the 22 states

which the winner spent more than other candidates, 13 were incumbents fighting successfully to retain their offices.[2] In fact, of the 18 incumbent governors seeking re-election, 14 were the largest spenders in the race, indicating that incumbency breeds more funds for a political campaign.[3]

A recent report indicates that running for lieutenant governor also is becoming expensive. A critical factor is whether the governor and lieutenant governor run as a team. In the 1982-84 election cycle where separate reports were available for those lieutenant governor candidates running jointly with a governor, the expenditures ranged from a high of $60,000, for the successful candidate in Wisconsin, to a low of $4,170 for a losing candidate in Connecticut. When the elections for the two top offices were held separately, the range was from $20,795 for an unsuccessful candidate in Vermont to $2.5 million for the winner in California. Losing candidates also spent considerable sums: $2.2 million in California and nearly $2 million in Texas. The range for most of the non-team election states was between $40,000 and $350,000, and in most cases it was the winning candidate spending the most.[4]

Gubernatorial Investigations

Since 1985, three governors have been the target of investigations in their states. In 1985, Gov. Bill Sheffield (D-Alaska) successfully defended his handling of a $9.1 million lease by the state before a special session of the state legislature called to consider impeaching him. Although Sheffield survived, he subsequently made a poor showing in the 1986 Democratic Party primary, losing to Fairbanks lawyer Steve Cowper by a substantial 15 percent margin. His re-election bid was also wounded deeply by the steep drop in oil prices in early 1986.

Gov. Edwin Edwards (D-Louisiana) successfully fought a 51 count grand jury indictment for fraud and racketeering in which he was charged with influence peddling in obtaining state hospital permits. The first trial ended with a hung jury, but in May 1986, the second jury acquitted him. Edwards attempted to bolster his battered image in the gubernatorial election campaign of 1987, but his popularity had clearly suffered from his legal ordeals. In October 1987, Edwards lost the Louisiana primary by about 5 percentage points to Democratic Congressman Buddy Roemer. Although

Table B
IMPEACHMENTS AND REMOVALS OF GOVERNORS

Name and state	Year	-------------- Process of Impeachment and Outcome --------------		
Charles Robinson (KS)	1862	Impeached	Acquitted	
Harrison Reed (FL)	1868	Impeached	Acquitted	
William Holden (NC)	1870	Impeached	Convicted	Removed
Powell Clayton (AR)	1871	Impeached	Acquitted	
David Butler (NE)	1871	Impeached	Convicted	Removed
Henry Warmoth (LA)	1872	Impeached		Term ended
Harrison Reed (FL)	1873	Impeached	Acquitted	
Adelbert Ames (MS)	1876	Impeached		Resigned
Alexander Davis (MS)	1876	Impeached	Convicted	Removed
William P. Kellogg (LA)	1876	Impeached	Acquitted	
William Sulzer (NY)	1913	Impeached	Convicted	Removed
James 'Pa' Ferguson (TX)	1917	Impeached	Convicted	Resigned
John C. Walton (OK)	1923	Impeached	Convicted	Removed
Henry S. Johnston (OK)	1928	Impeached	Acquitted	
Henry S. Johnston (OK)	1929	Impeached	Convicted	Removed
Huey P. Long (LA)	1929	Impeached	Acquitted	
Henry Horton (TN)	1931	Impeached	Acquitted	
Richard Leche (LA)	1939	Threatened		Resigned
Evan Mecham (AZ)	1988	Impeached	Convicted	Removed

OTHER REMOVALS OF INCUMBENT GOVERNORS

Name and state	Year	
John A. Quitman (MS)	1851	Resigned after federal criminal indictment
Lynn J. Frazier (ND)	1921	Recalled by voters during third term
Warren T. McCray (IN)	1924	Resigned after federal criminal conviction
William Langer (ND)	1934	Removed by North Dakota Supreme Court
Thomas L. Moodie (ND)	1935	Removed by North Dakota Supreme Court
J. Howard Pyle (AZ)	1955	Recall petition certified, but term ended before date set for recall election (1)
Marvin Mandel (MD)	1977	Removed after federal criminal conviction
Ray Blanton (TN)	1979	Term shortened in bipartisan agreement (2)

Notes:
(1) From a discussion with Sean Griffin, reporter for the *Phoenix Gazette*. March 31, 1988.
(2) See Lamar Alexander, *Steps Along the Way: A Governor's Scrapbook* (Nashville, TN: Thomas Nelson, 1986), pp. 21-29 for a discussion of this unique transition between governors.

---

the closeness of the vote and the fact that Roemer received only one-third of the total vote entitled Edwards to challenge Roemer to a run-off election, Edwards surprised Louisiana voters by conceding the election to Roemer.[2]

Over the course of 1987 and early 1988, the political opponents of Gov. Evan Mecham (R-Arizona) agonized over his performance in office and his controversial remarks, which offended a wide array of interests. A recall petition movement was started even prior to his inauguration and by fall 1987, less than a year after he had been elected, the necessary 400,000 signatures had been collected and a recall election was scheduled for May 1988.[3] Were Mecham removed from office by recall vote, he would have been only the second governor to meet this fate. North Dakota Gov. Lynn Frazier was the first in 1921 in a bitter fight within the state's Republican Party.[4]

To add to Mecham's troubles, a grand jury indicted him in January 1988 on six criminal charges relating to campaign finance violations, claiming that Mecham had failed to report a $350,000 campaign loan, had borrowed $80,000 from the Governor's Protocol Fund for his private car dealership and had interfered with a grand jury investigation involving the state police. In January, Mecham pled not guilty to the charges of fraud and perjury and was scheduled for trial in the spring.[5]

As a final blow to Mecham's political fortunes, the Arizona State House voted 46-14 on February 5 to impeach him for high crimes, misdemeanors and malfeasance of office. The 23 specific charges Mecham faced in his impeachment trial before the Arizona State Senate were almost all related to the criminal charges against him. The trial, held in March and April of 1988, focused on two charges: an obstruction of justice by blocking the probe of a death threat against an aide and of improperly loaning his automobile dealership $80,000 from a state fund. A third charge was set aside as it was the basis for the upcoming criminal prosecution.

Mecham was found guilty on both counts in a bipartisan vote of 21-9 on the first charge and

26-4 on the second. However, the Senate failed to impose the so-called "Dracula penalty" in which he would be barred from public office by failing to achieve the needed two-thirds vote by a close 17-13 decision.

After his impeachment, Mecham was removed from office and Secretary of State Rose Mofford assumed the position of acting governor under the dictates of the Arizona constitution.[6] Upon conviction, Mofford took the oath of office as governor. On April 12th, the Arizona Supreme Court canceled the May 17 recall, stating that Rose Mofford is not a "stop-gap governor," but is the new chief executive who should finish Mecham's four-year term.

These less than fine gubernatorial performances in several states has prompted one of the governorships' chief promoters to wonder if the governors in some states have declined in caliber.[7]

As can be seen from Table B, "Impeachments and Removals of Governors," Mecham was the 18th governor to be impeached and the eighth to be convicted.

Other elected executive branch officials also have had problems in the past two years. Attorney General Charlie Brown of West Virginia was acquitted of illegally soliciting campaign contributions from his employees. He argued that he simply provided his staffers with "an opportunity to give." Two of his three predecessors had been indicted and convicted of felony charges.[8]

Governors and Other Separately Elected Officials

Lieutenant Governors. For some lieutenant governors, one of the most perplexing issues has been how to reconcile their executive and legislative functions and roles. Constitutionally, most states call on their lieutenant governors to serve as the presiding officer of the state senate and to be the next-in-the-line of succession to the governor's office. Other constitutional responsibilities given some lieutenant governors include chairing a variety of boards, committees and commissions. However, little is said about the role of the lieutenant governor in the executive branch.[1] By statute, about two-thirds of the states have granted more responsibility to lieutenant governors mainly involving service on state boards and commissions. Alaska, Hawaii and Utah legislatures, however, have assigned their lieutenant governors duties normally performed by secretaries of state, thereby creating a dual role.[2]

Some of these state statutes require governors to initiate the assignment or delegation of responsibilities to the lieutenant governor. In effect, the governor defines the lieutenant governor's executive branch role.[3]

Compared to recent biennia, relationships between governors and their lieutenant governors remained relatively stable but often confusing. In Virginia, Gov. Gerald Baliles and Lt. Gov. L. Douglas Wilder, both Democrat, have clashed over use of the state's budget surplus. Wilder has seen the surplus as an opportunity to repeal the state sales tax on non-prescription medicine. Baliles wants the surplus held in reserve.[4]

In one of the latest episodes on the question of whether a lieutenant governor is a legislative or an executive officer, South Dakota voters rejected the proposed stripping of the lieutenant governor's legislative duties. The South Dakota legislature went one step further when the voters by conferring on the lieutenant governor the official position as leader of the Senate, complete with a full-time salary of $50,000. From the executive side, the governor has worked to expand the tasks of the lieutenant governor to include, for example, chairmanship of some important task forces.[5]

In a suit brought by a state senator, a Mississippi state court in 1986 struck down the practice of the lieutenant governor acting as legislative leader. The decision was based on separation of powers.[6]

Arizona now has no lieutenant governor. The secretary of state is next in the line of succession, but that office is clearly executive in nature and does not have a working relationship with the legislature.

A total of eight states do not have a lieutenant governor. Oregon, Arizona and Wyoming place the secretary of state next in the line of succession. Maine, New Hampshire, New Jersey, Tennessee and West Virginia place the president or speaker of the senate next in line. New Jersey Gov. Kean pushed for the creation of a lieutenant governor's office, but the proposal did not receive strong support in the legislature whose leaders stand next in the line of succession.[7] Of the remaining 42 states, 20 elect their lieutenant governors separately from their governors, setting up the potential for inter- or intra-party conflicts between the two officials once in office.[8]

A total of 22 states elect these officials as a team in the general elections, but only eight of these states link the two candidates together in the nomination process.[9] The need for a team approach beginning with the nomination process was amply demonstrated in the 1986 Democratic primary in Illinois when a disciple of Lyndon LaRouche captured the party's lieutenant governor's nomination. Democratic gubernatorial nominee Adlai Stevenson III resigned his position rather than standing jointly with the lieutenant governor nominee. Stevenson ran unsuccessfully as an independent candidate. With a team approach in the primary, such a situation would not have happened.[10]

In a March 1987 semi coup d'etat, opponents of Arkansas Gov. Clinton imposed a constitutional prerogative entitling them to gubernatorial duties, as both the governor and lieutenant governor were out of state, Clinton on his quest for the Democratic presidential nomination. They fired the governor's chief of staff and appointed 20 people to various state boards.[11]

Attorneys General. Several governors have had difficulty with their attorneys general. In Idaho, Democratic Gov. Andrus and Republican Attorney General Jim Jones battled over limiting state timber exports. Andrus, in the interest of protecting jobs, held that certain timber taken from state lands should not be sold for processing across state lines. Jones argued that Andrus' position was not legally tenable since the U.S. Supreme Court overruled a similar practice by Alaska.[12] In Georgia, Gov. Harris and Attorney General Mike Bowers differed over a suit Bowers brought against the state personnel board, as well as over a promotion issue. Although Harris lost the latter battle, a county Superior Court ruled against Bowers in the former case, which is now under appeal in the state's courts.[13]

In North Carolina, Republican Gov. James Martin and Democratic Attorney General Lacey Thornburgh have found themselves on both sides of the bench in law suits. In one state court suit concerning the governor's right to decide state real estate transactions rather than have the 10 member Council of State do so, Thornburgh sued on behalf of all the separately elected state officials and won.[14] The second suit, which the governor also lost, concerned the General Assembly's designation of the chief justice of the state Supreme Court to appoint the director of the Office of Administrative Hearings.[15] In a third case, Democrat Thornburgh is defending Republican Martin in a federal district court against a suit filed by three Democrats fired by the governor during his transition into office in 1985. They allege their First Amendment right of association was abridged by their "political firing." Thornburgh defended the need for the governor to be able to place his people into policy making positions upon assuming office.[16]

Arizona's attorney general's role in the Governor Mecham situation caused some problems as he was serving as prosecutor before a grand jury investigating the legality of a campaign loan while putatively in an attorney-client relationship with the governor.[17] Mecham countered by initiating an investigation of the attorney general's use of state resources to assist a private group.

The Texas attorney general has been in conflict with some of the state's powerful boards and commissions. The attorney general, the legal representative of the state's regulatory agencies, has taken stands on behalf of consumers before some of the major agencies. As of 1987, the attorney general was barred from continuing this consumer representation before the Railroad Commission, which regulates oil and gas, and the State Board of Insurance and Public Utility Commission.[18]

Superintendents of Public Instruction. How the states chief education are selected continues to be a problem. As of Jan. 1, 1986, 16 were separately elected; 29 were selected by the state's board of education - 23 directly, four with the approval of the governor and two with the approval of the legislature; and five were appointed by the governor - one directly and four with the approval of the legislature.

In 1986-87, several states addressed the issue of whether the state's chief educational officer should be elected or appointed. In 1986, the governor of Indiana called on the legislature to make the superintendent an appointed rather than elected post. The proposal followed the forced resignation of the superintendent for misusing the office for campaign purposes. The bill failed in the face of opposition from teachers, a coalition of moral groups and party leaders - all of whom feared loss of influence and patronage.[19] In 1987, the North Carolina legislature refused to place a proposed constitutional amendment on the general election ballot which would have changed the selection of the superintendent by popular election to appointment.[20] The Kentucky legislature placed a constitutional amendment before voters to shift the selection of the superintendent from an elected to an appointed post. The voters defeated the measure in the 1986 general election.[21]

Gubernatorial Powers

In a 1987 study, the National Governors' Association (NGA) analyzed "The Institutionalized Powers of the Governorship, 1965-85."[1] Based on previous studies by political scientists, the NGA study used a numerical scoring system to measure the governors' tenure potential, appointive powers, budget-making powers, veto powers, plus the legislatures' budget-changing authority and amount of party control the governor has in the legislature. The results indicate that over a 20-year period, the governor's power over the executive branch has increased while the powers over the legislative branch have declined.[2] The governors gaining the most power were in the less populous states. This may indicate the more populous states had already provided their governorships with greater powers.[3] Now for what happened in the past biennium.

Gubernatorial Tenure

The questions concerning gubernatorial tenure and succession still continue to be part of the political debate in the states.

Length of terms. All but three of the 50 states - New Hampshire, Rhode Island and Vermont - provide their governors with a four-year term. In 1986, Arkansas elected its first four-year governor. This is a reduction from 19 states in 1956.[4]

Number of terms allowed. Only three states continue to restrict their governors to a single four-year term - Kentucky, New Mexico and Virginia - down from 17 states in 1956.[5] But the Virginia General Assembly refused the governor's request for a constitutional amendment to be placed on the 1986 ballot, allowing the governor to seek two consecutive terms.[6] At the other end, 25 states now restrict their governors to no more than two, four-year terms, up from six in 1956.[7] Twenty-two states do not place any restriction on the number of terms a governor may serve.

Gubernatorial Veto

Currently, 43 states provide their governors with a general veto power in which the governor must either accept or reject a bill in its totality, while 47 state constitutions provide the governor with a form of the line item veto, usually limited to budget bills. Ten states provide for a more refined line item veto in which the governor can reduce amounts in the lines of budget rather than having to veto the line entirely. Seven states go even further by allowing a partial veto in which the governor can condition his or her approval of a bill with suggested rewording or amendments to the bill.[8]

The line item veto and its variants has proven to be the source of considerable controversy. A recent survey suggests there are at least four consequences which follow from the use of this veto: (1) It profoundly alters the relationship of the legislature to the governor, to the advantage of the latter; (2) It increases the number of formal confrontations between the two branches; (3) It spawns procedures to neutralize its impact; and (4) It precipitates litigation between the two branches, thereby introducing the judiciary into the law-making process at an early stage in its role as umpire.[9]

The role of the courts in this conflict over the line item veto has grown in recent years. Since 1893 there have been more than 113 court decisions on disputes between the branches over this veto, 50 of them in the last 15 years alone as the conflicts between the two political branches have escalated. These cases included a U.S. Supreme Court Decision and two federal appellate court decisions.[10]

Legislative leaders in Wisconsin have filed suit in the state's Supreme Court to invalidate Gov. Tommy Thompson's use of the partial veto 290 times in approving the 1987-89 biennial budget. The partial veto was adopted in 1930. Thompson's creative use of the veto allowed him to change legislative intent by excising isolated digits, letters and words even to the point of creating new words.[11]

The "separation of powers" war in North Carolina continues as the 1987 Democratic General Assembly again refused to approve a proposed constitutional amendment to provide the governor with veto powers.[12]

Gubernatorial Appointment and Removal Powers

Since 1945, states have been paying more

attention to the governor's power of removal as they rewrite or amend their constitutions. Afterall, to be able to appoint a person to a position, a governor must be able to remove the current holder of the position. Fifteen states have revised their organic documents or adopted new constitutions since WWII and only three, Connecticut (1965), Georgia (1982) and North Carolina (1971), have no explicit mention of the governor's right to remove officials. Several other states already had such a provision in their constitutions so that 22 states now provide their governors with a constitutionally based power of removal.[13] The Indiana governor's broad power of removal was granted by a state court decision. In two recent actions, Wyoming voters rejected an amendment providing their governor with this power in 1984, but adopted such an amendment in 1986.

Only eight of these constitutional provisions grant their governors complete power of removal. Restrictions placed on this power involve: the *cause*, (the reasons, or lack thereof, a governor must provide in removing someone from office); the *scope*, (which officers may or may not be removed); and the *process*, (how does the removal occur and who else must be involved). The most frequent constitutional restrictions relate to cause, followed by the process and lastly scope. This does not include the wide range of statutory provisions in the states, nor the array of state court cases addressing this power.[14]

Since 1976, governors have faced increasingly difficult problems in their ability to staff their administration. Three U.S. Supreme Court decisions have constrained the flexibility of elected officials to fire government employees from positions to which they want to appoint their own supporters. In the 1976 case, *Elrod v. Burns*, the court ruled patronage firing violates an individual's freedom to hold whatever political beliefs and to make whatever political associations he or she wants under the First Amendment of the U.S. Constitution; "political belief and association constitute the core of those activities protected by the First Amendment." Such dismissals were to be limited to policymaking positions only in order that "policies that the electorate has sanctioned are fully implemented."[15]

In the 1980 case, *Branti v. Finkel*, the court affirmed the earlier decision protecting a public employee from patronage firing based on what the employee believes. However, the court did provide some potential limitations on this restriction of the removal power by indicating that "the First Amendment rights may be required to yield to the state's vital interest . . . if an employee's private political beliefs would interfere with the discharge of his public duties."[16] In the 1983 case, *Connick v. Myers*, the court added another restriction by holding "the first Amendment does not protect from dismissal public employees who complain about their working conditions or their supervisor."[17]

These three decisions have led to several lawsuits in the states in which fired employees charge they were terminated for patronage or political reasons.

Gubernatorial Transitions

One of the unique aspects of our governmental systems, the peaceful transfer of executive power or transition between governors, appears to be occuring smoothly even in states undergoing a change in party control. Fewer horror stories are being told of empty files and offices, fights over which governor has the right to appoint a major official, two armed camps not communicating and other similar ills.

Some indicators of how the states and the governors involved are working for smoother transitions are the increase in meetings between the outgoing and incoming governors, lack of complaints by new governors about cooperation, preparation of manuals and briefing papers by the old administration for the new, a reduction of "lame-duck" appointments by the outgoing governors, newly elected governors being invited to become part of the budgetary process prior to their inauguration, and more willingness by new governors to retain professionally qualified individuals - even in positions to which political appointments can be made.[1]

In a 1986 move to ease transition problems, Louisiana voters agreed to shorten the period between the election of state officials and the date they take office. Effective in 1992, these officials will take office in January, two months earlier than they do now.

The National Governors' Association

The National Governors' Association has done much to assist new governors in their preparations to enter office by holding a New Governors' Seminar within two weeks of the general election in the even numbered years. The incumbent governors serve as staff. The subjects addressed in these seminars are of direct concern to the newly elected governor: organizing the governor's office; press and public relations; management of the executive branch; executive-legislative relations; the governorship as a partnership involving one's spouse; and the transition period.[1] In addition, printed materials and guidebooks have been prepared for the newly elected governors[2] and transition assistance is made available upon call. The transition assistance program has been an on-going responsibility of NGA since the early 1970s.

Within the last few years, NGA has taken additional steps to further governors' impact on public policy. Under the guidance of NGA Chairman Lamar Alexander (R-Tennessee, 1979-87), NGA and the governors conducted a 50-state assessment of the status of American education. Seven gubernatorial directed subcommittees assessed components of educational policy and presented their report at the NGA 1986 Annual Meeting, *Time for Results: The Governors' 1991 Report on Education*.[3] The report set an agenda for each governor to follow and, through 1991, they are to report at the annual meeting on the specific steps taken to achieve educational reform in each state.

The next NGA chairman, Bill Clinton (D-Arizona, 1979-1981, 1983-date), led a similarly focused effort on economic development and job creation which culminated in the report, *Making America Work: Productive People, Productive Policies*, at the 1987 NGA Annual Meeting.[4] The 1988 meeting will be focusing on the changing balance in the federal system under the direction of Chairman John Sununu (R-New Hampshire, 1983-date). Three separate concerns are involved: identifying changes in federal rules that would enable state governments to operate more effectively; examining the existing federal laws affecting states; and developing a broad, direct, overall approach to restoring the balance of power.[5]

References

Note: This chapter was prepared with the assistance of Joel Alan Boyette and Scott Mouw, graduate students in the Department of Political Science, University of North Carolina at Chapel Hill.

Introduction
[1] See Louis Harris, "Why the Odds Are Against a Governor's Becoming President," *Public Opinion Quarterly* 23:3 (Fall 1959), pp. 361-70.

Gubernatorial Elections
[1] See Gerald Benjamin, "The Power of Incumbency," *Empire State Report* (April 1987), pp. 33-37.

Gubernatorial Campaign Costs
[1] They were: Hunt, Alabama; Cowper, Alaska; Mecham, Arizona; Romer, Colorado; Martinez, Florida; Waihee, Hawaii; Hayden, Kansas; Blanchard, Michigan; Bellmon, Oklahoma; DiPrete, Rhode Island; McWherter, Tennessee; Clement, Texas; and Sullivan, Wyoming. DiPrete was the only incumbent governor.
[2] They were: Clinton, Arkansas; Deukmejian, California; O'Neill, Connecticut; Harris, Georgia; Thompson, Illinois; Branstad, Iowa; Dukakis, Massachusetts; Perpich, Minnesota; Bryan, Nevada; Sununu, New Hampshire; Cuomo, New York; Celeste, Ohio; and Kunin, Vermont.
[3] In addition to those listed in footnote 2 above: White of Texas. Incumbents who were outspent in the election were: Sheffield, Alaska; Blanchard, Michigan; DiPrete, Rhode Island; and Earl, Wisconsin. Sheffield lost in the Democratic Party primary, Earl in the general election.
[4] Gail B. Manning and Edward F. Feigenbaum, comp., *The Lieutenant Governor: The Office and Its Powers* (Lexington, Ky.: The National Conference of Lieutenant Governors by The Council of State Governments, 1987), p. 10.

Gubernatorial Investigations
[1] For a discussion of this saga see: Clive S. Thomas, "'The Thing' that Shook Alaska," *State Legislatures* 13:2 (February 1987), pp. 22-25.
[2] Bob Benenson, "The Edwards 'Hayride' Ends: Rep. Roemer to Be Governor," *Congressinal Quarterly Weekly Report* 45:44 (Oct. 31, 1987), pp. 2687-89.
[3] "The Governor's Problems in Arizona," *State Policy Reports* 6:3 (February 1988), pp. 23-26.
[4] Dave Kaplan, "Arizona's Mecham: The Troubles He's Seen," *Congressional Quarterly Weekly Report* 46:1 (Jan. 2, 1988), p. 6.
[5] Robert Lindsey, "What in the World Is Going

On in Arizona?," *New York Times* (Jan. 24, 1988).

[6]"Mecham Trial Starts Feb. 22," *Congressional Quarterly Weekly Report* 46:7 (Feb. 13, 1988), p. 291.

[7]Larry Sabato query at the "Symposium on the State of the States," Eagleton Institute, Rutgers University, Dec. 17, 1987. His book, *Good-bye to Goodtime Charlie* published by Lexington Books in 1978 and CQ Press in 1983, argued that not only was the governorship stronger in the states, but that many very able governors have served in recent decades.

[8]AP Wire story, "W. Va. attorney general acquitted in campaign-law case," (Raleigh) *News and Observer* (Nov. 20, 1986), p. 2A.

Governors and Other Separately Elected Officials
[1]Manning and Feigenbaum, pp. 3, 5.
[2]Ibid., pp. 5-7.
[3]Ibid., p. 6.
[4]"Some Governors Get No Respect," *Governing* 1:2 (November 1987), p. 67.
[5]*State Policy Reports* 5:10 (May 30, 1987), p. 10.
[6]"Lieutenant Governors as Legislative Leaders," *State Policy Reports* 4:23 (1986), p. 27.
[7]Alice Chasan Edelman, "Is There Room at the Top?," *New Jersey Reporter* (March 1986), pp. 8-12.
[8]Manning and Feigenbaum, p. 2.
[9]Ibid.
[10]Ibid., p. 7.
[11]Deborah Burroughs, "What Happens When a Governor Wants to be President," *Comparative State Politics Newsletter* 8:3 (June 1987), p. 25.
[12]"Some Governors Get No Respect."
[13]Ibid.
[14]*Martin v. Thornburgh*, (1987); see also Steve Riley and Jane Ruffin, "State high court rules against Martin in territorial tangles," *Raleigh News and Observer* (Sept. 4, 1987), pp. 1A ff.
[15]*Martin v. Melott*, (1987).
[16]Steve Riley, "Martin amasses bills for challenging laws," *Raleigh News and Observer* (Jan. 3, 1988), pp. 23A, 26A.
[17]"Attorneys General," *State Policy Reports* 5:20 (Nov. 9, 1987), p. 26.
[18]Ibid., pp. 25-26.
[19]Robert X. Browning, "1986 Indiana Legislative Report," *Comparative State Politics*

Newsletter 7:3 (June 1985), p. 13.
[20]Joel Thompson, "The 1987 North Carolina General Assembly," *Comparative State Politics Newsletter* 8:5 (October 1987), p. 3.
[21]*State Policy Reports* 4:8 (April 1986), p. 25.

Governors' Powers
[1]Office of State Services, *State Management Notes*, "The Institutionalized Powers of the Governorship, 1965-1985," (Washington, DC: National Governors' Association, 1987).
[2]Thad L. Beyle, "The Institutionalized Powers of the Governorship; 1965-1985," *Comparative State Politics Newsletter* 9:1 (February 1988), pp. 26-27.
[3]Ibid., pp. 26-29.
[4]Advisory Commission on Intergovernmental Relations, *The Question of State Government Capability* (Washington, DC: ACIR, 1985), p. 129.
[5]Ibid.
[6]John J. McGlennon, "The 1986 Session of the Virginia General Assembly," *Comparative State Politics Newsletter* 7:3 (June 1985), p. 19.
[7]Advisory Commission, p. 129.
[8]Ronald C. Moe, "Prospects for the Item Veto at the Federal Level: Lessons from the States," (Washington, DC: National Academy of Public Administration, 1988), pp. 3-5.
[9]Ibid., pp. 1-2.
[10]Ibid., pp. 17, 32.
[11]"Wis. Court Asked to Veto Vetoes," *Governing* 1:4 (January 1988), p. 58.
[12]Thompson, p. 4.
[13]Those states changing their constitutions since 1945 are Missouri (1945), New Jersey (1947), Hawaii (1950), Alaska (1956), Michigan (1963), Florida (1968), Pennsylvania (1968), Illinois (1970), Virginia (1971), Montana (1972) and Louisiana (1979). Other states with a constitutional provision are: Colorado, Delaware, Maryland, Mississippi, Nebraska, New Mexico, New York, South Carolina, South Dakota and West Virginia.
[14]Thad L. Beyle, "Report to the Attorney General's Office of the State of North Carolina re: *Stott v. Martin*," unpublished paper, September 1987.
[15]Elder Witt, "Patronage Firings," *Congressional Quarterly Weekly Report* 34:27 (July 3, 1976), p. 1726.
[16]Elder Witt, "Supreme Court Deals Blow to Public Employee Firings for Political Reasons," *Congressional Quarterly Weekly*

Report 38:14 (April 5, 1980), pp. 899-890

[17]Elder Witt, "Employee Rights," *Congressional Quarterly Report* 41:16 (April 6, 1983), pp. 791-792.

Gubernatorial Transitions

[1]"Transitions," State Policy Reports 4:23 (Dec. 16, 1986), p. 25.

The National Governors' Association

[1]Thad L. Beyle, "Gubernatorial Transitions: Lessons From the 1982-1983 Experience," *Publius* 14:3 (Summer 1984), p. 13.

[2]The National Governors' Conference, *The Critical Hundred Days: A Handbook for New Governors* (Washington, DC: NGC, 1975); National Governors' Association, *The Governor's Office* (Washington, DC: NGA, 1976); *Governing the American States: A Handbook for New Governors* (Washington, DC: NGA, 1978); *Transition and the New Governors: A Critical Overview* (Washington, DC: NGA, 1982); and, Office of State Service, *Management Note:* "The Transition: A View from Academia," (Washington, DC: NGA, 1986).

[3]National Governors' Association, *Time for Results: The Governors' 1991 Report on Education* (Washington, DC: NGA, 1986).

[4]National Governors' Association, *Making America Work: Productive People, Productive Policies* (Washington, DC: NGA, 1987).

[5]"Sununu Presents Agenda as New NGA Chairman," *Governors' Weekly Bulletin* 21:31 (August 7, 1987), pp. 1-2.

Table 2.1
THE GOVERNORS
1988

State or other jurisdiction	Name and party	Length of regular term in years	Date of first service	Present term ends	Number of previous terms	Maximum consecutive terms allowed by constitution	Joint election of governor and lieutenant governor (a)	Official who succeeds governor	Birthdate	Birth-place
Alabama	Harold Guy Hunt (R)	4	1/87	1/91		2	No	LG	6/17/33	Ala.
Alaska	Steve Cowper (D)	4	12/86	12/90		2	Yes	LG	8/21/38	N.C.
Arizona	Rose Mofford (D)	4	4/88	(u)			(b)	SS	6/10/22	Ariz.
Arkansas	Bill Clinton (D)	4	1/79	1/91	3(c)	2(c)	No	LG	8/19/46	Ark.
California	George Deukmejian (R)	4	1/83	1/91	1		No	LG	6/6/28	N.Y.
Colorado	Roy Romer (D)	4	1/87	1/91			Yes	LG	10/28/28	Colo.
Connecticut	William A. O'Neill (D)	4	12/80	1/91	1(d)	2(e)	Yes	LG	8/11/30	Conn.
Delaware	Michael N. Castle (R)	4	1/85	1/89		2	No	LG	7/2/39	Del.
Florida	Bob Martinez (R)	4	1/87	1/91		2	No	LG	12/25/34	Fla.
Georgia	Joe Frank Harris (D)	4	1/83	1/91			No	LG	2/26/36	Ga.
Hawaii	John D. Waihee III (D)	4	1/86	1/90		2	Yes	LG	5/19/46	Hawaii
Idaho	Cecil D. Andrus (D)	4	1/71	1/91	2(k)		No	LG	8/25/31	Ore.
Illinois	James R. Thompson (R)	4	1/77	1/91	3(f)		Yes	LG	5/8/36	Ill.
Indiana	Robert D. Orr (R)	4	1/81	1/89	1	2	Yes	LG	11/17/17	Ind.
Iowa	Terry Branstad (R)	4	1/83	1/91	1		No	LG	11/17/46	Iowa
Kansas	Mike Hayden (R)	4	1/87	1/91			Yes	LG	3/16/44	Kan.
Kentucky	Wallace G. Wilkinson (D)	4	1/88	1/92		(g)	No	LG	12/12/41	Ky.
Louisiana	Buddy Roemer (D)	4	3/88	3/92		2	No	LG	10/4/43	La.
Maine	John R. McKernan Jr. (R)	4	1/87	1/91		2	(b)	PS	5/20/48	Maine
Maryland	William Donald Schaefer (D)	4	1/87	1/91		2	Yes	LG	11/2/21	Md.
Massachusetts	Michael S. Dukakis (D)	4	1/75	1/91	2(h)		Yes	LG	11/3/33	Mass.
Michigan	James J. Blanchard (D)	4	1/83	1/91	1(i)		Yes	LG	8/8/42	Mich.
Minnesota	Rudy Perpich (DFL)	4	12/76	1/91			Yes	LG	6/27/28	Minn.
Mississippi	Ray Mabus (D)	4	1/88	1/92		1	No	LG	10/11/48	Miss.
Missouri	John Ashcroft (R)	4	1/85	1/89		2(e)	No	LG	5/9/42	Mo.
Montana	Ted Schwinden (D)	4	1/81	1/89	1		Yes	LG	8/31/25	Mont.
Nebraska	Kay A. Orr (R)	4	1/87	1/91	1	2	Yes	LG	1/2/39	Iowa
Nevada	Richard H. Bryan (D)	4	1/83	1/91	1	2	No	LG	6/16/37	D.C.
New Hampshire	John H. Sununu (R)	2	1/83	1/87	1		(b)	PS	7/2/39	Cuba
New Jersey	Thomas H. Kean (R)	4	1/82	1/90	1	2	(b)	PS	4/21/35	N.Y.
New Mexico	Garry E. Carruthers (R)	4	1/87	1/91	1	(g,v)	Yes	LG	8/29/39	Colo.
New York	Mario M. Cuomo (D)	4	1/83	1/91	1		Yes	LG	6/15/32	N.Y.
North Carolina	James G. Martin (R)	4	1/85	1/89		2(e)	No	LG	12/11/36	Ga.
North Dakota	George A. Sinner (D)	4	1/85	1/89			Yes	LG	5/29/28	N.D.
Ohio	Richard F. Celeste (D)	4	1/83	1/91	1	2	Yes	LG	11/11/37	Ohio

THE GOVERNORS—Continued

State or other jurisdiction	Name and party	Length of regular term in years	Date of first service	Present term ends	Number of previous terms	Maximum consecutive terms allowed by constitution	Joint election of governor and lieutenant governor (a)	Official who succeeds governor	Birthdate	Birthplace
Oklahoma	Henry Bellmon (R)	4	1/63	1/91	1(j)	2	No	LG	9/3/21	Okla.
Oregon	Neil Goldschmidt (D)	4	1/87	1/91		2(l)	(b)	SS	6/16/40	Ore.
Pennsylvania	Robert P. Casey (D)	4	1/87	1/91		2	Yes	LG	1/9/32	N.Y.
Rhode Island	Edward D. DiPrete (R)	2	1/85	1/89			No	LG	7/8/34	R.I.
South Carolina	Carroll A. Campbell Jr. (R)	4	1/87	1/91		2	No	LG	7/24/40	S.C.
South Dakota	George S. Mickelson (R)	4	1/87	1/91		2	Yes	LG	1/31/41	S.D.
Tennessee	Ned Ray McWherter (D)	4	1/87	1/91		2	No	SpS(n)	10/15/30	Tenn.
Texas	William P. Clements Jr. (R)	4	1/79	1/91	1(m)		No	LG	4/13/17	Texas
Utah	Norman H. Bangerter (R)	4	1/85	1/89			Yes	LG	1/4/33	Utah
Vermont	Madeleine Kunin (D)	2	1/85	1/89	1		No	LG	9/28/33	Switz.
Virginia	Gerald L. Baliles (D)	4	1/86	1/90		(g)	No	LG	7/8/40	Va.
Washington	Booth Gardner (D)	4	1/85	1/89			No	LG	8/21/36	Wash.
West Virginia	Arch A. Moore, Jr. (R)	4	1/69	1/89	2(o)	2(p)	(b)	PS	4/16/36	W.V.
Wisconsin	Tommy Thompson (R)	4	1/87	1/91			Yes	LG	11/19/41	Wis.
Wyoming	Michael (Mike) J. Sullivan (D)	4	1/87	1/91			(b)	SS	9/22/39	Neb.
American Samoa	A.P. Lutali (t)	4	1/85	1/89		2(r)	Yes	LG	12/24/19	A.S.
Guam	Joseph Ada (R)	4	1/87	1/91		3(s)	Yes	LG	12/11/27	Guam
No. Mariana Is.	Pedro P. Tenorio (R)	4	1/82	1/90	1		Yes	LG	4/18/34	Saipan
Puerto Rico	Rafael Hernandez-Colon (PDP)	4	1/73	1/89	1(x)		(b)	SS	10/24/36	P.R.
Virgin Islands	Alexander A. Farrelly (D)	4	1/87	1/91		2	Yes	LG	12/29/33	V.I.

(a) The following also choose candidates for governor and lieutenant governor through a joint nomination process: Florida, Kansas, Maryland, Minnesota, Montana, North Dakota, Ohio, Utah, American Samoa, and Guam.
(b) No lieutenant governor.
(c) Served 1979-81, 1983-85, and 1985-87. In 1984, a constitutional amendment passed which changes to four years the length of the governor's term, with a maximum of two terms (effective with the 1986 election).
(d) Succeeded to governor's office December 1980. Elected to first full term November 1982.
(e) Absolute two-term limit, but not necessarily consecutive.
(f) First term was for two years, four years thereafter.

(g) Successive terms forbidden.
(h) Served 1975-79 and 1983-87.
(i) Succeeded to governor's office December 1976 to serve remainder of unexpired term. Elected to first full term November 1982.
(j) Served 1963-67.
(k) Resigned in 1977 to accept appointment as U.S. Secretary of the Interior.
(l) Prohibited from serving more than eight years out of a twelve year period.
(m) Served 1979-83.
(n) Official bears the additional statutory title of "lieutenant governor."
(o) Served 1969-73, and 1973-77.
(p) Prohibited from serving in the term immediately following two consecutive terms regardless of whether the terms were filled in whole or in part.
(q) American Samoa has no political party system.
(r) Limit is statutory.
(s) Absolute three-term limitation, but not necessarily consecutive.
(t) Served 1973-77.
(u) Succeeded to governor's office April 1988 as a result of her predecessor's impeachment.
(v) Beginning in 1991, governor limited to 2 consecutive 4-year terms.

Key:
D—Democrat
DFL—Democrat-Farmer-Labor
I—Independent
PDP—Popular Democratic Party
R—Republican
LG—Lieutenant governor
SS—Secretary of state
PS—President of the senate
SpS—Speaker of the senate

Table 2.2
THE GOVERNORS: QUALIFICATIONS FOR OFFICE

State or other jurisdiction	Minimum age	State citizen (years)	U.S. citizen (years)	State resident (years)	Qualified voter (years)
Alabama	30	7	10	7	...
Alaska	30	...	7	7	★
Arizona	25	5	10	...	...
Arkansas	30	...	★	7	★
California	18	...	5	5	★
Colorado	30	...	★	2	...
Connecticut	30	...	...	...	★
Delaware	30	...	12	6	...
Florida	30	...	...	7	★
Georgia	30	6	15	6	...
Hawaii	30	...	★	5	★
Idaho	30	...	★	2	...
Illinois	25	...	★	3	...
Indiana	30	...	5	5	...
Iowa	30	...	★	2	...
Kansas	...	...	...	...	...
Kentucky	30	6	★	6	...
Louisiana	25	5	5	...	★
Maine	30	...	15	5	...
Maryland	30	...	(a)	5	5
Massachusetts	...	...	...	7	...
Michigan(b)	30	...	...	...	4
Minnesota	25	...	★	1	...
Mississippi	30	...	20	5	...
Missouri	30	...	15	10	...
Montana(c)	25	★	★	2	...
Nebraska	30	5	5	5	...
Nevada	25	2	...	2	★
New Hampshire	30	...	...	7	...
New Jersey	30	...	20	7	...
New Mexico	30	...	★	5	★
New York	30	...	★	5	...
North Carolina	30	...	5	2	...
North Dakota	30	...	★	5	★
Ohio(d)	...	...	...	...	★
Oklahoma	31	...	★	...	10
Oregon	30	...	★	3	...
Pennsylvania	30	...	★	7	...
Rhode Island(e)	...	...	...	...	★
South Carolina	30	5	★	5	...
South Dakota	...	...	2	2	...
Tennessee	30	7	★	...	...
Texas	30	...	★	5	...
Utah	30	5	...	5	★
Vermont	...	...	...	4	...
Virginia	30	...	★	5	5
Washington	18	...	★	...	★
West Virginia	30	5	★	★	★
Wisconsin	...	...	★	...	★
Wyoming	30	...	★	5	★
American Samoa	35	...	★(f)	5	...
Guam	30	...	5	5	★
No. Mariana Is.	30	...	...	7	...
Puerto Rico	35	5	5	5	...
Virgin Islands	30	...	5	5	★

Note: This table includes constitutional and statutory qualifications.
Key:
★—Formal provision; number of years not specified.
...—No formal provision.
(a) *Crosse v. Board of Supervisors of Elections* 243 Md. 555, 221A.2d431 (1966)—opinion rendered indicated that U.S. citizenship was, by necessity, a requirement for office.
(b) A person convicted of felony or breach of public trust is not eligible to the office for a period of 20 years after conviction.
(c) A person convicted of a felony is not eligible to hold office until his final discharge from state supervision.
(d) A person convicted of embezzlement of public funds is not eligible to hold office.
(e) A person convicted of bribery is not eligible to hold office.
(f) U.S. citizen or U.S. national.

Table 2.3
THE GOVERNORS: COMPENSATION

State or other jurisdiction	Salary	Governor's office staff(a)	Access to state transportation			Travel allowance	Official residence
			Automobile	Airplane	Helicopter		
Alabama	$70,223	22	★	★	★	(b)	★
Alaska	81,648	67	★	...	...	(b)	★
Arizona	75,000	23	★	★	...	(b)	...
Arkansas	35,000	48	★	...	...	(c)	★
California	85,000	84	★	...	...	(c)	(d)
Colorado	70,000	41.5	★	★	...	(e)	★
Connecticut	78,000	38	★	...	(f)	(e)	★
Delaware	70,000	22	★	...	★	$ 18,500(c)	★
Florida	96,646	122 (g)	★	...	...	(b)	★
Georgia	84,594	50	★	★	...	(e)	★
Hawaii	80,000	33	★	...	...	(e)	★
Idaho	55,000	15 (h)	★	★	...	(e)	★(i)
Illinois	93,266	135	★	★	★	220,000(b)	★
Indiana	77,200	34	★	★	★	0	★
Iowa	70,000	10	★	★	...	(b)	★
Kansas	65,693	22	★	★	...	(e)	★
Kentucky	68,364	78	★	★	★	(b)	★
Louisiana	73,400	46	★	★	★	32,000(c)	★
Maine	70,000	21	★	★	...	(e)	★
Maryland	85,000	109 (j)	★	★	★	(e)	★
Massachusetts	85,000	100	★	★	★	(e)	...
Michigan	100,077	45	★	★	★	(c)	★
Minnesota	94,204	30	★	★	★	(c)	★
Mississippi	63,000	39 (k)	★	★	★	24,017(c,e)	★
Missouri	81,000	33	★	★	...	(c)	★
Montana	50,452	23	★	★	★	(b)	★
Nebraska	58,000	13	★	★	★	(b)	★
Nevada	77,500 (l)	16	★	★	...	(c)	★
New Hampshire	68,005	25	★	...	...	(e)	★
New Jersey	85,000	60	★	...	★	(m)	★(i)
New Mexico	63,000	38	★	★	★	(c)	★
New York	130,000 (m)	216	★	★	★	(b)	★
North Carolina	105,000	84	★	★	★	11,500	★
North Dakota	60,856	15.25	★	★	...	(e)	★
Ohio	65,000	30	★	★	★	(e)	★
Oklahoma	70,000	34	★	★	...	(e)	★
Oregon	73,500	44	★	...	...	0	★
Pennsylvania	85,000	60	★	★	...	(b)	★
Rhode Island	69,900	49	★	★	★	8,500(c)	★(i)
South Carolina	81,600	28	★	★	...	20,000	★
South Dakota	57,324	26	★	★	...	(e)	★
Tennessee	85,000	40	★	★	★	(e)	★
Texas	91,600	178	...	★	★	(b)	★
Utah	60,000	14	★	★	...	(c)	★
Vermont	63,600	21	★	...	...	(e)	...
Virginia	85,000	36	★	★	★	(b)	★
Washington	83,800	37	★	★	...	N.A.	★
West Virginia	72,000	42	★	★	★	(n)	★
Wisconsin	86,149	34	★	★	...	(e)	★
Wyoming	70,000	8 (o)	★	★	...	(c)	★
American Samoa	50,000	25	★	...	...	(c)	★
Guam	50,000	N.A.	★	...	...	N.A.	★
Puerto Rico	45,000	N.A.	★	...	★	N.A.	★
Virgin Islands	64,400	N.A.	★	...	...	N.A.	★

Key:
★—Yes
. . . —No
N.A.—Not available

(a) Definitions of "governor's office staff" vary across the states—from general office support to staffing for various operations within the executive office.

(b) Reimbursed for travel expenses. Alabama—reimbursed up to $40/d in state; actual expenses out of state. Alaska—governor is reimbursed $80/d or if exceed for actual amount. Arizona—reimbursed for actual expenses to a maximum of $40/d in state and $75/d out of state. Florida—reimbursed at same rate as other state officials: in state, choice between per diem or actual expenses; out of state, actual expenses. Idaho—standard per diem, $15/d in state; $20/d out of state. Iowa—No set allowance. Kentucky—mileage at same rate as other state employees. Montana—reimbursed for actual and necessary expenses in state up to $55/d, and actual lodging plus meal allowance up to $30/d out of state (no annual limit). Nebraska—reasonable and necessary expenses. New York—reimbursed for actual and necessary expenses. Pennsylvania—reimbursed for reasonable expenses. Texas—reimbursed for actual expenses.

(c) Amount includes travel allowance for entire staff. Arkansas, Michigan, Missouri—amount not available. California—$130,000 in state;

$27,000 out of state. Nevada—$19,411 in state, $9,389 out of state. New Mexico—$67,400 in state, $48,400 out of state. Utah—$9,600 in state, $26,000 out of state. Wyoming—$45,536 in state; $46,158 out of state. American Samoa—$142,000.

(d) In California—provided by Governor's Residence Foundation, a non-profit organization which provides a residence for the governor of California. No rent is charged; maintenance and operational costs are provided by California Department of General Services.

(e) Travel allowance included in office budget.

(f) Emergency authorization for use of National Guard's.

(g) Does not include Office of Planning and Budgeting and a number of state commissions located within executive office of governor for budget purposes.

(h) Number on staff varies from 12 to 20 during the year.

(i) Governor does not occupy residence.

(j) Includes positions added when Criminal Justice Coordinating Council moved into governor's office.

(k) Currently 18; budget request is for 39.

(l) On employee/employer paid retirement system.

(m) Accepts $100,000.

(n) Included in general expense account.

(o) Also has state planning coordinator with staff of 9.

Table 2.4
THE GOVERNORS: POWERS

State or other jurisdiction	Budget-making power — Full responsibility	Budget-making power — Shares responsibility	Veto power(a) — No item veto	Veto power(a) — Item veto-2/3 legislators present to override	Veto power(a) — Item veto-majority legislators elected to override	Veto power(a) — Item veto-3/5 legislators elected to override	Veto power(a) — Item veto-at least 2/3 legislators elected to override	Authorization for reorganization through executive order(b)	Other statewide elected officials(c) — Number of officials	Other statewide elected officials(c) — Number of agencies
Alabama	★				★				17	8
Alaska	★						★	C	1	0(d)
Arizona	★						★		8	6
Arkansas	★				★				6	6
California		★					★	S	6	7
Colorado		★					★		4	16
Connecticut	★						★	C	5	5
Delaware	★					★		C	5	5
Florida	★						★	S	6	6
Georgia	★						★		12	8
Hawaii	★						★	(e)	14	2
Idaho	★						★		6	0
Illinois	★						★	C	14	5(f)
Indiana	★		★						6	6
Iowa	★						★		6	6
Kansas	★			★				C	15	6
Kentucky		★			★			S	7	7
Louisiana		★					★	S	21	10
Maine	★		★						0	0
Maryland	★					★		C	3	3
Massachusetts	★(g)			★				C	5	6
Michigan	★						★	C	35	7
Minnesota		★					★	S	5	5
Mississippi	★						★	S	13	9
Missouri	★			★				C	5	5
Montana	★						★		10	6
Nebraska	★					★		S	26	8
Nevada	★		★						23	7
New Hampshire	★		★						5	1
New Jersey	★						★		0	0
New Mexico		★		★					8	19
New York	★		(h)						3	3
North Carolina		★						C	9	9
North Dakota	★						★		13	11
Ohio	★					★			28	6

THE GOVERNORS: POWERS—Continued

State or other jurisdiction	Budget-making power		Veto power(a)					Authorization for reorganization through executive order(b)	Other statewide elected officials(c)	
	Full responsibility	Shares responsibility	No item veto	Item veto—2/3 legislators present to override	Item veto—majority legislators elected to override	Item veto—3/5 legislators elected to override	Item veto—at least 2/3 legislators elected to override		Number of officials	Number of agencies
Oklahoma	★	...	...	...	...	...	★	S	9	7
Oregon	★	...	...	★	...	...	...	...	5	5
Pennsylvania	★	...	...	...	...	...	★	...	4	4
Rhode Island	★	...	★	...	...	...	...	...	4	4
South Carolina	...	★	...	★	...	...	...	...	8	10(i)
South Dakota	★	...	...	...	...	...	★	C	9	7
Tennessee	★	...	...	...	★	...	...	S	3	1
Texas	...	★	...	★	...	...	...	...	29	8
Utah	★	...	...	...	...	...	★	...	14	4
Vermont	★	...	★	...	...	...	...	S	5	5
Virginia	★	...	...	★	...	...	...	S(j)	2	2
Washington	★	...	...	★	...	...	...	...	8	8
West Virginia	★	...	...	★	...	...	...	S	5	5
Wisconsin	★	...	...	...	★(k)	...	...	...	5	5
Wyoming	★	...	...	...	...	...	★	...	4	4
American Samoa	...	★	...	...	...	...	★	S	1	1
Guam	...	★	...	...	...	...	★	C	36	3
No. Mariana Is.	★	...	...	...	...	...	★	...	1	1
Puerto Rico	★	...	...	...	...	...	★	...	1	0
Virgin Islands	★	...	...	...	...	...	★	...	1	1

Sources: The National Governors' Association 1985 survey of governors' offices; The Council of State Governments; and state constitutions and statutes.

Key:
C—Constitutional
S—Statutory

(a) In all states, except North Carolina, governor has the power to veto bills passed by the state legislature. The information presented here refers to the governor's power to *item* veto—veto items within a bill—and the votes needed in the state legislature to override the item veto. For additional information on vetoes and veto overrides, as well as the number of days the governor is allowed to consider bills, see Table 3.14, "Enacting Legislation: Veto, Veto Overrides and Effective Date."

(b) For additional information on executive, orders, see Table 2.5, "Gubernatorial Executive Orders: Authorization, Provisions, Procedures."

(c) Includes only executive branch officials who are popularly elected either on a constitutional or statutory basis (elected members of state boards of education, public utilities commissions, university regents, or other state boards or commissions are also included); the number of agencies involving these officials is also listed.

(d) Lieutenant governor's office is part of governor's office.
(e) Implied through a broad interpretation of gubernatorial authority; no formal provision.
(f) Governor has administrative control over agencies.
(g) Full to propose; legislature adopts or revises; and governor signs or vetoes.
(h) Governor has no veto power.
(i) Divisions within governor's office.
(j) For shifting agencies between secretarial offices; all other reorganizations require legislative approval.
(k) For budget and supplemental appropriations bills, 2/3 legislators elected necessary to override.

Table 2.5

GUBERNATORIAL EXECUTIVE ORDERS: AUTHORIZATION, PROVISIONS, PROCEDURES

State or other jurisdiction	Authorization for executive orders	Provisions: Civil defense disasters, public emergencies	Provisions: Energy emergencies and conservation	Provisions: Other emergencies	Provisions: Executive branch reorganization plans and agency creation	Provisions: Create advisory, coordinating, study or investigative committees/commissions	Provisions: Respond to federal programs and requirements	Provisions: State personnel administration	Provisions: Other administration	Procedures: Filing and publication procedures	Procedures: Subject to administrative procedure act	Procedures: Subject to legislative review
Alabama	S,I(a)			★(b)	★	★				★(c,d)		
Alaska	C	★(a)	★(a)	★(a)	★	★	★			★(c)		
Arizona	S,I	★	★(a)	★	★	★	★	★	★	★(c)		
Arkansas	S,I(e)	★	★	★	★	★	★	★	★	★		
California	S	★	★	★(f)	★	★	★					
Colorado	S	★	★		★		★					
Connecticut	S	★	★	★	★	★	★		★(g,h)			
Delaware	C	★		★(i)	★	★	★		★	★		
Florida	C,S	★	★	★	★	★	★		★			
Georgia	S,I(e)				★		★					
Hawaii	I(a)		★	★	★				★(h,j)	★(c)		
Idaho	S		I	I	I	I	I			★(c)		
Illinois	C		I		★	I				★(c)		★(k)
Indiana	I											
Iowa	S	★	★		★	★	★	★	★			★
Kansas	S		★	★(n)	★				★(l)	★(c,d,m)		
Kentucky	S	★		★(n)	★	★	★	★	★(k,o,p,q)	★(c)		★(s,t)
Louisiana	S(r)			★(u,v)	★	★			★(j,s,t)	★(m)	★	★(s,t)
Maine	S				★		★		★(w)	★(d)		★(x)
Maryland	C,S	★	★	★(f,u)	★	★	★	★	★		★	
Massachusetts	C,I	★		★(f,u)	★	★	★		★(q)	★(m)	★	★(y)
Michigan	C,S	★			★	★	★		★(z)	★(c)		★(x)
Minnesota	S	★			★	★	★		★(q)	★(c,m)	★	
Mississippi	S	★			★	★	★			★(c)		
Missouri	C	★			★	★	★	★	★ (aa,bb)	★(x)		★(x,cc)
Montana	S,I	★	★		★	★	★	★	★(q)	★(c)		
Nebraska	S	★			★	★	★					
Nevada	I	★	★(a)	★(a)					★(q)			
New Hampshire	S	★							★(bb)	★		
New Jersey	S			★(dd)	★		★					

Sources: Massachusetts, Legislative Research Council, "Report Relative to Gubernatorial Executive Orders," House Document No. 6557, April 3, 1981, pp. 89-94; E. Lee Burnick, Department of Political Science, University of North Carolina at Greensboro; The Governors Center at Duke University (Survey, March 1984); The National Governors' Association 1985 survey; The Council of State Governments.

Key:
C—Constitutional
S—Statutory
I—Implied
★—Formal provision
...—No formal provision

(a) Broad interpretation of gubernatorial authority.
(b) To activate or veto environmental improvement authorities.
(c) Executive orders must be filed with secretary of state or other designated officer. In Idaho, must also be published in state general circulation newspaper.
(d) Governor required to keep record in office. In Maine, also sends copy to Legislative Counsel, State Law Library, and all county law libraries in state.
(e) Some or all provisions implied from constitution.
(f) To regulate distribution of necessities during shortages.

GUBERNATORIAL EXECUTIVE ORDERS—Continued

State or other jurisdiction	Authorization for executive orders	Provisions								Procedures		
		Civil defense, public emergencies	Energy emergencies and conservation	Other emergencies	Executive branch reorganization plans and agency creation	Create advisory, coordinating, study or investigative committees/commissions	Respond to federal programs and requirements	State personnel administration	Other administration	Filing and publication procedures	Subject to administrative procedure act	Subject to legislative review
New Mexico	S	★	★		S				S			
New York	I	S	S	S	S,C		S	S	S	S		★(x)
North Carolina	S,I	S	S	S		I	S	S	★(bb)	S		
North Dakota	S,I		★	★			★			★		
Ohio	S								★(bb)	★		★(x)
Oklahoma	S,I	★	★	★(u)					★(ee)	★(c)		
Oregon	S	★							★(ff)		★	★(x)
Pennsylvania	S	★	★	★(j,n,u,w)						★(c,m)		
Rhode Island	S(a)	★(bb)	★	★(h,i)					★(l)	★(c,d,gg)		
South Carolina	I(e)		★	★(h,i)	(hh)							
South Dakota	C		★	★		★			★(s)	★(c)		
Tennessee	S,I	★	★★	★★	★	★★	★★					★
Texas	S	★	★★	★								★
Utah	S		★★			★★		★★				
Vermont	S,I		★★		★				★(ii)	★(ii)		★(jj)
Virginia	S,I	★	★	★(r)	★(kk)	★	★	★	★(h,ff,ll,mm)	★(c)		
Washington	S	★★		★	★	★★	★		★(nn)	★(c,m)		
West Virginia	S,I(e)	★★		★	★	★★	★	★★				
Wisconsin	S								★(bb,oo,p)	★(c)		
Wyoming	I											
American Samoa	C,S	★	★	★	★	★★	★	★	★	★(pp)	★(pp)	
No. Mariana Is.	C											

(g) To reassign state attorneys and public defenders.
(h) To suspend certain officials and/or other civil actions.
(i) To declare water, crop and refugee emergencies.
(j) To designate game and wildlife areas or other public areas.
(k) Only if involves a change in statute.
(l) To transfer allocated funds.
(m) Included in state register or code.
(n) To give immediate effect to state regulations in emergencies.
(o) To control administration of state contracts and procedures.
(p) To impound or freeze certain state matching funds.
(q) To reduce state expenditures in revenue shortfall.
(r) Broad grant of authority.
(s) Appointive powers.
(t) To suspend rules and regulations of the bureaucracy.
(u) For fire emergencies.
(v) For financial institution emergencies.
(w) To control procedures for dealing with public.
(x) Reorganization plans and agency creation.
(y) Legislative appropriations committees must approve orders issued to handle a revenue shortfall.

(z) To assign duties to lieutenant governor, issue writ of special election.
(aa) To control prison and pardon administration.
(bb) To administer and govern the armed forces of the state.
(cc) For meeting federal program requirements.
(dd) To declare air pollution emergencies.
(ee) Relating to local governments.
(ff) To transfer funds in an emergency.
(gg) Must be published in register if they have general applicability and legal effect.
(hh) Can reorganize, but not create.
(ii) Filed with legislature.
(jj) Only executive branch reorganization.
(kk) To shift agencies between secretarial offices; all other reorganizations require legislative approval.
(ll) To control state-owned motor vehicles.
(mm) Delegate powers to secretaries and other executive branch officials.
(nn) Regarding annual reports of state agencies.
(oo) To transfer functions between agencies.
(pp) If executive order fits definition of rule.

Table 2.6
STATE CABINET SYSTEMS

State	Authorization for cabinet system				Criteria for membership			Number of members in cabinet (including governor)	Frequency of cabinet meetings	Open cabinet meetings
	Statute	Constitution	Governor	Tradition	Appointed to specified office	Elected to specified office	Gubernatorial appointment regardless of office			
Alabama	...	...	...	★	...	...	★	28	Twice monthly (a)	★
Alaska	...	...	★	...	★	...	...	17	Regularly	★(b)
Arizona	...	...	★	...	★	...	...	15	Weekly	...
Arkansas	★	...	...	...	★	...	...	17	Regularly	...
California	...	...	★	...	★	...	★	11	Every two weeks	...
Colorado	...	★	...	...	★	...	...	21	Twice monthly	★
Connecticut	★	...	...	...	★	...	...	24	Gov.'s discretion	...
Delaware	★	...	...	...	...	...	★(c)	19	Gov.'s discretion	★
Florida	...	★	...	...	...	★	...	7	Every two weeks	★
Georgia	----(d)----									
Hawaii	★	...	★	...	★	...	★	24	Gov.'s discretion	...
Idaho	----(d)----									
Illinois	...	...	...	★	★(c)	...	...	42 (e)	Gov.'s discretion(f)	★
Indiana	----(d)----									
Iowa	★	...	...	...	...	...	★	5	Weekly	★
Kansas	...	...	★	...	...	...	★	14	Monthly(a)	...
Kentucky	...	...	...	...	★	...	...	13	Weekly	...
Louisiana	★	★	...	...	★	★	...	21	Bi-annually	...
Maine	...	...	...	★	...	...	★(c)	21	Gov.'s discretion	(g)
Maryland	★	...	...	...	★(c)	...	...	23	Gov.'s discretion	...
Massachusetts	★	...	...	...	★	...	...	12	Twice monthly	...
Michigan	...	...	★	...	★	...	...	25	Gov.'s discretion	(h)
Minnesota	...	...	★	...	★	...	...	27 (i)	Regularly	...
Mississippi	----(d)----									
Missouri	...	★	...	★	★	...	...	16	Gov.'s discretion	...
Montana	...	...	★	...	★	...	...	16	6 times a year	★
Nebraska	...	...	★	...	★	...	...	27	Weekly	...
Nevada	----(d)----									
New Hampshire	----(d)----									
New Jersey	★	★	...	...	...	...	...	21	Once or twice monthly	...
New Mexico	★	...	...	...	...	...	...	15	Weekly	...
New York	...	...	...	★	★	...	...	16	Gov.'s discretion	...
North Carolina(j)	...	★	...	...	...	...	★	10	Monthly	...
North Dakota	----(d)----									
Ohio	★	...	...	...	...	...	★	27	Gov.'s discretion	(g)
Oklahoma	★	...	...	...	...	...	★	11 (k)	Gov.'s discretion	...
Oregon	...	...	★	...	...	...	★	21	As needed	...
Pennsylvania	★	...	...	...	★	...	...	20	Gov.'s discretion	★
Rhode Island	----(d)----									
South Carolina	----(d)----									
South Dakota	...	...	★	...	★	...	★	22	Gov.'s discretion	...
Tennessee	★	...	...	★	★	...	...	28	Gov.'s discretion	★
Texas	----(d)----									
Utah	...	...	★	(l)	★	...	...	26	Monthly	...
Vermont	★	...	...	...	★	...	...	6	Gov.'s discretion	...
Virginia	★	...	...	...	★	...	...	9	Gov.'s discretion	...
Washington	...	...	★	...	★	...	...	26	Twice monthly	...
West Virginia	----(d)----									
Wisconsin	★	...	...	...	★	...	...	9	Monthly	★
Wyoming	----(d)----									

Key:
★—Yes
. . .—No
(a) More often during legislative sessions. Kansas—bi-weekly.
(b) Except when in executive session.
(c) With the consent of the Senate.
(d) No formal cabinet system. In Idaho, however, sub-cabinets have been formed, by executive order; the chairmen report to the governor when requested.
(e) Includes directors of three independent bonding agencies.
(f) Sub-cabinets meet monthly.
(g) In practice, the media and others do not attend, but cabinet meetings have not been formally designated closed.
(h) Open cabinet meetings in the past; however, not all are open.
(i) Five sub-cabinets have been formed.
(j) Constitution provides for a Council of State made up of elective state administrative officials, which makes policy decisions for the state while the cabinet acts more in an advisory capacity.
(k) Each cabinet member is chair of a sub-cabinet (each state agency). These sub-cabinets meet quarterly.
(l) State Planning Advisory Committee, composed of all department heads serves as an informal cabinet. Committee meets at discretion of state planning coordinator.

Table 2.7
THE GOVERNORS: PROVISIONS AND PROCEDURES FOR TRANSITION

State or other jurisdiction	Legislation pertaining to gubernatorial transition	Appropriations available to gov-elect	Gov-elect's participation in state budget for coming fiscal year	Gov-elect to hire staff to assist during transition	State personnel to be made available to assist gov-elect	Office space in buildings to be made available to gov-elect	Acquainting gov-elect staff with office procedures and routine office functions	Transfer of information (files, records etc.)
Alabama............	...	...	•	(a)	•	•	•	...
Alaska..............	...	★	...	...	★	•	★	•
Arizona.............	...	...	•	...	•	•	•	•
Arkansas	★	60,000(b)	★	★	•	•	...	•
California..........	★	288,000(c)	★	★	★	★	•	•
Colorado	★	10,000	...	★	★	★	★	★
Connecticut	★	25,000	•	★	•	★	...	★
Delaware	★	49,000(d)	...	...	•	•	•	•
Florida	•	75,000	★	•	•	•	•	•
Georgia...........	★	★	•	★	★	★	•	•
Hawaii	★	50,000	•	★	★	★	★	★
Idaho	★	30,000	★	★	★	★	★	★
Illinois............	★	...	★	★(e)	★	★	★	★
Indiana	★	45,000	★	★	★	★	•	•
Iowa	★(f)	10,000	★	★	•(g)	•	•	★(h)
Kansas	★	100,000	★	★	★	★	★	•
Kentucky	★	Unspecified	★	★	★	★	★	•
Louisiana	★	10,000	★	★	...	★	•	•
Maine	★	5,000	★	★	★(i)	•	★	•
Maryland	★	50,000	★	★	★	★	•	•
Massachusetts	...	★	•	★	★	★	•	•
Michigan	★	1,000,000(c)	•	★	★	•	•	...
Minnesota	★	29,600	•	★	★	★	•	•
Mississippi	★	30,000	★	★	★	★	•	★
Missouri	★	100,000	★	★	•	★	•	...
Montana...........	★	5,000	★	★	★	★	★	★
Nebraska	...	44,000(j)	★	★	•	★	★	★
Nevada	...	5,000(k)	★	...	•	★	•	•
New Hampshire	★	5,000	★	★	★	★	★	...
New Jersey	★	150,000	★	★	★	★	•	★
New Mexico........	★	(l)	★	★	•	•	•	•
New York	...	...	•	•	•	•	•	•
North Carolina	★	50,000(d)	•(m)	★	•	★	•	•
North Dakota	...	...(n)	...	★	•	...	...	★
Ohio	★	(l)	...	★	•	★	...	•
Oklahoma	★	40,000	★	★	...	•	...	•
Oregon	★	20,000	★	★	★	★	★	★
Pennsylvania	★	100,000	...	★	•	★	•	•
Rhode Island	...	...	★	...	•	...	...	•
South Carolina	★	50,000	...	★	★	★	★	★
South Dakota	★	10,000(o)	...	★	•	★	•	★
Tennessee	★	★	•	...	•	•	•	•
Texas..............	...	...	★	★	•	...	...	•
Utah	...	...	...	...	•	•	...	...
Vermont	...	40,000	★(p)	•	•	•	...	(q)
Virginia	...	(j)	...	★(r)	★(r)	★(r)	★(r)	★(r)
Washington	★	80,000	•	•	•	•	•	•
West Virginia	...	...	...	•	•	•	•	★
Wisconsin..........	★	Unspecified	★	★	★	★	★	•
Wyoming	...	(l)	★	★	•	•	•	•
American Samoa	...	Unspecified	★(s)	•	•	•	•	•
Guam	...	...	...	...	...	...	...	...
No. Mariana Is.	...	...	...	...	...	...	...	...
Puerto Rico	...	250,000(d)	...	•	•	•	...	•
Virgin Islands	...	...	...	...	...	...	...	...

Sources: The National Governors' Association 1985 survey, and The Council of State Governments.
Key:
... .—No provisions or procedures
★—Formal provisions or procedures
•—No formal provisions, occurs informally
(a) Governor usually hires several incoming key staff during transition.
(b) Made available in 1983.
(c) Made available in 1982.
(d) Inaugural expenses are paid from this amount.
(e) On a contractual basis.
(f) Pertains only to funds.
(g) Provided on irregular basis.
(h) Arrangement for transfer of criminal files.

(i) Budget personnel.
(j) Determined prior to each election by legislature.
(k) Is not adequate and is augmented by legislature.
(l) Legislature required to make appropriation; no dollar amount stated in legislation. In New Mexico, $50,000 was made available in 1986.
(m) New governor can submit supplemental budget.
(n) If necessary, submit request to State Emergency Commission.
(o) Made available for 1987.
(p) Responsible for the preparation of the budget; staff made available.
(q) Not transferred but use may be authorized.
(r) Activity is traditional and routine, although there is no specific statutory provision.
(s) Can submit reprogramming or supplemental appropriation measure for current fiscal year.

Table 2.8
IMPEACHMENT PROVISIONS IN THE STATES

State or other jurisdiction	Governor and other state executive and judicial officers subject to impeachment	Legislative body which holds power of impeachment	Vote required for impeachment	Legislative body which conducts impeachment trial	Chief justice presides at impeachment trial(a)	Vote required for conviction	Official who serves as acting governor	Legislature may call special session for impeachment
Alabama	★(b)	H	2/3 mbrs.	S	★	2/3 mbrs.	LG	★
Alaska	★	S	maj. mbrs.	H	(c)	2/3 mbrs.	SS	★
Arizona	★(d)	H	...	S	★	2/3 mbrs.	SS	★
Arkansas	★	H	...	S	...	2/3 mbrs.	LG	...
California	★	H	maj. mbrs.	S	...	...	LG	★
Colorado	★(d)	H	maj. mbrs.	S	★	2/3 mbrs.	LG	...
Connecticut	★	H	2/3 mbrs.	S	★	2/3 mbrs. present	LG	...
Delaware	★	H	2/3 mbrs.	S	★	2/3 mbrs.	LG	★
Florida	★(e)	H	...	S	★	2/3 mbrs. present	...	★
Georgia	★(f)	H	...	S	★	2/3 mbrs. present	LG	★
Hawaii	★	H	...	S	★	2/3 mbrs.	LG	★
Idaho	★	H	maj. mbrs.	S	★	2/3 mbrs.	...	★
Illinois	★	H	2/3 mbrs.	S	...	2/3 mbrs.	LG	...
Indiana	★	H	...	S	...	2/3 mbrs. present	...	...
Iowa	★	H	...	S	...	...	...	...
Kansas	★	H	...	S	...	2/3 mbrs. present	LG	★
Kentucky	★	H	...	S	...	2/3 mbrs.	LG	★
Louisiana	★	H	...	S	...	2/3 mbrs.	PS	★
Maine	★	H	maj. mbrs.	S	...	2/3 mbrs. present	...	...
Maryland	★	H	maj. mbrs. present	(h)	...	2/3 mbrs.	LG	★
Massachusetts	★	H	maj. mbrs.	S	★	2/3 mbrs. present	LG	...
Michigan	★	H	maj. mbrs.	S(g)	★	2/3 mbrs.	LG	...
Minnesota	★	H	2/3 mbrs. present	S	...	2/3 mbrs.	...	...
Mississippi	★	H	...	S	(h)	2/3 mbrs.	...	...
Missouri	★	H	...	(h)	(h)	(h)	...	...
Montana	★	H	2/3 mbrs.	S	(j)	2/3 mbrs.	LG	★
Nebraska	★(d)	S(i)	maj. mbrs.	(j)	★	(j)	LG	...
Nevada	★	H	maj. mbrs.	S	★	2/3 mbrs.	...	...
New Hampshire	★	H	...	S	★	...	PS	...
New Jersey	★(k)	H	maj. mbrs.	S	★	2/3 mbrs.	PS	★

IMPEACHMENT PROVISIONS—Continued

State or other jurisdiction	Governor and other state executive and judicial officers subject to impeachment	Legislative body which holds power of impeachment	Vote required for impeachment	Legislative body which conducts impeachment trial	Chief justice presides at impeachment trial(a)	Vote required for conviction	Official who serves as acting governor	Legislature may call special session for impeachment
New Mexico	★	H	maj. mbrs.	S	★	2/3 mbrs.	LG	★★
New York	★	H	maj. mbrs.	(l)	...	2/3 mbrs. present	LG	★★
North Carolina	★(d)	H	...	S	★	2/3 mbrs. present	LG	...
North Dakota	★	H	maj. mbrs.	S	★	2/3 mbrs.	LG	★
Ohio	★	H	maj. mbrs.	S	...	2/3 mbrs.	...	★
Oklahoma	★(b)	H	...	S	★	2/3 mbrs. present	LG	★
Oregon					(m)			
Pennsylvania	★★	H	(n)	S	...	2/3 mbrs. present	LG	★
Rhode Island	★	H	...	S	★★	2/3 mbrs.	LG	...
South Carolina	★	H	2/3 mbrs.	S	★	2/3 mbrs.	LG	...
South Dakota	★(d)	H	maj. mbrs.	S	★	2/3 mbrs.	LG	★★
Tennessee	★	H	...	S	...	2/3 mbrs.(o)	LG	★★
Texas	★(d)	H	2/3 mbrs.	S	...	2/3 mbrs. present	LG	...
Utah	★	H	2/3 mbrs.	S	★	2/3 mbrs.	LG	...
Vermont	...	H	...	S	...	2/3 mbrs. present	...	...
Virginia	★(d)	H	maj. mbrs.	S	...	2/3 mbrs. present	...	★★
Washington	★	H	...	S	★★	2/3 mbrs.	...	★★
West Virginia	★(d)	H	maj. mbrs.	S	...	2/3 mbrs.	LG	★★
Wisconsin	★	H	maj. mbrs.	S	...	2/3 mbrs. present	...	...
Wyoming	★(d)	H	maj. mbrs.	S	★	2/3 mbrs.	SS	...
Dist. of Col.					(p)			
American Samoa	(q)	H	2/3 mbrs.	S	★	2/3 mbrs.	...	...
Guam					(p)			
No. Mariana Is.	★	H	2/3 mbrs.	S	...	2/3 mbrs.	...	★
Puerto Rico	(r)	H	2/3 mbrs.	S	★	3/4 mbrs.	...	...
Virgin Islands					(p)			

Sources: Legislative Drafting Research Fund, Columbia University, *Constitutions of the United States: National and State* (Dobbs Ferry, N.Y.: Oceana Press, 1982, 1985); *The Book of the States, 1984-85*; Public Administration Program, University of North Carolina at Chapel Hill; and The Council of State Governments.

Note: The information in this table is based on a literal reading of the state constitutions and statutes. For information on other methods for removing state officials, see Table 4.5, "Methods for Removal of Judges and Filling of Vacancies," and Table 5.16, "Provisions for Recall of State Officials."

Key:
★—Yes; provision for
...—Not specified, or no provision for
H—House or Assembly (lower chamber)
S—Senate
PS—President of the Senate
LG—Lieutenant governor
SS—Secretary of state

(a) Presiding justice of state court of last resort. In many states, provision indicates that chief justice presides only on occasion of impeachment of governor. Other judicial officers not subject to impeachment.
(b) Includes justices of Supreme Court.
(c) A Supreme Court justice designated by the court.
(d) With exception of certain judicial officers. In Arizona, Washington, and Wyoming—justices of courts not of record. In Colorado—county judges and justices of the peace. In Nevada and Utah—

justices of the peace. In North Dakota and South Dakota—county judges, justices of the peace, and police magistrates.
(f) Governor, lieutenant governor, and any appointive officer for whose removal the consent of the Senate is required.
(g) House elects three members to prosecute impeachment.
(h) All impeachments are tried before the state Supreme Court, except that the governor or a member of the Supreme Court is tried by a special commission of seven eminent jurists to be elected by the Senate. A vote of 5/7 of the court of special commission is necessary to convict.
(i) Court of impeachment is composed of chief justice and all district court judges in the state. A vote of 2/3 of the court is necessary to convict.
(k) All state officers while in office and for two years thereafter.
(l) Court for trial of impeachment composed of president of the Senate, senators (or major part of them), and judges of Court of Appeals (or major part of them).
(m) No provision for impeachment. Public officers may be tried for incompetency, corruption, malfeasance, or delinquency in office in same manner as criminal offenses.
(n) Vote of 2/3 members required for an impeachment of the governor.
(o) Vote of 2/3 of members sworn to try the officer impeached.
(p) Removal of elected officials by recall procedure only.
(q) Governor, lieutenant governor.
(r) Governor and Supreme Court justices.

THE EXECUTIVE BRANCH:
ORGANIZATION AND ISSUES, 1986-87

By Thad L. Beyle

Executive Branch Reorganization

In the past few years, there has been a slight reawakening of the drive to reorganize the executive branches of state governments - but not always with positive results. Over the course of the Twentieth Century, there have been three different waves of reorganization, usually following similar efforts at the national level: 1910-1913, The Taft Commission; 1937, the Brownlow Committee; and 1947-49, The Hoover Commission.[1]

While the goals of executive branch reorganization may vary from state to state, they generally include: a four year term for the governor plus other chief executive powers; adopting the short ballot by reducing the number of separately elected statewide officials to three - the governor, lieutenant governor, attorney general and possibly the auditor (although that office can be selected by the legislature); shift the control of state departments from commissions to a single removable appointee except in higher education and in the regulatory functions; and grouping state departments and agencies by consolidation or elimination of agencies and other units into 5 to 25 departments which report to the governor.[2] In a recent study of state government reorganizations, James Conant suggests that reorganization is more "a political rather than an administrative tool," and rather than reducing a large budget deficit, these reorganizations can be effective by slowing the growth of government by assisting in shifting budgetary and policy priorities, and by leading to some efficiencies.[3]

The 1986 Oklahoma legislature adopted what may be the most far reaching state reorganization plan seen in recent years, at least on paper. The general outlines of the plan included two major components: first, ending the

virtual independence of more than 200 agencies, boards and commissions by creating a centralized, cabinet form of government; and second, a new governor must, by executive order within 45 days of taking office, create his or her own cabinet and appoint cabinet secretaries subject to confirmation by the state Senate. The legislature also created a Reorganization Council to develop a statutory cabinet system; an Oklahoma Advisory Commission on Intergovernmental Relations; and abolished the Department of Economic and Community Affairs by reorganizing it into a Department of Commerce.

Upon taking office in 1987, Governor Henry Bellmon implemented the process by issuing executive orders creating an interim cabinet divided into 15 functional areas.[4] This step also meant that seven statewide elected Democratic officials lost their jobs.[5] However, many in the legislature felt the reorganization effort was a costly mistake and tried to dismantle it in the 1987 session. The bill passed the Oklahoma House 63-33, but was tabled in the Senate.[6]

Iowa began an effort to downsize and restructure its executive branch in 1986 by reducing the number of departments to 21 with five independent commissions. The governor was given the power of appointment over all departments except the Board of Regents. Fifty departments and 42 boards and commissions were eliminated as the executive branch was consolidated under the governor's control.[7]

However, after an extended study, the 1986 session of the Washington State legislature defeated a substantial executive branch reorganization plan which would have enhanced the powers of the governor. The plan was

Thad L. Beyle is Professor of Political Science at the University of North Carolina at Chapel Hill.

strongly supported by the governor and while there was support in the legislature for the plan, it foundered in the state Senate by a narrow vote on the question of whether it should be referred to the voters or not.[8] Some minor changes were adopted from the plan in shifting three functions into the Department of Community Development: historic preservation, emergency management and fire protection.[9]

Partial Reorganizations

As in each biennium, there have been partial reorganizations in the states. For the most part, the changes were minor and even cosmetic although there were some of import. Virginia separated the position of Secretary of Commerce and Resources into a Secretary of Economic Development and a Secretary of Natural Resources.[1] Following this change, there are now seven separate secretaries directing large "offices" or departments who report to the governor: administration, economic development, education, finance, human resources, transportation and public safety, and natural resources.[2]

The Maine legislature in 1986 split its Department of Finance and Administration into two departments, one to handle financial matters, the other to provide services to state agencies,[3] and in 1987, the legislature created a new Department of Economic and Community Development.[4]

The states were also active in establishing agencies and task forces to address current concerns such as AIDS, childrens' issues, the economy and economic development, the environment, low income housing, the organization of higher education and teenage pregnancy.

But not all partial reorganization attempts succeed. In a unique set of steps, the 1985 Minnesota state legislature passed legislation stripping the state treasurer of most duties by transferring nearly all of these duties to the finance department under the governor. However, the state Supreme Court held that this legislative attempt to abolish the treasurer's office violated the separation of powers doctrine in the state's constitution.[5] In 1986, the governor of Kansas attempted to reorganize the Board of Agriculture by bringing it into the governor's cabinet; the legislature did not give approval.[6] At the same time, the governor of Mississippi sought to reorganize the Highway Department into a Department of Transportation with the commissioners appointed by the governor rather than being elected; the legislature did not approve the proposal in a bizarre set of events.[7]

Futures Commissions

There have been several "blue ribbon" commissions working in the states developing analyses and reports concerning the state's future. In 1986, a Georgia 2000 committee addressed the disparity between urban and rural development,[1] which was followed by the creation of a Growth Strategies Commission in 1987.[2] The Kentucky Tomorrow Commission issued its report in 1986 which unfortunately was characterized as being long on rhetoric and short on specifics.[3] In 1986, Missouri's governor established a Missouri Opportunity 2000 Commission chaired by the secretary of state.[4]

A "Michigan Beyond 2000" study was prepared for that state's Senate in 1986,[5] followed by another report from a private organization on that state's economy.[6] A New Jersey State and Local Expenditures and Revenue Policy Commission has begun to report on its efforts by calling for a strong state role in economic development and the consolidation of some state agencies.[7] An Oklahoma Academy for State Goals was established in 1987 following a report on constructing a strategic plan for the state's future.[8] A "Competitive Wisconsin" group reported in 1986 on how state spending might be reduced to the U.S. average.[9] Finally, the first report of The Wyoming Futures Project in 1986 addresses that state's economic future.[10] There have been other commissions looking at indigent health care, liability and insurance, and infrastructure.

There is always a question of the effectiveness of such "blue ribbon" commission efforts especially when few attempts are made to analyze them. One recent study has evaluated such commissions in the higher education area and found a series of factors that can lead to the effectiveness of such commissions. Among these factors are: attainability of goals; time allotted to the study; frequency of commission meetings; accessability of the staff; an open process of comment; professional not political staff; solid background research; consideration of public comments at hearings; a positive media reaction; use of experts in addition to staff and commission members; recommendations that are substantiated; active involvement of the commission members in the commission activities; and consideration of those affected in the implementation process.[11]

Of course, tangible impacts may not be the only reasons to have such commissions, they may be vehicles to "coopt" members of the state's business and other elites into developing an understanding of particular problems the state and its governments face and/or to gain support for certain proposed policies; they can be used to put problems off by studying them for a while until the problem eases in the public mind, or an upcoming election is past; or they can even be used to further a particular actor's political ambitions. Then effectiveness becomes even harder to measure.

Ethics and Conflicts of Interest

There was the normal array of questionable behavior in some of the states raising questions about stricter laws to guide behavior. The problems that certain governors faced were discussed in "The Governors, 1986-87" essay. Among some of the questionable actions were: a banking commissioner accused of using inside information to sell stock (Oklahoma);[1] the chairman of the pardons board and the speaker of the house indicted for selling pardons (Louisiana);[2] misuse of state funds in traveling around the world (Minnesota);[3] and possible conflicts of interest of gubernatorial spouses (Arkansas and Kentucky).[4]

Some states responded to the particular situations in their state. The most extensive reaction appears to have taken place in New York in January 1987, when Governor Cuomo issued an executive order creating a corruption commission to investigate corruption in government and to suggest needed reforms.[5] The legislature passed legislation establishing a state ethics commission, a temporary state commission on local government ethics and a legislative ethics committee.[6]

References

State Government Organization

1. Advisory Commission on Intergovernmental Relations, *The Question of State Government Capability* (Washington, D.C.: ACIR, 1985), p. 144.
2. "State Government Reorganization," *State Policy Reports* 4:5 (March 11, 1986), pp. 16-17.
3. James Conant, "Reorganization and the Bot-

tom Line," *Public Administration Review* 46:1 (January/February 1986), p. 55.
4. Thomas H. Clapper, "Oklahoma Executive Government Reform," *Comparative State Politics Newsletter* 7:4 (August 1986), p. 13.
5. "People: GOP Gov. Bellmon Dumps Some Democratic Aides," *Governing The States and Localities* 1:3 (December 1987), p. 66.
6. Thomas H. Clapper and Thad L. Beyle, "Organizing State Government to Be Managed," in Beyle, ed., *State Government: CQ's Guide to Current Issues and Activities, 1987-88* (Washington, D.C.: CQ Press, 1987), p. 127.
7. James D. Carney, "Downsizing Government: Iowa's Challenge," *The Journal of State Government* 60:4 (July/August 1987), p. 189; "State Government Reorganization," pp. 17-18; and "State Reorganization," *State Policy Reports* 4:8 (April 26, 1986), p. 25.
8. Hugh A. Bone, "Productive Session in Washington State," *Comparative State Politics Newsletter* 7:3 (June 1986), p. 21.
9. "State Reorganization," ibid.

Partial Reorganizations

1. "Legislative Actions: Virginia raises gas tax," *State Government News* 29:10 (October 1986), p. 26.
2. *State Government Organization Charts*, The Council of State Governments, (Lexington, KY: 1988), p. 46.
3. Kenneth T. Palmer, "Maine Legislative Update," *Comparative State Politics Newsletter* 7:3 (June 1986), p. 14.
4. Kenneth T. Palmer, "Maine's Republican Governor and Democratic Legislature Have Generally Cooperative Session," *Comparative State Politics Newsletter* 8:4 (August 1987), p. 7.
5. "State Headlines: Treasurer's powers returned," *State Government News* 29:11 (November 1986), p. 21.
6. Mel Kahn, "Kansas' 1986 Legislative Session," *Comparative State Politics Newsletter* 7:4 (August 1986), p. 6.
7. Thomas H. Handy, "This Years Legislative Sessions in Mississippi," ibid., p. 6.

Blue Ribbon Commissions

1. "Georgia Development," *State Policy Reports* 4:4 (February 1986), p. 5.
2. "Georgia," *State Policy Reports* 5:12 (June 30, 1987), p. 25.

3. Kentucky Tomorrow Commission, *Meeting the Challenge: An Agenda Today for Kentucky's Tomorrow* (Lexington, KY: The Commission, 1986) as reported in "Kentucky Tomorrow," *State Policy Reports* 4:22 (Nov. 27, 1988), pp. 26-27.
4. "Missouri Development," *State Policy Reports* 4:4 (Feb. 28, 1986), pp. 9.
5. "Michigan Development," State Policy Reports 4:4 (Feb. 28, 1986), pp. 7-9.
6. "The Economic Future, Michigan Style," *State Policy Reports* 4:18 (Sept. 26, 1986), pp. 12-13.
7. "Economic Development and Reforms: New Jersey," *State Policy Reports* 5:21 (Nov. 16, 1987), pp. 10-11.
8. "Economic Development and Reforms: Oklahoma's Problem," Ibid., pp. 6-10.
9. "The Economic Future, Wyoming Style" *State Policy Reports* 4:18 (Sept. 26, 1986), pp. 11-12.
10. "Aspiring to be Average in Government Spending," *State Policy Reports* 4:20 (Oct. 25, 1986), pp. 24-28.
11. Janet Johnson and Laurence Marcus, *Blue Ribbon Commissions and Higher Education: Changing Academe from the Outside* (Washington, D.C.: Association for the Study of Higher Education, 1987).

Ethics and Conflicts of Interest

1. *State Government News* 30:5 (May 1987), p. 29.
2. "Selling Pardons in Louisiana?," *State Policy Reports* 4:18 (Sept. 26, 1986), p. 28.
3. "Official Globetrotting by State Officials," *State Policy Reports* 5:21 (Nov. 16, 1987), p. 28.
4. "Their Spouses' Businesses," *State Policy Reports* 4:12 (June 30, 1986), pp. 22-23.
5. "Corruption Commission Chartered," *National Civic Review* 76:2 (February 1987), p. 161.
6. Joseph F. Zimmerman, "More New York," *Comparative State Politics Newsletter* 8:5 (October 1987), pp. 4-5.

Table 2.9
CONSTITUTIONAL AND STATUTORY PROVISIONS FOR LENGTH AND NUMBER OF TERMS OF ELECTED STATE OFFICIALS

State or other jurisdiction	Governor	Lt. governor	Secretary of state	Attorney general	Treasurer	Auditor	Comptroller	Education	Agriculture	Labor	Insurance	Other
Alabama	4/2	4/2	4/2	4/2	4/2	4/2	...	...	4/2(a)	...	...	Bd. of Education—4/-; Public Service Commn.—4/-
Alaska	4/2(b)	4/2	(c)	...	...	...	...	...	...	...	...	
Arizona	4/-	(d)	4/-	4/-	4/2	...	...	4/-	...	...	...	Corporation Commn.—6/-; Mine inspector—2/-
Arkansas	4/-	4/-	4/-	4/-	4/-	4/-	(e)	...	...	...	...	Land Commr.—4/-
California	4/-	4/-	4/-	4/-	4/-	...	4/-	4/-	...	...	...	Bd. of Equalization—4/-
Colorado	4/-	4/-	4/-	4/-	4/-	...	...	...	...	...	...	Regents of Univ. of Colo.—6/-; Bd. of Education—6/-
Connecticut	4/-	4/-	4/-	4/-	4/-	...	4/-	...	...	...	...	
Delaware	4/2(f)	4/-	...	4/-	4/-	4/-	...	...	...	...	4/-	
Florida	4/2	4/-	4/-	4/-	4/-	...	4/-	4/-	4/-	...	(g)	
Georgia	4/2	4/-	4/-	4/-	...	...	4/-	4/-	4/-	4/-	(h)	Public Service Commn.—6/-
Hawaii	4/2	4/2	(c)	...	...	...	...	...	...	...	...	Bd. of Education—4/U
Idaho	4/-	4/-	4/-	4/-	4/-	4/-	(i)	4/-	...	...	...	
Illinois	4/-	4/-	4/-	4/-	4/-	...	4/-	...	...	...	...	Bd. of Trustees, Univ. of Ill.—6/-
Indiana	4/2(j)	4/-	4/2(j)	4/-	4/2(j)	4/2(j)	(i)	4/-	(c)	...	...	
Iowa	4/U	4/U	4/U	4/U	4/U	4/U	...	...	4/U	...	...	
Kansas	4/2	4/2	4/-	4/-	4/-	...	...	...	...	...	4/-	Bd. of Education—4/-
Kentucky	4/0	4/0	4/0	4/0	4/0	4/0	(e)	4/0	4/0	...	...	Railroad Commn.—4/-
Louisiana	4/2	4/-	4/-	4/-	4/-	...	(k)	...	4/-	...	4/-	Bd. of Education—4/-; Public Service Commn.—6/-; Elections Commr.—4/-
Maine	4/2	(l)	...	...	...	...	...	...	...	...	...	
Maryland	4/2(b)	4/-	...	4/U	...	...	4/-	...	...	...	...	
Massachusetts	4/-	4/-	4/-	4/-	4/-	4/-	...	...	...	...	...	Exec. Council—2/-
Michigan	4/-	4/-	4/-	4/-	...	...	(m)	...	...	...	...	Univ. Regents—8/-; Bd. of Education—8/-
Minnesota	4/-	4/-	4/-	4/-	4/-	4/-	...	...	...	...	...	
Mississippi	4/1	4/-	4/-	4/1	4/-	4/-	(i)	...	4/-	...	4/-	Public Service Commn.—4/-; Highway Commn.—4/-
Missouri	4/2(f)	4/-	4/-	4/-	4/2(f)	4/U	...	...	...	...	...	
Montana	4/-	4/-	4/-	4/-	...	4/-	...	4/-	...	...	(i)	Public Service Commn.—4/-
Nebraska	4/2(b)	4/-	4/-	4/-	4/2(n)	4/-	...	...	...	...	...	Regents of Univ. of Neb.—6/-; Bd. of Education—4/-; Public Service Commn.—6/-
Nevada	4/2	4/-	4/-	4/-	4/-	...	4/-	...	...	...	...	Bd. of Regents—6/-; Bd. of Education—4/3
New Hampshire	2/-	(l)	...	...	...	...	...	...	...	...	...	Exec. Council—2/-
New Jersey	4/2	(l)	...	...	...	...	...	...	...	...	...	

LENGTH AND NUMBER OF TERMS—Continued

State or other jurisdiction	Governor	Lt. governor	Secretary of state	Attorney general	Treasurer	Auditor	Comptroller	Education	Agriculture	Labor	Insurance	Other
New Mexico	4/1(o)	4/1(o)	4/1(o)	4/1(o)	4/1(o)	4/1(o)	...	...	...	...	...	Commr. of Public Lands—4/1(o); Bd. of Education—6/-; Corporation Commn.—6/-
New York	4/-	4/-	...	4/-	...	(p)	4/-	...	...	...	...	
North Carolina	4/2(f)	4/2(f)	4/-	4/-	4/-	4/-	(q)	4/-	4/-	4/-	4/-	
North Dakota	4/-	4/-	4/-	4/-	4/2	4/-	...	4/-	4/-(r)	4/-(r)	4/-	Public Service Commn.—6/-; Tax Commr.—4/-
Ohio	4/2	4/-	4/-	4/-	4/-	4/-	(m)	...	...	...	...	Bd. of Education—6/-
Oklahoma	4/2	4/U	...	4/U	4/U	4/U	...	4/U	...	...	4/-	Corporation Commn.—6/-
Oregon	4/2(j)	(d)	4/2(j)	4/-	4/2(j)	(s)	...	4/-	...	4/-	...	
Pennsylvania	4/2	4/2	...	4/2	4/2(t)	4/2	...	...	...	...	...	
Rhode Island	2/-	2/-	2/-	2/-	2/-	...	...	...	...	...	...	
South Carolina	4/2	4/-	4/-	4/-	4/-	...	4/-	4/-	4/-	...	...	Adjutant General—4/-
South Dakota	4/2	4/2	4/-	4/-	4/-	4/-	(i)	...	...	...	...	Commr. of School & Public Lands—4/-; Public Utilities Commn.—6/-
Tennessee	4/2	(l)	...	...	...	(p)	...	...	...	...	...	Public Service Commn.—6/-
Texas	4/-	4/-	...	4/-	4/-	...	4/-	...	4/-	...	...	Commr. of General Land Off.—6/-; Railroad Commn.—6/-
Utah	4/-	4/-	(c)	4/-	4/-	4/-	...	...	...	...	...	Bd. of Education—4/-
Vermont	2/-	2/-	2/-	2/-	2/-	2/-	...	...	...	...	...	
Virginia	4/0	4/U	...	4/U	...	...	...	...	...	...	...	
Washington	4/-	4/-	4/-	4/-	4/-	4/-	(m)	4/-	...	...	4/-	Commr. of Public Lands—4/-
West Virginia	4/2	(l)	4/-	4/-	4/-	4/-	(i)	...	4/-	...	...	
Wisconsin	4/-	4/-	4/-	4/-	4/-	...	(e)	4/-	...	...	...	
Wyoming	4/-	(d)	4/-	...	4/-	4/-	...	4/-	...	...	...	
Dist. of Col.	4/U(u)	...	...	...	...	...	...	...	...	...	...	Chmn. of Council of Dist. of Col.—4/U
American Samoa	4/2	4/2	(c)	...	...	...	(m)	...	...	...	...	
Guam	4/2(b)	4/-	(c)	...	...	...	...	...	...	...	(v)	Bd. of Education—4/-; Village Commr.—4/U
No. Mariana Is.	4/3	4/-	...	...	...	...	(e)	...	(w)	...	...	
Puerto Rico	4/-	(d)	...	...	...	...	...	...	...	...	...	
Virgin Islands	4/2(b)	4/-	(c)	...	(e)	...	...	...	...	...	(c)	

Note: First entry in a column refers to number of years per term. Entry following the slash refers to the maximum number of consecutive terms allowed. This table reflects a literal reading of the state constitutions and statutes. Blank cells indicate no specific administrative official performs function.

Key:

- —No provision specifying number of terms allowed.

0—Provision specifying officeholder may not succeed self.

U—Provision specifying individual may hold office for an unlimited number of terms.

...—Position is appointed or elected by governmental entity (not chosen by electorate).

(a) Commissioner of agriculture and industries.

(b) After two consecutive terms, must wait four years before being eligible again.

(c) Lieutenant governor performs function.

(d) Secretary of state is next in line of succession to the governorship.

(e) Finance administrator performs function.

(f) Absolute two-term limitation, but not necessarily consecutive.

(g) State treasurer also serves as insurance commissioner.

(h) Comptroller general is ex-officio insurance commissioner.

(i) State auditor performs function.

(j) Eligible for eight out of 12 years.

(k) Head of administration performs function.

(l) President of the senate is next in line of succession to the governorship. In Tennessee, speaker of the senate has the statutory title "lieutenant governor."

(m) State treasurer performs function.

(n) After two consecutive terms, must wait two years before being eligible again.

(o) Limited to two consecutive 4-year terms.

(p) Comptroller performs function.

(q) Budget administrator performs function.

(r) Constitution provides for a secretary of agriculture and labor. However, the legislature was given constitutional authority to provide for (and has provided for) a department of labor distinct from agriculture, and a commissioner of labor distinct from the commissioner of agriculture.

(s) Secretary of state's office performs function.

(t) Treasurer must wait four years before being eligible to the office of auditor general.

(u) Mayor.

(v) Taxation administrator performs function.

(w) Natural resources administrator performs function.

Table 2.10
SELECTED STATE ADMINISTRATIVE OFFICIALS: METHODS OF SELECTION

State or other jurisdiction	Governor	Lieutenant governor	Secretary of state	Attorney general	Treasurer	Adjutant general	Administration	Agriculture	Banking	Budget
Alabama	CE	CE	CE	CE	CE	G	...	CE	G	CS
Alaska	CE	CE	...	GB	GB	GB	A	A	A	A
Arizona	CE	...	CE	CE	CE	G	GS	B	GS	G
Arkansas	CE	CE	CE	CE	CE	G	G	(d)	AG	AG
California	CE	CE	CE	CE	CE	GS	...	GS	GS	GS
Colorado	CE	CE	CE	CE	CE	G	GS	GS	A	GS
Connecticut	CE	CE	CE	CE	CE	G	GE	GE	GE	A
Delaware	CE	CE	GS	CE	CE	GS	GS	GS	GS	GS
Florida	CE	CE	CE	CE	CE	GS	GS	CE	CE	A
Georgia	CE	CE	CE	CE	...	G	GS	CE	GS	G
Hawaii	CE	CE	...	GS	(a-9)	GS	G	GS	AG	GS
Idaho	CE	CE	CE	CE	CE	G	GS	GS	GS	G
Illinois	CE	CE	CE	CE	CE	G	GS	GS	GS	G
Indiana	CE	CE	CE	SE	CE	G	G	G	G	G
Iowa	CE	CE	CE	CE	CE	GS	G	SE	G	B
Kansas	CE	CE	CE	CE	SE	GS	GS	B	GS	CS
Kentucky	CE	CE	CE	CE	CE	G	G	CE	G	G
Louisiana	CE	CE	CE	CE	CE	GS	G	G	GS	GS
Maine	CE	...	CL	CL	CL	G	G	GLS	GLS	AG
Maryland	CE	CE	GS	CE	CL	GS	GS	GS	AGS	GS
Massachusetts	CE	CE	CE	CE	CE	G	G	G	G	AG
Michigan	CE	CE	CE	CE	GS	GS	GS	B	GS	GS
Minnesota	CE	CE	CE	CE	CE	G	GS	GS	B	GS
Mississippi	CE	CE	CE	CE	CE	GS	...	SE	GS	B
Missouri	CE	CE	CE	CE	CE	GS	GS	GS	AS	A
Montana	CE	CE	CE	CE	A	G	GS	GS	A	G
Nebraska	CE	CE	CE	CE	CE	GLS	(bb)	GS	GS	(bb)
Nevada	CE	...	CL	GC	CL	GC	GC	BG	GC	(a-6)
New Hampshire	CE	...	CL	GC	CL	GC	GC	GC	GC	(a-6)
New Jersey	CE	...	GS	GS	GS	GS	A	BG	GS	A
New Mexico	CE	CE	CE	CE	CE	GS	GS	BG	GS	GS
New York	CE	CE	GS	CE	(ii)	G	GS	GS	G	G
North Carolina	CE	CE	CE	CE	CE	G	G	CE	GS	AG
North Dakota	CE	CE	CE	CE	CE	G	AB	CE	GS	(ll)
Ohio	CE	CE	CE	CE	CE	G	GS	GS	A	GS
Oklahoma	CE	CE	GS	CE	CE	GS	G	GS	GS	G
Oregon	CE	...	CE	SE	CE	G	GS	GS	AG	A
Pennsylvania	CE	CE	GS	CE	CE	GS	G	GS	GS	G
Rhode Island	CE	CE	CE	CE	CE	G	GS	A	G	CS
South Carolina	CE	CE	CE	CE	CE	CE	B	CE	(a-4)	(a-6)
South Dakota	CE	CE	CE	CE	CE	GS	G	GS	A	A
Tennessee	CE	CE	CL	CT	CL	G	G	G	G	A
Texas	CE	CE	GS	CE	CE	GS	B	SE	BS	G
Utah	CE	CE	...	CE	CE	G	GS	GS	GS	G
Vermont	CE	CE	CE	SE	CE	SL	GS	GS	GS	GS
Virginia	CE	CE	GB	CE	GB	GB	GB	GB	B	GB
Washington	CE	CE	CE	CE	CE	GS	GS	GS	A	GS
West Virginia	CE	...	CE	CE	CE	GS	GS	CE	GS	GS
Wisconsin	CE	CE	CE	CE	CE	G	GS	B	GS	A
Wyoming	CE	...	CE	GS	CE	G	G	B	G	G

Note: The chief administrative officials responsible for each function were determined from information given by the states for the same function as listed in *State Administrative Officials Classified by Function 1987-88*, published by The Council of State Governments.

Key:
N.A.—Not available.
. . .—No specific chief administrative official or agency in charge of function.
CE—Constitutional, elected by public
CL—Constitutional, elected by legislature
SE—Statutory, elected by public
SL—Statutory, elected by legislature
L—Selected by legislature or one of its organs
CT—Constitutional, elected by state Supreme Court

Appointed by:
G —Governor
GS —Governor
GG —Governor
GB —Governor
GE —Governor
GC —Governor
GD —Governor
GLS —Governor

Approved by:
Senate
General Assembly
Both houses
Either house
Council
Departmental board
Appropriate legislative committee & Senate

GOC —Governor & Council or cabinet
LG —Lieutenant governor
AT —Attorney general
SS —Secretary of state

Appointed by:
A —Agency head
AB —Agency head
AG —Agency head
AGC —Agency head
AS —Agency head
AGS —Agency head
ASH —Agency head

Approved by:
Board
Governor
Governor & Council
Senate
Governor & Senate
Senate president & House speaker

B —Board or commission
BG —Board
BGC —Board
BGS —Board
BS —Board or commission
BA —Board or commission
CS —Civil Service
ACB —Nominated by audit committee

Approved by:
Governor
Governor & Council
Governor & Senate
Senate
Agency head
Both houses

SELECTED OFFICIALS: METHODS OF SELECTION—Continued

State or other jurisdiction	Civil rights	Commerce	Community affairs	Comptroller	Computer services	Consumer affairs	Corrections	Economic development	Education	Elections administration
Alabama	...	G	G	AG	CS	AT	G	G	B	(a-2)
Alaska	G	GB	GB	GB	A	AT	GB	A	BG	LG
Arizona	A	GS	(a-11)	AG	AG	AT	GS	(a-11)	CE	(a-2)
Arkansas	...	G	G	(a-6)	GS	AT	GS	(a-11)	BG	(a-2)
California	G	GS	GS	CE	G	GS	GS	(a-11)	CE	(a-2)
Colorado	A	A	A	A	...	AT	GS	GS	B	CE
Connecticut	B	G	A	CE	A	GE	GE	(a-11)	B	GE
Delaware	AGS	AGS	AG	L	A	A	GS	AG	B	GS
Florida	A	GS	GS	(a-8)	GS	A	GS	A	CE	SS
Georgia	...	B	G	CE	A	G	GD	(a-11)	CE	SS
Hawaii	...	GS	GS	G	A	G	A	(a-12)	B	LG
Idaho	BGS	G	AG	N.A.	(a-6)	(a-3)	BGS	(a-11)	CE	(a-2)
Illinois	GS	GS	(a-11)	CE	(a-6)	(a-3)	GS	(a-11)	B	GS
Indiana	G	(a-1)	A	N.A.	A	AT	G	LG	SE	B
Iowa	GS	GS	G	(a-9)	G	AT	GS	G	B	SS
Kansas	B	GS	A	A	A	A	GS	(a-11)	B	(a-2)
Kentucky	B	G	G	(a-9)	(a-9)	(a-3)	AG	AG	CE	(a-2)
Louisiana	(a-3)	GS	GS	(a-6)	A	...	GS	(a-11)	B	CE
Maine	B	GS	BG	BG	BG	GLS	AG	(a-11)	GLS	(a-2)
Maryland	GS	A	AG	CE	A	AT	AGS	G	B	G
Massachusetts	AT	G	G	G	A	G	G	G	B	SS
Michigan	B	G	A	(a-4)	A	A	B	CS	B	SS
Minnesota	GS	GS	A	(a-9)	A	GS	GS	A	BG	(a-2)
Mississippi	...	G	G	CE	B	(y)	B	(a-11)	BS	SS
Missouri	B	GS	(a-11)	A	A	...	GS	GS	B	SS
Montana	G	G	A	(a-6)	A	G	A	A	CE	SS
Nebraska	B	GS	A	(a-6)	A	AT	GS	GLS	(cc)	(a-2)
Nevada	G	G	G	CE	A	A	G	LG	B	(a-2)
New Hampshire	B	GC	GC	GOC	B	(a-3)	GOC	(a-11)	B	(a-2)
New Jersey	A	GS	GS	(a-9)	A	GS	GS	A	GS	(ff)
New Mexico	GS	GS	GS	(a-4)	A	AT	A	A	B	SS
New York	G	GS	(a-2)	(a-4)	(a-6)	GS	GS	(a-11)	B	G
North Carolina	A	G	A	A	AG	AT	G	A	CE	G
North Dakota	SE	G	A	(a-9)	A	AT	GS	(a-11)	CE	(a-2)
Ohio	GS	(hh)	A	(a-4)	A	B	GS	A	B	SS
Oklahoma	B	G	G	AG	A	B	B	(a-11)	CE	L
Oregon	CS	GS	A	(a-4)	A	A	AG	A	CE	SS
Pennsylvania	GS	GS	GS	AG	AG	A	AG	(a-11)	GS	G
Rhode Island	B	G	...	A	A	BS	GS	(a-11)	B	BG
South Carolina	B	G	A	CE	B	B	B	(a-11)	CE	BG
South Dakota	A	GS	GS	CE	(a-6)	AT	AG	(a-12)	B	(a-2)
Tennessee	B	G	(a-11)	CL	A	A	G	(a-11)	G	SS
Texas	B	G	GS	CE	B	AT	B	B	BS	SS
Utah	B	GS	(yy)	AG	AG	AG	BA	(yy)	B	(a-1)
Vermont	AT	A	GS	AGS	CS	(a-10)	GS	(a-11)	BG	(a-2)
Virginia	...	GB	A	GB	GB	A	GB	GB	GB	GB
Washington	B	GS	GS	(a-4)	B	AT	GS	A	CE	SS
West Virginia	GS	GS	G	CE	A	AT	GS	(a-11)	B	(a-2)
Wisconsin	A	GS	A	A	A	(ccc)	A	A	CE	BA
Wyoming	A	G	(a-11)	CE	A	AT	BG	(a-11)	CE	(a-2)

(a) Chief administrative official or agency in charge of function:
(a-1) Lieutenant governor
(a-2) Secretary of state
(a-3) Attorney general
(a-4) Treasurer
(a-5) Adjutant general
(a-6) Administration
(a-7) Agriculture
(a-8) Banking
(a-9) Budget
(a-10) Civil rights
(a-11) Commerce
(a-12) Community affairs
(a-13) Comptroller
(a-14) Computer services
(a-15) Consumer affairs
(a-16) Economic development
(a-17) Education (chief state school officer)
(a-18) Emergency management
(a-19) Employment services
(a-20) Energy resources
(a-21) Environmental protection
(a-22) Finance
(a-23) Fish and wildlife

(a-24) General services
(a-25) Health
(a-26) Highways
(a-27) Historic preservation
(a-28) Insurance
(a-29) Labor
(a-30) Mental health and retardation
(a-31) Natural resources
(a-32) Parks and recreation
(a-33) Personnel
(a-34) Planning
(a-35) Post audit
(a-36) Public utility regulation
(a-37) Public welfare
(a-38) Purchasing
(a-39) Revenue
(a-40) Social services
(a-41) Solid waste management
(a-42) Transportation
(b) Responsibilities shared by Director, Mental Health and Developmental Disabilities Division, Health and Social Services Department, and Program Administrator, same department.

SELECTED OFFICIALS: METHODS OF SELECTION—Continued

State or other jurisdiction	Emergency management	Employment services	Energy resources	Environmental protection	Finance	Fish & wildlife	General services	Health	Higher education	Highways
Alabama	CS	A	CS	G	G	G	A	B	B	G
Alaska	A	A	A	GB	GB	GB	A	A	BG	GB
Arizona	G	GS	GS	GS	(a-13)	B	GS	GS	B	GS
Arkansas	AG	G	GS	G	(a-6)	B	(a-6)	GS	BG	G
California	GS	GS	B	GS	(a-9)	GS	GS	GS	B	CS
Colorado	A	GS	G	GS	(a-13)	BA	(a-6)	GS	B	GS
Connecticut	GE	AG	...	GE	GE	GE	(a-6)	GE	B	A
Delaware	AG	GS	G	A	GS	A	(a-6)	AG	B	N.A.
Florida	A	A	A	GS	A	GS	GOC	A	B	GS
Georgia	(a-5)	A	G	A	A	A	(a-6)	BG	B	B
Hawaii	(a-5)	A	A	AG	(a-9)	(m)	(a-13)	GS	B	AG
Idaho	A	GS	A	GS	(a-9)	GS	A	A	BGS	BGS
Illinois	GS	A	GS	GS	GS	A	(a-6)	GS	B	GS
Indiana	GC	G	G	G	(a-9)	A	(a-6)	G	B	G
Iowa	A	G	G	G	(a-9)	G	(a-6)	GS	GS	A
Kansas	A	GS	GS	A	(a-9)	B	(a-6)	GS	B	GS
Kentucky	G	A	G	G	(a-9)	B	(a-9)	AG	B	G
Louisiana	GS	GS	GS	GS	(a-6)	GS	(a-6)	GS	B	G
Maine	AG	GLS	G	GLS	GLS	GLS	(a-22)	A	GLS	GLS
Maryland	G	GS	A	AG	(a-13)	G	GS	GS	B	AG
Massachusetts	G	G	G	G	(a-6)	G	G	G	B	G
Michigan	A	B	G	A	(a-9)	B	(a-9)	GS	CS	GS
Minnesota	G	B	GS	(w)	(a-9)	A	(a-6)	GS	GS	A
Mississippi	G	G	G	B	(a-9)	B	B	B	B	SE
Missouri	GS	A	A	A	(a-6)	B	(a-6)	GS	B	B
Montana	A	A	A	A	(a-9)	GS	(a-6)	GS	GS	GS
Nebraska	GS	A	GS	GS	N.A.	B	(a-6)	GS	B	GS
Nevada	G	G	...	A	(a-6,9,35,39)	G	G	A	B	B
New Hampshire	G	GC	G	GOC	(a-6)	B	(a-6)	GC	A	GC
New Jersey	A	A	GS	GS	(a-4)	AGC	(a-6)	GS	BG	GS
New Mexico	A	GS	GS	A	GS	A	(a-6)	GS	B	GS
New York	GS	GS	GS	G	(a-4)	(a-21)	(a-6)	(a-18)	(a-17)	GS
North Carolina	G	G	AG	G	(a-9)	A	A	G	BG	AG
North Dakota	A	G	(a-12)	A	(a-9)	G	(a-9)	G	B	G
Ohio	AG	GS	GS	GS	(a-9)	A	(a-6)	GS	BG	GS
Oklahoma	(a-5)	B	B	B	(a-9)	AB	A	B	B	B
Oregon	CS	AG	GS	B	(a-6,9)	B	GS	AG	B	AB
Pennsylvania	B	CS	GS	GS	GS	(rr)	GS	GS	G	GS
Rhode Island	(a-5)	G	GS	GS	G	B	A	GB	B	GS
South Carolina	A	B	G	AG	(a-6)	B	(a-13)	B	B	B
South Dakota	A	A	A	A	(a-9)	G	(a-6)	GS	B	A
Tennessee	A	G	BG	A	(a-6)	B	G	G	B	G
Texas	G	B	B	G	(a-13)	B	B	B	B	GS
Utah	BG	AG	A	B	(a-13)	BA	(a-6)	GS	N.A.	GS
Vermont	G	GS	G	GS	(a-13)	AS	(a-6)	GS	B	GS
Virginia	GB	GB	A	GB	GB	B	GB	GB	GB	GB
Washington	GS	GS	GS	GS	(a-9)	B	(a-6)	A	B	B
West Virginia	G	GS	B	GS	(a-6)	A	A	CS	BG	GS
Wisconsin	GS	A	A	A	A	A	A	GS	BG	A
Wyoming	G	G	...	G	(a-13)	A	(a-6)	G	G	B

(c) Responsibilities shared by Assistant Director, Developmental Disabilities Division, Department of Economic Security, and Director, Department of Health Services.

(d) Responsibilities shared by Director/Veterinarian, Livestock and Poultry Commission, $64,631, Director, Plant Board, and International Marketing Representative, Marketing Division, Industrial Development Commission.

(e) Responsibilities shared by Director, Department of Industrial Relations, and Supervisor, Conciliation, same department.

(f) Responsibilities shared by Director, Department of Mental Health, and Director, Developmental Services Department.

(g) Responsibilities shared by Auditor General, and Director, Department of Finance.

(h) Responsibilities shared by Director, Division of Mental Health, Department of Institutions, and Director, Division of Developmental Disabilities, same department.

(i) Responsibilities shared by Commissioner, Department of Mental Health, and Commissioner, Department of Mental Retardation.

(j) Responsibilities shared by two Auditors of Public Accounts.

(k) Responsibilities shared by Director, Division of Alcoholism, Drug Abuse & Mental Health, and Director, Division of Mental Retardation, Health and Social Services Department.

(l) Responsibilities shared by Secretary, Department of Services for Children, Youth, and Their Families, and Secretary, Department of Health & Social Services.

(m) Responsibilities shared by Director, Division of Aquatic Resources, Land and Natural Resources Department, and Acting Administrator, Division of Forestry and Wildlife, same department.

(n) Responsibilities shared by Chief, Mental Health Division, Department of Health, and Mental Retardation Administrator, Waimano Training School and Hospital, same department.

(o) Responsibilities shared by Chief Auditor and Legislative Auditor.

(p) Responsibilities shared by Commissioner, Department of Mental Health, and Assistant Commissioner, Developmental Disabilities Division, same department.

(q) Responsibilities shared by Assistant Secretary, Office of Mental Health, Health and Human Resources Department, and Assistant Secretary, Office of Mental Retardation, same department.

(r) Responsibilities shared by Budget Director, Division of Administration, and Legislative Auditor.

(s) Responsibilities shared by Commissioner, Division of Administration, and State Director of Purchasing, same division.

(t) Responsibilities shared by Director, Developmental Disabilities Administration, Health and Mental Hygiene Department, and Director, Mental Hygiene Administration, same department.

(u) Responsibilities shared by Commissioner, Department of Mental Health, and Commissioner, Department of Mental Retardation.

SELECTED OFFICIALS: METHODS OF SELECTION—Continued

State or other jurisdiction	Historic preservation	Insurance	Labor	Licensing	Mental health & retardation	Natural resources	Parks & recreation	Personnel	Planning	Post audit
Alabama	B	G	G	...	G	(a-23)	GB	B	...	L
Alaska	A	A	GB	A	(b)	GB	A	G	...	L
Arizona	B	GS	B	...	(c)	GS	B	AG	(a-11)	L
Arkansas	GS	AG	GS	...	AG	GS	GS	AG	...	L
California	G	GS	(e)	(a-15)	(f)	GS	GS	...	G	(g)
Colorado	GD	A	A	GS	(h)	GS	BA	GS	(a-9)	ACB
Connecticut	G	GE	GE	G	(i)	(a-21)	CS	G	A	(j)
Delaware	AG	CE	GS	AG	(k)	(a-21)	AG	(a-19)	G	CE
Florida	A	CE	A	GS	A	GOC	A	GS	(a-9)	L
Georgia	A	(a-13)	CE	SS	BG	(a-21)	A	G	(a-9)	GB
Hawaii	GS	AG	GS	(a-11)	(n)	(a-27)	AB	GS	GS	(o)
Idaho	B	GS	GS	G	A	...	GS	BGS	(a-11)	L
Illinois	GS	GS	GS	GS	GS	(a-20)	(a-23)	AG	GS	L
Indiana	G	G	G	G	(p)	G	A	G	LG	G
Iowa	G	G	G	G	A	G	A	N.A.	(a-16)	CE
Kansas	B	SE	(a-19)	...	AS	(a-21)	(a-23)	A	(a-9)	L
Kentucky	BG	G	G	G	G	(a-21)	G	G	(a-6)	L
Louisiana	GS	CE	GS	CS	(q)	GS	GS	B	GS	(r)
Maine	B	A	A	BG	BG	(a-21)	B	BG	G	SL
Maryland	A	GS	GS	GS	(t)	GS	A	(a-6)	GS	ASH
Massachusetts	N.A.	G	G	G	(u)	G	A	AG	G	CE
Michigan	CS	GS	GS	GS	GS	(a-23)	CS	B	...	CL
Minnesota	N.A.	BS	(x)	(a-29)	GS	GS	A	GS	G	CE
Mississippi	B	SE	...	...	(z)	B	AB	B	(a-12)	(a-13)
Missouri	AB	AS	GS	A	B	GS	A	G	(a-9)	CE
Montana	B	A	GS	A	(aa)	GS	A	AG	(a-12)	L
Nebraska	B	GS	(dd)	A	(ee)	B	(a-23)	GS	G	(bb)
Nevada	A	A	G	A	A	G	A	G	...	L
New Hampshire	GC	GC	GC	(a-2)	GC	(a-27)	GC	AGC	(a-12)	L
New Jersey	A	GS	GS	(a-15)	(gg)	GS	A	G	G	L
New Mexico	A	B	GS	G	(hh)	GS	A	G	...	CE
New York	GS	GS	(a-19)	(a-2)	(jj)	(a-21)	(a-27)	GS	(a-11)	(a-4)
North Carolina	G	CE	CE	...	G	(a-21)	G	G	N.A.	CE
North Dakota	B	CE	(a-10)	(a-2)	A	...	G	(a-6)	(a-12)	(mm)
Ohio	N.A.	GS	GS	...	(oo)	G	A	GS	(a-9)	CE
Oklahoma	B	CE	GS	...	(pp)	G	(a-31)	GS	...	CE
Oregon	A	AG	SE	(a-11)	(qq)	G	AB	A	G	A
Pennsylvania	BG	GS	GS	G	(ss)	(a-21)	CS	AG	G	CE
Rhode Island	B	G	G	G	(uu)	(a-21)	A	CS	CS	(vv)
South Carolina	B	B	GS	...	(ww)	N.A.	B	B	...	B
South Dakota	GS	A	GS	A	(xx)	GS	GS	GS	...	L
Tennessee	AB	G	G	A	G	G	A	G	G	(a-13)
Texas	B	B	G	...	B	G	(a-23)	...	G	L
Utah	AB	GS	GS	AG	(zz)	GS	BA	GS	(a-9)	CE
Vermont	A	(a-8)	GS	(a-2)	GS	(a-21)	A	GS	G	CE
Virginia	GG	(a-8)	GB	GB	GB	GB	A	GB	(a-9)	GB
Washington	GS	SE	GS	GS	(aaa)	CE	B	G	(a-9)	CE
West Virginia	A	GS	GS	...	(a-25)	(a-21)	A	GS	(a-11)	CE
Wisconsin	G	GS	GS	GS	(ddd)	B	A	GS	(a-9)	L
Wyoming	G	B	G	...	A	...	(a-27)	G	G	(a-8,13)

(v) Responsibilities shared by Deputy Treasurer, and Director of Local Finance Programs, same department.

(w) Responsibilities shared by Executive Director, Pollution Control Agency, and Executive Director, Environmental Quality Board.

(x) Responsibilities shared by Director, Licensing Unit, Department of Commerce, and Commissioner, Department of Labor and Industry.

(y) Responsibilities shared by Deputy Attorney General, and Director, Consumer Protection Division, Office of the Attorney General.

(z) Responsibilities shared by Director, Department of Mental Health, and Director, Mental Retardation Division, Department of Mental Health.

(aa) Responsibilities shared by Administrator, Mental Health Division, Department of Institutions, and Administrator, Developmental Disabilities Division, Social and Rehabilitation Services Department.

(bb) Also has finance responsibilities.

(cc) Responsibilities shared by Commissioner, Department of Education, and President of State Board of Education.

(dd) Responsibilities shared by Director, Labor Department, and Administrator, Commission on Industrial Relations.

(ee) Responsibilities shared by Director, Medical Services Division, Department of Public Institutions, and Director, Office of Mental Retardation, same department.

(ff) Responsibilities shared by Director, Election Division, Department of State, and Executive Director, Election Law Enforcement Commission, Department of Law and Public Safety.

(gg) Responsibilities shared by Director, Mental Health and Hospitals Division, Department of Human Services, and Director, Division of Developmental Disabilities, same department.

(hh) Responsibilities shared by Chief, Mental Health Bureau, Department of Health and Environment, and Chief, Developmental Disabilities Bureau, same department.

(ii) Responsibilities shared by Commissioner, Department of Taxation and Finance, and Comptroller. Comptroller also has Finance, Post audit, and Pre-audit responsibilities.

(jj) Responsibilities shared by Commissioner, Office of Mental Health, and Commissioner, Mental Retardation and Developmental Disabilities.

(kk) Commissioner, Department of Taxation and Finance (as discussed under Treasurer), has responsibilities in this area.

(ll) Budget, Comptroller, and Finance responsibilities are shared by Executive Budget Analyst, Office of Management and Budget, and Director, same office. The Director, Office of Management and Budget, also has General services and Pre-audit responsibilities.

(mm) Responsibilities shared by state Auditor, and Legislative Budget Analyst and Auditor.

(nn) Responsibilities shared by Director, Department of Commerce, and Director, Development Department.

(oo) Responsibilities shared by Director, Department of Mental Health, and Director, Department of Mental Retardation and Developmental Disabilities.

SELECTED OFFICIALS: METHODS OF SELECTION—Continued

State or other jurisdiction	Pre-audit	Public library	Public utility regulation	Public welfare	Purchasing	Revenue	Social services	Solid waste management	State police	Tourism	Transportation
Alabama	(a-13)	B	SE	G	CS	G	(a-37)	A	G	G	G
Alaska	A	A	GB	AG	(a-24)	AG	(a-25)	GB	A	GS	(a-26)
Arizona	AG	B	CE	GS	AG	GS	(a-30)	(a-21)	AG	(a-32)	(a-26)
Arkansas	A	B	GS	(a-30)	AG	AG	(a-30)	(a-21)	GS	(a-32)	(a-26)
California	(a-13)	GS	GS	GS	GS	BS	(a-37)	B	GS	G	GS
Colorado	(a-13)	A	GS	GS	A	GS	(a-37)	GS	A	G	...
Connecticut	(a-13)	B	GB	GE	A	GE	GE	CS	GE	CS	GE
Delaware	(a-35)	AG	GS	GS	AG	AG	(l)	N.A.	A	AG	GS
Florida	A	A	GS	A	A	GOC	A	GS	G	A	(a-26)
Georgia	(a-35)	A	CE	A	A	GS	(a-37)	GE	BG	A	(a-26)
Hawaii	A	B	GS	A	A	GS	GS	(a-21)	...	(a-12)	GS
Idaho	(a-13)	B	GS	GB	A	GS	GS	A	A	(a-11)	(a-26)
Illinois	(a-13)	A	G	GS	(a-6)	GS	A	(a-20)	GS	(a-11)	(a-26)
Indiana	(a-13)	B	G	G	(a-6)	G	(a-37)	A	A	G	G
Iowa	GS	...	G	A	G	G	GB	A	A	GS	GD
Kansas	(a-13)	GS	GS	GS	A	GS	GS	(a-21)	GS	A	(a-26)
Kentucky	(a-9)	G	G	AG	A	G	AG	AG	AG	G	G
Louisiana	(a-9)	B	CE	GS	(s)	GS	GS	A	GS	GS	GS
Maine	(a-13)	BG	G	A	BG	BG	(a-37)	(a-21)	AG	N.A.	(a-26)
Maryland	A	A	GS	AG	CS	(a-13)	(a-37)	A	GS	G	GS
Massachusetts	(a-13)	A	G	G	A	G	G	A	G	A	G
Michigan	(a-35)	...	GS	GS	CS	(v)	(a-37)	(a-21)	GS	GS	(a-26)
Minnesota	GS	A	GS	GS	A	GS	GS	A	A	B	GS
Mississippi	(a-13)	B	SE	G	A	GS	(a-37)	GS	A	GS	(a-20)
Missouri	(a-13)	B	GS	A	A	GS	GS	A	GS	B	(a-26)
Montana	...	B	SE	GS	A	(bb)	(a-37)	(a-21)	AT	A	B
Nebraska	(a-6)	B	CE	A	A	(bb)	(a-37)	(a-21)	G	A	(a-26)
Nevada	(a-6)	G	G	A	(a-24)	G	G	(a-21)	GC	A	(a-26)
New Hampshire	(a-6)	B	GC	A	AGC	GC	GC	A	A	A	(a-26)
New Jersey	GS	A	GS	AB	A	GS	GS	A	(a-18)	A	(a-26)
New Mexico	A	A	GS	A	GS	G	G	(a-21)	GD	A	GS
New York	(a-4)	(a-17)	GS	GS	(a-6)	(kk)	(a-37)	(a-21)	GS	GS	(a-26)
North Carolina	(a-35)	G	GB	G	AG	G	G	A	G	A	G
North Dakota	(a-9)	A	CE	G	A	G	G	A	AG	G	(a-26)
Ohio	(a-35)	B	GS	GS	A	G	(a-37)	GS	GS	(a-31)	(a-26)
Oklahoma	(a-9)	B	CE	GS	A	GS	(a-37)	A	GS	(a-31)	(a-26)
Oregon	...	B	G	AG	A	GS	GS	A	GS	A	G
Pennsylvania	(a-4)	A	GS	A	(a-24)	(a-22)	(tt)	CS	GS	(a-11)	(a-26)
Rhode Island	A	GS	(a-20)	A	CS	CS	GS	B	G	A	(a-26)
South Carolina	(a-13)	B	GS	B	B	GS	(a-37)	B	B	G	(a-26)
South Dakota	...	B	SE	AG	A	GS	GS	(a-20)	AG	A	GS
Tennessee	A	A	SE	G	A	G	A	A	A	G	(a-26)
Texas	(a-13)	B	GS	BS	(a-24)	(a-13)	(a-37)	A	B	B	(a-26)
Utah	(a-13)	AB	GS	GS	AG	GS	GS	A	AG	AB	(a-26)
Vermont	(a-13)	G	GS	GS	(a-14)	GS	GS	A	A	A	(a-26)
Virginia	(a-13)	GB	(a-8)	GB	A	G	(a-37)	A	GB	A	GB
Washington	...	B	GS	(bbb)	A	GS	(a-25)	A	GS	A	(a-26)
West Virginia	(a-6)	B	G	GS	A	GS	A	B	G	A	A
Wisconsin	A	A	GS	A	A	GS	GS	A	GS	A	GS
Wyoming	(a-13)	A	GS	A	A	G	(a-37)	A	AB	G	...

(pp) Responsibilities shared by Director, Mental Health Department, and Director, Developmental Disabilities Services.

(qq) Responsibilities shared by Administrator, Mental Health Division, Department of Human Resources, and Assistant Administrator, Mental Retardation and Developmental Disabilities Section, same department.

(rr) Responsibilities shared by Executive Director, Fish Commission, and Executive Director, Game Commission.

(ss) Responsibilities shared by Deputy Secretary, Office of Mental Health, Department of Public Welfare, and Deputy Secretary, Office of Mental Retardation, same department.

(tt) Responsibilities shared by Deputy Secretary for Children, Youth, and Their Families, and Deputy Secretary for Medical Assistance.

(uu) Responsibilities shared by Director, Mental Health, Retardation, and Hospitals Department, and Associate Director, Retardation Service, same department.

(vv) Responsibilities shared by Auditor General, and Director, Bureau of Audits.

(ww) Responsibilities shared by Commissioner, Department of Mental Health, and Commissioner, Department of Mental Retardation.

(xx) Responsibilities shared by Administrator, Developmental Disabilities, Department of Social Services, and Executive Director, Department of Charities and Corrections.

(yy) Responsibilities shared by Deputy Director, Division of Business and Economic Development, Community and Economic Development Department, and Deputy Director, Division of Community Development, same department. Deputy Director, Division of Business and Economic Development also has Economic development responsibilities.

(zz) Responsibilities shared by Director, Mental Health Division, Department of Social Services, and Director, Services to the Handicapped, same department.

(aaa) Responsibilities shared by Director, Division of Mental Health, Social and Health Services Department, and Acting Director, Division of Developmental Disabilities, same department.

(bbb) Responsibilities shared by Secretary, Department of Social and Health Services, listed under Health, and Director, Division of Income Assistance Services, same department.

(ccc) Responsibilities shared by Administrator, Trade and Consumer Protection Division, Agriculture, Trade, and Consumer Protection Department, and Unit Head, Consumer Protection and Antitrust Unit, Department of Justice.

(ddd) Responsibilities shared by Administrator, Division of Community Services, Health and Social Services, and Director, Developmental Disabilities Office, same department.

Table 2.11
SELECTED STATE ADMINISTRATIVE OFFICIALS: ANNUAL SALARIES

State or other jurisdiction	Governor	Lieutenant governor	Secretary of state	Attorney general	Treasurer	Adjutant general(a)	Adminis- tration	Agri- culture	Banking	Budget
Alabama	$70,223	$46,260	$36,234	$77,000	$49,500	$52,848	$ ...	$49,156	$52,848	$40,118(b)
Alaska	81,648	76,188		77,304	77,304	77,304	77,304	66,816	74,472	66,816
Arizona	75,000	...	50,000	70,000	50,000	58,000	65,975	61,275	72,910	67,173
Arkansas	35,000	22,500	22,500	26,500	22,500	48,419	68,448	(g)	60,998	39,754
California	85,000	72,500	72,500	77,500	72,500	84,957(h)	...	91,054	85,402	91,054
Colorado	70,000	48,500	48,500	60,000	48,500	72,155	65,000	65,000	55,680	N.A.
Connecticut	78,000	55,000	50,000	60,000	50,000	54,441(b)	71,617(b)	54,441(b)	57,627(b)	51,233(b)
Delaware	70,000	32,400	53,100	70,000	48,000	48,500	53,900	48,500	56,700	64,600
Florida	96,646	85,656	85,656	85,656	85,656	72,155	79,675	85,656	85,656	73,182
Georgia	84,594	51,328	64,494	66,092	...	83,680	62,361	64,493	62,361	69,810
Hawaii	80,000	76,000	...	68,400	(c-9)	81,822	68,400	68,400	61,404	68,400
Idaho	55,000	15,000	45,000	48,000	45,000	61,901	52,166	52,187	50,918	54,787
Illinois	93,266	65,835	82,294	82,294	71,321	40,598	68,578	65,835	68,250	70,400
Indiana	77,200	64,000	46,000	59,200	46,000	52,806	71,491	40,352	54,990	65,598
Iowa	70,000	23,900	50,000	62,500	50,000	56,810	43,500(b)	50,000	37,600(b)	49,000(b)
Kansas	65,693	19,128	52,530	60,417	52,530	45,900	64,370	50,870	43,954	63,598
Kentucky	68,364	58,101	58,101	58,101	58,101	64,983	64,983	58,101	58,452	64,983
Louisiana	73,400	63,367	60,169	66,566	60,169	74,556	66,492	60,169	50,000	49,596(b)
Maine	70,000	...	47,154	56,366	44,926	39,613	51,739	49,404	48,761	50,346
Maryland	85,000	72,500	45,000	72,500	72,500	55,900	70,700	70,700	58,000	72,700
Massachusetts	85,000	70,000	70,000	75,000	70,000	72,155	77,962	56,037	58,912	66,612
Michigan	100,077	67,377	89,000	89,000	65,700	68,698	65,700	64,100	27,833(b)	65,700
Minnesota	94,204	51,814	51,814	73,594	49,018	70,804	63,000	62,763	49,339(b)	73,500
Mississippi	63,000	34,000	45,000	51,000	45,000	42,000	...	45,000	41,000	57,939
Missouri	81,000	50,058	66,744	72,300	66,744	49,932	72,300	63,963	48,230	52,686
Montana	50,452	36,140	33,342	46,015	33,966	50,500	50,500	50,500	38,577	50,500
Nebraska	58,000	40,000	40,000	57,500	34,992	42,000	52,515(jj)	54,590	60,770	48,924(jj)
Nevada	77,500(nn)	11,494	50,500(nn)	57,471	49,000(nn)	39,282	55,344	43,613	46,350(nn)	(c-6)
New Hampshire	68,005	...	37,245(b)	60,708	37,245(b)	37,245(b)	60,708	35,625(b)	37,245(b)	(c-6)
New Jersey	85,000	...	90,000	90,000	90,000	90,000	72,050	90,000	90,000	85,000
New Mexico	63,000	40,425	40,425	46,200	40,425	51,604	58,814	58,814	45,609	50,220
New York	130,000(rr)	110,000	83,179	110,000	(ss)	83,179	87,578	83,179	83,179	92,059
North Carolina	105,000	64,092	64,092	64,092	64,092	55,656	64,092	64,092	61,656	73,656
North Dakota	60,856	49,992	46,000	52,000	46,000	73,512	45,864	46,000	46,500	(vv)
Ohio	65,000	42,536	50,000	50,000	50,000	57,595	54,392(b)	49,296(b)	49,296(b)	49,296(b)
Oklahoma	70,000	40,000	37,500	55,000	50,000	62,736	56,780	48,300	60,420	58,900
Oregon	73,500	...	55,000	60,996	55,000	52,848	74,316	58,224	52,848	64,248
Pennsylvania	85,000	67,500	58,000	65,000	58,000	58,000	65,000	58,000	58,000	65,000
Rhode Island	69,900	52,000	52,000	55,000	52,000	38,630(b)	61,619(b)	29,661(b)	33,624(b)	57,159(b)
South Carolina	81,600	35,700	69,360	69,630	69,630	69,630	82,214	69,360	(c-4)	(c-6)
South Dakota	57,324	50,003	38,937	48,672	38,937	54,080	49,920	50,128	45,073	62,400
Tennessee	85,000	24,200	65,000	65,650	65,000	57,500	65,000	55,500	58,000	60,444
Texas	91,600	7,200	64,890	73,233	73,233	55,826	59,699	73,233	79,310	65,000
Utah	60,000	50,000	...	49,000	45,000	38,628(b)	43,242(b)	36,498(b)	43,242(b)	40,883(b)
Vermont	63,600	26,500	40,000	48,000	40,000	43,618	56,202	48,922	48,006	50,502
Virginia	85,000	20,000	53,085	75,000	65,000	56,624	83,250	67,614	80,523	79,869
Washington	83,800	45,000	46,300	63,800	62,050	72,492	75,408	75,408	57,480	98,000
West Virginia	72,000	...	43,200	50,400	50,400	34,000	45,500	46,800	36,500	24,552(b)
Wisconsin	86,149	46,360	42,089	73,930	42,089	60,000	85,850	69,286	57,529	57,119
Wyoming	70,000	...	52,500	61,088	52,500	55,120	64,167	61,088	46,550	50,127
Dist. of Col.	83,010(ooo)	...	69,556	69,556	69,556	77,500	77,500	...	69,556	69,556
American Samoa	50,000	45,000	...	40,000	40,000	...	33,000	33,000	30,000	40,000
Guam	50,000	45,000	...	40,838	31,700	50,000	36,838	34,838	45,838	36,838
N. Marianas	50,000	45,000	...	42,000	28,000	...	36,000	25,000	30,000	36,000
Puerto Rico	45,000	...	50,500	50,000	50,000	49,375	49,375	50,000	47,500	50,000
Virgin Islands	64,400	57,600	N.A.	55,000	N.A.	55,000	55,000	55,000	(c-1)	55,000

Source: The Council of State Governments' survey of state personnel agencies, 1987.

Note: The chief administrative officials responsible for each function were determined from information given by the states for the same function as listed in *State Administrative Officials Classified by Function 1987-88*, published by The Council of State Governments. Salary figures (as of January 1988) are presented as submitted by the states. When necessary, figures have been rounded to the nearest dollar.

Key:
N.A.—Not available.
D.A.—Does not apply.
. . .—No specific chief administrative official or agency in charge of function.
(a) Salary listed may be of military grade.
(b) Minimum figure in range; top of range follows:
Alabama: Budget, $61,204; Comptroller, $61, 204; Computer services, $61,204; Consumer affairs, $48,906; Employment services, $56,758;

General services, $34,554; Parks and recreation, $52,702; Purchasing, $61,204; Solid waste management, $48,906; State police, $44,330; Transportation, $56,758
California: Highways, $70,536; Public library, $54,276
Connecticut: Adjutant general, $66,630; Administration, $87,547; Agriculture, $66,630; Banking, $70,370; Budget, $62,887; Civil rights, $70,370; Commerce, $75,219; Community affairs, $57,903; Computer services, $70,370; Consumer affairs, $75,219; Corrections, $80,898; Education, $87,547; Elections administration, $55,906; Emergency management, $50,424; Employment services, $70,370; Environmental protection, $80,898; Finance, $87,547; Fish and wildlife, $49,696; Health, $80,898; Highways, $70,370; Historic preservation, $45,944; Insurance, $70,370; Labor, $75,219; Licensing, 60,470; Parks and recreation, $49,696; Personnel, $70,370; Planning, $66,630; Public library, $66,630; Public utility regulation, $78,447; Public welfare, $80,898; Purchasing, $70,370; Revenue, $70,370; Social services, $75,219; Solid waste management, $53,754; State police, $80,898; Tourism, $47,785; Transportation, $87,547

SELECTED OFFICIALS: ANNUAL SALARIES—Continued

State or other jurisdiction	Civil rights	Commerce	Community affairs	Comptroller	Computer services	Consumer affairs	Corrections	Economic development	Education	Elections administration
Alabama	$ ...	$82,500	$52,848	$40,118(b)	$40,118(b)	$32,136(b)	$63,792	$82,500	$ 74,750	$ (c-2)
Alaska	69,276	77,304	77,304	64,620	69,276	71,880	77,304	77,304	77,304	66,816
Arizona	77,099	65,975	(c-11)	69,254	67,173	76,105	86,283	(c-11)	50,000	(c-2)
Arkansas	...	57,913	43,992	(c-6)	61,919	25,362	61,874	(c-11)	67,470	(c-2)
California	75,354	85,402	58,506	72,500	53,256	85,402	85,402	(c-11)	72,500	(c-2)
Colorado	58,464	58,464	55,680	58,464	...	57,204	68,000	70,000	82,500	34,188
Connecticut	57,627(b)	61,505(b)	47,376(b)	50,000	57,627(b)	61,505(b)	66,213(b)	(c-11)	71,617(b)	45,545(b)
Delaware	36,900	(c-2)	53,900	50,127(b)	57,800	36,900	64,600	64,700	86,300	34,900
Florida	45,072	79,675	79,675	(c-8)	59,122	50,474	79,675	53,594	85,656	46,236
Georgia	...	70,524	70,518	64,470	60,300	55,356	62,361	(c-11)	66,000	56,364
Hawaii	...	68,400	68,400	68,400	39,024(b)	68,400	68,400	(c-12)	76,000	35,580(b)
Idaho	33,613	46,176	36,171	45,000	(c-6)	(c-3)	52,354	(c-11)	45,000	(c-2)
Illinois	57,057	65,835	(c-11)	71,321	(c-6)	(c-3)	65,835	(c-11)	105,163	60,252
Indiana	44,538	(c-1)	47,320	45,994	63,128	56,004	68,302	45,656	63,102	32,474
Iowa	34,000(b)	43,500(b)	45,552(b)	(c-9)	45,552(b)	39,853(b)	49,700(b)	49,700(b)	49,700(b)	25,272(b)
Kansas	36,157	57,565	46,145	61,836	54,319(v)	33,611	62,094	(c-11)	71,900	(c-2)
Kentucky	55,289	64,983	50,488	(c-9)	(c-9)	(c-3)	64,983	60,000	58,101	(c-2)
Louisiana	(c-3)	53,353	52,366	(c-6)	37,836(b)	...	55,000	(c-11)	60,163	60,168
Maine	39,527	59,821	39,056	48,033	67,464	40,248	47,026	(c-11)	59,816	(c-2)
Maryland	57,400	52,400	52,400	72,500	58,000	58,000	61,300	97,400	72,700	58,000
Massachusetts	58,010	69,015	63,789	70,602	73,156	61,411	77,547	67,302	77,547	70,000
Michigan	60,000	64,100	27,833(b)	(c-4)	43,827(b)	51,302(b)	64,100	27,833(b)	70,900	39,401(b)
Minnesota	54,600	63,000	52,910(b)	(c-9)	47,606(b)	52,600(b)	62,753	41,259(b)	72,072	(c-2)
Mississippi	...	62,447	42,000	45,000	51,156	(gg)	40,000	(c-11)	62,447	44,936
Missouri	44,655	48,229	(c-11)	48,234	48,234	...	63,963	63,963	70,008	33,552
Montana	32,067	50,500	40,416	(c-6)	46,236	28,028	50,500	36,287	39,671	20,573
Nebraska	59,279	36,396	35,520	(c-6)	51,444	46,056	61,000	61,800	(kk)	(c-2)
Nevada	38,625(nn)	51,086	39,693	49,000(nn)	47,373	31,404	65,191(nn)	51,004	56,124	(c-2)
New Hampshire	28,568(b)	35,625(b)	45,000	37,245(b)	42,091(b)	(c-3)	42,091(b)	(c-11)	60,708	(c-2)
New Jersey	64,731	90,000	90,000	(c-9)	74,250	62,302	90,000	65,000	90,000	51,758(oo)
New Mexico	28,730(b)	58,814	58,814	(c-4)	48,858	46,175	58,814	58,814	61,161	40,683
New York	76,654	83,179	(c-2)	(c-4)	(c-6)	69,982	93,713	(c-11)	93,713	75,654
North Carolina	44,844	64,092	43,824	100,000	69,756	48,108	64,092	57,360	64,092	69,396
North Dakota	46,000	44,556	36,288	(c-9)	52,068	35,568	43,056	(c-11)	46,992	(c-2)
Ohio	33,363(b)	(xx)	32,115(b)	(c-4)	36,816(b)	40,560(b)	54,392(b)	35,381(b)	90,293	29,099(b)
Oklahoma	37,700	48,300	48,824(b)	55,000	43,242(b)	40,350	60,000	(c-11)	55,000	52,000
Oregon	47,904	58,224	52,848	(c-4)	52,848	58,224	64,248	74,316	55,000	41,388
Pennsylvania	59,032	61,500	58,000	54,000	51,951	51,951	61,500	(c-11)	65,000	35,345
Rhode Island	30,023(b)	57,159(b)	...	44,811(b)	42,693(b)	27,797(b)	61,619(b)	(c-11)	80,141	28,986
South Carolina	57,560	86,959	43,680	69,360	63,045	64,890	76,975	(c-11)	69,360	53,415
South Dakota	21,340	50,065	48,006	38,937	(c-6)	33,924	51,272	(c-12)	48,006	(c-2)
Tennessee	44,424	64,500	(c-11)	64,992	55,344	34,116	61,000	(c-11)	75,000	38,928
Texas	48,204	70,000	52,221	73,233	59,484	52,000	68,289	70,000	65,400	49,234
Utah	31,007(b)	40,883(b)	(iii)	40,883(b)	40,883(b)	29,462(b)	40,883(b)	(iii)	46,270(b)	(c-1)
Vermont	45,094	42,806	41,454	50,502	47,008	(c-10)	46,738	(c-11)	55,827	(c-2)
Virginia	...	83,250	61,467	78,000	74,941	32,689	75,028	80,000	86,489	55,208
Washington	56,560	75,408	75,408	(c-4)	81,096	56,400	75,408	53,376	66,600	38,712
West Virginia	38,992	63,600	63,600	46,800	40,788(b)	42,600	36,500	(c-11)	70,600	(c-2)
Wisconsin	46,922	74,740	56,649	51,404	55,752	(mmm)	69,558	44,328	66,536	46,936
Wyoming	51,375	61,088	(c-11)	52,500	43,222(b)	33,737(b)	43,222(b)	(c-11)	52,500	(c-2)
Dist. of Col.	69,556	69,556	55,753	69,556	59,469	(ppp)	69,556	(c-11)	83,010	69,556
Amer. Samoa	...	33,000	(c-11)	(c-4)	N.A.	30,576	17,921	(c-11)	35,000	31,595
Guam	...	34,838	45,000	(c-6)	(c-6)	...	34,838	(c-12)	50,000	35,000
N. Marianas	(uuu)	36,000	36,000	(c-4)	25,000	34,000	25,000	(vvv)	40,000	28,000
Puerto Rico	32,000(xxx)	50,000	43,750	50,500	47,500	50,000	47,500	N.A.	50,500	...
Virgin Islands	(c-3)	(c-7)	55,000	55,000	(c-9)	55,000	(c-3)	(c-7)	55,000	...

Delaware: Comptroller, $83,545; Solid waste management, $83,545; Tourism, $45,441

Florida: Public welfare, $67,000, Solid waste management, $65,000

Hawaii: Computer services, $64,176; Elections administration, $58,428; Employment services, $61,044; Energy resources, $61,044; Highways, $64,284; Parks and recreation, $61,044; Planning, $64,236; Pre-audit, $61,044; Public welfare, $64,284; Purchasing, $52,788

Indiana: Higher education, $78,000

Iowa: Administration, $57,000; Banking, $50,300; Budget, $66,200; Civil rights, $45,000; Commerce, $57,000; Community affairs, $57,574; Computer services, $57,574; Consumer affairs, $54,974; Corrections, $66,200; Economic development, $66,200; Education, $66,200; Elections administration, $32,198; Emergency management, $37,600; Employment services, $57,000; Energy resources, $57,574; Environmental protection, $57,574; Fish and wildlife, $57,574; Health, $57,000; Higher education, $66,200; Highways, $60,341; Historic preservation, $56,500; Insurance, $56,500; Labor, $56,500; Licensing, $37,600; Mental health and retarda-

tion, $63,232; Natural resources, $66,200; Parks and recreation, $50,024; Personnel, $57,000; Pre-audit, $66,200; Public utility regulation, $56,500; Public welfare, $43,472; Purchasing, $50,024; Revenue, $66,200; Social services, $63,232; Solid waste management, $57,574; State police, $60,341; Tourism, $43,472; Transportation, $66,200

Louisiana: Budget, $82,212; Computer services, $62,724; Highways, $87,972; Licensing, $47,844; Personnel, $82,212; Planning, $58,620

Maine: Tourism, $48,380

Maryland: Pre-audit, $41,003; Public library, $55,270; Purchasing, $47,826

Massachusetts: General services, $53,196

Michigan: Banking, $72,766; Community affairs, $67,317; Computer services, $58,715; Consumer affairs, $66,565; Economic development, $72,766; Elections administration, $54,351; Emergency management, $53,766; Energy resources, $72,766; Environmental protection, $77,924; Higher education, $58,715; Historic preservation, $72,766; Parks and recreation, $72,766; Personne, $83,290; Purchasing, $72,766; Tourism, $72,766

SELECTED OFFICIALS: ANNUAL SALARIES—Continued

State or other jurisdiction	Emergency management	Employment services	Energy resources	Environmental protection	Finance	Fish & wildlife	General services	Health	Higher education	Highways
Alabama.........	$52,848	$32,232 (b)	$ (d)	$52,848	$52,848	$52,848	$22,807 (b)	$100,976	$ 74,750	$52,848
Alaska...........	58,308	66,732	52,584	77,304	66,732	77,304	69,276	77,304	82,992	77,304
Arizona..........	47,69	55,920	38,393	65,975	(c-13)	58,000	43,481	76,125	96,425	83,551
Arkansas........	36,824	64,631	48,576	46,286	(c-6)	53,984	(c-6)	69,395	69,363	74,836
California........	75,354	85,402	81,635	91,054	(c-9)	85,402	85,402	85,402	91,409	64,140 (b)
Colorado	58,464	70,000	50,508	55,680	(c-13)	N.A.	(c-6)	80,803	88,176	74,000
Connecticut	41,281 (b)	57,627 (b)	...	66,213 (b)	71,617 (b)	40,488 (b)	(c-6)	66,213 (b)	95,000	57,627 (b)
Delaware	34,000	59,300	44,800	59,300	70,000	41,600	(c-6)	64,600	46,100	62,900
Florida	55,678	56,179	53,714	79,675	51,030	79,675	79,675	54,756	119,000	85,000
Georgia..........	(c-5)	53,544	55,356	70,980	58,428	63,130	(c-6)	87,790	123,000	88,654
Hawaii	(c-5)	37,236 (b)	37,236 (b)	55,404	(c-9)	(q)	(c-13)	68,400	95,000 (r)	42,864 (b)
Idaho	41,870	56,139	54,787	47,237	(c-9)	57,533	36,171	57,034	60,590	65,000
Illinois..........	40,598	71,321	57,057	65,835	54,862	65,835	(c-6)	71,321	96,000	71,321
Indiana	35,828	51,506	36,998	67,444	(c-9)	41,236	(c-6)	79,904	49,972 (b)	60,762
Iowa	22,600 (b)	43,500 (b)	45,552 (b)	45,552 (b)	(c-9)	45,552 (b)	(c-6)	43,500 (b)	49,700 (b)	47,736 (b)
Kansas	39,864	64,370	29,743	54,750	(c-9)	64,370	(c-5)	69,169	68,850	64,370
Kentucky	40,421	54,994	64,983	64,983	(c-9)	52,500	(c-9)	88,308	76,885	62,383
Louisiana	35,955	43,842	53,584	54,000	(c-6)	52,367	(c-6)	63,327	35,000	53,076 (b)
Maine	38,627	40,834	50,346	49,404	59,816	42,723	(c-22)	54,353	(z)	56,966
Maryland	47,900	52,400	52,400	70,700	(c-13)	54,600	70,700	72,700	72,700	72,700
Massachusetts	47,829	40,682	59,034	67,302	(c-6)	63,273	42,484 (b)	77,547	100,000 (bb)	77,547
Michigan	40,236 (b)	55,100	27,833 (b)	27,833 (b)	(c-9)	64,100	(c-9)	70,700	43,827 (b)	64,100
Minnesota	39,797 (b)	47,606 (b)	42,825 (b)	(ee)	(c-9)	35,580 (b)	(c-6)	62,753	65,000	51,072 (b)
Mississippi	28,000	48,000	40,000	36,254 (b)	(c-9)	45,145	51,928	77,767	87,000	45,000
Missouri	46,332	52,683	46,522	48,230	(c-6)	70,008	(c-6)	82,404	70,000	72,096
Montana.........	38,577	43,212	38,005	46,236	(c-9)	50,500	(c-6)	46,236	73,299	50,500
Nebraska	33,996	33,072	43,248	44,290	(c-6,9,35,39)	72,746	(c-6)	63,357	35,190	58,498
Nevada	35,897	48,248	39,439	45,690	(c-13)	45,410	48,637	47,005	102,000	57,614
New Hampshire ...	41,509	35,685 (b)	34,500	46,954 (b)	(c-6)	35,625 (b)	(c-6)	46,954 (b)	42,091 (b)	60,708
New Jersey	77,610	70,000	68,000	90,000	(c-4)	64,136	(c-6)	90,000	90,000	90,000
New Mexico......	58,814	58,814	54,873	51,604	58,814	48,858	(c-6)	58,814	53,050	54,873
New York	93,713	87,578	83,179	87,578	(c-4)	(c-21)	(c-6)	(c-18)	(c-17)	93,713
North Carolina	41,796	61,656	42,300	64,092	(c-9)	53,160	58,692	106,848	120,200	73,656
North Dakota	37,104	51,900	(c-12)	56,160	(c-9)	42,960	(c-9)	72,840	79,980	54,072
Ohio	37,336 (b)	44,720 (b)	32,115 (b)	54,392 (b)	(c-9)	37,336 (b)	(c-6)	54,392 (b)	97,011	54,392 (b)
Oklahoma	(c-5)	48,500	46,180	37,700	(c-9)	56,250	56,780	82,750	55,000	60,000
Oregon	43,440	58,224	58,224	58,224	(c-6,9)	58,224	61,188	55,452	98,160	61,188
Pennsylvania	54,240	56,500	56,607	65,000	61,500	(bbb)	61,500	65,000	54,000	65,000
Rhode Island	(c-5)	57,159 (b)	46,005 (b)	57,159 (b)	51,152 (b)	33,072 (b)	40,580 (b)	80,142	89,443	61,619 (b)
South Carolina	32,096 (b)	73,962	...	61,255 (b)	(c-6)	73,116	(c-13)	84,586	78,218	86,012
South Dakota	54,080	35,963	39,998	52,499	(c-9)	48,672	(c-6)	47,236	48,006	54,995
Tennessee	46,416	57,500	57,840	57,840	(c-6)	57,500	55,500	61,000	90,000	61,000
Texas............	44,136	59,251	60,976	55,200	(c-13)	62,830	59,699	66,640	110,100	68,701
Utah	32,656 (b)	43,242 (b)	32,656 (b)	38,628 (b)	(c-13)	36,498 (b)	(c-6)	52,952 (b)	N.A.	43,242 (b)
Vermont..........	34,570	48,755	55,141	53,997	(c-13)	45,406	(c-6)	63,752	35,942	59,010
Virginia..........	55,375	68,092	76,004	57,087	83,250	54,268	76,004	83,343	84,794	86,489
Washington	47,172	60,384	56,560	75,408	(c-9)	75,408	(c-6)	93,260	77,223	93,260
West Virginia	30,500	34,000	65,000	45,500	(c-6)	30,888 (b)	32,903	54,500	78,759	47,500
Wisconsin........	43,430	54,062	42,269	55,399	53,000	44,280	49,999	69,265	106,271	68,994
Wyoming	34,590	52,665	...	56,721	(c-13)	59,591	(c-6)	74,400	60,000	65,768
Dist. of Col.	69,556	69,556	53,717	65,386	69,556	(c-21)	69,556	69,556	(qqq)	69,556
American Samoa ..	27,000	...	30,000	29,536	(c-4)	30,000	30,000	35,000	(ttt)	24,000
Guam	34,838	34,838	34,838	34,838	(c-6)	(c-7)	(c-6)	36,838	50,000	36,838
N. Marianas	30,000	36,000	30,000	28,000	36,000	28,000	(c-6)	45,000	40,000	36,000
Puerto Rico	41,250	18,120 (xxx)	50,000	47,500	(c-9)	50,000	(c-13)	50,000	44,000 (xxx)	50,000
Virgin Islands	(c-5)	55,000	41,547	55,000	(c-13)	50,000	(c-21)	55,000	36,700	32,500

Minnesota: Banking, $65,480; Community affairs, $70,282; Computer services, $63,204; Consumer affairs, $67,800; Economic development, $54,831; Emergency management, $52,910; Employment services, $63,204; Energy resources, $56,814; Fish and wildlife, $47,606; Highways, $67,839; Mental health and retardation, $67,839; Parks and recreation, $58,882; Pre-audit, $63,204; Public library, $48,734; Public utility regulation, $52,910; Public welfare, $58,882; Purchasing, $58,882; Social services, $67,839; Solid waste management, $58,882; State police, $58,882; Tourism, $65,480

Mississippi: Environmental protection, $54,307; Purchasing, $46,752; Solid waste management, $49,153

New Hampshire: Secretary of state, $47,776; Treasurer, $47,776; Adjutant general, $47,776; Agriculture, $45,333; Banking, $47,776; Civil rights, $34,067; Commerce, $45,333; Comptroller, $47,776; Computer services, $54,230; Corrections, $54,230; Employment services, $42,959; Environmental protection, $59,097; Fish and wildlife, $45,333; Health, $59,097; Higher education, $54,230; Historic preservation, $35,624;

Labor, $45,333; Mental health and retardation, $59,097; Parks and recreation, $45,333; Personnel, $54,230; Post audit, $59,097; Public library, $45,333; Public welfare, $47,776; Purchasing, $47,776; Solid waste management, $45,333; State police, $45,333; Tourism, $35,888

New Mexico: Civil rights, $40,697; Labor, $52,133

North Carolina: Public library, $63,804

Ohio: Administration, $76,440; Agriculture, $70,803; Banking, $70,803; Budget, $70,803; Civil rights, $49,774; Community affairs, $47,424; Computer services, $54,392; Consumer affairs, $59,405; Corrections, $76,440; Economic development, $51,792; Elections administration, $43,410; Emergency management, $48,942; Employment services, $64,834; Energy resources, $47,424 Environmental protection, $76,440; Fish and wildlife, $48,942; Health, $76,440; Highways, $76,440; Insurance, $64,834; Labor, $64,834; Natural resources, $76,440; Parks and recreation, $48,942; Personnel, $49,774; Public library, $59,405; Public utility regulation, $76,440; Public welfare, $70,803; Purchasing, $49,774; Revenue, $64,834; Solid waste management, $48,942; State police, $59,405; Tourism, $43,410

SELECTED OFFICIALS: ANNUAL SALARIES—Continued

State or other jurisdiction	Historic preservation	Insurance	Labor	Licensing	Mental health & retardation	Natural resources	Parks & recreation	Personnel	Planning	Post audit
Alabama	$45,000	$52,848	$52,848	$ ...	$46,296	(c-23)	$34,554 (b)	$67,152	$ ...	$65,904
Alaska	51,012	66,816	77,304	64,620	(e)	77,304	71,880	66,816	...	71,928
Arizona	38,570	55,000	34,189	...	(f)	65,975	55,318	55,414	(c-11)	73,978
Arkansas	31,096	52,834	56,336	...	66,737	41,668	52,204	43,992	...	64,218
California	55,872	85,402	(i)	(c-15)	(j)	75,354	85,402	...	65,340	(k)
Colorado	54,800	60,000	58,464	65,000	(l)	N.A.	55,680	65,000	(c-9)	62,982
Connecticut	37,431 (b)	57,627 (b)	61,505 (b)	49,260 (b)	(m)	(c-21)	40,488 (b)	57,627 (b)	54,441 (b)	(n)
Delaware	45,900	48,500	53,900	34,000	(o)	(c-21)	41,600	(c-19)	51,500	48,500
Florida	50,052	85,656	61,820	45,156	53,246	79,675	65,000	55,755	(c-9)	79,800
Georgia	44,862	(c-13)	64,493	53,358	87,790	(c-21)	54,891	67,122	(c-9)	63,960
Hawaii	68,400	61,404	68,400	(c-11)	(s)	(c-27)	37,236 (b)	68,400	40,860 (b)	(t)
Idaho	41,870	59,966	48,485	41,870	37,981	...	48,485	52,187	(c-11)	48,485
Illinois	60,348	60,349	60,349	60,349	71,321	(c-20)	(c-23)	61,000	50,000	68,250
Indiana	30,290	54,964	46,592	48,568	(u)	65,026	51,896	64,246	D.A.	54,548
Iowa	43,800 (b)	43,800 (b)	43,800 (b)	22,600 (b)	50,024 (b)	49,700 (b)	39,582 (b)	43,500 (b)	(c-16)	50,000
Kansas	52,142	52,534	(c-19)	...	58,887	(c-21)	(c-23)	57,491	(c-9)	61,849
Kentucky	48,649	59,044	64,983	37,401	62,030	(c-21)	60,203	60,228	(c-6)	58,101
Louisiana	43,841	60,169	56,021	28,872 (b)	(w)	58,452	43,841	49,596 (b)	35,364	(x)
Maine	35,114	48,825	49,404	32,656	54,272	(c-21)	42,794	45,781	52,874	37,085
Maryland	46,400	61,300	58,000	70,700	(aa)	70,700	54,600	(c-6)	70,700	65,900
Massachusetts	N.A.	61,093	48,143	46,170	(cc)	69,015	41,818	73,156	62,626	70,000
Michigan	27,833 (b)	60,000	64,100	64,100	70,700	(c-23)	27,833 (b)	27,833 (b)	...	69,500
Minnesota	N.A.	62,753	(ff)	(c-29)	51,072 (b)	62,753	44,328 (b)	62,753	63,000	56,526
Mississippi	37,000	45,000	...	46,527	(hh)	51,928	32,017	48,902	(c-12)	(c-13)
Missouri	33,780	48,229	63,960	46,527	71,496	63,963	48,230	46,527	(c-9)	66,744
Montana	21,806	28,000	50,500	28,028	(ii)	50,500	37,232	41,479	(c-12)	50,500
Nebraska	45,000	51,499	(ll)	39,360	(mm)	47,153	(c-23)	43,000	43,264	34,992 (jj)
Nevada	31,582	46,350 (nn)	35,192	...	61,285 (nn)	49,743	39,148	46,208	...	50,981
New Hampshire	25,895 (b)	60,708	35,625 (b)	(c-2)	46,954 (b)	(c-27)	35,625 (b)	42,091 (b)	(c-12)	46,954 (b)
New Jersey	40,162	90,000	90,000	(c-15)	(pp)	72,000	56,639	90,000	70,000	65,000
New Mexico	36,575	42,717	40,294 (b)	58,814	(qq)	43,974	48,858	50,220	...	40,411
New York	83,179	83,179	(c-19)	(c-2)	(tt)	(c-21)	(c-27)	83,179	(c-11)	(c-4)
North Carolina	44,340	64,092	64,092	...	105,540	(c-21)	50,400	64,092	N.A.	64,092
North Dakota	37,116	46,000	(c-10)	(c-2)	47,340	...	39,708	(c-6)	(c-12)	(ww)
Ohio	N.A.	44,720 (b)	44,720 (b)	...	(yy)	54,392 (b)	37,336 (b)	33,363 (b)	(c-9)	50,000
Oklahoma	35,050	50,000	39,750	...	(zz)	48,300	(c-31)	50,000	...	50,000
Oregon	29,424	52,848	55,000	(c-11)	(aaa)	58,224	52,848	55,452	58,224	50,328
Pennsylvania	54,240	58,000	65,000	44,000	(ccc)	(c-21)	54,240	58,000	65,000	58,000
Rhode Island	31,210 (b)	41,541 (b)	50,465 (b)	27,551 (b)	(eee)	(c-21)	34,237 (b)	46,923 (b)	39,157 (b)	(fff)
South Carolina	29,673 (b)	74,039	60,739	...	(ggg)	51,000	60,739	63,754	...	69,257
South Dakota	23,504	34,507	48,609	23,878	(hhh)	52,499	48,672	48,609	...	47,257
Tennessee	34,116	57,500	55,500	23,988 (b)	61,000	57,500	46,416	55,500	58,008	(c-13)
Texas	46,968	60,873	55,002	...	72,615	66,024	(c-23)	...	65,000	72,228
Utah	32,656 (b)	36,498 (b)	38,628 (b)	29,462 (b)	(jjj)	43,242 (b)	36,498 (b)	40,883 (b)	(c-9)	45,000
Vermont	32,469	(c-8)	44,886	(c-2)	55,910	(c-21)	45,302	35,000 (b)	42,515	40,000
Virginia	58,768	(c-8)	58,213	51,784	83,064	83,250	58,768	71,537	(c-9)	43,930
Washington	44,904	53,700	75,408	49,572	(kkk)	66,600	70,032	75,408	(c-9)	55,250
West Virginia	31,740	35,000	34,000	...	(c-25)	(c-21)	47,600	36,500	(c-11)	30,997
Wisconsin	41,378	70,000	74,740	52,519	(nnn)	76,615	54,712	70,700	(c-9)	68,802
Wyoming	46,550	47,714	43,222	...	42,161	...	(c-27)	51,375	43,222	(c-8,13)
Dist. of Col.	52,135	65,043	(c-19)	47,397	69,556	(c-21)	(rrr)	69,556	69,556	69,556
American Samoa	21,028	25,000	...	...	25,000	...	33,000	35,000	(c-11)	35,000
Guam	34,838	...	34,838	(c-8)	34,838	(c-7)	(c-27)	(c-6)	34,838	(c-9)
N. Marianas	28,000	N.A.	(c-11)	18,000	30,000	32,000	25,000	(c-19)	(c-9)	36,000
Puerto Rico	43,750	47,500	50,000	13,224 (xxx)	30,324 (xxx)	(c-21)	50,000	(c-6)	50,000	(c-12)
Virgin Islands	(c-21)	(c-1)	(c-9)	(c-15)	(c-25)	(c-21)	55,000	55,000	(c-21)	33,171

Oklahoma: Community affairs, $55,000; Computer services, $57,745; Solid waste management, $56,384

Rhode Island: Adjutant general, $43,775; Administration, $68,312; Agriculture, $33,417; Banking, $38,081; Budget, $63,850; Civil rights, $33,985; Commerce, $63,850; Comptroller, $51,152; Computer services, $49,035; Consumer affairs, $31,436; Corrections, $68,312; Employment services, $63,850; Energy resources, $52,696; Environmental protection, $63,850; Finance, $57,495; Fish and wildlife, $37,298; General services, $46,923; Highways, $68,312; Historic preservation, $35,352; Insurance, $48,236; Labor, $57,159; Licensing, $31,000; Parks and recreation, $38,638; Personnel, $53,265; Planning, $44,811; Pre-audit, $22,094; Public library, $52,696; Public welfare, $51,152; Purchasing, $55,380; Revenue, $57,495; Social services, $68,312; Tourism, $36,719

South Carolina: Emergency management, $45,494; Environmental protection, $91,883; Historic preservation, $42,060; Purchasing, $60,780; Solid waste management, $55,798; State police, $90,629; Tourism, $55,798

Tennessee: Licensing, $35,640

Utah: Adjutant general, $56,418; Administration, $63,141; Agriculture, $53,307; Banking, $63,141; Budget, $59,675; Civil rights, $45,310; Commerce, $59,675; Comptroller, $59,675; Computer services, $59,675; Consumer affairs, $43,034; Corrections, $59,675; Education, $67,505; Emergency management, $47,627; Employment services, $63,141; Energy resources, $47,627; Environmental protection, $56,418; Fish and wildlife, $53,307; Health, $77,298; Highways, $63,141; Historic preservation, $47,627; Insurance, $53,307; Labor, $56,418; Licensing, $43,034; Natural resources, $63,141; Parks and recreation, $53,307; Personnel, $59,675; Public library, $47,627; Public utility regulation, $50,342; Public welfare, $53,307; Purchasing, $47,627; Revenue, $59,675; Social services, $63,141; Solid waste management, $53,307; State police, $50,342; Tourism, $47,627

Vermont: Personnel, $52,500

West Virginia: Budget, $43,843; Computer services, $58,157; Fish and wildlife, $55,473; Purchasing, $48,152; Social services, $45,960; Solid waste management, $38,135; Transportation, $36,397

Wyoming: Computer services, $69,096; Consumer affairs, $53,975; Corrections, $69,096; Tourism, $55,327

Guam: Public utility regulation, $28,000

SELECTED OFFICIALS: ANNUAL SALARIES—Continued

State or other jurisdiction	Pre-audit	Public library	Public utility regulation	Public welfare	Purchasing	Revenue	Social services	Solid waste management	State police	Tourism	Transportation
Alabama.........	$ (c-13)	$48,000	$44,550	$52,848	$40,118(b)	$52,848	$ (c-37)	$32,136(b)	$29,094(b)	$52,848	$37,232(b)
Alaska..........	40,356	62,508	66,816	69,276	(c-24)	71,880	(c-25)	60,228	64,620	66,816	(c-26)
Arizona..........	61,257	62,727	73,256	76,125	61,257	66,576	56,840	(c-21)	82,687	50,750	(c-26)
Arkansas........	31,096	47,725	53,770	(c-30)	43,992	50,140	(c-30)	(c-21)	45,701	(c-32)	(c-26)
California.......	(c-13)	49,416(b)	81,635	85,402	67,608	85,402	(c-37)	81,635	91,054	58,596	85,402
Colorado	(c-13)	53,710	48,400	65,000	58,464	58,464	(c-37)	58,464	58,464	55,680	. . .
Connecticut	(c-13)	54,441(b)	67,420(b)	66,213(b)	57,627(b)	57,627(b)	61,505(b)	43,794(b)	66,213(b)	38,929(b)	71,617(b)
Delaware	(c-35)	36,100	39,700	56,500	41,500	59,700	(p)	50,127(b)	54,800	27,265(b)	64,600
Florida	55,300	53,760	73,800	42,000(b)	57,750	79,657	66,800	41,000(b)	62,000	50,000	(c-26)
Georgia..........	(c-35)	63,930	61,900	69,442	58,218	63,920	(c-37)	57,991	68,802	66,840	(c-26)
Hawaii	37,236	68,400	61,560	42,864(b)	32,412(b)	68,400	68,400	(c-21)	(c-12)	(c-12)	68,400
Idaho	(c-13)	43,909	36,504	48,485	36,171	34,507	46,176	39,874	46,176	(c-11)	(c-26)
Illinois..........	(c-13)	54,996	70,455	71,321	(c-6)	71,321	65,835	(c-20)	65,835	(c-11)	(c-26)
Indiana	(c-13)	53,872	53,742	65,475	(c-6)	58,292	(c-37)	50,206	51,922	37,362	54,366
Iowa	49,700(b)	. . .	43,800(b)	34,362(b)	39,582(b)	49,700(b)	50,024(b)	45,552(b)	47,736(b)	34,362(b)	49,700(b)
Kansas	(c-13)	49,658	64,933	45,043	48,446	64,370	65,007	(c-21)	49,658	45,043	(c-26)
Kentucky	(c-9)	49,512	57,494	60,782	47,704	64,983	60,228	46,482	60,132	64,983	64,983
Louisiana	(c-9)	48,713	61,536	48,713	(y)	52,366	42,624	49,000	52,000	43,842	58,455
Maine	(c-13)	38,885	59,109	40,019	38,858	46,490	(c-37)	(c-21)	49,339	32,947(b)	(c-26)
Maryland	31,214(b)	42,078(b)	63,700	58,000	36,411(b)	(c-13)	(c-37)	54,600	70,700	61,300	97,400
Massachusetts	(c-13)	48,770	65,792	77,547	56,037	69,424	77,962	51,403	66,606	63,273	67,302
Michigan	(c-35)	. . .	60,000	70,700	27,833(b)	(dd)	(c-37)	(c-21)	64,100	27,833(b)	(c-26)
Minnesota	47,606(b)	36,122(b)	39,797(b)	44,328(b)	44,328(b)	63,000	51,072(b)	44,328(b)	44,328(b)	49,339(b)	73,500
Mississippi	(c-13)	37,000	40,000	45,000	31,224(b)	50,000	(c-37)	32,810(b)	40,000	35,899	(c-20)
Missouri	(c-13)	56,650	63,963	49,933	46,523	72,300	66,744	36,828	61,968	44,452	(c-26)
Montana.........	. . .	38,792	37,360	50,500	38,577	50,500	(c-37)	35,547	45,339	38,577	38,792
Nebraska	(c-6)	43,292	28,320	56,134	40,152	61,000(jj)	(c-37)	(c-21)	46,556	34,452	(c-26)
Nevada	(c-6)	41,500	52,979	55,620(nn)	(c-24)	49,194	59,606	(c-21)	44,687	54,075(nn)	(c-26)
New Hampshire ..	(c-6)	35,625(b)	60,708	37,245(b)	37,245(b)	60,708	60,708	35,625(b)	35,625(b)	29,855(b)	(c-26)
New Jersey	85,000	63,628	90,000	63,291	61,460	80,000	90,000	(c-18)	55,914	62,500	(c-26)
New Mexico......	43,974	38,378	53,050	42,276	42,276	58,814	42,276	(c-21)	55,628	45,714	58,814
New York	(c-4)	(c-17)	87,578	87,578	(c-6)	(uu)	(c-37)	(c-21)	87,578	83,179	(c-26)
North Carolina ...	(c-35)	39,012(b)	65,092	64,092	63,804	64,092	58,032	35,580	68,556	43,224	64,092
North Dakota	(c-9)	37,500	46,000	66,816	30,000	46,000	49,300	44,300	42,180	33,800	41,900
Ohio	(c-35)	40,560(b)	54,392(b)	49,296(b)	33,363(b)	44,720(b)	(c-37)	37,336(b)	40,560(b)	29,099(b)	(c-26)
Oklahoma	(c-9)	40,000	52,000	76,000	48,300	56,000	(c-37)	42,227(b)	49,360	(c-31)	(c-26)
Oregon	. . .	47,904	61,188	61,188	47,904	58,224	74,316	58,224	62,304	51,816	64,248
Pennsylvania	(c-4)	45,712	57,519	65,000	(c-24)	(c-22)	(ddd)	42,015	61,500	(c-11)	(c-26)
Rhode Island.....	19,646(b)	46,005(b)	(c-20)	44,811(b)	49,035(b)	51,152(b)	61,619(b)	N.A.	76,882	32,392	(c-26)
South Carolina ...	(c-13)	48,910	53,324	77,898	40,520(b)	58,662	(c-37)	39,051(b)	66,987(b)	39,051(b)	(c-26)
South Dakota	. . .	36,067	38,937	47,964	31,595	48,006	61,484	(c-20)	44,512	48,006	54,995
Tennessee........	48,504	60,444	57,490	57,500	46,416	55,500	42,504	48,504	55,500	57,500	(c-26)
Texas	(c-13)	48,410	55,620	68,289	(c-24)	(c-13)	(c-37)	45,940	66,641	49,500	(c-26)
Utah	(c-13)	32,656(b)	34,494(b)	36,498(b)	32,656(b)	40,883(b)	43,242(b)	36,498(b)	34,494(b)	32,656(b)	(c-26)
Vermont	(c-13)	41,392	57,300	50,690	(c-14)	47,861	50,939	49,005	39,374	45,843	(c-26)
Virginia..........	(c-13)	68,839	(c-8)	75,381	60,998	80,689	(c-37)	53,085	69,011	58,343	83,250
Washington	. . .	70,032	70,032	(lll)	50,796	75,408	(c-25)	49,572	75,408	53,376	(c-26)
West Virginia	(c-6)	56,758	44,675	45,500	26,916(b)	47,500	25,704(b)	21,456(b)	42,500	45,600	20,520(b)
Wisconsin........	47,220	58,508	60,001	64,974	49,999	74,740	82,315	55,745	63,774	53,500	78,780
Wyoming	(c-13)	42,161	52,665	48,900	41,142	59,591	(c-37)	43,222	44,303	34,590(b)	. . .
Dist. of Col.	(c-22)	69,556	. . .	55,753	69,556	69,556	69,556	69,556	69,556	69,556	(sss)	69,556
American Samoa .	. . .	25,000	. . .	. . .	(c-24)	25,000	. . .	N.A.	35,000	33,000	33,000
Guam	(c-9)	34,838	24,000(b)	(c-25)	(c-6)	(c-8)	(c-25)	(c-26)	36,838	42,500	36,000
N. Marianas	28,000	25,000	36,000	(c-12)	25,000	28,000	(c-12)	(www)	25,000	36,000	36,000
Puerto Rico	50,000	16,368(xxx)	38,000(xxx)	50,000	(c-13)(xxx)	23,556	(c-35)	47,500	21,048(xxx)	52,000(xxx)	50,000
Virgin Islands	(c-13)	(c-21)	27,250	(c-12)	(c-24)	38,640	(c-12)	55,000	55,000	(c-12)	(c-41)

(c) Chief administrative official or agency in charge of function:

(c-1) Lieutenant governor	(c-17) Education (chief state school officer)
(c-2) Secretary of state	(c-18) Emergency management
(c-3) Attorney general	(c-19) Employment services
(c-4) Treasurer	(c-20) Energy resources
(c-5) Adjutant general	(c-21) Environmental protection
(c-6) Administration	(c-22) Finance
(c-7) Agriculture	(c-23) Fish and wildlife
(c-8) Banking	(c-24) General services
(c-9) Budget	(c-25) Health
(c-10) Civil rights	(c-26) Highways
(c-11) Commerce	(c-27) Historic preservation
(c-12) Community affairs	(c-28) Insurance
(c-13) Comptroller	(c-29) Labor
(c-14) Computer services	(c-30) Mental health and retardation
(c-15) Consumer affairs	(c-31) Natural resources
(c-16) Economic development	(c-32) Parks and recreation
	(c-33) Personnel

SELECTED OFFICIALS: ANNUAL SALARIES—Continued

(c-34) Planning
(c-35) Post audit
(c-36) Public utility regulation
(c-37) Public welfare
(c-38) Purchasing
(c-39) Revenue
(c-40) Social services
(c-41) Solid waste management
(c-42) Transportation
(d) Salary varies; position vacant.
(e) Responsibilities shared by Director, Mental Health and Developmental Disabilities Division, Health and Social Services Department, $64,620, and Program Administrator, same department, $52,584.
(f) Responsibilities shared by Assistant Director, Developmental Disabilities Division, Department of Economic Security, $55,414, and Director, Department of Health Services (see Health).
(g) Responsibilities shared by Director/Veterinarian, Livestock and Poultry Commission, $64,631, Director, Plant Board, $39,998, and International Marketing Representative, Marketing Division, Industrial Development Commission, $41,236.
(h) Includes allowances (e.g., quarters, personal).
(i) Responsibilities shared by Director, Department of Industrial Relations, $91,054, and Supervisor, Conciliation, same department, $52,644-63,684.
(j) Responsibilities shared by Director, Department of Mental Health, $85,402, and Director, Developmental Services Department, $85,402.
(k) Responsibilities shared by Auditor General, $91,054, and Director, Department of Finance, $91,054.
(l) Responsibilities shared by Director, Division of Mental Health, Department of Institutions, $58,464, and Director, Division of Developmental Disabilities, same department, $58,464.
(m) Responsibilities shared by Commissioner, Department of Mental Health, $66,213-80,898, and Commissioner, Department of Mental Retardation, $66,213-80,898.
(n) Responsibilities shared by two Auditors of Public Accounts; both have salary range of $59,938-73,574.
(o) Responsibilities shared by Director, Division of Alcoholism, Drug Abuse & Mental Health, $68,000, and Director, Division of Mental Retardation, Health and Social Services Department, $56,500.
(p) Responsibilities shared by Secretary, Department of Services for Children, Youth, and Their Families, $59,300, and Secretary, Department of Health & Social Services, $64,600.
(q) Responsibilities shared by Director, Division of Aquatic Resources, Land and Natural Resources Department, $35,580-58,428, and Acting Administrator, Division of Forestry and Wildlife, same department, $35,580-58,428.
(r) Set by Board of Regents; cannot exceed this figure.
(s) Responsibilities shared by Chief, Mental Health Division, Department of Health, $57,156-62,592, and Mental Retardation Administrator, Waimano Training School and Hospital, same department, $37,236-61,044.
(t) Responsibilities shared by Chief Auditor, $37,236-61,044, and Legislative Auditor, $68,400.
(u) Responsibilities shared by Commissioner, Department of Mental Health, $71,986, and Assistant Commissioner, Developmental Disabilities Division, same department, $55,510.
(v) Ninety percent position; not fulltime.
(w) Responsibilities shared by Assistant Secretary, Office of Mental Health, Health and Human Resources Department, $56,784-94,128, and Assistant Secretary, Office of Mental Retardation, same department, $20,568.
(x) Responsibilities shared by Budget Director, Division of Administration, $49,596-82,212 (See Budget), and Legislative Auditor, $58,774.
(y) Responsibilities shared by Commissioner, Division of Administration, $66,492 (See Administration), and State Director of Purchasing, same division, $37,836-62,724.
(z) Receives $55 per diem plus expenses.
(aa) Responsibilities shared by Director, Developmental Disabilities Administration, Health and Mental Hygiene Department, $58,000, and Director, Mental Hygiene Administration, same department, $76,253.
(bb) Pending approval of Ways and Means; currently, $65,000.
(cc) Responsibilities shared by Commissioner, Department of Mental Health, $77,547, and Commissioner, Department of Mental Retardation, $74,839.
(dd) Responsibilities shared by Deputy Treasurer, $51,000, and Director of Local Finance Programs, same department, $51,000.
(ee) Responsibilities shared by Executive Director, Pollution Control Agency, $62,753, and Executive Director, Environmental Quality Board, $38,357-51,072.
(ff) Responsibilities shared by Director, Licensing Unit, Department of Commerce, $29,942-40,758, and Commissioner, Department of Labor and Industry, $63,000.
(gg) Responsibilities shared by Deputy Attorney General, $43,830, and Director, Consumer Protection Division, Office of the Attorney General, $27,550.
(hh) Responsibilities shared by Director, Department of Mental Health, $54,000, and Director, Mental Retardation Division, Department of Mental Health, $38,696-57,939.
(ii) Responsibilities shared by Administrator, Mental Health Division, Department of Institutions, $42,610, and Administrator, Developmental

Disabilities Division, Social and Rehabilitation Services Department, $40,416.
(jj) Also has finance responsibilities.
(kk) Responsibilities shared by Commissioner, Department of Education, $66,840, and President of State Board of Education (salary not available).
(ll) Responsibilities shared by Director, Labor Department, $41,400, and Administrator, Commission on Industrial Relations, $24,936.
(mm) Responsibilities shared by Director, Medical Services Division, Department of Public Institutions, $78,996, and Director, Office of Mental Retardation, same department, $43,608.
(nn) Employee on employee/employer paid retirement system; other employees on employer paid retirement pay schedule.
(oo) Responsibilities shared by Director, Election Division, Department of State, $51,758, and Executive Director, Election Law Enforcement Commission, Department of Law and Public Safety, $76,345.
(pp) Responsibilities shared by Director, Mental Health and Hospitals Division, Department of Human Services, $72,287, and Director, Division of Developmental Disabilities, same department, $65,385.
(qq) Responsibilities shared by Chief, Mental Health Bureau, Department of Health and Environment, $51,604, and Chief, Developmental Disabilities Bureau, same department, $51,604.
(rr) Accepts $100,000.
(ss) Responsibilities shared by Commissioner, Department of Taxation and Finance, $87,578, and Comptroller, $110,000. Comptroller also has finance, post audit, and pre-audit responsibilities.
(tt) Responsibilities shared by Commissioner, Office of Mental Health, $93,713, and Commissioner, Mental Retardation and Developmental Disabilities, $93,713.
(uu) Commissioner, Department of Taxation and Finance (as discussed under Treasurer), has responsibilities in this area.
(vv) Budget, Comptroller, and Finance responsibilities are shared by Executive Budget Analyst, Office of Management and Budget, $45,000, and Director, same office, $77,496. The Director, Office of Management and Budget, also has General services and Pre-audit responsibilities.
(ww) Responsibilities shared by state Auditor, $46,000, and Legislative Budget Analyst and Auditor, $55,900.
(xx) Responsibilities shared by Director, Department of Commerce, $44,720-64,834, and Director, Development Department, $54,392-76,440.
(yy) Responsibilities shared by Director, Department of Mental Health, $54,392-76,440, and Director, Department of Mental Retardation and Developmental Disabilities, $54,392-76,440.
(zz) Responsibilities shared by Director, Mental Health Department, $82,750, and Director, Developmental Disabilities Services, $55,200.
(aaa) Responsibilities shared by Administrator, Mental Health Division, Department of Human Resources, $64,248, and Assistant Administrator, Mental Retardation and Developmental Disabilities Section, same department, $47,904.
(bbb) Responsibilities shared by Executive Director, Fish Commission, $54,240, and Executive Director, Game Commission, $58,093.
(ccc) Responsibilities shared by Deputy Secretary, Office of Mental Health, Department of Public Welfare, $60,500, and Deputy Secretary, Office of Mental Retardation, same department, $59,000.
(ddd) Responsibilities shared by Deputy Secretary for Children, Youth, and Their Families, $56,000, and Deputy Secretary for Medical Assistance, $56,000.
(eee) Responsibilities shared by Director, Mental Health, Retardation, and Hospitals Department, $63,850-70,545, and Associate Director, Retardation Service, same department, $57,495-63,838.
(fff) Responsibilities shared by Auditor General, $68,266, and Director, Bureau of Audits, $40,580-46,923.
(ggg) Responsibilities shared by Commissioner, Department of Mental Health, $88,683, and Commissioner, Department of Mental Retardation, $76,202.
(hhh) Responsibilities shared by Administrator, Developmental Disabilities, Department of Social Services, $61,484, and Executive Director, Department of Charities and Corrections (See corrections).
(iii) Responsibilities shared by Deputy Director, Division of Business and Economic Development, Community and Economic Development Department, $32,656-47,627, and Deputy Director, Division of Community Development, same department, $32,656-47,627. Deputy Director, Division of Business and Economic Development also has Economic development responsibilities.
(jjj) Responsibilities shared by Director, Mental Health Division, Department of Social Services, $38,628-56,418, and Director, Services to the Handicapped, same department, $38,628-56,418.
(kkk) Responsibilities shared by Director, Division of Mental Health, Social and Health Services Department, $60,384, and Acting Director, Division of Developmental Disabilities, same department, $57,480.
(lll) Responsibilities shared by Secretary, Department of Social and Health Services, listed under Health, and Director, Division of Income Assistance Services, same department, $57,480.
(mmm) Responsibilities shared by Administrator, Trade and Consumer Protection Division, Agriculture, Trade, and Consumer Protection Department, $51,741, and Unit Head, Consumer Protection and Antitrust Unit, Department of Justice, $53,225.
(nnn) Responsibilities shared by Administrator, Division of Community Services, Health and Social Services, $64,974, and Director, Developmental Disabilities Office, same department, $38,020.
(ooo) Mayor.

SELECTED OFFICIALS: ANNUAL SALARIES—Continued

(ppp) Responsibilities shared by Chief, Office of Compliance, $47,397 and Acting Chief, Office of Consumer Education and Information, Consumer and Regulatory Affairs Department, $50,557.

(qqq) Responsibilities shared by Chairman, Board of Trustees, University of District of Columbia, (salary not available), and President, University of District of Columbia, $73,455.

(rrr) Responsibilities shared by Director, Recreation Department, $69,556, and Administrator, Public Space Maintenance Administration, $69,556.

(sss) Responsibilities shared by Executive Director, Washington Visitor's and Convention Association, (salary not available), and Director, D.C. Committee to Promote Washington, $40,111.

(ttt) Responsibilities shared by Chairman, Board of Higher Education, $35,000, and President, American Samoa Community College, $33,000.

(uuu) Responsibilities shared by Personnel Officer, Civil Service Commission, $36,000, and Special Assistant for Women's Affairs, $30,000.

(vvv) Responsibilities shared by Executive Director, Commonwealth Development Authority, $36,000, and Director, Department of Commerce and Labor, $36,000.

(www) Responsibilities shared by Chief, Environmental Quality Services, Public Health and Environmental Services, $28,000, and Executive Director, Commonwealth Utilities Corporation, Office of Governor, $36,000.

(xxx) Present salaries not available; figures based on 1987 information.

Table 2.12
LIEUTENANT GOVERNORS: QUALIFICATIONS AND TERMS

State or other jurisdiction	Minimum age	State citizen (years)	U.S. citizen (years)	State resident (years)	Qualified voter (years)	Length of term (years)	Maximum consecutive terms allowed
Alabama	30	7	10	7	...	4	2
Alaska	30	...	7	7	★	4	2
Arizona	--(a)--
Arkansas	30	...	★	7	★	2	...
California	18	...	5	5	★	4	...
Colorado	30	...	★	2	...	4	...
Connecticut	30	...	...	...	★	4	...
Delaware	30	...	12	6	...	4	...
Florida	30	...	...	7	★	4	...
Georgia	30	6	15	6	...	4	...
Hawaii	30	...	★	5	★	4	2
Idaho	30	...	★	2	...	4	...
Illinois	25	...	★	3	...	4	...
Indiana	30	...	5	5	...	4	...
Iowa	30	...	★	2	...	4	...
Kansas	...	...	★	...	...	4	2
Kentucky	30	6	★	6	...	4	(b)
Louisiana	25	5	5	...	★	4	...
Maine	--(a)--
Maryland	30	...	(c)	5	5	4	...
Massachusetts	...	...	...	7	...	4	...
Michigan(d)	30	...	...	...	4	4	...
Minnesota	25	...	★	1	...	4	...
Mississippi	30	...	20	5	...	4	...
Missouri	30	...	15	10	...	4	...
Montana	25	...	★	2	...	4	...
Nebraska	30	5	5	5	...	4	...
Nevada	25	2	...	2	★	4	...
New Hampshire	--(a)--
New Jersey	--(a)--
New Mexico	30	...	★	5	★	4	1(e)
New York	30	...	★	5	...	4	...
North Carolina	30	...	5	2	...	4	2
North Dakota	30	...	★	5	...	4	...
Ohio	...	...	...	...	★	4	...
Oklahoma	31	...	★	...	10	4	...
Oregon	--(a)--
Pennsylvania	30	...	★	7	...	4	2
Rhode Island	...	...	...	...	★	2	...
South Carolina	30	5	★	5	...	4	...
South Dakota	...	...	2	2	...	4	2
Tennessee	--(a)--
Texas	30	...	★	5	...	4	...
Utah	30	5	...	5	★	4	...
Vermont	...	...	...	4	...	2	...
Virginia	30	...	★	5	5	4	...
Washington	...	...	★	...	★	4	...
West Virginia	--(a)--
Wisconsin	...	...	★	...	★	4	...
Wyoming	--(a)--
American Samoa	35	...	★	5	...	4	2
Guam	30	...	5	★	★	4	...
No. Mariana Is.	30	...	...	7	★	4	...
Puerto Rico	--(a)--
Virgin Islands	30	...	5	★	★	4	...

Note: This table includes constitutional and statutory qualifications.
Key:
★—Formal provision; number of years not specified.
. . .—No formal provision.
(a) No lieutenant governor. In Tennessee, the speaker of the senate, elected from senate membership, has statutory title of "lieutenant governor."

(b) Successive terms forbidden.
(c) *Crosse v. Board of Supervisors of Elections* 243 Md. 555, 221 A.2d431 (1966)—opinion rendered indicated that U.S. citizenship was, by necessity, a requirement for office.
(d) A person who has been convicted of felony or breach of public trust is not eligible to the office for a period of 20 years after conviction.
(e) Limited to 2 consecutive 4-year terms.

Table 2.13
LIEUTENANT GOVERNORS: POWERS AND DUTIES

State or other jurisdiction	Presides over Senate	Appoints committees	Breaks roll-call ties	Assigns bills	Authority for governor to assign duties	Member of governor's cabinet or advisory body	Serves as acting governor when governor out of state
Alabama	★	★(a)	★	★	...	...	★(b)
Alaska	...	...	...	...	★	★	★(c)
Arizona	--------------------------(d)--------------------------						
Arkansas	★	...	★	★	...	...	★
California	★	...	★	...	★	...	★
Colorado	...	...	...	...	★	★	★
Connecticut	★	...	★	★	★	★	★
Delaware	★	...	★	★	★	★	...
Florida	...	...	...	...	★	...	...
Georgia	★	★(a)	...	★	★	...	...
Hawaii	...	...	...	...	★	★	★
Idaho	★	...	★	★	★	...	★
Illinois	...	...	...	...	★	...	...
Indiana	★	...	★	...	★	★	...
Iowa	★	★(a)	(e)	★	...	...	(f)
Kansas	...	...	...	...	★	(g)	(f)
Kentucky	★	...	★	(h)	★	★	★
Louisiana	...	...	...	...	★	...	★
Maine	--------------------------(d)--------------------------						
Maryland	...	...	...	...	★	★	★
Massachusetts	...	...	...	...	★	★	★
Michigan	★	...	★	...	★	★	★
Minnesota	...	...	...	...	★	...	...
Mississippi	★	★(a)	...	★	...	...	★
Missouri	★	...	★	...	★	...	★
Montana	...	...	...	...	★	★	★(b)
Nebraska	★(i)	...	★(j)	...	★	...	★
Nevada	★	...	★	...	...	...	★
New Hampshire	--------------------------(d)--------------------------						
New Jersey	--------------------------(d)--------------------------						
New Mexico	★	(l)	★	...	★	★	★
New York	★	...	★	...	★	★	★
North Carolina	★	★(a)	★	...	★	★	★
North Dakota	★	...	★	★	★	★	★
Ohio	...	...	...	...	(m)	★	(n)
Oklahoma	★	...	★	...	★	★	★
Oregon	--------------------------(d)--------------------------						
Pennsylvania	★	...	★(j)	★	★	★	...
Rhode Island	★	...	★	★	★	...	★
South Carolina	★	...	★	...	★	...	(f)
South Dakota	★	(o)	★	★	★	...	(p)
Tennessee	--------------------------(d)--------------------------						
Texas	★	★(a)	★	★	...	...	★
Utah	...	...	...	...	★	...	...
Vermont	★	★(a)	★	★	...	★	★
Virginia	★	...	★	...	★	★	...
Washington	★	(q)	★(j)	...	★	...	★
West Virginia	--------------------------(d)--------------------------						
Wisconsin	...	...	...	...	★	★	(r)
Wyoming	--------------------------(d)--------------------------						
American Samoa	...	...	...	...	★	...	★
Guam	...	...	...	...	...	...	★
No. Mariana Is.	...	...	...	...	★	★	★
Puerto Rico	--------------------------(d)--------------------------						
Virgin Islands	...	...	...	...	...	★	★

LIEUTENANT GOVERNORS, POWERS AND DUTIES—Continued

Key:

★—Provision for responsibility.

. . .—No provision for responsibility.

(a) Appoints all standing committees. Alabama—appoints some special committees; Georgia—appoints all Senate members of conference committees and all senators who serve on interim study committees; Mississippi—apppoints members of conference, joint and special committees; Texas—appoints subcommittees and temporary committees; Vermont— appoints special committees as a member of the Committee on Committees.

(b) After 20 days absence. In Montana, after 45 days.

(c) Alaska constitution identifies two types of absence from state: (1) temporary absence during which the lieutenant serves as acting governor; and (2) continuous absence for a period of six months, after which the governor's office is declared vacant and lieutenant governor succeeds to the office.

(d) No lieutenant governor; secretary of state is next in line of succession to governorship. In Tennessee, speaker of the Senate bears the additional statutory title of "lieutenant governor."

(e) Only on amendments.

(f) Only in emergency situations.

(g) Governor's cabinet is made up of heads of the state departments; since the state's statutes provide that the lieutenant governor may be assigned to serve as head of a department, the officeholder could become part of the official cabinet at some point during the tenure.

(h) As a member of Senate committee responsible for activity.

(i) Unicameral legislative body.

(j) Except on final enactments.

(k) Temporary committees to carry out duties in formal legislative ceremonies.

(l) Special committees only for joint sessions to inform the House and the governor.

(m) Presides over cabinet meetings in absence of governor.

(n) Only if governor asks the lieutenant to serve in that capacity, in the former's absence.

(o) Conference committees.

(p) Only in event of governor's continuous absence from state.

(q) In theory, lieutenant governor is responsible; in practice, appointments are made by majority caucus.

(r) Only in situations of an absence which prevents governor from discharging duties which need to be undertaken prior to his return.

Table 2.14
SECRETARIES OF STATE:
QUALIFICATIONS FOR OFFICE

State or other jurisdiction	Minimum age	U.S. citizen (years)	State resident (years)	Qualified voter (years)	Method of selection to office
Alabama	25	7	5	★	E
Alaska			----------(a)----------		
Arizona	25	10	5	★	E
Arkansas	18	★	★	★	E
California	18	★	★	★	E
Colorado	25	★	★	...	E
Connecticut	18	★	★	★	E
Delaware	..	...	..	...	A
Florida	30	...	7	★	E
Georgia	25	10	4	...	E
Hawaii			----------(a)----------		
Idaho	25	★	2	...	E
Illinois	25	★	3	...	E
Indiana	...	...	...	...	E
Iowa	...	...	★	...	E
Kansas	...	...	...	...	E
Kentucky	30	2	2(b)	...	E
Louisiana	25	5	(b)	★	E
Maine	...	...	...	...	(c)
Maryland	...	...	...	★	A
Massachusetts	...	...	5	...	E
Michigan(d)	...	...	...	★	E
Minnesota	21	★	★	★	E
Mississippi	25	★	5(b)	★	E
Missouri	18	★	★	★	E
Montana(e)	25	★	2	...	E
Nebraska(f)	18	★	...	...	E
Nevada	25	★	2	★	E
New Hampshire	18	★	★	★	(c)
New Jersey	...	...	...	...	A
New Mexico	30	★	★	★	E
New York	18	★	★	...	A
North Carolina	21	...	...	★	E
North Dakota	25	★	...	★	E
Ohio	18	★	★	★	E
Oklahoma	31	★	10	10	A
Oregon	18	★	...	★	E
Pennsylvania	...	...	...	...	A
Rhode Island	18	★	★	★	E
South Carolina	21	...	★	★	E
South Dakota	18	★	★	...	E
Tennessee	21	★	★	★	(c)
Texas	...	...	...	...	A
Utah			----------(a)----------		
Vermont	...	...	...	...	E
Virginia	...	...	...	...	A
Washington	18	★	30 da.	★	E
West Virginia	18	★	★	★	E
Wisconsin	18	...	10 da.	...	E
Wyoming	25	★	★	★	E
American Samoa			----------(a)----------		
Guam			----------(a)----------		
No. Mariana Is.			----------(a)----------		
Puerto Rico	35	★	★	★	A
Virgin Islands			----------(a)----------		

Note: This table contains constitutional and statutory provisions. "Qualified voter" provision may infer additional residency and citizenship requirements.

Key:
★—Formal provision; number of years not specified.
...—No formal provision.
A—Appointed by governor.
E—Elected by voters.
(a) No secretary of state.
(b) Additional state citizenship requirement. Kentucky-two years. Louisiana, Mississippi-five years.
(c) Chosen by joint ballot of state senators and representatives. In Maine and New Hampshire, every two years. In Tennessee, every four years.
(d) A person convicted of a felony or breach of public trust is not eligible to the office for a period of 20 years after conviction.
(e) No person convicted of a felony is eligible to hold public office until final discharge from state supervision.
(f) No person in default as a collector and custodian of public money or property shall be eligible to public office; no person convicted of a felony shall be eligible unless restored to civil rights.

Table 2.15
SECRETARIES OF STATE: ELECTION AND REGISTRATION DUTIES

State or other jurisdiction	Chief election officer	Determines ballot eligibility of political parties	Receives initiative and/or referendum petition	Files certificate of nomination or election	Supplies election ballots or materials to local officials	Files candidates' expense papers	Files other campaign reports	Conducts voter education programs	Prepares extradition papers or warrants of arrest	Registers corporations (a)	Processes and/or commissions notaries public	Registers securities	Registers trade names/marks
Alabama	★	★	...	★	★	★	★	★	★	★	...	...	★
Alaska(b)	★	★	★	★	★	★	★	★	...	...	★	...	★
Arizona	★	★	★	★	★	★	★	★	...	...	★	...	★
Arkansas	★	★	★	★	★	★	★	★	...	...	★	...	...
California	★	★	...	★	★	★	★	★	...	...	...	...	...
Colorado	★	★	★	★	★	...	★	★	...	...	...	...	★
Connecticut	★	★	...	★	★	★	★	★	...	★	★	...	★
Delaware	...	...	...	...	...	...	★	★	★	★	★	...	★
Florida	★	★	★	★	★	★	★	★	...	★	★	★	★
Georgia	★	★	...	★	★	★	★	★	...	★	★	...	★
Hawaii(b)	★	★	...	★	★	...	...	★	...	...	...	...	...
Idaho	★	★	★	★	★	★	...	...	★	★	★	...	★
Illinois	...	...	★	★	...	...	...	...(c)	★(d)	★	★	★	★
Indiana	...	...	★	...	...	...	★	...	...	★	★	★	★
Iowa	★	★	...	★	★	...	...	...	...	★	★	...	★
Kansas	★	★	...	★	★	★	...	★	...	★	★	...	★
Kentucky	★	★	...	★	★	...	...	...	...	★	★	...	★
Louisiana	★	★	★	★	★	★(e)	★	...	★	★	★	★	★
Maine	★	★	★	★	★	★	★	...	★	★	★	...	★
Maryland	...	★	★	...	...	...	...	...	...	...	★	...	★
Massachusetts	★	★	★	★	★	...	...	★	★	★	★	★	...
Michigan	★	★	★	★	★	★	★	★	★	★	★	...	★
Minnesota	★	★	★	★	★	...	...	...	...	★	★	★	★
Mississippi	(f)	★	...	★	★	...	★	...	★	★	...	★	★
Missouri	★	...	...	...	...	...	...	...	★	★	★	★	★
Montana	★	★	★	...	...	...	★	...	★	★	★	...	★
Nebraska	★	★	★	...	...	...	★	...	...	★	★	...	★
Nevada	★	★	★	★	★	★	★	...	...	★	★	...	★
New Hampshire	★	★	★	★	★	★	★	...	...	★	★	...	★
New Jersey	★	★	...	★	★	★	★	...	★	★	★	...	★
New Mexico	★	★	★	★	★	...	★	★	...	...	★	...	★
New York	...	...	...	...	...	...	...	...	...	★	★	★	★
North Carolina	...	...	...	...	...	...	...	...	...	★	★	★	★
North Dakota	★	★	★	★	★	★	★	...	...	★	★	...	★
Ohio	★	★	★	★	★	...	★	...	...	★	★	...	★
Oklahoma	...	...	...	...	...	...	...	...	...	★	★	...	★
Oregon	★	★	★	...	★	★	★	...	...	★	★	...	...
Pennsylvania	★	★	...	★	★	★	★	...	★	★	★	...	★
Rhode Island	★	★	...	★	★	...	★	★	...	★	★	...	★
South Carolina	...	...	...	...	...	...	...	...	...	...	★	★	...
South Dakota	★	★	★	★	★	★	★	★	★	★	★	...	★
Tennessee	(g)	★	...	★	★	★	★	...	...	★	★	...	★
Texas	★	★	...	★	★	★	★	★	...	...	★	...	...
Utah(b)	★	★	★	★	★	...	...	...	...	...	...	...	...
Vermont	★	★	...	★	★	★(h)	★	...	...	★	★	...	★
Virginia	...	...	...	...	...	...	...	...	★	...	★	...	★
Washington	★	★	★	...	★	...	...	...	★	★	★	...	★
West Virginia	★	★	...	★	★	★	★	...	★	★	★	...	★
Wisconsin	...	...	...	...	...	...	...	...	...	★	★	...	★
Wyoming	★	★	★	★	★	★	★	...	...	★	★	...	★
American Samoa(b)	...	...	...	...	...	...	...	...	N/A	N/A	★	N/A	N/A
Puerto Rico(i)	...	...	...	...	...	...	...	...	...	★	...	...	★
Virgin Islands(b)	...	...	...	...	★	...	...	...	...	★(j)	★	★	★

Key:
★—Responsible for activity.
...—Not responsible for activity.
N/A—Does not apply.
(a) Unless otherwise indicated, office registers domestic, foreign and non-profit corporations.
(b) No secretary of state. Duties indicated are performed by lieutenant governor.
(c) Does produce a brochure describing proposed amendments to the state constitution. State Board of Elections conducts most voter education programs.
(d) Secretary of State's office prepares, but Governor must sign.
(e) Receives these from federal candidates only.
(f) State Election Commission composed of governor, secretary of state and attorney general.
(g) Secretary appoints state coordinator of elections.
(h) Receives reports from statewide candidates only.
(i) Information based on 1985 survey.
(j)Both domestic and foreign profit; but only domestic non-profit.

Table 2.16
SECRETARIES OF STATE: CUSTODIAL, PUBLICATION AND LEGISLATIVE DUTIES

State or other jurisdiction	Custodial				Publication					Legislative			
	Archives state records and documents(a)	Files state agency rules and regulations	Administers uniform commercial code provisions	Files other corporate documents	State manual or directory	Session laws	State constitution	Statutes(a)	Administrative rules and regulations	Opens legislative sessions(b)	Enrolls or engrosses bills	Retains copies of acts	Registers lobbyists
Alabama	. . .	★	★	★	. . .	★	. . .	★	. . .	★	★	★	. . .
Alaska(c)	. . .	★	. . .	. . .	. . .	. . .	. . .	. . .	★	★	. . .	★	. . .
Arizona	. . .	★	★	★	★	. . .	★	★	★	★	. . .	★	★
Arkansas	. . .	. . .	★	★	★	U/A	★	. . .	U/A	. . .	. . .	★	. . .
California	★	★	★	★	★	. . .	. . .	. . .	. . .	. . .	. . .	★	★
Colorado	. . .	★	★	★	★	. . .	★	. . .	. . .	★	. . .	★	★
Connecticut	★	★	★	★	★	★	★	. . .	. . .	S	★	★	★
Delaware	★	★	★	★	. . .	. . .	. . .	. . .	. . .	N/A	N/A	N/A	. . .
Florida	★	★	★	. . .	. . .	★	★	★	★	. . .	. . .	★	. . .
Georgia	★	. . .	. . .	. . .	★	★	★	★	★	. . .	. . .	★	★
Hawaii(c)	(d)	★	. . .	. . .	. . .	. . .	. . .	(e)	. . .	. . .	. . .	★	. . .
Idaho	. . .	. . .	★	★	★	. . .	★	. . .	. . .	. . .	. . .	★	★
Illinois	★	★	★	★	★	. . .	★	. . .	★	H	. . .	★	★
Indiana	★	★	★	★	★	. . .	. . .	. . .	. . .	H	. . .	★	. . .
Iowa	(f)	. . .	★	★	. . .	. . .	★(g)	. . .	. . .	. . .	★	★	★
Kansas	★	. . .	★	★	★	. . .	★	. . .	. . .	★	. . .	★	★
Kentucky	★	★	★	★	. . .	. . .	★	. . .	. . .	. . .	. . .	★	★
Louisiana	★	. . .	N/A	★	. . .	. . .	★	. . .	. . .	. . .	. . .	★	★
Maine	★	★	★	★	. . .	. . .	★	. . .	. . .	. . .	. . .	★	★
Maryland	★(h)	. . .	. . .	. . .	. . .	. . .	★	. . .	★	. . .	. . .	★	. . .
Massachusetts	★	★	★	★	★	★	★	★	★	. . .	. . .	. . .	★
Michigan	★	★	★	★	. . .	★	★	. . .	. . .	. . .	. . .	. . .	★
Minnesota	★	★	★	★	★	. . .	★	. . .	. . .	H	. . .	★	★
Mississippi	. . .	★	★	★	★	★	★	. . .	. . .	. . .	★	★	★
Missouri	★	★	★	★	★	★	★	. . .	★	★	. . .	★	★
Montana	★(h)	★	★	★	★	. . .	★	. . .	★	H	★	★	★
Nebraska	★	★	★	★	★	★	★	. . .	. . .	(i)	★	★	★
Nevada	. . .	★	★	★	. . .	. . .	★	. . .	. . .	H	. . .	★	. . .
New Hampshire	★	. . .	★	★	★	. . .	★	. . .	. . .	. . .	★	★	. . .
New Jersey	★	. . .	★	★	★	. . .	★	. . .	. . .	. . .	. . .	★	. . .
New Mexico	★	. . .	★	★	★	. . .	★	. . .	. . .	H	. . .	★	★
New York	. . .	★	★	★	★	. . .	★	★	. . .	. . .	. . .	★	★
North Carolina	★	★(j)	★	★	★	★	★	. . .	★	. . .	. . .	★	★
North Dakota	. . .	. . .	★	★	★	★	★	. . .	★	. . .	. . .	★	★
Ohio	★	★	★	★	★	★	★	★	. . .	. . .	★	★	. . .
Oklahoma	. . .	★	★	★	. . .	. . .	. . .	. . .	. . .	. . .	. . .	★	. . .
Oregon	★	★	★	. . .	★	. . .	. . .	. . .	. . .	. . .	. . .	★	★
Pennsylvania	. . .	★	★	★	. . .	. . .	. . .	. . .	. . .	. . .	★	★	★
Rhode Island	★	★	★	★	. . .	. . .	★	★	. . .	. . .	. . .	★	★
South Carolina	★	. . .	★	★	. . .	. . .	. . .	. . .	. . .	. . .	. . .	. . .	★
South Dakota	★	★	★	★	★	. . .	★	. . .	. . .	H	. . .	★	★
Tennessee	★	★	★	★	. . .	. . .	★	. . .	★	. . .	. . .	★	★
Texas	★	★	★	★	. . .	. . .	. . .	★	★	. . .	. . .	★	★
Utah(c)	(d)	. . .	. . .	★	. . .	. . .	. . .	. . .	. . .	★	. . .	★	★
Vermont	★	★	★	★	★	★	★	. . .	★	H(k)	. . .	★	★
Virginia	. . .	. . .	. . .	★	. . .	. . .	. . .	. . .	. . .	. . .	. . .	. . .	★
Washington	★	. . .	. . .	★	. . .	. . .	. . .	. . .	. . .	. . .	. . .	. . .	. . .
West Virginia	★	★	★	★	. . .	. . .	. . .	. . .	★	. . .	. . .	★	. . .
Wisconsin	★	★	★	★	. . .	. . .	. . .	. . .	. . .	. . .	. . .	★	★
Wyoming	. . .	★	★	★	★	. . .	★	. . .	. . .	H	. . .	★	. . .
Puerto Rico	★	★	. . .	★	. . .	★	★	★	. . .	. . .	. . .	★	. . .
Virgin Islands(c)	U/A	★	★	★	. . .	. . .	. . .	U/A	. . .	. . .	. . .	★	. . .

Key:
★—Responsible for activity.
. . .—Not responsible for activity.
N/A—Does not apply.
U/A—Information not available.
(a) Data based on 1986-87 edition of *The Book of the States*; updated information not available.
(b) In this column only: ★ Both houses; H—House; S—Senate.
(c) No secretary of state. Duties indicated are performed by lieutenant governor.
(d) Limited responsibility.
(e) Distributes and sells session laws, statutes and administrative rules and regulations.
(f) Serves as chair of State Records Commission.
(g) In Redbook.
(h) As specified by law. In Maryland, Hall of Records is the archivist.
(i) Certifies and seats members of unicameral legislature.
(j) Only partial filing; the majority are filed with Attorney General's office.
(k) Until speaker is elected.

Table 2.17
ATTORNEYS GENERAL:
QUALIFICATIONS FOR OFFICE

State or other jurisdiction	Minimum age	U.S. citizen (years)	State resident (years)	Qualified voter (years)	Licensed attorney (years)	Membership in the state bar (years)	Method of selection to office
Alabama	25	7	5	...	...	...	E
Alaska	...	★	...	...	...	...	A
Arizona	25	10	5	...	...	...	E
Arkansas	...	★	★	★	...	...	E
California	18	...	...	...	(a)	(a)	E
Colorado	25	★	2	...	★	...	E
Connecticut	18	★	★	★	10	10	E
Delaware	...	...	...	...	...	...	E
Florida	30	...	7	★	5	5	E
Georgia	25	10	4	...	7	7	E
Hawaii	...	★	1	...	...	...	A
Idaho	30	★	2	...	★	★	E
Illinois	25	★	3	...	...	...	E
Indiana	...	...	(b)	...	★	...	E
Iowa	...	...	...	...	...	...	E
Kansas	...	★	...	...	8	2	E
Kentucky	30	2	2(b)	...	5	5	E
Louisiana	25	5	(b)	★	...	...	E
Maine	...	...	...	...	...	...	(c)
Maryland	...	★(d)	10(b)	★	10	10(e)	E
Massachusetts	...	...	5	...	...	★	E
Michigan(f)	...	...	...	★	...	...	E
Minnesota	21	...	30 da.	★	...	...	E
Mississippi	26	...	5(b)	...	5	5	E
Missouri	...	...	...	...	...	...	E
Montana(g)	25	★	2	...	5	★	E
Nebraska(h)	21(e)	...	(e)	...	(e)	...	E
Nevada	25	★	2(b)	★	★	...	A
New Hampshire	...	...	...	...	★	★	A
New Jersey	18(e)	...	★	...	★	★	A
New Mexico	30	★	5	...	★	★	E
New York	30	★	5	...	(e)	...	E
North Carolina	21	...	...	★	★	(e)	E
North Dakota	25	★	★	★	...	...	E
Ohio	18	★	★	★	...	...	E
Oklahoma	31	★	10	10	...	...	E
Oregon	...	...	...	★	...	...	E
Pennsylvania	30	★	7	...	★	★	E
Rhode Island	18	★	★	★	...	...	E
South Carolina	...	...	★	★	...	...	E
South Dakota	...	★	★	...	★	★	E
Tennessee	...	...	...	...	★	★	A(i)
Texas	...	...	...	...	★	★	E
Utah	25	...	5(b)	★	★	★	E
Vermont	...	...	...	...	...	...	E
Virginia	30	★	5(j)	...	...	5(j)	E
Washington	...	★	30 da.	★	★	★	E
West Virginia	25	★	(b)	★	...	...	E
Wisconsin	...	...	...	...	...	...	E
Wyoming	...	...	★	★	4	4	A
American Samoa	...	★	...	...	...	...	A
Guam	...	...	...	...	...	...	A
No. Mariana Is.	...	...	...	...	5	...	A
Puerto Rico	21(e)	★	...	...	(e)	(e)	A
Virgin Islands	...	★	...	...	(k)	...	A

Note: This table contains constitutional and statutory provisions. "Qualified voter" provision may infer additional residency and citizenship requirements.

Key:
★—Formal provision; number of years not specified.
...—No formal provision.
A—Appointed by governor.
E—Elected by voters.
(a) No statute specifically requires this, but the State Bar act can be interpreted as making this a qualification.
(b) Additional state citizenship requirement. Kentucky, Nevada—two years. Louisiana, Mississippi, Utah, West Virginia—five years.
(c) Chosen biennially by joint ballot of state senators and representatives.
(d) *Crosse v. Board of Supervisors of Elections* 243 Md. 555, 222 A.2d 431 (1966)—opinion rendered indicated that U.S. citizenship was, by necessity, a requirement for office.
(e) Implied.
(f) A person convicted of a felony or breach of public trust is not eligible to the office for a period of 20 years after conviction.
(g) No person convicted of felony is eligible to hold public office until final discharge from state supervision.
(h) No person in default as a collector and custodian of public money or property shall be eligible to public office; no person convicted of a felony shall be eligible unless restored to civil rights.
(i) Appointed by judges of state Supreme Court.
(j) Same as qualifications of a judge of a court of records.
(k) Must be admitted to practice before highest court.

Table 2.18
ATTORNEYS GENERAL: PROSECUTORIAL AND ADVISORY DUTIES

State or other jurisdiction	Authority in local prosecutions:				Issues advisory opinions:					Reviews legislation:	
	Authority to initiate local prosecutions	May intervene in local prosecutions	May assist local prosecutor	May supersede local prosecutor	To state executive officials	To legislators	To local prosecutors	On the interpretation of statutes	On the constitutionality of bills or ordinances	Prior to passage	Before signing
Alabama	A	A,D	A,D	A	★	★	★	★	★	★	...
Alaska	(a)	(a)	(a)	(a)	★	★	...	★	★	★	★
Arizona	A,B,C,D,F	B,D	B,D	B	★	★	★	★	★	★	...
Arkansas	...	D	D	...	★	★	★	★	★	★	★
California	A,E	A,D,E	A,B,D	A	★	★	★	★	★	★	★
Colorado	B,F	B	D,F(b)	B	★	...		★	★	★	★
Connecticut	...	...	...	...	★	...	...	★	★	★	★
Delaware					★	...	...	★	★	★	★
Florida	F	D	D	...	★	★	★	★	...	★	★
Georgia	A,B,F	A,B,D,G	A,B,D,F	B	★	★	★	★		★	★
Hawaii	E	A,D,G	A,D	A,G	★	★	★	★	★	★	★
Idaho	A,D,F	A	A,D	A	★	★	★	★	...	★	★
Illinois	A,D,E,F,G	A,D,E	A,D,E,F	F	★	★	★	★	★	(c)	(c)
Indiana	F(b)	...	A,D,E,F	G	★	★	★	★	★	★	...
Iowa	D,F	D	D	...	★	★	★	★	★	★	★
Kansas	B,C,D,F	D	D	A,F	★	★	★	★	★	...	★
Kentucky	A,B	B,D	B,D,F	G	★	★	★	★	★	★	★
Louisiana	G	G	D	G	★	★	★	★	★	★	...
Maine	A	A	A	A	★	★	...	★	★	★	★
Maryland	B,C,F	B,C,D	B,C,D	B,C	★	★	★	★	★	★	★
Massachusetts	A,B,C,D,E,F,G	A,B,C,D,E,G	A,B,C,D,E	A,B,C,E	★	★	...	★	★	★	★
Michigan	A	A	A	A	★	★	★	★	★	★	★
Minnesota	B	B,D,G	A,B,D	B	★	★	...	★	★	...	(c)
Mississippi	B,E,F	...	B,F	...	★	★	★	★	...	(c)	(c)
Missouri	F	...	B	...	★	★	★	★	...	★	★
Montana	C,F	A,B,C,D	A,B,C,D,F	A,C	★	★(d)	★	★	★	...	...
Nebraska	A	A	A,D	A	★	★	★	★	★	...	...
Nevada	D,F,G(e)	D(e)	(e,f)	G,F	★	...	...	★	★	★	★
New Hampshire	A	A	A	A	★	...	...	★	★	★	★
New Jersey	A	A,B,D,G	A,D	A,B,D,G	★	★	★	★	★	★	★
New Mexico	A,B,E,F,G	B,D,G	D	B	★	★	★	★	★	★	★
New York	B,F	B	D	B	★	★	...	★	★	...	★
North Carolina	...	D	D	...	★	★	★	★	★	★	...
North Dakota	A,G	A,D	A,D	A	★	★	★	★	★	...	(c)
Ohio	B,C,F	B,F	F	B,C	★	★(g)	★	★	...	...	...
Oklahoma	B,C	B,C	B,C	B,C	★	★	★	★	★	★	★
Oregon	B,F	B,D	B,D	B	★	★	★	★	★	(c)	(c)
Pennsylvania	A,D,G	D,G	D	G	★	...	...	★	...	★	★
Rhode Island	A	D	D	...	★	★	...	★	★	★	★
South Carolina	A	A,D	A,D	A	★	★	★	★	★	★	★
South Dakota	A(h)	A	A	A	★	★	★	★	...	★	★
Tennessee	D,F,G(b)	D,G(b)	D	F	★	★	★	★	★	(c)	(c)
Texas	F	...	D	...	★	★	★	★	★	★	★
Utah	A,B,D,E,F,G	E,G	D,E	E	★	...	★	★	★	(c)	(c)
Vermont	A	A	A	A	★	★	★	★	★	★	★
Virginia	B,F	A,B,D,F	B,D,F	B	★	★	★	★	★	★	★
Washington	B,D,G	B,D,G	D	B	★	★	★	★	★	★	★
West Virginia	...	...	D	...	★	★	★	★	★	(i)	(i)
Wisconsin	B,C,F	B,C,D	D	B,C(j)	★	★	★	★	★	(i)	(i)
Wyoming	B,D(e)	B,D	B,D	...	★	★	...	★	...	★	★
American Samoa	A,E	A,E	A,E	A,E	★	★	...	★	★	★	★
No. Mariana Is.	A	...	...	...	★	★	...	★	★	★	★
Puerto Rico	A,B,E	A,B,E	A,E	A,B,E	★	★	...	★	★	★	★
Virgin Islands	A	...	...	...	★	★	...	★	★	★	★

Source: The Council of State Governments, *The Book of the States 1987-88.*

Key:
A—On own initiative.
B—On request of governor.
C—On request of legislature.
D—On request of local prosecutor.
E—When in state's interest.
F—Under certain statutes for specific crimes.
G—On authorization of court or other body.
★—Has authority in area.
...—Does not have authority in area.
(a) Local prosecutors serve at pleasure of attorney general.

(b) Certain statutes provide for concurrent jurisdiction with local prosecutors.
(c) Only when requested by governor or legislature.
(d) To legislative leadership.
(e) In connection with grand jury cases.
(f) Will prosecute as a matter of practice when requested.
(g) To legislature as a whole not individual legislators.
(h) Has concurrent jurisdiction with states' attorneys.
(i) No legal authority, but sometimes informally reviews laws at request of legislature.
(j) If the governor removes the district attorney for cause.

Table 2.19
ATTORNEYS GENERAL: CONSUMER PROTECTION ACTIVITIES, SUBPOENA POWERS, AND ANTITRUST DUTIES

State or other jurisdiction	May commence civil proceedings	May commence criminal proceedings	Represents the state before regulatory agencies	Administers consumer protection programs	Handles consumer complaints	Subpoena powers (a)	Antitrust duties
Alabama	★	★	...	★	★	•	A, B
Alaska	★	★	★	★	★	★	B, C
Arizona	★	...	...	★	★	★	A, B, D
Arkansas	★	...	★	★	★	★	B, C, D
California	★	...	...	...	★	★	B, C, D
Colorado	★	★	★	★	★	•	B, C, D(b)
Connecticut	★	...	★	★	...	•	A, B, D
Delaware	★	★	★	★	...	★	A, B, C
Florida	★	★	...	★	★	★	A, B, C, D
Georgia	★	...	★	...	...	★	B, C, D
Hawaii	★	★	★	...	...	★	A, B, C, D
Idaho	★	...	★	★	★	•	D
Illinois	★	★	★	★	★	•	A, B, D
Indiana	★	...	...	★	★	...	B, C, D
Iowa	★	★	★	★	★	•	A, B, C, D
Kansas	★	★	★	★	★	(c)	B, C, D
Kentucky	★	★	★	★	★	(c)	A, B, D
Louisiana	★	...	★	...	★	•	B, C
Maine	★	★	★	★	★	•	B, C
Maryland	★	★	★	★	★	★	B, C, D
Massachusetts	★	★	★	★	★	•	A, B, C, D
Michigan	★	★	★	★	★	•	A, B, C, D
Minnesota	★	...	★	★	★	•	B, D
Mississippi	★	...	★	★	★	•	B, C
Missouri	★	...	...	★	★	•	A, B, C, D
Montana	★	★	★	...	...	★	B, C, D
Nebraska	★	...	★	★	★	•	A, B, C(d), D
Nevada	★	★	...	★	★	•	A, B, C, D
New Hampshire	★	★	★	...	★	•	B, C, D
New Jersey	★	★	★	★	★	★	A, B, C, D
New Mexico	★	★	★	★	★	•	A, C
New York	★	★	★	★	★	★	A, B, C, D
North Carolina	★	...	★	★	★	★	A, B, C, D
North Dakota	★	★	...	★	★	★	C, D
Ohio	★	★	★	★	★	•	B, C, D
Oklahoma	★	...	(e)	★	★	•	B, D
Oregon	★	★	(c)	★	★	•	A, B, C, D
Pennsylvania	★	...	★	★	★	•	D
Rhode Island	★	★	★	★	★	•	A, B, C, D
South Carolina	★	★	★	...	★	•	A, B, C, D
South Dakota	★	★	...	★	★	•	A, B, C, D
Tennessee	★	★	★(c)	★	★	•	A, B, C, D
Texas	★	...	★	★	★	•	B, D
Utah	★(d)	...	★(d,f)	...	★(f)	★	A(g), B, C, D(g)
Vermont	★	★	★	★	★	★	A, B, C, D
Virginia	★	(e)	★	★(f)	★(f)	•	A, B, C, D
Washington	★	...	★	★	★	•	A, B, D
West Virginia	★	...	★	★	★	★	A, B, D
Wisconsin	★	...	★	★	★	•	A, B, C, D
Wyoming	★	...	...	★	★	...	...
American Samoa	★	★	★	...	...	★	
No. Mariana Is.	★	★	★	★	★	★	B, C, D
Puerto Rico	★	★	★	★(e)	★(e)	★	A, B, C
Virgin Islands	★	★(h)	★	...	...	★	A, B(i), C, D

Source: The Council of State Governments, *The Book of the States 1987-88.*

Key:
A—Has *parens patriae* authority to commence suits on behalf of consumers in state antitrust damage actions in state courts.
B—May initiate damage actions on behalf of state in state courts.
C—May commence criminal proceedings.
D—May represent cities, counties and other governmental entities in recovering civil damages under federal or state law.
★—Has authority in area.
...—Does not have authority in area.
(a) In this column only: ★ broad powers and • limited powers.

(b) Only under Rule 23 of the Rules of Civil Procedure.
(c) When permitted to intervene.
(d) Attorney general has exclusive authority.
(e) To a limited extent.
(f) Attorney general handles legal matters only with no administrative handling of complaints.
(g) Opinion only, since there are no controlling precedents.
(h) May prosecute in inferior courts. May prosecute in district court only by request or consent of U.S. Attorney General.
(i) May initiate damage actions on behalf of jurisdiction in district court.

Table 2.20
ATTORNEYS GENERAL: DUTIES TO ADMINISTRATIVE AGENCIES AND OTHER RESPONSIBILITIES

State or other jurisdiction	Serves as counsel for state	Appears for state in criminal appeals	Duties to administrative agencies							
			Issues official advice	Interprets statutes or regulations	In behalf of agency	Conducts litigation: Against agency	Prepares or reviews legal documents	Represents the public before the agency	Involved in rule-making	Reviews rules for legality
Alabama	A, B, C	★(a)	★	★	★	★	★	(b)	...	★
Alaska	A, B, C	★	★	★	★	★	★	...	...	★
Arizona	A, B, C	(c,d)	★	★	★	★	★	...	★	★
Arkansas	A, B, C	★(a)	★	★	★	...	★	★	★	★
California	A, B, C	★(a)	★	★	★	★	★	...	...	...
Colorado	A, B, C	★(a)	★	★	★	★	★	...	★	...
Connecticut	A, B, C	...	★	★	★	★	★	...	★	★
Delaware	A, B, C	★(a)	★	★	★	...	★	★	★	★
Florida	A, B, C	★(a)	★	★	★	...	★	★	★	★
Georgia	A, B, C	(b,c)	★	★	★	★	★	...	★	★
Hawaii	A, B	(b,c)	★	★	★	★	★	★	★	★
Idaho	A, B, C	★(a)	★	★	★	★	★	...	★	★
Illinois	A, B*, C	(b,c,e)	★	★	★	★	★	★	...	...
Indiana	A, B, C	★(a)	★	★	★	...	★	...	★	...
Iowa	A, B, C	★(a)	★	★	★	★	★	...	...	★
Kansas	A, B, C	★(a)	★	★	★	★	★	...	...	★
Kentucky	A, B*, C	★	★	★	★	★	★	...	★	★
Louisiana	A, B, C	(c)	★	★	★	★	★	...	★	★
Maine	A, B, C	(b,d)	★	★	★	...	★	...	★	★
Maryland	A, B, C	★	★	★	★	(b)	★	★	★	★
Massachusetts	A, B, C	(b,c,d)	★	★	★	★	★	★	★	★
Michigan	A, B, C	(b,c,d)	★	★	★	★	★	★	★	★
Minnesota	A, B, C	(c)	★	★	★	★	★	★	...	★
Mississippi	A, B, C	★	★	★	★	...	★	...	★	★
Missouri	A, B, C	★	★	★	★	...	★	...	★	★
Montana	A, B, C	★	★	★	★	...	★	...	★	★
Nebraska	A, B, C	★	★	★	★	★	★	...	★	★
Nevada	A, B, C	★(d)	★	★	★	★	★	★	★	★
New Hampshire	A, B, C	★(a)	★	★	★	★	★	★	★	★
New Jersey	A, B, C	★(d)	★	★	★	★	★	...	★	★
New Mexico	A, B, C	★(a)	★	★	★	★	★	★	★	★
New York	A, B, C	(b)	★	★	★	★	...	★	...	...
North Carolina	A, B, C	★	★	★	★	★	★	(b)	...	★
North Dakota	A, B, C	(b)	★	★	★	...	★	...	★	★
Ohio	A, B, C	...	★	★	★	★	★	★	★	...
Oklahoma	A, B, C	(b)	★	★	★	★	★	★	★	★
Oregon	A, B, C	★	★	★	★	★	★	...	★	★
Pennsylvania	A, B, C	(c)	★	★	★	★	★	...	★	★
Rhode Island	A, B, C	★(a)	★	★	★	...	★	★	★	★
South Carolina	A, B, C	★(d)	★	★	★	...	★	...	★	★
South Dakota	A, B, C	★(a)	★	★	★	...	★	...	★	★
Tennessee	A, B, C	★(a)	★	★	★	...	★	(b)	★	★
Texas	A, B, C	(c)	★	★	★	...	★	...	★	★
Utah	A, B, C	★(a)	★	★	★	★	★	★	★	★
Vermont	A, B, C	(b)	★	★	★	★	★	(b)	...	★
Virginia	A, B, C	★(a)	★	★	★	★	★	★	★	★
Washington	A, B, C	(c,f)	★	★	★	★	★	★	★	★
West Virginia	A, B, C	★(a)	★	★	★	(f)	★	★	★	...
Wisconsin	A, B, C	(b)	★	★	★	★	★	(b)	★	...
Wyoming	A, B, C	★(a)	★	★	★	...	★	...	★	★
American Samoa	A, B, C	★(a)	★	★	★	...	★	...	★	★
No. Mariana Is.	A, B, C	★	★	★	★	...	★	...	★	★
Puerto Rico	A, B, C	★	★	★	★	...	★	...	★	★
Virgin Islands	A, B, C(g)	★	★	★	★	...	★	...	★	★

Source: The Council of State Governments, *The Book of the States* 1987-88.

Key: A—Defend state law when challenged on federal constitutional grounds.
B—Conduct litigation on behalf of state in federal and other states' courts.
C—Prosecute actions against another state in U.S. Supreme Court.
*Only in federal courts.
★—Has authority in area.
...—Does not have authority in area.

(a) Attorney general has exclusive jurisdiction.
(b) In certain cases only.
(c) When assisting local prosecutor in the appeal.
(d) Can appear on own discretion.
(e) In certain courts only.
(f) If authorized by the governor.
(g) Except in cases in which the U.S. Attorney is representing the Government of the Virgin Islands.

CHAPTER THREE

STATE LEGISLATIVE BRANCH

THE STATE LEGISLATURES

By William T. Pound

State legislatures in recent years have been affected by a variety of events. The legislative modernization movement and the growth in institutional capacity which took place in the 1960s and 1970s left the legislative branch in most states considerably changed from earlier years. Then the growth in the role of state government and the changed relationship of federal, state and local government in the 1980s had a major impact on the level of activity and the very issues themselves in state legislatures. And the decline of political parties, the increase in interest group activity and the increased commitment of time required to serve in most state legislatures have also affected the role and operations of these bodies.

The growth in the capacity and responsibilities of American state legislatures which has been taking place over the past 30 years continues unabated during the 1980s. The state legislature, which can be appropriately characterized as "the first branch of government," went through a period of revitalization between the late 1950s and the mid-1970s. In the early years of our federal system, most state legislatures met annually and enjoyed wide constitutional authority. From the mid-19th century, a movement developed which limited legislative sessions and placed many restrictions on the constitutional powers of the legislature.

The legislative reform movement affected virtually every state legislative body. This movement was stimulated not only by judicial decisions, active and effective citizen groups, and the changing nature of governmental responsibilities, but also by the state legislators themselves. The increase in legislative capacity and function has paralleled the overall growth in state governments' responsibilities and functions, but the state legislatures have been more affected by change than any other governmental institution.

The Modernization of the State Legislature

Legislative development during the past decade can best be characterized as a consolidation of previous reforms. The external relationships of the legislatures — with governors and the executive branch, with the federal government and with interest groups — have undergone considerable change. Trends toward decentralization within legislatures and greater autonomy for individual legislators are apparent. There is greater emphasis on the constituent service role of legislators, and computers and modern information systems are having a dramatic effect on the legislatures.

The eight years of President Ronald Reagan's administration have had a major impact on state government and the state legislatures. While Congress has not enacted "New Federalism" in any systematic statutory form, it has had a significant effect on state legislative responsibilities and the environment in which state legislatures function. Increasingly, the state legislatures are becoming the primary arena for policymaking and for financing governmental functions hitherto dominated by the federal and local governments.

The legislative modernization movement had several components. These include:

- the elimination or relaxation of many constitutional limitations on the legislature, including session and salary limitations,
- the development and expansion of professional staff,
- the increase in time spent by legislatures in both session and related activity,
- the expansion and improvement of legislative facilities,
- the reform of legislative rules and procedures,

William T. Pound is Executive Director of the National Conference of State Legislatures.

• the expansion of legislative budget review capacity,

• the tremendous growth of legislative information and analysis capability, especially utilizing modern computer systems, and

• the development of statutes on ethics, campaign finance, disclosure and conflict of interest.

Legislatures had begun to build their capacity in the postwar period. The Legislative Council movement, which had originated 20 years earlier, spread to many states. Specialized legislative staffs, particularly in the fiscal area, were established in states such as California and Texas. Legislatures began to move from biennial to annual sessions. At the beginning of World War II, only four states (New York, New Jersey, Rhode Island and South Carolina) held annual legislative sessions. By 1962, the number of legislatures meeting annually had increased to 19, by 1972 to 35, and by 1986 to 43.

Many of the changes in state legislatures required constitutional amendment. Constitutional restrictions on both regular and special sessions, on legislator salaries, and on legislative authority in the budget and oversight area were diluted or removed. Modifications were made to the restrictions on interim activity, the review of gubernatorial vetoes, and the legislature's ability to call itself into session or to determine matters that could be considered in certain sessions.

A critical stimulus to the legislative modernization movement was the series of state and federal judicial decisions that followed the U.S. Supreme Court rulings on legislative districting in *Baker v. Carr* (1963) and *Reynolds v. Sims* (1965) — decisions requiring equality of representation based on population in both houses of the state legislature. The result was a shift of power in many state legislatures from rural to urban, and especially suburban interests, and inevitably, a change in the composition of legislatures. The number of farmers and lawyers has declined, while the number of educators, urban professionals, women and racial minorities, has grown.

Legislative Operations, Organization, and Procedures

The increase in the capacity and willingness of legislatures to deal with modern societal problems has involved more than changes in patterns of representation. Legislative organization and procedures are constantly evolving. Many legislatures regularly review their structures and procedures, often through a Rules Committee or an interim study. Many procedural changes in recent years have had the objective either of opening and formalizing the process and providing more information to both the public and members of the legislative body, or of more effectively using legislative time.

Concern about legislative use of time has been motivated by at least two issues: How much time should a legislature spend in session, and should it be considered "full-time" or "part-time" in nature? And, how can the legislature most effectively use the time available and avoid the end-of-session logjam that occurs in many states?

Length of Legislative Sessions

Twelve states place no limit on session length, while 32 operate with constitutional limits (two of these, Colorado and Kansas, limit only the second year), and six states (Arizona, Iowa, Nevada, Rhode Island, Tennessee and Vermont) have statutory or indirect limitations based on cutoffs in legislator's salaries or per diem expense payments.

The argument about session limitations often is couched in terms of preserving the "citizen" nature of state legislatures, as opposed to developing "professional" or full-time legislatures on the congressional model. There is no question that the amount of time spent in session and the level of compensation affect the composition of the membership of the legislative bodies. Many argue it is desirable that the predominant occupation of members of the legislature not be that of "legislator," but that legislative bodies represent a broad spectrum of vocations. However, the growing demands on state legislatures and the greater legislative role in policy initiation, budgeting and program oversight have increased the pressure on legislative time.

The 1960s and 1970s were a time of elimination or relaxation of the limits on legislative sessions. More recently, however, there has been a mixed response to the question of session length. In 1984, Alaska adopted a 120-day limit, replacing its previously unlimited sessions. In 1982, Colorado adopted a limit of 140 days for the second year of the session, and in 1981, Washington included session limitations when it moved from biennial to annual sessions. In 1984, Utah lengthened its sessions by ten days per biennium when it changed from a 60-day (first year) 20-day (second year) system to 45 days per session. New Hampshire adopted annual sessions effective in 1986. Several legislatures, notably Arizona and Iowa, have limited their sessions by legislative rule or statute. Movements to adopt more restrictive session limits surface periodically. Michigan has experienced several attempts to limit sessions. Montana held annual sessions for one biennium in the 1970s, then returned to a biennial schedule. Colorado is considering further limitations on session days and there is a serious proposal in New Hampshire to return to biennial sessions.

"Full-time" Legislatures and Legislators

Whether a legislature is full-time in nature generally can be measured by factors such as time spent in session, level of compensation and occupational self-definition of members. Moreover, full-time legislatures are likely to have a pattern of considerable legislator time spent in district offices and a high priority placed on constituent service functions.

The legislatures of California, Illinois, Massachusetts, Michigan, New Jersey, New York, Ohio, Pennsylvania and Wisconsin have lengthy sessions, relatively high legislator salaries and many members whose primary occupation is "legislator." None of these states have constitutionally-imposed session limitations, although both California and Wisconsin adopt a systematic schedule of committee and floor activity, as well as recess periods at the beginning of each biennium. Many of the legislatures which have longer sessions meet only two or three days per week, while in other states with more restricted sessions, five- and six-day work weeks are common. Several of the medium-sized states spend as many actual days in session as do the full-time legislatures. Twenty-nine legislatures today have the authority to convene themselves in special session without being dependent on the governor.

The number of legislators who define their occupation as "legislator" is increasing. An occupational survey of state legislators conducted by the National Conference of State Legislatures in 1986 found that more than 60 percent of the legislators in New York and Pennsylvania define their occupation as "legislator," and more than half the legislators in the Middle Atlantic states are full-time. The study also indicated that in larger states the number of "business owners" who are members of the legislature is much smaller than it is in the states with more limited session lengths. Lawyer legislators exist in greatest numbers in the South, with Virginia having the largest number (45 percent). In a number of states, members engaged in "education" outnumber those coming from any other professional background. Individuals engaged in "agriculture" still are found in every legislature but are in greatest number in the rural Midwestern and mountain states. In rank order, the largest occupational categories are "attorney" (16 percent), "business owner" (14 percent), "full-time legislator" (11 percent), "agricultural occupations" (10 percent) and "educator" (8 percent).

The category of full-time legislator would exceed 20 percent if those who list themselves as "retired," "homemaker" or "student" were included. The increased time demands and complexity of legislative activity as well as stringent conflict of interest and disclosure laws have likely contributed to the continuing decline in lawyer legislators. The number of women and minorities in the legislatures continues to increase each biennium. In 1987, 1,157 of the 7,461 state legislators were female (15.5 percent). The number of women legislators is highest in New Hampshire, Colorado, Maine, Washington and Vermont. Female representation is smallest in Alabama, Kentucky, Louisiana, Mississippi and Pennsylvania. Minority membership in state legislatures now exceeds 400 (5.4 percent).

Legislative Scheduling

The effective use of time during legislative sessions is a continuing preoccupation of legislatures. A majority of the legislatures have experimented with committee and floor scheduling systems and the use of deadlines. There is increasing interest in deadline systems which establish specific dates for the introduction of bills, periods for committee consideration in each house and cutoff dates for floor consideration in the chambers. Such systems provide a more even flow of work during a legislative session and can avoid the end-of-session logjam. The logjam is not entirely eliminated, but instead is spread over several deadline periods during a session. Another effect of such deadlines is to kill bills at various stages of the legislative process — often providing a convenient excuse for inaction, rather than having all of the bills that have been introduced remain alive throughout a session. Most legislatures using deadlines have found them to be effective in managing sessions.

Bill Introductions

Another procedural tool for more effective use of legislative time is the limit on bill introductions. Colorado is the most restrictive, limiting legislators to six (in the first year) and four (in the second year) bill introductions. Other states are experimenting with limiting requests for bill drafts or with concept or committee bills (by which a number of bill ideas or requests may be combined into a single draft). The sheer number of bills introduced and considered each session has necessitated the implementation of such procedures.

Approximately 200,000 bills are introduced in the state legislatures each biennium — in recent years ranging from lows of less than 1,000 in Utah, Vermont and Wyoming to a high of more than 33,000 in New York during the 1984-85 biennium. States also vary widely in the number of bills which are enacted — from a low of fewer than 200 in Ohio to the more than 3,000 bills enacted in California. The two largest states, California and New York, enact the most legislation, but Rhode Island, Louisiana and Maryland also rank in the top five. Ohio, Alaska, Vermont and Utah pass the fewest bills.

Twenty-five legislatures permit bills introduced in the first session to carry over to the second year; approximately 50,000 bills carry over each biennium. The number of bills introduced in state legislatures in the mid-1980s actually declined by about 3,000 from the corresponding period a decade earlier. This is in part a result of the procedural changes mentioned above, but also was affected by the spread of home rule and a decline in local legislation and by tighter state budgets which impose a self-discipline on legislators.

Committee Work - Sessions and Interim Periods

The modernization of the legislatures has resulted in stronger committee systems in many states. Committee strength varies across the state legislatures, but in the most effective bodies, the primary shaping of legislation occurs in committee, not on the floor. Many legislatures now make committee assignments and arrange committee and floor schedules to eliminate meeting conflicts and maximize the time available to committees early in the session.

Legislatures also have become more active during the interim period — the period between sessions. Several states use committee weeks or weekends as a means of effectively performing interim work. By concentrating all interim committee meeting within a three- or four-day period each month, the time demands on legislators are minimized. However, even with limitations on formal legislative sessions, there is increasing pressure on legislators to devote considerable amounts of time to interim committee work, oversight activity and constituent service. This is particularly true as legislatures expand their budget power and develop policy in complex areas such as education finance and reform, children and family services and tort reform.

State legislatures have met in special session with great frequency during the 1980s. This reflects their growing agenda, state fiscal problems and the practice in several states of considering specific issues in special session for procedural purposes or to focus attention upon them. There has been a growing trend in states which have the constitutional ability to do so, of recessing subject to the call of the chair rather than adjourning *sine die*. This practice allows the legislature to react to changing situations and to consider gubernatorial vetoes more effectively.

Legislative Compensation

An important element of the legislative reform movement was the payment of adequate compensation to legislators. In recent years, legislators' salaries have been adjusted more frequently than in earlier periods. The removal of constitutional restrictions on legislator salaries has been accomplished in 41 states; in nine states, salaries still are set in the constitution. In at least 20 states, some form of compensation commission or advisory group has been established to make recommendations on legislative compensation. Most of these groups are advisory, but in four states (Hawaii, Idaho, Maryland and Michigan) compensation commission recommendations take effect unless specifically negated by the legislature.

The states that have retained constitutional salary limitations tend to be the ones that provide the lowest levels of compensation. As of early 1988, legislator salaries range from $100 per year in New Hampshire to $43,000 annually in New York. Five states will pay legislators more than $40,000 per year in 1989, with a high of $57,500 in New York. In eight states, salaries will exceed $30,000 annually. Legislator salaries have increased regularly in many states in recent years, with 10-15 states increasing compensation each biennium. Salaries are paid on an annual basis in 38 states, and on a daily or weekly rate (tied to time spent in session) in the remainder. Biennial salaries now total more than $40,000 in 15 states, while 12 pay salaries less than $10,000 per biennium. Legislators in all but six states receive a per diem allowance when the legislature is in session or during the interim when on legislative business. In some cases, these payments reflect actual expenses, and in others, a specific unvouchered sum.

Forty-two states provide some additional compensation for legislative leaders, and 11 provide extra compensation to some committee chairmen. In New York, nearly all members receive additional compensation. The variation in legislative practices makes it difficult to determine accurately the total amount of legislator compensation.

Legislative Staffing

The expansion of institutional resources which accompanied legislative modernization is continuing. This expansion of resources to support the legislative process can be seen in increased legislative staff and greater staff specialization, improved and expanded facilities, and greater informational resources. The development of permanent legislative research and library reference staff began early in the 20th century. Legislative staff in the early years were part-time, few in number and dedicated to the recording and administration of the legislative process. The offices of legislative clerk and secretary can be traced to our English parliamentary heritage. Permanent research staff grew out of the Legislative Council movement, which was initiated to enable the legislature to function during the interim and to provide independent research capability. Permanent staff for bill drafting and legal services also appeared in the early years of this century.

By the 1950s states had begun to develop their own fiscal and budget staffs, rather than relying solely on executive budget assistance. This trend toward independent budget analysis and information had reached all 50 states by 1975. Post audit and program evaluation also had become important legislative functions in a majority of the states by the late 1970s — agencies often characterized by large professional staff units. A study conducted by the National Conference of State Legislatures in 1981 found that there were approximately 16,000 full-time, permanent staff in the 50 state legislatures and about 9,000 session-only employees. Current estimates are that the permanent staff level is 18,000-20,000 persons. But by far the largest staff increase has occurred in leadership staff and personal staff for legislators.

The implications of the expansion of staff capacity for the legislature are many. Foremost, it has reduced the dependence of the legislatures on the executive branch, lobbyists and other external sources of information. Many legislatures once relied on the attorney general or private lawyers for bill drafting and on the executive for budget and fiscal data. In the budget area enhanced staff capacity has, in a majority of states, allowed the realization of the premier legislative power, that to raise and expend funds. The legislative branch has become more independent each biennium particularly in areas such as fiscal analysis, revenue estimation, program evaluation and the development and operation of information systems.

A by-product of this legislative independence has been the number of constitutional confrontations between the legislative and executive branches — often in challenges of legislative assertions of authority. The budget power, review of administrative regulations and conditioning executive actions on legislative approval are key areas of conflict. The appropriations bill in some states has increasingly become the vehicle for the enactment of substantive legislation. As legislatures develop this practice, governors have become more innovative in their use of the veto. A serious conflict between the legislature and the governor in Wisconsin in this area is now in the courts. Conflict over legislative assertions of authority is likely to increase in the future.

Legislative staff organizations originally were characterized by a high degree of centralization. This remains true in many states where staff is organized in one or a few central staff agencies performing all legislative support functions. Increasingly, the trend in recent years has been toward decentralization and more specialization. This is exemplified by the growth in staff who work for individual legislators, one house, a caucus, or a committee of the legislature, rather than the institution as a whole. Separate committee staffing now exists to some extent in many legislatures, although it is most highly developed in California, Florida, Pennsylvania and New York. Illinois, which had a highly diverse staff structure, has moved to a somewhat more centralized system with stronger leadership control.

In recent years, there also has been a growth in partisan staff. Until the 1960s, nearly all permanent legislative staff were hired on a non-partisan basis. But with the increase in leadership staff, caucus staff, and the partisan staffing of committees, there are now several states (including Connecticut, California, Hawaii, Illinois, Indiana, Michigan, Minnesota, New Jersey, New York, Pennsylvania and Washington) that are characterized by sizable partisan staffs.

In the past few years, there have been no major structural changes in legislative staff. Personal staff for legislators continues to be the area of greatest staff growth. Staff who provide direct constituent services and aid in election campaigns also are becoming increasingly prominent in state legislatures. A function of the professionalization of legislative staff is the growing attention to the development of personnel and compensation systems and professional development programs. Another aspect is national recruitment and the transfer of legislative staff between states.

Legislative Facilities

Accompanying this staff expansion has been an improvement in legislative facilities in most states. In a majority of states, legislators are now provided office space and no longer have to depend solely on their desks on the floor of the legislature. In a number of states, legislative office buildings have been constructed to house legislators and the expanded staff component. Most recently, legislative facilities in Alabama, Connecticut, Georgia, Michigan, Mississippi, Ohio and North Carolina have been improved or expanded.

Modern, functional space for committees frequently is found in these facilities or in the many state capitol buildings which have been modernized and restored in the past decade. These improved facilities affect the legislature in several ways: the public has better access to legislators and the legislative process, and the legislature works under much better condi-

tions. The improvement of legislative facilities has both enhanced the independence of the legislature and contributed toward the professionalism of legislative bodies. However, many observers feel that the interaction among legislators is affected in a negative way.

The institutional sense which accompanied the centralized, more confined working conditions of earlier years is no longer as strong in today's more decentralized working environment — one where legislators no longer spend as much time with each other. Instead, there is greater emphasis on the individual legislator, and the individual legislator has greater resources at his or her command. The addition of resources and their dispersal among the membership has made the legislator more independent, and in some cases, has weakened legislative leadership.

Information Systems

The evolution of computers and information system technology has greatly enhanced the capacity of legislatures to develop and analyze information and make it more readily available to the membership. The impact of the computer on the legislative process, and on constituent work and campaign technology, has been enormous. Information now available to the legislature, whether it be bill status, a statute database, budget analysis or the impact of alternative spending or taxation proposals, has made the legislative institution and individual legislators more effective participants in the policymaking process. Information technology has led to a dispersal of power within the legislature, to committees and to individual members, and also contributes to the power of incumbency and independence from the political party. Detailed fiscal analysis and tracking or modeling packages are now in use in many states. These newer systems allow more efficient and less expensive production of legislative journals and session laws, as well as improve bill drafting and make bill status information more quickly and widely available.

Information system technology also allows the rapid widespread dispersal of information about legislative actions. Two national firms now provide bill tracking information on a 50-state basis and several states provide access to their internal bill tracking and statutory databases for external users. Where word processing is available in the individual legislator's office, it alters the ability to communicate with constituents and changes the way in which (and the frequency with which) such communication takes place. Several legislatures now provide computer terminals in the office of every legislator. Such developments contribute to the independence of the individual legislator and the decentralization of the legislative process. Computers have also facilitated legislative campaigns and constituent service activity.

Party Control

Coalition control — crossing party lines — has occurred in several legislative bodies in recent years. Currently, coalitions exist in the Alaska, New Mexico and Florida Senates. The Montana Senate functions as a "shared power" situation in its current partisan tie. Cross-party coalitions to take control may occur in other chambers in 1989.

The partisan composition and control of the 99 state legislative chambers was little changed by legislative elections in 1986 and 1987. Four states, Louisiana, Mississippi, New Jersey and Virginia, hold legislative elections in odd years. The Democrats gained control in two states, far below the historic average gain of ten legislative chambers in the off-year election by the party not holding the presidency. Democratic dominance of state legislatures has decreased somewhat in the past decade. In 1976, Democrats held 67 percent of legislative seats; in 1987, they held 60 percent. In 1988, Democrats had majorities in both houses in 27 states and Republicans in ten. The others were in divided control, had a tied chamber, or were non-partisan. The Washington Senate moved from Democratic control to Republican as the result of a special election in November 1987.

The Evolving Legislature

The impact of legislative modernization has clearly been to make state legislatures more independent, analytical and capable of policy development. It has resulted in many states in a gradual decentralization of the legislature. This can be seen in the strengthening of committees and of specialized expertise, in the greater resources provided to individual legislators and party caucuses and in changes in legislative staffing patterns.

Two trends are evident in state legislative staff development in addition to the continued professionalization and emphasis on specializ-

ed expertise. The first of these is a decentralization of management control within legislatures, and sometimes within individual houses. The model for many years was of central service agencies working for both houses under some form of joint management control. The trend in the past decade has been toward separate house and senate staffs and the elimination or reduction in scope of joint central service agencies of the Legislative Council or Legislative Service Bureau type. Such decentralization is far along in the large states, with the exception of Ohio, but also is evident in states as diverse as Alaska, Louisiana, Minnesota, Oklahoma and South Carolina. Within individual houses there is evidence of further decentralization as committees are allowed to hire staff.

The second trend is in the type of staff. Staff growth is occurring significantly among personal staff for leaders and members or committees, and among partisan caucus staffs. Such staff are hired on a decentralized basis, in some states as a result of political ties, and are usually responsible only to individual legislators. An effect of these trends is to reduce the sense of the legislature as an institution and to reduce the opportunities and the need for two houses to work jointly and cooperatively together.

The growth of lobbying activity at the state level, with PACs and independent financing of legislative campaigns has also contributed to a fragmentation of the legislature. Developments in campaign funding present an interesting dichotomy in their impact on the legislature. On the one hand, they have contributed to candidate independence and a decline of party or leadership control; yet, where some control of PAC funding and overall fundraising can be gained by a legislative leader, he or she can use this to strengthen his or her leadership position and develop a more centralized, cohesive legislative party.

Another trend in legislatures today is the declining authority of legislative leadership. This trend is a result of many of the factors discussed above. The ability of leaders to control information, favors and finances is no longer as great as it once was. The tenure of leaders is often short, with a turnover rate in excess of 25 percent in recent years. But some strong, long serving leaders remain in places such as the Massachusetts and New York Senates and the House in Maine, Ohio and Georgia.

A trend is also evident toward increased constituent service and attention by state legislators. The professionalization of the legislature has accelerated this development. Nine state legislatures now provide district offices for members and expenditure allowances for district activity are growing.

Even with the trends noted above, the costs of state legislative operations remain small as a percentage of state government expenditures. According to U.S. Census data, legislatures expended slightly more than one billion dollars on their operations in Fiscal Year 1986. This represents less than 0.3 percent of total state government spending and exceeds the 0.5 percent level in only three states. Total dollar expenditures are greatest in the largest states, while per capita costs are highest in the smaller states. This reflects the fixed costs associated with operating a legislative body, regardless of state size.

Table 3.1
NAMES OF STATE LEGISLATIVE BODIES AND CONVENING PLACES

State or other jurisdiction	Both bodies	Upper house	Lower house	Convening place
Alabama	Legislature	Senate	House of Representatives	State Capitol
Alaska	Legislature	Senate	House of Representatives	State Capitol
Arizona	Legislature	Senate	House of Representatives	State Capitol
Arkansas	General Assembly	Senate	House of Representatives	State Capitol
California	Legislature	Senate	Assembly	State Capitol
Colorado	General Assembly	Senate	House of Representatives	State Capitol
Connecticut	General Assembly	Senate	House of Representatives	State Capitol
Delaware	General Assembly	Senate	House of Representatives	Legislative Hall
Florida	Legislature	Senate	House of Representatives	The Capitol
Georgia	General Assembly	Senate	House of Representatives	State Capitol
Hawaii	Legislature	Senate	House of Representatives	State Capitol
Idaho	Legislature	Senate	House of Representatives	State Capitol
Illinois	General Assembly	Senate	House of Representatives	State House
Indiana	General Assembly	Senate	House of Representatives	State House
Iowa	General Assembly	Senate	House of Representatives	State Capitol
Kansas	Legislature	Senate	House of Representatives	State House
Kentucky	General Assembly	Senate	House of Representatives	State Capitol
Louisiana	Legislature	Senate	House of Representatives	State Capitol
Maine	Legislature	Senate	House of Representatives	State House
Maryland	General Assembly	Senate	House of Delegates	State House
Massachusetts	General Court	Senate	House of Representatives	State House
Michigan	Legislature	Senate	House of Representatives	State Capitol
Minnesota	Legislature	Senate	House of Representatives	State Capitol
Mississippi	Legislature	Senate	House of Representatives	New Capitol
Missouri	General Assembly	Senate	House of Representatives	State Capitol
Montana	Legislature	Senate	House of Representatives	State Capitol
Nebraska	Legislature	(a)		State Capitol
Nevada	Legislature	Senate	Assembly	Legislative Building
New Hampshire	General Court	Senate	House of Representatives	State House
New Jersey	Legislature	Senate	General Assembly	State House
New Mexico	Legislature	Senate	House of Representatives	State Capitol
New York	Legislature	Senate	Assembly	State Capitol
North Carolina	General Assembly	Senate	House of Representatives	State Legislative Building
North Dakota	Legislative Assembly	Senate	House of Representatives	State Capitol
Ohio	General Assembly	Senate	House of Representatives	State House
Oklahoma	Legislature	Senate	House of Representatives	State Capitol
Oregon	Legislative Assembly	Senate	House of Representatives	State Capitol
Pennsylvania	General Assembly	Senate	House of Representatives	Main Capitol Building
Rhode Island	General Assembly	Senate	House of Representatives	State House
South Carolina	General Assembly	Senate	House of Representatives	State House
South Dakota	Legislature	Senate	House of Representatives	State Capitol
Tennessee	General Assembly	Senate	House of Representatives	State Capitol
Texas	Legislature	Senate	House of Representatives	State Capitol
Utah	Legislature	Senate	House of Representatives	State Capitol
Vermont	General Assembly	Senate	House of Representatives	State House
Virginia	General Assembly	Senate	House of Delegates	State Capitol
Washington	Legislature	Senate	House of Representatives	Legislative Building
West Virginia	Legislature	Senate	House of Delegates	State Capitol
Wisconsin	Legislature	Senate	Assembly(b)	State Capitol
Wyoming	Legislature	Senate	House of Representatives	State Capitol
Dist. of Col.	Council of the District of Columbia	(a)		District Building
American Samoa	Legislature	Senate	House of Representatives	Maota Fono
Guam	Legislature	(a)		Congress Building
No. Mariana Is.	Legislature	Senate	House of Representatives	Civic Center
Puerto Rico	Legislative Assembly	Senate	House of Representatives	The Capitol
Federated States of Micronesia	Congress	(a)		Congress Office Building
Virgin Islands	Legislature	(a)		Capitol Building

(a) Unicameral legislature. Except in Dist. of Col., members go by the title Senator.

(b) Members of the lower house go by the title Representative.

Table 3.2
LEGISLATIVE SESSIONS: LEGAL PROVISIONS

State or other jurisdiction	Regular sessions				Special sessions		
	Legislature convenes			Limitation on length of session(a)	Legislature may call	Legislature may determine subject of session	Limitation on length of session
	Year	Month	Day				
Alabama..............	Annual	Jan. Apr. Feb.	2nd Tues.(b) 3rd Tues.(c,d) 1st Tues.(e)	30 L in 105 C	No	Yes(f)	12 L in 30 C
Alaska...............	Annual	Jan. Jan.	3rd Mon.(c) 2nd Mon.(e)	120 C(g)	By 2/3 vote of members	Yes(h)	30 C
Arizona..............	Annual	Jan.	2nd Mon.	(i)	By petition, 2/3 members, each house	Yes(h)	None
Arkansas	Biennial-odd year	Jan.	2nd Mon.	60 C(g)	No	Yes(f,j)	(i)
California	(k)	Jan.	1st Mon.(d)	None	No	No	None
Colorado	Annual	Jan.	Wed. after 1st Tues.	(l)	By request, 2/3 members, each house	Yes(h)	None
Connecticut	Annual(m)	Jan. Feb.	Wed. after 1st Mon.(n) Wed. after 1st Mon.(o)	(p)	Yes(q)	(q)	None(r)
Delaware	Annual	Jan.	2nd Tues.	June 30	Joint call, presiding officers, both houses	Yes	None
Florida	Annual	Apr.	Tues. after 1st Mon.(d)	60 C(g)	Joint call, presiding officers, both houses	Yes	20 C(g)
Georgia..............	Annual	Jan.	2nd Mon.(d)	40 L	By petition, 3/5 members, each house	Yes(h)	(s)
Hawaii	Annual	Jan.	3rd Wed.	60 L(g)	By petition, 2/3 members, each house	Yes	30 L(g)
Idaho	Annual	Jan.	Mon. on or nearest 9th day	None	No	No	20 C
Illinois..............	Annual	Jan.	2nd Wed.	None	Joint call, presiding officers, both houses	Yes	None
Indiana	Annual	Jan.	2nd Mon.(d,t)	odd-61 L or Apr. 30; even-30 L or Mar. 15	No	Yes	30 L in 40 C
Iowa	Annual	Jan.	2nd Mon.	(u)	By petition, 2/3 members, both houses	Yes	None
Kansas	Annual	Jan.	2nd Mon.	odd-None; even-90 C(g)	Petition to governor of 2/3 members, each house	Yes	None
Kentucky	Biennial-even yr.	Jan.	Tues. after 1st Mon.(d)	60 L(v)	No	No	None
Louisiana	Annual	Apr.	3rd Mon.	60 L in 85 C	By petition, majority, each house	Yes(h)	30 C
Maine	(k,m)	Dec. Jan.	1st Wed.(b) Wed. after 1st Tues.(o)	100 L(g) 50 L(g)	Joint call, presiding officers, with consent of majority of members of each political party, each house	Yes(h)	None
Maryland	Annual	Jan.	2nd Wed.	90 C(g)	By petition, majority, each house	Yes	30 C

LEGISLATIVE SESSIONS: LEGAL PROVISIONS—Continued

State or other jurisdiction	Regular sessions				Special sessions		
	Legislature convenes			Limitation on length of session(a)	Legislature may call	Legislature may determine subject	Limitation on length of session
	Year	Month	Day				
Massachusetts	Annual	Jan.	1st Wed.	None	By petition(w)	Yes	None
Michigan	Annual	Jan.	2nd Wed.(d)	None	No	No	None
Minnesota	(x)	Jan.	Tues. after 1st Mon.(n)	120 L or 1st Mon. after 3rd Sat. in May(x)	No	Yes	None
Mississippi	Annual	Jan.	Tues. after 1st Mon.	125 C(g,y); 90 C(g,y)	No	No	None
Missouri	Annual	Jan.	Wed. after 1st Mon.	odd-June 30; even-May 15	No	No	60 C
Montana	Biennial-odd yr.	Jan.	1st Mon.	90 L(g)	By petition, majority, both houses	Yes	None
Nebraska	Annual	Jan.	Wed. after 1st Mon.	odd-90 L(g); even-60 L(g)	By petition, 2/3 members, each house	Yes	None
Nevada	Biennial-odd yr.	Jan.	3rd Mon.	60 C(u)	No	No	20 C(u)
New Hampshire	Annual	Jan.	Wed. after 1st Tues.(d)	45 L	By 2/3 vote of members	Yes	(u)
New Jersey...........	Annual	Jan.	2nd Tues.	None	By petition, majority, each house	Yes	None
New Mexico	Annual(m)	Jan.	3rd Tues.	odd-60 C; even-30 C	By petition, 3/5 members, each house	Yes(h)	30 C
New York	Annual	Jan.	Wed. after 1st Mon.	None	By petition, 2/3 members, each house	Yes(h)	None
North Carolina	(x)	Jan.	Wed. after 2nd Mon.(n)	None(x)	By petition, 3/5 members, each house	Yes	None
North Dakota	Biennial-odd yr.	Jan.	Tues. after Jan. 3, but not later than Jan. 11(d)	80 L(z)	No	Yes	None
Ohio	Annual	Jan.	1st Mon.	None	Joint call, presiding officers, both houses	Yes	None
Oklahoma	Annual	Jan.	Tues. after 1st Mon.	90 L	By 2/3 vote of members	Yes	None
Oregon	Biennial-odd yr.	Jan.	2nd Mon.	None	By petition, majority, each house	Yes	None
Pennsylvania	Annual	Jan.	1st Tues.	None	By petition, majority, each house	No	None
Rhode Island	Annual	Jan.	1st Tues.	60 L(u)	No	No	None
South Carolina	Annual	Jan.	2nd Tues.(d)	1st Thurs. in June(g)	No	Yes	None
South Dakota	Annual	Jan.	Tues. after 1st Mon.	odd-40 L; even-35 L	No	No	None
Tennessee	(x)	Jan.	(aa)	90 L(u)	By petition, 2/3 members, each house	Yes	30 L(u)

LEGISLATIVE SESSIONS: LEGAL PROVISIONS—Continued

State or other jurisdiction	Regular sessions				Special sessions		
	Legislature convenes			Limitation on length of session(a)	Legislature may call	Legislature may determine subject of session	Limitation on length of session
	Year	Month	Day				
Texas.............	Biennial-odd yr.	Jan.	2nd Tues.	140 C	No	No	30 C
Utah..............	Annual	Jan.	2nd Mon.	45 C	No	No	30 C
Vermont...........	(x)	Jan.	Wed. after 1st Mon.(n)	(u)	No	Yes	None
Virginia..........	Annual	Jan.	2nd Wed.	odd-30 C(g); even-60 C(g)	By petition, 2/3 members, each house	Yes	None
Washington........	Annual	Jan.	2nd Mon.	odd-105 C; even-60 C	By petition, 2/3 members, each house	Yes	30 C
West Virginia.....	Annual	Feb. / Jan.	2nd Wed.(c,d) / 2nd Wed.(e)	60 C(g)	By petition, 3/5 members, each house	Yes(bb)	None
Wisconsin.........	Annual(cc)	Jan.	1st Tues. after Jan. 8(d,n)	None	No	No	None
Wyoming...........	Annual(m)	Jan. / Feb.	2nd Tues.(n) / 2nd Tues.(o)	odd-40 L; even-20 L	No	Yes	None
Dist. of Col.....	(dd)	Jan.	2nd day	None			None
American Samoa	Annual	Jan. / July	2nd Mon. / 2nd Mon.	45 L / 45 L	No	No	None
Guam	Annual	Jan.	1st Mon.(ee)	None	No	No	None
Puerto Rico	Annual	Jan.	2nd Mon.	Apr. 30(g)	No	No	20 C
Virgin Islands ...	Annual	Jan.	2nd Mon.	75 L	No	No	15 C

Note: Some legislatures will also reconvene after normal session to consider bills vetoed by governor. Connecticut—if governor vetoes any bill, secretary of state must reconvene General Assembly on second Monday after the last day on which governor is either authorized to transmit or has transmitted every bill with his objections, whichever occurs first; General Assembly must adjourn *sine die* not later than three days after its reconvening. Hawaii—legislature may reconvene on 45th day after adjournment *sine die*, in special session, without call. Louisiana—legislature meets in a maximum five-day veto session on the 40th day after final adjournment. Missouri—if governor returns any bill on or after the fifth day before the last day on which legislature may consider bills (in even-numbered years), legislature automatically reconvenes on first Monday in September for a maximum 10 C session. New Jersey—legislature meets in special session (without call or petition) to act on bills returned by governor on 45th day after *sine die* adjournment of the first year of a two-year legislature; a special session may not be convened if the 45th day falls on or after the last day of the legislative year in which the second session occurs. Virginia—legislature reconvenes on sixth Wednesday after adjournment for a maximum three-day session (may be extended to seven days upon vote of majority of members elected to each house). Utah—if 2/3 of the members of each house favor reconvening to consider vetoed bills, a maximum five-day session is set by the presiding officers. Washington—upon petition of 2/3 of the members of each house, legislature meets 45 days after adjournment for a maximum five-day session.

Key:

C—Calendar day

L—Legislative day (in some states, called a session day or workday; definition may vary slightly, however, generally refers to any day on which either house of the legislature is in session)

(a) Applies to each year unless otherwise indicated.
(b) General election year (quadrennial election).
(c) Year after quadrennial election.
(d) Legal provision for organizational session prior to stated convening date. Alabama—in the year after quadremial election, on the second Tuesday in January for 10 C. California—in the even-numbered, general election year, on first Monday in December for an organizational session, recess until the first Monday in January of the odd-numbered year. Florida—in general election year, 14th day after election. Georgia—in odd-numbered year. Indiana—third Tuesday after first Monday in November. Kentucky—in odd-numbered year, Tuesday after first Monday in January for 10 L. Michigan—held in odd-numbered year. New Hampshire—in even-numbered year, first Wednesday in December. North Dakota—in even-numbered year, Tuesday after first Monday in December of three-day session. South Carolina—in even-numbered year, Tuesday after certification of election of its members for a maximum three-day session. West Virginia—in year after general election, on second Wednesday in January.
(e) Other years.
(f) By 2/3 vote each house.
(g) Session may be extended by vote of members in both houses. Alaska: 2/3 vote for 10-day extension. Arkansas: 2/3 vote. Florida: 3/5 vote. Hawaii: petition of 2/3 membership for maximum 15-day extension. Kansas: 2/3 vote. Maryland: 3/5 vote for maximum 30 C. Mississippi: 2/3 vote for 30-day extension, no limit on number of extensions. Nebraska: 4/5 vote. South Carolina: 2/3 vote. Virginia: 2/3 vote for 30-day extension. West Virginia: 2/3 vote (or if budget bill has not been acted upon three days before session ends, governor issues proclamation extending session). Puerto Rico: joint resolution.
(h) Only if legislature convenes itself. Special sessions called by the legislature are unlimited in scope in Arizona, Georgia, Maine, and New Mexico.

LEGISLATIVE SESSIONS: LEGAL PROVISIONS—Continued

(i) No constitutional or statutory provision; however, legislative rules require that regular sessions adjourn no later than Saturday of the week during which the 100th day of the session falls.

(j) After governor's business has been disposed of, members may remain in session up to 15 C by a 2/3 vote of both houses.

(k) Regular sessions begin after general election, in December of even-numbered year. In California, legislature meets in December for an organizational session, recesses until the first Monday in January of the odd-numbered year and continues in session until Nov. 30 of next even-numbered year. In Maine, session which begins in December of general election year runs into the following year (odd-numbered); second session begins in December of next even-numbered year.

(l) A 1982 constitutional amendment imposed a time limit of 140 C on regular sessions convening in even-numbered years.

(m) Second session limited to consideration of specific types of legislation. Connecticut—individual legislators may only introduce bills of a fiscal nature. Maine—budgetary matters; legislation in the governor's call; emergency legislation; legislation referred to committees for study. New Mexico—budgets, appropriations and revenue bills; bills drawn pursuant to governor's message; vetoed bills. Wyoming—budget bills.

(n) Odd-numbered years.

(o) Even-numbered years.

(p) Odd-numbered years—not later than Wednesday after first Monday in June; even-numbered years—not later than Wednesday after first Monday in May.

(q) Constitution provides for regular session convening dates and allows that sessions may also be held "...at such other times as the General Assembly shall judge necessary." Call by majority of legislators is implied.

(r) Upon completion of business.

(s) Limited to 40 days if called by governor and 30 days if called by petition of the legislature, except in cases of impeachment proceedings.

(t) Legislators may reconvene at any time after organizational meeting; however, second Monday in January is the final date by which regular session must be in process.

(u) Indirect limitation; usually restrictions on legislator's pay, per diem, or daily allowance.

(v) May not extend beyond April 15.

(w) Joint rules provide for the submission of a written statement requesting special session by a specified number of members of each chamber.

(x) Legal provision for session in odd-numbered year; however, legislature may divide, and in practice has divided, to meet in even-numbered years as well.

(y) A 1968 constitutional amendment calls for 90 C sessions every year, except the first year of a gubernatorial administration during which the legislative session runs for 125 C.

(z) No legislative day is shorter than a natural day.

(aa) Commencement of regular session depends on concluding date of organizational session. Legislature meets, in odd-numbered year, on second Tuesday in January for a maximum 15 C organizational session, then returns on the Tuesday following the conclusion of the organizational session.

(bb) According to a 1955 attorney general's opinion, when the legislature has petitioned to the governor to be called into session, it may then act on any matter.

(cc) The legislature, by joint resolution, establishes the session schedule of activity for the remainder of the biennium at the beginning of the odd-numbered year.

(dd) Each Council period begins on January 2 of each odd-numbered year and ends on January 1 of the following odd-numbered year.

(ee) Legislature meets on the first Monday of each month following its initial session in January.

Table 3.3
THE LEGISLATORS
Numbers, Terms, and Party Affiliations

State or other jurisdiction	Senate						House						Senate and House totals
	Demo-crats	Repub-licans	Other	Vacan-cies	Total	Term	Demo-crats	Repub-licans	Other	Vacan-cies	Total	Term	
All states	1,177	762	1	6	1,995		3,294	2,164	4	5	5,466		7,461
Alabama...........	30	5	...	...	35	4	89	16	...	...	105	4	140
Alaska.............	8	12	...	...	20	4	24	16	...	...	40	2	60
Arizona...........	11	19	...	...	30	2	24	36	...	...	60	2	90
Arkansas	31	4	...(a)	...	35	4	91	9	...	...	100	2	135
California..........	23	15	1(a)	1	40	4	44	36	...	...	80	2	120
Colorado	10	25	...	...	35	4	25	40	...	...	65	2	100
Connecticut	25	11	...	...	36	2	92	59	...	...	151	2	187
Delaware	13	8	...	...	21	4	19	22	...	...	41	2	62
Florida	25	15	...	...	40	4	75	45	...	...	120	2	160
Georgia...........	46	10	...	...	56	2	153	27	...	...	180	2	236
Hawaii	20	5	...	...	25	4	40	10	...	1	51	2	76
Idaho	16	26	...	...	42	2	20	64	...	...	84	2	126
Illinois.............	31	28	...	...	59	4(b)	67	51	...	...	118	2	177
Indiana	19	30	...	1	50	4	48	52	...	...	100	2	150
Iowa	30	20	...	...	50	4	58	42	...	...	100	2	150
Kansas	16	24	...	...	40	4	51	74	...	...	125	2	165
Kentucky	29	9	...	...	38	4	71	29	...	1	100	2	138
Louisiana	34	5	...	...	39	4	87	15	...	3	105	4	144
Maine	20	15	...	...	35	2	86	65	...	...	151	2	186
Maryland	40	7	...	...	47	4	124	17	...	...	141	4	188
Massachusetts	32	8	...	...	40	2	127	33	...	...	160	2	200
Michigan	18	20	...	...	38	4	64	46	...	...	110	2	148
Minnesota	47(c)	20(d)	...	...	67	4	83(c)	51(d)	...	...	134	2	201
Mississippi	45	7	...	...	52	4	113	9	...	...	122	4	174
Missouri	21	13	...	...	34	4	111	52	...	...	163	2	197
Montana...........	25	25	...	...	50	4(e)	49	51	...	...	100	2	150
Nebraska	----------Nonpartisan election----------				49	4	------------------------Unicameral------------------------						49
Nevada	9	12	...	...	21	4	29	13	...	...	42	2	63
New Hampshire	8	16	...	...	24	2	132	268	...	...	400	2	424
New Jersey..........	24	16	...	...	40	4(f)	39	41	...	...	80	2	120
New Mexico.........	21	21	...	...	42	4	47	23	...	...	70	2	112
New York	25	36	...	...	61	2	92	56	2(g)	...	150	2	211
North Carolina	40	10	...	...	50	2	84	36	...	...	120	2	170
North Dakota	27	26	...	...	53	4	45	61	...	...	106	2	159
Ohio	15	18	...	...	33	4	60	39	...	...	99	2	132
Oklahoma	30	17	...	1	48	4	70	31	...	...	101	2	149
Oregon	17	13	...	...	30	4	31	29	...	...	60	2	90
Pennsylvania	23	26	...	1	50	4	103	100	...	...	203	2	253
Rhode Island	38	12	...	...	50	2	80	20	...	...	100	2	150
South Carolina	36	10	...	...	46	4	92	32	...	...	124	2	170
South Dakota	11	24	...	...	35	2	22	48	...	...	70	2	105
Tennessee	23	10	...	...	33	4	61	38	...	...	99	2	132
Texas..............	25	6	...	...	31	4	94	56	...	...	150	2	181
Utah	8	21	...	...	29	4	27	48	...	...	75	2	104
Vermont	19	11	...	...	30	2	74	75	1(a)	...	150	2	180
Virginia............	30	10	...	...	40	4	64	35	1(a)	...	100	2	140
Washington	25	24	...	...	49	4	61	37	...	...	98	2	147
West Virginia	27	7	...	...	34	4	78	22	...	...	100	2	134
Wisconsin..........	20	11	...	2	33	4	54	45	...	...	99	2	132
Wyoming	11	19	...	...	30	4	20	44	...	...	64	2	94
Dist. of Col. (h)	11	1	1(i)	...	13	4	----------------------Unicameral----------------------						13
American Samoa	--------Nonpartisan election--------				18	4	-------- Nonpartisan election--------		21		21	2	39
Guam	13	8	...	...	21	2	----------------------Unicameral----------------------						21
No. Mariana Is.	2	7	...	...	9	4	6	9	...	...	15	2	24
Puerto Rico	18(j)	8(k)	1(l)	...	27	4	34(j)	16(k)	1(l)	...	51	4	78
Virgin Islands	7	1	7(a)	...	15	2	----------------------Unicameral----------------------						15

Note: This table reflects the legislatures as of January 1987, except for Louisiana, Mississippi, New Jersey and Virginia; information for those jurisdictions is as of January 1988; the Northern Mariana Islands (1985) and Puerto Rico (1984).

(a) Independent. In Virgin Islands, six Independent and one Independent Citizens Movement.

(b) The entire Senate is up for election every ten years, beginning in 1972. Senate districts are divided into three groups. One group elects senators for terms of 4-years, 4-years, and 2-years, the second group for terms of 4-years, 2-years, and 4-years, the third group for terms of 2-years, 4-years, and 4-years.

(c) Democratic-Farmer-Labor.

(d) Independent-Republican.

(e) After each decennial reapportionment, lots are drawn for half of the senators to serve an initial 2-year term. Subsequent elections are for 4-year terms.

(f) Senate terms beginning in January of second year following the U.S. decennial census are for 2 years only.

(g) Liberal.

(h) Council of the District of Columbia.

(i) Statehood Party.

(j) Popular Democratic Party.

(k) New Progressive Party.

(l) Independent Puerto Rican Party.

Table 3.4
MEMBERSHIP TURNOVER IN THE LEGISLATURES: 1986

State	Senate			House		
	Total number of members	Number of membership changes	Percentage change of total	Total number of members	Number of membership changes	Percentage change of total
Alabama	35	6	17	105	24	23
Alaska	20 (b)	5	25	40	12	30
Arizona	30	7	23	60	13	22
Arkansas	35 (b)	2	6	100	7	7
California	40 (b)	2	5	80	12	15
Colorado	35 (b)	7	20	65	22	34
Connecticut	36	15	42	151	46	30
Delaware	21 (b)	2	10	41	5	12
Florida	40 (b)	9	23	120	29	24
Georgia	56	7	13	180	24	13
Hawaii	25 (b)	5	25	51	12	24
Idaho	42	9	21	84	22	26
Illinois	59 (b)	10	17	118	17	14
Indiana	50 (b)	8	16	100	18	18
Iowa	50 (b)	10	20	100	23	23
Kansas	40	1	3	125	16	13
Kentucky	38 (b)	9	24	100	22	22
Louisiana	39 (a)	1	3	105 (a)	7	7
Maine	35	12	34	151	33	22
Maryland	47	9	19	141	41	29
Massachusetts	40	3	8	160	22	14
Michigan	38 (b)	7	18	110	18	16
Minnesota	67	11	16	134	31	23
Mississippi	52 (a)	2	4	122 (a)	3	2
Missouri	34 (b)	1	3	163	27	17
Montana	50 (b)	11	22	100	18	18
Nebraska	49 (b)	11	22	----------Unicameral----------		
Nevada	21 (b)	6	29	42	17	40
New Hampshire	24	6	25	400	134	34
New Jersey	40	3	8	80	23	29
New Mexico	42	2		70	18	26
New York	61	5	8	150	13	9
North Carolina	50	8	16	120	26	22
North Dakota	53 (b)	9	17	106	19	18
Ohio	33 (b)	7	21	99	16	16
Oklahoma	48 (b)	16	33	101	31	31
Oregon	30 (b)	6	20	60	11	18
Pennsylvania	50 (b)	4	8	203	16	8
Rhode Island	50	6	12	100	21	21
South Carolina	46	1	2	124	22	18
South Dakota	35	9	26	70	22	31
Tennessee	33 (b)	5	15	99	15	15
Texas	31 (b)	6	19	150	25	17
Utah	29 (b)	8	28	75	28	37
Vermont	30	5	17	150	39	26
Virginia	40	2	5	100	11	11
Washington	49 (b)	4	8	98	19	19
West Virginia	34 (b)	8	24	100	31	31
Wisconsin	33 (b)	4	12	99	13	13
Wyoming	30 (b)	6	20	64	18	28

Source: Survey conducted by The Council of State Governments, Lexington, Kentucky, 1987.

Note: *Turnover calculated after 1986 legislative elections. Data was obtained by comparing the 1985-86 and 1986-87 editions of *State Elective Officials and the Legislatures,* published by The Council of State Governments.

(a) No election held in 1986.
(b) Entire Senate membership not up for reelection in 1986.

Table 3.5
THE LEGISLATORS: QUALIFICATIONS FOR ELECTION

State or other jurisdiction	House					Senate				
	Minimum age	U.S. Citizen (years)	State resident (years)	District resident (years)	Qualified Voter (years)	Minimum age	U.S. Citizen (years)	State resident (years)	District resident (years)	Qualified Voter (years)
Alabama	21	…	3(a)	1	…	25	…	3(a)	1	★
Alaska	21	…	3	1	★	25	…	3	1	…
Arizona	25	★	3	1	…	25	★	3	1	★
Arkansas	21	★	2	1	★	25	★	2	1	★
California	18	3	3	1	★	18	3	3	1	★
Colorado	25	★	…	1	…	25	★	…	1	★
Connecticut	18	…	3(a)	★	★	18	…	3(a)	★	…
Delaware	24	…	2	1	…	27	…	2	1	★
Florida	21	★	(a)	★	★	21	★	(a)	1	★
Georgia	21	…	…	1	…	25	…	…	1	…
Hawaii	18	…	3	(b)	★	18	…	3	(b)	★
Idaho	18	★	…	1	★	18	★	…	1	★
Illinois	21	★	…	2(c)	…	21	★	…	2(c)	…
Indiana	21	★	2	…	…	25	★	2	…	…
Iowa	21	★	1	60 da.	…	25	★	1	60 da.	…
Kansas	18	…	2(a)	1	★	18	…	6(a)	★	★
Kentucky	24	…	2	1	★	30	…	2	1	★
Louisiana	18	5	1	(r)	★	18	…	…	(r)	…
Maine	21	5	1(a)	6 mo.(d)	★	25	5	1(a)	6 mo.(d)	★
Maryland	21	…	…	…	2	25	…	…	…	3
Massachusetts	18	★	…	1	★	18	…	5	★	★
Michigan(e)	21	…	…	(b)	★	21	…	1	(b)	★
Minnesota	21	…	1	6 mo.	★	21	…	1	6 mo.	★
Mississippi	21	…	4(a)	…	★	25	…	4	1(f)	4
Missouri	24	…	…	1(f)	2	30	…	…	1(f)	3
Montana(g)	18	…	1(a)	6 mo.(h)	★	18	…	1(a)	6 mo.(h)	★
Nebraska	U	U	U	U	U	21	…	1(a)	1	★
Nevada	21	…	1(a)	(b)	★	21	…	7(a)	(b)	★
New Hampshire	18	…	2	★	…	30	…	4(a)	★	★
New Jersey	21	…	2(a)	1	★	30	…	…	…	…
New Mexico	21	…	…	★	…	25	…	5	★	…
New York	18	★	5	1(i)	★	18	★	5	1(i)	★
North Carolina	(j)	★	1	1	★	25	…	2(a)	(b)	★
North Dakota	18	…	1	(b)	★	18	…	1	(b)	★
Ohio(k)	18	…	…	1	★	18	…	1	…	★

THE LEGISLATORS: QUALIFICATIONS FOR ELECTION—Continued

State or other jurisdiction	House					Senate				
	Minimum age	U.S. Citizen (years)	State resident (years)	District resident (years)	Qualified Voter (years)	Minimum age	U.S. Citizen (years)	State resident (years)	District resident (years)	Qualified Voter (years)
Oklahoma	21	...	...	(b)	★	25	...	...	(b)	★
Oregon	21	★	...	-	-	21	...	4(a)	-	...
Pennsylvania	21	...	4(a)	1	...	25	...	...	1	...
Rhode Island(l)	18	...	...	...	★	18	...	...	...	★
South Carolina	21	...	...	(b)	★	25	...	...	(b)	★
South Dakota(k,l)	25	★	2	(b)	★	25	★	2	(b)	★
Tennessee	21	★	(a)	1(b)	★	30	★	3	1(b)	★
Texas	21	★	2	1	★	26	★	5	1	★
Utah	25	...	3	6 mo.(b)	★	25	...	3	6 mo.(b)	★
Vermont	18	...	2	1	...	18	...	2	1	...
Virginia	21	...	...	★	★	21	...	...	★	★
Washington	18	★	...	(b)	★	18	...	...	(b)	★
West Virginia(l)	18	...	(a)	1	★	25	...	(a)	1	★
Wisconsin	18	...	1	(b)	★	18	...	(a)	(b)	★
Wyoming	21	★	(a)	1	...	25	★	(a)	1	...
Dist. of Col.	U	U	U	U	U	18	...	1	★	...
American Samoa(l)	25	★(m)	5	1	U	30(n)	★(m)	5	1	U
Guam(o)	U	U	U	U	U	25	★	5	...	U
No. Mariana Is.	21	...	3	...	U	25	...	5	...	★
Puerto Rico(p)	25	...	2(a)	1(q)	★	30	★	2(a)	1(q)	U
Virgin Islands(o)	U	U	U	U	U	21	★	3	...	U

Note: This table includes constitutional and statutory provisions.

Key:
U—Unicameral legislature; members are called senators, except in District of Columbia.
★—Formal provision; number of years not specified.
. . .—No formal provision.
(a) Additional state citizenship requirement. Alabama, Delaware—three years. Georgia, New Jersey, New Hampshire—seven years. House, two years; Senate, four years. Mississippi—four years. North Carolina—two years. Pennsylvania—four years. West Virginia—five years.
(b) Must be a qualified voter of the district; number of years not specified.
(c) Following redistricting, a candidate may be elected from any district that contains a part of the district in which he resided at the time of redistricting, and reelected if a resident of the new district he represents for 18 months prior to reelection.
(d) If the district was established for less than six months, residency is length of establishment of district.
(e) No person convicted of a felony or breach of public trust within preceding 20 years or convicted of subversion shall be eligible.
(f) Only if the district has been in existence for one year; if not, then legislator must have been a one year resident of the district(s) from which the new district was created.
(g) No person convicted of a felony is eligible to hold office until final discharge from state supervision.

(h) Shall be a resident of the county if it contains one or more districts or of the district if it contains all or parts of more than one county.
(i) After redistricting, must have been a resident of the county in which the district is contained for one year immediately preceding election.
(j) A conflict exists between two articles of the constitution, one specifying age for House members (i.e., "qualified voter of the state") and the other related to general eligibility for elective office (i.e., "every qualified voter . . . who is 21 years of age . . . shall be eligible for election").
(k) No person convicted of embezzlement of public funds shall hold any office.
(l) Disqualification for bribery. In South Dakota and West Virginia, disqualification also for perjury or other infamous crimes. In American Samoa, also for felony.
(m) Or U.S. national.
(n) Must be registered matai.
(o) Disqualification for felony or crime involving moral turpitude unless person received pardon restoring civil rights.
(p) Read and write the Spanish or English language.
(q) When there is more than one representative district in a municipality, residence in the municipality shall satisfy this requirement.
(r) Must be district resident at time of nomination.

Table 3.6
SENATE LEADERSHIP POSITIONS—METHODS OF SELECTION*

State or other jurisdiction	President	President pro tem	Majority leader	Assistant majority leader	Majority floor leader	Assistant majority floor leader	Majority whip	Majority caucus chairman	Minority leader	Assistant minority leader	Minority floor leader	Assistant minority floor leader	Minority whip	Minority caucus chairman
Alabama	(a)	ES	EC	…	…	…	…	…	EC	…	…	…	…	…
Alaska	ES	(b)	EC	EC	…	…	EC	…	EC	EC	…	…	EC	…
Arizona	(a)	ES	…	EC	…	…	EC	…	EC	…	…	…	EC	…
Arkansas	(a)	ES	…	…	…	…	…	…	…	…	…	…	…	…
California	(a)	ES	EC	EC	EC	…	EC	EC	EC	EC	EC	…	EC	EC
Colorado	ES	ES	EC	EC	…	…	AT/2	EC	EC	EC	…	…	…	EC
Connecticut	(a)	ES	AT	AT/6(c)	…	…	EC	…	EC	AL/8(c)	…	…	EC	…
Delaware	(a)	ES	EC	…	…	…	EC	…	EC	…	…	…	EC	…
Florida	(a)	ES	EC	EC(d)	…	…	EC	EC	EC	EC(d)	…	…	EC	EC
Georgia	(a)	ES	EC	…	…	…	EC	EC	EC	…	EC	…	EC	EC
Hawaii	ES	ES(e)	EC	EC	EC	EC	(f)	EC	EC	EC	EC	…	(f)	EC
Idaho	(a)	ES	EC	EC	EC	EC	AP/2	AP	EC	EC	EC	AL/3	AL	AL
Illinois	ES(g)	ES	(g)	AP/3	AT	AT	AT	AP	EC	AL/3	EC	EC	AL	EC
Indiana	(a)	ES	EC	EC/2	AT	AT	AT	EC	EC	EC/3	EC	AL	AL	EC
Iowa	(a)	ES	EC	EC/2	EC	EC	EC	EC	EC	EC/3	EC	…	…	…
Kansas	ES	ES(e)	EC	EC	EC	…	EC	EC	EC	EC	EC	…	EC	EC
Kentucky	(a)	ES	…	…	…	…	EC	EC	EC	…	EC	…	EC	EC
Louisiana	ES	ES	…	…	…	…	…	…	EC	…	EC	…	EC	…
Maine	ES	ES	AP	AP(h)	…	…	AP(h)	…	EC	EC	EC	EC	EC	…
Maryland	ES(i)	ES	EC	EC	AP	AP/2	AP	(i)	EC(i)	EC	EC(i)	AL/3	AL	(i)
Massachusetts	(a)	ES	EC	EC	AP	EC	AP	(i)	EC	EC	EC	EC/4	EC	EC
Michigan	ES	ES	EC	EC	EC	EC	EC	EC	EC	EC	EC	EC	EC	EC
Minnesota	(a)	ES	EC	EC	EC	…	EC/3	…	EC	…	EC	…	EC	…
Mississippi	(a)	ES	…	…	…	…	…	…	…	…	…	…	…	…
Missouri	ES	ES	EC	…	EC	…	EC	…	EC	…	EC	…	EC	…
Montana	(a)	ES(j)	AP	…	AP	…	…	…	AP	…	AP	…	EC	…
Nebraska(U)	(a)	ES(j)	…	…	…	…	…	…	…	…	…	…	…	…
Nevada	(a)	AP(e)	AP	AP	AP	…	AP	…	AP	…	AP	…	AL	…
New Hampshire	ES	AP(e)	EC	EC/3	EC	…	…	…	EC	EC/2	EC	…	EC	…
New Jersey	(a)	ES	EC	…	EC	…	…	…	EC	…	EC	…	EC	…
New Mexico	(a)	ES	(k)	AT	EC	…	EC/2	EC	AP	AL	EC	…	EC	EC
New York	(a)	ES(k)	EC	EC	EC	EC	AT	AT	EC	EC/2	EC	EC	AL/2	AL
North Carolina	(a)	ES	EC	EC	…	…	…	…	EC	AL	EC	…	EC	…
North Dakota	(a)	ES	EC	EC	…	…	ES	EC	EC	EC	…	EC	EC	EC
Ohio	ES(i)	ES	…	…	ES	…	ES	(i)	ES(i)	ES	…	…	ES	(i)

The Council of State Governments 93

SENATE LEADERSHIP POSITIONS—METHODS OF SELECTION—Continued

State or other jurisdiction	President	President pro tem	Majority leader	Assistant majority leader	Majority floor leader	Assistant majority floor leader	Majority whip	Majority caucus chairman	Minority leader	Assistant minority leader	Minority floor leader	Assistant minority floor leader	Minority whip	Minority caucus chairman
Oklahoma	(a)	ES	...	EC/2	EC	EC	EC/2	EC	EC	EC	EC	EC	EC	EC
Oregon	ES	ES	EC	...	...	...	EC	EC	EC	...	...	EC	EC	EC
Pennsylvania	(a)	ES	EC	EC/7	...	...	EC	...	EC	...	...	...	EC	EC
Rhode Island	(a)	ES	EC	...	...	...	...	...	...	EC/2	...	...	...	...
South Carolina	(a)	ES	.	...	...	...	...	EC	...	...	...	...	...	...
South Dakota	(a)	ES	EC	EC	...	...	EC/4	EC	EC	EC	...	...	EC	EC
Tennessee	ES(i)	EC	...	...	EC	...	...	...	...	EC	EC	EC	...	...
Texas	(a)	ES	EC	EC	...	...	EC	EC	EC	...	...	...	EC	EC
Utah	ES	...	EC	...	...	...	...	...	EC	EC	...	...	...	...
Vermont	(a)	ES	EC	EC	...	...	...	...	EC	...	...	...	...	...
Virginia	(a)	ES	EC	EC	...	...	EC	EC	EC	...	EC	EC	EC	EC
Washington	(a)	ES	AP	EC	...	...	EC	EC	EC	...	...	...	...	EC
West Virginia	ES	AP	EC	...	...	...	AP	EC	EC	...	...	...	...	EC
Wisconsin	ES	ES	EC	EC	...	...	...	(i)	EC(i)	EC	EC	...	EC(i)	(i)
Wyoming	ES	ES(e)	ES(o)	...	EC	...	...	...	(p)	...	...	...	...	...
Dist. of Col.(U)	(m)	(n)	...	...	...	...	...	...	...	...	...	...	...	...
American Samoa	ES	ES	...	...	...	...	...	...	...	...	...	...	...	...
Guam(U)	ES(j)	ES(e)	EC	...	EC	...	...	...	EC	EC	EC	EC	...	...
Puerto Rico	ES(i)	EC(i)	EC	...	...	...	(i)	(i)	EC(i)	EC	EC	...	...	(i)
Virgin Islands(U)	ES	ES(e)	ES(o)	...	...	...	...	...	(p)	...	...	...	...	...

Note: In some states, the leadership positions in the Senate are not empowered by the law or by the rules of the chamber, but rather by the party members themselves. Entry following slash indicates number of individuals holding specified position.

Key:
ES—Elected or confirmed by all members of the Senate.
EC—Elected by party caucus.
AP—Appointed by president.
AT—Appointed by president pro tempore.
AL—Appointed by party leader.
(U)—Unicameral legislative body.
...—Position does not exist or is not selected on a regular basis.
(a) Lieutenant governor is president of the Senate by virtue of the office.
(b) President *may* name any member as president pro tempore to serve during the former's absence. The appointment may extend throughout the session unless terminated by the Senate.
(c) Assistant majority leader: three deputy majority leaders and three assistant majority leaders. Assistant minority leader: deputy minority leader and seven assistant minority leaders.

(d) Official titles are majority leader pro tempore and minority leader pro tempore.
(e) Official title is vice president. In Guam, vice speaker.
(f) Majority policy leader; minority policy leader.
(g) President is also majority leader.
(h) Joint appointment by president and the majority leader.
(i) President and minority floor leader are also caucus chairmen. In Ohio and Puerto Rico, president and minority leader.
(j) Official title is speaker of the Senate. In Tennessee, officer has the statutory title of "lieutenant governor."
(k) President pro tempore is also majority leader.
(l) Minority whip is also majority leader.
(m) Chairman of the Council.
(n) Appointed by the chairman.
(o) Officer designated by a majority of the members.
(p) Any three or more senators may meet in order to select the minority leader.

Table 3.7
HOUSE LEADERSHIP POSITIONS—METHODS OF SELECTION

State or other jurisdiction	Speaker	Speaker pro tem	Majority leader	Assistant majority leader	Majority floor leader	Assistant majority floor leader	Majority whip	Majority caucus chairman	Minority leader	Assistant minority leader	Minority floor leader	Assistant minority floor leader	Minority whip	Minority caucus chairman
Alabama	EH	EH											EC	
Alaska	EH	EH	EC				EC		EC	EC			EC	
Arizona	EH	AS	EC				EC		EC	EC			EC	EC
Arkansas	EH	EH	(a)		AS(b)								EC/2	
California	EH							EC	EC		EC			EC
Colorado	EH		EC	EC			EC		EC	EC			EC	EC
Connecticut	EH	AS(c)	EC	AL/11(d)			AS		EC	AL/13(d)			AL/2	
Delaware	EH	EH	AS	AS/3			EC	AS	EC	EC(e)			AL/2	AL
Florida	EH	EH	EC				EC		EC				EC	EC
Georgia	EH	EH	EC				EC	EC	EC					
Hawaii	EH	EH(f)	EC		EC	EC/6		EC	EC	EC		EC/2		EC
Idaho	EH		EC	EC			AS/2		EC	EC			AL/2	EC
Illinois	EH	AS	AS	AS/4	EC		AS	AS	EC	AL/4			EC	AL
Indiana	EH		EC	EC/4	EC			EC	EC	EC/4		EC	EC	EC
Iowa	EH	EH			EC									
Kansas	EH	EH	EC	EC					EC				EC	EC
Kentucky	EH	EH	EC	EC			EC						EC	
Louisiana	EH	EH	EC	EC					EC					
Maine	EH		EC	EC	EC		EC		EC	EC		EC	EC	
Maryland	EH	EH	EC	EC			EC		EC	EC		EC	EC	
Massachusetts	EH(g)		AS	AS/2		EC/4		(g)	EC(g)	AL/2			EC	(g)
Michigan	EH	EH	EC	EC/5		EC/4	EC/16	EC	EC(g)	EC/4		EC	EC	EC
Minnesota	EH(g)						AS	(g)	EC(g)					(g)
Mississippi	EH													
Missouri	EH	EH					EC	EC	EC	EC	EC	EC	EC	EC
Montana	EH	EH			EC				EC			EC	EC	
Nebraska(h)	EH	EH												
Nevada	EH	EH	AS	AS	EC		AS		AS	AL			AL	
New Hampshire	EH		EC						EC		EC		AL	
New Jersey	EH	EH	EC	EC/4			EC/2		EC	EC/3			EC	EC

HOUSE LEADERSHIP POSITIONS—METHODS OF SELECTION—Continued

State or other jurisdiction	Speaker	Speaker pro tem	Majority leader	Assistant majority leader	Majority floor leader	Assistant majority floor leader	Majority whip	Majority caucus chairman	Minority leader	Assistant minority leader	Minority floor leader	Assistant minority floor leader	Minority whip	Minority caucus chairman
New Mexico	EH	AS	AS	...	EC	...	EC	EC/2	EC	...	EC	...	EC/2	EC
New York	EH	AS	(i)	...	...	...	AS	...	EC	...	...	...	AL	...
North Carolina	EH	EH(i)	(i)	EC	...	...	...	EC	EC	...	...	...	EC	EC
North Dakota	EH	EH	EC	...	...	...	EH	EC	EC	...	...	...	EH	EC
Ohio	EH	EH	EC	...	EH	EH	EH	EC	EH	EH	...	...	EH	...
Oklahoma	EH	EH	...	...	AS	AS/6(j)	AS	EC	EC	...	...	...	EC	EC
Oregon	EH	EC	EC	EC	...	...	EC	EC	EC	EC/3	...	EC/3	EC	EC
Pennsylvania	EH	AS	EC	...	...	...	EC	EC	EC	EC/5	...	...	EC	...
Rhode Island	EH	AS	EC	EC/9	...	...	EC	EC	EC	...	...	...	EC	...
South Carolina	EH	EH	EC	...	...	...	EC	EC	EC	...	...	...	EC	...
South Dakota	EH	EH	EC	...	EC	...	EC	EC	EC	EC	EC	...	EC	EC
Tennessee	EH	EH	EC	...	...	...	EC/6	EC	EC	...	...	...	EC	...
Texas	EH	AS	...	...	...	...	EC	EC	EC	...	...	...	EC	...
Utah	EH	...	EC	...	...	...	EC	EC	EC	...	...	...	EC	...
Vermont	EH	...	EC	...	EC	...	EC	EC	EC	...	EC	...	EC	EC
Virginia	EH	EH	EC	...	...	...	EC	EC	EC	...	EC	...	EC	EC
Washington	EH	AS	EC	AS/2(k)	...	...	(k)	(k)	EC	...	...	...	AL	EC
West Virginia	EH	EH	AS	EC	...	...	EC	EC	EC	...	...	...	EC	EC
Wisconsin	EH	EH	EC	...	...	...	EC	EC	EC	...	EC	...	EC	EC
Wyoming	EH	EH	...	EC	EC	...	EC	EC	EC	EC	...	...	EC(l)	(l)
Dist. of Col.(h)	EH	EH(f)	...	...	...	...	...	...	...	...	...	...	...	...
American Samoa	EH	EH(f)	...	...	...	...	...	...	...	...	...	...	...	...
Guam(h)	EH	...	EC	...	EC	...	...	(m)	EC(m)	...	...	...	...	(m)
Puerto Rico	EH(m)	EC(f)	EC	...	EC	...	...	(m)	EC(m)	...	...	EC	...	(m)
Virgin Islands(h)	...	...	...	...	...	...	...	...	...	...	...	...	...	...

Note: In some states, the leadership positions in the House are not empowered by the law or by the rules of the chamber, but rather by the party members themselves. Entry following slash indicates number of individuals holding specified position.

Key:
EH—Elected or confirmed by all members of the House.
EC—Elected by party caucus.
AS—Appointed by speaker.
AL—Appointed by party leader.
...—Position does not exist or is not selected on a regular basis.
(a) Outgoing speaker, by agreement of the House.
(b) Appointed by speaker, after consultation with members of supporting majority.
(c) Official title is deputy speaker.

(d) Assistant majority leader: two deputy majority leaders (appointed by majority leader), and nine assistant majority floor leaders. Assistant minority leader: deputy minority leader (appointed by minority leader) and 12 assistant minority leaders.
(e) Minority leader pro tempore.
(f) Official title is vice speaker.
(g) Speaker and minority leader are also caucus chairmen.
(h) Unicameral legislature; see entries in table on Senate leadership positions.
(i) Speaker pro tempore is also majority leader.
(j) Assistant majority floor leader: first assistant floor leader, five assistant floor leaders.
(k) One also serves as majority whip; the other also serves as majority caucus chairman.
(l) Minority whip is also caucus chairman.
(m) Also serves as caucus chairman.

Table 3.8

LEGISLATIVE COMPENSATION: REGULAR AND SPECIAL SESSIONS

State	Regular sessions Per diem salary	Regular sessions Limit on days	Salaries Annual salaries	Special sessions Per diem salary	Special sessions Limit on days	Travel allowance Cents per mile	Travel allowance Round trips home to capital during session	Per diem living expenses
Alabama	$10	105C		$10	30C	10	One	$40 (U)
Alaska			$22,140			0	One	$80 ($60 for Juneau legislators) (U)
Arizona			$15,000			22	Unlimited	$60 ($35 for those living inside Maricopa County, location of capital) (U) (a)
Arkansas	$20	(b)	$ 7,500	$20	(b)	21	Weekly	Up to $350/w (V)
California			$37,105(c)			...	One	$87 (U)
Colorado			$17,500			20 (24 for 4-wheel drive)	Weekly(d)	Actual and necessary (V)
Connecticut			$15,200			21	Unlimited	(e)
Delaware			$21,000			20	Unlimited	(f)
Florida			$19,848			20	Weekly	$50 (U)
Georgia			$10,125			21	Weekly	$59
Hawaii			$15,600			(g)	Unlimited	(g)
Idaho	$30	None	$32,500(h)	$30		20.5	Seven	$60 (U)
Illinois			$11,600	$80	20C	21	Weekly	$72 (U)
Indiana	$80	(b)		$40(i)	(b)	25	Weekly	None
Iowa			$14,600		(i)	21	Weekly	$40 ($25 for Polk County legislators (U) for office expenses (110 days odd-numbered years; 100 days even-numbered years)
Kansas	$55	None		$55	None	20.5	Weekly	$66 (U)
Kentucky	$100	(j)		$100	(j)	21	Weekly	$75 (U)
Louisiana	$75	60C	$16,800	$75	None	21	Weekly	None
Maine			(k)	$55	None	22	Weekly(l)	$26 for meals and $34 for lodging(l) (U)
Maryland			$22,000(m)			19	...	$78 in 1987 for lodging and meals (V); will rise as follows; 1988, $81; 1989, $84; 1990, $87
Massachusetts			$39,040				See living expense allowance	Amount covering mileage, meals, and lodging ranges from $5 to $50 depending on distance of legislator's district from capital (U)
Michigan			$39,881			26	Weekly	(n)
Minnesota			$24,174			27	Weekly	$36 outstate; $23 metro (U)
Mississippi			$10,000	$50	None	20	Weekly	$75 (U)
Missouri			$20,852			20.5	Weekly	$35 (U)
Montana	$52.13	90L	$ 4,800	$52.13	None	22.5	Four	$50 (U)
Nebraska	$130	60C		$130	20C	21	(o)	(o)
Nevada			$ 200/b	$3(q)	15L(q)	27(p)	Unlimited(p)	$57 (U)
New Hampshire						38 for first 45 mi., 19 thereafter	Unlimited	None
New Jersey			$25,000(r)			0	None	None

LEGISLATIVE COMPENSATION: REGULAR AND SPECIAL SESSIONS—Continued

State	Regular sessions			Special sessions		Cents per mile	Travel allowance	
	Per diem salary	Limit on days	Annual salaries	Per diem salary	Limit on days		Round trips home to capital during session	Per diem living expenses
New Mexico	$75	60C(odd yr) 30C(even yr)	...	$75	30C	25	One	None
New York	...	...	$43,000	...	...	0	Weekly	$75 (U)
North Carolina	...	...	$10,140	...	...	25	Weekly	$79 (V)
North Dakota	$90	(s)	$ 180/m(t)	$90	None	20.5	Weekly	$35 for lodging, not to exceed $600/m (V)
Ohio	...	...	$34,905	...	...	20.5	Weekly	
Oklahoma	(u)	(v)	$20,000	(u)	(v)	20.5	Weekly	Senators $35 for lodging
Oregon	$62	...	$ 919/m(w)	$62	...	21	One	
Pennsylvania	...	...	$35,000(x)	...	...	20	Weekly	$85 (U)
Rhode Island	$5	60L	$10,000	...	...	8	Unlimited	None
South Carolina	...	...	...	...	...	21	Weekly	$73 (V)
South Dakota	...	...	$ 3,200(odd yr) $ 2,800(even yr)	$80	...	20.5	Each weekend legislature is in session	$75 (U)
Tennessee	$30	...	$12,500	$30	30C	21	Weekly	$77 (U)
Texas	$65	140C	$ 7,200	$65	30L	21(y)	Weekly	None
Utah	...	45C	...	...	...	21	Weekly	$25 subsistence allowance and $50 lodging allowance for legislators residing outside Salt Lake or Davis counties (U)
Vermont	$340/w	...	...	$70	...	21	Weekly, if room rented in capital or vicinity; otherwise daily	$40 for room and $35 for meals if renting room in capital or vicinity; $31.25 for meals, if commuting (U)
Virginia	$77	...	$18,000	$77	30C	21	Weekly	None
Washington	$50	...	$16,500	$50	None	10	One	$30 for meals (U); $40 for lodging (V)
West Virginia	...	...	$ 6,500	$50	...	20	Weekly	$55 for legislators who establish temporary residence in state capital; otherwise, $27.50 (U),(aa)
Wisconsin	...	...	$29,997(z)	...	...	21.5	Weekly	$60 (U)
Wyoming	$75	None	...	$75	None	35	One	
American Samoa	(cc)	...	$15,000(bb)	(cc)	...	0	...	...
Puerto Rico	(cc)	...	$20,000	...	...	(dd)	...	...
Virgin Islands	$30	None	$35,000(ee)	$30	None	0	...	...

LEGISLATIVE COMPENSATION: REGULAR AND SPECIAL SESSIONS—Continued

Note: Compensation as of January 1, 1988. In many states, legislators who receive an annual salary or per diem salary also receive an additional per diem amount for living expenses. Consult appropriate columns for a more complete picture of legislative compensation during sessions. For information on interim compensation and other direct payments and services to legislators, see Table 3.9, "Legislative Compensation: Interim Compensation and Other Direct Payments."

Key:
C—Calendar day
L—Legislative day
(U)—Unvouchered
(V)—Vouchered
d—day
w—week
m—month
y—year
b—biennium
. . .—Not applicable
N.A.—Not available

(a) After 120 days reduced to $10 for Maricopa County legislators and $20 for out-of-county.
(b) Legislators receive per diem salary for each day of actual attendance at regular and special sessions.
(c) After December 5, 1988, will rise to $40,816.
(d) Paid only to those who do not live in the Denver metro area.
(e) Legislators receive $3,500/y expense allowance (U).
(f) Legislators receive $5,000/y expense allowance (U).
(g) Travel allowance to neighbor islands during a session on official legislative business, (excluding attendance at a legislative session for neighbor island legislators) to be equal to the maximum allowance for such expenses payable to any public officer or employee. Presently, this equals $50/d inter-island, $100/d out-of-state (U). On July 1, 1988, these rates will increase to $55 and $110, respectively.
(h) $35,661 all House and 39 Senators; difference due to midterm adjustment.
(i) Legislators receive $40/L ($25/L for Polk County legislators) during special sessions.
(j) While regular sessions are limited to 60L every other year, per diem amount is paid for every

calendar day of the session. Per diem amount is also paid for every calendar day of the special session (no limitation on length).
(k) Paid $9,000 first regular session and $6,000 second regular session.
(l) Plus one round-trip (in lieu of lodging) for each session day.
(m) Will increase in the following ways: 1988, $23,000; 1989, $24,000; 1990, $25,000.
(n) Legislators receive $6,700/y expense allowance (V).
(o) Legislators who live over 50 miles from capital receive $55 and mileage allowance for one round-trip per week; legislators who live less than 50 miles from capital receive $25, plus allowance for daily mileage.
(p) To a maximum of $5,000 per regular session, beginning in 1987.
(q) In addition to the biennial salary of $200, a legislator receives $3/d for up to 15L of the special session.
(r) Will rsie to $35,000 with beginning of 1990 legislative year.
(s) There is a constitutional limit on legislative sessions of 80 natural days during a biennium. The per diem is payable each calendar day during a session.
(t) $180 per month.
(u) $35 per diem in the House; none in the Senate.
(v) The limit is 4 legislative days in the House.
(w) $919 per month.
(x) Will increase to $47,000 on December 1, 1988.
(y) For travel in personally-owned automobiles. For travel in personally-owned or leased aircraft: 35 cents per highway mile in a single-engine aircraft, 55 cents per highway mile in a twin-engine aircraft, $1 per highway mile in a turbine-powered aircraft.
(z) $22,631 for senators elected prior to July 1984.
(aa) Legislators must sign statement listing days for which per diem is claimed.
(bb) Plus $5,000 allowance.
(cc) $72 if reside more than 50 kilometers from Capitol; otherwise $62.
(dd) 30/kilometer.
(ee) Will increase to $55,000 in January 1989.

Table 3.9
LEGISLATIVE COMPENSATION: INTERIM PAYMENTS AND OTHER DIRECT PAYMENTS

State	Compensation for committee or official business during interim			Other direct payments or services to legislators
	Per diem compensation for committee or official business	Travel allowance (cents per mile)	Per diem living expenses	
Alabama..........	$10	10(a)	$1,900 total (U)	:...
Alaska...........	$50-55(b)	25	...	$4,000 annual allowance during session (U)
Arizona..........	...	21	$60 ($35 for those living inside Maricopa County, location of capital) (U)	...
Arkansas	$60	21	...	$485/m for home office expenses (V)
California........	...	(c)	$82 (U)	...
Colorado	$75	20 (24 for 4-wheel drive)	Actual and necessary (V)	...
Connecticut	...	21	...	(d)
Delaware	...	20	...	(d)
Florida	...	20	$12/q for lodging and meals or actual cost of lodging and $3/breakfast, $6/lunch, $12/dinner (V)	...
Georgia..........	...	21	$59	$4,800/y expense allowance (V)
Hawaii	...	...	$10 on island; 50 inter-island travel; $100 out-of-state	...
Idaho	$30(e)	...	Actual expenses (V) (f)	Senators receive $45,000/y, representatives receive $35,000/y as district office allowance (g) (V)
Illinois	...	:21	$20 (U)	...
Indiana	$80	25	...	...
Iowa	$40(g)	21	Actual lodging expenses; $3/breakfast; $5/lunch; $8/dinner (House); $30 meals (Senate) (V)	...
Kansas	$55	20.5	$66 (U)	$600/m April through December to defray expenses (U)
Kentucky	$100	21	Actual (V)	$950/m interim expense allowance;$50/session stationery allowance
Louisiana	$75	21	...	$325/m allowance to cover rent, utilities and/or expenses for a district office (U); $1,000 initial furniture and equipment allowance, plus $250 (major equipment repair) for legislators who have served one or more four-year terms (U); $1,047/m (average) salary for legislative assistants (U)
Maine	$55	22	$26 for meals (V); actual expenses for lodging (V)	$500 constituent service allowance provided at beginning of session (U)
Maryland	...	19	$78 for lodging and meals (V) (i)	In-district travel allowance, $200 (U); also interim funds for staff and equipment for district offices

LEGISLATIVE COMPENSATION: INTERIM PAYMENTS AND OTHER DIRECT PAYMENTS—Continued

State	Compensation for committee or official business during interim		Per diem living expenses	Other direct payments or services to legislators
	Per diem compensation for committee or official business	Travel allowance (cents per mile)		
Massachusetts ...	Included in expense allowance	Included in expense allowance	Amount for mileage, ranges from $5 to $50 depending on distance legislator's district is from state capital	$2,400/y general expense allowance
Michigan	...	...	...	...
Minnesota	$48	15	$45/ for lodging (House) (V)	$600/y for telephone credit card (V) and postage allotment of $385 (U); senators $300 apartment allowance; Committee Chairs, $400/m apartment allowance (V)
Mississippi	$40	20	...	$500/m during interim
Missouri	...	20.5	Lodging and meals (V)	Representatives receive $600/m for office expenses (V), and $2,000/y mailing account (V)
Montana..........	$52.13	22	$14.50 for meals and $24.96 for lodging (V)	Health insurance $115/m; telephone credit card (amount varies)
Nebraska	...	21	...	...
Nevada	$130	24	$47.50 for three meals and lodging in-state (V)	$2,800 telephone allowance/regular session, postage allowance of $60/regular session (U)
New Hampshire .	...	38 for first 45 mi.; 19 thereafter	...	...
New Jersey.......	...	...	...	District office rent, office supplies, and telephone, postage allowances established at beginning of session
New Mexico.....	$75	25	...	...
New York	...	...	...	$252/m for expenses (rises to $265 with 1989 session) (U); postage and telephone allowance of $485 odd-numbered years and $146 even-numbered years; stationery allowance of 4,000 pieces for 2 year term
North Carolina ..	...	25	$79 in-state (U); $79 (U) or $20 for meals and actual cost of lodging for out-of-state	...
North Dakota ...	$62.50	20	$35 for lodging (V); $17 for meals	...
Ohio	...	...	...	...
Oklahoma	$25	20.5	...	Senators office supply allowance for session $350 (V), 1st class postage 8 rolls (U), telephone $600 (U)
Oregon	...	20	$50 (U)	$400-550 (depending on district size)/m for interim expenses (V); $12.50/d supplies during session (U); $2,785 staffing allowance during session (U); $9,600 staffing allowance during interim
Pennsylvania	...	21 (Senate); 20 (House)	$85 (V)	$10,000/y for accountable expenses (V). Senators recieve $17,500/y, representatives $10,000/y for home office expenses (V); representatives also receive $1,000/y postage allowance (V); car allowance, $6,600.

LEGISLATIVE COMPENSATION: INTERIM PAYMENTS AND OTHER DIRECT PAYMENTS—Continued

State	Compensation for committee or official business during interim			Other direct payments or services to legislators
	Per diem compensation for committee or official business	Travel allowance (cents per mile)	Per diem living expenses	
Rhode Island	...	...	...	...
South Carolina ..	$35	21	$73 (V)	...
South Dakota	$75	20.5	$21 (plus tax) for lodging (V); $16 for meals (V)	...
Tennessee	...	21	$77 in-state (U), $77 for meals and related expenses and actual cost for lodging and airfare (V)	$325/m home office expense allowance (U)
Texas...........	...	21(j)	$70 (V)	...
Utah	$65	21	$25 subsistence allowance on committee days; $50 lodging allowance if meeting is held in Salt Lake or Davis counties for legislators residing outside counties) (U)	...
Vermont	$70	21	Actual expenses (U)	...
Virginia.........	$100	21	Actual expenses (V)	$250/m for office expenses and supplies (U)
Washington	$50	21	...	$900/q for office expenses (V)
West Virginia ...	$50(l)	20	$30 for meals (U); $40 for lodging (V)	...
Wisconsin	...	21.5	$55 for legislators who must establish temporary residence in state capital; otherwise $27.50 (U)	Senators receive $75/m, representatives $25/m for interim expenses for full calendar months in which legislature is in actual session 3 days or less
Wyoming	$75	35	$60 (V)	...
American Samoa .	...	...	...	...
Puerto Rico	(m)	(n)	...	...
Virgin Islands	$30	0	...	...

LEGISLATIVE COMPENSATION: INTERIM PAYMENTS AND OTHER DIRECT PAYMENTS

Note: Compensation as of January 1, 1988. For more information on legislative compensation, see Table 3.8, "Legislative Compensation: Regular and Special Sessions."

Key:
(U)—Unvouchered
(V)—Vouchered
d—day
m—month
y—year

(a) For one round trip per week for interim committees. For other legislative business outside state capital, 22 cents per mile.
(b) Depends on location of permanent residence.
(c) Legislators are provided a leased vehicle gasoline credit card. Actual expenses or 15 cents per mile.
(d) See Table 3.8, "Legislative Compensation: Regular and Special Sessions" for information.
(e) For each day of authorized meetings. Plus $7/d for each day not in session.

(f) When not in session, legislators are permitted two round trips per month at $65/d (V).
(g) Allowance may be expended for additional staff, clerical help, office rent, printing, postage, etc.
(h) $60 for speaker.
(i) Of total amount, maximum $28/d for meals. Legislators may claim lodging only if meetings are scheduled on Consecutive days.
(j) For travel in personally-owned automobiles. For travel in personally-owned or leased aircraft: 40 cents per highway mile in a single-engine aircraft, 65 cents per highway mile in a twin-engine aircraft, $1.15 per highway mile in a turbine-powered aircraft.
(k) In emergency situations, the presiding officer and the majority and minority leaders of each chamber may authorize a $50/d lodging allowance for legislators residing in Salt Lake or Davis counties.
(l) Not to exceed $1,500 per member or a total of $65,000.
(m) $72 if reside more than 50 kilometers from Capitol; otherwise $62.
(n) 30/kilometer.

Table 3.10
ADDITIONAL COMPENSATION FOR SENATE LEADERS

State	President	President pro tem	Majority leader	Minority leader	Other
Alabama	$2/d(a)	0	. . .	. . .	
Alaska	$500/y	. . .	0	0	
Arizona	0	0	0	0	
Arkansas	$15,00/y(a,b)	$10,000/y(b)	. . .	. . .	
California	(a)	0	0	0	
Colorado	$75/d to max. $7,500/y	$75/d to max. $7,500/y	$75/d to max. $7,500/y	$75/d to max. $7,500/y	
Connecticut	(a)	$5,800/y	$4,800/y	$4,800/y	Dep. Maj. Ldrs., Dep. Min. Ldrs.: $3,500/y; Asst. Maj. Ldrs., Asst. Min. Ldrs.: $2,300/y; Cmte. Chmn.: $2,300/y; Ranking Min. Mbrs.: $1,300/y
Delaware	(a)	$300/m	$260/m	$260/m	Maj. Whip, Min. Whip: $225/m; Joint Finance Cmte. Mbrs.: $225/m; Chmn. Finance Room: $260/m
Florida	$7,716/y	0	0	0	
Georgia	(a)	$2,800/y	$2,400/y	$2,400/y	Admn. Floor Ldr.: $2,400/y; Asst. Admn. Floor Ldr.: $1,200/y
Hawaii	(a)	0(c)	0	0	
Idaho	(a)	0	0	0	
Illinois	$10,972/y(d)	. . .	(d)	$10,972/y	Asst. Maj. Ldrs., Asst. Min. Ldrs., Maj. Caucus Chmn., Min. Caucus Chmn., Maj. Whips, Min. Whip: $6,584/y
Indiana	(a)	$5,000/y	$3,500/y	$4,000/y	Maj. Caucus Chmn., Min. Caucus Chmn., Min. Asst. Fl. Ldr., Finance Cmte. Chmn.: $3,500/y; Budget Subcmte. Chmn.: $1,500/y; Maj. Whip: $1,000/y
Iowa	$7,300/y(a)	0	$2,500/y	$2,500/y	
Kansas	$8,705/y	$4,442/y(c)	$7,852/y	$7,852/y	Asst. Maj. Ldrs., Asst. Min. Ldrs.: $4,442/y; Ways & Means Cmte. Chmn.: $7,000/y
Kentucky	$25/d(a)	$25/d	$20/d	$20/d	Asst. Pres. Pro Tem, Maj. Whip, Min. Whip, Maj. Caucus Chmn., Min. Caucus Chmn.: $15/d; Standing and Interim Cmte. Chmn.: $10/meeting chaired
Louisiana	(o)	0	. . .	. . .	
Maine	(e)	. . .	(e)	(e)	Asst. Maj. Ldr., Asst. Min. Ldr.: (e)
Maryland	$7,500/y	0	0	0	
Massachusetts	$35,000/y	. . .	$22,500/y	$22,500/y	Asst. Maj. Fl. Ldr., Asst. Min. Fl. Ldr., 2nd Asst. Maj. Fl. Ldr., 2nd & 3rd Asst. Min. Fl. Ldrs., Post Audit & Oversight and Taxation Cmte. Chmn.: 15,000/y; Ways & Means Cmte. Chmn.: $25,000/y; Other Cmte. Chmn.: $7,500/y; Asst. V-Chmn. Ways & Means Cmte.: $7,500/y
Michigan	(a)	0	$21,000/y	$17,000/y	Maj. Fl. Ldr., Min. Fl. Ldr.: $10,000/y; Appropriations Cmte. Chmn.: $5,000/y
Minnesota	0	. . .	$9,670/y	$9,670/y	Tax and Finance Cmte. Chmn.: $4,835/y
Mississippi	(a)	0	. . .	. . .	
Missouri	(a)	$2,500/y	$1,500/y	$1,500/y	
Montana	$5/d	0	0	0	
Nebraska	(a)	0(f)	. . .	. . .	
Nevada	(a)	(o)	(o)	(o)	(o)
New Hampshire	$50/b	0(c)	0	0	
New Jersey	$8,333/y(g)	0	0	0	
New Mexico	(a)	0	0	0	
New York	(a)	$30,000/y(d)	(d)	$25,000/y	Dep. Maj. Ldr.: $24,500/y; Dep. Min. Ldr.: $15,000/y; Maj. Whip: $16,000/y; Min. Whip: $10,500/y; Maj. Conf. Chmn.: $18,000/y; Min. Conf. Chmn.: $12,000/y; Maj. Conf. Secy.: $16,000/y; Min. Conf. Secy.: $10,500/y; Cmte. Chmn. & Ranking Min. Mbrs.: Finance: $24,500/y & $15,000/y; Education, Judiciary, Codes: $13,000/y & $8,000/y; Banks, Health, Cities, Corporations: $11,000/y & $7,000/y; Other Cmtes., generally: $9,000/y & $6,500/y
North Carolina	(a)	$7,260/y	$2,316/y	$2,316/y	
North Dakota	(a)	0	$10/d	$10/d	Dep. Pres. Pro Tem: $5,244/y; Chmn.: $5/d
Ohio	$19,503/y	$15,737/y	. . .	$14,737/y	Asst. Pres. Pro Tem: $11,856/y; Asst. Min. Ldr.: $10,418/y; Maj. Whip: $8,978/y; Min. Whip: $6,100/y; Asst. Min. Whip: $1,611/y; Finance Cmte. Chmn.: $5,000/y; Other Standing Cmte. Chmn.: $2,783/y; Standing Subcmte. Chmn.: $1,392/y

ADDITIONAL COMPENSATION FOR SENATE LEADERS—Continued

State	President	President pro tem	Majority leader	Minority leader	Other
Oklahoma	(a)	$9,330/y	$6,440/y	$6,440/y	
Oregon	$919/m(j)	0	0	0	
Pennsylvania	(a)	$19,600/y(h)	$15,680/y(h)	$15,680/y(h)	Maj. Whip, Min. Whip: $11,900/y; Maj. Caucus Chmn., Min. Caucus Chmn.: $7,420/y; Maj. Appropriations Cmte. Chmn., Min. Appropriations Cmte. Chmn.: $7,420/y; Maj. Caucus Secy., Min. Caucus Secy., Maj. Policy Chmn., Min. Policy Chmn., Maj. Caucus Administr., Min. Caucus Administr.: $4,900/y
Rhode Island	(a)	0	0	0	Standing Cmte. Chmn.: $400 during interim
South Carolina	$1,575/y(a)	$7,500/y	. . .	. . .	
South Dakota	(a)	0	0	0	
Tennessee.........	$12,520/y(a)	0	0	0	
Texas	(a)	0	. . .	. . .	
Utah	$1,000/y	. . .	$500/y	$500/y	
Vermont..........	(a)	$400/w(i)	0	0	
Virginia	(a)	0	0	0	
Washington	(a)	0	0	0	
West Virginia	$50/d(j)	0	$25/d	$25/d	
Wisconsin	0	. . .	0	0	
Wyoming	$3/d	0(c)	0	0	
American Samoa ..	$5,000/y	0	. . .	. . .	
Puerto Rico.......	0	0	0	0	
Virgin Islands	$10,000	0	0	0	

Note: This table reflects the amount paid the leadership in addition to their regular legislative compensation.

Key:
d—day
w—week
m—month
y—year
b—biennium
. . .—Position does not exist or is not selected on a regular basis.
(a) Lieutenant governor is president of the Senate. Additional compensation noted is that which the lieutenant governor receives for services as president of the Senate. In Mississippi, constitution states that the salary of the lieutenant governor must be the same as that of the speaker of the House ($34,000), and that the lieutenant governor also receive the same per diem and expenses as members while in session. In Tennessee, lieutenant governor is a statutory title.

(b) Special public relations expense allowance of $10,000/y.
(c) Official title is vice-president.
(d) President also serves as majority leader. In New York, president pro tempore also serves as majority leader.
(e) Additional compensation for Senate leaders is calculated according to the following percentages of the base salaries during sessions: president, 50 percent; majority and minority leaders, 25 percent; and assistant majority and minority leaders, 12.5 percent.
(f) Official title is speaker of the Senate.
(g) Equal to one-third of regular annual salary.
(h) Will rise as of December 1, 1988.
(i) During session.
(j) President also receives $100/d for up to 80 days for attending to legislative business in the capitol office when the legislature is not in formal session.

Table 3.11
ADDITIONAL COMPENSATION FOR HOUSE LEADERS

State	Speaker	Speaker pro tem	Majority leader	Minority leader	Other
Alabama	$2/d	0	. . .	. . .	
Alaska	$500/y	. . .	0	0	
Arizona	0	0	0	0	
Arkansas	$10,000/y(a)	0	0	0	
California	0	0	0	0	
Colorado	$75/d to max. $7,500/y	$75/d to max. $7,500/y	$75/d to max. $7,500/y	$75/d to max. $7,500/y	
Connecticut	$5,800/y	$3,500/y(b)	$4,800/y	$4,800/y	Dep. Maj. Ldrs., Dep. Min. Ldr.s: $3,500/y; Asst. Maj. Ldrs., Asst. Min. Ldrs.: $2,300/y; Cmte. Chmn.: $2,300/y; Ranking Min. Mbrs.: $1,300/y
Delaware	$300/m	$260/m	$260/m	$260/m	Maj. Whip, Min. Whip: $225/m; Joint Finance Cmte. Mbrs.: $225/m; Chmn. Appropriations Cmte.: $260/m
Florida	$7,716/y	0	0	0	
Georgia	(c)	$2,800/y	$2,400/y	$2,400/y	Admn. Floor Ldr.: $2,400/y; Asst. Admn. Floor Ldr.: $1,200/y
Hawaii	0	0(d)	0	0	
Idaho	0	. . .	0	0	
Illinois	$10,972/y	. . .	$8,299/y	$10,972/y	Asst. Maj. Ldrs., Asst. Min. Ldrs., Maj. Whips, Min. Whips, Maj. Conf. Chmn., Min. Conf. Chmn.: $6,584/y
Indiana	$5,000/y	$3,500/y	$3,500/y	$4,000/y	Maj. Whip, Maj. Caucus Chmn., Min. Caucus Chmn., Asst. Min. Fl. Ldr., Ways & Means Cmte. Chmn.: $3,500/y
Iowa	$7,300/y	0	$2,500/y	$2,500/y	
Kansas	$8,705/y	$4,442/y	$7,852/y	$7,852/y	Asst. Maj. Ldrs., Asst. Min. Ldrs.: $4,442/y; Appropriations Cmte. Chmn.: $7,000/y
Kentucky	$25/d	$15/d	$20/d	$20/d	Maj. Whip, Min. Whip, Maj. Caucus Chmn., Min. Caucus Chmn.: $15/d; Standing and Interim Cmte. Chmn.: $10/meeting chaired
Louisiana	$15,200	0	. . .	. . .	
Maine	(e)	. . .	(e)	(e)	Asst. Maj. Ldr., Asst. Min. Ldr.: (e)
Maryland	$7,500/y	0	0	0	
Massachusetts	$35,000/y	. . .	$22,500/y	$22,500/y	Asst. Maj. Fl. Ldrs., Asst. Min. Fl. Ldrs., 2nd Asst. Maj. Fl. Ldrs., 2nd & 3rd Asst. Min. Fl. Ldrs., Post Audit & Oversight and Taxation Cmte. Chmn., Ways & Means Cmte. V-Chmn.: $15,000/y; Ways & Means Cmte. Chmn.: $25,000/y; Post Audit & Oversight Cmte. V-Chmn., Ways & Means Cmte. Asst. V-Chmn., Other Cmte. Chmn.: $7,500/y
Michigan	$23,000/y	0	$10,000/y	$17,000/y	Min. Fl. Ldr.: $8,000/y; Appropriations Cmte. Chmn.: $5,000/y
Minnesota	$9,298/y	. . .	$9,298/y	$9,208/y	
Mississippi	$34,000/y	. . .	. . .	. . .	
Missouri	$2,500/y	$1,500/y	$1,500/y	$1,500/y	
Montana	$5/d	0	0	0	
Nebraska	--Unicameral Legislature--				
Nevada	0	0	0	0	
New Hampshire	$50/b	. . .	0	0	
New Jersey	$8,333/y(f)	0	0	0	
New Mexico	0	. . .	0	0	
New York	$30,000/y	$18,000/y	$25,000/y	$25,000/y	Dep. Spkr.: $18,000/y; Min. Ldr. Pro Tem: $15,000/y; Cmte. on Cmtes. Chmn.: $18,000/y; Dep. Maj. Ldr., Asst. Maj. Ldr.: $14,000/y; Maj. Whip, Asst. Min. Ldr., Dep. Min. Ldr., Cmte. on Cmtes. Ranking Min. Mbrs.: $13,000/y; Min. Whip, Maj. Conf. Chmn.: $12,000/y; Min. Conf. Chmn.: $11,000/y; Maj. Conf. V-Chmn.: $9,000/y; Min. Conf. V-Chmn.: $8,000/y; Cmte. Chmn. & Ranking Min. Mbrs.: Ways & Means: $24,500/y & $15,000/y; Education, Judiciary, Codes: $13,000/y & $8,000/y; Banks, Cities, Health, Local Govts., Corporations: $11,000/y & $7,000/y; Labor: $10,000/y & $6,500/y; Other Cmte. Chmn., generally: $9,000/y & $6,500/y
North Carolina	$18,312/y	$4,512/y(g)	(g)	$2,316/y	
North Dakota	$10/d	. . .	$10/d	$10/d	Cmte. Chmn.: $5/d
Ohio	$19,503/y	$14,737/y	$11,856/y	$14,737/y	Asst. Maj. Fl. Ldr.: $8,978/y; Maj. Whip, Min. Whip: $6,100/y; Asst. Min. Ldr.: $10,418/y; Asst. Maj. Whip: $3,221/y; Asst. Min. Whip: $1,611/y; Finance/Appropriations Cmte. Chmn.: $5,000/y; Other Standing Cmte. Chmn.: $2,783/y; Standing Sub-Cmte. Chmn.: $1,392/y

ADDITIONAL COMPENSATION FOR HOUSE LEADERS—Continued

State	Speaker	Speaker pro tem	Majority leader	Minority leader	Other
Oklahoma	$9,330/y	0	$6,440/y	$6,440/y	
Oregon	$919/m	0	0	0	
Pennsylvania	$19,600/y(h)	. . .	$15,680/y(h)	$15,680/y(h)	Maj. Whip, Min. Whip: $11,900/y; Maj. Caucus Chmn., Min. Caucus Chmn.; Maj. Appropriations Cmte. Chmn., Min. Appropriations Cmte. Chmn.: $7,420/y; Maj. Caucus Secy., Min. Caucus Secy., Maj. Policy Chmn., Min. Policy Chmn., Maj. Caucus Administr., Min. Caucus Administr.: $4,900/y(h)
Rhode Island	$5/d	0	0	0	
South Carolina	$11,000/y	$3,600/y	0	0	
South Dakota	0	0	0	0	
Tennessee.........	$12,520/y	0	0	0	
Texas	0	0	. . .	. . .	
Utah	$1,000/y	. . .	$500/y	$500/y	
Vermont..........	$6,870/y	. . .	0	0	
Virginia	$10,000/y	. . .	0	0	
Washington	0	0	0	0	
West Virginia	$50/d(i)	0	$25/d	$25/d	
Wisconsin	$25/m	0	0	0	
Wyoming	$3/d	0	0	0	
American Samoa ..	$5,000/y	0	. . .	. . .	
Puerto Rico.......	0	0	0	0	
Virgin Islands	--Unicameral Legislature--				

Note: This table reflects the amount paid the leadership in addition to their regular legislative compensation.

Key:
d—day
m—month
y—year
b—biennium
. . .—Position does not exist or is not selected on a regular basis.
(a) Receives a special public relations expense allowance of $10,000/y.
(b) Official title is deputy speaker.
(c) Receives an annual salary of $22,800 plus a sum equal to the amount of salary over $30,000/y which is received by the lieutenant governor.

(d) Official title is vice speaker.
(e) Additional compensation for House leaders is calculated according to the following percentage of the base salaries during sessions: speaker, 50 percent; majority and minority leaders, 25 percent; and assistant majority and minority leaders, 12.5 percent.
(f) Equal to one-third of regular annual salary.
(g) Speaker pro tempore is also majority leader.
(h) Will rise as of December 1, 1988.
(i) Speaker also receives $100/d for up to 80 days for attending to legislative business in the capitol office when the legislature is not in formal session.

Table 3.12
TIME LIMITS ON BILL INTRODUCTION

State or other jurisdiction	Time limit on introduction of bills	Procedure for granting exception to time limits
Alabama	24th L day of regular session(a).	House: 4/5 vote of quorum present and voting. Senate: majority vote after consideration by Rules Committee.
Alaska	35th C day of 2nd regular session(b).	2/3 vote of membership (concurrent resolution).
Arizona	By 29th day of regular session; By 10th day of special session.	Permission of Rules Committee.
Arkansas	55th day of regular session (50th day for appropriations bills).	2/3 vote of membership.
California	March 8 of 1st year of regular session; Feb. 21 of 2nd year of regular session(c).	(c)
Colorado	45th L day in odd-year session; 25th L day in even-year session(d).	House, Senate Committees on Delayed Bills may extend deadline.
Connecticut	Depends on schedule set out by joint rules adopted for biennium(e).	2/3 vote of members present.
Delaware	House: no introductions during last 30 C days of 2nd session.	
Florida	House: noon 2nd day of regular session(b); Senate: noon 4th L day of regular session(d,f).	Senate committees on Rules and Calendar determine whether existence of emergency compels bill's consideration. House: 2/3 vote of members present.
Georgia	House: 30th L day of regular session because of Senate ruling; Senate: 33rd L day of regular session.	House: unanimous vote; Senate: 2/3 vote of membership.
Hawaii	Actual dates established during session.	Unanimous vote of membership.
Idaho	House: 20th day of session(b); 45th day of session(g). Senate: 12th day of session(b); 35th day of session(g).	
Illinois	April 10 of odd year of session(h).	House: rules governing limitations may not be suspended. Senate: rules may be suspended by affirmative vote of majority of members; suspensions approved by Rules Committee, adopted by majority of members present.
Indiana	House: 16th day of odd year of session; 4th day of even year. Senate: 10th day of odd year of session; 4th day of even year.	House: 2/3 vote of membership; Senate: consent of Rules and Legislative Procedures Committee.
Iowa	House: Friday of 7th week of 1st regular session; Friday of 3rd week of 2nd regular session(i,j). Senate: Friday of 7th week of 1st regular session(i,j); Friday of 2nd week of 2nd regular session(b,i).	Constitutional majority.
Kansas	31st C day of regular session for individuals(k); 45th day of regular session for committees(l).	Resolution adopted by majority of members of either house may make specific exceptions to deadlines.
Kentucky	House: 38th L day of regular session; Senate: no introductions during last 20 days of session.	Majority vote of membership each house.
Louisiana	15th C day of regular session(m).	2/3 vote of elected members of each house.
Maine	Last Friday in January of 1st regular session; deadlines for 2nd regular session established by Legislative Council(b,n).	Approval of majority of members of Legislative Council.
Maryland	No introductions during last 35 C days of regular session.	2/3 vote of elected members of each house.
Massachusetts	1st Wednesday in December even numbered years, preceeding regular session(o). 1st Wednesday in November odd numbered years, preceeding regular session(o).	Favorable vote of Rules Committee followed by 4/5 vote of members of each house.
Michigan	No limit.	
Minnesota	No limit.	
Mississippi	16th C day of 90-day session; 51st C day of 125-day session(d,p).	2/3 vote of members present and voting.
Missouri	60th L day of odd-year of session; 30th L day of even-year of session(d).	Majority vote of elected members each house; governor's request for consideration of bill by special message.
Montana	Individual introductions: 14th L day; revenue bills: 21st L day; committee bills: 78th L day; committee revenue bills: 66th L day(d,q).	2/3 vote of members.

TIME LIMITS ON BILL INTRODUCTION—Continued

State or other jurisdiction	Time limit on introduction of bills	Procedure for granting exception to time limits
Nebraska	10th L day of any session(d,r).	3/5 vote of elected membership (s).
Nevada	20th C day of regular session(t).	2/3 vote of members present; also standing committee of a house if request is approved by 2/3 members of committee. Consent to suspend rule may be given only by affirmative vote of majority members elected.
New Hampshire	Must file by title on or after May 5 and fully prepared by November 19.	2/3 vote of members present or approval of 3/5 of Rules Committee.
New Jersey	No limit.	
New Mexico	30th L day of regular session(d,u); appropriations bills: 50th L day of regular session.	2/3 vote of members present.
New York	Assembly: for unlimited introduction of bills, 1st Tuesday in March; for introduction of 10 or fewer bills, last Tuesday in March(v). Senate: not prior to the 1st Tuesday of March(w).	Unanimous vote(x).
North Carolina	House: April 6 for local bills or bills prepared to be introduced for departments, agencies or state institutions; Senate: same as House plus resolutions(y).	House: 2/3 of members present and voting; Senate: 2/3 vote of membership, except in case of deadline for local bills which may be suspended by 4/5 of senators present and voting.
North Dakota	15th L day(z); resolutions: 18th L day(aa); bills requested by executive agency or Supreme Court: Dec. 15 prior to regular session.	2/3 vote or approval of majority of Committee on Delayed Bills.
Ohio	After March 15 of 2nd regular session, either house by majority vote of its members may end bill introductions.	House majority vote on recommendation of bill by Reference Committee. Senate: 3/5 vote of elected members.
Oklahoma	27th L day for house of origin in 1st session(bb); 19th L day of 2nd session(cc).	2/3 vote of membership.
Oregon	House: 36th C day of session(dd); Senate: 36th C day following election of Senate president(ee).	
Pennsylvania	No limit(ff).	
Rhode Island	March 6(gg).	2/3 vote of members present.
South Carolina	House: April 15 of regular session; May 1 for bills first introduced in Senate(d,hh). Senate: May 1 of regular session for bills originating in House.	House: 2/3 vote of members present and voting; Senate: 2/3 vote of membership.
South Dakota	40-day session: 15th L day; committee bills and joint resolutions, 16th L day. 35-day session: 10th L day; committee bills and joint resolutions, 11th L day; bills introduced at request of department, board, commission, or state agency: 6th L day(ii).	2/3 of membership.
Tennessee	House: general bills, 10th L day of regular session(jj). Senate: general bills, 10th L day of regular session; resolutions, 40th L day.	House: 2/3 vote of members; Senate: 2/3 vote of members or unanimous consent of Committee on Delayed Bills.
Texas	60th C day of regular session(kk).	4/5 vote of members present and voting.
Utah	30th C day of session.	House: 2/3 vote of members present; Senate: majority of membership.
Vermont	House, Individual introductions: 1st session, March 1; 2nd session, Feb. 1. Committees: 10 days after 1st Tuesday in March(ll). Senate, Individual and committee: 1st session, 53rd C day; 2nd session, sponsor requests bill drafting 25 days before session and all bills are introduced on 1st day(mm).	Approval by Rules Committee.
Virginia	Deadlines may be set during session.	
Washington	(Constitutional limit) No introductions during final 10 days of regular session(d,nn).	2/3 vote of elected members of each house.
West Virginia	House: 50th day of regular session(b,d); Senate: 41st day of regular session(d).	2/3 vote of members present.

TIME LIMITS ON BILL INTRODUCTION—Continued

State or other jurisdiction	Time limit on introduction of bills	Procedure for granting exception to time limits
Wisconsin	No limit.	
Wyoming	15th L day of odd year of session(d).	2/3 of elected members of either house.
American Samoa	15th L day.	2/3 of elected members.
Guam	No limit.	
Puerto Rico	60th day.	Majority vote of membership.
Virgin Islands	No limit.	

Key:
C—Calendar
L—Legislative

(a) Not applicable to local bills that have been advertised or general bills of local application.

(b) Not applicable to bills sponsored by standing committees. In Florida, also does not apply to short-form bills.

(c) Not applicable to constitutional amendments, committee bills introduced pursuant to Assembly Rule 47 or Senate Rule 23, bills introduced in Assembly with permission of speaker or bills introduced in Senate with permission of Senate Rules Committee. Subject to these deadlines, bills may be introduced at any time, except when the houses are in joint summer, interim, or final recess.

(d) Not applicable to appropriations bills. In West Virginia, supplementary appropriations bills.

(e) Not applicable to (1) bills providing for current government expenditures; (2) bills the presiding officers certify are of an emergency nature; (3) bills the governor requests because of emergency or necessity; and (4) the legislative commissioners' revisor's bills and omnibus validating act.

(f) Not applicable to local bills and joint resolutions.

(g) Not applicable to House State Affairs, Appropriations, Revenue and Taxation, or Ways and Means committees, nor to Senate State Affairs, Finance, or Judiciary and Rules committees.

(h) Final day for introduction of bills: House and Senate—April 10 (except in the House if bill has been requested from Legislative Reference Bureau by March 13); final day for standing committee to report bills: House—April 17/Senate—May 8. Appropriation bills in even numbered years referred to Rules Committee. Non-applicable for emergency bills of the Rules Committee.

(i) Unless written request for drafting bill had been filed before deadline.

(j) Not applicable to bills co-sponsored by majority and minority floor leaders.

(k) Deadline for introduction by individual members may be changed to an earlier date in either house by resolution adopted by majority of members.

(l) Not applicable to Ways and Means and Federal and State Affairs committees, the select committees of either house or the House Committee on Calendar and Printing.

(m) Not applicable to concurrent resolutions proposing suspension of law and bills reported by substitute.

(n) Not applicable to bills intended to facilitate legislative business.

(o) Not applicable to messages from governor, reports required or authorized to be made to legislature, petitions filed or approved by voters of cities or towns (or by mayors and city councils) for enactment of special legislation and which do not affect the powers and duties of state departments, boards, or commissions.

(p) Not applicable to revenue, local, and private bills.

(q) Not applicable to interim study resolutions or joint resolutions concerning administration.

(r) Not applicable to "A" bills and those introduced at the request of the governor.

(s) For standing or special committee to introduce bill after 10th L day.

(t) Requests submitted to legislative counsel for bill drafting. Does not apply to standing committees or to member who had requested bill drafting before 21st C day.

(u) Not applicable to bills to provide for current government expenses; bills referred to legislature by governor by special message setting forth emergency necessitating legislation.

(v) Does not apply to bills introduced by Rules Committee, by message from the Senate, with consent of the speaker or by members elected at special election who take office on or after the first Tuesday of March.

(w) Bills recommended by state department or agency must be submitted to office of temporary president not later than March 1. Bills proposed by governor, attorney general, comptroller, department of education or office of court administration must be submitted to office of temporary president no later than first Tuesday in April.

(x) In no case may a bill be introduced on Fridays, unless submitted by governor or introduced by Rules Committee or by message from Senate.

(y) Not applicable to those honoring memory of the deceased.

(z) No member may introduce more than three bills as prime sponsor after 10th L day.

(aa) Not applicable to resolutions proposing amendments to U.S. Constitution or directing Legislative Council to carry out a study (deadline, 34th L day).

(bb) Final date for consideration on floor in house of origin during first session. Bills introduced after date are not placed on calendar for consideration until second session.

(cc) Not applicable to reapportionment bills.

(dd) Not applicable to measures approved by Committee on Legislative Rules and Operations or by speaker; appropriation or fiscal measures sponsored by Joint Committee on Ways and Means; true substitute measures sponsored by standing, special or joint committees, or measures drafted by legislative counsel.

(ee) Not applicable to measures approved by Rules Committee, appropriation or fiscal measures sponsored by Joint Committee on Ways and Means; measures requested for drafting by legislative counsel.

(ff) Resolutions fixing the last day for introduction of bills in the House are referred to the Rules Committee before consideration by the full House.

(gg) Not applicable to resolutions of condolence or congratulations, corporate charter renewals, claims bills or city and town bills.

(hh) Not applicable to joint resolutions approving or disapproving agency regulations.

(ii) Not applicable to governor's bills.

(jj) Not applicable to certain local bills or a bill correcting a typographical error or an earlier enactment of the Committee on Delayed Bills.

(kk) Not applicable to local bills, resolutions, emergency appropriations, all emergency matters submitted by governor in special messages to the legislature.

(ll) Not applicable to Appropriations or Ways and Means committees.

(mm) Not applicable to Appropriations or Finance committees.

(nn) Not applicable to substitute bills reported by standing committees for bills pending before such committees.

Table 3.13
BILL PRE-FILING, REFERENCE, AND CARRYOVER

State or other jurisdiction	Pre-filing of bills allowed(a)	Bills referred to committee by: Senate	Bills referred to committee by: House	Bill referral restricted by rule Senate	Bill referral restricted by rule House	Bill carryover allowed(b)
Alabama	★(c)	President(d)	Speaker			. . .
Alaska	★(e)	President	Speaker	★	★	★
Arizona	★	President	Speaker			. . .
Arkansas	★	Rules Cmte.	Speaker	★	★	
California	(f)	Rules Cmte.	Rules Cmte.	★		★(g)
Colorado	★	President	Speaker			. . .
Connecticut	★	President(d)	Speaker	★	★	. . .
Delaware	★	President(d)	Speaker		★	★
Florida	★	President	Speaker	★	★	. . .
Georgia	. . .	President(d)	Speaker			★
Hawaii	(h)	President	Speaker	★	★	★
Idaho	. . .	President(d)	Speaker			. . .
Illinois	★	Cmte. on Assignment	Cmte. on Assignment			★
Indiana	★	Pres. Pro Tempore	Speaker			. . .
Iowa	★	President(d)	Speaker	★		★
Kansas	★	President	Speaker	★	★	★
Kentucky	★	Cmte. on Cmtes.(i)	Cmte. on Cmtes.	★	★	. . .
Louisiana	★	President(j)	Speaker(j)	★	★	. . .
Maine	★(k)	--------Secy. of Senate and Clerk of House(l)--------				. . .
Maryland	★	President	Speaker	(m)	(m)	. . .
Massachusetts	★	Clerk(j)	Clerk(j)	★	★	. . .
Michigan	. . .	Majority Ldr.	Speaker			★
Minnesota	★(n)	President	Speaker	(m)	(m)	★
Mississippi	★	President(d)	Speaker			. . .
Missouri	★	Pres. Pro Tempore	Speaker	★	★	★
Montana	★	President	Speaker			★
Nebraska(U)	★	Reference Cmte.		★		. . .
Nevada	★	Majority Ldr.	Speaker	★		. . .
New Hampshire	★	President	Speaker	★	★	. . .
New Jersey	★(k)	President	Speaker			★
New Mexico	. . .	Pres. Pro Tempore	Speaker	(m)	(m)	. . .
New York	★	Pres. Pro Tempore(o)	Speaker			★
North Carolina	. . .	President(d)	Speaker	(m)	(m)	★
North Dakota	★	President(d)	Speaker	★	★	★
Ohio	★	Reference Cmte.	Reference Cmte.			★
Oklahoma	★	Pres. Pro Tempore	Speaker			★
Oregon	★	President	Speaker		★	★
Pennsylvania	★	President(d)	Speaker			★
Rhode Island	★	President(d)	Speaker			★
South Carolina	★	Pres. Pro Tempore	Speaker			★
South Dakota	★	President(d)	Speaker			. . .
Tennessee	★	Speaker	Speaker	★		★
Texas	★	President(d)	Speaker		★	. . .
Utah	★	President	Speaker			. . .
Vermont	★	President(d)	Speaker	★	★	★
Virginia	★	Clerk	Speaker	★	★	★
Washington	★	President	Speaker			★
West Virginia	★	President	Speaker			. . .
Wisconsin	★	Presiding Officer	Presiding Officer			★
Wyoming	★(k)	President	Speaker			. . .
American Samoa	★	President	Speaker	★	★	★
Guam(U)	★	Rules Cmte.		★		★
Puerto Rico	★	President	President	★	★	★
Virgin Islands(U)	★	President				★

BILL PRE-FILING, REFERENCE, AND CARRYOVER—Continued

Key:

. . .—Procedure not allowed.

(U)—Unicameral legislature.

(a) Unless otherwise indicated by footnote, bills may be introduced prior to convening each session of the legislature. In this column only: ★—pre-filing is allowed in both chambers (or in the case of Nebraska, Guam, and the Virgin Islands, in the unicameral legislature); . . .—pre-filing is not allowed in either chamber.

(b) Bills carry over from the first year of a legislature to the second (does not apply to legislatures meeting in session once every two years). Bills generally do not carry over after an intervening legislative election.

(c) Except between the end of the last regular session of the legislature in any quadrennium and the organizational session following the general election.

(d) Lieutenant governor is the president of the Senate.

(e) Maximum 10 bills.

(f) California has a continuous legislature. Members may introduce bills at any time during the biennium.

(g) Bills introduced in the first year of the regular session and passed by the house of origin on or before January 30 of the second year are "carryover bills."

(h) House only in even-numbered years.

(i) Lieutenant governor as president of the Senate is a member of committee.

(j) Subject to approval or disapproval. Louisiana—majority of members present. Massachusetts—by presiding officer.

(k) Prior to convening of first regular session only.

(l) For the joint standing committee system. Secretary of Senate and clerk of House, after conferring, suggest an appropriate committee reference for every bill, resolve and petition offered in either house. If they are unable to agree, the question of reference is referred to a conference of the president of the Senate and speaker of the House. If the presiding officers cannot agree, the question is resolved by the Legislative Council.

(m) Not restricted, except: Maryland—in House, local bills; in Senate, local bills and bills creating judgeships. Minnesota—bills on government structure and bills appropriating funds which are referred to Finance Committee. New Mexico—in House, bills referred to Appropriations and Finance Committee; in Senate, bills referred to Finance Committee. North Carolina—bills referred to Appropriations, Finance, and Ways and Means committees.

(n) Prior to convening of second regular session only.

(o) Also serves as majority leader.

Table 3.14
ENACTING LEGISLATION: VETO, VETO OVERRIDE, AND EFFECTIVE DATE

State or other jurisdiction	Governor may item veto appropriation bills — Amount	Other(b)	Days allowed governor to consider bill(a) — During session: Bill becomes law unless vetoed	After session: Bill becomes law unless vetoed	After session: Bill dies unless signed	Votes required in each house to pass bills or items over veto(c)	Effective date of enacted legislation(d)
Alabama	★	...	6		10A	Majority elected	Immediately(e)
Alaska	★(f)	★	15	20P		2/3 elected(g)	90 days after enactment
Arizona	★	...	5	10A		2/3 elected	90 days after adjournment
Arkansas	★	★	5	20A(h)		Majority elected	90 days after adjournment
California	★(f)	...	12(h,i)	(i)		2/3 elected	(j)
Colorado	★	★	10(h)	30A(h)		2/3 elected	Immediately(k)
Connecticut	★	...	5	15P(h)		2/3 elected	Oct. 1
Delaware	★	★	10		30A(h)	3/5 elected	Immediately
Florida	★	...	7(h)	15P(h)		2/3 elected	60 days after adjournment
Georgia(l)	★	...	6	40A(m)		2/3 elected	July 1(n)
Hawaii(l)	★(f)	...	10(o,p)	45A(o,p)	(p)	2/3 elected	Immediately
Idaho	★	★	5	10A		2/3 elected	July 1(n)
Illinois	★(f)	★	60(h)	60P(h)		3/5 elected(g)	Jan. 1(n)
Indiana		★	7	7A		Majority elected	(q)
Iowa	★	...	3	(r)	(r)	2/3 elected	July 1(n)
Kansas	★	★	10	10P		2/3 elected	Upon publication
Kentucky	★	★	10	10A		Majority elected	90 days after adjournment
Louisiana(l)	★(f)	★	10(h)	20P(h)		2/3 elected	60 days after adjournment
Maine	...(s)	★	10(h)	(m)		2/3 elected	90 days after adjournment
Maryland(l)	★	...	6	30P(m)		3/5 elected	June 1(t)
Massachusetts	★(f)	★	10(o)	10P	10P	2/3 present	90 days after enactment
Michigan	★	★	14(h)	14P(h)	14P	2/3 elected and serving	90 days after adjournment
Minnesota	★	...	3		14P	2/3 elected	Aug. 1(u)
Mississippi	★(f)	★	5	15P(m)		2/3 elected	60 days after enactment
Missouri	★(f)	★	15(r)	45P(m,r)		2/3 elected	90 days after adjournment(u,v)
Montana	★	★	5(h)	25A(h)		2/3 present	Oct. 1(u)
Nebraska	★(w)	...	5	5A		3/5 elected	3 months after adjournment
Nevada	...	...	5	10A		2/3 elected	July 1
New Hampshire	...	...	5		5P	2/3 elected	60 days after enactment
New Jersey	★(f)	...	(x)	(x)	(x)	2/3 elected	July 4
New Mexico	★	★	3	15A	20A	2/3 present	90 days after adjournment(u)
New York	★	...	10		30A	2/3 elected	20 days after enactment
North Carolina			(y)				30 days after adjournment
North Dakota	★(f)	★	3	15A		2/3 elected	July 1
Ohio	★	★	10	10A	15A	3/5 elected	90 days after filed with secretary of state
Oklahoma	★	...	5	20A		2/3 elected(g)	90 days after adjournment
Oregon	★(f)	★	5	30A(h)		2/3 present	90 days after adjournment
Pennsylvania	★(f)	...	10(h)	10A(h)		2/3 elected	60 days after enactment
Rhode Island	...	...	6	(m)		3/5 present	10 days after adjournment
South Carolina	★	★	5			2/3 present	20 days after enactment

VETO, VETO OVERRIDE, AND EFFECTIVE DATE—Continued

| State or other jurisdiction | Governor may item veto appropriation bills | | Days allowed governor to consider bill(a) | | | Votes required in each house to pass bills or items over veto(c) | Effective date of enacted legislation(d) |
	Amount	Other(b)	During session — Bill becomes law unless vetoed	After session — Bill becomes law unless vetoed	After session — Bill dies unless signed		
South Dakota	★	(f)	5	15A		2/3 elected	July 1(n)
Tennessee	★	...	10	10A		Majority elected	40 days after enactment
Texas	★	...	10	20A		2/3 present	90 days after adjournment
Utah	★	...	10(h)	20A(h)		2/3 elected	60 days after adjournment
Vermont	...	...	5		3A	2/3 present	July 1
Virginia	★	★	7(h)	20A	30A(h)	2/3 present(z)	July 1(u,aa)
Washington	★	★	5	15A(bb)		2/3 present	90 days after adjournment
West Virginia	★	(f) ★	5		6P	Majority elected(g)	90 days after enactment
Wisconsin	★	★	6	15A(h)		2/3 present	Day after publication
Wyoming	★	...	3			2/3 elected	Immediately
American Samoa	★	...	10		30P	2/3 elected	60 days after adjournment(cc)
Guam	★	(f)	10		30P	14 members	Immediately(dd)
No. Marianas	★	...	40(ee)			2/3 elected	Immediately
Puerto Rico	★	(f)	10		30P(h)	2/3 elected	Specified in act
Virgin Islands	★	★	10		30P(h)	2/3 elected	Immediately

Note: Some legislatures reconvene after normal session to consider bills vetoed by governor. Connecticut—if governor vetoes any bill, secretary of state must reconvene General Assembly on second Monday after the last day on which governor is either authorized to transmit or has transmitted every bill with his objections, whichever occurs first; General Assembly must adjourn *sine die* not later than three days after its reconvening. Hawaii—legislature may reconvene on 45th day after adjournment *sine die*, in special session, without call. Louisiana—legislature meets in a maximum five-day veto session on the 40th day after final adjournment. Missouri—if governor returns any bill on or after the fifth day before the last day on which legislature may consider bills (in even-numbered years), legislature automatically reconvenes on first Monday in September for a maximum 10C session. New Jersey—legislature meets in special session (without call or petition) to act on bills returned by governor on 45th day after *sine die* adjournment of the first year of a two-year legislature; a special session may not be convened if the 45th day falls on or after the last day of the legislative year in which the second session occurs. Virginia—legislature reconvenes on sixth Wednesday after adjournment for a maximum three-day session (may be extended to seven days upon vote of majority of members elected to each house). Utah—if 2/3 of the members of each house favor reconvening to consider vetoed bills, a maximum five-day session is set by the presiding officers. Washington—upon petition of 2/3 of the members of each house, legislature meets 45 days after adjournment for a maximum five-day session.

Key:
★—Yes
...—No
A—days after adjournment of legislature
P—days after presentation to governor
(a) Sundays excluded, unless otherwise indicated.
(b) Includes language in appropriations bill.

(c) Bill returned to house of origin with governor's objections.
(d) Effective date may be established by the law itself or may be otherwise changed by vote of the legislature. Special or emergency acts are usually effective immediately.
(e) Penal acts, 60 days.
(f) Governor can also reduce amounts in appropriations bills. In Hawaii, governor can reduce items in executive appropriations measures, but cannot reduce nor item veto amounts appropriated for the judicial or legislative branches.
(g) Different number of votes required for revenue and appropriations bills. Alaska—3/4 elected. Illinois—appropriations reductions, majority elected. Oklahoma—emergency bills, 3/4 vote. West Virginia—budget and supplemental appropriations, 2/3 elected.
(h) Sundays included.
(i) A bill presented to the governor that is not returned within 12 days becomes a law; provided that any bill passed before Sept. 1 of the second calendar year of the biennium of the legislative session and in the possession of the governor on or after Sept. 1 that is not returned by the governor on or before Sept. 30 of that year becomes law. The legislature may not present to the governor any bill after Nov. 15 of the second calendar year of the biennium of the session. If the legislature, by adjournment of a special session prevents the return of a bill with the veto message, the bill becomes law unless the governor vetoes within 12 days by depositing it and the veto message in the office of the secretary of state.
(j) For legislation enacted in regular sessions: Jan. 1 next following 90-day period from date of enactment. For legislation enacted in special sessions: 91 days after adjournment. Does not apply to statutes calling elections, statutes providing for tax levies or appropriations for the usual current state expenses or urgency statutes, all of which take effect immediately.
(k) An act takes effect on the date stated in the act, or if no date is stated in the act, then on its passage.
(l) Constitution withholds right to veto constitutional amendments.

VETO, VETO OVERRIDE, AND EFFECTIVE DATE—Continued

(m) Bills vetoed after adjournment are returned to the legislature for reconsideration. Georgia: bills vetoed during last three days of session and not considered for overriding, and all bills vetoed after *sine die* adjournment may be considered at next session. Maine: returned within three days after the next meeting of the same legislature which enacted the bill or resolution. Maryland: reconsidered at the next session. Mississippi: returned within four days of adjournment or later in first session are considered at beginning of second session; bills returned in second session are considered in automatic veto session. South Carolina: within two days after the next meeting.

(n) Effective date for bills which become law on or after July 1. Georgia—Jan. 1, unless a specific date has been provided for in legislation. Idaho—special sessions, 60 days after adjournment. Illinois—a bill passed after June 30 does not become effective prior to July 1 of the next calendar year unless legislature, by a 3/5 vote provided for an earlier effective date. Iowa—if governor signs bill after July 1, bill becomes law on Aug. 15; for special sessions, 90 days after adjournment. South Dakota—91 days after adjournment.

(o) Except Sundays and legal holidays. In Hawaii, except Saturdays, Sundays, holidays and any days in which the legislature is in recess prior to its adjournment.

(p) The governor must notify the legislature 10 days before the 45th day of his intent to veto a measure on that day. The legislature may convene on the 45th day after adjournment to consider the vetoed measures. If the legislature fails to reconvene, the bill does not become law. If the legislature reconvenes, it may pass the measure over the governor's veto or it may amend the law to meet the governor's objections. If the law is amended, the governor must sign the bill within 10 days after it is presented to him in order for it to become law.

(q) No act takes effect until it has been published and circulated in the counties, by authority, except in cases of emergency.

(r) Governor must sign or veto all bills presented to him. Iowa—any bill submitted to the governor for his approval during the last three days of a session must be deposited by him in the secretary of state's office within 30 days after adjournment with his approval or objections. Missouri—otherwise, legislature, by joint resolution, reciting fact of such failure, may direct the secretary of state to enroll the bill as an authentic act and it becomes law.

(s) Item veto on supplementary appropriations bills and capital construction bills only.

(t) Bills passed over governor's veto are effective in 30 days or on date specified in bill, whichever is later.

(u) Different date for fiscal legislation. Minnesota, Montana—July 1. Missouri, New Mexico—immediately.

(v) In event of a recess of 30 days or more, legislature may prescribe, by joint resolution, that laws previously passed and not effective shall take effect 90 days from beginning of recess.

(w) No appropriation can be made in excess of the recommendations contained in the governor's budget except by a 2/3 vote. The excess is not subject to veto by the governor.

(x) If a bill is not returned by the governor within 10 days after it is presented to him (excluding Sundays), it becomes law, unless the house of origin is in temporary adjournment. In that case, the bill becomes law on the day the house of origin reconvenes. If on the 10th day, the legislature is in adjournment *sine die*, the bill becomes law if the governor signs it within 45 days (excluding Sundays) after the adjournment. On the 45th day, the bill becomes law unless he returns it with his objections (1) on the 45th day if the house of origin has convened in regular or special session of the same two-year legislature; (2) on the day upon which the house reconvenes, if it is in temporary adjournment on the 45th day; or (3) on the 45th day (if the house is in adjournment *sine die*) at the special session which convenes on that day (without petition or call) for the sole purpose of acting on returned bills.

(y) Governor has no approval or veto power.

(z) Must include majority of elected members.

(aa) Special sessions—first day of fourth month after adjournment.

(bb) Five days for appropriations bills.

(cc) Laws required to be approved only by the governor. An act required to be approved by the U.S. Secretary of the Interior only after it is vetoed by the governor and so approved takes effect 40 days after it is returned to the governor by the secretary.

(dd) U.S. Congress may annul.

(ee) Twenty days for appropriations bills.

Table 3.15
BILL AND RESOLUTION INTRODUCTIONS AND ENACTMENTS:
1986 AND 1987 REGULAR SESSIONS

State	Duration of session*	Introductions		Enactments		Measures vetoed by governor	Length of session
		Bills	Resolu- tions	Bills	Resolu- tions		
Alabama...............	Jan. 14-April 28, 1986	1,577	985	280	344	N.A.	105C
	April 21-Aug. 3, 1987	1,883	755	537	689	12	105C
Alaska.................	Jan. 3-May 12, 1986	429	100	146	39	5	120C
	Jan. 9-May 20, 1987	637	96	178	67	3	122C
Arizona...............	Jan. 3-May 14, 1986	956	63	420	20	12	125C
	Jan. 2, May 19, 1987	937	34	369	8	5	127C
Arkansas	No regular session in 1986						
	Jan. 12-April 20, 1987	176	297	1,072	191	67	82C
California..............	Dec. 3, 1984-Nov. 30, 1986 (c)	3,062	560	3,128	322	361	(a)
	Dec. 1, 1986-Nov. 30, 1987 (c)	4,389	274	1,034	115	96 (b)	(a)
Colorado	Jan. 8-May 27, 1986	528	N.A.	262	N.A.	11 (b)	140C
	Jan. 7-Aug 13, 1987	634	N.A.	338	N.A.	18	219C
Connecticut	Feb. 5-May 7, 1986	1,736	207	493	N.A.	6	65L
	Jan. 7-June 3, 1987	3,877	252	701	N.A.	2	106L
Delaware	Jan. 4-June 30, 1986	640	300	300	N.A.	13	52L
	Jan. 13-June 30, 1987	682	436	194	16	7	53L
Florida	April 8-June 7, 1986	2,546	205	465	155	3 (b)	61C
	April 7-June 6, 1987	2,698	165	535	135	13	61C
Georgia...............	Jan. 5-March 7, 1986	1,250	839	907	748	6	40L
	Jan. 2-March 12, 1987	1,574	779	799	661	9	40L
Hawaii	Jan. 5-April 23, 1986	2,239	976	348	425	19	99C
	Jan. 21-April 30, 1987	3,716	1,185	384	504	34	100C
Idaho	Jan. 6-March 28, 1986	693	88	356	28	8	82C
	Jan. 12-April 1, 1987	619	88	367	49	3	80C
Illinois.................	Jan. 8, 1986-Jan. 13, 1987	1,926	1,887	373	1,791	76	51L
	Jan. 14-Nov. 6, 1987	4,497	1,882	784	1,753	254 (b)	69L
Indiana	Nov. 9, 1985-March 5, 1986	956	18 (d)	248	3 (d)	5 (b)	30L
	Nov. 18, 1986-April 29, 1987	1,420	19 (d)	371	6 (d)	2	61L
Iowa	Jan. 3-May 3, 1986	799	105	201	24	2	110C
	Jan. 2-May 10, 1987	609	149	234	45	9	119C
Kansas	Jan. 3-June 6, 1986	938 (e)	52 (e,f)	400	33 (f)	17 (g)	(a)
	Jan. 2-May 21, 1987	1,063	44 (f)	404	19 (f)	5 (g)	69L
Kentucky	Jan. 7-April 15, 1986	1,388	384	462	317	2	57L
	No regular session in 1987						
Louisiana	April 21-July 1, 1986	3,235	169	1,083	4	23	(a)
	April 20-July 3, 1987	2,525	116	944	5	6	(a)
Maine	Jan. 8-April 16, 1986	519	43	341	37	0	56L
	Dec. 3, 1986-June 30, 1987	1,883	51	692	48	11	92L
Maryland	Jan. 8-April 7, 1986	2,938	127	865	43	122	66C
	Jan. 14-April 13, 1987	2,668	113	778	25	95	65C
Massachusetts	Jan. 1, 1986-Jan. 6, 1987	8,824	(h)	712	N.A.	3 (b,g)	371C
	Jan. 7, 1987-(i)	(j)	(j)	(j)	(j)	(j)	(i)
Michigan	Jan. 8-Dec. 30, 1986	987	16 (k)	332	3 (k)	6	357C
	Jan. 14-Dec. 30, 1987	1,903	26 (k)	286	0	2	351C
Minnesota	Feb. 3-March 17, 1986	1,625	21	166	2	1	26L
	Jan. 6-May 18, 1987	3,241	38	405	9	1 (g)	55L
Mississippi	Jan. 7-April 15, 1986	2,390	500	514	200	10	99C
	Jan. 6-April 5, 1987	2,472	438	569	229	5 (b)	90C
Missouri	Jan. 8-May 5, 1986	1,193	66	244	6	15	128C
	Jan. 7-June 30, 1987	1,334	85	203	9	15 (l)	175C
Montana...............	No regular session in 1986						
	Jan. 5-April 23, 1987	1,308	86	738	57	4	90L
Nebraska	Jan. 8-April 16, 1986	531	143	316	97	14 (b)	60L
	Jan. 7-May 29, 1987	787	245	358	134	3 (b)	90L

1986 AND 1987 REGULAR SESSIONS—Continued

State	Duration of session*	Introductions		Enactments		Measures vetoed by governor	Length of session
		Bills	Resolu-tions	Bills	Resolu-tions		
Nevada	No regular session in 1986 Jan. 19-June 18, 1987	1,491	235	824	164	3	151C
New Hampshire	Jan. 8-June 10, 1986 Jan. 6-May 28, 1987	733 1,062	4 4	230 416	3 1	5 8	17L 29L
New Jersey.............	Jan. 14, 1986-Jan. 12, 1987 Jan. 13, 1987-Jan. 11, 1988	7,120 2,154	581 197	211 460	8 (d) 11 (d)	24 57	61L 43L
New Mexico............	Jan. 21, 1986-Feb. 20, 1987 Jan. 20-March 21, 1987	592 1,415	36 33	120 399	9 3	4 44	30C 60C
New York	Jan. 8-July 3, 1986 Jan. 7, 1987-(i)	5,842 15,095	3,896 3,667	939 855	3,883 3,651	65 26	(m) (i)
North Carolina	June 5-July 16, 1986 Feb. 9-Aug. 14, 1987	1,172 3,723	55 93	239 879	25 37	N.A. N.A.	(a) (a)
North Dakota	No regular session in 1986 Jan. 6-April 19, 1987	1,239	174	761	137	6	73L
Ohio .... (n)	Jan. 6-Dec. 30, 1986 N.A.	431 N.A.	N.A. N.A.	44 N.A.	N.A. N.A.	1 (n)	96L
Oklahoma	Jan. 7-June 13, 1986 Jan. 6-July 16, 1987	722 866	186 (o) 272	321 238	10 83	7 33	90L (a)
Oregon	No regular session in 1986 Jan. 12-June 28, 1987	2,571	144	906	60	15 (b)	168C
Pennsylvania	Jan. 7-Nov. 26, 1986 Jan. 6-(q)	1,349 3,312	231 (p) 405 (r)	275 145	152 234	6 (b) 2	(a) (a)
Rhode Island	Jan. 7-June 26, 1986 Jan. 6-June 25, 1987	3,263 3,601	279 276	931 1,083	279 276	59 (b) 55 (b)	82L 75L
South Carolina	Jan. 14-June 19, 1986 Jan. 13-June 25, 1987	1,047 2165 (h)	(h) (h)	328 791	(h) (h)	11 (b) 8 (b)	91L 94L
South Dakota	Jan. 14-March 17, 1986 Jan. 13-March 23, 1987	684 656	95 108	424 387	87 99	13 (b) 11	35L 40L
Tennessee	Jan. 15-May 14, 1986 Jan. 17-May 7, 1987	4,157 2,651	262 105	1,141 (s) 578 (s)	245 92	10 (b) 1	(a) (a)
Texas..................	No regular session in 1986 Jan. 13-June 1, 1987	4,179	2,070	1,185	1,649	52	140C
Utah	Jan. 13-Feb. 26, 1986 Jan. 12-Feb. 25, 1987	664 595	101 80	222 255	53 53	8 4	45C 45C
Vermont	Jan. 7-May 3, 1986 Jan. 7-May 22, 1987	493 698	108 110	116 136	79 85	3 0	70L 83L
Virginia................	Jan. 8-March 8, 1986 Jan. 14-Feb. 28, 1987	1,603 1,621	387 322	644 981	283 256	4 1	55C 46C
Washington	Jan. 13-March 12, 1986 Jan. 12-April 26, 1987	1,426 2,334	98 129	325 528	23 26	47 74	60C 105C
West Virginia	Jan. 8-March 9, 1986 Jan. 14-June 14, 1987	1,911 1,978	180 267	199 164	49 98	26 (b) 015 (b)	61C 60C (t)
Wisconsin..............	Jan. 7, 1985-Jan. 5, 1987 Jan. 5, 1987-Jan. 3, 1989 (u)	1,624 1,609	212 201	293 232 (v)	83 110	11 10	127L 730C
Wyoming	Feb. 17-March 15, 1986 Jan. 13-March 2, 1987	209 781	7 N.A.	130 242	7 4	6 4	N.A. 40L
American Samoa	Jan. 13-April 5, 1986 July 14-Sept. 20, 1986 Jan. 12-March 27, 1987 July 13-Sept. 25, 1987	N.A. N.A. 136 (w) N.A.	N.A. N.A. 91 (w) N.A.	N.A. N.A. 32 (w) N.A.	N.A. N.A. 44 (w) N.A.	N.A. N.A. 8 (w) N.A.	45L 45L N.A. N.A.
Puerto Rico	Jan. 13-June 5, 1986 Jan. 12-May 18, 1987	705 613	1,582 1,170	152 93	148 117	23 27	144C 127C
Virgin Islands	Jan. 13, 1986-Jan. 12, 1987 Jan. 16, 1987-Dec. 14, 1987	485 143	47 53	145 70	25 39	27 (b) 7	22C 22C

1986 AND 1987 REGULAR SESSIONS—Continued

*Actual adjournment dates are listed regardless of constitutional or statutory limitations. For more information on provisions, see Table 3.2, "Legislative Sessions: Legal Provisions."

Key:
C—Calendar day.
L—Legislative day (in some states, called a session or workday; definition may vary slightly, however, generally refers to any day on which either chamber of the legislature is in session).
N.A.—Not available.
(a) California: 1984-86 Senate = 254L; Assembly = 251L; 1986-87 Senate = 131L; Assembly = 228L; Kansas: 1986 Senate = 69L; House = 70L; Louisiana: 1986 Senate = 45L; House = 57L; North Carolina: 1986 Senate = 30L; House = 29L; 1987 Senate = 135L; House = 134L; Oklahoma: 1987 Senate = 89L (Adjourned on July 17, 1987); House = 90L; Pennsylvania: 1986 Senate = 64L; House = 72L; 1987 Senate = 86L; House = 82L; Tennessee: 1986 Senate = 37L; House = 36L; 1987 Senate = 44L; House = 43L.
(b) Number of vetoes overridden: California: 1987 - 1 (House); Colorado: 1986 - 5; Florida: 1986 - 1; Illinois: 1987 - 29; Indiana: 1986 - 1; Massachusetts: 1986-1987 - 1; Mississippi: 1987 - 2; Nebraska: 1986 - 6, 1987 - 3; Oregon: 1987 - 4; Pennsylvania: 1986 - 1; Rhode Island: 1986 - 2, 1987 - 2; South Carolina: 1986 - 5, 1987 - 4; South Dakota: 1986 - 3; Tennessee: 1986 - 6; West Virginia: 1986 - 1, 1987 - 5; Virgin Islands: 1986 - 10.
(c) After organizational session in December, legislature recesses until the first Monday in January of the odd-numbered year and continues in session until Nov. 30 of the next even-numbered year.
(d) Joint resolutions.

(e) Plus carryover legislation from the previous session. Kansas - 573 bills, 30 resolutions.
(f) Concurrent resolutions.
(g) Plus line item vetoes. Kansas: 1986 - 3, 1987 - 2; Massachusetts: 1986 - 4; Minnesota: 1987 - 1.
(h) Figures given under bill introductions include resolution introductions.
(i) Still in session as of November 30, 1987.
(j) Totals not available as still in session as of November 30, 1987.
(k) Includes joint.
(l) Veto information not available.
(m) Session is divided into "workdays" during which the legislature is actually meeting in session, and "legislative days" in which only one or two legislators perfunctorily open and adjourn for the day in order to speed up the bill consideration process. In 1986, the Senate meet for 151C and 73L.
(n) Final figures not available.
(o) Includes joint, concurrent, and single-house resolutions.
(p) Also, 13 Sunset Review Resolution Introductions.
(q) Senate adjourned on January 5, 1988; House on December 15, 1987.
(r) Also, 1 Sunset Review Resolution Introductions.
(s) Public and private acts.
(t) Extended 24 legislative days.
(u) Scheduled end of regular session. All information as of April 8, 1988.
(v) 194 bills pending action.
(w) Totals include those for special sessions as well.

Table 3.16
BILL AND RESOLUTION INTRODUCTIONS AND ENACTMENTS: 1986 AND 1987 SPECIAL SESSIONS

State	Duration of session*	Introductions		Enactments		Measures vetoed by governor	Length of session
		Bills	Resolu-tions	Bills	Resolu-tions		
Alabama...............	Sept. 8-Sept. 24, 1986	269	N.A.	57	79	N.A.	30C
	No special sessions in 1987						
Alaska.................	No special sessions in 1986						
	July 1-July 3, 1987	4	2	5	1	0(a)	3C
Arizona................	No special sessions in 1986						
	Jan. 21-Jan. 25, 1987	11	1	3	0	0	5C
	June 29-July 2, 1987	6	0	4	0	0	4C
	July 20-July 22, 1987	3	0	3	0	0	2C
Arkansas	No special sessions in 1986						
	June 2-June 5, 1987	100	18	61	15	1	4C
	Oct. 6-Oct. 9, 1987	10	6	3	3	0	4C
California..............	Sept. 8-Nov. 30, 1986	3	3	0	2	0	(b)
	Nov. 9-Nov. 10, 1987	17	2	4	1	0	2L
Colorado	Aug. 8-Sept. 3, 1986	18	N.A.	17	N.A.	0	27C
	No special sessions in 1987						
Connecticut	May 21-June 6, 1986	2	12	2	N.A.	1	2L
	June 11-June 13, 1986	1	7	1	N.A.	0	3L
	June 23,-June 30, 1986	2	28	2	N.A.	0	2L
	July 22-July 22, 1987	2	18	2	N.A.	0	1L
Delaware	Sept. 18-Sept. 18, 1986	0	0	1	0	0	1L
	July 2-Dec. 8, 1987(c)	N.A.	N.A.	N.A.	N.A.	N.A.	N.A.
Florida	June 19-June 19, 1986	15	0	9	0	0	1C
	Feb. 4-Feb. 4, 1987	5	1	2	1	0	1C
	Sept. 21-Oct. 8, 1987	45	6	12	6	1	18C
	Oct. 12-Oct. 15, 1987	5	1	2	1	0	4C
Georgia................	No special sessions in 1986/1987						
Hawaii	July 24-July 30, 1986	12	0	2	0	0	7C
	No special sessions in 1987						
Idaho	No special sessions in 1986/1987						
Illinois.................	Nov. 18, 1986-Jan. 13, 1987	19	13	0	13	0(d)	8L
	July 1-July 1, 1987	0	11	2	11	0	1L
Indiana	No special sessions in 1986						
	April 30-April 30, 1987	20	0	19	0	0	1L
Iowa	No special sessions in 1986						
	June 4-June 6, 1987	2	8	1	2	0	3C
	Oct. 27-Oct. 27, 1987	2	1	1	1	0	1C
Kansas	No special sessions in 1986						
	Aug. 31-Sept. 5, 1987	10	9(e)	0	3(e)	0	6L
Kentucky	No special sessions in 1986						
	Oct. 14-Oct. 23, 1987	3	50	2	50	0	8L
Louisiana	Dec. 4-Dec. 9, 1986	238	16	38	0	2	(b)
	No special sessions in 1987						
Maine	May 28-May 30, 1986	25	0	25	1	0	4L
	Oct. 28-Oct. 28, 1986	10	1	10	1	0	1L
	Oct. 9-Oct. 9, 1987	33	0	28	0	2	1L
	Oct. 21-Nov. 20, 1987	19	0	12	0	2	4L
Maryland	No special sessions in 1986/1987						
Massachusetts	No special sessions in 1986/1987						
Michigan	No special sessions in 1986/1987						
Minnesota	April 2-April 2, 1986	4	0	3	0	0	1L
	June 25-June 25, 1987	13	0	5	0	0	1L
Mississippi	May 28-June 1, 1986	14	13	1	9	0	5L
	Aug. 27-Aug. 29, 1987	38	20	21	19	0	3C
Missouri	No special sessions in 1986/1987						

1986 AND 1987 SPECIAL SESSIONS—Continued

State	Duration of session*	Introductions		Enactments		Measures vetoed by governor	Length of session
		Bills	Resolutions	Bills	Resolutions		
Montana...............	March 24-March 29, 1986	33	5	17	5	0	6L
	June 16-July 1, 1986	77	5	45	2	0	14L
	No special sessions in 1987						
Nebraska	Nov. 12-Nov. 20, 1986	3	6	3	5	0	7L
	Dec. 5-Dec. 12, 1986	5	3	3	3	0	7L
	No special sessions in 1987						
Nevada	No special sessions in 1986/1987						
New Hampshire	No special sessions in 1986/1987						
New Jersey..............	No special sessions in 1986/1987						
New Mexico.............	June 23-June 24, 1986	10	0	2	0	0	2C
	July 11-July 12, 1987	2	1	2	1	0	2C
New York	(f)						
	No special sessions in 1987						
North Carolina	Feb. 18-Feb. 18, 1986	13	1	7	1	N.A.	1L
	No special sessions in 1987						
North Dakota	Dec. 2-Dec. 5, 1986	10	2	7	2	0	4L
	No special sessions in 1987						
Ohio	No special sessions in 1986/1987						
Oklahoma	No special sessions in 1986						
	July 6-July 6, 1987	1	1	N.A.	N.A.	N.A.	1L
	July 7-July 14, 1987 (g)	1	1	N.A.	N.A.	N.A.	2L
Oregon	No special sessions in 1986/1987						
Pennsylvania	No special sessions in 1986						
	Nov. 9-Nov. 30, 1987	61	2	0	0	0	(b)
Rhode Island	No special sessions in 1986						
	Sept. 8-Sept. 8, 1987	6	2	6	2	0	1L
South Carolina	No special sessions in 1986/1987						
South Dakota	No special sessions in 1986						
	July 16-July 16, 1987	3	1	3	1	0	1L
Tennessee	No special sessions in 1986/1987						
Texas...................	Aug. 6-Sept. 4, 1986	157	19	254	197	0	30C
	Sept. 8-Sept. 30, 1986	142	273	33	231	1	23C
	June 2-June 3, 1987	16	10	6	6	0	2C
	June 22-July 21, 1987	286	524	78	418	1	30C
Utah	May 13-May 14, 1986	23	5	16	4	0	2L
	June 18-June 18, 1986	1	1	1	1	0	1L
	Nov. 18-Nov. 25, 1986	14	1	5	1	0	4L
	May 20-June 17, 1987	22	0	20	0	0	2L
Vermont	No special sessions in 1986/1987						
Virginia.................	Sept. 15-Sept. 27, 1986	41	21	16	19	0	12C
	April 8-April 8, 1987	2	9	2	9	0	1L
Washington	No special sessions in 1986						
	April 27-May 21, 1987 (h)	2 (h)	5 (h)	14 (h)	8 (h)	0 (h)	27C
	Aug. 10-Aug. 10, 1987 (h)						
	Oct. 10-Oct. 10, 1987 (h)						
West Virginia	May 15-May 30, 1986	100	13	25	12	5 (i)	10L
	July 18-Sept. 9, 1986	24	35	7	14	1	9L
	Dec. 8-Dec. 8, 1987	3	7	2	5	2	1L
Wisconsin...............	Jan. 27-May 30, 1986	1	4	1	3 (j)	1	34L
	March 24-March 26, 1986	1	1	1	1	0	3L
	May 20-May 29, 1986	44	3	12	3	0	6L
	July 15-July 15, 1986	3	1	2	1	0	1L
	Sept. 15-Sept. 16, 1987	2	1	2	1	0	2C
	Nov. 18-(k)	6 (l)	3 (l)	0 (l)	2 (l)	2 (l)	(k)

1986 AND 1987 SPECIAL SESSIONS—Continued

State	Duration of session*	Introductions		Enactments		Measures vetoed by governor	Length of session
		Bills	Resolu-tions	Bills	Resolu-tions		
Wyoming	June 16-June 19, 1986	8	3	6	2	N.A.	4C
	May 19-May 22, 1987	10	0	5	0	0	4C
American Samoa	March 13-March 22, 1986	N.A.	N.A.	N.A.	N.A.	N.A.	N.A.
	April 21-April 25, 1986	N.A.	N.A.	N.A.	N.A.	N.A.	N.A.
	May 14-May 20, 1986	N.A.	N.A.	N.A.	N.A.	N.A.	N.A.
	June 10-June 11, 1986	N.A.	N.A.	N.A.	N.A.	N.A.	N.A.
	Nov. 24-Dec. 5, 1986	N.A.	N.A.	N.A.	N.A.	N.A.	N.A.
	March 27-April 6, 1987	(m)	(m)	(m)	(m)	(m)	N.A.
Puerto Rico	June 6-June 23, 1986	18	35	5	2	N.A.	18L
	Aug. 13-Sept. 1, 1986	19	23	11	6	2	20L
	Dec. 18-Dec. 24, 1986	3	6	8	0	N.A.	7L
	May 19-May 19, 1987	0	0	0	1	N.A.	1L
	June 4-June 23, 1987	14	13	10	40	N.A.	20L
	Sept. 8-Sept. 27, 1987	21	16	9	1	N.A.	20L
	Oct. 26-Oct. 26, 1987	1	1	N.A.	4	N.A.	1L
Virgin Islands	March 25-March 25, 1986 (h)	4	0	4	0	0	1C
	Oct. 24-Oct. 24, 1986 (h)	(h)	(h)	(h)	(h)	(h)	1C
	No special sessions in 1987						

*Actual adjournment dates are listed regardless of constitutional or statutory limitations. For more information on provisions, see Table 3.2, "Legislative Sessions: Legal Provisions."
Key:
C—Calendar day
L—Legislative day
N.A.—Not available
(a) 2 line items overridden.
(b) California: 1986 Senate 65L, Assembly 69C. Louisiana: 1986 Senate 13L, House 16L. Pennsylvania: 1987 Senate 14L, House 13L.
(c) Final data not available.
(d) 11 vetoes overridden; includes amendatory and item vetoes and restore reductions.

(e) Concurrent resolutions.
(f) Special session was held Dec. 6 - Dec. 31, 1986; information not available.
(g) Senate adjourned July 7.
(h) Figures given include totals for all special sessions.
(i) 5 vetoes overridden.
(j) Partial veto.
(k) In session as of April 8, 1988.
(l) Totals as of April 8, 1988.
(m) Included in numbers given in Table 3.15, "Bill and Resolution Introductions and Enactments: 1986 and 1987." Separate figures not available.

Table 3.17
STAFF FOR INDIVIDUAL LEGISLATORS

	Senate			House		
	Capitol			Capitol		
State	Personal	Shared	District	Personal	Shared	District
Alabama	...	YR	...	YR	YR	...
Alaska	YR	...	...	YR	...	...
Arizona	...	...	...	...	...	...
Arkansas	...	YR(a)	...	...	YR(a)	...
California	YR	...	YR	YR	...	YR
Colorado	(b)	YR/3(c)	...	(b)	YR/5(c)	...
Connecticut	(b)	YR/1.6	(b)	(b)	YR/3	...
Delaware	SO	YR	...	SO	YR	...
Florida	...	...	YR	...	...	YR
Georgia	...	YR/2	...	...	YR/6	...
Hawaii	YR	(e)	...	YR	(f)	...
Idaho	...	SO/10	...	...	SO/12	...
Illinois	YR	...	(f)	...	YR	(f)
Indiana	...	YR/4	...	...	YR/4	...
Iowa	SO	...	...	SO	...	...
Kansas	SO	...	...	...	SO/3	...
Kentucky	...	YR/15	...	...	YR/46	...
Louisiana	SO	YR	YR	...	...	YR
Maine	(b)	SO/7.5	...	(b)	SO/24.3	...
Maryland	YR	...	(f)	YR	YR/3	(f)
Massachusetts	YR	...	...	YR	...	...
Michigan	YR	...	...	YR	...	...
Minnesota	YR	...	...	(g)	YR/3	...
Mississippi	...	YR	...	...	SO	...
Missouri	YR	...	YR	SO	IO/6	...
Montana	...	...	...	...	...	...
Nebraska	YR	...	...	----------Unicameral----------		
Nevada	...	YR/3	...	...	YR/6	...
New Hampshire	...	SO/8	...	...	YR/30	...
New Jersey	YR(d)	...	(d)	YR(d)	...	(d)
New Mexico	SO	SO/3.5	...	SO	SO/7.5	...
New York	YR	...	YR	YR	...	YR
North Carolina	SO	...	...	SO	...	...
North Dakota	...	SO/10	...	...	SO/13	...
Ohio	YR	YR	...	...	YR/0.8	...
Oklahoma	SO	IO/5	...	SO	YR/2	...
Oregon	YR	...	(f)	YR	...	(f)
Pennsylvania	YR	...	YR	YR	...	YR
Rhode Island	...	YR/8	...	...	YR/7	...
South Carolina	YR	YR/2	...	...	YR/10	...
South Dakota	...	YR	...	...	YR	...
Tennessee	YR	...	YR	YR	...	...
Texas	YR	...	YR	YR	YR(c,h)	YR
Utah	...	SO/4	...	...	SO/4	...
Vermont	...	YR(c)	...	...	YR(c)	...
Virginia	YR	SO/2	YR	YR	SO/2	YR
Washington	YR(i)	YR/1	(i)	YR	YR/2	YR
West Virginia	SO	...	...	...	SO/20	...
Wisconsin	YR(i)	...	(i)	YR	...	...
Wyoming	...	SO(j)	...	...	SO(j)	...
American Samoa	...	...	...	...	...	...
Puerto Rico	YR	...	...	YR	...	...
Virgin Islands	YR	YR	YR	----------Unicameral----------		

Note: For entries under column heading "Shared," figure after slash indicates approximate number of legislators per staff person, where available.

Key:
...—Staff not provided for individual legislators.
YR—Year-round.
SO—Session only.
IO—Interim only.
(a) Permanent year-round staff and additional staff during sessions. Number of legislators for whom a single staff member will work varies from one staff member to another.
(b) Personal staff provided to leadership only (may include specific committee chairmen).
(c) Staff sizes are reduced during interim.
(d) Personal and district staff are the same.
(e) Majority and minority offices provide staff year-round. Number increases during session.

(f) Expense allowance may be used for staffing. Illinois—legislators may employ staff from district office allowance. Maryland—legislators may employ staff from discretionary funds in expense account. Oregon—biennial allowance may be used for session and/or interim staffing, depending on legislator's needs.
(g) Each committee chairman has a committee secretary and committee administrator. The secretary also serves as the primary administrative support person for the chairman on non-committee business.
(h) House research organization.
(i) Senators may choose to have some or all personal staff in a district office. In Wisconsin, the total of all employees' salaries for each senator must be within the limits established by the Senate.
(j) During sessions, legislators are served by temporary sessional staff; during interim period, by Legislative Service Office.

Table 3.18
STAFF FOR LEGISLATIVE STANDING COMMITTEES

| State or other jurisdiction | Committee staff assistance | | | | Source of staff services* | | | | | | | |
| | Senate | | House | | Joint central agency(a) | | Chamber agency(b) | | Caucus or leadership | | Committee or committee chairman | |
	Prof.	Cler.	Prof.	Cler.	Prof.	Cler.	Prof.	Cler.	Prof.	Cler.	Prof.	Cler.
Alabama	(c)	★	(c)	★	B						B	B
Alaska	★	★	★	★	B			B	B	B	B	B
Arizona	★	★	★	★	(d)		B	B	B		B	
Arkansas	★	★	★	★	B	B		B				
California	★	★	★	★			B	B				
Colorado	★	...	★	...	B							
Connecticut	★(e)	★(e)	★(e)	★(e)	(e)	(e)						
Delaware	(c)	★(f)	(c)	★(f)	B	B		B	B			
Florida	★	★	★	★							B	H
Georgia	★	★(f)	★	★(f)	B		S			B		
Hawaii	(g)	★	(g)	★	B	B	B	B	B	B	B	B
Idaho	(c)	★	(c)	★	B				B	B		
Illinois	★	★	★	★						S		
Indiana	★	★	★	...	B				B			
Iowa	★	★	★	★	B			B(h)	B			B(h)
Kansas	★	★	★	★	B	B		B		B		B
Kentucky	★	★	★	★	B	B						
Louisiana	★	★	★	★				B			B	B
Maine	★(e)	★(e)	★(e)	★(e)	(e)							(e)
Maryland	★	★	★	★	B							B
Massachusetts	★	★	★	★	B		B		B	B	B	B
Michigan	★	★	★	★				H	B		B	B
Minnesota	★	★	★	★							B	B
Mississippi	•	★	•	★	B	B					B	B
Missouri	(c,f)	★	(c,f)	★					B	B	B	B
Montana	★	★	★	★	B	B					U	U
Nebraska	★	★					U	U				
Nevada	(c)	★	(c)	★	B	B			H			
New Hampshire	•	★(f)	•	★(f)	B	B						
New Jersey	★	★	★	★	B	B						
New Mexico	•	★	•	★				B				
New York	★	★	★	★	B	B	B	B	B	B	B	B
North Carolina	•	★	•	★	B		B	B	B			
North Dakota	(c)	★	(c)	★	B			B				
Ohio	★	★	★	★	B				B	B		
Oklahoma	•	★	•	★			B	B			B	B
Oregon	★	★	★	★							B	B
Pennsylvania	★	★	★	★			B	B				
Rhode Island	★	★	★	★							B	B
South Carolina	•	★	•	★	B	B	B	B		B	B	B
South Dakota	★	★	★	★	B					B		B
Tennessee	★	★	★	★	B				B	B	S	B
Texas	★	★	★	★	B	B	B(f)			B	B	B
Utah	★	★	★	★	B					B		
Vermont	★	★	★	★	B	B						
Virginia	★	★	★	★	B			B				B(h)
Washington	★	★	★	★			B	B	B	B	B	B
West Virginia	★	★	★	★	B	B	B	B			B	B
Wisconsin	★	★	★	★	B			B				
Wyoming	★(f)	★	★(f)	★	B							
American Samoa	★(f)	...	★(f)	...	B							
Guam	★	★			B	U			U	U	B	U
Puerto Rico	★	★	★	★	B	U						U
Virgin Islands	★	★			U	U						

*Multiple entries reflect a combination of organizational location of services.

Key:
★—All committees
•—Some committees
...—No committees
B—Both chambers
H—House
S—Senate
U—Unicameral

(a) Includes legislative council or service agency or central management agency.
(b) Includes chamber management agency, office of clerk or secretary and House or Senate research office.
(c) Money committees only.
(d) Joint Legislative Budget Committee provides staff assistance to the fiscal committees of both houses.
(e) Standing committees are joint House and Senate committees.
(f) Provided on a pool basis.
(g) All professional committee staff (except Finance committees) during session only. During interim, assistance provided by year-round majority and minority research offices.
(h) The Senate secretary and House clerk maintain supervision of committee clerks. Iowa: during the session each committee selects its own clerk.

Table 3.19
STANDING COMMITTEES: APPOINTMENT AND NUMBER

State or other jurisdiction	Committee members appointed by:		Committee chairpersons appointed by:		Number of standing committees during regular 1987 session(a)	
	Senate	House	Senate	House	Senate	House
Alabama	P(b)	S	P(b)	S	17	24
Alaska...........	CC(c)	CC(c)	CC(c)	CC(c)	9(d)	9(d)
Arizona..........	P	S	P	S	11(d)	16(d)
Arkansas	CC	S	CC	S	10(d)	10(d)
California........	CR	S	CR	S	22(d)	26(d)
Colorado	MjL,MnL(e)	S,MnL(e)	MjL	S	11(d)	12(d)
Connecticut	PT	S	PT	S	(f)	(f)
Delaware	PT	S	PT	S	20(d)	20(d)
Florida	P	S	P	S	16(d)	28(d)
Georgia..........	P(b)	S	P(b)	S	24	28
Hawaii	P(g)	(h)	P(g)	(h)	20	17
Idaho	PT(i)	S	PT	S	11	14
Illinois...........	CC	S,MnL	P	S	18	25
Indiana	PT	S	PT	S	19	26
Iowa	P(b)	S	P(b)	S	15(d)	15(d)
Kansas	CC	S	CC	S	18(d)	21(d)
Kentucky	CC	CC	CC	CC	15	17
Louisiana	P	S	P	S	15	15
Maine	P	S	P	S	(f)	(f)
Maryland	P	S	P	S	9(d)	10(d)
Massachusetts	P	S	P	S	7(d)	6(d)
Michigan	MjL	S	MjL	S	15	30
Minnesota	(j)	S	(j)	S	18	21
Mississippi	P(b)	S	P(b)	S	28(d)	30(d)
Missouri	PT	S	PT	S	23(d)	49(d)
Montana.........	CC	S	CC	S	16	14
Nebraska(U)	CC		(k)		13	
Nevada	(l)	S(m)	MjL	S	9	13
New Hampshire ...	P	S	P	S	15(d)	23(d)
New Jersey.......	P	S	P	S	17(d)	27(d)
New Mexico.......	CC	S	CC	S	8	15
New York	PT(n)	S	PT(n)	S	32(d)	37(d)
North Carolina	P(b)	S	P(b)	S	35	58
North Dakota	CC	S	CC	S	15(d)	15(d)
Ohio	CC	S	CC	S	11	26
Oklahoma	PT(o)	S	PT	S	18(d)	28(d)
Oregon	P	S	P	S	14(d)	15(d)
Pennsylvania	PT	CC(p)	PT	S	20	21
Rhode Island	MjL	S	MjL	S	6(d)	6(d)
South Carolina	E(q)	S	E	E	18	11
South Dakota	(r)	S	(r)	S	13(d)	13(d)
Tennessee.........	S	S	S	S	9(d)	11(d)
Texas............	P(b)	S(s)	P(b)	S	12	34
Utah	P	S	P	S	10(d)	10(d)
Vermont..........	P(b)	S	P(b)	S	12(d)	15(d)
Virginia..........	E	S	(t)	S	11	20
Washington	P(b,u)	S(u)	(u)	S(u)	13	19
West Virginia	P	S	P	S	15(d)	13(d)
Wisconsin.........	(v)	S	(v)	S	14(d)	26(d)
Wyoming	P(w)	S(w)	P(w)	S(w)	12(d)	12(d)
Dist. of Col.(U) ...	(x)		(x)		11	
American Samoa ..	P,E	S,E	P	S	16	11
Guam(U)	(y)		E		10	
Puerto Rico	P	S	P	S	19(d)	22(d)
Virgin Islands(U) ..	P		P		9	

STANDING COMMITTEES: APPOINTMENT AND NUMBER—Continued

Note: Standing committees are those which regularly consider legislation during the legislative session.

Key:
CC—Committee on Committees
CR—Committee on Rules
E—Election
MjL—Majority leader
MnL—Minority leader
P—President
PT—President pro tempore
S—Speaker
(U)—Unicameral legislature
(a) Taken from state legislative rulebooks 1988, 1987, and 1986.
(b) Lieutenant governor is president of the Senate.
(c) Report of Committee on Committees is subject to approval by majority vote of chamber's membership.
(d) Also, joint standing committees. Alaska, 1; Arizona, 4; Arkansas, 4; California, 12; Colorado, 5; Delaware, 2; Florida, 2; Iowa, 1; Kansas, 6; Maryland, 2 (and 9 joint statutory); Massachusetts, 21; Mississippi, 6; Missouri, 5; New Hampshire, 5; New Jersey, 3; New York, 15; North Dakota, 1; Oklahoma, 3; Oregon, 4; Rhode Island, 8; South Dakota, 2; Tennessee, 1; Utah, 10; Vermont, 4; West Virginia, 2; Wisconsin, 7; Wyoming, 1; and Puerto Rico, 2.
(e) Minority leader appoints committee members from minority party.
(f) Substantive standing committees are joint committees. Connecticut, 20; Maine, 19.
(g) President appoints committee members and chairpersons; minority members on committees are nominated by minority party caucus.
(h) By resolution, with members of majority party designating the chairmen, vice-chairmen and majority party members of committees, and members of minority party designating minority party members.
(i) Committee members appointed by the Senate leadership under the direction of the president pro tempore, by and with the Senate's advice.
(j) Subcommittee on Committees of the Committee on Rules and Administration.
(k) Secret ballot by legislature as a whole.
(l) Committee composition and leadership usually determined by party caucus.
(m) For Committee on Ethics, minority leader appoints one member of minority party.
(n) President pro tempore is also majority leader.
(o) Minority floor leader appoints minority members of committees (subject to Senate approval).
(p) Committee on Committees recommends to House for approval the names of committee members.
(q) Seniority system is retained in process.
(r) Presiding officer announces committee membership after selection by president pro tempore, majority and minority leaders.
(s) A maximum of one-half of the membership on each standing committee, exclusive of the chair and vice chair, is determined by seniority; the remaining membership is appointed by the speaker.
(t) Senior member of the majority party on the committee is the chair.
(u) With majority caucus.
(v) Committee on Senate Organization.
(w) With the advice and consent of the Rules and Procedures Committee.
(x) Chairman of the Council.
(y) Chairman of each committee.

Table 3.20
STANDING COMMITTEES: PROCEDURE

State or other jurisdiction	Uniform rules of committee procedure			Open to public		Advance notice required (number of days)		Recorded roll call on vote to report bill to floor	
	Senate	House	Joint	Senate	House	Senate	House	Senate	House
Alabama	...	★		★	★	...	...	Al	Nv
Alaska	...	...		★	★	...	...	Sm	Sm
Arizona	...	★		★	★	5	(a)	Nv	Nv
Arkansas	★	★	★	★	★	2	2	Sm	Sm
California	★	★	★	★	★	4	4	Al	Al
Colorado	★	★		★	★	...	...	Al	Al
Connecticut	...	...	★	★(b)	★(b)	1	1	Al	Al
Delaware	★	★	...	★	★	(c)	(c)	Al	Al
Florida	★	★		★	★	7	2(d)	Al	Al
Georgia	...	...		★	★	...	...	Nv	Nv
Hawaii	★	★		★	★	2	2	Al	Al
Idaho	★	★		★	★	...	...	Us	Us
Illinois	★	★	...	★	★	6	6.5	Al	Al
Indiana	...	...		★	★	3	1	Al	Al
Iowa	★	★		★	★	...	...	Al	Al
Kansas	★	★		★	★	...	(c)	Sm	Sm
Kentucky	...	...		★	★	...	3	Al	Al
Louisiana	★	★		★	★	1(e)	1(e)	Sm	Al
Maine	...	...	★	★	★	(c)	(c)	Sm	Sm
Maryland	★	★		★	★	(c)	(c)	Al	Al
Massachusetts	...	...	...	★	★	...	...	Nv	Nv
Michigan	★	★		★	★	(f)	(f)	Al	Al
Minnesota	★	★	★	★	★	3	3	Sm	Sm
Mississippi	...	...	...	★	★	...	...	Sm	Sm
Missouri	★	★	★	★	★	1	1	Al	Al
Montana	...	...		★	★	(g)	(g)	Al	Al
Nebraska(U)	★			★		5-7		Al	
Nevada	★	★		★	★	(c)	5(h)	Al	Al
New Hampshire	...	★		★	★	3	3	Al	Al
New Jersey	★	★		★	★	5	5	Al	Al
New Mexico	...	...		★	★	...	...	Sm	Al
New York	★	★		★	★	7	7	Al	Al
North Carolina	...	...	...	★(b)	★(b)	(c)	(c)	Sm	Sm
North Dakota	...	...		★	★	(i)	(i)	Al	Al
Ohio	★	★		★	★	5	(c)	Al	Al
Oklahoma	★	★		★	★	(c)	(c)	Sm	Sm
Oregon	★	★		★	★	1(j)	1(k)	Al	Al
Pennsylvania	...	...		★	★	3	3	Al	Al
Rhode Island	★	★	★	★	★	...	...	Sm	Sm
South Carolina	★	★	★	★	★	1	1	Sm	Sm
South Dakota	★	★		★	★	2	2	Al	Al
Tennessee	★	★		★	★	(l)	(l)	Al	Sm
Texas	...	★		★	★	1	5	Sm	Al
Utah	★	★	★	★	★	1	1	Al	Al
Vermont	★	★	★	★	★	...	...	Sm	Sm
Virginia	★	★		★	★(m)	(c)	(c)	Al	Al
Washington	★	★		★	★	5	5	Sm	Sm
West Virginia	...	...		★	★	...	...	Sm	Sm
Wisconsin	★	★	★	★	★	7	7	Al	Al
Wyoming	...	...	...	★	★	...	...	Sm	Sm
American Samoa	...	...	...	★	★	(d)	1.5	Nv	Nv
Guam(U)	★			★(b)		7		Al	
Puerto Rico	★	★		★(b)	★	...	...	Nv	Nv
Virgin Islands(U)	★			★		7(n)		Us	

STANDING COMMITTEES: PROCEDURE—Continued

Key:
★—Yes
. . .—No
Al—Always
Us—Usually
Sm—Sometimes
Nv—Never
(U)—Unicameral legislature

(a) Rules: Thursday of previous week. Statute: 24 hours.

(b) Certain matters specified by statute can be discussed in executive session. Connecticut—upon a 2/3 vote of committee members present and voting and stating the reason for such executive session. North Carolina—appropriations committees are required to sit jointly in open session. Guam—hearings are open to the public, but meetings may be closed.

(c) No specified time. Kansas—"due notice" required by House rules. Maine—usually seven days notice given. Maryland—"from time to time," usually seven days. Nevada—"adequate notice." North Carolina—notice must be given in the House or Senate; two methods to waive notice in the Senate. Ohio—"due notice," usually seven days. Virginia—notice published in the daily calendar.

(d) During session—two days notice for first 45 days, two hours thereafter.

(e) One day during session, five days during interim.

(f) Committees meet on regular schedule during sessions. For rescheduled or special meetings 18 hours notice, unless legislature is adjourned or recessed for less than 18 hours.

(g) There is an informal agreement to give three days notice.

(h) Public hearings on bills or resolutions of "high public importance" must receive five calendar days notice. All other committee meetings must have 24 hours notice.

(i) Rules require posting of bills and resolutions to be considered at each meeting and provide deadlines for such posting depending upon the schedules for particular committees.

(j) Except in case of meeting to resolve conflicts or inconsistencies among two or more measures, in which case posting and notice to the public shall be given immediately upon call of the meeting, and notice of the meeting shall be announced on the floor if the Senate is in session.

(k) In case of actual emergency, a meeting may be held upon such notice as is appropriate to the circumstances.

(l) Committees meet on a fixed schedule during sessions. Five days notice required during interim.

(m) Committee meetings are required to be open for final vote on bill.

(n) Advance notice may be waived if the committee determines there is cause to conduct a meeting sooner. In that case, notice must be given at least 48 hours in advance. Items on the agenda may be considered by unanimous consent.

Table 3.21
LEGISLATIVE APPROPRIATIONS PROCESS:
BUDGET DOCUMENTS AND BILLS

	Budget document submission							Budget bill introduction		
	Legal source of deadline		Submission date relative to convening							
State or other jurisdiction	Consti-tutional	Statutory	Prior to session	Within one week	Within two weeks	Within one month	Over one month	Same time as budget document	Another time	Not until committee review of budget document
Alabama............	...	★	...	2nd day	...	...	...	★	...	...
Alaska............	...	★	...	★	...	...	...	★	...	...
Arizona...........	...	★	...	★	...	...	...	...	...	(a)
Arkansas..........	...	...	...	...	(b)	...	...	...	...	★
California........	★	...	...	...	...	...	(c)	★	...	...
Colorado	...	★	...	...	★(d)	...	...	...	...	★
Connecticut	...	★	...	...	...	★(e)	...	...	...	...
Delaware	...	★	...	...	...	Feb. 1	...	★(f)	...	...
Florida	...	★	30 days	...	...	...	...	...	...	★(g)
Georgia...........	★	...	...	★	...	...	...	★	...	...
Hawaii	...	★	20 days	...	...	...	...	...	★	...
Idaho	...	★	...	★	...	...	...	...	...	★
Illinois..........	...	★	...	...	...	...	★	...	★	...
Indiana...........	...	★	7 days(h)	...	...	...	...	★	...	...
Iowa	...	★	...	...	...	★	...	...	...	★(g)
Kansas	...	★	...	...	...	★(e)	...	...	★(i)	...
Kentucky	...	...	...	...	...	...	(j)	★	(k)	...
Louisiana	...	★	...	1st day	...	...	...	...	...	...
Maine	...	★	...	...	★(l)	...	...	★	...	...
Maryland	★	...	...	★(l)	...	...	...	★(m)	...	...
Massachusetts ...	★	...	...	...	...	★(l)	...	★(a)	...	...
Michigan	...	★	...	...	★(n)	...	...	★	...	...
Minnesota	...	★	...	...	...	★	...	...	...	★
Mississippi	...	★	Dec. 15	...	...	...	...	...	...	★
Missouri	★	...	...	...	...	★	...	★	...	...
Montana..........	...	★	...	1st day	...	...	...	...	★	...
Nebraska	...	★	...	★	...	...	...	...	...	★(f)
Nevada	...	★	...	★	...	...	...	...	...	★
New Hampshire .	...	★	...	...	...	...	★	...	...	★
New Jersey......	...	★	...	...	...	★(l)	...	...	...	★
New Mexico.....	...	★	...	(o)	...	...	...	★	...	...
New York	★	...	...	...	★(l)	...	...	★(p)	...	...
North Carolina ..	...	...	...	(b)	...	...	...	★	...	...
North Dakota ...	...	★	...	3rd day(q)	...	...	...	★	...	...
Ohio	...	★	...	...	...	★(l)	...	★	...	...
Oklahoma	...	★	...	★	...	...	...	★	...	...
Oregon	...	★	Dec. 1(l)	...	...	...	...	★	...	...
Pennsylvania	...	★	...	...	...	...	★(l,r)	...	...	★
Rhode Island	...	★	...	...	...	...	(s)	★	...	...
South Carolina ..	...	★	1st Tues. in Jan.	...	...	...	...	...	...	★
South Dakota ...	...	★	Dec. 1	...	...	...	...	...	...	★
Tennessee	...	★	...	...	★(l)	...	...	★	...	...
Texas............	...	★	...	★	...	...	...	★	...	...
Utah	...	★	(t)	...	★(e)	...	...	...	...	★
Vermont	...	★	...	...	...	★	...	...	...	★
Virginia..........	...	★	...	★	...	...	...	★	...	...
Washington	...	★	Dec. 20	...	...	...	...	★	★	...
West Virginia ...	★	...	...	1st day(l)	...	...	...	★	...	...
Wisconsin	...	...	...	...	...	★(u)	...	★	...	...
Wyoming	...	★	Jan. 1	...	...	...	...	...	...	★
American Samoa .	...	...	(b)	...	...	...	...	...	★	...
Guam	...	★	...	...	...	★	...	★	...	...
Puerto Rico	★	...	...	...	...	...	...	...	...	★
Virgin Islands ...	...	★	...	...	...	★(v)	...	★	...	...

LEGISLATIVE APPROPRIATIONS PROCESS—Continued

Key:
★—Yes
. . .—No

(a) General appropriations bill only.

(b) By custom only. No statutory or constitutional provisions.

(c) Session begins in December. Within the first 10 days of each calendar year.

(d) Copies of agency budgets to be presented to the legislature by November 1. Governor's budget usually is presented in January.

(e) Even year. Connecticut—first day; Kansas—second day; Utah—first day.

(f) Executive budget bill is introduced and used as working tool for committee. Delaware: after hearings on executive bill, a new bill is then introduced. The committee bill is considered by the legislature.

(g) Executive submits bill, but it is not introduced; used as a working tool by committee.

(h) Budget document submitted prior to session does not necessarily reflect budget message which is given sometime during the first three weeks of session.

(i) Within one month for most bills; however, some are introduced later.

(j) No set time.

(k) Subject to same 15-day limit as other bills.

(l) Later for first session of a new governor. Maine—six weeks; Maryland—10 days; Massachusetts—two months; New Jersey—February 15;

New York—February 1; Ohio—March 16; Oregon—February 1; Pennsylvania—first full week in March; Tennessee—March 1; West Virginia—one month.

(m) Appropriations bills other than the budget bill (supplementary) may be introduced at any time. They must provide their own tax source and may not be enacted until the budget bill is enacted.

(n) Long-range capital budget: 30 days.

(o) Statutes provide for submission by 25th legislative day; however, the executive budget is usually presented by the first day of the session. The legislative budget is usually presented on the first day or at the pre-legislative session conference of the standing finance committees.

(p) Governor has 30 days to amend or complete submission bills which enact the recommendations contained in this executive budget, computed from the designated submission date for the budget.

(q) For whole legislature. The Legislative Council only receives budget on December 1.

(r) Submitted by governor as soon as possible after General Assembly organizes, but not later than the first full week in February.

(s) Twenty-fourth legislative day.

(t) Must submit to fiscal analyst 30 days prior to session.

(u) Last Tuesday in January. A later submission date may be requested by the governor.

(v) Organic Act specifies at opening of each regular session; statute specifies on or before May 30.

Table 3.22
FISCAL NOTES: CONTENT AND DISTRIBUTION

	Content						Distribution — Legislators			Appropriations committee			
State or other jurisdiction	Intent or purpose of bill	Cost involved	Projected future cost	Proposed source of revenue	Fiscal impact on local government	Other	All	Available on request	Bill sponsor	Members	Chairman only	Fiscal staff	Executive budget staff
Alabama	...	★	...	★	★(a)		★(b)	...	...	...	...	...	...
Alaska	...	★	★	★(c)	...		★(d)	...	...	...	...	...	...
Arizona	...	★	★	★	★		★	...	...	...	...	...	...
Arkansas	(e)	(e)	(e)	...	(e)		(e)	...	...	...	...	★	★
California	★	★	★	★	★		★	...	...	...	...	★	★
Colorado	★	★	★	★	★		★	...	...	...	...	...	...
Connecticut	...	★	★	...	★		★	...	...	...	...	★	...
Delaware	...	★	★	...	...	★(f)	...	★	...	★	...	★	★
Florida	★	★	★	★	★	★(g)	★	...	...	...	...	★	★
Georgia	...	★	★	★	★		...	★	...	...	...	...	...
Hawaii													
Idaho	★	★	★	★(h)	★		★	...	...	...	...	...	...
Illinois	...	★	★	★	★	(i)	...	★(j)	★(j)	...	...	...	...
Indiana	★	★	★	★	★		★	...	...	...	...	★	★
Iowa	...	★	★	★	★		★	...	...	...	...	...	...
Kansas	★	★	★	★	★		...	★	...	...	★(k)	★	...
Kentucky	★	★	★	★	...		...	★	★	★	...	★	...
Louisiana	...	★	★	...	★		...	★	★	...	...	★(l)	...
Maine	...	★	★	...	...		★	...	...	...	...	★	...
Maryland	★	★	★	★	★		...	★	★	★(k)	...	★	★
Massachusetts	...	★(m)	...	...	...		★	★	...	...	...	★	...
Michigan	★	★	★	★	★	★(n)	★(o)	★	...	...	...	★	...
Minnesota	★	★	★	★	★		...	★	★	★	...	★	...
Mississippi	★	★	★	...	★		...	★	...	...	★	...	...
Missouri	...	★	★	★	★		★	...	...	...	...	...	...
Montana	★(p)	★	★	★	★	★(g)	★	...	...	...	...	...	...
Nebraska	...	★	★	★	★		★	...	...	...	...	★	★
Nevada	★	★	★	★	★		★	...	...	...	...	★	★
New Hampshire	★	★	★	★	★		★	...	...	...	...	★	★
New Jersey	★	★	★	...	★	★	★(q)	...	...	...	...	★	★
New Mexico	★	★	★	...	(h)	★(r)	...	(s)	...	...	★(s)	...	...
New York	★	★(t)	...	...	★		...	★	★	★	...	★	...
North Carolina	★	★	★	...	★	★(u)	...	★	★	...	★	★	...
North Dakota	★	★	★(v)	★	...		...	★	...	...	★	★	...
Ohio	★	★	★	...	...		★(w)	★	★	★	...	★	...
Oklahoma													
Oregon	...	★	★	★	★		★	...	...	...	...	...	...
Pennsylvania	...	★	★	★	★	★(i)	★	...	...	...	...	★	★
Rhode Island	...	★	★	...	★	★(x)	...	★	...	★	...	★	★
South Carolina	...	★	★	...	...		...	★	★	...	...	...	...
South Dakota	...	★	★	★	★		...	★	...	...	...	...	...
Tennessee	★	★	★	★	★	★(y)	...	...	...	...	...	★	★
Texas	...	★	★	★	★		...	★	★	★(k)	...	...	★
Utah	...	★	★	★	★		★	...	...	...	...	...	...
Vermont	★	★	★	★			...	★	...	...	★	...	...
Virginia	★	★	★	★(z)	...	★	...	★	★	★	...	...	...
Washington	★	★	★	★	★		...	★	...	...	...	★	★
West Virginia	★	★	★	★	★(aa)		★	...	...	...	...	...	...
Wisconsin	...	★	★	★	★		★	...	...	...	...	...	...
Wyoming	...	★	★	★	★		★	...	...	...	...	...	...
American Samoa													
Guam	★	★	★	★	★		★	...	...	...	...	★	★
Puerto Rico	...	★	...	...	★		★	...	...	...	...	...	...
Virgin Islands	★	★	...	★	...		★	...	...	...	...	...	...

FISCAL NOTES: CONTENT AND DISTRIBUTION—Continued

Key:

★—Yes

. . .—No

(a) Senate only.

(b) Fiscal notes are included in bills for final passage calendar.

(c) Contained in the bill, not in the fiscal note.

(d) Fiscal notes are attached to the bill before it is reported to the Rules Committee. Governor's bills must have fiscal note before introduction.

(e) Required on retirement and local government bills and distributed to all legislators.

(f) Relevant data and prior fiscal year cost information.

(g) Mechanical defects in bill and effective date.

(h) Occasionally.

(i) Bill proposing changes in retirement system of state or local government must have an actuarial note.

(j) A summary of the fiscal note is attached to the summary of the relevant bill in the Legislative Synopsis and Digest. Fiscal notes are prepared for the sponsor of the bill and are attached to the bill on file in either the office of the clerk of the House or the secretary of the Senate.

(k) Or to committee to which referred.

(l) Prepared by Legislative Fiscal Office; copies sent to House and Senate staff offices respectively.

(m) Fiscal notes are prepared only if cost exceeds $100,000 or matter has not been acted upon by the Joint Committee on Ways and Means.

(n) Other revelant data.

(o) Analyses prepared by Senate Fiscal Agency, distributed to Senate members only; analyses prepared by House Fiscal Agency, distributed to House members only.

(p) Comment or opinion on the merits of the bills is prohibited.

(q) Sponsor may disapprove fiscal note; if disapproved, fiscal note is not printed or distributed.

(r) Impact of revenue bills reviewed by Legislative Council Service and executive agencies.

(s) Legislative Finance Committee staff prepared fiscal notes for Appropriations Committee chairman; other fiscal impact statements prepared by Legislative Council Service and executive agencies are available to anyone upon request.

(t) Rules of the Assembly require sponsors' memoranda to include estimate of cost to state and/or local government. Fiscal note required by law to be included on all pension bills.

(u) Fiscal note required in Senate. In House, staff prepares a summary.

(v) A two-year projection.

(w) If a bill comes up for floor consideration.

(x) Technical or mechanical defects may be noted.

(y) Effects of revenue bills.

(z) The Department of Taxation prepares revenue impact notes including the intent and revenue impact.

(aa) House of Delegates only.

Table 3.23
LEGISLATIVE REVIEW OF ADMINISTRATIVE REGULATIONS:
STRUCTURES AND PROCEDURES

State	Type of reviewing committee	All rules reviewed	Time limits for submission of rules for review
Alabama............	Joint	★	60 days
Alaska.............	Joint	★	45 days
Arizona............	(a)	(b)	Must have attorney general certification and filed with secretary of state
Arkansas	Joint	★	10 days before agency hearing
California	--(a)--		
Colorado	Joint	(c)	20 days after approval by attorney general
Connecticut	Joint bipartisan	★	After approval by attorney general
Delaware	--(a)--		
Florida	Joint statutory	★	21 days
Georgia............	Standing cmtes.	★	30 days
Hawaii	(d)	(c)	None
Idaho	Standing cmtes. & germane jt. sub-cmtes.	★	Beginning of each session or upon adoption
Illinois.............	Joint bipartisan	★	45 days
Indiana	Joint bipartisan	(e)	
Iowa	Joint	★	35 days(f)
Kansas	Joint	★	By Dec. 15 of each year
Kentucky	Joint subcmte.	★	None(g)
Louisiana	Standing cmtes.	★	15 days before adoption(h)
Maine	Joint standing cmtes.	(i)	20 days or within 10 days following adoption of an emergency rule
Maryland	Joint standing cmtes.(j)	★	30 days before proposal (publication), 45 days from proposal to adoption
Massachusetts	Joint standing cmtes.(j)	. . .	None(k)
Michigan	Joint	★	Within 2 years of last public hearing
Minnesota	Joint bipartisan	★(l)	None
Mississippi	--(a)--		
Missouri	Joint	★	None (prefer to review proposed rules; 30 day limit)
Montana	Joint	★	None
Nebraska	Standing cmtes.	★	None
Nevada	Joint	★	30 days before agency hearing
New Hampshire	Joint	★	120 days to file final text
New Jersey..........	--(a)--		
New Mexico.........	--(a)--		
New York	Joint	★	45 days before adoption
North Carolina	--(a,m)--		
North Dakota	Joint interim	★	None
Ohio	Joint	(n)	60 days before adoption
Oklahoma	Independent Regulatory Review Commission & standing cmtes.	★	10 days after adoption
Oregon	Joint	(o)	Within 10 days after filing adopted rule with secretary of state
Pennsylvania	Administrative review cmte. & standing cmtes.	★	None
Rhode Island	--(a,p)--		
South Carolina	Standing cmtes.	★	None(q)
South Dakota	Joint interim	★	10 days before regular rules become effective; 3 days before emergency rules become effective
Tennessee	Standing cmtes.(r)	★	45 days before effective date
Texas..............	--(a)--		
Utah	Joint bipartisan	★	30 days before effective date
Vermont	Joint	★	30 days after filing with legis. cmte. and secretary of state
Virginia............	Standing cmtes.	★	60 days before public hearing
Washington	Joint	★	Immediately upon filing with code revisor
West Virginia	Joint	★	None
Wisconsin	Joint(s)	★	None
Wyoming	Joint	★	60 days before filing

Note: Even though a state legis. may not have a formal mechanism in place to take action on admin. rules and reg., rules could be submitted and standing cmtes. could review on an informal basis. In some states, the courts' determinations that statutes providing for formal legis. rev. of admin. rules were unconstitutional led the legis. to reenact or revise those procedures. Consult annotated state statutes and court actions for more details.

Key:
★—Yes
. . .—No
(a) No formal mechanism for legislative review of administrative rules.
(b) Only for legis. review of those rules promulgated by State Parks Board.
(c) Reviews rules when adopted, amended, or repealed.
(d) Review is by office of legislative auditor which submits reports to the legislature for appropriate action.
(e) Rules are not routinely submitted for review.
(f) Published in Iowa Administrative Code 35 days prior to adoption.
(g) Legislation passed in 1986 states that all regulations shall expire 90 days after the adjournment of the next General Assembly. Those regs. that an admin. body wishes to remain in effect must be enacted into the statutes.
(h) Thirty days before the regular session, agencies must submit an annual report to the legislature on all rules adopted over the previous year.

(i) Legislation pending on whether all rules are reviewed.
(j) Joint standing committees have the power but are not exercising it as a practical matter.
(k) Except in selected statutory provisions for particular rules.
(l) Commission reviews only those rules brought to its attention by specific complaints.
(m) The Rules Commission is an Executive Branch Agency, however the members are appointed by the General Assembly, and reports on action are made to the General Assembly when there is an objection to a rule.
(n) Certain rules exempt from review.
(o) Cmte. may review or may direct the legis. counsel to review a rule. Review is not automatic.
(p) Auditor reviews rules, is empowered by General Assembly.
(q) But rule cannot go into effect until 90 days after submission. During interim, emergency regs. can be issued with an immediate effective date.
(r) House and Senate Government Operations committees.
(s) All standing committees review proposed rules. If there is an objection, it is referred to the Joint Committee for Review of Administrative Rules. The joint committee can review all existing rules.

Table 3.24
LEGISLATIVE REVIEW OF ADMINISTRATIVE REGULATIONS: POWERS

State	Reviewing committee's powers:				Legislative powers:		
	Review of proposed rules	Review of existing rules	No objection constitutes approval of proposed rule	Committee may suspend rule	Legislature must sustain committee action	Time limit for legislative action	Legislature can amend or modify rule
Alabama	★	★	★	★	★	End of regular session	...
Alaska	★	★	★	★	★	30 days after convening of regular session	...
Arizona	——————(a)——————						
Arkansas	★	★	...	...	——(a)——		...
California	——————(a)——————						
Colorado	...	★	...	...	(b)	(b)	★(c)
Connecticut	★	★	★	★	——(a)——		
Delaware	——————(a)——————						
Florida	★	★	...	...	...		...
Georgia	★	...	★	...	...	30 days after convening of regular session	...
Hawaii	(d)	★	...	...	...	End of regular session	...
Idaho	★	★	★	...	★	150 days	★
Illinois	★	★	★	★	★		
Indiana	(e)	★	...	...	★	End of regular session	...
Iowa	★	★	★	★	★	End of regular session	...
Kansas	★	★	...	...	(f)		...
Kentucky	★	★	★	...	...		...
Louisiana	★	★	★	★(g)	...		★
Maine	★	★	★	★(h)	...		...
Maryland	★(i)	★	★(i)	...	★	Practices vary	...
Massachusetts	★(i)	★	...	...	(l)	(m)	...
Michigan	★	...	(j)	(k)	(o)	End of next regular session	...
Minnesota	(n)	★	...	★	...		...
Mississippi	——————(a)——————						
Missouri	★	★	...	★	...	None	★
Montana	★	★	...	...	★	Next regular session	...
Nebraska	...	★	...	...	★	30 session days	...
Nevada	★	...	★	(p)	★		...
New Hampshire	★	★	★	(q)	...		...
New Jersey	——————(a)——————						
New Mexico	——————(a)——————						
New York	★	★	★	...	...		...
North Carolina	——————(a,r,s)——————						
North Dakota	...	★	★	...	★	60 days	...
Ohio	★	...	★	★	★	30 legislative days	...
Oklahoma	★	★	★	...	...		...
Oregon	★	...	★	...	...		...
Pennsylvania	(n)	★(t)	...	...	...	20 days for proposed regulations from date published in Pennsylvania Bulletin	...
Rhode Island	——————(a,u)——————						
South Carolina	★	...	★	...	★	Next regular session	...
South Dakota	★	★	★	★	★	End of next regular session	★
Tennessee	★	★	★	★	...		...
Texas	——————(a)——————						
Utah	★	★	...	...	...		...
Vermont	★	★	★	...	...	End of regular session	...
Virginia	★	...	★	...	...		...
Washington	★	★	★	(v)	...		★
West Virginia	★	★	...	...	★	End of session	...
Wisconsin	★	★	...	★	★	End of next regular session	★(w)
Wyoming	★	★	...	...	★		...

Note: See note Table 3.23.

Key:
★—Yes
...—No

(a) No formal mechanism for legislative review of administrative rules.

(b) It is not mandatory for legislature to approve or disapprove committee action. However, disapproval of a rule implementing a federally subsidized program must be sustained by legislature before end of the regular session or committee's action is reversed.

(c) Committee may disapprove a part of a rule.

(d) Reviews rules when adopted, amended, or repealed.

(e) Committee shall receive and may review complaints regarding an agency rule or practice. Committee may also review an agency rule or practice on its own motion, and may recommend that a rule be modified, repealed, or adopted.

(f) Legislation passed in 1986 states that all regulations shall expire 90 days after the adjournment of the next General Assembly. Those regulations that an administrative body wishes to remain in effect must be enacted into the statutes.

(g) If committee determines that rule is unacceptable, it submits a report to the governor. The governor has five days to accept or reject the report.

(h) May suspend for 30 days.

(i) Provided in statute for certain rules but not others.

(j) Committee must approve rules before they take effect.

(k) Committee may suspend rules during interim only, if granted authorization to do so by legislature.

(l) Legislature may overrule committee disapproval of rules by passing a Joint Resolution adopting the rules.

(m) Legislature has 60 days to pass a Joint Resolution approving rules which the commitee has disapproved.

(n) Some rules may be submitted for "review and comment."

(o) Yes, if the commission action is to suspend a rule; otherwise its recommendations are self-executing.

(p) Constitutional amendment pending 3-88 authorizing legislation review of regulations.

(q) Committee may object to rule. Rule may be adopted over committee objection, but committee can shift burden of proof to agency.

(r) Committee abolished.

(s) The Rules Commission is an Executive Branch Agency, however the members are appointed by the General Assembly, and reports on actions are made to the General Assembly when there is an objection to a rule.

(t) Then recommendation goes to existing Agency.

(u) Auditor is empowered by legislature to review rules.

(v) By a two-third's vote, the committee may request the governor to approve suspension of a rule upon which the committee has made an adverse finding. If suspended, the rule must be stayed until 90 days following the next legislative session.

(w) For a proposed rule, the Legislature can amend or modify with the agreement of the promulgating Agency. However it cannot do so for an existing rule.

Table 3.25
SUMMARY OF SUNSET LEGISLATION

State or other jurisdiction	Scope	Preliminary evaluation conducted by	Other legislative review	Other oversight mechanisms in bill	Phase-out period	Life of each agency (in years)	Other provisions
Alabama.........	C	Select Jt. Cmte.	Dept. of Examiners of Public Accounts	Zero-base budgeting	180/d	4	1-hour time limit on floor debate on each bill.
Alaska............	R	Standing cmtes.	...	Perf. audit	1/y	Varies (usually 4)	Specific programs authorized for termination by Legis. Budget & Audit Cmte.
Arizona..........	C	Off. of the Auditor General	Committees of reference appointed at beginning of legislative term	Perf. audit	(a)	10	1984 legislation allows Jt. Legis. Oversight Cmte. to establish priorities for and reschedule sunset audits. Cmte. may also request special performance audits not required by sunset schedule.
Arkansas	(b)	...	...	...	...	...	...
California	(c)	...	...	...	...	...	...
Colorado	C	Dept. of Regulatory Agencies reports to Joint Legis. Sunrise & Sunset Cmte. by July 1, preceding year of termination	Standing cmtes.	Perf. audit	1/y	10	There also is legislation requiring a study of 20 principal depts. of state government on a schedule concluding in 1994.
Connecticut	R(d)	Legis. Prog. Review & Investigations Cmte.	Govt. Admin. & Elections Cmte.	Perf. audit	1/y	5	...
Delaware	C	Agencies under review submit report to Del. Sunset Comm. based on criteria for review and set forth in statute. Comm. staff conducts separate review	...	Perf. audit	Dec. 31 of next succeeding calendar year	4	Yearly Sunset Review schedules must include at least 9 agencies. If the number automatically scheduled for review or added by the General Assembly is less than a full schedule, additional agencies shall be added in order of their appearance in the Del. Code to complete the review schedule.
Florida	R	Appropriate substantive cmte. shall begin review 15 months prior to repeal date	...	...	1/y	10	Provides for periodic review of limitations on the initial entry into a profession, occupation, business, industry, or other endeavor.

Key:
C—Comprehensive
R—Regulatory
S—Selective
D—Discretionary
d—day
m—month
y—year

SUNSET LEGISLATION—Continued

State or other jurisdiction	Scope	Preliminary evaluation conducted by	Other legislative review	Other oversight mechanisms in bill	Phase-out period	Life of each agency (in years)	Other provisions
Georgia	R	Dept. of Audits	Standing Cmtes.	Perf. audit	1/y	1-6	A performance audit of each regulatory agency must be conducted at least once every 6 years.
Hawaii	R	Legis. Auditor	Consumer Protection Cmte. of each house	...	None	6	Proposed new regulatory measures must be referred to the Auditor for sunrise analysis.
Idaho				———No program———			
Illinois	(e)	...	Off. of Auditor General; standing cmtes. of each house	...	...	...	...
Indiana	C	Off. of Fiscal Review	Interim Legislative Cmtes.	Governor submits recommendations	None(f)		Each newly-established agency subject to termination with 10-year life span. Agencies established by exec. order, terminate when a Governor leaves office. Agencies established by concurrent resolution by General Assembly terminate after adjournment of the 2nd session.
Iowa	(c)	...	...	...	...	...	...
Kansas	R(d)	Standing cmtes. of each house	Legis. Post Audit, if directed by legislative cmte., or Legis. Post Audit Cmte.	Perf. audit	1/y	Subject to legislative discretion	Act terminates in July 1992 unless reenacted.
Kentucky				———No program———			
Louisiana	C	Standing cmtes. of the two houses which have usual jurisdiction over the affairs of the entity. Process begins 2 years prior to the termination date	Bill authorizing re-creation referred to cmte. performing initial review	Zero budget review (g)	1/y	9	Standing cmtes. may conduct a more extensive evaluation of selected statutory entities under their jurisdiction or of particular programs of such entities.
Maine	C	Off. of Fiscal & Prog. Review	...	Perf. eval.	1/y	10	Performance reviews also scheduled for executive departments (no terminations).
Maryland	R	Dept. of Fiscal Services	Standing cmtes.	...	None	10	Sunset cycle was completed in 1983 and will resume again in 1989.
Massachusetts				———No program———			

Key:
C—Comprehensive
R—Regulatory
S—Selective
D—Discretionary
d—day
m—month
y—year

SUNSET LEGISLATION—Continued

State or other jurisdiction	Scope	Preliminary evaluation conducted by	Other legislative review	Other oversight mechanisms in bill	Phase-out period	Life of each agency (in years)	Other provisions
Michigan	(c)	...	...	...	...	...	...
Minnesota	(c)	...	...	...	...	...	...
Mississippi	S	Jt. Cmte. on Performance Evaluation and Expenditure Review	...	...	...	...	Sunset Act terminated Dec. 31, 1984.
Missouri				----No program----			
Montana	D	Legis. Audit Cmte.	Standing cmtes.	...	1/y	...	Prior to each legislative session, the Governor may recommend by September 1 a prioritized list of agencies for review to the Legis. Audit Cmte. who must then introduce legislation before a review can occur.
Nebraska	(h)	...	...	...	...	...	...
Nevada	(i)	...	...	...	...	...	...
New Hampshire	(j)	...	...	...	...	...	...
New Jersey	(c)	...	...	...	...	...	...
New Mexico	R	Legis. Finance Cmte.	...	...	(a)	6	Legis. Finance Cmte. is responsible for introducing legislation to continue any agency reviewed.
New York				----No program----			
North Carolina	(k)	...	...	...	...	...	...
North Dakota				----No program----			
Ohio	(c)	...	...	...	...	...	...
Oklahoma	R	Jt. Cmte. on Sunset Review	Standing cmtes.	...	1/y	6	Rules & regulations of terminated agencies continue in effect unless terminated by law; includes agencies established by exec. order.
Oregon	R	Interim cmte.	Standing cmtes.	...	None	8	...
Pennsylvania	S	Legis. Budget and Finance Cmte.	Standing cmtes.	Perf. eval.	6/m	10	...
Rhode Island	C	Auditor General	Auditor General	Zero-base budgeting	1/y	(m)	Oversight Comm. established to conduct sunset reviews.

Key:
C—Comprehensive
R—Regulatory
S—Selective
D—Discretionary
d—day
m—month
y—year

SUNSET LEGISLATION—Continued

State or other jurisdiction	Scope	Preliminary evaluation conducted by	Other legislative review	Other oversight mechanisms in bill	Phase-out period	Life of each agency (in years)	Other provisions
South Carolina	R	Legis. Audit Council	Reorganization Comm.; standing cmtes.	Perf. audit	1/y	6	...
South Dakota	S	Special interim cmte.	Legis. Research Council	Perf. audit	180/d	10	The sunset review cycle pertains only to an agency's administrative rules. Only through legislation can an agency be terminated.
Tennessee	C	Special evaluation cmte. in each house	State Auditor	Perf. audit	1/y	8	Establishment of new agencies subject to review by Govt. Operations cmtes. of each house.
Texas	C	Sunset Advisory Comm.	...	Perf. eval.	1/y	12	Initial review conducted by agencies themselves.
Utah	R	Interim study cmte.	Off. of Legis. Research & General Counsel	Interim cmte.'s discretion	1/y	Varies (usually not more than 10)	Legis. Audit Cmte. may at its discretion coordinate the audit of state agencies with the interim cmte's sunset review.
Vermont	R	Legis. Council staff	Standing cmtes.	...	None	13	...
Virginia	(n)	...	...	...	...	...	...
Washington	C	Legis. Budget Cmte.	Standing cmtes.	Prog. review	1/y	(m)	Select jt. cmte. prepares termination legislation.
West Virginia	S	Jt. Cmte. on Govt. Operations	Legis. Post Audit Div.	Perf. audit	1/y	6	Jt. Cmte. on Govt. Operations composed of 5 House members, 5 Senate members & 5 citizens appointed by Governor. Agencies may be reviewed more frequently.
Wisconsin	(c)	...	...	...	...	...	...
Wyoming	S	Legis. Service Office	11-mbr. joint cmte.	...	1/y	Subject to legislative discretion	Every 2 years, the legislature selects a group of agencies to undergo sunset review.

Key:
C—Comprehensive
R—Regulatory
S—Selective
D—Discretionary
d—day
m—month
y—year

(a) Agency termination is scheduled on July 1 of the year prior to the scheduled termination of statutory authority for that agency.
(b) Arkansas' sunset law terminated on June 30, 1983.
(c) While they have not enacted sunset legislation in the same sense as the other states with detailed information in this table, the legislatures in California, Iowa, Michigan, Minnesota, New Jersey, Ohio, and Wisconsin have included sunset clauses in selected programs.
(d) Primarily.
(e) Illinois sunset law remains on the books but without any staff support since summer 1985.
(f) Through an executive order, the governor may provide a terminated agency with one year to wind up its affairs.

(g) Louisiana no longer uses zero based budgeting, but the sunset law has not been revised.
(h) Nebraska's Sunset Act terminated in 1985.
(i) Nevada law provided for a one-cycle pilot program under which three agencies were reviewed in 1980. No further expansion of the law has been enacted.
(j) New Hampshire's Sunset Committee was sunsetted July 1, 1987.
(k) North Carolina's sunset law terminated on July 30, 1981. Successor vehicle, The Legislative Cmte. on Agency Review, operated until June 30, 1983.
(l) Joint Committee on Sunset Review makes a recommendation by drafting legislation to either recreate or sunset an agency. Sunset bills are then assigned to standing commitees of the two houses which have usual jurisdiction over the affairs of the agency.
(m) Subject to legislative discretion.
(n) By joint resolution, Senate and House of Delegates establish a schedule for review of "functional areas" of state government. Program evaluation is carried out by Joint Legislative Audit and Review Commission. Agencies are not scheduled for automatic termination. Commission reports are made to standing committees which conduct public hearings.

Table 3.26
LEGISLATIVE ACTIVITIES PERFORMED WITH THE USE OF COMPUTERS

State or other jurisdiction	Statutory, bill systems, legal applications							Fiscal, budget, economic applications											Legislative management			
	Statutory retrieval	Bill drafting	Bill status report	Statutory revision	Case law retrieval	Redistricting	Other	Revenue forecasting	Revenue analysis	Budget comparison	Budget effects of legislation	Fiscal notes	Local fiscal notes	Economic impact note	Impact of salary and fringe changes	State aid formulas	Tracking federal dollars	Other	Computer printing	Legislative accounting	Mailing lists	Other
Alabama	★	★	★	★		★		★	★	★		★	★		★	★			★	★		
Alaska	★	★	★	★				★	★	★					★		★		★			
Arizona	★	★	★												★							
Arkansas	★(a)	★	★	★	★(a)	★	★(a)										★(a)		★	★	★	
California																						(b,c)
Colorado	★	★	★	★	★		★	★	★	★	★	★	★		★	★	★		★	★	★	
Connecticut	★	★	★	★		★		★	★	★	★	★	★	★	★	★	★		★	★	★	
Delaware	★	★	★	★						★									★	★	★	
Florida	★	★	★	★	★	★		★	★	★	★	★		★	★	★	★		★	★	★	
Georgia	★	★	★	★		★		★	★	★	★	★	★	★	★	★	★		★	★	★	
Hawaii	★	★	★							★	★			D.A.								(e)
Idaho	★	★	★	DA			(d)			★	★									★	★	(f)
Illinois	★	★	★	★				★	★	★	★	★	★		★	★	★		★	★	★	
Indiana	★	★	★	★		★		★	★	★	★	★	★		★	★	★			★	★	
Iowa	★	★	★	★	★	★		★	★	★	★	★	★		★	★	★		★	★	★	
Kansas	★	★	★	★			(g,h)	★	★	★	★	★	★	★	★	★	★		★	★	★	(i,j)
Kentucky	★	★	★	★	★	★		★	★	★	★	★	★	★	★	★	★		★	★	★	
Louisiana	★	★	★	★												★			★	★	★	
Maine	★	★	★	★	★	★		★	★	★	★	★			★	★	★		★	★	★	
Maryland	★	★	★	★		★(a)		★(a)	★(a)	★(a)	★(a)	★(a)	★(a)	★	★	★(a)	★(a)	(p)	★	★	★	(e,k,l) (h,m) (e,m,n,o)
Massachusetts	★(a)	★(a)	★	★		★(a)																
Michigan	★	★	★	★	★	★		★	★	★	★	★	★	★	★	★	★		★	★	★	
Minnesota	★	★	★	★	★	★		★	★	★	★	★	★	★	★	★			★	★	★	
Mississippi	★	★	★	★		★		★	★	★	★	★	★		★	★			★	★	★	
Missouri	★	★	★	★	★	★	(e,l,q,r)	★	★	★	★	★	★	★	★	★	★		★	★	★	
Montana	★	★	★	★	★	★		★	★	★	★	★	★	★	★	★	★	(s)	★	★	★	(e,l,s)
Nebraska	★	★	★	★	★	★	(l,u,v,w)	★	★	★	★	★			★	★	★	(t)	★	★	★	(m)
Nevada	★	★	★	★	★	★		★	★	★	★	★			★	★	★		★	★	★	
New Hampshire	★	★	★	★		★													★	★	★	
New Jersey	★	★	★	★	★	★		★	★	★	★	★	★	★	★	★	★		★	★	★	(w)
New Mexico	★	★	★	★			(e,x)	★(a)	★(a)	★(a)	★	★	★	★	★	★	★		★	★	★	
New York	★	★	★	★			(y)													★		
North Carolina	★	★	★	★			(z)								★					★		
North Dakota	★	★	★	★	★	★											★		★	★	★	(l)
Ohio	★	★	★	★	★	★	(aa)								★				★	★	★	(l,bb)

LEGISLATIVE ACTIVITIES PERFORMED WITH THE USE OF COMPUTERS

State or other jurisdiction	Statutory, bill systems, legal applications							Fiscal, budget, economic applications											Legislative management			
	Statutory retrieval	Bill drafting	Bill status report	Statutory revision	Case law retrieval	Redistricting	Other	Revenue forecasting	Revenue analysis	Budget comparison	Budget effects of legislation	Fiscal notes	Local fiscal notes	Economic impact note	Impact of salary and fringe changes	State aid formulas	Tracking federal dollars	Other	Computer printing	Legislative accounting	Mailing lists	Other
Oklahoma	★	★	★	★(a)	★(a)	★(a)	(n,y,cc)	★	★	★	★(a)	★	...	...	★(a)	...	★	...	★	★(a)	★	
Oregon	★	★	★	★	...	★	(l,u,z,dd)	★	★	...	★	★	★	★	★	★	...	...	★	★	★	(ee,ff)
Pennsylvania	★	★	★	★	...	★	(l)	★	★	...	★	★	...	...	★	★	...	...	★	★	...	(l)
Rhode Island	★	★	★	★	...	...		...	...	...	...	...	...	...	...	★	...	...	...	...	★	
South Carolina	★	★	★	★	★	...		★	★	...	★	★	...	★	★	★	★	...	★	★	★	
South Dakota	★	★	★	★	...	...		★	★	...	★	★	...	...	...	...	...	...	★	★	★	
Tennessee	★	★	★	...	...	...	(h,l,q,gg)	...	...	...	...	★	...	★	★	★	...	...	...	...	★	(k,o)
Texas	★	★	★	★	...	...	(d)	★	★	★	★	★	★	★	★	★(a)	★	...	...	★	★	(e,q,hh)
Utah	★	★	★	★	...	...		★	★	...	★	★	...	...	★	★	...	...	...	...	★	
Vermont	★	★	★	★	★	...		★	★	...	★	★	...	...	★	★	★	...	...	...	★	
Virginia	★	★	★	★	...	...		★	★	...	★	★	★	★	★	★	★	...	★	...	★	
Washington	★	★	★	★	...	...	(ii)	★	★	★	★	★	★	...	★	★	★	★	★	...	★	
West Virginia	★	★	★	★	...	...	(e)	★	★	...	★	★	...	...	★	★	...	...	★	...	★	
Wisconsin	...	...	★	...	★	...		...	...	...	...	★	...	...	★	...	★	...	★	★	★	
Wyoming	★	★	★	...	★	...		★	★	★	★	★	★	★	★	★(a)	★	...	★	★	★	
American Samoa	...	...	...	...	...	...		★(a)	★(a)	★(a)	★(a)	★	...	...	...	...	...	...	...	...	...	
Puerto Rico	...	...	...	...	...	...	(d)	★	...	...	...	...	...	...	★	★(a)	★	...	...	...	...	
Virgin Islands	★	★	★	★	★	...		★	★	★	★	★	★	★	★	★	...	...	★	★	★	(l)

Key:
★—Existing application.
...—Not an existing application.
DA—Does not apply.
(a) Reported use in one chamber or agency.
(b) Payroll.
(c) Timekeeping and purchasing.
(d) Legal and/or database searches.
(e) Textual composition and/or general word processing.
(f) Work flow tracking.
(g) Civil code.
(h) Indexing of bills, journals.
(i) Lists of publications.
(j) Tracking for legislators.
(k) Payroll.
(l) Preparation/printing of journals, calendars, public laws and/or supplements/annotations.
(m) Electronic mail.
(n) Scheduling.
(o) Personnel.
(p) Appropriation bill writing.
(q) Committee activities. In Florida: committee bill reference, proposed committee bills. In Texas: committee bill status and hearing schedules.
(r) Bill amendments.
(s) For general budget development and analyses, and for internal comparison between executive and legislative budgets.
(t) Local government budgets.
(u) Photo composition.
(v) Daily history.
(w) Workload analysis.
(x) Bill tracking and/or registry.
(y) Retrieval/access to Administrative Codes/Rules and/or Attorney General's opinions.
(z) Roll call votes and/or chamber resolutions.
(aa) Caseload forecasting.
(bb) Legislative analysis.
(cc) Publication distribution.
(dd) Tracking only.
(ee) Executive nominations.
(ff) Listing of registered lobbyists.
(gg) Word searching of bills and/or existing statutes.
(hh) Correspondence.
(ii) Daily journals.

Table 3.27
LOBBYISTS: AS DEFINED IN STATE STATUTES*

State	"Lobbyist" includes:				"Lobbyist" does not include:						
	Anyone receiving compensation to influence legislative action	Anyone spending money to influence legislation	Anyone representing someone else's interests	Anyone attempting to influence legislation(a)	Public officials acting in an official capacity	Anyone who speaks only before committees or boards	Anyone with professional knowledge acting as a professional witness	Members of the media	Representatives of religious organizations(b)	Anyone performing professional bill drafting services(c)	Others
Alabama	★	...	...	...	(d)	★	★	...	...	...	...
Alaska(e)	★	★	...	...	★	★	...	★	...	★	...
Arizona	★	...	★	★	★	★	...	...	...	★	(f,g)
Arkansas	★	...	★	...	(d)	...	...	...	...	...	...
California	★	★(k)	...	...	★(h)	...	...	★	...	...	...
Colorado	★	...	...	...	★	★(i)	...	...	...	...	(f,j)
Connecticut	★(k)	★(k)	...	...	★	★	...	★	...	...	(l)
Delaware	★	...	★	...	★	★	★	...	★	★	...
Florida	...	...	...	★(m)	(d)	★	...	...	...	★	...
Georgia	★	...	...	★	★	★	...	...	...	★	...
Hawaii	★(k)	★(k)	★	...	★	★	★	★	...	★	...
Idaho	★	...	...	...	★	★	★	★	★	...	...
Illinois	★	...	★	...	(d)	★	★	★	★	★	(n)
Indiana	★(k)	★(k)	...	...	★	★	...	★	...	...	(o)
Iowa	★	★	★	...	★	...	★	★	...	...	(o)
Kansas	★	★(k)	★	...	★	...	...	...	...	...	(p)
Kentucky	★	★	...	★(q)	...	★	...	★	...	...	...
Louisiana	★(k)	...	★	...	★	★	...	★	...	...	...
Maine	★(k)	★	★	...	★	★	...	★	...	...	(j)
Maryland	★(k)	★(k)	...	...	★	★	★	★	★	★	(r)
Massachusetts	★	...	...	...	...	...	...	...	...	...	...
Michigan	★(k)	★(k)	...	...	★(s)	...	★	★	...	...	...
Minnesota	★(k)	★(k)	...	...	★	...	★	★	...	...	(t)
Mississippi	★	...	...	...	...	★	...	★	★	...	...
Missouri	★	...	...	...	(d)	...	...	...	...	...	...
Montana	★	★(k)	...	...	★(u)	★	...	...	...	...	...
Nebraska	...	...	★	...	★(u)	...	...	...	...	...	...
Nevada	...	...	★	★	★	★	★	★	...	...	(n,v)
New Hampshire	★	...	...	...	...	...	...	...	...	...	...
New Jersey	★(k)	...	...	...	★	...	...	★	★	...	(o,v)
New Mexico	★	...	...	...	★	★	★	...	...	...	(n)
New York	★	...	...	...	★(u)	...	★	★	★	★	(f,j)
North Carolina	★	...	...	...	★(d)	★	★	★	...	★	(j,v)
North Dakota	...	...	...	★	★(d)	★	...	...	...	...	(v)
Ohio	★	...	★	★	...	★	...	★	...	...	...
Oklahoma	★(k)	★(k)	★	...	★	★	★	...	...	...	(f,v)
Oregon	★(k)	★(k)	★	★(m)	(d,w)	★	...	★	...	...	...
Pennsylvania	★	★(k)	★	...	★	★	...	...	...	...	...
Rhode Island	★(k)	★(k)	★	...	★	...	...	...	...	...	...
South Carolina	★	...	★	★(q)	★	★	...	★	★	★	(v)
South Dakota	★	...	...	★(q,m)	...	★	★	...	★	...	(x)
Tennessee	...	★(k)	...	★(m)	★	★	...	★	...	...	(f,j)
Texas	★(k)	★(k)	...	...	★	...	...	★	...	...	(y)
Utah	★	★	...	...	★	★	...	★	★	★	(f,o)
Vermont	★	...	...	...	★	★	...	★	...	...	...
Virginia	...	...	★	...	★	★	...	...	...	...	...
Washington	...	★(k)	...	★	★	★	...	★	...	...	...
West Virginia	★	...	★	★	...	...	...	...	...	...	(o)
Wisconsin	★	★(k)	...	...	★	★	★	★	...	...	(j)
Wyoming	★	...	★	...	★	...	...	...	...	...	...

*Definitions used to determine who is required to register and, in most cases, report as lobbyist.

Note: Entries reflect a literal reading of statutes. Consult lobbyist regulation provisions in each state for more details.

Key:

★—Specifically included or excluded in statute wording.

. . .—Not specifically included or excluded in statute wording.

LOBBYIST: AS DEFINED IN STATE STATUTES—Continued

(a) Does not link activity to compensation or expenditures.

(b) Persons representing a bona fide church or religious society for the purpose of protecting the public right to practice the doctrines of such church.

(c) Or advising clients as to the construction or effects of proposed legislation.

(d) Specifically excludes members of the state legislature. In Missouri, stipulates only elected officials.

(e) An individual who lobbies without compensation or who limits lobbying activities to appearances before the legislature, its committees or other public hearings may elect to register with and report to the secretary of state.

(f) Attorneys representing clients before any court or quasi-judicial body or proceedings.

(g) Anyone contacting an official for the sole purpose of acquiring information.

(h) Also does not apply to any state employee acting within the scope of employment, provided that an employee (other than a legislative official) who attempts to influence legislative action and who would otherwise be required to register as a lobbyist is not allowed to make gifts of more than $10/month to an elected state officer or legislative official.

(i) Unless person makes more than three such appearances in a calendar year.

(j) Communications by person in response to an inquiry or request for information. Lobbying as an activity in Colorado does not include communications made by a person in response to a statute, rule, regulation or order requiring such a communication. In Wisconsin, requests from agencies for information is exempt, however, requests from legislators for information is not exempt.

(k) Compensation and/or expenditures or time spent lobbying must exceed a specific amount before individual is required to register as a lobbyist. California—anyone spending $5,000 in a given quarter must file. Connecticut—compensation, reimbursement or expenditures (or combined total) of $500 or more/year. Hawaii—anyone who spends more than five hours/month or $275/six months for lobbying activities. Indiana—compensation or expenditures of $500 or more/year. Kansas—expenditures of $100 or more/year. Maine—anyone who spends more than eight hours/month on lobbying activities. Maryland—compensation of $500 or more/reporting period; expenditures of $2,000/reporting period. Michigan—"lobbyist agent" is an individual who receives at least $250/year in compensation; "lobbyist" is an individual who spends more than $1,000/year on activities (more than $250/year, if amount is spent on a single public official). Minnesota—anyone who spends more than five hours/month or more than $250/year. Montana—anyone who spends more than $1,000/year. New Jersey—anyone who is reimbursed over $100/three months. Oklahoma—compensation or expenditures over $250/quarter. Oregon—anyone who spends over 16 hours/quarter or over $50/quarter. Pennsylvania—anyone who spends over $300/month. Rhode Island—compensation or expenditures over $100/year. Tennessee—anyone who spends more than $200/report period. Texas—compensation or expenditures over $200/quarter. Washington—anyone who spends more than four days/three months and over $25. Wisconsin—anyone who spends over $500/year.

(l) Lobbying as an activity does not include communications by or on behalf of a public service company in connection with public utilities control authority's rate hearings.

(m) Any public official who lobbies. In Florida, includes state executive and judicial or quasi-judicial department employees. In South Dakota, executive employees register as "public employee lobbyists."

(n) Legislative employees.

(o) Officers, employees, or representatives of state political parties.

(p) Non-profit organizations that are interstate in their operations.

(q) Specifies legislation affecting private pecuniary interests.

(r) Appearances (as part of official duties) by an officer, director, member, or employee of an association engaged exclusively in lobbying for counties and municipalities.

(s) Although all elected and appointed officials of state or local government are excluded, the categorization itself does not refer to the employees of colleges and universities, townships and other local governments, the state executive departments, the judicial branch, or appointed members of state-local boards and commissions.

(t) Individuals engaged in selling goods or services to be paid for by public funds; stockholders of family farm corporations not spending over $250/year in communication with public officials.

(u) College officials and employees are not excluded from lobbyist definition. In Nebraska, the University of Nebraska is specified.

(v) Persons who express a personal opinion to their legislators.

(w) Governor, secretary of state, treasurer, attorney general (and attendant deputies for the latter three officers), superintendent of public instruction, and the commissioner of the Bureau of Labor and Industries.

(x) Public corporations.

(y) Persons whose only activity is to encourage or solicit members, employees, or stockholders of an entity by which individual is employed to communicate with legislative members to influence legislation; persons whose only activity is to compensate another to act on their behalf; persons whose only activity is to attend meetings or entertainment events attended by executive or legislative branch members.

Table 3.28
LOBBYISTS: REGISTRATION AND REPORTING

State	Lobbyist registers with	Frequency	Total expenditures	Expenditures by category	Sources of income	Monies or gifts to individual officials	Legislation supported/opposed by lobbyist	Other	Penalties
Alabama	Ethics Comm.	Monthly(c)	★	...	...	★	★	(d)	Fine of not more than $10,000 or imprisonment for not more than 10 years, or both.
Alaska	Public Offices Comm.	Monthly(e)	★	...	★	★	★	(d)	For failure to register or file report on time: $10/day until filed; for violation of provisions: fine of not more than $1,000 or imprisonment for not more than 1 year, or both.
Arizona	Secy. of State	Annually(f)	★	...	...	★	...	...	Prosecuted as a Class 1 misdemeanor.
Arkansas	Clerk of House; Secy. of Senate	+ + +	...	...	...	...	...	...	None specified.
California	Secy. of State	Quarterly	...	...	★	★	★	(d)	Prosecuted as misdemeanor, subject to civil fines.
Colorado	Secy. of State	Monthly(g)	★	...	★	★	★	(h)	Fine of not more than $5,000 or imprisonment in county jail for 1 year, or both; revocation of registration at discretion of secretary of state.
Connecticut	Ethics Comm.	Quarterly(i)	★	...	...	★	...	(j)	Fine of not more than $1,000 or imprisonment for 1 year, or both.
Delaware	Legislative Council	Quarterly	★	...	...	★	...	...	For failure to register or for furnishing false information: prosecuted as a Class C misdemeanor; for failure to file report: deemed voluntary cancellation of registration.
Florida	Clerk of House; Secy. of Senate(k)	Semi-annually	★	...	★	...	...	...	For violation of provisions: reprimand, censure, prohibition from lobbying for or part of the legislative biennium during which violation occurred (l); for false swearing to material fact: prosecuted as 2nd degree misdemeanor.
Georgia	Secy. of State	+ + +	...	...	...	...	★	...	For violation of provisions or non-compliance: prosecuted as a misdemeanor.
Hawaii	Ethics Comm.	Semi-annually	★	★	...	...	★	...	For failure to file statement or for falsifying statement: prosecuted as a misdemeanor.
Idaho	Secy. of State	Annually(i)	★	★	★	★	★	...	For registration and reporting violations: prosecuted as a misdemeanor and liable to max. civil fine of $250 or max. 6 months imprisonment, or both; for late filing of report: $10/day at discretion of secretary of state; for violation of statutory duties of lobbyists: possible revocation of registration.
Illinois	Secy. of State	Jan., Apr., July(m)	★	...	...	★	...	...	Prosecuted as a Class 3 felony(n).
Indiana	Secy. of State	Semi-annually	★	★	...	★	★	(o)	For failure to file report: $10/day (to max. of $100) until filed; for violation of provisions or false reporting: prosecuted as a Class D felony.
Iowa	Clerk of House; Secy. of Senate	Monthly	★	★	★	...	★	...	For failure to file report: cancellation of registration.
Kansas	Secy. of State	Monthly(p)	★	★	★	★	...	...	Prosecuted as a Class B misdemeanor.
Kentucky	Attorney General	After session	★	★	★	...	★	...	Fine of not more than $5,000 or imprisonment for not more than 5 years, or both.
Louisiana	Clerk of House; Secy. of Senate	+ + +	...	...	...	...	...	...	Prosecuted as a misdemeanor, punishable by fine of not more than $500 or imprisonment for not more than 6 months, or both.
Maine	Secy. of State	Monthly(c)	★	...	★	★	★	...	For failure to register or report: fine of $50.
Maryland	Ethics Comm.	Semi-annually	★	★	★	★	★	(o)	Prosecuted as a misdemeanor.

Note: Entries reflect a literal reading of statutes. Consult lobbyist regulation provisions in each state for more details.

Key:
. . .—Not required in report.
+ + +—Report not required.

LOBBYISTS: REGISTRATION AND REPORTING—Continued

State	Lobbyist registers with	Frequency	Activity reports(a) Total expenditures	Expenditures by category	Information required(b) Sources of income	Monies or gifts to individual officials	Legislation supported/ opposed by lobbyist	Other	Penalties:
Massachusetts	Secy. of State	Semi-annually	★	...	...	★	...	...	For failure to register or report: fine of not less than $100 nor more than $5,000; additionally, for legislative agent, disqualification until end of 3rd regular session of legislature after conviction.
Michigan	Secy. of State	Annually(q)	...	★	...	★	...	(o)	For failure to register or file report: $10/day (to max. $300); for failure to register over 30 days: prosecuted as a misdemeanor, with fine of not more than $1,000.
Minnesota	Ethical Practices Bd.	Quarterly	...	★	★	★	...	(o)	For late registration or failure to report after first notice: $5/day (to max. $100); for failure to report after second notice: prosecuted as a misdemeanor.
Mississippi	Secy. of State	Annually	...	...	★	★	★	...	For first violation: fine of $1,000 or imprisonment for not more than 6 months, or both; for second offense: $5,000, imprisonment for not more than 3 years, or both.
Missouri	Clerk of House; Secy. of Senate	3 times during session.	★	★	...	★	★	...	Prosecuted as a misdemeanor; may not register for 2 years.
Montana	Commr. of Political Practices	(r)	...	★	...	★	★	...	For violation of licensing provision: revocation. Prosecuted as a misdemeanor; subject to civil penalties of not less than $250 nor more than $7,500.
Nebraska	Clerk of Legislature	Monthly(c,s)	★	★	★	★	★	(o)	For violation of gifting provision: prosecuted as Class III misdemeanor.
Nevada	Dir., Legislative Counsel Bureau	After session(t)	★	★	...	...	...	...	For late reports: $5/day for first 30 days; $100 after period at discretion of Director. Prosecuted as a misdemeanor.
New Hampshire	Secy. of State	(u)	...	★	★	★	★	(o)	Prosecuted as a misdemeanor. For filing false statement: punished as perjury.
New Jersey	Attorney General	Quarterly(g)	...	★	★	★	★	...	Prosecuted as a misdemeanor.
New Mexico	Secy. of State	(v)	...	...	★	★	...	...	Prosecuted as a misdemeanor; fine of not more than $1,000.
New York	Temporary State Comm. on Lobbying	(w)	...	★	★	★	★	...	Prosecuted as a Class A misdemeanor.
North Carolina	Secy. of State	Annually	...	...	...	...	★	...	Prosecuted as a misdemeanor: fine of not less than $50 nor more than $1,000 or imprisonment for not more than 2 years, or both; upon conviction, may not lobby for 2 years.
North Dakota	Secy. of State	Annually	★	...	...	★	...	...	Prosecuted as a Class B misdemeanor.
Ohio	Jt. Cmte. on Agency Rule Review	Semi-annually	★	...	...	★	★	...	Prosecuted as a misdemeanor of the 4th degree.
Oklahoma	Jt. Legislative Ethics Cmte.	Semi-annually	★	...	...	★	...	...	For violation of provisions: prosecuted as a misdemeanor; for failure to register or report, liable for amount equal to 3 times the expenditure; for third violation: prohibited from lobbying for 5 years. Either house of legislature may prescribe penalty.
Oregon	Govt. Ethics Comm.	Quarterly	...	★	...	★	...	...	Prosecuted as a 3rd degree misdemeanor.
Pennsylvania	Clerk of House; Secy. of Senate	Semi-annually	...	★	...	★	...	...	For person, corporation, or association engaging lobbyist: fine of not less than $200 nor more than $5,000; for legislative counsel or agent: fine of not less than $100 nor more than $1,000 and disqualification for 3 years.
Rhode Island	Secy. of State	3 times during session	...	...	...	★	★	(x)	
South Carolina	Secy. of State	Annually	★	★	...	★	★	...	Prosecuted as a misdemeanor; upon conviction, disqualification for 2 years.

Note: Entries reflect a literal reading of statutes. Consult lobbyist regulation provisions in each state for more details.

Key:
. . .—Not required in report.
+ + +—Report not required.

LOBBYISTS: REGISTRATION AND REPORTING—Continued

State	Lobbyist registers with	Activity reports(a) Frequency	Information required(b) Total expenditures	Expenditures by category	Sources of income	Monies or gifts to individual officials	Legislation supported/ opposed by lobbyist	Other	Penalties:
South Dakota	Secy. of State	Annually							Disqualification from lobbying for 3 years.
Tennessee	State Librarian & Archivist	Annually				★★		(d)	For late filing: suspension of registration; for violation of registration or reporting provisions: prosecuted as a misdemeanor.
Texas	Secy. of State	Monthly(s)		★			★	(h)	For late filing: civil liability of $100; for failure to register or report: amount equal to 3 times the compensation or expenditure; for violation of provisions: prosecuted as a Class A misdemeanor.
Utah	Lieutenant Governor	+ + +	★						For violation of provisions: prosecuted as a Class C misdemeanor.
Vermont	Secy. of State	Annually(y)	★		★	★			Fine of not more than $500.
Virginia	Secy. of Commonwealth	After session	★						For failure to report: $50/day until filed; for violation of provisions: prosecuted as a misdemeanor.
Washington	Public Disclosure Comm.	Monthly		★	★	★			Determined by Comm. No individual penalty may exceed $250; for multiple violations: max. aggregate penalty of $5,000.
West Virginia	Clerk of Senate(z)	After session	★	★					None specified.
Wisconsin	Secy. of State	Semi-annually	★	★					Fine of not more than $5,000 depending on offense.
Wyoming	Dir., Legislative Service Office	+ + +					★		For failure to register: prosecuted as a misdemeanor, subject to $200 fine.

Key:
. . . —Not required in report.
+ + +—Report not required.

(a) When activity or financial reports are required, they are filed with the official or entity responsible for registering lobbyist.
(b) Reports must contain the stated information; however, additional information may be volunteered by the lobbyist or principal responsible for reporting.
(c) During legislative session.
(d) Statement of business association or partnership with any official; may include entities with which lobbyist has engaged in exchange.
(e) As long as individual continues to engage in lobbying activities.
(f) Supplemental reports filed monthly to show any single expenditure over $25 occurring during month.
(g) Also, annual cumulative disclosure statement.
(h) Media expenditures.
(i) Also, interim monthly reports of lobbying activities during legislative session.
(j) Terms of any contracts, agreements, or promises.
(k) As defined by statute, a central office designated jointly by the president of the Senate and the speaker of the House and under the immediate responsibility of the secretary of the Senate and the clerk of the House.
(l) If a legislative committee finds there has been a violation of the lobbying provisions, it reports its findings to the presiding officer along with a recommended penalty. The presiding officer brings committee report and recommendations to entire chamber for determination by a majority of members.
(m) April and July of the year during which legislature is in regular session; within 20 days after adjournment of special session; and January each year for the preceding year during which the legislature was not in session.
(n) Corporations violating provisions are guilty of a business offense and receive a maximum fine of $10,000. Any individual convicted of violation is prohibited from lobbying (for compensation) for three

years.
(o) Update of information required at registration.
(p) Only required for months during which expenditures are made, or gifts, payments, or honoraria given.
(q) On Jan. 31, covering the calendar year ending Dec. 31, and on Aug. 31 covering immediately preceding Dec. 31 to July 31.
(r) Before Feb. 16 when legislature is in session; before the 16th day of the calendar month when principal spent $5,000 or more in the previous month; 60 days after adjournment.
(s) Also, during the interim. In Nebraska, once during interim. In Texas, quarterly during interim.
(t) Monthly during session if lobbyist is attempting to influence legislative action.
(u) If registered for regular session—file April and Aug. 15 of each odd year; if regular session days are held after Aug. 1 of odd year, must file 30 days after each calendar day in which legislative business is conducted. If registered for special session—15 days after conclusion.
(v) Upon filing registration statement for all pre-session expenditures and 60th day after regular or special session.
(w) Any lobbyist who receives, spends, or incurs over $2,000/year files by the 15th day following reporting period in which cumulative total equalled amount (reporting periods—Jan. 1-May 31; June 1-Aug. 31) and files an annual cumulative report.
(x) Monthly expenses incurred on behalf of each person in whose interest individual engaged in lobbying.
(y) Also after two months of legislative session.
(z) Copies of registration and report sent to clerk of House.
(aa) By principal.

CHAPTER FOUR

STATE JUDICIAL BRANCH

STATE OF THE JUDICIARY

By Erick B. Low

The administration of justice of state courts across the nation is marked by a mixture of innovation and caution as the courts respond to changes in demographics, social structure, and economic conditions. Courts in many states are trying to do more with less as sparse or shrinking public resources constrict judicial budgets. To stretch budget dollars, state courts have tested or implemented innovative programs in court finance, personnel administration, caseflow management, appellate review, and alternatives to the judicial process. State courts have recognized a variety of programs designed to relieve congested dockets and to extend informal justice to citizens who are not accustomed to resolving their problems in court. As they have continued to modernize their internal operations, the courts also have begun to use technology in evolving areas of public concern such as the protection of child witnesses.

While the courts have extended their range of operations and experimented with new procedures in response to social change and limited resources, they have proceeded with caution in a period that has been marked as much by uncertainty as by progress. Some innovations in court procedures in recent years have been made in response to a "litigation explosion" that is itself a matter of uncertainty and controversy. The existence of an explosion in the rate of civil filings has been questioned by some commentators.[1] Data on state court filings, recently released by the National Center for State Courts, failed to demonstrate national patterns or strong demographic trends in civil litigation rates, including tort filings, from 1984 to 1985.[2] Since there is considerable controversy concerning national rates of litigation, the responses of court officials to uncertain national trends are apt to be controlled by perceptions of their local conditions. Judges and court administrators in jurisdictions with heavy caseloads and crowded dockets, for example, are likely to agree that a litigation explo-

sion does exist in the United States.

Other uncertainties exist as well. Extraordinary events in society at large have influenced the day-to-day procedures of the courts. Violence in the courtrooms, the demands of women and minorities for equal treatment in the justice system, and the specter of AIDS have forced the courts to examine their central purposes and to reformulate their goals. The following discussion summarizes some of the areas of continuing concern to court administrators and focuses upon several areas of special challenge.

Alternative Court Funding

The assessment of fees at increased rates and surcharges has become institutionalized in many courts as a means of generating revenues to offset court costs and to provide funding for special programs. The findings of a 1985 survey by the Conference of State Court Administrators (COSCA) revealed that 19 states and Puerto Rico impose surcharges on civil filing fees.[3] A total of 34 states, the District of Columbia, and Puerto Rico assess criminal court surcharges. Monies generated by increased fees and surcharges are used to support a variety of traditional court operations and specialized programs. In many states that impose surcharges, receipts are returned to the state general fund or to a local county or municipality. In other states, monies are earmarked for specific programs such as training, retirement, and victim/witness or indigent defense funds. Frequent recipients of revenues from surcharges on the civil side are local law libraries.

In some jurisdictions, offenders are assessed increased fees or fines that support programs directly related to particular offenses, such as the diversion of fines for driving while intoxicated (DWI) to traffic safety programs. Legisla-

---

Erick B. Low is the Librarian for the National Center for State Courts in Williamsburg, Virginia.

tion enacted by the California Assembly in 1980 provides for increased surcharges on drunk driving fines to help cover the costs of blood/alcohol tests, county alcoholism programs, and laboratory drug tests.[4]

Increased fees and surcharges are also used to support basic court functions. Montgomery County, Penn., finances its court automation system through court user fees. Illinois statutes direct revenues from surcharges assessed against civil filing fees to a court automation fund. Surcharges and increased fee amounts are also used to maintain local court facilities, which few jurisdictions, including those with state financing, fund at the state level.[5] Maine enacted legislation in 1987 that provides a 10 percent surcharge on fines, forfeitures, and penalties imposed by state courts. The monies are collected by the courts and are deposited into a Jail Operations Surcharge Fund.[6] In New York state, plans submitted to the legislature to finance improvements in court facilities include the use of increased court fees.[7]

In recent years, court officials have voiced concern over the imposition of increased fees and surcharges as revenue-producing measures.[8] Despite the need for increased revenues to support special programs, some judges and court administrators contend that the practice of increasing fees and imposing surcharges may limit access to the courts and may increase the administrative burden of the courts in processing and managing monies.[9] The COSCA *Cost Standards* may meet with opposition by groups that appreciate COSCA's position, but fear that state financing may not be made available to support programs traditionally funded by user fees.[10]

Collection of Fines and Fees

The collection of fines and fees is an issue of major concern to the courts since they often lack sufficient manpower or information systems to collect the fines they have assessed. In general, the trial courts have a legal responsibility for the collection and distribution of court fines, fees, and forfeitures.[11] The percentage of court revenues generated by fees and fines in a court of limited jurisdiction such as a municipal or traffic court may be very substantial.

Traditional collection methods have included the use of card or tickler files to monitor payment of assessments and delinquent cases, and lock-box systems in which payments are mailed to a post office box and processed by a bank. Recent initiatives in court revenue collection have included the use of credit card payment. Credit card payment has been seen as a convenient payment option for offenders and as a means for the courts to ensure collection of fines and assessed costs, but it has met with limited success in some jurisdictions. The state of Maine permits payment of fines up to $500 by credit card. Experimental use of bank credit cards in the Augusta District Court has been discontinued, however, since defendants lacking cash to pay fines often lack credit as well.[12] Several other jurisdictions, including Boulder, Douglas and Fremont Counties in Colorado, have found that the charge option has been less popular than anticipated by court planners. Credit card payment in these jurisdictions has been largely confined to payment of traffic fines and bail bonds.

Court experimentation with credit card payment of fines and fees has continued, however. In addition to Maine and Colorado, jurisdictions in at least 10 other states, including Alaska, Arkansas, California, Hawaii, Nevada, New Jersey, North Dakota, Ohio, Texas, and Virginia, have instituted or obtained authorization to institute credit card or other charge payment programs for fines and fees, or for the posting of bonds. Most of the jurisdictions that permit credit card payment of court costs receive credit card services from local banks without charge or at reduced rates.

Courts in some jurisdictions are also applying various get tough measures to ensure the payment of fines and forfeitures. Guidelines for trial courts recommended by the Kentucky Judicial Council provide that failure to pay assessed fines for traffic violations may result in suspension of the delinquent offender's driver's license.[13] California has enacted legislation that authorizes the Department of Motor Vehicles to refuse to reissue a driver's license to an applicant who has outstanding parking tickets.[14] Several states submit the names of motorists who fail to pay parking tickets to law enforcement agencies who are authorized to locate a delinquent motorist's car and attach a boot to one of the wheels. Removal of the boot incurs additional costs in addition to payment of outstanding fines. In another process that depends upon information transfer between departments, Utah uses computers to identify individuals with outstanding court warrants who file for tax refunds.[15]

Some courts have turned to the private sector for aid in collecting outstanding fines and fees. A New York-based computer firm, Datacom Systems Corporation, collects parking fines for Detroit, Michigan and New York City.[16] Other jurisdictions that have utilized private collection agencies include Kitsap and Franklin Counties in Washington.[17] Cincinnati also considered the use of a private agency to collect outstanding parking fines. By improving its recordkeeping and information management systems instead, the Traffic Court increased its internal capacity to monitor delinquent traffic fines and to inform offenders of delinquency. The number of outstanding fines has dramatically decreased in Cincinnati's Traffic Court as a result of improved internal recordkeeping systems.

Alternative Dispute Resolution

In response to the needs of individuals and corporations for timely and affordable justice, a wide variety of informal programs for dispute resolution have grown outside the courtroom as alternatives to formal judicial procedures.[18] Initially, many programs were developed at the neighborhood or local level without recognition by the courts. Neighborhood justice centers, operating outside the court system, promised a means of relieving overcrowded dockets and providing a form of justice that could adapt to the needs of individuals who were unschooled in the adversarial process.[19]

The trend in recent years has been toward a reconciliation of informal and formal justice. Many courts have annexed alternative dispute resolution (ADR) programs and woven them into the fabric of a multi-dimensional approach to public justice. The array of ADR programs administered, authorized or recognized by the courts ranges from arbitration and mediation to informal trial techniques, such as summary jury trials and minitrials that enable litigants to evaluate their cases and that encourage settlement of commercial disputes.

One of the first forms of alternative dispute resolution to be adopted by the courts was arbitration. By amendment of an 18th century statute providing for referral of trial cases to arbitrators, the first court-administered arbitration program was established in Philadelphia in 1952.[20] Court-annexed arbitration programs spread across Pennsylvania in the 1960s, and similar programs were established in other states in the 1970s and 1980s. At present, 22 states and the District of Columbia have court-annexed arbitration programs. The total number of programs is estimated at about 200. In the majority of states, programs are mandatory and require participation by litigants in civil damage suits that fall within prescribed jurisdictional limits. An award given by an arbitrator or neutral decision maker has the effect of a court judgment and may be appealed by trial de novo by an unsatisfied litigant. Many court-annexed arbitration programs discourage litigants from appealing awards, however, by imposing a variety of disincentives, such as assessing costs or opposing counsel fees if the appeal is unsuccessful or if the party bringing the case to trial does not substantially better his or her position.

Despite the apparent pervasiveness of court-annexed arbitration in the nation's trial courts, a recent survey of members of the Conference of State Court Administrators (COSCA) has indicated that arbitration programs within the courts are less widespread than aggregate numbers would suggest and that the rate of growth of court-annexed arbitration and other ADR programs has declined in recent years. The survey data demonstrated that arbitration programs tend to be concentrated in a small number of highly populated states, and that only a few states, California, New Jersey, New York, and Pennsylvania, have adopted court-annexed arbitration on a statewide basis rather than in selected trial courts. The study also showed that subject-matter or dollar-amount jurisdiction limitations upon arbitration programs lessened the potential impact of court-annexed arbitration on trial dockets. In New York, for example, all civil cases are subject to arbitration, but monetary limits are low ($6,000), effectively excluding the majority of complex and time-consuming cases.

The COSCA study also revealed a lack of national patterns in the estimated 500 mediation programs operated by the courts to resolve disputes in domestic relations, contracts, motor vehicle, consumer, landlord/tenant, and other forms of potential litigation. Analysis of the survey results did not reveal a correlation between program acceptance and population size or urban/rural patterns.

One area of litigation where ADR programs have had substantial acceptance in the courts is domestic relations. Courts in 27 states, the District of Columbia, and Puerto Rico operate ADR programs for domestic relations cases including family relations, child custody, and divorce. Several of the domestic relations programs are mandatory, and some states have implemented domestic relations ADR programs on a statewide basis. A sign of growing acceptance of ADR in domestic relations has been the development of professional standards for attorneys who serve as domestic relations mediators.[21]

Trial Court Delay Reduction

Despite the prevailing interest of the public in the rulings of federal courts, the bulk of judicial activity in the United States is performed in state courts. Caseload data for all state courts providing complete and comparable data in 1985 indicated that more than 14.3 million new civil cases and more than 9.3 million new criminal cases were filed in limited and general jurisdiction state courts during the year.[22]

To provide timely justice, the state courts have given considerable attention to programs for delay reduction. A recent survey of state court administrators showed trial court delay in general jurisdiction trial courts was perceived as a significant problem in 20 states and as a serious problem in 4 states. Delay problems were viewed with less concern in limited and special jurisdiction courts, where only one state reported a serious problem in the lower trial courts.[23]

Factors causing delay are usually identified as (1) local traditions under which lawyers and litigants control the pace of litigation, (2) lax continuance policies, (3) lack of adequate case monitoring, and (4) lack of commitment by judges to control the dockets. These attitudinal and procedural factors that courts can control are more likely to cause delay, than factors beyond judicial control that have been traditionally assumed to cause delay, such as court size, judicial caseloads, case complexity, or jury trial rates.[24]

Techniques that have been implemented with success in a number of trial court delay reduction plans include (1) commitment to delay reduction by the state's judicial leadership, (2) commitment to delay reduction by the trial bench, (3) education and training of judicial personnel, (4) implementation of effective case monitoring systems, and (5) collection and dissemination of data on the court's progress toward its improved case processing goals.

A commitment to reduce court delays is often expressed by a trial court or state court system with the establishment of time standards for processing civil and criminal cases. While speedy trial rules for criminal cases may be imposed by statute, civil time standards are usually adopted voluntarily by the courts by order or rule. A total of 22 states and the District of Columbia have adopted some form of time standard to reduce court delays, and additional states are developing case processing goals based upon local aspirations or upon national time standards adopted by the Conference of State Court Administrators (1983) or by the National Conference of State Trial Judges of the American Bar Association (1985).[25]

Strict time standards are also an essential element of differentiated case management, which recently was tested in Anchorage, Alaska, Phoenix, Washington, D.C., Aroostook, Cumberland, Kennebec, and Oxford counties in Maine, and Bergen County, N.J.[26]

Differentiated case management (DCM) distinguishes between cases at an early stage of development on the basis of their probable impact on judicial resources. An essential ingredient of differentiated case management systems is the establishment of multiple, separate case tracks that reflect the complexity of cases and anticipated levels of judicial resources required to achieve disposition.[27] Separate time requirements are developed for each case track, as in Bergen County's Expedited Track for actions that can be tried promptly with minimal pretrial procedures, Standard Track, and Complex Track for actions that appear likely to require disproportionate expenditure of resources to prepare for trial.

Connecticut has begun the first statewide differentiated case management program. As of Jan. 1, 1988, one judicial district was operating a DCM program with statewide implementation scheduled to begin by June 1988. Four tracks have been established for civil actions, and motion practice will be regulated under differing standards for each track. Strict time standards will be observed, and judges will play a controlling role in the pace of litigation.[28]

Another area of trial court management that has come under scrutiny in recent years and for which comprehensive, national standards have been developed is jury management. In 1979, a task force of judges, court administrators, and representatives of judicial organizations began to design a series of standards regarding management of petit juries in state courts. The American Bar Association adopted the recommendations of the task force in 1983 and began to seek adoption of its *Standards Relating to Juror Use and Management* by each state. The jury standards deal primarily with the principles of jury system management and the mechanics of juror selection and term of service rather than with trial issues, but they provide a framework in which courts may conduct trials in a just and efficient manner. As of March, 1988, six states, Idaho, Kansas, Minnesota, Oregon, Virginia and Washington, have adopted the jury standards, and an additional 13 states, Alaska, Arizona, Colorado, Illinois, Indiana, Louisiana, Massachusetts, Nebraska, New Jersey, North Dakota, Pennsylvania, Vermont and Wyoming, have begun jury standards adoption procedures.

The first set of trial court standards that focus upon the goals and social impact of the courts is currently under development through a joint project of the Bureau of Justice Assistance and the National Center for State Courts. A Commission on Trial Court Performance Standards has been formed and development has begun of a set of standards that may be used to assess the performance of general jurisdiction trial courts. The commission has identified five broad areas of trial court activity that support the end goals of the courts and that are conducive to measurement and evaluation. These concept areas include predictability; regularity and timeliness; equity, fairness and equality; integrity of court action and judicial decisions; fiscal and professional responsibility; and public acceptance or institutional integrity. The concept of institutional integrity focuses upon the effect courts have on participants in court processes, public satisfaction with the courts, the impact of courts upon society as a whole, and the accessibility of the courts.

Appellate Court Time Standards

While time standards have become an integral part of programs to reduce trial court delay, a similar interest in case processing goals has risen in appellate courts as well. In 1986, Idaho and Florida became the first states to adopt appellate time standards. The Idaho Time Standards for Appeals prescribe specific time limits for each step in the appellate process, with a total time, filing to disposition, of 418-508 days.[29] The appellate time standards adopted by court rule in Florida were announced in an unsigned opinion of the Supreme Court and indicate that a decision should be rendered in cases before the five District Courts

of Appeal and the Supreme Court within 180 days of oral argument or submission of the case for decision without oral argument.[30]

Time standards are used to measure progress toward court- or system-wide goals, but appellate courts also set time limits on specific events in the appellate process, during the normal course of daily operations. Time limits are commonly set on filing the intent to appeal, certification of the trial record, filing legal briefs, and production of opinions by judges or justices.[31] Time requirements enable the court to monitor case progress effectively, and the requirements serve as essential building blocks in a variety of programs to expedite appellate cases. In New Hampshire, for example, appellate reforms that gave discretionary review to the Supreme Court and created a multi-track case processing system also recognized eight major events in the appellate process and set a total disposition time of 270-360 days.[32]

The adoption of national appellate time standards recently took a major step forward with the adoption of the final draft of the Time Standards Committee of the Appellate Judges Conference by the American Bar Association's House of Delegates. The time standards are divided into three subdivisions: administrative time, lawyer time and judge time. The total time for the normal appeal has been set at 280 days, a goal considered achievable by most courts and a substantial improvement over average completion times of 420 to 480 days.[33] In recognition of the ambitious efforts of the American Bar Association to reduce costs and delays in trial and appellate courts and to develop time standards for appellate courts, the Conference of Chief Justices recently adopted a resolution urging all state chief justices to encourage the adoption of time standards for appellate courts in their states.[34]

Judicial Compensation

Inadequate judicial compensation continues to be a major problem for state courts.[35] Although statistics are unavailable on the number of judges who have resigned from the bench for salary reasons, numerous articles indicate that dissatisfaction with compensation has been a contributing factor in the decisions of numerous judges who have returned to private law practice.[36] In Minnesota, an alarmingly high number of judges left the bench in the early 1980s and attributed their resignations to low judicial salaries.[37] A demographic change in the judiciary that may be attributable to low salaries has been observed in Indiana, where an informal study by the Indiana Judicial Center revealed a decline in the ages of sitting judges. Thirty-eight percent of sitting judges were found to be under 40 years of age, and nearly 60 percent of the judges elected or appointed after 1980 were under 40. The trend toward a youthful bench is disturbing since it indicates that the bench has become less attractive to seasoned attorneys.[38]

In order to preserve an experienced judiciary, the American Bar Association has developed a handbook on state judicial salaries that outlines strategies to secure higher salaries for judges.[39] Economic indicators that justify judicial salary increases include the consumer price index and per capita personal income. Reasonable salary levels may also be determined through salary comparisons with attorneys, law deans and professors, nonjudicial state and local government officials, judges of other states, and federal judges.

Salary comparisons with any one group are difficult, since judging, in terms of skills, career path and objectives, and professional commitment to public service, is a unique calling. Salary comparisons with attorneys are especially difficult because of wide variations in salary and method of compensation of members of the private bar. In general, judicial salaries need not equal those of private attorneys, but should bear a reasonable relationship to the compensation of experienced attorneys in the private sector.[40]

In the absence of firm measures of reasonable salary levels for state judges, the American Bar Association adopted a resolution in 1981 recommending parity between federal and state judicial salaries. Several states have adopted this resolution as their goal, and some states achieved parity with federal salaries before the most recent increases in federal judicial salaries.[41]

One of the difficulties faced by state court judges has been the sporadic nature of salary increases and uncertainty whether judicial salaries will keep pace with inflation or with rates of increase of other state employees. Some states, the District of Columbia and American Samoa provide automatic adjustments in salary based upon increases in the cost of living as measured by the consumer price index or upon increases in the compensation of other state civil service employees.[42] Several states take longevity in a position into consideration

in their salary scales. In Rhode Island, judicial salaries, as well as the salaries of other state employees, include longevity increments ranging from 5 to 20 percent. In North Carolina, state court judges receive a salary supplement of 4.8 percent after 5 years on the bench and 9.6 percent after 10 years.

In order to ensure stability in judicial compensation and orderly adjustments in judicial salaries, a number of states have formed compensation commissions that examine the adequacy of compensation levels for judges, or for state employees including judges, on a periodic basis. In 1985, at least 19 states, including Alabama, Arizona, Arkansas, Colorado, Connecticut, Delaware, Georgia, Hawaii, Illinois, Maine, Michigan, Minnesota, Missouri, New Mexico, Ohio, Oregon, Rhode Island, South Dakota and Washington, had committees or commissions that made recommendations to the legislature concerning judicial salaries. In Alabama, the Judicial Compensation Committee's recommendations to the legislature become effective automatically unless rejected by both houses.

The success of efforts to raise judicial salaries often can be attributed to the support of leaders in the business community and the bar for an independent judiciary. Prominent business leaders serve on judicial compensation commissions in a number of states. In Delaware, for example, the legislature is usually sympathetic to the recommendations of the Compensation Committee in deference to the support for higher judicial salaries demonstrated by members of the business community that serve on the committee. Support of the bar is also vital to successful campaigns for adequate judicial compensation. At least 16 states, Connecticut, Florida, Hawaii, Indiana, Kansas, Maine, Massachusetts, Missouri, Nevada, New York, North Carolina, Ohio, Oklahoma, South Dakota, Vermont and Virginia, have bar committees that deal with judicial salaries. In a large number of states, bar associations have lobbied the legislature or shown other forms of support for higher salaries for judges. A particularly successful lobbying effort was waged by the Missouri Bar, which created a legislative network in 1984 among attorneys, judges, lay public and legislators in order to secure passage of a judicial pay raise and to create a permanent vehicle to support key initiatives, selected on a year-to-year basis, of vital importance to the administration of justice.

New Developments

Tort Reform. In 1986 and 1987, many state legislatures enacted laws to ease the apparent liability insurance crisis.[43] A number of states passed legislation setting caps on punitive damage awards. Oregon put the limit at $500,000, Florida at $450,000, Alabama and Idaho at $400,000, Virginia at $350,000, Georgia and Kansas at $250,000, and Texas at $200,000. In addition to caps on awards, several states also diverted a proportion of awards from plaintiffs to state programs. Missouri now requires 50 percent of punitive damages, less attorneys' fees, be awarded to the state and deposited in the Tort Victims Compensation Fund. Georgia requires 75 percent of punitive damages be paid to the state.

Several states approved legislation that allows reduction of a judgment based on the amount of collateral benefits the plaintiff has received. Alabama, Georgia, Iowa, Maryland, Missouri, North Dakota and Oregon have adopted procedures that permit judges or arbitration panels to subtract various collateral benefits from a judgment.

Joint and several liability (which allows a victim to collect full damages from whichever defendant is at fault, even one only partially at fault) was abolished in several western and central states in 1987, including Arizona, Idaho, Montana, North Dakota, Nevada and Texas, except in cases involving intentional torts, concerted actions or hazardous wastes.

Although some state legislatures are still confronted with proposed changes in their tort systems, the focus of attention in 1988 appears to be turning from tort reform to a re-examination of the extent of the liability insurance crisis. Attorneys general representing nine states recently filed suit against major American and British insurance carriers, charging them with conspiracy and manipulation of the commercial liability insurance market during the insurance crisis of 1984 and 1985. Numerous other states assisted in the investigation, headed by the California attorney general's office, that led to the filing of actions in U.S. District Court in California and state court in Texas. Some of these states are expected to file separate actions in the near future.[44]

Court Security. The increase in threats to the physical safety of judges, court officers, litigants and other court participants has received a considerable amount of media attention.[45] Guidelines for court security have been developed in several states, including Illinois, which convened a court security committee in the wake of several violent incidents in its courtrooms. Guidelines were developed for daily court security, prisoner/defendant security, judicial and witness security, security for the sequestered jury, and responses to hostage situations.

The selection and training of court security personnel is one of the most critical determinants of the success of a court security plan. To assist court officials in developing training programs, the National Sheriffs' Association has issued guidelines for the development of training programs for court security officers. The U.S. Marshals Service also provides court security training programs to local law enforcement officials.

Plans to assist court personnel maintain security and order in the courthouse must take into consideration the physical features of public buildings. Architects and court planners have begun to pay serious attention to court security in the design of new facilities and the renovation of existing buildings. Courthouses throughout the country also have begun to employ various types of technical equipment to increase security. Courthouses are installing emergency lighting in case of power outages, and marshals are reinforcing judges' benches, witness stands and other courtroom furniture with armor to protect against bullets and explosive devices.

Other technical courthouse security devices include card access control systems, hand-held metal detectors, hand-held radios, and post and rope railings. Walk-through screening stations similar to those at airports have been installed in the Maricopa County Central Courthouse building in Phoenix and proven to be effective. After three months of operation, 4 guns, 54 knives and 10 other potential weapons were confiscated by security officials as a result of the recently installed walk-through screening stations.

AIDS. The Acquired Immune Deficiency Syndrome (AIDS) epidemic has held special significance for court personnel who may be exposed to AIDS carriers in a variety of settings.[46] To protect court personnel and the public and to protect the rights of litigants and defendants with AIDS Related Complex (ARC), written policies have been developed in a few jurisdictions regarding the treatment of court participants who have been exposed to the AIDS virus.

The San Francisco Sheriff's Department has written guidelines on handling detainees suspected of having AIDS. In January 1988, the New York Office of Court Administration promulgated guidelines for conducting court proceedings involving people afflicted with infectious diseases, including AIDS. The New York guidelines permit a judge to establish whether a person appearing in court and suspected of having AIDS has a highly contagious disease. This information may be conveyed to counsel and to court personnel. The judge may seek the waiver of the person's presence in the courtroom if there is reason to believe that he or she has been exposed to the AIDS virus. If the person does not waive the right to attend trial, he or she may be informed that court proceedings will be routine except for the possibility that court personnel may be repositioned, seating arrangements changed, and potentially injurious courtroom objects removed or secured. Surgical gloves may be worn under dress white gloves with a uniform blouse by court security officers who are in the courtroom with the AIDS infected person or who are responsible for the infected person's custody. The guidelines recommend that antiseptics and disinfectants be kept accessible for use in case of blood spills, and that objects (e.g. hypodermic needles) containing blood or semen or its residue that will be offered into evidence at trial or in a proceeding be placed inside a sealed, transparent envelope and not removed or circulated except under judicial instruction. Since the release of the guidelines, a storm of controversy has arisen about whether the recommendations violate the civil rights of the AIDS infected person.

AIDS guidelines also have been adopted for the judicial departments in Alaska and Connecticut. The judicial departments of Massachusetts, New Jersey and Oregon also are considering promulgating AIDS guidelines. Alaska, Arizona, Connecticut, Delaware, the District of Columbia, Florida, Iowa, Missouri, Montana, New York, North Carolina, Oregon and South Dakota have reported efforts to educate employees about AIDS, and educational programs for court employees are under consideration in Tennessee and New Jersey.

Since the known circumstances under which AIDS may be transmitted are not commonly present in the courtroom, the Center for Disease Control has not recommended any special precautions for courtroom proceedings where one or more of the participants has AIDS.

Conclusion

The breadth of issues confronting the state courts includes many more areas of justice system management.

In many states, an independent judiciary is threatened not only by a lack of adequate compensation and an uncertain financial future for judges, but also by the need for judicial pension reform, paid judicial sabbaticals, improved commitments to judicial education, and reform of selection/retention procedures. A recent study by the Institute for Judicial Administration has indicated that statutory authorization of judicial sabbaticals has only been provided in two states (Alaska and Oregon) and Puerto Rico.[47] Even in these jurisdictions, however, sabbatical leave must be taken without pay. The institute has developed a model plan for judicial sabbaticals that places emphasis upon the opportunities offered by judicial leave for restoration, education and public service in nonjudicial capacities.

A major purpose of paid judicial sabbaticals would be to provide opportunities for judicial education. In 1987, the National Conference on Judicial Education in Williamsburg, Virginia, explored major educational issues. These included relationships among those who provide judicial education and training: law schools, states and national educational groups, such as the National Judicial College and the National Center for State Courts. Future trends, including sequenced educational programs for judges and implementation of mandatory judicial education in an increasing number of states, also were explored at the conference.

Another issue of special concern to the judiciary is the partisan election of judges. National attention was recently focused on Texas, where members of the Supreme Court are required to raise large sums of money from the public and the legal fraternity in order to conduct successful election and retention campaigns. The chief justice of Texas recently resigned from the Supreme Court in order to actively support reform of the state's partisan judicial election system and to lobby for adoption of a merit plan of judicial selection. Announcing that he would not seek re-election, the chief justice of Alabama recently voiced similar concern over the continuing practice in

Alabama of selecting judges in partisan popular elections. The chief justice expressed his hope that the state would consider a merit selection process that would be free from all political considerations. At present, nominating commissions and merit selection are employed to some degree in 33 states and the District of Columbia. Although popular elections are still in use and a matter of controversy in some states, particularly for judicial vacancies in the lower courts, no states exclusively use popular elections for all phases of selection and retention of judges at all jurisdictional levels.[48]

As leaders of the judiciary and court administration have examined ways to improve the quality of judging, they have also begun to focus on a wide variety of areas that affect, or are affected by, the work of the courts. The role of women in the courts as members of the judiciary,[49] court officials and officers, litigants, offenders and users of court services has been expanded in recent years as more women have entered the professions and the workplace and as family units have dissolved in increasing numbers. Twenty states have undertaken formal initiatives to determine the extent of gender bias in their court systems and to seek a goal of equal justice under law for all court participants regardless of race or sex.[50]

In the area of child support, a wave of changes in state laws has swept the country following federal revisions in Title IV-D programs (named for Title IV-D of the Social Security Act, which created the nationwide subsidized child support enforcement system). In view of changes in state and federal law, recommendations have been offered that outline a model child support system in which courts play a central role in determining and modifying the amount of child support orders, establishing paternity, enforcing support orders and collecting support payments.

Following the decline in federal funding of state court improvement projects in the early 1980s due to the elimination of Law Enforcement Assistance Administration (LEAA) programs, a substantial portion of remaining federal support for state courts has been provided by the Bureau of Justice Assistance and the National Institute of Justice. A major new force in the development of court improvement initiatives has been the State Justice Institute (SJI). State Justice Institute Act of 1984 authorized the institute to award grants and contracts to state and local courts and court-related organizations to improve the administration and quality of justice. Some of the areas that SJI is currently interested in funding include judicial career enhancement, judicial education and training, alternative dispute resolution, court technology and management systems, enforcement of fines and orders, courthouse security and the implications of AIDS for the courts.

One of the initiatives that the State Justice Institute proposes to explore is the future and the courts. This research would focus upon the changing demands that will be placed upon the courts in the 21st century and the modifications that may be necessary in court organization, procedures and services to dispense fair and equal justice. As state courts approach the end of the present decade, they are faced with many new and familiar issues. Despite the inherent caution of the courts, they will need to demonstrate a capacity for change to solve problems of increasing complexity and to prepare for the challenges of the 21st century.

Notes

1. *State Court Caseload Statistics: Annual Report 1984* (National Center for State Courts 1986): 172. See also, Deborah R. Hensler, *Trends in Tort Litigation: The Story Behind the Statistics* (Institute for Civil Justice 1987); Stephen J. Carroll, *Assessing the Effects of Tort Reforms* (Institute for Civil Justice 1987): 2.

2. *State Court Caseload Statistics: Annual Report 1985* (National Center for State Courts 1987).

3. Table 4, "Imposition of Surcharge on Civil Filing Fees," *Standards Relating to Court Costs: Fees, Miscellaneous Charges and Surcharges and a National Survey of Practice* (Conference of State Court Administrators 1986).

4. Dena Cochran, "The Rising Costs of Justice, Compliments of Proposition 13," *California Journal* 30 (January 1981).

5. According to an article entitled "New Publication Covers Importance of Accounting Skills for Managers." *National Center for State Courts Report* 8:2 (May 1981), seven states fund all, or almost all, trial court expenses, including court facilities: Alaska, Connecticut, Delaware, Hawaii, Kentucky, Massachusetts and Rhode Island. For a discussion of state assumption of court system costs, or state financing, see Marcia J. Lim, "State of the Judiciary," *The Book of the States* 1986-87) 146.

6. Dana R. Baggett, Memorandum to Marilyn Roberts, "Update on Maine Court Administration Activities," Sept. 10, 1987, 1.

7. "Court Facilities Financing Plan Introduced," *Modern Courts* 3: 1 (Spring 1987).

8. Bruce A. Kotzan, "Court Fees and Funding of Court Programs," *Benchmarks* 14:2: (Fall 1985).

9. *Standards Relating to Court Costs: Fees, Miscellaneous Charges and Surcharges and a National Survey of Practice (Conference of State Court Administrators 1986)*, sec. 3.1.

10. "AALL Executive Board Adopts Resolution on Standards Relating to Court Costs," *American Association of Law Libraries Newsletter* 19:108 (December 1987).

11. Robert Tobin, *Financial Management* (National Institute of Law Enforcement and Criminal Justice 1979):2.

12. Dana R. Baggett, "Memorandum to Marilyn Roberts, Update on Maine Court Administration Activities," Sept. 10, 1987, 2.

13. "Judicial Council Recommends Guidelines for Collection of Fines and Costs," *Accent on Courts* 3:15 (January/February 1981).

14. Cal. Vehicle Code sec. 4760 (West 1987).

15. "National Center Researchers Report New Trends in State Courts," *National Center for State Courts Report* 14:2 (July 1987).

16. "Cincinnati May Hire Agency to Collect Old Fines," *Judicial Notice* 4:3 (August-September 1984).

17. "National Center Researchers Report New Trends in State Courts," *National Center for State Courts Report* 14:2 (July 1987).

18. Unless otherwise noted, the remarks in this section are based upon an upcoming article in the *State Court Journal* by Susan Keilitz, Geoff Gallas, and Roger Hanson, "What's Been Going on in the States with Alternative Dispute Resolution?".

19. Deborah R. Hensler, "What We Know and Don't Know About Court-Administered Arbitration," *Judicature* 69:270 (February-March 1986).

20. Ibid, 271.

21. "Standards of Practice for Lawyer Mediators in Family Disputes," *Family Law Quarterly*, 18:363 (Fall 1984).

22. *State Court Caseload Statistics: Annual Report 1985* (National Center for State Courts 1987).

23. Unless otherwise noted, the remarks in this section are based upon the fourth in a series of annual surveys of state court administrators on caseload management, Howard P. Schwartz, Delay Reduction Efforts: *Conference of State Court Administrators Survey* (Conference of State Court Administrators 1987) sec. 1:1.

24. Thomas Church, Jr., *Justice Delayed: The Pace of Litigation in Urban Trial Courts* (National Center for State Courts 1978):5.

25. Alaska, California, Connecticut, Delaware, District of Columbia, Florida, Hawaii, Idaho, Iowa, Kansas, Massachusetts, Minnesota, Nebraska, New Jersey, New York, North Dakota, Ohio, Oregon, Rhode Island, South Carolina, Texas, Vermont and West Virginia.

26. Chuck Ray, "Judges Say Fast Track Works," *Alaska Bar Rag* 11: 1 (May 1987); "Advisory Committee's Explanatory Memorandum Concerning Administrative Order in Regard to Civil Case Flow Expedition," *Maine Bar Bulletin* 267 (November 1984); "Bergen County Pilot Rules Re: Differentiated Civil Case Management," *New Jersey Law Journal* 117:1 (Jan. 23, 1986).

27. Differentiated case management is an umbrella term that has been applied to a number of caseflow management programs that share certain characteristics, most notably multiple case tracks. The definition offered in the text closely follows that of the EMT Group, Inc., which is conducting a project to pilot test components of criminal and civil differentiated case management systems in 4 jurisdictions under the sponsorship of the Bureau of Justice Assistance. Economical Litigation Projects (ELP), such as the pioneer programs in several California and Kentucky counties, are similar to differentiated case management programs in that they provide expedited procedures for specific case types. For additional information on ELP projects, see *Attacking Litigation Costs and Delay: Project Reports and Research Findings* (American Bar Association 1984). For additional information on differentiated case management, see Marcia J. Lim, "State of the Judiciary," in *The Book of the States 1986-87*, 148.

28. George Gombossy, "Connecticut Courts Hoping to Speed Handling of Suits," *National Law Journal* 9:10 (Feb. 9, 1987).

29. "Idaho Court System is First to Adopt Appellate Time Standards," *News Release* (Idaho Administrative Office of the Courts, May 14, 1986).

30. The Florida Bar Re: Amendment to Rules, 493 So.2d 423, 425 (Fla. 1986).

31. See tables 13 through 17, Robert T. Roper, Mary E. Elsner, and Victor E. Flango, *1984 State Appellate Court Jurisdiction Guide for Statistical Reporting: Summary Tables* (Joint project, Conference of State Court Administrators and National Center for State Courts 1985).

32. Charles G. Douglas III, "Summary Disposition: The New Hampshire Supreme Court's Innovative and Unique Approach to Appellate Case Processing," *New Hampshire Bar Journal* 27:211 (Summer 1986).

33. According to Douglas K. Somerlot, project director, American Bar Association Judicial Administration Division, Lawyers Conference Task Force on Reduction of Litigation Cost and Delay, late amendments to the final draft of the Appellate Judges Conference Time Standards Committee before adoption by the ABA House of Delegates reduced the total disposition time from 300 to 280 days.

34. Resolution 22, "Appellate Court Time Standards," adopted as proposed by the Delay Reduction Committee of the Conference of Chief Justices, Williamsburg, Virginia, Jan. 28, 1988.

35. For a general discussion of judicial compensation, see Marcia J. Lim, "State of the Judiciary," The *Book of the States* 1986-87, 146.

36. Francis J. Flaherty, "Judges are Militant, Bitter Over Pay," *National Law Journal* 6:1 (April 16, 1984); "Crisis in Judicial Morale Generates Study and Action," *Benchmarks* 1 (August-September 1981); Martha Middleton, "Higher Pay for Judges: Bars Called Upon to Lead the Fight," *Bar Leader* 8:4 (July-August 1982); Bruce S. Rosen, "Edwards: Quality of Judicial Candidates Declining, *New Jersey Law Journal* 117:1 (April 3, 1986).

37. In 1982, Chief Justice Douglas K. Amdahl reported to the Minnesota State Bar Association that the judiciary had lost substantial numbers of trial judges through resignations attributable to insufficient compensation. In 1983, however, the chief justice indicated that, through the support of the bar association, substantial salary increases had been won in the state legislature and a 16-member Com-pensation Council had been created to make continuing recommendations concerning judicial salary levels.

38. "Crisis in Judicial Morale Generates Study and Action," *Benchmarks* 1 (August-September 1981).

39. *A Handbook on State Judicial Salaries* (American Bar Association 1986).

40. Statement of Edward B. McConnell, president, National Center for State Courts, to the Joint Select Committee to Study Judicial Compensation in Ohio, March 5, 1987, Columbus, Ohio, 2.

41. Ibid, 6.

42. According to a survey conducted by the National Center for State Courts in 1980, the salaries of judges in California, Ohio and Tennessee were adjusted in accordance with changes in the consumer price index. The salaries of judges in Maryland and Missouri were increased automatically on the basis of salary increases received by other state government employees.

43. This section is based upon a recent report on tort reform compiled by the National Center for State Court's Information Service, Jan. 20, 1988.

44. "Eight States Sue U.S., British Insurers," *Washington Post*, March 23, 1988.

45. This section is based upon a report on court security compiled by the National Center for State Court's Information Service, Sept. 16, 1987.

46. This section is based upon a report on AIDS and the court community compiled by the National Center for State Court's Information Service, Feb. 5, 1988.

47. "IJA Study Advocates Judicial Sabbaticals," *IJA Report* 19:1 (Spring/Summer 1987).

48. *State Court Organization* 1987 (National Center for State Courts 1988).

49. There are approximately 950 fulltime, law-trained women judges in the state and federal courts in 1988.

50. For additional information on gender bias, see Marcia J. Lim, "State of the Judiciary," *The Book of the States* 1986-87, 152.

Table 4.1
STATE COURTS OF LAST RESORT

State or other jurisdiction	Name of court	Justices chosen(a) At large	Justices chosen(a) By district	No. of judges(b)	Term (in years)(c)	Chief justice Method of selection	Chief justice Term of service as chief justice
Alabama	S.C.	★		9	6	Popular election	6 years
Alaska	S.C.	★		5	10	By court	3 years(d)
Arizona	S.C.	★		5	6	By court	5 years
Arkansas	S.C.	★		7	8	Popular election	8 years
California	S.C.	★		7	12	Appointed by governor(e)	12 years
Colorado	S.C.	★		7	10	By court	At pleasure of court
Connecticut	S.C.	★		7	8	Nominated by governor, appointed by General Assembly	8 years
Delaware	S.C.	★		5	12	Appointed by governor with consent of Senate	12 years
Florida	S.C.	★		7	6	By court	2 years
Georgia	S.C.	★		7	6	By court	4 years
Hawaii	S.C.	★		5	10	Appointed by governor, with consent of Senate	10 years
Idaho	S.C.	★		5	6	By court	4 years
Illinois	S.C.		★	7	10	By court	3 years
Indiana	S.C.	★		5	10(f)	Selected by judicial nominating commission from S.C. members	5 years
Iowa	S.C.	★		9	8	By court	Remainder of term
Kansas	S.C.	★		7	6	By seniority of service(g)	Remainder of term
Kentucky	S.C.		★★	7	8	By court	4 years
Louisiana	S.J.C.		★★	7	10	By seniority of service	Remainder pf term
Maine	C.A.		★	7	7	Appointed by governor, with consent of Senate	7 years
Maryland				7	10	Designated by governor	Remainder of term
Massachusetts	S.J.C.	★		7	To age 70	Appointed by governor	To age 70
Michigan	S.C.	★★		7	8	By court	2 years
Minnesota	S.C.	★★		7	6	Popular election	6 years
Mississippi	S.C.		★	9	8	By seniority of service	Remainder of term
Missouri	S.C.	★		7	12	By court	2 years
Montana	S.C.	★		7	8	Popular election	8 years
Nebraska	S.C.		★(h)	7	6	Appointed by governor	Life
Nevada	S.C.	★★		5	6	By seniority of service(i)	1-2 years
New Hampshire	S.C.	★★		5	To age 70	Appointed by governor and Council	To age 70
New Jersey	S.C.	★		7	7(j)	Appointed by governor, with consent of Senate	7 years(j)
New Mexico	S.C.	★		5	8	By court	2 years
New York	C.A.	★★		7	14(j)	Appointed by governor, with consent of Senate	14 years(j)
North Carolina	S.C.	★★		7	8	Popular election	8 years
North Dakota	S.C.	★		5	10	By Supreme and district court judges	5 years(k)
Ohio	S.C.	★		7	6	Popular election	6 years
Oklahoma	S.C.			9	6	By court	2 years
Oklahoma	C.C.A.			3	6	By court	2 years
Oregon	S.C.		★★	7	6	By court	6 years
Pennsylvania	S.C.		★★	7	10	By seniority of service	Remainder of term
Rhode Island	S.C.		★★	5	Life	By legislature	Life
South Carolina	S.C.	★		5	10	Joint public vote of General Assembly	10 years

STATE COURTS OF LAST RESORT—Continued

State or other jurisdiction	Name of court	Justices chosen(a) At large	Justices chosen(a) By district	No. of judges(b)	Term (in years)(c)	Chief justice Method of selection	Chief justice Term of service as chief justice
South Dakota	S.C.		★(l)	5	8	By court	4 years
Tennessee	S.C.	★		5	8	By court	18 months
Texas	S.C.	★		9	6	Popular election	6 years
Texas	C.C.A.	★		9	6	Popular election(m)	6 years(m)
Utah	S.C.	★		5	10(n)	By court	4 years
Vermont	S.C.	★		5	6	Appointed by governor, with consent of Senate	6 years
Virginia	S.C.	★		7	12	By seniority of service	Remainder of term
Washington	S.C.	★		9	6	By seniority of service	2 years
West Virginia	S.C.	★		5	12	By seniority of service	1 year
Wisconsin	S.C.	★		7	10	By seniority of service(o)	Remainder of term
Wyoming	S.C.	★		5	8	By court	2 years
Dist. of Col.	C.A.	★		9	15	Designated by President(p)	4 years
American Samoa	H.C.	★			8 years(q)	Appointed by Secretary of the Interior	(r)
Puerto Rico	S.C.	★		8	To age 70	Appointed by President with consent of Senate	To age 70

Sources: National Center for State Courts, *State Court Organization 1987*; state constitutions and statutes.

Key:
S.C.—Supreme Court
S.C.A.—Supreme Court of Appeals
S.J.C.—Supreme Judicial Court
C.A.—Court of Appeals
C.C.A.—Court of Criminal Appeals
H.C.—High Court
(a) See Table 4.4, "Selection and Retention of Judges," for details.
(b) Number includes chief justice.
(c) The initial term may be shorter. See Table 4.4, "Selection and Retention of Judges," for details.
(d) A justice may serve more than one term as chief justice, but may not serve consecutive terms in that position.

(e) Subsequently, must run on record for retention.
(f) Initial 2 years; retention 10 years.
(g) If two or more qualify, then senior in age.
(h) Chief justice chosen statewide; associate judges chosen by district.
(i) If two or more qualify, then determined by lot.
(j) May be reappointed to age 70.
(k) Or expiration of term, whichever is first.
(l) Initially chosen by district; retention determined statewide.
(m) Presiding judge of Court of Criminal Appeals.
(n) Initial 3 years; retention 10 years.
(o) If two or more qualify, then justice with least number of years remaining in term.
(p) From list of nominees submitted by Judicial Nominating Commission.
(q) Chief judges and associate judges sit on appellate and trial divisions.
(r) For good behavior.

Table 4.2
STATE INTERMEDIATE APPELLATE COURTS
AND GENERAL TRIAL COURTS: NUMBER OF JUDGES AND TERMS

State or other jurisdiction	Intermediate appellate court			General trial court		
	Name of court	No. of judges	Term (years)	Name of court	No. of judges	Term (years)
Alabama	Court of Criminal Appeals	5	6	Circuit courts	124	6
	Court of Civil Appeals	3	6			
Alaska	Court of Appeals	3	8	Superior courts	29	6
Arizona	Court of Appeals	18	6	Superior courts	101	4
Arkansas	Court of Appeals	6	8	Chancery courts	30	4
				Circuit courts	32	6
California	Courts of Appeal	77	12	Superior courts	724	6
Colorado	Court of Appeals	10	8	District Court	107	6
Connecticut	Appellate Court	9	8	Superior courts	139	8
Delaware	. . .			Superior courts	13 (a)	12
Florida	District Court of Appeals	46	6	Circuit courts	362	6
Georgia	Court of Appeals	9	6	Superior courts	131	4 (b)
Hawaii	Intermediate Court of Appeals	3	10	Circuit courts	24	10
Idaho	Court of Appeals	3	6	District courts	33	4
Illinois	Appellate Court	34	10	Circuit courts	780 (c)	6
Indiana	Court of Appeals	12	10 (d)	Circuit courts	89	6
Iowa	Court of Appeals	6	6	District courts	100 (e)	6
Kansas	Court of Appeals	10	4	District courts	146 (f)	4
Kentucky	Court of Appeals	14	8	Circuit courts	91	8
Louisiana	Court of Appeals	48	10	District courts	192	6
Maine	. . .			Superior Court	16	7
Maryland	Court of Special Appeals	13	10	Circuit courts	109 (g)	15
Massachusetts	Appeals Court	10	To age 70	Trial Court	281	To age 70
Michigan	Court of Appeals	18	6	Circuit courts	167	6
Minnesota	Court of Appeals	12	6	District courts	224	6
Mississippi	. . .			Chancery courts	39	4
				Circuit courts	40	4
Missouri	Court of Appeals	32	12	Circuit courts	133 (h)	6
Montana	. . .			District courts	36	6
Nebraska	. . .			District courts	48	6
Nevada	. . .			District courts	35	6
New Hampshire	. . .			Superior Court	25	To age 70
New Jersey	Appellate Division of Superior Court	28	7	Superior Court	321	7

STATE INTERMEDIATE APPELLATE COURTS AND GENERAL TRIAL COURTS—Continued

State or other jurisdiction	Intermediate appellate court			General trial court		
	Name of court	No. of judges	Term (years)	Name of court	No. of judges	Term (years)
New Mexico	Court of Appeals	7	8	District courts	59	6
New York	Appellate Division of Supreme Court	47	5(i)	Supreme Court	484(j)	14(i)
North Carolina	Court of Appeals	12	8	Superior Court	72	8
North Dakota	. . .			District courts	26	6
Ohio	Court of Appeals	53	6	Courts of common pleas	330	6
Oklahoma	Court of Appeals	12	6	District Court	71(k)	4
Oregon	Court of Appeals	10	6	Circuit courts	85	6
	Tax Court	1	6			
Pennsylvania	Superior Court	15	10	Courts of common pleas	330	10
	Commonwealth Court	9	10			
Rhode Island	. . .			Superior Court	19	Life
South Carolina	Court of Appeals	6	6	Circuit Court	31	6
South Dakota	. . .			Circuit courts	35	8
Tennessee	Court of Appeals	12	8	Chancery courts	33	8
	Court of Criminal Appeals	9	8	Circuit courts	92(l)	8
Texas	Courts of Appeals	80	6	District courts	374	4
Utah	Court of Appeals	7	10(m)	District courts	29	6
Vermont	. . .			Superior courts	10	6
				District courts	15	6
Virginia	Court of Appeals	10	8	Circuit courts	122	8
Washington	Court of Appeals	16	6	Superior courts	133	4
West Virginia	. . .			Circuit courts	60	8
Wisconsin	Court of Appeals	13	6	Circuit courts	197	6
Wyoming	. . .			District courts	17	6
Dist. of Col.	. . .			Superior Court	51	15
American Samoa	. . .			High Court: trial level	8(n)	(o)
Guam	. . .			Superior Court	6	7
Puerto Rico	. . .			Superior Court	92	12

Sources: National Center for State Courts, *State Court Organization 1987;* state statutes and court administration offices.

Key:

. . .—Court does not exist in jurisdiction.
(a) President judge, three resident judges and nine associate judges.
(b) For judges of the Superior Court of the Atlanta Judicial Court, term of office is eight years.
(c) Includes circuit and associate circuit judges.
(d) 2 years initial; 10 years retention.
(e) Plus 39 district associate judges and 14 senior judges.
(f) Plus 69 district associate judges and 71 district magistrates.

(g) Includes judges of Circuit Court for Baltimore City.
(h) Plus 170 associate circuit judges.
(i) To age 70.
(j) Trial divisions, 272 justices; certified retired justices, 51.
(k) Plus 72 associate judges and 56 special judges.
(l) With civil jurisdiction, 66 judges; with criminal jurisdiction, 26.
(m) 3 years initial; 10 years retention.
(n) Chief justice and associate judges sit on appellate and trial divisions.
(o) For good behavior.

Table 4.3
QUALIFICATIONS OF JUDGES OF STATE APPELLATE COURTS AND GENERAL TRIAL COURTS

State or other jurisdiction	U.S. citizenship (years)		Years of minimum residence				Minimum age		Member of state bar (years)		Other	
			In state		In district							
	A	T	A	T	A	T	A	T	A	T	A	T
Alabama	5	5	(a)	(a)	...	1	25	25	★	★	...	...
Alaska	★	★	5(a)	5(a)	...	...	...	...	★(b)	★(b)	...	...
Arizona	...	...	10(c)	5	3(d,e)	...	30(d)	30	10(c)	5	(f,g)	(f,g)
Arkansas	★	★	2	2	...	...	30	28	(h,i)	(h,i)	(f)	(f)
California	...	...	...	...	...	...	...	...	10(i)	10(i)	...	...
Colorado	...	...	(e)	...	...	(e)	...	...	5	5	(g)	(g)
Connecticut	...	...	...	...	...	...	18	...	★	★	...	...
Delaware	...	...	(a)	(a)	...	...	...	...	(h)	(h)	...	...
Florida	...	...	(e)	(e)	★	★	...	...	10	5	(g)	(g)
Georgia	3	3	(a)	(a)	...	...	30	...	7	7	...	...
Hawaii	★	★	★(a)	★(a)	...	...	...	...	10	10	...	...
Idaho	★	★	2	2	...	(e)	30	30	★	(h)	...	...
Illinois	★	★	...	...	★	★	...	...	★	★	...	...
Indiana	★	★	...	...	★	★	...	...	10(i)	★	...	...
Iowa	...	...	...	...	...	...	...	...	★	★	...	...
Kansas	...	...	...	...	...	★	30	30	★(i)	★(i)	...	...
Kentucky	★	★	2	2	2	2	...	...	8	8	...	...
Louisiana	...	...	5	...	2	2	25	...	5	5	...	...
Maine	...	...	...	...	...	...	...	...	(h)	(h)	(f)	(f)
Maryland	...	...	5(a,e)	5(a,e)	6 mo.	6 mo.	30	30	★	★	(f)	(f)
Massachusetts	...	...	...	...	...	...	...	...	...	...	...	...
Michigan	...	...	(e)	...	(e)	(e)	...	...	★	★	(g,j)	(g,j)
Minnesota	...	...	...	...	...	...	...	...	(h)	(h)	...	...
Mississippi	...	...	(a)	(a)	...	...	30	26	5	5	...	...
Missouri	15	10	(e)	(e)	★	1	30	30	★	★	...	...
Montana	★	★	2	2	...	...	30	30	5	5	...	...
Nebraska	★	★	3	...	★(e)	★	30	30	5(i)	5(i)	...	...
Nevada	...	...	2(e)	2(e)	...	...	25	25	★	★	(k)	(k)
New Hampshire	...	...	...	...	...	...	...	...	...	...	(l)	(l)
New Jersey	...	...	...	...	...	...	...	...	10	10	...	...
New Mexico	...	...	3	3	...	★	30	30	3(h,i)	3(h,i)	...	...
New York	...	...	...	...	...	...	...	...	10	10	...	...
North Carolina	...	...	1	...	...	...	21	...	★	★	...	...
North Dakota	★	★	★	★	...	...	...	...	★(h)	★(h)	...	...
Ohio	...	...	...	...	...	★	...	...	6(i)	6(i)	(g)	(g)
Oklahoma	...	...	(e)	...	(e)	(e)	30	...	5(i)	4(i)	...	...
Oregon	★	★	3	★	(e)	★	...	...	★	★	...	...
Pennsylvania	★	★	1(a)	(a)	...	1	...	...	★	★	...	...
Rhode Island	...	...	...	...	...	...	...	...	...	...	...	...
South Carolina	★	★	5(a)	5(a)	...	★(e)	26	26	5	5	...	...
South Dakota	★	★	★	★	★(e)	★(e)	...	...	★	★	...	...
Tennessee	...	...	5(a)	5	...	1	35(m)	30	★	★	...	...
Texas	★	★	(a)	(a)	(d)	2	35	25	★(i)	★(i)	...	...
Utah	...	...	5	3	...	★	30	25	★	★	...	...
Vermont	...	...	★	★	...	...	...	...	★(i)	★(i)	...	...
Virginia	...	...	★	★	...	...	...	...	5	5	...	...
Washington	...	...	1	...	1	1	...	...	★(n)	★	...	...
West Virginia	...	...	5	5	...	...	30	30	★(i)	★(i)	...	...
Wisconsin	...	...	(e)	...	...	(e)	...	...	5	5	...	...
Wyoming	★	★	3	2	...	...	30	28	1(h,i)	1(h)	...	...
Dist. of Col.	★	★	...	...	90 days	...	...	...	5(i)	5(i)	...	...
American Samoa	★	★	...	...	...	...	...	...	★	★	...	...
Guam	...	★	...	...	...	...	...	...	...	(h)	...	...
No. Mariana Is.	...	★	...	...	...	...	...	30	...	(h)	...	...
Puerto Rico	★	★	...	...	...	...	...	25	★(i)	★(i)	...	...

QUALIFICATIONS OF JUDGES—Continued

Sources: National Center for State Courts, *State Court Organization 1987;* state constitutions and statutes.

Note: The information in this table is based on a literal reading of the state constitutions and statutes. Requirements that an individual be a member of the state bar or a qualified elector may imply additional requirements.

Key:

A—Judges of courts of last resort and intermediate appellate courts.

T—Judges of general trial courts.

★—Provision; length of time not specified.

. . .—No specific provision.

(a) Citizen of the state. In Alabama, Mississippi and Tennessee (court of criminal appeals), five years; in Georgia, three years.

(b) Must have been engaged in active practice of law for specific number of years. Alaska: appellate—eight years; trial—five years.

(c) For court of appeals, five years.

(d) For court of appeals judges only.

(e) Qualified elector. For Arizona court of appeals, must be elector of county of residence. For Michigan Supreme Court, elector in state; court of appeals, elector of appellate circuit. For Missouri Supreme and appellate courts, electors for nine years; for circuit courts, electors for three years. For Oklahoma Supreme Court and Court of Criminal Appeals, elector for one year; court of appeals and district courts, elector for six months. For Oregon court of appeals, qualified elector in county.

(f) Specific personal characteristics. Arizona, Arkansas—good moral character. Maine—sobriety of manners. Maryland—integrity, wisdom and sound legal knowledge.

(g) Nominee must be under certain age to be eligible. Arizona—under 65. Colorado—under 72, except when name is submitted for vacancy. Florida—under 70, except upon temporary assignment or to complete a term. Michigan, Ohio—under 70.

(h) Learned in law.

(i) Years as a practicing lawyer and/or service on bench of court of record in state may satisfy requirement. Arkansas—appellate: eight years; trial: six years. Indiana—10 years admitted to practice or must have served as a circuit, superior or criminal court judge in the state for at least five years. Kansas—appellate: 10 years; trial: five years (must have served as an associate district judge in state for two years). Texas—appellate: 10 years; trial: four years. Vermont—five of 10 years preceding appointment. West Virginia—appellate: 10 years; trial: five years. Puerto Rico—appellate: 10 years; trial: five years.

(j) A person convicted of a felony or breach of public trust is not eligible to the office for a period of 20 years after conviction.

(k) May not have been previously removed from judicial office.

(l) Except that record of birth is required.

(m) Thirty years for judges of court of appeals and court of criminal appeals.

(n) For court of appeals, admitted to practice for five years.

Table 4.4
SELECTION AND RETENTION OF JUDGES

Alabama . . . . Appellate, circuit, district and probate judges elected on partisan ballots. Municipal court judges appointed by the governing body of the municipality (majority vote of its members).

Alaska . . . . Supreme Court, court of appeals, superior court and district court judges appointed by governor from nominations submitted by Judicial Council. Supreme Court, court of appeals and superior court judges approved or rejected at first general election held more than three years after appointment. Reconfirmation every 10 and six years, respectively. District court judges approved or rejected at first general election held more than one year after appointment. Reconfirmation every four years. District court magistrates appointed by and serve at pleasure of presiding judge of superior court in each judicial district.

Arizona . . . . Supreme Court justices and court of appeals judges appointed by governor from a list of not less than three nominees submitted by a nine-member Commission on Appellate Court Appointments. Superior court judges (in counties with population of at least 150,000) appointed by governor from a list of not less than three nominees submitted by a nine-member commission on trial court appointments. Judges initially hold office for term ending 60 days following next regular general election after expiration of two-year term. Judges who file declaration of intention to be retained in office run at next regular general election on non-partisan ballot. Superior court judges in counties having population less than 150,000 elected on non-partisan ballot; justices of the peace elected on partisan ballot; police judges and magistrates selected as provided by charter or ordinance; Tucson city magistrates appointed by mayor and council from nominees submitted by non-partisan Merit Selection Commission on magistrate appointments.

Arkansas . . . . All elected on partisan ballot.

California . . . . Supreme Court and courts of appeal judges appointed by governor, confirmed by Commission on Judicial Appointments. Judges run unopposed on non-partisan ballot at next general election after appointment. Superior court judges elected on non-partisan ballot or selected by method described above; judges elected to full term at next general election on non-partisan ballot. Municipal court and justice court judges initially appointed by governor and county board of supervisors, respectively, retain office by election on non-partisan ballot.

Colorado . . . . Supreme Court and court of appeals judges appointed by governor from nominees submitted by Supreme Court Nominating Commission. Other judges appointed by governor from nominees submitted by Judicial District Nominating Commission. After initial appointive term of two years, judges run on record for retention. Municipal judges appointed by municipal governing body. Denver County judges appointed by mayor from list submitted by nominating commission; judges run on record for retention.

Connecticut . . . . All nonelected judges appointed by legislature from nominations submitted by governor exclusively from candidates submitted by the Judicial Selection Commission. Judicial Review Council makes recommendations on nominations for reappointment. Probate judges elected on partisan ballots.

Delaware . . . . All appointed by governor with consent of majority of senate.

Florida . . . . Supreme Court and district court of appeals judges appointed by governor from nominees submitted by appropriate judicial nominating commission. Judges run for retention at next general election preceding expiration of term. Circuit and county court judges elected on non-partisan ballots.

Georgia . . . . Supreme Court, court of appeals and superior court judges elected on non-partisan ballots. Probate judges and justices of peace elected on partisan ballots. Other county and city court judges appointed.

Hawaii . . . . Supreme Court and intermediate court of appeals justices and circuit court judges nominated by Judicial Selection Commission (on list of at least six names) and appointed by governor with consent of senate. District court judges nominated by Commission (on list of at least six names) and appointed by chief justice.

Idaho . . . . Supreme Court and court of appeals justices and district court judges elected on non-partisan ballot. Magistrates appointed on non-partisan merit basis by District Magistrates Commission and run for retention in first general election next succeeding the 18-month period following initial appointment; thereafter, run every four years.

Illinois . . . . Supreme Court, appellate court and circuit court judges nominated at primary elections or by petition and elected at general or judicial elections on partisan ballot. Circuit court associate judges appointed by circuit judges for four-year terms.

Indiana . . . . Supreme Court justices and court of appeals judges appointed by governor from list of three nominees submitted by seven-member Judicial Nominating Commission. Judges serve until next general election after two years from appointment date; thereafter, run for retention on record. Circuit, superior and county judges in most counties run on partisan ballot. Marion County municipal judges appointed by governor from nominees submitted by county nominating commission.

Iowa . . . . Supreme Court, court of appeals and district court judges appointed by governor from lists submitted by nominating commissions. Judges serve initial one-year term and until January 1 following next general election, then run on records for retention. Full-time judicial magistrates appointed by district judges in judicial election district from nominations submitted by county judicial magistrate appointing commission. Part-time magistrates appointed by county judicial magistrate appointing commission.

Kansas . . . . Supreme Court and court of appeals judges appointed by governor from nominations submitted by Supreme Court Nominating Commission. Judges serve until second Monday in January following first general election after one year in office; thereafter run on record for retention every six (Supreme Court) and four (court of appeals) years. District judges in most judicial districts selected by non-partisan commission plan.

Kentucky . . . . All judges elected on non-partisan ballot.

Louisiana . . . . All justices and judges (except Orleans Parish District and Family Court judges) elected on non-partisan ballot.

Maine . . . . All appointed by governor with confirmation of the senate, except probate judges who are elected on partisan ballot.

Maryland . . . . Court of Appeals and special appeals judges nominated by Judicial Nominating Commission, and appointed by governor with advice and consent of senate. Judges run on record for retention after one year of service. Judges of circuit courts and Supreme Bench of Baltimore City nominated by Commission and appointed by governor. Judges run in first general election after year of service (may be challenged by other candidates). District court judges nominated by Commission and appointed by governor, subject to senate confirmation.

SELECTION AND RETENTION OF JUDGES—Continued

Massachusetts ..... All nominated and appointed by governor with advice and consent of Governor's Council. Judicial Nominating Commission, established by executive order, submits names on non-partisan basis to governor.

Michigan .... All elected on non-partisan ballot, except remaining municipal judges who are selected in accordance with local procedures for selecting public officials.

Minnesota .... All elected on non-partisan ballot.

Mississippi .... All elected on partisan ballot, except municipal court judges who are appointed by governing authority of each municipality.

Missouri .... Judges of Supreme Court, court of appeals and several circuit courts appointed initially by governor from nominations submitted by judicial selection commissions. Judges run for retention after one year in office. All other judges elected on partisan ballot.

Montana .... All elected on non-partisan ballot. Judges unopposed in reelection effort, run for retention.

Nebraska .... All judges appointed initially by governor from nominees submitted by judicial nominating commissions. Judges run for retention on non-partisan ballot in general election following initial three-year term; subsequent terms are six years.

Nevada .... All elected on non-partisan ballot.

New Hampshire ... All appointed by governor and confirmed by majority vote of five-member Executive Council.

New Jersey .... All appointed by governor with advice and consent of senate, except judges of municipal courts serving a single municipality who are appointed by the governing body.

New Mexico .... All elected on partisan ballot.

New York .... All elected on partisan ballot, except judges of Court of Appeals who are appointed by governor with advice and consent of senate. Governor also appoints judges of court of claims and designates members of appellate division of supreme court. Mayor of New York City appoints judges of criminal and family courts in the city.

North Carolina .... All elected on partisan ballot, except special judges of superior court who are appointed by governor.

North Dakota ..... All elected on non-partisan ballot.

Ohio .... All elected on non-partisan ballot, except court of claims judges who may be appointed by chief justice of Supreme Court from ranks of Supreme Court, court of appeals, court of common pleas or retired judges.

Oklahoma .... Supreme Court justices and Court of Criminal Appeals judges appointed by governor from lists of three submitted by Judicial Nominating Commission. Judges run for retention on non-partisan ballot at first general election following completion of one year's service. Judges of court of appeals, and district and associate district judges elected on non-partisan ballot. Special judges appointed by district judges within judicial administrative districts. Municipal judges appointed by governing body of municipality.

Oregon .... All judges elected on non-partisan ballot for six-year terms, except municipal judges who are generally appointed and serve as prescribed by city council.

Pennsylvania ...... All initially elected on partisan ballot and thereafter on non-partisan retention ballot, except judges of traffic court and magistrates (Pittsburgh) who are appointed by mayor.

Rhode Island ...... Supreme Court justices elected by legislature. Superior, district and family court judges appointed by governor with advice and consent of senate. By executive order, governor selects appointees from names submitted by a judicial nominating commission. Probate and municipal court judges appointed by city or town councils.

South Carolina .... Supreme Court, court of appeals, circuit court and family court judges elected by legislature from names submitted on a non-partisan basis by judiciary committee of legislature. Probate judges elected on partisan ballot. Magistrates appointed by governor with advice and consent of senate. Municipal judges appointed by mayor and alderman of city.

South Dakota ..... Supreme Court justices appointed by governor from nominees submitted by Judicial Qualifications Commission. Justices run for retention at first general election after three years in office. Circuit court judges elected on non-partisan ballot. Magistrates appointed by presiding judge of judicial court.

Tennessee .... Judges of intermediate appellate courts appointed initially by governor from list of three nominees submitted by Appellate Court Nominating Commission. Judges run for election to full term at biennial general election held more than 30 days after occurrence of vacancy. Supreme Court judges and all other judges elected on partisan ballot, except some municipal judges who are appointed by governing body of city.

Texas .... All elected on partisan ballot (method of selection for municipal judges determined by city charter or local ordinance).

Utah .... Supreme Court, district court, circuit court and juvenile court judges appointed by governor from list of at least three nominees submitted by Judicial Nominating Commission. Judges run unopposed for retention in general election following initial three-year term; thereafter run on record for retention every 10 (Supreme Court) and six (other courts of record) years.

Vermont .... Supreme Court justices, superior court and district court judges nominated by Judicial Nominating Board and appointed by governor with advice and consent of senate. Judges retained in office unless legislature votes for removal.

Virginia .... All full-time judges elected by majority vote of legislature.

Washington .... All elected on non-partisan ballot (method of selection for some municipal judges locally determined).

West Virginia ..... Supreme Court of Appeals judges, circuit court judges and magistrates elected on partisan ballot.

Wisconsin .... Supreme Court, court of appeals and circuit court judges elected on non-partisan ballot. Method of selection for municipal judges determined locally.

SELECTION AND RETENTION OF JUDGES—Continued

Wyoming	Supreme Court justices, district and county court judges appointed by governor from list of three nominees submitted by judicial nominating commission. Judges run for retention on non-partisan ballot at first general election occurring more than one year after appointment. Justices of the peace elected on non-partisan ballot. Municipal (police) judges appointed by mayor with consent of council.
Dist. of Col.	Court of appeals and superior court judges nominated by president of the United States from a list of persons recommended by District of Columbia Judicial Nominating Commission; appointed upon advice and consent of U.S. Senate.
American Samoa ..	Chief justice and associate justice(s) appointed by the U.S. Secretary of the Interior pursuant to presidential delegation of authority. Associate judges appointed by governor of American Samoa on recommendation of the chief justice, and subsequently confirmed by the senate of American Samoa.
Guam	All appointed by governor with consent of legislature from list of nominees submitted by Judicial Council; thereafter, run on record for retention every seven years.
No. Mariana Is. ...	All appointed by governor with advice and consent of senate.
Puerto Rico	All appointed by governor with advice and consent of senate.
Virgin Islands	All appointed by governor with advice and consent of legislature.

Sources: Larry Berkson, Scott Beller and Michele Grimaldi, *Judicial Selection in the United States: A Compendium of Provisions* (Chicago: American Judicature Society) and update; Donna Vandenberg, "Judicial Merit Selection: Current Status," American Judicature Society; and state constitutions and statutes.

Table 4.5
METHODS FOR REMOVAL OF JUDGES AND FILLING OF VACANCIES

State or other jurisdiction	How removed	Vacancies: how filled
Alabama	Judicial Inquiry Commission investigates, receives or initiates complaints concerning any judge. Complaints are filed with the Court of the Judiciary which is empowered to remove, suspend, censure or otherwise discipline judges in the state.	By gubernatorial appointment. At next general election held after appointee has been in office one year, office is filled for a full term. In some counties, vacancies in circuit and district courts are filled by gubernatorial appointment on nominations made by judicial commission.
Alaska	Justices and judges subject to impeachment for malfeasance or misfeasance in performance of official duties. On recommendation of Judicial Qualifications Commission or on its own motion, Supreme Court may suspend judge without salary when judge pleads guilty or no contest or is found guilty of a crime punishable as felony under state or federal law or of any other crime involving moral turpitude under that law. If conviction is reversed, suspension terminates and judge is paid salary for period of suspension. If conviction becomes final, judge is removed from office by Supreme Court. On recommendation of Judicial Qualifications Commission, Supreme Court may censure or remove a judge for action (occurring not more than six years before commencement of current term) which constitutes willful misconduct in office, willful and persistent failure to perform duties, habitual intemperance or conduct prejudicial to the administration of justice that brings the judicial office into disrepute. The Court may also retire a judge for a disability that seriously interferes with the performance of duties and is (or is likely to become) permanent.	By gubernatorial appointment, from nominations submitted by Judicial Council.
Arizona	Judges subject to recall election. Electors, equal in number to 25% of votes cast in last election for judge, may petition for judge's recall. All Supreme Court, court of appeals and superior court judges (judges of courts of record) are subject to impeachment. On recommendation of Commission on Judicial Qualifications or on its own motion, Supreme Court may suspend without salary, a judge who pleads guilty or no contest or is found guilty of a crime punishable as felony or involving moral turpitude under state or federal law. If conviction is reversed, suspension terminates and judge is paid salary for period of suspension. If conviction becomes final, judge is removed from office by Supreme Court. Upon recommendation of Commission on Judicial Qualifications, Supreme Court may remove a judge for willful misconduct in office, willful and persistent failure to perform duties, habitual intemperance or conduct prejudicial to the administration of justice that brings the office into disrepute. The Court may also retire a judge for a disability that seriously interferes with performance of duties and is (or is likely to become) permanent.	Vacancies on Supreme Court, court of appeals and superior courts (in counties with population over 150,000) are filled as in initial selection. Vacancies on superior courts in counties of less than 150,000 may be filled by gubernatorial appointment until next general election when judge is elected to fill remainder of unexpired term. Vacancies on justice courts are filled by appointment by county board of supervisors.
Arkansas	Supreme, appellate, circuit and chancery court judges are subject to removal by impeachment or by the governor upon the joint address of 2/3 of the members elected to each house of General Assembly.	By gubernatorial appointment. Appointee serves remainder of unexpired term if it expires at next general election.
California	All judges subject to impeachment for misconduct. All judges subject to recall election. On recommendation of the Commission on Judicial Performance or on its own motion, the Supreme Court may suspend a judge without salary when the judge pleads guilty or no contest or is found guilty of a crime punishable as a felony or any other crime that involves moral turpitude under that law. If conviction is reversed, suspension terminates and judge is paid salary for period of suspension. If conviction becomes final, judge is removed from office by Supreme Court. Upon recommendation of Commission on Judicial Performance, Supreme Court may remove judge for willful misconduct in office, persistent failure or inability to perform duties, habitual intemperance or conduct prejudicial to the administration of justice that brings the office into disrepute. The Court may also retire a judge for disability that seriously interferes with performance of duties and is (or is likely to become) permanent.	Vacancies on appellate courts are filled by gubernatorial appointment with approval of Commission on Judicial Appointments until next general election at which appointee has the right to become a candidate. Vacancies on superior courts are filled by gubernatorial appointment until next election. Vacancies on municipal courts are filled by gubernatorial appointment for remainder of unexpired term; on justice courts by appointment of county board of supervisors or by nonpartisan special election.
Colorado	Supreme, appeals and district court judges are subject to impeachment for high crimes and misdemeanors or malfeasance in office by 2/3 vote of senate. Supreme Court, on its own motion or upon petition, may remove a judge from office upon final conviction for a crime punishable as felony under state or federal law or of any other crime involving moral turpitude under that law. Upon recommendation of Commission on Judicial Discipline, Supreme Court may remove or discipline a judge for willful misconduct in office, willful or persistent failure to perform the duties of office, intemperance or violation of judicial conduct, or for disability that seriously interferes with performance and is (or is likely to become) permanent. Denver county judges are removed in accordance with charter and ordinance provisions.	By gubernatorial appointment (or mayoral appointment in case of Denver county court) from names submitted by appropriate judicial nominating commission.

METHODS FOR REMOVAL OF JUDGES—Continued

State or other jurisdiction	How removed	Vacancies: how filled
Connecticut	Supreme and superior court judges are subject to removal by impeachment or by the governor on the address of 2/3 of each house of the General Assembly. On recommendation of Judicial Review Council or on its own motion, the Supreme Court may remove or suspend a judge of the Supreme or superior court after an investigation and hearing. If the investigation involves a Supreme Court justice, such judge is disqualified from participating in the proceedings. If a judge becomes permanently incapacitated and cannot adequately fulfill the duties of office, the judge may be retired for disability by the Judicial Review Council on its own motion or on application of the judge.	If General Assembly is in session, vacancies are filled by gubernatorial nomination and legislative appointment. Otherwise vacancies are filled temporarily by gubernatorial appointment.
Delaware	Judges are subject to impeachment for treason, bribery or any high crime or misdemeanor. The Court on the Judiciary may (after investigation and hearing) censure or remove a judge for willful misconduct in office, willful and persistent failure to perform the duties of office or an offense involving moral turpitude or other persistent misconduct in violation of judicial ethics. The Court may also retire a judge for permanent mental or physical disability interfering with the performance of duties.	Vacancies are filled as in initial selection.
Florida	Supreme Court, district courts of appeal and circuit court judges are subject to impeachment for misdemeanors in office. On recommendation of Judicial Qualifications Commission, Supreme Court may discipline or remove a judge for willful or persistent failure to perform duties or for conduct unbecoming to a member of the judiciary, or retire a judge for a disability that seriously interferes with the performance of duties and is (or is likely to become) permanent.	By gubernatorial appointment, from nominees recommended by appropriate judicial nominating commission.
Georgia	Judges are subject to impeachment for cause. Upon recommendation of the Judicial Qualifications Commission (after investigation of alleged misconduct), the Supreme Court may retire, remove or censure any judge.	By gubernatorial appointment (by executive order) on nonpartisan basis from names submitted by Judicial Nominating Commission.
Hawaii	Upon recommendation of the Commission on Judicial Discipline (after investigation and hearings), the Supreme Court may reprimand, discipline, suspend (with or without salary), retire or remove any judge as a result of misconduct or disability.	Vacancies on Supreme, intermediate court of appeals and circuit courts are filled by gubernatorial appointment (subject to consent of senate) from names submitted by Judicial Selection Committee. Vacancies on district courts are filled by appointment by chief justice from names submitted by Committee.
Idaho	Judges are subject to impeachment for cause. Upon recommendation by Judicial Council, Supreme Court (after investigation) may remove judges of Supreme Court, court of appeals and district court judges. District court judges (or judicial district sitting en banc), by majority vote in accordance with Supreme Court rules, may remove magistrates for cause. District Magistrate's Commission may remove magistrates without cause during first 18 months of service.	Vacancies on Supreme Court, court of appeals and district courts are filled by gubernatorial appointment from names submitted by Judicial Council for unexpired term. Vacancies in magistrates' division of district court are filled by District Magistrate's Commission for remainder of unexpired term.
Illinois	Judges are subject to impeachment for cause. The Judicial Inquiry Board receives (or initiates) and investigates complaints, and files complaints with the Courts Commission which may remove, suspend without pay, censure or reprimand a judge for willful misconduct in office, persistent failure to perform duties or other conduct prejudicial to the administration of justice or that brings the judicial office into disrepute. The Commission may also suspend (with or without pay) or retire a judge for mental or physical disability.	Vacancies on Supreme, appellate and circuit courts are filled by appointment by Supreme Court until general election. Associate judge vacancies on circuit courts are filled as in initial selection.
Indiana	Upon the recommendation of the Judicial Qualifications Commission or on its own motion, the Supreme Court may suspend or remove an appellate judge for pleading guilty or no contest to a felony or crime involving moral turpitude. The Supreme Court may also retire, censure or remove a judge for other matters. The Supreme Court may also discipline or suspend without pay a non-appellate judge.	Appellate vacancies are filled as in initial selection. Vacancies on circuit courts are filled by gubernatorial appointment until general election. Vacancies on most superior courts are filled by gubernatorial appointment.
Iowa	Supreme and district court judges are subject to impeachment for misdemeanor or malfeasance in office. Upon recommendation of Commission on Judicial Qualifications, the Supreme Court may retire a Supreme, district or associate district judge for permanent disability, or remove such judge for failure to perform duties, habitual intemperance, willful misconduct, conduct which brings the office into disrepute or substantial violations of the canons of judicial ethics. Judicial magistrates may be removed by a tribunal in the judicial election district of the magistrate's residence.	Vacancies are filled as in initial selection.

METHODS FOR REMOVAL OF JUDGES—Continued

State or other jurisdiction	How removed	Vacancies: how filled
Kansas	All judges are subject to impeachment for treason, bribery or other high crimes and misdemeanors. Supreme Court justices are subject to retirement upon certification to the governor (after a hearing by the Supreme Court nominating commission) that such justice is so incapacitated as to be unable to perform adequately the duties of office. Upon recommendation of the Judicial Qualifications Commission, the Supreme Court may retire for incapacity, discipline, suspend or remove for cause any judge below the Supreme Court level.	Vacancies on Supreme Court and court of appeals are filled as in initial selection. Vacancies on district courts (in areas where commission plan has not been adopted) are filled by gubernatorial appointment until next general election, when vacancy is filled for remainder of unexpired term; in areas where commission plan has been adopted, vacancies are filled by gubernatorial appointment from names submitted by judicial nominating commission.
Kentucky	Judges are subject to impeachment for misdemeanors in office. Retirement and Removal Commission, subject to rules of procedure established by Supreme Court, may retire for disability, suspend without pay or remove for good cause any judge. The Commission's actions are subject to review by Supreme Court.	By gubernatorial appointment (from names submitted by appropriate judicial nominating commission) or by chief justice if governor fails to act within 60 days. Appointees serve until next general election after their appointment at which time vacancy is filled.
Louisiana	Judges are subject to impeachment for commission or conviction of felony or malfeasance or gross misconduct. Upon investigation and recommendation by Judiciary Commission, Supreme Court may censure, suspend (with or without salary), remove from office or retire involuntarily a judge for misconduct relating to official duties, willful and persistent failure to perform duties, persistent and public conduct prejudicial to the administration of justice that brings the office into disrepute, or conduct while in office which would constitute a felony or conviction of felony. The Court may also retire a judge for disability which is (or is likely to become) permanent.	Vacancies are filled by Supreme Court appointment if remainder of unexpired term is six months or less; if longer than six months, vacancies are filled in special election.
Maine	Judges are subject to removal by impeachment or by governor upon the joint address of the legislature. Upon recommendation of the Committee on Judicial Responsibility and Disability, the Supreme Judicial Court may remove, retire or discipline any judge.	Vacancies are filled as in initial selection.
Maryland	Judges are subject to impeachment. Judges of Court of Appeals, court of special appeals, trial courts of general jurisdiction and district courts are subject to removal by governor on judge's conviction in court of law, impeachment, or physical or mental disability. Judges are also subject to removal upon joint address of the legislature. Upon recommendation of the Commission on Judicial Disabilities (after hearing), the Court of Appeals may remove or retire a judge for misconduct in office, persistent failure to perform duties, conduct prejudicial to the proper administration of justice, or disability that seriously interferes with the performance of duties and is (or is likely to become) permanent. Elected judges convicted of felony or misdemeanor relating to public duties and involving moral turpitude may be removed from office by operation of law when conviction becomes final.	Vacancies are filled as in initial selection.
Massachusetts	Judges are subject to impeachment. The governor, with the consent of the Executive Council, may remove judges upon joint address of the legislature, and may also (after a hearing and with consent of the Council) retire a judge because of advanced age or mental or physical disability. The Commission on Judicial Conduct, using rules of procedure approved by the Supreme Judicial Court, may investigate the action of any judge that may, by consequence of willful misconduct in office, willful or persistent failure to perform his duties, habitual intemperance or other conduct prejudicial to the administration of justice, bring the office into disrepute.	Vacancies are filled as in initial selection.
Michigan	Judges are subject to impeachment. With the concurrence of 2/3 of the members of the legislature, the governor may remove a judge for reasonable cause insufficient for impeachment. Upon recommendation of Judicial Tenure Commission, Supreme Court may censure, suspend (with or without salary), retire or remove a judge for conviction of a felony, a physical or mental disability, or a persistent failure to perform duties, misconduct in office, habitual intemperance or conduct clearly prejudicial to the administration of justice.	Vacancies in all courts of record are filled by gubernatorial appointment from nominees recommended by a bar committee. Appointee serves until next general election at which successor is selected for remainder of unexpired term. Vacancies on municipal courts are filled by appointment by city councils.

METHODS FOR REMOVAL OF JUDGES—Continued

State or other jurisdiction	How removed	Vacancies: how filled
Minnesota	Supreme and district court judges are subject to impeachment. Upon recommendation of Board of Judicial Standards, Supreme Court may censure, suspend (with or without salary), retire or remove a judge for conviction of a felony, physical or mental disability, or persistent failure to perform duties, misconduct in office, habitual intemperance or conduct prejudicial to the administration of justice.	As a result of executive order, by gubernatorial appointment from names submitted by appropriate committee on judicial nominations. Appointee serves until general election occurring more than one year after appointment at which time a successor is elected to serve a full term.
Mississippi	Judges are subject to impeachment. For reasonable cause which is not sufficient for impeachment, the governor may, on joint address of legislature, remove judges of Supreme and inferior courts. Upon recommendation of Commission on Judicial Performance, Supreme Court may remove, suspend, fine, publicly censure or reprimand a judge for conviction of a felony (in a court outside the state), willful misconduct, willful and persistent failure to perform duties, habitual intemperance or conduct prejudicial to the administration of justice which brings the office into disrepute. The Commission may also retire any judge for physical or mental disability that seriously interferes with performance of duties and is (or is likely to become) permanent.	By gubernatorial appointment, from names submitted by a nominating commission. The office is filled for remainder of unexpired term at next state or congressional election held more than seven months after vacancy.
Missouri	Upon recommendation of Commission on Retirement, Removal and Discipline, Supreme Court may retire, remove or discipline any judge.	Vacancies on Supreme Court, court of appeals and circuit courts which have adopted commission plan are filled as in initial selection. Vacancies on other circuit courts and municipal courts are filled, respectively, by special election and mayoral appointment.
Montana	All judges are subject to impeachment. Upon recommendation of Judicial Standards Commission, Supreme Court may suspend a judge and remove same upon conviction of a felony or other crime involving moral turpitude. The Supreme Court may retire any judge for a disability that seriously interferes with the performance of duties, and that is (or may become) permanent. The Court may also censure, suspend, or remove any judge for willful misconduct in office, willful and persistent failure to perform duties, violation of canons of judicial ethics adopted by the Supreme Court, or habitual intemperance.	Vacancies on Supreme and district courts are filled by gubernatorial appointment (with confirmation by senate) from names submitted by judicial nominating commission. Vacancies on municipal and city courts are filled by appointment by city councils for remainder of unexpired term.
Nebraska	Judges are subject to impeachment. In case of impeachment of Supreme Court justice, judges of district court sit as court of impeachment with 2/3 concurrence required for conviction. In case of other judicial impeachments, Supreme Court sits as court of impeachment. Upon recommendation of the Commission on Judicial Qualifications, the Supreme Court may reprimand, discipline, censure, suspend or remove a judge for willful misconduct in office, willful failure to perform duties, habitual intemperance, conviction of crime involving moral turpitude, disbarment or conduct prejudicial to the administration of justice that brings the office into disrepute. The Supreme Court also may retire a judge for physical or mental disability that seriously interferes with performance of duties and is (or is likely to become) permanent.	Vacancies are filled as in initial selection.
Nevada	All judges, except justices of peace, are subject to impeachment. Judges are also subject to removal by legislative resolution and by recall election. The Commission on Judicial Discipline may censure, retire or remove a Supreme Court justice or district judge for willful misconduct, willful or persistent failure to perform duties or habitual intemperance, or retire a judge for advanced age which interferes with performance of duties or for mental or physical disability that is (or is likely to become) permanent.	Vacancies on Supreme or district courts are filled by gubernatorial appointment from among three nominees submitted by Commission on Judicial Selection. Vacancies on justice courts are filled by appointment by board of county commissioners or by special election.
New Hampshire	Judges are subject to impeachment. Governor, with consent of Executive Council, may remove judges upon address of both houses of legislature.	Vacancies are filled as in initial selection.

METHODS FOR REMOVAL OF JUDGES—Continued

State or other jurisdiction	How removed	Vacancies: how filled
New Jersey........	Supreme and superior court judges are subject to impeachment by the legislature. Except for Supreme Court justices, judges are subject to a statutory removal proceeding that is initiated by the filing of a complaint by the Supreme Court on its own motion or the governor or either house of the legislature acting by a majority of its total membership. Prior to institution of the formal proceedings, complaints are usually referred to the Supreme Court's Advisory Committee on Judicial Conduct, which conducts a preliminary investigation, makes findings of fact and either dismisses the charges or recommends that formal proceedings be instituted. The Supreme Court's determination is based on a plenary hearing procedure, although the Court is supplied with a record created by the Committee. The formal statutory removal hearing may be either before the Supreme Court sitting en banc or before three justices or judges (or combination thereof) specifically designated by chief justice. If Supreme Court certifies to governor that it appears a Supreme Court or superior court judge is so incapacitated as to substantially prevent the judge from performing the duties of office, the governor appoints a commission of three persons to inquire into the circumstances. On their recommendation, the governor may retire the justice or judge from office, on pension, as may be provided by law.	Vacancies on Supreme, superior, appellate division of superior, county, district, tax and municipal courts are filled as in initial selection.
New Mexico.......	Judges are subject to impeachment. The Judicial Standards Commission may discipline or remove a judge for willful misconduct in office, willful and persistent failure to perform duties or habitual intemperance, or retire a judge for disability that seriously interferes with performance of duties and is (or is likely to become) permanent.	Vacancies on Supreme and district courts are filled by gubernatorial appointment (may use nominating commission). Appointee serves until next general election when a successor is elected for remainder of unexpired term. Vacancies on court of appeals are filled by gubernatorial appointment (may use nominating commission), with appointee serving until Dec. 31 following general election or the remainder of the unexpired term, whichever is longer.
New York	All judges are subject to impeachment. Court of Appeals and supreme court judges may be removed by 2/3 concurrence of both houses of legislature. Court of claims, county court, surrogate's court, family court, civil and criminal court (NYC) and district court judges may be removed by 2/3 vote of the senate on recommendation of governor. Commission on Judicial Conduct may determine that a judge be admonished, censured or removed from office for cause, or retired for disability, subject to appeal to the Court of Appeals.	Vacancies on Court of Appeals and appellate division of supreme court are filled as in initial selection. Vacancies in elective judgeships (outside NYC) are filled at the next general election for full term; until election, governor makes appointment (with consent of senate if in session).
North Carolina	Upon recommendation of Judicial Standards Commission, Supreme Court may censure or remove a court of appeals or trial court judge for willful misconduct in office, willful and persistent failure to perform duties, habitual intemperance, conviction of a crime involving moral turpitude, conduct prejudicial to the administration of justice that brings the office into disrepute, or mental or physical incapacity that interferes with the performance of duties and is (or is likely to become) permanent. Upon recommendation of Judicial Standards Commission, a seven-member panel of the court of appeals may censure or remove (for the above reasons) any Supreme Court judge.	Vacancies on Supreme, appeals and superior courts are filled by gubernatorial appointment until next general election. Superior court judges are selected from names submitted by judicial nominating commission.
North Dakota	Supreme and district court judges are subject to impeachment for habitual intemperance, crimes, corrupt conduct, malfeasance or misdemeanor in office. Governor may remove county judges after hearing. All judges are subject to recall election. On recommendation of Commission on Judicial Qualifications or on its own motion, Supreme Court may suspend a judge without salary when judge pleads guilty or no contest or is found guilty of a crime punishable as a felony under state or federal law or any other crime involving moral turpitude under that law. If conviction is reversed, suspension terminates and judge is paid salary for period of suspension. If conviction becomes final, judge is removed by Supreme Court. Upon recommendation of Commission on Judicial Qualifications, Supreme Court may censure or remove a judge for willful misconduct, willful failure to perform duties, willful violation of the code of judicial conduct or habitual intemperance. The Court may also retire a judge for disability that seriously interferes with the performance of duties and is (or is likely to become) permanent.	Vacancies on Supreme and district courts are filled by gubernatorial appointment from nominees submitted by Judicial Nominating Committee until next general election, unless governor calls for a special election to fill vacancy for remainder of term. Vacancies on county courts are filled by appointment by board of county commissioners from names submitted by nominating commission.

METHODS FOR REMOVAL OF JUDGES—Continued

State or other jurisdiction	How removed	Vacancies: how filled
Ohio	Judges are subject to impeachment. Judges may be removed by concurrent resolution of 2/3 members of both houses of legislature or removed for cause upon filing of a petition signed by 15% of electors in preceding gubernatorial election. The Board of Commissioners on Grievances and Discipline of the Judiciary may disqualify a judge from office when judge has been indicted for a crime punishable as felony under state or federal law. Board may also remove or suspend a judge for willful and persistent failure to perform duties, habitual intemperance, conduct prejudicial to the administration of justice or which would bring the office into disrepute, or suspension from practice of law, or retire a judge for physical or mental disability that prevents discharge of duties. Judge may appeal action to Supreme Court.	Vacancies are filled by gubernatorial appointment until next general election when successor is elected to fill unexpired term. If unexpired term ends within one year following such election, appointment is made for unexpired term.
Oklahoma	Judges are subject to impeachment for willful neglect of duty, corruption in office, habitual intemperance, incompetency or any offense involving moral turpitude. Upon recommendation of Council on Judicial Complaints, chief justice of Supreme Court may bring charges against any judge in the Court on the Judiciary. Court on the Judiciary may order removal of judge for gross neglect of duty, corruption in office, habitual intemperance, an offense involving moral turpitude, gross partiality in office, oppression in office, or any other ground specified by law. Judge may also be retired (with or without salary) for mental or physical disability that prevents performance of duties, or for incompetence to perform duties.	Vacancies on Supreme Court and Court of Criminal Appeals are filled as in initial selection. Vacancies on court of appeals and district courts are filled by gubernatorial appointment from nominees submitted by Judicial Nominating Commission. For court of appeals vacancies, judge is elected to fill unexpired term at next general election.
Oregon	On recommendation of Commission on Judicial Fitness, Supreme Court may remove a judge for conviction of a felony or crime involving moral turpitude, willful misconduct in office, willful or persistent failure to perform judicial duties, habitual intemperance, illegal use of narcotic drugs, willful violation of rules of conduct prescribed by Supreme Court or general incompetence. A judge may also be retired for mental or physical disability after certification by Commission. Judge may appeal action to Supreme Court.	Vacancies on Supreme Court, court of appeals and circuit courts are filled by gubernatorial appointment, until next general election when judge is selected to fill unexpired term.
Pennsylvania	All judges are subject to impeachment for misdemeanor in office. Upon recommendation of Judicial Inquiry and Review Board, a judge may be suspended, removed or otherwise disciplined by Supreme Court for specific forms of misconduct, neglect of duty or disability.	By gubernatorial appointment (with advice and consent of senate), from names submitted by appropriate nominating commission. Appointee serves until next election if the election is more than 10 months after vacancy occurred.
Rhode Island	All judges are subject to impeachment. The Supreme Court on its own motion may suspend a judge who pleaded guilty or no contest or was found guilty of a crime punishable as felony under state or federal law or any other crime involving moral turpitude. Upon recommendation of the Commission on Judicial Tenure and Discipline, the Supreme Court may censure, suspend, reprimand or remove from office a judge guilty of a serious violation of the canons of judicial ethics or for willful or persistent failure to perform duties, a disabling addiction to alcohol, drugs or narcotics, or conduct that brings the office into disrepute. The Supreme Court may also retire a judge for physical or mental disability that seriously interferes with performance of duties and is (or is likely to become) permanent. Whenever the Commission recommends removal of a Supreme Court justice, the Supreme Court transmits the findings to the speaker of the house of representatives, recommending the initiation of proceedings for the removal of the justice by resolution of the legislature.	Vacancies on Supreme Court are filled by the two houses of the legislature in grand committee until the next election. In case of a judge's temporary inability, governor may appoint a person to fill vacancy. Vacancies on superior, family and district courts are filled by gubernatorial appointment (with advice and consent of senate) from names submitted by nominating commission.
South Carolina	Judges are subject to removal by impeachment or by governor on address of 2/3 of each house of legislature. Supreme Court may retire judges for mental and/or physical disability. Judicial Standards Commission enforces code of judicial conduct.	Vacancies are filled as in initial selection for remainder of unexpired term; if remainder is less than one year, vacancy is filled by gubernatorial appointment. Vacancies on probate courts are filled by gubernatorial appointment until next general election.
South Dakota	Supreme Court justices and circuit court judges are subject to removal by impeachment. Upon recommendation of Judicial Qualifications Commission, Supreme Court may remove a judge from office.	Vacancies on Supreme and circuit courts are filled by gubernatorial appointment from names submitted by Judicial Qualifications Commission for balance of unexpired term.

METHODS FOR REMOVAL OF JUDGES—Continued

State or other jurisdiction	How removed	Vacancies: how filled
Tennessee.........	Judges are subject to impeachment for misfeasance or malfeasance in office. Upon recommendation of the Court on the Judiciary, the legislature (by concurrent resolution) may remove a judge for willful misconduct in office or physical or mental disability.	Vacancies on Supreme, circuit, criminal and chancery courts are filled by gubernatorial appointment until next biennial election held more than 30 days after vacancy occurred. At election, successor is chosen as in initial selection. Vacancies on court of appeals and court of criminal appeals are filled as in initial selection.
Texas.............	Supreme Court, court of appeals and district court judges are subject to removal by impeachment or by joint address of both houses. Supreme Court may remove district judges from office. District judges may remove county judges and justices of the peace. Upon charges filed by the State Commission on Judicial Conduct, the Supreme Court may remove a judge for willful or persistent violation of the code of judicial conduct, and willful or persistent conduct that is clearly inconsistent with the proper performance of duties, or casts public discredit upon the judiciary or administration of justice. The Court may also retire a judge for disability.	Vacancies on appellate and district courts are filled by gubernatorial appointment until next general election, at which time a successor is chosen. Vacancies on county courts are filled by appointment by county commissioner's court until next election when successor is chosen. Vacancies on municipal courts are filled by governing body of municipality for remainder of unexpired term.
Utah	All judges, except justices of the peace, are subject to impeachment. Following investigations and hearings, the Judicial Conduct Commission may order the reprimand, censure, suspension, removal, or involuntary retirement of any judge for willful misconduct, final conviction of a crime punishable as a felony under state or federal law, willful or persistent failure to perform judicial duties, disability that seriously interferes with performance, or conduct prejudicial to the administration of justice that bring the judicial office into disrepute. Prior to implementation, the Supreme Court reviews the order. Lay justices of the peace may be removed for willful failure to participate in judicial education program.	Vacancies on Supreme, district and circuit courts are filled by gubernatorial appointment from candidates submitted by appropriate nominating commission.
Vermont..........	All judges are subject to impeachment. Supreme Court may discipline, impose sanctions on, or suspend from duties any judge in the state.	Vacancies on Supreme, superior and district courts are filled as in initial selection if senate is in session. Otherwise, by gubernatorial appointment from nominees submitted by judicial nominating board.
Virginia...........	All judges are subject to impeachment. Upon certification of charges against judge by Judicial Inquiry and Review Commission, Supreme Court may remove a judge.	Vacancies are filled as in initial selection if General Assembly is in session. Otherwise, by gubernatorial appointment, with appointee serving until 30 days after commencement of next legislative session.
Washington	A judge of any court of record is subject to impeachment. After notice, hearing and recommendation of Judicial Qualifications Commission, Supreme Court may censure, suspend or remove a judge for violating a rule of judicial conduct. The Supreme Court may also retire a judge for disability that seriously interferes with the performance of duties and is (or is likely to become) permanent.	Vacancies on appellate and general trial courts are filled by gubernatorial appointment until next general election when successor is elected to fill remainder of term.
West Virginia......	Judges are subject to impeachment for maladministration, corruption, incompetency, gross immorality, neglect of duty or any crime or misdemeanor. The Supreme Court of Appeals may censure or suspend a judge for any violation of the judicial code of ethics or retire a judge who is incapable of performing duties because of advancing age, disease or physical or mental infirmity.	Vacancies on appellate and general trial courts are filled by gubernatorial appointment (from names submitted by nominating commission). If unexpired term is less than two years (or such additional period not exceeding three years), appointee serves for remainder of term. If unexpired term is more than three years, appointee serves until next general election, at which time successor is chosen to fill remainder of term.

METHODS FOR REMOVAL OF JUDGES—Continued

State or other jurisdiction	How removed	Vacancies: how filled
Wisconsin........	All judges are subject to impeachment. Supreme Court, court of appeals and circuit court judges are subject to removal by address of both houses of legislature with 2/3 of members concurring, and by recall election. As judges of courts of record must be licensed to practice law in state, removal of judge may also be by disbarment. Upon petition of Judicial Commission or on its own motion, Supreme Court may declare a judgeship vacant for judge's misconduct or disability. In case of disability, judge receives salary and benefits for balance of term or until temporary vacancy terminates, whichever comes first.	Vacancies on Supreme Court, court of appeals and circuit courts are filled by gubernatorial appointment from nominees submitted by nominating commission.
Wyoming	All judges, except justices of peace, are subject to impeachment. Upon recommendation of Judicial Supervisory Commission, the Supreme Court may retire or remove a judge. After a hearing before a panel of three district judges, the Supreme Court may remove justices of the peace.	Vacancies are filled as in initial selection. Vacancies on justice of the peace courts are filled by appointment by county commissioners until next general election.
Dist. of Col.	Commission on Judicial Disabilities and Tenure may remove a judge upon conviction of a felony (including a federal crime), for willful misconduct in office, willful and persistent failure to perform judicial duties or for other conduct prejudicial to the administration of justice which brings the office into disrepute.	Vacancies are filled as in initial selection, unless president of the United States fails to nominate candidate within 60 days of receipt of list of nominees from D.C. Judicial Nominating Commission; then Commission nominates and appoints, wth advice and consent of U.S. Senate.
American Samoa ...	U.S. Secretary of the Interior may remove chief and associate justices for cause. Upon recommendation of governor, chief justice may remove associate judges for cause.	Vacancies are filled as in initial selection.
Guam	On recommendation of Judicial Qualifications Commission, a special court of three judges may remove a judge for misconduct or incapacity.	By gubernatorial appointment.
No. Mariana Is.	Judges are subject to impeachment for treason, commission of a felony, corruption or neglect of duty. Upon recommendation of an advisory commission on the judiciary, the governor may remove, suspend or otherwise sanction a judge for illegal or improper conduct.	By gubernatorial appointment.
Puerto Rico	Supreme Court justices are subject to impeachment for treason, bribery, other felonies and misdemeanors involving moral turpitude. Supreme Court may remove other judges for cause (as provided by judiciary act) after a hearing on charges brought by order of chief justice, who disqualifies self from final proceedings.	Vacancies are filled as in initial selection.

Sources: American Judicature Society, 1984 (used with permission); and update by The Council of State Governments.

Table 4.6
COMPENSATION OF JUDGES OF APPELLATE COURTS
AND GENERAL TRIAL COURTS

State or other jurisdiction	Appellate courts					General trial courts	Salary
	Court of last resort	Salary	Intermediate appellate court	Salary			
Alabama	Supreme Court	$ 77,420(a)	Court of Criminal Appeals	$ 76,420(b)		Circuit courts	$54,000(c)
			Court of Civil Appeals	76,420(b)			
Alaska............	Supreme Court	85,728(d)	Court of Appeals	79,992		Superior courts	77,304(d)
Arizona...........	Supreme Court	75,000	Court of Appeals	72,500		Superior courts	70,000
Arkansas	Supreme Court	66,010(a)	Court of Appeals	63,763(b)		Chancery courts	61,513
						Circuit courts	61,513
California........	Supreme Court	103,469(a)	Courts of Appeal	97,003		Superior courts	84,765
Colorado	Supreme Court	72,000(a,r)	Court of Appeals	67,500(b,r)		District Court	63,000(r)
Connecticut	Supreme Court	77,283(a,c)	Appellate Court	71,860(b,c)		Superior courts	68,647(c)
Delaware	Supreme Court	81,900(a)	. . .	. . .		Superior courts	77,600(b)
Florida	Supreme Court	88,825	District Court of Appeals	83,600		Circuit courts	78,375
Georgia...........	Supreme Court	75,564	Court of Appeals	74,982		Superior courts	62,172(c)
Hawaii	Supreme Court	78,500(a)	Intermediate Court	73,500(b)		Circuit courts	69,500
Idaho	Supreme Court	59,750(a)	Court of Appeals	58,750		District courts	56,000
Illinois...........	Supreme Court	93,266	Appellate Court	87,780		Circuit courts	75,113(b)
Indiana	Supreme Court	66,000(a,e)	Court of Appeals	61,000(b,e)		Circuit courts	56,000(c)
						Superior courts	56,000(c)
Iowa	Supreme Court	65,200(a)	Court of Appeals	61,900(b)		District courts	57,800(b)
Kansas	Supreme Court	65,553(a)	Court of Appeals	63,213(b)		District courts	(g)
Kentucky	Supreme Court	65,633(a)	Court of Appeals	62,954(b)		Circuit courts	60,275
Louisiana	Supreme Court	76,166	Court of Appeals	72,967		District courts	69,769
Maine	Supreme Judicial Court	71,746(a,r)	. . .	. . .		Superior Court	68,715(b,r)
Maryland	Court of Appeals	78,500(a)	Court of Special Appeals	75,500(b)		Circuit courts	74,000
Massachusetts	Supreme Judicial Court	80,500(a)	Appeals Court	74,500(b)		Trial Court(i)	71,520(b)
Michigan	Supreme Court	100,000	Court of Appeals	96,000		Circuit courts	55,000(c)
						Recorder's Court (Detroit)	86,480
Minnesota	Supreme Court	73,981(a)	Court of Appeals	68,248(b)		District courts	65,436
Mississippi	Supreme Court	59,000(a)	. . .	. . .		Chancery courts	51,000
						Circuit courts	51,000
Missouri	Supreme Court	80,649(a)	Court of Appeals	75,087		Circuit courts	61,182(b,s)
						Municipal division of circuit courts	up to 60,180
Montana..........	Supreme Court	50,452(a)	. . .	. . .		District courts	49,178
Nebraska	Supreme Court	63,512	. . .	. . .		District courts	57,038
Nevada	Supreme Court	73,500	. . .	. . .		District courts	67,000
New Hampshire ...	Supreme Court	66,078(a)	. . .	. . .		Superior Court	64,350(b)
New Jersey.......	Supreme Court	93,000(a)	Appellate division of Superior Court	90,000		Superior Court	85,000(k)
New Mexico.......	Supreme Court	60,375(a)	Court of Appeals	57,330(b)		District courts	54,350
New York	Court of Appeals	115,000(a)	Appellate divisions of Supreme Court	102,500(q)		Supreme Court	95,000
North Carolina	Supreme Court	76,236(a,l)	Court of Appeals	72,180(b,l)		Superior Court	64,092(b,l)
North Dakota	Supreme Court	59,140(a)	. . .	. . .		District courts	55,519(b)
Ohio	Supreme Court	83,250(a)	Court of Appeals	77,500		Courts of common pleas	59,750(c)
Oklahoma	Supreme Court	68,006(a)	Court of Appeals	63,756		District Court	(n)
	Court of Criminal Appeals	68,006(a)					
Oregon	Supreme Court	69,552(a)	Court of Appeals	67,896(b)		Circuit courts	63,096
			Tax Court	65,172			
Pennsylvania	Supreme Court	91,500(a)	Superior Court	89,500(b)		Courts of common pleas	80,000(b)
			Commonwealth Court	89,500(b)			
Rhode Island	Supreme Court	78,642(a,o)	. . .	. . .		Superior Court	70,443(b,o)
South Carolina	Supreme Court	80,657(a)	Court of Appeals	76,625(b)		Circuit Court	76,625
South Dakota	Supreme Court	56,975(a)	. . .	. . .		Circuit courts	53,210(b)
Tennessee	Supreme Court	65,650(a)	Court of Appeals	63,125(b)		Chancery courts	60,600
			Court of Criminal Appeals	63,125(b)		Circuit courts	60,600
						Criminal courts	60,600
Texas............	Supreme Court	78,795(a)	Court of Appeals	70,916(b,c)		District courts	56,135(c)
	Court of Criminal Appeals	78,795(a)					
Utah	Supreme Court	58,000(a)	Court of Appeals	55,100(b)		District courts	54,000
Vermont	Supreme Court	60,300(a)	. . .	. . .		Superior courts	57,300(b)
						District courts	57,300(b)
Virginia..........	Supreme Court	83,304(a)	Court of Appeals	79,139(b)		Circuit courts	77,334
Washington	Supreme Court	82,700(r)	Court of Appeals	78,600(r)		Superior courts	74,600(r)
West Virginia	Supreme Court of Appeals	55,000	. . .	. . .		Circuit courts	50,000
Wisconsin.........	Supreme Court	76,859(a)	Court of Appeals	70,947		Circuit courts	66,512
Wyoming	Supreme Court	63,500	. . .	. . .		Distict courts	61,000
Dist. of Col.	Court of Appeals	95,000(a)	. . .	. . .		Superior Court	89,500
American Samoa ..	High Court	69,000(a)	. . .	. . .		(p)	(p)
Guam	. . .	. . .	. . .	. . .		Superior Court	60,000(b)
Puerto Rico	Supreme Court	60,000(a)	. . .	. . .		Superior Court	48,000
						District Court	42,000
Virgin Islands	. . .	. . .	. . .	. . .		Territorial Court	62,000

COMPENSATION OF JUDGES—Continued

Source: National Center for State Courts, *Survey of Judicial Salaries.*
Note: Compensation is shown according to most recent legislation, even though laws may not yet have taken effect.

(a) These jurisdictions pay the following additional amounts to the chief justice or presiding judge of court of last resort:
Alabama, Utah—$1,000.
Arkansas—$5,860.
California—$5,034.
Colorado, Missouri, Pennsylvania—$2,500.
Connecticut—$7,200.
Delaware—$3,200.
Hawaii, Maryland, Idaho—$1,500.
Indiana, New Jersey, South Dakota—$2,000.
Iowa—$5,700.
Kansas—$1,817.
Kentucky—$1,339.
Maine—$3,587.
Massachusetts—$3,000.
Minnesota—$5,732.
Mississippi—chief justice, $1,000; presiding judge, $500.
Montana—$1,270.
New Hampshire—$2,562.
New Mexico—$1,050.
New York—$5,000.
North Carolina—$1,608.
North Dakota—$1,645.
Ohio—$5,250.
Oklahoma—$3,036.
Oregon—$1,740.
Rhode Island—$7,231.
South Carolina—$4,245.
Tennessee—$2,525.
Texas—$515.
Vermont—$2,900.
Virginia—$5,508 (plus $4,000 in lieu of travel expenses).
Wisconsin—$8,477.
District of Columbia—$500.
American Samoa—$17,000.
Puerto Rico—$2,600.

(b) Additional amounts paid to various judges:
Alabama—presiding judge, $500.
Arkansas—chief judge, $1,240.
Colorado—chief judge, $2,500.
Connecticut—state court administrator who is also a judge of superior court, $4,436.
Delaware—presiding judge, $3,200.
Hawaii—chief judge, $2,000.
Illinois—chief judge, $5,486.
Indiana—chief judge, $2,000.
Iowa—chief judge of court of appeals, $1,400; chief judge of district court, $2,700.
Kansas—chief judge, $1,724.
Kentucky—chief judge, $670.
Maine—chief justice, $3,436.
Maryland—chief judge of court of special appeals, $1,500.
Massachusetts—chief justice of appeals court, $2,900; chief administrative justice, $3,180.

Minnesota—chief judge, $2,921.
Missouri—chief judge, $8,343.
New Hampshire—chief judge of superior court, $1,728.
New Mexico—chief judge, $1,102.
New York—presiding judge of appellate division of supreme court, $5,000.
North Carolina—chief judge of court of appeals, $1,620; senior judge of superior court, $2,112.
North Dakota—presiding judge, $1,516.
Oregon—chief judge, $1,656.
Pennsylvania—presiding judges of superior court and commonwealth court, $1,500; president judges of courts of common pleas, additional amounts to $2,500, depending on number of judges and population.
Rhode Island—presiding judge of superior court, $6,867.
South Carolina—chief judge, $3,225.
South Dakota—presiding circuit judge, $1,000.
Tennessee—presiding judge of intermediate appeals courts, $1,010.
Texas—chief judge, $463.
Utah—Chief Judge, $1,000.
Vermont—administrative judges of superior and district courts, $3,000.
Virginia—chief judge, $1,000.
District of Columbia—chief judge of superior court, $500.
Guam—presiding judge, $2,500.
Virgin Islands—presiding judge of territorial court, $4,000.

(c) Plus local supplements, if any. In Texas, for court of appeals, supplements to salary $1,000 less than salary for supreme court justice; for district court, supplements to salary $1,000 less than salary of court of appeals judge.
(d) Salaries range from $85,728 to $97,728 for supreme court justices and $77,304 to $90,828 for superior court judges, depending on location and cost-of-living differentials.
(e) Plus $3,000 subsistence allowance.
(f) Salaries range from $47,000 to $50,000.
(g) Salary varies according to designation: district judge designated administrative judge, $57,638; district judge, $56,989; associate district judge, $51,779; district magistrate judge, $27,316; associate district judge designated as administrative judge, $56,989.
(h) Base figure.
(i) Superior court department of the trial court.
(j) Circuit court associate judges receive $59,400.
(k) Assignment judges recieve $88,000.
(l) Plus 4.8 percent after 5 years, 9.6 percent after 10 years, 14.4 percent after 15 years, and 19.2 percent after 20 years.
(m) Salaries range from $57,500 to $64,500.
(n) District judges, $56,672. Associate district judges paid on basis of population ranges: over 30,000—$51,005; 10,000 to 30,000—$45,338; under 10,000—$42,504.
(o) Salary varies depending on longevity.
(p) General trial court responsibilities handled by the chief justice or associate judges of the High Court.
(q) Appellate Division of the Supreme Court in the 1st, 2nd, 3rd, and 4th departments, the Presiding Justice, $107,500 and the Associate Justice, $102,500. Appellate Terms of the Supreme court, 1st, 2nd, 9th, 10th, 11th, and 12th Districts, $97,500.
(r) Effective July 1, 1988.
(s) State may pay if municipality elects to transfer jurisdiction of municipal ordinance violations to Circuit Court.

Table 4.7
SELECTED DATA ON COURT ADMINISTRATIVE OFFICES

State or other jurisdiction	Title	Established	Appointed by(a)	Salary
Alabama	Administrative Director of Courts (b)	1971	CJ	$65,884
Alaska	Administrative Director	1959	CJ(b)	83,728
Arizona	Court Administrator	1960	SC	73,588
Arkansas	Executive Secretary, Judicial Department	1965	CJ(c)	50,763
California	Administrative Director of the Courts	1960	JC	93,272
Colorado	State Court Administrator	1959	SC	58,500
Connecticut	Chief Court Administrator (d)	1965	CJ	80,717
Delaware	Director, Delaware Court System	1971	CJ	54,500
Florida	State Courts Administrator	1972	SC	61,473
Georgia	Director, Administrative Office of the Courts	1973	JC	57,825
Hawaii	Administrative Director of the Courts	1959	CJ(b)	68,400
Idaho	Administrative Director of the Courts	1967	SC	60,637
Illinois	Administrative Director of the Courts	1959	SC	87,780
Indiana	Executive Director, Division of State Court Administration	1975	SC	55,440
Iowa	Court Administrator	1971	SC	49,700 to 66,200
Kansas	Judicial Administrator	1965	CJ	55,872
Kentucky	Administrative Director of the Courts	1976	CJ	55,125
Louisiana	Judicial Administrator	1954	SC	69,769
Maine	Court Administrator	1975	CJ	55,000
Maryland	State Court Administrator (b)	1955	CJ	70,100
Massachusetts	Administrator, Supreme Judicial Court (b)	1978	SC	77,400
Michigan	State Court Administrator	1952	SC	90,240
Minnesota	Director, State Court Administration	1963	SC	not to exceed 65,436
Mississippi	Executive Assistant to the Supreme Court	1974	SC	45,100
Missouri	Court Administrator	1970	SC	63,963
Montana	State Court Administrator	1975	SC	38,216
Nebraska	State Court Administrator	1972	CJ	50,484
Nevada	Director, Office of Court Administration	1971	SC	53,470
New Hampshire	Director of Administrative Services	1980	SC	60,883
New Jersey	Administrative Director of the Courts	1948	CJ	90,000
New Mexico	Director, Administrative Office of the Courts	1959	SC	52,920
New York	Chief Administrator of the Courts (e)	1978	CJ(f)	110,000
North Carolina	Director, Administrative Office of the Courts	1965	CJ	66,204
North Dakota	Court Administrator (g)	1971	CJ	53,568
Ohio	Administrative Director of the Courts	1955	SC	66,872
Oklahoma	Administrative Director of the Courts	1967	SC	63,756
Oregon	Court Administrator	1971	CJ	63,096
Pennsylvania	Court Administrator	1968	SC	79,000
Rhode Island	Court Administrator	1969	CJ	61,619 (h)
South Carolina	Director of Court Administration	1973	CJ	59,160
South Dakota	State Court Administrator	1974	SC	36,616 to 54,496
Tennessee	Executive Secretary of the Supreme Court	1963	SC	63,125
Texas	Administrative Director of the Courts (i)	1977	SC	56,135
Utah	Court Administrator	1973	SC	54,000
Vermont	Court Administrator (j)	1967	SC	57,300
Virginia	Executive Secretary to the Supreme Court	1952	SC	77,334
Washington	Administrator for the Courts	1957	SC(k)	57,000
West Virginia	Administrative Director of the Supreme Court of Appeals	1975	SC	51,000
Wisconsin	Director of State Courts	1978	SC	70,947
Wyoming	Court Coordinator	1974	SC	39,857
Dist. of Columbia	Executive Officer of D.C. Courts	1971	(l)	89,500
American Samoa	Court Administrator	1977	CJ	26,000
Guam	Administrative Director of Superior Court	N.A.	CJ(m)	43,000
Puerto Rico	Administrative Director of Court Administration	1952	CJ	50,000

Key:
Source: Salary information was taken from *Survey of Judicial Salaries,* published by National Center for State Courts.
Key:
SC—State court of last resort.
CJ—Chief justice or chief judge of court of last resort.
JC—Judicial council.
(a) Term of office for all court administrators is at pleasure of appointing authority.
(b) With approval of Supreme Court.
(c) With approval of Judicial Council.

(d) Administrator is an associate judge of the Supreme Court.
(e) If incumbent is a judge, the title is Chief Administrative Judge of the Courts.
(f) With advice and consent of Administrative Board of the Courts.
(g) Serves as executive secretary to Judicial Council.
(h) Base pay supplemented by increments for length of service.
(i) Serves as executive director of judicial council.
(j) Also clerk of the Supreme Court.
(k) Appointed from list of five submitted by governor.
(l) Joint Committee on Judicial Administration.
(m) Presiding judge of Superior Court (general trial court).

CHAPTER FIVE

STATE ELECTIONS

ELECTION LEGISLATION: 1986-87

By Richard Smolka

State authority in election law was limited during the past two years by two Supreme Court decisions and by other cases decided at the appellate court level. In *Bandemer vs. Davis*, the Supreme Court, by a 6-3 vote, ruled that political gerrymandering may violate the Constitution when it consistently degrades a group's influence. In that decision, however, the court, by a 7-2 vote, found that an Indiana state legislative districting plan did not violate the new Constitutional standard established by the court.

The Supreme Court also limited the power of the states to regulate primary elections when it struck down a Connecticut law requiring the Republican Party to conduct a closed party primary election. The court decided the Republican Party rules which permitted independent voters to vote for certain offices in the Republican primary, prevailed over state law.

The court's decision opened-up to challeng all closed primary elections if either party adopts rules allowing a more open system than state law permits. The decision in *Tashjian vs. Republican Party of Connecticut* (December, 1986) did not indicate whether a party could close its primary election if the state law prescribed an open primary.

The courts also are beginning to consider whether judicial elections are covered by Sec. 2 of the Voting Rights Act and if so, whether at-large judicial elections discriminate against minorities. Section 2 of the Voting Rights Act prohibits any practice or procedure that is not equally open to participation by minorities or one in which minorities have less opportunity than others to elect representatives of their choice. Federal appellate courts in the 5th and 6th Circuits ruled early in 1988 that judicial elections are covered by the Voting Rights Act. (See *Mallory vs. Eyrich*, 6th Cir., No. 87-3838, 1988 and *Chisom vs. Edwards*, 5th Cir., No. 87-3463, 1988.) Lawsuits have also been filed challenging the entire method of electing judges in Illinois and other states.

Plaintiffs are seeking smaller judicial districts to enable more minority judges to be elected. If the court finds that at-large elections in states, counties, or cities discriminate against minorities, it could overturn state constitutional provisions regarding election to judicial office.

A three-judge panel of the Ninth Federal Circuit Court in February 1988 also limited state powers to prohibit exit polls within 300 feet of the polls (*Daily Herald Company vs. Munro.*) The court said the law, which was drafted to prevent network projections from exit polls, was an unconstitutional infringement on First Amendment rights. The decision overturned the state law, but did not diminish the power of the state to prohibit conduct that disrupts the polling place.

Presidential Primaries

The number of states providing for presidential primaries in 1988 increased substantially over 1984 when southern state legislators helped establish "Super Tuesday," a regional primary on March 8, 1988. A total of 20 states held either a primary or a caucus that day. In 1988, a total of 37 states held presidential primaries for at least one of the two major political parties.

Super Tuesday added an election date to the calendar for most of the states introducing the presidential primary. With few exceptions, primary elections for state and local offices remained scheduled later in the year. Although the regional primary drew some attention from candidates who otherwise might have ignored the political concerns of the South, voter turnout was not exceptional and political leaders in some of these states indicated they will not repeat the experiment in 1992. At the same time, state legislatures in other parts of the

Richard G. Smolka is Professor of Government at The American University in Washington, D.C. and Editor of Election Administration Reports.

country were at least considering the possibility of simultaneous presidential primaries in their regions.

Super Tuesday at one time was viewed as a potential predecessor to a national primary election. Enthusiasm for a national primary, however, was reduced somewhat because the division of the vote among several Democratic candidates on Super Tuesday indicated that a national primary also might not produce clear winner.

Absentee Ballot Procedures

For the past two decades most states have eased absentee ballot procedures to make more people eligible for absentee ballots and to make it easier to obtain and cast an absentee ballot. Some states place no restriction on who may apply for an absentee ballot. Others have dropped requirements for medical verification on applications made because of illness, notarization of absentee ballot requests or on absentee ballot envelopes, or restrictions on who distribute absentee ballot applications or return voted absentee ballots to the election office. Recent events, however, have caused a few states to begin to tighten up absentee ballot procedures.

Experience with vote fraud has caused certain states, among them California, Connecticut and Virginia to change their laws. California, which permits anyone to apply for an absentee ballot as a matter of convenience, found absentee voting in some municipal and special elections to exceed 50 percent of the total votes cast. Because of charges of fraud, intimidation, and illegal assistance to absentee voters, several states recently imposed new restrictions on how absentee ballots may be procured or returned, or passed specific laws prescribing more regulated absentee voting by residents of nursing homes, hospitals or other institutions.

The liberal absentee ballot laws, it is contended, allow campaign workers to solicit absentee ballot requests, then have them mailed to the party or candidate headquarters where they are hand delivered to the voter. The campaign worker assists the voter in completing the ballot and takes the voted ballot from the voter for delivery to the election office.

One example of an absentee ballot controversy occurred in a 1987 election in Inglewood, Calif. An incumbent city councilman who received only 30 percent of the vote at the polls,

won the election by 17 votes after receiving 86 percent of the votes cast by absentee ballot. A court found at least five instances in which the man who came to pick up the absentee ballots from voters insisted that the envelope be returned unsealed. In several cases, the person who came to pick up the ballot requested that someone other than the person named on the absentee ballot mark the ballot, and persons soliciting absentee ballot applications and voted ballots were charged with misrepresenting absentee ballot procedures to voters. Based on the absentee ballot irregularities, a court overturned the election.

Despite such examples, states which have little history of vote fraud are likely to continue easing absentee ballot procedures, especially for elderly, disabled, students, vacationers and others for whom in person may be inconvenient. At the same time, legislatures have been fairly quick to respond if it appears that fraud may occur under less restrictive laws.

Voter Registration

During the past two years, states continued a 25-year trend to make voter registration easier. State initiatives were most noticeable through administrative action rather than legislative. At least 15 states now provide for voter registration through non-election agency employees of state and local government, including departments of motor vehicles, social service agencies, employment agencies and other public offices.

States with agency registration include Alaska, Arizona, Colorado, Iowa, Maryland, Michigan, Minnesota, Montana, Nevada, New York, Oregon, Ohio, Oklahoma, Vermont and Washington. Taking advantage of permissive state legislation, many cities also introduced public agency voter registration. Among them were New York, San Francisco, Minneapolis, Houston, Los Angeles, San Antonio and Des Moines.

Connecticut, in 1987, joined 23 states and the District of Columbia by permitting voters to register by mail. Through administrative action many states increased the number of deputy registrars. Others expanded voter registration practices by increasing registration sites and operating hours and engaging in imaginative voter-outreach programs such as drive-in registration locations.

Handicapped Access to the Polls.

The states, in response to a new federal law, made 73 percent of all polling places accessible to the handicapped. However, 22 states had previously passed some form of polling place accessibility legislation. Others had relied on absentee voting or curbside voting to accommodate persons who were physically unable to get to the polls.

In its first report to Congress on the subject, the Federal Election Commission (FEC) said state compliance with the Voting Accessibility for the Elderly and Handicapped Act was generally good, although non-uniform reporting practices made comparisons among the states difficult. The new federal law allowed states to define "accessibility," but definitions varied widely. Statistics from the states, however, indicated that attention was focused on unramped stairs, inadequate door widths, obstructed walkways or pathways and inadequate parking for the handicapped.

The FEC report indicated that those states that employed the most demanding criteria for accessibility reported the most difficulty in achieving 100 percent compliance. States with more general definitions of accessibility tended to report complete or substantial compliance with the law.

The federal law and supervision of implementation by state election agencies had an impact on the number and location of polling places. Some local governments shifted polls from private homes or other private locations to public schools or other public buildings which were already accessible. In some jurisdictions, the number of polling places was reduced due to the limited number of accessible locations available.

By making accessibility to the handicapped a higher criteria for polling place selection than geographical location, local officials expressed concern that some people might have to travel greater distances to vote.

Election Technology

State legislatures are paying more attention to the continued expansion of computerized vote counting and electronic voting machines. Although not a single case of computer vote fraud was identified as of January 1988, enough inaccurate vote counts because of human error occurred to draw legislative and public attention.

The Texas Legislature passed a 1987 law that imposed greater scrutiny on voting systems and procedures used for electronic vote counting. The Texas law requires that a voting system may not be used unless it can be audited. The law also requires depositing program codes and related documentation with the secretary of state and no modem access to tabulation equipment during the counting function. Other provisions include complete tests "using all applicable ballot formats," procedures for reconciling discrepancies and provisions for partial manual recounts to check the accuracy of a system.

Texas required recertification of all electronic vote counting systems used in the state after the passage of the law.

The Federal Election Commission's National Clearinghouse on Election Administration, assisted by its advisory panel of state and local election officials, has been developing proposed voluntary standards and management guidelines for computerized vote-counting systems. The project has received strong endorsement from the chief election officers of several states and recommendations are likely to generate state legislation and changes in procedures for jurisdictions using electronic vote-counting systems.

To achieve these results, states are continuing to centralize responsibility for administering elections.

Federal Overseas Write-in Ballot

The Uniformed and Overseas Citizens Absentee Voting Act passed by Congress in August 1986 imposes some changes on state election practices but does not enfranchise any new voters. The law, passed in response to complaints by citizens overseas, was designed to protect the voting rights of military and overseas citizens. Many citizens reported that although they had applied for ballots well before the election, they had not received the absentee ballot in time to return it prior to the deadline and thereby lost their vote.

The new federal law permits overseas citizens to use the write-in ballot after they have made a timely application for an absentee ballot from their home state, but did not receive it in time to return it prior to the deadline.

The federal ballot is a blank conditional ballot for use only in general elections. An overseas citizen may cast a vote by writing in the name of a candidate or a political party. Regardless of state write-in laws, the federal ballot cannot be voided for misspellings, abbreviations, or other minor variations in the form of a candidate's name.

The federal write-in ballot may not be counted if the ballot is submitted from any location within the U.S.; if the application of the overseas voter for a state absentee ballot is received less than 30 days prior to an election; or if a state absentee ballot of the overseas voter is received by the appropriate state election official not later than the deadline for absentee ballots.

The federal write-in ballot form was developed by the Federal Voting Assistance Program in the Department of Defense after consultation with chief election officers in each state. The ballot, to be printed by the federal agency, will be made available overseas through the same government officials who now distribute federal post card application for registration and absentee ballots.

Selected references

Brace, Kimball W. *Voting Equipment by County, 1986*. A national map of use of voting equipment usage by types, Washington D.C.: Election Data Services, 1987.

Congressional Research Service, "Voter Registration and Turnout: 1948-1986," Washington, D.C., Library of Congress, Report 88-247 GOV, March 29, 1988.

Davis vs. Bandemer, 106, S. Ct. 2797 (1986).

Everson, David, ed. *Comparative State Politics Newsletter*. A bimonthly publication of the Illinois Legislative Studies Center, Sangamon State University, Springfield, Ill.

Federal Election Commission, *Polling Place Accessibility in the 1986 General Election*, Washington, D.C., 1987.

Palmer, James A. and Edward D. Feigenbaum, *Campaign Finance Law 1986*. Federal Election Commission, Washington, D.C.,

Smolka, Richard G. *Election Administration Reports*, A biweekly newsletter for election officials, Washington, D.C.

Tashjian vs. Republican Party of Connecticut (107 S. Ct. 544, 1986).

Table 5.1
STATE OFFICIALS TO BE ELECTED: 1988 AND 1989

State or other jurisdiction	Date of general elections in 1988(a)	Governor	Lieutenant governor	Secretary of state	Attorney general	Treasurer	Auditor	Judges of court of last resort(b)	Judges of intermediate appellate court(b)	Board of educ. members	Public utilities commissioners	Superintendent of public instruction	Other	State legislatures: members to be elected — Senate	State legislatures: members to be elected — House
Alabama	Nov. 8							5	2(c)					1/2(d)	All
Alaska	Nov. 8							1	8					All	All
Arizona	Nov. 8							2	3		1	★	State mine inspector; corporation commr.	1/2(d)	All
Arkansas	Nov. 8							1	3					1/2(d)	All
California	Nov. 8													1/2	All
Colorado	Nov. 8							1	3	3				1/2(d)	All
Connecticut	Nov. 8													All	All
Delaware	Nov. 8	★	★										Insurance commr.	1/2(d)	All
Florida	Nov. 8								1			★		1/2	All
Georgia	Nov. 8								1		1	★		All	All
Hawaii	Nov. 8													1/2(d)	All
Idaho	Nov. 8													All	All
Illinois	Nov. 8													1/3(d)	All
Indiana	Nov. 8	★	★	★	★	★	★					★		1/2	All
Iowa	Nov. 8													1/2	All
Kansas	Nov. 8							1						All	All
Kentucky	Nov. 8							2	4					1/2	All
Louisiana	(e)												Public service commr.		
Maine	Nov. 8							1		4				All	All
Maryland	Nov. 8								3						
Massachusetts	Nov. 8							2						All	All
Michigan	Nov. 8							1	13	4					All
Minnesota	Nov. 8							1	1	4					All
Mississippi	Nov. 8					N.A.		4							
Missouri	Nov. 8	★	★	★	★	★	★	1	2	4				1/2	All
Montana	Nov. 8	★	★	★	★		★	2			3	1		1/2(d)	All
Nebraska	Nov. 8							1	1		2			1/2(d)	U
Nevada	Nov. 8							1					3 university regents	All	All
New Hampshire	Nov. 8	★											5 executive councillors		All
New Jersey (1989)	Nov. 7	★													17.5%
New Mexico	Nov. 8							1	1				Corporation commr.	All	1/2
New York	Nov. 8													All	All
North Carolina	Nov. 8	★	★	★	★	★	★	1	2		1	1	Commr. of agriculture; commr. of insurance; commr. of labor	All	All
North Dakota	Nov. 8	★	★	★	★	★	★	1			1	1	Commr. of insurance; commr. of agriculture; tax commr.	1/2	All
Ohio	Nov. 8							2	All					1/2	All

STATE OFFICIALS TO BE ELECTED: 1988 AND 1989—Continued

State or other jurisdiction	Date of general elections in 1988(a)	Governor	Lieutenant governor	Secretary of state	Attorney general	Treasurer	Auditor	Judges of court of last resort(b)	Judges of intermediate appellate court(b)	Board of education members	Public utilities commissioners	Superintendent of public instruction	Other	State legislatures: Senate	State legislatures: House
Oklahoma	Nov. 8	...	...	...	...	...	...	3	4	...	...	★	Corporation commr.	1/2	All
Oregon	Nov. 8	...	...	★	★	★	...	3	5	...	...	...	...	1/2(d)	All
Pennsylvania	Nov. 8	...	...	...	...	★	★	2	...	...	...	...	...	1/2	All
Rhode Island	Nov. 8	★	★	★	★	★	...	...	...	...	...	...	...	All	All
South Carolina	Nov. 8	...	...	...	...	...	...	...	...	...	...	...	...	All	All
South Dakota	Nov. 8	...	...	...	...	...	...	...	...	...	1	...	...	All	All
Tennessee	Nov. 8	...	...	...	...	...	...	1	6	...	...	...	...	1/2(d)	All
Texas	Nov. 8	...	...	...	...	...	...	3	3	15	...	...	Railroad commr. (2)	1/2(d)	All
Utah	Nov. 8	...	...	...	...	...	...	2	...	3	...	...	...	1/2(d)	All
Vermont	Nov. 8	★	★	★	★	★	★	...	...	...	...	...	...	All	All
Virginia ....(1989)	Nov. 8	★	★	...	★	...	...	...	...	...	...	...	...	1/2(d)	All
Washington	Nov. 8	★	★	★	★	★	★	3	...	...	...	...	...	1/2	All
West Virginia	Apr. 1	★	...	★	★	★	★	...	...	★	★	★	...	1/2(d)	2/3(d)
Wisconsin	Nov. 4	...	...	...	...	...	...	...	2	...	...	★	...	1/2(d)	All
Wyoming ....(1989)	Apr. 7	...	...	...	...	...	...	1	2	...	...	1	...	1/2	All
Dist. of Col.	Nov. 8	...	...	...	...	...	...	...	...	...	...	...	...	(i)	U
American Samoa	Nov. 8	★	★	...	...	...	...	...	...	...	...	...	...	...	All
Guam	Nov. 8	...	...	...	...	...	...	...	...	3	...	...	Village commrs.	All	U
No. Mariana Is.	Nov. 3	★	★	...	...	...	...	...	...	...	...	...	...	...	All
Puerto Rico	Nov. 8	★	...	...	...	...	...	...	...	...	...	...	...	...	...
Virgin Islands	Nov. 8	★	★	...	...	...	...	...	...	...	...	...	...	1/2	All (U)

Source: State election administration offices.

Note: In several states, elections for some state offices do not occur in 1988 or 1989. When a number appears in a column instead of a star, the figure indicates the number of individuals on the state court or other government body up for election in 1988 or 1989. The information in this table is current as of February 1988.

Key:
★—Office up for election.
...—Office not up for election.
U—Unicameral legislative body.

(a) Elections for 1989 are indicated by (1989) before date for general election.
(b) For some states, information on number of judges facing election in 1988 or 1989 is tentative given the nature of the selection and retention processes.

(c) Court of Civil Appeals-1; Criminal Court of Appeals-1.
(d) Actual number of seats up for election: Alaska (11); Arkansas (12); Colorado (18); Delaware (10); Hawaii (13); Illinois (20); Nebraska (25); Nevada (10); Oregon (16); Tennessee (16); Utah (14); Washington (24); Wisconsin (S-15, H-64).
(e) Under Louisiana's election law, candidates of all parties run together on a single ballot in September; if no candidate for an office wins a majority of the vote, the top two finishers oppose each other in a November runoff. In 1988, the elections will be held on Sept. 27, 1988 and Nov. 8, 1988. In 1989, the elections will be held on Oct. 24, 1989 and Nov. 21, 1989.
(f) Supreme Court (5); Court of Criminal Appeals (1).
(g) Mayor.
(h) Six members of the Council of the District of Columbia.

Table 5.2
METHODS OF NOMINATING CANDIDATES FOR STATE OFFICES

State or other jurisdiction	Method(s) of nominating candidates
Alabama...................	Primary election; however, the state executive committee or other governing body of any political party may choose instead to hold a state convention for the purpose of nominating candidates (meetings must be held at least 60 days prior to the date on which primaries are conducted).
Alaska.....................	Primary election.
Arizona....................	Primary election.
Arkansas	Primary election.
California.................	Primary election.
Colorado	Primary election; however, a political party may hold a pre-primary convention (at least 55 days before the primary) for the designation of candidates. Each candidate who receives at least 20 percent of the convention delegates' votes is listed on the primary ballot, with the candidate receiving the most votes listed first.
Connecticut	Convention/primary election. Political parties hold state conventions (convening not earlier than the 61st day and closing not later than the 43rd day before the date of the primary) for the purpose of endorsing candidates. If no one challenges the endorsed candidate, no primary election is held. However, if anyone (who received at least 20 percent of the delegate vote) challenges the endorsed candidate, a primary election is held to determine the party nominee for the general election.
Delaware	Primary election.
Florida	Primary election.
Georgia....................	Primary election.
Hawaii	Primary election.
Idaho	Primary election.
Illinois....................	Primary election; however, state conventions are held for the nomination of candidates for trustees of the University of Illinois.
Indiana	Primary election held for the nomination of candidates for governor and U.S. senator; state party conventions held for the nomination of candidates for other state offices.
Iowa	Primary election; however, if there are more than two candidates for any nomination and none receives at least 35 percent of the primary vote, the primary is deemed inconclusive and the nomination is made by party convention.
Kansas	Primary election; however, candidates of any political party whose secretary of state did not poll at least 5 percent of the total vote cast for all candidates for that office in the preceding general election are restricted to nomination by delegate or mass convention.
Kentucky	Primary election.
Louisiana	Primary election. Open primary system requires all candidates, regardless of party affiliation, to appear on a single ballot. Candidate who receives over 50 percent of the vote in the primary is elected to office; if no candidate receives a majority vote, a runoff election is held between the two candidates who received the most votes.
Maine	Primary election.
Maryland	Primary election.
Massachusetts	Primary election.
Michigan	Primary election held for the nomination of candidates for governor, U.S. congressional seats and state senators and representatives; state conventions held for the nomination of candidates for lieutenant governor, secretary of state and attorney general.
Minnesota	Primary election.
Mississippi	Primary election.
Missouri	Primary election.
Montana...................	Primary election.

METHODS OF NOMINATING CANDIDATES FOR STATE OFFICES—Continued

State or other jurisdiction	Method(s) of nominating candidates
Nebraska	Primary election.
Nevada	Primary election.
New Hampshire	Primary election.
New Jersey	Primary election.
New Mexico	Primary election.
New York	Convention/primary election. The person who receives the majority vote at the state party committee meeting becomes the designated candidate for nomination; however, all other persons who received at least 25 percent of the convention vote may demand that their names appear on the primary ballot as candidates for nomination.
North Carolina	Primary election.
North Dakota	Primary election.
Ohio	Primary election.
Oklahoma	Primary election.
Oregon	Primary election.
Pennsylvania	Primary election.
Rhode Island	Primary election.
South Carolina	Primary election for republicans and democrats; party conventions held for four minor parties. All must file with proper election commission by varying dates depending on office.
South Dakota	Primary election. Any candidate who receives a plurality of the primary vote becomes the nominee; however, if no individual receives at least 35 percent of the vote for the candidacy for the offices of governor, U.S. Senator, or U.S. congressman, a runoff election is held 2 weeks later.
Tennessee	Primary election.
Texas	Primary election.
Utah	Convention/primary election. Delegates from the county primary conventions are elected to the state primary convention for the purpose of selecting the political party nominees to run at the regular primary election.
Vermont	Primary election.
Virginia	Primary election; however, the state executive committee or other governing body of any political party may choose instead to hold a state convention for the purpose of nominating candidates (party opting for convention can only do so within 32 days prior to date on which primary elections are normally held).
Washington	Primary election.
West Virginia	Primary election.
Wisconsin	Primary election.
Wyoming	Primary election.
Dist. of Col.	Primary election.

Note: The nominating methods described here are for state offices; procedures may vary for local candidates. Also, independent candidates may have to petition for nomination. For more information on primaries, see Table 5.3, "Primary Election Information."

Table 5.3
PRIMARY ELECTION INFORMATION

State or other jurisdiction	Dates of 1988 primaries for state officials(a)		Party affiliation for primary voting		Voters receive ballot of:	
	Primary	Runoff primary(b)	Voters must declare/change affiliation prior to election day	Voters select party on election day	One party (c)	All parties participating(d)
Alabama	June 7	June 28	...	★	★	...
Alaska	Aug. 23	...	...	(e)	...	★(e)
Arizona	Sept. 13	...	At least 50 days before	...	★	...
Arkansas	March 8	March 22	...	★	★	...
California	June 7	...	At least 29 days before	...	★	...
Colorado	Aug. 9	...	At least 32 days before	...	★	...
Connecticut	Sept.14	...	At least 6 months before(f)	...	★	...
Delaware	Sept. 10	...	At least 21 days before	...	★	...
Florida	Sept. 6	Oct. 4	At least 30 days before	...	★	...
Georgia	Aug. 9	Aug. 30	...	★	★	...
Hawaii	Sept. 17	...	...	★	...	★
Idaho	May 24	...	...	★	...	★
Illinois	March 15	...	...	★	★	...
Indiana	May 3	...	...	★	★	...
Iowa	June 7	...	...	★	★	...
Kansas	Aug. 2	...	At least 20 days before(f)	(f)	★	...
Kentucky	May 27	...	At least 30 days before	...	★	...
Louisiana	Oct. 1(g)	Nov. 8(g)	...	(g)	...	(g)
Maine	June 14	...	At least 90 days before(f)	(f)	★	...
Maryland	March 8	...	At least 4 months before(f)	...	★	...
Massachusetts	Sept. 15	...	At least 28 days before(f)	(f)	★	...
Michigan	Aug. 2	...	...	★	...	★
Minnesota	Sept. 13	...	...	★	...	★
Mississippi	March 8	March 29	...	★	★	...
Missouri	Aug. 2	...	...	★	★	...
Montana	June 7	...	...	★	...	★
Nebraska	May 10	...	At least 10 days before	...	★	...
Nevada	Sept. 6	...	At least 30 days before	...	★	...
New Hampshire	Sept. 13	...	At least 10 days before	...	★	...
New Jersey	June 7	...	At least 50 days before(f)	(f)	★	...
(1989)	June 10					
New Mexico	June 7	...	At least 42 days before(h)	...	★	...
New York	Sept. 15	...	At least 1 year before(f)	...	★	...
North Carolina	May 3	May 31	At least 21 days before(i)	...	★	...
North Dakota	June 14	...	...	★	...	★
Ohio	May 3	...	...	★	★	...
Oklahoma	Aug. 23	Sept. 20	(j)	(j)	★	...
Oregon	May 17	...	At least 20 days before(f)	...	★	...
Pennsylvania	April 26	...	At least 30 days before	...	★	...
Rhode Island	Sept. 14	...	At least 90 days before(f)	(f)	★	...
South Carolina	June 14	June 28	...	★	★	...
South Dakota	June 7	...	At least 15 days before	...	★	...
Tennessee	Aug. 4	...	...	★	★	...
Texas	March 8	April 12	...	★	★	...
Utah	Sept. 13	...	...	★	...	★
Vermont	Sept. 13	...	...	★	...	★
Virginia	June 14	...	...	★	★	...
(1989)	June 13					
Washington	Sept. 20	...	...	(e)	...	★(e)
West Virginia	May 10	...	At least 30 days before	...	★	...
Wisconsin	Sept. 13	...	...	★	...	★
Wyoming	Aug. 16	...	...	★	★	...
Dist. of Col.	Sept. 13	...	At least 30 days before	...	★	...
Guam	Sept. 2	...	...	★	...	★
Virgin Islands	Sept. 2	...	At least 30 days before	...	★	...

PRIMARY ELECTION INFORMATION—Continued

Sources: Federal Election Commission; League of Women Voters, *Vote! The First Steps;* state election administration offices.

(a) Primaries for state offices in 1989 have (1989) before the date.

(b) A runoff election between the top two candidates is held if the leading candidate does not get a majority of the votes cast in the first primary.

(c) The type of primary in which voters receive only the ballot of their party choice in a primary (voters must declare their affiliation on, or prior to, election day) is generally referred to as a *closed* primary.

(d) The type of primary in which voters receive a ballot for all parties and select the party of their choice in the privacy of the voting booth is generally referred to as an *open* primary.

(e) Voters are not restricted to one party. In Alaska and Washington, voters participate in a *blanket* primary. As in regular open primaries, voters receive a ballot that contains the primary ballot for all parties. However, a voter in the blanket primary may pick and choose among the parties in moving through the lists of candidates for various offices. The only restriction is that the voter can indicate only one preference for each office.

(f) Applies to previously affiliated registered voters. In Connecticut, unaffiliated voters may now vote in some Republican primaries but not in Democratic primaries. In Kansas, Maine, Massachusetts, New Jersey (new voters), and Rhode Island, unaffiliated voters may declare party at the polls. In Maryland and Oregon, new registrants declare at time of registration. In New York, new voters declare affiliation at least 30 days before, while previously eligible voters declare at least 60 days before.

(g) Louisiana has an open primary which requires all candidates, regardless of party affiliation, to appear on a single ballot. If a candidate receives over 50 percent of the vote in the primary, he is elected to the office. If no candidate receives a majority vote, then a single election is held between the two candidates receiving the most votes.

(h) Previously affiliated voters may not change party affiliation after proclamation of primary.

(i) Business days.

(j) New registrants declare at time of registration; however, no changes in party affiliation are allowed between July 1 and Sept. 30 in an even-numbered year.

Table 5.4
CAMPAIGN FINANCE LAWS: GENERAL FILING REQUIREMENTS
(As of January 1986)

State or other jurisdiction	Statements required from	Statements filed with	Time for filing
Alabama	Political committees.	Secy. of state for statewide and judicial offices. Secy. of state and probate judge in county of residence for legislative office.	15 days after primary or runoff and 30 days after any other election.
Alaska	Candidates; groups and individuals who contribute $250 or more per year to any group or candidate; a business entity, labor organization or municipality making a contribution or expenditure; suppliers receiving more than $250 from a candidate or group.	Alaska Public Offices Commission, central office.	30 days and 1 week before and 10 days after election; annually on Dec. 31 for contributions and expenditures received but not reported that year.(a)
Arizona	Candidates, committees and continuing political organizations.	Secy. of state.	10-15 days before and 20 days after primary; 10-15 days before and 20 days after general or special election; supplemental reports annually by Apr. 1 for contributions and expenditures subsequent to post-election report.
Arkansas	Candidates and persons acting on their behalf receiving contributions in excess of $250/election from any person.	Secy. of state and county clerk in county of residence.	Contributions: 25 and 7 days before and 30 days after election. Expenditures: 30 days after election. Supplemental reports for expenditures subsequent to post-election report.
California	Candidates receiving or spending more than $500 in an election; certain committees; elected officers.	Secy. of state, registrar of Los Angeles and San Francisco and clerk of county of residence; legislative candidates also file with clerk of county with largest number of registered voters in district.	Semiannual: July and Jan. 31; periodic: March and Sept. 22 and 12 days before 1st Tues. after 1st Mon. in June and Nov.; 40 and 12 days before and 65 days after any election not held on the 1st Tues. after the 1st Mon. of June or Nov.(b)
Colorado	Candidates; certain political committees; persons making independent expenditures of more than $100.	Secy. of state.	11 days before and 30 days after election. Supplemental reports annually on the anniversary of the election until no unexpended balance or deficit.(c)
Connecticut	Candidates, political committees, and party committees receiving or spending over $500 in a single election.	Secy. of state.	2nd Thurs. of Jan., Apr., July, Oct.; 7 days before and 30 days after primary (45 days after general election). Supplemental reports for deficits: 90 days after election and within 30 days after any change and within 7 days after distribution of surplus funds.
Delaware	Candidates, committees.	State election commissioner.	20 days before election, Dec. 31 of election year, Dec. 31 of post-election year and annually by Dec. 31 until fund closes.
Florida	Candidates; political committees; committees of continuous existence; party executive committees; persons making independent expenditures of $100 or more.	Qualifying officer and supervisor of elections in county of residence for candidates. Division of elections and supervisor of elections in county where election is held for statewide committees.	Pre-election: 10th day of each calendar quarter from time treasurer is appointed through last day of qualifying for office; the 4th, 18th and 32nd days preceding the first and second primaries, and the 4th and 18th days preceding the general election for unopposed candidates. Post-election report 10 days after each quarter until no unexpended surplus.
Georgia	Candidates, committees, and certain other individuals or organizations.	Secy. of state and copy to probate judge in candidate's county of residence.	45 and 15 days before and 10 days after primary and 15 days before general or special election; Dec. 31 of election year; and annually on Dec. 31 for winning candidates with additional contributions or expenditures since filing post-election report.
Hawaii	Candidates, parties, committees.	Campaign Spending Commission.	10 working days before each election; 20 days after primary and 30 days after general or special election. Supplemental reports in event of surplus or deficit over $250 on 5th day after the last day of election year, and every 6 months thereafter.

GENERAL FILING REQUIREMENTS—Continued

State or other jurisdiction	Statements required from	Statements filed with	Time for filing
Idaho	Candidates; political committees; organizations which contribute more than $500 to a political committee; persons making independent expenditures of more than $50.	Secy. of state.	By 7 days before election and 30 days after.(d) Supplemental reports on 10th day of Jan., Apr., July and Oct. annually in the event of an unexpended balance or expenditure deficit.
Illinois	Political committees.	State Board of Elections.	Contributions: 15 days before election and 90 days after each general election. Annual reports of contributions and expenditures: July 31.
Indiana	Political committees and any person making an independent expenditure.	State Election Board; legislative candidate committees file duplicate with elections board of candidate's county of residence.	10 days (if postmarked) or 8 days (if hand-delivered) before election or convention; 20 days after convention, if no pre-convention report is filed; annually by Jan. 15.
Iowa	Candidates and committees receiving contributions of or spending more than $250.	Campaign Finance Disclosure Commission.	20th day of Jan., May, July, and Oct. annually. In years in which the candidate does not stand for election, the May and July reports are not required of a candidate committee.
Kansas	Candidates; political committees; party committees; persons making independent expenditures of more than $100.	Secy. of state.	6 days before election and Dec. 10 of election years.
Kentucky	Candidates, campaign committees, political party executive committees, permanent committees.	Kentucky Registry of Election Finance with duplicates to clerk of county where candidate resides. Campaign committees file with appropriate central campaign committees.	Candidates and campaign committees: 32 and 12 days before and 30 days after election. Political party executive committees: 30 days after election. Permanent committees: last day of each calendar quarter. Semiannual supplemental reports June 30 and Dec. 31 until fund shows a zero balance.
Louisiana	Candidates; political committees; any person (not a candidate) making independent expenditures or accepting contributions (other than to or from a candidate) of more than $500.	Supervisory Committee.	Candidates and committees: 180, 90, 30, and 10 days before primary; 10 days before and 40 days after general election; Jan. 15 annually until a deficit has been paid, or if the candidate or committee has received contributions or made expenditures during the year.(e)
Maine	Candidates; political committees; state party committees; political action committees; any person (not a candidate) making expenditures of more than $50.	Commission on Governmental Ethics and Election Practices.	7 days before and 42 days after election; gubernatorial candidates also file Jan. 15 after non-election years if they received or spent more than $1,000 in that year, and 42 days before election. Disposition of surplus or deficit in excess of $50 on 1st day of each quarter of fiscal year until eliminated.(f)
Maryland	Candidates receiving contributions of or spending $300 or more; political committtees; political clubs spending more than $50.	Board at which candidate filed certificate of candidacy. Central committees and political committees file with State Administrative Board of Election Laws.	4th Tues. before primary; 2nd Fri. before any election; 3rd Tues. after general election or before taking office, whichever is earlier. Disposition of surplus or deficit 6 months after general election and annually on anniversary of election until eliminated.
Massachusetts	Candidates and political committees.	Director of campaign and political finance.	8 days before election and Jan. 10 of year after general election for General Assembly candidates; 3rd business day after designating depository and Jan. 10 of year after general election for others.
Michigan	Candidates; political committees; party committees; persons making independent expenditures of $100 or more.	Secy. of state.	11 days before and 30 days after election; committees other than independent committees by Jan. 31 of each year.(g)

GENERAL FILING REQUIREMENTS—Continued

State or other jurisdiction	Statements required from	Statements filed with	Time for filing
Minnesota	Candidates; political committees; party committees; and individuals making independent expenditures over $100.	Ethical Practices Board. Legislative candidates file copies with auditor of each county in district.	10 days before election and Jan. 31 annually.(h)
Mississippi	Candidates and political committees.	Secy. of state.	Contributions: 5th day of each month of candidacy and Sat. before election. Expenditures: candidates report within 60 days after election; committees, within 30 days.
Missouri	Candidates who spend or receive more than $1,000 or who receive a single contribution in excess of $250; committees; and persons making independent expenditures of $500 or more.	Secy. of state for statewide candidates and committees, and candidates for Supreme Court or appellate court; candidates for legislature file with secy. of state and election authority of candidate's place of residence.	40 and 7 days before and 30 days after election. Supplemental reports each Jan. 15 if contributions or expenditures of $500 or more were made or received since last report. Quarterly reports if post-election report shows outstanding debts of more than $500, until deficit is below $500.(i)
Montana	Candidates and political committees.	Commissioner of political practices and county clerk or recorder where candidate resides or political committee has headquarters.	Statewide office: March 10 and Sept. 10 in election years. 15 and 25 days before and 20 days-after election; supplemental reports March 10 and Sept. 10 until all debts and obligations are extinguished and no more contributions are accepted or expenditures made. Legislative office: 10 days before and 20 days after election.(j)
Nebraska	Candidate committees, political party committees, and certain other committees.	Nebraska Accountability and Disclosure Commission and election commissioner or clerk of candidate's county of residence.	30 and 10 days before and 40 days after election. June 1 annually for certain committees.(k)
Nevada	Candidates, party committees, and other committees spending over $500.	Officer with whom candidate filed declaration of candidacy.	15 days before primary and 15 days before and 30 days after general election.
New Hampshire	Candidates, and political committees spending over $500.	Secy. of state.	Wed. 3 weeks before and Wed. immediately before election; 2nd Fri. after election and every 6 months thereafter until outstanding debt or obligation is satisfied or surplus depleted.(l)
New Jersey	Candidates and political committees.	Election Law Enforcement Commission.	29 and 11 days before and 20 days after election; every 60 days after election (starting with the 19th day after election) until no balance remains.(m)
New Mexico	Candidates receiving or spending more than $500; political committees.	Secy. of state.	10 days before and 30 days after election; 6 months after if any contributions are unspent or debt remains unpaid, and 12 months after an election (and annually thereafter) if debt remains unpaid.
New York	Candidates and political committees spending or receiving more than $1,000 in a filing period.	State Board of Elections.	Primary election reports filed on the 32nd and 11th day before, and 10th day after; general election reports filed 32nd and 11th day before, and 27th day after. Additional statements on Jan. 15 and July 15 until satisfaction of all liabilities and disposition of all assets.(n)
North Carolina	Candidates, political committees, and individuals making independent expenditures over $100.	State Board of Elections for statewide and multicounty district offices. County board of elections for others.	10 days before and after election (losing candidates in primary file 10 days after election). Supplemental reports due Jan. 7 after general election and annually following years in which contributions are received or expenditures made. Independent expenditure reports are filed within 10 days after expenditure is made.
North Dakota	Candidates receiving more than $100 in contributions; political parties receiving contributions of more than $100 or contributing more than $100 to a candidate; political committees.	Secy. of state. Legislative candidates file with county auditor of candidate's county of residence.	Candidates: 10 days before election and 30 days after close of calendar year. Political committees: by Oct. 15, with supplemental report 30 days after close of calendar year. Political parties: 30 days after close of calendar year.(o)

GENERAL FILING REQUIREMENTS—Continued

State or other jurisdiction	Statements required from	Statements filed with	Time for filing
Ohio	Candidate campaign committees, political committees, political parties.	Secy. of state. Legislative candidates file with Board of Elections for county with largest population.	12 days before and 45 days after election and last business day of Nov. annually.
Oklahoma	Candidates, political parties, and organizations.	State Election Board.	10 days before election and 40 days after general election. Supplemental reports within 6 months and 10 days after general election if any contributions are received or expenditures made within 6 months after general election.
Oregon	Candidates, political committees.	Secy. of state.	29-39 and 4-7 days before and 30 days after election. If post-election statement shows an unexpended balance of contributions or a deficit, supplemental reports are required annually on Sept. 10 until there is no balance or deficit.(p)
Pennsylvania	Candidates and political committees receiving or spending over $250.	Secy. of the commonwealth.	6th Tues. and 2nd Fri. before and 30 days after election. Annual reports required on Jan. 31 until there is no balance or debt in the report.
Rhode Island	Candidates, political action committees, and political party committees spending more than $5,000 or receiving any contribution in excess of $200; and those making independent expenditures of $200 or more.	State Board of Elections; independent expenditures are to be reported to the appropriate candidate or party committee.	28 and 7 days before and 28 days after election. Party committees also file by March 1 annually. Supplemental reports are required at 90-day intervals commencing 120 days after election until dissolution.
South Carolina	Candidates and committees.	State Ethics Commission; Senate or House Ethics Committee for legislative office.	30 days after election and 10 days after end of each calendar quarter in which funds are received or spent.
South Dakota	Candidates and certain committees.	Secy. of state.	Last Tues. before election and Feb. 1 of each year (for statewide offices); July 1 and Dec. 31 of each year (for legislative office).(q)
Tennessee	Candidates and political campaign committees.	Secy. of state; copy filed with county election commission of residence for legislative office.	7 days before any election and 48 days after general election. Supplemental report one year after election (or sooner if no surplus or deficit).
Texas	Candidates and political committees.	Secy. of state.	30 and 7 days before and 30 days after election; annually on Jan. 15 if contributions are received or expenditures made.(r)
Utah	Personal campaign committees for gov., state auditor, state treasurer, atty. gen.; state senate or house of representatives candidates; party committees.	Lt. governor.	10th day of July, Oct., and Dec. of election year and 5th day before election for state office candidates and for political parties 30 days after election for legislative candidates.
Vermont	Candidates, political parties, and political committees.	Secy. of state for state office, political parties, and political committees. Senatorial or representative district clerk for legislative office.	State office, political parties, and political committees: 40 and 10 days before any election and 10 days after general election. Legislative office: within 10 days before any election and within 30 days after general election. Supplemental reports for all candidates annually on July 15 until all expenditures are accounted for and all deficits are eliminated.
Virginia	Candidates, political action committees, and political party committees meeting certain thresholds.	State Board of Elections and election board where candidate resides.	8 days before and 30 days after election. Statewide candidates and committees also report 30 days before election.(s)
Washington	Candidates and political committees.	Public Disclosure Commission and county auditor in county of candidate's residence. Continuing political committees: commission and auditor in county where committee maintains its office.	Initial report at time of appointment of treasurer; 21 and 7 days before election and 21 days after any election; 10th day of each month in which no other report is filed if total contributions or expenditures since last report exceed $200.(t)

GENERAL FILING REQUIREMENTS—Continued

State or other jurisdiction	Statements required from	Statements filed with	Time for filing
West Virginia	Candidates and their financial agents; party committees, persons, and treasurers supporting or opposing any candidate.	Secy. of state for multicounty office. Clerk of county commission for single-county office.	Last Sat. in March or 15 days after that day before a primary; 7-10 days before and 25-30 days after any election.
Wisconsin	Candidates; political party committees, political committees, and others receiving or spending over $25.	State Elections Board. Legislative candidates also file duplicate with county clerk of counties in district.	8-14 days before election; continuing reports by committees and individuals, Jan. 1-31 and July 1-10 annually.(u)
Wyoming	Candidates, political party committees, and political action committees.	Secy. of state. Legislative candidates also file with county clerk.	10 days after election. Non-party committees: 14 days after election; party committees: 7 days after election. Committees formed after election report July 1 and Dec. 31 of odd-numbered years until all debts are paid.
Dist. of Col.	Candidates spending more than $250; political committees; and individuals making independent expenditures of $50 or more.	Director of campaign finance.	Each year: Jan. 31. Election years: 10th day of March, June, Aug., Oct., and Dec. and 8 days before election. Non-election years: July 31.(v)

Source: James A. Palmer and Edward D. Feigenbaum, *Campaign Finance Law 1986* (Washington, D.C.: National Clearinghouse on Election Administration, Federal Election Commission, 1986).

Note: This table deals with filing requirements for statewide and legislative offices in general terms. For detailed legal requirements or requirements for county and local offices, state statutes should be consulted.

(a) Contributions exceeding $250 made within one week before the election must be reported within 24 hours.

(b) Contributions or independent expenditures of $1,000 or more received after the final pre-election report must be reported within 48 hours.

(c) Contributions exceeding $500 received within 16 days before the election must be reported within 48 hours.

(d) Winning candidates in a primary do not file a post-primary report.

(e) Special report is required within 48 hours after receipt of a contribution of more than $2,000, or a candidate's expenditure of more than $200 to any candidate, committee, or other person required to file disclosure reports who makes endorsements during the period from 20 days before any election through election day.

(f) Contributions to or expenditures by candidates of $1,000 or more made after the 11th day and more than 48 hours before any election must be reported within 48 hours.

(g) Contributions of $200 or more received after the closing date of a pre-election statement, but before the second day prior to the election, must be reported within 48 hours after receipt.

(h) Contributions of $2,000 or more ($200 or more for a legislative candidate) received between the closing date of the last pre-election report and the election must be reported within 48 hours after receipt.

(i) Contributions of more than $1,000 ($500 for a legislative candidate) received after the closing date of the last pre-election report but before election day must be reported within 48 hours after receipt.

(j) Contributions of $500 or more received by a statewide candidate between the 10th day before the election and election day must be reported within 24 hours. Contributions of $100 or more received by a legislative candidate between the 15th day before the election and election day must

be reported within 24 hours.

(k) Contributions of $500 or more received after last pre-election statement must be reported within five days after receipt.

(l) Contributions exceeding $500 received after Wednesday before any election must be reported within 24 hours.

(m) Contributions of $250 or more received by a candidate or political committee between the 13th day before and the election day must be reported within 48 hours.

(n) Contributions of more than $1,000 received after the final pre-election statement must be reported within 24 hours after receipt.

(o) Contributions of $500 or more received by a candidate in the 15-day period before any election must be reported within 48 hours of receipt.

(p) Contributions of $500 or more received after the eighth day before the day preceding the election must be reported on the day before the election.

(q) Contributions of $500 or more received within the nine days immediately prior to the election must be reported within 48 hours after receipt.

(r) Aggregate contributions of more than $1,000 for a Senate candidate or more than $200 for a House candidate accepted between the ninth and second day before an election must be reported within 48 hours of acceptance.

(s) Contributions of $1,000 or more received between the 11th day before any nomination or election and the day of nomination or election must be reported within 72 hours, but no later than the day prior to the day of nomination or election.

(t) Contributions of $500 or more made or received after the last pre-election report and before any election must be reported within 24 hours after the contribution is made or received. Candidates and committees may also qualify for abbreviated reporting.

(u) Contributions of more than $500 received after the last pre-election report must be reported within 24 hours after receipt.

(v) Contributions of $200 or more received after last pre-election report must be reported within 24 hours.

Table 5.5
CAMPAIGN FINANCE LAWS: LIMITATIONS ON CONTRIBUTIONS
BY ORGANIZATIONS
(As of January 1986)

State or other jurisdiction	Corporate	Labor union	Separate segregated fund— political action committee (PAC)	Regulated industry	Political party
Alabama............	Limited to $500 to any one candidate, political committee, or political party per election.	Unlimited.	Unlimited.	Public utility regulated by public service commission may only contribute through a PAC.	Unlimited.
Alaska(a)	Limited to $1,000 per year for each elective office.	Same as corporate.	Same as corporate.	. . .	Unlimited.
Arizona............	Prohibited.	Prohibited.	Unlimited.	Prohibited.	Unlimited.
Arkansas(a)	Limited to $1,500 per candidate, per election.	Same as corporate.	Same as corporate.	. . .	Limited to $2,500 per candidate, per election.
California(a)	Unlimited.	Unlimited.	Unlimited.	. . .	Unlimited.
Colorado(a)	Unlimited.	Unlimited.	Unlimited.	. . .	Unlimited.
Connecticut(a)	Prohibited.	Prohibited.	Labor organization PAC limited to an aggregate of $50,000 per election, and same limits per candidate as individuals. Corporate PAC limited to an aggregate of $100,000 per election, and twice the limits per candidate as individuals.	Prohibited.	Unlimited.
Delaware(a)	Limited to $1,000 per statewide candidate per election, $500 per non-statewide candidate, per election.	Same as corporate.	Same as corporate.	. . .	. . .
Florida(a)	Limited to $3,000 for statewide office candidate per election; $2,000 for candidate for retention as district court of appeal judge; $1,000 for any other candidate or committee, per election.	Same as corporate.	Same as corporate.	. . .	Unlimited, except that party may not contribute to a candidate for judicial office.
Georgia............	Unlimited.	Unlimited.	Unlimited.	Public utility corporation regulated by public service commission may not contribute, directly or indirectly.	Unlimited.
Hawaii(a)	Limited to $2,000 in any election period.	Same as corporate.	Same as corporate.	. . .	Sliding scale percentage limit based upon candidate expenditure limits.
Idaho	Unlimited.	Unlimited.	Unlimited.	. . .	Unlimited.
Illinois.............	Unlimited.	Unlimited.	Unlimited.	. . .	Unlimited.

LIMITATIONS ON CONTRIBUTIONS BY ORGANIZATIONS—Continued

State or other jurisdiction	Corporate	Labor union	Separate segregated fund—political action committee (PAC)	Regulated industry	Political party
Indiana	Limited to an aggregate of $5,000 for statewide candidates; an aggregate of $5,000 for state party central committees; an aggregate of $2,000 for other offices; and an aggregate of $2,000 for other party committees.	Same as corporate.	Unlimited.	...	Unlimited.
Iowa	Prohibited.	Unlimited.	Unlimited.	Prohibited for insurance companies.	Unlimited.
Kansas	Limited to $3,000 per statewide candidate per election, and $750 per candidate, per election for other offices.	Same as corporate.	Same as corporate.	Same as corporate.	Unlimited.
Kentucky(a)	Prohibited.	Unlimited.	Unlimited.	Prohibited.	Unlimited.
Louisiana(a)	Unlimited.	Unlimited.	Unlimited.	...	Unlimited.
Maine	Limited to $5,000 per candidate per election.	Same as corporate.	Same as corporate.	Same as corporate.	Same as corporate.
Maryland(a)	Limited to an aggregate of $2,500 per election and $1,000 per candidate, per election.	Same as corporate.	Unlimited.	...	Unlimited.
Massachusetts(a)	Prohibited.	Unlimited.	Unlimited.	Prohibited.	Unlimited.
Michigan(a)	Prohibited for candidate elections. Corporations may contribute up to $40,000 to a ballot question committee.	Limited to $1,700 for a statewide office, $450 for state senator, $250 for state representative candidates per election.	Same as labor union.	Prohibited.	State central committee is limited to $34,000 for a statewide office, $4,500 for a state senator, $2,500 for state representative candidates, per election. Local party is limited to $17,000 for a statewide office, $4,500 for a state senator, $2,500 for state representative candidates, per election.
Minnesota	Prohibited.	Limited to $60,000 per election year for governor/lt. governor ($12,000 in non-election years); $10,000 per election year for attorney general ($2,000 in non-election years); $5,000 per election year for other statewide offices ($1,000 in non-election years); $1,500 per election year for state senator ($300 in non-election years); $750 per election year for state representative ($150 in non-election years).	Same as labor union.	Prohibited for insurance companies.	Limited to $300,000 per election year for governor/lt. governor ($60,000 in non-election years); $50,000 per election year for attorney general ($10,000 in non-election years); $25,000 per election year for other statewide offices ($5,000 in non-election years); $7,500 per election year for state senator ($1,500 in non-election years); $3,750 per election year for state representative ($750 in non-election years).

LIMITATIONS ON CONTRIBUTIONS BY ORGANIZATIONS—Continued

State or other jurisdiction	Corporate	Labor union	Separate segregated fund—political action committee (PAC)	Regulated industry	Political party
Mississippi	Limited to $1,000 per candidate per year and $250 for judicial office primary candidates.	Unlimited, except in contributions to judicial office primary candidates ($250 limit).	Same as labor union.	Generally prohibited.	Same as labor union.
Missouri(a)	Unlimited.	Unlimited.	Unlimited.	. . .	Unlimited.
Montana	Prohibited.	Limited for all elections in a campaign to $1,500 for governor/lt. governor; $750 for other statewide candidates; $400 for public service commissioner or state senator; $250 for other candidates.	Limited for all elections in a campaign to $8,000 for governor/lt. governor; $2,000 for other statewide candidates; $1,000 for public service commissioner; $600 for state senator ($1,000 total from all nonparty political committees); $300 for other candidates ($600 total for house candidates from all nonparty political committees).	Prohibited.	Contributions to judicial candidates are prohibited; otherwise, same as PAC.
Nebraska(a)	Unlimited.	Unlimited.	Unlimited.	. . .	Unlimited.
Nevada	Unlimited.	Unlimited.	Unlimited.	. . .	Unlimited.
New Hampshire	Prohibited.	Prohibited.	Limited to $5,000.	Prohibited.	Unlimited.
New Jersey(a)	Unlimited, except in contributions to governor in any primary or general election ($800 limit).	Same as corporate.	Same as corporate.	Prohibited for insurance corporations or associations and certain other corporations.	Unlimited, except state committee contribution to governor in general election ($800 limit).
New Mexico	Unlimited.	Unlimited.	Unlimited.	. . .	Prohibited in primary elections, otherwise unlimited.
New York(a)	Limited to an aggregate of $5,000 per calendar year.	Unlimited.	Unlimited.	Public utilities may not contribute from public service revenues unless cost is charged to shareholders.	Unlimited.
North Carolina(a)	Prohibited.	Prohibited.	Limited to $4,000 per committee or candidate, per election.	Prohibited.	Unlimited.
North Dakota	Prohibited.	Prohibited.	Unlimited.	Prohibited.	Unlimited.
Ohio(a)	Prohibited.	Unlimited.	Prohibited for corporate PAC; otherwise, unlimited.	Prohibited for public utilities.	Unlimited.
Oklahoma	Prohibited.	Limited to $5,000 to a political party or organization or a state office, and $1,000 for a local office candidate.	Same as labor union.	Prohibited.	Same as labor union.
Oregon	Unlimited.	Unlimited.	Unlimited.	Generally prohibited.	Unlimited.
Pennsylvania(a)	Prohibited.	Prohibited.	Unlimited.	Prohibited.	Unlimited.
Rhode Island	Unlimited.	Unlimited.	Unlimited.	. . .	Unlimited.

LIMITATIONS ON CONTRIBUTIONS BY ORGANIZATIONS—Continued

State or other jurisdiction	Corporate	Labor union	Separate segregated fund— political action committee (PAC)	Regulated industry	Political party
South Carolina	Unlimited.	Unlimited.	Unlimited.	. . .	Unlimited.
South Dakota	Prohibited.	Prohibited if union is a corporation; otherwise, unlimited.	Unlimited.	Prohibited.	Unlimited.
Tennessee	Prohibited.	Unlimited.	Unlimited.	Prohibited.	Unlimited.
Texas(a)	Prohibited.	Prohibited.	Unlimited.	Prohibited.	Unlimited.
Utah	Unlimited.	Unlimited.	Unlimited.	Unlimited.	Unlimited.
Vermont(a)..........	Limited to $1,000 per candidate or committee, per election.	Same as corporate.	Limited to $5,000 per candidate or committee per election.	Same as corporate.	Same as corporate.
Virginia.............	Unlimited.	Unlimited.	Unlimited.	. . .	Unlimited.
Washington(a)	Unlimited, except aggregate contributions of more than $5,000 may not be made to a candidate or political committee within 21 days of a general election.	Same as corporate.	Same as corporate.	Same as corporate.	Same as corporate.
West Virginia(a)	Prohibited.	Limited to $1,000 per candidate, per election.	Same as labor union.	Prohibited.	Same as labor union.
Wisconsin(a)	Prohibited.	Limited according to formula for statewide candidates; and $1,000 for state senator; $500 for state representative; and $6,000 for political parties.	Same as labor union.	Public utilities may not offer special privileges to candidates.	Certain specified percentage limits per candidate.
Wyoming	Prohibited.	Prohibited.	Unlimited.	Prohibited.	Prohibited in primary elections.
Dist. of Col.(a)	Limited to an aggregate of $4,000 per election and $2,000 for mayor, $1,500 for council chairman, $1,000 for council member at-large, $400 for council member from a district and board of education member at-large, $200 for board of education member from a district or a party official, $25 for neighborhood advisory commission member.	Same as corporate.	Same as corporate.	. . .	. . .

Source: James A. Palmer and Edward D. Feigenbaum. *Campaign Finance Law 1986.* (Washington, D.C.: National Clearinghouse on Election Administration, Federal Election Commission, 1986).
Note: Consult state statutes for more details.
Key:
. . .—No reference to contribution in the law.
(a) Restriction on cash contributions. In Alaska, Arkansas, Florida, Kentucky, Maryland, Missouri, New York, North Carolina, Ohio, and Texas (no limit for general purpose committee): must be $100 or less. In California and Colorado: must be less than $100. In Connecticut, Delaware, Massachusetts, Nebraska, Vermont, Washington, West Virginia, and Wisconsin: must be $50 or less. In Hawaii: cash contribution of more than $100 requires a receipt to the donor and a record of the transaction. In Louisiana: cash contributions of more than $300 must be by written instrument; all cash contributions by corporations, labor organizations, and associations must be by check. In New Jersey: cash contributions are prohibited unless in response to public solicitation, or a written contributor statement is filed (cumulative maximum of $100). In Pennsylvania: must be $100 or less per candidate. In District of Columbia: must be less than $50.

Table 5.6
CAMPAIGN FINANCE LAWS: LIMITATIONS ON CONTRIBUTIONS
BY INDIVIDUALS
(As of January 1986)

State or other jurisdiction	Individual	Candidate	Candidate's family member	Government employees	Anonymous or in name of another
Alabama...........	Unlimited.	Unlimited.	Unlimited.	No solicitation of state employees for state political activities. City employees may contribute to county/state political activities; county employees may contribute to city/state political activities.	. . .
Alaska(a)	Limited to $1,000 per year for each elective office.	Unlimited.	Same as individual.	Contribution may not be required of state employees.	Prohibited.
Arizona............	Unlimited.	Unlimited.	Unlimited.	. . .	. . .
Arkansas(a)	Limited to $1,500 per candidate, per election.	Unlimited.	Same as individual.	Contribution may not be required of state employees. State division of social services/county board of public welfare employees may not solicit, nor may certain judges solicit for campaigns other than their own.	Anonymous contribution must be less than $50 per year. Contribution in the name of another prohibited.
California(a)	Unlimited.	Unlimited.	Unlimited.	Local agency employees may not solicit employees of their agency except incidentally through a large solicitation.	Anonymous contribution must be less than $100 per year. Contribution in the name of another prohibited.
Colorado(a)	Unlimited.	Unlimited.	Unlimited.	. . .	Contribution in the name of another prohibited.
Connecticut(a)	Limited to an aggregate of $15,000 per election and $2,000 for governor; $1,500 for other statewide office; $1,000 for sheriff; $500 for state senator or probate judge; $250 for state representative, town, city or borough office; $5,000 per year to state party.	Unlimited.	Unlimited.	May not be required. State department heads and deputy department heads may not solicit.	Anonymous contribution must be less than $15. Contribution in the name of another prohibited.
Delaware(a)	Limited to $1,000 per statewide candidate, per election; $500 per non-statewide candidate per election.	Limited to $5,000 per election.	Same as candidate.	. . .	Prohibited.
Florida(a)	Limited to $3,000 for statewide office candidate per election; $2,000 for candidate for retention as district court of appeal judge; $1,000 for any other candidate or committee per election.	Unlimited.	Same as individual.	Judges not elected in public elections between competing candidates may not make contributions. Solicitation generally prohibited for state employees. Judges may not solicit contributions.	Contribution in the name of another prohibited.

LIMITATIONS ON CONTRIBUTIONS BY INDIVIDUALS—Continued

State or other jurisdiction	Individual	Candidate	Candidate's family member	Government employees	Anonymous or in name of another
Georgia.............	Unlimited.	Unlimited.	Unlimited.	State employee may not coerce another state employee into contributing.	Anonymous contribution prohibited.
Hawaii(a)...........	Limited to $2,000 in any election period.	Limited to an aggregate of $50,000 in any election year.	Same as candidate.	Solicitation of contributions prohibited. Contribution to other employees is prohibited.	Prohibited.
Idaho	Unlimited.	Unlimited.	Unlimited.	Contributions permitted. State employee may not coerce another state employee into contributing.	Anonymous contribution must be $50 or less. Contribution in the name of another prohibited.
Illinois..............	Unlimited.	Unlimited.	Unlimited.	Generally prohibited.	Prohibited.
Indiana	Unlimited.	Unlimited.	Unlimited.	Contribution may not be required. Employees may not solicit or receive contributions.	Contribution in the name of another prohibited.
Iowa	Unlimited.	Unlimited.	Unlimited.	. . .	Prohibited.
Kansas	Limited to $3,000 per statewide candidate, per election; and $750 per candidate per election for other offices.	Unlimited.	Spouse is unlimited.	Contribution may not be required.	Anonymous contribution must be $10 or less. Contribution in the name of another prohibited.
Kentucky(a).........	Limited to $3,000 per candidate per election.	Unlimited.	Same as individual.	Contribution may not be required. Contribution may be prohibited, depending on who is recipient.	Anonymous contribution must be $50 or less. Contribution in the name of another prohibited.
Louisiana(a).........	Unlimited.	Unlimited.	Unlimited.	Contribution may not be solicited.	Anonymous contribution generally prohibited if more than $25. Contribution in the name of another prohibited.
Maine	Limited to an aggregate of $25,000 in a calendar year and $1,000 per candidate, per election.	Unlimited.	Spouse is unlimited.	State employee may not coerce another state employee into contributing.	Contribution in the name of another prohibited.
Maryland(a).........	Limited to an aggregate of $2,500 per election and $1,000 per candidate per election.	Unlimited.	Spouse is unlimited.	Contribution may not be required.	Prohibited.
Massachusetts(a).....	Limited to $1,000 per candidate, per year. Minors limited to $25 per year.	Unlimited.	Same as individual.	Contribution may not be required. Solicitation generally prohibited.	Contribution in the name of another prohibited.
Michigan(a).........	Limited to $1,700 for statewide office, $450 for state senator, $250 for state representative candidates per election.	Limited to $25,000 per gubernatorial campaign.	Same as candidate.	Contribution may not be required.	Prohibited.

LIMITATIONS ON CONTRIBUTIONS BY INDIVIDUALS—Continued

State or other jurisdiction	Individual	Candidate	Candidate's family member	Government employees	Anonymous or in name of another
Minnesota	Limited to $60,000 per election year for governor/lt. governor ($12,000 in non-election years); $10,000 per election year for attorney general ($2,000 in non-election years); $5,000 per election year for other statewide offices ($1,000 in non-election years); $1,500 per election year for state senate ($300 in non-election years); $750 per election year for state representative ($150 in non-election years).	Unlimited.	Same as individual.	Contribution may not be required. Solicitation prohibited during hours of employment.	Anonymous contribution must be less than $20. Contribution in the name of another prohibited.
Mississippi	Unlimited, except in contributions to judicial office primary candidates ($250 limit).	Same as individual.	Same as individual.	Contribution may not be required. Highway patrol or correctional system employees may not contribute. Solicitation prohibited for state correctional system employees.	. . .
Missouri(a)	Unlimited.	Unlimited.	Unlimited.	. . .	Anonymous contribution must be $10 or less. Contribution in the name of another prohibited.
Montana	Limited for all elections in a campaign to $1,500 for governor/lt. governor; $750 for other statewide candidates; $400 for public service commissioner, district court judge, or state senator; $250 for other candidates.	Unlimited.	Same as individual.	Contributions by municipal employees in city with municipal commission form of government prohibited. Solicitation by municipal government employees prohibited.	Prohibited.
Nebraska(a)	Unlimited.	Unlimited.	Unlimited.	Solicitation prohibited during hours of employment.	Prohibited.
Nevada	Unlimited.	Unlimited.	Unlimited.	Employees may not solicit from other employees.	. . .
New Hampshire	Limited to $5,000.	Unlimited.	Same as individual.	Contribution may not be solicited or required from classified state employees.	Prohibited.
New Jersey	Unlimited, except in contribution to governor in any primary or general election ($800 limit). Contributor's spouse may contribute up to $800 for governor in general election.	Unlimited, but if receiving public funds for governor, limited to $25,000 per election from own funds.	Unlimited, except in contribution to governor in any primary or general election ($800 limit).	Prohibited to demand from other public employees.	Prohibited.

LIMITATIONS ON CONTRIBUTIONS BY INDIVIDUALS—Continued

State or other jurisdiction	Individual	Candidate	Candidate's family member	Government employees	Anonymous or in name of another
New Mexico........	Unlimited.	Unlimited.	Unlimited.	Solicitation prohibited while on duty.	Anonymous contribution in excess of $50 subject to special report.
New York(a)	Limited to an aggregate of $150,000 in a calendar year and a maximum aggregate per office. Statewide: $0.025 x voters (voters in party in primaries). Senate or assembly: $0.05 x voters in district (voters in party in primaries) with $2,500 min./ $50,000 max. for assembly member, and $4,000 min./ $50,000 max. for senator.	Unlimited.	Spouse is unlimited. Other family member contributions are aggregated and subject to a maximum aggregate per office. Statewide: $0.025 x voters (voters in party in primaries). Senate or assembly: $0.25 x voters in district (voters in party in primaries) with $20,000 min./ $100,000 max. for senator; $12,500 min./$100,000 max. for assembly member.	Contributions permitted, but may not be required. Judicial candidates may not solicit government employees or receive contributions from them. Police force members may not solicit for contributions from government employees. State employees may not coerce other state employees into contributing.	Prohibited.
North Carolina(a)....	Limited to $4,000 per committee or candidate, per election.	Unlimited.	Unlimited.	State employee may not coerce another state employee into contributing.	Prohibited.
North Dakota	Unlimited.	Unlimited.	Unlimited.	. . .	Prohibited.
Ohio(a)	Unlimited.	Unlimited.	Unlimited.	Classified service employees may not solicit or be solicited. Judge may not contribute to a political party in the year of candidacy. Court employees may not be solicited for a judicial candidate.	Anonymous contribution generally prohibited. Contribution in the name of another prohibited.
Oklahoma	Limited to $5,000 to a political party or organization or a state office, and $1,000 for a local office candidate, per person or family.	Unlimited.	Same as individual.	State employee may not solicit. Certain state employees may not receive contributions.	Prohibited.
Oregon	Unlimited.	Unlimited.	Unlimited.	Contribution may not be required. Solicitation prohibited during hours of employment.	Prohibited.
Pennsylvania(a)	Unlimited.	Unlimited.	Unlimited.	State employees may not be solicited, and may not solicit from other state employees.	Prohibited.
Rhode Island	Unlimited.	Unlimited.	Unlimited.	State classified employees may not be solicited, and may not solicit other state employees.	Prohibited.
South Carolina	Unlimited.	Unlimited.	Unlimited.	. . .	. . .
South Dakota	Limited to $1,000 for any statewide candidate; $250 for any other candidate; or $3,000 to a political party in any calendar year.	Unlimited.	Unlimited.	. . .	. . .

LIMITATIONS ON CONTRIBUTIONS BY INDIVIDUALS—Continued

State or other jurisdiction	Individual	Candidate	Candidate's family member	Government employees	Anonymous or in name of another
Tennessee	Unlimited.	Unlimited.	Unlimited.	Superiors may not solicit their employees. Certain government contractors may not be solicited.	. . .
Texas..............	Unlimited.	Unlimited.	Unlimited.	. . .	Contribution in the name of another prohibited unless there is disclosure.
Utah	Unlimited.	Unlimited.	Unlimited.	Solicitation prohibited during hours of employment.	. . .
Vermont(a).........	Limited to $1,000 per candidate or committee, per election.	Unlimited.	Unlimited.	Solicitation by employees prohibited.	. . .
Virginia............	Unlimited.	Unlimited.	Unlimited.	. . .	. . .
Washington	Unlimited, except aggregate contributions of more than $5,000 may not be made to a candidate or political committee within 21 days of a general election.	Same as individual.	Unlimited.	. . .	Prohibited.
West Virginia(a)	Limited to $1,000 per candidate, per election.	Same as individual.	Same as individual.	Contribution may not be solicited.	Anonymous contribution prohibited. Contributor disclosure required for contribution in the name of another.
Wisconsin..........	Limited to $10,000 for statewide candidates; $1,000 for state senator; $500 for state representative; other offices by formula, with an aggregate limit of $10,000.	Unlimited, unless candidate receives a grant from the election campaign fund, then limited to 200% of individual limit.	Unlimited as to funds or property owned jointly or as marital property by candidate and spouse.	Contribution and solicitation prohibited during hours of employment, or while engaged in official duties.	Anonymous contribution must be less than $10. Contribution in the name of another prohibited.
Wyoming	Limited to an aggregate of $25,000 and $1,000 per candidate in any general election and the year preceding.	Unlimited.	Unlimited.	. . .	. . .

LIMITATIONS ON CONTRIBUTIONS BY INDIVIDUALS—Continued

State or other jurisdiction	Individual	Candidate	Candidate's family member	Government employees	Anonymous or in name of another
Dist. of Col.(a)	Limited to an aggregate of $4,000 per election and $2,000 for mayor, $1,500 for council chairman, $1,000 for council member at-large, $400 for council member from a district or board of education member at-large, $200 for board of education member from a district or a party official, $25 for neighborhood advisory commission member.	Same as individual.	Same as individual.	Contributions permitted, but district employees may not solicit or collect political contributions.	Contribution in the name of another prohibited.

Source: James A. Palmer and Edward D. Feigenbaum. *Campaign Finance Law 1986.* (Washington, D.C.: National Clearinghouse on Election Administration, Federal Election Commission, 1986).

Note: Consult state statutes for more details.

Key:

. . .—No reference to contribution in the law.

(a) Restriction on cash contributions. In Alaska, Arkansas, Florida, Kentucky, Maryland, New York, North Carolina, and Ohio: must be $100 or less. In California and Colorado: must be less than $100. In Connecticut, Delaware, Massachusetts, Nebraska, Vermont, West Virginia: must be $50 or less. In Hawaii and Missouri: cash contribution of more than $100 requires a receipt to the donor and a record of the transaction. In Louisiana: cash contributions of more than $300 must be by written instrument. In Michigan: must be $20 or less. In Pennsylvania: must be $100 or less per candidate. In District of Columbia: must be less than $50.

Table 5.7
CAMPAIGN FINANCE LAWS: LIMITATIONS ON EXPENDITURES
(As of January 1986)

State or other jurisdiction	Who may make expenditures	Total expenditures allowed	Expenditures prior to first filing	For certain purposes	Use of surplus funds(a)
Alabama	Committee named and designated by candidate.	...	...	Candidate's travel, filing fees, stenographic work, clerks for mailings, communications and stationery, voter lists, office rent, broadcast, advertising, campaign literature, compensation to those distributing literature, rent for rally halls, bands.	...
Alaska(b)	Candidate, treasurer, deputy treasurer.	Gov./lt. gov.: $.40 x total population (with no more than 50% spent in any one primary or general election); senate/house: $1 x district population divided by number of seats in district.	None permitted, except for personal travel expenses and public opinion surveys/polls.	...	May be given to charity, used to repay contributors, spent on a future campaign, used to repay candidate or used as income, contributed to another committee, or transferred to office allowance fund.
Arizona	...	...	None permitted until registration form is properly filed.	...	...
Arkansas(b)	...	...		...	...
California(b)	Must have authorization of treasurer or treasurer's designated agents.	...	...	...	...
Colorado(b)	...	...	...	Must be reasonably related to election, voter registration, or political education.	May be contributed to a non-profit or charitable organization or to the state or political subdivision, but not to candidate or party.
Connecticut(b)	...	...	None permitted until treasurer and campaign depository have been properly designated.	Polls, meeting halls and rally expenses, printing and advertising, professional services fee, travel, staff salaries, rent, supplies, voter transportation, communications, expenses incurred in circulating nominating petitions, and other necessary expenses.	May be donated to another committee(c) or distributed on a pro rata basis to contributors or used for transition expenses. Ballot question committees may distribute surplus to government agencies or tax exempt organizations.
Delaware	Those with candidate's written approval.	Primary: statewide candidates: $.25 x qualified voters; senate: greater of $.25 x qualified voters or $4,000; house: greater of $.25 x qualified voters or $2,000. General election: all figures doubled.	None permitted until registration form is properly filed.	Staff salaries, travel expenses, communications, filing fees, printing, food, office supplies, voter lists and canvasses, poll watchers, rent, advertising, rallies, state licensed counsel.	May be contributed to tax-exempt charitable or political organization with candidate's authorization.

LIMITATIONS ON EXPENDITURES—Continued

State or other jurisdiction	Who may make expenditures	Total expenditures allowed	Expenditures prior to first filing	For certain purposes	Use of surplus funds(a)
Florida(b)	...	...	...	Expenditures only to influence results of election.	May be used to reimburse a candidate for his contributions; transferred to a public office account in amount up to $10,000 for statewide candidate, $5,000 for multi-county candidate, and $2,500 x number of years in term of office for which legislative candidate is elected; returned pro rata to contributors; donated to a non-profit or charitable organization; or given to state or political subdivision.
Georgia	...	...	...	...	...
Hawaii	Campaign treasurer and deputy treasurer.	Voluntary election year limits: gov.: $1.25 x qualified voters; lt. gov.: $.70 x qualified voters; mayor: $1 x qualified voters; house/senate/council/ prosecutor: $.70 x qualified voters; others: $.10 x qualified voters.	...	Donations to community, youth, social, or recreational organizations; reports, surveys, or polls.	May be used for fundraising; candidate-sponsored politically-related activity; ordinary and necessary officeholder expenses; or donated to any community service, scientific, educational, youth, recreational, charitable, or literary organization.
Idaho(b)	...	...	...	...	...
Illinois	...	...	...	...	Must be returned to contributors or transferred to other political or charitable organizations.
Indiana	Treasurer.	...	...	...	May be transferred to one or more political party committees or to the state election board.(d)
Iowa	...	...	...	Only for legitimate campaign purposes in general elections, including salaries, rent, advertising, supplies, travel, campaign paraphernalia, contributions to other candidates, and the like.	(e)
Kansas	...	...	None permitted until registration form is properly filed.	...	...
Kentucky	Treasurer must make or authorize all expenditures on behalf of candidate.	...	None permitted until primary campaign depository is designated.	...	May be returned pro rata to all contributors, transferred to candidate's party committee, or retained for election to the same office.

LIMITATIONS ON EXPENDITURES—Continued

State or other jurisdiction	Who may make expenditures	Total expenditures allowed	Expenditures prior to first filing	For certain purposes	Use of surplus funds(a)
Louisiana(b)	...	...	None aggregating in excess of $500 until statement of organization is properly filed.	...	...
Maine	Candidate, treasurer.	Political action committee limited to $5,000 per candidate or political committee in any election.		...	...
Maryland(b)	Public funds may only be spent upon authority of candidate or treasurer; other expenditures must be made by or through treasurer.	Publicly-financed candidates limited per primary or general elections: gov./lt. gov./senate: $.10 x qualified voters; atty. gen./comptr.: $.025 x qualified voters; house: $.05 x qualified voters; state's atty.: greater of $2,500 or $.025 x qualified voters; other: greater of $1,000 or $.01 x qualified voters.(f)	None permitted until registration form is properly filed.	Public contributions may only be used to further candidate's nomination or election, for legal purposes, and for expenses not incurred later than 30 days after election.	Surplus public contributions must be paid not later than 60 days after the election for which the funds were granted. Other funds must be returned on a pro rata basis to contributors, paid to a party central committee, or donated to a local board of education, recognized non-profit educational organization, or charitable organization.
Massachusetts(b)	...	...	...	Candidates; limited to reasonable and necessary expenses directly related to candidate's campaign. Other committees: for enhancement of political future of candidate or principle.	Pro rata portion of public funds revert to state. Other funds must be donated to local aid fund.
Michigan(b)	Expenditure may only be made with authorization of treasurer or treasurer's designee.	Publicly-financed candidates limited to $1 million per election.(g)	...	Public funds may be spent only on services, facilities, materials, or other things of value to further candidate's election during election year.	Surplus public funds must be promptly repaid and may not be used in subsequent election. Other funds may be transferred to another committee, party, tax-exempt charitable institution or returned to contributors.
Minnesota(b)	Authorized by treasurer or deputy treasurer of committee or fund.	Publicly-financed candidates limited in election year to greater of following amounts. Gov./lt. gov.: $.125 per capita or $600,000; atty. gen.: $.025 per capita or $100,000; secy. of state, treas., aud.: $.0125 per capita or $50,000; senate: $.20 per capita or $15,000; house: $.20 per capita or $7,500. In non-election year, to 20% of applicable limit.	...	Salaries, wages, fees, communications, mailing, transportation and travel, advertising and printing, office space and furnishings, supplies, and other expenses reasonably related to election.	...

LIMITATIONS ON EXPENDITURES—Continued

State or other jurisdiction	Who may make expenditures	Total expenditures allowed	Expenditures prior to first filing	For certain purposes	Use of surplus funds(a)
Mississippi	...	...	...	...	...
Missouri(b)	Expenditures must be made by or through treasurer; when treasurer's office is vacant candidate serves as treasurer.	...	...	...	...
Montana(b)	Campaign treasurers, authorized deputy campaign treasurers of candidates and political committees.	...	...	...	...
Nebraska(b)	Treasurers or treasurer's designees; however candidates and agents also permitted to make expenditures.	...	None may be made by committee until it files statement of organization and has treasurer.	Committee (other than political party committee) may use funds for goods, materials, services, or facilities to assist or oppose candidate or ballot question.(h)	...
Nevada	...	...	...	...	...
New Hampshire	Candidate or fiscal agent, treasurer of political committee.	...	None may be made by non-party political committee until registration statement is filed and (if organized to support a candidate) written consent of candidate or financial agent has been secured and filed.	...	...
New Jersey	Treasurer or deputy treasurer of candidate, political party committee, political committee, and continuing political committees.	Max. amount for gov. in primary: $.35 x number of voters in preceding presidential election; in general election: $.70 x number of voters in preceding presidential election.	...	...	...
New Mexico	Treasurer of candidate or political committee.	...	None permitted until treasurer appointed.	...	...
New York(b)	Treasurer of candidate or political committee.	...	None may be made by a political committee until designation of treasurer and depository have been filed.	Any lawful purpose.	Surplus campaign funds may be used for any lawful purpose, including transfer to political party committee, return to donor, or held for use in subsequent campaign.
North Carolina(b)	Treasurer or asst. treasurer of candidate or political committee.(i)	...	None permitted until treasurer appointed and certified.(i)	...	...
North Dakota	...	...	...	...	...

LIMITATIONS ON EXPENDITURES—Continued

State or other jurisdiction	Who may make expenditures	Total expenditures allowed	Expenditures prior to first filing	For certain purposes	Use of surplus funds(a)
Ohio	Campaign treasurer, authorized deputy campaign treasurers for a campaign committee.	…	None may be made by candidate's campaign committee until candidate designates treasurer.	…	…
Oklahoma	Agents and sub-agents in the case of candidates and political parties.	…	…	Only to defray campaign expenditures or ordinary and necessary expenses incurred in connection with duties of public officeholder.	…
Oregon(b)	…	…	…	…	…
Pennsylvania	…	…	…	No expenditures except as provided by law.	…
Rhode Island	Campaign treasurers, deputy campaign treasurers.	…	…	…	…
South Carolina	…	…	…	…	…
South Dakota	…	…	…	Necessary expenditure of money for ordinary or usual expense of conducting political campaign unless expressly forbidden.	…
Tennessee	Political treasurer of candidate and political campaign committee.	…	None permitted until candidate and political committee certify name and address of treasurer.	Clerical/office force, dissemination of literature, public speakers, newspaper announcement of candidacy and transportation of voters unable to go to polls.	…
Texas	Candidate and campaign treasurer or asst. campaign treasurer, and campaign treasurer or asst. campaign treasurer of political committee.	Independent expenditures by individuals limited to $100(j), unless contribution is made or individual reports as a political committee.	None permitted until name of campaign treasurer has been filed.	…	…
Utah	Candidate and secretary and members of personal campaign committee in case of candidate.	…	None permitted until state office candidate files statement of appointment of personal campaign committee.	Any expenditures may be made, except those prohibited by law.	…
Vermont(b)	Designated treasurer.	…	…	…	May be used by candidate to reduce personal campaign debts.
Virginia(b)	…	…	(k)	…	After filing of final report, surplus funds may be used for next election.

LIMITATIONS ON EXPENDITURES—Continued

State or other jurisdiction	Who may make expenditures	Total expenditures allowed	Expenditures prior to first filing	For certain purposes	Use of surplus funds(a)
Washington(b)	Campaign treasurer or candidate or person on authority of campaign treasurer or candidate.	...		...	...
West Virginia	Candidates, financial agents, political party committee treasurers.	...	None may be made by political party committee until treasurer appointed.	...	...
Wisconsin(b)	Treasurer of candidate, political committee, political group, or individual.	...	None permitted until registration statement is filed. State office candidates who receive election campaign fund grant may not spend more for campaign than amount specified in authorized disbursement schedule.	For any lawful purpose.	
Wyoming	...	...	...	...	
Dist. of Columbia(b)	Chairman, treasurer, or designated agents.	...	...	...	May be contributed to a political party for political purposes; returned to donors; transferred to a scientific, technical, or literacy or educational organization; or used for constituent services with certain limitations.

Source: James A. Palmer and Edward D. Feigenbaum, *Campaign Finance Law 1986.* (Washington, D.C.: National Clearinghouse on Election Administration, Federal Election Commission, 1986).

Note: Consult state statutes for more details.

Key:

... —No reference in the law.

(a) Post election.

(b) Restrictions on cash expenditures. In Alaska, California, Colorado, Connecticut, Louisiana, and New York: may not exceed $100. In Arkansas, Massachusetts, Michigan, Nebraska, Oregon, Washington, and the District of Columbia: may not exceed $50. In Florida: must be less than $30. In Idaho and Maryland: must be less than $25. In Minnesota: petty cash expenditures limited to $100 per week for statewide elections and $20 per week for legislative elections. In Missouri: single cash expenditures from petty cash fund may not exceed $50; aggregate calendar year expenditures may not exceed the lesser of $5,000 or 10 percent of the committee's total calendar year expenditures. In Montana: petty cash fund may be established to pay for office supplies, transportation expenses and other necessities of less than $10. In North Carolina: cash expenditures permitted for non-media expenses of $50 or less. In Vermont: expenditures by a candidate who has made expenditures or received contributions of $500 or more and by a political committee must be paid by the treasurer by check from a single checking account. In Virginia: petty cash expenditures of less than $25 are permitted; otherwise, only by check.

In Wisconsin: cash expenditures are prohibited.

(c) Except one established to further the candidate's future campaigns.

(d) Unless otherwise provided by the committee in its statement of organization.

(e) Public funds may not be used to lease or purchase any item whose benefits extend beyond the time within which the funds must be spent.

(f) In general election, parties are limited to expenditures for greater of $250 or $.0025 per qualified voter in addition to the candidate limits.

(g) Except up to $200,000 more can be spent to solicit contributions, and additional expenditures are authorized in response to editorials, endorsements, and the like.

(h) After an election, a committee may expend or transfer funds for: continued operation of campaign offices; social events for workers and volunteers; obtaining public input and opinion; repayment of campaign loans; newsletters and other political communications; gifts of acknowledgement; and candidate-related meals, lodging, and travel by officeholder and family.

(i) Except for independent expenditures.

(j) Plus donated services and personal traveling expenses.

(k) Candidate must appoint one campaign treasurer no later than upon acceptance of a contribution, expenditure of funds, or qualification as a candidate, whichever occurs first.

Table 5.8
FUNDING OF STATE ELECTIONS: TAX PROVISIONS AND PUBLIC FINANCING
(As of January 1986)

State or other jurisdiction	Tax provisions relating to individuals				Public financing	
	Credit	Deduction	Checkoff	Surcharge	Source of funds	Distribution of funds
Alabama............	...	...	...	$1(a)	Surcharge	To political party designated by taxpayer
Alaska.............	$50	...	...	...	...	...
Arizona............	...	$100(a)	...	...	...	...
Arkansas	...	$25	...	...	...	...
California..........	...	$100	...	$1, $5, $10, or $25(b)	Surcharge and an equal amount matched by state	To political parties for party activities and distribution to statewide general election candidates
Hawaii	...	$100 for contributions to central or county party committees or $500 for contributions to candidates who abide by expenditure limits, with max. of $100 of a total contribution to a single candidate deductible	$2(a)	...	Checkoff, appropriated funds, other moneys	To candidates for all non-federal elective offices
Idaho	50% of contribution to max. $5(a)	...	$1	...	Checkoff	To political party designated by taxpayer
Indiana............	...	...	...	...	Revenue from personalized motor vehicle license plates	Percentage divided equally between the qualified political parties
Iowa	...	...	$1(a)	$2(a)	Checkoff/surcharge	To political party designated by taxpayer; if not specified, amount divided among qualifying parties for party activities and distribution to general election candidates
Kentucky	...	...	$2(a)	...	Checkoff	To political party designated by taxpayer for party activities and distribution to general election candidates
Maine	...	...	...	$1	Surcharge	To political party designated by taxpayer
Maryland	...	...	...	...	Direct appropriations	To candidates for state or county office; Baltimore city offices
Massachusetts	...	...	...	$1(a)	Surcharge	To candidates in statewide primary and general elections
Michigan	...	...	$2(a)	...	Checkoff and an equal amount matched by state	To candidates in gubernatorial primaries and candidates for governor and lt. governor in general election
Minnesota	50% of contribution to max. $50(a)	...	$2(a)	...	Checkoff and excess anonymous contributions	To candidates for governor, lt. governor, attorney general, secretary of state, state auditor, state treasurer, state senator and representative in primary and general elections

FUNDING OF STATE ELECTIONS—Continued

State or other jurisdiction	Tax provisions relating to individuals				Public financing	
	Credit	Deduction	Checkoff	Surcharge	Source of funds	Distribution of funds
Montana	...	$100(a)	$1(a)	$1(a) for those with no tax liability	Checkoff/surcharge	To candidates opposed in elections for governor, lt. governor, Supreme Court chief justice and justices
New Jersey	...	...	$1(a)	...	Direct appropriations and checkoff	To gubernatorial candidates
North Carolina	...	$25	$1(a)	...	Checkoff	Divided among political parties according to registration; of amount—50% goes to party, 50% for other purposes
Oklahoma	...	$100	$1(a)	...	Checkoff	50% to political parties(c) and 50% to eligible general election candidates(d)
Oregon	Lesser of 50% of contribution to max. $25(a) or the taxpayer's tax liability	...	...	...	...	...
Rhode Island	(e)	...	$2(a)	...	Credit/checkoff	To political party designated by taxpayer; other funds allocated to parties based on number of elected state officials and of votes in most recent election
Utah	...	...	$1	...	Checkoff	To political party designated by taxpayer; allocated 50% to county central committees
Virginia	...	...	...	$2(a)	Surcharge	To political party designated by taxpayer
Wisconsin	...	...	$1(a)	...	Checkoff	According to formula, to general election candidates for state executive office, Supreme Court, and legislative offices(f)
Dist. of Col.	50% of contribution to max. $50(a)	...	...	...	...	...

Source: James A. Palmer and Edward D. Feigenbaum, *Campaign Finance Law 1986.* (Washington, D.C.: National Clearinghouse on Election Administration, Federal Election Commission, 1986).

Note: This table shows only those states that have a tax provision relating to individuals or a provision for public financing of state elections. Credits and deductions may be allowed only for certain types of candidates and/or political parties. Consult state laws for further details.

Key:
... —No provision.
(a) For joint returns, amount indicated above may be doubled.

(b) And a separate designation of $1, $5, $10, or $25.
(c) 10 percent to each party and remainder divided according to registration figures.
(d) 20 percent for governor, 15 percent for lieutenant governor, 15 percent for attorney general and 10 percent each for state treasurer, state auditor and inspector, commissioner of insurance, superintendent of public instruction, and corporation commissioner.
(e) See checkoff.
(f) Candidates must meet certain qualifications.

Table 5.9
VOTER REGISTRATION INFORMATION

State or other jurisdiction	Mail registration allowed for all voters	Minimum state residence requirement (days)	Closing date for registration before general election (days)	Persons eligible for absentee registration(a)	Automatic cancellation of registration for failure to vote after _____ years
Alabama		1	10	B,D,S,T	-
Alaska	★	30	30	(b)	2
Arizona		30(c)	50	B,C,D,E,R,S,T	1 general election
Arkansas		. . .	20	B,D,S,T	4
California	★	29	29	(b)	-
Colorado		32	25	B,C,D,E,R,S,T	2 general elections
Connecticut	★	. . .	21(d)	D,R,T	-
Delaware	★	. . .	3rd Sat. in Oct.(d)	B,D,E,R,S,T	2 general elections
Florida		. . .	30	B,D,E,R,S,T	2
Georgia		30	30	B,D,E,R,S,T	3
Hawaii	★	. . .	30	B,D,R,S,T	2
Idaho		30	17/10(f)	B,D,E,S,T	4
Illinois		30	28	B,D,E,R,S,T	4
Indiana		30	29	B,D,E,S,T	2
Iowa	★	. . .	10	(b)	4
Kansas	★	1	20	(b)	2 general elections
Kentucky	★	30	30	B,D,E,S,T	4
Louisiana		. . .	24	D,E,S,T	4
Maine	★	. . .	Election day	B,D,E,R,S,T	-
Maryland	★	30	30	D(e)	5
Massachusetts		. . .	28	B,D,E,R,S,T	1
Michigan		30	30	B,D,T	10
Minnesota	★	20	Election day(h)	B,D,E,R,S,T	4
Mississippi		30	30	B,D,S	4
Missouri		. . .	28	B,D,E,R,S,T	-
Montana	★	30	30	D(e)	4
Nebraska	★	. . .	(k)	B,D,E,R,S,T	-
Nevada		30	30	B,D,E,R,S,T	1 general election
New Hampshire		10	10	D(e)	10
New Jersey	★	30	29	B,D,E,R,S,T	4
New Mexico		. . .	29	B,C,D,E,R,T	1 general election
New York	★	30	30(d)	D,T	4
North Carolina		30	21(i)	(e)	8
North Dakota(j)		30	(b)	-	
Ohio	★	30	30	B,C,D,R,S,T	4
Oklahoma		. . .	10	B,D,T	8
Oregon	★	20	21	(b)	2
Pennsylvania	★	30	30	B,D,E,R,S,T	2
Rhode Island		30	30	B,D,E,O,R,S	5
South Carolina	★	. . .	30	B,D,E,S,T	2 general elections
South Dakota	★	15	15	B,D,E,R,S,T	4
Tennessee	★	20	29	B,D,R,S,T	4
Texas	★	30	30	C(b)	-
Utah	★	30	5(l)	B,D,R,S,T	4
Vermont		. . .	17	(e)	4
Virginia		. . .	31	B,D,E,R,S,T	4
Washington		30	30	(b)	2
West Virginia	★	30	30	B,D,S,T	2 general elections
Wisconsin	★	10	Election day(l)	C(b)	2 general elections
Wyoming		. . .	(h)	B,D,E,R,S,T	1 general election
Dist. of Col.	★	. . .	30	(b)	4
Guam	★	N.A.	10	N.A.	1 general election
Puerto Rico	★	. . .	50	(g)	1 general election
Virgin Islands	★	45	30	S	2 general elections

Source: Adapted from *Vote! The First Steps.* League of Women Voters Education Fund, 1730 M St., N.W., Washington, D.C. (Copyright 1988), and state election administration officials.

Key:
. . .—No residence requirement
——No automatic cancellation.
N.A.—Not available.
(a) In this column: B-Absent on business; C-Senior citizen; D-Disabled persons; E-not absent, but prevented by employment from registering; O-Out of state; R-Absent for religious reasons; S-Students; T-Temporarily out of jurisdiction.
(b) All voters. See column on mail registration.

(c) 30 for state office, 55 for presidential.
(d) Closing date differs for primary election. In Connecticut, 1 day; Delaware, 21 days; New York, 60 days.
(e) Anyone unable to register in person.
(f) With precinct registrar, 17 days before; with county clerk, 10 days.
(g) No one is eligible to register absentee.
(h) Minnesota-20 days or election day; Wyoming-30 days or election day.
(i) Business days.
(j) No voter registration.
(k) 2nd Friday before election day.
(l) By mail: Utah, 20 days; Wisconsin, 13 days.

Table 5.10
POLLING HOURS: GENERAL ELECTIONS

State or other jurisdiction	Polls open	Polls close	Notes on hours(a)
Alabama	No later than 8 a.m.	Between 6 and 8 p.m.	Polls must be open at least 10 consecutive hours; hours set by county commissioner.
Alaska	7 a.m.	8 p.m.	
Arizona	6 a.m.	7 p.m.	
Arkansas	Between 7 and 8 a.m.	7:30 p.m.	
California	7 a.m.	8 p.m.	
Colorado	7 a.m.	7 p.m.	
Connecticut	6 a.m.	8 p.m.	
Delaware	7 a.m.	8 p.m.	
Florida	7 a.m.	7 p.m.	
Georgia	7 a.m.	7 p.m.	
Hawaii	7 a.m.	6 p.m.	
Idaho	8 a.m.	8 p.m.	Polls may open earlier at option of county clerk. Polls may close earlier if all registered electors in a precinct have voted.
Illinois	6 a.m.	7 p.m.	
Indiana	6 a.m.	6 p.m.	
Iowa	7 a.m.	9 p.m.	
Kansas	Between 6 and 7 a.m.	Between 7 and 8 p.m.	Hours may be changed by county election officer, but polls must be open at least 12 consecutive hours between 6 a.m. and 8 p.m.
Kentucky	6 a.m.	6 p.m.	Persons in line may vote only until 7 p.m.
Louisiana	6 a.m.	8 p.m.	
Maine	Between 6 and 9 a.m.	8 p.m.	Opening hour is determined by municipal election officer. Towns with population less than 100 may open and close at any time.
Maryland	7 a.m.	8 p.m.	
Massachusetts	7 a.m.	8 p.m.	
Michigan	7 a.m.	8 p.m.	
Minnesota	7 a.m.	8 p.m.	Municipalities of less than 1,000 may establish hours of no later than 9 a.m. to 8 p.m.
Mississippi	7 a.m.	6 p.m.	
Missouri	6 a.m.	7 p.m.	
Montana	7 a.m. noon	8 p.m. 8 p.m.	In precincts of over 200 registered voters. In precincts of less than 200 registered voters, polls may close when all registered electors have voted.
Nebraska	7 a.m. 8 a.m.	7 p.m. 8 p.m.	Mountain Time Zone. Central Time Zone.
Nevada	7 a.m.	7 p.m.	
New Hampshire	Varies	Varies	Cities: Polls open not less than 8 hours and may be opened not earlier than 6 a.m. nor later than 8 p.m. Small towns: In towns of less than 700 population the polls must be open at least five consecutive hours. On written request of seven registered voters the polls shall be kept open until 6 p.m. In towns of less than 100 population, the polls close if all registered voters have appeared. Other towns: Polls may not open later than 10 a.m. and may not close earlier than 6 p.m. On written request of 10 registered voters the polls may close at 7 p.m.
New Jersey	7 a.m.	8 p.m.	
New Mexico	7 a.m.	7 p.m.	
New York	6 a.m.	9 p.m.	
North Carolina	6:30 a.m.	7:30 p.m.	In precincts where voting machines are used, county board of elections may permit closing at 8:30 p.m.
North Dakota	Between 7 and 9 a.m.	Between 7 and 9 p.m.	In precincts where less than 75 votes were cast in previous election, polls may open at noon.
Ohio	6:30 a.m.	7:30 p.m.	
Oklahoma	7 a.m.	7 p.m.	
Oregon	8 a.m.	8 p.m.	
Pennsylvania	7 a.m.	8 p.m.	
Rhode Island	Between 7 a.m. and noon	9 p.m.	Opening hours vary across cities and towns.

POLLING HOURS: GENERAL ELECTIONS—Continued

State or other jurisdiction	Polls open	Polls close	Notes on hours(a)
South Carolina	7 a.m.	7 p.m.	
South Dakota	7 a.m. 8 a.m.	7 p.m. 8 p.m.	Mountain Time Zone. Central Time Zone.
Tennessee	Varies.	7 p.m. (CST); 8 p.m. (EST)	Counties with population over 120,000 may not open later than 8 a.m. Must be open at least 10 hours and no more than 12 hours.
Texas	7 a.m.	7 p.m.	Counties with population over one million may open polls at 6 a.m.
Utah	7 a.m.	8 p.m.	
Vermont	Between 6 and 10 a.m.	7 p.m.	
Virginia	6 a.m.	7 p.m.	
Washington	7 a.m.	8 p.m.	
West Virginia	6:30 a.m.	7:30 p.m.	
Wisconsin	7 a.m. Between 7 and 9 a.m.	8 p.m. 8 p.m.	1st class cities. 2nd, 3rd and 4th class cities, towns and villages.
Wyoming	7 a.m.	7 p.m.	
Dist. of Col.	7 a.m.	8 p.m.	
American Samoa	6 a.m.	6 p.m.	
Guam	8 a.m.	8 p.m.	
Puerto Rico	9 a.m.	3 p.m.	
Virgin Islands	8 a.m.	6 p.m.	

Sources: State statutes and state election administration offices.

Note: Hours for primary, municipal and special elections may differ from those noted.

(a) In all states, voters standing in line when the polls close are allowed to vote; however, provisions for handling those voters vary across jurisdictions.

Table 5.11
VOTING STATISTICS FOR GUBERNATORIAL ELECTIONS*

State	Primary election			General election						
	Republican	Democrat	Total votes	Republican	Per-cent	Democrat	Per-cent	Other	Per-cent	Total votes
Alabama.........	29,194	940,088 (a)	969,282	696,203	56.3	537,163	43.5	2,864	0.2	1,236,230
Alaska...........	84,004	63,486	147,490	76,515	42.6	84,943	47.3	18,097	10.1	179,555
Arizona..........	226,296	210,688	436,984	343,913	39.7	298,986	34.5	224,085	25.8	866,984
Arkansas.........	22,346	520,628	542,974	248,427	36.1	439,882	63.9	242	0.0	688,551
California........	2,059,413	2,168,625	4,228,038	4,506,601	60.5	2,781,714	37.4	155,236	2.1	7,443,551
Colorado	187,820	unopposed	187,820	434,420	41.0	616,325	58.2	8,183	0.8	1,058,928
Connecticut	94,536	(b)	94,536	408,489	41.1	575,638	57.9	9,565	1.0	993,692
Delaware‡	unopposed	34,658	34,658	135,250	55.5	108,315	44.5	0	0.0	243,565
Florida	554,663 (a)	1,006,662 (a)	1,561,325	1,847,525	54.6	1,538,620	45.4	26	0.0	3,386,171
Georgia..........	unopposed	611,463	611,463	346,512	29.5	828,465	70.5	137	0.0	1,175,114
Hawaii	41,001	231,560	272,561	160,460	48.0	173,655	52.0	0	0.0	334,115
Idaho	unopposed	unopposed	0	189,794	49.0	193,429	49.9	4,203	1.1	387,426
Illinois..........	497,982	791,180	1,289,162	1,655,849	52.7	208,830 (c)	6.6	1,279,299	40.7	3,143,978
Indiana‡	446,667	611,261	1,057,928	1,146,497	52.2	1,036,922	47.2	14,569	0.7	2,197,988
Iowa	unopposed	134,191	134,191	472,712	51.9	436,987	48.0	924	0.1	910,623
Kansas	276,126	unopposed	276,126	436,267	51.9	404,338	48.1	0	0.0	840,605
Kentucky†	97,836	658,454	756,290	454,650	44.1	561,674	54.5	14,347	1.4	1,030,671
Louisiana†	(d)	(d)	(d)	(d)	(d)	(d)	(d)	(d)	(d)	(d)
Maine	116,129	118,436	234,565	170,312	39.9	128,744	30.2	127,805	29.9	426,861
Maryland	unopposed	639,964	639,964	194,185	17.6	907,291	82.4	0	0.0	1,101,476
Massachusetts	64,373	unopposed	64,373	525,364	31.2	1,157,786	68.7	929	0.1	1,684,079
Michigan	582,337	457,087	1,039,424	753,647	31.4	1,632,138	68.1	10,779	0.4	2,396,564
Minnesota	192,153	510,495	702,648	606,755	42.9	790,138	55.8	19,096	1.3	1,415,989
Mississippi†	unopposed	828,211 (a)	828,211	288,764	38.9	409,209	55.1	44,764	6.0	742,737
Missouri‡	363,638	514,845	878,483	1,194,506	56.7	913,700	43.3	4	0.0	2,108,210
Montana‡.........	unopposed	99,056	99,056	100,070	26.4	266,578	70.3	12,322	3.3	378,970
Nebraska	192,851	145,057	337,908	298,325	52.9	265,156	47.0	941	0.2	564,422
Nevada	68,236	89,960	158,196	65,081	25.0	187,268	71.9	8,026	3.1	260,375
New Hampshire ...	58,105	36,109	94,214	134,824	53.7	116,142	46.3	141	0.1	251,107
New Jersey§ ...	unopposed	326,403	326,403	1,372,631	69.6	578,402	29.3	21,191	1.1	1,972,224
New Mexico.......	89,107	unopposed	89,107	209,455	53.0	185,378	47.0	0	0.0	394,833
New York	unopposed	unopposed	0	1,363,810	31.8	2,775,229	64.6	155,085	3.6	4,294,124
North Carolina‡	140,354	955,799 (a)	1,096,153	1,208,167	54.3	1,011,209	45.4	7,351	0.3	2,226,727
North Dakota‡	unopposed	41,641	41,641	140,460	44.7	173,922	55.3	0	0.0	314,382
Ohio	730,946	unopposed	730,946	1,207,264	39.4	1,858,372	60.6	975	0.0	3,066,611
Oklahoma	158,899	517,310 (a)	676,209	431,762	47.5	405,295	44.5	72,868	8.0	909,925
Oregon	284,937	317,517	602,454	506,986	47.8	549,456	51.9	3,188	0.3	1,059,630
Pennsylvania	unopposed	973,210	973,210	1,638,268	48.4	1,717,484	50.7	32,523	1.0	3,388,275
Rhode Island	unopposed	57,244	57,244	208,822	64.7	104,508	32.4	9,394	2.9	322,724
South Carolina	unopposed	329,496	329,496	384,565	51.0	361,325	47.9	7,861	1.0	753,751
South Dakota	116,098	71,944	188,042	152,543	51.8	141,898	48.2	0	0.0	294,441
Tennessee	236,141	740,469	976,610	553,449	45.7	656,602	54.2	288	0.0	1,210,339
Texas............	544,719	1,096,552	1,641,271	1,813,779	52.7	1,584,515	46.0	43,166	1.3	3,441,460
Utah‡	167,287	82,723	250,010	351,792	55.9	275,669	43.8	2,158	0.3	629,619
Vermont	unopposed	unopposed	0	75,162	38.2	92,379	47.0	29,175	14.8	196,716
Virginia§..........	(b)	(b)	(b)	601,652	46.2	700,438	53.8	153	0.0	1,302,243
Washington‡	250,656	654,221	904,877	881,994	46.7	1,006,993	53.3	0	0.0	1,888,987
West Virginia‡	128,337	371,609	499,946	394,937	53.3	346,565	46.7	0	0.0	741,502
Wisconsin........	301,118	268,169	569,287	805,090	52.7	705,578	46.2	16,292	1.1	1,526,960
Wyoming	94,068	41,265	135,333	75,841	46.0	88,879	54.0	0	0.0	164,720

*Figures are for 1986, except where indicated: † 1983; ‡ 1984; § 1985.
Source: *America Votes*.
(a) Total shown is for first primary. Total votes for runoff election:
Alabama, 931,346; Florida, Republican 390,985, Democrat 848,041;
Mississippi, 773,301; North Carolina, 678,629; Oklahoma, 446,763.
(b) Candidates nominated by convention.
(c) No Democratic candidate for Governor on ballot; Fairchild "paired" Democrat for Lieutenant Governor; Democratic vote cast for "no name" and Fairchild.

(d) Louisiana has an open primary which requires all candidates, regardless of party affiliation, to appear on a single ballot. If a candidate receives over 50 percent of the vote in the primary, he is elected to the office. If no candidate receives a majority vote, then a single election is held between the two candidates receiving the most votes.

Table 5.12
VOTER TURNOUT IN NON-PRESIDENTIAL ELECTION YEARS:
1978, 1982 AND 1986
(In thousands)

State or other jurisdiction	1986 Voting age population (a)	1986 Number registered	1986 Number voting (b)	1982 Voting age population (a)	1982 Number registered	1982 Number voting (b)	1978 Voting age population (a)	1978 Number registered	1978 Number voting (b)
United States	182,628	121,089	64,803	169,339	110,477	67,592	158,373	104,829	61,038
Alabama..........	3,010	2,362	1,236	2,812	2,136	1,128 (c)	2,669	1,938	730 (d)
Alaska............	385	292	181	287	266	195 (c)	269	238	130
Arizona..........	2,605	1,598	867	2,061	1,141	726 (c)	1,766	969	551
Arkansas	1,761	1,189	695	1,650	1,116	789 (c)	1,575	1,047	524 (c)
California	20,8785	12,834	7,444	18,277	11,559	7,876 (c)	16,546	10,130	7,132
Colorado	2,489	1,822	1,061	2,225	1,456	956 (c)	1,974	1,345	848
Connecticut	2,492	1,673	994	2,378	1,647	1,084 (c)	2,254	1,626	1,061
Delaware	490	296	161	443	286	191 (d)	426	278	166
Florida	9,614	5,631	3,430	8,169	4,866	2,689 (c)	6,862	4,217	2,530
Georgia..........	4,665	2,576	1,225	4,040	2,316	1,169 (c)	3,667	2,183	663 (c)
Hawaii	824	420	334	716	405	312 (c)	657	395	293
Idaho	701	550	387	661	541	3,691 (f)	612	526	297
Illinois..........	8,550	6,004	3,144	8,346	5,965	3,691 (f)	8,132	5,809	3,343
Indiana	4,068	2,878	1,556	3,904	2,937	1,817 (c)	3,812	2,851	1,405
Iowa	2,068	1,622	911	2,094	1,586	1,038 (c)	2,075	1,588	843 (c)
Kansas	1,829	1,173	841	1,759	1,186	763 (c)	1,681	1,182	749 (d)
Kentucky	2,746	1,999	677	2,620	1,827	700 (e)	2,528	1,666	477 (d)
Louisiana	3,175	2,179	1,370	3,055	1,965	(g)	2,760	1,821	840
Maine	893	790	427	831	766	460 (c)	791	692	375 (d)
Maryland	3,491	2,140	1,113	3,190	1,968	1,139 (c)	3,014	1,888	1,012 (c)
Massachusetts	4,535	3,006	1,684	4,394	3,027	2,051 (d)	4,213	2,920	2,044
Michigan	6,791	5,791	2,397	6,554	5,625	3,040 (c)	6,406	5,230	2,985
Minnesota	3,161	2,615	1,416	2,988	2,668	1,805 (d)	2,823	2,511	1,625
Mississippi	1,867	1,652	524	1,745	1,508	645 (d)	1,672	1,150 (h)	584 (d)
Missouri	3,821	2,769	1,477	3,640	2,749	1,544 (d)	3,499	2,579	1,546 (i)
Montana..........	586	444	318	569	446	321 (d)	548	410	297
Nebraska	1,167	850	564	1,144	832	548 (c)	1,108	833	511
Nevada	780	368	262	661	322	240 (d)	520	268	195
New Hampshire ...	823	551	251	697	462	285 (c)	638	489	279
New Jersey........	5,943	3,777	1,554	5,544	3,681	2,194 (d)	5,326	3,602	2,060
New Mexico.......	1,101	633	395	936	583	407 (c)	841	598	357
New York	13,480	8,071	4,294	13,153	7,635	5,222 (c)	12,912	7,801	4,929
North Carolina	4,913	3,081	1,591	4,417	2,675	1,321 (e)	4,088	2,430	1,136 (d)
North Dakota	483	(j)	289	473	(j)	262 (d)	455	(j)	235
Ohio	7,970	5,987	3,121	7,793	5,674	3,395 (c)	7,638	5,222	3,018
Oklahoma	2,404	2,018	910	2,299	1,614	883 (c)	2,081	1,366	801
Oregon	2,051	1,502	1,060	1,954	1,517	1,042 (c)	1,808	1,473	911 (c)
Pennsylvania	9,060	5,847	3,388	8,883	5,703	3,684 (c)	8,673	5,590	3,742 (c)
Rhode Island	764	525	323	726	534	343 (d)	707	534	332
South Carolina	2,534	1,299	754	2,291	1,229	672 (c)	2,104	1,098	633 (d)
South Dakota	509	428	296	482	426	279 (c)	480	421	260 (c)
Tennessee.........	3,661	2,446	1,210	3,375	2,273	1,260 (d)	3,179	2,138	1,190 (c)
Texas.............	12,270	7,287	3,441	10,793	6,415	3,191 (c)	9,350	5,682	2,370 (c)
Utah	1,078	763	435	986	749	531 (d)	858	667	385
Vermont	412	328	197	379	316	169 (c)	353	286	125
Virginia..........	4,544	2,610	1,043	4,078	2,234	1,415 (d)	3,794	2,027	1,251
Washington	3,417	2,230	1,337	3,154	2,106	1,368 (d)	2,792	1,961	1,029
West Virginia	1,398	946	396	1,408	948	565 (d)	1,363	1,021	493
Wisconsin	3,563	(j)	1,527	3,464	(j)	1,580 (c)	3,263	1,682	1,501 (c)
Wyoming	351	235	165	354	230	169 (c)	296	201	142
Dist. of Col.	489	282	132	487	361	111 (e)	515	250	103

Sources: U.S. Department of Commerce, Bureau of the Census, *Statistical Abstract of the United States* and unpublished data from the Republican National Committee.

(a) Estimated as of November 1 of the year indicated. Includes armed forces stationed in each state, aliens and institutional population.

(b) Number represents total voting in general election for all races for the year indicated, except where noted. Total persons voting restricted to number of ballots recorded by secretaries of state as having been cast. 1986-Highest number if votes cast for the Senatorial election, the gubernatorial election or all races for the U.S. House of Representatives.

(c) Total vote for largest race—governor.

(d) Total vote for largest race—senator.

(e) Total vote for largest race—congressional.

(f) Total vote for largest race—secretary of state.

(g) Under Louisiana's election law, candidates of all parties run together on a single non-partisan ballot in September. If no candidate wins a majority of the vote, the top two finishers, regardless of party, oppose each other in a November runoff. In 1982, the congressional incumbents were reelected in the September race.

(h) Estimated.

(i) Total vote for largest race—state auditor.

(j) No required statewide registration.

(k) Total vote for largest race—mayor.

Table 5.13
VOTER TURNOUT FOR PRESIDENTIAL ELECTIONS: 1976, 1980 AND 1984
(In thousands)

State or other jurisdiction	1984 Voting age population (a)	1984 Number registered	1984 Number voting (b)	1980 Voting age population (a)	1980 Number registered	1980 Number voting (b)	1976 Voting age population (a)	1976 Number registered	1976 Number voting (b)
United States	173,937	123,842	92,708	164,473	112,929	86,485	152,309	105,838	82,645
Alabama	2,875	2,343	1,442	2,755	2,132	1,342	2,554	1,865	1,183
Alaska...........	345	305	207	276	259	158	257	207	128
Arizona..........	2,200	1,463	1,026	1,962	1,121	874	1,611	980	765
Arkansas	1,694	1,160	884	1,626	1,186	838	1,502	1,021	768
California........	19,063	13,074	9,559	17,525	11,362	8,586	15,598	9,982	8,137
Colorado	2,365	1,621	1,295	2,121	1,434	1,184	1,838	1,349	1,082
Connecticut	2,404	1,809	1,467	2,304	1,719	1,405	2,201	1,669	1,408
Delaware	457	314	255	431	301	236	412	301	236
Florida	8,529	5,574	4,180	7,566	4,810	3,686	6,408	4,094	3,151
Georgia..........	4,204	2,732	1,776	3,872	2,467	1,597	3,494	2,302	1,467
Hawaii	755	419	336	696	403	303	624	363	309
Idaho	681	582	411	645	581	437	567	520	355
Illinois..........	8,410	6,470	4,819	8,230	6,230	4,749	7,939	6,252	4,839
Indiana	3,969	3,050	2,233	3,890	2,944	2,242	3,692	3,010	2,279
Iowa	2,119	1,763	1,320	2,097	1,747	1,317	2,026	1,407	1,279
Kansas	1,794	1,113	1,022	1,728	1,159	980	1,628	1,113	958
Kentucky	2,700	2,023	1,369	2,594	1,821	1,296	2,434	1,713	1,167
Louisiana	3,147	2,244	1,707	2,916	2,015	1,549	2,623	1,866	1,278
Maine	848	811	553	810	760	523	759	696	486
Maryland	3,259	2,253	1,676	3,082	2,065	1,540	2,920	1,950	1,440
Massachusetts	4,422	3,254	2,559	4,277	3,157	2,520	4,132	2,912	2,594
Michigan	6,530	5,889	3,802	6,529	5,726	3,909	6,214	5,202	3,722
Minnesota	3,044	2,893	2,084	2,931	2,787	2,046	2,726	2,566	1,979
Mississippi	1,810	1,670	941	1,722	1,486	893	1,603	(c)	769
Missouri	3,682	2,969	2,123	3,576	2,845	2,099	3,408	2,553	1,954
Montana.........	591	527	384	560	496	364	519	455	339
Nebraska	1,163	903	652	1,130	856	640	1,081	841	624
Nevada	689	356	287	602	297	244	457	251	206
New Hampshire ...	722	544	389	671	551	384	593	478	359
New Jersey........	5,659	4,073	3,218	5,418	3,761	2,976	5,220	3,770	3,037
New Mexico.......	997	651	514	899	653	456	783	527	426
New York	13,326	9,044	6,807	12,929	7,898	6,201	12,892	8,199	6,668
North Carolina	4,559	3,271	2,176	4,272	2,775	1,856	3,907	2,554	1,679
North Dakota	491	(c)	309	466	(c)	302	442	(c)	309
Ohio	7,846	6,359	4,563	7,738	5,927	4,284	7,461	4,693	4,195
Oklahoma	2,452	1,929	1,256	2,202	1,469	1,150	1,990	1,401	1,108
Oregon	1,961	1,609	1,227	1,928	1,569	1,180	1,679	1,420	1,049
Pennsylvania	8,989	6,194	4,845	8,783	5,754	4,562	8,531	5,750	4,621
Rhode Island	733	542	409	709	547	416	689	545	411
South Carolina	2,386	1,396	969	2,213	1,236	890	1,993	1,113	803
South Dakota	498	443	318	487	448	328	469	426	301
Tennessee	3,476	2,580	1,712	3,320	2,359	1,617	3,033	1,912	1,476
Texas............	11,487	7,900	5,398	10,117	6,640	4,541	8,789	6,319	4,072
Utah	1,040	840	630	938	782	604	791	705	548
Vermont	391	334	235	370	312	213	337	284	194
Virginia..........	4,203	2,544	2,147	3,924	2,302	1,866	3,613	2,124	1,716
Washington	3,202	2,458	1,875	3,037	2,237	1,742	2,601	2,065	1,585
West Virginia	1,433	1,025	736	1,398	1,035	738	1,314	1,084	751
Wisconsin........	3,490	(c)	2,212	3,375	(c)	2,272	3,163	2,566	2,104
Wyoming	365	240	184	332	219	177	267	195	160
Dist. of Col.	482	282	210	494	289	173	525	268	171

Sources: Republican National Committee, *1985 Republican Almanac*; U.S. Department of Commerce, Bureau of the Census, *Statistical Abstract of the United States, 1982-83*. (Compiled from U.S. Bureau of the Census, *Current Population Reports* and unpublished data from the National Republican Congressional Committee.)

(a) Estimated population as of November of year indicated. Includes armed forces in each state, aliens and institutional population.

(b) For 1980 and 1984, "number voting" is number of ballots cast in presidential race. For 1976, "number voting" is restricted to number of ballots recorded by secretaries of state as having been cast for any electoral office or referendum; or in those states which do not count total number of ballots, the largest number of votes cast for a particular office.

(c) No statewide registration required. Excluded from totals for persons registered.

Table 5.14
INITIATIVE PROVISIONS FOR STATE LEGISLATION

State or other jurisdiction	Type(a)	Basis for number of signatures required on petition(b)
Alaska...............	D	10% of votes cast in last general election and resident in at least 2/3 of election districts
Arizona...............	D	10% of qualified electors based on votes cast in last general election for governor
Arkansas	D	8% of legal voters based on votes cast in last general election for governor
California.............	D	5% of votes cast in last general election for governor
Colorado	D	5% of votes cast in last general election for secretary of state
Idaho	D	10% of votes cast in last general election for governor
Maine	I	10% of votes cast in last general election for governor
Massachusetts	I	3% of votes cast in last general election for governor
Michigan	I	8% of votes cast in last general election for governor
Missouri	D	5% of voters in each of 2/3 of congressional districts
Montana..............	D	5% of qualified electors in each of at least 1/3 of legislative representative districts; total must be at least 5% of the total qualified electors in state
Nebraska	D	7% of votes cast in last general election for governor; petition must include 5% of electors of each of 2/5 of counties in state
Nevada	I	10% of votes cast in last general election in at least 75% of counties in state
North Dakota	D	2% of state's resident population at last federal decennial census
Ohio	B	3% of electors
Oklahoma	D	8% of legal voters based on total vote cast in last general election for state office receiving largest number of votes
Oregon	D	6% of total votes cast in last election for governor
South Dakota	I	5% of qualified voters based on votes cast in last general election for governor
Utah	B	10% (direct) or 5% (indirect) of total votes cast in last general election for governor with same percentage required from a majority of counties in state
Washington	B	8% of votes cast in last general election for governor
Wyoming	D	15% of qualified voters based on votes cast in last general election and resident in at least 2/3 of counties in state
Dist. of Col.	D	5% of registered qualified voters; total must include 5% of registered voters in each of five or more of the wards in the district
Guam	D	20% of voters in last general election for governor
No. Mariana Is.	D	20% of qualified voters

Note: This table refers only to those jurisdictions that allow proposed state laws to be placed on a state ballot by citizen petition and enacted or rejected by the electorate.

(a) The initiative may be direct or indirect. The direct type, designated D in this column, allows proposed measures to be placed on the ballot by securing a specific number of signatures on a petition—no legislative action is required. The indirect type, designated I, requires that the petition for a proposed measure first be submitted to the legislature allowing the legislators an opportunity to enact or alter the measure before it is placed on the ballot for consideration by the electorate. In some states, both types, designated B, are used.

(b) A majority of the popular vote is required to enact a measure in every jurisdiction except the Northern Mariana Islands where enactment requires approval by 2/3 of the votes cast. In Massachusetts and Nebraska, apart from satisfying the requisite majority vote, the measure must receive, respectively, 30 and 35 percent of the total votes cast in favor.

Table 5.15
PROVISIONS FOR REFERENDUM ON STATE LEGISLATION

State or other jurisdiction	Basis of referendum(a)	Basis for number of signatures on citizen petition(b)
Alaska...............	Citizen petition	10% of votes cast in last general election for governor and resident in at least 2/3 of election districts
Arizona..............	Citizen petition Submission by legislature	5% of qualified voters
Arkansas	Citizen petition	6% of legal voters based on votes cast in last general election for governor
California.............	Citizen petition Constitutional requirement(c)	5% of votes cast in last general election for governor
Colorado	Citizen petition Submission by legislature	5% of votes cast in last general election for secretary of state
Connecticut	Submission by legislature	
Florida	Constitutional requirement(c)	
Georgia...............	Constitutional requirement(c)	
Idaho	Citizen petition	10% of votes cast in last general election for governor
Illinois...............	Submission by legislature(c)	
Iowa	Constitutional requirement(c)	
Kansas	Constitutional requirement(c)	
Kentucky	Citizen petition(d) Submission by legislature(d) Constitutional requirement(d)	5% of legal voters based on votes cast in last general election for governor
Maine	Citizen petition Submission by legislature Constitutional requirement(c)	10% of votes cast in last general election for governor
Maryland	Citizen petition	3% of qualified voters based on votes cast in last general election for governor; not more than 1/2 can be residents of Baltimore or any one county
Massachusetts	Citizen petition	2% of votes cast in last general election for governor
Michigan	Citizen petition Submission by legislature Constitutional requirement(c)	5% of votes cast in last general election for governor
Missouri	Citizen petition Submission by legislature	5% of legal voters in each of 2/3 of congressional districts
Montana..............	Citizen petition Submission by legislature	5% of total qualified electors and 5% in at least 1/3 of legislative districts
Nebraska	Citizen petition	5% of votes cast in last general election for governor
Nevada	Citizen petition	10% of votes cast in last general election
New Jersey............	Submission by legislature Constitutional requirement(c)	
New Mexico...........	Citizen petition Constitutional requirement(c)	10% of qualified electors of each of 3/4 of counties; total must be at least 10% of qualified electors in state
New York	Constitutional requirement(c)	
North Carolina	Constitutional requirement(c)	
North Dakota	Citizen petition	2% of state's resident population from last federal decennial census
Ohio	Citizen petition Constitutional requirement(c)	6% of electors

PROVISIONS FOR REFERENDUM—Continued

State or other jurisdiction	Basis of referendum(a)	Basis for number of signatures on citizen petition(b)
Oklahoma	Citizen petition	5% of votes cast for state office receiving largest number of votes in last general election
	Submission by legislature Constitutional requirement(c)	
Oregon	Citizen petition	4% of votes cast in last election for governor
Pennsylvania	Constitutional requirement(c)	
Rhode Island	Constitutional requirement(c)	
South Dakota	Citizen petition	5% of votes cast in last general election for governor
Utah	Citizen petition	10% of votes cast in last general election for governor and same percentage required from a majority of the counties
Virginia	Submission by legislature Constitutional requirement(c)	
Washington	Citizen petition	4% of voters registered and voting in last general election for governor
	Submission by legislature Constitutional requirement(c)	
Wisconsin	Submission by legislature Constitutional requirement(c)	
Wyoming	Citizen petition	15% of voters in last general election and resident in at least 2/3 of counties
Dist. of Col.	Citizen petition	5% of registered qualified voters; total must include 5% of registered voters in each of five or more wards in district
Guam	Citizen petition	20% of persons voting in last general election for governor
	Submission by legislature	
No. Mariana Is.	Citizen petition	20% of qualified voters
Puerto Rico	Citizen petition	20% of persons voting in last general election for governor
	Submission by legislature	

Note: This table refers only to those jurisdictions which provide for a process whereby a state law passed by the legislature may be referred to the voters before it goes into effect.

(a) Three forms of referendum exist: (1) Citizen petition—the people may petition for a referendum, usually with the intention of rejecting an act passed by the legislature (in many states, the right to petition for referendum may not extend to specific types of legislation); (2) Submission by legislature—the legislature may voluntarily submit laws to the voters for their approval; (3) Constitutional requirement—the state constitution may require that certain questions, such as debt authorization, be submitted to the voters.

(b) A majority of the popular vote is required to enact a referendum measure in every jurisdiction. In Massachusetts, the measure must also receive at least 30 percent of the total ballots cast in the election.

(c) Applies to laws regarding state debt authorization: California, Il-linois (debt may be incurred by law passed by legislature or by submission of question to voters), Iowa, Kansas, New Jersey, New Mexico, New York, North Carolina, Oklahoma, Pennsylvania, Rhode Island, Virginia, Washington, Wisconsin; state bond issuance: Florida, Maine; taxation: Georgia (exemptions from ad valorem taxes), Michigan (taxing and spending over prescribed limits); and authorization of banking powers for associations: Iowa, Ohio.

(d) Applies only to referendum on legislation classifying property and providing for taxation on the same. The referendum, required by the state constitution, may be ordered by citizen petition or submitted by the legislature.

Table 5.16
PROVISIONS FOR RECALL OF STATE OFFICIALS

State or other jurisdiction	Officers to whom applicable	Basis for number of signatures on petition(a)
Alaska............	All elective officials except judicial officers	25% of voters in last general election in jurisdiction of official sought to be recalled
Arizona..........	All elective officials	25% of votes cast in last election for office of official sought to be recalled
California........	All elective officials	Statewide officers: 12% of votes cast in last election for officer sought to be recalled; signatures must be obtained from at least five different counties equal in number to 1% of last vote for office in each of the five counties. State legislators, members of Board of Equalization and courts of appeals justices: 20% of last vote for office
Colorado	All elective officials	25% of votes cast in last election for office of official sought to be recalled
Georgia...........	All elective officials	Statewide officers: 15% of electors registered and qualified to vote at the last general election for office of official sought to be recalled. At least 1/15 of electors must reside in each of the U.S. congressional districts in state. Others: 30% of electors registered and qualified to vote in last general election for office of official sought to be recalled
Idaho	All elective officials except judicial officers	Statewide officers: 20% of number of electors registered to vote in last general election for governor. Others: 20% of electors registered to vote in last general election in jurisdiction of official sought to be recalled
Kansas	All elective officials except judicial officers	40% of votes cast at last general election for office of official sought to be recalled
Louisiana	All elective officials except judicial officers	25% of electors in jurisdiction of official sought to be recalled
Michigan	All elective officials except judges of courts of records and courts of like jurisdiction	25% of voters in last election for governor in district of official sought to be recalled
Montana..........	All public officials elected or appointed(b)	Statewide officers: 10% of registered voters at last general election. Others: 15% of number registered to vote in last election in jurisdiction of official sought to be recalled
Nevada	All elective officials	25% of voters in last election in jurisdiction of official sought to be recalled
North Dakota	All elective officials	25% of electors voting in last general election for governor in jurisdiction of official sought to be recalled
Oregon	All elective officials	15% of votes cast in last gubernatorial election
Washington	All elective officials except judges of courts of record	25% or 35% of qualified voters depending on office
Wisconsin........	All elective officials	25% of votes cast in last general election for governor in jurisdiction of official sought to be recalled
Dist. of Col.	All elective officials except D.C. delegate to U.S. Congress	At-large officers: 10% of registered electors in each of five or more of the city's wards. Others: 10% of registered electors in ward of official sought to be recalled
Guam	Governor	50% of votes cast in last gubernatorial election(c)
No. Mariana Is. ...	All elective officials	40% of persons qualified to vote for official sought to be recalled
Virgin Islands	Governor	50% of votes cast in last gubernatorial election(c)

Note: This table refers only to those jurisdictions that allow the voters to remove state elective officials from office in a recall election.

(a) A majority of the popular vote is required to recall an official in every jurisdiction except the Northern Mariana Islands where recall requires approval by 2/3 of votes cast. In Guam and the Virgin Islands, apart from satisfying the requisite majority vote, the "yes" votes must total 2/3 of the votes cast in the last gubernatorial election.

(b) An elective official may be recalled by qualified voters entitled to vote for individual's successor. An appointed official may be recalled by qualified voters entitled to vote for the successor(s) of the elective officer(s) authorized to appoint an individual to the position.

(c) Referendum on governor (recall) may be initiated by petition described above or by 2/3 vote of members of legislature.

CHAPTER SIX

STATE FINANCES

STATE GOVERNMENT FINANCES

By Dr. James Leigland

The Intergovernmental System

The 1930s marked the emergence of the modern system of fiscal relations between federal, state and local governments. Up to the time of the Great Depression, there had been little movement of funds from one tier of government to another. With increases in federal income taxes and other revenue sources, and the establishment of a host of social programs, the federal government began to take a leadership role in the fiscal system. States began receiving matching grants and seed monies from the federal government, and in turn began providing funds to their localities. A new era of intricately entwined fiscal relationships between different levels of government began to take shape.

Along with this new, truly intergovernmental fiscal system, came a relatively new form of government financing entity, which marked a second major shift in the federal system — and continues as a major feature of the system today. Semi-independent government corporations, often called public authorities, proliferated across the U.S. beginning in the 1930s and 1940s. Although they have existed in the U.S. since the early 19th Century, their use was promoted heavily by the federal government during the New Deal years as mechanisms for financing public works. These entities continue to grow in numbers today because they offer freedom from regular government operating regulations and, above all, minimal restrictions on the issuance of debt. This is especially important today, when 42 states require some kind of voter approval prior to the issuance of state general obligation (or full faith and credit) bonds. State and local government corporations are principally responsible for the 80-fold increase in the issuance of non-guaranteed, or revenue-backed, debt since 1945. As housing authorities, port authorities, turnpike authorities, etc., these entities build and run public works, provide essential services and finance capital spending by other governmental entities.

New Fiscal Realities

The intergovernmental fiscal system has changed significantly during the 1980s. Because of mounting budget deficits, the federal government has sought to shift planning and operational responsibility for many programs to state and local levels, while at the same time reducing federal financial support for those programs. In general, federal aid as a percentage of state-local outlays has dropped from 25 percent in 1981 to an estimated 19 percent in 1987. Federal grants-in-aid for public works needs alone, have declined in constant dollars by almost $4 billion from 1979 to 1987.

During 1986-87, many states have been forced to cut spending and raise taxes because of federal cutbacks and sluggish economic growth, as well as the impacts of a variety of policy shifts, such as the extension of Medicare coverage to all state and local government employees not already covered. During fiscal 1987, nearly half of the states reduced expenditures from budgeted levels, and 33 states adopted new taxes. The ending general fund balance for all states during fiscal 1987 was $5.2 billion, or just 2.5 percent of total state expenditures. State budgets for 1988 show almost no growth and promise dangerously small year-end budgetary surpluses, well below the 5 percent ending balances recommended by the financial community as necessary to protect against financial contingencies. Fourteen states reported deficits or balances of 1 percent or less at the end of fiscal 1987.

In response to declining revenues, growing responsibilities and increasing limits on their

---

Dr. James Leigland is a Visiting Scholar with The Council of State Governments and an advisor to the Policy Analysis Services Division.

ability to issue debt, states and localities continue to create and use government corporations as mechanisms for financing public works and government operations of many kinds.

State Government Revenues, Expenditures and Debt

The latest available comprehensive figures from the U.S. Census Bureau tend to support the contention that, although state revenues continue to show short-term increases, the rates of growth in those revenue categories — and overall state financial condition — have begun to deteriorate.

Revenue Trends. The accompanying tables indicate that, except for utility revenues, and a number of miscellaneous revenue categories, most types of state revenue showed increases in fiscal 1986. Utility revenues decreased by .5 percent after a gain of 10.7 percent in 1985. This was primarily because of a 3.5 percent decline in electric revenues.

Total state revenues increased by 9.5 percent with general revenues increasing by 7.6 percent. In some cases, percentage increases in 1986 were higher than those in 1985. For example, revenue from charges for education and hospital services showed increasing rates of growth, as did insurance and trust fund revenues.

However, for the most part, the rate of increase slowed significantly in 1986. For example, the increase in total revenues slowed from 10.7 percent in 1985, to 9.5 percent in 1986. The percentage increase in federal aid for highways dropped from 22.4 percent to 9.1 percent. Federal aid to education dropped from a 9.5 percent increase in 1985 to a 7.9 percent increase in 1986.

The rate of growth in other kinds of state revenues declined significantly as well. The percentage increases for charges, taxes, intergovernmental revenues and miscellaneous general revenues, all slowed in 1986, as compared with 1985.

Traditional Revenue Categories. Traditionally, the largest source of state revenues are the so-called general revenues, consisting of taxes, intergovernmental revenues, charges and miscellaneous revenues. In fiscal 1986, taxes provided states with $228.1 billion, or about 58 percent of all general revenues. General sales and gross receipts taxes continue to account for the largest proportion of tax revenues at the state level. In 1986, these taxes provided states

with $112.3 billion in revenues, followed by individual income taxes, at $67.5 billion.

In recent years, income taxes and general sales taxes have increased in their relative importance for states as sources of revenue, while corporation and severance taxes have become less important. Because personal income and sales taxes more closely track inflation and increases in the gross national product, they are considered relatively stable sources of revenue. However, they are also somewhat more income-elastic than other kinds of revenue, and greater reliance on them makes states more vulnerable to economic fluctuations and fiscal stress during recessions.

Intergovernmental revenues primarily federal government aid, represents the second largest portion of state general revenues, at $98.6 billion in fiscal 1986, with almost half of these federal funds going for public welfare services. Charges represent the third largest portion of state general revenues at $66.8 billion, with the single largest sub-category of these revenues coming through charges related to higher education, at $17 billion. Various miscellaneous general revenues, including revenue from interest earnings, rents and royalties and donations, represent the fourth and smallest component of general revenues, at $36.9 billion.

Expenditure Trends. Most expenditure categories showed increases in 1986 over 1985. Significant exceptions to this trend however included public works categories such as capital spending for sewerage and housing — down 11.8 percent and 15.8 percent respectively — as well as spending for airports and water transport and terminals — down 6.1 percent and 4.5 percent respectively.

In the vast majority of functional categories, percentage increases declined in 1986 from what they had been in 1985. In 1985 total expenditures increased by 11.2 percent, but that growth rate dropped to 8.6 percent in 1986. This declining rate of growth was experienced in every general expenditure sub-category (education, transportation, public safety, environment and housing), except for social services, which experienced a slightly larger percentage increase in 1986 over 1985, and governmental administration, which went from a 11.1 percent increase in 1985 to a 16.7 percent increase in 1986.

Traditional Expenditure Categories. Among general expenditure categories, education accounted for more state spending than any other category, with $140.2 billion in 1986. Federal grants channeled through states to local public schools represented the single largest type of state education spending, at $81.9 billion.

After education, social services accounted for the largest type of general expenditure, with direct payments to public welfare service providers the single largest type of spending in this category, at $35.6 billion in 1986.

Expenditure on highways amounted to $36.7 billion, with about $28.6 billion of this total spent on regular state highway facilities. Capital spending for highways amounted to $19.7 billion, by far the largest single functional area of state capital spending.

Indebtedness. Debt outstanding at the end of fiscal 1986 totaled $247.7 billion. Only $1.6 billion of this total was short-term debt; the remaining long-term debt consisted of $181.5 billion in revenue-backed (or non-guaranteed) debt, and $64.6 billion in general obligation (or fullfaith and credit debt). Debt issued for higher education purposes, at $29.8 billion, represented the single largest functional type of long-term debt outstanding at the end of 1986. That total was followed closely by debt for hospitals, at $26.4 billion.

The amount of outstanding non-guaranteed debt, backed primarily by project revenues, largely reflects the continuing use by states of government corporations as revenue debt-issuing mechanisms. This debt increased by 18.1 percent in 1985, and 22 percent in 1986, indicating a rapidly growing reliance by states on these debt issuing entities. In contrast, general obligation, or full faith and credit, debt, backed primarily by taxing power and limited by statute constitutions in virtually every state, increased by only 7 percent.

The Census Bureau publishes special reports on "independent special districts," and the financial activities of many government corporations are listed separately from state finances in those reports. Much of the revenue debt issuing activity indicated in the Bureau's state government financial tables (some of which are summarized in the following sec-

tions) is actually activity undertaken by government corporations deemed "subordinate agencies" (and thus not separate and independent) by the Census Bureau. This is a definitional questions. Readers should simply keep in mind that most of the revenue debt indicated as having been issued by states, has actually been issued through entities that are defined by the states as legally distinct government corporations.

Emerging Financial Issues

The Tax Reform Act of 1986, with its sweeping new restrictions on what may be considered tax-exempt municipal debt, has resulted in substantial reductions in bond issuance by states and localities. New municipal debt issues in 1987 declined to $100.1 billion from $147.1 billion in 1986, and $201 billion in 1985. Many Wall Street investment firms began in 1987 to make drastic cuts in their municipal units. Salomon Brothers, Inc., the leading underwriter of municipal bonds in 1987 and 1986, completely closed its municipal operation, laying off over 200 public finance experts.

The stock market crash of 1987 affected state finances directly only in terms of impacts on pension fund investments and other state equity holdings. But federal efforts to slash the budget deficit and increase federal revenues — precipitated by the crash — may endanger the tax-exempt status of municipal securities not affected by tax reform, and may pre-empt state efforts to raise money through gasoline and other highway taxes. Municipal borrowing may also face new, tougher disclosure requirements as a result of increased general interest in protecting investors.

Most important perhaps, the stock market crash may have signaled the beginning of a new national economic slow-down that will restrict the ability of states to respond to federal cutbacks, as well as respond to growing economic development and infrastructure improvement needs.

6.1
STATE BUDGETARY CALENDARS

State or other jurisdiction	Budget guidelines to agencies	Agency requests submitted to Governor	Agency hearings held	Governor's Budget sent to legislature	Legislature adopts budget	Fiscal year begins	Frequency of legislative/ budget cycles
Alabama............	July/Aug	Oct/Nov	Dec/Jan	Jan/Feb/Ap	May/July	October 1	Annual/Annual
Alaska.............	...	...	...	...	...	...	...
Arizona............	June	September	Oct/Nov	January	April	July 1	Annual/Annual
Arkansas	May	August	Aug/Sept	Sept/Dec	April	July 1	Biennial/Biennial
California..........	July	Sept/Nov	Nov/Dec	January	March/June	July 1	Annual/Annual
Colorado	June	August	Dec/Jan	November	March/April	July 1	Annual/Annual
Connecticut	July	September	December	January	May	July 1	Annual/Annual
Delaware	August	Sept/Oct	Oct/Dec	January	June	July 1	Annual/Annual
Florida............	July/Aug	Oct/Nov	...	February	June	July 1	Annual/Biennial
Georgia............	June	September	Oct/Dec	January	March	July 1	Annual/Annual
Hawaii	May/June	August	November	January	April 1	July 1	Annual/Biennial
Idaho	May	September	...	January	March	July 1	Annual/Annual
Illinois.............	July	Nov/Dec	Nov/Dec	March	June	July 1	Annual/Annual
Indiana	June	September	Oct/Nov	January	April/May	July 1	Annual/Biennial
Iowa	June	September	December	January	April	July 1	Annual/Annual
Kansas	July	Sept/Oct	November	January	April	July 1	Annual/Annual
Kentucky	July	October	December	January	March	July 1	Biennial/Biennial
Louisiana	October	December	January	April	July	July 1	Annual/Annual
Maine	July	September	December	Jan/Feb	June	July 1	Annual/Biennial
Maryland	July	Sept/Oct	Oct/Dec	January	April	July 1	Annual/Annual
Massachusetts	July	September	Oct/Nov	January	June	July 1	Annual/Annual
Michigan	May	Sept/Oct	Oct/Nov	January	June	October 1	Annual/Annual
Minnesota	June/July	October	...	January	May	July 1	Annual/Biennial
Mississippi	June	August	September	November	March	July 1	Annual/Annual
Missouri	June/July	October	Oct/Nov	January	April/June	July 1	Annual/Annual
Montana...........	June	Aug/Sept	...	December	April	July 1	Biennial/Biennial
Nebraska	July	September	January	January	March	July 1	Biennial/Biennial
Nevada	July	September	Sept/Dec	January	June	July 1	Biennial/Biennial
New Hampshire	May	October 1	December	February 15	June	July 1	Annual/Biennial
New Jersey.........	May/June	October	...	January	June	July 1	Annual/Annual
New Mexico........	June/July	September	Oct/Nov	January	Feb/March	July 1	Annual/Annual
New York	June/July	September	November	January	March	April 1	Annual/Annual
North Carolina	June	September	October	February	July	July 1	Biennial/Biennial
North Dakota	March	July/Aug	July/Sept	December	April	July 1	Biennial/Biennial
Ohio	July	September	October	February	June	July 1	Annual/Biennial
Oklahoma	July	September	Sept/Oct	January	May/June	July 1	Annual/Annual
Oregon	April	September	Sept/Nov	December 1	June	July 1	Biennial/Biennial
Pennsylvania	August	Oct/Nov	December	February	June	July 1	Annual/Annual
Rhode Island	June	October	November	Feb/March	June	July 1	Annual/Annual
South Carolina	July	August	August	January	June	July 1	Annual/Annual
South Dakota	July	September	September	December	March	July 1	Annual/Annual
Tennessee	August	October	November	January	May	July 1	Annual/Annual
Texas..............	March/Ap	June/July	Aug/Oct	January	May	September 1	Biennial/Biennial
Utah	July	September	October	December	February	July 1	Annual/Annual
Vermont	June	September	Sept/Oct	January	May	July 1	Annual/Biennial
Virginia............	May	September	Oct/Dec	January	March	July 1	Annual/Biennial
Washington	April	Aug/Sept	October	December	May	July 1	Annual/Biennial
West Virginia	July	August	...	...	...	July 1	Annual/Annual
Wisconsin..........	April	October	March	June	July	July 1	Annual/Biennial
Wyoming	August	September	November	December	March	July 1	Annual/Biennial

Source: National Association of State Budget Officers, *Budgetary Process in the States* (July 1987).

Table 6.2
OFFICIALS OR AGENCIES RESPONSIBLE FOR BUDGET
PREPARATION, REVIEW AND CONTROLS

State or other jurisdiction	Official/agency responsible for preparing budget document	Special budget review agency in legislative branch	Agency(ies) responsible for budgetary and related accounting controls
Alabama	Budget Officer, Dept. of Finance	Legis. Fiscal Off., Joint Fiscal Cmte.	Dept. of Finance
Alaska	Director, Off. of Mgt. & Budget	Div. of Legis. Finance, Legis. Budget & Audit Cmte.	Div. of Treasury, Dept. of Revenue
Arizona	Director, Finance Div.. Dept. of Admin.	Joint Legis. Budget Cmte.	Div. of Finance, Dept. of Admin.
Arkansas	Administrator, Off. of Budget, Dept. of Finance & Admin.	Research & Fiscal Services, Legis. Council	Dept. of Finance & Admin.
California	Director, Dept. of Finance	Legis. Budget Cmte.	Dept. of Finance, Off. of Controller
Colorado	Exec. Director, Off. of State Planning & Budgeting	Joint Budget Cmte.	Div. of Accounts & Control, Dept. of Admin.
Connecticut	Budget Director, Off. of Policy & Mgt.	Off. of Fiscal Analysis, Joint Cmte. on Legis. Mgt.	Off. of Policy & Mgt., Comptroller
Delaware	Director, Off. of the Budget	Off. of Controller General, Legislative Council	Dept. of Finance; Off. of Controller General
Florida	Director, Off. of Planning & Budgeting	Senate, House Appropriations cmtes.	Comptroller; Finance Div., Dept. of Banking & Finance
Georgia	Director, Off. of Planning & Budget	Legis. Budget Analyst, Legis. Budget Off., Legislative Services Cmte.	Fiscal Div., Dept. of Administrative Services; Comptroller General
Hawaii	Director, Dept. of Budget & Finance	Senate Ways & Means, House Finance cmtes., Off. of the Legis. Auditor	Dept. of Budget & Finance; Dept. of Accounting & General Services
Idaho	Administrator, Div. of Financial Mgt., Off. of the Governor	Legis. Budget Off., Joint Finance-Appropriations Cmte.	Div. of Financial Mgt., Off. of the Governor; Off. of State Auditor
Illinois	Director, Bur. of the Budget	Senate, House Appropriations cmtes.	Off. of the Comptroller; Dept. of Financial Institutions
Indiana	Director, Budget Agcy.	Off. of Fiscal & Mgt. Analysis, Legis. Services Agcy.	Budget Agcy.; Off. of State Auditor
Iowa	Dir., Dept. of Mgt.	Legis. Fiscal Bur.	Dept. of Mgt.
Kansas	Director, Div. of the Budget, Dept. of Admin.	Fiscal Analyst, Legis. Research Dept., Jt. Legis. Budget Cmte.	Div. of Accounts & Reports, Dept. of Admin.
Kentucky	Secretary, Finance & Admin. Cabinet	Budget Review, Legis. Research Comm.	Finance & Admin. Cabinet
Louisiana	Budget Director, Div. of Admin., Off. of the Governor	Legis. Fiscal Off., Joint Legis. Cmte. on the Budget; Fiscal Svcs., Senate Research Svcs; Fiscal Affairs Div., House Legis. Svcs.	Div. of Admin., Off. of the Governor
Maine	State Budget Officer, Bur. of the Budget, Dept. of Finance & Admin.	Legis. Finance Off., Joint Appropriations & Financial Affairs Cmte., Office of Fiscal & Program Review, Legislative Council	Bur. of Accounts & Control, Dept. of Finance
Maryland	Secretary, Dept. of Budget & Fiscal Planning	Div. of Budget Review; Div. of Fiscal Research, Dept. of Fiscal Services, Senate Budget & Taxation Cmte., House Appropriations Cmte.	Comptroller of the Treasury
Massachusetts	Budget Director, Exec. Off. for Admin. & Finance	Senate, House Ways & Means cmtes., Senate, House Post Audit & Oversight Cmtes.	Comptroller's Div., Exec. Off. for Admin. & Finance
Michigan	Director, Dept. of Mgt. & Budget	Senate, House Fiscal Agencies	Dept. of Treasury; Dept. of Mgt. & Budget
Minnesota	Commissioner, Dept. of Finance	Senate Finance Cmte.; House Appropriations Cmte.	Dept. of Finance
Mississippi	State Fiscal Officer, Fiscal Mgt. Bd.	Joint Legis. Budget Off. Joint Legis. Budget Cmte.	Fiscal Mgt. Bd.; Off. of State Auditor

BUDGET OFFICIALS OR AGENCIES—Continued

State or other jurisdiction	Official/agency responsible for preparing budget document	Special budget review agency in legislative branch	Agency(ies) responsible for budgetary and related accounting controls
Missouri	Director, Div. of Budget & Planning, Off. of Admin.	Senate Appropriations Cmte.; House Budget Cmte., Oversight Div., Cmte. on Legis. Res., Sen. State Budget Control Cmte.	Div. of Accounting, Off. of Admin.
Montana	Director, Budget & Program Planning Off.	Off. of Legis. Fiscal Analyst	Dept. of Admin.; Budget & Program Planning Off.
Nebraska	Budget Administrator, Budget Div., Administrative Services Dept.	Off. of Legis. Fiscal Analyst	Dept. of Administrative Services; State Auditor
Nevada	Director, Dept. of Admin.	Fiscal Analysis Div., Legis. Counsel Bur.	Off. of the Controller
New Hampshire	Commissioner, Admin. Services Dept.	Off. of Legis. Budget Analyst, Fiscal Cmte. of the General Court, Jt. Advisory Budget Control Cmte.	Div. of Accounting, Dept. of Admin. Services
New Jersey	Director, Off. of Mgt. & Budget, Dept. of Treasury	Legis. Budget & Finance Off., Off. of Legis. Services	Dept. of Treasury
New Mexico	Director, Budget Div., Dept. of Finance & Admin.	Legis. Finance Cmte.	Dept. of Finance & Admin.; Off. of Treasurer
New York	Director, Div. of Budget, Exec. Dept.	Senate Finance Cmte.; Assembly Ways & Means Cmte.	Office of the State Comptroller
North Carolina	Budget Officer, Off. of Budget & Mgt.	Fiscal Research Div., Legis. Services Off.	State Controller's Off.; Off. of Budget & Mgt.
North Dakota	Director; Exec. Budget Analyst, Off. of Mgt. & Budget	Legis. Budget Analyst & Auditor, Legis. Council	Off. of Mgt. & Budget
Ohio	Director, Off. of Budget & Mgt.	Legis. Budget Off.	Office of Budget & Mgt.; Off of Treasurer
Oklahoma	Director, Off. of State Finance	Joint Fiscal Operations Cmte.; House of Rep. Research, Legal & Fiscal Divs., Appropriations Cmte. Coord. Sen. Fiscal Staff	Off. of State Finance
Oregon	Administrator, Budget & Mgt. Div., Exec. Dept.	Legis. Fiscal Off.	Budget & Mgt. Div., Exec. Dept; Off. of State Treasurer
Pennsylvania	Secretary, Off. of Budget, Off. of the Governor	Legis. Budget & Finance Cmte., Senate, House Appropriations Cmtes.	Comptroller Operations, Off. of the Budget; Dept. of Revenue
Rhode Island	Finance & Planning, Dept. of Admin.	Senate, House Finance cmtes.	Accounts & Control, Dept. of Admin.
South Carolina	Director, State Budget Division	State Auditor; Joint Appropriations Review Cmte.	Off. of Comptroller General; State Budget & Control Bd.
South Dakota	Commissioner, Bur. of Finance & Mgt.	Off. of Fiscal Analysis, Legis. Research Council	Bur. of Finance & Mgt.; Off. of State Auditor
Tennessee	Commissioner, Budget Div., Dept. of Finance & Admin.	Fiscal Review Cmte.	Dept. of Finance & Admin.; Off. of Comptroller of the Treasury
Texas	Director, Governor's Off. of Budget & Planning	Legis. Budget Bd.	Comptroller, Public Accounts
Utah	Director, Off. of Planning & Budget	Off. of Legis. Fiscal Analyst, Legis Mgt. Cmte.	Div. of Finance, Admin. Services Dept.
Vermont	Commissioner, Dept. of Finance & Mgt.	Joint Fiscal Cmte.	Finance & Mgt. Dept., Agcy. of Admin.
Virginia	Director, Dept. of Planning & Budget	Senate Finance Cmte.; House Appropriations Cmte.	Comptroller, Dept. of Accounts; Off. of Finance
Washington	Director, Off. of Financial Mgt.	Legis. Auditor, Legis. Budget Cmte.; Legis. Evaluation & Accountability Prog. Cmte.	Off. of Financial Mgt.; State Treasurer
West Virginia	Director, Budget Div.; Commissioner, Dept. of Finance & Admin.	Off. of Legis. Auditor, Joint Cmte. on Government & Finance	Dept. of Finance & Admin.; Off. of State Auditor

BUDGET OFFICIALS OR AGENCIES—Continued

State or other jurisdiction	Official/agency responsible for preparing budget document	Special budget review agency in legislative branch	Agency(ies) responsible for budgetary and related accounting controls
Wisconsin	Administrator, State Exec. Budget & Planning, Dept. of Admin.	Legis. Fiscal Bur.	Bur. of Financial Operations; State Finance & Program Mgt., Dept. of Admin.
Wyoming	Administrator, Budget Div., Admin. & Fiscal Control Dept.	Budget Analysis Div., Legis. Service Off.	Off. of State Auditor
Dist. of Col.	Director, Off. of the Budget	Acct. Unit, Off. of the Sec. of Council	Off. of Controller
American Samoa	Director, Program Planning & Budget Development	Fiscal Officer, Legis. Financial Off.	Dept. of Treasury
Guam	Director, Bur. of Budget & Mgt. Research	Ways & Means Cmte.	Dept. of Admin.
No. Mariana Is.	Planning & Budget, Off. of the Governor	Senate Fiscal Affairs Cmte.; House Appropriations Cmte.	Dept. of Finance & Accounting
Puerto Rico	Director, Off. of Budget & Mgt.	Economics Div., Off. of Legis. Services	Off. of Budget & Mgt.; Off. of Comptroller
Virgin Islands	Director, Off. Mgt. & Budget	Legis. Finance Cmte., Off. of Post Audit	Accounting Div., Dept. of Finance

Table 6.3
STATE BALANCED BUDGETS AND DEFICIT LIMITATIONS:
CONSTITUTIONAL AND STATUTORY PROVISIONS

State or other jurisdiction	Governor must submit a balanced budget	Legislature must pass a balanced budget	Governor must sign a balanced budget	May carry over deficit for one year maximum	Cannot carry over deficit into next biennium	Cannot carry over deficit into next fiscal year	Constitutional limit on general obligational debt (a)
Alabama............	C,S	★	★	...	...	★	★
Alaska(b)..........	U/A	C,S	U/A	U/A	...	...	...
Arizona............	S	S	S	...	...	★	$ 350,000
Arkansas	S	...	...	...	★	★	...
California..........	★	...	★	★(c)	...	★(c)	300,000
Colorado	S	C	C	C	C	C	★
Connecticut	★	★	★	...	...	...	...
Delaware	C	C	C	...	★	★	...
Florida	S	C	...	...	...	★	...
Georgia............	★	★	★	...	...	...	(d)
Hawaii	C,S	...	C,S	...	...	...	(e)
Idaho	C	C	...	...	...	★	2,000,000
Illinois.............	C	C	...	...	...	...	...
Indiana	C	C	C	...	★	★	0
Iowa	C	C	...	...	...	...	250,000
Kansas	S	S	...	...	★	★	1,000,000
Kentucky	C	C	C	...	★	★	500,000
Louisiana	★	★	★	...	...	...	(f)
Maine	★	...	...	...	...	...	2,000,000
Maryland	C	C	...	★(g)	★(g)	★(g)	...
Massachusetts	C,S	...	...	...	...	...	...
Michigan	C	C	C	...	★	★	0
Minnesota	C,S	C,S	C,S	S	C,S	...	...
Mississippi	S	...	...	...	...	...	(h)
Missouri	C	C	C	...	...	★	0
Montana...........	C	C	...	★	★	★	100,000
Nebraska	C	C	C	...	...	...	AV
Nevada	S	C	...	...	...	...	...
New Hampshire	S	...	★	...	★	★	...
New Jersey.........	C	C	C	...	★	★	(i)
New Mexico........	...	...	★	...	...	★	AV
New York	C	...	C	C	...	...	V
North Carolina	C	C	C	...	★	★	★
North Dakota	★	★	★	...	★	...	...
Ohio	★	★	★	...	★	★	(j)
Oklahoma	S	...	...	...	★	★	V
Oregon	C,S	C,S	C,S	...	...	...	50,000
Pennsylvania	C	C	S	C	...	...	★
Rhode Island	C,S	C,S	C,S	...	...	★	V
South Carolina	C	C	C	...	★	★	(k)
South Dakota	C	C	C	...	...	★	100,000
Tennessee..........	C	C	C	...	...	★	...
Texas..............	C	C	C	...	...	★	200,000
Utah	S	C	...	...	★	★	AV
Vermont	...	...	...	...	...	...	...
Virginia............	S	...	...	...	S	S	V,T
Washington	S	...	...	...	★	...	T
West Virginia(b)	...	C	...	...	...	C	...
Wisconsin..........	...	...	...	...	...	...	AV
Wyoming...........	★	★	★	...	★	★	AV

Source: National Association of State Budget Officers, *Budgetary Processes in the States, 1987.*

Key:
C—Constitutional provision
S—Statutory provision
V—Popular vote required for any debt
T—Percentage of taxes
AV—Percentage of property value
★—Yes
...—No provision
U/A—Information not available
(a) Different provisions may apply to other long and short term debts; repayment periods may vary.
(b) Based on 1986 information.

(c) May carry over only with legislative concurrence.
(d) Not more than 10 percent of prior year's net general revenues.
(e) Not to exceed 20 percent of average of General Fund revenues for 3 fiscal years preceeding; may not be exceeded by popular vote.
(f) Limited to 10 percent of 3 year average of Bond Security and Redemption Fund.
(g) General Fund must have positive balance at end of fiscal year of proposed budget.
(h) 5 percent of General Fund.
(i) 1 percent of expenditures.
(j) Highway, $500 million; Coal, $100 million.
(k) Limited to 5 percent of last completed fiscal year revenue for Capital Improvement Bonds.

Table 6.4
SUMMARY FINANCIAL AGGREGATES, BY STATE: 1985
(In millions of dollars)

State or other jurisdiction	Revenue				Expenditure				Debt outstanding at end of fiscal year	Cash and security holdings at end of fiscal year
	Total	General	Utilities and liquor store	Insurance trust	Total	General	Utilities and liquor store	Insurance trust		
United States	$438,954	$365,344	$5,702	$67,907	$390,828	$345,133	$7,755	$37,940	$211,904	$519,014
Alabama	6,601	5,535	136	930	6,082	5,544	122	416	3,240	6,921
Alaska	5,918	5,453	1	463	4,950	4,606	123	221	5,692	15,483
Arizona	5,330	4,293	7	1,031	4,599	4,251	7	340	684	6,254
Arkansas	3,342	2,925	0	418	3,018	2,797	0	221	825	3,596
California	57,894	46,047	182	11,665	51,840	45,775	5	6,060	16,057	65,833
Colorado	5,298	4,133	0	1,164	4,817	4,251	0	566	1,520	7,060
Connecticut	6,268	5,698	18	552	5,429	4,871	78	480	6,389	6,636
Delaware	1,682	1,542	4	136	1,335	1,251	9	75	1,832	1,926
Florida	13,798	11,882	6	1,910	12,854	12,148	16	691	5,014	13,748
Georgia	8,760	7,572	0	1,188	7,618	7,087	0	531	2,158	8,960
Hawaii	2,677	2,245	0	432	2,539	2,081	0	458	2,710	3,834
Idaho	1,610	1,299	37	275	1,440	1,256	29	155	629	1,858
Illinois	17,573	15,377	0	2,196	16,491	14,781	0	1,709	9,787	16,125
Indiana	7,917	7,102	0	814	7,084	6,624	0	460	1,730	5,693
Iowa	4,697	4,004	125	569	4,630	4,229	87	314	1,326	4,159
Kansas	3,714	3,142	0	572	3,248	3,002	0	246	319	3,167
Kentucky	6,178	5,396	0	782	5,447	4,982	0	465	3,633	6,302
Louisiana	8,156	6,961	0	1,195	7,581	6,562	0	1,019	8,095	8,574
Maine	2,137	1,848	45	244	1,948	1,705	44	198	1,225	2,035
Maryland	8,221	7,093	78	1,050	7,365	6,381	184	799	5,091	8,184
Massachusetts	11,485	10,417	3	1,066	11,028	10,171	24	833	10,101	10,247
Michigan	17,262	15,165	430	1,667	15,634	14,063	386	1,185	5,904	18,589
Minnesota	9,378	8,261	0	1,118	8,121	7,492	0	629	3,503	11,587
Mississippi	3,923	3,303	110	510	3,561	3,204	93	265	1,007	3,430
Missouri	6,682	5,786	0	896	5,817	5,442	0	375	3,319	8,075
Montana	1,738	1,388	39	312	1,557	1,318	35	205	745	2,598
Nebraska	2,144	2,003	0	140	2,137	2,067	0	70	1,028	1,800
Nevada	1,909	1,398	39	473	1,643	1,318	40	285	1,108	3,243
New Hampshire	1,361	1,068	154	138	1,195	1,012	125	58	1,979	1,567
New Jersey	15,905	13,245	269	2,391	14,080	11,858	621	1,601	13,365	20,678
New Mexico	3,579	3,124	0	455	3,041	2,861	0	180	1,277	7,411
New York	46,762	37,432	1,779	7,551	40,106	33,359	3,478	3,270	32,355	60,419
North Carolina	9,879	8,288	0	1,591	8,492	7,828	0	664	2,157	11,190
North Dakota	1,651	1,472	0	179	1,541	1,440	0	101	586	1,872
Ohio	21,242	14,776	317	6,150	17,568	14,071	298	3,199	8,204	31,057
Oklahoma	5,672	4,933	125	613	5,077	4,367	272	438	3,581	6,946
Oregon	5,337	4,079	139	1,119	4,812	3,986	84	742	6,605	11,552
Pennsylvania	20,337	16,662	589	3,086	18,067	15,088	564	2,416	7,289	18,842
Rhode Island	2,129	1,860	8	261	2,010	1,787	26	197	2,814	2,953
South Carolina	5,825	4,545	430	850	5,254	4,400	481	373	3,403	7,175
South Dakota	1,082	929	0	152	1,005	964	0	40	1,086	2,024
Tennessee	6,142	5,351	0	791	5,439	5,025	0	414	1,913	6,550
Texas	21,346	18,796	0	2,550	19,074	17,536	0	1,539	5,193	30,617
Utah	3,133	2,583	68	483	2,818	2,564	48	206	1,333	3,693
Vermont	1,109	984	28	96	1,034	954	27	53	887	1,136
Virginia	9,030	7,687	240	1,103	7,833	7,234	201	399	3,317	9,156
Washington	9,781	7,407	207	2,166	9,012	7,402	177	1,433	3,030	9,585
West Virginia	3,672	2,964	60	648	3,343	2,780	44	520	1,628	3,622
Wisconsin	9,740	8,185	0	1,555	8,718	7,994	0	725	4,473	11,145
Wyoming	1,946	1,704	30	211	1,497	1,365	28	105	757	3,907

Source: U.S. Bureau of the Census, *State Government Finances in 1985.*
Notes: Detail may not add to totals due to rounding. Data presented are statistical in nature and do not represent an accounting statement. Therefore, a difference between an individual government's total revenues and expenditures does not necessarily indicate a "budget" surplus or deficit.

Table 6.5
SUMMARY FINANCIAL AGGREGATES, BY STATE: 1986
(In millions of dollars)

State or other jurisdiction	Revenue				Expenditure				Debt outstanding at end of fiscal year	Cash and security holdings at end of fiscal year
	Total	General	Utilities and liquor store	Insurance trust	Total	General	Utilities and liquor store	Insurance trust		
United States	$481,174	$393,476	$5,714	$81,984	$424,216	$376,519	$7,948	$39,749	$247,715	$610,975
Alabama............	6,801	5,718	141	942	6,438	5,900	135	403	3,752	8,244
Alaska.............	6,115	5,444	3	669	4,221	3,888	82	250	6,961	18,216
Arizona............	6,038	4,605	7	1,426	5,074	4,688	9	377	1,473	8,484
Arkansas	3,623	3,172	0	451	3,355	3,133	0	223	1,087	3,996
California..........	63,987	50,234	142	13,612	57,370	50,791	6	6,573	20,122	81,193
Colorado	5,995	4,550	0	1,445	4,952	4,376	0	577	1,998	8,261
Connecticut	6,966	6,364	18	584	6,009	5,404	92	513	7,317	7,798
Delaware	1,807	1,553	4	250	1,415	1,319	9	87	2,635	2,094
Florida	15,815	13,319	6	2,490	13,740	12,967	18	755	5,680	17,896
Georgia............	9,391	8,044	0	1,347	8,530	7,974	0	556	2,451	10,363
Hawaii	2,945	2,430	0	515	2,472	2,241	0	231	2,828	4,400
Idaho	1,744	1,354	37	352	1,517	1,323	30	164	658	2,102
Illinois............	19,437	16,294	0	3,144	17,823	16,108	0	1,715	11,988	20,033
Indiana	8,485	7,617	0	868	7,548	7,111	0	437	2,180	6,833
Iowa	5,314	4,350	114	850	4,852	4,451	83	319	1,601	5,049
Kansas	3,948	3,235	0	713	3,522	3,240	0	282	352	3,536
Kentucky	6,710	5,706	0	1,004	5,791	5,372	0	419	4,110	7,357
Louisiana	8,359	7,035	0	1,325	8,218	7,151	0	1,067	10,479	10,444
Maine	2,389	2,039	46	304	2,156	1,914	45	198	1,558	2,562
Maryland	9,140	7,763	52	1,325	8,132	7,154	205	773	5,410	9,650
Massachusetts	13,121	12,050	26	1,045	12,449	11,445	25	979	11,844	12,796
Michigan	20,507	16,608	429	3,470	17,563	15,602	365	1,596	7,084	22,024
Minnesota	9,540	8,077	0	1,463	8,581	7,858	0	723	3,760	12,537
Mississippi	4,434	3,586	115	733	3,836	3,483	93	260	1,184	4,532
Missouri	7,491	6,304	0	1,187	6,477	6,064	0	413	3,751	9,527
Montana...........	1,754	1,388	38	328	1,643	1,396	30	216	1,240	3,131
Nebraska	2,334	2,165	0	169	2,205	2,122	0	83	1,309	2,140
Nevada	2,391	1,614	43	734	1,917	1,539	42	336	1,224	3,685
New Hampshire	1,548	1,247	164	137	1,348	1,159	133	57	2,384	2,021
New Jersey.........	17,558	14,485	287	2,786	16,043	13,616	768	1,660	16,899	26,277
New Mexico........	3,925	3,380	0	546	3,300	3,098	0	202	2,137	8,547
New York	50,909	40,932	1,697	8,280	43,139	36,364	3,460	3,315	36,371	68,230
North Carolina	10,801	8,904	0	1,897	9,369	8,649	0	720	2,606	13,709
North Dakota	1,565	1,380	0	184	1,537	1,427	0	111	743	2,064
Ohio	23,021	15,801	323	6,897	19,010	15,372	296	3,343	8,859	35,196
Oklahoma	5,905	5,032	161	712	5,629	4,801	324	503	3,830	7,452
Oregon	5,524	4,179	139	1,206	4,925	4,233	88	605	7,142	12,564
Pennsylvania	22,120	17,886	605	3,629	19,278	16,322	579	2,377	7,802	21,373
Rhode Island	2,362	1,960	8	393	2,167	1,925	40	202	2,950	3,225
South Carolina	6,362	4,919	455	988	5,641	4,812	450	378	3,726	8,953
South Dakota	1,241	1,038	0	204	1,074	1,029	0	45	1,303	2,397
Tennessee...........	6,813	5,886	0	927	6,080	5,671	0	409	2,156	7,624
Texas..............	23,103	19,904	0	3,198	20,782	18,918	0	1,864	5,432	33,895
Utah	3,311	2,727	69	516	3,071	2,793	50	228	1,325	3,997
Vermont	1,185	1,048	30	107	1,095	1,014	29	52	984	1,304
Virginia............	9,964	8,406	253	1,304	8,873	8,239	210	424	3,843	10,541
Washington	10,668	8,013	213	2,442	9,669	8,100	184	1,384	3,572	11,107
West Virginia	3,822	3,170	58	593	3,621	3,065	41	515	2,132	4,081
Wisconsin	10,886	8,832	0	2,054	9,125	8,424	0	701	4,660	13,162
Wyoming	2,004	1,732	31	241	1,633	1,476	28	129	825	4,374

Source: U.S. Bureau of the Census, State Government Finances in 1986.
Notes: Detail may not add to totals due to rounding. Data presented are statistical in nature and do not represent an accounting statement. Therefore, a difference between an individual government's total revenues and expenditures does not necessarily indicate a "budget" surplus or deficit.

Table 6.6
NATIONAL TOTALS OF STATE GOVERNMENT FINANCES FOR SELECTED YEARS: 1972-86

Item	Amount (in millions)										Percentage change 1985 to 1986	Percentage change 1984 to 1985	Per capita 1986	Per capita 1985
	1986	1985	1984	1983	1982	1980	1978	1976	1974	1972				
Revenue total	$481,174	$439,416	$397,087	$357,660	$330,898	$276,962	$225,011	$183,821	$140,816	$112,309	9.5	10.7	$2,001.13	$1,845.38
General revenue	393,476	365,835(r)	330,740	290,480	275,111	233,592	189,099	152,118	122,327	98,632	7.6	10.6	1,636.41	1,536.37
Taxes total	228,054	215,893(r)	196,795	171,464	162,607	137,075	113,261	89,256	74,207	59,870	5.6	9.7	948.44	906.67
Intergovernmental revenue	98,574	89,887	81,450	72,704	69,166	64,326	53,461	44,717	33,170	27,981	9.7	10.4	409.95	377.49
From federal government	92,666	84,434	76,140	68,962	66,026	61,892	50,200	42,013	31,632	26,791	9.7	10.9	385.38	354.59
Public welfare	41,802	38,664	35,423	32,949	31,510	24,680	20,007	16,867	13,320	12,289	8.1	9.1	173.85	162.37
Education	16,523	15,307	13,975	13,185	13,149	12,765	9,819	8,661	6,720	5,984	7.9	9.5	68.72	64.28
Highways	13,855	12,702	10,380	8,927	8,304	8,860	6,301	6,262	4,503	4,871	9.1	22.4	57.62	53.34
General revenue sharing	(b)	(b)	(b)	(b)	(b)	2,278	2,255	2,102	2,045	0	0.0	0.0	(b)	(b)
Employment security administration	2,790	2,594	2,606	2,531	2,352	2,050	1,887	1,658	1,295	1,148	7.6	-.5	11.60	10.89
Other	17,696	15,167	13,756	11,370	10,711	11,258	9,931	6,463	3,749	2,499	16.7	11.0	73.60	63.70
From local governments	5,908	5,453	5,310	3,742	3,139	2,434	3,261	2,704	1,538	1,191	8.3	2.7	24.57	22.90
Charges and miscellaneous revenue	66,848	60,055(r)	52,495	46,312	43,338	32,190	22,377	18,145	14,950	10,780	11.3	14.4	278.01	252.21
Utility revenue(a)	2,907	2,921(r)	2,638	2,390	2,085	1,304	962	0	0	0	-.5	10.7	12.09	12.27
Liquor stores revenue	2,807	2,753	2,759	2,819	2,854	2,765	2,388	2,196	2,049	1,904	2.0	-.2	11.67	11.56
Insurance trust revenue	81,984	67,907	60,950	61,971	50,848	39,301	32,562	29,508	16,439	11,773	20.7	11.4	340.96	285.18
Unemployment compensation	18,173	17,596	16,671	21,480	16,854	13,468	13,083	15,068	5,711	3,588	3.3	5.5	75.58	73.90
Employee retirement	56,820	43,993	38,564	35,236	29,035	21,146	16,026	12,171	8,919	6,827	29.2	14.1	236.31	184.75
Other	6,991	6,319	5,715	5,255	4,959	4,686	3,452	2,269	1,809	1,359	10.6	10.6	29.07	26.54
Debt outstanding at end of fiscal year, total	247,715	211,917(r)	186,377	167,291	147,470	121,958	102,569	84,825	65,296	53,833	16.9	13.7	1,030.53	889.97
Long-term	246,109	209,125(r)	183,208	164,696	143,702	119,821	99,671	78,814	61,697	50,379	17.7	14.1	1,023.53	878.24
Non-guaranteed	181,469	148,693	125,859	109,617	92,195	70,457	53,336	39,972	30,842	25,314	22.0	18.1	754.70	624.45
Full-faith and credit	64,640	60,432	57,349	55,079	51,507	49,364	46,316	38,842	30,855	25,065	7.0	5.4	268.83	253.79
Short-term	1,606	2,792	3,169	2,595	3,768	2,137	2,897	6,011	3,599	3,454	-42.5	-11.9	6.68	11.73
Net long-term	129,119	110,361	101,681	94,779	87,047	79,810	72,089	62,488	53,847	45,082	17.0	8.5	536.99	463.47
Full-faith and credit only	50,212	47,894	46,976	41,442	39,766	39,357	39,147	33,708	26,967	21,932	4.8	2.0	208.82	201.14
Expenditure and debt redemption	439,793	402,450	361,810	345,162	317,482	263,494	208,533	184,511	134,948	111,933	9.3	11.2	1,829.03	1,690.14
Debt redemption	15,577	11,708	10,364	11,143	7,190	5,682	4,701	3,585	2,814	2,690	33.1	13.0	64.78	49.17
Expenditure, total	424,216	390,742(r)	351,446	334,019	310,292	257,812	203,832	180,926	132,134	109,243	8.6	11.2	1,764.25	1,640.97
General expenditure	380,346	349,685	309,684	285,042	269,490	228,223	179,802	153,690	119,891	98,810	8.8	12.9	1,581.80	1,468.54
Education	140,189	128,604	116,058	107,703	102,984	87,939	69,702	59,630	46,860	38,348	9.0	8.8	583.03	540.09
Intergovernmental expenditure	81,929	74,937	67,485	63,118	60,684	52,688	40,125	34,084	27,107	21,195	8.3	10.8	340.73	314.71
State institutions of higher education	47,928	44,264	40,016	36,496	34,296	27,927	23,259	19,707	15,395	13,381	8.3	11.0	199.33	185.89
Other	10,332	9,403	8,557	8,089	8,005	7,324	6,318	5,839	4,358	3,773	9.9	10.6	42.97	39.49
Public welfare	72,554	67,263(r)	62,749	57,544	55,257	44,219	35,776	29,633	22,558	19,191	7.9	7.2	301.74	282.48
Intergovernmental expenditure	16,298	14,629	13,628	13,091	13,744	10,977	10,047	9,476	7,369	6,944	11.4	7.3	67.78	61.44
Cash assistance, categorical programs	9,277	8,388	8,297	7,461	7,337	6,831	5,712	5,203	4,984	5,089	10.6	1.1	38.58	35.23
Cash assistance, other	1,161	1,148	1,154	1,200	875	687	623	353	212	192	1.1	-.5	4.83	4.82
Other public welfare	45,817	43,099	39,670	35,792	33,301	25,725	19,393	14,601	9,974	6,967	6.3	8.6	190.55	181.00
Highways	36,661	33,154(r)	28,937	26,431	25,131	25,044	18,479	18,100	15,847	15,380	10.6	15.0	152.47	139.23
Regular state highway facilities	28,598	25,791	21,971	19,961	19,078	19,652	13,970	14,223	11,887	12,089	10.9	17.9	118.93	108.31
State toll highway facilities	1,593	1,343	1,278	1,193	1,025	1,009	687	636	749	658	18.6	5.1	6.63	5.64
Intergovernmental expenditure	6,470	6,019	5,688	5,277	5,028	4,383	3,821	3,241	3,211	2,633	7.5	5.8	26.91	25.28

NATIONAL TOTALS OF STATE GOVERNMENT FINANCES—Continued

Item	Amount (in millions) 1986	1985	1984	1983	1982	1980	1978	1976	1974	1972	Percentage change 1985 to 1986	Percentage change 1984 to 1985	Per capita 1986	Per capita 1985
Health and hospitals	30,131	27,595	24,982	23,926	22,284	17,855	13,883	11,110	8,443	6,963	9.2	10.4	125.31	115.89
State hospitals and institutions for handicapped	16,962	15,802	15,068	14,663	13,681	11,015	8,979	7,572	5,957	4,825	7.3	4.9	70.54	66.36
Other	13,169	11,793	9,914	9,263	8,603	6,840	4,905	3,538	2,486	2,138	11.7	19.0	54.77	49.53
Natural resources	7,312	6,758	5,945	5,834	5,485	4,346	3,411	3,863	3,053	2,595	8.2	13.7	30.41	28.38
Corrections	10,771	9,171	7,732	6,743	5,889	4,449	3,275	2,480	1,812	1,389	17.4	18.6	44.79	38.51
Financial administration	5,855	5,019(r)	4,517	4,206	3,735	3,031	2,482	1,955	1,594	1,235	16.7	11.1	24.35	21.08
General control	5,767	5,231	4,654	4,271	3,909	3,232	2,331	1,688	1,273	944	10.3	12.4	23.98	21.97
Employment security administration	2,697	2,582(r)	2,546	2,464	2,278	2,001	1,757	1,570	1,304	1,133	4.5	1.4	11.22	10.84
Police	3,714	3,518	3,140	3,002	2,730	2,263	1,826	1,569	1,262	983	5.6	12.0	15.45	14.77
Interest	16,876	14,982	13,137	11,252	9,015	6,763	5,268	4,140	2,863	2,135	12.6	14.0	70.18	62.92
Veteran's services	122	113	99	75	64	61	54	64	156	51	8.0	14.1	.51	.47
Utility expenditure(a)	5,530	5,364	4,817	4,417	3,730	2,401	1,544	0	0	0	3.1	11.4	23.00	22.53
Liquor expenditure	2,418	2,391	2,313	2,380	2,408	2,206	1,991	1,781	1,653	1,495	1.1	3.4	10.06	10.04
Insurance trust expenditure	39,749	37,940	34,632	42,180	34,664	24,981	20,495	25,455	10,590	8,938	4.8	9.6	165.31	159.33
Unemployment compensation	14,821	14,928	13,987	24,068	18,027	12,006	10,672	17,780	4,673	4,722	-.7	6.7	61.64	62.69
Employee retirement	19,878	18,230	16,467	14,204	13,133	10,257	7,811	6,045	4,591	3,175	9.0	10.7	82.67	76.56
Other	5,051	4,782	4,178	3,908	3,503	2,718	2,011	1,629	1,326	1,041	5.6	14.5	21.01	20.08
Total expenditure by character and object	424,216	390,742(r)	351,446	334,019	310,292	257,812	203,832	180,926	132,134	109,243	8.6	11.2	1,764.25	1,640.97
Direct expenditure	292,249	269,171(r)	243,073	232,710	211,549	173,307	136,545	123,069	86,193	72,483	8.6	10.7	1,215.42	1,130.41
Current operation	186,188	172,124(r)	156,734	144,018	133,152	108,131	86,153	68,175	50,803	39,790	8.2	9.7	774.33	722.85
Capital outlay	34,550	30,657	25,583	23,351	23,466	23,325	16,064	18,009	15,417	15,283	12.7	20.3	143.69	128.75
Construction	26,557	23,877(r)	19,671	18,616	19,560	19,736	13,260	15,285	12,655	13,022	11.2	22.4	110.45	100.27
Purchase of land and existing structures	2,177	1,833	1,816	1,507	1,316	1,345	1,171	1,274	1,540	1,369	18.8	-2.7	9.05	7.70
Equipment	5,816	4,947	4,096	3,228	2,590	2,243	1,633	1,450	1,222	892	17.6	20.8	24.19	20.78
Assistance and subsidies	14,162	12,842	12,386	11,452	10,867	9,818	8,341	7,290	6,521	6,337	10.3	3.7	58.90	53.93
Interest on debt	17,601	15,608	13,738	11,708	9,400	7,052	5,493	4,140	2,863	2,135	12.8	13.6	73.20	65.55
Insurance benefits and repayments	39,749	37,940	34,632	42,181	34,664	24,981	20,495	25,455	10,590	8,938	4.8	9.6	165.31	159.33
Intergovernmental expenditure	131,966	121,571	108,373	101,309	98,743	84,504	67,287	57,858	45,941	36,759	8.6	12.2	548.83	510.55
Cash and security holdings at end of fiscal year	610,975	519,014(r)	443,366	391,224	338,274	273,047	212,107	157,210	134,493	99,769	17.7	17.1	2,540.95	2,179.66
Unemployment fund balance in U.S. Treasury	18,019	8,629	5,707	4,811	6,789	11,945	7,450	4,425	10,773	8,942	108.8	51.2	74.94	36.24
Cash and deposits	47,164	44,569	45,232	39,288	35,400	30,782	25,345	18,477	18,387	12,372	5.8	22.1	196.15	187.17
Securities	534,481	453,128(r)	392,427	347,125	296,084	230,320	179,312	134,308	105,332	78,456	18.0	15.5	2,222.83	1,902.96
Total by purpose: Insurance trust	377,152	318,204	274,378	246,022	211,493	166,656	124,371	94,679	80,840	62,947	18.5	16.0	1,547.73	1,336.33
Debt offsets	116,990	98,764	81,527	69,915	56,655	40,011	27,582	15,880	7,849	5,309	18.5	21.1	486.54	414.77
Other	116,833	102,046	87,461	75,287	70,126	66,381	60,154	46,651	45,804	31,514	14.5	16.7	485.89	428.55

Sources: U.S. Bureau of the Census, annual reports on State Government Finances and Historical Statistics on Governmental Finances and Employment (vol. 6, no. 4, of the 1977 Census of Governments).
(a) Reported separately only since 1977, previously included with general revenue or general expenditure.
(b) State participation ended September 1980.
(r) Revised.

Table 6.7
STATE GENERAL REVENUE, BY SOURCE AND BY STATE: 1985
(In thousands of dollars)

State	Total general revenue(a)	Taxes Total(b)	Sales and gross receipts Total(b)	General	Motor fuels	Licenses Total(b)	Motor vehicle	Individual income	Corporation net income	Intergovernmental revenue	Charges and miscellaneous general revenue
United States	$365,344,398	$215,319,951	$105,324,694	$69,629,340	$13,351,590	$13,546,077	$7,045,280	$63,643,517	$17,637,037	$89,922,140	$60,102,307
Alabama	5,535,054	2,924,048	1,611,284	818,927	252,339	220,338	59,532	710,195	212,261	1,545,381	1,065,625
Alaska	5,453,073	1,885,811	112,908	0	35,842	56,708	15,229	1,268	204,600	398,694	3,168,568
Arizona	4,292,969	2,945,482	1,809,637	1,359,395	224,408	197,122	146,226	608,611	202,301	775,858	571,689
Arkansas	2,924,952	1,744,945	989,532	690,561	151,260	114,061	70,817	471,448	130,231	818,143	361,864
California	46,046,986	28,952,494	12,105,062	9,682,886	1,157,881	974,342	552,848	10,762,213	3,658,093	11,429,201	5,665,291
Colorado	4,133,456	2,284,417	1,081,766	762,484	186,619	133,062	68,868	907,619	101,654	997,202	851,837
Connecticut	5,697,963	3,497,970	2,379,145	1,538,542	204,975	165,213	102,561	291,640	489,507	1,067,610	1,132,383
Delaware	1,541,758	816,328	98,240	0	39,647	238,796	34,664	365,589	77,060	238,731	486,699
Florida	11,882,029	8,328,869	6,501,496	4,672,404	595,602	535,085	321,266	0	454,088	2,408,396	1,144,764
Georgia	7,572,067	4,525,038	2,207,367	1,532,811	385,768	138,611	64,986	1,718,326	418,251	2,194,722	852,307
Hawaii	2,245,293	1,362,595	851,297	683,630	35,593	19,061	9,413	429,398	48,717	407,016	475,682
Idaho	1,298,527	733,575	361,870	238,550	79,051	67,968	29,916	258,230	42,682	368,402	196,550
Illinois	15,377,208	9,227,777	4,950,229	3,180,453	609,780	706,093	548,504	2,600,864	706,009	3,835,912	2,313,519
Indiana	7,102,450	4,336,068	2,632,614	2,112,932	335,237	153,135	115,439	1,287,050	178,346	1,636,226	1,130,156
Iowa	4,004,037	2,307,406	1,071,146	757,766	182,417	196,442	136,058	824,551	154,412	997,358	699,273
Kansas	3,141,972	1,915,199	862,879	546,933	148,825	121,159	75,148	603,459	159,670	738,994	487,779
Kentucky	5,396,063	3,012,713	1,352,422	820,482	196,170	156,477	92,298	776,569	211,284	1,460,369	922,981
Louisiana	6,961,177	3,855,780	1,946,644	1,192,214	361,822	306,436	61,574	526,684	293,598	1,585,052	1,520,345
Maine	1,847,770	1,005,216	550,555	353,976	88,872	76,859	42,193	297,233	53,537	568,508	274,046
Maryland	7,093,148	4,321,772	1,949,496	1,098,445	297,015	153,449	93,255	1,768,256	246,123	1,534,171	1,237,205
Massachusetts	10,417,026	6,620,595	2,225,515	1,438,003	280,759	195,733	116,829	3,158,971	851,283	2,391,623	1,404,808
Michigan	15,164,596	8,684,163	3,519,875	2,542,053	620,308	413,442	297,687	3,048,512	1,391,863	4,020,532	2,459,901
Minnesota	8,260,655	5,228,004	2,163,282	1,348,222	349,965	319,899	230,623	2,233,467	383,264	1,802,232	1,230,419
Mississippi	3,303,269	1,811,598	1,190,037	932,174	131,462	151,369	54,180	259,447	106,484	1,035,478	456,193
Missouri	5,785,785	3,352,482	1,831,397	1,418,212	205,701	277,578	165,174	1,053,598	160,564	1,500,690	932,613
Montana	1,388,045	640,750	139,683	0	81,483	56,232	27,232	181,057	62,671	433,770	313,525
Nebraska	2,003,297	1,040,064	566,078	341,429	127,565	90,669	50,452	318,848	48,959	554,325	408,908
Nevada	1,397,858	940,622	803,902	458,311	74,361	104,441	36,608	0	0	277,228	180,008
New Hampshire	1,067,753	433,873	200,416	0	64,087	62,686	35,839	24,480	95,421	334,418	299,462
New Jersey	13,244,732	7,718,790	4,056,410	2,260,827	303,395	534,006	312,627	1,937,007	923,166	2,794,368	2,731,574

GENERAL REVENUE, BY SOURCE: 1985—Continued

State	Total general revenue(a)	Taxes Total(b)	Sales and gross receipts Total(b)	General	Motor fuels	Licenses Total(b)	Motor vehicle	Individual income	Corporation net income	Intergovernmental revenue	Charges and miscellaneous general revenue
New Mexico	3,123,960	1,439,312	819,410	607,193	104,170	69,783	39,482	84,980	64,056	563,261	1,121,387
New York	37,432,447	20,702,069	6,910,616	4,229,025	408,761	756,025	457,566	10,395,165	1,859,979	12,081,750	4,648,628
North Carolina	8,288,109	5,198,024	2,161,583	1,159,614	407,561	365,082	188,543	2,023,463	490,296	2,039,201	1,050,884
North Dakota	1,471,930	692,213	293,574	187,457	53,727	57,253	32,078	76,182	84,445	363,635	416,082
Ohio	14,775,850	8,651,690	4,625,294	2,880,548	622,579	749,816	320,613	2,781,658	437,129	3,411,827	2,712,333
Oklahoma	4,933,429	2,982,106	1,123,120	630,522	190,754	270,152	189,878	727,100	104,522	964,834	986,489
Oregon	4,079,361	1,982,956	237,419	0	119,026	218,744	139,387	1,310,731	153,822	1,056,594	1,039,811
Pennsylvania	16,662,092	10,162,436	5,056,989	3,019,349	621,648	1,037,136	376,959	2,588,913	942,971	4,127,915	2,371,741
Rhode Island	1,859,583	862,070	454,392	274,239	45,864	32,548	23,568	281,742	70,504	478,263	519,250
South Carolina	4,544,945	2,732,346	1,497,892	1,010,796	247,004	136,480	48,380	850,814	199,771	1,083,303	729,296
South Dakota	929,400	355,452	293,444	184,559	55,240	30,453	12,573	0	16,938	313,821	260,127
Tennessee	5,351,295	2,998,373	2,292,690	1,738,375	288,486	303,268	120,749	61,825	259,198	1,648,068	704,854
Texas	18,795,846	11,540,836	7,612,317	4,244,826	986,869	1,602,675	530,754	0	0	3,858,259	3,396,751
Utah	2,582,538	1,323,699	728,433	555,415	112,322	57,904	31,811	430,711	52,191	756,122	502,717
Vermont	984,361	458,654	231,055	87,950	37,391	39,173	27,997	145,149	34,958	306,300	219,407
Virginia	7,687,100	4,469,391	1,845,506	927,908	327,830	269,929	186,455	1,948,199	287,747	1,630,212	1,587,497
Washington	7,407,484	4,585,551	3,449,085	2,680,599	348,992	249,056	127,158	0	0	1,914,123	907,810
West Virginia	2,964,217	1,855,583	1,136,514	795,025	158,911	91,812	62,603	503,186	98,766	748,838	359,796
Wisconsin	8,185,352	5,066,390	2,203,026	1,453,526	370,427	211,117	122,890	2,009,109	413,645	1,996,841	1,122,121
Wyoming	1,704,131	806,416	230,151	179,792	35,819	61,199	37,790	0	0	428,363	469,352

Source: U.S. Bureau of the Census, State Government Finances in 1985.
Note: Detail may not add to totals due to rounding.
(a) Total general revenue equals total taxes plus intergovernmental revenue plus charges and miscellaneous revenue.
(b) Total includes other taxes not shown separately in this table.

Table 6.8
STATE GENERAL REVENUE, BY SOURCE AND BY STATE: 1986
(In thousands of dollars)

State	Total general revenue(a)	Taxes Total(b)	Sales and gross receipts Total(b)	Sales and gross receipts General	Sales and gross receipts Motor fuels	Licenses Total(b)	Licenses Motor vehicle	Individual income	Corporation net income	Intergovernmental revenue	Charges and miscellaneous general revenue
United States	$393,475,517	$228,053,889	$112,342,667	$74,821,130	$14,086,947	$14,904,172	$7,679,189	$67,469,185	$18,362,904	$98,573,784	$66,847,844
Alabama	5,717,701	2,997,093	1,661,142	838,347	254,355	260,162	100,073	757,289	156,745	1,549,087	1,171,521
Alaska	5,443,686	1,856,488	67,254	0	22,651	63,835	17,676	556	177,751	418,991	3,168,207
Arizona	4,604,929	3,195,720	1,969,299	1,459,253	257,445	225,714	168,290	701,998	170,821	806,831	602,378
Arkansas	3,171,659	1,826,701	1,044,978	696,866	197,668	120,798	70,207	509,872	113,205	931,920	413,038
California	50,233,596	30,878,427	13,023,355	10,405,892	1,193,698	1,041,300	651,907	11,368,059	3,833,261	12,411,304	6,943,865
Colorado	4,549,639	2,344,375	1,075,062	736,649	194,444	142,817	72,935	955,931	116,937	1,192,455	1,012,809
Connecticut	6,363,783	3,836,804	2,491,269	1,624,938	241,861	205,561	135,600	300,687	616,824	1,187,370	1,339,609
Delaware	1,553,404	882,666	92,801	0	33,054	265,451	40,553	393,705	88,923	280,580	390,158
Florida	13,319,466	9,120,166	7,062,173	5,027,376	739,000	620,928	348,020	0	486,925	2,709,768	1,489,532
Georgia	8,043,815	4,917,070	2,339,383	1,640,401	392,913	153,976	71,202	1,945,188	418,119	2,245,797	880,948
Hawaii	2,429,803	1,490,665	945,431	746,697	44,070	25,858	15,061	467,789	43,661	418,131	521,007
Idaho	1,354,011	744,739	375,065	250,475	77,667	67,305	30,656	255,974	42,652	403,513	205,759
Illinois	16,293,640	9,800,757	5,288,629	3,366,226	618,868	734,305	567,529	2,645,364	859,707	4,077,635	2,415,248
Indiana	7,617,073	4,458,168	2,727,274	2,161,337	369,405	144,631	101,788	1,326,861	183,565	1,832,384	1,326,521
Iowa	4,330,091	2,459,172	1,158,962	768,564	230,549	236,417	168,854	864,475	138,588	1,066,868	824,051
Kansas	3,234,844	1,911,548	886,507	560,718	151,651	124,780	74,990	582,158	156,344	807,100	516,196
Kentucky	5,706,009	3,216,343	1,434,204	881,274	194,546	187,482	96,024	819,893	233,524	1,537,151	952,515
Louisiana	7,034,730	3,629,513	1,891,334	1,135,007	335,619	351,664	68,699	457,636	263,815	1,768,820	1,636,897
Maine	2,039,026	1,101,381	600,443	383,324	91,445	81,876	42,969	337,129	51,870	610,973	326,672
Maryland	7,762,963	4,669,561	2,099,614	1,189,603	308,768	158,002	98,039	1,929,547	250,331	1,695,914	1,397,488
Massachusetts	12,050,047	7,668,440	2,524,673	1,721,345	291,247	205,783	121,110	3,617,300	1,067,987	2,526,385	1,855,222
Michigan	16,607,657	9,314,194	3,763,451	2,687,022	593,425	534,095	329,516	3,248,238	1,449,598	4,487,230	2,806,233
Minnesota	8,077,295	4,898,456	2,209,443	1,359,015	336,122	341,013	245,720	1,948,595	367,312	1,916,005	1,262,834
Mississippi	3,586,331	1,917,330	1,307,982	1,030,745	124,542	153,585	55,506	272,612	97,301	1,172,009	496,992
Missouri	6,304,144	3,608,083	1,975,585	1,530,176	214,924	304,369	179,157	1,116,470	174,199	1,550,109	1,145,952
Montana	1,387,763	617,108	140,716	0	79,380	61,240	30,487	172,216	58,585	468,100	302,555
Nebraska	2,164,881	1,119,382	605,090	349,884	146,546	93,757	49,381	351,828	54,559	590,242	455,257
Nevada	1,613,707	1,048,301	896,958	519,535	79,687	117,624	45,934	0	0	353,113	212,293
New Hampshire	1,246,782	484,478	219,495	0	70,022	82,101	39,020	24,853	99,063	359,857	402,447
New Jersey	14,484,709	8,360,193	4,565,571	2,614,372	339,001	519,611	308,672	2,052,592	954,885	3,066,194	3,058,322

GENERAL REVENUE, BY SOURCE: 1986—Continued

State	Total general revenue(a)	Taxes Total(b)	Sales and gross receipts Total(b)	General	Motor fuels	Licenses Total(b)	Motor vehicle	Individual income	Corporation net income	Intergovernmental revenue	Charges and miscellaneous general revenue
New Mexico	3,379,527	1,462,123	845,121	625,873	104,535	64,790	33,262	102,629	72,130	630,638	1,286,766
New York	40,931,527	22,747,419	7,479,297	4,760,919	468,946	776,163	420,073	11,582,305	1,901,879	13,276,386	4,907,722
North Carolina	8,903,826	5,579,710	2,312,029	1,384,069	424,208	391,692	195,300	2,206,749	512,095	2,141,705	1,182,411
North Dakota	1,380,323	616,076	279,573	177,042	50,470	55,567	31,143	73,368	56,312	365,659	398,588
Ohio	15,800,846	9,062,151	4,937,604	3,165,994	663,692	804,217	333,818	2,776,884	477,794	3,926,726	2,811,969
Oklahoma	5,032,412	2,959,632	1,216,862	656,048	205,681	326,204	237,628	687,646	107,077	1,073,996	998,784
Oregon	4,178,916	1,931,346	272,603	0	133,807	242,740	156,772	1,193,767	161,728	1,099,486	1,148,084
Pennsylvania	17,886,012	10,683,238	5,314,474	3,241,419	635,896	1,137,078	395,830	2,655,677	963,228	4,701,448	2,501,326
Rhode Island	1,960,356	885,557	469,520	291,377	47,451	34,289	25,815	286,649	67,656	531,846	542,953
South Carolina	4,918,662	2,887,103	1,627,834	1,111,500	253,161	158,379	64,374	907,285	149,465	1,210,191	821,368
South Dakota	1,037,611	403,741	319,138	198,929	57,477	43,693	24,967	0	23,617	349,743	284,127
Tennessee	5,886,272	3,271,963	2,517,290	1,865,934	369,323	332,259	126,719	67,432	268,618	1,852,921	761,388
Texas	19,904,369	11,124,708	7,669,750	4,327,698	1,011,478	1,783,357	643,590	0	0	4,558,617	4,221,044
Utah	2,726,829	1,364,835	740,493	558,581	117,668	57,498	31,781	451,543	66,450	835,226	526,768
Vermont	1,048,283	499,519	252,932	98,576	38,499	42,912	30,692	160,507	30,531	300,592	248,172
Virginia	8,406,083	4,846,627	1,961,999	1,020,192	307,637	306,482	197,925	2,174,272	280,768	2,052,707	1,506,749
Washington	8,012,646	5,219,292	3,966,927	3,113,204	393,643	263,843	125,689	0	0	1,771,313	1,022,041
West Virginia	3,169,860	1,848,552	1,144,965	811,147	152,120	109,749	65,150	478,590	88,909	891,472	429,836
Wisconsin	8,832,243	5,491,530	2,332,903	1,543,347	389,523	286,745	155,306	2,239,067	407,590	2,113,675	1,227,038
Wyoming	1,731,730	795,445	238,210	184,240	37,159	60,475	37,780	0	0	447,601	488,684

Source: U.S. Bureau of the Census, *State Government Finances in 1986.*
Note: Detail may not add to totals due to rounding.
(a) Total general revenue equals total taxes plus intergovernmental revenue plus charges and miscellaneous revenue.
(b) Total includes other taxes not shown separately in this table.

Table 6.9
STATE EXPENDITURE, BY CHARACTER AND OBJECT AND BY STATE: 1985
(In thousands of dollars)

State	Intergovernmental expenditure	Direct expenditure		Capital outlay				Assistance and subsidies	Interest on debt	Insurance benefits and repayments	Exhibit: Total salaries and wages
		Total	Current operation	Total	Construction	Land and existing structures	Equipment				
United States	$121,571,151	$269,257,171	$172,210,077	$30,656,897	$23,877,199	$1,832,800	$4,946,898	$12,841,719	$15,608,441	$37,940,037	$70,626,629
Alabama	1,492,642	4,589,547	3,100,742	695,314	457,439	55,480	182,395	153,058	224,035	416,398	1,269,686
Alaska	1,573,744	3,375,999	1,775,563	730,863	661,402	23,823	45,638	58,130	590,750	220,693	755,017
Arizona	1,793,077	2,805,705	1,928,907	390,489	292,684	46,937	50,868	104,176	41,856	340,277	790,946
Arkansas	900,887	2,117,325	1,496,704	255,763	185,759	15,502	54,502	78,875	65,022	220,961	676,524
California	22,176,573	29,663,381	20,023,007	2,063,106	1,545,718	197,631	319,757	339,435	1,177,888	6,059,945	7,185,901
Colorado	1,562,837	3,254,328	2,223,576	294,407	208,541	29,306	56,560	29,706	140,620	566,019	1,096,989
Connecticut	1,066,940	4,361,748	2,704,630	433,787	373,147	30,169	30,471	262,567	480,914	479,850	1,203,028
Delaware	238,756	1,096,450	699,679	145,998	119,928	1,771	24,299	38,136	138,017	74,620	327,931
Florida	5,211,019	7,642,938	4,884,231	1,507,647	1,169,728	218,018	119,901	286,343	273,957	690,760	2,802,055
Georgia	2,254,410	5,363,961	3,533,925	910,476	721,785	69,531	119,160	228,521	159,606	531,433	1,606,586
Hawaii	24,637	2,514,056	1,503,874	262,687	213,248	12,126	37,313	102,501	187,078	457,916	797,838
Idaho	390,299	1,049,722	633,166	182,823	142,711	11,978	28,134	29,279	49,283	155,171	270,644
Illinois	4,320,715	12,169,789	6,939,060	1,469,477	1,268,175	27,826	173,476	1,383,996	668,188	1,709,068	2,409,999
Indiana	2,475,262	4,608,758	3,320,346	624,141	477,987	40,041	106,113	79,791	124,543	459,937	1,286,596
Iowa	1,411,917	3,217,868	2,119,643	504,270	419,182	12,051	73,037	215,826	64,171	313,958	953,791
Kansas	923,348	2,324,307	1,600,486	347,188	298,557	5,785	42,846	117,587	13,314	245,732	782,736
Kentucky	1,297,089	4,149,935	2,687,187	571,347	437,516	49,468	84,363	168,685	257,886	464,830	1,186,368
Louisiana	1,589,533	5,991,279	3,665,465	670,290	535,957	71,796	62,537	189,736	447,192	1,018,596	1,698,878
Maine	376,750	1,571,017	1,052,356	112,727	78,482	21,409	12,836	105,974	101,622	198,338	366,827
Maryland	1,732,295	5,632,427	3,502,215	668,084	471,930	68,332	127,822	338,249	324,399	799,480	1,422,344
Massachusetts	2,977,536	8,050,501	5,210,371	683,678	565,740	25,885	92,053	606,250	717,526	832,676	2,057,606
Michigan	4,429,263	11,204,627	7,271,422	779,244	614,464	9,017	155,763	1,533,651	435,569	1,184,741	2,877,216
Minnesota	2,928,387	5,192,625	3,597,886	609,051	526,515	34,956	47,580	81,785	275,175	628,728	1,520,013
Mississippi	1,147,165	2,414,245	1,694,191	286,990	235,981	9,412	41,597	89,811	78,281	264,972	632,149
Missouri	1,703,603	4,113,374	2,659,096	593,010	483,921	32,650	76,439	223,513	262,546	375,209	1,176,188
Montana	307,582	1,249,842	702,526	237,981	212,593	5,525	19,863	39,450	64,714	205,171	394,654
Nebraska	546,944	1,589,636	1,090,535	272,202	221,573	12,605	38,024	78,895	78,295	69,709	587,422
Nevada	503,270	1,139,647	599,357	152,963	132,703	2,734	17,526	14,387	87,827	285,113	293,828
New Hampshire	165,050	1,029,626	685,177	129,725	108,755	6,239	14,731	34,984	121,883	57,857	306,141
New Jersey	4,426,816	9,653,363	6,007,146	952,145	754,400	73,640	124,105	106,201	987,116	1,600,755	2,243,356

EXPENDITURE, BY CHARACTER AND OBJECT: 1985—Continued

State	Intergovernmental expenditure	Direct expenditure						Assistance and subsidies	Interest on debt	Insurance benefits and repayments	Exhibit: Total salaries and wages
		Total	Current operation	Capital outlay							
				Total	Construction	Land and existing structures	Equipment				
New Mexico	1,088,172	1,952,707	1,302,342	309,211	250,292	25,637	33,282	63,355	98,007	179,792	552,698
New York	13,396,972	26,709,131	17,047,949	3,127,234	1,935,649	119,159	1,072,426	644,723	2,619,462	3,269,763	6,446,733
North Carolina	3,024,220	5,467,833	3,818,700	600,995	458,862	10,515	131,618	238,520	145,972	663,646	1,839,467
North Dakota	394,367	1,146,750	812,408	161,055	136,864	2,043	22,148	25,004	47,460	100,823	303,600
Ohio	5,114,504	12,453,913	6,729,640	1,126,070	916,181	42,338	167,551	835,225	564,301	3,198,677	2,689,612
Oklahoma	1,332,122	3,745,032	2,406,283	490,675	394,351	24,624	71,700	153,312	256,499	438,263	1,055,474
Oregon	1,099,969	3,711,743	2,005,047	349,506	269,695	21,997	57,814	135,853	479,403	741,934	896,476
Pennsylvania	4,971,177	13,096,173	7,787,887	919,438	766,024	6,206	147,208	1,436,781	536,380	2,415,687	2,732,563
Rhode Island	298,113	1,711,570	1,050,438	166,995	142,633	5,212	19,150	85,277	211,692	197,168	419,915
South Carolina	1,373,468	3,880,487	2,659,663	461,411	317,260	20,265	123,886	111,905	274,138	373,370	1,144,603
South Dakota	187,686	816,829	513,976	157,427	127,902	3,229	26,296	19,667	85,734	40,025	218,234
Tennessee	1,276,127	4,162,899	2,881,980	598,963	503,402	27,707	67,854	131,481	136,789	413,686	1,219,021
Texas	6,111,188	12,963,233	8,814,197	1,719,908	1,352,836	100,229	266,843	507,518	382,786	1,538,824	3,669,671
Utah	728,783	2,089,425	1,342,598	371,307	309,778	10,150	51,379	68,332	100,960	206,228	580,741
Vermont	147,911	885,913	616,241	86,796	68,104	2,891	15,801	57,242	72,568	53,066	218,548
Virginia	2,161,501	5,671,329	4,124,426	661,861	533,941	40,877	87,043	226,692	259,699	398,651	1,864,775
Washington	2,441,588	6,569,969	3,730,260	780,763	630,019	39,919	110,825	377,325	249,114	1,432,507	1,638,644
West Virginia	799,474	2,543,794	1,491,365	339,009	286,341	15,025	37,643	97,532	96,270	519,618	578,070
Wisconsin	3,125,629	5,592,857	3,662,342	443,398	315,399	89,844	38,155	478,332	284,183	724,602	1,330,331
Wyoming	549,834	947,558	499,866	247,002	225,145	3,290	18,567	28,145	67,751	104,794	248,196

Source: U.S. Bureau of the Census, State Government Finances in 1985.
Note: Detail may not add to totals due to rounding.

Table 6.10
STATE EXPENDITURE, BY CHARACTER AND OBJECT AND BY STATE: 1986
(In thousands of dollars)

State	Intergovernmental expenditure	Direct expenditure Total	Current operation	Capital outlay Total	Construction	Land and existing structures	Equipment	Assistance and subsidies	Interest on debt	Insurance benefits and repayments	Exhibit: Total salaries and wages
United States	$131,966,258	$292,249,386	$186,188,033	$34,549,903	$26,557,244	$2,176,569	$5,816,090	$14,162,129	$17,600,707	$39,748,614	$76,095,575
Alabama	1,563,108	4,874,508	3,450,551	595,607	444,927	34,150	116,530	164,187	261,247	402,916	1,441,447
Alaska	863,981	3,356,897	1,861,105	467,432	400,420	19,814	47,198	70,020	708,341	249,999	794,655
Arizona	1,913,685	3,160,467	2,054,610	562,376	365,048	130,774	66,554	116,592	49,954	376,935	896,560
Arkansas	988,755	2,366,648	1,632,679	339,547	289,393	7,327	42,827	86,738	85,120	222,564	752,239
California	24,929,013	32,441,207	21,603,898	2,396,644	1,714,088	232,219	450,337	443,129	1,424,084	6,573,452	7,888,388
Colorado	1,459,018	3,493,040	2,308,667	403,899	316,206	25,386	62,307	31,608	172,362	576,504	1,118,145
Connecticut	1,147,052	4,862,052	2,997,427	533,121	465,542	29,211	38,368	266,183	551,847	513,474	1,323,734
Delaware	254,127	1,161,198	769,930	131,452	98,711	3,193	29,548	34,805	137,645	87,366	360,841
Florida	5,198,824	8,540,938	5,782,411	1,249,341	887,980	185,514	175,847	435,505	319,012	754,669	3,167,348
Georgia	2,604,968	5,925,085	3,964,703	985,535	769,366	75,275	140,894	247,284	171,131	556,432	1,744,336
Hawaii	30,034	2,441,920	1,589,560	316,270	253,841	14,544	47,885	99,473	205,990	230,627	857,934
Idaho	399,356	1,117,223	663,632	205,246	166,983	9,777	28,486	29,484	55,052	163,809	283,706
Illinois	4,797,568	13,025,199	7,516,929	1,543,024	1,274,023	39,378	129,623	1,467,987	782,562	1,714,697	2,627,513
Indiana	2,591,875	4,956,146	3,611,506	683,151	512,291	44,747	126,113	83,460	141,050	436,979	1,381,277
Iowa	1,457,094	3,395,300	2,264,134	483,935	381,851	15,762	86,322	225,340	103,337	318,554	991,624
Kansas	994,956	2,526,858	1,693,374	412,730	344,207	4,847	63,676	124,900	13,571	282,283	836,497
Kentucky	1,415,742	4,375,420	2,933,691	587,355	429,064	47,087	111,204	172,968	262,722	418,684	1,283,913
Louisiana	1,867,466	6,350,525	3,683,937	832,884	669,062	83,482	80,340	211,198	555,158	1,067,348	1,420,042
Maine	427,857	1,728,581	1,146,344	147,045	41,356	83,601	22,088	120,225	117,150	197,817	395,732
Maryland	1,854,629	6,277,298	3,805,765	967,169	720,561	117,577	129,031	361,246	369,916	773,202	1,545,711
Massachusetts	3,325,747	9,123,504	5,990,749	671,198	552,841	41,925	76,432	658,602	823,994	978,961	2,300,566
Michigan	4,842,870	12,719,959	8,112,478	898,484	669,051	27,808	201,625	1,606,786	506,187	1,596,024	3,108,164
Minnesota	3,124,133	5,457,115	3,750,852	620,491	525,692	43,151	51,648	93,943	268,743	723,086	1,791,145
Mississippi	1,237,181	2,598,507	1,810,272	322,517	267,326	12,369	42,822	108,445	97,724	259,549	691,292
Missouri	1,915,955	4,560,966	2,892,202	735,161	591,355	38,167	105,639	229,598	290,591	413,414	1,344,414
Montana	319,790	1,322,946	717,596	256,027	232,010	2,648	21,369	45,377	87,917	216,029	334,592
Nebraska	537,476	1,667,448	1,149,610	248,500	195,542	11,699	41,259	78,923	107,413	83,002	601,469
Nevada	590,225	1,326,442	685,401	184,501	151,258	2,811	30,432	23,527	96,824	336,189	330,542
New Hampshire	174,711	1,173,449	831,270	102,792	83,654	4,040	15,098	35,685	146,821	56,881	339,948
New Jersey	4,803,345	11,239,753	6,739,785	1,596,192	1,329,492	148,039	118,661	122,250	1,121,992	1,659,534	2,422,398

EXPENDITURE, BY CHARACTER AND OBJECT: 1986—Continued

State	Intergovernmental expenditure	Total	Current operation	Direct expenditure: Capital outlay Total	Construction	Land and existing structures	Equipment	Assistance and subsidies	Interest on debt	Insurance benefits and repayments	Exhibit: Total salaries and wages
New Mexico	1,119,486	2,180,653	1,475,164	315,627	261,377	18,567	35,683	63,042	124,468	202,352	592,082
New York	15,182,153	27,956,814	17,943,679	3,223,064	1,968,917	90,946	1,163,201	648,281	2,826,873	3,314,917	7,021,357
North Carolina	3,402,507	5,966,984	4,116,561	686,319	496,392	12,276	177,651	272,535	171,573	719,996	2,059,374
North Dakota	399,352	1,137,838	813,451	131,492	111,486	2,085	17,921	27,464	54,835	110,596	322,389
Ohio	5,536,665	13,473,630	7,215,771	1,389,352	1,138,173	62,407	188,772	889,908	635,979	3,342,620	2,870,949
Oklahoma	1,478,351	4,150,724	2,634,527	567,692	463,182	23,900	80,610	165,878	279,139	503,488	1,178,414
Oregon	1,105,928	3,819,352	2,189,641	358,624	277,782	23,283	57,559	153,059	513,236	604,792	969,118
Pennsylvania	5,364,037	13,914,294	8,363,802	1,227,829	991,282	46,515	190,032	1,481,183	464,447	2,377,033	2,682,765
Rhode Island	347,862	1,819,179	1,120,254	178,220	135,526	7,749	34,945	91,845	226,446	202,414	432,016
South Carolina	1,429,440	4,211,128	2,867,520	540,782	392,527	18,132	130,123	130,770	293,819	378,237	1,294,875
South Dakota	194,507	879,527	545,605	163,365	133,572	1,412	28,381	25,564	100,220	44,773	220,902
Tennessee	1,430,475	4,649,729	3,247,297	688,512	576,439	32,488	79,585	152,346	152,259	409,315	1,301,940
Texas	6,147,106	14,634,638	9,281,005	2,504,997	2,014,923	165,815	324,259	624,733	359,945	1,863,958	3,774,811
Utah	782,272	2,288,642	1,512,824	365,452	289,039	14,542	61,871	72,758	110,026	227,582	645,689
Vermont	158,962	935,754	651,491	92,613	67,168	3,678	21,767	58,453	81,133	52,064	225,343
Virginia	2,513,086	6,359,653	4,440,266	938,051	726,895	57,111	154,045	249,423	307,743	424,170	2,068,956
Washington	3,011,346	6,657,225	3,838,266	649,864	513,983	26,289	109,592	445,982	339,201	1,383,912	1,739,789
West Virginia	855,734	2,765,580	1,639,870	380,586	335,485	7,417	37,684	120,959	109,518	514,647	624,137
Wisconsin	3,286,305	5,838,613	3,709,830	420,620	289,800	22,841	107,979	665,108	341,751	701,304	1,432,660
Wyoming	590,143	1,042,830	566,141	247,216	230,155	2,794	14,267	27,370	72,639	129,464	261,837

Source: U.S. Bureau of the Census, State Government Finances in 1986.
Note: Detail may not add to totals due to rounding.

Table 6.11
STATE GENERAL EXPENDITURE, BY FUNCTION AND BY STATE: 1985
(In thousands of dollars)

State or other jurisdiction	Total general expenditure(a)	Education	Public welfare	Highways	Hospitals	Natural resources	Health	Corrections	Financial administration	Employment security administration	Police
All states	$345,132,879	$128,604,436	$67,317,011	$33,186,443	$15,982,007	$6,757,844	$11,612,831	$9,171,052	$4,995,535	$2,605,593	$3,517,932
Alabama	5,544,133	2,427,464	659,853	670,015	383,486	113,137	172,950	113,621	94,496	31,836	43,631
Alaska	4,605,555	1,143,566	200,154	611,312	25,167	186,037	190,630	124,942	82,795	9,662	61,257
Arizona	4,251,280	1,915,896	466,608	610,359	57,052	56,312	97,618	141,411	76,723	18,783	69,202
Arkansas	2,797,251	1,232,669	461,509	363,441	125,027	83,098	91,230	53,182	53,762	28,989	27,102
California	45,774,836	17,904,476	11,000,955	2,296,534	1,331,274	1,204,074	1,778,090	1,237,968	645,326	242,175	500,247
Colorado	4,251,146	1,833,724	675,957	473,537	231,662	107,358	117,641	81,895	82,915	26,389	31,311
Connecticut	4,871,035	1,279,610	953,287	443,415	360,143	38,647	118,684	128,997	71,592	49,039	53,903
Delaware	1,251,097	481,488	117,386	124,316	40,697	23,154	40,347	40,140	30,377	5,316	21,527
Florida	12,147,670	4,976,742	1,546,774	1,209,796	255,672	420,325	694,783	411,997	111,593	55,677	151,094
Georgia	7,086,938	3,034,575	1,135,368	940,348	335,531	182,458	268,390	230,337	96,132	57,247	71,815
Hawaii	2,080,777	729,962	287,048	84,542	102,972	47,293	76,523	43,559	31,523	15,033	2,452
Idaho	1,258,047	539,240	139,564	206,295	22,312	61,289	44,049	21,006	19,636	21,333	13,990
Illinois	14,781,436	4,916,620	3,489,101	1,850,702	495,376	168,201	430,006	401,045	237,617	151,601	144,460
Indiana	6,624,083	2,908,024	1,009,370	769,020	263,390	119,493	182,607	145,760	72,326	53,709	60,271
Iowa	4,228,661	1,789,860	734,993	693,685	265,293	74,791	57,501	84,181	46,574	38,103	30,409
Kansas	3,001,923	1,352,679	457,307	461,377	187,866	82,201	53,378	72,278	53,391	13,202	18,074
Kentucky	4,982,194	2,015,844	862,512	629,412	153,233	149,853	134,944	97,498	82,746	35,443	64,427
Louisiana	6,562,216	2,361,362	1,098,273	681,750	534,317	167,868	167,710	175,522	71,663	26,730	96,547
Maine	1,705,482	547,113	436,295	185,498	41,160	49,869	50,249	27,136	20,708	16,429	17,001
Maryland	6,380,869	1,964,693	1,199,007	809,306	242,991	133,499	264,204	270,381	103,006	24,620	158,439
Massachusetts	10,171,442	2,546,465	2,459,568	469,172	552,842	71,374	424,446	220,147	146,132	63,743	59,746
Michigan	14,063,002	4,185,009	3,885,099	1,114,350	703,333	185,486	917,373	366,695	112,663	152,128	135,131
Minnesota	7,492,284	2,695,769	1,479,501	713,899	381,181	197,356	130,332	101,250	85,087	76,142	53,890
Mississippi	3,203,645	1,285,217	482,160	410,301	167,487	104,814	98,578	62,977	26,994	36,699	35,268
Missouri	5,441,768	2,200,860	937,252	697,890	294,105	123,211	179,119	103,927	82,037	54,725	62,706
Montana	1,317,682	435,947	183,879	238,970	31,192	83,789	48,020	29,043	40,848	8,766	16,629
Nebraska	2,066,871	692,501	328,762	369,291	114,349	78,543	62,375	45,828	20,326	18,859	20,207
Nevada	1,317,938	464,617	117,390	198,783	25,445	22,302	29,842	44,887	36,468	19,708	10,351
New Hampshire	1,011,885	200,806	185,046	162,906	43,864	14,888	55,604	29,584	20,548	11,406	12,161
New Jersey	11,858,056	3,472,447	2,127,951	952,203	517,713	107,716	267,762	265,095	170,343	55,116	156,954

GENERAL EXPENDITURE, BY FUNCTION: 1985—Continued

State or other jurisdiction	Total general expenditure(a)	Education	Public welfare	Highways	Hospitals	Natural resources	Health	Corrections	Financial administration	Employment security administration	Police
New Mexico	2,861,087	1,263,590	252,481	312,923	131,845	58,537	96,574	82,430	43,926	23,867	29,483
New York	33,358,620	9,448,898	9,621,260	1,514,160	2,210,010	182,482	1,046,360	1,139,288	529,799	287,684	261,262
North Carolina	7,828,407	3,826,940	945,221	804,942	411,962	183,763	264,267	258,502	83,036	38,394	101,019
North Dakota	1,440,294	540,545	177,129	212,092	60,992	49,699	32,594	10,159	16,107	5,347	5,919
Ohio	14,071,365	5,431,414	3,134,228	1,424,765	737,236	180,589	389,796	329,694	239,172	131,377	85,359
Oklahoma	4,366,858	1,950,213	701,178	523,122	261,923	77,315	112,881	136,104	74,596	34,143	39,380
Oregon	3,986,054	1,264,086	501,820	481,001	187,511	123,420	101,538	86,823	111,864	27,102	47,489
Pennsylvania	15,088,135	4,840,697	3,927,081	1,770,360	790,851	235,495	433,175	244,029	211,915	110,609	182,591
Rhode Island	1,786,915	489,448	431,764	117,231	107,900	12,241	71,673	37,711	31,726	16,500	17,625
South Carolina	4,399,862	2,076,648	505,108	381,574	270,446	101,392	216,642	149,397	58,565	44,670	44,773
South Dakota	964,490	254,936	119,877	181,058	31,554	50,515	27,796	17,573	21,931	10,691	9,038
Tennessee	5,025,340	2,002,990	852,837	700,620	252,606	87,499	191,376	155,683	53,466	48,823	35,299
Texas	17,535,597	9,545,476	2,145,603	1,650,470	1,014,477	305,670	371,724	464,312	222,218	170,921	148,706
Utah	2,563,524	1,174,019	310,476	378,052	107,987	65,078	90,126	54,672	38,054	28,847	24,022
Vermont	953,729	314,291	171,530	119,655	20,748	30,047	37,352	20,557	16,698	8,588	16,182
Virginia	7,233,655	3,026,592	953,185	997,075	520,606	78,013	224,645	360,906	127,306	38,855	134,165
Washington	7,401,755	3,291,974	1,208,519	863,099	261,540	206,091	227,937	221,626	112,825	72,816	56,320
West Virginia	2,779,542	1,192,378	355,305	426,094	54,743	73,055	87,469	24,268	63,935	19,088	24,423
Wisconsin	7,993,884	2,716,007	1,794,896	590,484	233,185	151,684	311,477	186,159	87,943	56,658	41,656
Wyoming	1,364,564	418,049	89,584	295,229	27,753	46,823	32,444	18,870	24,106	12,005	13,019

Source: U.S. Bureau of the Census, State Government Finances in 1985.
Note: Totals may not add due to rounding.
(a) Does not represent sum of state figures because total includes miscellaneous expenditure not shown separately.

Table 6.12
STATE GENERAL EXPENDITURE, BY FUNCTION AND BY STATE: 1986
(In thousands of dollars)

	Total general expenditure(a)	Education	Public welfare	Highways	Hospitals	Natural resources	Health	Corrections	Financial administration	Employment security administration	Police
All states	$376,518,948	$140,189,241	$72,554,362	$36,661,0?4	$17,151,495	$7,312,177	$12,979,666	$10,770,764	$5,855,221	$2,696,787	$3,713,694
Alabama	5,899,645	2,666,833	737,610	658,145	413,739	126,638	203,012	128,163	105,193	34,028	46,493
Alaska	3,888,487	927,250	259,345	436,608	21,161	163,731	82,688	107,960	84,881	18,927	37,529
Arizona	4,688,190	2,069,595	480,456	739,305	60,620	65,308	131,152	224,756	103,454	15,242	71,192
Arkansas	3,132,839	1,341,968	502,571	469,774	129,162	90,149	92,982	60,448	57,483	28,952	26,429
California	50,791,107	20,086,649	11,412,273	2,485,11?4	1,424,858	1,236,154	2,041,542	1,798,721	937,329	247,859	548,362
Colorado	4,375,554	1,841,680	761,831	538,081	216,903	106,681	148,080	118,398	83,960	19,131	40,288
Connecticut	5,403,791	1,388,518	1,018,805	514,206	406,681	55,487	140,024	154,296	86,496	50,018	66,591
Delaware	1,318,705	522,865	122,573	135,792	44,271	26,520	47,888	45,726	33,341	5,463	24,407
Florida	12,967,355	5,310,058	1,680,897	1,395,264	367,863	449,335	752,088	437,979	164,533	31,551	168,424
Georgia	7,973,621	3,497,639	1,284,104	926,612	383,433	198,189	286,105	267,020	119,263	65,378	75,698
Hawaii	2,241,327	805,666	281,767	94,399	107,890	54,153	82,523	69,872	33,157	16,922	2,800
Idaho	1,322,888	566,673	144,529	218,4?1	22,546	65,003	45,749	23,841	20,319	11,019	12,909
Illinois	16,108,070	5,524,244	3,656,149	1,835,618	513,515	201,297	505,168	423,814	293,960	152,320	165,635
Indiana	7,111,042	3,108,013	1,118,388	855,098	293,936	146,540	206,449	157,547	85,454	57,255	64,787
Iowa	4,450,728	1,871,781	788,801	679,785	276,151	98,704	60,406	89,906	48,205	38,758	31,844
Kansas	3,239,531	1,447,835	484,527	507,473	205,011	85,385	62,815	78,123	60,307	14,160	19,670
Kentucky	5,372,478	2,133,925	926,796	717,976	155,626	158,817	150,060	106,008	97,148	38,740	69,741
Louisiana	7,150,643	2,697,457	984,930	777,021	578,058	215,650	177,105	184,885	56,827	50,549	98,374
Maine	1,913,806	646,814	475,929	202,533	43,562	54,187	53,369	32,036	29,380	16,820	19,598
Maryland	7,153,702	2,106,590	1,283,729	1,034,744	260,213	149,741	304,011	335,287	118,169	27,462	166,323
Massachusetts	11,445,499	2,734,538	2,867,738	557,507	592,668	113,258	509,007	249,681	174,765	69,309	84,046
Michigan	15,602,259	4,842,812	4,031,015	1,162,003	817,551	222,576	1,030,759	498,532	150,746	127,070	150,195
Minnesota	7,858,162	2,909,487	1,511,523	796,129	404,887	195,922	135,927	107,401	91,099	76,150	55,229
Mississippi	3,483,399	1,419,727	508,982	439,699	176,813	110,242	109,697	72,539	31,871	45,222	36,141
Missouri	6,063,507	2,433,973	998,033	837,560	359,693	136,927	193,703	122,967	89,112	53,283	68,323
Montana	1,396,274	446,618	195,228	270,354	31,841	76,822	49,736	27,924	44,807	7,703	18,831
Nebraska	2,121,922	689,890	360,877	352,843	124,938	74,204	63,328	44,026	21,932	20,968	20,413
Nevada	1,538,763	572,941	127,876	218,912	28,977	28,747	32,958	55,449	43,920	20,498	12,460
New Hampshire	1,158,511	265,858	209,285	170,157	39,978	23,371	72,114	22,648	19,368	12,451	13,951
New Jersey	13,615,557	3,918,191	2,364,561	1,290,215	575,743	143,980	361,480	343,850	176,227	54,211	187,915

GENERAL EXPENDITURE, BY FUNCTION: 1986—Continued

	Total general expenditure(a)	Education	Public welfare	Highways	Hospitals	Natural resources	Health	Corrections	Financial administration	Employment security administration	Police
New Mexico........	3,097,787	1,392,178	282,324	328,673	135,652	66,216	104,214	78,527	47,995	22,854	28,631
New York.........	36,363,680	10,415,869	10,566,994	1,699,055	2,363,633	183,281	1,069,371	1,225,679	565,618	304,523	297,547
North Carolina....	8,649,495	4,227,289	1,074,954	875,757	431,689	196,581	305,747	290,031	83,755	66,269	91,480
North Dakota.....	1,426,500	559,764	173,507	185,465	61,233	54,081	33,457	10,079	14,501	5,984	5,206
Ohio.............	15,372,007	5,887,775	3,579,213	1,495,691	757,244	153,360	383,450	404,872	264,842	122,956	87,146
Oklahoma........	4,801,238	2,155,226	790,556	575,407	250,804	87,090	135,526	137,672	95,808	36,412	40,565
Oregon..........	4,232,590	1,325,659	558,869	494,871	192,873	130,168	110,948	90,434	128,485	29,956	51,674
Pennsylvania.....	16,321,836	5,232,331	4,154,001	1,956,553	842,097	245,631	463,998	289,555	223,385	125,566	193,981
Rhode Island.....	1,924,906	529,381	466,057	130,993	107,765	13,692	77,185	39,996	62,029	16,653	15,601
South Carolina....	4,812,153	2,219,599	594,024	379,523	287,770	111,739	250,440	170,426	72,916	46,586	54,696
South Dakota.....	1,029,261	281,939	136,114	175,633	28,860	55,185	39,862	18,363	24,059	12,949	10,319
Tennessee........	5,670,889	2,229,420	1,011,510	799,577	251,461	90,210	231,618	188,669	59,687	49,415	41,819
Texas...........	18,917,786	9,728,150	2,252,964	2,533,231	1,021,638	292,018	404,284	530,721	240,742	189,036	136,995
Utah............	2,793,218	1,327,450	355,206	324,983	134,025	72,338	111,903	69,103	40,284	34,023	25,340
Vermont.........	1,014,070	340,437	183,560	120,837	19,722	31,944	35,356	19,058	19,452	9,417	15,724
Virginia.........	8,238,896	3,356,547	961,804	1,204,716	621,458	127,621	298,981	405,771	143,313	56,478	80,492
Washington.......	8,100,450	3,675,073	1,324,669	672,196	245,701	229,101	303,070	239,711	120,812	47,408	63,281
West Virginia.....	3,065,281	1,268,193	447,585	473,122	54,230	80,912	95,946	23,437	58,418	20,555	24,499
Wisconsin........	8,423,614	2,774,978	1,957,532	619,458	237,437	160,665	339,418	128,054	95,375	59,344	30,754
Wyoming.........	1,475,929	465,895	101,791	297,865	27,915	56,626	52,967	20,803	26,039	12,984	13,346

Source: U.S. Bureau of the Census, State Government Finances in 1986.
Note: Totals may not add due to rounding.
(a) Includes miscellaneous expenditures not shown separately in this table.

Table 6.13
STATE DEBT OUTSTANDING AT END OF FISCAL YEAR, BY STATE: 1985
(In thousands of dollars, except per capita amounts)

State	Total	Per capita	Long-term Total	Long-term Full faith and credit	Long-term Non-guaranteed	Short-term	Net long-term(a) Total	Net long-term(a) Full faith and credit
All states	$211,903,730	$ 889.92	$209,111,998	$60,431,886	$148,680,112	$2,791,732	$110,348,059	$47,778,899
Alabama...........	3,239,853	805.73	3,232,419	691,470	2,540,949	7,434	2,125,762	675,921
Alaska.............	5,692,101	10,925.34	5,692,101	1,929,813	3,762,288	0	1,625,072	791,765
Arizona...........	683,889	214.59	683,889	0	683,889	0	281,172	0
Arkansas	824,708	349.60	824,708	0	824,708	0	135,249	0
California..........	16,056,548	609.01	16,053,648	4,779,496	11,274,152	2,900	8,641,261	3,233,990
Colorado	1,520,473	470.59	1,520,003	0	1,520,003	470	108,912	0
Connecticut	6,389,163	2,012.97	6,355,503	2,280,335	4,075,168	33,660	4,095,744	2,044,241
Delaware	1,831,524	2,944.57	1,822,542	561,710	1,260,832	8,982	1,452,886	561,710
Florida	5,014,494	441.18	5,014,414	1,565,576	3,448,838	80	2,734,690	785,165
Georgia............	2,157,591	361.04	2,157,591	1,233,226	924,365	0	1,548,275	1,188,206
Hawaii	2,709,596	2,570.77	2,642,069	1,697,636	944,433	67,527	2,071,230	1,668,729
Idaho	629,247	626.12	629,247	220	629,027	0	141,382	91
Illinois............	9,787,199	848.48	9,603,883	3,487,000	6,116,883	183,316	5,380,549	3,367,722
Indiana	1,730,339	314.66	1,624,038	0	1,624,038	106,301	785,362	0
Iowa	1,325,543	459.62	873,141	0	873,141	452,402	262,439	0
Kansas	318,865	130.15	318,860	0	318,860	5	260,170	0
Kentucky	3,633,273	975.11	3,633,273	186,260	3,447,013	0	2,380,961	136,966
Louisiana	8,094,673	1,806.44	8,094,513	2,946,372	5,148,141	160	4,991,865	2,939,992
Maine	1,224,601	1,052.06	1,223,850	285,934	937,916	751	261,226	285,934
Maryland	5,091,055	1,159.17	5,065,824	2,242,390	2,823,434	25,231	2,726,919	2,207,105
Massachusetts	10,100,950	1,734.96	9,760,161	3,556,674	6,203,487	340,789	4,475,760	3,553,463
Michigan	5,903,899	649.64	5,871,780	651,605	5,220,175	32,119	2,164,498	624,905
Minnesota	3,502,627	835.35	3,502,627	1,144,308	2,358,319	0	1,271,030	957,320
Mississippi	1,006,930	385.35	1,006,930	537,787	469,143	0	569,596	471,264
Missouri	3,319,406	660.05	3,249,249	315,515	2,933,734	70,157	1,288,437	301,418
Montana...........	744,503	901.34	744,503	100,835	643,668	0	157,225	85,010
Nebraska	1,028,066	640.14	1,025,253	0	1,025,253	2,813	171,813	0
Nevada	1,108,496	1,184.29	1,108,394	269,965	838,429	102	469,173	256,556
New Hampshire	1,979,239	1,983.21	1,979,239	415,805	1,563,434	0	1,322,528	402,924
New Jersey.........	13,364,830	1,767.37	13,364,752	2,435,760	10,928,992	78	8,460,937	2,427,063
New Mexico........	1,277,455	881.00	1,274,686	23,951	1,250,735	2,769	288,824	1,437
New York	32,355,192	1,819.45	31,748,551	4,176,616	27,571,935	606,641	17,325,277	2,724,296
North Carolina	2,156,628	344.78	2,145,810	827,298	1,318,512	10,818	1,365,641	807,612
North Dakota	585,866	855.28	585,091	3,650	581,441	775	55,214	0
Ohio	8,204,063	763.59	8,095,449	2,621,980	5,473,469	108,614	6,426,664	2,617,598
Oklahoma	3,581,385	1,084.94	3,576,685	106,655	3,470,030	4,700	1,526,514	82,985
Oregon	6,605,048	2,458.15	6,275,048	5,535,043	740,005	330,000	593,544	352,813
Pennsylvania	7,289,221	614.97	7,253,914	4,120,475	3,133,439	35,307	5,604,435	4,021,528
Rhode Island	2,814,124	2,907.15	2,637,766	298,345	2,339,421	176,358	1,188,152	298,345
South Carolina	3,402,857	1,016.69	3,383,308	626,833	2,756,475	19,549	2,234,909	433,226
South Dakota	1,086,446	1,534.53	1,086,446	0	1,086,446	0	31,722	0
Tennessee	1,913,389	401.80	1,755,419	610,897	1,144,522	157,970	764,768	534,632
Texas..............	5,192,530	317.20	5,192,530	1,713,683	3,478,847	0	2,826,053	658,651
Utah	1,333,302	810.52	1,333,302	229,715	1,103,587	0	308,682	174,058
Vermont	887,416	1,658.72	887,298	269,696	617,602	118	340,553	269,696
Virginia............	3,316,926	581.30	3,314,806	423,087	2,891,719	2,120	641,775	413,475
Washington	3,029,948	687.22	3,029,232	2,494,595	534,637	716	2,564,839	2,455,673
West Virginia	1,628,348	841.09	1,628,348	721,140	907,208	0	910,641	703,257
Wisconsin..........	4,473,094	936.77	4,473,094	2,312,535	2,160,559	0	2,943,717	2,262,157
Wyoming	756,811	1,486.86	756,811	0	756,811	0	44,012	0

Source: U.S Bureau of the Census, *State Government Finances in 1985.*
Note: Debt figures include revenue bonds and other special obligations
of state agencies as well as state general obligations.
(a) Long-term debt outstanding minus long-term debt offsets.

Table 6.14
STATE DEBT OUTSTANDING AT END OF FISCAL YEAR, BY STATE: 1986
(In thousands of dollars, except per capita amounts)

State	Total	Per capita	Long-term Total	Full-faith and credit	Non-guaranteed	Short-term	Net long-term(a) Total	Full-faith and credit
All states	$247,715,163	$ 1,030.21	$246,108,919	$64,640,182	$181,468,737	$1,606,244	$129,119,122	$50,211,978
Alabama............	3,751,658	925.65	3,751,005	1,987,083	1,763,922	653	2,155,821	1,705,095
Alaska.............	6,961,334	13,036.21	6,961,334	1,934,848	5,026,486	0	2,086,386	673,062
Arizona............	1,472,580	443.95	1,471,833	0	1,471,833	747	708,835	0
Arkansas	1,086,677	458.13	1,086,677	0	1,086,677	0	186,306	0
California..........	20,122,437	745.80	20,122,437	5,238,659	14,883,778	0	11,217,621	2,821,248
Colorado	1,998,327	611.67	1,998,082	0	1,998,082	245	405,398	0
Connecticut	7,317,104	2,294.48	7,314,012	2,186,945	5,127,067	3,092	4,585,502	1,938,400
Delaware	2,634,531	4,161.98	2,625,905	489,258	2,136,647	8,626	2,187,911	489,258
Florida	5,679,591	486.47	5,679,093	1,553,356	4,125,737	498	2,954,772	993,691
Georgia............	2,450,622	401.48	2,450,622	1,430,661	1,019,961	0	1,860,943	1,429,824
Hawaii	2,828,037	2,662.94	2,760,231	1,734,972	1,025,259	67,806	2,134,722	1,710,169
Idaho	658,164	656.20	658,164	100	658,064	0	141,250	99
Illinois.............	11,987,958	1,037.65	11,978,582	3,757,855	8,220,727	9,376	6,266,654	3,636,150
Indiana	2,180,275	396.13	2,069,803	0	2,069,803	110,472	917,726	0
Iowa	1,600,792	561.48	1,137,760	0	1,137,760	463,032	338,649	0
Kansas	352,393	143.19	352,388	0	352,388	5	306,739	0
Kentucky	4,109,579	1,102.35	4,109,579	164,650	3,944,929	0	2,709,528	148,727
Louisiana	10,478,904	2,491.42	10,478,824	3,123,326	7,355,498	80	6,716,849	2,968,170
Maine	1,558,447	1,327.47	1,558,447	289,830	1,268,617	0	394,189	289,830
Maryland	5,410,424	1,212.28	5,394,148	2,120,878	3,273,270	16,276	2,655,355	2,071,088
Massachusetts	11,843,997	2,030,86	11,664,824	3,953,324	7,711,500	179,173	4,947,495	3,914,823
Michigan	7,084,150	774.65	7,050,241	621,700	6,428,541	33,909	2,728,001	594,700
Minnesota	3,759,541	892.15	3,759,541	1,215,917	2,543,624	0	1,514,773	1,021,777
Mississippi	1,183,841	450.99	1,183,659	456,285	727,374	182	567,778	400,746
Missouri	3,750,916	740.41	3,750,916	308,920	3,441,996	0	1,262,694	255,690
Montana............	1,240,239	1,514.33	1,177,800	106,814	1,070,986	62,439	182,335	79,755
Nebraska	1,309,164	819.25	1,275,785	0	1,275,785	33,379	316,652	0
Nevada	1,224,223	1,271.26	1,224,215	329,080	895,135	8	516,567	302,990
New Hampshire	2,383,510	2,320.85	2,379,566	472,436	1,907,130	3,944	1,531,459	284,663
New Jersey.........	15,899,079	2,217.73	16,899,079	2,479,055	14,420,024	0	11,120,470	2,468,611
New Mexico........	2,137,298	1,445.10	2,116,698	82,851	2,033,847	20,600	392,953	-27,944
New York	36,371,158	2,046.54	36,045,020	4,198,602	31,846,418	326,138	19,982,508	2,742,191
North Carolina	2,605,893	411.61	2,593,392	767,736	1,825,656	12,501	1,511,125	726,006
North Dakota	742,822	1,093.99	742,822	1,880	740,942	0	53,071	0
Ohio	8,858,693	823.91	8,841,086	2,656,985	6,184,101	17,607	6,631,423	2,652,716
Oklahoma	3,829,963	1,158.84	3,828,990	100,751	3,728,239	973	1,798,987	100,751
Oregon	7,141,919	2,647.12	7,141,919	6,376,368	765,551	0	1,577,112	1,319,431
Pennsylvania	7,801,523	656.20	7,790,194	4,186,132	3,604,062	11,329	6,066,739	4,124,155
Rhode Island	2,949,547	3,025.18	2,917,247	332,295	2,584,952	32,300	1,307,805	332,295
South Carolina	3,725,616	1,102.91	3,724,863	658,703	3,066,160	753	2,246,371	418,086
South Dakota	1,303,054	1,840.47	1,303,040	0	1,303,040	14	35,790	0
Tennessee	2,156,403	448.97	1,978,103	753,050	1,225,053	178,300	886,188	678,266
Texas..............	5,432,198	325.63	5,432,198	1,969,678	3,462,520	0	2,538,531	527,746
Utah	1,325,214	795.92	1,325,142	217,975	1,107,167	72	322,019	186,469
Vermont	984,145	1,819.12	982,095	273,704	708,391	2,050	353,958	273,704
Virginia............	3,842,665	664.02	3,833,138	393,727	3,439,411	9,527	678,914	378,543
Washington	3,572,162	800.39	3,572,024	2,865,715	706,309	138	2,931,437	2,822,867
West Virginia	2,131,681	1,110.83	2,131,681	670,488	1,461,193	0	1,221,334	617,209
Wisconsin	4,659,656	973.80	4,659,656	2,177,590	2,482,066	0	2,897,432	2,140,921
Wyoming	825,059	1,627.34	825,059	0	825,059	0	66,045	0

Source: U.S Bureau of the Census, *State Government Finances in 1986.*
Note: Debt figures include revenue bonds and other special obligations
of state agencies, as well as state general obligations.
(a) Long-term debt outstanding minus long-term debt offsets.

TRENDS IN STATE TAXATION: 1986-87

By John Gambill

In 1986 and 1987, many states increased their tax rates - especially for sales taxes and taxes on motor fuel, cigarettes, and tobacco products. Only nine states increased their individual and/or corporation income tax rates, while a slightly larger number reduced their rates or adopted flatter rate structures. Many states increased their personal exemption and standard deduction amounts.

General Sales Taxes

1986 actions

Sales tax rates were increased in Idaho (4 to 5 percent from April 1, 1986, through June 30, 1987), Kansas (3 to 4 percent), Nebraska (3.5 to 4 percent), New Mexico (3.75 to 4.75 percent), North Dakota (4 to 5 percent), and Virginia (3 to 3.5 percent). Hawaii exempted prescription medicine from its tax. Voters in Washington and West Virginia rejected increases in their sales tax rates.

1987 actions

Sales tax rates were increased in Florida (5 to 6 percent, effective Feb. 1, 1988), North Dakota (5 to 5.5 percent, effective July 1, 1987 - June 30, 1989), Oklahoma (3.25 to 4 percent), South Dakota (4 to 5 percent, effective May 1, 1987 - April 30, 1988), Texas (5.25 to 6 percent), and Utah (4 19/32 to 5 3/32 percent, effective April 1, 1987 - Dec. 31, 1989). Idaho and Vermont made permanent sales tax rates that were originally adopted as temporary. Florida, Minnesota, and Texas extended their sales taxes to cover a variety of services that were previously exempt or excluded from the sales tax. Later in the year, Florida repealed the tax on services and raised the sales tax rate as described above.

Individual Income Taxes

1986 actions

Income tax rates were increased in New Mexico, North Dakota, and Utah (a one-time surtax). Income tax rates were reduced in Delaware, Massachusetts (repeal of a surtax), Ohio, and Pennsylvania. Michigan advanced the date of its tax rate reduction. Rhode Island and Vermont provided for adjusting the state tax rate to offset the revenue effects of federal tax reform.

1987 actions

Income tax rates were increased in Idaho, Indiana, Montana (a surtax), and North Dakota (a surtax). Rates were decreased in California, Iowa and Wisconsin. Legislation to narrow the rate range was adopted in Delaware, Minnesota, New York, Oregon, West Virginia and the District of Columbia. Colorado adopted a flat rate income tax. Virginia moved its dividing line between the highest and second highest tax rates upwards over several years. Hawaii eliminated its top rate and South Carolina eliminated its lowest tax rate.

Personal exemptions were increased in Delaware, Georgia, Maryland, Michigan, New York, Utah, Virginia, West Virginia and the District of Columbia. Arkansas and California increased the amounts of personal credits (which they use in place of personal exemptions).

The standard deduction was increased in California, Delaware, Georgia, Hawaii, Iowa, Maine, Maryland, New York, Utah, Virginia, West Virginia and the District of Columbia.

Colorado and Minnesota will base their personal income taxes on federal taxable income

John Gambill is Senior Research Associate and Director of Publications, The Federation of Tax Administrators. Linda Spencer, FTA Research Attorney, assembled the information on tax amnesty programs.

rather than federal adjusted gross income. Nebraska changed its tax from a percentage of federal tax liability to a set of rates to be applied to adjusted gross income.

Colorado, Delaware, Minnesota and Utah repealed the deduction for federal income taxes. The Delaware deduction had been limited in amount and the Minnesota deduction had been restricted to taxpayers who paid the higher of two income tax schedules. Oregon reduced the maximum amount of its deduction from $7,000 to $3,000.

Corporation Income Taxes

1986 actions

Colorado raised its corporate rates to 6 percent for tax years beginning July 1, 1986, through June 30, 1987, and to 5.5 percent for tax years beginning July 1, 1987, and thereafter. New Mexico increased its rates from a range of 4.8 to 7.2 percent to a range of 4.8 to 7.6 percent, with lower thresholds for rates after the first tax rate. Pennsylvania reduced its rate from 9.5 to 8.5 percent.

1987 actions

Idaho raised its rate from 7.7 to 8 percent. Indiana raised its adjusted gross income tax from 3 to 3.4 percent and its supplemental net income tax from 4 to 4.5 percent. Montana imposed a 4 percent surtax. North Carolina raised its rate from 6 to 7 percent.

California reduced its rate from 9.6 to 9.3 percent. Hawaii reduced its rates to a range of 4.4 to 6.4 percent. New York State its tax rate from 10 to 9 percent and established an 8 percent rate for corporation incomes of less than $200,000. Oregon reduced its rate from 7.5 to 6.6 percent. South Carolina reduced its rate from 6 to 5.5 percent for 1988 and to 5 percent for subsequent years. The District of Columbia reduced its surtax from 5 to 2.5 percent.

Colorado set its rate at 5.5 recent on the first $50,000 of income and 6 percent on additional amounts between July 1, 1987, and June 30, 1988. The rates will gradually be reduced to a flat 5 percent.

Motor Fuel Taxes

1986 actions

Motor fuel tax rates were increased in Colo-

rado (12 to 18 cents per gallon for gasoline and 13 to 20.5 cents for diesel fuel), Delaware (11 to 13 cents), Kentucky (10 to 15 cents for gasoline and 10 to 12 cents for diesel fuel), Montana (15 to 17 cents for gasoline), North Carolina (12 to 15.5 cents), Tennessee (13 to 17 cents for gasoline and 13 to 16 cents for diesel fuel), and Virginia (11 to 17.5 cents, as a result of two measures with different effective dates). Hawaii ended its additional 1 cent tax on diesel fuel. Virginia repealed its gross receipts tax on oil companies.

The Nebraska tax rate fluctuated quarterly, ranging between 16.7 and 19.0 cents per gallon, as a result of its variable rate law. Wisconsin's rate increased from 16.5 to 17.5 cents on April 1, 1986, as a result of its variable rate law.

1987 actions

Motor fuel tax rates were increased in Delaware (from 13 to 16 cents), Maryland (13.5 to 18.5 cents), Mississippi (9 to 15 cents, July 1, 1987; 17 cents Jan. 1, 1988, and 18 cents, Jan. 1, 1989). Missouri (7 to 11 cents), Montana (17 to 20 cents), Nevada (gasoline 13 to 16 cents, July 1, 1987; 18 cents, July 1, 1988 and diesel fuel, 13 to 17 cents July 1, 1987; 20 cents, July 1, 1988), New Mexico (gasoline 11 to 14 cents and diesel fuel 11 to 16 cents), North Dakota (13 to 17 cents), Ohio (12 to 14.7 cents), Oklahoma (gasoline 10 to 16 cents and diesel fuel, 10 to 13 cents), Oregon (12 to 14 cents, Jan. 1, 1988; 16 cents, Jan. 1, 1989, and 18 cents on Jan. 1, 1990), South Carolina (13 to 15 cents July 1, 1987; 16 cents, Jan. 1, 1989), Utah (14 to 19 cents), and Wisconsin (18 to 20 cents). Texas made its 15 cents per gallon tax rate permanent.

Variable-rate laws caused rates to change in four states in 1987: Nebraska's rate changed quarterly, ranging from 17.6 to 19 cents. North Carolina's rate increased from 15.5 to 15.8 cents, effective Jan. 1, 1988. Ohio removed a limit on its tax rate, thereby increasing from 12 to 14.7 cents on July 1, 1987, and by up to 0.8 cents on March 1 annually beginning in 1988. The Wisconsin tax increased from 17.5 to 18 cents on April 1, 1987, before the legislature raised the rate to 20 cents.

Cigarette and Tobacco Taxes

1986 actions

Cigarette tax rates were increased in Colorado

(15 to 20 cents), Florida (21 to 24 cents), New Mexico (12 to 15 cents), Rhode Island (23.4 to 25 cents), and Washington State (23 to 31 cents). Colorado, Maine and New Mexico enacted taxes on tobacco products other than cigarettes, and Utah and Washington raised their rates on tobacco products.

1987 actions

Cigarette tax rates were increased in Idaho (9.1 to 18 cents), Indiana (10.5 to 15.5 cents), Michigan (21 to 25 cents, effective Jan. 1, 1988), Minnesota (23 to 38 cents), Nebraska (23 to 27 cents), Nevada (15 to 20 cents), New Jersey (25 to 27 cents), North Dakota (18 to 27 cents), Ohio (14 to 18 cents), Oklahoma (18 to 23 cents), Texas (20.5 to 26 cents), Utah (12 to 23 cents), Wisconsin (25 to 30 cents), and the District of Columbia (13 to 17 cents).

New taxes were imposed on other tobacco products in Indiana and Nebraska and tax rates on tobacco products were increased in Minnesota, North Dakota and Texas. Arkansas extended its tax on tobacco products to include snuff and imposed a tax on cigarette papers.

Alcoholic Beverage Taxes

1986 actions

Tax rates on distilled spirits, wine, or beer were increased in Hawaii (all beverages), Iowa (beer and wine), and Maine (all beverages).

1987 actions

Tax rates on distilled spirits, wine, or beer were increased in Minnesota (all beverages), Montana (wine), North Carolina (spirits), Oklahoma (spirits and wine), South Dakota (all beverages), and Washington (wine).

Tax Amnesty Programs

Tax amnesty programs were conducted in 11 states and the District of Columbia in 1986 or 1987. As a result, 27 states and the District of Columbia had conducted tax amnesty programs by the end of 1987. The names of the states, the dates of the programs, and the amounts collected are reported in one of the tables.

Table 6.15
AGENCIES ADMINISTERING MAJOR STATE TAXES
(As of January 1, 1988)

State or other jurisdiction	Income	Sales	Gasoline	Motor vehicle
Alabama	Dept. of Revenue	Dept. of Revenue	Dept. of Revenue	Dept. of Revenue
Alaska	Dept. of Revenue	. . .	Dept. of Revenue	Dept. of Public Safety
Arizona	Dept. of Revenue	Dept. of Revenue	Dept. of Transportation	Dept. of Transportation
Arkansas	Dept. of Fin. & Admin.	Dept. of Fin. & Admin.	Dept. of Fin. & Admin.	Dept. of Fin. & Admin.
California	Franchise Tax Bd.	Bd. of Equalization	Bd. of Equalization	Dept. of Motor Vehicles
Colorado	Dept. of Revenue	Dept. of Revenue	Dept. of Revenue	Dept. of Revenue
Connecticut	Dept. of Revenue Serv.	Dept. of Revenue Serv.	Dept. of Revenue Serv.	Dept. of Motor Vehicles
Delaware	Div. of Revenue	. . .	Dept. of Public Safety	Dept. of Public Safety
Florida	Dept. of Revenue	Dept. of Revenue	Dept. of Revenue	Div. of Motor Vehicles
Georgia	Dept. of Revenue	Dept. of Revenue	Dept. of Revenue	Dept. of Revenue
Hawaii	Dept. of Taxation	Dept. of Taxation	Dept. of Taxation	County Treasurer
Idaho	Dept. of Revenue & Tax.	Dept. of Revenue & Tax.	Dept. of Revenue & Tax.	Transportation Dept.
Illinois	Dept. of Revenue	Dept. of Revenue	Dept. of Revenue	Secretary of State
Indiana	Dept. of Revenue	Dept. of Revenue	Dept. of Revenue	Bur. of Motor Vehicles
Iowa	Dept. of Revenue & Finance	Dept. of Revenue & Finance	Dept. of Revenue & Finance	Dept. of Transportation
Kansas	Dept. of Revenue	Dept. of Revenue	Dept. of Revenue	Dept. of Revenue
Kentucky	Revenue Cabinet	Revenue Cabinet	Revenue Cabinet	Transportation Cabinet
Louisiana	Dept. of Revenue & Tax.	Dept. of Revenue & Tax.	Dept. of Revenue & Tax.	Dept. of Public Safety
Maine	Bur. of Taxation	Bur. of Taxation	Bur. of Taxation	Secretary of State
Maryland	Comptroller	Comptroller	Comptroller	Dept. of Transportation
Massachusetts	Dept. of Revenue	Dept. of Revenue	Dept. of Revenue	Reg. of Motor Vehicles
Michigan	Dept. of Treasury	Dept. of Treasury	Dept. of Treasury	Secretary of State
Minnesota	Dept. of Revenue	Dept. of Revenue	Dept. of Revenue	Dept. of Public Safety
Mississippi	Tax Comm.	Tax Comm.	Tax Comm.	Tax Comm.
Missouri	Dept. of Revenue	Dept. of Revenue	Dept. of Revenue	Dept. of Revenue
Montana	Dept. of Revenue	. . .	Dept. of Revenue	Reg. of Motor Vehicles
Nebraska	Dept. of Revenue	Dept. of Revenue	Dept. of Revenue	Dept. of Motor Vehicles
Nevada	. . .	Dept. of Taxation	Dept. of Taxation	Dept. of Motor Vehicles
New Hampshire	Dept. of Revenue Admin.	. . .	Dept. of Safety	Dept. of Safety
New Jersey	Dept. of Treasury	Dept. of Treasury	Dept. of Treasury	Dept. of Law & Public Safety
New Mexico	Tax & Revenue Dept.	Tax & Revenue Dept.	Tax & Revenue Dept.	Tax & Revenue Dept.
New York	Dept. of Tax. & Finance	Dept. of Tax. & Finance	Dept. of Tax. & Finance	Dept. of Motor Vehicles
North Carolina	Dept. of Revenue	Dept. of Revenue	Dept. of Revenue	Dept. of Transportation
North Dakota	Tax Commr.	Tax Commr.	Tax Commr.	Dept. of Motor Vehicles
Ohio	Dept. of Taxation	Dept. of Taxation	Dept. of Taxation	Bur. of Motor Vehicles
Oklahoma	Tax Comm.	Tax Comm.	Tax Comm.	Tax Comm.
Oregon	Dept. of Revenue	. . .	Dept. of Transportation	Dept. of Transportation
Pennsylvania	Dept. of Revenue	Dept. of Revenue	Dept. of Revenue	Dept. of Transportation
Rhode Island	Dept. of Administration	Dept. of Administration	Dept. of Administration	Dept. of Transportation
South Carolina	Tax Comm.	Tax Comm.	Tax Comm.	Dept. of Hwys. & Pub. Transportation
South Dakota	. . .	Dept. of Revenue	Dept. of Revenue	Dept. of Revenue
Tennessee	Dept. of Revenue	Dept. of Revenue	Dept. of Revenue	Dept. of Revenue
Texas	. . .	Comptroller	Comptroller	Dept. of Hwys. & Pub. Transportation
Utah	Tax Comm.	Tax Comm.	Tax Comm.	Tax Comm.
Vermont	Commr. of Taxes	Commr. of Taxes	Dept. of Motor Vehicles	Dept. of Motor Vehicles
Virginia	Dept. of Taxation	Dept. of Taxation	Dept. of Motor Vehicles	Dept. of Motor Vehicles
Washington	. . .	Dept. of Revenue	Dept. of Licensing	Dept. of Licensing
West Virginia	Tax Dept.	Tax Dept.	Tax Dept.	Dept. of Motor Vehicles
Wisconsin	Dept. of Revenue	Dept. of Revenue	Dept. of Revenue	Dept. of Transportation
Wyoming	. . .	Dept. of Revenue & Tax.	Dept. of Revenue & Tax.	Dept. of Revenue & Tax.
Dist. of Col.	Dept. of Fin. & Revenue	Dept. of Fin. & Revenue	Dept. of Fin. & Revenue	Dept. of Fin. & Revenue

Source: The Federation of Tax Administrators

AGENCIES ADMINISTERING MAJOR STATE TAXES—Continued

State or other jurisdiction	Tobacco	Death	Alcoholic beverage	Number of agencies administering taxes
Alabama	Dept. of Revenue	Dept. of Revenue	Alcoh. Bev. Control Bd.	2
Alaska	Dept. of Revenue	Dept. of Revenue	Dept. of Revenue	2
Arizona	Dept. of Revenue	Dept. of Revenue	Dept. of Revenue	2
Arkansas	Dept. of Fin. & Admin.	Dept. of Fin. & Admin.	Dept. of Fin. & Admin.	1
California	Bd. of Equalization	Controller	Bd. of Equalization	4
Colorado	Dept. of Revenue	Dept. of Revenue	Dept. of Revenue	1
Connecticut	Dept. of Revenue Serv.	Dept. of Revenue Serv.	Dept. of Revenue Serv.	2
Delaware	Div. of Revenue	Div. of Revenue	Div. of Revenue	2
Florida	Dept. of Business Reg.	Dept. of Revenue	Dept. of Business Reg.	3
Georgia	Dept. of Revenue	Dept. of Revenue	Dept. of Revenue	1
Hawaii	Dept. of Taxation	Dept. of Taxation	Dept. of Taxation	2
Idaho	Dept. of Revenue & Tax.	Dept. of Revenue & Tax.	Dept. of Revenue & Tax.	2
Illinois	Dept. of Revenue	Attorney General	Dept. of Revenue	3
Indiana	Dept. of Revenue	Dept. of Revenue	Dept. of Revenue	2
Iowa	Dept. of Revenue & Finance	Dept. of Revenue & Finance	Dept. of Revenue & Finance	2
Kansas	Dept. of Revenue	Dept. of Revenue	Dept. of Revenue	1
Kentucky	Revenue Cabinet	Revenue Cabinet	Revenue Cabinet	2
Louisiana	Dept. of Revenue & Tax.	Dept. of Revenue & Tax.	Dept. of Revenue & Tax.	2
Maine	Bur. of Taxation	Bur. of Taxation	Liquor Comm.	3
Maryland	Comptroller	Local	Comptroller	3
Massachusetts	Dept. of Revenue	Dept. of Revenue	Dept. of Revenue	2
Michigan	Dept. of Treasury	Dept. of Treasury	Liquor Control Comm.	3
Minnesota	Dept. of Revenue	Dept. of Revenue	Dept. of Revenue	2
Mississippi	Tax Comm.	Tax Comm.	Tax Comm.	1
Missouri	Dept. of Revenue	Dept. of Revenue	Dept. of Revenue	1
Montana	Dept. of Revenue	Dept. of Revenue	Dept. of Revenue	2
Nebraska	Dept. of Revenue	Dept. of Revenue	Liquor Control Comm.	3
Nevada	Dept. of Taxation	. . .	Dept. of Taxation	2
New Hampshire	Dept. of Revenue Admin.	Dept. of Revenue Admin.	Liquor Comm.	3
New Jersey	Dept. of Treasury	Dept. of Treasury	Dept. of Treasury	2
New Mexico	Tax & Revenue Dept.	Tax & Revenue Dept.	Tax & Revenue Dept.	1
New York	Dept. of Tax. & Finance	Dept. of Tax. & Finance	Dept. of Tax. & Finance	2
North Carolina	Dept. of Revenue	Dept. of Revenue	Dept. of Revenue	2
North Dakota	Tax Commr.	Tax Commr.	Treasurer	3
Ohio	Dept. of Taxation	Dept. of Taxation	Dept. of Taxation	2
Oklahoma	Tax Comm.	Tax Comm.	Tax Comm.	1
Oregon	Dept. of Revenue	Dept. of Revenue	Liquor Control Comm.	3
Pennsylvania	Dept. of Revenue	Dept. of Revenue	Dept. of Revenue	2
Rhode Island	Dept. of Administration	Dept. of Administration	Dept. of Administration	2
South Carolina	Tax Comm.	Tax Comm.	Tax Comm.	2
South Dakota	Dept. of Revenue	Dept. of Revenue	Dept. of Revenue	1
Tennessee	Dept. of Revenue	Dept. of Revenue	Dept. of Revenue	1
Texas	Comptroller	Comptroller	Alcoh. Bev. Comm.	3
Utah	Tax Comm.	Tax Comm.	Tax Comm.	1
Vermont	Commr. of Taxes	Commr. of Taxes	Commr. of Taxes	2
Virginia	Dept. of Taxation	Dept. of Taxation	Dept. of Taxation	2
Washington	Dept. of Revenue	Dept. of Revenue	Liquor Control Bd.	3
West Virginia	Tax Dept.	Tax Dept.	Alcoh. Bev. Control Commr.	3
Wisconsin	Dept. of Revenue	Dept. of Revenue	Dept. of Revenue	2
Wyoming	Dept. of Revenue & Tax.	Dept. of Revenue & Tax.	Liquor Comm.	2
Dist. of Col.	Dept. of Fin. & Revenue	Dept. of Fin. & Revenue	Dept. of Fin. & Revenue	1

Table 6.16
STATE TAX AMNESTY PROGRAMS
November 22, 1982 - December 15, 1987

State or other jurisdiction	Amnesty Period	Legislative Authorization	Major Taxes Covered	Accounts Receivable Included	Collections ($ Millions)(a)	Installment Arrangements Permitted(b)
Alabama............	01/20/84 - 04/01/84	No(c)	All	No	3.15	No
Arizona.............	11/22/82 - 01/20/83	No(c)	All	No	6.0	Yes
Arkansas	09/01/87 - 11/30/87	Yes	All	No	1.2 (d)	Yes
California..........	12/10/84 - 03/15/85	Yes	Individual Income	Yes	154.0	Yes
		Yes	Sales	No	43.0	Yes
Colorado	09/16/85 - 11/15/85	Yes	All	No	6.4	Yes
Florida	01/01/87 - 06/30/87	Yes	Intangibles	No	13.0	No
Idaho	05/20/83 - 08/30/83	No(c)	Individual Income	No	.3	No
Illinois.............	10/01/84 - 11/30/84	Yes	All	Yes	152.4	No
Iowa	09/02/86 - 10/31/86	Yes	All	Yes	35.1	No
Kansas	07/01/84 - 09/30/84	Yes	All	No	.6	No
Louisiana	10/01/85 - 12/31/85	Yes	All	No	1.2	Yes(e)
	10/01/87 - 12/15/87	Yes	All	No	.24(d)	Yes(e)
Maryland	09/01/87 - 11/02/87	Yes	All	Yes	34.6 (f)	No
Massachusetts	10/17/83 - 01/17/84	Yes	All	Yes	85.2	Yes(g)
Michigan	05/12/86 - 06/30/86	Yes	All	Yes	109.8	No
Minnesota	08/01/84 - 10/31/84	Yes	All	Yes	12.1	No
Mississippi	09/01/86 - 11/30/86	Yes	All	No	1.0	No
Missouri	09/01/83 - 10/31/83	No(c)	All	No	.85	No
New Jersey	09/10/87 - 12/08/87	Yes	All	Yes	182.0 (d)	Yes
New Mexico........	08/15/85 - 11/13/85	Yes	All(h)	No	13.6	Yes
New York	11/01/85 - 01/31/86	Yes	All(i)	Yes	401.3	Yes
North Dakota	09/01/83 - 11/30/83	No(c)	All	No	.15	Yes
Oklahoma	07/01/84 - 12/31/84	Yes	Income Sales	Yes	13.9	No(j)
Rhode Island	10/15/86 - 01/12/87	Yes	All	No	1.9	Yes
South Carolina	09/01/85 - 11/30/85	Yes	All	Yes	7.1	Yes
Texas..............	02/01/84 - 02/29/84	No(c)	All(k)	No	.5	No
West Virginia	10/01/86 - 12/31/86	Yes	All	Yes	10.1 (d)	Yes
Wisconsin...........	09/15/85 - 11/22/85	Yes	All	Yes(l)	27.3	Yes
Dist. of Col.	07/01/87 - 09/30/87	Yes	All	Yes	12.2	Yes

Source: The Federation of Tax Administrators.

(a) Where applicable, figure includes local portions of certain taxes collected under the state tax amnesty program.

(b) "No" indicates requirement of full payment by the expiration of the amnesty period. "Yes" indicates allowance of full payment after the expiration of the amnesty period.

(c) Authority for amnesty derived from pre-existing statutory powers permitting the waiver of tax penalties.

(d) Preliminary figure.

(e) Amnesty taxpayers were billed for the interest owed, with payment to be made within 30 days of notification.

(f) Figure includes $1.1 million for the separate program conducted by the Department of Natural Resources for the boat excise tax.

(g) The amnesty statute was construed to extend the amnesty to those who applied to the department before the end of the amnesty period, and permitted them to file overdue returns and pay back taxes and interest at a later date.

(h) The severance taxes, including the six oil and gas severance taxes, the resources excise tax, the corporate franchise tax, and the special fuels tax were not subject to amnesty.

(i) Availability of amnesty for the corporation tax, the oil company taxes, the transportation and transmissions companies tax, the gross receipts oil tax, and the unincorporated business tax restricted to entities with 500 or fewer employees in the United States on the date of application. In addition, a taxpayer principally engaged in aviation, or a utility subject to the supervision of the State Department of Public Service was also ineligible for amnesty.

(j) Full payment of tax liability required before the end of the amnesty period to avoid civil penalties.

(k) Texas does not impose a corporate or individual income tax. In practical effect, the amnesty was limited to the sales tax and other excises.

(l) Waiver terms varied depending upon the date of tax liability was assessed.

Table 6.17
STATE EXCISE RATES
(As of January 1, 1988)

State or other jurisdiction	Sales and gross receipts (percent)	Cigarettes (cents per pack of 20)	Distilled spirits(a) (dollars per gallon)	Motor fuel(b) (cents per gallon)	
				Gasoline	Diesel
Alabama	4	16.5	...	13(c)	14(c)
Alaska	...	16	$5.60	8	8
Arizona	5(d)	15	3.00	16	16
Arkansas	4	21	2.50	13.5	12.5
California	4.75	10	2.00(e)	9	9
Colorado	3	20	2.28(f)	18	20.5
Connecticut	7.5	26	3.00	19	19
Delaware	...	14	2.25	16	16
Florida	5(g)	24	6.50(h)	9.7(i)	9.7(i)
Georgia	3	12	3.79(f)	7.5	7.5
Hawaii	4(j)	40% of wholesale price	5.20	11	11
Idaho	5	18	...	14.5	14.5
Illinois	5	20	2.00	13	15.5
Indiana	5	15.5	2.68	14(k)	15(k)
Iowa	4	26	...	16	18.5
Kansas	4	24	2.50	11	13
Kentucky	5	3.1	1.92	15(l)	12(l)
Louisiana	4	16	2.50(f)	16	16
Maine	5	28	...	14	14
Maryland	5	13	1.50(f)	18.5	18.5
Massachusetts	5	26	4.05	11	11
Michigan	4	25	...	15	15
Minnesota	6(m)	38	5.03	17	17
Mississippi	6(n)	18	...	17	17
Missouri	4.225	13	2.00	11	11
Montana	...	16	...	20	20
Nebraska	4	27	3.00	18.3	18.3
Nevada	5.75(o)	20	2.05	16	17
New Hampshire	...	17	...	14	14
New Jersey	6	27	2.80	8	11
New Mexico	4.75	15	3.94(f)	14	16
New York	4	21	4.09(f)	8	10
North Carolina	3(p)	2	...	15.8	15.8
North Dakota	5.5(q)	27	2.50	17	17
Ohio	5	18	...	14.7	14.7
Oklahoma	4	23	5.56(f)	16	13
Oregon	...	27	...	14	14
Pennsylvania	6	18	...	12(r)	12(r)
Rhode Island	6	25	2.50	15	15
South Carolina	5	7	2.96(f,s)	15	15
South Dakota	5	23	3.93	13	13
Tennessee	5.5(t)	13.05(u)	4.00	17	16
Texas	6	26	2.40	15	15
Utah	5.093	23	...	19	19
Vermont	4	17	...	13	14
Virginia	3.5	2.5	...	17.5(v)	16(v)
Washington	6.5(w)	31	...	18	18
West Virginia	5(x)	17	...	15.35(i)	15.35(i)
Wisconsin	5	30	3.25(f)	20	20
Wyoming	3	8	...	8	8
Dist. of Col.	6(y)	17	1.50	15.5	15.5

STATE EXCISE RATES—Continued

Source: The Federation of Tax Administrators (based on legislation enacted at the 1987 sessions).

Key:
. . .—Not applicable.

(a) Seventeen states have liquor monopoly systems: Alabama, Idaho, Iowa, Maine, Michigan, Mississippi, Montana, New Hampshire, Ohio, Oregon, Pennsylvania, Utah, Vermont, Virginia, Washington, West Virginia, and Wyoming. North Carolina has county-operated stores on a local option basis. Some of the monopoly states impose taxes, generally expressed in terms of percentage of retail price. Only gallonage taxes imposed by states with license systems are reported in the table.

(b) In some states, different tax rates apply to liquefied petroleum gas, compressed natural gas, and gasohol. Several states have variable-rate motor fuel taxes, under which the motor fuel tax rate is changed periodically by administrative action according to a statutory formula. Connecticut, New York, and Pennsylvania have gross receipts or franchise taxes on oil companies, which are not covered in this table.

(c) Includes a 2 cent per gallon inspection fee.

(d) This rate is for retailers. Selected other businesses are taxed at rates ranging from 0.46875 to 5 percent.

(e) If not over 50 percent alcohol by weight. If over 50 percent, $4.00 per gallon.

(f) Several states express the tax rate dollars per liter (one gallon = 3.7854 liters): Colorado, $0.6026; Georgia, $1.00; Louisiana, $0.66; Maryland, $0.3963; Minnesota, $1.33; New Mexico, $1.04; New York, $1.08; Oklahoma, $1.47; South Carolina, $0.7828925 (includes 9 percent surcharge, but excludes case charges); and Wisconsin, $0.8586.

(g) Self-propelled or power-driven farm equipment is taxed at 3 percent.

(h) On beverages containing 17.259 to 55.78 percent alcohol. The tax rate on beverages containing more than 55.78 percent alcohol is $9.53 per gallon. Lower (but variable) rates apply to beverages made from citrus products and sugarcane.

(i) The rates shown include a motor fuel sales tax, imposed on a cents-per-gallon basis and adjusted annually to reflect changes in motor fuel prices.

(j) Wholesalers and manufacturers, 0.5 percent; retailers, 4 percent.

(k) An additional tax of 8 cents per gallon is imposed on motor carriers on a use basis.

(l) Heavy equipment motor carriers pay a 17.2 cents per gallon tax on a use basis.

(m) Farm machinery is taxed at 2 percent, and special tooling and capital equipment is taxed at 4 percent.

(n) Among other rates imposed under the tax: aircraft, automobiles, trucks, and truck tractors—3 percent; manufacturing machinery—1.5 percent; farm tractors—1 percent; contractors (on compensation exceeding $10,000)—3.5 percent.

(o) Includes mandatory, statewide, state-collected 3.75 percent county and school sales tax.

(p) Motor vehicles, boats, railway cars and locomotives, and airplanes—2 percent (maximum tax is $300). A tax of 1 percent is imposed on various items used in agriculture and industry; on some items, this tax is limited to $80.

(q) The tax on farm machinery, agricultural irrigation equipment, and mobile homes is 3 percent. A 6 percent tax is imposed on alcoholic beverages.

(r) An additional tax of 6 cents per gallon is imposed on alcoholic beverages.

(s) Includes a 9 percent surtax. In addition, there is a tax of $5.84 ($5.36 + 9 percent surtax) per case on wholesale sales.

(t) Among other rates imposed under the tax: water sold to or used by manufacturers—1 percent; various fuels used by farmers and nurserymen; sales through vending machines—1.5 percent (2.5 percent for tobacco products).

(u) Includes a 0.05 cent per pack enforcement and administrative fee.

(v) A 19.5 cent per gallon tax is imposed on motor carriers of property on a use basis.

(w) Also has a gross income tax with rates varying from 0.011 percent to 1.5 percent (including surtax), according to type of business. Retailers are subject to a 0.471 percent business and occupation tax.

(x) Sales of mobile homes to be used by purchasers as their principal year-round residence and dwelling—3 percent.

(y) Parking charges—12 percent; hotel accommodations—10 percent; food or drink for immediate consumption—8 percent; rental vehicles—8 percent.

Table 6.18
FOOD AND DRUG SALES TAX EXEMPTIONS
(As of January 1, 1988)

State or other jurisdiction	Tax rate	Exemptions		Related income tax credit	State or other jurisdiction	Tax rate	Exemptions		Related income tax credit
		Food	Prescription drugs				Food	Prescription drugs	
Alabama	4		★		New Jersey	6	★	★	
Arizona	5	★	★		New Mexico	4.75			★
Arkansas	4		★		New York	4	★	★	
California	4.75	★	★		North Carolina	3		★	
Colorado	3	★	★		North Dakota	5.5	★	★	
Connecticut	7.5	★	★		Ohio	5	★	★	
Florida	5	★	★		Oklahoma	4		★	
Georgia	3		★		Pennsylvania	6	★	★	
Hawaii	4		★	★	Rhode Island	6	★	★	
Idaho	5		★	★	South Carolina	5		★	
Illinois	5	★	★		South Dakota	5		★	
Indiana	5	★	★		Tennessee	5.5		★	
Iowa	4	★	★		Texas	6	★	★	
Kansas	4		★		Utah	5.093		★	
Kentucky	5	★	★		Vermont	4	★	★	★
Louisiana	4	★	★		Virginia	3.5		★	
Maine	5	★	★		Washington	6.5	★	★	
Maryland	5	★	★		West Virginia	5	★	★	
Massachusetts	5	★	★		Wisconsin	5	★	★	
Michigan	4	★	★		Wyoming	3		★	
Minnesota	6	★	★		Dist. of Col.	6	★	★	
Mississippi	6		★						
Missouri	4.225		★						
Nebraska	4	★	★						
Nevada	5.75	★	★						

Source: The Federation of Tax Administrators (based on legislation enacted at the 1987 sessions).

Table 6.19
STATE INDIVIDUAL INCOME TAXES
(As of January 1, 1988)

State or other jurisdiction	Rate range(a) (percent)	Income brackets Lowest (ends)	Income brackets Highest (over)	Personal exemptions Single	Personal exemptions Married	Personal exemptions Dependents	Federal income tax deductible
Alabama	2.0 - 5.0(3)	$ 500(c)	$ 3,000(c)	$1,500	$ 3,000	$ 300	★
Arizona(b)	2.0 - 8.0(7)	1,183(c)	7,098(c)	2,045	4,090	1,227	. . .
Arkansas	1.0 - 7.0(6)	3,000	25,000	20(d)	40(d)	20(d)	. . .
California(b)	1.0 - 9.3(6)	3,650	23,950	52(d)	104(d)	52(d)	. . .
Colorado	5.0	--------------Flat rate--------------		1,950(e)	3,900(e)	1,950(e)	. . .
Delaware	3.2 - 7.7(7)	5,000(a)	40,000(a)	1,250	2,500	1,250	. . .
Georgia	1.0 - 6.0(6)	750(f)	7,000(f)	1,500	3,000	1,500	. . .
Hawaii	2.25 - 10.0(8)	1,200(c)	20,200(c)	1,040	2,080	1,040	. . .
Idaho	2.0 - 8.2(8)(g)	1,000(g)	20,000(g)	1,950(e,g)	3,900(e,g)	1,900(e,g)	. . .
Illinois	2.5	--------------Flat rate--------------		1,000	2,000	1,000	. . .
Indiana	3.4	--------------Flat rate--------------		1,000	2,000	1,000	. . .
Iowa(b)	0.4 - 9.98(9)(h)	1,000	45,000	20(d)	40(d)	20(d)	★
Kansas	2.0 - 9.0(8)	2,000(c)	25,000(c)	1,000	2,000	1,000	★
Kentucky	2.0 - 6.0(5)	3,000	8,000	20(d)	40(d)	20(d)	★
Louisiana	2.0 - 6.0(3)	10,000	50,000	4,500(i)	9,000(i)	1,000	★
Maine(b)	1.0 - 10.0(8)	2,000(c)	25,000(c)	1,000	2,000	1,000	. . .
Maryland	2.0 - 5.0(4)	1,000	3,000	1,000	2,000	1,000	. . .
Massachusetts	5.0(j)	--------------Flat rate--------------		2,200	4,400(k)	1,000	. . .
Michigan	4.6	--------------Flat rate--------------		1,800	3,600	1,800	. . .
Minnesota(b)	6.0 - 8.0(2)	13,000(l)	13,000(l)	1,950(e)	3,900(e)	1,950(e)	. . .
Mississippi	3.0 - 5.0(3)	5,000	10,000	6,000	9,500	1,500	. . .
Missouri	1.5 - 6.0(10)	1,000	9,000	1,200	2,400	400	★
Montana(b)	2.0 - 11.0(10)(m)	1,400	48,100	1,100	2,200	1,100	★
Nebraska	2.0 - 5.9(4)	1,500	27,000	1,130	2,260	1,130	. . .
New Jersey	2.0 - 3.5(3)	20,000	50,000	1,000	2,000	1,000	. . .
New Mexico	1.8 - 8.5(7)	5,200(n)	41,600(n)	2,000	4,000	2,000	. . .
New York	3.0 - 8.75(7)	3,000(c)	17,000(c)	1,000	2,000	1,000	. . .
North Carolina	3.0 - 7.0(5)	2,000	10,000	1,100	3,300	800	. . .
North Dakota	2.67 - 12.0(8)(o)	3,000	50,000	1,950(e)	3,900(e)	1,900(e)	★(o)
Ohio	0.743- 6.9(8)	5,000	100,000	1,000(p)	2,000(p)	1,000(p)	. . .
Oklahoma	0.5 - 6.0(7)(q)	1,000	7,500	1,000	2,000	1,000	(q)
Oregon(b)	5.0 - 9.0(3)	2,000	5,000	86(d)	172(d)	86(d)	★(r)
Pennsylvania	2.1	--------------Flat rate--------------		. . .	. . .	. . .	. . .
Rhode Island	22.96% of U.S. tax	. . .	. . .	. . .	. . .	. . .	. . .
South Carolina	3.0 - 7.0(5)	4,000	10,000	1,950(e)	3,900(e)	1,950(e)	. . .
Utah	2.75 - 7.75(6)	750(c)	3,750(c)	1,462.50(e)	2,925(e)	1,462.50(e)	. . .
Vermont	25% of U.S. tax(s)	. . .	. . .	. . .	. . .	. . .	. . .
Virginia	2.0 - 5.75(4)	3,000	15,000	800	1,600	800	. . .
West Virginia	3.0 - 6.5(5)	10,000	60,000	2,000	4,000	2,000	. . .
Wisconsin	4.9 - 6.93(3)	7,500	15,000	. . .	. . .	50(d)	. . .
Dist. of Col.	6.0 - 9.5(3)	10,000	20,000	1,025	2,050	1,025	. . .

STATE INDIVIDUAL INCOME TAXES—Continued

Source: The Federation of Tax Administrators, on the basis of legislation enacted at the 1987 sessions.

Note: This table excludes the following state taxes: Connecticut taxes interest and dividends at 1 to 12 percent and capital gains at 7 percent. New Hampshire taxes interest and dividends at 5 percent. Tennessee taxes interest and dividends at 6 percent.

Key:

. . .—Not applicable.

(a) The figure in parentheses is the number of steps in the range. For Delaware, the amount shown for the lowest bracket incvludes zero bracket amount and lowest positive bracket.

(b) Seven states have statutory provisions for automatic adjustment of tax brackets or personal exemptions, as well as other features, to reflect changes in price levels. Adjustments to be made for 1988 tax years will generally not be known until the latter part of 1987. The 1987 amounts are shown.

(c) For joint returns, the tax is twice the tax imposed on half the income.

(d) Tax credits.

(e) These states by definition allow personal exemptions provided in the Internal Revenue Code. Utah specifies that its personal exemptions are equal to three-fourths of the federal personal exemption.

(f) The range reported is for single persons. For joint returns and heads of households, the same rates are applicable to income brackets ranging from $1,000 to $10,000. For married persons filing separately, the income brackets range from $500 to $5,000.

(g) In the case of joint returns, the tax is twice the tax imposed on half the income. A filing fee of $10 is imposed on each return. A credit of $15 is allowed for each personal exemption.

(h) 1987 rates. No tax is imposed on married persons and others whose net income does not exceed $7,500, or on single persons whose income does not exceed $5,000.

(i) Combined personal exemption and standard deduction.

(j) A 10 percent rate applies to interest and dividends (other than from savings deposits) and net capital gains. The 5 percent rate applies to all other income, including earned income and income from savings deposits.

(k) Maximum allowance; spouse's exemption is $1,000 plus the amount of earnings, but the total exemption for taxpayer and spouse may not exceed $4,400.

(l) These are the rate brackets for single persons. The end of the lower tax bracket for married couples comes at $19,000, and for heads of households at $16,000. In addition, there is a tax equal to 10 percent of the federal 15 percent rate and personal exemption phase-out for taxpayers above certain income levels.

(m) Plus a 10 percent surtax.

(n) The rate range reported is for single persons. For joint returns and heads of households, tax rates range from 2.4 percent on income not over $8,000 to 8.5 percent on income over $64,000. For married persons filing separately, another set of rates and brackets applies.

(o) Taxpayers have the option of paying 14 percent of adjusted federal income tax liability. No deduction for federal income taxes is provided to these taxpayers.

(p) Or, at taxpayer's option, $650 deduction plus $20 credit per exemption.

(q) The rate range shown is for single persons not deducting federal income tax. Married persons filing jointly, surviving spouses, and heads of households have the same rate and brackets that are twice as wide. Separate schedules, with rates ranging from 0.5 to 17 percent, apply to taxpayers deducting federal income taxes.

(r) The federal tax deduction is limited to $3,000.

(s) If Vermont tax liability for any taxable year exceeds Vermont tax liability determinable under federal tax law in effect on January 1, 1987, the taxpayer will be entitled to a credit equal to the excess, plus 6 percent of that amount. A credit is allowed for taxpayers with an adjusted gross income under $7,000.

Table 6.20
STATE PERSONAL INCOME TAXES: FEDERAL STARTING POINTS

State or jurisdiction	Relation to Internal Revenue Code	Tax Base
Alabama	. . .	. . .
Arizona	1/1/87	federal adjusted gross income
Arkansas	. . .	. . .
California	1/1/87	federal adjusted gross income
Colorado	Current	federal taxable income
Delaware	Current	federal adjusted gross income
Georgia	1/1/87	federal adjusted gross income
Hawaii	12/31/86	federal taxable income
Idaho	1/1/87	federal taxable income
Illinois	Current	federal adjusted gross income
Indiana	1/1/87	federal adjusted gross income
Iowa	1/1/87	federal adjusted gross income
Kansas	Current	federal adjusted gross income
Kentucky	12/31/85	federal adjusted gross income
Louisiana	Current	federal adjusted gross income
Maine	Current	federal adjusted gross income
Maryland	Current	federal adjusted gross income
Massachusetts	1/1/85	federal adjusted gross income
Michigan	Current(a)	federal adjusted gross income
Minnesota	12/31/86	federal taxable income
Mississippi	. . .	. . .
Missouri	Current	federal adjusted gross income
Montana	Current	federal adjusted gross income
Nebraska	Current	federal adjusted gross income
New Jersey	. . .	. . .
New Mexico	Current	federal adjusted gross income
New York	Current	federal adjusted gross income
North Carolina	. . .	. . .
North Dakota	Current(b)	federal liability(b)
Ohio	Current	federal adjusted gross income
Oklahoma	Current	federal taxable income
Oregon	12/31/86	federal taxable income
Pennsylvania	. . .	. . .
Rhode Island	Current	federal liability
South Carolina	12/31/86	federal taxable income
Utah	Current	federal taxable income
Vermont	Current(c)	federal liability
Virginia	Current	federal adjusted gross income
West Virginia	1/1/87	federal adjusted gross income
Wisconsin	12/31/86	federal adjusted gross income
Dist of Col.	10/22/86	federal adjusted gross income

Source: The Federation of Tax Administrators (based on legislation enacted at the 1987 session).
Key:
. . .—state does not employ a federal starting point
Current—state has adopted IRC provisions as currently in effect. Dates indicate state has adopted IRC as amended to that date.

(a) or 1/1/87, taxpayer's option.
(b) or federal taxable income based on IRC of 12/31/86.
(c) not to exceed tax computed using IRC as of 1/1/87.

Table 6.21
RANGE OF STATE CORPORATE INCOME TAX RATES
(As of January 1, 1988)

State or other jurisdiction	Tax rate(a) (percent)	Federal income tax deductible	State or other jurisdiction	Tax rate(a) (percent)	Federal income tax deductible
Alabama		★	**Mississippi**		. . .
Business corporations	5		$0 to $5,000	3	
Banks & financial corps.	6		Over $10,000	5(3)	
Alaska		. . .	**Missouri**		★
$0 to $10,000	1		Business corporations	5	
Over $90,000	9.4(10)		Banks & trust companies	7	
Arizona		★	**Montana**	6.75(m)	. . .
$0 to $1,000	2.5		**Nebraska**		. . .
Over $6,000	10.5(7)(b)		$0 to $50,000	4.75	
Arkansas		. . .	Over $50,000	6.65(2)	
$0 to $3,000	1		**New Hampshire**	8(n)	
Over $25,000	6(5)		**New Jersey**	9(o)	. . .
California		. . .	**New Mexico**		. . .
Business corporations	9.3(c)		$0 to $500,000	4.8	
Banks & financial corps.	11.058(c)		Over $1 million	7.6(3)	
Colorado		. . .	**New York**		. . .
$0 to $50,000	5.5		Business corporations	9(p)	
Over $50,000	6		Banks & financial corps.	9(p)	
Connecticut	11.5(d)		**North Carolina**		. . .
Delaware	8.7	. . .	Business corporations	7	
Florida	5.5(e)	. . .	Banks	4.5(q)	
Georgia	6	. . .	**North Dakota**		★
Hawaii		. . .	Business corporations		
Business corporations			$0 to $3,000	3	
$0 to $25,000	4.4(f)		Over $50,000	10.5(6)	
Over $100,000	6.4(3)		Banks & financial corps.	7(r)	
Banks & financial corps.	11.7		**Ohio**		. . .
Idaho	8(g)		$0 to $25,000	5.1(s)	
Illinois	6.5(h)	. . .	Over $25,000	8.9(2)(s)	
Indiana	7.9(i)	. . .	**Oklahoma**		. . .
Iowa		(j)	Business corporations	5	
Business corporations			Banks	4	
$0 to $25,000	6		**Oregon**	6.6(q)	
Over $250,000	12(4)		**Pennsylvania**	8.5	. . .
Financial institutions	5		**Rhode Island**	8(t)	. . .
Kansas		. . .	**South Carolina**		. . .
Business corporations	4.5(k)		Business corporations	6	
Banks	4.25(k)		Banks	4.5	
Trust companies & savings & loan associations	4.5(k)		Financial associations	6	
Kentucky		. . .	**South Dakota**		★
$0 to $25,000	3		Banks & financial corps.	6(u)	
Over $250,000	7.25(5)		**Tennessee**	6	. . .
Louisiana		★	**Utah**	5(v)	. . .
$0 to $25,000	4		**Vermont**		. . .
Over $200,000	8(5)		$0 to $10,000	5.5	
Maine		. . .	Over $250,000	8.25(4)(w)	
$0 to $25,000	3.5		**Virginia**	6	
Over $250,000	9.93(4)		**West Virginia**	9.75	. . .
Maryland	7		**Wisconsin**	7.9	. . .
Massachusetts		. . .			
Business corporations	9.4962(l)		**Dist. of Col.**	10(x)	. . .
Banks & trust companies	12.54				
Utility corporations	6.5				
Minnesota	9.5	. . .			

RANGE OF STATE CORPORATE INCOME TAX RATES—Continued

Source: The Federation of Tax Administrators (based on legislation enacted at 1987 sessions.)

Note: Michigan imposes a single business tax (sometimes described as a business activities tax or value added tax) of 2.35 percent on the sum of federal taxable income of the business, compensation paid to employees, dividends, interest, and royalties paid, and other items.

(a) Figure in parenthesis is number of steps in range.

(b) Not more than 6.4 percent on capital gains.

(c) Minimum tax is $300. Banks and corporations electing a water's edge method of apportioning income must pay a tax of 0.3 percent of the sum of property, payroll, and sales in California.

(d) Or 3.1 mills per dollar of capital stock and surplus (maximum tax $500,000) or $100.

(e) An exemption of $5,000 is allowed.

(f) Taxes capital gains at 4 percent.

(g) Minimum tax is $20. An additional tax of $10 is imposed on each return.

(h) Includes 2.5 percent personal property replacement tax.

(i) Consists of 3.4 percent on income from sources within state plus a 4.5 percent supplemental income tax.

(j) 50 percent of federal income tax deductible.

(k) Plus a surtax of 2.25 percent of taxable income in excess of $25,000 (2.125 percent for banks).

(l) Rate includes a 14 percent surtax, as does the following: an additional tax of $2.60 per $1,000 on taxable tangible property (or net worth allocable to state, for intangible property corporations); minimum tax of $228.

(m) 7 percent tax on taxpayers using water's edge combination. A 4 percent surtax is imposed on all. Minimum tax is $50; for small business corporations, $10.

(n) Business profits tax imposed on both corporations and unincorporated associations.

(o) This is the business franchise tax rate; there is also a net worth tax at rates ranging from 0.2 mills to 2 mills; minimum tax is $25 for domestic corporations, $50 for foreign corporations. Corporations not subject to the franchise tax are subject to a 7.25 percent income tax. Savings institutions are subject to a 3 percent tax.

(p) Or $250; 1.78 mills per dollar of capital (up to $350,000); or 3.5 percent of "minimum taxable income"; if any of these is greater than the tax computed on net income. Businesses with income under $200,000 are taxed at 8 percent; a surtax is imposed on income between $250,000 and $290,000.

(q) Minimum tax is $10.

(r) Minimum tax is $50; plus an additional 2 percent privilege tax.

(s) Or 5.82 mills times the value of the taxpayer's issued and outstanding shares of stock as determined according to the value of capital surplus, undivided profits, and reserves; minimum tax $50. An additional litter tax is imposed equal to 0.11 percent on the first $25,000 of taxable income, 0.22 percent on income over $25,000, or 0.14 mills on net worth. Corporations manufacturing or selling litter stream products are subject to an additional 0.22 percent tax on income over $25,000 or 0.14 mills on net worth.

(t) Or, for business corporations, the tax is 40 cents per 4100 of net worth, if greater than the tax computed on net income. For banks, if a greater tax result, the alternative tax is $2.50 per $10,000 of capital stock; minimum tax is $100.

(u) Minimum tax is $200 per authorized location.

(v) Minimum tax is $100.

(x) A 2.5 percent surtax is also imposed. Minimum tax is $100.

Table 6.22
STATE SEVERANCE TAXES: 1987

State	Title and application of tax(a)	Rate
Alabama..........	Iron Ore Mining Tax	$.03/ton
	Forest Products Severance Tax	Varies by species and ultimate use
	Oil and Gas Conservation & Regulation of Production Tax	2% of gross value at point of production
	Oil and Gas Production Tax	8% of gross value at point of production; 4% if wells produces 25 bbl. or less oil per day or 200,000 cu. ft. or less gas per day; 6% of gross value at point of production for certain on-shore and off-shore wells; 2% of gross value of occluded natural gas from coal seams at point of production for well's first five years
	Coal Severance Tax(b)	$.135/ton
	Coal and Lignite Severance Tax	$.20/ton in addition to Coal Severance Tax
Alaska...........	Fisheries Business Tax	3% to 5% of fish value based on type of fish
	Oil and Gas Production Tax	The greater of $.60/bbl. for old crude oil ($.80 for all other) or 15% of gross value at production point (multiplied by economic limit factor); the greater of $.064/1,000 cu. ft. of gas or 10% of gross value at production point (multiplied by economic limit factor). Additional $.00125/bbl. of oil and $.00125/50,000 cu. ft. of gas (oil and gas conservation tax)
Arizona..........	Severance Tax(c)	2.5% of net severance base for mining; 1.5% of value for timbering
Arkansas	Natural Resources Severance Tax	Separate rate for each substance
	Oil and Gas Conservation Tax	Maximum 25 mills/bbl. of oil and 5 mills/1,000 cu. ft. of gas
California........	Oil and Gas Production Tax	Rate determined annually by Department of Conservation(d)
Colorado	Severance Tax(e)	Separate rate for each substance
	Oil and Gas Conservation Tax	Maximum 1.5 mills/$1 of market value at wellhead(f)
Florida	Oil, Gas and Sulfur Production Tax	8% (oil); additional 12.5% for escaped oil and 5% (gas) of gross value at point of production. $2.79/long-ton produced or recovered sulfur. Wells producing less than 100 bbls./day or oil produced by tertiary methods are taxed at 5% of gross value at point of production
	Solid Minerals Tax(g)	5% of market value at point of severance, except $1.35/ton phosphate rock and $.84/ton heavy minerals
Georgia..........	Tax on Phosphates	$1/ton
Idaho	Ore Severance Tax	2% of net value
	Oil and Gas Production Tax	Maximum of 5 mills/bbl. of oil and 5 mills/50,000 cu. ft. of gas(h)
	Additional Oil and Gas Production Tax	2% of market value at site of production
Illinois...........	Timber Fee	4% of purchase price(i)
Indiana	Petroleum Production Tax(j)	1% of value
Kansas	Severance Tax(k)	8% of gross value of oil and gas; $1/ton of coal; $.04 ton of salt
	Oil and Gas Assessments	$.008/bbl. of oil and $.00024/1,000 cu. ft. of gas, in addition to $.0125/bbl. of oil or petroleum and $.0033/1,000 cu. ft. of gas produced, sold, marketed or used(l)
	Mined-Land Conservation & Reclamation Tax	$50, plus per ton fee of between $.03 and $.10
Kentucky	Oil Production Tax	4.5% of market value
	Coal Severance Tax	4.5% of gross value
	Natural Resource Severance Tax(m)	4.5% of gross value, less transportation expenses
Louisiana	Natural Resources Severance Tax	Rate varies according to substance
Maine	Mining Excise Tax	The greater of a tax on facilities and equipment or a tax on gross proceeds
Maryland	Mine Reclamation Surcharge	$.09/ton (as per state authority) and $.06/ton (as per county authority) of coal removed by open-pit or strip method
	Coal and Gas Severance Taxes(n)	$.30/ton of surface-mined coal; greater of 7% of wholesale market value of gas or 11/150 of 1%/1,000 cu. ft. of gas
Michigan	Gas and Oil Severance Tax	5% (gas), 6.6% (oil), and 4% (oil from stripper wells and marginal properties) of gross cash market value of the total production. Maximum additional fee of 1% of gross cash market value on all oil and gas produced in state in previous year
Minnesota	Iron Severance Tax(o)	14% of value (minus credits)
	Ore Royalty Tax	14% of royalty received (minus credits)
	Taconite, Iron Sulphides and Agglomerate Taxes	$1.90/ton ($.05/ton for agglomerates)
	Semi-Taconite Tax	$.10/ton ($.05/ton if agglomerated or sintered in state), plus $.001/ton depending on percentage of iron content
	(p)	

STATE SEVERANCE TAXES—Continued

State	Title and application of tax(a)	Rate
Mississippi	Oil and Gas Severance Tax	6% of value at point of production; also, maximum 20 mills/bbl. oil or 2 mills/1,000 cu ft. gas (Oil and Gas Board maintenance tax).
	Timber Severance Tax	Varies depending on type of wood and ultimate use
	Salt Severance Tax	3% of value of entire production in state
Missouri	Surface Coal Mining Permittee Assessment	$.30/ton for first 50,000 tons sold (shipped, or otherwise disposed of) in calendar year, and $.20/ton for next 50,000 tons
Montana..........	Coal Severance Tax	Varies by quality of coal and type of mine
	Metalliferous Mines License Tax(q)	Progressive gross value tax from 0.5% to 1.5%
	Oil or Gas Producers' Severance Tax	5% of total gross value of petroleum and other mineral or crude oil(r), 3% of total gross value of petroleum and other mineral or crude oil, and 2.65% of total gross value of natural gas (license tax); maximum 0.2% of market value/bbl. of oil and of each 10,000 cu. ft. of gas (conservation tax)(h)
	Micaceous Minerals License Tax	$.05/ton
	Cement License Tax(s)	$.22/ton of cement, $.05/ton of cement, plaster, gypsum or gypsum products
	Mineral Mining Tax	$25 plus 0.5% of gross value over $5,000
Nebraska	Oil and Gas Severance Tax	3% of value of nonstripper oil and natural gas; 2% of value of stripper oil
	Oil and Gas Conservation Tax	Maximum 4 mills/$1 of value at wellhead(h)
	Uranium Tax	2% of gross value over $5 million
Nevada	Net Proceeds of Mine Tax	Total property tax rate of place where mine is located
	Oil and Gas Conservation Tax	50 mills/bbl. of oil and 50 mills/50,000 cu. ft. of gas
New Hampshire ...	Refined Petroleum Products Tax	0.1% of fair market value
New Mexico.......	Resources Excise Tax(t)	Varies according to substance
	Severance Tax(t)	Varies according to substance
	Oil and Gas Severance Tax	3.75% of value of oil, other liquid hydrocarbons and carbon dioxide; greater of 3.75% of value or $.163/mcf at 60°F and pressure base 15.025 lbs./square inch absolute (new wells at 3.75%)
	Oil and Gas Privilege Tax	3.15% of value
	Natural Gas Processor's Tax	0.45% of value of products
	Oil and Gas Ad Valorem Production Tax	Varies
	Oil and Gas Conservation Tax(u)	Percentage varies (v)
North Carolina	Oil and Gas Conservation Tax	Maximum 5 mills/bbl. of oil and 0.5 mill/1,000 cu. ft. of gas(h)
	Primary Forest Product Assessment Tax	$.40 or $.50/1,000 board ft. and $.12 or $.20/cord depending on type of wood and use
North Dakota	Oil and Gas Gross Production Tax	5% of gross value at well
	Coal Severance Tax	$.75/ton plus $.02/ton from July 1, 1987 to June 30, 1989 (w)
	Oil Extraction Tax	6.5% of gross value at well (with exceptions due to price and date of well completion)
Ohio	Resource Severance Tax(x)	$.10/bbl. of oil; $.025/1,000 cu. ft. of gas; $.04/ton of salt; $.01/ton of sand, gravel, limestone and dolomite; $.07/ton of coal
Oklahoma	Oil, Gas, and Mineral Gross Production Tax(y)	Separate rate for each substance
	Natural Gas and Casinghead Gas Conservation Excise Tax	$.07/1,000 cu. ft., less 7% of gross value of each 1,000 cu. ft. of gas
Oregon	Forest Products Harvest Tax	$.05/1,000 board ft. (privilege tax); $.15/1,000 board ft. (harvest tax)(z)
	Oil and Gas Production Tax	6% of gross value at well
	Severance Tax on Eastern Oregon Timber	5% of immediate harvest value and additional severance tax on reforestation land
	Severance Tax on Western Oregon Timber	6.5% of value and additional severance tax on reforestation land
South Dakota	Precious Metals Severance Tax	2% of gross yield from sale of metals plus 8% on net profits or royalties from sale of precious metals
	Energy Minerals Severance Tax	4.5% of taxable value of any energy minerals
	Conservation Tax	2.4 mills of taxable value of any energy minerals
Tennessee	Oil and Gas Severance Tax	3% of sales price
	Coal Severance Tax (aa)	$.20/ton
Texas.............	Natural Gas Production Tax	7.5% of market value
	Oil Production Tax	The greater of 4.6% of market value or $.046/bbl.
	Sulphur Production Tax	$1.03/long ton or fraction thereof
	Cement Production Tax	$.0275/100 lbs. or fraction thereof
Utah	Mining Occupation Tax(bb)	1% of gross value for metals; 4% of value for oil, gas and other hydrocarbons at wellhead
	Oil and Gas Conservation Tax	2 mills/$1 of market value at wellhead
Virginia...........	Forest Products Tax	Varies by species and ultimate use
	Coal Surface Mining Reclamation Tax	Varies depending on balance of Coal Surface Mining Reclamation Fund
	Oil Severance Tax (cc)	0.5% of gross receipts from sale

STATE SEVERANCE TAXES—Continued

State	Title and application of tax(a)	Rate
Washington	Uranium and Thorium Milling Tax Enhanced Food Fish Tax	$.05/lb. 0.07% to 5% of value (depending on species) at point of landing
West Virginia	(dd)	(dd)
Wisconsin	Metalliferous Minerals Occupation Tax	Progressive net proceeds tax from 3% to 15%
Wyoming	Oil and Gas Production Tax Mining Excise and Severance Taxes	Maximum 0.8 mill/$1 of value at wellhead(h,ee) Varies by substance from 1.5% to 7.25% of value; some additional excise taxes of 2% to 3%

Source: Commerce Clearing House, *State Tax Guide.*

(a) Application of tax is same as that of title unless otherwise indicated by a footnote.

(b) Tax scheduled to terminate upon the redemption of, and payment of all accrued interest on, bonds issued by the Alabama State Docks Department.

(c) Timber, metalliferous minerals.

(d) For 1986, $.01673/bbl. of oil or per 10,000 cu. ft. of gas.

(e) Metallic minerals, coal, oil shale, oil and gas.

(f) Currently set at 1 mill.

(g) Clay, gravel, phosphate rock, lime, shells, stone, sand, heavy minerals and rare earths.

(h) Actual rate set by administrative actions.

(i) Buyer deducts amount from payment to grower; amount forwarded to Department of Conservation.

(j) Petroleum, oil, gas and other hydrocarbons.

(k) Coal, salt, oil and gas.

(l) Figures are total parts of tax designed for pollution and conservation.

(m) Coal and oil excepted.

(n) Limited to certain counties. Coal tax expires June 30, 1989.

(o) All ores; tax repealed after December 31, 1989..

(p) State also has two related taxes; Mining Occupation Tax and Proceeds Tax.

(q) Metals, precious and semi-precious stones and gems.

(r) Except 2.5% of gross value of incremental petroleum and other mineral or crude oil produced in tertiary recovery projects. Over $250,000 gross value to over $1 million.

(s) Cement and gypsum or allied products.

(t) Natural resources except oil, natural gas, liquid hydrocarbons or carbon dioxide.

(u) Oil, coal, gas, liquid hydrocarbons, geothermal energy, carbon dioxide and uranium.

(v) Currently, rate is .19%.

(w) Rate reduced by 50% if burned in cogeneration facility using renewable resources as fuel to generate at least 10% of its energy output.

(x) Oil, gas, coal, salt, limestone, dolomite, sand and gravel.

(y) Asphalt, oil, gas, uranium and metals.

(z) Additional $.26/1,000 board ft. ($.16 is part of privilege and $.10 is for administering State Forest Practices Act) on forest products harvested until July 1, 1989.

(aa) Counties and municipalities also authorized to levy severance taxes on sand, gravel, sandstone, chert, and limestone and a privilege tax on nuclear materials.

(bb) Metals, oil, gas, other hydrocarbons, and uranium.

(cc) May be levied by counties and cities, until July 1, 1992.

(dd) Severance tax on coal, limestone, sandstone, natural gas, sand, gravel and other mineral products became effective July 1, 1987; tax rates on gross value of articles will vary each year, until 1992.

(ee) Currently, rate is .2 mill/$1.

STATE TAX COLLECTIONS IN 1987

By Vance Kane

State tax collections reached $247 billion in fiscal 1987, a healthy 8 percent increase from 1986. As usual, sales and income taxes remained the major sources of state tax revenue (88 percent). Income taxes (corporate and individual) reached a new high of 39 percent of total state taxes. An undetermined amount of growth was related to avoidance of the capital gain tax increase, effective in the Tax Reform Act of 1987.

Table A
Percent Distribution of State Tax Collections By Major Tax Category

Year	Sales & Gross Receipts Taxes	Income Taxes	License Taxes	Other
1957	58.1	17.6	15.1	9.2
1967	58.2	22.4	11.4	8.0
1977	51.8	34.3	7.1	6.8
1982	48.5	36.7	6.2	8.6
1983	48.9	36.7	6.2	8.2
1984	48.7	37.8	6.1	7.4
1985	48.8	37.8	6.4	7.0
1986	49.2	37.6	6.5	6.7
1987	48.5	39.2	6.5	5.8

Selective sales taxes totaled $40 billion, an increase of 7 percent since 1986. Motor fuel taxes increased 11 percent, to $16 billion, the largest of selective sales taxes.

Tobacco taxes showed a 3.5 percent increase; alcohol taxes registered a 1 percent growth. Twelve states increased the cigarette rate in 1987. These increases offset any decline in consumption.

Severance taxes dropped 33 percent in 1987 to a five year low of $4 billion compared to $7.4 billion in 1983. Nationwide, the decline in energy costs (primarily oil and gas) was easily absorbed. However, for particular states, the stagnation in energy production verged on the catastrophic and contributed to a reduction in all major tax sources.

Individual State Tax Collections

State government per capita taxes reached a new high of $1,018 in 1987. Nine states collected $9 billion or more in 1987. Table B ranks these states by dollars and per capita amounts.

Table B
Selected States' Tax Collections: 1987

Name	Amount of Taxes (in millions)	Per Capita Amount	Rank
California	35,791	1,294	8
New York	24,676	1,384	5
Pennsylvania	11,379	953	24
Texas	11,228	669	48
Illinois	10,430	900	29
Michigan	9,857	1,071	16
Florida	9,846	819	37
Ohio	9,717	901	28
New Jersey	9,491	1,237	11

Taxes for the nine states listed were $132 billion or 54 percent of the total. Their collective populations were 125 million or 52 percent of the U.S. total. Their per capita tax burden, however, was $1,055, which exceeded the national average of $1,018. Individually, only New York ($1,384), California ($1,294), New Jersey ($1,237) and Michigan ($1,071) exceeded the national per capita averages.

Five states reported state tax collections in 1987 which exceeded a 15 percent increase from the previous year: Rhode Island (18.6 percent), Maine (17 percent), Oregon (15.7 percent), South Carolina (15.7 percent) and California (15.2 percent). (See Table 6.24).

Rhode Island not only enjoyed the general prosperity of the New England area but received some windfall from the Federal Tax Reform Act of 1987.

Vance Kane is Assistant Division Chief for Programs, and was assisted by Sharon Meade, Social Science Analyst, both of the Governments Division, U.S. Bureau of the Census.

Maine enjoyed a sharp increase in individual income from $337 million to $423 million, a 26 percent increase. Oregon received $1.5 billion compared to $1.2 billion in 1986 for a 22.4 percent increase. South Carolina owes most of its tax growth to an 18 percent jump in sales tax collections and, to a lesser degree, 27 percent growth in corporate income taxes. California experienced a 23 percent increase from both corporate and individual income tax collections.

On the reverse side of the ledger, seven states reported a percentage drop in 1987 tax collection from the previous year.

Alaska	-43.2%
Wyoming	-20.6%
Oklahoma	- 9.8%
North Dakota	- 6.9%
Louisiana	- 5.0%
Montana	- 4.2%
West Virginia	- 1.0%

In Alaska, which relies heavily on oil and gas revenues, corporate net income declined $37 million, taxes on oil and gas properties by $11 million and severance taxes by $766 million. The depressed economy limited the increase in sales taxes to only $1 million.

Wyoming mirrored Alaska in that severance taxes dropped $128 million from fiscal 1986. Property taxes also declined $6 million and total sales taxes $27 million.

Oklahoma lost $201 million in severance taxes, $23 million in corporate net income and $47 million in sales taxes due to the continued depression of the oil and gas industry.

Although North Dakota experienced only a 6.9 percent total tax decline, it lost $51 million in severance taxes and $23 million in corporation net income. West Virginia, which almost broke even in tax collections, did lose $37 million in business and occupation sales taxes levied in lieu of a severance tax and $13 million in death and gift taxes. Other revenue sources remained even or showed a modest growth.

States continued to develop amusement and tourism activities for additional taxes. New Jersey collected $247 million in amusement taxes and licenses on its casinos. This compares to $271 million in Nevada collected from amusement sales taxes and licenses. Several states collect substantial sums from hunting and fishing licenses. California received $55 million; Pennsylvania, $36.5 million; Texas, $32 million; Wisconsin, $31 million; and Michigan, $31 million. Some small states collect significant amounts, such as Idaho with $15 million.

Tax Burden

While all states rely on various types of selective sales taxes, Alaska, Delaware, Montana, New Hampshire and Oregon do not levy a general sales tax. Six states — Florida, Nevada, South Dakota, Texas, Washington and Wyoming — do not utilize individual income taxes. Four states — Nevada, Texas, Washington and Wyoming — exclude corporation net income taxes. Therefore, the burden of who actually pays state taxes in a particular state varies. Locating the actual taxpayer is even more confusing in states with a high degree of tourism.

Caution should be used in any per capita ranking of states.

Against a national state per capita average of $1,018, Alaska still leads with $2,203. Hawaii is second ($1,567) and Delaware third ($1,536). However, New York has the highest per capita personal income tax, $700 compared to an average of $313. New Hampshire has the lowest with $8.21. (Discount Alaska's $0.81 as these are residual amounts collected for an income tax law now repealed). However, New York ranks 34th in general sales tax.

Because states utilize a variety of sources to support their programs, no comparison should be made or inferences drawn without a background analysis of their general economy.

Table 6.23
NATIONAL SUMMARY OF STATE GOVERNMENT TAX REVENUE, BY TYPE OF TAX: 1985 TO 1987

Tax source	Amount (in thousands of dollars)			Percent change year-to-year		Percent distribu-tion, 1987	Per capita, 1987 (in dollars)
	1987 (preliminary)	1986	1985	1986 to 1987	1985 to 1986		
Total collections	$247,148,658	$228,294,540	$215,893,158	8.3	5.7	100.0	$1,018.00
Sales and gross receipts	119,970,060	112,352,643	105,419,355	6.8	6.6	48.5	494.16
General	79,818,707	74,927,418	69,632,708	6.5	7.6	32.3	328.77
Selective	40,151,353	37,425,225	35,786,647	7.3	4.6	16.2	165.38
Motor fuels	15,661,127	14,101,182	13,344,397	11.1	5.7	6.3	64.51
Public utilities	5,982,998	6,022,529	6,202,564	-0.7	-2.9	2.4	24.64
Insurance	6,382,557	5,488,885	4,361,762	16.3	25.8	2.6	26.29
Tobacco products	4,605,543	4,449,007	4,534,346	3.5	-1.9	1.9	18.97
Alcoholic beverages	3,090,589	3,062,102	3,031,347	0.9	1.0	1.3	12.73
Other...................	4,428,539	4,301,520	4,312,231	3.0	-0.2	1.8	18.24
Licenses	16,002,130	14,919,384	13,766,118	7.3	8.4	6.5	65.91
Motor vehicles............	8,308,761	7,677,046	7,162,686	8.2	7.2	3.4	34.22
Corporations in general.....	3,171,598	3,064,843	2,812,524	3.5	9.0	1.3	13.06
Motor vehicle operators	728,329	695,192	617,248	4.8	12.6	0.3	3.00
Hunting and fishing........	667,984	629,719	589,579	6.1	6.8	0.3	2.75
Alcoholic beverages	251,931	239,720	234,735	5.1	2.1	0.1	1.04
Other.....................	2,873,527	2,612,864	2,349,346	10.0	11.2	1.2	11.84
Individual income...........	76,037,916	67,469,485	63,907,951	12.7	5.6	30.8	313.20
Corporation net income	20,740,041	18,462,149	17,631,194	12.3	4.7	8.4	85.43
Severance	4,047,878	6,038,399	7,211,178	-33.0	-16.3	1.6	16.67
Property...................	4,613,690	4,354,702	3,984,180	5.9	9.3	1.9	19.00
Death and gift..............	3,022,580	2,736,509	2,327,515	10.5	17.6	1.2	12.45
Other......................	2,714,363	1,961,269	1,645,667	38.4	19.2	1.1	11.18

Source: U.S. Bureau of the Census, *State Government Tax Collections in 1987.*

Note: Because of rounding, detail may not add to totals. Population figures as of July 1, 1987 were used to calculate per capita amounts; see Table 6.28.

Table 6.24
SUMMARY OF STATE GOVERNMENT TAX REVENUE, BY STATE:
1985 TO 1987

| | Amount (in thousands of dollars) | | | Percent change year-to-year | | |
State	1987 (preliminary)	1986	1987	1986 to 1987	1985 to 1986	Per capita, 1987 (in dollars)
All states	$247,148,658	$228,294,540	$215,893,158	8.3	5.7	$1,018.00
Alabama..................	3,222,201	2,997,093	2,941,336	7.5	1.9	789.17
Alaska....................	1,062,391	1,869,913	1,885,811	-43.2	-0.8	2,023.60
Arizona...................	3,469,477	3,195,720	2,945,422	8.6	8.5	1,024.65
Arkansas	1,889,066	1,826,733	1,744,954	3.4	4.7	791.07
California.................	35,790,750	31,078,383	28,952,494	15.2	7.3	1,293.81
Colorado	2,561,477	2,344,375	2,287,738	9.3	2.5	777.15
Connecticut	4,359,175	3,836,804	3,529,194	13.6	8.7	1,357.58
Delaware	989,298	882,666	818,579	12.1	7.8	1,536.18
Florida	9,846,189	9,120,166	8,334,433	8.0	9.4	818.95
Georgia...................	5,323,689	4,917,070	4,525,038	8.3	8.7	855.62
Hawaii	1,697,424	1,490,665	1,362,595	13.9	9.4	1,567.34
Idaho	829,698	744,739	733,575	11.4	1.5	831.36
Illinois...................	10,429,524	9,800,757	9,227,777	6.4	6.2	900.49
Indiana...................	4,774,190	4,458,168	4,336,068	7.1	2.8	863.17
Iowa	2,662,110	2,459,172	2,307,406	8.3	6.6	939.35
Kansas	2,085,490	1,911,548	1,915,199	9.1	-0.2	842.28
Kentucky	3,520,409	3,216,343	3,012,713	9.5	6.8	944.57
Louisiana	3,448,641	3,629,513	3,855,780	-5.0	-5.9	773.06
Maine	1,288,480	1,101,381	1,005,216	17.0	9.6	1,085.49
Maryland	5,204,499	4,669,561	4,321,772	11.5	8.0	1,147.63
Massachusetts	8,463,874	7,668,440	6,620,595	10.4	15.8	1,445.58
Michigan	9,857,122	9,314,194	9,141,953	5.8	1.9	1,071.43
Minnesota	5,546,422	4,898,456	5,228,004	13.2	-6.3	1,306.27
Mississippi	1,943,388	1,917,330	1,811,598	1.4	5.8	740.34
Missouri	3,942,295	3,608,083	3,352,482	9.3	7.6	772.54
Montana..................	591,001	617,082	640,750	-4.2	-3.7	730.53
Nebraska	1,203,344	1,119,382	1,040,064	7.5	7.6	754.92
Nevada	1,118,326	1,048,301	940,622	6.7	11.4	1,110.55
New Hampshire	562,712	494,454	434,048	13.8	13.9	532.37
New Jersey................	9,491,417	8,360,193	7,718,790	13.5	8.3	1,237.15
New Mexico...............	1,574,692	1,462,123	1,440,312	7.7	1.5	1,049.79.
New York.................	24,676,346	22,766,888	20,702,069	8.4	10.0	1,384.37
North Carolina	6,235,163	5,579,710	5,198,024	11.7	7.3	972.27
North Dakota	573,465	616,076	692,213	-6.9	-11.0	853.37
Ohio	9,717,146	9,059,970	8,651,690	7.3	4.7	901.07
Oklahoma	2,669,188	2,959,632	2,982,106	-9.8	-0.8	815.77
Oregon	2,235,073	1,931,346	1,982,956	15.7	-2.6	820.51
Pennsylvania	11,378,764	10,683,238	10,162,436	6.5	5.1	953.31
Rhode Island	1,050,144	885,557	861,836	18.6	2.8	1,065.05
South Carolina	3,339,515	2,887,103	2,732,346	15.7	5.7	975.04
South Dakota	416,386	403,741	355,452	3.1	13.6	587.29
Tennessee	3,603,331	3,271,963	2,998,373	10.1	9.1	742.19
Texas.....................	11,227,796	11,124,708	11,556,056	0.9	-3.7	668.76
Utah	1,438,325	1,364,835	1,323,699	5.4	3.1	856.15
Vermont	537,905	499,519	458,654	7.7	8.9	981.58
Virginia...................	5,526,557	4,846,627	4,469,391	14.0	8.4	936.07
Washington	5,639,369	5,219,292	4,585,551	8.0	13.8	1,242.70
West Virginia	1,830,168	1,848,552	1,848,439	-1.0	0.0	964.77
Wisconsin.................	5,673,577	5,491,530	5,113,133	3.3	7.4	1,180.27
Wyoming..................	631,669	795,445	806,416	-20.6	-1.4	1,289.12

Source: U.S. Bureau of the Census, *State Government Tax Collections in 1987.*

Note: Because of rounding, detail may not add to totals. Population figures as of July 1, 1987 were used to calculate per capita amounts; see Table 6.28.

Table 6.25
STATE GOVERNMENT TAX REVENUE, BY TYPE OF TAX: 1987
(In thousands of dollars)

State	Total	Sales and gross receipts	Licenses	Individual income	Corporation net income	Severance	Property	Death and gift	Documentary and stock transfer	Other
Number of states using tax	50	50	50	44	46	33	42	49	29	14
All states	$247,148,658	$119,970,060	$16,002,130	$76,037,916	$20,740,041	$4,047,878	$4,613,690	$3,022,580	$2,633,171	$81,192
Alabama	3,222,201	1,740,745	279,291	887,807	161,832	53,342	68,640	16,351	14,193	...
Alaska	1,062,391	81,725	68,737	427	141,068	666,870	102,491	1,073	...	...
Arizona	3,469,477	2,124,694	243,162	762,128	198,948	...	114,852	25,693	...	...
Arkansas	1,889,066	1,081,990	124,624	535,317	115,620	15,130	5,669	6,010	3,992	714
California	35,790,750	13,758,531	1,426,331	13,874,104	4,758,950	22,847	1,668,447	281,540	...	...
Colorado	2,561,477	1,216,438	141,839	1,034,676	124,085	9,694	7,570	18,254	93,741	8,921
Connecticut	4,359,175	2,696,144	246,200	465,968	680,242	...	...	176,868	31,169	1,137
Delaware	989,298	93,909	297,579	431,685	120,993	...	...	12,826	543,737	...
Florida	9,846,189	7,588,430	662,708	...	596,434	81,268	221,959	151,653	16,863	3,736
Georgia	5,323,689	2,487,090	169,623	2,149,111	449,176	...	17,801	30,289	...	...
Hawaii	1,697,424	1,040,995	27,802	543,093	76,793	...	...	5,178	3,563	...
Idaho	829,698	438,696	76,272	265,336	47,308	426	138	1,522	13,001	...
Illinois	10,429,524	5,388,013	767,214	3,095,177	862,435	...	222,432	81,252	...	...
Indiana	4,774,190	2,856,221	132,918	1,454,886	235,709	556	39,957	53,943	3,000	...
Iowa	2,662,110	1,245,335	255,572	955,232	149,602	...	...	53,369	...	...
Kansas	2,085,490	1,062,093	126,185	634,479	137,061	63,601	30,426	31,645	2,606	...
Kentucky	3,520,409	1,563,175	254,499	920,968	267,378	211,203	251,246	49,334	...	...
Louisiana	3,448,641	1,954,964	369,550	438,643	191,189	449,576	4,552	40,167	13,785	...
Maine	1,288,480	668,494	87,018	423,209	68,336	...	8,156	19,482	77,108	...
Maryland	5,204,499	2,305,755	168,568	2,181,080	270,489	...	128,523	46,892	...	26,084
Massachusetts	8,463,874	2,757,566	251,056	3,979,026	1,203,940	...	1,689	211,450	59,147	...
Michigan	9,857,122	4,092,375	563,591	3,208,459	1,644,692	53,362	205,113	89,530	...	...
Minnesota	5,546,422	2,407,445	367,875	2,312,044	422,999	8,266	6,180	21,601	12	...
Mississippi	1,943,388	1,301,047	164,131	315,449	102,865	49,190	285	10,421	...	1,023
Missouri	3,942,295	2,093,344	322,716	1,247,536	235,352	21	9,872	32,431	...	...
Montana	591,001	148,705	61,010	194,675	34,568	101,453	41,957	7,212	...	1,421
Nebraska	1,203,344	663,649	99,599	359,803	67,423	2,396	3,574	4,480	2,420	...
Nevada	1,118,326	956,296	123,485	...	...	3	38,542	...	...	...
New Hampshire	562,712	243,189	84,326	8,678	151,793	85	11,307	21,186	42,148	...
New Jersey	9,491,417	4,911,270	576,744	2,603,334	1,088,311	...	29,827	190,368	91,563	...

TAX REVENUE, BY TYPE OF TAX: 1987—Continued

State	Total	Sales and gross receipts	Licenses	Individual income	Corporation net income	Severance	Property	Death and gift	Documentary and stock transfer	Other
New Mexico	1,574,692	924,356	66,894	242,622	99,139	235,044	3,260	3,377	...	...
New York	24,676,346	7,876,098	733,000	12,476,941	2,143,390	...	78,316	392,687	1,054,230	...
North Carolina	6,235,163	2,530,090	415,486	2,565,878	566,480	1,436	2,215	77,477	...	...
North Dakota	573,465	299,667	60,241	80,150	33,442	95,808	...	1,942	...	...
Ohio	9,717,146	5,131,010	822,529	3,217,989	474,588	9,528	16,136	45,366	...	...
Oklahoma	2,669,188	1,169,464	305,972	678,828	83,703	370,178	...	47,381	5,351	8,311
Oregon	2,235,073	302,113	266,236	1,461,609	136,376	33,309	176	33,670	1,584	...
Pennsylvania	11,378,764	5,733,514	1,168,468	2,749,784	1,015,814	...	137,521	371,860	201,803	...
Rhode Island	1,050,144	531,499	40,527	359,005	87,675	...	7,156	18,462	5,762	58
South Carolina	3,339,515	1,921,034	167,592	1,008,938	190,474	...	8,465	26,981	16,031	...
South Dakota	416,386	326,504	50,097	...	24,212	5,469	...	10,104	...	...
Tennessee	3,603,331	2,785,525	351,296	68,123	298,644	1,581	...	31,757	52,276	14,129
Texas	11,227,796	8,116,106	1,816,263	...	...	1,181,685	...	113,742	...	...
Utah	1,438,325	752,813	68,792	531,674	60,891	21,548	289	2,318	...	...
Vermont	537,905	277,525	46,552	161,971	38,445	...	430	2,554	9,676	752
Virginia	5,526,557	2,259,632	329,803	2,445,816	320,598	1,714	23,510	32,800	104,775	7,909
Washington	5,639,369	4,244,763	295,315	...	...	40,483	889,069	22,189	147,550	...
West Virginia	1,830,168	1,134,027	111,390	482,205	89,890	...	1,944	6,761	3,890	61
Wisconsin	5,673,577	2,475,212	287,348	2,224,053	470,689	1,071	104,469	85,604	18,195	6,936
Wyoming	631,669	210,785	58,104	...	...	259,735	99,517	3,528	...	...

Source: U.S. Bureau of the Census, State Government Tax Collections in 1987.
Key:
. . .—Not applicable.

Table 6.26
STATE GOVERNMENT SALES AND GROSS RECEIPTS TAX REVENUE: 1987
(In thousands of dollars)

State	Total	General sales or gross receipts	Selective sales and gross receipts								
			Total	Motor fuels	Public utilities	Tobacco products	Insurance	Alcoholic beverages	Parimutuels	Amusements	Other
Number of states using tax	50	45	50	50	40	50	50	50	31	25	36
All states	$119,970,060	$79,818,707	$40,151,353	$15,661,127	$5,982,998	$4,605,543	$6,382,557	$3,090,589	$642,522	$479,877	$3,306,140
Alabama	1,740,745	883,762	856,983	262,744	246,038	71,351	125,401	97,309	…	67	54,073
Alaska	81,725	…	81,725	32,117	1,985	9,875	23,659	12,580	…	…	1,509
Arizona	2,124,694	1,547,425	577,269	309,534	84,808	51,220	79,269	40,819	10,882	737	…
Arkansas	1,081,990	715,636	366,354	206,457	…	63,060	52,189	24,093	20,555	…	18,816
California	13,758,531	10,934,653	2,823,878	1,248,218	35,146	268,337	1,008,887	131,319	113,155	…	…
Colorado	1,216,438	718,646	497,792	291,575	7,321	80,207	82,331	23,173	8,721	534	3,930
Connecticut	2,696,144	1,823,025	873,119	254,123	252,320	88,803	140,323	32,934	65,459	14,948	24,209
Delaware	93,909	…	93,909	33,322	16,614	12,249	23,158	5,129	63	…	3,374
Florida	7,588,430	5,478,278	2,110,152	716,019	202,333	330,498	254,760	445,817	118,809	2,734	39,182
Georgia	2,487,090	1,739,304	747,786	385,698	…	91,058	154,462	116,568	…	…	…
Hawaii	1,040,995	817,525	223,470	48,089	61,792	19,060	36,463	34,547	…	…	23,519
Idaho	438,696	297,896	140,800	82,227	1,819	11,954	32,519	10,079	483	8,391	1,719
Illinois	5,388,013	3,405,309	1,982,704	740,786	586,242	251,426	178,752	67,287	52,159	…	97,661
Indiana	2,856,221	2,252,060	604,161	397,254	…	75,761	96,520	34,562	…	64	…
Iowa	1,245,335	826,107	419,228	252,041	…	77,590	76,490	13,107	…	…	…
Kansas	1,062,093	726,833	335,260	156,753	765	61,645	64,986	45,450	…	774	4,887
Kentucky	1,563,175	892,042	671,133	294,472	…	17,114	136,642	49,109	7,985	283	165,528
Louisiana	1,954,964	1,189,690	765,274	357,400	32,472	78,786	182,435	52,137	22,048	196	39,800
Maine	668,494	439,399	229,095	97,278	28,960	39,618	28,167	33,490	1,582	1,533	…
Maryland	2,305,755	1,302,463	1,003,292	328,335	93,058	66,042	120,653	29,063	2,450	…	362,158
Massachusetts	2,757,566	1,866,748	890,818	310,397	…	171,024	215,088	80,693	35,679	7,909	70,028
Michigan	4,092,375	2,828,516	1,263,859	717,796	…	253,828	160,952	106,323	24,960	…	…
Minnesota	2,407,445	1,468,608	938,837	356,870	114,950	80,189	107,091	54,370	…	…	225,367
Mississippi	1,301,047	1,015,402	285,645	128,125	1,202	53,638	66,358	37,139	…	385	…
Missouri	2,093,344	1,624,025	469,319	215,212	…	82,784	145,047	25,074	…	…	…
Montana	148,705	…	148,705	85,490	9,857	12,616	25,304	13,794	166	…	1,478
Nebraska	663,649	390,546	273,103	161,842	1,811	35,892	30,895	15,434	5,405	…	16,843
Nevada	956,296	552,995	403,301	97,900	2,912	21,052	40,700	13,266	9	4,981	3,539
New Hampshire	243,189	…	243,189	83,615	6,427	31,674	30,219	11,276	10,518	223,923	69,460
New Jersey	4,911,270	2,911,780	1,999,490	343,542	1,018,560	210,955	147,891	57,886	7,379	199,844	13,433

SALES AND GROSS RECEIPTS TAX REVENUE: 1987—Continued

State	Total	General sales or gross receipts	Selective sales and gross receipts								
			Total	Motor fuels	Public utilities	Tobacco products	Insurance	Alcoholic beverages	Parimutuels	Amusements	Other
New Mexico	924,356	699,564	224,792	107,684	6,108	18,621	41,854	17,480	2,253	99	30,693
New York	7,876,098	5,097,847	2,778,251	495,922	969,056	406,235	458,965	156,384	83,836	1,123	206,730
North Carolina	2,530,090	1,456,024	1,074,066	554,254	207,465	16,141	139,941	131,437	...	...	24,828
North Dakota	299,667	193,779	105,888	55,441	10,304	11,276	12,203	5,608	...	...	11,056
Ohio	5,131,010	3,382,985	1,748,025	641,771	620,111	181,350	223,044	69,395	12,354	...	...
Oklahoma	1,169,464	613,769	555,695	204,931	12,549	74,515	121,208	52,299	1,498	...	88,695
Oregon	302,113	...	302,113	150,345	2,283	77,750	55,704	11,214	4,817	...	...
Pennsylvania	5,733,514	3,568,903	2,164,611	651,124	543,624	229,927	306,497	137,702	9,454	262	286,021
Rhode Island	531,499	350,811	180,688	52,666	56,106	29,748	27,523	7,684	6,605	111	245
South Carolina	1,921,034	1,356,473	564,561	262,054	27,504	30,303	87,537	106,614	9,876	40,673	...
South Dakota	326,504	205,480	121,024	56,751	600	14,878	22,294	6,918	3,583	...	16,000
Tennessee	2,785,525	1,994,313	791,212	489,224	20,336	82,516	126,575	62,335	...	180	10,226
Texas	8,116,106	4,601,385	3,514,721	1,273,136	210,474	370,843	460,963	326,192	...	...	872,933
Utah	752,813	559,208	193,605	127,378	4,629	15,955	28,990	16,653	239	...	...
Vermont	277,525	109,450	168,075	40,208	19,971	11,891	14,708	14,822	...	...	66,236
Virginia	2,259,632	1,102,670	1,156,962	438,691	144,132	17,175	158,495	95,257	9,244	188	303,024
Washington	4,244,763	3,284,378	960,385	448,682	163,748	129,240	91,876	105,493	...	91	12,011
West Virginia	1,134,027	790,406	343,621	161,649	...	34,512	43,803	7,401	...	644	96,256
Wisconsin	2,475,212	1,651,907	823,305	418,527	156,606	129,083	73,857	44,588	172	...	...
Wyoming	210,785	150,682	60,103	35,458	...	4,278	18,909	1,286	...	...	...

Source: U.S. Bureau of the Census, State Government Tax Collections in 1987.
Key:
... —Not applicable.

Table 6.27
STATE GOVERNMENT LICENSE TAX REVENUE: 1987
(In thousands of dollars)

State	Total	Motor vehicle	Motor vehicle operators	Corporations in general	Occupations and businesses, n.e.c.	Hunting and fishing	Alcoholic beverages	Public utilities	Amusements	Other
Number of states using tax	50	50	49	49	50	50	48	31	35	48
All states	$16,002,130	$8,308,761	$728,329	$3,171,598	$2,297,659	$667,984	$251,931	$255,214	$139,520	$181,134
Alabama	279,291	104,077	8,467	88,748	63,596	11,645	1,289	1,469	...	...
Alaska	68,737	17,688	600	896	37,630	9,979	1,666	...	249	29
Arizona	243,162	179,582	6,924	3,838	19,866	12,318	2,134	...	29	18,471
Arkansas	124,624	69,443	7,576	4,238	22,027	13,069	747	7,008	348	168
California	1,426,331	946,287	72,940	7,799	249,055	55,183	31,936	56,336	470	6,325
Colorado	141,839	77,538	4,823	2,495	21,656	27,971	2,436	...	330	4,590
Connecticut	246,200	174,696	22,306	8,758	27,842	2,622	5,937	...	87	3,952
Delaware	297,579	42,604	1,372	152,152	94,985	833	581	4,368	131	553
Florida	662,708	363,139	58,709	21,642	156,247	11,770	22,423	14,497	6,381	7,900
Georgia	169,623	73,123	14,092	17,873	27,141	13,465	1,824	...	...	22,105
Hawaii	27,802	17,604	...	1,048	6,378	194	...	2,510	...	68
Idaho	76,272	32,821	3,481	253	20,839	15,194	1,007	2,155	...	522
Illinois	767,214	579,787	34,593	74,401	58,541	15,279	1,707	...	987	1,919
Indiana	132,918	89,468	...	4,620	19,202	8,000	9,730	107	238	1,553
Iowa	255,572	176,462	11,554	13,879	14,995	10,984	8,609	5,487	10,793	2,809
Kansas	126,185	73,915	6,164	10,650	21,045	9,335	1,395	2,756	19	906
Kentucky	254,499	140,422	6,146	65,896	20,994	10,559	1,945	4,446	871	3,220
Louisiana	369,550	71,286	13,527	241,685	26,582	9,402	2,322	4,329	107	310
Maine	87,018	46,657	6,583	950	20,351	9,633	1,804	...	272	768
Maryland	168,568	85,544	8,008	3,907	61,999	7,223	350	...	33	1,504
Massachusetts	251,056	131,605	47,553	16,160	40,829	3,653	1,448	16,640	1,200	8,608
Michigan	563,591	339,746	13,968	89,099	49,522	30,834	16,039	...	34	7,709
Minnesota	367,875	265,234	8,921	61,557	61,557	23,590	528	...	...	4,858
Mississippi	164,131	57,714	5,894	61,041	28,644	7,272	1,215	2,274	...	77
Missouri	322,716	185,017	11,901	49,847	46,858	14,149	2,447	7,507	1,051	3,939
Montana	61,010	30,464	1,972	769	9,274	15,819	1,468	1,158	...	86
Nebraska	99,599	50,586	2,927	4,419	22,334	7,385	259	...	...	11,689
Nevada	123,485	49,919	3,075	4,351	12,650	4,508	22	...	46,590	2,370
New Hampshire	84,326	43,051	4,471	4,508	21,148	4,677	2,056	1,500	514	2,401
New Jersey	576,744	324,080	25,898	127,002	36,375	7,233	3,697	2,507	47,346	2,606

LICENSE TAX REVENUE: 1987—Continued

State	Total	Motor vehicle	Motor vehicle operators	Corporations in general	Occupations and businesses, n.e.c.	Hunting and fishing	Alcoholic beverages	Public utilities	Amusements	Other
New Mexico	66,894	36,631	3,200	5,581	11,523	7,058	1,020	87	1,794	...
New York	733,000	410,000	70,000	20,031	113,008	22,524	33,558	57,409	3,115	3,355
North Carolina	415,486	204,414	33,132	106,048	54,363	10,738	2,529	...	3,100	1,162
North Dakota	60,241	31,093	1,876	645	20,667	4,644	260	10	1,026	20
Ohio	822,529	339,154	12,834	329,578	101,360	15,717	16,779	3,797	...	3,310
Oklahoma	305,972	218,025	9,902	33,339	24,600	9,644	3,266	4	1,042	6,150
Oregon	266,236	170,821	12,251	3,898	47,043	20,190	1,574	6,875	1,632	1,952
Pennsylvania	1,168,468	404,895	41,466	478,111	164,870	36,514	11,534	25,927	25	5,126
Rhode Island	40,527	27,463	...	2,262	9,968	508	157	...	103	66
South Carolina	167,592	73,300	7,085	19,792	34,559	9,185	6,154	...	6,726	10,791
South Dakota	50,097	33,837	1,123	666	7,200	6,449	222	...	...	600
Tennessee	351,296	130,347	14,469	155,329	33,160	11,477	1,383	2,638	...	2,493
Texas	1,816,263	697,428	48,537	892,607	107,638	32,031	24,189	4,389	2,392	7,052
Utah	68,792	39,860	4,746	...	10,213	13,243	350	...	...	380
Vermont	46,552	32,429	1,831	566	6,083	3,552	545	...	201	1,345
Virginia	329,803	227,709	20,976	18,564	43,074	12,313	4,960	...	36	2,171
Washington	295,315	137,838	16,024	6,425	89,678	24,184	8,157	9,014	248	3,747
West Virginia	111,390	68,401	...	4,565	16,770	7,782	6,041	6,386	...	1,445
Wisconsin	287,348	149,107	13,776	4,996	80,333	31,171	232	13	...	7,720
Wyoming	58,104	36,450	656	2,484	1,387	15,282	...	1,611	...	234

Source: U.S. Bureau of the Census, State Government Tax Collections in 1987.
Key:
. . .—Not applicable.

Table 6.28
FISCAL YEAR, POPULATION AND PERSONAL INCOME, BY STATE

State	Date of close of fiscal year in 1987	Total population (excluding armed forces overseas)(a) (in thousands)		Personal income, calendar year 1986(b)		State government portion of state-local tax revenue in fiscal 1985-86(c) (percent)
		July 1, 1987 (provisional)	July 1, 1986	Amount (in millions of dollars)	Per capita (in dollars)	
United States	...	242,778	240,471	3,517,380	14,629	61.1
Alabama..................	September 30	4,083	4,050	45,939	11,336	72.4
Alaska....................	June 30	525	532	9,495	17,796	77.5
Arizona...................	June 30	3,386	3,279	44,719	13,474	65.3
Arkansas	June 30	2,388	2,371	26,268	11,078	76.2
California.................	June 30	27,663	27,001	456,078	16,904	66.3
Colorado	June 30	3,296	3,296	49,771	15,234	48.3
Connecticut	June 30	3,211	3,193	218,635	19,600	61.8
Delaware	June 30	644	633	9,498	15,010	83.9
Florida	June 30	12,023	11,694	170,980	14,646	61.3
Georgia...................	June 30	6,222	6,100	82,078	13,446	62.9
Hawaii	June 30	1,085	1,065	15,814	14,886	78.6
Idaho	June 30	998	1,002	11,250	11,223	70.5
Illinois....................	June 30	11,582	11,551	180,052	15,586	55.0
Indiana...................	June 30	5,531	5,503	72,294	13,136	66.0
Iowa	June 30	2,834	2,850	38,053	13,348	60.9
Kansas	June 30	2,476	2,459	36,042	13,789	55.7
Kentucky	June 30	3,727	3,726	41,902	11,238	78.2
Louisiana	June 30	4,461	4,499	50,382	11,193	64.3
Maine	June 30	1,187	1,172	15,007	12,790	66.4
Maryland	June 30	4,535	4,461	75,272	16,864	60.1
Massachusetts	June 30	5,853	5,834	103,353	17,722	68.0
Michigan	September 30	9,200	9,139	135,113	14,775	59.8
Minnesota	June 30	4,246	4,213	63,184	14,994	67.8
Mississippi	June 30	2,625	2,624	25,504	9,716	75.7
Missouri	June 30	5,103	5,064	69,856	13,789	61.8
Montana..................	June 30	809	817	9,666	11,803	54.8
Nebraska	June 30	1,594	1,598	21,957	13,742	52.3
Nevada	June 30	1,007	967	14,870	15,437	69.8
New Hampshire	June 30	1,057	1,027	16,339	15,911	38.8
New Jersey................	June 30	7,672	7,625	141,919	18,626	58.7
New Mexico...............	June 30	1,500	1,479	16,894	11,422	79.6
New York	March 31	17,825	17,795	304,095	17,111	50.4
North Carolina	June 30	6,413	6,331	78,763	12,438	72.1
North Dakota	June 30	672	679	8,470	12,472	70.6
Ohio	June 30	10,784	10,748	149,807	13,933	59.7
Oklahoma	June 30	3,272	3,306	40,595	12,283	61.8
Oregon	June 30	2,724	2,702	35,955	13,328	49.9
Pennsylvania	June 30	11,936	11,894	169,392	14,249	61.6
Rhode Island	June 30	986	975	14,213	14,579	59.3
South Carolina	June 30	3,425	3,381	38,153	11,299	75.1
South Dakota	June 30	709	708	8,364	11,814	50.0
Tennessee	June 30	4,855	4,800	57,645	12,002	63.3
Texas.....................	August 31	16,789	16,689	224,877	13,478	51.6
Utah	June 30	1,680	1,664	18,288	10,981	63.5
Vermont	June 30	548	541	7,220	13,348	62.6
Virginia...................	June 30	5,904	5,795	89,169	15,408	59.7
Washington	June 30	4,538	4,463	66,978	15,009	73.6
West Virginia	June 30	1,897	1,917	20,289	10,576	79.3
Wisconsin.................	June 30	4,807	4,783	66,549	13,909	66.3
Wyoming	June 30	490	507	6,485	12,781	59.7

Source: U.S. Bureau of the Census, State Government Tax Collections in 1987.
Note: Because of rounding, detail may not add to totals.
(a) U.S. Bureau of the Census, Current Population Reports, Series P-25, January 1988.
(b) U.S. Department of Commerce, Survey of Current Business, August 1987.
(c) U.S. Bureau of the Census, Government Finances in 1985-86, November 1987.

CHAPTER SEVEN

STATE MANAGEMENT AND ADMINISTRATION

DEVELOPMENTS IN STATE ADMINISTRATION AND MANAGEMENT

By Doug Roederer

Changing issues in the workplace, including pay discrimination based on sex, family policies and substance abuse and AIDS testing, were dealt with by states struggling to adapt their personnel policies over the biennium.

State governments updated their administrative and central management programs to meet the challenges of an increasingly complex state bureaucracy. State services covering personnel, purchasing, facilities, data processing, fleets, risk management, telecommunications, printing, and training and development are generally directed by departments of administration or general services. Debate continued on the value of centralizing these services. For example, integrating new technology in data processing, telecommunications and printing in government is a new challenge for states. Attracting and developing state managers is a struggle for states which have inevitable turnovers in political leadership. This article reviews these and other developments in state management and administration.

Personnel Management

Trends affecting and shaping the future state work force include comparable worth, family issues and workplace privacy. Comparable worth emerged as a remedy for sex discrimination against women in pay practices. Today, women, minorities and men in traditionally female-dominated jobs are affected. Unlike the equal pay for equal work principle, comparable worth requires equal pay for work of comparable value based on objective evaluation criteria.

Comparable worth studies typically use either an economic analysis or a job content analysis. In an economic analysis, the relationship between selected employee characteristics and pay differentials are examined. The study reviews worker education, training and experience, job concentration of women or racial minorities, regional variations and internal personnel policies. A job content analysis places a value on the important attributes of various jobs and examines whether the total values are consistent with pay practices. Point factor evaluation, the method used most often in comparable worth studies, is the system used by Washington, Minnesota and Montana, three of the leaders in comparable worth implementation.

Comparable worth has been considered by some 40 states since 1981, most recently Oregon, Connecticut and North Dakota. Oregon state agencies adopted a method of determining the comparability of the value of work and reported to the legislature with a system to upgrade undervalued classifications. The legislature then created a pay equity adjustment fund to pay for needed adjustments. Connecticut amended a 1979 law to eliminate sex-based inequities in unclassified positions held by employees in collective bargaining units. North Dakota authorized a study on the desirability of comparable worth legislation.

Personnel policies that center on personal and family needs are becoming important parts of state benefits packages.

Parental leave policies of some form are available in 29 states for the birth, adoption or serious illness of a child. As a result of 1987, legislative actions, more states now allow employees varying periods of paid/unpaid leave and guarantee reinstatement to the same or similar job upon return to the workplace. Connecticut provides up to 24 weeks leave for state employees. Other 1987 leave laws include Minnesota (six weeks), Oregon, (12 weeks), Rhode Island (13 weeks) and Tennessee (four months

Doug Roederer is Director of the Center for Management and Administration at The Council of State Governments. He was assisted by center staff Diana Bryan, Linda Carroll, Kevin Devlin and Jack Gallt.

for a mother only). Forty-six states' formal maternity leave policies treat absence for the care of a new baby (included an adopted one) as sick/annual leave or leave without pay. California allows up to 12 months of unpaid parental leave. States are also helping their employees find and pay for child care.

Some states now require any new public buildings to provide child day care facilities on site. Other new options include wage and benefit plans such as income reduction for child care expenses and temporary disability insurance for maternity leave.

Connecticut, Washington and Wisconsin fund child care facilities for public employees. States see the investment in child care for employees as being cost effective in that absenteeism, tardiness and workday interruptions among parents who work for the state will be curtailed because children are cared for in facilities near their place of work. Connecticut authorized bond funds for state agencies and municipalities to establish child care centers. Washington appropriated $450,000 in 1987 to construct a state child care center. In addition, California, Illinois and Wisconsin require that child care space be included in new and remodeled state buildings. New Jersey, Oregon and Washington offer an income reduction plan for child care expenses to state employees. The federal tax code allows deduction of child care expenses on gross income which can result in tax savings for employees.

States are also keeping pace with changes in workplace privacy issues, including substance abuse testing, smoking in the workplace, asbestos abatement, chemical hazards and AIDS education. Each of these potentially can invade an employee's privacy or adversely affect employee health. States now offer substance abuse help through employee assistance programs.

Substance abuse testing was reviewed by more than half the state legislatures meeting in 1987. Testing policies in 24 states are applied most frequently affect state police and corrections officers, but may also apply to health officials. Testing laws passed in 1987 in Connecticut, Iowa, Louisiana, Minnesota, Montana, Rhode Island, Utah and Vermont.

Laws restricting smoking in the workplace passed in Arkansas, Arizona, California, Connecticut, Hawaii, Indiana, Massachusetts, Maine, New York, Oklahoma and Vermont in 1987. Connecticut required employers, including the state and municipalities, to establish nonsmoking work areas upon worker request. Employers must post signs which distinguish smoking and nonsmoking areas. Broad restrictions by the New York State Public Health Council limiting smoking at work sites and public places are in litigation. An appeal is pending of a state Supreme Court Justice's ruling that the Council exceeded its authority in issuing the regulations.

States further regulated chemical and health hazards in 1987 due to federal Occupational Safety and Health Administration asbestos standards, effective Jan. 17, 1987. Fifteen states adopted and two amended legislation pertaining to asbestos abatement work and/or workplace knowledge of chemical hazards.

States are increasing health education initiatives in response to the Acquired Immune Deficiency Syndrome (AIDS) epidemic. States' aggressive pro-active approach includes extensive campaigns to educate employees about the manner in which AIDS is spread. AIDS education is usually provided to high-risk professions such as corrections officers and health care specialists.

Facilities Management

The facility management field encompasses, but is not restricted to, maintenance, construction, renovation, architecture and design, provision of office space, leasing of equipment, and other services concerning the state's physical plant. It has expanded to include strategic long-range planning, the implementation of computer-generated aids, office automation and similar concerns.

Of increasing concern to state facility managers is the availability of funds to properly operate and maintain state buildings. Scheduled and preventive maintenance are frequently targets of budget cuts. Deferred maintenance has become the norm.

Asbestos abatement continues to be a volatile issue in state governments. U.S. Environmental Protection Agency (EPA) standards provided under the 1973 Clean Air Act, U.S. Occupational Safety and Health Administration (OSHA) regulations, and court orders for asbestos removal affect state facilities management policies. Many state governments have responded by licensing asbestos removal contractors and establishing asbestos health hazard assessment criteria.

Aging physical plants are another vital concern. Most state facilities are over 20 years old, and some are a century old. Adapting these structures to house rapidly advancing technologies is difficult, but due to fiscal austerity new construction projects are a low priority.

Many facilities managers are considering innovative energy cost-savings programs, including using alternative energy resources and performance contracting. Use of the private sector is of increasing importance to facilities managers as states consider contracting for custodial services and maintenance.

These problems concern all state facilities managers. Increased funding and long-range capital planning could cure many ills, but budget cuts will most likely continue.

Risk Management

In recent years, states have been forced to consider alternatives to commercial liability insurance coverage because of rising costs and declining availability. Some states have been plagued with substantial premium rate increases, contract cancellations and the discontinuation of insurance underwriting programs by private companies.

Solutions, such as self-insurance for liability coverage, are being considered by state risk managers. A 1987 survey by the State Risk and Insurance Management Association (STRIMA) revealed that 32 of the 35 states responding use some degree of self-insurance, 27 use self-insurance extensively and three states are totally self-insured.

Most risk management offices are units of central departments of administration, although a few are in financial management or insurance departments. Most states have centralized risk management programs, with the average risk management office little more than a decade old. State recognition of the importance of risk management is relatively new.

Risk managers are reducing the vulnerability of state government to civil action and thus controlling insurance costs by using resources such as loss history records, inspections, surveys and expert opinions. Nevertheless, risk managers are hampered by inadequate financial resources, insufficient centralization of risk management responsibilities and state policymakers limited knowledge of risk management.

Many states employ such loss prevention methods as statutory dollar limits for liability. To decrease the possibility of lawsuits by those injured on state property, states are instituting employee safety standards and training employees to prevent hazardous situations.

Risk managers must contend with vast areas of legal liability, covering state automobiles, law enforcement and even claims of civil rights violations. While states face a crisis in tort liability, there are other types of risk they must consider. For example, states may be liable for breaches of contracts for services rendered for or provided by the state. States are subject to fidelity risk over the loss of money or property by theft or fraud by a government employee or official. States also may suffer damage to property because of vandalism, fire or natural disasters.

The crisis in insurance coverage has forced state governments to strengthen and reform their risk management programs. States are likely to continue to centralize risk management functions.

Purchasing

State purchasing officials perform complex duties, including the purchase of equipment, supplies, materials and services. In recent years, changes in state legislatures, agency offices and technology suggest a continuing evolution of the role of the state purchasing office.

All states have some form of central purchasing; however, the degree and manner of centralization differs substantially. In some states, central purchasing offices largely approve prices, not contracting or buying. Centralization of the purchasing function continues throughout the country. In the past six years, four additional state purchasing offices issued purchase orders centrally, bringing the total number of states to 29. The duties of central purchasing also continue to expand with 25 states now supervising agency inventories and surplus property disposal.

Data processing will have the most impact on the administration of state purchasing and the buying workload which occurs in the states. Thirty-six states, under legislative or agency directive, are exploring computerized procurement systems. Automated administrative support systems allow 20 states to track dollars spent by type of contract, maintenance, construction, architectural design, etc. Historically states could identify dollars spent by broad categories, but now increased automation allows some 15 states to track dollars spent and the number of items purchased by specific commodity code.

Despite anticipated administrative state procurement changes, the basic charge for the purchasing official remains to increase competition and competitiveness among state bidders. Purchasing officials have maintained the position that preference policies prevent acceptance of the lowest and best monetary bid from a responsible bidder. Over objections from procurement professionals, some 36 states have adopted policies that give preference to in-state products and services. The preference may apply to meat, coal, autos, recycled paper or bidders who represent a minority or small business or some other specialized provider. Not all states have a preference policy for all products. Of the 36 with an official policy, only 10 have a preference policy in place for all items.

Recent changes in the ordinary treatment of bidders include fees by seven states for placing potential bidders on appropriate state bidder lists. The fee offsets the administrative costs of mailing, printing and maintaining the list. As states look to alternative revenue sources, this policy may become more widespread. As another cost reduction policy 20 states now delete bidders from their list who fail to respond to two bids.

Printing

State printing operations changed radically in the last few years. New technology has revolutionized the graphic communications industry, requiring many states to reassess the most effective and efficient ways to meet their needs.

Most states have some form of centralized printing control and more than half have a centralized printing facility. The type and volume of work done at each of these central operations varies widely from state to state. Most central shops are responsible for providing basic printing services such as typesetting, forms printing, presswork, etc. to the state agencies they serve. States often contract out jobs to commercial printers that require specialized equipment or services that the central shop can not provide economically. Several states use correctional agency printing facilities as well. Many states also have departmental printing operations that serve a particular agency. These departmental shops are often little more than quick copy facilities, although a number of

states such as Florida, Mississippi, New Jersey and New York still have a significant number of agency shops that can provide a variety of printing and graphic arts services to their customers.

Legislative print shops often have very different priorities and needs than their counterparts in the executive branch. These operations are usually faced with strict deadlines and are therefore more concerned with speed and convenience rather than with cost control. Many jobs must be done in less than 12 hours to be ready for the next morning's sessions. The unusual demands placed on these shops and the cyclical nature of these operations can be problematic as well.

All state printing operations share common concerns on such issues as state in-house print shops vs. private sector contracting; rapid advances in technology which potentially outdates new equipment; pressure to control printing costs vs. demands of quality and service; labor relations and union issues; drugs in the workplace; contracting and purchasing guidelines/restrictions in dealing with the private sector; evaluating vendor performance; and the impact of desktop publishing systems on state printing capabilities.

Telecommunications

No area of American industry has undergone a more rapid and dramatic change than telecommunications. As a result, state governments have been able to improve the facilities and operations of telecommunications to better transmit voice, data and video. Some of the initial developments of the decade include: teleconferencing systems designed to save money; centralized information processing resources for more effective operations; statewide communications networks connected with high-tech enterprises and universities; establishment of special warning telecommunications systems used in emergency situations, such as a natural disaster; and satellite and cable television networks designed to carry coverage of state government meetings for public viewing.

The most debated telecommunications issues came as a result of the breakup of American Telephone and Telegraph (AT&T) in 1984. The divestiture of the world's largest telecommunications company raised several policy issues including how state agencies should encourage competition and handle applications for certificates of public convenience and necessity; how rate requests should be handled; what requirements telephone companies and phone equipment dealers should have; how state agencies should regulate new businesses in the industry; and how new service boundaries should be drawn — such as local access and transport areas (LATAs) and local measured services (LMS) for equitable rates. Moreover, the lifeline program, designed to provide basic services at reduced rates to needy subscribers, also became a major issue.

In addition to policy issues that posed problems, the new economic climate created by the divestiture brought about major developments in manufacturing, information services and long distance services. There is now a large variety of carriers and equipment suppliers from which the states can choose. Both carriers and suppliers are listening more to their users as new product lines and services reflect.

Some states have converted to state-owned telecommunications systems to achieve cost savings over continued use of common carriers' facilities. For example, Arizona will soon begin replacing more than half of its 700 leased lines with a private, statewide T-1 network to save an estimated $20 million over the next decade.

Other states are taking advantage of offerings created by new competition in the industry. Wisconsin contracted with AT&T to replace its statewide network with an integrated voice/data system. The 10-year, customized contract protects the state from tariffed rate increases and is projected to avoid $163 million in increased costs.

In coming years, state telecommunications officials will continue to face tough issues including the need for long-range planning to combat obsolescence; management improvement, particularly in inventory and cost accounting techniques; upgraded personnel classification and updated purchasing practices; streamlined systems of technical assistance to state agencies; and development of a statewide program to ensure security and public safety.

Fleet Administration

The number of state-owned and leased vehicles is as high as 30,000 in the largest states. With the average number of vehicles held by states in the 6,000 to 7,000 range, the need for professional fleet management practices is essential.

State fleets include passenger automobiles, vans, pick up trucks, buses, police and other emergency vehicles, heavy equipment, aircraft, watercraft and a wide range of special purpose vehicles. Fleet administration includes assessing needs, writing specifications, purchasing, assignment, recordkeeping, maintenance and repair, determination of lease/rental rates, utilization review and disposal.

A number of issues concern state fleet managers today. One is the structure of state fleet management programs and, in particular, the degree to which all vehicles will be managed by a single central agency. Some states operate successful programs with a totally centralized structure. Others operate separate fleet programs in a number of state agencies.

A continuing issue is the operating efficiency of state fleets as measured by vehicle life cycle. Timetables for scheduled maintenance, frequency of unplanned maintenance and replacement intervals measured in time or accumulated mileage determine total fleet operations costs.

Two environmental issues are of particular concern to state fleet managers. One is a pending requirement that state fleets that operate in metropolitan areas which have high levels of air pollution utilize alternative fuels. The additional cost of purchasing or retro-fitting such vehicles could be significant for some state fleets.

Another environmental issue involves the required replacement of leaking underground storage tanks. A high percentage of older metal tanks can be expected to deteriorate and leak. States are faced with costs for testing for leaks and for replacement of tanks.

Training and Development

The states have been slow to recognize the value and importance of training and development programs to enhance the skills of state employees. Because of the austere fiscal condition of many state governments, state training and development programs have not retained the levels of funding enjoyed by their private sector counterparts.

Training and development in state governments is a function of state personnel offices in over 30 states. Many state programs are based in state colleges or universities, as is the case in Alabama and Kentucky, or are dispersed among a variety of state agencies, as is the case in Illinois and Kansas. Only a handful of states do not have a central office for training and development.

The primary function of state training and development offices is to provide courses and workshops to help state employees improve their skills. A 1987 National Association of State Training and Development Directors survey of state training programs revealed the variety of courses and workshops which are available to state employees. The types of skills offered by training and development programs range from computer training workshops to management development training. Courses emphasize such diverse topics as typing and proof reading, assertiveness training and coping with job stress. Training programs serve virtually all classifications of personnel, running the gamut from secretaries to high-ranking career managers, and may take the form of one-day workshops or semester-length semi-nars. Some states even train elected officials. For example, the University of Texas has an annual training program for state legislators.

A growing training effort in the United States today is the Certified Public Manager program, which 17 states have adopted. CPM programs are comprised of extensive course work for career managers in state government administrative positions. Those who complete the CPM curriculum earn the title of "Certified Public Manager" or "CPM."

Training and development officials have introduced instructional techniques to state government which have improved the productivity of state employees. Nevertheless, increased funding and a commitment to the development of the state workforce are needed for training and development programs to have a profound impact upon state government.

Table 7.1
THE OFFICE OF STATE PERSONNEL ADMINISTRATOR

State or other jurisdiction	Method of selection	Primary responsibilities:							
		Reports to governor	Reports to personnel board	Directs departmental employees	Administers policies of personnel board	Administers merit tests, establishes qualifications for classified state employees	Maintains roster of state employees, classification and compensation plans	Makes budget recommendations to legislature	Other(a)
Alabama	B		★	★	★	★	★	★	★
Alaska	G	★		★		★	★	★	★
Arizona	D			★			★	★	
Arkansas	D	★		★	★	★	★	★	★
California									
State Personnel Bd.	B		★	★	★	★	★	★	★
Dept. of Personnel Admin.	G	★					★		
Colorado	G	★		★	★	★	★		★
Connecticut	G		★	★		★	★		★★
Delaware	G	★		★	★	★	★	★	★★
Florida	G	★		★		★(n)	★	★	★★
Georgia	G			★	★	★	★		
Hawaii	G	★	★	★	★	★	★	★	★
Idaho	B	★		★		★	★	★	★
Illinois	D	★★		★★		★★	★★	★★	★
Indiana	G	★		★		★	★		★
Iowa	G	★		★		★	★		★
Kansas	G	★	★	★	★	★	★	★	★
Kentucky	G	★	★	★	★	★	★	★	★
Louisiana	(c)			★		★	★		★
Maine	G	★	★	★	★	★	★	★	★
Maryland	G	★		★	★	★	★	★	★
Massachusetts	(d)		★		★	★	★		★
Michigan	B			★	★	★	★	★	★
Minnesota	B			★	★	★	★	★	★
Mississippi	B		★			★	★		★
Missouri	G(e)	★			★	★	★	★	★
Montana	(f)			★		★	★		
Nebraska	G	★		★	★	★	★	★	★
Nevada	G	★		★		★	★		★
New Hampshire	D	★		★	★	★	★	★	★
New Jersey	G	★	★	★	★	★	★	★	

THE OFFICE OF STATE PERSONNEL ADMINISTRATOR—Continued

State or other jurisdiction	Method of selection	Reports to governor	Reports to personnel board	Directs departmental employees	Administers policies of personnel board	*Primary responsibilities:* Administers merit tests, establishes qualifications for classified state employees	Maintains roster of state employees, classification and compensation plans	Makes budget recommendations to legislature	Other(a)
New Mexico	B(b)	★	★	★	★	★	★	★	★
New York	G	★		★	★	★	★	★	★
North Carolina	G	★	★	★	★	★	★		
North Dakota	D(g)	★	★	★	★	★	★		★
Ohio	G	★		★	★	★	★	★	
Oklahoma	G	★		★	★	★	★	★	★
Oregon	D			★		★	★	★	★
Pennsylvania									
Civil Service Comm.	(h)		★	★	★	★	★	★	★
Bur. of Personnel	G	★		★	★	★	★		★
Rhode Island	(h)		★	★	★	★	★		★
South Carolina	(i)	★		★	★	★	★	★	
South Dakota	G	★		★	★	★	★	★	★
Tennessee	G	★		★	(j)	★	★	★	★
Texas									
Utah	G	★		★		★	★	★	★
Vermont	G	★		★	★	★	★	★	★
Virginia	G	★	★	★		★	★	★	
Washington	G(k)		★	★	★	★	★	★	
West Virginia	G(l)	★	★	★	★	★	★	★	
Wisconsin	G		★			★	★		
Wyoming	G	★		★		★	★		
Guam	G					(m)			
Puerto Rico	G			★			★		

THE OFFICE OF STATE PERSONNEL ADMINISTRATOR—Continued

Source: Information derived from survey of state personnel offices conducted by The Council of State Governments (March 1986) for the National Association of State Personnel Executives.

Key:
B—Appointment by personnel board
D—Appointment by department head
G—Appointment by governor
(a) Other responsibilities specified:

Alabama—appoints employees of Personnel Board; serves as secretary to Board.

Arizona—administers personnel rules and policies.

California—(State Personnel Board)—(oversees all aspects of merit employment. (Department of Personnel Administration)—represents governor in bargaining with employee representatives; administers training, performance evaluation, benefit, labor relations, and staff reduction programs.

Connecticut—supervises affirmative action activities; conducts collective bargaining negotiations and labor management programs; administers management relations and personnel development programs, job analysis and evaluation, workers' compensation.

Delaware—administers affirmative action programs; development and training; directs labor relations for the executive branch; coordinates affirmative action; administers statewide staff development/training program, employee incentive, performance evaluation; publishes employee newsletter; coordinates state labor-management cooperate programs.

Florida—represents governor in collective bargaining negotiations; supports state agency employee training programs; administers group insurance, retirement benefit programs.

Georgia—administers health insurance plan; coordinates training programs, deferred compensation plan; serves as secretary to Personnel Board; central payroll.

Hawaii—conducts recruitment and examinations, training and safety programs, classification and compensation review, employee services, labor relations.

Illinois—negotiates collective bargaining agreements.

Indiana—administers affirmative action, rules, medical-dental plans for employees, training and continuing education; publishes newsletter; processes applications; performance appraisals; approves payroll; establishes new personnel programs and policies.

Maine—administers all aspects of employee relations and collective bargaining, workers' compensation program, and training and development programs.

Maryland—administers equal opportunity employment program; adjudicates employee grievances and appeal of disciplinary actions; administers state employee training and development program, and health benefits.

Michigan—administers employee benefits, rules of employment conditions, employee development and assistance, grievance and unfair labor practices charges, technical appeals (including selection and classification issues); regulates collective bargaining system; conducts representation elections for exclusive collective bargaining agents.

Minnesota—negotiates contracts with 16 bargaining units; represents state in labor disputes.

Missouri—recommends pay plan revisions for approval by the Board and governor; directs central training function for all state agencies; participates in central labor relations; develops standard performance appraisal system for the state.

Montana—collective bargaining supervisor; administers health benefits, deferred compensation, training and award programs, affirmative action.

Nebraska—promulgates system rules and regulations; administers health and life insurance benefits; coordinates labor relations programs.

New York—oversees agency affirmative action programs under governor's order; administers health insurance programs.

North Dakota—administers statewide appeal mechanism.

Oregon—maintains personnel system statewide.

Pennsylvania—(Civil Service Commission)—appoints staff; attends Commission meetings; recommends rules and amendments; investigates impact of Civil Service Act; appoints deputy; makes biennial report. (Bureau of Personnel)—develops personnel policy for all agencies under governor's jurisdiction; reviews and evaluates personnel programs; develops and administers senior management executive programs; administers training programs; negotiates collective bargaining.

Tennessee—administers provisions of Civil Service Act, rules of the Department of Personnel, including employment practices, classification, compensation, job performance planning and evaluation, attendance and leave, affirmative action, appeals and grievance procedures; acts as secretary of Civil Service Commission.

Utah—establishes rules and regulations.

Vermont—negotiates collective bargaining agreements; administers employee benefits; handles employee grievances.

(b) With approval by Governor.

(c) Appointed by the Louisiana Civil Service Commission following a competitive examination.

(d) Massachusetts' Civil Service Commission submits three names to the secretary of administration and finance who appoints the personnel administrator with the governor's consent. The personnel administrator serves a four-year term.

(e) From candidates certified by the Personnel Advisory Board.

(f) Selected through procedures specified in the Montana recruitment and selection rules.

(g) Director of Office of Management and Budget makes final choice from among the candidates presented by the State Personnel Board.

(h) Appointed by director of administration following a competitive examination.

(i) Selected by State Budget and Control Board, a five-member board chaired by the governor.

(j) Decentralized personnel system.

(k) From three candidates recommended by the Personnel Board.

(l) From list of eligible candidates following competitive examination.

(m) Information not available.

(n) Personnel office in Florida no longer administers merit tests.

Table 7.2
STATE PERSONNEL ADMINISTRATION: STRUCTURE AND FUNCTIONS

State or other jurisdiction	Legal basis for personnel department	Organizational status		Functions(a):												
		Separate agency	Part of a larger agency	Human resource planning	Classification	Recruitment	Selection	Performance evaluation	Promotion	Employee assistance and counseling	Human resource development and training	Affirmative action	Labor and employee relations	Grievance and appeals	Compensation	Retirement
Alabama	C,S	★			•	★		★	★	★		★	★	★	★	★	
Alaska	C,S		★		•	★		★	•	★		•	★			•	
Arizona	S		★		★	•		•	•	•		•		•		★	
Arkansas	C,S		★		•	•		•	•	•		•	•	•	•	•	•
California:																
State Personnel Bd.	C,S,E	★			★	•		•	★	★		•	★	★	★	★	
Dept. of Personnel Admin.	S	★			★	★								★	★		
Colorado	C,S,E	★			★	★		★	★	★	★	★	★	★	★	★	•
Connecticut	S			★	★	★		★	★	★	★	★	★	•	•	•	
Delaware	S	★		•	•	•		•	•	•	★	•	★	•	★	•	★
Florida	S	★		•	★	★		•	★	•	★	•	•	•	•	•	★
Georgia	C,S	★		•	★	★		•	★	•	★	★	★	★	★	★	★
Hawaii	C,S	★	★		★	•		•	•	•	•	•	•		•	•	
Idaho	S	★			•	•		•	•	•		•	•		•	•	
Illinois	S		★	★	★	★		★	★	★	★	•	★	★	★	★	★★
Indiana	S		★		★	★		★	★	•	•	★	★	★	★	★	
Iowa	S	★	★	•	•	★		•	★	★	★	★	•	•	•	•	
Kansas	S		★	★	★	★		•	★	★	•	★	★	•	★	★	
Kentucky	C	★	★	★	•	★		•	★★	★	★	•	★	★	•	•	
Louisiana	C	★	★	•	•	★		•	★	★	•	•	★	•	★	★	★★
Maine	S	★		•	•	★		•	★	•	•	•	•	•	★	•	
Maryland	S			•	★	•		•	★	★	•	•	★	•	•	•	
Massachusetts	S	★		★	•	★		•	★	★	★	★	★	★	★	★	
Michigan	C	★		★	•	★		★	★	★	★	★	★	★	★	★	
Minnesota	C	★		★	•	★		•	★	•	★	•	★	•	•	•	
Mississippi	S	★			•	★		•	•	•	•	•	★	•	★	★	
Missouri	C,S			•	•	★		•	★	•	★	★	★	•	★	•	
Montana	S	★		★	•	(c)		(c)	(c)	(c)	•	•	•	•	•	•	
Nebraska	S	★		•	•	★		•	★	★	•	★	•	★	★	★	
Nevada	S		★		•	•		★	★★	★	★★	•	★	★★	★★	★	★★
New Hampshire	C,S		★		•	•		•	•	•	•	•	•	•	•	•	
New Jersey	C,S	★		•	•	★		•	★	★	★	•	★	•	•	•	
New Mexico	S	★			•	•		★	•	★	★	★	★	•	•	★	
New York	C,S,E(b)	★			•	•		•	★	•	•	•	★	•	★	★	
North Carolina	S	★			•	•		•	•	★	★	•	★	★★	★	★	
North Dakota	S		★		•	•		•	•	•	★	•	•	•	•	★	
Ohio	C		★		•	•		•	•	★	★	•	★	★	★	★	★

STATE PERSONNEL ADMINISTRATION: STRUCTURE AND FUNCTIONS—Continued

State or other jurisdiction	Legal basis for personnel department	Organizational status: Separate agency	Organizational status: Part of a larger agency	Human resource planning	Classification	Recruitment	Selection	Performance evaluation	Promotion	Employee assistance and counseling	Human resource development and training	Affirmative action	Labor and employee relations	Grievance and appeals	Compensation	Retirement
Oklahoma	S	★		★	★	●	★	★	●	★	★	★	★	●	●	
Oregon	S		★	●	★	●	★	★	●	●	★		★	★	★	
Pennsylvania																
Civil Service Comm.	S	★		★		★	★			★		●	●	●	●	
Bur. of Personnel	E		●	★	●	★	★	★	★	★	★	●	●	●	★	
Rhode Island	S		●	★	●	★	★		●	●	★	●	●	●	●	
South Carolina	S		●	★	●	★	●	★	●	●	●	●	●	★	●	
South Dakota	S	★		●	●	●	(c)★	●	●	●	●	●	●	●	●	
Tennessee	S	★		★	●	●	★	●	●	●	★	●	★	★	●	
Texas											(c)					
Utah	S	★		★	●	★	★	★	●	★	★	★	●	●	●	
Vermont	S		●	★	●	●	●	●	●		●	●	●	●	●	
Virginia	S	★		●	●	●		●	●	●	●	●	●		●	
Washington	S	★		★	●	●		★	●	★	★	●	★	●	●	
West Virginia	S	★		★	●	●	●	●	●	●	★	●	★	★	●	
Wisconsin	S		★		●	●		●	●	●	★	●	●	●	●	
Wyoming																
Guam	S		●	★	●	★	●	●	●	●	●	★	★	★	★	
Puerto Rico	S		★	●	●	●	●	●	●	★	●	●	●	●	●	

Source: Information derived from survey of state personnel offices conducted by The Council of State Governments (March 1986) for the National Association of State Personnel Executives.

Key:
C—Constitution
S—Statute
E—Executive order
(a) In these columns: ★—function centralized in personnel department;
●—function performed in personnel department.
(b) Also, Civil Service Commission regulations.
(c) Decentralized system.

Table 7.3
CLASSIFICATION AND COMPENSATION PLANS

State or other jurisdiction	Classification plan: Legal basis for plan	Current number of classifications	Requirement for periodic comprehensive review of plan(a)	Date of most recent comprehensive review	Legal basis for compensation plan
Alabama................	(b)	1,340	★/5	1982	S,R
Alaska.................	S	1,000	. . .	1985	S
Arizona................	S,R	1,450	. . .	1987(c)	S,R
Arkansas	S	2,100	. . .	1980	S
California..............	C,S	4,400	★/2	. . .	S
Colorado	C,S	1,600	. . .	1975(d)	C,S
Connecticut	S	2,500	. . .	1986(c)	S,CB
Delaware	S	1,100	. . .	1986	S
Florida	S	1,651	. . .	1985	S
Georgia................	S	1,500	. . .	1978	S
Hawaii	S,R	1,605	. . .	1987	S,R
Idaho	S	1,100	★/2	. . .	S
Illinois.................	S	1,620	. . .	1987(c)	S
Indiana	S	1,525	. . .	1986(c)	S
Iowa	S	1,116	. . .	1985	S,CB
Kansas	S,R	1,200	. . .	1986(c)	S,R
Kentucky	S,R	1,442	. . .	1982	S,R
Louisiana	C	3,764	. . .	1987	C
Maine	S	1,497	★/10	1982	CB
Maryland	S	3,000	. . .	1982	S
Massachusetts	S	1,000	. . .	1987	S,CB
Michigan	C	1,766	. . .	1980	C
Minnesota	S	1,600	. . .	1986(c)	S,CB
Mississippi	S	1,700	. . .	1987(c)	S
Missouri	S,R	1,080(e)	. . .	(f)	S
Montana...............	S,R	1,500	. . .	1985	S,R
Nebraska	S	1,300	. . .	1969	S
Nevada	S	1,200	★/5	1986(c)	S
New Hampshire	S	1,470	. . .	1987	S
New Jersey.............	S,R	6,500	. . .	1986(c)	S,R
New Mexico............	S	800	. . .	. . .	S
New York	S	7,300	. . .	1954	S
North Carolina	S	3,012	. . .	1949	S
North Dakota	S	960	. . .	1986(c)	S
Ohio	S	1,832	. . .	1987-88	S
Oklahoma	S	1,136	. . .	1981	S
Oregon	S	1,185	. . .	(c)	S
Pennsylvania	S,R,E	2,700	. . .	1970	S,R,E
Rhode Island	S	1,500	. . .	1957	S
South Carolina	S	2,400	. . .	1979	S
South Dakota	S,R	579	. . .	1986	S,R
Tennessee	S	1,451	. . .	1984	S
Texas..................	S	1,288(e)	★/1	(g)	S
Utah	S	2,100	★/(c)	1986(c)	S
Vermont...............	S	1,063	. . .	1986(c)	S
Virginia................	S	2,100	. . .	1980	S
Washington	S	2,400	. . .	1986(c)	S
West Virginia	S	950	. . .	1986	S
Wisconsin..............	S	2,011	. . .	1947	S
Wyoming	S	1,375	. . .	1976	S
Guam	S	900	★/2	1984	S,R
Puerto Rico	S	1,131	. . .	1986(c)	S

Source: Information derived from survey of state personnel offices conducted by The Council of State Governments (March 1986) for the National Association of State Personnel Executives.

Key:
C—Constitution
S—Statute
R—Regulation
E—Executive order
CB—Collective bargaining
N.A.—Not available
(a) In this column, number after slash represents frequency (in years)

of required review.
(b) Authorization from state personnel board rules.
(c) Ongoing review. In Illinois, ongoing since 1969.
(d) Incremental reviews have been conducted, based on 1975 comprehensive review.
(e) Legal limit on number of classifications. Missouri—1,100; Texas—1,288.
(f) No comprehensive reviews; only reviews of sections of plan.
(g) In Texas, budget reviewed biennially by classification compensation salary administration.

Table 7.4
SELECTED EMPLOYEE LEAVE POLICIES

State or other jurisdiction	Annual leave accrual (in days per year) first year	Annual leave accrual (in days per year) fifth year	Sick leave accrual (in days per year)	Maternity leave — Treated as sick leave and/or annual leave or leave without pay	Maternity leave — Other provision(a)	Paternity leave — Treated as sick leave and/or annual leave or leave without pay	Paternity leave — Other provision(b)
Alabama	13	16.25	13	★	...	...	...
Alaska	15	18	15	...	★	...	...
Arizona	12	15	12	★	...	(c)	...
Arkansas	12	18	12	★	...	...	...
California	10	15	12	...	★	...	...
Colorado	12	15	15	★	...	★	...
Connecticut	12	15	15	★	...	★(c)	★
Delaware	15	15	15	★	...	★	...
Florida	19.5	22.75	6.5	★	...	...	...
Georgia	15	15	15	★	...	...	...
Hawaii	21	21	21	...	★	...	★
Idaho	12	15	12	★	...	...	...
Illinois	10	10	12	(g)	...	...	...
Indiana	12	15	6(d)	★	...	...	...
Iowa	12	17	18	...	★	...	★
Kansas	12	15	12	★	...	...	★
Kentucky	11	11	12	★	...	...	★
Louisiana	12	18	12	...	...	...	...
Maine	12	15	12	...	★	...	...
Maryland	10	10	15	★	...	...	...
Massachusetts	10	15	15	(g)	★(h)	...	...
Michigan	13	15	13	...	...	...	...
Minnesota	13(e)	13(e)	13	★	...	★	...
Mississippi	18	21	12	★	...	...	...
Missouri	15	15	15	★	...	...	...
Montana	15	15	12	★	...	...	...
Nebraska	12	15	12	★	...	...	★
Nevada	15	15	15	★	...	★	...
New Hampshire	12	15	15	★	...	...	...
New Jersey	12	15	15	★	...	★	...
New Mexico	15	15	12	...	...	...	...
New York	14	18	13	★	...	★	...
North Carolina	11.75	16.75	12	★	...	...	★
North Dakota	12	15	12	★	...	...	...
Ohio	10	10	7	★	...	★	...
Oklahoma	15	18	15	★	...	★	...
Oregon	12	15	12	★	★	★	★
Pennsylvania	5.2(f)	15.6(f)	13	★	...	★	...
Rhode Island	10	15	15	★	...	★	...
South Carolina	15	15	15	★	...	...	...
South Dakota	15	15	14	★	...	...	...
Tennessee	12	18	12	★	...	...	...
Texas	10.5	13.5	12	★	...	★	...
Utah	13	16.25	13	★	...	...	...
Vermont	12	15	12	...	★	★	...
Virginia	12	15	15	★	...	★	...
Washington	12	15	12	★	...	★	...
West Virginia	15	18	18	★	...	...	...
Wisconsin	10	15	13	★	...	★	...
Wyoming	12	15	12	★	...	...	...
Guam	13	19.5	13	★	...	★	...
Puerto Rico	30	30	18	...	★	...	...

Source: Information derived from survey of state personnel offices conducted by The Council of State Governments (March 1986) for the National Association of State Personnel Executives.

Note: For information on holidays, see Table 7.5, "State Employees: Paid Holidays."

(a) Formal provision for maternity leave—Alaska, California, Vermont, Puerto Rico. After using sick leave, employee can acquire "child care" leave—Hawaii. Determined by union contract—Maine. In addition to sick leave and annual leave, union contract covered employees are entitled to a minimum months maternity leave without pay—Iowa.

(b) After using sick leave, employee can acquire "child care" leave—Hawaii. Annual leave available for family needs—Kansas (five days), Kentucky (varies). Contingent upon approval of agency head—Nebraska, North Carolina. In addition to annual leave and leave without pay, employees are entitled to use 5 days per year of sick leave for care of im-

mediate family members—Iowa.

(c) Three days of sick leave as paternity leave in Connecticut; treated as annual leave or leave without pay in Arizona.

(d) Full-time employees with over five years of service, who have used all annual and sick leave, may apply for special sick leave at the rate of one week for each year of service.

(e) Managerial personnel receive 19 1/2 days.

(f) As part of a collective bargaining agreement, new state employees (those hired since July 1, 1985) receive only 5.2 annual leave days in their first year of employment, and 10.4 in their fifth year.

(g) Employee may be eligible for ordinary disability (half-pay) through retirement system.

(h) Massachusetts provides maternity leave, and also offers parental and adoptive leave through collective bargaining agreements.

Table 7.5
STATE EMPLOYEES: PAID HOLIDAYS*

State or other jurisdiction	Major holidays(a)	Martin Luther King's Birthday(b)	Lincoln's Birthday	President's Day(c)	Washington's Birthday(c)	Good Friday	Memorial Day(d)	Columbus Day(e)	Veteran's Day	Day after Thanksgiving	Day before or after Christmas	Day before or after New Year's	Election Day(f)	Other(g)
Alabama	★	★(h)	...	...	★	...	★	★	★	...	...	...	...	★
Alaska (i)	★	...	...	★	...	...	★	...	★	...	Before	...	...	★
Arizona	★	(h)	★	...	★	...	★	★	★	...	...	...	...	...
Arkansas	★	★	★	...	★	...	★	...	★	★	...	...	...	★
California	★	★	★	★	...	...	★	★	★	...	...	...	...	...
Colorado	★	★	...	★	★	★	★	★	★	...	...	...	★	★
Connecticut	★	★	★	...	★	★	★	★	★	...	...	...	...	...
Delaware	★	★	...	★	...	...	★	★	★	★	(j)	...	★	★
Florida	★	★	★	...	★	...	★	★	★	(j)	...	...	...	★
Georgia	★	★	...	...	★	...	★	★	★	...	...	...	...	★
Hawaii	★	...	...	★	...	★	★	...	★	...	...	...	...	★
Idaho	★	...	★	...	★(j)	★	★	★(k)	...	...	...	...	★	★
Illinois	★	(j)	★	...	★	...	★	★	★	...	...	...	★	★
Indiana	★	★	★	★	★(j)	★	★	★	★	★	...	...	★(l)	★
Iowa	★	★★	...	...	...	...	★	★	★	...	...	...	...	...
Kansas	★	★	★	★	...	...	★	...	★	★	...	...	...	★
Kentucky	★	...	★	...	★	(m)★	★	...	★	(n)	(n)	(n)	(o)	★(p)
Louisiana	★	(h)	★★	★	...	★	★	★	★	★	...	...	★	★
Maine	★	★	...	...	★	...	★	★	...	...	...	...	...	★
Maryland	★	★	...	★	★	★	★	★	★	★	...	...	★	★
Massachusetts	★	(r)	...	...	...	...	★	...	★	...	...	...	...	★
Michigan	★	★	★	★	...	...	★	★	★	★	Before	Before	...	★(p)
Minnesota	★	★	...	★	...	...	★(q)	(s)	★	★	...	...	(s)	...
Mississippi	★	★	...	...	★	...	★	★	★	★	...	...	★	★★
Missouri	★	...	...	★	...	...	★	★	★	★	(j)	...	★	★★★
Montana	★	...	...	...	★(j)	...	★	★	★	...	...	...	...	★(s)
Nebraska	★	★	★	★	...	...	★	...	★	★	Before	Before	...	...
Nevada	★	★	...	...	...	★(t)	★	★	★	(j)	(j)	...	(s)★	...
New Hampshire	★	★	...	...	...	★★	★	★	★	★	...	...	★	★★★
New Jersey	★	★	...	★	...	★	★	★	★	...	Before	...	...	★(s)
New Mexico	★	...	...	...	...	...	★	...	★	...	...	...	...	...
New York	★	★	★	...	★	...	★	★	★	...	...	...	...	...
North Carolina	★	...	...	...	...	...	★	...	★	...	...	...	...	...
North Dakota	★	★	...	...	★	...	★	★	★	...	...	...	...	...
Ohio	★	★	...	★★	...	...	★	★	★	...	...	...	...	...

STATE EMPLOYEES: PAID HOLIDAYS—Continued

State or other jurisdiction	Major holidays(a)	Martin Luther King's Birthday(b)	Lincoln's Birthday	President's Day(c)	Washington's Birthday(c)	Good Friday	Memorial Day(d)	Columbus Day(e)	Veteran's Day	Day after Thanksgiving	Day before or after Christmas	Day before or after New Year's	Election Day(f)	Other(g)
Oklahoma	★	★		★			★		★	★	★			
Oregon	★	★		★			★		★		After			
Pennsylvania	★	★		★			★	★	★				★	
Rhode Island	★	★			★		★	★	★	★			★	★
South Carolina	★						★		★					★
South Dakota	★			★	★		★	★(u)	★					★
Tennessee	★	★(v)			★	★(w)	★		★	★				
Texas	★	★(x)		★	★		★	★	★					★
Utah	★	★(v)	★(v)		★		★	★	★					★
Vermont	★						★		★					★
Virginia	★	★(y)		★			★	★(z)	★				★	★
Washington	★	★	★		★		★		★			Before	★(l)	★
West Virginia	★	★					★	★	★		Before	Before		★
Wisconsin	★	★		★	★	★(m)	★						★	
Wyoming	★						★		★					
Dist. of Col.	★	★					★	★	★	★				★
American Samoa	★	★		★	★	★	★	★	★					★
Guam	★	★		★	★	★	★	★	★				★	★
No. Mariana Is.	★			★	★	★	★	★	★					★
Puerto Rico	★	★	★			★	★	★	★		(bb)		★	★
Virgin Islands	★	★		★		★	★	★(aa)	★			Before(cc)	★	★

STATE EMPLOYEES: PAID HOLIDAYS—Continued

*Holidays in addition to any other authorized paid personal leave granted state employees.

Note: In some states, the governor may proclaim additional holidays or select from a number of holidays for observance by state employees. In some states, the list of paid holiday's is determined by the personnel department at the beginning of each year; as a result, the number of holidays may change from year to year. Number of paid holidays may also vary across some employee classifications. Dates given are for 1988 and may change slightly for 1989. If holiday falls on a weekend, generally employees get the day preceding or following.

Key:

. .—Paid holiday not granted.

(a) New Year's Day, Independence Day, Labor Day, Thanksgiving Day, and Christmas Day.

(b) Third Monday in January.

(c) Generally, third Monday in February; Washington's Birthday or Presidents' Day. In some states, the holiday is called Presidents' Day or Washington-Lincoln Day. Most frequently, this day recognizes Washington and Lincoln.

(d) Last Monday in May in all states indicated, except New Hampshire where holiday is observed on May 30. Generally, states follow the Federal Government's observance (last Monday in May) rather than the traditional Memorial Day (May 30).

(e) Second Monday in October.

(f) General election day only, unless otherwise indicated.

(g) Additional holidays:

Alabama — Robert E. Lee and Martin Luther King's Birthdays (Jan. 18), Mardi Gras Day (varies, Feb. 16), Thomas Jefferson's birthday (April 13), Confederate Memorial Day (April 25), Jefferson Davis's Birthday (June 6).

Alaska — Seward's Day (last Mon. in March), Alaska Day (Oct. 18), one floating holiday.

Arkansas — Robert E. Lee's Birthday (and Martin Luther King's) (Third Monday in Jan.), employee's birthday.

Colorado — Colorado Day (Aug. 1).

Georgia — Robert E. Lee's Birthday (Jan. 19; observed on Nov. 25), Confederate Memorial Day (Apr. 26).

Hawaii — Prince Jonah Kuhio Kalanianaole Day (March 25), King Kameh ameha Day (June 10), Admission Day (August 9).

Kansas — Discretionary day (taken whenever employee chooses with supervisor's approval).

Louisiana — Mardi Gras Day (day before Ash Wednesday), Inauguration Day (every four years, in Baton Rouge only).

Maine — Patriot's Day (April 18).

Maryland — Maryland Day (March 25), Defenders' Day (Sept. 12).

Massachusetts — Evacuation Day (March 17), Patriot's Day (Apr. 18; always on Monday), Bunker Hill Day (June 17; all three in Suffolk County only.

Mississippi — Confederate Memorial Day (Apr. 25; last Monday in April), Jefferson Davis's Birthday (May 30; last Monday in May).

Missouri — Harry Truman's Birthday (May 8).

Montana — Heritage Day (varies; set annually).

Nebraska — Arbor Day (April 22).

Nevada — Nevada Day (Oct. 31).

New Hampshire — Fast Day (in April; date varies).

Rhode Island — Victory Day (2nd Mon. in Aug.)

South Carolina — Discretionay day (taken whenever employee chooses with supervisor's approval).

South Dakota — Pioneer Day (2nd Mon. in Oct.)

Texas — Confederate Heroes Day (Jan. 19), Texas Independence Day (March 2), Lyndon Johnson's Birthday (Aug. 27), Sanjacinto Day (April 21), Emancipation Day (June 19); offices remain open; none observed on another day if it falls on weekend.

Utah — Pioneer Day (July 24).

Vermont — Town Meeting Day (1st Tues. in March), Battle of Bennington Day (Aug. 16).

Virginia — Lee/Jackson Day (3rd Mon. in Jan., same as Martin Luther King's Birthday).

West Virginia — West Virginia Day (June 20).

District of Columbia — Inauguration Day (every 4 years).

American Samoa — Flag Day (April 17); Manu'a Islands Cession Day (normally July 16).

Guam — Guam Discovery Day (1st Mon. in March), Liberation Day (July 21), Lady of Camarin Day (Dec. 8),

Northern Mariana Islands — Commonwealth Day (Jan. 8), Covenant Day (March 24), Citizenship Day (Nov. 4), Constitution Day (Dec. 8),

Puerto Rico — Three Kings Day (Jan. 6), DeHostos' Birthday (Jan. 11), Abolition of Slavery Day (March 25), Jose de Diego's Birthday (April 16), Luis Munoz Rivera's Birthday (July 17), Commonwealth Constitution Day (July 25), Jose C. Barbosa's Birthday (July 27), Discovery of Puerto Rico Day (Nov. 19).

Virgin Islands — Three Kings Day (Jan. 6), Transfer Day (March 31), Holy Thursday (varies), Easter Monday, Carnival in St. Thomas (3rd Fri. after Easter), Organic Act Day (3rd Mon. in June), Emancipation Day (July 3), Hurricane Supplication Day (4th Mon. in July), Local Thanksgiving and End of Hurricane Season (3rd Mon. in Oct.), Liberty Day (varies; early Nov.).

(h) Also for Robert E. Lee's Birthday.

(i) Bargaining process over dates of observance continues; thus, some holidays may move to floating ones.

(j) Robert E. Lee's and Washington's birthdays in Georgia and Lincoln's and Washington's birth-days in Indiana will be observed instead on Nov. 25 (day after Thanksgiving) and Dec. 23 (day before Christmas); in New Mexico, President's Day and Martin Luther King's birthday will be observed on Nov. 25 (day after Thanksgiving) and December 23 (day before Christmas); also in Indiana, Martin Luther King's birthday will be observed on Dec. 31 (New Year's Eve).

(k) Discoverer's Day.

(l) Also, primary election day.

(m) Half days.

(n) One extra day designated for each holiday.

(o) Presidential election day only.

(p) One floating holiday.

(q) Also for Jefferson Davis' Birthday.

(r) Work; but called Day of Observance.

(s) State offices remain open; employees receive three floating holidays in lieu of these statutory holidays.

(t) Called Easter Friday.

(u) May observe on day after Thanksgiving.

(v) Offices open; employee may take on another day.

(w) Good Friday is optional for Martin Luther King's Birthday.

(x) Called Human Rights Day; celebrates Martin Luther King and others who worked for human rights.

(y) Martin Luther King's Birthday and Lee/Jackson Day.

(z) And Yorktown Victory Day.

(aa) And Puerto Rico Friendship Day.

(bb) Half day before and full day after.

(cc) Called Old Year's Day.

Table 7.6
SUMMARY OF STATE GOVERNMENT EMPLOYMENT: 1952-1986

	Employment (in thousands)						Monthly payrolls (in millions of dollars)			Average monthly earnings of full-time employees		
	Total, full-time and part-time			Full-time equivalent								
Year	All	Educa-tion	Other	All	Educa-tion	Other	All	Educa-tion	Other	All	Educa-tion	Other
October:												
1986.............	4,068	1,800	2,267	3,437	1,256	2,181	$6,801.4	$2,583.4	$4,226.9	$2,052	$2,263	$1,956
1985.............	3,984	1,764	2,220	2,990	945	2,046	6,328.6	2,443.7	3,884.9	1,935	2,155	1,834
1984.............	3,898	1,708	2,190	3,177	1,091	2,086	5,814.9	2,178.0	3,637.0	1,825	1,991	1,740
1983.............	3,816	1,666	2,150	3,116	1,072	2,044	5,345.5	1,989.0	3,357.0	1,711	1,850	1,640
1982.............	3,747	1,616	2,131	3,083	1,051	2,032	5,027.7	1,874.0	3,153.7	1,625	1,789	1,551
1981.............	3,726	1,603	2,123	3,087	1,063	2,024	4,667.5	1,768.0	2,899.5	1,507	1,671	1,432
1980.............	3,753	1,599	2,154	3,106	1,063	2,044	4,284.7	1,608.0	2,676.6	1,373	1,523	1,305
1979.............	3,699	1,577	2,122	3,072	1,046	2,026	3,869.3	1,451.4	2,417.9	1,257	1,399	1,193
1978.............	3,539	1,508	2,032	2,966	1,016	1,950	3,483.0	1,332.9	2,150.2	1,167	1,311	1,102
1977.............	3,491	1,484	2,007	2,903	1,005	1,898	3,194.6	1,234.4	1,960.1	1,096	1,237	1,031
1976.............	3,343	1,434	1,910	2,799	973	1,827	2,893.7	1,111.5	1,782.1	1,031	1,163	975
1975.............	3,271	1,400	1,870	2,744	952	1,792	2,652.7	1,021.7	1,631.1	964	1,080	909
1974.............	3,155	1,357	1,798	2,653	929	1,725	2,409.5	932.7	1,476.9	906	1,023	855
1973.............	3,013	1,280	1,733	2,547	887	1,660	2,158.2	822.2	1,336.0	843	952	805
1972.............	2,957	1,267	1,690	2,487	867	1,619	1,936.6	746.9	1,189.7	778	871	734
1971.............	2,832	1,223	1,609	2,384	841	1,544	1,741.7	681.5	1,060.2	731	826	686
1970.............	2,755	1,182	1,573	2,302	803	1,499	1,612.2	630.3	981.9	700	797	605
1969.............	2,614	1,112	1,501	2,179	746	1,433	1,430.5	554.5	876.1	655	743	597
1968.............	2,495	1,037	1,458	2,085	694	1,391	1,256.7	477.1	779.6	602	687	544
1967.............	2,335	940	1,395	1,946	620	1,326	1,105.5	406.3	699.3	567	666	526
1966.............	2,211	866	1,344	1,864	575	1,289	975.2	353.0	622.2	522	614	483
1965.............	2,028	739	1,289	1,751	508	1,243	849.2	290.1	559.1	484	571	450
1964.............	1,873	656	1,217	1,639	460	1,179	761.1	257.5	503.6	464	560	427
1963.............	1,775	602	1,173	1,558	422	1,136	696.4	230.1	466.3	447	545	410
1962.............	1,680	555	1,126	1,478	389	1,088	634.6	201.8	432.8	429	518	397
1961.............	1,625	518	1,107	1,435	367	1,068	586.2	192.4	393.8	409	482	383
1960.............	1,527	474	1,053	1,353	332	1,021	524.1	167.7	356.4	386	439	365
1959.............	1,454	443	1,011	1,302	318	984	485.4	136.0	349.4	373	427	352
1958.............	1,408	406	1,002	1,259	284	975	446.5	123.4	323.1	355	416	333
April 1957	1,300	375	925	1,153	257	896	372.5	106.1	266.4	320	355	309
1956.............	1,268	353	915	1,136	250	886	366.5	108.8	257.7	321	358	309
1955.............	1,199	333	866	1,081	244	837	325.9	88.5	237.4	302	334	290
1954.............	1,149	310	839	1,024	222	802	300.7	78.9	221.8	294	325	283
1953.............	1,082	294	788	966	211	755	278.6	73.5	205.1	289	320	278
1952.............	1,060	293	767	958	213	745	260.3	65.1	195.2	271	298	262

Source: U.S. Bureau of the Census, annual *Public Employment* reports.
Note: Because of rounding, detail may not add to totals.

Table 7.7
EMPLOYMENT AND PAYROLLS OF STATE AND LOCAL GOVERNMENTS, BY FUNCTION: OCTOBER 1985

Function	All employees, full-time and part-time (in thousands)			October payrolls (in millions of dollars)			Average October earnings of full-time employees
	Total	State governments	Local governments	Total	State governments	Local governments	
All functions	13,669	3,984	9,685	$21,365	$6,329	$15,036	$1,885
Education:							
Higher education	2,011	1,639	371	2,669	2,229	440	2,193
Instructional personnel only	696	511	185	1,328	1,067	261	2,990
Elementary/secondary schools	4,994	25	4,969	7,839	39	7,800	1,877
Instructional personnel only	3,306	15	3,291	6,158	29	6,129	2,093
Local libraries	113	0	113	110	0	110	1,442
Other education	100	100	0	176	176	0	1,895
Selected functions:							
Highways	549	252	296	908	460	448	1,719
Public welfare	418	186	232	621	307	314	1,591
Hospitals	1,102	548	554	1,666	859	807	1,626
Health..............................	288	130	158	468	232	236	1,782
Police protection.....................	694	81	613	1,328	175	1,153	2,129
Police officers only	510	52	458	1,109	125	984	2,282
Fire protection	317	0	317	554	0	554	2,346
Firefighters only	291	0	291	523	0	523	2,370
Natural resources	202	163	39	308	258	50	1,799
Correction	357	231	126	639	421	218	1,837
Social insurance administration	106	106	0	189	189	0	1,881
Financial administration	320	131	190	491	229	262	1,704
General control	593	138	455	857	295	562	1,926
Local utilities.......................	420	26	394	914	70	844	2,263

Source: U.S. Bureau of the Census, *Public Employment in 1985*.
Note: Statistics for local governments are estimates subject to sampling variation. Because of rounding, detail may not add to totals.

Table 7.8
EMPLOYMENT AND PAYROLLS OF STATE AND LOCAL
GOVERNMENTS, BY FUNCTION: OCTOBER 1986

Function	All employees, full-time and part-time (in thousands)			October payrolls (in millions of dollars)			Average October earnings of full-time employees
	Total	State govern-ments	Local govern-ments	Total	State govern-ments	Local govern-ments	
All functions	13,913	4,068	9,846	$23,109	$6,810	$16,298	$2,009
Education:							
Higher education	2,049	1,675	374	2,831	2,357	474	2,306
Instructional personnel only	704	520	184	1,426	1,149	277	3,185
Elementary/secondary schools	5,090	24	5,065	8,662	40	8,622	2,038
Instructional personnel only	3,375	16	3,359	6,814	30	6,784	2,276
Local libraries	117	1	116	119	1	119	1,512
Other education	101	101	0	187	187	0	1,996
Selected functions:							
Highways	550	253	297	956	485	471	1,801
Public welfare	430	190	239	677	333	343	1,678
Hospitals	1,099	554	544	1,737	914	822	1,699
Health...............................	291	128	163	499	245	255	1,879
Police protection.....................	704	79	625	1,410	183	1,227	2,220
Police officers only	515	53	462	1,170	137	1,033	2,378
Fire protection	326	0	326	603	0	603	2,503
Firefighters only	299	0	299	566	0	566	2,536
Natural resources	195	157	38	322	269	52	1,977
Correction	376	244	132	713	469	244	1,940
Social insurance administration	105	105	0	197	197	0	1,950
Financial administration	328	134	194	526	247	280	1,792
General control......................	610	140	470	908	316	592	2,032
Local utilities.......................	426	26	400	959	75	883	2,335

Source: U.S. Bureau of the Census, *Public Employment in 1986.*
Note: Statistics for local governments are estimates subject to sampling variation. Because of rounding, detail may not add to totals.

Table 7.9
STATE AND LOCAL GOVERNMENT EMPLOYMENT, BY STATE: OCTOBER 1985

State or other jurisdiction	All employees (full-time and part-time)		Full-time equivalent employment					
			Number			Number per 10,000 population		
	State	Local	Total	State	Local	Total	State	Local
United States	3,983,689	9,685,325	10,567,675	2,990,470	7,577,205	443	125	317
Alabama................	80,162	146,024	184,951	62,673	122,278	460	156	304
Alaska..................	25,838	23,476	39,436	20,926	18,510	757	402	355
Arizona................	53,109	130,145	136,047	34,767	101,280	427	109	318
Arkansas	44,369	81,748	101,727	35,159	66,568	431	149	282
California	328,182	1,123,851	1,044,404	235,012	809,392	396	89	307
Colorado	62,090	140,167	142,934	36,665	106,269	442	113	329
Connecticut	61,891	107,133	135,714	49,206	86,508	428	155	273
Delaware	20,980	17,558	30,338	15,644	14,694	488	252	236
Florida	138,945	428,776	480,730	110,394	370,336	423	97	326
Georgia................	97,881	266,080	304,315	80,202	224,113	509	134	375
Hawaii	47,583	12,744	47,768	36,076	11,692	453	342	111
Idaho	18,858	41,663	42,838	12,909	29,929	426	128	298
Illinois.................	155,062	471,899	462,279	109,419	352,860	401	95	306
Indiana	95,515	217,458	226,369	62,578	163,791	412	114	298
Iowa	59,003	130,021	129,331	39,528	89,803	448	137	311
Kansas	53,513	117,642	120,170	35,792	84,378	490	146	344
Kentucky	70,803	113,906	149,788	56,906	92,882	402	153	249
Louisiana	106,497	166,528	225,859	83,047	142,812	504	185	319
Maine	24,594	44,039	49,584	17,876	31,708	426	154	272
Maryland	88,715	159,624	194,654	68,652	126,002	443	156	287
Massachusetts	93,991	215,779	252,002	76,597	175,405	433	132	301
Michigan	155,534	389,461	375,928	101,534	274,394	414	112	302
Minnesota	75,034	183,285	172,684	47,463	125,221	412	113	299
Mississippi	50,404	107,340	129,505	40,118	89,387	496	154	342
Missouri	74,497	185,250	204,967	58,265	146,702	408	116	292
Montana...............	21,436	35,778	39,555	14,329	25,226	479	173	305
Nebraska	34,413	79,244	82,599	26,166	56,433	514	163	351
Nevada	15,820	36,712	42,525	12,609	29,916	454	135	320
New Hampshire	21,287	37,568	39,176	13,805	25,371	393	138	254
New Jersey.............	104,980	319,435	350,802	87,639	263,163	464	116	348
New Mexico............	42,287	53,253	75,998	30,160	45,838	524	208	316
New York	288,462	906,461	987,216	256,538	730,678	555	144	411
North Carolina	107,216	256,968	283,788	86,110	197,678	454	138	316
North Dakota	19,261	35,244	31,342	12,297	19,045	458	180	278
Ohio	150,812	427,999	431,940	101,694	330,246	402	95	307
Oklahoma	71,525	124,263	157,550	53,283	104,267	477	161	316
Oregon	55,531	113,069	116,773	36,753	80,020	435	137	298
Pennsylvania	144,407	390,433	422,813	113,363	309,450	357	96	261
Rhode Island	25,285	26,023	40,085	17,535	22,550	414	181	233
South Carolina	74,156	119,885	158,809	59,711	99,098	474	178	296
South Dakota	16,835	32,947	32,127	11,202	20,925	454	158	296
Tennessee	78,719	171,095	207,788	62,610	145,178	436	131	305
Texas..................	229,342	674,115	763,535	177,625	585,910	466	109	358
Utah	37,347	59,435	67,991	27,737	40,254	413	169	245
Vermont	12,957	18,693	23,469	10,523	12,946	439	197	242
Virginia................	119,216	212,467	259,353	88,432	170,921	455	155	300
Washington	97,258	161,504	192,091	65,324	126,767	436	148	288
West Virginia	43,000	66,014	93,436	35,026	58,410	483	181	302
Wisconsin	76,413	221,521	203,235	53,031	150,204	426	111	315
Wyoming	12,674	31,725	32,298	9,560	22,738	635	188	447

Source: U.S. Bureau of the Census, *Public Employment in 1985.*
Note: Statistics for local governments are estimates subject to sampling variation. Because of rounding, detail may not add to totals.

Table 7.10
STATE AND LOCAL GOVERNMENT EMPLOYMENT, BY STATE:
OCTOBER 1986

State or other jurisdiction	All employees (full-time and part-time)		Full-time equivalent employment					
			Number			Number per 10,000 population		
	State	Local	Total	State	Local	Total	State	Local
United States	4,067,587	9,845,538	11,852,532	3,437,458	8,415,074	492	143	349
Alabama...............	80,191	147,506	201,434	70,431	131,003	497	174	323
Alaska.................	23,744	23,732	41,132	20,989	20,143	770	393	377
Arizona................	55,710	137,106	161,202	42,520	118,682	486	128	358
Arkansas	44,900	83,063	109,492	38,672	70,820	462	163	299
California.............	337,324	1,155,504	1,244,316	279,451	964,865	461	104	358
Colorado	62,468	142,972	172,957	50,488	122,469	529	155	375
Connecticut	62,242	107,652	150,525	55,790	94,735	472	175	297
Delaware	21,553	17,806	33,175	17,198	15,977	524	272	252
Florida	141,520	449,456	530,364	123,589	406,775	454	106	348
Georgia...............	102,500	256,669	329,486	90,743	238,743	540	149	391
Hawaii	49,068	12,736	53,272	41,268	12,004	502	389	113
Idaho	19,524	42,084	50,791	17,508	33,283	506	175	332
Illinois...............	158,458	475,748	514,732	130,147	384,585	446	113	333
Indiana	96,132	220,047	256,828	75,125	181,703	467	136	330
Iowa	58,665	129,747	158,074	56,761	101,313	554	199	355
Kansas	54,026	120,130	138,821	42,839	95,982	564	174	390
Kentucky	72,459	116,890	165,914	63,421	102,493	445	170	275
Louisiana	100,334	166,532	237,227	85,748	151,479	527	191	337
Maine	25,066	46,018	55,793	19,758	36,035	475	168	307
Maryland	90,062	163,251	222,912	79,571	143,341	499	178	321
Massachusetts	100,587	219,006	279,803	88,203	191,600	480	151	329
Michigan	158,299	397,059	443,391	128,356	315,035	485	140	344
Minnesota	76,024	180,105	198,417	60,919	137,498	471	145	326
Mississippi	48,931	109,960	137,852	42,382	95,470	525	161	364
Missouri	77,881	185,857	222,824	65,784	157,040	440	130	310
Montana...............	20,934	35,880	44,285	15,718	28,567	541	192	349
Nebraska	34,592	82,664	94,412	29,375	65,037	591	184	407
Nevada	16,278	36,543	47,840	14,823	33,017	497	154	343
New Hampshire	22,017	38,281	47,012	17,715	29,297	458	172	285
New Jersey	109,756	323,035	378,982	95,837	283,145	497	126	372
New Mexico............	42,172	54,390	83,343	34,174	49,169	564	231	332
New York	292,930	918,499	1,082,111	272,056	810,055	609	153	456
North Carolina	111,376	259,304	308,909	92,804	216,105	488	147	341
North Dakota	19,821	34,722	36,660	15,053	21,607	540	222	318
Ohio	157,121	435,209	486,700	121,620	365,080	453	113	340
Oklahoma	71,519	124,277	173,248	64,434	108,814	524	195	329
Oregon	57,476	115,121	135,281	44,018	91,263	501	163	338
Pennsylvania	143,260	392,908	464,180	124,030	340,150	390	104	286
Rhode Island	25,233	26,621	42,867	18,975	23,892	440	195	245
South Carolina	77,825	123,121	177,842	68,918	108,924	526	204	322
South Dakota	16,661	34,654	35,888	12,531	23,357	507	177	330
Tennessee	81,347	175,160	227,659	70,591	157,068	474	147	327
Texas.................	225,050	692,915	825,603	192,633	632,970	495	115	379
Utah	38,656	61,272	80,007	32,850	47,157	481	197	283
Vermont	12,999	19,175	26,015	11,427	14,588	481	211	270
Virginia...............	123,266	217,539	296,780	102,146	194,634	513	177	336
Washington	103,335	166,343	222,089	79,086	143,003	498	177	320
West Virginia	40,339	66,884	95,311	34,468	60,843	497	180	317
Wisconsin..............	93,331	219,952	241,780	73,736	168,044	505	154	351
Wyoming	12,625	31,334	35,843	10,779	25,064	707	213	494
District of Col.	0	53,099	51,151	0	51,151	817	0	817

Source: U.S. Bureau of the Census, *Public Employment in 1986.*
Note: Statistics for local governments are estimates subject to sampling variation. Because of rounding, detail may not add to totals.

Table 7.11
STATE AND LOCAL GOVERNMENT PAYROLLS AND
AVERAGE EARNINGS OF FULL-TIME EMPLOYEES,
BY STATE: OCTOBER 1985

State or other jurisdiction	Amount of payroll (in thousands of dollars)			Percentage of October payroll		Average earnings of full-time state and local government employees (dollars)		
	Total	State government	Local governments	State government	Local governments	All	Education employees	Other
United States.........	$21,364,692	$6,328,586	$15,036,106	29.6	70.4	$1,885	$1,940	$1,837
Alabama...............	313,237	126,056	187,181	40.2	59.8	1,606	1,695	1,520
Alaska.................	129,235	66,604	62,631	51.5	48.5	3,101	3,257	2,997
Arizona...............	298,353	77,241	221,112	25.9	74.1	2,050	2,083	2,015
Arkansas	151,876	61,918	89,958	40.8	59.2	1,418	1,483	1,344
California.............	2,777,231	669,195	2,108,036	24.1	75.9	2,424	2,507	2,358
Colorado	315,995	99,075	216,920	31.4	68.6	2,008	1,973	2,041
Connecticut	287,535	108,877	178,658	37.9	62.1	2,016	2,030	2,002
Delaware	57,569	29,424	28,145	51.1	48.9	1,791	1,907	1,686
Florida	855,304	198,085	657,220	23.2	76.8	1,696	1,713	1,682
Georgia...............	487,282	146,151	341,130	30.0	70.0	1,527	1,588	1,477
Hawaii	92,177	69,393	22,785	75.3	24.7	1,816	1,883	1,766
Idaho	74,344	25,916	48,428	34.9	65.1	1,575	1,571	1,579
Illinois...............	987,051	258,419	728,633	26.2	73.8	1,969	2,065	1,885
Indiana	412,450	137,561	274,889	33.4	66.6	1,665	1,880	1,422
Iowa	252,362	92,660	159,702	36.7	63.3	1,716	1,752	1,673
Kansas	212,586	65,619	146,967	30.9	69.1	1,621	1,677	1,557
Kentucky	252,068	97,070	144,998	40.1	59.9	1,533	1,604	1,454
Louisiana	367,101	147,361	219,740	40.1	59.9	1,543	1,590	1,502
Maine	82,388	32,392	49,996	39.3	60.7	1,538	1,537	1,539
Maryland	426,765	143,910	282,855	33.7	66.3	2,035	2,262	1,843
Massachusetts	516,129	157,601	358,528	30.5	69.5	1,950	1,998	1,913
Michigan	890,120	252,869	637,251	28.4	71.6	2,144	2,234	2,044
Minnesota	401,303	125,556	275,748	31.3	68.7	2,059	2,108	2,013
Mississippi	178,609	62,337	116,272	34.9	65.1	1,295	1,343	1,247
Missouri	353,373	97,041	256,332	27.5	72.5	1,620	1,687	1,558
Montana	74,453	28,534	45,919	38.3	61.7	1,722	1,857	1,591
Nebraska	143,470	41,191	102,279	28.7	71.3	1,587	1,549	1,624
Nevada	92,140	26,734	65,406	29.0	71.0	2,027	1,973	2,061
New Hampshire	68,270	25,717	42,554	37.7	62.3	1,573	1,609	1,534
New Jersey............	737,345	189,720	547,625	25.7	74.3	2,016	2,211	1,838
New Mexico...........	132,101	56,942	75,159	43.1	56.9	1,634	1,671	1,597
New York	2,271,241	584,733	1,686,508	25.7	74.3	2,185	2,258	2,146
North Carolina	509,753	174,842	334,911	34.3	65.7	1,663	1,801	1,518
North Dakota	63,145	24,279	38,867	38.4	61.6	1,832	2,070	1,542
Ohio	834,924	213,391	621,533	25.6	74.4	1,791	1,914	1,672
Oklahoma	263,512	101,433	162,079	38.5	61.5	1,568	1,628	1,508
Oregon	245,111	80,752	164,359	32.9	67.1	1,886	1,897	1,875
Pennsylvania	821,690	218,913	602,778	26.6	73.4	1,839	1,925	1,761
Rhode Island	84,784	35,503	49,281	41.9	58.1	2,017	2,218	1,848
South Carolina	253,702	106,766	146,936	42.1	57.9	1,510	1,597	1,416
South Dakota	50,185	18,968	31,218	37.8	62.2	1,436	1,485	1,379
Tennessee	337,208	111,124	226,084	33.0	67.0	1,549	1,617	1,492
Texas.................	1,374,916	357,424	1,017,492	26.0	74.0	1,723	1,714	1,733
Utah	132,370	53,626	78,744	40.5	59.5	1,794	1,760	1,839
Vermont	40,581	18,865	21,715	46.5	53.5	1,604	1,649	1,548
Virginia...............	483,541	170,913	312,628	35.3	64.7	1,721	1,788	1,650
Washington	423,991	144,673	279,318	34.1	65.9	2,042	1,970	2,100
West Virginia	144,977	53,464	91,513	36.9	63.1	1,495	1,645	1,315
Wisconsin.............	431,983	121,867	310,117	28.2	71.8	1,929	2,047	1,806
Wyoming	65,863	19,883	45,980	30.2	69.8	1,867	2,000	1,744
District of Columbia	120,990	. . .	120,990	. . .	100.0	2,477	2,774	2,382

Source: U.S. Bureau of the Census, *Public Employment in 1985.*
Note: Statistics for local governments are estimates subject to sampling variation. Because of rounding, detail may not add to totals.

Table 7.12
STATE AND LOCAL GOVERNMENT PAYROLLS AND AVERAGE EARNINGS OF FULL-TIME EMPLOYEES, BY STATE: OCTOBER 1986

State or other jurisdiction	Amount of payroll (in thousands of dollars)			Percentage of October payroll		Average earnings of full-time state and local government employees (dollars)		
	Total	State government	Local governments	State government	Local governments	All	Education employees	Other
United States..........	$23,108,804	$6,810,358	$16,298,446	29.5	70.5	$2,009	$2,090	$1,937
Alabama...............	325,306	128,153	197,152	39.4	60.6	1,652	1,746	1,562
Alaska.................	130,327	65,150	65,177	50.0	50.0	3,275	3,302	3,257
Arizona...............	333,764	86,099	247,665	25.8	74.2	2,170	2,289	2,050
Arkansas	160,974	64,112	96,862	39.8	60.2	1,504	1,589	1,410
California.............	3,060,800	737,885	2,322,915	24.1	75.9	2,583	2,636	2,544
Colorado	350,472	112,785	237,687	32.2	67.8	2,106	2,111	2,100
Connecticut	316,469	124,233	192,236	39.3	60.7	2,178	2,145	2,211
Delaware	62,045	30,988	31,057	49.9	50.1	1,890	2,030	1,758
Florida	964,146	212,204	751,942	22.0	78.0	1,844	1,917	1,787
Georgia...............	533,025	161,823	371,202	30.4	69.6	1,650	1,738	1,580
Hawaii	97,553	73,674	23,880	75.5	24.5	1,884	1,969	1,823
Idaho	77,835	27,592	50,244	35.4	64.6	1,607	1,612	1,600
Illinois................	1,077,351	271,001	806,350	25.2	74.8	2,165	2,287	2,056
Indiana	442,616	145,339	297,278	32.8	67.2	1,788	2,042	1,497
Iowa	264,264	96,469	167,796	36.5	63.5	1,832	1,923	1,727
Kansas	227,032	68,375	158,657	30.1	69.9	1,696	1,787	1,593
Kentucky	261,649	101,893	159,755	38.9	61.1	1,617	1,725	1,496
Louisiana	365,690	141,282	224,408	38.6	61.4	1,558	1,636	1,488
Maine	89,450	33,714	55,736	37.7	62.3	1,635	1,663	1,603
Maryland	462,944	156,363	306,581	33.8	66.2	2,167	2,415	1,958
Massachusetts	563,266	174,624	388,642	31.0	69.0	2,067	2,108	2,035
Michigan	995,213	300,698	694,516	30.2	69.8	2,387	2,494	2,268
Minnesota	450,796	133,763	317,033	29.7	70.3	2,348	2,617	2,089
Mississippi	184,560	60,426	124,134	32.7	67.3	1,356	1,447	1,266
Missouri	383,414	105,745	277,669	27.6	72.4	1,766	1,914	1,632
Montana	76,015	28,482	47,533	37.5	62.5	1,776	1,923	1,628
Nebraska	154,826	43,514	111,313	28.1	71.9	1,698	1,680	1,716
Nevada	96,063	28,751	67,312	29.9	70.1	2,093	1,997	2,160
New Hampshire	77,004	28,787	48,217	37.4	62.6	1,721	1,765	1,674
New Jersey............	812,398	216,533	595,866	26.7	73.3	2,180	2,405	1,973
New Mexico............	138,948	59,111	79,837	42.5	57.5	1,724	1,787	1,658
New York	2,415,041	633,785	1,781,256	26.2	73.8	2,289	2,424	2,217
North Carolina	526,624	175,474	351,150	33.3	66.7	1,744	1,881	1,597
North Dakota	67,086	25,707	41,379	38.3	61.7	1,931	2,231	1,579
Ohio	911,613	231,798	679,815	25.4	74.6	1,928	2,097	1,768
Oklahoma	273,280	103,256	170,025	37.8	62.2	1,642	1,713	1,573
Oregon	264,117	85,804	178,313	32.5	67.5	2,004	2,059	1,950
Pennsylvania	880,736	229,223	651,513	26.0	74.0	1,960	2,095	1,836
Rhode Island	89,220	37,430	51,790	42.0	58.0	2,140	2,373	1,943
South Carolina	281,068	115,593	165,475	41.1	58.9	1,614	1,762	1,462
South Dakota	53,338	20,345	32,993	38.1	61.9	1,526	1,601	1,438
Tennessee	362,078	120,957	241,121	33.4	66.6	1,612	1,706	1,531
Texas.................	1,450,007	360,803	1,089,205	24.9	75.1	1,788	1,821	1,749
Utah	138,207	52,950	85,257	38.3	61.7	1,796	1,782	1,815
Vermont	43,592	20,243	23,349	46.4	53.6	1,737	1,781	1,681
Virginia...............	525,309	188,477	336,832	35.9	64.1	1,824	1,892	1,750
Washington	465,688	168,656	297,032	36.2	63.8	2,167	2,132	2,196
West Virginia	151,565	53,547	98,018	35.3	64.7	1,606	1,763	1,399
Wisconsin..............	476,422	146,971	329,451	30.8	69.2	2,062	2,193	1,914
Wyoming	67,549	19,776	47,774	29.3	70.7	1,954	2,170	1,736
District of Col.	130,046	. . .	130,046	. . .	100.0	2,594	2,788	2,538

Source: U.S. Bureau of the Census, *Public Employment in 1986.*
Note: Statistics for local governments are estimates subject to sampling variation. Because of rounding, detail may not add to totals.

Table 7.13
STATE GOVERNMENT EMPLOYMENT (FULL-TIME EQUIVALENT), FOR SELECTED FUNCTIONS, BY STATE: OCTOBER 1985

State	All functions	Education		Selected functions							
		Higher education(a)	Other education(b)	High-ways	Public welfare	Hospi-tals	Correc-tion	Police protection	Natural resources	Financial adminis-tration	General control
All states	3,983,689	1,639,015	100,247	252,495	186,183	548,237	230,679	81,002	162,951	130,807	137,951
Alabama........	80,162	35,426	4,809	3,819	3,961	11,662	3,338	1,001	3,382	2,418	2,369
Alaska.........	25,838	5,633	474	3,249	1,413	445	965	494	2,420	1,364	1,723
Arizona........	53,109	28,468	2,382	3,293	2,637	769	3,624	1,484	1,719	1,866	1,203
Arkansas	44,369	16,607	2,700	3,694	2,323	5,333	1,707	769	2,990	1,558	447
California......	328,182	160,463	4,552	14,793	2,875	34,586	19,418	11,229	15,000	10,745	6,232
Colorado	62,090	35,218	1,242	3,191	1,255	7,205	1,852	845	1,996	2,031	2,968
Connecticut	61,891	18,883	3,693	4,549	2,801	11,868	4,775	1,484	990	2,966	3,597
Delaware	20,980	8,689	251	1,409	1,753	1,567	1,472	641	518	786	1,092
Florida	138,945	41,434	2,433	8,369	7,825	18,106	15,003	2,924	7,797	4,587	8,544
Georgia.........	97,881	35,907	3,581	6,096	5,656	13,548	7,643	1,743	5,155	2,081	1,556
Hawaii	47,583	10,268	145	814	1,020	2,792	1,054	...	1,533	734	1,744
Idaho	18,858	8,378	534	1,860	907	967	629	268	1,836	660	485
Illinois.........	155,062	71,845	2,650	8,661	11,555	16,204	10,136	3,311	4,645	6,953	4,886
Indiana	95,515	54,851	4,645	5,546	1,301	10,226	4,650	1,708	2,820	2,344	1,381
Iowa	59,003	27,582	1,315	3,334	3,612	9,644	2,116	839	2,960	1,720	1,715
Kansas	53,513	25,385	1,395	3,522	2,846	6,614	2,358	723	2,514	2,519	2,149
Kentucky	70,803	26,016	4,103	6,677	3,196	6,854	4,174	1,681	3,544	2,585	4,045
Louisiana	106,497	41,261	5,100	6,722	6,237	20,223	5,630	1,118	4,862	2,738	3,306
Maine	24,594	9,181	1,276	2,729	1,849	1,943	872	537	1,610	918	894
Maryland	88,715	29,747	2,249	4,997	6,329	9,290	7,207	2,156	2,817	3,475	4,952
Massachusetts ...	93,991	28,287	1,406	4,809	8,617	20,233	5,463	1,835	1,325	4,788	6,152
Michigan	155,534	80,745	2,206	3,912	13,406	18,810	8,120	2,967	5,506	2,300	4,045
Minnesota	75,034	40,860	1,629	4,937	1,536	9,553	1,877	853	3,591	2,212	1,501
Mississippi	50,404	18,788	1,444	2,996	2,986	7,641	2,333	1,017	4,166	1,223	578
Missouri	74,497	25,006	2,066	6,280	5,625	12,904	3,861	1,825	2,832	2,547	3,529
Montana	21,436	8,807	409	1,908	1,148	1,346	743	312	2,895	1,178	694
Nebraska	34,413	16,564	765	2,267	2,617	3,801	1,305	571	2,071	556	1,002
Nevada	15,820	6,354	212	1,340	661	683	1,217	281	872	706	571
New Hampshire .	21,287	10,397	406	1,894	1,228	1,623	444	295	758	354	880
New Jersey......	104,980	29,324	3,013	8,645	5,414	18,099	7,177	4,622	2,352	3,487	4,893
New Mexico.....	42,287	21,232	644	2,546	1,714	4,608	2,218	664	1,633	1,463	1,451
New York	288,462	61,249	5,345	14,933	7,055	74,336	24,196	5,598	3,537	12,373	20,639
North Carolina ..	107,216	42,533	3,087	11,093	1,036	15,585	8,548	2,609	5,630	2,828	4,625
North Dakota ..	19,261	9,759	553	973	455	2,571	300	249	1,502	354	518
Ohio	150,812	80,824	2,553	8,651	1,573	20,768	6,999	2,062	4,342	4,224	2,663
Oklahoma	71,525	31,514	1,987	3,676	7,052	7,613	3,871	1,659	2,801	1,907	1,765
Oregon	55,531	22,760	919	3,521	3,325	6,030	1,968	1,170	3,732	2,108	2,524
Pennsylvania	144,407	41,205	1,884	14,169	10,623	27,564	5,109	4,964	7,776	5,783	6,297
Rhode Island	25,285	10,316	1,385	1,042	1,691	1,518	1,022	222	606	933	1,196
South Carolina ..	74,156	30,127	2,931	4,801	4,130	9,955	4,356	1,425	2,162	1,977	1,329
South Dakota ...	16,835	6,874	517	1,237	1,203	1,528	531	308	1,079	426	830
Tennessee	78,719	33,739	2,188	5,009	5,360	9,345	5,310	1,121	2,929	2,633	1,563
Texas...........	229,342	103,612	3,751	15,612	12,483	35,007	15,119	2,987	11,147	6,662	3,547
Utah	37,347	19,958	944	1,912	2,007	3,681	1,325	514	1,265	1,136	1,111
Vermont	12,975	4,646	235	1,390	763	777	570	489	586	546	600
Virginia.........	119,216	51,994	2,987	10,836	1,091	19,302	8,105	2,125	3,508	3,615	2,890
Washington	97,258	48,346	1,859	5,723	5,266	10,065	4,923	1,460	4,799	2,413	1,515
West Virginia ...	43,000	14,449	1,561	5,521	2,677	4,017	951	860	2,164	1,510	1,203
Wisconsin.......	76,413	42,972	1,607	1,736	1,570	8,383	3,616	730	3,326	2,784	2,144
Wyoming	12,674	4,532	225	1,802	520	1,045	479	253	951	733	408

Source: U.S. Bureau of the Census, *Public Employment in 1985.*
(a) Includes instructional and other personnel.
(b) Includes instructional and other personnel in elementary secondary schools.

Table 7.14
STATE GOVERNMENT EMPLOYMENT (FULL-TIME EQUIVALENT), FOR SELECTED FUNCTIONS, BY STATE: OCTOBER 1986

| State | All functions | Education | | Selected functions | | | | | | | |
		Higher educa-tion(a)	Other educa-tion(b)	High-ways	Public welfare	Hospi-tals	Correc-tion	Police protection	Natural resources	Financial adminis-tration	General control
All states	3,437,458	1,140,435	115,928	249,656	186,571	529,586	241,655	78,490	139,299	130,373	130,979
Alabama........	70,431	25,294	4,343	4,354	3,873	11,920	3,391	1,090	3,574	2,510	2,310
Alaska..........	20,989	3,812	3,486	2,945	1,351	420	992	385	2,045	957	1,516
Arizona........	42,520	16,747	2,692	3,028	3,160	800	4,899	1,001	1,997	1,716	1,132
Arkansas.......	38,672	12,111	1,891	3,744	2,684	5,232	1,709	805	2,572	1,590	501
California......	279,451	97,743	4,190	14,406	3,001	32,710	21,971	9,558	12,831	10,756	6,092
Colorado	50,488	24,927	983	3,065	1,284	7,067	1,973	877	1,754	2,020	2,802
Connecticut	55,790	12,877	3,276	4,339	2,831	12,425	4,426	1,557	959	3,143	3,706
Delaware	17,198	5,099	244	1,266	1,706	1,631	1,492	653	466	752	1,048
Florida	123,589	30,836	2,286	7,769	7,796	14,923	14,950	3,025	6,698	4,646	8,310
Georgia........	90,743	26,025	3,399	6,389	5,978	13,167	8,175	1,890	4,847	2,081	1,259
Hawaii	41,268	6,289	17,710	783	1,018	2,690	1,066	...	1,329	742	2,008
Idaho	17,508	7,851	505	1,823	856	822	682	268	1,252	859	391
Illinois........	130,147	47,462	2,721	8,703	11,877	14,813	10,234	3,689	3,703	7,687	5,164
Indiana........	75,125	35,550	5,061	5,562	1,353	10,040	4,602	1,747	2,438	2,283	863
Iowa	56,761	26,048	1,236	3,258	3,445	9,887	2,018	794	2,675	1,444	2,501
Kansas	42,839	16,139	1,074	3,500	2,812	6,473	2,093	752	2,278	2,401	2,002
Kentucky	63,421	18,653	4,011	6,844	3,684	6,445	4,402	1,738	3,351	2,618	3,898
Louisiana	85,748	24,133	3,900	6,341	5,902	20,997	5,613	1,050	4,416	2,811	2,160
Maine	19,758	4,618	1,253	2,689	1,871	1,940	909	589	1,415	1,022	782
Maryland	79,571	21,626	2,184	5,204	5,945	8,849	7,446	2,161	2,464	3,591	3,849
Massachusetts ...	88,203	21,885	1,307	5,065	8,413	19,446	5,693	1,789	1,389	4,770	6,065
Michigan	128,356	55,846	2,142	3,930	13,054	17,454	9,729	3,037	4,231	2,302	3,886
Minnesota	60,919	29,867	1,521	4,940	1,492	7,762	1,855	835	3,268	2,126	1,172
Mississippi	42,382	13,153	1,441	2,904	2,401	7,175	2,359	922	3,679	1,152	419
Missouri	65,784	15,792	2,090	6,242	5,713	13,552	4,371	1,851	2,697	2,695	3,346
Montana........	15,718	4,707	352	1,781	1,085	1,264	672	303	2,264	971	434
Nebraska	29,375	11,802	718	2,211	2,537	4,007	1,252	572	1,908	578	1,144
Nevada	14,823	5,312	225	1,377	664	721	1,265	281	759	724	526
New Hampshire .	17,715	6,843	370	1,774	1,207	1,629	718	329	787	342	901
New Jersey......	95,837	21,771	3,048	8,780	5,334	17,174	7,257	3,618	1,881	3,358	4,923
New Mexico.....	34,174	14,072	641	2,584	1,728	4,723	2,196	620	1,458	1,395	1,250
New York	272,056	46,398	5,233	14,070	7,698	71,762	25,566	5,453	3,642	12,037	20,652
North Carolina ..	92,804	31,653	3,063	10,913	958	14,676	8,627	2,657	3,685	2,817	4,620
North Dakota ...	15,053	6,206	308	1,086	411	2,304	301	250	1,293	333	344
Ohio	121,620	53,221	2,446	8,604	1,657	19,533	7,401	2,062	4,222	4,293	2,591
Oklahoma	64,434	24,441	2,014	3,647	6,730	8,225	3,761	1,600	2,820	1,854	2,091
Oregon	44,018	13,262	827	3,525	3,180	5,600	1,960	1,048	2,942	2,115	2,292
Pennsylvania	124,030	27,924	1,859	14,481	10,486	25,001	5,281	4,990	5,309	5,690	5,613
Rhode Island ...	18,975	4,998	1,123	1,025	1,685	2,611	1,048	258	605	1,005	1,083
South Carolina ..	68,918	22,582	3,097	4,613	4,510	11,758	5,535	1,450	2,099	2,166	1,209
South Dakota ...	12,531	3,784	487	1,179	1,049	1,442	511	302	760	396	553
Tennessee	70,591	25,387	2,114	5,201	5,500	9,347	5,803	1,169	2,476	2,750	1,502
Texas..........	192,633	73,462	3,653	15,152	12,798	33,367	15,733	2,894	7,222	6,418	2,981
Utah	32,850	16,135	858	1,835	1,883	3,793	1,297	666	1,167	1,226	935
Vermont	11,427	3,711	220	1,116	749	766	434	447	450	584	598
Virginia........	102,146	36,545	2,747	10,665	1,389	19,015	7,937	2,053	3,613	3,530	2,688
Washington	79,086	31,036	2,397	5,583	5,287	9,847	4,970	1,543	3,953	2,171	1,478
West Virginia ...	34,468	9,958	1,540	5,710	2,546	3,789	811	851	1,863	1,463	1,116
Wisconsin......	73,736	41,863	1,448	1,966	1,466	7,574	3,769	758	2,943	2,742	1,839
Wyoming	10,779	2,979	194	1,685	534	1,018	500	253	850	741	434

Source: U.S. Bureau of the Census, *Public Employment in 1986.*
(a) Includes instructional and other personnel.
(b) Includes instructional and other personnel in elementary and seconadary schools.

Table 7.15
STATE GOVERNMENT PAYROLLS
FOR SELECTED FUNCTIONS, BY STATE: OCTOBER 1985
(In thousands of dollars)

| State | All functions | Education | | Selected functions | | | | | | | |
		Higher education(a)	Other education(b)	High-ways	Public welfare	Hospi-tals	Correc-tion	Police protection	Natural resources	Financial adminis-tration	General control
All states	$6,328,586	$2,228,859	$214,844	$459,835	$307,006	$858,641	$420,855	$174,738	$258,100	$228,842	$294,905
Alabama........	126,056	51,966	8,398	6,444	6,638	17,923	5,656	2,024	5,455	4,121	4,349
Alaska.........	66,604	12,457	10,552	8,607	3,106	987	2,943	1,800	7,065	3,144	5,099
Arizona........	77,241	35,571	3,886	6,223	4,131	1,177	6,153	3,284	2,493	2,654	2,467
Arkansas	61,918	21,727	3,896	6,270	3,338	6,750	2,480	1,284	3,915	2,223	692
California......	669,195	299,080	11,175	38,262	6,313	74,633	47,578	25,715	29,237	22,961	15,231
Colorado	99,075	44,272	1,989	7,574	2,628	12,381	4,606	2,144	4,297	4,309	6,434
Connecticut	108,877	25,786	5,744	7,290	5,619	23,857	9,952	3,437	1,984	5,201	7,546
Delaware	29,424	9,935	515	2,326	2,279	2,394	2,358	1,394	808	1,140	1,893
Florida	198,085	55,373	3,538	14,684	8,978	22,288	23,142	5,665	9,619	7,359	16,858
Georgia.........	146,151	49,981	5,758	8,940	9,412	19,009	11,615	3,384	7,235	3,343	3,218
Hawaii	69,393	12,805	30,015	1,467	1,557	4,195	1,528	0	2,387	1,424	3,651
Idaho	25,916	8,911	852	3,053	1,508	1,279	959	487	2,637	1,165	962
Illinois..........	258,419	98,542	5,091	18,351	19,707	28,970	18,727	8,157	9,684	10,986	12,890
Indiana	137,561	76,636	5,954	8,470	1,764	15,415	6,048	3,523	4,088	3,506	2,864
Iowa	92,660	40,372	2,368	5,586	6,026	14,928	3,938	2,053	4,163	2,985	3,456
Kansas	65,619	24,865	1,772	6,111	2,651	7,929	3,933	1,416	3,962	3,692	3,487
Kentucky	97,070	30,868	7,012	9,903	4,665	8,320	6,150	3,090	4,917	3,732	6,298
Louisiana	147,361	45,687	7,794	10,679	9,422	27,422	11,332	1,887	7,098	4,509	6,835
Maine	32,392	8,347	2,101	4,488	2,918	2,715	1,381	1,051	2,268	1,355	1,242
Maryland	143,910	42,419	4,511	8,479	10,070	14,668	13,143	4,821	4,684	6,295	8,563
Massachusetts ...	157,601	35,810	2,994	10,064	16,210	30,995	10,213	4,799	2,637	8,779	14,519
Michigan	252,869	98,809	4,928	9,203	27,777	37,119	18,137	7,598	8,778	4,954	9,727
Minnesota	125,556	58,269	3,539	10,971	2,828	15,642	4,099	1,990	6,728	4,273	3,936
Mississippi	62,337	22,268	2,154	3,953	3,617	7,731	2,676	1,714	5,264	1,994	1,056
Missouri	97,041	26,776	3,090	10,715	7,035	14,035	5,528	3,864	4,008	3,336	6,371
Montana........	28,534	9,207	663	3,749	1,716	1,978	1,130	640	3,274	1,718	1,078
Nebraska	41,191	16,311	1,268	3,596	3,386	4,678	1,881	1,123	2,365	830	1,693
Nevada	26,734	7,914	451	2,799	1,219	1,344	2,532	543	1,424	1,296	1,324
New Hampshire .	25,717	10,375	632	2,450	1,773	2,188	636	543	817	540	1,525
New Jersey	189,720	49,708	6,800	17,969	9,644	27,069	13,780	9,203	4,014	5,880	12,456
New Mexico.....	56,942	23,891	1,049	4,318	2,669	5,965	3,519	1,122	2,603	2,367	2,561
New York	584,733	101,459	11,366	28,681	15,688	139,122	51,333	13,970	7,610	23,133	53,781
North Carolina ..	174,842	68,626	5,681	17,073	1,928	23,345	13,413	5,395	8,848	4,995	8,588
North Dakota ...	24,279	10,630	869	1,611	659	3,096	470	461	1,874	579	779
Ohio	213,391	99,157	4,577	15,374	2,626	30,425	12,212	4,109	7,175	7,198	4,520
Oklahoma	101,433	37,122	3,441	5,767	10,646	10,810	6,031	2,939	4,578	3,426	4,009
Oregon	80,752	26,823	1,533	6,270	5,487	8,769	3,398	2,854	4,759	3,511	4,600
Pennsylvania	218,913	47,957	3,597	23,721	19,070	42,271	9,179	10,866	9,575	9,464	11,922
Rhode Island	35,503	9,209	1,778	1,846	3,051	2,499	2,056	644	1,007	1,837	2,174
South Carolina ..	106,766	39,925	5,016	6,064	5,830	13,020	6,203	2,571	3,141	3,169	2,736
South Dakota ...	18,968	6,738	581	1,948	1,275	1,601	660	463	1,125	639	808
Tennessee	111,124	43,329	3,427	7,517	7,722	12,829	8,490	2,171	3,935	4,047	3,250
Texas...........	357,424	140,041	6,979	30,702	20,977	50,688	27,393	5,904	17,553	13,579	8,129
Utah	53,626	24,276	1,614	3,902	3,306	4,710	2,291	1,035	2,270	1,831	1,974
Vermont	18,865	6,794	352	1,792	1,054	1,015	851	912	983	805	994
Virginia.........	170,913	69,288	4,638	15,605	1,757	26,001	12,074	3,910	5,866	5,620	5,464
Washington	144,673	56,595	3,322	13,551	8,386	14,385	9,163	3,436	8,390	4,977	3,356
West Virginia ...	53,464	17,007	2,259	7,603	3,398	4,326	804	1,401	3,028	2,028	1,747
Wisconsin.......	121,867	63,489	2,919	4,214	2,751	12,283	6,343	1,443	4,770	4,840	4,909
Wyoming	19,883	5,457	406	3,600	884	1,465	739	499	1,704	1,273	882

Source: U.S. Bureau of the Census, *Public Employment in 1985.*
Note: Because of rounding, detail may not add to totals.
(a) Includes instructional and other personnel.
(b) Includes instructional and other personnel in elementary and secondary schools.

Table 7.16
STATE GOVERNMENT PAYROLLS
FOR SELECTED FUNCTIONS, BY STATE: OCTOBER 1986
(In thousands of dollars)

| State | All functions | Education | | Selected functions | | | | | | | |
		Higher education(a)	Other education(b)	High-ways	Public welfare	Hospi-tals	Correc-tion	Police protection	Natural resources	Financial adminis-tration	General control
All states	$6,810,358	$2,357,046	$226,385	$484,714	$333,434	$914,463	$468,582	$182,880	$269,244	$246,842	$315,709
Alabama........	128,153	50,478	8,673	7,122	6,632	17,876	7,084	2,185	5,702	4,280	4,658
Alaska..........	65,150	10,869	10,338	10,427	3,441	1,100	3,110	1,640	6,396	2,979	4,765
Arizona........	86,099	38,197	4,866	6,502	5,454	1,340	8,452	2,571	3,152	2,861	2,746
Arkansas	64,112	22,501	3,175	6,475	4,121	6,997	2,538	1,545	3,949	2,365	1,067
California.......	737,885	263,850	11,434	41,951	7,397	77,514	58,277	25,984	37,646	25,052	17,713
Colorado	112,785	55,293	1,963	7,465	2,774	14,380	4,923	2,264	4,281	4,516	6,556
Connecticut	124,233	26,880	6,722	8,756	6,498	29,828	9,337	4,301	2,220	5,985	9,754
Delaware	30,988	10,278	557	2,255	2,395	2,292	2,542	1,668	802	1,160	2,080
Florida	212,204	60,572	3,612	14,655	9,966	22,261	23,827	5,557	10,163	7,548	18,520
Georgia........	161,823	52,902	6,131	10,794	10,267	20,103	12,688	3,856	8,319	3,921	3,688
Hawaii	73,674	13,989	30,567	1,467	1,670	4,277	1,697	. . .	2,552	1,324	4,046
Idaho	27,592	10,921	888	2,826	1,470	1,290	1,034	487	2,151	1,516	1,067
Illinois.........	271,001	101,874	5,555	19,552	21,723	28,261	20,172	10,178	8,537	12,993	13,669
Indiana	145,339	79,826	6,924	8,687	1,937	16,492	7,917	3,698	4,833	3,657	1,946
Iowa	96,469	41,845	2,598	5,736	6,900	15,744	4,578	2,064	4,778	2,685	2,784
Kansas	68,375	25,296	1,890	6,283	4,091	8,383	3,344	1,504	4,073	3,778	3,654
Kentucky	101,893	31,859	7,475	10,509	5,553	8,483	6,831	3,242	4,982	3,846	6,714
Louisiana	141,282	44,845	7,115	9,857	9,058	28,819	9,039	1,831	7,368	4,796	5,076
Maine	33,714	8,411	2,229	4,428	3,110	2,980	1,513	1,143	2,441	1,597	1,368
Maryland	156,363	45,735	4,736	9,199	10,315	15,203	15,089	4,840	4,751	7,021	8,568
Massachusetts ...	174,624	42,499	3,036	11,851	16,926	31,893	11,821	4,603	2,262	10,012	13,047
Michigan	300,698	118,691	5,668	11,071	32,046	41,566	23,835	8,678	9,486	6,433	11,116
Minnesota	133,763	64,020	3,731	11,751	3,111	15,221	4,285	2,079	7,102	4,688	4,100
Mississippi	60,426	22,039	2,023	3,754	2,983	7,348	2,928	1,522	5,332	1,837	1,134
Missouri	105,745	27,381	3,236	11,257	8,055	18,056	6,492	4,083	4,120	3,971	6,758
Montana........	28,482	9,217	661	3,671	1,775	1,973	1,139	656	3,314	1,573	1,054
Nebraska	43,514	16,517	1,227	3,691	3,732	6,005	1,714	1,025	2,454	871	2,103
Nevada	28,751	8,574	505	2,977	1,343	1,472	2,686	543	1,491	1,386	1,376
New Hampshire .	28,787	10,913	675	2,940	1,975	2,235	1,350	731	1,104	586	1,687
New Jersey......	216,533	57,319	7,941	20,001	10,891	29,927	15,383	9,115	4,230	6,688	14,372
New Mexico.....	59,111	24,868	1,163	4,554	2,909	7,085	3,589	1,188	2,861	2,387	2,566
New York	633,785	112,685	12,186	29,892	17,553	146,689	58,543	14,198	8,352	24,770	59,672
North Carolina ..	175,474	66,321	6,148	16,956	1,869	24,513	14,388	5,818	6,882	5,354	9,455
North Dakota ...	25,707	11,736	554	1,687	711	3,020	480	465	1,932	570	798
Ohio	231,798	107,218	4,934	16,248	3,066	32,325	13,982	4,472	7,654	8,000	5,373
Oklahoma	103,256	37,604	3,509	5,822	10,201	12,508	5,939	2,850	4,541	3,373	4,640
Oregon	85,804	29,466	1,598	6,446	5,508	9,317	3,867	2,910	4,538	3,803	4,997
Pennsylvania	229,223	52,729	3,762	25,036	19,547	41,938	10,089	11,400	9,914	10,074	12,344
Rhode Island	37,430	9,924	1,801	1,870	3,065	5,346	2,305	764	1,047	1,948	2,300
South Carolina ..	115,593	42,648	5,355	5,970	6,718	16,690	8,020	2,677	3,282	3,545	2,660
South Dakota ...	20,345	7,104	761	1,984	1,388	1,666	715	483	1,136	670	1,053
Tennessee	120,957	48,267	3,807	8,100	8,421	13,980	8,703	2,324	3,816	4,449	3,578
Texas...........	360,803	146,638	7,002	29,591	21,667	49,646	28,808	5,880	14,326	13,400	7,751
Utah	52,950	24,541	1,639	3,148	3,358	5,098	2,074	1,465	2,004	1,930	2,054
Vermont........	20,243	7,372	371	1,899	1,133	1,079	778	988	719	1,926	1,111
Virginia.........	188,477	78,056	4,987	16,837	2,391	27,670	12,085	4,118	7,001	6,144	6,197
Washington	168,656	69,877	4,945	14,038	9,088	17,204	9,566	3,691	9,203	4,854	3,867
West Virginia ...	53,547	18,366	2,461	8,599	3,397	4,359	1,076	1,434	3,147	2,127	1,964
Wisconsin.......	146,971	82,583	2,869	4,647	2,912	13,569	7,177	1,654	5,234	5,299	5,187
Wyoming	19,776	5,452	382	3,479	921	1,442	772	510	1,663	1,292	956

Source: U.S. Bureau of the Census, *Public Employment in 1986.*
(a) Includes instructional and other personnel.
(b) Includes instructional and other personnel in elementary and secondary schools.

FINANCES OF STATE-ADMINISTERED PUBLIC EMPLOYEE RETIREMENT SYSTEMS

By Vance Kane

At the end of fiscal 1985-86, there were 198 state-administered public employee retirement systems. These systems encompassed 10.4 million members and held assets of $347 billion. In 1983-84, there were 202 state-administered systems with 10.0 million members' assets of $257 billion. Receipts totaled $69 billion, compared to $49 billion in 1983-84, an increase of 42 percent during the two years. However, benefits and withdrawals totaled $19.9 billion in 1985-86, compared to $16.5 in 1983-84, or an increase of 21 percent. Obviously, benefits and withdrawal payments seem to be within a margin of tolerance during this period.

Membership Size

Of the 10.4 million members, 9.1 million were active (still employed) and 1.3 were classified as "other," which indicates no longer employed but taking a deferred retirement. Because state systems often include local government employees, they are sizable. Of the 198 systems, 96 cover 10.2 million members or 98 percent. Thirteen systems, each having a membership of between 5,000 and 9,999, had a total membership of 96,000. Twenty-four systems had a total of 65,000 members and nine systems had 6,000.

In 1986, 2.8 million persons received retirement fund payments. Persons retired for age or service totaled 2.4 million; 146,000 were on disability and 177,000 received survivor payments (see Table 7.20). In 1984, 2.6 million persons received monthly benefits; of those, 130,000 were on disability.

California had the most members, 994,000; New York was second with 751,000; and Texas third with 665,000. Vermont had 24,000 and Delaware 26,000, for the two smallest systems.

Benefit Payments

Benefits paid in fiscal 1986 reached $18.2 billion, compared to $14.6 billion in fiscal 1984 (see Table 7.19). Receipts over payments (which include benefits, withdrawals, and miscellaneous expenditures) were $48.5 billion, an increase of $16.5 billion from 1984. However, earnings from investments totaled $38.4 billion, an increase of $15.5 billion from 1984.

The average monthly payment for all beneficiaries was $504 in 1986. In 1985, it was $475, and in 1984, it was $453. Persons retired for service received average monthly payments of $520; those on disability, $527, and survivors, $271 (see table 7.18).

California had the largest number of beneficiaries (331,000), followed by New York (260,000) and Ohio (209,000). Vermont had the least number (4,830) next to North Dakota (5,212) and Nebraska (5,944).

States exceeding the $700 average benefit payment were Alaska ($944), Colorado ($704), Connecticut ($777) and Nevada ($702). States with less than $300 per month average payment were Iowa, $236; Kansas, $242; Nebraska, $156; North Dakota, $253; and South Dakota, $241.

A variety of factors may influence the payment levels of former public employees. These include general wage levels for the area, and whether the state retirement system is supplemental to other retirement programs (such as social security, deferred compensation or investment programs). It is not uncommon for a state to maintain a two-tiered benefit program whereby new employees have different lengths of service to qualify for benefits and different payment schedules compared to senior employees with more service years.

Vance Kane is Assistant Division Chief for Programs, and was assisted by Helen Smith, Senior Financial Statistical Examiner, both in the Governments Division, U.S. Bureau of the Census.

Revenues

Receipts for state-administered retirement systems totaled $69 billion of which $9 billion came from employees (13 percent), $12 billion from state governments (18 percent), $10 billion from local governments (14 percent), and $38 billion from earnings on investments (56 percent) (see Table 7.22).

The lower the relationship of benefits to receipts, the higher the probability a retirement system is in a healthy fiscal condition. However, further review must be made of any system before generalizations as to relative solvency can be made. In 1986, four states states had annual benefit payments less than 15 percent of total annual receipts: Alaska, 14.7 percent; Arizona, 14.9 percent, Nebraska 11.9 percent and South Dakota, 11.9 percent.

Investments and Assets

Cash and security holdings total $347 billion, an increase of $91 billion or 35 percent, from fiscal 1984.

More than $244 billion (70 percent) were invested in nongovernmental securities with $92 billion (27 percent) in federal securities. The distribution of investments was almost unchanged from fiscal 1984 when 71 percent, or $181 billion, was nongovernmental securities and 26 percent, or $46 billion, was in federal securities.

Two states had annual benefit payments less than 3 percent of cash and security holdings: Nebraska (2.4 percent) and South Dakota (2.9 percent).

Favorable investment markets have reduced the relative share of employee/employer contributions to the retirement fund. In 1984, employees contributed 15 percent, state employers 16.5 percent and local employers 21.5 percent. In 1985-86, employees provided 13 percent, state employers 14 percent and local governments 18 percent. This was a substantial drop for all in terms of relative contributions.

NOTE

1. The U.S. Bureau of the Census defines a publicly administered retirement system as a system sponsored by a recognized unit of government whose membership is comprised of public employees compensated with public funds. There must be an identifiable retirement fund financed in whole or in part with public contributions. Direct payments to retired or disabled individuals by appropriation of general funds do not constitute a retirement system. Payments to a private trustee or insurance carrier also are excluded as a publicly administered employee retirement system.

Table A
Number and Membership of State Government
Employee Retirement Systems by Size-Group: 1985-86

Number of Systems with Membership of —

Total	10,000 or More	5,000 to 9,999	1,000 to 4,999	500 to 999	200 to 499	100 to 199	Less Than 100
198	96	13	24	9	23	10	23

Number of Members in Systems with Membership of —

Total	10,000 or More	5,000 to 9,999	1,000 to 4,999	500 to 999	200 to 499	100 to 199	Less Than 100
10,378,470	10,201,709	96,008	64,752	6,204	7,542	1,542	713

Table 7.17
NUMBER, MEMBERSHIP AND MONTHLY BENEFIT PAYMENTS
OF STATE ADMINISTERED EMPLOYEE-RETIREMENT SYSTEMS:
1983-84 THROUGH 1985-86

Item	1985-86	1984-85	1983-84
Number of systems	198	203	202
Membership, last month of fiscal year:			
Total number	10,378,470	10,263,598	10,044,368
Active members	9,049,425	8,817,896	8,676,214
Other	1,329,045	1,445,702	1,368,154
Percent distribution	100.0	100.0	100.0
Active members	87.2	85.9	86.4
Other	12.8	14.1	13.6
Beneficiaries receiving periodic benefits:			
Total number	2,760,304	2,661,215	2,579,174
Persons retired on account of age or length of service	2,437,191	2,355,031	2,300,605
Persons retired on account of disability	146,315	140,299	130,280
Survivors of deceased former members	176,798	165,885	148,289
Percent distribution	100.0	100.0	100.0
Persons retired on account of age or length of service	88.3	88.5	89.1
Persons retired on account of disability	5.3	5.3	5.1
Survivors of deceased former members	6.4	6.2	5.8
Recurrent benefit payments for last month of fiscal year:			
Total amount (in thousands)	$1,392,523	$1,263,427	$1,169,579
To persons retired on account of age or length of service	$1,267,546	$1,149,860	$1,071,542
To persons retired on account of disability	$77,068	$69,236	$60,701
To survivors of deceased former members	$47,908	$44,331	$37,336
Percent distribution	100.0	100.0	100.0
For persons retired on account of age or length of service	91.0	91.0	91.6
For persons retired on account of disability	5.5	5.5	5.2
For survivors of deceased former members	3.4	3.5	3.2
Average monthly payment for beneficiaries:			
Average for all beneficiaries (in dollars)	$504	$475	$453
For persons retired on account of age or length of service	$520	$488	$466
For persons retired on account of disability	$527	$493	$466
For survivors of deceased former members	$271	$267	$252
Lump-sum survivors' benefits for the month:			
Amount (in thousands)	$18,938	$20,764	$19,775(a)
Number of beneficiaries (payees)	2,976	2,705	5,618(a)
Average amount of payments (in dollars)	$6,364	$7,676	$3,520(a)

Source: U.S. Bureau of the Census, *Finances of Employee-Retirement Systems of State and Local Governments in 1985-86.*
Note: Because of rounding, detail may not add to totals.

(a) Revised from totals appearing in the *Book of the States 1986-87* and *Finances of Employee Retirement Systems of State and Local Government 1983-84.*

Table 7.18
NATIONAL SUMMARY OF FINANCES OF STATE-ADMINISTERED EMPLOYEE RETIREMENT SYSTEMS: SELECTED YEARS, 1980-1986

	Amount (in millions of dollars)							Percentage distribution			
	1985-86	1984-85	1983-84	1982-83	1981-82	1980-81	1979-80	1985-86	1984-85	1983-84	1982-83
Receipts	$68,982	$56,313	$48,724	$45,124	$37,944	$33,340	$28,603	100.0	100.0	100.0	100.0
Employee contributions	8,939	7,913	7,306	7,196	6,674	5,982	5,285	13.0	14.1	15.0	15.9
Government contributions	21,693	20,920	18,521	17,197	15,777	14,749	13,010	31.4	37.1	38.0	38.1
From state governments	12,162	11,976	10,458	9,611	8,898	8,353	7,399	17.6	21.3	21.5	21.3
From local governments	9,531	8,944	8,063	7,585	6,879	6,395	5,611	13.8	15.9	16.5	16.8
Earnings on investments	38,350	27,480	22,897	20,734	15,492	12,609	10,308	55.6	48.8	47.0	45.9
Benefits and withdrawal payments	19,878	17,987	16,492	14,204	13,134	11,393	10,257	100.0	100.0	100.0	100.0
Benefits	18,187	16,189	14,594	12,757	11,430	9,964	8,809	91.5	90.0	88.5	89.8
Withdrawals	1,691	1,798	1,898	1,447	1,704	1,429	1,448	8.5	10.0	11.5	10.2
Cash and security holdings at end of fiscal year, total	347,361	296,692	256,583(r)	223,262(r)	193,295	164,624	144,682	100.0	100.0	100.0	100.0
Cash and deposits	10,867	12,279	8,065(r)	5,893(r)	2,427	2,611	2,647	3.1	4.1	3.1	2.6
Governmental securities	92,485	86,373	67,646(r)	54,265(r)	44,216	34,292	26,724	26.6	29.1	26.4	24.3
Federal	92,139	85,992	66,961(r)	53,526(r)	43,368	33,716	26,213	26.5	29.0	26.1	24.0
U.S. Treasury	68,900	61,225	45,840(r)	33,032(r)	24,494	19,503	13,814	19.8	20.6	17.9	14.8
Federal agency	23,239	24,767	21,121(r)	20,494(r)	18,874	14,212	12,399	6.7	8.3	8.2	9.2
State and local	346	381	685(r)	739(r)	848	577	511	0.1	0.1	0.3	0.3
Nongovernmental securities	244,009	198,040	180,872(r)	163,104(r)	146,652	127,721	115,311	70.2	66.7	70.5	73.1
Corporate bonds	77,138	67,208	60,646(r)	60,563(r)	68,948	65,246	60,871	22.2	22.7	23.6	27.1
Corporate stocks	110,721	84,331	66,201(r)	54,296(r)	44,025	36,438	31,146	31.9	28.4	25.8	24.3
Mortgages	29,572	23,902	22,301(r)	23,312(r)	17,742	14,174	11,966	8.5	8.1	8.7	10.5(r)
Other securities	15,721	16,541	23,422(r)	14,777(r)	12,525	9,684	10,677	4.5	5.6	9.1	6.5(r)
Other investments	10,858	6,058	8,301(r)	10,156(r)	3,412	2,179	651	3.1	2.0	3.2	4.6(r)

(r) Revised.

Sources: U.S. Bureau of the Census, Census of Governments reports for 1977 and 1982: *Employee Retirement Systems of State and Local Governments* (Volume 6, No. 1); annual reports for other years: *Finances of Employee Retirement Systems of State and Local Governments.*

Table 7.19
MEMBERSHIP AND BENEFIT OPERATIONS OF STATE-ADMINISTERED EMPLOYEE RETIREMENT SYSTEMS: LAST MONTH OF FISCAL YEAR 1985-86

Benefit Operations, last month of fiscal year

		Beneficiaries receiving periodic benefit payments				Periodic benefit payment for the month (in thousands of dollars)				Lump-sum survivors benefit payments during the month (in thousands of dollars)
State	Membership, last month of the fiscal year	Total(a)	Persons retired on account of age or length of service	Persons retired on account of disability	Survivors of deceased former members (no. of payees)	Total(a)	Persons retired on account of age or length of service	Persons retired on account of disability	To survivors of deceased former members	
United States	11,907,289	3,519,182	3,029,881	222,210	267,091	1,891,016	1,662,392	148,657	79,967	25,191
Alabama	172,353	38,642	32,932	2,694	3,016	37,005	35,356	1,025	624	10
Alaska	49,996	6,929	6,276	263	390	6,657	6,098	339	221	51
Arizona	162,863	33,027	31,719	660	648	15,940	15,339	293	308	0
Arkansas	82,748	20,360	16,946	1,987	1,427	7,397	6,459	615	323	1
California	1,264,260	454,423	363,412	51,678	39,333	320,684	265,509	40,458	14,717	3,743
Colorado	125,590	35,340	29,900	3,799	1,641	23,161	19,757	2,696	708	4
Connecticut	122,460	43,590	38,026	2,788	2,776	30,974	27,810	1,934	1,230	149
Delaware	27,848	10,057	7,138	1,254	1,665	4,505	3,229	588	687	6
Florida	464,683	108,872	89,593	7,833	11,446	44,899	38,604	3,036	3,260	99
Georgia	275,662	54,291	44,416	3,991	5,884	31,539	27,157	2,296	2,086	24
Hawaii	55,166	17,026	15,938	1,033	55	9,384	9,021	345	18	161
Idaho	50,934	14,697	13,025	327	1,345	4,992	4,488	197	307	48
Illinois	573,993	187,703	144,848	6,561	36,294	94,954	82,295	3,905	8,754	3,154
Indiana	213,354	61,036	55,705	3,135	2,196	24,785	23,044	814	928	7
Iowa	151,580	44,968	43,747	526	695	11,589	10,882	453	254	0
Kansas	128,953	37,440	33,643	1,601	2,196	9,377	8,247	647	483	126
Kentucky	157,730	40,792	36,179	2,596	2,017	18,477	16,648	1,145	684	0
Louisiana	259,142	67,240	57,489	4,280	5,471	43,844	38,343	2,709	2,792	115
Maine	67,640	20,375	18,731	852	792	10,781	9,926	682	172	45
Maryland	200,036	54,252	50,973	2,055	1,224	35,328	33,621	1,463	244	291
Massachusetts	344,731	123,253	106,860	6,476	9,917	77,436	67,570	6,183	3,684	281
Michigan	447,961	134,738	122,796	6,937	5,005	68,333	64,067	2,566	1,700	8
Minnesota	248,792	64,273	55,566	2,079	6,628	30,082	27,296	1,316	1,471	56
Mississippi	175,913	29,693	24,980	1,846	2,867	10,055	8,447	632	976	30
Missouri	170,180	51,020	42,810	3,353	4,857	20,376	17,915	1,312	1,150	216
Montana	60,466	15,254	13,434	1,154	666	7,052	6,231	537	284	85
Nebraska	44,870	9,122	8,110	309	703	2,800	2,329	202	269	1,101
Nevada	66,273	9,499	7,504	507	1,488	6,666	5,800	309	557	0
New Hampshire	31,666	8,034	8,034	0	0	2,602	2,602	0	0	36
New Jersey	402,722	99,821	99,273	143	405	61,440	61,286	66	88	940
New Mexico	123,140	18,886	16,953	1,209	724	9,397	8,844	370	183	0
New York	1,072,757	477,520	407,349	35,356	34,815	266,059	221,762	36,199	8,098	4,811
North Carolina	346,403	72,073	71,953	91	29	35,313	35,256	50	8	1
North Dakota	34,521	5,540	5,096	53	391	1,466	1,349	27	90	1
Ohio	663,691	212,702	173,516	16,204	22,982	113,446	94,982	11,148	7,316	322

MEMBERSHIP AND BENEFIT OPERATIONS—Continued

Benefit Operations, last month of fiscal year

State	Membership, last month of the fiscal year	Beneficiaries receiving periodic benefit payments				Periodic benefit payment for the month (in thousands of dollars)				Lump-sum survivors benefit payments during the month (in thousands of dollars)
		Total(a)	Persons retired on account of age or length of service	Persons retired on account of disability	Survivors of deceased former members (no. of payees)	Total(a)	Persons retired on account of age or length of service	Persons retired on account of disability	To survivors of deceased former members	
Oklahoma	133,715	42,786	38,574	1,551	2,661	23,028	21,480	889	659	401
Oregon	128,902	47,545	43,962	3,312	271	17,917	16,218	1,505	194	0
Pennsylvania	438,208	197,704	169,206	11,906	16,592	97,346	86,684	6,236	4,426	5,313
Rhode Island	38,493	14,645	14,213	149	283	8,777	8,521	119	136	115
South Carolina	243,884	35,230	29,381	3,213	2,636	15,979	13,802	1,341	836	9
South Dakota	31,315	8,653	7,445	188	1,020	2,154	1,875	68	211	0
Tennessee	200,514	60,427	53,679	2,677	4,071	25,028	22,660	921	1,446	1,451
Texas	721,454	145,467	120,925	8,243	16,299	82,740	73,984	4,047	4,709	1,217
Utah	77,091	15,321	14,489	832	0	5,354	5,124	230	0	0
Vermont	24,243	5,025	4,565	49	411	1,968	1,835	29	104	47
Virginia	333,323	61,692	50,581	8,008	3,103	26,582	22,675	3,473	434	205
Washington	233,154	77,696	75,864	1,033	799	43,149	42,145	508	496	9
West Virginia	109,697	35,190	29,992	1,794	3,404	12,938	11,573	667	699	192
Wisconsin	293,212	73,069	66,474	3,505	3,090	32,001	29,507	1,998	497	273
Wyoming	47,406	7,355	6,777	120	458	2,534	2,034	71	430	29
Dist. of Col.	11,60	18,889	8,884	0	5	14,725	14,707	0	18	0

Source: U.S. Bureau of the Census, Finances of Employee Retirement Systems of State and Local Governments in 1985-86.
(a) Detail may not add to totals because of rounding.

Table 7.20

FINANCES OF STATE-ADMINISTERED EMPLOYEE RETIREMENT SYSTEMS, BY STATE: 1985-86

(In thousands of dollars)

State	Total	Receipts during fiscal year				Payments during fiscal year			
		Government contributions							
		Employee contributions	From state	From local governments	Earnings on investments	Total	Benefits	Withdrawals	Other
All states	$68,982,371	$8,939,295	$12,162,195	$9,530,722	$38,350,159	$20,472,028	$18,186,951	$1,690,550	$594,527
Alabama...........	880,150	138,598	250,084	302	491,166	232,501	201,657	26,959	3,885
Alaska.............	668,309	72,585	111,544	87,536	396,644	116,872	98,226	12,476	6,170
Arizona............	1,149,941	159,562	48,196	117,711	824,472	222,436	171,810	42,183	8,443
Arkansas	433,527	46,340	126,032	19,667	241,488	94,177	81,735	9,554	2,888
California..........	11,073,544	1,471,381	1,580,482	1,650,095	6,371,586	2,975,676	2,695,994	212,108	67,574
Colorado	1,029,205	185,214	4,911	195,559	643,521	274,552	229,607	37,145	7,800
Connecticut	822,497	102,729	417,863	13,324	288,581	313,368	295,533	17,394	441
Delaware	262,238	15,979	80,792	0	165,467	55,262	46,924	2,046	6,292
Florida	2,270,865	11,499	261,742	733,419	1,264,205	488,976	468,985	4,979	15,012
Georgia............	1,409,947	192,660	392,832	99,476	724,979	365,078	315,663	34,476	14,939
Hawaii	578,692	53,834	145,986	47,050	331,822	182,003	170,233	5,335	6,435
Idaho	258,232	42,459	26,333	49,291	140,149	78,949	62,366	12,180	4,403
Illinois............	2,604,834	484,999	435,364	143,802	1,540,669	844,956	743,438	74,318	27,200
Indiana	808,965	104,962	219,064	82,020	402,919	267,683	238,464	23,373	5,846
Iowa	640,611	76,856	39,455	87,056	437,244	150,415	119,330	24,357	6,728
Kansas	582,242	81,615	66,771	33,201	400,655	132,126	106,394	17,718	8,014
Kentucky	940,642	159,364	197,472	67,028	516,778	253,365	215,658	19,164	18,543
Louisiana	1,236,019	249,386	349,988	33,242	603,403	559,823	510,500	43,124	6,199
Maine	337,786	47,673	116,266	24,631	149,216	143,940	127,405	9,648	6,887
Maryland	1,296,104	120,161	482,272	18,988	674,683	448,411	400,891	45,472	2,048
Massachusetts	892,140	279,597	375,508	0	237,035	591,601	479,807	49,589	62,205
Michigan	2,372,574	201,794	350,457	402,040	1,418,283	815,541	800,400	6,219	8,922
Minnesota	1,341,870	189,980	183,365	100,865	867,660	323,677	276,867	33,640	13,170
Mississippi	641,818	111,948	65,790	99,533	364,547	184,379	132,249	29,428	22,702
Missouri	983,054	132,368	139,491	145,531	565,664	217,559	178,074	27,656	11,829
Montana...........	236,715	56,789	25,616	40,211	114,099	98,036	83,810	13,001	1,225
Nebraska	114,132	22,878	8,680	23,049	59,525	20,301	13,633	5,262	1,406
Nevada	451,339	16,126	33,280	110,746	291,187	96,901	78,146	16,952	1,803
New Hampshire	101,609	31,162	8,980	11,267	50,200	44,538	30,946	10,827	2,765
New Jersey..........	2,232,055	363,680	586,498	343,846	938,031	771,744	720,698	42,215	8,831
New Mexico........	526,063	104,278	64,510	73,548	283,727	135,993	106,073	26,455	3,465
New York	6,597,885	161,085	649,420	1,605,342	4,182,038	1,853,859	1,724,029	79,076	50,754
North Carolina	1,798,831	312,347	402,030	74,908	1,009,546	482,285	420,996	57,942	3,347
North Dakota	104,464	22,518	8,346	16,822	56,778	27,669	17,848	7,291	2,530
Ohio	5,412,458	857,971	355,413	1,144,875	3,054,199	1,699,548	1,561,841	109,179	28,528
Oklahoma	743,204	126,901	282,839	28,464	305,000	277,196	255,718	17,147	4,331
Oregon	692,606	135,220	86,235	153,955	317,196	253,946	214,867	36,082	2,997
Pennsylvania	3,428,491	476,422	888,902	415,326	1,647,841	1,315,749	1,178,307	59,973	77,469
Rhode Island	281,252	51,012	71,570	40,403	118,267	87,254	81,775	4,520	959
South Carolina	902,866	158,887	95,545	121,911	526,523	230,234	196,047	30,360	3,827
South Dakota	193,392	26,562	10,678	15,401	140,751	30,448	23,041	6,241	1,166
Tennessee	984,376	71,700	308,432	39,947	564,297	225,947	204,645	21,302	0
Texas..............	3,182,569	735,100	858,518	77,058	1,511,893	1,009,658	823,190	169,063	17,405
Utah	365,085	86,080	18,637	57,820	202,548	90,927	65,288	22,210	3,429
Vermont	86,226	2,092	32,367	852	50,915	25,391	22,352	408	2,631
Virginia............	1,263,878	48,568	223,353	356,577	635,380	300,757	251,442	35,163	14,152
Washington	1,417,313	245,561	429,978	108,380	633,394	517,118	467,414	40,614	9,090
West Virginia	302,379	75,157	67,706	17,265	142,251	155,822	140,214	13,910	1,698
Wisconsin	1,872,187	9,493	146,174	362,877	1,353,643	347,408	309,508	35,602	2,298
Wyoming	175,190	8,163	30,428	38,505	98,094	39,973	26,913	9,214	3,846

Source: U.S. Bureau of the Census, *Finances of Employee Retirement Systems of State and Local Governments in 1985-86*.
Note: Because of rounding, detail may not add to totals.

FINANCES OF STATE-ADMINISTERED EMPLOYEE RETIREMENT SYSTEMS, BY STATE: 1985-86—Continued
(In thousands of dollars)

			Cash and security holdings at end of fiscal year				
				Governmental securities			Non-governmental securities
				Federal securities		State and local	
State	Total	Cash and deposits	Total	U.S. Treasury	Federal agency		
All states	$437,229,289	$16,383,059	$118,045,879	$88,307,270	$29,738,609	$1,195,521	$301,604,830
Alabama................	5,188,032	50,407	371,799	204,393	167,406	0	4,765,826
Alaska.................	2,727,085	122,767	948,351	948,351	0	0	1,655,967
Arizona................	5,970,254	143,379	1,985,044	1,791,903	193,141	0	3,841,831
Arkansas	2,316,141	165,837	909,995	790,340	119,655	11	1,240,298
California..............	76,661,282	3,774,055	11,013,985	7,648,535	3,365,450	30,073	61,843,169
Colorado	6,474,552	149,039	968,661	833,921	134,740	145	5,356,707
Connecticut	4,903,361	375,566	1,046,239	547,933	498,306	907	3,480,649
Delaware	1,065,240	14,401	18,309	10,825	7,484	0	1,032,530
Florida	11,944,444	387,876	2,169,783	1,691,636	478,147	2,165	9,384,620
Georgia................	7,974,435	462,386	3,185,570	3,117,854	67,716	135	4,326,344
Hawaii	2,672,949	37,558	915,385	148,553	766,832	0	1,720,006
Idaho	940,305	63,530	167,278	121,505	45,773	0	709,497
Illinois................	19,176,593	1,853,391	5,654,486	4,266,254	1,388,232	4,676	11,664,040
Indiana................	3,185,482	160,126	1,889,360	1,416,251	473,109	0	1,135,996
Iowa	3,520,892	42,460	1,090,108	863,458	226,650	0	2,388,324
Kansas	2,701,812	122,230	769,893	606,913	162,980	10,011	1,799,678
Kentucky	4,460,769	609,631	1,616,360	1,133,352	483,008	122	2,234,656
Louisiana	5,550,573	569,516	2,441,356	2,013,648	427,708	10	2,539,691
Maine	1,030,076	100,759	255,950	138,833	117,117	984	672,383
Maryland	7,097,845	403,525	2,088,288	1,400,632	687,656	865	4,605,167
Massachusetts	5,843,793	596,243	1,750,423	630,056	1,120,367	13,098	3,484,029
Michigan	19,091,303	865,863	1,761,499	1,028,976	732,523	4,330	16,459,611
Minnesota	8,766,631	579,940	1,622,548	1,474,146	148,402	1,822	6,562,321
Mississippi	2,947,312	371,561	1,540,859	1,117,302	423,557	0	1,034,892
Missouri	6,656,148	107,120	1,616,912	602,615	1,014,297	3,199	4,928,917
Montana...............	1,064,659	60,966	144,918	113,991	30,927	1,319	857,456
Nebraska	1,052,600	40,402	359,475	286,877	72,598	497	652,226
Nevada	1,753,955	644	451,413	180,470	270,943	0	1,301,898
New Hampshire	926,237	19,890	232,070	169,535	62,535	0	674,277
New Jersey.............	13,796,060	2,246	1,724,958	104,997	1,619,961	188	12,068,668
New Mexico............	2,333,214	178,527	1,292,715	855,631	437,084	0	861,972
New York	69,581,992	545,634	23,591,782	20,109,855	3,481,927	978,167	44,466,409
North Carolina	10,086,339	16,252	3,068,914	2,255,897	813,017	0	7,001,173
North Dakota	613,403	105,024	248,224	147,391	100,833	12	260,143
Ohio	26,642,862	169,995	8,731,759	6,434,849	2,296,910	126,109	17,614,999
Oklahoma	3,337,103	511,520	1,602,852	670,108	932,744	82	1,222,649
Oregon	3,954,598	101,632	694,464	646,352	48,112	0	3,158,502
Pennsylvania	17,199,939	657,287	6,003,886	4,825,914	1,177,972	445	10,538,321
Rhode Island	1,245,342	30,742	525,309	520,598	4,711	0	689,291
South Carolina	6,170,291	4,322	4,773,205	3,828,278	944,927	1,668	1,391,096
South Dakota	824,213	3,334	280,745	146,415	134,330	100	540,034
Tennessee	6,040,161	113,422	1,708,839	1,614,240	94,599	0	4,217,900
Texas..................	20,665,810	303,210	7,832,381	5,575,108	2,257,273	15	12,530,204
Utah	2,195,862	296,065	650,609	635,324	15,285	0	1,249,188
Vermont................	457,317	45,820	42,631	33,606	9,025	419	368,447
Virginia................	6,691,318	317,630	2,150,248	1,550,147	600,101	415	4,223,025
Washington	7,310,370	297,425	1,250,047	958,630	291,417	738	5,762,160
West Virginia	1,266,145	133,792	573,625	569,384	4,241	4,682	554,046
Wisconsin..............	11,625,125	78,208	1,807,772	1,459,207	348,565	8,112	9,731,033
Wyoming	907,519	90,473	504,597	66,281	438,316	0	312,449
Dist. of Col.	619,546	129,431	0	0	0	0	490,115

Table 7.21
COMPARATIVE STATISTICS FOR STATE-ADMINISTERED PUBLIC EMPLOYEE RETIREMENT SYSTEMS: 1985-86

| State | Percent of receipts paid by | | | Annual benefit payments as a percentage of | | Average benefit pay-ments(a) | Investment earnings as a percentage of cash and security holdings | Cash and deposits | Percentage distribution of cash and security holdings | | |
| | Employee contri-bution | State gov-ernment | Local gov-ernment | Annual receipts | Cash and security holdings | | | | Governmental securities | | Nongov-ernmental securities |
									Federal	State and local	
All states	13.0	17.6	13.8	26.4	5.2	$504	11.0	3.1	26.5	0.1	70.2
Alabama.............	15.7	28.4	0.0	22.9	4.3	431	10.4	0.2	2.8	0.0	97.1
Alaska..............	10.9	16.7	13.1	14.7	3.8	944	15.2	4.7	34.9	0.0	60.4
Arizona.............	13.9	4.2	10.2	14.9	3.1	487	15.0	2.6	32.8	0.0	64.6
Arkansas............	10.7	29.1	4.5	18.9	3.6	360	10.8	6.3	39.1	0.0	54.6
California...........	13.3	14.3	14.9	24.3	4.9	637	11.6	4.5	8.5	0.0	87.1
Colorado............	18.0	0.5	19.0	22.3	4.2	704	11.7	1.1	4.0	0.0	84.9
Connecticut.........	12.5	50.8	1.6	35.9	7.9	777	7.7	7.3	25.2	0.0	67.5
Delaware............	6.1	30.8	0.0	17.9	4.7	442	16.4	0.6	0.7	0.0	98.8
Florida..............	0.5	11.5	32.3	20.7	4.8	387	13.0	1.8	14.8	0.0	83.4
Georgia.............	13.7	27.9	7.1	22.4	4.5	594	10.2	5.4	37.2	0.0	57.4
Hawaii..............	9.3	25.2	8.1	29.4	6.4	551	12.4	1.4	34.2	0.0	64.3
Idaho...............	16.4	10.2	19.1	24.2	6.7	338	15.0	6.5	17.8	0.0	75.7
Illinois..............	18.6	16.7	5.5	28.5	6.3	460	13.2	9.0	27.2	0.0	63.8
Indiana.............	13.0	27.1	10.1	29.5	7.6	371	12.8	4.8	59.5	0.0	35.7
Iowa................	12.0	6.2	13.6	18.6	3.9	236	14.2	0.2	25.1	0.0	74.7
Kansas..............	14.0	11.5	5.7	18.3	4.3	242	16.1	4.6	27.9	0.4	67.1
Kentucky............	16.9	21.0	7.1	22.9	5.2	446	12.4	13.7	37.0	0.0	49.3
Louisiana...........	20.2	28.3	2.7	41.3	10.1	661	11.9	10.6	43.5	0.0	45.9
Maine	14.1	34.4	7.3	37.7	12.4	529	14.5	9.8	24.8	0.1	65.3
Maryland............	9.3	37.2	1.5	30.9	7.6	675	12.9	6.0	31.2	0.0	62.8
Massachusetts	31.3	42.1	0.0	53.8	14.4	698	7.1	6.9	31.8	0.4	61.3
Michigan	8.5	14.8	16.9	33.7	6.2	441	11.0	2.5	5.3	0.0	92.2
Minnesota	14.2	13.7	7.5	20.6	3.8	410	11.9	6.0	20.5	0.0	73.6
Mississippi	17.4	10.3	15.5	20.6	4.6	331	12.6	11.3	52.9	0.0	35.7
Missouri	13.5	14.2	14.8	18.1	3.4	415	10.9	0.1	25.9	0.0	74.0
Montana............	24.0	10.8	17.0	35.4	7.9	463	10.7	5.7	13.6	0.0	80.6
Nebraska	20.0	7.6	20.2	11.9	2.4	156	10.6	2.2	35.3	0.1	62.4
Nevada	3.6	7.4	24.5	17.3	4.5	702	6.6	0.0	25.7	0.0	74.2
New Hampshire	30.7	8.8	11.1	30.5	3.4	322	5.4	2.0	25.1	0.0	72.8
New Jersey..........	16.3	26.3	15.4	32.3	5.2	618	6.8	0.0	12.5	0.0	87.5

COMPARATIVE STATISTICS: 1983-84—Continued

State	Percent of receipts paid by			Annual benefit payments as a percentage of		Average benefit payments(a)	Investment earnings as a percentage of cash and security holdings	Cash and deposits	Percentage distribution of cash and security holdings		
									Governmental securities		Nongovernmental securities
	Employee contribution	State government	Local government	Annual receipts	Cash and security holdings				Federal	State and local	
New Mexico	19.8	12.3	14.0	20.2	4.5	499	12.2	7.6	55.4	0.0	37.0
New York	2.4	9.8	24.3	26.1	4.0	467	9.8	0.1	33.1	0.4	66.4
North Carolina	17.4	22.3	4.2	23.4	4.2	489	10.1	0.1	30.4	0.0	69.4
North Dakota	21.6	8.0	16.1	17.1	3.1	253	9.9	16.9	41.7	0.0	41.5
Ohio	15.9	6.6	21.2	28.9	6.0	533	11.7	0.6	33.0	0.5	65.9
Oklahoma	17.1	38.1	3.8	34.4	8.1	550	9.6	15.5	48.8	0.0	35.7
Oregon	19.5	12.5	22.2	31.0	5.4	354	8.0	2.4	17.6	0.0	80.0
Pennsylvania	13.9	25.9	12.1	34.4	8.0	493	11.2	3.5	39.0	0.0	57.5
Rhode Island	18.1	25.4	14.4	29.1	7.5	593	10.8	1.8	43.8	0.0	54.3
South Carolina	17.6	10.6	13.5	21.7	3.2	453	8.6	0.0	77.4	0.0	22.5
South Dakota	13.7	5.5	8.0	11.9	2.9	241	17.9	0.3	33.6	0.0	66.1
Tennessee	7.3	31.3	4.1	20.8	4.4	373	12.0	0.2	28.9	0.0	70.9
Texas	23.1	27.0	2.4	25.9	4.6	559	8.4	0.4	40.7	0.0	58.9
Utah	23.6	5.1	15.8	17.9	3.0	349	9.2	13.5	29.6	0.0	56.9
Vermont	2.4	37.5	1.0	25.9	5.1	390	11.7	10.5	7.9	0.1	81.5
Virginia	3.8	17.7	28.2	19.9	4.9	426	12.5	3.8	35.4	0.0	60.8
Washington	17.3	30.3	7.6	33.0	6.9	554	9.4	3.8	16.6	0.0	79.7
West Virginia	24.9	22.4	5.7	46.4	11.4	364	11.6	9.6	46.1	0.0	44.3
Wisconsin	0.5	7.8	19.4	16.5	3.0	430	13.3	0.3	17.0	0.1	82.6
Wyoming	4.7	17.4	22.0	15.4	3.0	342	11.0	9.3	55.8	0.0	34.9

Source: U.S. Bureau of Census, *Finances of Employee Retirement Systems of State and Local Governments in 1985-86.*

(a) Average benefit payment for last month of fiscal year.

PRIVATIZATION AND CONTRACTING FOR STATE SERVICES

By Keon S. Chi

Privatization has emerged as a trend-setting issue to be reckoned with in only a few years. Privatization has been debated at every level of government, in the private sector and academic community. Indications are that privatizing public services will continue to be of major concern to policymakers.

Local governments long have used private businesses extensively. Privately operated local services encompass solid waste collection, street repair, custodial and security services. According to a 1987 survey by Touche Ross, nearly 80 percent of responding local governments used or planned to use private firms to deliver services. The survey showed major contributing factors to privatization were greater demand for services, citizen resistance to tax increases and elimination of the federal revenue sharing program.

The federal government, through the use of OMB Circular A-76, "Performance of Commercial Activities," has also used private firms for various programs considered to be commercial activities. During the 1950s, the federal government conceived A-76 as part of a policy to rely on private firms for goods and services, instead of government competing with the private sector. A-76 received a great deal of attention when the Reagan administration attempted to privatize commercial activities performed by federal workers. The Reagan administration's efforts include the Task Force on the Private Sector Initiatives in 1981, the President's Private Sector Survey on Cost Control (Grace Commission) in 1984 and the President's Commission on Privatization in 1987. An executive order issued in November 1987, required all federal agencies by April 1988 to identify their commercial activities for possible further privatization.

States have not been as quick to privatize as local governments or the federal government. States commonly rely on the private sector for some in-house services and legal, medical, engineering and technical professional services. Now states are considering private vendors for public services traditionally performed by government employees. Several states have conducted comprehensive privatization feasibility studies, established legislative committees on privatization and enacted privatization laws to implement alternative methods of delivering services.

Forms of Privatization

Definitions of privatization vary: the transfer of government assets or functions to the private sector, the shifting of government services and state enterprises to private sector owners and/or suppliers, a shift from publicly to privately produced goods and services, and governmental reliance on the private sector to satisfy the needs of society. Some use the term privatization and the phrase alternative service delivery synonymously. In essence, however, privatization means the use of the private sector in government management and delivery of public services.

Privatization may take several forms. The 10 forms of privatization used or available in state government are as follows:

1. *Contracting.* The state enters into agreements with private firms, for profit or non-profit, to provide goods or services. The state funds private provision of public services. Contracting is used for in-house and professional services, transportation, health care and social services and to a lesser degree employment and training, mental health and mental retardation, fleet management and corrections.

Dr. Chi is a senior policy analyst for The Council of State Governments in Lexington, Kentucky.

2. *Vouchers.* The government provides vouchers which allow the public to purchase services from private firms available in the market. As in contracting, government pays for the service. Several states use vouchers for social services and educational programs. Examples include day care programs in Massachusetts and New Jersey, training and employment programs in Illinois and Massachusetts, and the distinguished scholar program in New Jersey.

3. *Grants and Subsidies.* The state makes monetary contributions to help private organizations provide a service. A good example is the Employer Training Assistance Program in Illinois which provides grants and loans to companies to help cover employee training costs.

4. *Franchise.* The state gives monopoly privileges to a private firm to provide a service in a given geographical area. Franchises are used in operating concession services in state parks, such as food services, stores, sporting equipment rentals and recreational facilities.

5. *Asset Sale.* The state sells or "cashes out" its assets to private firms or individuals to shift government functions to the private sector. Examples include surplus real estate disposition sales in California, Illinois, New York and Pennsylvania.

6. *Deregulation.* The state lifts regulations on a service. In 1980, Florida deregulated the motor carrier industry in favor of a free market. Similar deregulations occurred in Arizona, Kansas, Maine and Wisconsin.

7. *Volunteerism.* States use volunteers to provide public services. Most states now have offices to coordinate volunteer action programs. Volunteers provide a variety of services, such as visitor services in state parks; geological studies in California; tutors, interpreters, drivers and shopping assistants in Florida; and the adoption program called "One Church and One Child" in Illinois.

8. *Private Donation.* The state may rely on the private sector for assistance in providing public services. Private firms may loan personnel, facilities or equipment to state agencies. The private sector also may make monetary or in-kind contributions to states for correctional services, state parks and employment and training programs.

9. *Public-Private Partnership.* The state conducts projects in cooperation with private firms, relying on private resources instead of tax monies. Examples include private sector advisory commissions for cost control and efficiency studies, and vocational education and employment training programs.

10. *Service Shedding.* The state drastically reduces or eliminates a service so the private sector can assume the function. Some state health, human services and recreational programs have been considered as candidates for this form of privatization. Private charitable organizations may pick up such services with the help of taxpayers' contributions.

Reasons for Privatization

Why privatize? Reasons for privatizing state services vary greatly, but there are four major incentives: cost savings, administrative expediency, management improvement and ideology.

First, privatization is often considered by state government as a cost-saving measure. Proponents contend that privatization is a more efficient and less costly way of delivering services. Cost-savings may be achieved through either economies of scale by consolidating administration of services, for example, or through competition among private providers.

Second, privatization may be favored for administrative or political reasons. When agencies lack resources, or the state has a freeze on hiring, or the state has to meet certain deadlines, privatization has been called into use. Under these circumstances, cost-savings is not necessarily the prime motive for privatization.

Third, the state may consider privatization as a management and productivity improvement tool. One of the benefits of the private sector is that it has less red tape and bureaucracy. It is usually easier for the private sector to make quick investments in technology and to improve workforce productivity. Privatization may also spur state employees to greater productivity when competing with the private sector.

And, fourth, ideology also plays a role in privatization. Big government is seen as a threat to some people. To them, privatization is regarded as a way to cut the size of government. Proponents contend that government should not be involved in producing or providing commercial activities. Thus conservatives often perceive privatization as a policy innovation aiming at efficiency, while liberals tend to oppose privatization, expressing concerns about equity and accountability issues.

Privatization study

A state-wide or agency-wide privatization study may be initiated either by the legislature, the governor's executive order or a state agency to identify opportunities for greater use of private firms in delivering state services. Such a study may be conducted by a state agency, other public organizations or a private consultant. The following are a few examples of such studies.

• In 1984, Virginia produced one of the most comprehensive state privatization studies, *Contracting Services in Virginia,* conducted by the Department of Planning and Budget. In 1986, Virginia's General Assembly mandated a privatization feasibility study for mental health and mental retardation facilities and the Department of Planning and Budget prepared a report, *The Feasibility of Contracting in Virginia's Mental Health and Mental Retardation Facilities.*

• The Wisconsin Expenditure Commission, charged to study the potential benefits of privatization by the governor, submitted a report in 1986 entitled *Privatization in Wisconsin State and Local Governments.* The study made a list of alternatives state and local governments could consider to further privatize public services.

• The Texas Commission on Economy and Efficiency in State Government sponsored a privatization study and the Lyndon B. Johnson School of Public Affairs at the University of Texas, Austin in 1986 produced a report, *Contracting Selected State Government Functions: Issues and Next Step.* The LBJ School prepared another report in 1987 entitled *Contracting Selected State Government Functions: Legislation and Implementation.*

• In June of 1986, the Connecticut Public/Private Partnership Commission produced a report, *Contracting-Out Selected Functions of the Connecticut Department of Motor Vehicles and Other State Agencies.* The study, conducted by a private consultant, was designed to test a methodology for "the routine application of privatization techniques to functions and services" performed by state workers.

• The New Jersey State and Local Expenditure and Revenue Policy Commission in 1987 completed a privatization study, *Alternative Methods for Delivering Public Services in New Jersey.* The study dealt with the extent of the use of contracts, intergovernmental agreements, vouchers, and use of voluntary organiza-

tions in state and local governments in New Jersey.

• In 1986 and 1987, a study team of researchers from The Urban Institute (UI) and The Council of State Governments (CSG) conducted two *Alternative Service Delivery* studies for Delaware and Maryland. Unlike other studies, in these privatization studies, state policymakers and administrators identified opportunities for greater use of private firms. The UI-CSG study team held a series of workshops for participating state agency representatives over a period of several months to develop specific recommendations for future privatization opportunities.

Privatization Laws

Privatization has been implemented in some state governments under the existing statutory provisions. In many states, however, minor revisions or a complete overhaul of the statute are necessary. By 1987, more than 20 states enacted legislation removing legal barriers to privatization. State privatization laws may be grouped into three broad categories: general legislation applicable to all state agencies, legislation for specific state services and legislation for specific local services.

• *General legislation for all state agencies.* A good example is Colorado's privatization legislation (Colo. Rev. Stat. Ann. 24-113-101) effective July 1988. This legislation prohibits state agencies from competing with private enterprises by engaging in the manufacturing, processing, sale, offering for sale, rental, leasing, delivery, dispensing, distributing, or advertising of goods or services to the public which are also offered by private enterprise, unless specifically authorized by law.

• *Legislation for selected state services.* Several states enacted legislation to authorize certain state agencies to privatize selected services. For example, in 1987, Texas Senate Bill 251 allowed the Department of Corrections to contract with private firms for the financing, construction, operation, maintenance and management of four correctional facilities.

• *Legislation authorizing local governments to privatize selected services.* Many state laws allow their political subdivisions to contract with private firms to handle wastewater and solid waste treatment facility. Other areas of local services authorized by states to contract include fire protection, water and electric power facility management and public works. Indiana's House Bill 1353, introduced in 1987, is designed to authorize local governments to negotiate contracts for design, construction, operation, financing, ownership and maintenance of certain structures. A bill (LRB 5190/1) was introduced in the Wisconsin legislature in 1987 to allow local school districts to contract for the performance of teaching services by licensed teachers who are not employed by the district.

State Contracts

Of the 10 forms of privatization described above, contracting is most frequently used in state government. In fact, privatization in most states means contracting. States vary greatly in the frequency and service areas of contracting. A few examples illustrate this trend.

• In 1981, California wrote nearly 6,000 contracts worth more than $1.4 billion to carry out certain state administrative and public services. The largest share of the contracts went to health care services.

• In Minnesota, the largest number of contracts (2,178 worth more than $454 million) were let for transportation in 1983, followed by economic security (1,729 contracts) and energy and economic development (694 contracts).

• In fiscal year 1982-83, Virginia spent $954.5 million on contracts for in-house services and $18.4 million for public services, including individual and family services.

• In Wisconsin, the top four areas of contracted services have been health and social services, the University of Wisconsin system, labor and human relations, and transportation. In 1984-85, state agencies issued 39,538 non-construction or engineering contracts worth more than $186 million.

• According to the 1987 privatization study in New Jersey, the state departments of Banking, Civil Service, Community Affairs, Corrections, Education, Labor and State Treasury contracted out less than 5 percent of their operating budgets to private firms, while the Health Department spent about half, and the departments of Agriculture, and Energy and Environmental Protection spent 25 percent. About 75 percent of the Department of Transportation's budget was spent for contracting for designing, building and maintaining roads and highways.

• A survey of participants at the 1987 annual meeting of the National Association of State Purchasing Officials showed that some

states (for example, New Jersey, South Carolina, Utah, West Virginia and Wisconsin) have contracted part of mental health and mental retardation, health care, employment training, transportation, facility management and maintenance, and professional and administrative services, while other states (for example, Tennessee and Washington) have not used contractors to provide such services except administrative services. A majority of states, however, have contracted a few selected public services.

Currently, according to a recent survey of the 50 states released in 1988 by the National Association of State Purchasing Officials, all but two states have or are actively developing a purchasing policy, rules, regulations or administrative procedures manual, and 44 states have a contract procedures manual used in the central purchasing office. All states but one now have a central purchasing office which contracts for most or all state agencies.

Guidelines for Contracting

In order to determine whether a state service should be contracted to a private firm, the state needs to develop comprehensive guidelines for contracting ranging from preparing a Request-for-Proposal to contract monitoring and evaluation. Guidelines should also address the three most tricky issues: specific reasons for contracting, cost comparison method and employee union relations.

Oregon has comprehensive guidelines offering suggestions for contracting state services. In 1987, the state's Executive Department and Department of General Services published a document, *Guidelines for Contracting State Work,* to help state agencies conduct a feasibility study to determine potential costs and benefits of contracting a state service. The guidelines cover three areas in contract decisionmaking: specific conditions necessitating contracting, cost comparison and employee (union) relations. But the guidelines were not intended as administrative rules or policies; rather these were designed to be general advice to state agencies for contract decisionmaking.

In 1987, the UI-CSG study team developed a detailed review process for state agencies for *Analysis of Service Delivery Alternatives.* The process covers selection of programs and agencies for review, workshops for representatives from participating agencies, group efforts to examine alternative service delivery approaches, cost comparison and provision of motivation, and incentives to agency managers to undertake a feasibility study.

Conditions Conducive to Contracting

According to the Oregon guidelines, state agencies are encouraged to consider contracting as an option when any of the following conditions exist:
- Newly-created services with significant start-up costs.
- Specialized services and equipment.
- Worn out and obsolete equipment in need of replacement.
- Geographic location of client or customer base.
- Budget reductions or projected revenue shortfalls.
- Limited position availability.
- Hiring freeze.
- Lack of fund source or mechanism to replace equipment and facilities.
- A readily available market of service providers.
- Pay practices bar paying market wages to get needed services.
- Variable or uncertain workload.
- Labor intentive work that requires routine procedures and limited supervision and performance can be easily monitored.
- Skills to write work specifications, draft contracts and set up performance monitoring are present.
- If legislative or other mandates require it.

The UI-CSG guidelines suggest criteria for assessing feasibility of using contracting (or other privatization forms) focusing more on future conditions than current ones. The following is a list of slightly modified criteria:
- To what extent do the state laws or regulations prevent or preclude contracting for the program or service relating to procurement and personnel?
- To what extent do federal laws or regulations make it difficult for the agency to contract the service?
- Is contracting consistent with the goals and policy direction of the agency's leadership?
- Is contracting consistent with the goals and policy direction of the governor's office?
- Is contracting consistent with the goals and policy direction of the legislature?
- Is there likely to be positive or negative reaction by the public to contracting a service?

- Will current personnel be displaced?
- Are there likely to be important consequences of failures?
- Are the number and quality of needed personnel likely to be available in the private sector?
- Are qualified personnel or organizations likely to be available in the labor market, both initially and in the future?
- Are new facilities, major new equipment, and/or major rehabilitation likely to be required?
- Are agency managers frustrated in their attempts to make desired changes in the program because of red tape, etc.?
- Are current state employees dissatisfied with program conditions and environment?
- Does the contracting provide a constructive competitive environment?
- Is the agency experienced in administering and monitoring a contracting arrangement?
- Is there opportunity for corruption, i.e. fraud, bribes, payoffs, etc.?
- Are there interrelationships with other programs or other agencies that would be affected positively or negatively?
- Are there substantial fluctuations or changes in workload both from month to month and over various times of the day or days of the week?
- Have there been any recent crises, major problems, or adverse publicity with the service, thus making contracting more feasible?

Cost Comparison

One of the most difficult tasks state officials face when contracting a state service is comparing in-house and contracting costs. Among the questions often asked is, "What costs need to be compared?" The Oregon guidelines offer cost comparison elements as well as cost comparison worksheet. In-house costs include salaries and other personnel expenses, equipment (capital outlay) costs and services and supplies. Administrative overhead costs include service charges assessed on the basis of the agency's number of full-time equivalent positions.

Estimates for contracting costs include contract management and monitoring costs as well as one-time costs, including staff time to prepare the bid, the cost of training staff to administer the contract, the cost to set up a contract monitoring system, buyout of unused employee leave benefits, disposing of unused equipment, and unemployment expense if the work is done by staff and former employees who don't remain with the contractor.

Along with cost comparison analysis, state officials must also decide cost savings size and when the savings must be realized. The Oregon guidelines suggest use of a reasonable break-even point of no more than three biennia in deciding if contracting is cost effective.

Employee Union Relations

Contracting is often viewed by government employee union leaders as "union busting." The American Federation of State, County and Municipal Employees (AFSCME), for example, has led fights against privatization efforts at all levels of government. In Oregon, as in several other states, state agencies may not be able to contract out state work without employee union approval. The contracting process provided in the contract between the state and the Oregon Public Employes Union (OPEU) is as follows:

• A state agency considering contracting work must conduct a formal feasibility study to determine the potential cost and benefits.

• The agency must notify the union within one week of its decision to do the study and indicate job classifications and work areas affected.

• OPEU must be given 30 days notice before an agency issues bids if contracting the work will displace bargaining unit workers.

• The agency must also tell the union the results of the feasibility study such as assumptions used, cost detail, projected cost savings, and expected quality changes, if any.

• OPEU may submit an alternative proposal, such as a productivity improvement program, during the 30 day notice period.

• The union proposal must be put into effect if it shows greater cost savings and quality improvements.

• The agency and OPEU are required to discuss the effect of contracting the work on bargaining unit workers if any full time bargaining union employee will lose their job.

• Once an agency decides to contract the work, it must either require the contractor to hire displaced workers or place the employees elsewhere in state government.

• Workers hired by the contractor must be paid the same rate of pay for at least six months subject only to "just cause" terminations.

• The agency will provide workers hired by the contractor with health and dental insurance coverage through the Bargaining Unit Benefits Board for six months.

Incentives for Privatization and Contracting

In an effort to reduce employee resistance and give incentives to federal employees to participate in privatization initiatives, the President's Council on Management Improvement established the Privatization Concerns Task Group. The task Group in July of 1986 released a report, "Employee Incentives for Privatization." Many of the suggested incentives can be considered by state government. The following is a summary of selected policy options under five approaches taken from the report.

• *Employee-owned business.* Agencies would encourage employees to privatize commercial activities by converting them to employee-owned businesses, by transferring the capital assets of the government activity to the employee-owned businesses or by providing employee-owned businesses with services to organize and create businesses.

• *Pay and benefit policy revisions.* Revise the retirement and severance pay systems to allow displaced employees to continue to be eligible for Civil Service Retirement System benefits. The approach would return to employees payments made by their employing agencies to the Civil Service Retirement Trust Fund, or provide inflation protection to employees who elect to remain eligible for retirement, or give severance pay to employees, or provide employees the option of early retirement.

• *Job placement and retraining.* Employ displaced workers in the private sector by instituting outside hiring restrictions, by using savings from contracting to retrain workers for jobs in other government agencies, by placing displaced workers with training vouchers or stipends to help transition to new occupations, or by soliciting private sector and contractor's assistance in finding jobs for displaced workers.

• *Employee and organized incentives.* Individuals and agencies would receive monetary rewards for their efforts to privatize by tying performance appraisal, incentive bonuses and other forms of recognition to progress toward privatization. Employees would be given a share of the savings from privatization activities, or agencies could be allowed to retain a percentage of their savings in a revolving

fund for further privatization.
* *Contractor purchase of functions.* Agencies could raise funds to pay for displaced employees by selling commercial functions to private businesses.

The Prospects

Privatization is a multi-dimensional issue and presents new challenges to state policymakers.

First, in the next few years privatization will be examined more closely than ever before as a cost-saving and productivity improvement approach to meet growing demands in state and local services. Yet no one should claim that privatization is a panacea for inefficient government management or that privatization is inherently superior to government services. The cost effectiveness of privatization may be highly situational.

Second, although several forms of privatization are available, contracting is likely to be more widely used than other forms. It is interesting to see how extensively states will make use of the private sector in providing other state services currently performed by government employees. Obviously, not every state function can be easily contracted. Certain functions, such as maintaining bank data and tax records, might not easily be contracted to private firms for the reasons of security and confidentiality. Defining such inherent government functions that should not be contracted and those commercial functions that can be performed by the private sector may be a challenging task.

Third, privatization might not be successfully implemented unless existing institutional and administrative hurdles are cleared. Agency managers' orientations are also important. Decentralized government authority in contracting government services, the intransigence of government agencies, application of the Davis-Bacon Act (which requires the contractor to pay prevailing labor wages), and unrealistic cost comparison procedures can impede privatization.

And, fourth, the success or failure of privatization depends on the public and private sectors. For state policymakers and administrators, a thorough pre-analysis of contracting opportunities, a carefully prepared Request-for-Proposal, and a well-devised contract administration, monitoring and performance evaluation are essential for successful privatization.

For successful contracting, the private sector must have qualified and capable providers who can compete with each other in the labor market, who can provide prescribed goods or services without interruptions or mismanagement, and who will reject fraud, bribery, kickbacks, pay-offs and other illegal actions that state managers and employee unions are concerned about. The public and private sectors together can improve government management and delivery of state services through privatization.

References:

American Federation of State, County and Municipal Employees, AFL-CIO. *When Public Services Go Private*, 1987.
Chi, Keon S. "Privatization: A Public Option?" *State Government News*, June 1985.
_____. "Private-Public Alliances Grow," *State Government News*, January 1986.
Butler, Stuart. *Privatizing Federal Spending: A Strategy to Eliminate the Deficit*, New York: Universe Books, 1985.
Council of State Governments and National Association of State Purchasing Officials. *A Guide to Buying Professional and General Services*, 1986.
Council of State Governments and National Association of State Purchasing Officials. *State and Local Government Purchasing*, Third Edition, 1988.
Hatry, Harry, et al. *Opportunities for the Greater Use of the Private Sector in Delivering State Services*, The Urban Institute and Council of State Governments, December 31, 1987.
Lyndon B. Johnson School of Public Affairs, The University of Texas at Austin. *Contracting Selected State Government Functions: Issues and Next Steps*, Policy Research Project Report Number 75, 1986.
_____. *Contracting Selected State Government Functions: Legislation and Implementation*, Policy Research Project Report Number 81, 1987.
National Institute of Justice. "Contracting for the Operation of Prisons and Jails," *Research in Brief*, June 1987.
New Jersey State and Local Expenditure and Revenue Policy Commission. *Alternative Methods for Delivering Public Services in New Jersey*, February 1987.

Office of Management and Budget. *OMB Circular No. A-76 (Revised): Performance of Commercial Activities*, August 1983.

Oregon Department of General Services and Executive Department. *Guidelines for Contracting State Work*, 1987.

Privatization Concerns Task Group, The President's Council on Management Improvement. *Employee Incentives for Privatization*, July 1986.

Savas, E. S. *Privatization: The Key to Better Government*, Chatham House, 1987.

Short, John. *The Contract Cookbook for Purchase of Service*, The Council of State Governments and National Association of State Purchasing Officials, 1987.

Touche Ross, Inc. *Privatization in America*, Washington, D. C., 1987.

Urban Institute and Council of State Governments. *Analysis of Service Delivery Alternatives: Building Innovation Into Program Reviews*, October 1987.

Virginia Department of Planning and Budget. *Contracting Services in Virginia*, November 1984.

Virginia Department of Planning and Budget. *The Feasibility of Contracting in Virginia's Mental Health and Mental Retardation Facilities*, March 1987.

Wisconsin Expenditure Commission. *Privatization in Wisconsin State and Local Governments*, October 1986.

Table 7.22
FUNCTIONS AND RESPONSIBILITIES OF STATE LIBRARY AGENCIES

State	Library services to state governments							Statewide library services development															
	Documents	Information and reference service	Legislative reference	Law library	Genealogy and state history	Archives	Liaison with institutional libraries	Coordination of academic libraries	Coordination of public libraries	Coordination of school libraries	Coordination of institutional libraries	Research	Coordination of library systems	Consulting services	Interlibrary loan, reference and bibliographic service	Statistical gathering and analysis	Library legislation review	Interstate library compacts and other cooperative efforts	Specialized resource centers	Direct service to the public	Annual reports	Public relations	Continuing education
Alabama	★	★	†	†	…	…	★	…	★	†	★	★	★	★	★	★	★	★	★	†	★	★	★
Alaska	★	★	†	…	…	…	★	†	★	†	★	★	★	★	★	★	†	★	★	★	★	†	★
Arizona	★	★	★	★	★	★	★	★	★	★	★	★	★	★	★	★	★	★	★	★	★	†	★
Arkansas	★	★	…	…	…	…	★	†	★	†	★	★	★	★	★	★	★	★	★	…	★	★	★
California	★	★	★	★	…	…	★	†	★	…	†	★	★	★	★	★	†	★	†	…	★	†	†
Colorado	★	…	…	…	…	…	★	†	★	★	★	★	†	★	★	★	★	†	…	★	†	★	†
Connecticut	★	★	★	★	★	†	★	…	★	†	★	★	★	★	★	★	★	★	★	★	★	★	★
Delaware	†	★	†	†	…	†	★	†	★	†	★	†	★	★	★	†	★	†	★	★	★	★	★
Florida	★	★	…	…	…	…	★	…	★	…	★	★	★	★	★	★	★	★	★	★	★	†	★
Georgia	†	★	…	…	…	…	★	…	★	†	★	†	★	★	★	★	★	★	★	★	★	★	†
Hawaii	★	★	…	…	★	★	★	…	★	★	†	†	†	★	†	★	…	…	★	★	†	†	†
Idaho	†	★	†	…	†	…	★	…	★	★	★	★	★	★	★	★	★	★	★	★	★	★	★
Illinois	★	★	†	†	…	†	†	†	★	†	★	†	★	★	★	★	★	★	†	…	★	★	†
Indiana	★	★	†	★	†	…	★	†	★	†	★	†	★	★	★	†	★	★	★	…	★	★	†
Iowa	★	★	…	★	…	†	★	†	★	†	★	†	★	★	★	★	★	★	★	★	★	★	†
Kansas	★	★	★	…	…	†	★	†	★	†	★	†	★	★	★	★	★	†	★	★	†	★	†
Kentucky	†	★	…	…	†	★	★	†	★	…	†	★	★	★	★	★	★	†	†	★	†	★	†
Louisiana	†	★	†	…	…	★	★	†	★	†	★	★	★	★	★	★	★	★	★	†	†	★	†
Maine	★	★	†	…	…	★	★	†	★	★	★	†	★	★	★	★	★	†	★	★	†	★	†
Maryland	†	†	…	…	…	…	★	†	★	★	★	★	★	★	★	★	†	★	★	★	★	★	★
Massachusetts	…	†	…	…	…	…	★	…	★	†	★	★	★	†	★	†	★	★	…	…	★	†	★
Michigan	★	★	†	★	★	★	★	†	★	†	†	★	★	★	★	★	★	★	†	★	★	★	★
Minnesota	…	†	…	…	…	…	★	†	★	†	†	★	†	★	★	★	†	★	★	★	★	★	★
Mississippi	★	★	†	…	…	…	★	†	★	†	★	★	★	★	★	★	†	★	†	★	★	★	★
Missouri	†	†	†	…	…	…	★	†	★	†	★	…	★	★	★	★	★	†	★	★	★	★	★
Montana	†	★	…	…	…	…	★	†	★	†	★	★	★	★	★	★	★	★	★	★	★	★	★
Nebraska	★	★	†	…	…	…	★	†	★	†	★	★	★	★	★	★	★	★	★	★	★	★	★
Nevada	★	★	†	…	†	★	★	†	★	†	★	★	★	★	★	★	★	★	★	★	★	★	★
New Hampshire	★	★	★	★	★	…	★	…	★	†	★	†	★	★	★	★	★	†	…	★	★	★	★
New Jersey	★	★	†	★	★	…	★	†	★	★	★	★	★	★	†	★	†	★	†	★	†	★	†
New Mexico	★	★	†	†	★	★	★	†	†	†	★	†	★	★	★	★	†	★	†	★	★	†	★
New York	★	★	†	★	★	†	★	★	★	†	★	†	★	★	★	★	†	★	★	★	★	†	★
North Carolina	★	★	†	†	†	…	★	†	†	†	★	†	★	★	★	★	†	†	★	†	★	★	★
North Dakota	★	★	…	…	†	…	★	★	★	★	★	★	★	★	★	★	★	★	★	†	★	★	★
Ohio	★	★	†	…	†	…	★	†	★	†	★	★	★	★	★	★	†	★	†	†	†	†	†
Oklahoma	★	★	★	★	†	★	★	†	★	†	★	★	★	★	★	★	★	★	†	★	★	★	★
Oregon	★	★	†	…	†	…	★	†	★	†	★	★	★	★	★	★	★	★	…	★	★	★	★
Pennsylvania	★	★	†	★	†	…	★	★	★	★	★	★	★	★	★	★	★	★	★	…	★	★	★
Rhode Island	†	…	…	…	…	…	★	★	★	…	★	★	★	★	★	†	★	★	★	†	★	★	†
South Carolina	†	★	★	…	†	…	★	…	★	†	★	†	★	★	★	★	★	★	★	…	★	★	★
South Dakota	★	★	★	…	†	†	★	†	†	★	★	★	★	★	★	★	†	†	★	★	★	★	★
Tennessee	★	†	†	…	★	★	†	…	★	†	★	★	★	★	★	★	†	†	†	★	†	★	★
Texas	★	★	…	…	★	★	★	†	★	†	†	★	★	★	★	★	†	†	†	★	★	★	★
Utah	★	★	…	…	…	…	★	†	★	†	★	★	★	★	★	★	†	†	★	★	★	★	★
Vermont	★	★	†	★	†	…	★	…	★	★	†	★	★	★	★	★	†	★	★	★	★	★	★
Virginia	★	†	†	…	★	★	★	…	★	…	★	†	★	★	★	★	★	★	★	†	†	†	†
Washington	★	★	★	…	†	†	★	†	†	★	★	†	★	★	★	★	†	★	★	★	★	★	★
West Virginia	†	†	†	…	…	…	★	†	★	†	★	★	★	★	★	★	★	…	★	★	★	★	★
Wisconsin	†	†	…	…	…	…	★	†	★	★	★	†	★	★	★	★	★	†	★	★	†	★	★
Wyoming	★	★	…	…	…	†	★	★	★	†	★	…	★	★	★	★	…	†	★	†	★	★	†

Note: For additional information, see *Standards for Library Functions at the State Level*, 3rd edition. (American Library Association, 1985).

Key:
★—Primary.
†—Shared.
. . .—None.

FUNCTIONS AND RESPONSIBILITIES—Continued

State	Statewide development of library resources										Statewide development of information networks				Financing library programs		
	Long-range planning	Determination of size and scope of collections in the state	Mobilization of resources	Subject and reference centers	Resources—books	Resources—other printed materials	Resources—multimedia	Resources—materials for the blind and handicapped	Coordination of resources	Little-used materials	Planning of information networks	Provision of centralized facilities	Exchange of information and materials	Interstate cooperation	Administration of federal aid	Administration of state aid	Financing of library systems and networks
Alabama	★	★	★	★	★	★	★	★	★	★	★	†	★	★	★	★	★
Alaska	★	†	†	†	†	†	★	★	★	...	★	†	★	†	★	★	†
Arizona	★	★	★	★	★	★	★	★	★	...	★	★	★	★	★	★	★
Arkansas	★	★	★	★	★	★	★	★	★	★	★	★	★	★	★	★	★
California	★	†	†	†	†	†	†	†	★	†	†	†	†	★	★	★	★
Colorado	★	†	†	†	†	†	†	★	†	†	†	†	†	★	★	★	★
Connecticut	★	★	★	†	★	★	★	★	★	★	★	★	★	★	★	★	★
Delaware	★	†	★	†	★	★	★	★	★	★	★	★	★	★	★	★	★
Florida	★	†	†	★	†	†	†	†	★	★	★	★	★	★	★	★	★
Georgia	★	★	★	★	★	★	★	★	★	★	★	★	★	★	★	★	★
Hawaii	†	†	†	★	†	†	†	★	†	★	†	†	†	†	†	†	†
Idaho	★	†	★	†	★	★	★	★	★	★	†	†	★	†	★	...	†
Illinois	†	†	†	†	†	†	†	†	†	...	†	†	†	★	★	★	★
Indiana	★	...	†	†	†	†	†	†	†	...	†	†	†	★	★	★	★
Iowa	★	★	★	★	★	★	★	★	★	★	★	★	★	★	★	★	★
Kansas	★	★	†	†	†	†	†	†	†	†	★	★	★	★	★	★	★
Kentucky	★	†	†	†	†	†	†	†	★	†	★	★	★	★	★	★	★
Louisiana	†	†	†	†	†	†	†	★	†	...	★	†	★	★	★	★	★
Maine	★	★	★	†	★	★	★	★	†	†	★	†	★	★	★	★	★
Maryland	★	...	...	★	...	...	...	★	★	...	★	†	★	★	★	★	★
Massachusetts	†	...	†	...	†	†	†	†	†	†	★	...	†	★	★	★	★
Michigan	★	...	†	†	†	†	†	★	★	†	★	...	†	★	★	★	★
Minnesota	★	†	★	†	†	†	†	★	★	★	★	†	†	★	★	★	†
Mississippi	★	★	★	★	★	★	†	★	★	★	★	†	★	★	★	★	†
Missouri	★	†	★	★	★	★	†	†	★	★	★	†	†	†	★	★	†
Montana	★	★	★	★	★	★	★	★	†	†	★	†	★	★	★	★	★
Nebraska	★	...	★	★	★	★	★	★	†	...	★	...	★	★	★	★	★
Nevada	★	†	†	†	†	†	†	★	★	★	★	†	★	★	★	★	★
New Hampshire	★	★	★	†	†	†	†	★	★	★	★	★	★	★	★	★	★
New Jersey	★	†	★	†	†	†	†	★	†	†	★	★	★	★	★	★	★
New Mexico	★	†	★	...	†	†	†	★	★	★	★	★	★	★	†	★	★
New York	★	†	†	†	★	★	★	†	★	★	★	★	★	†	★	★	★
North Carolina	★	†	†	†	★	★	★	★	★	†	★	★	★	★	★	★	★
North Dakota	★	...	★	★	★	★	★	★	★	†	★	★	★	★	★	★	★
Ohio	★	†	†	†	†	†	†	†	★	★	★	...	★	★	★	★	★
Oklahoma	★	†	★	★	†	†	★	★	★	★	★	★	†	★	★	★	†
Oregon	★	★	★	...	†	★	★	★	†	†	★	†	†	★	★	★	†
Pennsylvania	★	†	†	†	★	†	†	†	★	†	★	★	★	...	★	★	★
Rhode Island	★	†	★	†	†	†	†	★	★	...	★	★	★	★	★	★	★
South Carolina	★	†	...	★	†	†	†	★	★	...	★	★	★	★	★	★	...
South Dakota	★	†	★	★	†	†	★	★	†	★	★	★	†	★	★	...	★
Tennessee	★	...	†	†	†	†	†	†	†	★	★	†	★	★	★	★	★
Texas	★	†	†	†	★	★	†	★	★	†	★	†	†	★	★	★	★
Utah	★	†	†	†	†	†	†	★	†	...	★	†	★	★	★	★	†
Vermont	★	†	†	†	†	†	★	★	★	†	†	†	★	★	★	★	†
Virginia	★	†	†	†	†	†	†	†	†	†	★	†	★	★	★	★	†
Washington	★	...	★	†	...	...	...	†	...	...	★	★	★	★	★	...	†
West Virginia	★	...	...	†	★	...	★	★	†	★	★	★	★	★	★	†	†
Wisconsin	★	†	†	†	†	†	†	★	†	†	★	†	★	★	★	★	★
Wyoming	★	†	†	†	†	†	†	†	★	★	†	†	★	★	★	...	...

Key:
★—Primary.
†—Shared.
... —None.

CHAPTER EIGHT

SELECTED STATE ACTIVITIES, ISSUES AND SERVICES

UNIFORM STATE LAWS: 1986-87

By John M. McCabe

In 1986 and 1987, the Uniform Law Commissioners produced 10 acts for adoption by the states. Included is a major new article to the Uniform Commercial Code and a new commercial act, the Uniform Franchise and Business Opportunities Act. Another significant statute is a revised organ donor law which replaces the original 1969 Act.

Uniform Anatomical Gift Act (1987)

The 1987 Uniform Anatomical Gift Act retains the principal provisions of the earlier act which empowered a competent adult to donate his or her body or organs for medical purposes after death in a properly executed document of gift and included a list of relatives who may consent to donation after an individual has died without a document of gift. The 1987 act simplifies the document of gift by eliminating the requirement for witnesses. The act also requires medical institutions to ask incoming patients about organ donations and to discuss organ donation with a deceased person's relatives. The act also permits medical authorities to remove organs from a body in their custody when specifically requested by a physician and when a reasonable inquiry shows no one objects to the removal of the organs.

Uniform Commercial Code, Article 2A — Leases

The Uniform Commercial Code, Article 2A — governs any lease of personal property or goods, whether the transaction is a true lease or a finance lease. A true lease occurs when the lessor gives the lessee the right to use the personal property for a fixed period in return for rent. The title to the property remains with the lessor. A finance lease occurs when the lessor is not the fundamental supplier of the goods leased, but leases goods to lessees as a means of financing their sale. Article 2A is largely derived from the sales article of the Uniform Commercial Code. It provides basic contract rules, including matters of offer and acceptance, statutes of frauds, warranties, assignment of interests, and remedies upon breach of contract.

Uniform Construction Lien Act

The Uniform Construction Lien Act is intended to replace the mechanic's or materialman's lien found in every jurisdiction. It permits contractors, subcontractors and materials suppliers to attach a lien for the value of unpaid services and materials upon real property improved by those services or materials. The act provides a Notice of Commencement, which the landowner may file to establish the time the lien becomes effective as well as set priorities between lienholders. Landholders are protected under this act in the event contractors are paid, but then do not pay subcontractors and materialmen. The act provides for a security bond in lieu of a lien and establishes a statutory trust in construction funds that may be used to prevent the dissipation of such funds before they are properly paid to those entitled to them under a construction contract. The Construction Lien Act was derived from Article 5 of the Uniform Simplification of Land Transfers Act.

Uniform Criminal-History Records Act

The Uniform Criminal-History Records Act governs the gathering, maintenance and disclosure of information regarding a person's criminal record. The act establishes a central agency for gathering information from all law enforcement agencies in a state. Law enforcement agencies have primary access to this information for their work. All citizens may have access to conviction information and to other

---

John M. McCabe is Legislative Director of the National Conference of Commissioners of Uniform State Laws.

records that are no more than one year old. A person may review his or her own records and can demand to know who else has reviewed these records. A process for correcting erroneous records also is provided. If authorized access is blocked by the central agency, the right of access may be enforced in court. There are civil and criminal penalties for unauthorized access to records.

Uniform Custodial Trust Act

The Uniform Custodial Trust Act allows any person to place property in a custodial trust. A custodial trust is distinguished from other trusts by the control beneficiaries exercise over the powers of the trustee to manage and expend trust assets and income for the beneficiaries. When beneficiaries become incapacitated, however, the trustee has the full powers of a trustee over any inter vivos, discretionary trust. The act, in addition, provides for a springing trust that commences upon a future event such as the incapacity of the donor. A non-probate transfer of property in trust can also be made to other designated persons at the death of a beneficiary.

Uniform Dormant Mineral Interests Act

The Uniform Dormant Mineral Interests Act establishes the criteria by which a severed mineral interest in real estate becomes dormant. Once a mineral interest becomes dormant, it may be merged with the surface interest in an action to quiet title. A mineral interest becomes dormant if there is not actual use of the interest for 20 years or more. The term "use" means exploring for or taking minerals generally, but includes such exercises of ownership as paying taxes on the interest or recording a judgment pertaining to it. Even if a holder of a mineral interest does not use it, the interest can be kept current by filing a notice of intent to preserve in the real property records.

Uniform Franchise and Business Opportunities Act

This act governs franchise and business opportunity contracts by balancing the bargaining position of franchisors and franchisees and of promoters and purchasers. In a franchise contract, the franchisee pays a fee to use a franchisor's marketing scheme and public symbols.

In a business opportunity contract, a promoter sells a business to a purchaser for an initially large payment, while representing that the promoter must refund payments if the business is unsuccessful, buy produced goods and services from the purchaser, or assist the purchaser so that the business will not fail. The act subjects both franchise and business opportunity contracts to good faith and unconscionability requirements. Both franchisors and promoters must provide adequate disclosure of information pertaining to the opportunity to prospective franchisees or purchasers. Both kinds of contracts are subject to investigative and enforcement powers of the administering agency. However, business opportunity contracts are also subject to registration requirements, to rescission rights, to bonding requirements in certain instances, and to certain prohibitions.

Uniform Rules of Criminal Procedure (1987)

The Uniform Rules of Criminal Procedure, originally promulgated in 1974, were amended in 1987 to reflect changes in the American Bar Association's *Standards for Criminal Justice* since 1974, and to incorporate concepts from the American Bar Association's *Criminal Justice Mental Health Standards*, which was completed in 1984. New provisions include more specific standards for pre-trial release with or without bond and detention of criminal suspects before arrest, citation or release from custody. The newest provisions come from the *Criminal Justice Mental Health Standards*. For example, a criminal defendant can petition for court assistance in paying for mental health examinations. There are extensive new procedures for evaluating a criminal defendant's capacity to stand trial.

Uniform Rules of Evidence (1986)

In 1986, amendments affected eight Sections of the Uniform Rules of Evidence promulgated originally in 1974. These amendments came from the Federal Rules of Evidence, from cases interpreting the Federal Rules (and Uniform Rules) since 1974, and from new policy concerns not raised in 1974. These amendments:

(1) Limit evidence of a victim's past sexual behavior in criminal actions involving sexual offenses; (2) Include communication to anyone employed to pro-

vide legal representation under lawyer-client privilege; (3) Limit the husband and wife privilege in criminal cases to the defendant's spouse; (4) Provide for evidence of a witness' bias, prejudice or interest to attack the witness' credibility; (5) Add a new category of nonhearsay statement identifying a person shortly after perceiving that person; (6) Allow an accused person to introduce public records and police investigative reports in a criminal action; (7) Allow an audio-visual statement or written deposition of a minor under 12 in a sexual abuse case or physical abuse case to be introduced in evidence when direct testimony would cause severe emotional or psychological distress; and, (8) Establish the certification requirements for introducing foreign or domestic records without "extrinsic evidence of authenticity."

Uniform Statutory Rule Against Perpetuities

The Uniform Statutory Rule Against Perpetuities validates nonvested future interests in property as the common-law Rule Against Perpetuities does, by measuring the time for vesting in terms of lives in being plus 21 years. In contrast to the common-law rule, the statutory rule does not automatically invalidate future interests that may not necessarily vest within the prescribed time. They are given 90 years to vest, and extinguish only if they don't vest in that time. The Uniform Statutory Rule also provides a judicial procedure to vest interests within the allotted 90-year time. In addition, the Uniform Statutory Rule carefully sets out the kinds of interests that are excluded from the operation of the perpetuities rule.

A large number of drafting projects continue to occupy the ULC. Further revisions of the Uniform Commercial Code are contemplated, and work on the Commercial Code may continue for the next decade. Other topics concerning drafting committees are parentage rules for children conceived by such techniques as in vitro fertilization and pursuant to contracts with surrogate mothers, employment termination and more amendments to the Uniform Probate Code.

Table 8.1
RECORD OF PASSAGE OF UNIFORM ACTS
(As of September 1, 1987)

State or other jurisdiction	Alcoholism and Intoxication Treatment (1971)	Anatomical Gift (1968)(1987)	Arbitration (1956)	Attendance of Out of State Witnesses (1931)(1936)	Audio-Visual Deposition (1978)	Certification of Questions of Law (1967)	Child Custody Jurisdiction (1968)	Class Actions (1976)(1987)	Commercial Code (1951)(1957)(1962)(1966)	Commercial Code—Article 2A (1986)	Commercial Code—Article 8 (1977)	Commercial Code—Article 9 (1972)	Common Interest Ownership (1982)	Common Trust Fund (1938)(1952)	Comparative Fault (1977)(1979)	Condominium (1977)(1980)
Alabama	..	★		●	...	...	★	...	●	...	...	...		★	...	...
Alaska	★	★	★	●	...	...	★	...	●	...	...	...	★	★	★	...
Arizona	...	★	★	●	...	...	★	...	●	...	...	★	...	★	...	...
Arkansas	...	★	★	★	...	...	★	...	●	...	★	★	...	★	...	...
California	...	☆	☆	●	...	...	★	...	●	...	★	★	...	★	...	...
Colorado	★	★	★	●	...	★	★	...	●	...	★	★	...	★	...	...
Connecticut	☆	★	☆	●	...	★	★	...	●	...	★	★	★	★	...	...
Delaware	★	★	★	●	...	...	★	...	●	...	★	★	...	★	...	...
Florida	☆	★	★	●	...	☆	★	...	●	...	...	★	...	★	...	...
Georgia	★	★	...	●	...	...	★	...	●	...	...	...	...	...	...	...
Hawaii	...	★	☆	●	...	...	★	...	●	...	★	...	...	★	...	...
Idaho	★	★	★	★	...	...	★	...	●	...	...	★	...	★	...	...
Illinois	★	★	★	●	...	...	★	...	●	...	...	★	...	★	...	...
Indiana	...	★	★	★	...	...	★	...	●	...	...	★	...	●	...	...
Iowa	★	★	★	☆	...	★	★	★	●	...	...	...	...	●	...	...
Kansas	★	★	★	●	...	★	★	...	●	...	...	★	...	★	...	...
Kentucky	...	★	★	●	...	...	★	...	●	...	...	...	...	...	☆	...
Louisiana	...	☆	★	●	...	...	★	...	...	...	...	...	...	...	...	...
Maine	★	★	★	●	...	☆	★	...	●	...	...	★	...	...	★	●
Maryland	☆	★	★	●	...	★	★	...	●	...	...	★	...	...	...	...
Massachusetts	☆	★	★	●	...	★	☆	...	●	...	★	★	...	●	★	...
Michigan	☆	★	☆	☆	...	...	★	...	●	...	...	★	...	★	★	★
Minnesota	☆	★	★	●	...	★	★	...	●	...	...	★	...	★	★	●
Mississippi	...	★	...	●	...	...	★	...	●	...	...	...	...	★	★	●
Missouri	...	★	☆	●	...	...	★	...	●	...	...	...	...	★	...	...
Montana	★	★	★	●	...	...	★	...	●	...	...	★	...	★	...	●
Nebraska	...	★	★	●	...	...	★	...	●	...	★	★	...	★	...	...
Nevada	...	★	☆	●	...	...	★	...	●	...	...	★	...	●	...	★
New Hampshire	...	★	☆	●	...	★	★	...	●	...	...	★	...	...	...	...
New Jersey	...	★	☆	●	...	...	★	...	●	...	...	★	...	...	...	...
New Mexico	...	★	★	●	...	...	★	...	●	...	...	...	...	★	...	●
New York	...	★	☆	●	...	...	★	...	●	...	★	★	...	...	...	...
North Carolina	...	★	★	●	...	...	★	...	●	...	★	★	...	...	...	...
North Dakota	...	★	★	★	★	★	★	★	●	...	★	★	...	...	...	...
Ohio	...	★	☆	●	...	...	★	...	●	...	...	...	...	●	...	...
Oklahoma	★	★	★	●	...	★	★	...	●	...	★	★	...	●	...	...
Oregon	...	★	☆	●	...	★	★	...	●	...	★	★	...	...	...	...
Pennsylvania	...	★	★	●	...	...	★	...	●	...	...	...	...	...	...	★
Rhode Island	☆	★	☆	★	...	★	★	...	●	...	...	★	...	...	...	●
South Carolina	...	★	★	●	...	...	★	...	●	...	...	...	...	...	...	...
South Dakota	★	★	★	●	...	...	★	...	●	...	★	★	...	★	...	...
Tennessee	...	★	★	●	...	...	★	...	●	...	★	★	...	★	...	...
Texas	...	★	☆	●	...	...	★	...	●	...	★	★	...	★	...	...
Utah	...	★	☆	●	...	...	★	...	●	...	★	...	...	★	...	...
Vermont	...	★	...	●	...	...	★	...	●	...	...	...	...	...	...	...
Virginia	...	★	★	●	★	...	★	...	●	...	★	★	...	★	...	☆
Washington	★	★	☆	●	...	☆	★	...	●	...	★	★	★	★	☆	★
West Virginia	...	★	...	●	...	★	★	...	●	...	...	★	...	...	...	★
Wisconsin	★	★	☆	●	...	★	★	...	●	...	★	★	...	★	...	...
Wyoming	...	★	★	★	...	...	★	...	●	...	★	★	...	★	...	...
Dist. of Col.	☆	★	★	●	...	★	★	...	●	...	...	★	...	★	...	...
Puerto Rico	...	...	☆	★	...	...	●	...	...	...	...	...	...	...	...	...
Virgin Islands	...	...	☆	●	...	...	●	...	...	...	...	...	...	...	...	...

Source: National Conference of Commissioners on Uniform State Laws, *1985-86 Reference Book*, and update.

Key:
★—Enacted
●—Amended version enacted
☆—Substantially similar version enacted
. . .—Not enacted

PASSAGE OF UNIFORM ACTS—Continued

State or other jurisdiction	Conflict of Laws—Limitations (1982)	Conservation Easement (1981)	Consumer Credit Code (1968) (1974)	Consumer Sales Practices (1970) (1971)	Construction Lien (1987)	Controlled Substances (1970) (1973)	Crime Victims Reparations (1973)	Criminal History Records (1986)	Criminal Procedures, Rules of (1974) (1987)	Custodial Trust (1987)	Deceptive Trade Practices (1964) (1966)	Declaratory Judgments (1922)	Determination of Death (1978) (1980)	Disclaimer of Property Interests (1973) (1978)	Disclaimer of Transfers by Will, Intestacy or Appt. (1973) (1978)	Disclaimer of Transfers under Nontestamentary Instruments (1973) (1978)
Alabama						★						★		•		
Alaska						★						★	•		•	
Arizona		★				★						★	★			
Arkansas	★	★				☆						★	•		•	
California						☆						★	•			
Colorado	★		★								•	★	•			
Connecticut												★	•	•		
Delaware						★					★	★	★			
Florida						☆						★	•			
Georgia						☆					•	★		•		
Hawaii						☆					•	•		★		
Idaho			★			★						★	•			
Illinois						☆						★	•		★	
Indiana		★	★									★	•			
Iowa			★			★						★				
Kansas			★	★		★	☆						•			
Kentucky						☆	★						•		★	
Louisiana						★						★				
Maine		★	★									★	•	•	★	★
Maryland						★						★	☆		★	
Massachusetts						★						★				
Michigan						★						★				
Minnesota		★				☆	☆				•	★				
Mississippi		★				★						★	•			
Missouri						★						★				
Montana						★	★					★	•			
Nebraska						★					•	★	•			
Nevada		★				★					•	★	•			
New Hampshire												★	•			
New Jersey						★	★					★			★	★
New Mexico						★					☆	★				
New York						★						★	☆			
North Carolina						☆						★	★			
North Dakota	★					★	★					★	★			★
Ohio				☆							•	★	☆			
Oklahoma			★	☆		★					★	★	•			
Oregon		★				★						★	•	•	★	★
Pennsylvania						★						★	•			
Rhode Island						☆						★	•		☆	
South Carolina			☆			★						★	•			
South Dakota		★				★						★				
Tennessee						★	☆					★	•			
Texas		★				★	☆					★				
Utah			★	•		★						★				
Vermont												★	•		★	
Virginia						☆	★					★				
Washington	★					★						★	•			
West Virginia						★						★	★			
Wisconsin		★	☆			★						★	•	•		
Wyoming			★			★						★	★			
Dist. of Col.		★				☆						☆	•			
Puerto Rico						★						★				
Virgin Islands						★						★				

Key:
★—Enacted
•—Amended version enacted
☆—Substantially similar version enacted
. . .—Not enacted

PASSAGE OF UNIFORM ACTS—Continued

State or other jurisdiction	Disposition of Community Property Rights at Death (1971)	Division of Income for Tax Purposes (1957)	Dormant Mineral Interests (1986)	Drug Dependence Treatment and Rehabilitation (1973)	Durable Power of Attorney (1979)	Duties to Disabled Persons (1972)	Enforcement of Foreign Judgments (1948) (1964)	Evidence, Rules of (1953) (1974) (1986)	Exemptions (1976) (1979)	Extradition and Rendition (1980)	Facsimile Signatures of Public Officials (1958)	Federal Lien Registration (1978) (1982)	Fiduciaries (1922)	Foreign Money Judgments Recognition (1962)	Franchise and Business Opportunities (1987)	Fraudulent Conveyance (1918)
Alabama					★		•						★			
Alaska	★	★			★		•		•				★	★		
Arizona					★		•	•					★			
Arkansas	★	★			★		★	•				★		★		
California		★			★		?	★				★	★	★		
Colorado	★	★			★	★	•	•					★	★		
Connecticut	★	☆	★		☆	★	•	•				★				
Delaware		☆			★		•	•				★				
Florida		☆			☆		•	•						★		
Georgia		☆				☆	•									
Hawaii	★	★			★		•	•					★			
Idaho		★			★		•	•					★			
Illinois							•	★					★	★		
Indiana		★			★		•						★			
Iowa					★											
Kansas		★			★			★								
Kentucky	★	★			☆							•	★			
Louisiana												•	★			
Maine		★			★		•	•								
Maryland					★		•					★	★	★	★	
Massachusetts		★			★									★		
Michigan	★	★			★		•	•						★		
Minnesota		☆			★	★	•	•				★	★	★	★	
Mississippi					☆								★	★	★	
Missouri		★			★		★						★	★	★	
Montana					★		•	•				★	•			
Nebraska					★		★	•					★			
Nevada					★		•	•				★	★	★		
New Hampshire		☆			☆							★				
New Jersey					★			★					★			
New Mexico		★			★							★	★			
New York	★				☆		•	•					☆	★		
North Carolina	★	★			☆	★	•	•					★			
North Dakota		★			★	★	•	•		★			★			
Ohio		☆			★	★	•	•					★			
Oklahoma						★	•	•				★		★		
Oregon	★	★			☆		•	•					★	★		
Pennsylvania		★			★	☆	•					★	★			
Rhode Island		☆			★		•					★		☆		
South Carolina		☆			★											
South Dakota		★			★		•	•					★			
Tennessee		☆			★		•	★					★			
Texas		★			☆		•	•					★			
Utah		☆			★		•						★			
Vermont		★			★								★			
Virginia	★	☆	☆		☆								★			
Washington		★	☆		★		•	•								
West Virginia					☆		•	•				★				
Wisconsin		☆			★		•	•				★	★	★		
Wyoming	★						•	•				★	★			
Dist. of Col.		★											★			
Puerto Rico							★	•					★			
Virgin Islands								★					★			

Key:
★—Enacted
•—Amended version enacted
☆—Substantially similar version enacted
. . .—Not enacted

PASSAGE OF UNIFORM ACTS—Continued

State or other jurisdiction	Fraudulent Transfer (1984)	Guardianship and Protective Proceedings (1982) (1987)	Health Care Information (1985)	Information Practices Code (1980)	International Wills (1977)	Interstate Arbitration of Death Taxes (1943)	Interstate Compromise of Death Taxes (1943)	Jury Selection and Service (1970) (1971)	Land Security Interests (1985)	Land Transactions (1975) (1977) (1983)	Limited Partnership (1976) (1983) (1985)	Management of Institutional Funds (1972)	Mandatory Disposition of Detainers (1958)	Marital Property (1983)	Marriage and Divorce (1970) (1973)
Alabama	...	★	★	★	...	...	...	...	...	...	★	...	...	...	...
Alaska	...	...	...	...	...	...	...	...	...	...	...	...	...	...	...
Arizona	...	...	...	...	...	...	...	...	...	...	★	...	★	...	★
Arkansas	★	...	...	...	...	...	...	...	...	...	★	...	...	...	...
California	★	...	...	...	★	★	★	...	...	...	☆	☆	...	...	...
Colorado	...	...	...	...	...	★	★	★	...	...	★	★	★	...	★
Connecticut	...	...	...	...	★	★	★	...	...	...	★	★	...	...	...
Delaware	...	...	...	...	...	...	...	...	...	...	★	★	...	...	...
Florida	★	...	...	...	...	...	...	...	...	...	●	★	...	...	...
Georgia	...	...	...	...	...	...	...	...	...	...	...	★	...	...	☆
Hawaii	★	...	...	...	...	...	...	...	...	...	...	...	...	...	...
Idaho	★	...	...	...	...	...	...	★	...	...	★	...	★	...	★
Illinois	...	...	...	...	...	...	☆	...	...	...	●	...	★	...	...
Indiana	...	...	...	...	...	...	...	☆	...	...	...	...	...	...	...
Iowa	...	...	...	...	...	...	...	...	...	...	★	...	...	...	...
Kansas	...	...	...	...	...	...	...	...	...	...	●	☆	★	...	...
Kentucky	...	...	...	...	...	...	...	...	...	...	...	★	...	...	★
Louisiana	...	...	...	...	...	...	...	...	...	...	...	★	...	...	...
Maine	★	...	...	...	...	★	★	★	...	...	...	★	...	...	...
Maryland	...	...	...	...	...	★	★	...	...	...	...	★	...	...	...
Massachusetts	...	...	...	...	...	★	★	...	...	...	★	★	...	...	...
Michigan	...	...	...	...	...	★	★	★	...	...	★	★	...	...	...
Minnesota	★	...	...	...	★	☆	★	●	...	...	●	★	★	...	☆
Mississippi	...	...	...	...	...	...	...	☆	...	...	●	...	...	...	...
Missouri	...	...	...	...	...	...	...	...	...	...	★	★	...	...	...
Montana	...	...	...	...	...	...	...	...	...	...	★	★	...	...	●
Nebraska	...	...	...	...	...	★	★	...	...	...	★	...	...	...	...
Nevada	★	...	...	...	...	...	...	...	...	...	●	...	...	...	...
New Hampshire	★	...	...	...	...	...	...	...	...	...	★	★	...	...	...
New Jersey	...	...	...	...	...	...	...	★	...	...	★	★	...	...	...
New Mexico	...	...	...	...	...	...	...	...	...	...	...	...	...	...	...
New York	...	...	...	...	...	★	...	...	...	...	...	☆	...	...	...
North Carolina	...	...	...	...	...	...	...	...	...	...	●	★	...	...	...
North Dakota	★	...	...	...	★	...	...	★	...	...	★	★	★	...	...
Ohio	...	...	...	...	...	...	...	...	...	...	★	☆	...	...	...
Oklahoma	★	...	...	...	...	...	...	...	...	...	★	...	...	...	...
Oregon	★	...	...	...	...	...	...	...	...	...	●	★	...	...	...
Pennsylvania	...	...	...	...	★	★	★	...	...	...	...	...	...	...	...
Rhode Island	★	...	...	...	...	...	...	...	...	...	●	★	★	...	...
South Carolina	...	...	...	...	...	...	...	...	...	...	★	★	...	...	...
South Dakota	★	...	...	...	...	...	...	...	...	...	★	...	...	...	...
Tennessee	...	...	...	...	...	☆	☆	...	...	...	...	★	...	...	...
Texas	★	...	...	...	...	...	...	...	...	...	●	...	...	...	...
Utah	...	...	...	...	...	...	...	...	...	...	...	★	★	...	...
Vermont	...	...	...	...	★	★	...	...	...	...	...	★	...	...	...
Virginia	...	...	...	...	...	★	★	...	...	...	●	★	...	...	...
Washington	★	...	...	...	...	★	★	...	...	...	★	★	...	...	☆
West Virginia	★	...	...	...	...	★	★	...	...	...	●	★	...	...	...
Wisconsin	...	...	...	...	...	...	...	★	...	...	★	★	...	★	...
Wyoming	...	...	...	...	...	...	...	...	...	...	★	...	...	...	...
Dist. of Col.	...	☆	☆	☆	...	...	...	...	...	...	...	★	...	...	...
Puerto Rico	...	...	...	...	...	...	...	...	...	...	...	...	...	...	...
Virgin Islands	...	...	...	...	...	...	...	...	...	...	...	...	...	...	...

Key:
★—Enacted
●—Amended version enacted
☆—Substantially similar version enacted
...—Not enacted

PASSAGE OF UNIFORM ACTS—Continued

State or other jurisdiction	Motor Vehicle Accident Reparations (1972)	Notarial Acts (1982)	Parentage (1973)	Partnership (1914)	Photographic Copies as Evidence (1949)	Planned Communities (1980)	Post-Conviction Procedure (1980)	Premarital Agreement (1983)	Principal and Income (1931) (1962)	Probate Court (1969) (1975) (1982) (1987)	Public Assembly (1972)	Reciprocal Enforcement of Support (1950) (1958) (1968)	Residential Landlord and Tenant (1972)	Rights to the Terminally Ill (1985)	Securities (1985)
Alabama	...	...	★	☆	★	...	...	...	★	...	...	●	...	...	...
Alaska	...	...	...	★	★	...	...	...	★	★	...	●	★	★	...
Arizona	...	...	...	★	...	...	...	...	●	★	...	●	★	...	...
Arkansas	...	...	...	★	★	...	...	★	●	...	...	●	...	●	...
California	...	...	★	★	★	...	...	★	●	...	...	●	...	...	...
Colorado	...	...	★	★	★	...	...	...	★	●	...	●	...	...	...
Connecticut	...	...	...	★	...	...	...	...	●	...	...	●	★	...	...
Delaware	...	★	★	★	...	...	...	...	...	...	...	●	★	...	...
Florida	...	...	...	★	★	...	...	...	●	...	...	●	★	...	...
Georgia	...	...	...	★	...	...	...	...	...	...	...	●	...	...	...
Hawaii	...	...	★	★	★	...	...	★	●	...	...	●	★	...	...
Idaho	...	...	...	★	★	...	...	...	●	★	...	●	...	...	...
Illinois	...	...	●	★	...	...	...	...	★	...	...	●	...	...	...
Indiana	...	...	...	★	...	...	...	...	...	...	...	●	...	...	...
Iowa	...	...	...	★	★	...	...	...	...	...	...	●	...	★	...
Kansas	...	★	★	★	★	...	...	...	...	★	...	●	☆	...	...
Kentucky	...	...	...	★	★	...	...	...	★	...	...	●	★	...	...
Louisiana	...	...	...	...	...	...	...	...	★	...	...	●	...	...	...
Maine	...	...	...	★	★	...	...	★	...	...	...	●	...	★	...
Maryland	...	...	...	★	★	...	...	...	...	...	...	●	...	...	...
Massachusetts	...	...	...	★	★	...	...	...	...	...	...	●	★	...	...
Michigan	...	...	...	★	...	...	...	...	●	☆	...	●	...	☆	...
Minnesota	...	★	★	★	★	...	...	...	●	★	...	●	...	...	...
Mississippi	...	...	...	★	...	...	...	...	...	...	...	●	...	...	...
Missouri	...	...	...	★	...	...	...	...	...	...	...	●	...	...	...
Montana	...	...	★	★	...	...	...	★	●	★	...	●	★	★	...
Nebraska	...	...	...	☆	★	...	...	...	●	★	...	●	★	...	...
Nevada	...	...	★	★	★	...	...	...	●	...	...	●	...	...	★
New Hampshire	...	...	...	★	★	...	...	...	...	...	...	●	...	...	...
New Jersey	...	...	★	★	★	...	...	...	...	☆	...	●	...	...	...
New Mexico	...	...	...	★	★	...	...	...	●	★	...	●	★	...	★
New York	...	...	...	★	★	...	...	...	●	...	...	●	...	...	...
North Carolina	...	...	...	★	★	...	★	...	●	...	...	●	...	...	...
North Dakota	...	...	★	★	★	...	★	...	●	●	...	●	...	...	...
Ohio	...	...	☆	★	...	...	...	...	...	...	...	●	...	...	...
Oklahoma	...	★	...	★	...	...	...	...	★	●	★	●	★	...	...
Oregon	...	★	...	★	...	...	...	★	●	...	...	●	★	...	...
Pennsylvania	...	...	...	★	...	...	...	★	●	☆	...	●	...	...	...
Rhode Island	...	...	★	★	★	...	...	★	●	...	...	●	...	...	★
South Carolina	...	...	...	★	...	...	...	...	●	★	...	●	...	...	...
South Dakota	...	...	...	★	★	...	...	...	●	...	...	●	...	★	...
Tennessee	...	...	...	★	★	...	...	...	●	...	...	●	...	...	...
Texas	...	...	...	★	...	...	...	★	★	...	...	●	...	...	...
Utah	...	...	...	★	...	...	...	...	●	★	★	●	...	...	...
Vermont	...	...	★	★	★	...	...	...	...	★	...	☆	...	...	...
Virginia	...	...	...	★	★	...	★	...	★	...	...	●	★	...	...
Washington	...	...	★	★	★	...	...	...	●	...	...	●	☆	...	...
West Virginia	...	...	★	★	★	...	...	...	★	...	...	●	...	...	...
Wisconsin	...	★	...	★	★	...	...	...	★	...	...	●	...	...	...
Wyoming	...	...	★	★	★	...	...	...	●	...	...	●	...	...	...
Dist. of Col.	...	...	...	★	...	...	...	...	...	...	...	●	...	...	...
Puerto Rico	...	...	...	...	...	...	...	...	...	...	...	●	...	...	...
Virgin Islands	...	...	...	★	★	...	...	...	...	...	...	●	...	...	...

Key:
★—Enacted
●—Amended version enacted
☆—Substantially similar version enacted
. . .—Not enacted

PASSAGE OF UNIFORM ACTS—Continued

State or other jurisdiction	Simplification of Fiduciary Security Transfers (1958)	Simplifications of Land Transfers (1976) (1977) (1983)	Simultaneous Death (1940) (1953)	State Antitrust (1973) (1979)	Status of Convicted Persons (1964)	Statutory Rule Against Perpetuities (1986)	Statutory Will (1984)	Succession Without Administration (1983)	Supervision of Trustees for Charitable Purposes (1954)	Testamentary Additions to Trusts (1960)	Trade Secrets (1979) (1985)	Transboundary Pollution Reciprocal Access (1982)	Transfers to Minors (1983) (1986)	Trustees' Powers (1964)	Unclaimed Property (1981)
Alabama	★	...	...	...	...	...	...	...	...	☆	...	...	★	...	...
Alaska	...	...	...	...	...	...	...	...	...	★	...	...	...	...	★
Arizona	★	...	...	★	...	...	...	...	...	★	...	...	...	...	★
Arkansas	...	...	...	...	...	...	...	...	...	★	...	...	★	★	★
California	★	...	...	...	...	...	...	...	★	★	★	...	★	...	...
Colorado	★	...	...	...	...	...	...	...	...	☆	●	★	★	...	★
Connecticut	...	...	...	...	...	...	...	...	...	★	★	●	★	...	...
Delaware	★	...	...	...	...	...	...	...	...	★	★	●	...	...	...
Florida	★	...	...	...	...	...	...	...	...	☆	★	...	...	...	...
Georgia	★	...	...	...	...	...	...	...	...	★	...	...	★	★	★
Hawaii	★	...	...	...	★	...	...	...	...	★	...	...	★	...	...
Idaho	★	...	...	...	...	...	...	...	...	★	★	...	★	★	★
Illinois	★	...	...	...	...	...	...	...	★	☆	...	...	★	★	★
Indiana	★	...	...	...	...	...	...	...	...	☆	★	...	★	...	...
Iowa	★	...	...	★	...	...	...	...	...	★	...	...	★	...	...
Kansas	★	...	...	...	...	...	...	...	...	★	★	...	★	★	...
Kentucky	...	...	...	...	...	...	...	...	...	★	★	...	★	★	...
Louisiana	★	...	...	...	...	...	...	...	...	★	...	★	...	●	★
Maine	★	...	...	...	...	...	...	...	...	★	...	●	...	...	...
Maryland	★	...	...	...	...	...	...	...	...	☆	...	...	...	...	...
Massachusetts	...	...	...	...	...	...	...	...	...	★	★	...	★	...	...
Michigan	★	...	...	★	...	...	...	...	★	★	...	...	★	...	...
Minnesota	★	...	...	...	...	...	...	...	...	★	★	●	★	☆	...
Mississippi	★	...	...	...	...	...	...	...	...	☆	...	...	★	...	...
Missouri	★	...	...	...	...	...	...	...	...	...	...	...	...	★	...
Montana	★	...	...	...	☆	...	...	...	...	☆	★	★	★	★	☆
Nebraska	★	...	...	...	...	...	...	...	...	★	...	...	...	...	...
Nevada	★	...	...	...	...	...	...	...	...	★	...	●	★	...	★
New Hampshire	...	...	...	...	★	...	...	...	...	★	...	...	★	★	★
New Jersey	★	...	...	...	...	...	...	...	...	☆	...	★	●	...	...
New Mexico	...	...	...	...	...	...	...	...	...	★	...	...	...	...	...
New York	★	...	...	...	...	...	...	...	...	☆	...	...	...	...	...
North Carolina	★	...	...	...	...	...	...	...	...	☆	...	...	...	●	...
North Dakota	★	...	...	...	...	...	...	...	...	★	★	...	★	...	★
Ohio	...	...	...	●	...	...	...	...	...	☆	...	...	...	...	...
Oklahoma	...	...	...	...	...	...	...	...	...	★	★	...	★	...	...
Oregon	...	...	...	...	...	...	...	...	★	★	★	●	★	★	★
Pennsylvania	...	...	...	...	...	...	...	...	...	☆	...	●	...	...	★
Rhode Island	★	...	...	...	...	...	...	...	...	...	...	●	★	...	...
South Carolina	★	...	...	...	...	...	...	...	...	★	...	...	★	...	★
South Dakota	★	...	...	...	...	...	...	...	...	★	...	...	★	...	...
Tennessee	★	...	...	...	...	...	...	...	...	★	...	...	...	...	...
Texas	★	...	...	...	...	...	...	...	...	☆	...	...	...	...	...
Utah	★	...	...	...	...	...	...	...	...	☆	...	...	...	★	★
Vermont	...	...	...	...	...	...	...	...	...	★	...	...	...	...	...
Virginia	★	...	...	...	...	...	...	...	...	...	...	●	...	...	★
Washington	★	...	...	...	...	...	...	...	...	☆	★	...	...	...	★
West Virginia	★	...	...	...	...	...	...	...	...	★	...	●	★	...	★
Wisconsin	★	...	...	...	...	...	...	...	...	...	...	●	●	...	★
Wyoming	★	...	...	...	...	...	...	...	...	☆	...	...	●	★	...
Dist. of Col.	★	...	...	...	...	...	...	...	...	☆	...	...	★	...	...
Puerto Rico	...	...	...	...	...	...	...	...	...	...	...	...	...	...	...
Virgin Islands	...	...	...	...	...	...	...	...	...	...	...	...	...	...	...

Key:
★—Enacted
●—Amended version enacted
☆—Substantially similar version enacted
...—Not enacted

Table 8.2
RECORD OF PASSAGE OF MODEL ACTS
(As of September 1, 1987)

State or other jurisdiction	Act to Provide for the Appointment of Commissioners (1944)	Anti-Discrimination (1966)	Class Actions (1976) (1987)	Eminent Domain Code (1974)	Insanity Defense and Post-Trial Disposition (1984)	Juvenile Court (1968)	Land Sales Practices (1966)	Minor Student Capacity to Borrow (1969)	Periodic Payment of Judgments (1980)	Post-Mortem Examinations (1954)	Public Defender (1970) (1974)	Real Estate Cooperative (1981)	Real Estate Time-Share (1980) (1982)	State Administrative Procedures (1981)	Statutory Construction (1965)	Water Use (1958)
Alabama	★			★			★									
Alaska							★									
Arizona	★							★						★		
Arkansas	★															
California																
Colorado															★	
Connecticut							★	★								
Delaware							★									
Florida						☆	★									
Georgia						☆	☆									
Hawaii		★					★									☆
Idaho																
Illinois																
Indiana										☆						
Iowa	★		★												★	
Kansas	★						★									
Kentucky	★															
Louisiana													☆			
Maine	★										☆		☆			
Maryland										☆			☆			
Massachusetts																
Michigan																
Minnesota																
Mississippi	★															
Missouri																
Montana	★						★	☆								
Nebraska	★															
Nevada																
New Hampshire	★															
New Jersey																
New Mexico																
New York																
North Carolina																
North Dakota	★		★		☆	★		★								
Ohio																
Oklahoma	★	★						★					★			
Oregon	★												★			
Pennsylvania																
Rhode Island														★		
South Carolina																
South Dakota										★						
Tennessee																
Texas	★									★						
Utah																
Vermont																
Virginia												★				
Washington								★								
West Virginia										☆						
Wisconsin	★														★	
Wyoming																
Dist. of Col.																
Puerto Rico																
Virgin Islands																

Source: National Conference of Commissioners on Uniform State Laws.
Key:
★—Enacted
☆—Substantially similar version enacted
. . .—Not enacted

Table 8.3
MINIMUM AGE FOR SPECIFIED ACTIVITIES

State or other jurisdiction	Age of majority (a)	Minimum age for marriage with consent(b) male	Minimum age for marriage with consent(b) female	Minimum age for making a will	Minimum age for buying(c) liquor	Minimum age for buying(c) beer or wine	Minimum age for serving on a jury	Minimum age for leaving school(d)
Alabama	19	14(e)	14(e)	19	21	21	19	16
Alaska	18	16(f)	16(f)	18	21	21	18	16
Arizona	18	16(f)	16(f)	18	21	21	18	(g)
Arkansas	18	17(f)	16(f)	18	21	21	18	15
California	18	(h)	(h)	18(i)	21	21	18	18
Colorado	18	16(f)	16(f)	18	21	18(j)	18	16
Connecticut	18	16(f)	16(f)	18	21	21	18	16(k,l)
Delaware	18	18(f,m)	16(f,m)	18	21	21	18	16
Florida	18	16(f)	16(f)	18	21	21	18	16
Georgia	18	16(f,m)	16(f,m)	18	21	21	18	16
Hawaii	18	16	16(f)	18	21	21	18	18(l)
Idaho	18	16(f)	16(f)	18(i)	21	21	18	16
Illinois	18	16(f)	16(f)	18	21	21	18	16
Indiana	18	17(f)	17(f)	18	21	21	18	16
Iowa	18	16	16	18	21	21	18	16(k,l)
Kansas	18	(h)	(h)	18	21	21	18	16
Kentucky	18	(h)	(h)	18	21	21	18	16
Louisiana	18	18(f)	16(f)	16(i)	21	21	18	17
Maine	18	16(f)	16(f)	18	21	21	18	17(n)
Maryland	18	16(f)	16(f)	18	21	21	18	16
Massachusetts	18	(h)	(h)	18	21	21	18	16
Michigan	18	16	16	18	21	21	18	16
Minnesota	18	16(o)	16(o)	18	21	21	18	16
Mississippi	18	17(f)	15(f)	18	21	21	21	17(p)
Missouri	18	15(f)	15(f)	18	21	21	21	16
Montana	18	18(f)	18(f)	18	21	21	18	16(q)
Nebraska	19	17	17	18	21	21	19	16
Nevada	18	16(f)	16(f)	18	21	21	18	17
New Hampshire	18	14(o)	13(o)	18	21	21	18	16
New Jersey	18	16(r)	16(r)	18	21	21	18	16
New Mexico	18	16(f)	16(f)	18	21	21	18	18(s)
New York	(t)	16	14(o)	18	21	21	18	17(u)
North Carolina	18	16	16(f)	18	21	21	18	16
North Dakota	18	16	16	18	21	21	18	16
Ohio	18	18(f)	16(f)	18	21	19	18	18
Oklahoma	18	16(f)	16(f)	18	21	21	18	16
Oregon	18	17	17	18	21	21	18	16(v)
Pennsylvania	21	16(f)	16(f)	18	21	21	18	16(v)
Rhode Island	18	18(f)	16(f)	18	21	21	18	16
South Carolina	18	18(f)	14(f)	18	21	21	18	16
South Dakota	18	16(f)	16(f)	18	21	19(j)	18	16
Tennessee	18	16(f)	16(f)	18	21	21	18	16
Texas	18	14(o)	14(o)	18(i)	21	21	18	17
Utah	18	(h)	(h)	18	21	21	18	18
Vermont	18	16(f)	16(f)	18	21	21	18	18
Virginia	18	16(f)	16(f)	18	21	21	18	17
Washington	18	17(f)	17(f)	18	21	21	18	18(v)
West Virginia	18	(w)	(w)	18	21	21	18	16
Wisconsin	18	16	16	18	21	21	18	16(v)
Wyoming	19	16(f)	16(f)	19	19	19	19	16
Dist. of Col.	18	16	16	18	21	18	18	16(l)

(a) Generally, the age at which an individual has legal control over own actions and business (e.g. ability to contract) except as otherwise provided by statute. In many states, age of majority is arrived at upon marriage if minimum legal marrying age is lower than prescribed age of majority.

(b) With parental consent. Minimum age for marrying without consent is 18 years in all states, except Mississippi (21 years) and Wyoming (19 years).

(c) As of early 1986. Legislation enacted; may not yet be effective.

(d) Without graduating.

(e) Bond is required if under 18.

(f) Legal procedure for younger persons to obtain license.

(g) To 10th grade, effective with 1986-87 school year.

(h) Statute provides that any unmarried male or female under 18 may marry with consent (usually with order of court granting permission).

(i) Age may be lower for a minor who is living apart from parents or legal guardians and managing own financial affairs, or who has contracted a lawful marriage.

(j) In Colorado and South Dakota, 3.2 beer only.

(k) Unless parent or guardian is able to show child is receiving equivalent instruction.

(l) Younger, if lawfully employed. Connecticut, Iowa, District of Columbia, 14 years; Hawaii, 15 years.

(m) Parental consent not required when female is pregnant or applicants are parents of a living child.

(n) Does not apply to those who have reached age 15 or completed ninth grade, or who otherwise have permission to leave.

(o) Parental consent and judicial consent required.

(p) Effective 1989-90 school year.

(q) Or completion of eighth grade, whichever is earlier.

(r) Parental consent required for ages 16 to 18; judicial approval for individuals under 16.

(s) Does not apply to those who have completed 10th grade and have consent of parents and school officials.

(t) As defined in general obligations (for purposes of contracting) and civil rights codes, 18 years.

(u) In cities having over 4,500 population and union-free school districts.

(v) With certain exceptions.

(w) Under 16, must have parental consent and approval of circuit judge.

Table 8.4
GENERAL REVENUE OF PUBLIC SCHOOL SYSTEMS BY SOURCE: 1985-86
(In thousands of dollars)

State or other jurisdiction	Total(a)	Intergovernmental(a) Total	Directly from federal government	From state: Federal aid distributed by state	From state: Other	From other local governments	From own sources: Total	Taxes	Parent government contributions	Current charges: School lunch	Current charges: Other	Other
United States	$157,978,274	$85,931,576	$1,460,169	$8,196,684	$73,947,152	$2,327,571	$72,046,698	$48,001,569	$12,649,993	$2,782,387	$3,799,559	$4,813,190
Alabama	1,714,794	1,415,103	21,581	196,328	1,064,333	132,861	299,691	177,711	0	66,789	11,595	43,596
Alaska	963,173	696,386	51,302	25,037	620,047	0	266,787	0	230,718	7,849	7,467	20,753
Arizona	2,324,863	1,348,866	74,342	111,412	1,091,476	71,636	975,997	771,343	156	37,264	74,988	92,246
Arkansas	1,160,029	741,174	7,718	109,804	621,080	2,572	418,855	317,814	0	21,817	39,435	39,789
California	18,630,875	13,500,776	152,156	1,030,450	12,149,234	168,936	5,130,099	3,787,924	180,916	230,872	300,848	629,539
Colorado	2,280,584	987,299	10,727	80,444	893,973	2,155	1,293,285	1,057,951	0	40,150	62,606	132,578
Connecticut	1,942,553	918,486	7,436	81,431	663,219	66,400	1,024,067		986,188	26,388	8,061	3,430
Delaware	397,680	299,360	4,487	26,764	268,109		98,320	81,581	0	8,002	341	8,396
Florida	6,801,823	4,067,779	56,796	421,426	3,588,678	879	2,734,044	2,065,690	0	135,983	318,905	213,466
Georgia	3,474,599	2,057,533	26,907	174,837	1,855,789	0	1,417,066	1,107,052	0	75,045	22,793	212,176
Hawaii	536,250	514,350	58,523		455,827		21,900	0	0	10,136	10,333	1,431
Idaho	502,547	331,235	8,106	34,794	288,284	51	171,312	140,324	0	11,805	6,751	12,432
Illinois	7,215,124	3,208,609	58,464	350,968	2,790,578	8,599	4,006,515	3,317,833	0	113,113	243,956	331,613
Indiana	3,181,586	1,838,419	7,477	140,073	1,666,660	24,209	1,343,167	1,131,552	0	92,420	27,371	91,824
Iowa	1,934,228	982,619	9,368	64,799	908,417	35	951,609	759,958	0	68,992	83,236	39,423
Kansas	1,735,972	867,081	16,541	35,828	715,786	98,926	868,891	687,987	0	39,525	62,378	79,001
Kentucky	1,561,991	1,122,793	8,408	170,681	942,714	990	439,198	328,875	0	33,974	12,858	63,491
Louisiana	2,424,126	1,509,957	15,247	232,237	1,251,931	10,542	914,169	724,960	0	37,006	30,004	122,199
Maine	657,404	340,312	4,629	36,161	299,522		317,092	109,054	179,789	8,678	7,525	12,046
Maryland	2,866,757	1,059,182	28,298	140,655	889,946	283	1,807,575	0	1,611,654	55,236	101,667	39,018
Massachusetts	3,761,052	1,760,260	14,508	181,127	1,344,404	220,221	2,000,792	0	1,901,276	67,827	15,154	16,535
Michigan	7,094,563	2,505,353	55,419	312,971	1,998,581	138,382	4,589,210	3,955,808	0	122,068	276,701	234,633
Minnesota	3,033,619	1,735,865	22,056	127,291	1,556,271	30,247	1,297,754	1,013,885	0	67,385	107,926	108,558
Mississippi	1,340,399	940,632	18,954	185,025	736,533	92	399,767	244,897	0	23,930	54,778	75,013
Missouri	2,703,766	1,703,177	15,269	144,028	1,053,259	490,621	1,000,589	759,570	1,149	54,791	105,860	80,368
Montana	640,838	431,877	25,008	19,029	225,132	162,708	208,961	170,585	0	8,907	2,766	26,703
Nebraska	1,099,800	358,519	13,529	44,643	230,433	69,914	741,281	603,580	0	22,657	74,062	40,982
Nevada	565,641	389,738	2,854	19,763	367,121	491	175,903	146,402	0	10,461	2,925	16,115
New Hampshire	543,250	56,285	2,636	16,718	36,440	9,560	486,965	354,976	104,243	14,205	3,970	9,571
New Jersey	5,975,230	2,527,429	20,688	274,569	2,222,612		3,447,801	2,653,419	482,134	86,764	101,483	124,001
New Mexico	972,706	858,431	50,162	72,695	735,574		114,275	67,295	0	13,511	4,103	29,366
New York	15,373,649	6,885,998	30,091	583,689	6,270,873	1,345	8,487,651	4,549,810	3,202,645	153,848	320,383	260,965
North Carolina	3,765,816	2,681,596	28,868	254,211	2,397,759	758	1,084,220	0	802,675	111,495	47,337	122,713
North Dakota	434,022	260,548	12,842	19,588	218,985	9,133	173,474	130,995	0	9,549	12,631	20,299
Ohio	6,812,631	3,326,304	34,113	293,537	2,992,996	5,658	3,486,327	2,876,715	0	164,745	222,873	221,994

GENERAL REVENUE OF PUBLIC SCHOOL SYSTEMS: 1985-86—Continued

State or other jurisdiction	Total(a)	Intergovernmental(a) Total	From state: Directly from federal government	Federal aid distributed by state	Other	From other local governments	From own sources: Total	Taxes	Parent government contributions	Current charges: School lunch	Current charges: Other	Other
Oklahoma	1,931,507	1,270,648	31,035	112,728	1,087,557	39,328	660,859	545,661	0	35,341	7,634	72,223
Oregon	2,089,528	727,333	46,501	77,845	563,490	39,497	1,362,195	1,170,251	0	27,824	94,925	69,195
Pennsylvania	7,573,014	3,447,419	100,508	312,765	3,031,551	2,595	4,125,595	3,536,182		128,302	218,870	242,241
Rhode Island	558,557	244,466	5,390	20,726	209,662	8,688	314,091	0	311,489	0	638	1,964
South Carolina	1,743,620	1,092,024	5,876	155,535	878,754	51,859	651,596	502,081	0	40,565	54,663	54,287
South Dakota	419,493	168,167	19,642	24,346	117,121	7,058	251,326	214,918	0	7,616	2,600	26,192
Tennessee	1,926,460	1,249,539	25,302	187,088	809,484	227,665	676,921	0	560,131	52,021	16,726	48,043
Texas	11,672,854	5,903,569	87,659	646,633	5,149,253	20,024	5,769,285	4,780,978	0	197,276	378,429	412,602
Utah	1,102,546	680,609	10,996	52,051	617,562	0	421,937	339,863	0	23,221	7,141	51,712
Vermont(b)	325,204	105,464	475	10,165	94,724	100	219,740	203,144	0	6,125	1,221	9,250
Virginia	3,519,153	1,750,429	31,816	181,968	1,535,378	1,267	1,768,724	0	1,635,428	88,973	23,115	21,208
Washington	2,737,103	2,144,664	32,494	139,802	1,971,516	852	592,439	401,308	0	43,403	82,357	65,371
West Virginia	1,171,438	831,728	5,491	107,495	718,742	0	339,710	267,423	0	17,252	2,880	52,155
Wisconsin	3,539,625	1,668,127	20,850	140,082	1,466,723	40,472	1,871,498	1,642,903	0	51,471	91,064	86,060
Wyoming	719,570	366,186	10,753	14,414	283,059	57,960	353,384	301,311	0	8,299	22,531	21,243
Dist. of Col.	524,662	51,873	49,871	0	0	2,002	472,789	0	459,402	1,511	8,695	3,181

Source: U.S. Bureau of the Census, Finances of Public School Systems in 1985-86.
Note: Because of rounding, detail may not add to totals. Revenue from state sources for state dependent school systems is included as intergovernmental revenue from state rather than as parent government contributions.
(a) To avoid duplication, interschool system transactions are excluded.
(b) Vermont data were estimated. Actual data were not available from the state education agency.

Table 8.5
GENERAL EXPENDITURES OF PUBLIC SCHOOL SYSTEMS: 1985-86
(In thousands of dollars)

State or other jurisdiction	Total(a)	Elementary and secondary					Higher education					Interest on debt	Intergovern-mental(a)
		Total	Current operation		Capital outlay		Total	Current operation		Capital outlay			
			Salaries and wages	Other	Construction	Other		Salaries and wages	Other	Construction	Other		
United States	$156,277,024	$144,513,235	$91,340,228	$43,389,767	$6,073,407	$3,709,833	$8,605,285	$5,195,682	$2,850,253	$244,098	$315,252	$2,769,596	$388,908
Alabama	1,720,274	1,699,853	1,287,873	308,820	56,427	46,733	0	0	0	0	0	13,248	7,173
Alaska	966,877	914,143	525,179	265,385	108,772	14,807	0	0	0	0	0	52,065	669
Arizona	2,428,601	2,092,244	1,130,911	571,147	285,890	104,296	249,365	143,755	78,121	14,252	13,237	86,992	0
Arkansas	1,298,193	1,271,461	747,440	292,361	227,671	3,989	0	0	0	0	0	26,732	0
California	17,868,372	15,689,787	10,350,449	4,658,229	234,625	446,484	2,114,872	1,381,659	616,375	50,793	66,045	51,793	11,920
Colorado	2,279,916	2,177,981	1,319,705	608,188	146,156	103,932	35,491	21,862	12,155	803	671	66,444	0
Connecticut	1,957,773	1,922,921	1,316,543	556,390	20,618	29,370	0	0	0	0	0	34,722	130
Delaware	407,709	406,584	241,879	152,864	5,518	6,323	0	0	0	0	0	1,125	0
Florida	6,722,918	6,116,953	3,527,822	2,022,915	300,855	165,361	551,934	352,582	153,186	23,381	22,785	54,031	0
Georgia	3,263,472	3,200,895	2,112,528	802,964	211,445	73,958	25,152	14,897	9,102	0	1,153	36,681	744
Hawaii	536,251	536,251	355,447	132,846	37,518	10,440	22,910	12,837	8,762	492	819	11,196	0
Idaho	517,871	483,765	331,189	106,255	32,758	13,563	0	0	0	0	0	137,560	0
Illinois	7,043,692	6,267,067	4,098,737	1,812,078	180,016	176,236	639,065	387,359	214,397	9,556	27,753	33,994	167,280
Indiana	3,103,642	2,902,368	1,988,817	698,946	163,560	51,045	182,262	99,341	71,537	4,127	7,257	22,258	0
Iowa	1,828,702	1,624,182	1,006,367	519,169	56,659	41,987	0	0	0	0	0		0
Kansas	1,685,633	1,508,709	967,197	435,367	56,947	49,198	150,657	83,489	59,939	1,055	6,174	26,267	0
Kentucky	1,642,267	1,601,987	1,001,383	511,085	43,782	45,737	8,968	4,235	3,867	722	144	40,280	0
Louisiana	2,419,038	2,339,905	1,457,548	678,258	152,368	51,731	0	0	0	0	0	70,165	0
Maine	665,631	652,014	413,660	195,165	20,337	22,852	0	0	0	0	0	13,617	0
Maryland	2,811,735	2,527,045	1,771,666	622,583	89,660	43,136	262,584	161,173	88,181	3,702	9,528	22,106	0
Massachusetts	3,508,488	3,445,394	2,114,636	1,254,952	35,945	39,861	3,509	2,435	1,043	0	31	59,585	0
Michigan	7,092,135	6,466,349	4,118,442	2,091,750	97,341	158,816	485,777	289,995	176,429	3,277	16,076	140,009	0
Minnesota	3,018,969	2,963,597	1,950,052	804,713	113,698	95,134	157,796	92,571	57,620	2,869	4,736	55,372	0
Mississippi	1,320,095	1,147,902	768,518	351,087		28,297	0	0	0	0	0	14,397	0
Missouri	2,755,208	2,562,187	1,669,497	733,617	89,255	69,818	149,453	82,551	55,836	4,743	6,323	43,568	0
Montana	642,203	623,308	358,041	228,703	20,233	16,331	8,470	4,487	3,600	245	138	10,425	0
Nebraska	1,079,287	982,258	586,157	346,826	24,909	24,366	79,986	41,499	33,309	2,006	3,172	17,043	0
Nevada	541,153	529,394	344,570	157,559	7,285	19,980	0	0	0	0	0	11,759	0
New Hampshire	562,722	554,872	307,913	198,961	30,524	17,474	0	0	0	0	0	7,850	0
New Jersey	5,845,890	5,421,398	3,345,202	1,809,983	178,522	87,691	295,494	173,823	106,747	3,881	11,043	92,862	36,136
New Mexico	987,937	972,566	505,845	344,664	109,265	12,792	0	0	0	0	0	15,371	0
New York	14,885,950	13,828,885	8,162,431	5,038,825	398,148	229,481	806,164	499,591	284,642	4,734	17,197	250,901	0
North Carolina	3,704,770	3,298,388	2,129,095	1,016,822	120,572	31,899	386,069	235,215	118,267	15,938	16,649	20,313	1,551
North Dakota	425,512	420,254	250,617	140,801	17,456	11,380	0	0	0	0	0	3,707	0
Ohio	6,744,595	6,531,767	4,157,203	2,051,007	130,130	193,427	143,018	73,093	62,506	2,325	5,094	69,810	0

GENERAL EXPENDITURES OF PUBLIC SCHOOL SYSTEMS: 1985-86—Continued

State or other jurisdiction	Total(a)	Elementary and secondary					Higher education						
		Total	Current operation		Capital outlay		Total	Current operation		Capital outlay		Interest on debt	Inter-governmental(a)
			Salaries and wages	Other	Construction	Other		Salaries and wages	Other	Construction	Other		
Oklahoma	1,963,024	1,933,766	1,220,536	459,760	159,848	93,622	0	0	0	0	0	29,258	0
Oregon	2,071,163	1,803,636	1,032,349	684,948	51,173	35,166	217,909	124,953	84,858	2,001	6,097	49,618	0
Pennsylvania ...	7,488,264	6,892,573	4,246,981	2,330,578	213,166	101,848	257,741	143,443	98,251	433	15,614	184,513	153,437
Rhode Island ...	553,664	548,258	370,271	170,524	2,395	5,068	0	0	0	0	0	5,406	0
South Carolina ...	1,755,672	1,687,438	1,170,564	388,093	116,127	12,654	0	0	0	0	0	67,671	563
South Dakota ...	405,256	402,714	241,330	138,823	11,254	11,307	0	0	0	0	0	2,542	0
Tennessee	1,987,920	1,926,405	1,292,138	436,929	88,113	109,225	0	0	0	0	0	61,515	0
Texas	11,987,389	10,657,329	7,071,489	2,148,718	1,098,053	339,069	825,229	473,632	278,013	35,514	38,070	504,831	0
Utah	1,133,231	1,097,194	629,045	323,136	106,309	8,704	0	0	0	0	0	36,037	0
Vermont(b)	329,110	322,241	182,680	130,645	3,206	5,710	0	0	0	0	0	6,715	154
Virginia	3,598,087	3,550,471	2,178,493	1,177,589	122,319	72,070	0	0	0	0	0	47,616	0
Washington	2,803,412	2,733,506	1,703,996	791,694	145,964	91,852	0	0	0	0	0	69,906	0
West Virginia ...	1,152,401	1,143,625	788,918	289,513	36,878	28,316	0	0	0	0	0	8,776	0
Wisconsin	3,516,194	3,078,078	1,850,009	1,104,485	36,118	87,466	375,604	199,369	127,140	34,697	14,398	55,179	7,333
Wyoming	722,042	611,813	320,044	210,454	54,059	27,256	84,464	35,816	24,631	20,961	3,056	25,765	0
Dist. of Col.	526,714	439,554	320,826	82,593	23,560	12,575	85,342	60,020	21,739	1,591	1,992	0	1,818

Source: U.S. Bureau of the Census, Finances of Public School Systems in 1985-86.
Note: Because of rounding, detail may not add to totals.
(a) To avoid duplication, interschool system transactions are excluded.
(b)Vermont data were estimated. Actual data were not available from the state education agency.

Table 8.6
FEDERAL FUNDS OBLIGATED FOR CHILD NUTRITION PROGRAMS, BY STATE: FISCAL YEAR 1986
(In thousands of dollars)

State or other jurisdiction	Total	Special Milk	School lunch	School breakfast	State administrative expense	Child care	Summer food service
United States	$1,473,993,145	$15,422,789	$509,991,736	$386,381,702	$38,465,051	$425,027,061	$98,704,806
Alabama...........	37,631,427	39,482	12,554,633	11,457,071	1,186,219	9,384,942	3,009,080
Alaska.............	4,460,579	21,447	1,310,767	656,768	278,484	2,190,602	2,511
Arizona...........	20,496,101	268,812	5,880,184	5,304,481	647,737	7,699,248	695,639
Arkansas	16,321,178	28,507	6,582,495	5,402,680	632,373	3,581,105	94,018
California..........	162,179,548	1,084,017	46,450,621	55,097,996	2,011,933	47,412,418	10,122,563
Colorado	19,979,699	82,911	5,958,936	2,198,487	436,065	10,703,162	600,138
Connecticut	12,392,106	498,824	5,015,100	998,470	485,665	4,360,574	1,033,473
Delaware	4,755,868	36,481	1,119,806	937,163	264,929	1,728,734	668,755
Florida	65,992,807	120,597	22,346,802	20,114,139	1,894,488	16,244,884	5,271,897
Georgia...........	50,389,559	56,528	19,334,254	14,881,477	1,011,596	12,220,745	2,884,959
Hawaii	7,625,581	9,134	3,493,366	2,142,375	312,675	1,373,983	294,048
Idaho	4,772,549	67,999	2,472,197	384,223	266,183	1,525,309	56,638
Illinois.............	56,930,645	2,487,481	20,240,873	11,305,417	1,848,224	17,476,920	3,571,730
Indiana	23,972,749	223,223	12,554,497	3,075,258	748,985	5,870,141	1,500,645
Iowa	14,478,309	137,395	7,588,568	1,249,239	517,215	4,480,088	505,804
Kansas	13,780,619	88,047	5,936,293	766,597	446,003	6,242,963	300,716
Kentucky	30,081,787	106,177	10,832,473	12,837,255	699,920	4,619,770	986,192
Louisiana	45,873,285	83,771	15,090,665	13,487,201	1,409,168	13,745,737	2,056,743
Maine	6,486,806	72,978	2,411,638	760,728	332,193	2,706,294	202,975
Maryland	20,712,376	309,069	7,317,900	4,490,352	699,576	6,759,204	1,136,275
Massachusetts	31,517,216	421,967	10,158,072	4,919,305	52,586	14,394,883	1,570,403
Michigan	41,231,970	1,001,512	14,938,369	4,164,515	1,374,537	15,387,912	4,365,125
Minnesota	30,325,049	366,180	9,363,307	1,619,054	910,459	16,914,872	1,151,177
Mississippi	39,545,573	14,054	9,334,078	13,064,983	1,128,311	12,823,270	3,180,877
Missouri	26,010,767	349,703	11,238,557	5,585,140	634,122	7,256,195	947,050
Montana...........	4,999,148	54,578	1,794,401	653,822	333,019	2,010,892	152,436
Nebraska	9,249,353	99,207	3,849,390	694,650	319,875	4,100,366	185,865
Nevada	3,137,663	23,267	1,187,048	1,058,594	238,461	587,789	42,504
New Hampshire	4,063,138	222,239	1,793,514	459,924	260,389	1,157,226	169,846
New Jersey..........	31,726,214	828,792	11,846,687	4,733,558	1,073,988	9,619,712	3,623,477
New Mexico........	13,752,215	27,770	3,798,231	3,040,166	566,275	5,377,631	942,142
New York	126,172,729	1,860,060	33,496,756	32,276,173	684,836	33,686,530	24,168,374
North Carolina	49,069,271	103,335	17,360,730	19,253,814	928,793	9,421,747	2,000,852
North Dakota	6,520,085	16,412	1,868,880	375,871	316,420	3,779,038	163,464
Ohio	52,762,671	1,120,248	21,103,696	14,787,264	1,625,569	12,417,787	1,708,107
Oklahoma	20,225,985	9,126	7,609,282	5,436,416	695,703	6,088,529	386,929
Oregon	12,064,643	168,426	4,818,901	2,100,803	500,020	4,035,722	440,771
Pennsylvania	50,017,988	563,580	21,367,594	6,282,103	1,518,137	13,730,363	6,556,211
Rhode Island	4,302,539	82,011	1,278,453	794,376	259,379	1,214,292	674,028
South Carolina	27,794,679	32,370	10,428,704	8,315,754	927,377	5,090,046	3,000,428
South Dakota	5,861,689	33,000	2,040,031	1,358,661	283,935	1,665,250	480,812
Tennessee	33,363,476	33,925	12,812,701	12,310,614	1,055,725	5,938,985	1,211,526
Texas..............	122,884,627	112,128	39,625,630	53,887,734	3,272,029	22,811,955	3,175,151
Utah	11,031,311	23,392	4,984,213	554,505	257,281	5,127,301	84,619
Vermont	2,383,548	163,869	929,421	83,214	246,621	926,149	34,274
Virginia............	27,779,947	139,424	12,995,639	6,116,931	683,923	6,431,699	1,412,331
Washington	23,438,870	286,282	7,153,274	3,006,501	406,981	12,159,032	426,800
West Virginia	16,105,373	29,462	4,689,746	8,050,390	528,502	2,323,963	483,310
Wisconsin...........	19,421,524	1,374,663	9,283,541	2,174,270	682,233	5,293,582	613,235
Wyoming	2,965,466	23,878	1,150,149	120,838	255,982	1,402,712	11,907
Dist. of Col.	4,954,840	15,049	1,200,673	1,554,382	313,952	1,524,808	345,976

Source: U.S. Department of Agriculture, Food and Nutrition Service, Budget Division, unpublished data.

Table 8.7
AVERAGE ANNUAL SALARY OF INSTRUCTIONAL STAFF
IN PUBLIC ELEMENTARY AND SECONDARY SCHOOLS: 1939-40 to 1986-87

State or other jurisdiction	Average annual salary for: (in unadjusted dollars)					
	1939-40	1949-50	1959-60	1969-70	1979-80 (a)	1986-87 (a)
Alabama	$ 744	$2,111	$4,002	$ 6,954	$13,338	$24,480
Alaska	N.A.	N.A.	6,859	10,993	27,697	46,082
Arizona	1,544	3,556	5,590	8,975	16,180	28,971
Arkansas	584	1,801	3,295	6,445	12,704	21,067
California	2,351	N.A.	6,600	9,980	18,626	32,230
Colorado	1,393	2,821	4,997	7,900	16,840	28,400
Connecticut	1,861	3,558	6,008	9,400	17,062	30,193
Delaware	1,684	3,273	5,800	9,300	16,873	28,440
Florida	1,012	2,958	5,080	8,600	14,875	25,552
Georgia	770	1,963	3,904	7,372	14,547	25,600
Hawaii	N.A.	N.A.	5,390	9,829	20,436	27,646
Idaho	1,057	2,481	4,216	7,257	14,110	22,299
Illinois	1,700	3,458	5,814	9,950	18,271	29,399
Indiana	1,433	3,401	5,542	9,574	16,256	26,557
Iowa	1,017	2,420	4,030	8,200	15,600	23,434
Kansas	1,014	2,628	4,450	7,811	14,513	25,297
Kentucky	826	1,936	3,327	7,624	15,350	23,560
Louisiana	1,006	2,983	4,978	7,220	14,020	21,736
Maine	894	2,115	3,694	8,059	13,743	21,943
Maryland	1,642	3,594	5,557	9,885	18,308	29,940
Massachusetts	2,037	3,338	5,545	9,175	22,500	30,810
Michigan	1,576	3,420	5,654	10,125	19,277	32,800
Minnesota	1,276	3,013	5,275	9,957	16,654	30,190
Mississippi	559	1,416	3,314	6,012	12,274	20,050
Missouri	1,159	2,581	4,536	8,091	14,543	24,383
Montana	1,184	2,962	4,425	8,100	15,080	24,370
Nebraska	829	2,292	3,876	7,855	14,236	24,138
Nevada	1,557	3,209	5,693	9,689	17,290	27,340
New Hampshire	1,258	2,712	4,455	8,018	12,930	22,625
New Jersey	2,093	3,511	5,871	9,500	18,851	30,770
New Mexico	1,144	3,215	5,382	8,125	15,406	26,892
New York	2,604	3,706	6,537	10,200	20,400	33,500
North Carolina	946	2,688	4,178	7,744	14,445	24,395
North Dakota	745	2,324	3,695	6,900	13,839	22,533
Ohio	1,587	3,088	5,124	8,594	16,100	27,379
Oklahoma	1,014	2,736	4,659	7,139	13,500	22,770
Oregon	1,333	3,323	5,535	9,200	16,996	28,000
Pennsylvania	1,640	3,006	5,308	9,000	17,060	28,042
Rhode Island	1,809	3,294	5,499	8,900	18,425	32,026
South Carolina	743	1,891	3,450	7,000	13,670	24,043
South Dakota	807	2,064	3,725	6,700	13,010	19,518
Tennessee	862	2,302	3,929	7,290	14,193	23,231
Texas	1,079	3,122	4,708	7,503	14,729	26,255
Utah	1,394	3,103	5,096	8,049	17,403	26,908
Vermont	981	2,348	4,466	8,225	13,300	23,293
Virginia	899	2,328	4,312	8,200	14,655	26,401
Washington	1,706	3,487	5,643	9,500	19,735	28,746
West Virginia	1,170	2,425	3,952	7,850	14,395	22,428
Wisconsin	1,379	3,007	4,870	9,150	16,335	29,000
Wyoming	1,169	2,798	4,937	8,532	16,830	28,230
Dist. of Col.	2,350	3,920	6,280	11,075	23,027	41,467

Sources: U.S. Department of Education, National Center for Education Statistics, *Statistics of State School Systems;* National Education Association, *Estimates of School Statistics, 1986-87* (Copyright 1987). Reprinted with permission.

Note: Includes supervisors, principals, classroom teachers, and other instructional staff.

Key:
N.A.—Not available.
(a) Estimated.

Table 8.8
MEMBERSHIP AND ATTENDANCE IN PUBLIC ELEMENTARY AND SECONDARY SCHOOLS, BY STATE: 1985-86 AND 1986-87

State or other jurisdiction	1985-86			1986-87		
	Estimated average daily membership (ADM)	Average daily attendance (ADA)	ADA as a percent of ADM	Estimated average daily membership (ADM)	Estimated average daily attendance (ADA)	ADA as a percent of ADM
United States	38,705,754	36,642,002	94.7	38,901,740	36,837,858	94.7
Alabama	724,327	687,127	94.9	727,575	690,208	94.9
Alaska	103,124	93,431	90.6	105,388	95,785	90.9
Arizona	524,481	494,505	94.3	540,817	510,088	94.3
Arkansas	428,668	405,403	94.6	428,689	406,817	94.9
California	N.A.	4,242,400	UD	N.A.	4,300,242	UD
Colorado	529,154	508,357	96.1	535,134	514,065	96.1
Connecticut	459,200	441,250	96.1	458,700	449,100	97.9
Delaware	91,251	84,936	93.1	92,937	86,526	93.1
Florida	1,563,443	1,444,934	92.4	1,601,832	1,488,422	92.9
Georgia	1,048,300	993,200	94.7	1,050,600	995,430	94.7
Hawaii	161,764	151,193	93.5	162,195	151,596	93.5
Idaho	N.A.	200,699	UD	N.A.	200,800	UD
Illinois	1,707,117	1,595,977	93.5	1,683,199	1,575,186	93.6
Indiana	949,256	898,134	94.6	929,703	881,295	94.8
Iowa	476,240	453,402	95.2	471,148	448,868	95.3
Kansas	385,551	366,203	95.0	392,130	372,452	95.0
Kentucky	612,078	577,190	94.3	611,082	576,250	94.3
Louisiana	756,550	713,805	94.4	760,000	715,000	94.1
Maine	205,412	194,341	94.6	209,185	196,840	94.1
Maryland	668,217	614,326	91.9	672,383	618,156	91.9
Massachusetts	844,625	761,017	90.1	845,000	761,500	90.1
Michigan	N.A.	1,543,100	UD	N.A.	1,542,840	UD
Minnesota	699,109	662,594	94.8	703,372	666,093	94.7
Mississippi	450,898	442,330	98.1	487,000	473,640	97.3
Missouri	N.A.	714,229	UD	N.A.	719,100	UD
Montana	146,229	139,356	95.3	146,091	139,200	95.3
Nebraska	262,431	250,934	95.6	262,912	251,434	95.6
Nevada	148,836	143,900	96.7	148,704	142,682	96.0
New Hampshire	154,345	145,392	94.2	157,823	148,669	94.2
New Jersey	1,111,000	1,030,200	92.7	1,096,456	1,029,836	93.9
New Mexico	264,748	251,511	95.0	268,765	255,327	95.0
New York	2,558,000	2,325,800	90.9	2,544,000	2,312,900	90.9
North Carolina	1,075,289	1,014,795	94.4	1,073,330	1,013,723	94.4
North Dakota	116,790	112,119	96.0	116,733	112,005	95.9
Ohio	1,775,167	1,660,757	93.6	1,772,653	1,658,140	93.5
Oklahoma	585,000	553,000	94.5	582,227	551,550	94.7
Oregon	442,300	414,900	93.8	443,000	415,500	93.8
Pennsylvania	1,671,800	1,568,100	93.8	1,648,000	1,535,900	93.2
Rhode Island	132,707	122,109	92.0	131,466	123,417	93.9
South Carolina	583,170	558,736	95.8	590,000	572,200	97.0
South Dakota	123,457	118,192	95.7	124,000	118,375	95.5
Tennessee	808,303	762,225	94.3	814,086	770,460	94.6
Texas	N.A.	2,933,122	UD	N.A.	2,977,345	UD
Utah	400,667	379,359	94.7	413,273	391,294	94.7
Vermont	88,500	83,000	93.8	88,400	82,980	93.9
Virginia	960,292	904,347	94.2	966,176	909,889	94.2
Washington	743,172	696,724	93.8	756,153	708,893	93.7
West Virginia	N.A.	333,849	UD	N.A.	328,172	UD
Wisconsin	749,842	683,291	91.1	751,829	679,551	90.4
Wyoming	101,098	95,548	94.5	101,451	95,921	94.5
Dist. of Col.	84,962	76,653	90.2	84,350	76,196	90.3

Source: National Education Association, *Estimates of School Statistics 1986-87.* (Copyright 1987). Reprinted with permission.
Key:
N.A.—Not available
UD—Undefined

Table 8.9
ENROLLMENT, AVERAGE DAILY ATTENDANCE, AND CLASSROOM TEACHERS IN PUBLIC ELEMENTARY AND SECONDARY SCHOOLS, BY STATE: 1985-86

State or other jurisdiction	Enrollment	Estimated average daily attendance	Classroom teachers	Pupils per teacher based on enrollment	Pupils per teacher based on average daily attendance
United States ..	39,529,922	36,642,002	2,209,955	17.9	16.6
Alabama.......	730,460	687,127	36,971	19.8	18.6
Alaska.........	107,506	93,431	5,140	20.9	18.2
Arizona........	593,783	494,505	28,988	20.5	17.1
Arkansas	433,410	405,403	23,699	18.3	17.1
California......	4,255,554	4,242,400	186,017	22.9	22.8
Colorado	550,642	508,357	29,895	18.4	17.0
Connecticut	472,427	441,250	33,125	14.3	13.3
Delaware	92,901	84,936	5,745	16.2	14.8
Florida	1,559,507	1,444,934	88,973	17.5	16.2
Georgia	1,064,600	993,200	57,370	18.6	17.3
Hawaii	163,899	151,193	8,362	19.6	18.1
Idaho	211,425	200,699	10,256	20.6	19.6
Illinois.........	1,826,478	1,595,977	102,568	17.8	15.6
Indiana	966,057	898,134	51,971	18.6	17.3
Iowa	485,443	453,402	30,897	15.7	14.7
Kansas	410,229	366,203	26,847	15.3	13.6
Kentucky	643,833	577,190	33,670	19.1	17.1
Louisiana	792,700	713,805	42,610	18.6	16.8
Maine	206,827	194,341	12,884	16.1	15.1
Maryland	671,560	614,326	37,860	17.7	16.2
Massachusetts ...	841,203	761,017	56,825	14.8	13.4
Michigan	1,677,300	1,543,100	80,240	20.9	19.2
Minnesota	705,242	662,594	40,837	17.3	16.2
Mississippi	464,280	442,330	25,610	18.1	17.3
Missouri	795,107	714,229	48,113	16.5	14.8
Montana........	153,661	139,356	9,705	15.8	14.4
Nebraska	265,819	250,934	17,574	15.1	14.3
Nevada	155,000	143,900	7,751	20.0	18.6
New Hampshire .	160,974	145,392	10,251	15.7	14.2
New Jersey......	1,116,194	1,030,200	74,236	15.0	13.9
New Mexico.....	264,748	251,511	14,935	17.7	16.8
New York	2,605,363	2,325,800	173,400	15.0	13.4
North Carolina ..	1,092,893	1,014,795	57,638	19.0	17.6
North Dakota ...	117,970	112,119	7,852	15.0	14.3
Ohio	1,794,000	1,660,757	95,465	18.8	17.4
Oklahoma	596,000	553,000	36,000	16.6	15.4
Oregon	447,500	414,900	25,740	17.4	16.1
Pennsylvania ...	1,683,221	1,568,100	101,665	16.6	15.4
Rhode Island	133,450	122,109	8,755	15.2	13.9
South Carolina ..	605,790	558,736	34,324	17.6	16.3
South Dakota ...	123,875	118,192	8,153	15.2	14.5
Tennessee	815,423	762,225	41,103	19.8	18.5
Texas..........	3,149,380	2,933,122	179,800	17.5	16.3
Utah	403,305	379,359	17,084	23.6	22.2
Vermont	90,157	83,000	6,397	14.1	13.0
Virginia.........	968,104	904,347	58,667	16.5	15.4
Washington	748,694	696,724	36,193	20.7	19.3
West Virginia ...	357,923	333,849	22,733	15.7	14.7
Wisconsin.......	768,234	683,291	46,500	16.5	14.7
Wyoming	102,779	95,548	7,296	14.1	13.1
Dist. of Col.	87,092	76,653	5,265	16.5	14.6

Source: National Education Association, *Estimates of School Statistics, 1986-87.* (Copyright 1987.) Used with permission.

Table 8.10
STATE COURSE REQUIREMENTS FOR HIGH SCHOOL GRADUATION

State or other jurisdiction	All courses	English/ language arts	Social studies	Mathe-matics	Science	Physical education /health	Electives	Other courses	First gradua-ting class to which require-ments apply
Alabama(a,b)									
Standard diploma ..	22	4	3	2	2	1½	9	½ home and personal management	1989
Advanced diploma .	22	4	4	3	3	1½	4	2½ home and personal management, 2 foreign language	1989
Alaska	21	4	3	2	2	1	9	. . .	1985
Arizona(b)	20	4	3	2	2	. . .	9		1991
Arkansas(c)	20	4	3	----------5----------		1	6½	½ fine arts	1988
California(b)	13	3	3	2	2	2	. . .	1 visual or performing arts or foreign language	1987
Colorado(d)	. . .	. . .	. . .	. . .	. . .	. . .	. . .	. . . .	. . .
Connecticut	20	4	3	3	2	1	6	1 arts or vocational education	1988
Delaware(b)	19	4	3	2	2	1½	6½	. . .	1987
Florida(b,e,f)									
Standard diploma ..	24	4	3	3	3	1	9	½ practical or exploratory vocational education, ½ performing fine arts, or speech and debate	1989
Academic scholars .	26	4	3	4	4	1	7	2 foreign language, 1 fine arts	1984
Georgia(b)									
Standard diploma ..	21	4	3	2	2	1	8	1 fine arts, vocational education, computer technology, or ROTC	1988
Advanced diploma .	21	4	3	3	3	1	4	2 foreign language, 1 fine arts, vocational education, computer technology, or ROTC	1988
Hawaii(b)	20	4	4	2	2	1½	6	½ guidance	1983
Idaho(g)	21	4	2	2	2	1½	6	½ reading, ½ speech, ½ consumer education, 1 humanities, 1 history/ government	1988
Illinois(h)	16	3	2	2	1	4½	2¼	¼ consumer education, 1 art, foreign language, music or vocational education	1988
Indiana									
Standard diploma ..	19½	4	2	2	2	1½	8	. . .	1989
Academic honors ..	24	4	3	4	4	1	4 or 5	3 or 4 in foreign language	1990
Iowa(f,i)	. . .	. . .	1½	. . .	1	. . .	. . .	. . .	. . .
Kansas	21	4	3	2	2	1	8	1 local board determines	1989
Kentucky(b)									
Standard diploma ..	20	4	2	3	2	1	7	1 additional mathematics science, social studies, or vocational education	1987
Commonwealth diploma	22	5	2	----------6----------		1	. . .	1 foreign language in advanced placement	1986
Louisiana									
Standard diploma ..	23	4	3	3	3	2	7½	½ computer literacy	1989
Louisiana scholar(j) .	23	4	3	3	3	2	7½	½ computer literacy	1987
Regent's scholar ...	24	4	3½	3	3	2	4½	3 foreign language, 1 fine arts	1983
Maine(a)	16	4	2	2	2	1½	3½	1 fine arts	1989
Maryland(b)	20	4	3	3	2	1 P.E.	5	1 fine arts, 1 practical arts	1989
Massachusetts(i)	. . .	. . .	1	. . .	. . .	4	. . .	. . .	. . .
Michigan(i)	. . .	. . .	½	. . .	. . .	. . .	. . .	. . .	. . .
Minnesota(f)	20	4	3	1	1	1	9½	. . .	1982
Mississippi(b)	18	4	2	2	2	. . .	8	. . .	1989
Missouri									
Standard diploma ..	22	3	2	2	2	1	10	1 practical arts, 1 fine arts	1988
College preparatory studies certificate (k)	24	4	3	3	3	1	8	1 practical arts, 1 fine arts	. . .

STATE COURSE REQUIREMENTS—Continued

State or other jurisdiction	All courses	English/ language arts	Social studies	Mathe- matics	Science	Physical education /health	Electives	Other courses	First graduating class to which requirements apply
Montana............	20	4	1½ or 2	2	1	1	10½ or 10	...	1986
Nebraska(l)	...	...	...	...	...	...			1991
Nevada(b)..........	22½	4	2	2	2	2½	8½	1 arts/humanities, ½ computer literacy	1992
New Hampshire(m) ..	19 3/4	4	2½	2	2	1¼	4	½ arts, ½ computer science, 3 from 2 of the following: arts, foreign language, practical arts, and vocational education	1989
New Jersey(b)	21½	4	2	3	2	4	4	1 fine, practical or performing arts, ½ career exploration, 1 world history and cultures	1992
New Mexico(a,g).....	23	4	3	3	2	1	9	1 communication skills	1990
New York(b)									
Local diploma.....	18½	4	4	2	2	½	varies	1 art and/or music	1989
Regent's diploma ..	18½	4	4	2	2	½	varies	3 to 5 in a sequence of specific courses (varying on type of diploma) chosen by the student	1989
North Carolina(b)....									
Standard diploma ..	20	4	2	2	2	1	9	...	1987
Scholars program ..	22	4	4	3	3	2	1	1 vocational education, 1 arts education	1984
North Dakota	17	4	3	2	2	1	5	...	1984
Ohio(b).............	18	3	2	2	1	1	9	...	1988
Oklahoma									
Standard diploma ..	20	4	2	2	2	...	10	...	1987
College preparatory	15	4	2	3	2	...	...	4 from: foreign language, computer science, economics, English, geography, government, math, history, sociology, science, speech, or psychology. Total hour requirement is less, but curriculum is more rigorous and restrictive.	1988
Oregon(b)..........	22	3	3½	2	2	2	8	½ career development, 1 applied arts, fine arts, or foreign language	1988
Pennsylvania	21	4	3	3	3	1	5	2 arts and humanities	1989
Rhode Island									
Standard diploma ..	16	4	1	1	1	...	9	...	1989
Career bound	16	4	2	2	2	...	6	...	1989
College bound.....	18	4	2	3	2	...	4	2 foreign languages, ½ arts, ½ computer literacy	1988
South Carolina(b,f,n)									
Standard diploma ..	20	4	3	3	2	1	7	...	1987
Academic achieve- ment honors	22	4	3	3	2	1	7	2 foreign language	1986
South Dakota	20	4	3	2	2	...	8	½ computer studies, ½ fine arts	1989
Tennessee(b)									
Standard diploma ..	20	4	1½	2	2	1½	9	...	1987
Honors	20½	4	3	3	3	1½	2	2 in same foreign language, 2 fine/visual/ performing arts (general honors) or 4 in same voca- tional education program (vocational education honors)	1987
Texas(b,f)									
Standard diploma ..	21	4	2½	3	2	2	7	½ economics/free enterprise	1988
Advanced programs	22	4	2½	3	3	1½	2	½ economics/free enterprise, 2 foreign language, 1 computer science, 1 fine arts	1988
Utah	24	3	3	2	2	2	9½	1½ arts, 1 vocational education, ½ computer science	1988
Vermont(c)..........	14½	4	3	----------5----------		1½	...	1 arts	1989

STATE COURSE REQUIREMENTS—Continued

State or other jurisdiction	All courses	English/ language arts	Social studies	Mathe- matics	Science	Physical education /health	Electives	Other courses	First gradua- ting class to which require- ments apply
						Years of instruction in . . .			
Virginia(b,f)									
Standard diploma . .	21	4	3	2	2	2	6	1 additional science or mathematics, 1 fine or practical arts	1989
Advanced studies diploma	23	4	3	3	3	2	4	3 foreign languages, 1 fine or practical arts	1989
Washington	19	3	2½	2	2	2	5½	1 occupational education, 1 fine, visual, or performing arts	1991
West Virginia	21	4	3	2	2	2	7	1 applied, fine, or performing arts or second language	1989
Wisconsin(n)	13	4	3	2	2	2	. . .	. . .	1989
Wyoming(i)	18	. . .	1	. . .	. . .	. . .	. . .	. . .	. . .
Dist. of Col.									
Comprehensive	20½	4	2	2	2	1½	8	1 foreign language	1985
Career/vocational . .	23	4	2	2	2	1½	1½	1 foreign language, 9 specialized preparation	1985

Source: Education Commission of the States, *Clearinghouse Notes* (August, 1987).

Key:

. . .—No requirement.

(a) Must be computer literate before graduation.

(b) Minimum competency test is required for graduation. In Ohio and South Carolina, effective by 1990. In Oregon, effective by 1992. In Maryland, a writing test and passage of a quiz on citizenship is also required.

(c) Arkansas and Vermont have combined the math and science requirements in an effort to allow more flexibility for both vocational education students and for smaller or more rural districts.

(d) Colorado requires total of 300 semester hours (30 units) with local boards determining requirements as well as use of the competency test for graduation. State has constitutional prohibition against state requirements.

(e) Florida students in vocational programs may substitute certain sequences of vocational courses to satisfy up to two of the required credits in each of the areas of English, mathematics, and science.

(f) Florida, Iowa, Minnesota, South Carolina, Texas and Virginia allow students in the junior and senior classes to receive dual credits for college courses.

(g) Idaho and New Mexico have available state level minimum competency tests which districts have the option to use. If students pass the test, a special proficiency endorsement is included in their high school diploma.

(h) Illinois school boards may excuse pupils in 11th and 12th grades from physical education for: (1) participation in interscholastic athletics; or (2) enrollment in an academic class required for admission to college or to meet graduation requirements. Pupils in Grades 9-12 may elect to take a State Board of Education-developed consumer education proficiency test. If passed, pupils will be excused from this requirement.

(i) Legislative requirements in effect for many years. Local districts determine remaining requirements.

(k) For college preparation, specific core subjects must be taken and 3 electives must be in advanced courses.

(j) Must have ACT score of 29 or above, 3½ GPA with no semester grade lower than a "B", no unexcused absences and no high school suspensions to receive a Scholar Program Gold Seal on diploma.

(l) Local boards determine specific requirements. For graduation, state requires 200 credit hours (20 units), with at least 80 percent in core curriculum courses.

(m) Use of minimum competency test as requirement for graduation is option of the local district.

(n) South Carolina students who earn one unit in science and six or more in a specific occupational service area will fulfill the science requirements for a standard diploma. Certain vocational programs may count prevocational education as one of the six required units.

Table 8.11
NUMBER OF INSTITUTIONS OF HIGHER EDUCATION AND BRANCHES, BY TYPE, CONTROL OF INSTITUTION, AND STATE: 1986-87

State or other jurisdiction	All institutions			Universities		All other 4-year institutions		2-year institutions	
	Total	Public	Private	Public	Private	Public	Private	Public	Private
United States	3,406	1,533	1,873	94	62	479	1,435	960	376
Alabama................	79	53	26	2	0	14	17	37	9
Alaska.................	15	12	3	1	0	2	3	9	0
Arizona................	32	19	13	2	0	1	9	16	4
Arkansas	34	20	14	1	0	9	10	10	4
California..............	299	138	161	2	4	30	134	106	23
Colorado	52	29	23	2	1	12	13	15	9
Connecticut	49	24	25	1	1	6	20	17	4
Delaware	10	5	5	1	0	1	4	3	1
Florida	89	37	52	2	1	7	39	28	12
Georgia................	81	36	45	1	1	17	28	18	16
Hawaii	14	9	5	1	0	2	5	6	0
Idaho	10	6	4	1	0	3	3	2	1
Illinois.................	163	59	104	3	4	9	87	47	13
Indiana	76	29	47	4	1	11	37	14	9
Iowa	61	21	40	2	1	1	34	18	5
Kansas	52	29	23	3	0	5	20	21	3
Kentucky	56	21	35	2	0	6	22	13	13
Louisiana	32	20	12	1	2	13	8	6	2
Maine	31	13	18	1	0	7	13	5	5
Maryland	56	32	24	1	1	12	20	19	3
Massachusetts	121	31	90	1	7	13	65	17	18
Michigan	91	44	47	3	1	12	42	29	4
Minnesota	73	33	40	1	0	9	33	23	7
Mississippi	42	25	17	2	0	7	11	16	6
Missouri	92	28	64	1	2	12	51	15	11
Montana...............	17	10	7	2	0	4	3	4	4
Nebraska	33	18	15	1	1	6	13	11	1
Nevada	9	6	3	1	0	1	2	4	1
New Hampshire	28	12	16	1	0	3	12	8	4
New Jersey.............	61	31	30	1	2	13	24	17	4
New Mexico............	21	18	3	2	0	4	3	12	0
New York	308	86	222	2	12	40	163	44	47
North Carolina	125	74	51	2	2	14	35	58	14
North Dakota	19	14	5	2	0	4	4	8	1
Ohio	142	60	82	8	1	14	62	38	19
Oklahoma	47	29	18	2	1	12	13	15	4
Oregon	45	21	24	2	0	6	23	13	1
Pennsylvania	212	62	150	3	4	23	105	36	41
Rhode Island	13	3	10	1	0	1	10	1	0
South Carolina	62	33	29	2	0	10	20	21	9
South Dakota	18	8	10	2	0	6	7	0	3
Tennessee	82	24	58	1	1	9	43	14	14
Texas..................	163	100	63	6	4	33	51	61	8
Utah	14	9	5	2	1	2	1	5	3
Vermont	22	6	16	1	0	3	14	2	2
Virginia................	75	39	36	3	0	12	31	24	5
Washington	52	32	20	2	0	4	18	26	2
West Virginia	29	16	13	1	0	11	9	4	4
Wisconsin..............	62	29	33	1	1	12	30	16	2
Wyoming	9	8	3	1	0	0	0	7	1
Dist. of Columbia	18	2	16	0	5	2	11	0	0
U.S. Service Schools	10	10	0	0	0	9	0	1	0
American Samoa	1	1	0	0	0	0	0	1	0
Guam	2	2	0	0	0	1	0	1	0
Northern Marianas.......	1	1	0	0	0	0	0	1	0
Puerto Rico	42	14	28	1	0	9	22	4	6
Virgin Islands	1	1	0	0	0	1	0	0	0

Source: U.S. Department of Education, Center for Education Statistics, *Integrated Postsecondary Education Data System, Institutional Characteristics* survey.

Table 8.12
ESTIMATED UNDERGRADUATE TUITION AND FEES AND
ROOM AND BOARD RATES IN INSTITUTIONS OF HIGHER EDUCATION,
BY CONTROL OF INSTITUTION AND BY STATE: 1986-87

State or other jurisdiction	Public institutions				Private institutions			
	Total	Tuition (in state)	Room	Board	Total	Tuition	Room	Board
United States	$4,178	$1,396	$1,318	$1,464	$ 8,467	$6,781	$1,686	$1,800
Alabama...............	3,445	1,269	1,037	1,139	6,809	4,276	1,186	1,347
Alaska................	4,029	974	1,397	1,658	7,244	3,627	1,588	2,029
Arizona...............	3,902	1,136	1,365	1,401	4,417	2,292	924	1,201
Arkansas	2,848	933	784	1,131	5,396	3,349	794	1,253
California.............	5,008	819	1,960	2,229	12,696	8,751	1,747	2,198
Colorado	4,568	1,522	1,373	1,673	10,977	8,130	1,375	1,472
Connecticut	4,383	1,524	1,371	1,488	12,578	8,488	1,948	2,142
Delaware	3,544	2,148	1,396	. . .	8,475	5,115	1,726	1,634
Florida	3,954	1,055	1,261	1,638	8,889	8,889	. . .	. . .
Georgia...............	3,665	1,362	955	1,348	9,136	5,955	1,418	1,763
Hawaii	4,347	975	1,309	2,063	5,234	3,792	1,442	. . .
Idaho	3,832	1,037	847	1,948	8,695	5,837	900	1,958
Illinois...............	4,532	1,712	1,344	1,476	10,160	6,700	1,714	1,746
Indiana	4,886	1,633	1,883	1,370	9,659	6,817	1,347	1,495
Iowa	3,510	1,385	1,008	1,117	8,422	5,948	1,063	1,411
Kansas	3,590	1,275	1,151	1,164	6,814	4,445	1,007	1,362
Kentucky	3,340	1,153	889	1,298	6,433	3,846	1,077	1,510
Louisiana	3,631	1,340	1,049	1,242	10,475	6,849	1,759	1,867
Maine	4,602	1,550	1,475	1,577	11,232	7,489	1,765	1,978
Maryland	5,409	1,680	1,891	1,838	11,242	7,297	1,902	2,043
Massachusetts	4,286	1,392	1,289	1,605	13,787	9,089	2,336	2,362
Michigan	4,855	1,908	1,212	1,735	7,702	5,007	1,194	1,501
Minnesota	4,075	1,819	1,112	1,144	9,510	6,847	1,223	1,440
Mississippi	3,906	1,600	1,039	1,267	5,598	3,903	652	1,043
Missouri	3,465	1,280	1,160	1,025	8,151	5,413	1,302	1,436
Montana..............	4,208	1,210	1,206	1,792	6,432	3,852	928	1,652
Nebraska	3,473	1,364	870	1,239	7,468	4,960	1,173	1,335
Nevada	3,577	984	1,300	1,293	4,900	3,100	1,800	. . .
New Hampshire	4,769	2,379	1,424	966	12,351	8,338	1,981	2,032
New Jersey	4,976	1,850	1,766	1,360	12,584	8,759	1,942	1,883
New Mexico............	3,734	959	1,122	1,653	6,513	3,576	1,173	1,764
New York	4,779	1,427	1,647	1,705	11,425	7,357	2,044	2,024
North Carolina	3,115	818	1,131	1,166	8,075	5,599	1,070	1,406
North Dakota	3,192	1,199	682	1,311	5,874	4,102	682	1,090
Ohio	4,897	1,970	1,408	1,519	9,001	6,153	1,317	1,531
Oklahoma	3,000	765	948	1,287	6,713	4,143	1,118	1,452
Oregon	4,031	1,306	1,051	1,674	10,319	7,085	1,320	1,914
Pennsylvania	5,218	2,501	1,407	1,310	10,745	7,186	1,836	1,723
Rhode Island	5,476	1,833	1,798	1,845	12,016	8,173	1,953	1,890
South Carolina	4,304	1,739	1,100	1,465	7,073	4,516	1,285	1,272
South Dakota	3,505	1,444	798	1,263	7,614	4,804	1,221	1,589
Tennessee..............	3,439	1,133	1,027	1,279	7,791	5,149	1,397	1,245
Texas.................	3,904	879	1,440	1,585	8,870	5,693	1,325	1,852
Utah	4,017	1,164	1,644	1,209	3,578	1,528	1,000	1,050
Vermont	6,418	2,933	1,987	1,498	9,443	6,404	1,528	1,511
Virginia...............	5,047	2,069	1,479	1,499	8,918	5,669	1,702	1,547
Washington	4,056	1,388	1,268	1,400	10,140	6,790	1,608	1,742
West Virginia	4,178	1,008	1,621	1,549	9,026	6,108	1,242	1,676
Wisconsin.............	3,659	1,270	1,128	1,261	9,162	6,147	1,315	1,700
Wyoming	1,866	778	1,088	. . .	. . .	. . .	. . .	. . .
Dist. of Col.	634	634	. . .	. . .	11,526	7,100	2,362	2,064

Source: U.S. Department of Education, Center for Education Statistics.
Note: Data are for the entire academic year and are average charges.
Tuition and fees are calculated on the basis of full-time-equivalent students
but are not adjusted to reflect student residency. Room and board were
based on full-time students.
. . . - Data not reported or not applicable.

Table 8.13
TOTAL ROAD AND STREET MILEAGE: 1986
(Classified by jurisdiction)

State or other jurisdiction	Rural mileage				Urban mileage			Total rural and urban mileage
	Under state control	Under local control(a)	Under federal control(b)	Total rural roads	Under state control	Under local control(a)	Total urban mileage	
United States	703,900	2,243,143	231,081	3,178,124	94,415	605,960	701,414	3,879,538
Alabama...................	9,384	63,034	919	73,337	1,601	13,041	14,642	87,979
Alaska (c).................	11,936	...	...	11,936	1,539	164	1,703	13,639
Arizona...................	6,194	25,689	35,205	67,088	567	9,659	10,226	77,314
Arkansas	14,925	53,069	1,439	69,433	1,199	6,418	7,617	77,050
California	14,998	61,735	30,968	107,701	3,343	64,039	67,391	175,092
Colorado	8,498	49,808	7,098	65,404	847	10,067	10,914	76,318
Connecticut	2,200	6,726	4	8,930	1,699	9,059	10,758	19,688
Delaware	3,559	228	3	3,790	1,177	365	1,542	5,332
Florida	7,518	59,572	...	67,090	4,075	27,909	31,984	99,074
Georgia	15,555	70,276	931	86,762	2,227	17,611	19,845	106,607
Hawaii	870	1,727	61	2,658	185	1,173	1,382	4,040
Idaho	4,855	26,788	37,517	69,160	251	2,123	2,384	71,544
Illinois...................	13,133	90,246	304	103,683	4,432	26,647	31,095	134,778
Indiana	9,609	64,324	...	73,933	1,578	15,951	17,529	91,462
Iowa	9,288	94,471	114	103,873	910	7,711	8,625	112,498
Kansas	10,092	113,834	...	123,926	608	8,108	8,716	132,642
Kentucky	23,305	38,461	297	62,063	1,872	5,475	7,533	69,596
Louisiana	14,833	30,600	587	46,020	1,643	10,566	12,209	58,229
Maine	7,660	11,729	169	19,558	286	2,114	2,410	21,968
Maryland	3,983	11,746	303	16,032	1,427	10,153	11,706	27,738
Massachusetts	1,750	11,367	87	13,204	1,860	18,710	20,599	33,803
Michigan	7,697	83,032	...	90,729	1,881	25,054	26,935	117,664
Minnesota	12,323	104,687	1,672	118,682	1,154	12,808	13,962	132,644
Mississippi	9,635	54,862	301	64,798	724	6,260	7,020	71,818
Missouri	30,772	72,876	709	104,357	1,535	13,506	15,041	119,398
Montana..................	7,740	53,783	7,886	69,409	166	2,128	2,297	71,706
Nebraska	10,013	77,115	133	87,261	321	4,617	4,938	92,199
Nevada	4,932	22,909	13,356	41,197	301	2,938	3,241	44,438
New Hampshire	3,744	8,250	142	12,136	348	2,007	2,355	14,491
New Jersey................	1,595	10,018	21	11,634	1,588	20,800	22,406	34,040
New Mexico...............	11,513	30,441	6,432	48,386	918	4,292	5,210	53,596
New York	12,276	60,645	...	72,921	4,099	33,116	37,215	110,136
North Carolina	69,665	3,404	2,514	75,583	7,561	10,232	18,047	93,630
North Dakota	7,151	76,624	704	84,479	202	1,492	1,694	86,173
Ohio	16,681	65,639	29	82,349	3,794	27,145	30,939	113,288
Oklahoma	12,014	86,561	20	98,595	1,002	11,404	12,406	111,001
Oregon	10,075	33,857	42,156	86,088	774	7,679	8,490	94,578
Pennsylvania	39,039	46,568	988	86,595	7,163	21,905	29,068	115,663
Rhode Island	185	1,435	...	1,620	1,610	2,767	4,377	5,997
South Carolina	34,760	18,624	598	53,982	5,902	3,412	9,314	63,296
South Dakota	7,766	62,021	1,956	71,743	169	1,556	1,725	73,468
Tennessee	12,517	56,355	510	69,382	2,017	12,452	14,469	83,851
Texas.....................	65,567	145,930	964	212,461	6,211	67,290	73,501	285,962
Utah	5,053	22,061	17,528	44,642	655	4,640	5,296	49,938
Vermont	2,694	10,320	71	13,085	106	849	964	14,049
Virginia...................	49,209	800	1,469	51,478	5,901	8,167	14,324	65,802
Washington	17,454	38,166	9,419	65,039	1,055	14,384	15,439	80,478
West Virginia	30,130	643	1,400	32,173	1,200	1,770	2,970	35,143
Wisconsin.................	11,145	83,266	184	94,595	1,351	12,721	14,072	108,667
Wyoming..................	6,410	26,821	3,913	37,144	279	1,506	1,787	38,931
Dist. of Columbia	...	...	...	...	1,102	...	1,102	1,102

Source: Federal Highway Administration, U.S. Department of Transportation. Compiled for calendar year ending Dec. 31, 1986 from reports of state authorities.

Note: This table does not include mileage of non-public roads.

(a) Includes mileage not identified by administrative authority.

(b) Mileage in federal parks, forests, and reservations that is not a part of the state and local highway systems.

(c) Incomplete 1986 data submitted for these states; 1985 data used. Because of factoring procedures used, individual data components for Alaska may not be compatible among the various mileage tables.

Table 8.14
STATE RECEIPTS FOR HIGHWAYS: 1986
(In thousands of dollars)

State or other jurisdiction	State highway user tax revenues	Roads and crossing tolls(a)	Other state imposts, general fund revenues	Miscellaneous income	Federal funds — Federal Highway Administration	Federal funds — Other agencies	Transfers from local governments	Bond proceeds (b)	Total receipts
United States	$22,178,016	$2,079,792	$2,454,355	$1,460,374	$12,892,014	$396,065	$474,031	$3,925,986	$45,860,633
Alabama.........	361,276	...	83,627	31,944	285,724	2,698	10,074	...	775,343
Alaska...........	34,396	14,350	178,809	18,543	146,981	1,138	...	...	394,217
Arizona..........	462,552	...	204,955	36,992	271,596	4,820	7,195	294,163	1,282,273
Arkansas........	309,308	...	18,148	20,460	166,467	4,333	2,746	...	521,462
California........	1,881,428	67,531	...	156,080	856,499	41,614	122,143	...	3,125,295
Colorado	299,266	...	71,720	19,824	230,315	3,476	16,706	...	641,307
Connecticut	281,092	31,542	...	43,660	197,765	1,062	...	149,039	704,160
Delaware	79,688	42,637	28,611	9,717	48,230	661	...	25,773	235,317
Florida..........	782,402	156,524	115,433	77,823	486,532	6,499	1,000	371,550	1,997,763
Georgia..........	353,325	1,028	177,506	76,774	396,469	3,677	...	82,001	1,090,780
Hawaii	70,135	6,523	25,214	1,257	46,871	783	25	11,820	156,105
Idaho	125,687	...	...	87	85,319	5,112	952	...	217,157
Illinois..........	1,151,417	179,160	134,070	28,556	605,263	7,048	24,882	524,870	2,655,266
Indiana	611,655	49,778	98,559	16,087	103,564	2,755	14,242	...	896,640
Iowa	393,311	560	86,373	32,720	202,815	2,269	2,419	...	720,467
Kansas	211,568	30,453	48,472	28,742	198,070	2,839	13,885	9,004	543,033
Kentucky	512,922	20,329	30,086	85,831	276,413	3,538	398	103,445	1,032,962
Louisiana	413,852	...	102,836	6,445	287,192	3,665	...	60,925	874,915
Maine	136,877	27,336	1,154	4,668	57,393	1,872	1	16,300	245,601
Maryland	707,521	72,912	...	49,064	247,181	1,885	370	102,674	1,181,607
Massachusetts	379,574	101,197	27,840	34,802	110,959	2,770	593	178,900	836,635
Michigan	825,877	9,043	102,268	46,050	395,455	5,564	15,436	758	1,400,451
Minnesota	558,101	...	55,990	48,441	272,631	6,329	12,423	143	954,058
Mississippi	182,910	...	160,249	18,550	178,678	9,238	4,201	...	553,826
Missouri	378,500	...	114,146	10,378	326,537	3,400	3,694	...	836,655
Montana.........	112,397	...	3,729	21,749	119,122	8,835	383	...	266,215
Nebraska	188,143	...	59,703	3,765	127,359	3,023	11,636	...	393,629
Nevada	116,541	...	...	2,105	107,166	926	1,082	35,000	262,820
New Hampshire ...	107,279	22,263	...	9,533	56,295	839	5,861	20,125	222,195
New Jersey.......	423,306	307,584	...	96,424	358,842	2,650	...	359,266	1,548,072
New Mexico......	186,268	...	39,751	21,444	119,504	23,703	1,606	20,300	412,576
New York	812,613	435,537	5,574	93,735	663,682	7,278	...	194,891	2,213,310
North Carolina ...	674,466	1,094	...	41,798	276,819	3,447	3,409	1,241	1,002,274
North Dakota	81,401	...	4,489	1,323	79,008	2,685	4,883	...	173,789
Ohio	937,092	73,392	3,169	65,232	411,611	5,148	34,085	100,477	1,630,206
Oklahoma	382,548	44,420	29,567	14,218	173,337	2,375	5,956	...	652,421
Oregon	281,168	2,067	...	5,472	177,061	57,798	9,856	...	533,422
Pennsylvania	1,445,143	207,456	505	48,257	743,984	9,865	7,759	785,133	3,248,102
Rhode Island	65,731	7,480	...	1,489	78,023	1,065	...	28,440	182,228
South Carolina	319,694	...	...	1,122	137,672	3,116	240	...	461,844
South Dakota	79,281	...	23,522	2,806	71,788	1,455	1,157	...	180,009
Tennessee	511,420	...	47,974	2,948	314,656	2,703	12,011	...	891,712
Texas............	1,585,850	19,066	192,285	64,638	896,518	24,249	62,550	...	2,845,156
Utah	142,000	...	20,802	3,512	147,989	5,366	4,300	...	323,969
Vermont	89,037	...	...	519	66,810	565	...	...	156,931
Virginia..........	726,461	73,682	33,135	5,432	370,964	7,895	17,205	...	1,234,774
Washington	553,796	53,333	...	12,480	355,940	19,323	4,383	82,273	1,081,528
West Virginia	240,119	28,038	76,986	28,095	208,655	19,400	137	133,190	734,620
Wisconsin........	492,356	...	...	3,277	195,139	3,377	30,648	204,018	928,815
Wyoming	62,249	...	47,098	5,202	89,964	49,112	1,499	...	255,124
Dist. of Col.	57,017	...	...	304	63,187	822	...	30,267	151,597

Source: Federal Highway Administration, U.S. Department of Transportation. Compiled for calendar year ending Dec. 31, 1986 from reports of state authorities.

(a) Toll receipts allocated for non-highway purposes are excluded.
(b) Par value of bonds issued and redeemed by refunding is excluded.

Table 8.15
STATE DISBURSEMENTS FOR HIGHWAYS: 1986
(In thousands of dollars)

State or other jurisdiction	Capital outlay — Federal-aid Systems — Interstate	Other federal aid systems	Other roads & streets	Total	Maintenance & traffic services	Administration & highway police	Bond interest	Grants-in-aid to local governments	Bond retirement(a)	Total disbursements
United States	$7,172,173	$12,194,280	$2,031,694	$22,049,734	$6,717,034	$5,659,468	$1,489,810	$6,324,397	$1,959,067	$44,199,510
Alabama	134,925	241,240	50,605	426,770	52,986	69,543	16,519	151,590	54,650	772,058
Alaska	47,126	112,258	9,692	169,076	91,457	37,888	13,444	51,990	30,361	394,216
Arizona	216,826	263,946	65,830	546,602	48,674	78,349	31,865	303,087	18,476	1,027,053
Arkansas	74,239	180,761	44,451	299,451	105,125	42,211	. . .	39,369	. . .	536,156
California	348,233	723,267	55,962	1,127,462	393,351	653,435	8,890	767,001	13,988	2,964,127
Colorado	136,078	143,639	36,809	316,526	112,623	52,212	. . .	143,978	. . .	625,339
Connecticut	162,860	194,590	40,181	397,631	64,526	95,253	60,729	25,268	61,458	704,865
Delaware	14,787	68,418	16,019	99,224	31,952	51,293	29,161	2,500	26,583	240,713
Florida	342,817	384,743	288,916	1,016,476	155,896	214,498	72,442	185,542	133,557	1,778,411
Georgia	283,529	331,606	. . .	615,135	204,813	121,065	35,113	9,807	122,499	1,108,432
Hawaii	20,372	33,625	6,523	60,520	13,571	16,236	14,462	23,061	12,502	140,352
Idaho	55,312	50,101	2,959	108,372	39,876	27,314	. . .	44,371	. . .	219,933
Illinois	257,111	751,101	117,182	1,125,394	240,881	262,349	97,368	325,018	63,276	2,114,286
Indiana	133,103	324,205	14,590	471,898	166,450	57,417	22,708	250,976	. . .	969,449
Iowa	51,065	196,664	18,079	265,808	93,952	79,809	113	285,253	210	725,145
Kansas	90,223	205,664	30,116	326,003	74,037	70,786	21,652	71,004	17,692	581,174
Kentucky	131,539	327,538	15,709	474,786	137,286	86,780	182,641	75,662	47,104	1,004,259
Louisiana (b)	. . .	. . .	. . .	651,587(b)	47,271	115,296	114,449	51,424	74,996	1,055,023
Maine	30,651	50,905	11,453	93,009	80,900	28,611	7,655	15,286	9,245	234,706
Maryland	230,375	223,150	39,509	493,034	131,466	142,900	68,242	277,263	180,437	1,293,342
Massachusetts	57,884	169,388	76,408	303,680	113,179	160,218	53,266	95,313	74,735	800,391
Michigan	238,355	203,328	50,976	492,659	152,688	195,362	17,634	524,306	31,808	1,414,457
Minnesota	173,486	176,680	154,948	505,114	109,183	68,918	13,434	225,809	39,192	961,650
Mississippi	55,722	220,355	66,224	342,301	61,502	57,627	18,555	64,249	142,812	687,046
Missouri	137,143	284,843	9,274	431,260	172,350	139,286	. . .	125,227	. . .	868,123
Montana	52,115	97,881	50,602	200,598	35,204	22,711	7,123	24,253	25,925	315,814
Nebraska	37,912	128,103	13,346	179,361	48,345	28,206	230	125,213	1,000	382,355
Nevada	59,337	105,317	. . .	164,654	29,782	39,614	1,432	15,390	5,000	255,872
New Hampshire	31,633	36,046	8,044	75,723	65,598	43,837	9,017	409	9,250	203,834
New Jersey	289,972	323,588	190,651	804,211	211,751	264,567	132,088	. . .	104,470	1,517,087
New Mexico	55,268	138,482	28,148	221,898	72,115	80,947	8,283	14,683	14,650	412,576
New York	364,781	673,139	58,468	1,096,388	405,405	304,168	53,944	179,001	144,553	2,183,459
North Carolina	129,783	257,046	22,080	408,909	270,728	177,336	28,891	54,703	14,500	955,067
North Dakota	24,621	66,176	6,593	97,390	24,732	16,176	. . .	33,544	. . .	171,842
Ohio	218,623	415,935	22,564	657,122	235,104	256,783	25,279	351,335	67,850	1,593,473
Oklahoma	96,827	189,619	20,003	306,449	102,099	108,098	9,528	121,322	5,914	653,410
Oregon	69,777	172,892	2,410	245,079	68,353	91,665	1,994	142,767	3,300	553,158
Pennsylvania	604,795	692,710	. . .	1,297,505	572,214	275,352	109,663	204,958	148,873	2,608,565
Rhode Island	25,038	65,309	33,123	123,470	20,443	13,461	8,397	390	24,259	190,420
South Carolina	105,260	117,013	11,037	233,310	116,435	64,441	1,315	17,800	7,850	441,151
South Dakota	10,989	74,489	20,713	106,191	31,399	29,785	. . .	18,128	. . .	185,503
Tennessee..........	108,739	258,216	68,003	434,958	131,783	63,997	3,389	178,890	11,220	824,237
Texas	530,689	1,233,406	104,413	1,868,508	468,383	333,835	29,890	80,528	1,625	2,782,769
Utah	135,629	65,708	8,200	209,537	40,092	38,892	1,561	33,246	10,915	334,243
Vermont..........	11,875	66,166	6,830	84,871	24,543	20,715	4,435	19,218	7,710	161,492
Virginia	270,288	322,712	85,110	678,110	363,841	157,528	16,371	118,744	4,663	1,339,257
Washington	250,288	228,938	6,858	486,084	151,588	126,367	54,751	214,916	58,970	1,092,676
West Virginia	121,533	201,152	. . .	322,685	126,928	50,501	41,742	. . .	51,030	592,886
Wisconsin	56,008	263,380	21,088	340,476	113,991	84,288	21,586	181,296	21,269	762,906
Wyoming..........	69,226	95,821	13,063	178,110	65,183	25,368	. . .	9,309	. . .	277,970
Dist. of Col.	17,406	43,021	7,932	68,359	25,000	16,174	18,559	. . .	58,690	186,782

Source: Federal Highway Administration, U.S. Department of Transportation. Compiled for calendar year ending Dec. 31, 1986 from reports of state authorities.

(a) Par value of bonds issued and redeemed by refunding is excluded.
(b) Segregation by federal-aid systems not identified by state.

Table 8.16
APPORTIONMENT OF FEDERAL-AID HIGHWAY FUNDS: FISCAL 1987
(In thousands of dollars)

State or other jurisdiction	Highway systems funds					Total highway systems funds	Highway safety pro-grams(d)	Total highway safety funds(a,d)	Total(e)
	Consoli-dated primary(a)	Rural secondary (a)	Urban system (a)	Interstate (b)	Interstate resurfacing (c)				
United States(f)....	$2,300,392 (g)	$584,115	$730,511	$2,623,950	$2,541,292	$8,780,260	$125,335	$1,372,400	$11,917,173
Alabama.........	41,509	12,180	9,465	111,637	47,425	222,216	2,241	26,611	257,825
Alaska..........	74,660	32,262	3,657	13,126	21,602	145,307	630	3,431	152,882
Arizona..........	31,521	9,927	9,446	17,531	55,922	124,347	1,687	3,431	148,369
Arkansas	28,381	10,593	4,464	13,126	27,618	84,182	1,515	19,880	125,130
California........	167,084	23,967	92,603	287,964	246,581	818,199	10,808	38,493	969,771
Colorado	34,374	11,030	9,801	54,861	49,643	159,709	1,748	15,565	187,149
Connecticut	25,239	3,851	10,494	66,013	32,907	138,504	1,394	48,102	273,222
Delaware	11,335	2,925	3,657	13,126	12,724	43,767	630	3,431	49,391
Florida	75,267	14,826	34,887	146,770	89,522	361,272	4,665	20,555	429,370
Georgia..........	55,429	15,743	13,914	61,619	89,682	236,387	3,012	39,578	323,112
Hawaii	11,335	2,925	3,657	98,051	12,724	128,692	630	3,435	134,217
Idaho	18,308	7,235	3,657	24,312	23,195	76,707	918	4,041	84,554
Illinois...........	89,741	16,992	40,130	13,126	90,911	250,900	5,615	40,287	374,647
Indiana	52,531	13,837	14,534	17,862	56,511	155,275	2,906	24,121	253,889
Iowa	35,240	12,699	6,652	13,126	36,700	104,417	2,043	30,954	166,278
Kansas	33,225	11,995	6,218	13,126	37,178	101,742	1,979	32,821	144,260
Kentucky	39,494	12,183	7,437	19,445	45,525	124,084	2,004	31,909	165,291
Louisiana	38,806	9,831	11,859	112,322	45,168	217,986	2,134	33,327	260,126
Maine	14,458	5,115	3,657	13,126	12,724	49,080	630	5,347	57,057
Maryland	33,957	5,583	14,387	104,431	38,409	196,767	1,899	19,301	275,749
Massachusetts	44,577	5,993	20,391	367,326	32,222	470,509	2,554	44,216	532,423
Michigan	82,564	17,527	27,574	40,733	83,572	251,970	4,617	19,883	318,963
Minnesota	43,607	14,557	11,058	58,004	46,636	173,862	2,620	20,257	207,934
Mississippi	31,796	10,714	4,663	13,126	32,097	92,396	1,567	25,615	128,562
Missouri	51,720	15,700	13,687	13,126	71,504	165,737	2,894	60,829	253,429
Montana.........	26,672	11,020	3,657	13,126	40,916	95,391	874	8,648	107,958
Nebraska	25,218	9,389	4,025	13,126	21,773	73,531	1,347	22,121	103,447
Nevada	18,903	7,110	3,657	13,126	22,478	65,274	662	3,431	71,272
New Hampshire ...	11,335	2,925	3,657	13,126	12,724	43,767	630	8,099	54,219
New Jersey........	53,435	5,240	28,088	96,374	30,112	213,249	3,205	65,486	317,858
New Mexico.......	25,888	9,755	3,846	13,126	42,529	95,144	939	5,198	103,956
New York	134,682	17,439	63,285	13,126	88,691	317,223	7,869	137,240	639,665
North Carolina	64,684	17,510	11,330	43,072	47,066	183,662	3,077	38,852	292,280
North Dakota	17,499	7,116	3,657	13,126	20,565	61,963	933	6,792	73,962
Ohio	93,769	18,277	33,398	29,675	104,158	279,277	5,193	49,189	422,638
Oklahoma	34,570	11,798	8,137	13,126	36,266	103,897	2,073	35,079	191,941
Oregon	29,445	9,909	7,272	16,303	38,468	101,397	1,787	11,244	128,408
Pennsylvania	107,743	22,152	34,318	150,550	66,537	381,300	5,640	95,611	506,915
Rhode Island	11,335	2,925	3,657	13,126	12,724	43,767	630	3,850	101,743
South Carolina	32,937	9,074	6,717	16,846	40,662	106,236	1,741	9,979	149,916
South Dakota	17,793	7,325	3,474	12,470	24,156	65,218	849	9,253	78,413
Tennessee	46,888	13,456	11,431	13,126	62,203	147,104	2,488	54,155	244,549
Texas.............	132,584	37,363	47,234	125,010	202,915	545,106	7,886	57,261	857,926
Utah	19,825	6,571	5,141	35,487	39,331	106,355	963	3,431	113,555
Vermont	11,335	2,925	3,657	13,126	12,870	43,913	630	6,345	52,588
Virginia..........	49,847	12,861	14,816	65,352	69,792	212,668	2,646	17,936	241,669
Washington	39,771	10,196	12,669	107,904	55,317	225,857	2,283	26,353	261,273
West Virginia	23,695	7,528	3,657	13,126	19,199	67,205	1,053	35,374	106,945
Wisconsin.........	48,134	13,576	12,314	13,126	34,557	121,707	2,727	31,722	196,997
Wyoming	15,454	6,739	3,474	12,470	31,769	70,906	630	3,431	76,941
Dist. of Col.	11,335	...	3,657	34,779	12,724	62,495	630	7,471	83,102
American Samoa ..	...	...	...	...	...	...	315	...	732
Guam	...	...	...	...	...	...	315	...	732
N. Marianas	...	...	...	...	...	...	315	...	732
Puerto Rico	28,455	3,742	8,342	...	12,088	52,627	1,353	3,431	60,505
Virgin Islands	...	...	...	...	...	...	315	...	732

Source: Federal Highway Administration, U.S. Department of Transportation, *Highway Statistics 1986.*
Note: This table does not include funds from the mass transit account of the Highway Trust Fund.
(a) Apportioned pursuant to the surface transportation and uniform relocation assistance act of 1987.
(b) Resurfacing, rehabilitation, restoration, and reconstruction.
(c) In 1985, interstate highway substitute and 85 percent minimum allocation funds were inluded in this category. They are now reported separately by Federal Highway Admnistration.
(d) Includes $9.8 million administered by the Federal Highway Ad-

ministration and $115.6 million set-aside for commercial vehicle driver licensing programs.
(e) Does not include funds from the following programs: Emergency relief, forest highways, public lands highways, parkways and park highways, Indian reservation roads, interstate and intersate 4-R discretionary, bridge discretionary, truck and bus safety grants, allocated interstate highway substitute, or section 149 demonstration funds. These funds are allocated from the Highway Trust Fund.
(f) May not add due to rounding.
(g) Does not include $11.3 million apportioned to the territories considered as one state.

Table 8.17
STATE MOTOR VEHICLE REGISTRATIONS: 1986

State or other jurisdiction	Automobiles(a)	Motorcycles(a)	Buses(a,b)	Trucks(a)	Comparison of total motor vehicle registrations		Percentage change
					1985	1986	
United States	135,431,112	5,262,322	593,728	40,166,499	171,688,878	176,191,339	2.6
Alabama..................	2,522,043	59,222	8,361	926,530	3,337,831	3,456,934	3.6
Alaska...................	226,665	9,736	1,987	134,027	353,015	362,679	2.7
Arizona..................	1,647,879	81,031	4,162	693,480	2,235,021	2,345,521	4.9
Arkansas	929,254	24,114	5,170	491,823	1,383,699	1,426,247	7.1
California	15,364,800	709,746	35,812	4,359,648	18,899,221	19,760,260	4.6
Colorado	2,015,917	108,509	5,575	741,460	2,758,878	2,762,952	0.1
Connecticut	2,402,332	58,053	8,648	151,369	2,464,850	2,562,349	4.0
Delaware	378,639	10,233	1,762	99,264	465,091	479,665	3.1
Florida	8,263,294	229,687	34,208	2,064,010	9,864,835	10,361,512	5.0
Georgia..................	3,507,096	120,463	15,936	1,317,816	4,580,020	4,840,848	5.7
Hawaii	601,868	17,986	3,995	83,171	650,879	689,034	5.9
Idaho	535,142	47,847	3,315	318,869	853,639	857,326	0.4
Illinois...................	6,060,698	218,610	19,218	1,339,619	7,526,738 (c)	7,419,535	-1.4
Indiana	3,115,437	125,538	18,846	1,039,331	4,024,032	4,173,614	3.7
Iowa	1,894,724	230,200	8,241	735,211	2,695,792	2,638,176	-2.1
Kansas	1,496,336	90,029	3,820	675,867	2,147,923	2,176,023	1.3
Kentucky	1,809,057	41,939	9,629	866,576	2,614,767	2,685,262	2.7
Louisiana	1,938,267	52,002	19,669	931,722	3,012,090	2,889,658	-4.1
Maine	645,316	45,393	2,632	224,482	840,011	872,430	3.9
Maryland	2,774,029	76,507	10,839	576,433	3,275,713	3,361,301	2.6
Massachusetts	3,350,007	116,568	10,629	480,341	3,738,050	3,840,977	2.8
Michigan	5,421,198	238,404	22,123	1,388,441	6,726,678	6,831,762	1.6
Minnesota	2,391,990	137,225	13,408	681,582	3,385,331	3,086,980	-8.8
Mississippi	1,350,114	24,594	8,257	411,402	1,745,956	1,769,773	1.4
Missouri	2,686,800	78,573	10,022	986,572	3,557,869	3,683,394	3.5
Montana..................	433,234	27,912	1,849	237,464	652,182	672,547	3.1
Nebraska	852,669	32,694	4,275	423,702	1,258,189 (c)	1,280,646	1.8
Nevada	555,785	19,344	1,725	211,566	709,429	769,076	8.4
New Hampshire	893,733	64,354	1,572	175,942	973,893	1,071,247	10.0
New Jersey(d)	4,769,000	128,000	16,058	482,431	5,163,569 (c)	5,267,489	2.0
New Mexico	828,715	46,241	3,820	487,586	1,175,701	1,320,121	12.3
New York	8,321,210	240,477	31,742	1,162,423	9,041,825	9,515,375	5.2
North Carolina	3,461,293	64,299	32,473	1,245,190	4,450,383	4,738,956	6.5
North Dakota	380,244	28,118	1,988	265,431	655,127	647,663	-1.1
Ohio	6,719,345	292,863	31,138	1,408,688	8,101,612	8,159,171	0.7
Oklahoma	1,877,256	69,281	12,251	1,012,884	2,863,748	2,902,391	1.3
Oregon	1,628,730	82,073	9,362	625,897	2,203,685	2,263,989	2.7
Pennsylvania	6,090,520	208,156	28,560	1,357,937	7,209,093	7,477,017	3.7
Rhode Island	531,663	25,714	1,563	98,592	610,074	631,818	3.6
South Carolina	1,737,037	36,234	13,360	553,811	2,221,598	2,304,208	3.7
South Dakota	408,778	36,117	1,991	253,291	650,352	664,060	2.1
Tennessee.................	3,097,473	114,234	12,499	822,248	3,753,926	3,932,220	4.7
Texas....................	8,499,972	252,382	55,360	3,851,276	12,444,187	12,406,608	-0.3
Utah	749,633	50,180	1,141	359,859	1,098,797	1,110,633	1.1
Vermont	313,725	20,818	1,360	103,106	397,608	418,191	5.2
Virginia..................	3,610,396	79,346	14,648	906,736	4,253,295	4,531,780	6.5
Washington	2,610,890	141,911	7,770	1,133,582	3,526,362	3,752,242	6.4
West Virginia	810,743	32,757	3,639	355,756	1,143,388 (c)	1,170,138	2.3
Wisconsin.................	2,397,418	191,422	12,128	710,480	3,186,991	3,120,026	-2.1
Wyoming	250,714	21,605	2,404	187,037	499,583	440,155	-11.9
Dist. of Col.	272,034	3,581	2,788	14,538	306,352 (c)	289,360	-5.5

Source: Federal Highway Administration, U.S. Department of Transportation, *Highway Statistics 1986*. Compiled for the calendar year ending December 31, 1986 from reports of state authorities.

Note: Where the registration year is not more than one month removed from the calendar year, registration-year data are given. Where the registration year is more than one month removed, registrations are given for the calendar year.

(a) Includes federal, state, county, and municipal vehicles. Vehicles owned by the military service are not included.

(b) The numbers of private and commercial buses given here are estimates by the Federal Highway Administration of the numbers in operation, rather than the registration counts of the states.

(c) The 1985 data were revised due to additional information.

(d) Unable to provide motor-vehicle registration data for 1986. The figures shown here are estimates by the Federal Highway Administration.

Table 8.18
MOTOR VEHICLE LAWS
(As of 1987)

State or other jurisdiction	Minimum Age for driver's license(a)			Liability laws(b)	Vehicle inspection (c)	Transfer of plates to new owner	Child restraints mandatory for passengers under ___ years(d)	Mandatory seat belt law(e)
	Regular	Learner's	Restrictive					
Alabama	16	15(f)	14(g)	S	(h)	★	4	...
Alaska	16	14(i)	14(i)	S	spot	★	7	...
Arizona	18	15+7mo.(f,i)	16(i)	C	(j)	★	5	...
Arkansas	16	(f)	14(i,k)	S,NF	★	...	6	...
California	18	15(k,l)	16(l)	(m)	(j)	★	5(n)	★(o)
Colorado	21	15+6mo.(f,p)	16(i)	S,NF	(j)	...	4(n)	...
Connecticut	18	(q)	16(l)	S,NF	★	★	4	★
Delaware	18	15+10mo.(f,k,l)	16(l)	S,NF	★	★	5	★
Florida	16	(f)	15(i)	(r)	...	...	6	★
Georgia	21	15	16(i)	C,NF	(j)	★	4	...
Hawaii	18	(f)	15(i)	S,NF	★	...	4	★
Idaho	16	(f)	14(l)	S,C	...	...	4	★
Illinois	18	(f)	16(i,l)	S	(s)	...	6	★
Indiana	18	15(l,p)	16+1mo.(i,l)	S,C	...	...	5	★
Iowa	18	14	16(l)	S	spot	...	6	★
Kansas	16	...	14(k)	NF	spot	...	4	★
Kentucky	18	(f)	16(i)	C,NF	...	★	(n)	...
Louisiana	17	...	15(t)	C	★	★	5	★
Maine	17	(f,k)	15(l)	S	★	...	5	...
Maryland	18	15+9mo.(f,k)	16(i,l,t)	NF	(u)	...	5	★
Massachusetts	18	16(f)	16+6mo.(i,l,t)	C,NF	★	...	5	...
Michigan	18	(f)	16(i,l,v)	C,NF	spot	...	4	★
Minnesota	18	(f)	16(l)	NF	spot(h)	★	4	★(o)
Mississippi	15	(f)	...	S,F	★	...	2	...
Missouri	16	...	15(p)	S	★	...	4	★
Montana	18	(f)	15(i,l)	C	...	...	4(n)	...
Nebraska	16	15(f,k)	(v)	F	...	...	4	★
Nevada	18	15+6mo.	16(i)	F,C	(u)	...	5	...
New Hampshire	18	(q)	16(l)	S,F	★	...	5	...
New Jersey	17	(k)	(v)	S,NF,UJ	★	...	5	★(o)
New Mexico	16	15(k)	15(i,l)	S,UM	...	...	11	★
New York	18	(f,k)	16(i,t)	S,C,NF,UM	★	...	5	★(o)
North Carolina	18	15(k,l)	...	S,C	★	...	7	★
North Dakota	16	(f)	14(l)	S,C,NF,UM,UJ	spot	★	4	...
Ohio	18(w)	(k)	(v)	S,C	spot	...	5(n)	★
Oklahoma	16	(p)	15+6mo.(l)	S,C	★	★	5	★
Oregon	16	15(f)	(v)	F,C,NF	spot(j)	★	16	...
Pennsylvania	18	(f)	16(i,t)	(x)	★	...	4	...
Rhode Island	18	(f)	16(l)	S	★	...	4	...
South Carolina	16	15(k)	15	C,NF,UM	★	★	4	...
South Dakota	16	14(k)	14(t)	F,UM	...	★	5	...
Tennessee	16	15(f)	...	S,F	(h)	...	4	★
Texas	18	15(k,p)	16(l,v)	S,F,C,NF,UM	★	★	4	★
Utah	16(l)	(f)	...	S,NF	★	...	5	★
Vermont	18	15(k)	16(k)	S	★	...	4	...
Virginia	18	15+8mo.(f,i,k)	16(i,l)	S,NF	★	...	5	...
Washington	18	15(f,p)	16(l)	S,F	(j)	★	5	★(o)
West Virginia	18	(f)	16(i)	S,C	★	...	5	...
Wisconsin	18	(f)	16(l)	S	spot	...	4	...
Wyoming	18	15(k)	16(i)	S,C	...	...	3	...
Dist. of Col.	18	(f)	16(i)	NF	★	...	7	★(o)
American Samoa	18	(f,k)	16(i,l)	C	★	★	...	...
Guam	18	15(i,k)	16(i)	S	★	...	...	...
Puerto Rico	18	(f)	16(i)	(x)	★	★	...	★
Virgin Islands	18	...	16(l)	C	★	★	...	...

MOTOR VEHICLE LAWS—Continued

Sources: American Automobile Association, *Digest of Motor Laws,* (1987).

Note: All jurisdictions except Guam have chemical test laws for intoxication. All except the District of Columbia have an implied consent provision. (Colorado has expressed consent law).

Key:

★—Provision.

. . .—No provision.

(a) See Table 8.20, "Motor Vehicle Operators and Chauffeurs Licenses 1986" for additional information on driver licenses.

(b) All jurisdictions except Colorado, Hawaii, District of Columbia, American Samoa, Guam, Puerto Rico, and the Virgin Islands have a non-resident service of process law. Alabama, Arkansas, California, Georgia, Illinois (applicable to hitchhikers only), New Mexico, Oregon, Texas, Utah, Virginia, Wyoming, and the Virgin Islands each have a guest suit law. In this column only: S—"Security-type" financial responsibility law (following accident report, each driver/owner of the vehicles involved must show ability to pay damages which may be charged in subsequent legal actions arising from accident); F—"Future-proof type" financial responsibility law (persons who have been convicted of certain serious traffic offenses or who have failed to pay a judgment against them for damages arising from an accident must make a similar showing of financial responsibility); C—"Compulsory insurance" law (motorists must show proof of financial responsibility—liability insurance—usually as a condition of vehicle registration); NF—"No-fault insurance" law (vehicle owner looks to own insurance company for reimbursement for accident damages, rather than having to prove in court that the other party was responsible); UJ—"Unsatisfied judgment funds" law (financed with fees from motorists unable to provide evidence of insurance or from assessments levied on auto insurance companies to cover pedestrians and others who do not have no-fault insurance); UM—"Uninsured motorist" law (insurance companies must offer coverage against potential damage by uninsured motorists).

(c) "Spot" indicates spot check, usually for reasonable cause, or random roadside inspection for defective or missing equipment.

(d) The type of child restraint (safety seat or seat belt) required may differ depending upon the age of the child.

(e) These states have enacted mandatory seat belt legislation; effective dates of legislation range from 1985 to 1987. Unless otherwise specified, legislation covers driver and front-seat passengers.

(f) Permit required. In Arkansas, for 30 days prior to taking driving test. In Delaware, for up to two months prior to 16th birthday. In Michigan, for 30 days prior to application for first license. In Minnesota, not required if driver can pass road test. In Oregon, not required if applicant can already drive.

(g) Restricted to mopeds.

(h) Cities have authority to maintain inspection stations. In Alabama, state troopers also authorized to inspect at their discretion.

(i) Guardian or parental consent required.

(j) Emission inspections. In Arizona, Colorado, Georgia, and Washington, mandatory annual emission inspections in certain counties. In California, biennial inspections are required in portions of counties which do not meet federal clean air standards. In Oregon, biennial inspections in Portland metro area and Jackson County. In Washington, also other checks (e.g., out of state purchases, salvaged).

(k) Driver must be accompanied by licensed operator. In California and Vermont (learner's permit), a licensed operator 25 years or older.

In Kansas, may drive to school or work without licensed operator. In Maine, New York, Texas, Vermont (restrictive license), Virginia and Wyoming, a licensed operator 18 years or older. In Maryland, individual, 21 years or older, licensed to drive vehicle of that class, and licensed for 3 or more years. In Nebraska, a licensed operator 19 years or older. In New Jersey, an individual licensed for same classification as the learner's permit. In South Carolina, a licensed operator 21 years or older. In American Samoa, must be accompanied by parent, legal guardian, or safety instructor. In Guam, must be accompanied by parent or legal guardian.

(l) Must have successfully completed approved driver education course.

(m) Financial responsibility required of every driver/owner of motor vehicle at all times.

(n) Other restrictions. In California, Colorado, Montana, and Ohio, age restriction or child under 40 pounds. In Kentucky, 40 inches in height or under.

(o) Covers other passengers in vehicle. California, Washington, and District of Columbia, all passengers. In Minnesota, driver, front seat passengers, and anyone under 11. New Jersey, all passengers between 5 and 18 years, as well as driver and all front-seat passengers over 18 years. New York, all back seat occupants under 10 years and over 3 years, as well as all front-seat occupants.

(p) Must be enrolled in driver education course. In Colorado, if not in such course, wait until 15 + 9 mo.

(q) Required for motorcyclists only. In New Hampshire, otherwise, unlicensed persons who are being taught to drive must be accompanied by licensed operator 21 years or older.

(r) Proof of personal injury protection is required. In event of an accident in which operator is charged with a moving violation, the operator must prove liability insurance in force on date of accident.

(s) Trucks, buses, and trailers only.

(t) Driving hours restricted. In Louisiana, drivers under 17 not permitted to operate vehicles between hours of 11 p.m. and 5 a.m. Monday through Thursday; between midnight and 5 a.m. Friday through Sunday. In Maryland, drivers prohibited from driving between midnight and 5 a.m. unless accompanied by licensed driver 21 years or older. In Massachusetts, drivers prohibited from driving between 1 a.m. and 4 a.m., unless accompanied by parent or legal guardian. In New York, drivers may operate certain classes of vehicles alone during the daylight hours and with a parent or guardian at night; may drive alone during darkness if on direct route between home and school or to place of business. In Pennsylvania, drivers prohibited from driving between midnight and 5 a.m., unless accompanied by parent or spouse 18 years or older or in possession of employer's affidavit. In South Dakota, driver not permitted to operate vehicle between 8 p.m. and 6 a.m., unless accompanied by licensed driver in front seat.

(u) Mandatory inspection only under certain circumstances. In Maryland, all used cars upon resale or transfer. In Nevada, used cars registered to new owner and emissions test for first-time registration in Clark and Washoe counties.

(v) License will be granted at lower age under special conditions. In Michigan (extenuating circumstances), 14. In Nebraska (school permit), 14. In New Jersey (agriculture pursuit), 16. In Ohio (proof of hardship), 14. In Oregon, (special conditions), 14. In Texas (proof of hardship), 15.

(w) Probationary license issued to persons 16-18 upon completion of approved driver education course.

(x) Has financial responsibility law; details not available.

Table 8.19
STATE NO-FAULT MOTOR VEHICLE INSURANCE LAWS

State or other jurisdiction	Pur-chase of first-party benefits	Minimum tort liability threshold(a)	Maximum first-party (no-fault) benefits			
			Medical	Income loss	Replacement services	Survivors/funeral benefits
Arkansas	O	None	$5,000 if incurred within 2 yrs. of accident	70% of lost income up to $140/wk. beginning 8 days after accident, for up to 52 wks.	Up to $70/wk. beginning 8 days after accident, for up to 52 wks.	$5,000
Colorado	M	$2,500	$50,000 if incurred within 5 yrs. (additional $50,000 for rehabilitation expenses incurred within 5 yrs. of accident)	100% of first $125/wk., 70% of next $125/wk., 60% of remainder up to $400, for up to 52 wks.	Up to $25/day for up to 52 wks.	$1,000
Connecticut	M	$400	————$5,000 overall max. on first-party benefits————			
			Limited only by total benefits limit	85% of lost income up to $200/wk.	85% of replacement services up to $200/wk.	85% of actual loss for income and replacement services up to $200/wk. Funeral benefit: $2,000
Delaware	M	None, but amt. of no-fault benefits received cannot be used as evidence in suits for general damage	————$15,000 per person, $30,000 per accident overall max. on first-party benefits————			
			Limited only by total benefits limit, but must be incurred within 2 yrs. of accident	Limited only by total benefits limit, but must be incurred within 2 yrs. of accident	Limited only by total benefits limit, but must be incurred within 2 yrs. of accident	Funeral benefit: $3,000 (must be incurred within 2 yrs. of accident)
Florida	M	No dollar threshold(b)	————$10,000 overall max. on first-party benefits————			
			80% of all costs	60% of lost income	Limited only by total benefits limit	Funeral benefit: $1,750
Georgia........	M	$500	————$5,000 overall max. on first-party benefits————			
			$2,500	85% of lost income up to $200/wk.	$20/day	Max. wage loss and replacement services amounts. Funeral benefit: $1,500
Hawaii	M	$5,000 modified annually by percentage change in CPI for Honolulu metro area	————$15,000 overall max. on first-party benefits————			
			Limited only by total benefits limit	Up to $900/mo. for income loss and replacement services		Up to $900/mo. Funeral benefit: $1,500
Kansas	M	$2000 (b)	$4,500 (additional $4,500 for rehabilitation)	85% of lost income up to $900/mo. for 1 yr.	$25/day for 365 days	Up to $900/mo. for lost income and $25/day for replacement services for up to 1 yr., less disability payments received before death. Funeral benefit: $2,000
Kentucky	(c)	$1,000	————$10,000 overall max. on first-party benefits————			
			Limited only by total benefits limit	85% of lost income (more if tax advantage is less than 15%) up to $200/wk.	Up to $200/wk.	Up to $200/wk. each for survivors' economic loss and survivors' replacement services loss. Funeral benefit: $1,000
Maryland	M	None	————$2,500 overall max. on first-party benefits————			
			————for expenses incurred within 3 yrs. of accident————			
			Limited only by total benefits limit	Limited only by total benefits limit	Limited only by total benefits limit; payable only to non-wage earners	Funeral benefit: limited only by total benefits limit

NO-FAULT INSURANCE LAWS—Continued

State or other jurisdiction	Purchase of first-party benefits	Minimum tort liability threshold(a)	Maximum first-party (no-fault) benefits			
			Medical	Income loss	Replacement services	Survivors/funeral benefits
Massachusetts ...	M	$500	—————————$2,000 overall max. on first-party benefits—————————			
			Limited only by total benefits limit, if incurred within 2 yrs.	Up to 75% of lost income	Limited only by total benefits limit; payments made to nonfamily members for services that would have been performed by victim	Funeral benefit: limited only by total benefits limit
Michigan(d)	M	No dollar threshold(e)	Unlimited	85% of lost income up to $1,475/30-day period for up to 3 yrs.; max. amt. adjusted annually for cost of living	$20/day for up to 3 yrs.	Up to $1,475/30-day period for lost income for up to 3 yrs. and $20/day for replacement services. Funeral benefits: $1,000
Minnesota	M	$4,000	—————————$20,000 max. for first-party benefits other than medical—————————			
			$20,000	85% of lost income up to $250/wk.	$200/wk., beginning 8 days after accident	Up to $200/wk. ea. for survivors' economic loss and survivors' replacement services loss. Funeral benefit: $2,000
New Jersey......	M	$200 or $1,500 (f)	Unlimited	Up to $100/wk. for one yr.	Up to $12/day for a max. of $4,380/person	Max. amount of benefits victim would have received. Funeral benefit: $1,000
New York	M	No dollar threshold(g)	—————————$50,000 overall max. on first-party benefits—————————			
			Limited only by total benefits limit	80% of lost income up to $1,000/mo. for 3 yrs.	$25/day for 1 yr.	$2,000 in addition to other benefits
North Dakota ...	M	$2,500	—————————$30,000 overall max. on first-party benefits—————————			
			Limited only by total benefits limit	85% of lost income up to $150/wk.	Up to $15/day	Up to $150/wk. for survivors income loss and $15/day for replacement services. Funeral benefit: $1,000
Oregon	M	None	$5,000 if incurred within 1 yr. of accident	If victim is disabled at least 14 days, 70% of lost income up to $750/mo. for up to 52 wks.	If victim is disabled at least 14 days, up to $18/day for up to 52 wks.	Funeral benefit: $1,000
Pennsylvania(h)..	M	None	$10,000	After 5 workdays, up to $5,000, limited to $1,000/mo. and 80% of actual lost income(i)	None	Funeral benefit: $1,500
South Carolina ..	O	None	—————————$1,000 overall max. on first-party benefits—————————			
			Limited only by total benefits limit if incurred within 3 yrs. of accident	Limited only by total benefits limit	Limited only by total benefits limit	Funeral benefit: limited only by total benefits limit
South Dakota ...	O	None	$2,000 if incurred within 2 yrs. of accident	$60/wk. for up to 52 wks. for disability extending beyond 14 days of date of accident	None	$10,000 if death occurs within 90 days of accident

NO-FAULT INSURANCE LAWS—Continued

State or other jurisdiction	Pur-chase of first-party benefits	Minimum tort liability threshold(a)	Maximum first-party (no-fault) benefits			
			Medical	Income loss	Replacement services	Survivors/funeral benefits
Texas..........	O	None	—————————$2,500 overall max. on first-party benefits—————————			
			Limited only by total benefits limit if incurred within 3 yrs. of accident	Limited only by total benefits limit if incurred within 3 yrs. of accident	Limited only by total benefits limit if incurred within 3 yrs. of accident. Payable only to non-wage earners	Limited only by total benefits limit if incurred within 3 yrs. of accident
Utah	M	$3,000	$3,000	85% of lost income up to $250/ wk. for up to 52 wks. subject to 3-day waiting period which does not apply if disability lasts longer than 2 wks.	$20/day for up to 365 days subject to 3-day waiting period which does not apply if disability lasts longer than 2 wks.	$3,000 survivors benefit. Funeral benefit: $1,500
Virginia.........	O	None	$2,000 if incurred within 1 yr. of accident	100% of lost income up to $100/ wk. for up to 52 wks.	None	Funeral benefit: included in medical benefit
Dist. of Col.	O	(j)	$50,000 or $100,000 (medical and rehabilitation)	$12,000 or $24,000	Max. of $24,000	Funeral benefit: $4,000

Source: No Fault Press Reference Manual, State Farm Insurance Companies.

Key: O—Optional; M—Mandatory.

(a) Refers to minimum amount of medical expenses necessary before victim can sue for general damages ("pain and suffering"). Lawsuits allowed in all states for injuries resulting in death and permanent disability. Some states allow lawsuits for one or more of the following: serious and permanent disfigurement, certain temporary disabilities, loss of body member, loss of certain bodily functions, certain fractures, or economic losses (other than medical) which exceed stated limits.

(b) Victim cannot sue for general damages unless injury results in significant and permanent loss of important body function, permanent injury, significant and permanent scarring or disfigurement, or death.

(c) Accident victim is not bound by tort restriction if (1) he has rejected the tort limitation in writing or (2) he is injured by a driver who has rejected the tort limitation in writing. Rejection bars recovery of first-party benefits.

(d) Liability for property damage for all states with no-fault insurance is under the state tort system. Michigan has no tort liability for vehicle damage.

(e) Victim cannot sue for general damages unless injuries result in death, serious impairment of bodily function, or serious permanent disfigurement.

(f) Motorist chooses one of two optional limitations.

(g) Victim cannot recover general damages unless injury results in in-ability to perform usual daily activities for at least 90 days during the 180 days following the accident; dismemberment; significant disfigurement; fracture; permanent loss of use of a body organ, member, function, or system; permanent consequential limitation of use of a body organ or member; significant limitation of use of a body function or system; or death.

(h) Pennsylvania repealed its no-fault act on February 12, 1984 and replaced it with a law that requires motorists to carry certain first-party coverages but places no restriction on the right to sue for general damages.

(i) May be waived by policyholder who has no expectation of actual income loss because of age, disability, or lack of employment history. Amount includes benefits for hiring substitute to perform self-employment services and hiring special help to enable victim to work.

(j) Person can choose "Personal Injury Protection" option. If person chooses this coverage, victims who are covered by no-fault benefits have 60 days after accident to decide whether to receive no-fault benefits. Victims who choose to get no-fault benefits cannot recover damages unless injury resulted in substantial permanent scarring or disfigurement; substantial and medically demonstrable permanent inpairment which has significantly affected the ability of the victim to perform professional activities or usual and customary daily activities; a medically demonstrable impairment that prevents victim from performing substantially all of his usual customary daily activities for more than 180 continuous days; or medical and rehabilitation expenses or work loss exceeding the amount of no-fault benefits available.

Table 8.20
MOTOR VEHICLE OPERATORS AND CHAUFFEURS LICENSES: 1986

State or other jurisdiction	Operators licenses			Chauffeurs licenses			Estimated total licenses in force during 1986 (in thousands) (a)
	Years for which issued	Renewal date	Amount of fee	Years for which issued	Renewal date	Amount of fee	
Alabama..........	4	Birthday	$15.00(b)				2,545
Alaska...........	5	Birthday	10.00				310
Arizona..........	4	Birthday	7.00	4	Birthday	$10.00	2,163
Arkansas	2 or 4	Birth month	7.00 or 13.00	2 or 4	Birth month	11.00 or 21.00	1,646
California*.......	4	Birthday	10.00				18,017
Colorado*	4	Birthday	6.50				2,292
Connecticut*.....	4	Birthday	31.00(b)				2,335
Delaware*	4(d)	Birthday	10.00(d)				455
Florida	4	Birthday	15.00	4	Birthday	15.00	8,335
Georgia*.........	4(e)	Birthday	4.50				4,081
Hawaii*	2 and 4(f)	Birthday	5.50 or 8.50(f)				612
Idaho	3	Birthday	12.00	3	Birthday	14.00	684
Illinois*.........	3 and 4(g)	Birthday	8.00 or 10.00(h)				7,093
Indiana	3 and 4	Birth month	3.00 or 6.00(h)	2 or 4	Birth month	4.00 or 8.00	3,761
Iowa*	2, 4, or 6(i)	Birthday	7.00 or 20.00(i)	2, 4, or 6(i)	Birthday	14.00 or 40.00(i)	1,883
Kansas*	4	Birthday	8.00				1,651
Kentucky	4	Birth month	8.00	4	Birth month	8.00	2,298
Louisiana*.......	4	Birthday	10.00				2,700
Maine*	2 or 4(l)	Birthday	18.00(l)				817
Maryland*	4	Birthday	6.00(k)				2,949
Massachusetts*	4	Birthday	25.00(b)				3,922
Michigan*	4(l)	Birthday	6.00(k)	4(k)	Birthday	14.50(k)	6,332
Minnesota*	4	Birthday	10.00(m)				2,455
Mississippi	4	Birth month	13.00				1,744
Missouri	3	Issuance	7.50	3	Issuance	15.00	3,430
Montana.........	4	Birthday	12.00	4	Birthday	12.00	591
Nebraska*	4(n)	Birthday	10.00(n)				1,097
Nevada*	4	Birthday	10.00(h)				707
New Hampshire* ..	4	Birthday	20.00				762
New Jersey*......	4(o)	Issuance	17.50(o)				5,904
New Mexico*.....	4(p)	30 days after Birthday	10.00(p)				1,024
New York*	4	Birthday	16.00				9,947
North Carolina* ...	4	Birthday	10.00				4,244
North Dakota*	4	Birthday	8.00				438
Ohio	4	Birthday	5.00(q)	4	Birthday	5.00(q)	7,386
Oklahoma	2 and 4	Birth month	7.00 or 14.00(r)	2 and 4	Birth month	11.00 or 22.00(r)	2,137
Oregon	4	Birthday	13.00(k)	4	Birthday	5.00(k)	1,943
Pennsylvania*	4	Birth month	21.50(j)				7,691
Rhode Island*	5	Birthday	20.00(s)				627
South Carolina* ...	4	Birthday	10.00				2,168
South Dakota	4	Birthday	6.00				485
Tennessee	4	Birthday	13.00	4	Birthday	21.00	3,106
Texas*...........	4	Birthday	16.00				11,129
Utah*	4	Birthday	10.00				970
Vermont	2 or 4	Birthday	10.00 or 16.00(b)				397
Virginia*.........	5	Birth month	12.00(s)				3,973
Washington*	4	Birthday	14.00(b)				3,029
West Virginia	4	Issuance	10.00	4	Issuance	15.00	1,297
Wisconsin*........	4	Birthday	9.00(b)	1	Birthday	9.00(b,k)	3,229
Wyoming	4	Birthday	5.00(t)				326
Dist. of Col.	4	Issuance	15.00				388

MOTOR VEHICLE LICENSES—Continued

Sources: Highway Statistics 1986, Federal Highway Administration, U.S. Department of Transportation. Compiled from reports of state authorities and other sources. Status of requirements as of December 31, 1986.

Key:

*—Classified drivers licenses are issued; permit qualified persons to operate specified vehicles on the public highways.

(a) Compiled for calendar year ending Dec. 31, 1986 from reports of state authorities and other sources. For Alabama, Arizona, Arkansas, and Michigan, data were estimated by (and for Louisiana, data were adjusted by) the Federal Highway Administration.

(b)The following examination fees are in addition to the fee shown for an original license: Connecticut-$15 for operator and $3.50 for public service licenses; Kansas-$3; Alabama, Massachusetts, Rhode Island, and Wisconsin-$5; Washington-$7; Vermont-written examination fee is $10 with original learner permit. No further examination fee unless driving test is failed, then $5 additional for additional test.

c) Beginning in 1984, a portion of all applicants were issued new four-year licenses. Replacement of three-year licenses will be complete by Jan. 1, 1987.

(d) An indefinite term license ($35 fee) is issued for drivers meeting specified requirements, but a reexamination (with a $1 photo fee) is required every five years.

(e) A permanent free drivers license is issued to veterans who entered the Armed Forces as a resident of the state.

(f) Licenses issued for two years to persons 15-24 years and 65 years and over. Cost varies depending on place of issuance; fees shown are for Honolulu.

(g) Beginning in 1984, licenses were issued for both three- and four-year terms to phase-in use of four-year term.

(h) Illinois—$4 for persons 69 years and over; Indiana—$3 for two-year renewal license for persons 75 years and over; Nevada—$5 for original or renewal license for persons over 70 years.

(i) Two years at $7 for operator license and $14 for chauffeur license issued to persons under 18 and over 70 years old; 6-year license is mandatory for persons 18 to 70 years old.

(j) Two-year license for persons 65 years and over at $11.50.

(k) Maryland—$20 for original operators license; Michigan—$7.50 for original operators, $16 for original chauffeurs (expires first birthday after issue date); Oregon—$21 for original operators and $10 for original chauffeurs; Wisconsin—$6.50 for original school bus.

(l) Persons with unsatisfactory driving records renew for two-year term.

(m) For persons under 19 years old, $6.

(n) Original license expires on licensee's birthday in the first year after issuance that licensee's age is divisible by four. Fees are: $3.50 for one year; $5.50 for two years; $8 for three years.

(o) New Jersey is phasing in a 4-year term. All original licenses will be 4-year photo licenses. Approximately half of all renewals will be 2-year nonphoto licenses at basic fee $8. Original 4-year fees are $17.50 for photo or $16 for nonphoto at licensee's option.

(p) Persons 75 years or over renew annually at no charge.

(q) A $1.50 deputy issuance fee and $1.00 eye exam fee are charged for licenses and permits.

(r) There is an additional $4 fee for the license application before obtaining the original license. Both 2 and 4-year licenses are being issued to phase in a 4-year term.

(s) In Rhode Island, effective January 1, 1985, licenses are being issued for terms varying from 1 to 5 years at $4 per year to phase in a 5 year term. In Virginia, effective January 1, 1985, licenses are issued for terms varying from 3 to 7 years at $2.40 per year for the basic license and $1 per year for each endorsement. This will phase in a new 5-year term with licenses expiring in a year when the licensee's age is divisible by 5.

(t) Original license is $10.

Table 8.21
STATE PUBLIC UTILITY COMMISSIONS

State or other jurisdiction	Regulatory authority	Members		Selection of chair	Length of commissioners' terms (in years)	Number of full-time employees
		Number	Selection			
Alabama............	Public Service Commission	3	E	E	4	139
Alaska.............	Public Utilities Commission	5	GL	G(a)	6	40
Arizona............	Corporation Commission	3	E	C	6	219
Arkansas	Public Service Commission	3	GS	G	6	114
California..........	Public Utilities Commission	5	GS	G	6	1024
Colorado	Public Utilities Commission	3	GS	G	6	92
Connecticut	Department of Public Utilities Control	5	GL	C	4	151
Delaware	Public Service Commission	5	GS	G	5	20
Florida	Public Service Commission	5	GS	C	4	332
Georgia............	Public Service Commission	5	E	C	6	133
Hawaii	Public Utilities Commission	3	GS	G	6	22
Idaho	Public Utilities Commission	3	GS	G	6	56
Illinois.............	Commerce Commission	7	G	G	5	312
Indiana	Utility Regulatory Commission	5	GS	G	4	121
Iowa	State Utilities Board	3	GS	G	6	99.5
Kansas	State Corporation Commission	3	GS	C	4	272.5
Kentucky	Public Service Commission	3	GS	G	4	129
Louisiana	Public Service Commission	5	E	C	6	108
Maine	Public Utilities Commission	3	GL	G	6	72
Maryland	Public Service Commission	5	GS	G	5	133
Massachusetts	Department of Public Utilities	3	G	G	4(b)	130
Michigan	Public Service Commission	3	GS	G	6	236
Minnesota	Public Utilities Commission	5	GS	G	6	28
Mississippi	Public Service Commission	3	E	C	4	112
Missouri	Public Service Commission	5	GS	G	5	191
Montana...........	Public Service Commission	5	E	C	4	46
Nebraska	Public Service Commission	5	E	C	6	61
Nevada	Public Service Commission	5	G	G	4	91
New Hampshire	Public Utilities Commission	3	G	G	6	57
New Jersey.........	Board of Public Utilities	3	GS	G	6	361
New Mexico........	Public Service Commission	3	GS	G	6	52
New York	Public Service Commission	7	GS	G	6	654
North Carolina	Utilities Commission	7	GL	G	8	134
North Dakota	Public Service Commission	3	E	C	6	57
Ohio	Public Utilities Commission	5	GS	G	5	544
Oklahoma	Corporation Commission	3	E	C	6	438
Oregon	Public Utility Commissioner	3	GS	C	4	425
Pennsylvania	Public Utility Commission	5	GS	G	10	590
Rhode Island	Public Utilities Commission	3	GS	G	6	38
South Carolina	Public Service Commission	7	L(f)	C(c)	4(d)	141
South Dakota	Public Utilities Commission	3	E	C	6	26
Tennessee..........	Public Service Commission	3	E	C	6	236
Texas..............	Public Utility Commission	3	GS	C	6	187
Utah	Public Service Commission	3	GS	G	6	82
Vermont	Public Service Board	3	GS	G	6	18
Virginia............	State Corporation Commission	3	L	C	6	474
Washington	Utilities & Transportation Commission	3	GS	G	6	234
West Virginia	Public Service Commission	3	GS	G	6	214
Wisconsin..........	Public Service Commission	3	GS	G(e)	6	179
Wyoming	Public Service Commission	3	GS	C	6	37
District of Col.	Public Service Commission	3	MC	C	4	58
Puerto Rico	Public Service Commission	5	GS	GS	4	454
Virgin Islands	Public Service Commission	9(g)	GS(g)	C	3	2

Source: National Association of Regulatory Utility Commissioners, *Annual Report on Utility and Carrier Regulation*, 1986. (Washington, D.C.: 1987 and updates).

Key:
G—Appointed by Governor.
GC—Appointed by Governor, with consent of the Governor's Council.
C—Elected by the Commission.
GS—Appointed by Governor, with consent of Senate.
L—Appointed by the Legislature.
GL—Appointed by Governor, with consent of entire Legislature.
MC—Appointed by the Mayor, with consent of City Council.
E—Elected by the public.

(a) Chairman serves in that position for four years.
(b) Co-terminous with Governor's.
(c) Chairmanship rotates every two years.
(d) Concurrent terms.
(e) Chairman serves in that position for two years.
(f) Upon recommendation of State Merit Selection Panel.
(g) 7 voting, 2 non-voting. Voting members appointed by Governor and confirmed by Senate, nonvoting appointed by President of Senate.

Table 8.22
SELECTED REGULATORY FUNCTIONS OF STATE PUBLIC UTILITIES COMMISSIONS*

State or other jurisdiction	Controls rates of privately owned utilities on sales to ultimate consumers of				Prescribe temporary rates, pending investigation			Require prior authorization of rate changes			Suspend proposed rate changes			Initiate rate investigation on its own motion		
	Electric	Gas	Telephone	CATV	Electric	Gas	Telephone	Electric	Gas	Telephone	Electric	Gas	Telephone	Electric	Gas	Telephone
Alabama	★	★	★	...	★	★	...	★	★	...	★	★	★	★	★	★
Alaska	★	★	★	★	★	★	★	★	★	★	★	★	★	★	★	★
Arizona	★	★	★	...	★	★	★	★	★	★	(a)	(a)	(a)	★	★	★
Arkansas	★	★	★	...	★	★	★	★	★	★	★	★	★	★	★	★
California	★	★	★	★	★	★(b)	★(b)	★	★	★	★	★	★	★	★	★
Colorado	★	★	★	...	★(c)	★(c)	★(c)	★	★	★	★	★	★	★	★	★
Connecticut	★	★	★	★	★	★	★	★	★	★	★	★	★	★	★	★
Delaware	★	★	★	...	★	★	★	★	★	★	★	★	★	★	★	★
Florida	★	★	★	...	★	★	★	★	★	★	★	★	★	★	★	★
Georgia	★	★	★	...	★	★	★	★	★	★	★	★	★	★	★	★
Hawaii	★	★	★	(d,q)	★	★	★	★	★	★	...	...	...	★	★	★
Idaho	★	★	★	★	★	★	★	★(e)	★(e)	★(e)	★	★	★	★	★	★
Illinois	★	★	★	...	★	★	★	★	★	★	★	★	★	★	★	★
Indiana	★	★	★	...	...	...	...	★	★	★	★	★	★	★	★	★
Iowa	★	★	★(f)	...	★(g)	★(g)	★(f,s)	★	★	★(f)	★	★	★(f)	★	★	★(f)
Kansas	★	★	★	...	★	★	★	★	★	★	★	★	★	★	★	★
Kentucky	★	★	★	★	★	★	★	★	★	★	★	★	★	★	★	★
Louisiana	★	★(h)	★	...	★	★	★	★	★	★	★	★	★	★	★	★
Maine	★	★	★	★	★	★	★	★	★	★	★	★	★	★	★	★
Maryland	★	★	★	★	★	★	★	★	★	★	★	★	★	★	★	★
Massachusetts	★	★	★	★(r)	★	★	★	★	★	★	★	★	★	★	★	★
Michigan	★	★	★	...	★(i)	★(i)	★(i)	★	★	★	(j)	(j)	(j)	★	★	★
Minnesota	★	★(k)	★(l)	...	★	★	★	★	★	★(l)	★	★	★(l)	★	★	★(l)
Mississippi	★	★	★	...	★	★	★	★	★	★	★	★	★	★	★	★
Missouri	★	★	★	...	★	★	★	★	★	★	★	★	★	★	★	★
Montana	★	★	★	...	★	★	★	★	★	★	★	★	★	★	★	★
Nebraska(m)	...	...	★	...	...	...	★	...	...	★	...	...	★	...	...	★
Nevada	★	★	★	...	★	★	★	★	★	★	★	★	★	★	★	★
New Hampshire	★	★	★	...	★	★	★	★	★	★	★	★	★	★	★	★
New Jersey	★	★	★	★	★	★	★	...	★	★	★	★	★	★	★	★
New Mexico Public Service Comm.	★	★	...	...	★	★	...	★	★	...	★	★	...	★	★	...
State Corp. Comm.	...	...	★	★	...	...	★	...	...	★	...	...	★	...	...	★
New York	★	★	★	...	★	★	★	★	★	★	★	★	★	★	★	★
North Carolina	★	★	★	...	★	★	★	★	★	★	★	★	★	★	★	★
North Dakota	★	★	★	...	★	★	★	★	★	★	★	★	★	★	★	★
Ohio	★	★	★	★	★	★	★	★	★	★	★	★	★	★	★	★
Oklahoma	★	★	★	...	★	★	★	★	★	★	★	★	★	★	★	★
Oregon	★	★	★	★	★	★	★	★	★	★	★	★	★	★	★	★
Pennsylvania	★	★	★	★	★	★	★	★	★	★	★	★	★	★	★	★
Rhode Island	★	★	★	...	★	★	★	★	★	★	★	★	★	★	★	★
South Carolina	★	★	★	...	★	★	★	★	★	★	...	...	★	★	★	★
South Dakota	★	★	★(n)	...	★	★	★	★	★	★	★	★	★	★	★	★
Tennessee	★	★	★	★	★(o)	★(o)	★	★	★	★	★	★	★	★	★	★
Texas Pub. Utilities Comm.	★	...	★	...	★	...	★	★	...	★	★	...	★	★	...	★
Railroad Comm.	...	★	...	...	...	★	...	...	★	...	...	★	...	...	★	...
Utah	★	★	★	★	★	★	★	★	★	★	★	★	★	★	★	★
Vermont	★	★	★	★	★	★	★	★	★	★	★	★	★	★	★	★
Virginia	★	★	★	...	...	...	...	★	★	★	★	★	★	★	★	★
Washington	★	★	★	...	★	★	★	★	★	★	★	★	★	★	★	★
West Virginia	★	★	★	...	★	★	★	★	★	★	★	★	★	★	★	★
Wisconsin	★	★	★	...	★	★	★	★	★	★	(j)	(j)	(j)	★	★	★
Wyoming	★	★	★	...	★	★	★	★	★	★	★	★	★	★	★	★
Dist. of Col.	★	★	★	★	...	...	...	★	★	★	★	★	...	★	★	★
Puerto Rico	(q)	★	(p)	★	...	...	(p)	...	...	(p)	...	...	(p)	...	★	(p)
Virgin Islands	(q)	...	★	★	★	★	★	★	★	★	...	...	★	...	...	★

SELECTED REGULATORY FUNCTIONS—Continued

*Full names of commissions are shown on Table 8.21.

Source: National Association of Regulatory Utility Commissioners, *Annual Report on Utility and Carrier Regulation*, 1986 (Washington, D.C.: 1987).

Key:

★—Yes

. . .—No

(a) Rates cannot be increased without hearings and a subsequent order of the Commission; consequently no suspension is required.

(b) May fix temporary rates, but practice is not followed.

(c) No specific statutory authority.

(d) Regulated by the Cable Television Division of the Department of Regulatory Agencies.

(e) Rates become effective after seven months if Commission does not take action.

(f) Not for companies with less than 15,000 customers and less than 15,000 access lines.

(g) Interim rates must be approved and are collected under bond, subject to refund.

(h) Except no authority over rates charged to industrial customers by any gas company.

(i) Commission has authority to grant partial and immediate rate relief during pendency of final order, after statutory requirements are met.

(j) Specific authority required to change rates. Rates do not become effective after a specified period; consequently, no suspension is required.

(k) Rates not regulated for gas utilities serving fewer than 650 customers.

(l) Has authority only at the election of the cooperative.

(m) Telephone is the only regulated utility.

(n) PUC does not regulate rates of rural telephone cooperatives.

(o) Emergency only.

(p) The Puerto Rico Telephone Authority, a state public corporation, purchased the Puerto Rico Telephone Company.

(q) Commission did not respond to request for updated information.

(r) Act conferring jurisdiction to regulate pole attachments effective March 31, 1989.

LABOR LEGISLATION: 1986-87

By Richard R. Nelson

The 1986-87 biennium was marked by a surge in the volume of labor standards legislation introduced and enacted by the states. Along with the increased volume, several legislatures grappled with difficult and controversial headline-producing issues such as employee drug and AIDS testing, parental leave, plant closings and restrictions on workplace smoking. Differing approaches to these emerging issues resulted in legislation reflecting a general lack of consensus among those seeking solutions.

In addition to these issues, attention also was given to other more traditional subjects including minimum wage protection, bans on employment discrimination, collection of unpaid wages, and child labor restrictions. In the newer areas of regulation lawmakers also looked at issues such as asbestos abatement work and background clearance of child care workers. First time laws were enacted prohibiting the wrongful discharge of employees.

Wages and Hours

Minimum wages

Minimum wage was one of the most active subjects of legislation in 1986 and 1987 with bills to increase rates introduced in a majority of the states. Hourly wage rates were increased either through new legislation or by administrative action in 14 states[1] and were increased for certain occupations in the District of Columbia and Puerto Rico[2]. Additionally, wage rates rose in Maine, Montana, and Vermont because of increases mandated by prior laws. Under a new wage order, issued by the California Industrial Welfare Commission, the minimum hourly wage in that state will rise to $4.25 on July 1, 1988.

Legislation enacted in Hawaii, Massachusetts, Minnesota, New Hampshire, and Rhode Island increased rates in those states above the $3.35 per hour federal standard. The federal rate, in effect since 1981, was exceeded in 10 jurisdictions on January 1, 1988, including the 6 New England states (see table 8.27). This number will increase to 11 when the California rate becomes effective on July 1, 1988. Bills to further increase the rate in Maine and to raise the Wisconsin rate above the federal level passed those legislatures in 1987 but were vetoed by the governors. On January 1, 1988, 24 jurisdictions had minimum wage rates at or near $3.35 per hour for some or all occupations. Rates were significantly lower than $3.35 in 11 states, and 9 states did not have minimum wage laws.

Other noteworthy wage actions included the addition of an overtime pay standard to the New Hampshire wage law which requires payment of time-and-one-half the regular rate after 40 hours per week for employment not covered by the Federal Fair Labor Standards Act (FLSA); an administrative change made in New York providing for overtime pay of time-and-one-half the employee's regular rate rather than time-and-one-half the state minimum rate as before, and the elimination of various subminimum rates; and a requirement in Wyoming for overtime pay on public works projects for hours worked in excess of 10 a day or 40 a week instead of after 8 hours a day. Montana included its existing tip credit prohibition into

Richard R. Nelson is a State Standards Adviser in the Division of State Employment Standards Programs, Office of State Liaison and Legislative Analysis, Employment Standards Administration, U.S. Department of Labor. The portion of the Occupational Safety and Health section reporting on federal developments was prepared by Arlene Perkins, Project Officer, Directorate of Federal-State Operations, Office of State Programs, Occupational Safety and Health Administration, U.S. Department of Labor. The Workers' Compensation section was prepared by Ruth Brown, State Standards Adviser, Division of State Workers' Compensation Programs, Office of State Liaison and Legislative Analysis, Employment Standards Administration, U.S. Department of Labor.

its minimum wage law and extended coverage to employees covered by the FLSA if the state minimum rate is higher. Indiana repealed its tip credit allowance, the allowance was reduced in Maine, and employers in Delaware were prohibited from taking any part of an employee's tips. The tip credit allowance in Minnesota will be eliminated Jan. 1, 1989. The new California wage order reinstitutes tip credits by establishing a $3.50 minimum rate for employees who receive at least $60 a month in tips, whereas others are to receive $4.25 an hour.

Separate U.S. circuit court decisions in Hawaii and New York held that the Federal Motor Carrier Act, which authorizes the Secretary of Transportation to establish requirements for maximum hours of service for employees of interstate carriers, does not preempt state requirements for overtime pay for these workers.

Wage payment and collection

A comprehensive new wage payment law applicable to both public and private sector employers was enacted in South Carolina and Kansas extended coverage of its wage payment and collection law to public employers. Labor departments in Delaware, Washington, and Wisconsin were authorized to collect unpaid wages for all underpaid employees of an employer rather than only for those who filed wage claims, and the ceiling was removed on acceptance of wage claims by the Utah Industrial Commission. The Commission also was authorized to enter into reciprocal agreements with other states for wage claim collection[3].

Civil penalties, previously authorized for certain violations under the New York minimum wage and wage payments acts, may now be assessed for violations concerning minimum wage standards for farmwork and for nonmonetary violations involving recordkeeping, posting, and wage statements. In other wage payment legislation, Rhode Island specified that vacation pay accrued by workers separated after 1 year's service, must be paid. Wisconsin will bar contractors from state public works contracts for 3 years, if they have failed to pay prevailing wage or overtime rates. New Jersey enacted a Construction Workers' Fringe Benefit Security Act to ensure payments to fringe benefit funds. And New Hampshire amended reporting requirements under a similar law.

Prevailing wage

Several measures were introduced to repeal or modify state prevailing wage laws which specify that wage rates paid on publicly funded construction projects be not less than those prevailing in the locality. While only a few of these were enacted into law, there were some significant actions. The Kansas prevailing wage and public work 8-hour-day law was repealed (the eighth state to repeal a prevailing wage law since 1979), leaving 33 states with laws of this kind[4]. Amendments to the Montana law provide for rate determination for each of 10 districts rather than the county or locality in which the work is performed, define the prevailing wage to be a weighted average based on hours worked by craft or classification in the district including both private and public projects, and establish a $25,000 threshold amount for coverage. Other amendments changed rate-setting procedures in Massachusetts, bid advertisement requirements in Oregon, and the definition of locality in Wyoming. Washington extended coverage of its prevailing wage law to facilities built by private parties for lease to state agencies.

An effort to repeal the Massachusetts prevailing wage law has received enough petition signatures to place the question on the November 1988 general election ballot for referendum vote.

Pay equity

The subject of equal pay for jobs of comparable value in state government received less legislative attention during this biennium than in recent years, but there were a few noteworthy developments. Each branch of the Oregon state government was directed to adopt a method to determine the comparable value of different types of jobs and report to the legislature on proposals to upgrade undervalued classifications. A Pay Equity Adjustment Fund was created to pay for needed adjustments. Coverage under a Connecticut law designed to eliminate sex-based inequities in state service was expanded and studies of the need for similar legislation were initiated in Hawaii and North Dakota. Money for implementation continued to be appropriated in some other states which enacted pay equity legislation in prior years.

Employee Drug Testing

The highly controversial and emotionally charged issue of substance abuse testing of job applicants or employees was the subject of proposed legislation in more than half of the legislatures. The divergence of opinion on such matters as employee right of privacy and workplace safety concerns was reflected in the bills introduced and the laws enacted. The 8 state laws which were passed (Connecticut, Iowa, Louisiana, Minnesota, Montana, Rhode Island, Utah, and Vermont) vary between those permitting testing provided certain conditions are met and those prohibiting testing except for probable cause or other specified reasons or for certain employees. Louisiana and Utah permit testing of employees in a number of situations within the terms of a written employer policy provided certain safeguards are met with respect to sample collection and testing procedures, and permit test results to be used as the basis for discharge or other adverse personnel actions (the Utah law also applies to applicants). Testing in the event of probable cause is permitted in each of the other 6 states. Testing is also permitted as part of a regularly scheduled physical exam with advance notice for job applicants or employees in Connecticut, Iowa, Minnesota, and Vermont and for applicants for certain high risk or sensitive occupations in Montana. Testing of high risk employees in high risk or sensitive occupations also is permitted in Connecticut and Minnesota.

Job applicants and employees are covered by the laws in 6 of the states, with the laws of Louisiana and Rhode Island covering only employees. Most of the laws provide the right to a re-test in the event of a positive test finding (usually using a different test method), provide the right to explain a positive test result, and specifically protect the confidentiality of results. Employees in Iowa, Minnesota, Rhode Island, and Vermont may not be discharged for a first time positive drug test and must be given the opportunity to participate in counseling or rehabilitation.

AIDS testing of applicants or employees is another subject of great controversy raising questions of privacy and discrimination. Only a few measures have been adopted addressing this subject. Wisconsin and Massachusetts prohibited employers from requesting or requiring a test for the presence of the AIDS antibody as a condition of employment. San Francisco adopted an ordinance prohibiting drug testing and employer interference in an employee's personal relationships, organizations, or activities.

Parental Leave

Parental leave for the birth, adoption or serious illness of a child emerged as an issue during the biennium. The issue was hastened, in part, by changing workforce demographics, especially the increasing numbers of women in the workforce with young children who must reconcile the demands of work and families. Bills were introduced in nearly half the legislatures to require employers to grant unpaid leave of varying durations and to guarantee returning employees reinstatement to the same job or a similar one. Laws applicable to private and public sector employers were enacted in Minnesota (up to 6 weeks' leave), Oregon (12 weeks), Rhode Island (13 weeks), and Tennessee (4 months for female employees only). A law applicable to state employees only was adopted in Connecticut providing up to 24 weeks parental leave or time off for the employee's serious illness or the illness of a parent. In addition, a task force was established to study various aspects of parental leave in private sector employment.

Related legislation was passed for all employees in New York and for public employees in Missouri requiring adoptive parents be given the same opportunities for leave as biological parents. Also, a leave of absence because of disability on account of pregnancy or related medical condition was authorized for up to eight weeks in Iowa and for up to four months in Louisiana.

Wrongful Discharge

Over the past several years there has been considerable litigation concerning "employment-at-will" and limits on an employers right to discharge workers. While some legislation had been introduced previously, the Virgin Islands in 1986 and Montana in 1987 became the first jurisdictions to enact wrongful discharge laws.

Under these two laws, the discharge of an employee for reasons other than those specifically authorized is considered to be wrongful and remedies are provided. The Montana law, which establishes an exclusive remedy for redress, allows wrongfully discharged employees to file an action for recovery of lost wages and interest and to recover punitive damages where employer fraud or malice is discovered. The Virgin Islands law authorizes the commissioner of Labor to order reinstatement and back pay and permits employees to bring court action for compensatory and punitive damages.

Child Labor

New or amending legislation regulating the employment of children was enacted in 23 states in 1986 and 1987 with most of the laws easing work restrictions.

Amendments to the Arizona law permitted the labor department to grant individual variances, added detailed definitions of prohibited occupations similar to those under federal law, and extended the permitted work hours by those under age 16 on days preceding days when school is not in session. Night work restrictions also were eased for children under age 16 in Delaware and Rhode Island. In other actions, proof-of-age certificates will no longer be required in Connecticut for persons over age 18 employed in hazardous occupations and the minimum age for employment was lowered for certain work in mercantile establishments; the age at which children may sell or deliver newspapers was lowered from 12 to 9 in Massachusetts; and the minimum age was reduced for detasseling corn and similar farming operations in Michigan.

Several changes were made in the Alabama child labor law which was amended to conform to federal law regarding night work, daily, and weekly hours restrictions of children under age 16 and to add restrictions on permissible night work hours for 16-and-17-year olds. Florida, for the first time, imposed limits on the daily and weekly hours of 16-and-17-year-old students during the school year. Also, permissible weekly hours were reduced for minors under age 16 during the school year and night work hours revised for those 17 and under. Night work hours also were reduced for minors under 16 in Minnesota.

The labor commissioner in Iowa was given new rule making authority and in Tennessee the labor commissioner's authority was expanded. Provisions were enacted in Arkansas and Vermont regulating the employment of children as actors.

Compulsory school attendance laws were amended in Louisiana to require attendance until age 17, rather than 16, and in Mississippi, to require attendance to age 17 by the 1989-90 school year.

Equal Employment Opportunity

Amendments to the Federal Age Discrimination in Employment Act effective January 31, 1987, included removal of the age-70 upper limit for prohibitions on employment discrimination because of age and mandatory retirement[5]. This law applies to private and public sector employment with the exception of federal employees. Following this action, mandatory retirement provisions for public sector employees in Ohio were specifically conformed to the federal law. The age-70 upper limit also was removed from age discrimination and mandatory retirement provisions for various public sector employees by amendments to laws in Louisiana, Minnesota, Nebraska, South Dakota, Vermont, and Virginia, and for public and private sector employees in Illinois, Nevada, Oregon, and Utah. In West Virginia, an age-65 upper limit was removed from the law prohibiting age discrimination in public and private employment. In other actions, age discrimination was banned in Colorado under the state civil rights law, and the Illinois Human Rights Act was amended to prohibit age discrimination between 18 and 40 in apprenticeship or training programs.

Laws addressing other forms of employment discrimination, primarily on the basis of sex or handicap, were enacted in a majority of these states. A Virginia human rights act was enacted making it unlawful to discriminate on the basis of race, color, religion, national origin, sex, age, marital status, or disability. In Missouri, separate laws pertaining to discrimination in employment, housing, and places of public accommodation were repealed and replaced with a law consolidating all of these measures, and provisions were repealed which had permitted sex-based differences in employment under certain conditions, in the age of retirement, and in annuity, death, and survivors benefits. Sexual harassment of employees was specified as a form of sex discrimination and prohibited in Massachusetts. In Iowa, criminal penalties were added for sex discrimination violations.

Discrimination in employment because of physical or mental disability unrelated to job performance was banned under the South Dakota Human Relations Act. The prohibition against discrimination in public employment on the basis of handicap was extended to include private employers in Tennessee. Ohio enacted a Bill of Rights for mentally retarded and developmentally disabled persons. The Rhode Island Fair Employment Practices Act was amended to add failure by an employer to reasonably accommodate a worker's handicap to the list of unlawful employment practices. And in Alaska, mental disability was added to physical disability as a prohibited form of discrimination.

Occupational Safety and Health

Various worker safety and health subjects drew considerable attention with laws dealing with one or more aspects enacted in 40 jurisdictions. Of these, asbestos abatement, restrictions on smoking in the workplace, and the right of workers to be informed and given training regarding chemical hazards in the workplace were the 3 subjects with the most enactments. Asbestos abatement laws regulate various aspects of this work, generally including the regulation or licensing of contractors, safety training of workers and advance notification of asbestos work to be performed. A few laws of this kind had been enacted in prior years, but this became a major area of legislative activity in 1986 and 1987 with new legislation adopted in 19 states and amendments made to the laws of 2 others[6]. Some of this activity was likely in response to the Federal Asbestos Hazard Emergency Response Act of 1986, which requires, among other things, state certification of contractors performing asbestos abatement work in schools by the Environmental Protection Agency and Federal Occupational Safety and Health Administration (OSHA) asbestos standards effective Jan. 17, 1987, requiring training (but not licensing or certification) of people working with asbestos in the private sector. Laws regulating smoking in the workplace were enacted in 10 states[7] and amendments were made to some previously enacted. These laws usually require employers to implement policies prohibiting or restricting smoking in the workplace. If reasonable accommodation between smokers and nonsmokers cannot be achieved, preference is generally given to nonsmokers. The amount of legislation concerning hazardous chemical right-to-know declined from past years, perhaps as the result of court-mandated expansion of federal jurisdiction and preemption of state coverage. Of the 16 enactments, 12 were amendments to existing legislation. Among these, an amendment incorporated the Federal OSHA's Hazard Communication Standard by reference into the Michigan state law, workers in New Mexico will now be given hazardous substance information, and laws were enacted in Kansas and Utah to provide for carrying out the requirements of the Federal Emergency Planning and Community Right-to-Know Act of 1986.

The Federal OSHA's 1983 Hazard Communication Standard provides for federal preemption of state laws or standards, unless part of a federally approved state occupational safety and health program, or "state plan," is operated in accordance with the requirements of the Occupational Safety and Health Act of 1970. In conformance with a March 1985 U.S. Circuit Court decision, in August 1987, OSHA expanded coverage of the Hazard Communication Standard from industries in the manufacturing sector to include all industries where employees are exposed to hazardous chemicals. The expanded coverage will go into effect in 1988. The revised rule also included a specific statement regarding preemption of state standards, including an indicator of the types of provisions the agency would consider to be preempted in states without OSHA-approved state plans.

Of the 25 "state plan" jurisdictions with occupation safety and health programs (see table 8.25), 23 operate programs covering both private and public sector employees. Two states, Connecticut and New York, cover public employees only. Of these 25 states, Indiana and South Carolina were granted "final approval" status during the biennium, bringing to 13 the number of state plans which have been granted final approval by OSHA. California Gov. George Deukmejian, in a letter to the Secretary of Labor, announced his intent to end California's participation as an OSHA approved State. This matter was still under dispute in the state courts in February 1988.

Among other significant developments, a new comprehensive Occupational Safety and Health Act was enacted in West Virginia for state employees with provision for optional coverage by political subdivisions of the state. Public agencies in Texas may now consider the safety record of bidders in the awarding of public works construction contracts. Other laws were enacted concerning boiler, mine, elevator, and amusement ride safety.

Plant Closings

Efforts continued to be made to lessen the impact on communities and workers when an employer suddenly closes, significantly reduces operations, or relocates. New laws were enacted in Hawaii and the Virgin Islands. The Hawaii law requires advance notice of a closing or out-of-state relocation be given to employees and the Director of Labor and Industrial Relations and that employees receive a dislocated worker allowance to supplement unemployment compensation benefits for 4 weeks. The Virgin Islands law requires advance notice of a closing or major reduction in the work force be given to the employees, their union, and the Commissioner of Labor. Affected employees are to receive severance pay, continuation of disability insurance, a preference in hiring at other employer facilities and have the opportunity to purchase a facility being closed. A task force was established in Missouri to help alleviate the problems associated with plant closings and to facilitate the creation of replacement jobs. Massachusetts will develop sanctions for employers who fail to notify laid-off workers of their right to extended health insurance. Connecticut extended the time for continuation of employee health benefit coverage, and New York established a temporary program to assist dislocated workers with the payment of health insurance premiums. Also, in New York, the governor and business and labor leaders signed an agreement to improve labor-management cooperation in the private sector and to deal with the problems of plant closings and layoffs. In related legislation, laws were passed in Michigan and Oregon to encourage the formation of employee-owned enterprises, and Washington enacted a law authorizing and regulating employee cooperative corporations.

Workers' Compensation

Nearly 400 laws to improve or modify state workers' compensation programs were passed during 1986-1987. Among these, maximum benefit levels for temporary total disability were increased in 46 states, the District of Columbia, and the Virgin Islands (see table 8.23), and 23 states[8] made significant changes in their statutes covering medical care and vocational rehabilitation.

Five states made legislative changes in the area of occupational disease. Georgia deleted the schedule of compensable occupational diseases and the statute of limitations for such diseases from the law. Kentucky provided that all claims for asbestos-related disease must be filed within 20 years of exposure. Nevada's law was amended to allow employers the option to provide occupational disease coverage to employees who were previously excluded. In Oregon, the statute of limitations for filing

claims was reduced from 5 years to 1. Coverage was broadened in Virginia to include diseases not ordinarily considered job related if it can be established that suchdisease arose out of and in the course of employment.

In other actions, amendments to allow workers' compensation coverage of sole proprietors and partners were enacted in Alaska, Iowa, Minnesota, Nevada, New York and West Virginia, and the laws of 10 states[9] were amended to cover persons performing community service work such as volunteer public safety workers. Coverage was eliminated for licensed real estate agents in Kansas and New York and for certain inmates in Maine and Montana.

In Connecticut and Vermont the percentage of the state average weekly wage used for computing disability and death benefits was increased from 100 to 150 percent, while New Mexico reduced its percentage of the average weekly wage from 100 to 85 percent.

Oklahoma now will increase its weekly wage once every 3 years rather than annually; burial allowances were raised in 9 states[10]; and in November 1986, a ratified constitutional amendment in New Mexico changed the workers' compensation system from a court-administered to an administrative system.

Montana, New Hampshire and North Dakota enacted first-time legislation providing for the garnishment of compensation benefits for the support of dependent children of workers' compensation recipients.

Other Legislation

Other notable laws, covering an array of labor standards, were enacted during the biennium. Among these, 13 jurisdictions[11] enacted or amended "whistleblower" laws designed to protect employees from employer retaliation for reporting violations to a public body, or for participating in an investigation, hearing, or court action. Several states passed legislation requiring background clearance checks of child care operators or workers. Nebraska enacted a new comprehensive State Employees Collective Bargaining Act, and collective bargaining laws in Delaware, Illinois, Maryland, Washington and Wisconsin were either enacted or amended to expand public sector coverage. Nebraska also enacted a Farm Labor Contractor Registration Act. The Texas Labor Agency Law was repealed and several other states amended laws regulating private employment agencies including a measure in Montana transferring administration of its law from the Department of Labor and Industry to the Department of Commerce. Laws prohibiting polygraph examinations as a condition of employment were amended in Maryland, Massachusetts, Rhode Island and Tennessee.

New York enacted an apparel industry registration law establishing a special task force to enforce labor standards in the industry. Measures enacting or amending contractor or resident preferences in the awarding of public contracts were adopted in several states, and New Mexico passed a law creating a single, consolidated cabinet-level Labor Department.

Notes

1. Arkansas, Connecticut, Delaware, Hawaii, Kentucky, Massachusetts, Minnesota, Nebraska, Nevada, New Hampshire, Rhode Island, Texas, West Virginia, and Wisconsin.

2. Revised wage orders issued by the District of Columbia Wage-Hour Board raised minimum wage rates in 1986 for beauty culture and building service occupations, and in 1987 for occupations not covered by other industry wage orders. In Puerto Rico, revised mandatory decrees issued by the Commonwealth Minimum Wage Board raised minimum rates in 1986 in the chemical, petroleum, rubber, and related products industry, the commercial services industry, and motor vehicle storage, custody, or parking services employees, and in 1987 in the paper, paper products, printing, and publishing industry, the alcoholic beverage and industrial alcohol industry, and the food and related products industry.

3. Currently 17 states have the necessary authorizing legislation to enter into reciprocal agreements with other states for mutual assistance in the collection of unpaid wages. These states are: Alaska, Arkansas, California, Hawaii, Illinois, Iowa, Kansas, Maryland, Montana, Nevada, New York, North Dakota, Oregon, South Dakota, Utah, Washington, and Wyoming.

4. Alaska, Arkansas, California, Connecticut, Delaware, Hawaii, Illinois, Indiana, Kentucky, Louisiana, Maine, Maryland, Massachusetts, Michigan, Minnesota, Missouri, Montana, Nebraska, Nevada, New Jersey, New Mexico, New York, Ohio, Oklahoma, Oregon, Pennsylvania, Rhode Island, Tennessee, Texas, Washington, West Virginia, Wisconsin and Wyoming. Guam and the Virgin Islands also have prevailing wage laws.

5. The Age Discrimination in Employment Act of 1986 (Public Law 99-592, generally effective Jan. 1, 1987) amended the Age Discrimination Act of 1967 (as amended) to extend group health plan coverage to individuals beyond age 69, and to remove the age 70 upper limit for purposes of prohibitions on employment discrimination because of age and mandatory retirement. Temporary exceptions remain for firefighters and law enforcement officers and for certain tenured faculty members. The Secretary of Labor and the Equal Employment Opportunity Commission are to jointly conduct a study and submit recommendations on the use of physical and mental fitness tests as valid measurements of the ability and competency of police officers and firefighters to perform their jobs. The extension of group health plan coverage to individuals beyond age 69 was also provided for in the Consolidated Omnibus Budget Reconciliation Act of 1986 (Public Law 99-272, generally effective Jan. 1, 1987). The Omnibus Budget Reconciliation Act of 1986 (Public Law 99-509, generally effective Jan. 1, 1988) amended the Age Discrimination Act of 1967 (as amended) to prohibit discrimination on the basis of age in employee pension benefit plans.

6. New asbestos abatement laws were enacted in Arizona, Colorado, Connecticut, Delaware, Florida, Hawaii, Illinois, Maine, Massachusetts, Michigan, Minnesota, Missouri, New Hampshire, North Dakota, Ohio, Oregon, Texas, Vermont and Virginia. Amendments were made to prior laws in Arkansas and Georgia.

7. Arizona, Arkansas, Hawaii, Indiana, Maine, New Hampshire, Oklahoma, Rhode Island, Utah, and Vermont.

8. Arizona, Arkansas, Colorado, Connecticut, Delaware, Florida, Iowa, Kansas, Louisiana, Maine, Maryland, Minnesota, Montana, Nebraska, New Mexico, New York, North Dakota, Oklahoma, Oregon, Rhode Island, Texas, Virginia and Washington.

9. Arkansas, Delaware, Georgia, Hawaii, Iowa, Kentucky, New Jersey, New York, North Dakota and Virginia.

10. Arkansas, Colorado, Idaho, New Mexico, North Carolina, Rhode Island, Tennessee, Vermont, and West Virginia.

11. California, Connecticut, Florida, Hawaii, Illinois, Indiana, Kentucky, Minnesota, Missouri, New Hampshire, New Jersey, Pennsylvania, and Puerto Rico.

Table 8.23
MAXIMUM BENEFITS FOR TEMPORARY TOTAL DISABILITY
PROVIDED BY WORKERS' COMPENSATION STATUTES
(As of January 1988)

State or other jurisdiction	Maximum percentage of wages	Maximum payment per week		Maximum period		Total maximum stated in law
		Amount	Based on*	Duration of disability	Number of weeks	
Federal (FECA)(a) ..	66-2/3(b)	$1,029.48	75% of the pay of specific grade level in federal civil service(b)	★	. . .	. . .
(LS/HWCA)(a)	66-2/3	616.96	200% of NAWW	★	. . .	. . .
Alabama...........	66-2/3	331.00	100% of SAWW	★	. . .	. . .
Alaska.............	80 of worker's spendable earnings	1,094.00(c)	200% of SAWW	★	. . .	. . .
Arizona...........	66-2/3	253.19(d)	. . .	★	. . .	. . .
Arkansas	66-2/3	189.00	. . .	. . .	450	. . .
California..........	66-2/3	224.00	. . .	★	. . .	. . .
Colorado	66-2/3	357.63(e)	80% of SAWW	★	. . .	. . .
Connecticut	66-2/3	643.00(f)	150% of SAWW	★	. . .	. . .
Delaware	66-2/3	250.53	66-2/3% of SAWW	★	. . .	. . .
Florida	66-2/3	344.00(c)	100% of SAWW	. . .	350	. . .
Georgia............	66-2/3	175.00	. . .	★	. . .	. . .
Hawaii	66-2/3	334.00	100% of SAWW	★	. . .	. . .
Idaho	69-90	282.60 – 392.50(g)	90% of SAWW		52(h)	. . .
Illinois.............	66-2/3	554.27	133-1/3% of SAWW	★	. . .	. . .
Indiana	66-2/3	190.00	. . .	. . .	500	95,000
Iowa	80 of worker's spendable earnings	632.00	200% of SAWW	★	. . .	. . .
Kansas	66-2/3	256.00	75% of SAWW	★	. . .	100,000
Kentucky	66-2/3	330.53	100% of SAWW	★	. . .	. . .
Louisiana	66-2/3	262.00(i)	75% of SAWW	★	. . .	. . .
Maine	66-2/3	447.92(i,j)	166-2/3% of SAWW	★	. . .	. . .
Maryland	66-2/3	382.00	100% of SAWW	★	. . .	. . .
Massachusetts	66-2/3	411.00(k)	100% of SAWW	. . .	260	(l)
Michigan	80 of worker's spendable earnings	397.00(m)	90% of SAWW	★	. . .	. . .
Minnesota	66-2/3	376.00	100% of SAWW	★	. . .	. . .
Mississippi	66-2/3	140.00	. . .	. . .	450	63,000
Missouri	66-2/3	269.81	75% of SAWW	. . .	400	. . .
Montana...........	66-2/3	299.00(e,n)	100% of SAWW	★	. . .	. . .
Nebraska	66-2/3	235.00	. . .	★	. . .	. . .
Nevada	66-2/3	353.01	100% of SAWW	★	. . .	. . .
New Hampshire	66-2/3(p)	525.00	150% of SAWW	★	. . .	. . .
New Jersey..........	70	320.00	75% of SAWW	. . .	400	. . .
New Mexico.........	66-2/3	270.97	85% of SAWW	. . .	700	(q)
New York	66-2/3	300.00	. . .	★	. . .	. . .
North Carolina	66-2/3	356.00	100% of SAWW	★	. . .	. . .
North Dakota	66-2/3	299.00(r,s)	100% of SAWW	★	. . .	. . .
Ohio	72 for first 12 weeks; 66-2/3 thereafter	385.00(t)	100% of SAWW	★	. . .	. . .
Oklahoma	66-2/3	231.00(u)	66-2/3% of SAWW	. . .	300	. . .
Oregon	66-2/3	355.04	100% of SAWW	★	. . .	. . .
Pennsylvania	66-2/3	377.00	100% of SAWW	★	. . .	. . .
Rhode Island	66-2/3	337.00(v)	100% of SAWW	★	. . .	. . .
South Carolina	66-2/3	319.20	100% of SAWW	★	500	. . .
South Dakota	66-2/3	272.00	100% of SAWW	★	. . .	. . .
Tennessee	66-2/3	210.00	. . .	★	. . .	84,200
Texas..............	66-2/3	231.00(w)	. . .	. . .	401	. . .
Utah	66-2/3	335.00(x)	100% of SAWW	. . .	312	. . .
Vermont	66-2/3	486.00(y)	150% of SAWW	★	. . .	. . .
Virginia............	66-2/3	344.00	100% of SAWW	. . .	500	. . .
Washington	60-75	288.70.(e)	75% of SAMW	★	. . .	. . .
West Virginia	70	350.83	100% of SAWW	. . .	208	. . .
Wisconsin...........	66-2/3	348.00(e)	100% of SAWW	★	. . .	. . .
Wyoming	66-2/3	352.70	100% of SAMW	★	. . .	. . .
Dist. of Col.	66-2/3 or 80 of worker's spendable earnings	481.92	100% of SAWW	★	. . .	. . .
Puerto Rico	66-2/3	45.00	. . .	. . .	312	. . .
Virgin Islands	66-2/3	193.00	66-2/3% of SAWW	★	. . .	. . .

MAXIMUM BENEFITS—Continued

Source: Division of State Workers' Compensation Programs, Office of State Liaison and Legislative Analysis, Employment Standards Administration, U.S. Department of Labor.

*SAWW—State's average weekly wage; AWW—Worker's aveage weekly wage; SAMW—State's average monthly wage.; NAWW—National average weekly wage.

(a) Federal Employees' Compensation Act (FECA) and the Longshoremen's and Harbor Workers' Compensation Act (LHWCA). LHWCA benefits are for private-sector maritime employees (not seamen) who work on navigable waters of the U.S., including dry docks.

(b) Benefits under FECA are computed at a maximum of 75 percent of the pay of a specific grade level in the federal civil service.

(c) Payments subject to Social Security and Unemployment Insurance benefits offsets.

(d) Additional $10 monthly added to benefits of dependents residing in the U.S.

(e) Payments subject to Social Security benefit offsets.

(f) Additional $10 weekly for each dependent child under 18 years of age, up to 50 percent of basic benefit, not to exceed 75 percent of worker's wage.

(g) Additional 7 percent ($20.23) of SAWW is payable for each dependent child up to five children.

(h) After 52 weeks, payments are 60 percent of SAWW for duration of disability.

(i) Payments subject to Unemployment Insurance benefit offsets.

(j) Benefit payments are frozen at $447.92 until August 1, 1988.

(k) Additional $6 will be added per dependent if weekly benefits are below $150.

(l) Total maximum payable not to exceed 250 times the SAWW in effect at time of injury.

(m) Payments subject to reduction by Unemployment Insurance and Social Security benefits, in addition to benefits paid by an employer disability, retirement or pension plan.

(n) Benefit payments are frozen at $299 for injuries occurring on or after 7/1/87 until 7/1/89.

(o) Effective July 1, 1988, maximum weekly benefit will be $245.

(p) If the employee's AWW exceeds 40 percent of the SAWW, compensation will increase to 66-2/3 percent of the employee's AWW (not to exceed 150 percent of the SAWW).

(q) Total maximum equals the sum of 700 multiplied by the maximum weekly benefit payable at time of injury.

(r) Additional $5 per week for each dependent child, not to exceed worker's net wage.

(s) Payments are reduced by 50 percent of Social Security benefits.

(t) Payments are subject to offset if concurrent and/or duplicate with those under employer non-occupational benefits plan.

(u) Benefit payments are frozen at $231 from November 1, 1987 until November 1, 1990.

(v) Additional $9 for each dependent; including a non-working wife; aggregate not to exceed 80 percent of worker's AWW.

(w) Each cummulative $10 increase in the AWW for manufacturing production workers will increase the maximum weekly benefit by $7 per week.

(x) Additional $5 for dependent spouse and each dependent child up to four, but not to exceed 100 percent of SAWW.

(y) Additional $10 will be paid for each dependent under age 21.

Table 8.24
ESTIMATES OF WORKERS' COMPENSATION PAYMENTS, BY STATE AND TYPE OF INSURANCE: 1984-85*
(In thousands of dollars)

State or other jurisdiction	1984				1985				Percentage change in total payment from 1984 to 1985
	Total	Insurance losses paid by private insurance(a)	State and federal fund disbursements(b)	Self insurance payments(c)	Total	Insurance losses paid by private insurance(a)	State and federal fund disbursements(b)	Self insurance payments(c)	
United States	$19,685,368	$10,609,775	$5,404,553	$3,671,040	$22,470,112	$12,334,404	$5,873,584	$4,262,124	14.1
Alabama	166,350	118,850	...	47,500	202,577	144,577	...	58,000	21.8
Alaska	92,842	77,342	...	15,500	109,413	91,113	...	18,300	17.8
Arizona	165,243	92,518	57,703	15,022	197,571	108,643	70,967	17,961	19.6
Arkansas	133,735	89,135	...	44,600	142,170	99,270	...	42,900	6.3
California	2,655,267	1,538,604	319,663	797,000	3,243,307	1,866,429	402,878	974,000	22.1
Colorado	250,812	105,890	112,622	32,300	281,046	130,008	114,838	36,200	12.1
Connecticut	266,155	215,463	...	50,692	304,811	249,880	...	54,931	14.5
Delaware	36,208	27,308	...	8,900	40,057	30,757	...	9,300	10.6
Florida	685,085	482,115	...	202,970	814,546	560,982	...	253,564	18.9
Georgia	295,929	255,129	...	40,800	360,028	310,328	...	49,700	21.7
Hawaii	121,878	91,128	...	30,750	126,228	90,278	...	35,950	3.6
Idaho	56,048	38,688	11,260	6,100	66,031	45,935	13,146	6,950	17.8
Illinois	824,872	601,872	...	223,000	911,839	665,576	...	246,263	10.5
Indiana	133,984	116,784	...	17,200	152,301	132,801	...	19,500	13.7
Iowa	119,491	107,591	...	11,900	124,888	112,488	...	12,400	4.5
Kansas	125,791	107,441	...	18,350	141,700	120,800	...	20,900	12.6
Kentucky	193,854	145,354	...	48,500	225,279	168,779	...	56,500	16.2
Louisiana	431,448	345,148	...	86,300	465,971	372,771	...	93,200	8.0
Maine	169,547	127,747	...	41,800	210,969	158,969	...	52,000	24.4
Maryland	272,152	186,432	35,020	50,700	305,775	210,080	38,095	57,600	12.4
Massachusetts	451,329	414,029	...	37,300	509,661	468,361	...	41,300	12.9
Michigan	733,051	392,627	32,424	308,000	782,054	435,605	38,449	308,000	6.7
Minnesota	373,478	313,835	43	59,600	431,420	360,349	2,171	68,900	15.5
Mississippi	82,826	74,623	...	8,203	97,589	89,243	...	8,346	17.8
Missouri	195,316	158,916	...	36,400	233,248	189,748	...	43,500	19.4
Montana	78,651	31,651	38,666 (d)	8,334	102,356	40,142	52,835 (d)	9,379	30.1
Nebraska	60,832	53,132	...	7,700	65,443	57,143	...	8,300	7.6
Nevada	106,090	1,121	91,658	13,311	123,434	920	105,950	16,564	16.3
New Hampshire	76,595	67,298	...	9,297	90,964	80,599	...	10,365	18.8
New Jersey	443,733	377,233	...	66,500	501,382	422,482	...	78,900	13.0
New Mexico	113,851	107,451	...	6,400	139,522	131,622	...	7,900	22.5
New York	857,969	467,272	238,295	152,402	985,156	533,024	271,842	180,290	14.8
North Carolina	201,232	150,232	...	51,000	241,699	180,699	...	61,000	20.1
North Dakota	28,860	166	28,694	...	32,731	480	32,251	...	13.4
Ohio	1,259,348	4,022	818,726	436,600	1,440,672	4,921	931,751	504,000	14.4

ESTIMATES OF WORKERS' COMPENSATION PAYMENTS—Continued

State or other jurisdiction	1984				1985				Percentage change in total payment from 1984 to 1985
	Total	Insurance losses paid by private insurance(a)	State and federal fund disbursements(b)	Self insurance payments(c)	Total	Insurance losses paid by private insurance(a)	State and federal fund disbursements(b)	Self insurance payments(c)	
Oklahoma	266,197	186,700	37,897	41,600	291,039	201,822	43,817	45,400	9.3
Oregon	345,838	123,373	165,665	56,800	406,611	156,380	182,631	67,600	17.6
Pennsylvania	888,046	631,466	53,580(d)	203,000	998,343	716,951	52,392(d)	229,000	12.4
Rhode Island	85,041	78,541	...	6,500	97,132	89,632	...	7,500	14.2
South Carolina	127,908	105,970	...	21,938	155,853	129,153	...	26,700	21.8
South Dakota	20,863	18,163	...	2,700	26,063	22,663	...	3,400	24.9
Tennessee	174,511	158,611	...	15,900	204,255	185,655	...	18,600	17.0
Texas	1,293,089	1,293,089	...	...	1,563,778	1,563,778	...	...	20.9
Utah	66,205	27,512	28,393	10,300	80,296	30,738	37,058	12,500	21.3
Vermont	25,250	23,150	...	2,100	30,328	27,828	...	2,500	20.1
Virginia	243,375	204,517	...	38,858	268,971	229,890	...	39,081	10.5
Washington	627,009	15,906	471,103	140,000	784,518	23,513	586,005	175,000	25.1
West Virginia	248,582	1,231	162,278	85,073	285,156	1,887	185,047	98,222	14.7
Wisconsin	238,577	196,377	47,296	42,200	287,303	228,381	...	58,922	20.4
Wyoming	47,753	457	47,296	...	47,043	988	46,055	...	-1.5
Dist. of Col.	73,705	60,565	...	13,140	74,179	59,343	...	14,836	.6
Federal:									
Civilian Employee Program(e)	1,003,563	...	1,003,563	...	1,055,285	...	1,055,285	...	5.2
Black Lung Program(f)	1,641,131	...	1,641,131	...	1,602,977	...	1,602,977	...	-2.3
Other(g)	8,873	...	8,873	...	7,144	...	7,144	...	-19.5

*Data for 1985 preliminary; data for 1984 are revised figures. Calendar year figures, except for Montana, Nevada, and West Virginia, for Federal civilian employees and "other" Federal workers' compensation, and for state fund disbursements in Maryland, North Dakota, and Wyoming, represent fiscal years ended in 1984 and 1985. Includes benefit payments under the Longshoremen's and Harbor Workers' Compensation Act and extensions for the states in which such payments are made.

Source: Social Security Administration, *Social Security Bulletin*, January 1988.

Note: The above figures are the most recent ones available for workers' compensation payment estimates.

(a) Net cash and medical payments paid during calendar year by private insurance carriers under standard workers' compensation policies. Data primarily from A.M. Best Company, a national data-collecting agency for private insurance.

(b) Net cash and medical benefits paid by state funds compiled from state reports (published and unpublished); estimated for some states.

(c) Cash and medical benefits paid by self-insurers, plus the value of medical benefits paid by employers carrying workers' compensation policies that do not include standard medical coverage. Estimated from available state data.

(d) Includes payment of supplemental pensions from general funds.

(e) Payments to civilian Federal employees (including emergency relief workers) and their dependents under the Federal Employees' Compensation Act.

(f) Includes $594,061,000 in 1984 and $574,527,000 in 1985 paid by the Department of Labor.

(g) Primarily payments made to dependents of reservists who died while on duty in the Armed Forces, to individuals under the War Hazards Act, War Claims Acts, and Civilian War Benefits Act, and to Civil Air Patrol and Reserve Officers Training Corps personnel, persons involved in maritime war risks, and law enforcement officers (Public Law 90-921).

Table 8.25
STATUS OF APPROVED STATE PLANS DEVELOPED IN ACCORDANCE WITH THE FEDERAL OCCUPATIONAL SAFETY AND HEALTH ACT
(As of January 1988)

State or other jurisdiction	Opera-tional status agreement(a)	Different standards(b)	7(c)(l)On-site consultation agreements(c)	On-shore maritime coverage	Date of initial approval	Date certified(d)	Date of 18(e) final approval(e)
Alaska............	...	★	★	...	7/31/73	9/09/77	9/26/84
Arizona...........	...	★	...	...	10/29/74	9/18/81	6/20/85
California........	★	★	★	★	4/24/73	8/12/77	
Connecticut(f)	...	...	★	...	10/02/78		
Hawaii	...	★	★	...	12/28/73	4/26/78	4/30/84
Indiana	...	...	...	...	2/25/74	9/24/81	9/26/86
Iowa	...	...	★	...	7/20/73	9/14/76	7/02/85
Kentucky	...	...	...	...	7/23/73	2/08/80	6/13/85
Maryland	...	...	★	...	6/28/73	2/15/80	7/18/85
Michigan	★	★	★	...	9/24/73	1/16/81	
Minnesota	...	...	★	★	5/29/73	9/28/76	7/30/85
Nevada	★	...	...	...	12/28/73	8/13/81	
New Mexico.......	★	...	...	...	12/04/75	12/04/84	
New York(f)	...	...	★	...	6/01/84		
North Carolina	★	...	★	...	1/26/73	9/29/76	
Oregon	★	★	★	★	12/22/72	9/15/82	
South Carolina	...	...	★	...	11/30/72	7/28/76	12/15/87
Tennessee........	...	...	★	...	6/28/73	5/03/78	7/22/85
Utah	...	...	★	...	1/04/73	11/11/76	7/16/85
Vermont..........	★	...	★	★	10/01/73	3/04/77	
Virginia..........	★	...	★	...	9/23/76	8/15/84	
Washington	★	★	...	★	1/19/73	1/26/82	
Wyoming	...	...	★	...	4/25/74	12/18/80	6/27/85
Puerto Rico	★	...	...	...	8/30/77	9/07/82	
Virgin Islands	...	...	...	...	9/11/73	9/22/81	4/17/84

Source: Directorate of Federal-State Operations, Office of State Programs, Occupational Safety and Health Administration, U.S. Department of Labor.
Key:
★—Yes
...—No
(a) Concurrent federal jurisdiction suspended.

(b) Standards frequently not identical to the federal.
(c) On-site consultation is available in all states either through a 7(c)(l) Agreement or under a State Plan.
(d) Developmental steps satisfactorily completed.
(e) Concurrent federal jurisdiction relinquished (supersedes Operational Status Agreement).
(f) Plan covers only state and local government employees.

Table 8.26
SELECTED STATE CHILD LABOR STANDARDS AFFECTING MINORS UNDER 18
(As of January 1988)
(Occupational coverage, exemptions and deviations usually omitted)

State or other jurisdiction	Documentary proof of age required up to age indicated(a) (c)	Maximum daily and weekly hours and days per week for minors under 16 unless other age indicated(b)	Nightwork prohibited for minors under 16 unless other age indicated(b)
Federal (FLSA)....	(c)	8-40, non-school period. Schoolday/week: 3-18(d)	7 p.m. (9 p.m. June 1 through Labor Day) to 7 a.m.
Alabama..........	17; 19 in mines and quarries.	8-40-6. Schoolday/week: 3-18.	7 p.m. (9 p.m. during summer vacation) to 7 a.m. 10 p.m. before non-schoolday to 5 a.m., 16 and 17 if enrolled in school.
Alaska...........	18	6-day week, under 18. Schoolday/week: 9(e)-23.	9 p.m. to 5 a.m.
Arizona..........	(f)	8-40.	9:30 p.m. (11 p.m. before non-schoolday; 7 p.m. in door-to-door sales or deliveries) to 6 a.m.
Arkansas	16	8-48-6. 10-54-6, 16 and 17.	7 p.m. (9 p.m. before non-schoolday) to 6 a.m. 11 p.m. before schoolday to 6 a.m., 16 and 17.
California.......	18	8-48-6, under 18. Schoolday/week: 4-28(g) under 18, except 8 before non-schoolday, 16 and 17.	10 p.m. (12:30 a.m. before non-schoolday) to 5 a.m., under 18.
Colorado	16	8-40, under 18. Schoolday: 6.	9:30 a.m. to 5 a.m., before schoolday.
Connecticut	18	9-48, under 18. 8-48-6, under 18 in stores, and under 16 in agriculture. (Overtime permitted in certain industries.)	10 p.m. (midnight before non-schoolday in supermarkets) to 6 a.m., under 18. 11 p.m. (midnight before non-schoolday or if not attending school) to 6 a.m., 16 and 17 in restaurants or as usher in non-profit theater.
Delaware	18	8-48-6.	7 p.m. (10 p.m. on Friday, Saturday and before non-schoolday) to 6 a.m.
Florida	18	10-30-6, during school year, under 18. Schoolday: 4 when followed by schoolday, except if enrolled in vocational program.	9 p.m. to 6:30 a.m. before schoolday. Midnight to 5 a.m., before schoolday, 16 and 17
Georgia	18	8-40. Schoolday: 4.	9 p.m. to 6 a.m.
Hawaii	18	8-40-6. Schoolday: 10(e). 9-54.	7 p.m. to 7 a.m. (9 p.m. to 6 a.m. June 1 through day before Labor Day).
Idaho	(f)		9 p.m. to 6 a.m.
Illinois	16	8-48-6. Schoolday/week: 3 [8(e)]-23(g).	7 p.m. (9 p.m. June 1 through Labor Day) to 7 a.m.

SELECTED STATE CHILD LABOR STANDARDS—Continued

State or other jurisdiction	Documentary proof of age required up to age indicated(a)	Maximum daily and weekly hours and days per week for minors under 16 unless other age indicated(b)	Nightwork prohibited for minors under 16 unless other age indicated(b)
Indiana	17	8-40-6, under 17, except minors of 16 not enrolled in school. 9-48 during summer vacation, minors of 16 enrolled in school. Schoolday/week: 3-23.	7 p.m. (9 p.m. before non-schoolday) to 6 a.m.
Iowa	18	8-40. Schoolday/week: 4-28.	10 p.m. (midnight before non-schoolday) to 6 a.m., minors of 16 enrolled in school.
Kansas	16(f)	8-40.	7 p.m. (9 p.m. June 1 through Labor Day) to 7 a.m.
Kentucky	18	8-40 Schoolday/week: 3-18, under 16. 6 (8 Saturday and Sunday)-40, 16 and 17 if attending school.	7 p.m. (9 p.m. June 1 through Labor Day) to 7 a.m. 11:30 p.m. (1 a.m. Friday and Saturday) to 6 a.m. when school in session, 16 and 17.
Louisiana	18	8-40-6. Schoolday: 3.	10 p.m. before schoolday to 7 a.m.
Maine	16	8-48-6. Schoolday/week: 4-28.	10 p.m. to 7 a.m.
Maryland	18	8-40. Schoolday/week:4-23(g), under 16. 12(e), under 18.	9 p.m. to 7 a.m., under 15. 10 p.m. to 7 a.m., 15.
Massachusetts	18	8-48-6. 4-24 in farmwork, under 14. 9-48-6, 16 and 17.	8 p.m. (9 p.m. Memorial Day through Labor Day) to 7 a.m. 8 hours of non-work, non-school time required in each 24-hour day, 16 and 17.
Michigan	18	10-48-6, under 18. Schoolweek: 48(e), under 18.	6 p.m. to 6:30 a.m. 10 p.m. (midnight in restaurants on Friday, Saturday and vacation) to 6 a.m., 16 and 17.
Minnesota	18	8-40.	9 p.m. to 7 a.m. 10:30 p.m. to 6 a.m., 16 and 17 if attending school. 11:30 p.m. to 6 a.m., 16 and 17 if not attending school.
Mississippi	(f)	8-44 in factory, mill, cannery or workshop.	9 p.m. to 7 a.m.
Missouri	16	8-40-6.	7 p.m. to 6 a.m. in factory, mill, cannery or workshop.
Montana	18	...	7 p.m. (10 p.m. before non-schoolday and for minors not enrolled in school) to 7 a.m.
Nebraska	16	8-48.	8 p.m. to 6 a.m. under 14. 10 p.m. (beyond 10 p.m. before non-schoolday with special permit) to 6 a.m., 14 and 15.
Nevada	17(f)	8-48.	...

SELECTED STATE CHILD LABOR STANDARDS—Continued

State or other jurisdiction	Documentary proof of age required up to age indicated(a)	Maximum daily and weekly hours and days per week for minors under 16 unless other age indicated(b)	Nightwork prohibited for minors under 16 unless other age indicated(b)
New Hampshire	18	8 on non-schoolday, 48-hour week during vacation, if enrolled in school. 10-48 at manual or mechanical labor in manufacturing. 10¼-54 at such labor in other employment, under 16 if not enrolled in school, and 16 and 17. Schoolday/week: 3-23 if enrolled in school.	9 p.m. to 7 a.m. if enrolled in school.
New Jersey	18	8-40-6, under 18. 10-hour day, 6-day week in agriculture. Schoolday: 8(e).	6 p.m. to 7 a.m. 11 p.m. to 6 a.m., 16 and 17 during school term, with specified variations.
New Mexico	16	8-44 (48 in special cases), under 14.	9 p.m. to 7 a.m., under 14.
New York	18	8-40-6. 8-48-6, 16 and 17. Schoolday/week: 3-23, under 16. 4-28, 16 if attending school.	7 p.m. to 7 a.m. Midnight to 6 a.m., 16 and 17.
North Carolina	18	8-40. Schoolday/week: 3-18(g).	7 p.m. (9 p.m. before non-schoolday) to 7 a.m.
North Dakota	16	8-48-6, under 18. Schoolday/week: 3-24 if not exempted from school attendance.	7 p.m. (9 p.m. June 1 through Labor Day) to 7 a.m.
Ohio	18	8-40. Schoolday/week: 3-18.	7 p.m. (9 p.m. June 1 through September 1 or during school holidays of 5 days or more) to 7 a.m.
Oklahoma	16	8-48.	6 p.m. to 7 a.m. in factories, factory workshops, pool halls or steam laundries.
Oregon	18	10-44 (emergency overtime with permit)-6. 44-hour week (emergency overtime with permit), 16 and 17.	6 p.m. to 7 a.m., except with special permit.
Pennsylvania	18	8-44-6, under 18. Schoolday/week: 4-26(g), under 16. 28 in schoolweek, 16 and 17 if enrolled in regular day school.	7 p.m. (10 p.m. during vacation from June to Labor Day) to 7 a.m. 11 p.m. (midnight before non-schoolday) to 6 a.m., 16 and 17 if enrolled in regular day school
Rhode Island	18	8-40. 9-48, 16 and 17.	7 p.m. (9 p.m. during school vacation) to 6 a.m. 11:30 p.m. (1:30 a.m. before non-schoolday) to 6 a.m., 16 and 17 if regularly attending school.
South Carolina	(f)	8-40. Schoolday/week: 3-18.	7 p.m. (9 p.m. June 1 through Labor Day) to 7 a.m.
South Dakota	16	8-40.	After 7 p.m. in mercantile establishments, under 14.
Tennessee	18	8-40. Schoolday/week: 3-18.	7 p.m. to 6 a.m. (9 p.m. to 6 a.m. before non-schooldays).
Texas	(f)	8-48.	10 p.m. (midnight before non-school day or in summer if not enrolled in summer school) to 5 a.m.

SELECTED STATE CHILD LABOR STANDARDS—Continued

State or other jurisdiction	Documentary proof of age required up to age indicated(a)	Maximum daily and weekly hours and days per week for minors under 16 unless other age indicated(b)	Nightwork prohibited for minors under 16 unless other age indicated(b)
Utah	(f)	8-40 Schoolday: 4.	9:30 p.m. to 5 a.m. before schoolday.
Vermont	16(f)	8-48-6. 9-50, 16 and 17.	7 p.m. to 6 a.m.
Virginia	16	8-40-6.	7 p.m. (9 p.m. before non-schoolday and June 1 to Labor Day or with special permit) to 7 a.m.
Washington	18	8-hour day, 5-day week, under 18. Schoolday/week: 3-18.	7 p.m. (9 p.m. during summer vacation) to 7 a.m. After 9 p.m. on consecutive nights preceding school-day, 16 and 17.
West Virginia	18	8-40-6.	8 p.m. to 5 a.m.
Wisconsin	18	8-24-6 when school in session and 8-40-6 in non-schoolweek. 8-40-6 when school in session and 8-48-6 in non-schoolweek (voluntary overtime per day and week permitted in non-schoolweek up to 50-hour week), 16 and 17 if required to attend school.	8 p.m. (9:30 p.m. before non-schoolday) to 7 a.m. 12:30 a.m. to 6 a.m., except where under direct adult supervision, and with 8 hours rest between end of work and schoolday, 16 and 17 if required to attend school.
Wyoming	16	8-56.	10 p.m. (midnight before non-schoolday and for minors not enrolled in school) to 5 a.m. Midnight to 5 a.m., females 16 and 17.
Dist. of Col.	18	8-48-6, under 18.	7 p.m. (9 p.m. June 1 through Labor Day) to 7 a.m. 10 p.m. to 6 a.m., 16 and 17.
Guam	16	8-40-6, under 18. Schoolday: 9(e), under 18.	After 10 p.m. on schoolday, under 18.
Puerto Rico	18	8-40-6, under 18. Schoolday: 8(e).	6 p.m. to 8 a.m. 10 p.m. to 6 a.m., 16 and 17.

Source: Division of State Employment Standards Programs, Office of State Liaison and Legislative Analysis, Employment Standards Administration, U.S. Department of Labor.

(a) Many states require an employment certificate for minors under 16 and an age certificate for 16 and 17 year olds; in a few states other types of evidence are acceptable as proof of age. In most states the law provides that age certificates may be issued upon request for persons above the age indicated, or although not specified in the law, such certificates are issued in practice.

(b) State hours limitations on a schoolday and in a schoolweek usually apply only to those enrolled in school. Several states exempt high school graduates from the hours and/or nightwork or other provisions, or have less restrictive provisions for minors participating in various school-work programs. Separate nightwork standards in messenger service and street trades are common, but are not displayed in table.

(c) Not required. State age or employment certificates which show that the minor has attained the minimum age for the job are accepted under the Fair Labor Standards Act.

(d) Students of 14 and 15 enrolled in approved Work Experience and Career Exploration programs may work during school hours up to three hours on a schoolday and 23 hours in a schoolweek.

(e) Combined hours of work and school.

(f) Proof of age is not mandatory under state law in Arizona, Idaho, Mississippi, South Carolina, Texas and Utah; or in Kansas for minors enrolled in secondary schools, and in Nevada and Vermont for employment outside school hours. For purposes of the Fair Labor Standards Act (FLSA), federal age certificates are issued upon request by the State Department of Labor in South Carolina and by Federal Wage and Hour Offices in Mississippi and Texas. In Utah, state law directs schools to issue age certificates upon request.

Wage and Hour Offices will also issue federal age certificates upon request in Florida, Georgia, Kentucky, and Tennessee, where the states' required proof-of-age documents do not conform to those of Federal Child Labor Regulation No. 1. Also, for FLSA purposes, birth or baptismal certificates are accepted in lieu of age certificates in Alaska and Guam.

(g) More hours are permitted when school is in session less than five days.

Table 8.27
CHANGES IN BASIC MINIMUM WAGES IN NON-FARM EMPLOYMENT UNDER STATE LAW: SELECTED YEARS 1968 TO 1988

State or other jurisdiction	1968(a)	1970(a)	1972	1976(a)	1979	1980	1981	1984	1985	1986	1987	1988
Federal (FLSA)	$1.15 & $1.60	$1.30 & $1.60	$1.60	$2.20 & $2.30	$2.90	$3.10	$3.35	$3.35	$3.35	$3.35	$3.35	$3.35
Alabama	...	...	...	...	...	...	...	...	...	...	...	...
Alaska	2.10	2.10	2.10	2.80	3.40	3.60	3.85	3.85	3.85	3.85	3.85	3.85
Arizona	18.72-26.40/wk.(b)	18.72-26.40/wk.(b)	18.72-26.40/wk.(b)	...	...	...	...	...	...	...	...	...
Arkansas	1.25/day(b)	1.60	1.20	1.90	2.30	2.55	2.70	3.05	3.15	3.15	3.15	3.25(c)
California	1.65(b)	1.65(b)	1.65(b)	2.00	2.90	2.90	3.35	3.35	3.35	3.35	3.35	3.35(c)
Colorado	1.00-1.25(b)	1.00-1.25(b)	1.00-1.25(b)	1.00-1.25(b)	1.90	1.90	1.90	2.50	3.00	3.00	3.00	3.00
Connecticut	1.40	1.60	1.85	2.21 & 2.31	2.91	3.12	3.37	3.37	3.37	3.37	3.37	3.37(c)
Delaware	1.25	1.25	1.60	2.00	2.00	2.00	2.00	3.00	3.00	3.00	3.00	3.35
Florida	...	...	...	...	...	...	...	...	...	...	...	...
Georgia	...	...	1.25	1.25	1.25	1.25	1.25	1.25	3.25	3.25	3.25	3.25
Hawaii	1.25	1.60	1.60	2.40	2.65	2.90	3.10	3.35	3.35	3.35	3.35	3.85
Idaho	1.15	1.25	1.40	1.60	2.30	2.30	2.30	2.30	2.30	2.30	2.30	2.30
Illinois	...	...	1.40	2.10	2.30	2.30	2.30	2.65	3.00	3.35	3.35	3.35
Indiana	1.15	1.25	1.25	1.25	2.00	2.00	2.00	2.00	2.00	2.00	2.00	2.00
Iowa	...	...	...	...	...	...	...	...	...	...	...	...
Kansas	.65-.75(b)	.65-.75(b)	.65-.75(b)	1.60	1.60	1.60	1.60	1.60	1.60	1.60	1.60	1.60
Kentucky	...	...	...	...	2.00	2.15	2.15	2.60	2.60	2.60	3.35	3.35
Louisiana	...	...	...	...	...	...	...	...	...	...	...	...
Maine	1.40	1.60	1.40-1.80	2.30	2.90	3.10	3.35	3.35	3.45	3.55(c)	3.65	3.65
Maryland	1.00 & 1.15	1.30	1.60	2.20 & 2.30	2.90	3.10	3.35	3.35	3.35	3.35	3.35	3.35
Massachusetts	1.60	1.60	1.75	2.10	2.90	3.10	3.35	3.35	3.35	3.35(c)	3.55	3.65(c)
Michigan	1.25	1.25	1.60	2.20	2.90	3.10	3.35	3.35	3.35	3.35	3.35	3.35
Minnesota	.70-1.15(b)	.70-1.15(b)	.75-1.60	1.80	2.30	2.90	3.10	3.35	3.35	3.35	3.35	3.55 & 3.50(c)
Mississippi	...	...	...	...	...	...	...	...	...	...	...	...
Missouri	...	...	...	...	...	...	...	...	...	...	...	...
Montana	1.00	1.00	1.00	1.80	2.00	2.00	2.00	2.75	2.75	3.05(c)	3.35	3.35
Nebraska	1.25	1.30	1.00	1.60	1.60	1.60	1.60	1.60	1.60	1.60	1.60	3.35
Nevada	1.40	1.45-1.60	1.60	2.20 & 2.30	2.75	2.75	2.75	2.75	2.75	2.75	2.75	3.35
New Hampshire	1.45-1.60	1.50	1.60	2.20-2.30	2.90	2.70	2.75	3.35	3.35	3.35	3.45	3.55(c)
New Jersey	1.40	1.50	1.50	2.20	2.50	3.10	3.35	3.35	3.35	3.35	3.35	3.35

CHANGES IN BASIC MINIMUM WAGE—Continued

State or other jurisdiction	1968(a)	1970(a)	1972	1976(a)	1979	1980	1981	1984	1985	1986	1987	1988
New Mexico	1.15-1.40	1.30-1.60	1.30-1.60	2.00	2.30	2.65	2.90	3.35	3.35	3.35	3.35	3.35
New York	1.60	1.60	1.85	2.30	2.90	3.10	3.35	3.35	3.35	3.35	3.35	3.35
North Carolina	1.00	1.25	1.45	2.00	2.50	2.75	2.90	3.35	3.35	3.35	3.35	3.35
North Dakota	1.00-1.25	1.00-1.45	1.00-1.45	2.00-2.20	2.10-2.30	2.60-3.10	2.80-3.10	2.80-3.10	2.80-3.10	2.80-3.10	2.80-3.10	2.80-3.10
Ohio	.75-1.25(b)	.75-1.25(b)	.75-1.25(b)	1.60	2.30	2.30	2.30	2.30	2.30	2.30	2.30	2.30
Oklahoma	1.00	1.00	1.40	1.80	2.00	2.00	3.10	3.35	3.35	3.35	3.35	3.35
Oregon	1.25	1.25	1.25	2.30	2.30	2.90	3.10	3.10	3.10	3.35	3.35	3.35
Pennsylvania	1.15	1.30	1.60	2.20	2.90	3.10	3.35	3.35	3.35	3.35	3.35	3.35
Rhode Island	1.40	1.60	1.60	2.30	2.30	2.65	2.90	3.35	3.35	3.35	3.55	3.65
South Carolina	. . .	. . .	. . .	. . .	. . .	. . .	. . .	. . .	. . .	. . .	. . .	. . .
South Dakota	17.00-20.00/wk.	1.00	1.00	2.00	2.30	2.30	2.30	2.80	2.80	2.80	2.80	2.80
Tennessee	. . .	. . .	1.40	1.40	1.40	1.40	1.40	1.40	1.40	1.40	1.40	3.35
Utah	1.00-1.15(b)	1.00-1.15(b)	1.20-1.35(b)	1.55-1.70(b)	2.20-2.45(b)	2.35-2.60(b)	2.50-2.75(b)	2.50-2.75(b)	2.50-2.75(b)	2.50-2.75(b)	2.50-2.75(b)	2.50-2.75(b)
Vermont	1.40	1.60	1.60	2.30	2.90	3.10	3.35	3.35	3.35	3.35(c)	3.45	3.55(c)
Virginia	. . .	. . .	. . .	2.00	2.35	2.35	2.65	2.65	2.65	2.65	2.65	2.65
Washington	1.60	1.60	1.60	2.20-2.30	2.30	2.30	2.30	2.30	2.30	2.30	2.30	2.30
West Virginia	1.00	1.00	1.20	2.00	2.20	2.20	2.75	3.05	3.05	3.05	3.35	3.35
Wisconsin	1.25(b)	1.30(b)	1.45(b)	2.10	2.80	3.00	3.25	3.25	3.25	3.25	3.25	3.35
Wyoming	1.20	1.30	1.50	1.60	1.60	1.60	1.60	1.60	1.60	1.60	1.60	1.60
Dist. of Col.	1.25-1.40	1.60-2.00	1.60-2.25	2.25-2.75	2.46-3.00	2.50-3.50	2.50-3.75	3.50-3.90	3.50-3.95	3.50-3.95	3.50-4.50	3.50-4.85
Puerto Rico	.43-1.60	.43-1.60	.65-1.60	.76-2.50	1.20-2.50	1.20-2.50	1.20-3.35	1.20-3.35	1.20-3.35	1.20-3.35	1.20-3.35	1.20-3.35

Source: Prepared by the Division of State Employment Standards Programs, Office of State Liaison and Legislative Analysis, Employment Standards Administration, U.S. Department of Labor.

Note: Rates are for January 1 of each year, except in 1968 and 1972 which show rates as of February. The rates are per hour unless otherwise indicated. A range of rates, as in North Dakota and a few other states, reflects rates which differ by industry, occupation, geographic zone or other factors, as established under wage-board type laws or by statute.

(a) Under the federal Fair Labor Standards Act (FLSA), the two rates shown in 1968, 1970, and 1976 reflect the former multiple-track minimum wage system in effect from 1961 to 1978. The lower rate applied to newly-covered persons brought under the act by amendments, whose rates were gradually phased in. A similar dual-track system was also in effect in certain years under the laws in Connec-ticut, Maryland and Nevada.

(b) The law applies only to women and minors.

(c) Scheduled future increases have been enacted in Arkansas, California, Connecticut, Massachusetts, Minnesota, New Hampshire, and Vermont as follows: Arkansas to $3.30 on January 1, 1989; California, $4.25 on July 1, 1988; Connecticut, $4.25 on October 1, 1988; Massachusetts, $3.75 on July 1, 1988; New Hampshire, $3.65 on January 1, 1989; and Vermont, $3.65 on July 1, 1988. Minnesota adopted a two-tier wage schedule effective in 1988: the higher rate applies to employers covered by the FLSA; the lower rate to employers not covered by the FLSA. These rates will increase to $3.85 and $3.65 on January 1, 1989, and to $3.95 and $3.80 on January 1, 1990.

STATE REGULATION OF OCCUPATIONS AND PROFESSIONS

By Frances Stokes Berry and Pamela L. Brinegar

Occupational licensure is an exercise of the state's inherent police power to protect the health, safety and welfare of its citizens. More than 800 occupations and professions are licensed in one or more states today, and the majority of the states license about 60 professions in common. Five generally accepted criteria indicate when licensure is appropriate: unregulated practice of the occupation poses a serious risk to a consumer's life, health, safety or economic well-being, and the potential for harm is recognizable and likely to occur; the practice of the occupation requires a high degree of skill, knowledge and training; the functions and responsibilities of the practitioner require independent judgment and the members of the occupational group practice independently; the scope-of-practice of the occupation is distinguishable from other licensed and unlicensed occupations; and the economic impact on the public of regulating this occupational group is justified. Failure to meet these criteria, in general, indicates that licensure is not justified or that some less restrictive type of regulation, such as registration or certification, may be appropriate.[1]

Occupational and professional groups seek licensure for many reasons: It offers practitioners an opportunity for increased status; it can lead to increased economic benefits (for example, licensure is sometimes a prerequisite for third-party reimbursement); and licensure offers mechanisms for keeping unqualified or unscrupulous practitioners from engaging in the occupations or professions.

The benefits of protecting the public from incompetent practitioners can have negative side effects, however. Several pitfalls of occupational regulation are now recognized. By restricting the number of people entering a profession, licensure may result in increased costs to consumers of some professional services. This restriction can also result in a shortage of licensed professional services in certain geographic areas. In many fields, auxiliary professions have been underused or their ability to work independently has been hampered. Licensure often focuses on testing applicants for the initial license and is less concerned about the competence and performance of practitioners after the license is granted. State laws frequently place restrictions on advertising and on various business structures and practices.

State officials concerned with occupational and professional licensing today face at least four major issues: 1) setting appropriate criteria for determining which of the growing number of groups requesting licensure should receive it; 2) evaluating the organization, structure, composition and performance of licensure boards; 3) assessing the continuing competence of licensed practitioners; and 4) creating mechanisms for exchanging information.

Sunrise

State legislatures each year are approached by numerous occupations requesting state regulation. Since 1950, the number of newly licensed allied health professions has expanded rapidly with the addition of such groups as physical therapists, psychologists, social workers, radiologic technicians, emergency medical personnel, physicians' assistants, and many others. (See Table 8.28 for a list of selected health professions regulated by the states.)

To help legislators establish licensure criteria, 14 states in the last 10 years have instituted formal sunrise processes. Under sunrise programs, professional groups usually

Frances Stokes Berry is Deputy Director for Secretariat Services and Pamela L. Brinegar is a Research Associate in the Center for Health and Regulation at The Council of State Governments.

draft legislation providing for regulation of the profession and then attempt to convince legislators of its necessity. A legislative or executive body reviews applications for state regulation from representatives of the occupation. Generally, the process includes questions designed to measure the costs, benefits and need for regulation. The reviewing body then recommends to the legislature whether regulation and what type of regulation is appropriate.[2]

Sunset

The sunset law was a precursor of sunrise, first proposed by Colorado in 1976 and later passed by 38 states. Sunset's unique feature was an automatic termination provision for boards and agencies unless the legislature took positive measures to re-enact them. Without exception, state sunset laws included occupational and professional licensing boards in their review cycles. Many people believed sunset would lead to the wholesale deregulation of the professions but this did not occur. Only a few occupational and professional licensing boards have been terminated under sunset, and most of those eliminated were non-functioning or relatively obscure. A few small agencies have been sunseted through reorganization into other agencies.[3]

While administrative and structural reforms were more common outcomes of sunset performance reviews, sunset laws have come under scrutiny by state legislatures as unnecessary, ineffective or costly to administer. Mississippi, Nebraska, New Hampshire and North Carolina have repealed their sunset laws. Other states, such as Kansas and Illinois, have essentially inactivated the sunset reviews while leaving the laws on the books. Still other states (e.g., Connecticut and New Hampshire) have completed the initial review of occupational and professional licensing boards and will not resume another cycle of reviews until the late 1980s. (See Table 3.25 for a summary of sunset legislation in the states.)

Enforcement and Disciplinary Procedures

At the state and federal level, incompetent practitioners — and how to find them and how to deal with them — has emerged as a priority for state legislators and regulators. Legislatures have increased funding for enforce-

ment functions and amended practice acts to expand the disciplinary sanctions available to regulators beyond suspension and revocation. The most frequent additional sanctions include administrative fines, reprimand and probation. State licensing boards are increasingly developing policies on dealing with practitioners who abuse drugs or alcohol, referring abusers to treatment programs for rehabilitation when possible, and tracking practitioners' successes and failures after treatment.

Investigative series in leading newspapers continue to draw attention to state licensing responsibilities. The *Washington Post*, for instance, gave extensive coverage in 1987 and 1988 to state health licensing systems judged either to be exemplary or lacking in suitable disciplinary procedures.

The *New York Times* in 1984 drew attention to cases involving individuals who purchased phony medical degrees from Caribbean medical schools. It is estimated that there may be as many as 10,000 persons practicing medicine as hospital residents or licensed physicians with these fraudulently obtained medical degrees. State medical boards and central licensing agencies (especially in California, Florida and New York) have developed detailed procedures for checking individual credentials and the legitimacy of non-American medical schools.

Examinations

State regulators are aware of the professional and legal standards which a licensing exam must meet.[4] Licensure examinations must be job-related and based upon an empirically conducted job analysis; they must accurately measure the domains relevant to a given profession; and they must have a point at which individuals pass or fail. This point, known as the cut score, should be established by objective criteria determined prior to the administration of the examination.

Since licensing board members may not have the expertise to independently develop and administer valid and reliable examinations, states including California, Florida, Michigan and Wisconsin have established central testing offices staffed by exam specialists to assist board members. Such states use nationally developed licensing exams to provide some assurance the exam was properly designed. Many boards that do not have access to state testing experts work with independent testing consultants.

A landmark U.S. Supreme Court decision involving licensure examinations — *Hoover vs. Ronwin* — was decided in 1984. In this case, an unsuccessful candidate for admission to the Arizona Bar sued members of the Committee on Examinations and Admissions charging that the bar examiners established a cutoff score at an artificially high level in order to exclude competitors of current Arizona lawyers, rather than to protect the public against incompetent practitioners. The court ruled that the particular bar examiners were immune from suit under federal antitrust law, but said its finding was limited to the bar examiners and would not necessarily apply to health and other regulatory boards. Although the court's decision does provide some assurance to boards relative to their immunity under federal antitrust laws, examinations must still be developed and administered in a manner which is psychometrically sound.

Organization of Licensure Boards

Historically, most licensure boards have been autonomous.[5] More than 35 states have established a central agency for some or all licensure boards. Frequently, the health boards are organized in a separate agency. However, central agencies differ widely in their statutory responsibilities and the extent of the authority exercised over board decisions.[6] In a majority of states, the central agency is responsible for administrative functions such as processing applications, issuing licenses, record keeping, fee collection and routine correspondence, while the boards continue to exercise primary policy-making powers such as conducting examinations, exercising disciplinary authority and drafting administrative regulations. In other states, such as Illinois, New York, Florida and Connecticut, the central agency has authority over board personnel, budgets, investigations and examinations. The trend since the late 1970s to centralize administrative services for licensing boards continues at a reduced pace since 1984.

The composition of licensure boards is changing as well. Traditionally, boards have been comprised exclusively of members of the regulated profession. Most states now place one or more public members on licensure boards. The California Public Members Act requires that boards be made up of a majority of lay members except for health and accountancy boards which are to have one-third lay members. A related trend adds to board membership practitioners who are specialists or auxiliaries to the profession regulated by the board, such as adding a dental hygienist to a board of dentistry.

While states continue to add public members to licensing boards, the debate continues about whether public members are effective. A Michigan study found public members had limited impact on licensing policies and procedures.[7]

Opponents of the trend toward centralization of licensure contend that it adds to bureaucracy and red tape, and reduces the responsiveness of the licensure authority to both licensee needs and citizen complaints. Further, they argue that individual licensure boards with professional members best understand the issues of examinations, professional practice and discipline.

Exchanging Information

Responding to the expressed need for a forum to share information and discuss common problems, state licensing officials formed the National Clearinghouse on Licensure, Enforcement and Regulation (CLEAR) in 1980.

CLEAR, with staff support from The Council of State Governments, maintains an information library on state licensing practices and procedures. Sixteen publications provide comparative state information on model investigative practices, licensing structures, sunset audits, public membership and financing patterns. An annual national conference, regional meetings, training programs for investigators and a newsletter provide forums for information exchange on mutual problems and innovative solutions.

To assist states with their needs to exchange enforcement information, CLEAR has established the National Disciplinary Information System, which provides information on disciplinary actions taken by states against licensed practitioners.

Footnotes

1. "Licensure" is the most restrictive form of state regulation. Under licensure laws, it

is illegal for a person to practice a profession without first meeting the standards imposed by the state. Under "certification," the state grants title protection to persons meeting predetermined standards. Those without the title may perform the services of the occupation but may not use the title. "Registration" is the least restrictive form of regulation which usually takes the form of requiring individuals to file their name, address and qualifications with a government agency before practicing the occupation. See *Occupational Licensing: Questions A Legislator Should Ask* (Lexington, Ky: The Council of State Governments, 1978) for further information on the types of regulation and the questions to answer in deciding among them.

2. For detailed information on state sunrise programs, see State Sunrise Programs: *Deciding When to Regulate Occupations* (Lexington, Ky: The Council of State Governments, 1986).

3. For a discussion of sunset outcomes, see *Ten Years of Sunset* (Columbia, SC: The State Reorganization Commission, 1986).

4. Nationally accepted guidelines are contained in *The Standards for Educational and Psychological Testing* (Washington, D.C.: American Psychological Association, 1985).

5. For a brief description of the regulatory system and a cogent discussion of key occupational licensing issues, see Benjamin Shimberg, *Occupational Licensing, A Public Perspective* (Princeton, N.J: Educational Testing Service, 1982).

6. See *Centralizing State Licensing Functions* (Lexington, Ky: The Council of State Governments, 1980).

7. See *"A Report on the Role and Effectiveness of Public Members on Licensing Boards,"* Michigan Department of Licensing and Regulation, 1980.

Table 8.28
STATE REGULATION OF HEALTH OCCUPATIONS AND PROFESSIONS: 1988

State or other jurisdiction	Acupuncturist	Chiropractor	Counselor, Professional	Counselor, Alcoholism	Counselor, Drug	Counselor, Pastoral	Counselor, Substance Abuse	Dentist	Dental Assistant	Dental Hygienist	Denturist	Dietitian	Emergency Medical Technologist	Hearing Aid Dealer & Fitter	Homeopath
Alabama		L	L					L		L			R	L	
Alaska	BA	L						L		L			L	R	
Arizona		L						L	C	L	C			L	L
Arkansas		L	L					L	C	L			R	L	
California	L	L						L	L	L			R	L	
Colorado		L						L		L			L		L
Connecticut		L						L	C	L			L	L	
Delaware		L						L	C	L			L	L	
Florida	L	L	L	C		L		L	C	L		C	L	L	
Georgia	BA	L	L					L		L		C	L	L	
Hawaii	L	L						L		L	L		L	L	
Idaho		L		C				L		L			L	L	
Illinois		L						L		L			L	L	
Indiana	**	L						L	C	L		L	L	L	
Iowa		L						L	C	L		L	L	L	
Kansas		L	L					L	C	L			L	L	
Kentucky		L						L		L			R	L	
Louisiana	**	L						L		L			R	L	
Maine		L					R	L	C	L	L	R	R	L	
Maryland	R	L	L					L	C	L		*		L	
Massachusetts	L	L						L	C	L			L	L	
Michigan		L						L	C	L			L	L	
Minnesota		L						L	C	L		L	L	L	
Mississippi		L	L					L		L		L	L	L	
Missouri		L	L					L		L			L	L	
Montana	L	L	L					L	C	L	L	R	L	L	
Nebraska		L	L					L		L			L	L	L
Nevada	L	L						L	C	L			L	L	
New Hampshire		L				C		L	L	L			L	L	
New Jersey	L	L						L		L			L	L	
New Mexico	L	L						L	C	L			L	L	
New York	L	L						L	C	L			L	R	
North Carolina	(a)	L	C					L		L		C	L	L	
North Dakota		L						L		L		L	L	L	
Ohio		L	L					L		L		L	L	L	
Oklahoma		L	C					L	C	L		L	L	L	
Oregon		L						L	C	L	C		L	L	
Pennsylvania	R**	L						L		L			L	L	
Rhode Island	L	L						L		L			L	L	
South Carolina	(b)	L	L					L	C	L			L	L	
South Dakota		L						L		L			L	L	
Tennessee		L	C					L	C	L		C	L	L	
Texas		L	L					L		L		C	L	L	
Utah	L	L						L	C	L		C	L	L	
Vermont	R	L						L	L	L			L		
Virginia	BA/R	L	L	C	C	C		L		L			L	L	
Washington	C	L						L		L			L	L	
West Virginia	BA/R	L	L					L		L	C		L	L	
Wisconsin		L						L		L	C		L	L	
Wyoming		L	*				C	L		L			L	L	
Dist. of Col.	L	L						L		L			L	L	
Puerto Rico		L						L	L	L		L			

Source: Health Professions Licensure Information System/Council of State Governments; May, 1987 — Updated March, 1988
Key:
C = Certification / L = Licensure / R = Registration
*—Enabling legislation
**—Practice under the supervision of licensed M.D.
+—Licensed in New York City, but not in New York
++—Identified in practice act, but not recognized

BA—Board approval submitted by licensed physician
NR—No current state regulation
(a) Must be licensed M.D.; certain exceptions exist.
(b) Practice under supervision of licensed M.D. or dentist.

STATE REGULATION OF HEALTH OCCUPATIONS AND PROFESSIONS: 1988
—Continued—

State or other jurisdiction	Medical Technologist	Nuclear Medicine Technologist	Nurse, Licensed Practical	Nurse Midwife	Nurse Practitioner	Nurse, Registered	Nursing Home Administrator	Occupational Therapist	Occupational Therapy Assistant	Optician	Optometrist	Pharmacist	Pharmacist Assistant	Physical Therapist
Alabama	...	...	L	C	C	L	L	(c)	(c)	...	L	L	...	L
Alaska	...	...	L	C	C	L	L	L	L	L	L	L	...	L
Arizona	...	...	L	C	C	L	L	...	...	L	L	L	...	L
Arkansas	...	...	L	C	C	L	L	...	...	L	L	L	...	L
California	L	*	L	C	C	L	L	C	C	L	L	L	...	L
Colorado	...	...	L	C	C	L	L	...	...		L	L	...	L
Connecticut	...	...	L	C	C	L	L	L	L	L	L	L	...	L
Delaware	...	*	L	C	C	L	L	L	L	...	L	L	...	L
Florida	L	L	L	C	C	L	L	L	L	L	L	L	...	L
Georgia	...	...	L	C	C	L	L	L	L	L	L	L	...	L
Hawaii	L	...	L	C		L	L	C	C	L	L	L	...	L
Idaho	...	...	L	C	C	L	L	L	L	...	L	L	...	L
Illinois	C	L	L	C	...	L	L	L	L	...	L	L	...	L
Indiana	...	*	L	C	*	L	L	L	L	...	L	L	...	L
Iowa	...	*	L	C	C	L	L	L	L	L	L	L	...	L
Kansas	...	...	L	C	C	L	L	R	R	...	L	L	...	L
Kentucky	...	*	L	C	C	L	L	L	L	L	L	L	...	L
Louisiana	...	L	L	C	C	L	L	L	L	...	L	L	...	L
Maine	...	L	L	C	C	L	L	L	L	...	L	L	...	L
Maryland	...	...	L	C	C	L	L	L	L	...	L	L	...	L
Massachusetts	...	...	L	C	C	L	L	L	L	L	L	L	...	L
Michigan	L	*	L	C	C	L	L	(c)	(c)	...	L	L	...	L
Minnesota	...	*	L	C	...	L	L	(c)	(c)	...	L	L	...	L
Mississippi	...	...	L	C	C	L	L	(c)	(c)	...	L	L	...	L
Missouri	...	...	L	C	...	L	L	(c)	(c)	...	L	L	...	L
Montana	...	...	L	C	C	L	L	L	L	...	L	L	...	L
Nebraska	...	...	L	C	C	L	L	L	L	...	L	L	...	L
Nevada	...	...	L	C	C	L	L	...	...	L	L	L	...	L
New Hampshire	...	...	L	C	C	L	L	L	L	...	L	L	...	L
New Jersey	...	L	L	C	C	L	L	(c)	(c)	L	L	L	...	L
New Mexico	...	*	L	C	C	L	L	L	L	...	L	L	...	L
New York	+	...	L	C	C	L	L	L	L	L	L	L	...	L
North Carolina	...	...	L	C	...	L	L	L	L	L	L	L	...	L
North Dakota	...	...	L	C	C	L	L	L	L	...	L	L	...	L
Ohio	...	...	L	C	...	L	L	L	L	L	L	L	...	L
Oklahoma	...	...	L	C	C	L	L	L	L	...	L	L	...	L
Oregon	...	...	L	C	C	L	L	L	L	...	L	L	...	L
Pennsylvania	...	*	L	C	C	L	L	L	L	...	L	L	...	L
Rhode Island	...	...	L	C	...	L	L	L	L	L	L	L	...	L
South Carolina	...	...	L	C	C	L	L	L	L	L	L	L	...	L
South Dakota	...	...	L	C	C	L	L	L	L	...	L	L	...	L
Tennessee	L	*	L	C	C	L	L	L	L	L	L	L	...	L
Texas	...	...	L	C	C	L	L	L	L	...	L	L	...	L
Utah	...	...	L	C	C	L	L	L	L	...	L	L	...	L
Vermont	...	L	L	C	C	L	L	...	...	L	L	L	...	L
Virginia	...	...	L	C	C	L	L	L	L	...	L	L	...	L
Washington	...	...	L	C	C	L	L	L	L	L	L	L	L	L
West Virginia	...	...	L	C	...	L	L	L	L	...	L	L	...	L
Wisconsin	...	...	L	C	...	L	L	(c)	(c)	...	L	L	...	L
Wyoming	...	L	L	C	C	L	L	...	...	L	L	L	...	L
Dist. of Col.	...	...	L	C	C	L	L	L	L	...	L	L	...	L
Puerto Rico	...	L	L	C	...	L	L	L	L	...	L	L	...	L

Key:
C = Certification / L = Licensure / R = Registration
*—Enabling legislation
**—Practice under the supervision of licensed M.D.
+—Licensed in New York City, but not in New York
+ +—Identified in practice act, but not recognized

BA—Board approval submitted by licensed physician
NR—No current state regulation
(c) To begin regulation this year (legislation pending).

STATE REGULATION OF HEALTH OCCUPATIONS AND PROFESSIONS: 1988
—Continued—

State or other jurisdiction	Physical Therapy Assistant	Physician	Physician Assistant	Podiatrist	Psychologist	Radiologic Technologist	Radiation Therapy Technologist	Respiratory Therapist	Sanitarian	Social Worker	Speech-Language Pathologist & Aud.	Therapist, Marriage & Family	Veterinarian	Veterinary Technician
Alabama	L	L	C	L	L	...	...	...	...	L	L	...	L	R
Alaska	L	L	C	L	...	...	...	...	...	...	...	...	L	R
Arizona	...	L	C	L	C	L	L	...	L	...	...	...	L	C
Arkansas	C/R	L	C	L	L	...	...	R	L	L	L	L	L	C
California	R	L	L	L	L	L	L	C	L	L	L	L	L	R
Colorado	...	L	C	L	L	...	...	*	...	L/R	...	C	L	++
Connecticut	...	L	...	L	L	*	*	...	L	L	L	C	L	C
Delaware	L	L	R	L	L	...	...	C	C	L	L	L	L	...
Florida	L	L	C	L	L	L	L	...	C	L	L	L	L	C/R
Georgia	L	L	L	L	L	...	...	C	L	L	L	...	L	R
Hawaii	...	L	C	L	L	L	L	*	L	L	L	...	L	...
Idaho	R	L	R	L	L	L	L	*	L	C	R	(4)	L	C
Illinois	...	L	C	L	C	L	*	*	L	...	L	...	L	R
Indiana	C	L	C	L	L	L	*	...	...	L	L	...	L	R
Iowa	...	L	C	L	L	L	*	C	...	...	L	L	L	...
Kansas	C/R	L	R	L	C	...	...	R	C	L	L	...	L	R
Kentucky	C	L	C	L	C/L	...	*	...	L	L	L	L	L	C
Louisiana	...	L	C	L	L	L	L	L	...	L	R	L	L	...
Maine	R	L	R	L	L	L	L	*	L	L	R	...	L	R
Maryland	L	L	C	L	L	*	*	*	...	L	L	...	L	R
Massachusetts	L	L	R	L	L	*	*	L	L	L	L	...	L	...
Michigan	...	L	L	L	...	*	*	...	C	R	*	C	L	C
Minnesota	...	L	C	L	L	*	*	*	C	C	(4)	L	L	R
Mississippi	...	L	...	L	L	...	...	*	...	L	L	...	L	R
Missouri	...	L	...	L	L	...	...	*	C	...	...	...	L	R/C
Montana	...	L	C	L	L	L	*	...	L	L	L	...	L	C
Nebraska	C	L	C	L	L	...	...	L	*	L	L	C	L	L
Nevada	L	L	C	L	C	...	...	...	...	...	C	...	L	...
New Hampshire	R	L	C	L	C	...	...	...	...	...	...	L	L	...
New Jersey	R	L	...	L	L	L	L	...	L	...	L	L	L	R
New Mexico	L	L	C	L	C	*	*	L	...	L	L	...	L	R
New York	C/R	L	R	L	L	L	L	**	C	C	L	C	L	R/L
North Carolina	L	L	R	L	L	...	...	...	L	...	L	...	L	R
North Dakota	L	L	C	L	L	...	...	L	*	L	L	...	L	R
Ohio	L	L	R	L	L	...	...	*	L	L/R	...	...	L	R
Oklahoma	L	L	C	L	L	...	...	...	L	L	L	...	L	C
Oregon	L	L	C	L	L	*	*	*	L	R	...	...	L	C
Pennsylvania	R	L	C	L	L	...	...	C	C	C	R	L	L	...
Rhode Island	...	L	R	L	C	...	...	C	C	R	L	...	L	R
South Carolina	L	L	R	L	L	...	...	C	C	R	L	...	L	...
South Dakota	R	L	C	L	L	...	...	...	...	L	L	...	L	R
Tennessee	C	L	R	L	L	L	L	L	C	L	L/C	L	L	L
Texas	L	L	R	L	C/L	...	...	C	*	L	L	L	L	...
Utah	...	L	R	L	L	...	...	...	...	...	L	...	L	...
Vermont	L	L	L	L	L	L	L	...	...	...	L	...	L	...
Virginia	L	L	R	L	L	...	...	C	*	L	L	C	L	C
Washington	...	L	R	L	L	...	...	*	C	C	L	C	L	R
West Virginia	L	L	C	L	L	L	L	...	L	L	...	...	L	R
Wisconsin	...	L	C	L	L	...	...	*	...	L	(4)	...	L	C
Wyoming	R	L	C	L	L	L	L	...	...	...	L	C	L	R
Dist. of Col.	...	L	L	L	L	...	...	*	...	...	L	L	L	...
Puerto Rico	R	L	...	L	L	...	...	...	...	...	L	...	L	L

Key:
C = Certification / L = Licensure / R = Registration
*—Enabling legislation
**—Practice under the supervision of licensed M.D.
+—Licensed in New York City, but not in New York
+ +—Identified in practice act, but not recognized

BA—Board approval submitted by licensed physician
NR—No current state regulation
(d) Regulation pending.

Table 8.29
STATE HEALTH AGENCIES: ORGANIZATIONAL CHARACTERISTICS AND SELECTED PUBLIC HEALTH RESPONSIBILITIES—FISCAL 1985

State or other jurisdiction	Organizational structure		Responsibilities:					
	Freestanding independent agency	Component of superagency	State crippled children's agency (Title V, SSA)	Mental health authority (PL 94-63)	Medicaid single state agency (Title XIX, SSA)	State health planning & development agency (PL 93-641)	Lead environmental agency	Operates institutions
Total	32	23	42	13	9	33	14	18
Alabama............	★	...	...	...	...	...	...	...
Alaska..............	...	★	★	...	...	...	...	...
Arizona.............	★	...	★	★	...	...	...	...
Arkansas	★	...	...	...	...	★	★	★
California	...	★	★	...	★	...	...	...
Colorado	★	...	★	★	...	★	★	...
Connecticut	★	...	★	...	...	...	...	...
Delaware	...	★	★	...	...	...	...	★
Florida	...	★	...	...	...	...	...	★
Georgia	...	★	★	...	...	...	...	...
Hawaii	★	...	★	★	...	★	★	★
Idaho	...	★	★	...	...	...	...	...
Illinois.............	★	...	...	...	...	★	...	...
Indiana	★	...	...	...	...	★	★	...
Iowa	★	...	...	...	...	★	...	...
Kansas	★	...	★	...	...	★	★	...
Kentucky	...	★	...	...	...	...	...	...
Louisiana	...	★	★	...	...	...	...	...
Maine	...	★	★	...	...	...	...	...
Maryland	★	...	★	★	...	★	★	★
Massachusetts	...	★	★	...	...	★	...	★
Michigan	★	...	★	★	...	...	...	★
Minnesota	★	...	★	...	...	...	...	...
Mississippi	★	...	★	...	...	...	...	...
Missouri	...	★	★	...	...	★	...	★
Montana	★	...	★	...	...	★	★	...
Nebraska	★	...	...	★	...	★	...	...
Nevada	...	★	★	...	...	...	...	...
New Hampshire	...	★	★	...	...	...	...	...
New Jersey..........	★	...	★	★	...	★	...	...
New Mexico.........	...	★	★	★	...	★	★	★
New York	★	...	★	...	...	★	★	★
North Carolina	...	★	★	...	...	...	...	★
North Dakota	★	...	...	...	...	★	★	★
Ohio	★	...	★	...	...	...	...	...
Oklahoma	★	...	...	...	...	...	★	...
Oregon	...	★	...	...	...	...	...	...
Pennsylvania	★	...	★	★	...	★	...	...
Rhode Island	★	...	★	...	...	...	...	...
South Carolina	★	...	★	...	...	★	★	...
South Dakota	★	...	★	...	...	★	...	...
Tennessee	★	...	★	...	...	...	★	...
Texas...............	★	...	★	...	★	★	...	★
Utah	★	...	★	...	★	★	★	...
Vermont	...	★	★	...	...	...	...	...
Virginia.............	★	...	★	...	...	★	...	...
Washington	...	...	★	...	...	★	...	...
West Virginia	★	...	...	★	...	★	...	★
Wisconsin...........	...	★	...	...	★	★	...	...
Wyoming...........	...	★	★	...	★	★	...	...
Dist. of Col.	...	★	★	★	...	...	...	...
American Samoa	★	...	★	★	...	...	...	★
Guam	...	★	★	...	★	...	...	★
Puerto Rico	★	...	★	...	★	...	...	★
Virgin Islands	...	★	★	★	★	★	★	★

Source: Public Health Foundation, Washington, D.C.
Key:
★—Yes
...—No

Table 8.30
PUBLIC HEALTH PROGRAM EXPENDITURES
OF STATE HEALTH AGENCIES, BY PROGRAM: FISCAL 1985
(In thousands of dollars)

State or other jurisdiction	Total	Personal health	Environmental health	Health resources	Laboratory	General administration	Funds to LHDs not allocated to program areas
United States	$6,844,344 (a)	$5,000,636 (a)	$466,987 (a)	$626,714 (a)	$229,247 (a)	$418,393 (a)	$102,367 (a)
Alabama..................	75,042	53,898	1,943	3,612	4,828	3,586	7,176
Alaska...................	30,452	19,165	86	8,038	2,250	913	0
Arizona..................	119,138	91,571	14,076	5,268	2,053	6,170	0
Arkansas	62,066	46,578	6,245	1,929	2,085	5,229	0
California................	675,886	301,864	55,481	237,628	25,786	55,126	0
Colorado	75,640	48,863	10,687	3,943	2,527	5,516	4,104
Connecticut	60,852	40,247	2,097	9,030	5,967	2,428	1,083
Delaware	38,368	33,802	2,211	551	746	1,057	0
Florida	227,039	159,696	33,726	10,212	8,058	8,800	6,546
Georgia..................	149,556	102,894	870	3,896	3,587	1,317	36,990
Hawaii	171,016	145,015	6,696	14,432	1,644	3,228	0
Idaho	21,448	16,284	87	2,229	1,853	994	0
Illinois..................	126,238	85,744	6,314	11,777	3,487	11,745	7,171
Indiana..................	74,243	38,056	22,368	3,135	3,069	7,515	100
Iowa	39,756	33,666	704	4,409	0	977	0
Kansas	35,746	18,748	7,623	3,613	2,153	3,609	0
Kentucky	105,120	66,886	4,151	5,656	2,333	16,745	9,349
Louisiana	118,286	96,828	11,395	3,947	4,959	1,156	0
Maine	18,842	15,288	1,339	524	1,433	257	0
Maryland	572,747	490,922	34,234	12,454	8,982	26,156	0
Massachusetts	230,693	209,780	6,826	3,740	5,977	4,370	0
Michigan	249,475	198,544	16,734	11,916	10,286	11,995	0
Minnesota	67,693	42,548	4,870	10,247	3,626	6,401	0
Mississippi	91,946	79,679	3,862	3,030	1,032	4,344	0
Missouri	78,170	67,084	3,573	3,739	1,982	1,793	0
Montana(b)	...	...	...	...	...	642	0
Nebraska	22,976	14,318	1,483	5,775	759	642	0
Nevada	16,286	11,489	1,127	1,717	905	295	751
New Hampshire	20,237	13,032	2,687	2,874	978	665	0
New Jersey...............	122,085	81,315	6,981	17,541	7,683	8,565	0
New Mexico..............	154,545	127,328	10,490	4,943	3,005	8,780	0
New York	537,573	368,860	13,107	81,294	42,709	31,603	0
North Carolina	148,943	128,926	7,747	2,076	6,472	3,721	0
North Dakota	15,084	7,134	3,425	1,398	1,329	1,196	602
Ohio	150,288	123,963	2,522	9,037	4,042	8,406	2,319
Oklahoma	84,832	57,833	16,593	3,857	1,217	5,332	0
Oregon	35,986	23,199	2,233	4,217	2,583	2,833	922
Pennsylvania	235,301	197,940	3,291	25,260	3,486	5,324	0
Rhode Island	27,338	13,458	3,454	5,101	3,762	1,562	0
South Carolina	150,130	108,604	21,413	4,395	4,261	11,457	0
South Dakota(b)	...	...	...	...	...	...	...
Tennessee	148,040	104,835	22,062	8,358	5,114	7,673	0
Texas....................	289,877	216,096	21,066	23,283	5,900	15,811	7,720
Utah	47,663	23,885	15,847	2,679	2,759	2,494	0
Vermont	18,900	14,868	1,128	1,438	1,167	299	0
Virginia..................	183,600	127,210	24,535	8,478	1,675	16,510	5,191
Washington	62,147	40,911	12,002	4,405	3,177	1,652	0
West Virginia	141,133	121,951	1,344	4,620	2,272	6,646	4,302
Wisconsin................	76,784	37,717	3,482	10,126	1,766	15,654	8,040
Wyoming(b)...............	...	...	...	...	...	...	...
Dist. of Col.	107,341	90,196	265	406	1,741	14,733	0
American Samoa(b)	...	...	...	...	...	...	...
Guam(b).................	...	...	...	...	...	...	...
Puerto Rico	402,680	352,419	3,148	7,003	1,230	38,879	0
Virgin Islands	64,351	43,269	487	1,619	5,764	13,212	0

Source: Public Health Foundation, Washington, D.C.
Note: The data in this table relate only to expenditure of official state health agencies. The public health expenditures of other agencies, such as separate mental health authorities, environmental agencies, and hospital authorities are not reflected.

(a) Estimated.
(b) Not reporting.

Table 8.31

PUBLIC HEALTH EXPENDITURES OF STATE HEALTH AGENCIES, BY SOURCE OF FUNDS: FISCAL 1985

(In millions of dollars)

Source of funds	Total	Personal health		Environmental health	Health resources	Laboratory	General administration	Funds to LHDs not allocated to program areas
		Noninstitutional	SHA-operated institutions					
Total	$6,844.3	$3,926.3	$1,074.3	$467.0	$626.7	$229.2	$418.4	$102.4
Subtotal, excluding federal grant and contract funds	4,294.0	1,719.0	1,030.7	348.4	534.2	205.3	370.4	86.0
State funds	3,744.4	1,471.3	893.0	283.1	492.8	186.6	331.7	85.9
Local funds	149.2	105.1	...	29.3	2.0	1.4	11.3	0.1
Fees	302.3	120.3	110.7	30.6	21.4	10.6	8.8	...
Patient fees & reimbursements from Medicaid	83.4	35.0	47.2	0.3	0.1	0.1	0.8	...
Patient fees & reimbursements from other sources	155.6	76.0	63.5	9.4	3.9	0.6	2.2	...
Other fees	63.3	9.3	...	20.9	17.4	9.9	5.8	...
Other	98.2	22.4	27.0	5.4	18.0	6.7	18.7	...
Subtotal, federal grant and contract funds(a)	2,550.3	2,207.3	43.6	118.6	92.5	23.9	48.0	16.3
Department of Health and Human Services	953.2	756.1	37.2	13.2	87.0	15.4	27.9	16.3
Public Health Service	790.2	679.4	15.2	13.1	39.9	13.7	12.5	16.3
Alcohol, Drug Abuse & Mental Health Administration	82.5	81.0	...	...	0.5	0.1	0.9	...
ADAMHA Block Grant (PL 97-35)	68.7	67.5	...	...	0.4	0.1	0.7	...
Other ADAMHA	13.7	13.5	...	...	0.1	...	0.2	...
Centers for Disease Control	150.4	108.5	...	10.6	18.2	4.4	3.9	4.9
Preventive Health & Health Services Block Grant (PL 97-35)	84.8	50.7	...	8.0	15.8	3.3	2.3	4.8
Immunization (PHSA Sec. 317)	17.9	16.5	...	...	...	0.1	1.2	...
Refugee Assistance Act of 1980 (Sec. 412C3)	7.8	5.2	...	...	2.2	0.1	0.2	0.1
Venereal Disease (PHSA Sec. 318)	21.8	21.3	...	...	...	0.4	0.1	...
Diabetes Control (PHSA Sec. 301)	3.8	3.8	...	...	...	...	...	...
Tuberculosis (PHSA Sec. 317)	3.0	3.0	...	...	...	...	...	...
Other CDC	11.3	8.0	...	2.6	0.2	0.4	0.1	...
Food & Drug Administration	1.7	...	...	1.7	...	...	...	...

PUBLIC HEALTH EXPENDITURES—Continued

Source of funds	Total	Personal health						Funds to LHDs not allocated to program areas
		Noninstitutional	SHA-operated institutions	Environmental health	Health resources	Laboratory	General administration	
Health Resources and Services Administration	529.7	487.8	1.2	0.8	15.0	6.4	7.0	11.5
Maternal and Child Health Services Block Grant (PL 97-35)	399.4	372.9	0.8	0.7	1.1	6.4	6.1	11.5
Community Health Centers (PHSA Sec. 330)	6.7	6.7	…	…	…	…	…	…
Family Planning (PHSA Title X)	88.4	88.2	…	…	…	…	0.1	…
Migrant Health (PHSA Sec. 319)	4.8	4.7	…	0.1	…	…	…	…
National Health Planning & Resources Development Act (PL 93-641)	13.0	…	…	…	12.4	…	0.6	…
Other HRSA	17.5	15.3	0.4	…	1.5	…	0.2	…
National Institutes of Health	21.0	2.0	14.0	…	1.7	2.9	0.4	…
National Center for Health Statistics	4.8	0.1	…	…	4.5	…	0.3	…
Health Care Financing Administration	112.9	42.2	21.4	…	45.3	1.3	2.7	…
Medicaid grants and contracts (SSA Title XIX)	70.7	36.2	9.8	…	22.7	…	2.0	…
Medicare grants and contracts (SSA Title XVIII)	38.6	5.1	11.6	…	19.9	1.3	0.6	…
Other HCFA	3.6	0.9	…	…	2.7	…	0.1	…
Social Security Administration	14.2	1.0	…	…	0.5	0.1	12.5	…
Office of Human Development Services	26.2	25.1	0.5	…	1.0	…	0.1	…
Developmental Disabilities (PL 91-517, PL 94-103)	10.5	9.5	…	0.0	0.9	0.0	0.0	…
Grants for Services (SSA Title XX)	12.6	12.6	…	…	…	…	0.1	…
Other OHDS	3.1	3.0	…	…	0.1	…	…	…
Other DHHS	9.7	8.5	0.5	0.1	0.1	0.3	…	…
Other federal agencies	1,579.3	1,448.4	5.9	101.9	3.9	6.8	12.5	…
Department of Agriculture	1,455.1	1,443.3	…	4.8	1.2	0.1	5.7	…
WIC	1,437.9	1,431.1	…	…	1.2	0.1	5.6	…
Other	17.2	12.2	…	4.8	…	1.6	0.1	…
Department of Labor	7.5	…	…	5.7	0.1	0.3	0.1	…
Department of Transportation	2.9	0.9	…	…	1.4	…	0.4	…
Consumer Product Safety Commission	82.3	…	0.8	76.5	…	3.2	1.7	…
Environmental Protection Agency	0.6	0.1	…	0.4	0.2	…	0.1	…
Nuclear Regulatory Commission	1.5	1.4	…	…	0.1	…	…	…
Regional Commissions	…	…	…	…	…	…	…	…
Other	29.4	2.7	5.0	14.5	1.0	1.7	4.4	…
Unidentified federal	17.8	2.8	0.6	3.6	1.6	1.7	7.6	…

Source: Public Health Foundation, Washington D.C.

Key:

- Dollar amounts less than $50,000.

(a) State health agency expenditures of federal grant and contract funds may not equal the amounts appropriated or allotted since they reflect only SHA expenditures during the state fiscal year, and do not include federal funds provided directly to local health agencies or direct assistance in lieu of cash (e.g., provision of personnel, supplies, vaccines).

ISSUES IN CORRECTIONS

By Timothy H. Matthews

The American correctional system has as its purpose the dual responsibility of protecting the public from criminals and rehabilitating those individuals in its care. The system has been hampered in its efforts to accomplish these responsibilities because of an overcrowding crisis which plagues all of its components — prisons, probation and parole. Many observers of the correctional system have acknowledged that corrections officials have their backs against the wall. Under increasing pressure from an alarmed public's demands to incarcerate more offenders for longer periods of time, officials have had to balance the need between protecting the public and providing for decent and humane care of the individuals under their supervision. Overcrowding has forced officials to redirect their priorities, develop innovative alternatives and, above all, make judicious use of existing limited resources which have inevitably dictated many adverse realities.

Correctional Populations

Incarceration rates have skyrocketed in the 1980's. Mandatory sentencing, determinate sentencing and the abolition of parole are but a few of the many independent, interacting variables that have led to tremendous inmate increases in many states. In addition, the "baby boom" generation is widely believed to have contributed to population growth in the prisons. In 1986, 502,251 inmates were incarcerated in state prisons, an increase of 8.6 percent over the previous year (*Prisoners in 1986*). This number represents an increase of 65.7 percent since 1980. According to the Bureau of Justice Statistics, these prisoners had the following characteristics:
• Over four-fifths were repeat offenders;
• Two-thirds were serving a sentence for a violent crime (i.e., murder, robbery, and assault);
• About 13 percent were first-time offenders

in for a violent crime;
• Over a third (35 percent) were under the influence of a drug at the time of their offense;
• More than half (54 percent) were under the influence of drugs and/or alcohol at the time of their offense;
• 62.3 percent used drugs on a regular basis prior to incarceration;
• 95.6 percent were male;
• 49.7 percent were white and 46.9 percent were black;
• 12.6 percent were hispanic;
• 72.4 percent were between the ages of 18-34; and
• 61.6 percent had less than 12 years of education (*Profile of State Prison Inmates 1986*).

Thus, the typical prisoner is a white or black male repeat offender, between the ages of 18-34, who has been incarcerated for a violent crime, used drugs on a regular basis and has less than a high school education.

Although most of the attention concerning our nation's correctional crowding crisis is focused on the prison dilemma, probation and parole are system components which have experienced significant crowding problems as well. In 1986, state agencies were supervising 2,035,235 probationers (an increase of 6.4 percent over the previous year) and 309,440 parolees (an increase of 9.3 percent over the previous year). In fact, the community-based populations increased at a higher rate from 1983 to 1986. Probation and parole caseloads increased by 32.4 percent over the four-year period as compared to a 24 percent increase for prisons and jails. It is not uncommon for a probation officer to have caseload of more than 200 clients.

More than 3.2 million offenders were supervised by the correctional system in 1986 (this

---

Timothy H. Matthews is a research associate with the Center for Law and Justice at The Council of State Governments.

figure includes the number in jails and under federal supervision). That represents one out of every 55 Americans. Three out of four convicted offenders are supervised in the community (*Probation and Parole, 1986*).

Table A
Offenders Under Correctional Supervision - 1986

Supervised in the community	74.7%
Probation	64.6
Parole	10.1
Incarcerated	25.3%
Jail	8.4
Prison	16.9
TOTAL	100.0%

Source: Probation and Parole 1986

State Responses to Overcrowding

Officials have responded to the continuing correctional crisis by initiating change in their operations. Many of those changes have occurred and are continually evolving in the community corrections setting. Three primary solutions exist to the problem of prison crowding — building more prisons, sentencing fewer people to prison, and releasing people from prison (either by discretionary parole release, early release or mandatory release). All of these solutions have been and will continue to be implemented.

Construction

In determining the extent of overcrowding, one need only look at the number of inmates for which an institution was designed and the number it actually holds. The average rate of overcrowding was 16.2 percent, and 35 states reported prison populations greater than their rated capacities. The National Institute of Justice reported that states would have to build 1000 new beds each week just to keep pace with the increase in prisoners. This figure does not account for those deficiences in beds mentioned above.

In 1986, 39 new prisons were opened in 25 states. Built at an average cost of $48,739 per bed and $17,134,325 per facility, these prisons were designed to hold an average of 598 inmates. In addition to the new prisons constructed, 14,691 more beds were added to 129

prisons in 29 states at an average cost of $13,135 per bed. It also was reported that 131 prisons and additions to prisons are currently under construction in 33 states and the federal system. This construction will provide 56,115 new beds at a total cost approximating $2.5 billion. Finally, 60,424 beds are in the planning stages in 40 states and the federal system (*Corrections Yearbook, 1987*). These figures do not include the estimated $22 billion being spent for the addition of 300,000 new jail beds.

Intermediate Sanctions

Front-door options available to judges for ameliorating the prison overcrowding problem have taken the form of intermediate sanctions. These are criminal sanctions that exist on the continuum of penalties between incarceration and regular probation. They are typically reserved for those offenders who are on the edge of the "in/out" decision. They pose too great a risk to be placed on regular probation, but at the same time could benefit from community supervision. Were it not for the availability of intermediate sanctions, it must be assumed that these individuals would be sentenced to a prison term. The three most common forms of intermediate sanctions are intensive probation supervision, house arrest and electronic monitoring. These sanctions may be used independently or in combination.

Intensive probation supervision. The most widely used intermediate sanction is intensive probation supervision (IPS). It has become popular as a sanction because it appears to satisfy two seemingly contradictory goals: reducing the extent of prison overcrowding by closely monitoring offenders in the community and meeting the public's demand that offenders be punished for their crimes. The IPS model widely replicated is the Georgia program. Among the strict supervision standards are:
- Five face-to-face contacts per week;
- 132 hours of mandatory community service;
- Mandatory curfew;
- Mandatory employmemt;
- Weekly check of local arrest records;
- Automatic notification of any arrests; and
- Routine and unannounced alcohol and drug testing.

By closely monitoring offenders in the community, Georgia and other states where IPS has been implemented, such as New Jersey, Oregon and Kentucky, IPS has demonstrated that offenders can be diverted from prison to probation without unacceptable risk to the community. Another major attraction leading to the increase in IPS programs is the capacity for significantly reducing the high cost associated with incarceration. Georgia reportedly saved $6,775 for each offender placed in IPS instead of sent to prison. That represented a yearly savings of more than $13 million (*New Dimensions in Probation, 1987*).

House Arrest. House arrest refers to a sentence imposed by the court in which offenders are required to stay in their homes at all times, except for periods of time permitted by the court to perform special functions such as community service or attend treatment programs. Restricted to their homes during evening hours and on weekends, they are usually entitled to leave only to go to their jobs or for medical reasons. Several states including Utah, Michigan, Illinois and California have begun to use this form of sentence as an alternative. The more restrictive programs were modeled after Florida's "Community Control Program" where as many as 5,000 criminals may be confined to their homes on a given day. Florida reported significant cost savings, reducing the cost of supervision from $28 a day for imprisonment to $3 a day for home confinement (*House Arrest, 1987*).

In addition to reducing the cost of supervision, which averages $15,000 per inmate per year to as low as $1,500 per offender per year in some jurisdictions, house arrest appears to have several advantages. One advantage is that it minimizes the adverse social consequences by allowing offenders to keep their jobs, maintain family ties and avoid the stigmatizing effects commonly associated with imprisonment. Another advantage is its flexibility in application and responsiveness to offender needs. It can be used at any point in the criminal justice system — pretrial, sentencing, parole; and it can be applied to a variety of special populations enabling courts to establish appropriate guidelines for each particular offender's needs. Perhaps the most common use of house arrest has been with DWI offenders in an attempt to keep them off the highways during non-working hours. A final advantage is that it is easy to implement since it does not require new construction, an increase in personnel or legislative change. Violations are easy to detect (either a person is at home or he is not), making revocation of one's house arrest status relatively easy to process.

Electronic Monitoring. Often used in conjunction with a house arrest sentence, electronic monitoring is another alternative used to verify the presence of an offender in a specified location. The advantages of electronic monitoring are largely the same as for house arrest. It is the use of an electronic tracking device that makes this alternative unique. It was the willingness of correctional administrators to consider, in light of prison overcrowding, such an innovation that led private manufacturers to pursue and make improvements to the technology. As many as 20 states are presently using electronic bracelets, anklets and other devices to detect violations of the house arrest conditions imposed by courts.

Although several types of technologies are currently available, the two most common involve the use of technologies which are "continuously signaling" or allow for programmed contact. Continuously signaling systems are those that broadcast signals at regular intervals from a transmitter worn by the offender through a receiver located in the offender's home to a central host computer in the probation office. Those systems which provide for programmed contact enable the probation department to call the offender at home at random or at scheduled intervals to verify the offender's presence. Two of the newer and more sophisticated electronic monitoring technologies in use involve voice verification and visual verification as an additional means for monitoring the offender's whereabouts.

Although the corrections field has become fascinated by the capabilities of the new technology, it is not without critics. It is still quite new and too untried to be hailed as a panacea. Many administrative, legal and technological questions remain to be answered before it becomes widely implemented. Cautionary hope exists, however, that the technology will bring about a cost-effective means for reducing prison overcrowding.

Parole Release

Parole systems have undergone drastic changes in several states. The question of whether it should be abolished has concerned many state officials. Eleven states have made major modifications to their parole structure since 1976 (*Observations on Parole, 1987*). The most commonly stated reason for these changes was erosion of support for rehabilitation and a greater emphasis on punishment and incapacitation.

The parole issue is closely related to the sentencing structure; some states have implemented a determinate sentencing scheme in which discretionary release by a parole board has been eliminated or reduced. Although discretionary release has been eliminated in some states, most states retained some type of post-release supervision. Four-fifths of those released in 1984 were released on the condition that they follow specified rules or face revocation of their community status.

Twenty-one states reported the implementation of emergency release programs to ease the prison overcrowding problem. Thirteen of these programs are provided by statute. North Carolina, South Carolina, Delaware and Tennessee were the most frequent users of the programs (*Corrections Yearbook, 1987*). Other than emergency release, which is used only in emergencies, the typical avenue is for an inmate to be released from prison on discretionary release (i.e., a parole board determines release dates and conditions) or mandataory release (i.e., dates are determined by the original sentence minus any good time earned). During 1986, 188,132 inmates were released from state prisons by one of these mechanisms. The time served for those released on parole may be summarized as follows (summary is for 1984, the latest year in which statistics are available):

• median time served (including jail time) for all offenses was 17 months or 45.4% of their original sentences;
• median time served for violent offenses was 28 months;
• median time served for murder and non-negligent manslaughter was 78 months;
• median time served for rape was 44 months;
• median time served for robbery was 30 months;
• median time served for burglary was 17 months;
• median time served for drug trafficking was 16 months;
• average amount of time spent in prison and jail and on parole was 60 months for a violent offense, 42 months for a drug offense and 37 months for a property offense (*Time Served in Prison and on Parole 1984*).

Privatization

Perhaps the single biggest issue that has con-

fronted corrections during the last two years has been privatization. Several states have pursued the use of private contracts for the operation of prisons and jails as a means of reducing the governments average operational costs of $41.70 per inmate per day or $15,221 per inmate per year (*Corrections Yearbook 1987*). The most activity in this area has occurred in Kentucky, Tennessee, Florida and Texas where legislation was enacted authorizing privately run prisons and jails.

Many variations occur in the use of privatization. It may be used for a dministrative, financial, construction or service-oriented functions. Contracting for such services as medical and mental health care, drug treatment and education has been a mainstay of the correctional system for many years. The total operation of entire facilities, however, represents a somewhat radical departure from the norm. Myriad legal, moral and philosophical issues and controversies have been addressed by state officials when discussing privatization. The pros and cons of the debate over privatization will certainly continue into the 1990's.

BIBLIOGRAPHY

House Arrest. U.S. Department of Justice, National Institute of Justice.

New Construction Methods for Correctional Facilities. U.S. Department of Justice, National Institute of Justice, 1986.

New Dimensions in Probation: Georgia's Experience With Intensive Probation Supervision (IPS). U.S. Department of Justice, National Institute of Justice, 1987.

Observations on Parole: A Collection of Readings From Western Europe, Canada and the United States. Association of Paroling Authorities International, 1987.

Prisoners in 1986. U.S. Department of Justice, Bureau of Justice Statistics, 1987.

Probation and Parole 1986. U.S. Department of Justice, Bureau of Justice Statistics, 1987.

Profile of State Prison Inmates 1986. U.S. Department of Justice, Bureau of Justice Statistics, 1988.

The Corrections Yearbook. Criminal Justice Institute, Inc., 1987.

Time Served in Prison and on Parole 1984. U.S. Department of Justice, Bureau of Justice Statistics, 1987.

Table B
NEW PRISONS OPENED IN 1986

State or other jurisdiction	New Institutions	New Beds	Cost (in thousands)
Alaska	1	74	$4,500
Arizona	8	2,064	36,559
Arkansas	1	108	13,525
California	4	2,620	182,000
Connecticut	1	600	15,000
Delaware	1	300	2,100
District of Columbia	1	208	9,300
Florida	2	266	2,892
Georgia	1	300	10,550
Illinois	1	896	33,700
Kentucky (a)	1	200	
Massachusetts	1	216	18,933
Michigan	2	566	69,500
Minnesota	1	144	15,000
Mississippi	1	580	25,000
Missouri	1	950	37,000
New York	2	1,286	
North Carolina	1	50	60
Oregon	1	400	10,146
Pennsylvania	1	180	7,960
South Carolina	1	696	25,572
Tennessee	1	180	3,821
Virginia	1	512	26,412
Washington	1	500	48,843
Wisconsin	2	750	67,000
Federal System	1	902	18,000

Source: *Corrections Yearbook, 1987.*
(a) Privately operated. Total cost figure includes privately owned and operated under contract with the state.

Table C
FACILITIES TO BE OPENED IN THE FUTURE

State or other jurisdiction	Under Construction Facilities	Beds	Cost (in thousands)	Planned Beds
Alabama	1	611		1,548
Alaska	2	328	$50,000	
Arizona	4	1,758	53,000	1,914
Arkansas	1	700	11,000	500
California	12	13,146	647,200	6,560
Colorado	3	842	40,000	1,532
Connecticut				2,100
Delaware	1	200	450	
District of Columbia	1	400	18,420	804
Florida	2	1,628	36,000	2,749
Georgia	4	2,164	44,775	1,835
Hawaii	3	654	73,056	252
Idaho				348
Illinois	1	128	3,400	2,405
Indiana	2	806	43,000	1,104
Kansas	1	352	10,800	634
Kentucky	3	700	50,100	
Louisiana	3	310	5,116	3,228
Maine	1	100	877	113
Maryland	1	1,440	100,000	50
Massachusetts	1	229	32,960	2,543
Michigan	3	401		1,417
Mississippi	3	303	1,908	1,500
Missouri	5	2,140	82,700	
Nebraska				160
Nevada	3	364	2,500	3,044
New Hampshire	2	262		480
New Jersey	6	2,156	156,000	210
New Mexico				464
New York		897		3,800
North Carolina	6	692	20,433	2,400
North Dakota	2	95	5,809	
Ohio	13	8,695	460,000	1,930
Oklahoma				500
Oregon				1,661
Pennsylvania	5	2,398	112,250	806
Rhode Island				550
South Carolina	5	2,496	117,500	1,826
Tennessee				1,104
Texas	12	4,644	92,100	
Utah	3	1,096	40,000	2,000
Vermont				40
Virginia	2	344	7,050	2,180
Wisconsin				663
Wyoming				100
Federal System	14	2,636	107,905	3,370

Source: *Corrections Yearbook, 1987.*

Table D
SPACE PROVIDED THROUGH ADDITIONS AND RENOVATIONS
TO EXISTING FACILITIES DURING 1986

State or other jurisdiction	Additions and Renovations	Beds Added	Cost (in thousands)
Alabama		587	
Arizona	3	304	$1,524
California	2	244	
Colorado		365	18,000
Connecticut	3	250	4,600
Florida	10	1,187	1,277
Georgia			2,400
Hawaii	2	45	250
Illinois	2	388	12,200
Indiana	4	898	8,147
Kansas	3	126	1,100
Kentucky	1	100	633
Louisiana	5	1,812	24,000
Michigan	7	1,252	28,330
Mississippi	4	397	3,193
Montana	14	204	15,567
Nevada	3	174	341
New Hampshire (a)	2	262	21,000
New Jersey	1	50	4,000
New York	31	2,282	
North Carolina	1	26	130
Ohio	5	925	8,980
Oklahoma	1	122	225
Pennsylvania	3	531	16,516
South Carolina	6	576	2,317
Texas	3	168	2,808
Virginia	1	50	31
Washington		52	432
Wyoming	4	98	
Federal System	8	1,216	14,718

Source: Corrections Yearbook, 1987.
(a) 510 beds were added and 248 were deleted.

Table E
ADULTS ON PROBATION, 1986

State or other jurisdiction	Probation population 1/1/86	1986(a) Entries	1986(a) Exits	Probation population 12/31/86	Percent change in probation population 1985-86	1986 probationers per 100,000 adult residents
Alabama(a)	16,520	5,400	4,895	17,025	3.1	579
Alaska..............	2,606	1,308	1,029	2,885	10.7	797
Arizona.............	18,068	9,241	7,026	20,283	12.3	842
Arkansas	9,268	2,526	1,659	10,135	9.4	587
California	210,449	126,155	115,862	220,742	4.9	1,111
Colorado	17,612	10,585	10,980	17,217	-2.2	717
Connecticut	38,805	30,237	25,168	41,874	13.8	1,723
Delaware	7,139	4,624	3,778	7,985	11.9	1,688
Florida	130,399	152,522	142,672	140,249	7.6	1,551
Georgia............	94,461	57,738	51,636	100,563	6.5	2,290
Hawaii	7,986	5,102	4,684	8,404	5.2	1,082
Idaho	3,414	2,130	1,774	3,770	10.4	546
Illinois.............	74,156	46,992	44,945	76,203	2.8	897
Indiana(b)	42,800	45,345	38,880	49,265	15.1	1,224
Iowa	12,063	12,108	11,587	12,584	4.3	598
Kansas	16,204	9,093	9,344	15,953	-1.5	879
Kentucky	6,594	4,916	4,669	6,841	3.8	252
Louisiana	26,638	11,767	10,728	27,677	3.9	877
Maine	4,451	4,661	4,492	4,620	3.8	530
Maryland	67,138	40,648	38,652	69,134	3.0	2,062
Massachusetts	86,597	50,925	46,359	91,163	5.3	2,030
Michigan	99,365	77,732	72,235	104,862	5.5	1,571
Minnesota	32,986	28,332	26,091	35,227	6.8	1,135
Mississippi	6,636	3,018	3,196	6,458	-2.7	354
Missouri(c)	26,081	20,474	15,633	30,922	18.6	823
Montana............	2,637	1,277	971	2,943	11.6	501
Nebraska	10,720	12,264	11,719	11,265	5.1	963
Nevada(c)	5,365	2,593	2,440	5,518	2.9	762
New Hampshire	3,096	2,477	1,955	3,618	16.9	472
New Jersey.........	47,483	28,077	22,530	53,030	11.7	916
New Mexico........	4,130	3,831	3,786	4,175	1.1	403
New York	99,183	41,168	32,794	107,557	8.4	803
North Carolina	56,207	32,123	29,686	58,644	4.3	1,245
North Dakota	1,569	802	827	1,544	-1.6	316
Ohio	66,810	43,975	38,863	71,922	7.7	911
Oklahoma	21,480	11,237	9,726	22,991	7.0	956
Oregon	23,000	13,589	13,934	22,655	-1.5	1,126
Pennsylvania	75,591	39,183	35,789	78,985	4.5	874
Rhode Island	7,536	4,416	3,778	8,174	8.5	1,093
South Carolina	17,979	10,210	9,948	18,241	1.5	748
South Dakota	2,249	3,967	3,990	2,226	-1.0	436
Tennessee	26,205	16,399	16,313	26,291	.3	740
Texas..............	269,909	139,033	118,868	290,074	7.5	2,468
Utah	6,330	3,559	3,511	6,378	.8	610
Vermont	5,298	2,852	2,788	5,362	1.2	1,337
Virginia............	17,447	6,730	6,448	17,729	1.6	408
Washington	45,399	31,630	25,873	51,156	12.7	1,547
West Virginia	3,905	2,289	2,220	3,974	1.8	281
Wisconsin..........	23,877	11,257	10,486	24,648	3.2	701
Wyoming	1,716	1,181	1,110	1,787	4.1	506
Dist. of Col.	11,777	10,253	9,723	12,307	4.5	2,522

Source: U.S. Department of Justice, Bureau of Justice Statistics, *Probation and Parole 1986.*
(a) Alabama estimated 1986 exit data.
(b) Indiana reported 1985 data for 1986.
(c) State estimated all data.

Table F
ADULTS ON PAROLE, 1986

State or other jurisdiction	Parole population 1/1/86	1986 Entries	1986 Exits	Parole population 12/31/86	Percent change in parole population 1985-86	1986 parolees per 100,000 adult residents
Alabama............	2,425	1,723	1,157	2,991	23.3	102
Alaska.............	155	114	150	119	-23.2	33
Arizona............	1,717	2,613	2,296	2,034	18.5	85
Arkansas	3,891	1,743	1,793	3,841	-1.3	222
California..........	30,127	45,553	42,518	33,162	10.1	167
Colorado	2,003	2,013	2,025	1,991	-.6	83
Connecticut	695	166	258	603	-13.2	25
Delaware	864	522	408	978	13.2	207
Florida	4,214	3,011	3,747	3,478	-17.5	39
Georgia............	8,538	9,480	7,597	10,421	22.1	237
Hawaii	716	292	123	885	23.6	114
Idaho	483	274	226	531	9.9	77
Illinois.............	11,421	8,358	7,468	12,311	7.8	145
Indiana............	2,797	4,836	4,360	3,273	17.0	81
Iowa	1,971	1,592	1,634	1,929	-2.1	92
Kansas	2,282	1,255	1,177	2,360	3.4	130
Kentucky	3,694	2,637	2,779	3,552	-3.8	131
Louisiana	3,346	2,795	1,975	4,166	24.5	132
Maine(a)...........	0	0	0	0		0
Maryland	7,308	4,924	4,738	7,494	2.5	224
Massachusetts	4,496	3,382	3,880	3,998	-11.1	89
Michigan	6,639	4,238	4,975	5,902	-11.1	88
Minnesota	1,364	1,390	1,317	1,437	5.4	46
Mississippi	3,392	1,644	1,582	3,454	1.8	189
Missouri	4,485	3,166	2,455	5,196	15.9	138
Montana...........	634	312	278	668	5.4	114
Nebraska	246	440	390	296	20.3	25
Nevada(b)..........	1,313	1,446	1,230	1,529	16.5	211
New Hampshire	453	207	121	539	19.0	70
New Jersey.........	13,385	7,565	6,886	14,064	5.1	243
New Mexico........	1,092	1,162	1,107	1,147	5.0	114
New York	28,289	13,444	12,408	29,325	3.7	219
North Carolina	3,184	5,522	5,384	3,322	4.3	71
North Dakota	166	158	165	159	-4.2	33
Ohio	6,509	4,932	5,294	6,147	-5.5	78
Oklahoma	1,625	611	494	1,742	7.2	72
Oregon	1,894	2,084	1,839	2,139	12.9	106
Pennsylvania	34,785	19,762	15,539	39,008	12.1	432
Rhode Island	402	414	358	458	13.9	61
South Carolina	3,261	879	1,236	2,904	-10.9	119
South Dakota	415	407	414	408	-1.7	80
Tennessee..........	7,899	6,828	6,127	8,600	8.9	242
Texas	47,471	27,255	17,217	57,509	21.1	489
Utah	1,169	678	659	1,188	1.6	114
Vermont	344	199	206	337	-2.0	84
Virginia............	5,640	5,506	5,376	5,770	2.3	133
Washington(b).......	6,039	2,105	478	7,666	26.9	232
West Virginia	638	505	437	706	10.7	50
Wisconsin..........	3,427	2,450	2,222	3,655	6.7	104
Wyoming	332	190	194	328	-1.2	93
Dist. of Col.	3,504	1,651	1,435	3,720	6.2	762

Source: U.S. Department of Justice, Bureau of Justice Statistics, *Probation and Parole 1986.*
(a) Maine abolished parole in 1976, so the number of persons remaining on parole is negligible.
(b) Nevada and Washington estimate their parole population counts.

CRIMINAL JUSTICE

Table 8.32
TRENDS IN STATE PRISON POPULATION

State or other jurisdiction	Total population			Population by maximum length of sentence					
				More than a year			Year or less and unsentenced		
	1986	1985	Percentage change	1986	1985	Percentage change	1986	1985	Percentage change
United States	502,251	463,048	8.5	487,391	448,698	8.6	14,860	14,350	3.6
Alabama...................	11,710	11,015	6.3	11,504	10,749	7.0	206	266	-22.6
Alaska....................	2,460	2,329	5.6	1,666	1,530	8.9	794	799	-0.6
Arizona...................	9,434	8,531	10.6	9,038	8,273	9.2	396	258	53.5
Arkansas	4,701	4,611	2.0	4,701	4,611	2.0	0	0	ND
California.................	59,484	50,111	18.7	57,725	48,279	19.6	1,759	1,832	-4.0
Colorado	3,673	3,369	9.0	3,673	3,369	9.0	0	0	ND
Connecticut	6,905	6,149	12.3	4,043	4,326	-6.5	2,862	1,823	57.0
Delaware	2,828	2,553	10.8	2,026	1,759	15.2	802	794	1.0
Florida...................	32,228	28,600	12.7	32,219	28,482	13.1	9	118	-92.4
Georgia...................	17,363	16,014	8.4	16,291	15,115	7.8	1,072	899	19.2
Hawaii	2,180	2,111	3.3	1,521	1,428	6.5	659	683	-3.5
Idaho	1,451	1,294	12.1	1,451	1,294	12.1	0	0	ND
Illinois...................	19,456	18,634	4.4	19,456	18,634	4.4	0	0	ND
Indiana	10,175	9,904	2.7	9,963	9,615	3.6	212	289	-26.6
Iowa	2,777	2,832	-1.9	2,777	2,832	-1.9	0	0	ND
Kansas	5,425	4,732	14.6	5,425	4,732	14.6	0	0	ND
Kentucky	6,322	5,801	9.0	6,322	5,801	9.0	0	0	ND
Louisiana	14,580	13,890	5.0	14,580	13,890	5.0	0	0	ND
Maine	1,316	1,226	7.3	1,165	967	20.5	151	259	-41.7
Maryland	13,326	13,005	2.5	12,559	12,303	2.1	767	702	9.3
Massachusetts	5,678	5,390	5.3	5,678	5,390	5.3	0	0	ND
Michigan	20,742	17,755	16.8	20,742	17,755	16.8	0	0	ND
Minnesota	2,462	2,343	5.1	2,462	2,343	5.1	0	0	ND
Mississippi	6,747	6,392	5.6	6,565	6,208	5.8	182	184	-1.1
Missouri	10,485	9,915	5.7	10,485	9,915	5.7	0	0	ND
Montana..................	1,111	1,129	-1.6	1,111	1,129	-1.6	0	0	ND
Nebraska	1,953	1,814	7.7	1,863	1,733	7.5	90	81	11.1
Nevada	4,505	3,771	19.5	4,505	3,771	19.5	0	0	ND
New Hampshire	782	683	14.5	782	683	14.5	0	0	ND
New Jersey................	12,020	11,335	6.0	12,020	11,335	6.0	0	0	ND
New Mexico...............	2,701	2,313	16.8	2,545	2,112	20.5	156	201	-22.4
New York	38,449	34,712	10.8	38,449	34,712	10.8	0	0	ND
North Carolina	17,762	17,344	2.4	16,460	16,007	2.8	1,302	1,337	-2.6
North Dakota	421	422	-0.2	361	375	-3.7	60	47	27.7
Ohio	22,463	20,864	7.7	22,463	20,864	7.7	0	0	ND
Oklahoma	9,596	8,330	15.2	9,596	8,330	15.2	0	0	ND
Oregon	4,737	4,454	6.4	4,737	4,454	6.4	0	0	ND
Pennsylvania	15,201	14,227	6.8	15,165	14,119	7.4	36	108	-66.7
Rhode Island..............	1,361	1,307	4.1	1,010	964	4.8	351	343	2.3
South Carolina	11,676	10,510	11.1	11,022	9,908	11.2	654	602	8.6
South Dakota	1,045	1,047	-0.2	1,014	1,035	-2.0	31	12	158.3
Tennessee	7,182	7,127	0.8	7,182	7,127	0.8	0	0	ND
Texas....................	38,534	37,532	2.7	38,534	37,532	2.7	0	0	ND
Utah	1,845	1,633	13.0	1,817	1,623	12.0	28	10	180.0
Vermont..................	676	677	-0.1	476	443	7.4	200	234	-14.5
Virginia..................	12,930	12,073	7.1	12,545	11,717	7.1	385	356	8.1
Washington	6,603	6,909	-4.4	6,603	6,909	-4.4	0	0	ND
West Virginia	1,482	1,725	-14.1	1,482	1,725	-14.1	0	0	ND
Wisconsin.................	5,697	5,442	4.7	5,678	5,412	4.9	19	30	-36.7
Wyoming	865	758	14.1	865	758	14.1	0	0	ND
Dist. of Col.	6,746	6,404	5.3	4,786	4,604	4.0	1,960	1,800	8.9

Source: U.S. Department of Justice, Bureau of Justice Statistics,
Prisoners in 1986.
Key:
ND—Not definable.

Table 8.33
STATE DEATH PENALTY
(As of December 1986)

State or other jurisdiction	Capital offenses	Minimum age	Persons on death row	Method of execution
Alabama	Murder during kidnaping, robbery, rape, sodomy, burglary, sexual assault, or arson; murder of peace officer, correctional officer, or public official; murder while under a life sentence; murder for pecuniary gain or contract murder; multiple murders; aircraft piracy; murder by a defendant with a previous murder conviction; murder of a witness to a crime	None	83	Electrocution
Alaska	...			
Arizona	First-degree murder	None	59	Lethal gas
Arkansas	Murder during rape, kidnaping, arson, vehicular piracy, robbery, burglary, or escape; murder of any law enforcement officer, jailer, prison official, firefighter, judge, or other court official, probation officer, parole officer, or military personnel; multiple murders; contract murder; murder for pecuniary gain; murder while under sentence of life imprisonment, life imprisonment without parole, or death	15	26	Lethal injection or electrocution
California	Treason; aggravated assault by a prisoner serving a life term; first-degree murder with special circumstances; train wrecking	18	176	Lethal gas
Colorado	First-degree murder; first-degree kidnaping	18	1	Lethal gas
Connecticut	Murder of a public safety or correctional officer; murder for pecuniary gain; murder in the course of a felony; murder by a defendant with a previous conviction for intentional murder; murder while under a life sentence; murder during a kidnaping; illegal sale of cocaine; methadone, or heroin to a person who dies from using these drugs; murder during first-degree sexual assault; multiple murders	18	0	Electrocution
Delaware	First-degree murder with aggravating circumstances	None	4	Lethal injection or hanging
Florida	First-degree murder	None	254	Electrocution
Georgia	Murder; kidnaping with bodily injury when the victim dies; aircraft hijacking; treason	17	111	Electrocution
Hawaii	...			
Idaho	First-degree murder; aggravated kidnaping	18	14	Lethal injection or firing squad
Illinois	Murder	18	101	Lethal injection
Indiana	Murder	10	40	Electrocution
Iowa	...			
Kansas	...			
Kentucky	Aggravated murder; kidnaping when victim is killed	16	31	Electrocution
Louisiana	First-degree murder	15	39	Electrocution
Maine	...			
Maryland	First-degree murder, either premeditated or during the commission of a felony	14	18	Lethal gas
Massachusetts	...			
Michigan	...			
Minnesota	...			
Mississippi	Capital murder includes murder of a peace officer or correctional officer, murder while under a life sentence, murder by bomb or explosive, contract murder, murder committed during specific felonies (rape, burglary, kidnaping, arson, robbery, sexual battery, unnatural intercourse with a child, non-consensual unnatural intercourse), and murder of an elected official; capital rape is the forcible rape of a child under 14 years by a person 18 years or older	13	38	Lethal injection or lethal gas (a)
Missouri	First-degree murder	14	43	Lethal gas

STATE DEATH PENALTY—Continued

State	Offenses	Minimum age	Number on death row	Method
Montana	Deliberate homicide; aggravated kidnaping when victim dies; attempted deliberate homicide, aggravated assault, or aggravated kidnaping by a state prison inmate with a prior conviction for deliberate homicide or who has been previously declared a persistent felony offender	None	5	Lethal injection or hanging
Nebraska	First-degree murder	18	14	Electrocution
Nevada	First-degree murder	16	35	Lethal injection
New Hampshire	Contract murder; murder of a law enforcement officer; murder of a kidnap victim	17	0	Hanging
New Jersey	Purposeful or knowing murder; contract murder; murder during a kidnaping	18	23	Lethal injection
New Mexico	First-degree murder	18	0	Lethal injection
New York	. . .			
North Carolina	First-degree murder	14	63	Lethal injection or lethal gas
North Dakota	. . .			
Ohio	Assassination; contract murder; murder during escape; murder while in a correctional facility; murder after conviction of a prior purposeful killing or prior attempted murder; murder of a peace officer; murder arising from specified felonies (rape, kidnaping, arson, robbery, burglary); murder of a witness to prevent testimony in a criminal proceeding	18	69	Electrocution
Oklahoma	Murder with malice aforethought; murder arising from specified felonies (forcible rape, robbery with a dangerous weapon, kidnaping, escape from lawful custody, first-degree burglary, arson); murder when the victim is a child	None	72	Lethal injection
Oregon	Aggravated murder	16(b)	2	Lethal injection
Pennsylvania	First-degree murder	None	74	Electrocution
Rhode Island	. . .			
South Carolina	Murder with statutory aggravating circumstances	None	47	Electrocution
South Dakota	First-degree murder; kidnaping with gross permanent physical injury inflicted on the victim	None(c)	0	Lethal injection
Tennessee	First-degree murder	None	53	Electrocution
Texas	Murder of a public safety officer, fireman, or correctional employee; murder during the commission of specified felonies (kidnaping, burglary, robbery, aggravated rape, arson); murder for remuneration; multiple murders	17	236	Lethal injection
Utah	First-degree murder	None	7	Lethal injection or firing squad
Vermont	Murder of a police officer or correctional officer; kidnaping for ransom	None	0	Electrocution
Virginia	Murder during the commission of specified felonies (abduction, armed robbery, rape); contract murder; murder by a prisoner while in custody; murder of a law enforcement officer; multiple murders; murder of a child under 12 years old during an abduction	15	33	Electrocution
Washington	First-degree premeditated murder	None	7	Lethal injection or hanging
West Virginia	. . .			
Wisconsin	. . .			
Wyoming	First-degree murder including felony murder	None	3	Lethal injection or lethal gas
Dist. of Col.	. . .			

Source: U.S. Department of Justice, Bureau of Justice Statistics, *Capital Punishment, 1986*; and update by The Council of State Governments.
Key:
. . . - State has no capital punishment statute.

(a) Mississippi authorizes lethal injection for those convicted after 7/1/84; executions of those convicted prior to that date are to be carried out with lethal gas.
(b) After removal to adult court.
(c) Must be tried as an adult.

IMPLEMENTATION OF THE RESOURCE CONSERVATION AND RECOVERY ACT OF 1976: THE ROLE OF THE STATES

By James P. Lester

A new federal-state partnership exists in environmental policy today, a relationship that can best be described as regulatory federalism. Also termed partial preemption, the procedure allows the federal government to return program responsibility to the states while retaining the authority to decide on the acceptability of states' actions. States are given the latitude to design and implement their own laws, but these laws must meet minimum federal standards and objectives. Thus, partial preemption is a delegation of authority but not an abdication of federal control.[1]

Recent environmental statutes enacted by Congress and implemented by the Environmental Protection Agency (EPA) are examples of partial preemption: the Clean Air Act Amendments of 1970, the Safe Drinking Water Act of 1974, and the Resource Conservation and Recovery Act of 1976, among others. These acts and their reauthorization amendments contain a unique partial preemption scheme which environmental enforcement agents refer to as primacy. This technique attempts to encourage states to implement the provisions of the acts by applying for primary enforcement responsibility. In order to receive this delegation of authority (or authorization), state laws must be at least as stringent as the applicable federal statutes.

From a national perspective, authorization (primacy) is desirable because it promotes minimal federal standards nationwide as opposed to stringency in states and laxity in others. From the state perspective, primacy allows a state to have some control over its environmental programs. The EPA is responsible for enforcing the federal statutes in states that elect not to seek primacy. Furthermore, if a state is not in compliance with minimum federal standards and procedures, the EPA can revoke its grant of primacy.

RCRA Authorization

The Resource Conservation and Recovery Act of 1976 (RCRA) established the first comprehensive federal regulatory program for controlling hazardous waste and provided grants and technical assistance to help states improve waste management techniques. From 1976-1980, federal efforts were primarily concerned with establishing the regulatory framework for hazardous waste management. These regulations established standards for identifying and listing hazardous wastes, for generators of hazardous waste, for transporters, for hazardous waste managers awaiting administrative disposition of their permits, and for managers with permits.[2] Initially, many states attempted to achieve comply with RCRA standards and objectives.[3] By January, 1988, 41 states received EPA authorization to manage hazardous waste programs under RCRA. Specifically, Section 3006 of RCRA provides guidelines describing conditions under which states can be authorized to carry out their own programs.[4]

The law provides for two stages in establishing state programs that meet federal standards. The first stage is interim authorization which give states two years to upgrade their programs. The second stage is full, or final, authorization. Final authorization has three main criteria: a state program must be equivalent to federal programs, a state program must be consistent with federal or other state programs, and a state must provide for adequate enforcement. For equivalence, EPA requires state programs to have a manifest tracking

The author is a Visiting Scholar at The Council of State Governments during 1987-1988. Dr. Lester is on leave from Colorado State University, where he is an Associate Professor of Political Science. He has written extensively on comparative state environmental politics and policy.

system, criteria standards, adequate resources and legal authority, a designated lead agency and a public participation effort. For consistency, EPA forbids states from banning imports of hazardous waste from other states. Regulations allow withdrawal of federal approval based on inadequate legal authority, unsatisfactory program operations or enforcement programs, and modifications of a state program that interfere with the free movement of hazardous waste across state borders.[5]

States' Record

Of the 41 states that have received final authorization for their pre-Hazardous and Solid Waste Amendments program, 11 were approved in 1984, 19 in 1985, 10 in 1986, and one in 1987 (See Table A). Only Alaska, California, Connecticut, Hawaii, Idaho, Iowa, Maine, Ohio and Wyoming have not yet received final authorization as of March 1988. Maine was one the verge of receiving final authorization.

Research in the area of intergovernmental policy implementation provides insight into why some states achieve primacy quickly and why others do not. According to a 50 state study, RCRA implementation has been slowed by difficulty in measuring the seriousness of the hazardous waste problem, by the scope of those affected by RCRA regulations, by dissension over state policy goals, and by administrative fragmentation. RCRA has been promoted, on the other hand, by the availability of fiscal resources, by the receptivity of the state's implementing agency to RCRA goals, and by the commitment and leadership of state government officials involved.[6]

For example, state efforts to assess the magnitude of the hazardous waste problem have floundered due to discrepancies between EPA and state estimates of the total number of waste sites. Moreover, critics point out that some potentially serious sites are omitted simply because adequate information about them is unavailable.

The sheer enormity of the hazardous waste problem has been another constraining factor. Since the responsible management of hazardous waste involves a large regulated community, including waste generators, waste carriers and waste disposers, as well as the federal, state and local governments, the process of policy implementation moves slowly. Thus, the greater the scope of those affected by the regulations, the slower the implementation.

A third factor that appears to influence the speed of RCRA implementation is whether or not the state had a single agency in charge of hazardous waste policy implementation. Some states have had as many as four separate agencies involved in implementation. This type of fragmented organizational structure appears to slow down the process.

Some states, on the other hand, are able to achieve authorization relatively quickly. Support from the governor and legislators, as well as the commitment and leadership skills of affected agency officials, apparently speeds RCRA authorization.

A recent study by The Council of State Governments (1987) found that RCRA authorization depends heavily on the nature of federal-state communication and the support of implementing officials at the regional and state levels. State officials implemented RCRA more quickly if they considered the directive to be clear, consistent and flexible. Moreover, the greater the involvement of regional EPA officials, governors, legislators, judicial officials and local officials in the RCRA implementation process, the more rapid the compliance by the states. The adequacy of state resources (e.g., Full Time Employees or budget size), on the other hand, was found to be of little consequence in the speed of RCRA implementation.[7]

There are also individual factors that are important in a given state. For example, the reasons why California and Wyoming are not authorized to manage hazardous waste programs are vastly different. California has opted to move slowly and deliberately in designing its regulations. Wyoming, on the other hand, sees primacy as not a cost-effective way to manage its relatively minor hazardous waste problem.

With the passage of the Hazardous and Solid Waste Amendments of 1984 (HSWA), even Wyoming may reconsider the authorization issue. HSWA expands the regulated community from producers of 1000 kilograms of hazardous waste per month to include producers of 100 kilograms (or more) per month. This change may mean that it makes sense for states with lesser hazardous waste problems to seek authorization.

Hazardous Wastes and Policy Redesign

Lessons learned from intergovernmental policy implementation should be taken into account as Congress considers re-authorizing RCRA in 1988 as well as any other environmental legislation that states must implement. Congress should consider how states are likely to implement any such new federal mandates. Indeed, according to the Domestic Policy Council's Working Group on Federalism, writing in its report, The Status of Federalism in America, Congress should provide a "federalism impact" statement for every new law it enacts.[8]

This means that, as future hazardous waste legislation is designed (or redesigned), Congress should take in account how federal-state relations evolved during RCRA (and HSWA) implementation. Moreover, state experiences with implementation of the Clean Air Act, the Clean Water Act, and the Safe Drinking Water Act, should also provide insight into regulatory federalism, and the nature of federal-state relations. The states and Congress should then be able to redesign policies that work.

Moreover, if primacy succeeds in encouraging the states to supplement federal enforcement efforts, then Congress seems likely to expand its use. Consequently, insight into primacy's viability is gained by identifying the factors that have promoted or inhibited RCRA implementation in the states. To the extent that these constraints may be relieved by careful planning or policy redesign, intergovernmental policy implementation may be greatly improved.

Notes

1. *Regulatory Federalism: Policy, Process, Impact and Reform* (Washington, D.C.: Advisory Commission on Intergovernmental Relations, 1984). See also, Patricia McGee Crotty, "The New Federalism Game: Primacy Implementation of Environmental Policy," *Publius* 17 (Spring, 1987).

2. *Environmental Quality 1984: The 15th Annual Report of the Council on Environmental Quality* (Washington, D.C.: U.S. Government Printing Office): 161.

3. James P. Lester, James L. Franke, Ann O'M. Bowman, and Kenneth W. Kramer, "Hazardous Wastes, Politics, and Public Policy: A Comparative State Analysis', *Western Political Quarterly* 36 (June, 1983).

4. U.S. Environmental Protection Agency, Office of Solid Waste and Emergency Response, State Programs Branch, Jan. 1, 1988.

5. James P. Lester and Ann O'M. Bowman, eds., *The Politics of Hazardous Waste Management* (Durham, NC: Duke University Press, 1983). See also, J. Ward Wright, *Managing Hazardous Wastes: A Programmatic Approach* (Lexington: The Council of State Governments, 1986).

6. James P. Lester and Ann O'M. Bowman, "Implementing Intergovernmental Policy: A Test of the Sabatier-Mazmanian Model," *Polity 21* (Summer 1989).

7. James P. Lester, "Implementing Intergovernmental Regulatory Policy: A Comparative State Analysis," (Lexington: The Council of State Governments, 1988).

8. The Status of Federalism in America, A Report of the Working Group on Federalism of the Domestic Policy Council, November 1986.

Table A
STATES GRANTED FINAL AUTHORIZATION FOR PRE-HSWA PROGRAM
(As of January 1, 1988)

State or other jurisdiction	Date authorized	FR page number	
Alabama	December 23, 1987	46466	(December 8)
Arizona	December 4, 1985	47736	(November 20)
Arkansas	January 25, 1985	1513	(January 11)
Colorado	November 2, 1984	41036	(October 19)
Revisions Approved	November 7, 1986	37729	(October 24)
Delaware	June 22, 1984	23837	(June 8)
Florida	February 12, 1985	3908	(January 29)
Georgia	August 21, 1984	31417	(August 7)
Illinois	January 31, 1986	3778	(January 30)
Indiana	January 31, 1986	3953	(January 31)
Kansas	October 17, 1985	40377	(October 3)
Kentucky	January 31, 1985	2550	(January 17)
Louisiana	February 7, 1985	3348	(January 24)
Maryland	February 11, 1985	3511	(January 25)
Massachusetts	February 7, 1985	3344	(January 24)
Michigan	October 30, 1986	36804	(October 16)
Minnesota	February 11, 1985	3756	(January 28)
Mississippi	June 27, 1984	24377	(June 13)
Missouri	December 4, 1985	47740	(November 20)
Montana	July 25, 1984	28245	(July 11)
Nebraska	February 7, 1985	3345	(January 24)
Nevada	November 1, 1985	42181	(October 18)
New Hampshire	January 3, 1985	49092	(December 18)
New Jersey	February 21, 1985	5260	(February 7)
New Mexico	January 25, 1985	1515	(January 11)
New York	May 29, 1986	17737	(May 15)
North Carolina	December 31, 1984	48694	(December 14)
Revisions Approved	April 8, 1986	10211	(March 25)
North Dakota	October 19, 1984	39328	(October 5)
Oklahoma	January 10, 1985	50362	(December 27)
Oregon	January 31, 1986	3779	(January 30)
Pennsylvania	January 30, 1986	1791	(January 15)
Rhode Island	January 31, 1986	3780	(January 30)
South Carolina	November 22, 1985	46437	(November 8)
South Dakota	November 2, 1984	41038	(October 19)
Tennessee	February 5, 1985	2820	(January 22)
Texas	December 26, 1984	48300	(December 12)
Revisions Approved	October 4, 1985	3952	(January 31)
Utah	October 24, 1984	39683	(October 10)
Vermont	January 21, 1985	775	(January 7)
Virginia	December 18, 1984	47391	(December 4)
Washington	January 31, 1986	3782	(January 30)
West Virginia	May 29, 1986	17739	(May 15)
Wisconsin	January 31, 1986	3783	(January 30)
Dist. of Col.	March 22, 1985	9427	(March 8)
Guam	January 27, 1986	1370	(January 13)

Source: U.S. Environmental Protection Agency, Office of Solid Waste and Emergency Response, January 1, 1988.

ENVIRONMENT

Table B
STATE CAPABILITY IN THE AREA OF SUPERFUND IMPLEMENTATION

State or other jurisdiction	As of June 30, 1986				Projected Additional through 1990				Projected Percentage Increase through 1990			
	Tech	Mgmt	Others	Total	Tech	Mgmt	Others	Total	Tech	Mgmt	Others	Total
Alabama	0	0	0	0	0	0	0	0	0	0	0	0
Arizona	12	6	2	20	18	8	3	29	150	133	150	145
Arkansas	0.75	0.06	0.06	0.09	...	...	...	...	0	0	0	0
California	112	85	142	339	90	45	90	225	80	53	63	66
Colorado	0	1.25	0	1.25	...	...	...	...	...	...	...	...
Connecticut	0.50	0.25	0.10	0.9	...	...	...	...	...	...	...	...
Delaware	2	1	0.5	3.5	3	0	1	4	150	0	200	114
Florida	33	10	...	43	...	...	...	...	...	...	...	...
Georgia	0	2	0	2	1	3	0	4	...	150	0	200
Illinois	26	11	5	42	5	1	2	8	19	9	40	19
Indiana	14	4	2	20	25	8	4	37	179	200	200	185
Iowa	1	0.5	0.5	2	...	...	...	...	...	...	...	...
Kansas	13	5	2	20	3.5	0	0	3.5	27	0	0	18
Kentucky	2		0.25	0.25	2.5	0	0	2	100	0	0	80
Maine	6	2	0.5	8.5	0	0	0	0	0	0	0	0
Maryland	8	4	2	14	3	1	1	5	38	25	50	36
Massachusetts	65	20	15	100	65	20	15	100	100	100	100	100
Michigan	19	6	10	35	10	3	5	18	53	50	50	51
Minnesota	32	10	5	47	34	13	7	54	106	130	140	115
Mississippi	1	0	0	1	0	0	0	0	0	0	0	0
Missouri	20	5	4	29	5	3	2	10	25	60	50	34
Montana	...	...	...	...	...	...	...	...	...	...	...	...
Nebraska	0	1	0	1	4	1	1	6	...	100	...	600
New Hampshire	13	2	31	46	13	4	41	58	100	200	132	126
New Jersey	...	...	...	...	...	...	...	...	...	...	...	...
New Mexico												
New York	53	17	0	70	75	25	4	104	142	147	...	149
North Carolina	0	0	0	0	...	...	...	...	...	...	...	...
North Dakota	0	0	0	0	...	...	...	...	...	...	...	...
Ohio	12	4	1	17	...	...	...	...	0	0	0	0
Oklahoma	0	0	0	0	5	3	2	10	...	...	...	...
Oregon	1	1	0	2	15	4	3	22	1333	400	...	1035
Pennsylvania	15	6	1	22	10	...	2	12	67	0	200	55
Rhode Island	...	...	...	...	...	...	...	...	...	...	...	...
South Carolina	5	2	1	8	7	3	2	12	140	150	200	150
South Dakota	0	0	0	0	0	0	0	0	0	0	0	...
Tennessee	26	6	2	34	9	3	4	16	35	50	200	47
Texas	4	1	2	7	...	0	0	0	0	0	0	0
Utah	1	2	2	5	5	0	0	5	500	0	0	100
Vermont	7	2	1	10	10	2	2	14	143	100	200	140
Virginia	4	2	...	6	8	3	1	12	200	150	...	200
Washington	38.2	16.7	5.8	60.7	19.7	1	3	23.7	52	6	52	39
West Virginia	0	0.25	0	0.25	2	1	0	3	...	400	...	1200
Wisconsin	8	1	0.5	9.5	12	...	...	12	150	0	0	126
Wyoming	0	0	0	0	0	0	0	0	...	...	...	...

Source: Association of State and Territorial Solid Waste Management Officials, *State Programs for Hazardous Waste Site Assessments and Remedial Actions*, June 1987.
Key:
... - Information unavailable.

Table 8.34
SUPERFUND SITES NATIONAL PRIORITY LIST AND STATUS, BY STATE
(As of September 30, 1987)

State or other jurisdiction	NPL Sites: Proposed final or deleted	Sites at RI/FS stage	Sites at RD stage	Sites with RA start	Site work completed
United States	964	494	94	89	29
Alabama	10	6	0	3	0
Alaska	1	0	0	0	1
Arizona	9	5	0	0	1
Arkansas	10	3	2	3	0
California	63	47	2	6	1
Colorado	15	8	3	2	0
Connecticut	8	3	1	2	0
Delaware	18	8	3	0	0
Florida	39	23	6	3	0
Georgia	8	3	0	0	1
Hawaii	6	0	0	0	0
Idaho	4	3	0	0	0
Illinois	27	10	3	4	1
Indiana	29	15	4	4	0
Iowa	13	7	0	2	1
Kansas	8	4	0	0	1
Kentucky	10	6	3	0	0
Louisiana	8	2	3	2	0
Maine	7	4	0	2	0
Maryland	10	5	0	0	2
Massachusetts	21	12	4	3	0
Michigan	70	31	5	6	2
Minnesota	41	16	4	5	1
Mississippi	3	2	0	0	1
Missouri	19	10	2	2	0
Montana	9	3	1	2	0
Nebraska	5	2	0	1	0
Nevada	0	0	0	0	0
New Hampshire	13	6	2	2	1
New Jersey	101	52	16	8	2
New Mexico	4	4	0	0	0
New York	67	32	9	5	0
North Carolina	12	9	0	0	1
North Dakota	1	0	1	0	0
Ohio	31	21	2	1	2
Oklahoma	6	3	1	0	1
Oregon	6	4	0	1	0
Pennsylvania	82	39	6	11	2
Rhode Island	8	5	1	1	0
South Carolina	15	7	1	0	0
South Dakota	1	1	0	0	0
Tennessee	10	7	0	0	0
Texas	26	13	7	2	2
Utah	10	5	0	0	1
Vermont	2	1	0	0	0
Virginia	19	10	1	0	1
Washington	28	11	0	3	1
West Virginia	6	2	1	1	0
Wisconsin	33	17	0	1	0
Wyoming	1	0	0	1	0
Guam	1	1	0	0	0
N. Mariana Islands . .	1	0	0	0	1
Puerto Rico	8	6	0	0	0
Trust Territories	1	0	0	0	1

Source: U.S. Environmental Protection Agency, Office of Solid Waste
and Emergency Response, September 30, 1987.
Key:
RI/FS - Remedial Investigation and Feasibility Studies
RD - Remedial Design
RA - Remedial Action

Table 8.35
INTERSTATE WATER AGENCIES

State or other jurisdiction	Delaware River Basin Comm. (1961)	Great Lakes Comm. (1955)	Interstate Comm. on the Potomac River Basin (1940)	Interstate Sanitation Comm. (1936)	Klamath River Compact Comm. (1957)	Missouri Basin States Assn. (1981)	New England Governors' Conf., Inc. (1936)	New England Interstate Water Pollution Control Comm. (1947)	Ohio River Basin Comm. (1981)	Ohio River Valley Water Sanitation Comm. (1948)	Susquehanna River Basin Comm. (1971)	Tahoe Regional Planning Agency (1969)	Upper Colorado River Comm. (1948)	Upper Mississippi River Basin Assn. (1981)	Western States Water Council (1965)
Alabama															
Alaska															★
Arizona															★
Arkansas															
California					★							★			★
Colorado						★							★		★
Connecticut				★			★	★							
Delaware	★														
Florida															
Georgia															
Hawaii															
Idaho															★
Illinois		★							★	★				★	
Indiana		★							★	★					
Iowa						★								★	
Kansas						★									★
Kentucky									★	★					
Louisiana															
Maine							★	★							
Maryland			★								★				
Massachusetts							★	★							
Michigan		★													
Minnesota		★				★								★	
Mississippi															
Missouri						★								★	
Montana						★									★
Nebraska						★									★
Nevada												★			★
New Hampshire							★	★							
New Jersey	★			★											
New Mexico													★		★
New York	★	★		★				(a)	★	★	★				
North Carolina															
North Dakota						★									★ (b)
Ohio		★							★	★					

INTERSTATE WATER AGENCIES—Continued

State or other jurisdiction	Delaware River Basin Comm. (1961)	Great Lakes Comm. (1955)	Interstate Comm. on the Potomac River Basin (1940)	Interstate Sanitation Comm. (1936)	Klamath River Compact Comm. (1957)	Missouri Basin States Assn. (1981)	New England Governors' Conf., Inc. (1936)	New England Interstate Water Pollution Control Comm. (1947)	Ohio River Basin Comm. (1981)	Ohio River Valley Water Sanitation Comm. (1948)	Susquehanna River Basin Comm. (1971)	Tahoe Regional Planning Agency (1969)	Upper Colorado River Comm. (1948)	Upper Mississippi River Basin Assn. (1981)	Western States Water Council (1965)
Oklahoma	.	.	.	.	.	.	.	.	.	.	.	.	.	.	★
Oregon	.	.	.	.	★	.	.	.	.	.	.	.	.	.	.
Pennsylvania	★	★	★	.	.	.	.	.	★	★	★	.	.	.	.
Rhode Island	.	.	.	.	.	.	.	.	.	.	.	.	.	.	.
South Carolina	.	.	.	.	.	.	.	.	.	.	.	.	.	.	.
South Dakota	.	.	.	.	.	★	.	.	.	.	.	.	.	.	★
Tennessee	.	.	.	.	.	.	.	.	.	.	.	.	★	.	★
Texas	.	.	.	.	.	.	.	.	.	.	.	.	.	.	★
Utah	.	.	.	.	.	.	.	.	.	.	.	.	★	.	.
Vermont	.	.	.	.	.	.	★	★	.	.	.	.	.	.	.
Virginia	.	.	★	.	.	.	.	.	★	★	.	.	.	.	★
Washington	.	.	.	.	.	.	.	.	.	.	.	.	.	.	.
West Virginia	.	.	★	.	.	.	.	.	★	★	.	.	.	.	★
Wisconsin	.	★	.	.	.	★	.	.	.	.	.	.	.	★	.
Wyoming	.	.	.	.	.	★	.	.	.	.	.	.	★	.	.
Dist. of Col.	.	.	★	.	.	.	.	.	.	.	.	.	.	.	.
Other information about agency:															
Federal membership	•	.	.	.	.	.	.	.	.	.	.	.	•(d)	.	.
Advisory only	.	•	•	.	.	•	•	.	•	.	.	.	.	•	•
Enforcement powers	.	.	.	•	•	.	.	•(c)	.	•	•	•	.	.	.
Funding state	.	•	•	•	•	•	•	.	.	•	.	•	•	•	•
Funding federal/state	•	.	.	.	.	.	.	•	•	.	•	.	.	.	.

Key:
★ —Membership in agency
. —Not applicable
• —Yes

(a) Not a formal member; cooperates on water issues through the New England/New York Water Council which is part of this conference.
(b) Associate member.
(c) Primarily advisory; has the power to enforce water quality regulations on interstate rivers.
(d) Allocates water from Colorado River.

STATE ASSISTANCE FOR LOCAL PUBLIC WORKS

By Terry Busson, Judith Hackett and John Daily

Economic development has become the dominant state and local policy issue of the 1980s and investment in infrastructure improvements is seen by many as a critical component of the development process. Local, state and national leaders, as well as the private sector, are examining the changing role of the states in providing assistance to local governments regarding infrastructure needs.

Since 1980, a number of studies have been conducted on the condition of capital facilities in America. A major initial finding of one study conducted by the National Council on Public Works Improvement was that the infrastructure issue has matured since 1980.

> Public concern has moved beyond simple physical evidence of deterioration to include the economic importance of public works facilities. Increasingly, it is understood that the condition, safety, and responsiveness of the nation's infrastructure are a reflection of national commitment to maintaining a healthy and competitive business climate, improving the quality of life, and providing a sound economic future for generations to come.[1]

During 1987 The Council of State Governments undertook a study for the National Council on Public Works Improvements to examine the role of states in providing assistance to local governments for public works. The study involved an inventory of programs in 50 states. A researcher in each state conducted interviews with more than 300 state officials.

THE CHANGING ROLE OF THE STATES IN THE FEDERAL SYSTEM

Since 1982, when federal grants for public works began to decline, the role of the states in relation to local governments underwent a gradual change. Throughout the 1980s, federal aid for local public works has declined significantly, except in the field of transportation where federal trust funds have supported a fairly stable level of programs. At the same time, state aid to local governments has been increasing modestly, overall while remaining stable in some states and declining in others. New types of state aid and programs to support local public works have appeared. However, the lack of precise information about the evolving state role in assisting local public works since 1982 makes it difficult to answer key questions about the future role of federal, state and local governments in the provision, upgrading, or repair of infrastructure.

State and Local Fiscal Conditions. The difficulties state and local governments face in addressing the nation's infrastructure needs can best be understood by reviewing the financial condition of state and local governments. According to the National Association of State Budget Officers, 21 states in fiscal year 1982 and 39 states in fiscal year 1983 were forced to cut state budgets after they had been adopted. More recent figures indicate that 18 states in 1986 and 24 states in 1987 reduced spending levels.[2]

This reduction comes at a time when financial demands placed on state and local governments have never been greater. In the face of this adversity, state and local governments have continued to find ways to provide needed services. Most of the states raised taxes. Thirty-nine have increased gasoline taxes since 1981, 22 raised taxes in 1986, and 27 raised some taxes in 1987.[3]

Terry Busson is a visiting scholar at The Council of State Governments and director of The Institute of Government at Eastern Kentucky University. Judith Hackett is director of the Center for Agriculture and Rural Development at The Council of State Governments. John Daily is professor of Political Science and Public Administration at Georgia Southern College.

State Assistance Strategies. The methods chosen by states to provide assistance for local public works were examined and compared with the federal patterns. There were 392 federal grant-in-aid programs as of Jan. 1, 1984. There were also 12 block grant programs which provided assistance to state and local governments.[4] State and local finance for public works, however, tends to vary by category of infrastructure.

Roads and bridges are often financed on a pay-as-you-go basis from dedicated taxes. Solid waste, water and wastewater treatment maintenance and operation programs have most often been financed by user fees. New facilities for water, wastewater treatment and expansion and development of mass transit operations have been financed through the sale of bonds or long-term loans, which are paid back from user fees or, in some cases, increased levels of taxation.[5]

During this study of 1986 spending by individual states, we have confirmed the concluding statement of the ACIR report, *Financing Public Physical Infrastructures,* which found the problems to be "both diverse and localized. The problems are complex and require differing solutions. No single national or state program will meet the needs for every state to build, rebuild or maintain their public works facilities."[6] State and local governments have met the challenge by adopting innovative new programs, increasing gasoline and other taxes, and setting new borrowing limits.

STATE ASSISTANCE PROGRAMS

Traditions play a major role in the different approaches to funding local public works. And traditions die hard, especially if they are based in the state constitution. While most states in 1986 provided more support for local public works than five years earlier, that support varied widely and followed previous traditions of state assistance even though the focus of that assistance may have changed.

The diversity of the 50 states is clearly seen in their approaches to assisting local public works. While all states provide some type of assistance to local governments, the types of programs they support, their financing mechanisms, the authority, responsibility and type of spending differ widely from state to state and from program to program.

There are 700 individual state programs which provide assistance for local public works.

The map indicates the range for each state in terms of total programs. The smallest number of programs in any state is five while the largest number of programs is 34 (see Figure 1).

FINANCING MECHANISMS

States use two principal financing methods: grants and non-loan programs (including taxes, user fees, technical assistance and income generating activities), and loans and bonds.

More than 544 of the 700 programs discovered during the study are grants and other non-loan programs. These programs occur in every region of the country, and there are very few regional differences. The regions with the largest number of programs per state include the mid-East, the Great Lakes and the Plains. Those with the fewest number of programs per state are the Far West, New England and the Southwest.

Grants. Grant programs are the predominant type of state assistance to local public works, with a majority of the programs in six of the 10 categories, funded through grants. The largest number of grant programs are for highways, followed by public buildings, airports, wastewater treatment and water supply. These programs are usually funded with general fund dollars, but a number of states have been adding other revenues, which sometimes come from the sale of bonds. This money is often part of a package including a grant, dedicated tax dollars, federal and local money.

Taxes. Often dedicated to specific types of public works, taxes are the second most popular funding mechanism. More than half of the total state tax programs are in the category Highways, Roads and Bridges. These areas are usually funded by some type of dedicated tax — fuel, motor vehicle, drivers license — or other taxes that must be spent for construction, maintenance and upkeep of highways, roads and bridges. Only two other categories have significant numbers of programs: airports and mass transit. Several new programs have been developed using dedicated taxes to support water and wastewater programs. These are discussed in more detail in the section on trends.

User Fees. Relatively few state assistance programs impose user fees — most often assessed at the local level. The principal role of states has been to allow or in some cases mandate the enactment of user fees by local governments to support public works. Highways, airports and

Figure 1
INFRASTRUCTURE ASSISTANCE
Total Number of Programs

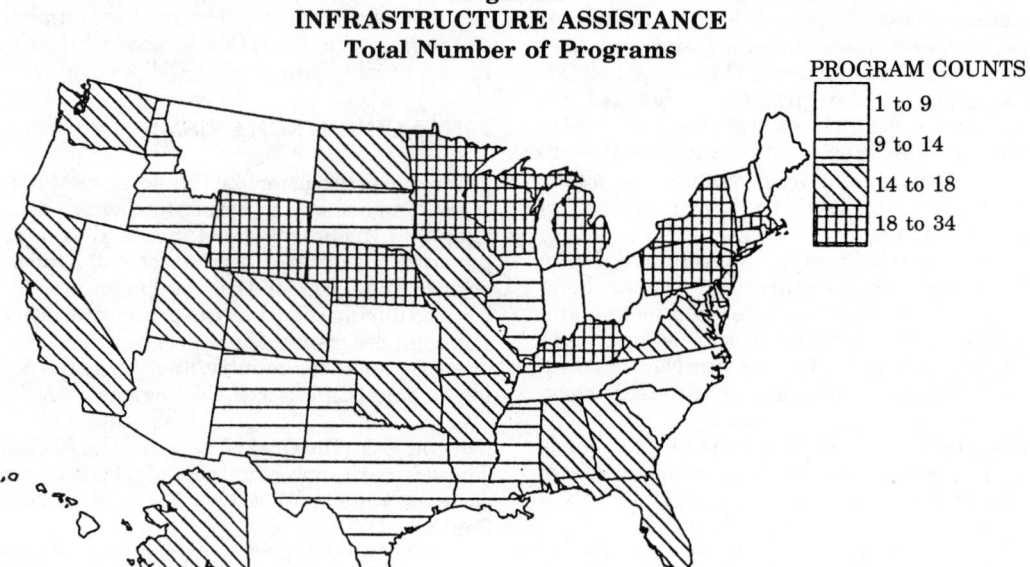

PROGRAM COUNTS

1 to 9

9 to 14

14 to 18

18 to 34

mass transit programs account for nearly all state user fees.

Technical Assistance. Very few state technical assistance programs were identified. In almost every state, however, technical assistance is an important part of state assistance to local governments. When asked to place a dollar amount on technical assistance, most state officials say that it is provided in conjunction with other duties and not as a specific budgeted line item. In cases where individuals provide assistance on a full-time basis, their salary and support would not reflect the actual contribution to local public works programs. Those programs which could be specified are included.

Income-Generating Activities. There are only a small number of programs in this category, and most have been established in the last five years. They may, however, be more prevalent in the future for local public works development. Several states have established a trust fund or development fund that receives money from a state lottery. This money can often be used by local communities for a variety of public works projects. Other trust funds have been established using money from rents, royalties or other payments received by the state.

Bonds. Water and wastewater programs use

bonds as the funding source more frequently than any other state assistance program. Many state bond programs were established to provide matching funds for the EPA Construction Grant Program, while others were created or expanded to meet the cut in the federal percentage of funds available for these projects. Still others were created to assist communities that were either low on priority lists but still had a need or were not able to raise their part of the federal match. The use of bonds for highways and buildings is also very common.

Loans. Water and wastewater programs again dominate the loan category. Many states have established revolving loan funds to support local community efforts in these areas. States also provide combined general fund money with bonds to create a revolving loan fund.

Public works problems addressed by loans seem to be those requiring a long-term effort to solve, those not expecting an increase in support from the federal government, and those with insufficiently funded state general revenues. Loan programs also are becoming more important for highways, as states seek an alternative to raising the gasoline tax to support increased costs and needs. This trend is most noticeable in states seeking to expand their efforts in economic development and in those which have major highway and bridge projects as a part of that effort.

STATE SPENDING FOR PUBLIC WORKS

Total state spending for public works assistance varies from a high of $896,664,000 to a low of $2,898,000. These large differences are due, in part, to differences in population. (See Tables B and C for total spending by states for each program.) However, in order to provide data reflecting the magnitude of state assistance for local public works, total *per capita* spending is provided for grant to loan dollars for each state. These figures are derived by dividing total state dollars for grants to loans by total state population. The range of per capita spending is $2 to $524. Only Alaska and Wyoming exceed $100 per capita.

When per capita spending for grants is examined, Wyoming and Alaska again rank high, $510 and $190 respectively. The other states range from $0, in Hawaii which has no grant programs, to Iowa, with $89 per capita (see Figure 2).

The states tend to be closely divided on per capita spending for loan and bond programs.

Eleven states have no loan or bond programs and thus have $0 per capita while only three, Alaska, Mississippi and Ohio, are above $30.00 per capita (see Figure 3).

The majority of states tend to fall into three categories when comparing loan and bond per capita spending with per capita spending for grants. (See Table A).

Table A
Patterns of State Spending for Public Works
Per Capita Grants, Per Capita Loans & Bonds

States Which Rank High on One Low on Other	States Which Rank Low on Both	States Which Rank High on Both
Arizona	Alabama	Alaska
Connecticut	Kansas	Arkansas
Delaware	Louisiana	Colorado
Georgia	Nevada	Kentucky
Hawaii	New Hampshire	Maryland
Idaho	North Carolina	Mississippi
Indiana	Oregon	North Dakota
Iowa	Rhode Island	Utah
Maine	South Carolina	Wyoming
Massachusetts	Tennessee	
Minnesota	West Virginia	
Montana		
Nebraska		
New Jersey		
New York		
Wisconsin		

Figure 2
INFRASTRUCTURE ASSISTANCE
Grant Dollars Per Capita

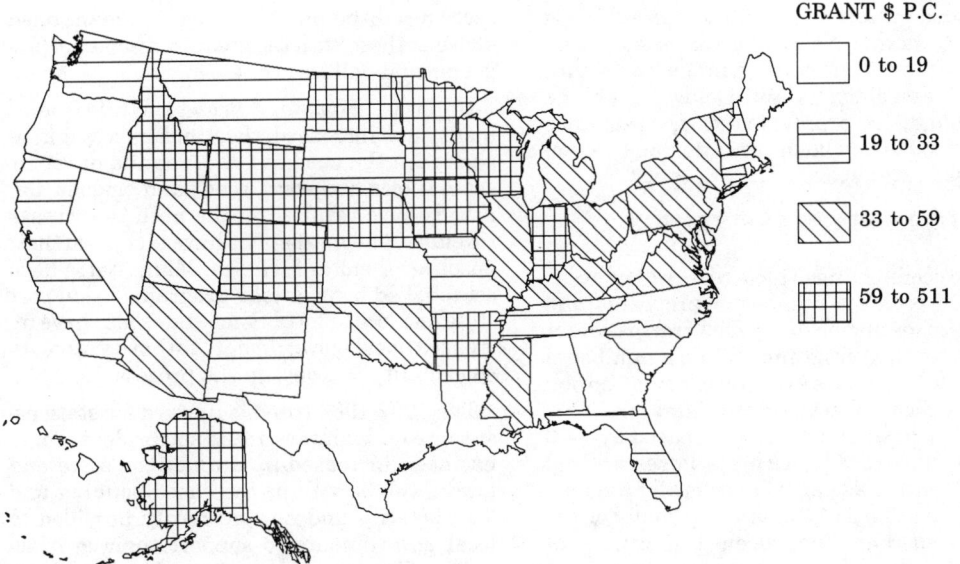

GRANT $ P.C.

0 to 19

19 to 33

33 to 59

59 to 511

Figure 3
INFRASTRUCTURE ASSISTANCE
Loan Dollars Per Capita

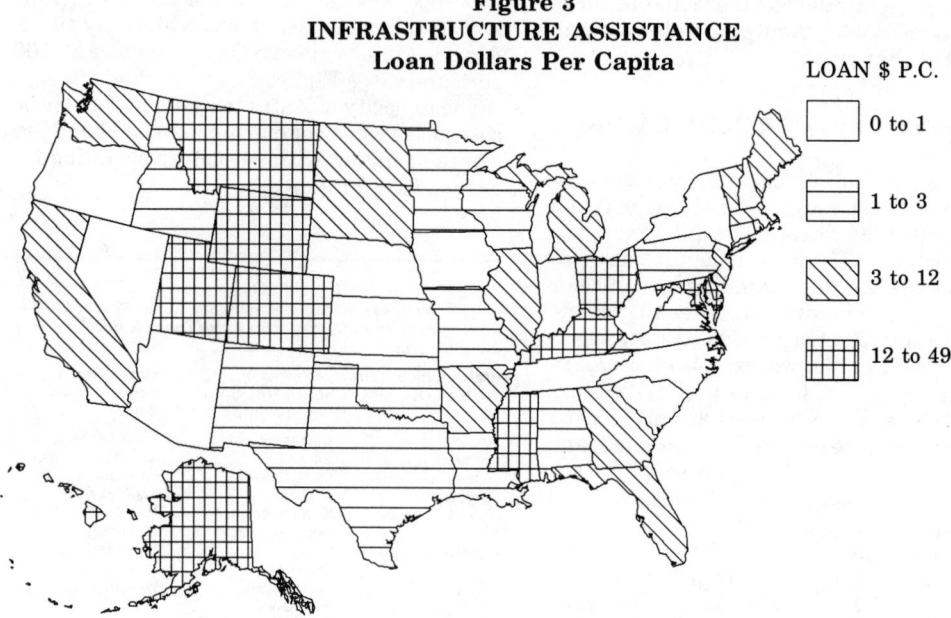

LOAN $ P.C.

☐	0 to 1
☰	1 to 3
⧄	3 to 12
▦	12 to 49

The majority of states with low per capita spending (six of 11) are from the Southeast. The majority of states with high per capita spending (five of nine) are from the far-West, but do not tend to be those in the best economic condition.

A mix of states rank high on one scale and low on the other. Most seem to be following traditional patterns of state assistance. This is true of Iowa and Nebraska, which have continued to provide grants even in the face of hard times. Massachusetts and Delaware, on the other hand, have provided more assistance through loans and bonds even during times of increased revenues.

TRENDS IN STATE ASSISTANCE

Most recent changes have occurred in areas with the greatest number of programs and dollars: roads and bridges, mass transit, water and wastewater programs. While a number of programs for airports exist, little new attention has been focused on these programs (probably because federal money has increased by 44.6 percent since 1982). Airports have received some attention as part of an overall economic development package created by many of the states, but have not been the center of attention.

The only other infrastructure category that has a significant number of programs and state dollars for local public works is public buildings. Little or no federal money is involved in these programs, therefore, changes have not come as a result of federal cutbacks. Most of the new effort by states to assist local governments has been in funding for jails. The focus of this section will be on the categories mentioned above as those with the greatest number of programs and dollars spent.

Highways, Roads and Bridges. While federal money has increased, the funds have not kept pace with the need to build, rebuild or repair the nation's highways, roads and bridges. Demands have resulted in the need to increase revenues, and most states have increased their gasoline or motor fuels tax. Many states have established bond or loan programs to support state and local efforts. Some states also have increased local government authority and responsibility to assist in the process.

The 1982-1986 trend is upward for state assistance for highways, roads and bridges. There has been increased funding at the state and local level, as well as increased bonding and loan activity and new authority provided to local governments to support their own activities. The method used depends primarily on tradition. The availability of general revenues may play an important role in deciding what mechanism will be used.

In regions of the country where most state economies are doing fairly well, much of the assistance has been in the form of grants from the general fund and increased gasoline taxes. States which are having financial problems are doing less, but what they have done is often related to economic development which includes raising gas taxes and other fees, improving water and wastewater facilities and increasing state efforts to improve business development.

Mass Transit. Few new state efforts have been made on behalf of mass transit due to the loss of 27.6 percent of the federal monies in urban mass transit programs over the past five years. Several interviews with state officials indicated that states would not replace federal money, systems would live and die on the local government's ability and the willingness of the local people to support the system. In many states, local governments support these systems if they are really essential to the community. The states which have increased their efforts have done so by expanding bond and loan funds to include more money for mass transit and by giving local governments more authority to raise revenues for their needs.

Water and Wastewater Treatment Programs. Water supply and wastewater treatment facilities assistance programs are often considered together in packages by states. Federal assistance for these programs has been cut by 42.8 percent since 1982. The major impact has been the reduction in the federal share of program costs from 75 percent to 55 percent in the EPA Construction Grants Program. This means that projects must receive increased funds from the state or the local government. Since all states are under a mandate to meet clean water standards by 1989, they are concerned about this problem.

Between 1981 and 1986, 25 states either created a bond bank, a bond program or a revolving loan fund. Thirteen others had such proposals under study or before the legislature for consideration. In addition a number of states picked up all or part of the 20 percent in federal cuts rather than pass the increase along to the local governments, many of whom would not have been able to afford the increase and thus could not have participated in the federal program. Most states provided some increased support to local governments either through more general fund monies, bond or loan programs. Some provided more authority to local governments to raise user fees, expand bond limits or use option taxes to support water and wastewater efforts. A few provided considerable amounts of money to assist local efforts through new state taxes and innovative programs.

KEY INFRASTRUCTURE QUESTIONS

Several key questions need consideration by the states as they examine their needs and options for local public works assistance.

To what extent is state aid filling the gap left by declining federal aid?

Since 1982 nearly every state has experienced a revenue shortfall. Some states have never fully recovered from the recession of 1981-1983, while others have suffered recent setbacks due to falling energy prices and decreased demand for oil. Most states have revised plans for financing of capital projects. Historically, most states have operated their capital financing programs on a pay as-you-go basis. State efforts to assist local governments with their public works needs are funded in the same manner. Thirty-three states had limits on their short or long term debt.

Both state and local governments rely on federal funds to assist them in their efforts to build, rebuild, expand and maintain their public infrastructure. Programs such as the Federal Highway Trust Fund, EPA Wastewater Construction Grants, EDA Grants, the ARC and other regional organizations provided important funds which, when combined with state and local dollars, made it possible for state and local governments to develop and expand their economic health and well-being. In 1982, some programs actually received fewer dollars — and this trend continues.

The tax revolt in the states, aimed largely at local property taxes, has compounded problems in some local public works financing. Beginning with Proposition 13 in California in 1978 and carrying through the property tax freeze in Montana in 1986, local governments are finding their ability to raise revenues through traditional sources (such as the property tax) severely limited. States which are reducing their existing budgets because of revenue shortfalls caused by the farm recession, international competition, energy prices, or conflicting spending and revenue policies, can offer little help to these local governments.

Despite federal budget cuts and state revenue shortfalls, states have continued to provide funds for local public works and in many cases have increased their efforts. This has resulted in a growing state debt. It is interesting to note the rapid growth in state and local debt, up from $260 million in 1978 to $595 million in 1986. There has been a similar growth of debt that is not guaranteed: 45 percent in 1978 versus 67 percent in 1986.[7] While many states are not incurring more debt than they can handle in the near future, some states could have problems financing future programs, and other states could experience severe fiscal stress if they should encounter a long term economic decline.

What state innovations are available for meeting local public works needs?

There has been a noticeable increase in state innovations for local public works during the 1980s. This process is encouraging and holds great promise for the future. States have completed inventories of total public works needs. Trust funds for special categories of needed infrastructure, as well as general purpose funding, are beginning to emerge.

State targeting of assistance is quite different than that of national programs. Special rural infrastructure funds have been created in urban states (California) while states with economic problems in agriculture (Illinois) have mounted a statewide initiative. Innovations seem to be closely related to state economic well-being, as in the case of Arkansas and Alabama which have established innovations that cannot be implemented.

The political dynamics necessary for adopting innovations are as follows:
• There must be a problem that innovation could solve.
• The innovation must be brought to the attention of political leaders.
• The executive and legislative branches of state government must agree on an approach that has a reasonable chance of success.

As state assistance replaces federal aid, what changes are occurring in the program purposes and structure?

Most states had developed a pattern of providing assistance to local governments for public works, and they continued to support these programs in the face of federal budget cuts. Some funds that were received as outright grants by the federal government now came from the states as loans or were financed through a bond program that the local governments were expected to help pay off. For the most part, however, few changes in program purposes or structure were found.

If states followed a pay-as-you-go philosophy, they increased the burden placed on local citizens to pay for public works programs by increasing user fees or by authorizing local governments to expand fees or incur higher levels of debt. If states provided grants, they continued to do so even if they had to raise taxes or create bond programs to provide the assistance.

States wanting additional information on infrastructure would benefit from several of the recent reports.[8] These reports provide information on the public works problem, recommend actions for federal, state and local governments, as well as specific information on state programs and funding options.

References

1. National Council on Public Works Improvement, *The Nation's Public Works: Defining the Issues* (Washington, D.C.: September 1986).

2. National Association of State Budget Officers. *Fiscal Survey Of The States*. (Washington, D.C.: March 1987), 4-7.

3. National Association of State Budget Officers, *State Budget and Tax News, and State Policy Data Book*, 1987.

4. Advisory Commission on Intergovernmental Relations. *A Catalog of Federal Grant-in-aid Programs to State and Local Governments* (M139), (Washington D.C.: GPO, December 1984), pp. 1-3.

5. Municipal Finance Officers Association. *Building Prosperity: Financing Public Infrastructure For Economic Development*. (Washington D.C.: Government Finance Research Center, 1984), pp. 24-49.

6. Advisory Commission on Intergovernmental Relations. *Financing Public Physical Infrastructure*. P.32.

7. J. Richard Aronson and John L. Hilley. *Financing State and Local Governments*, 4th edition. (Washington, D.C. The Brookings Institution, 1986), p.162, and; The State Policy Data Book, 1987. (Alexandria, VA; State Policy Research, Inc., March 1987), Table C-15.

8. Busson, Terry and Judith Hackett. *State Assistance for Local Public Works*, Lexington, KY: The Council of State Governments, 1988; *Fragile Foundations: A Report on America's Public Works*, National Council on Public Works Improvement, Washington, D.C.: Government Printing Office, 1988.

Table B
STATE ASSISTANCE FOR LOCAL PUBLIC WORKS, BY STATE, FOR FISCAL YEAR 1986
GRANTS, TAXES, USER FEES, TECHNICAL ASSISTANCE, AND INCOME-GENERATING ACTIVITIES*
(In thousands of dollars)

State or other jurisdiction	Airports	Highways	Mass transit	Dams	Inter-model	Public buildings	Hazardous waste	Solid waste	Waste-water	Water	Other
Alabama	$ 434	$ 64,715	...	...	...	$ 665	$ 75	$ 1,130	$ 648	...	...
Alaska	100	250	.	.	.	179	...	...	...	$ 3,367	$ 82,428
Arizona	3,400	67,300	$ 23,500	.	.	...	...	...	8,822	26,728	...
Arkansas	2,892	101,267	300	...	...	52,302	...	4,112	...	3,336	...
California	4,000	608,914	83,000	$34,950	...	...	...	...	...	...	...
Colorado	...	126,491	78,300	...	...	2,687	...	50	276	2,623	12,840
Connecticut	220	53,992	...	...	...	...	50	1,973	...	15,254	...
Delaware	10	2,475	770	125	...	...	...	...	...	...	...
Florida	23,010	181,657	12,400	...	...	...	...	...	45,135	...	...
Georgia	2,653	76,600	1,166	5,630	...	2,387	...	2,000	...	6,000	...
Hawaii	...	...	...	...	...	...	...	...	...	...	...
Idaho	200	60,100	...	132	...	...	...	38,000	6,050	50	...
Illinois	...	345,152	...	771	...	...	...	...	70,900	...	...
Indiana	806	294,895	2,630	...	...	...	...	3,280	9,769	45,062	...
Iowa	660	253,045	...	...	...	1,981	...	360	1,590	...	...
Kansas	...	7,441	...	1,000	...	...	...	...	...	...	...
Kentucky	1,000	112,139	600	4,000	...	4,480	...	246	96	1,205	...
Louisiana	2,400	38,239	6,300	22,000	...	...	...	...	...	...	15,445
Maine	171	15,217	...	...	...	...	...	...	485	...	...
Maryland	261	231,564	14,627	5,546	...	...	...	...	...	...	...
Massachusetts	813	18,470	2,600	...	...	...	...	345	115,000	25,700	23,000
Michigan	598	254,252	112,980	1,085	12	...	...	...	...	...	...
Minnesota	5,410	239,824	929	...	...	730	250	3,819	15,758	...	...
Mississippi	82,048	...	1,800	...	...	...	...	...	2,750	...	...
Missouri	1,904	90,306	...	2,192	...	50	...	...	27,257	5,273	...
Montana	...	14,000	...	5,160	...	875	...	630	...	...	...
Nebraska	354	100,112	1,056	895	...	...	...	500	2,294	130	...
Nevada	12,000	...	...	...	...	...	...	...	...	...	...
New Hampshire	21	13,310	...	...	...	80	...	...	...	9,980	...
New Jersey	1,131	69,200	18,000	1,940	...	10,065	31,400	...	...	...	...
New Mexico	857	10,174	...	1,105	...	...	...	...	21,059	...	4,000
New York	...	179,074	18,825	1,329	...	300,274	...	19,812	122,224	2,640	...
North Carolina	3,400	71,763	...	314	...	...	...	...	2,843	4,304	...
North Dakota	762	34,475	...	1,650	...	2,500	...	15	379	8,188	...
Ohio	1,113	164,162	...	1,000	...	...	...	...	...	...	314,500
Oklahoma	575	155,423	...	...	...	...	...	...	488	1,168	...
Oregon	...	13,429	1,342	...	...	...	...	...	11,820	1,180	...
Pennsylvania	2,832	382,400	279,700	...	...	...	...	500	22,510	6,000	258
Rhode Island	...	390	...	...	...	904	...	...	40	...	...
South Carolina	158	56,250	...	...	...	...	...	...	1,140	...	6,000
South Dakota	66	14,941	...	...	...	...	...	...	3,167	5,070	...
Tennessee	2,385	137,608	2,977	1,459	50	...	...	...	...	...	...
Texas	5,713	118,803	4,911	...	...	...	...	...	...	...	49,000
Utah	3,842	32,248	23,500	...	...	...	...	...	...	...	...
Vermont	...	17,531	235	407	...	...	...	...	4,850	...	...
Virginia	1,072	226,000	31,795	1,149	...	3,770	...	...	5,313	...	...
Washington	650	30,650	200	...	...	12,800	...	2,322	47,900	...	...
West Virginia	368	...	...	...	...	169	...	...	111	68,000	3,000
Wisconsin	2,833	192,922	38,357	1,000	...	...	...	72,447	694	...	...
Wyoming	1,974	14,251	48,800	...	...	21,537	...	194	12,053	161,068	...

Source: Information derived from survey of key state officials conducted by The Council of State Governments (1987) for the National Council on Public Works Improvement.

Key:

*—Income-Generating Activities includes monies received from lotteries, rents, royalties or other payments received by the state and dedicated to local public works programs.

Table C
STATE ASSISTANCE FOR LOCAL PUBLIC WORKS
BY STATE, FOR FISCAL YEAR 1986
BONDS & LOANS
(In thousands of dollars)

State or other jurisdiction	Airports	Highways	Mass transit	Dams	Inter-model	Public buildings	Hazardous waste	Solid waste	Waste-water	Water	Other
Alabama	$ ...	...	9,582(b)	...	...	...	...	...	...	17,283(b,l)	...
Alaska	...	4,700(l)	...	2,700(l)	...	...	...	...	...	...	...
Arizona	...	...	...	...	...	...	...	...	...	...	...
Arkansas	...	...	...	...	...	...	...	...	15,000(b)	...	...
California	...	30,000(l)	...	...	...	121,500(b)	...	...	...	47,300(b)	50,000(b)
Colorado	...	...	...	72,000(l)	...	...	...	...	...	...	...
Connecticut	...	...	...	90(b)	...	...	...	...	...	...	...
Delaware	975(b)	...	...	2,600(b)	300(b)	4,650(b)	...	...	27,500(b)	...	...
Florida	...	30,200(b,l)	...	...	...	...	...	...	20,752(l)	...	...
Georgia	...	...	...	...	...	...	...	...	...	...	...
Hawaii	...	4,115(b)	...	25(b)	...	2,723(b)	...	...	3,833(b)	3,656(b)	...
Idaho	...	...	...	2,309(b)	...	...	...	...	...	...	...
Illinois	3,400(b)	36,000(b,l)	79,900(b)	...	...	9,500(b,l)	8,800(b)	...	...	...	...
Indiana	...	...	...	...	...	...	...	...	...	...	...
Iowa	...	...	...	...	...	...	...	...	...	...	...
Kansas	...	...	...	...	...	28,000(b)	...	1,100(b,l)	21,520(b,l)	10,773(b,l)	...
Kentucky	...	2,600(b)	...	...	...	4,275(b)	...	...	...	...	...
Louisiana	...	...	...	...	...	...	...	...	5,100(b)	...	...
Maine	451(b)	...	...	...	...	64,956(b)	...	...	16,000(b)	3,558(b)	...
Maryland	...	...	...	...	...	...	...	...	...	...	...
Massachusetts	...	60,500(b)	1,000(b)	...	...	...	...	950(l)	4,000(b) 65,000(b)	6,500(b)	...
Michigan	...	...	...	...	...	...	...	...	...	...	...
Minnesota	575(l)	7,036(b)	...	...	...	...	...	...	3,500(l)	2,200(b)	...
Mississippi	...	100,000(l)	3,000(b)	1,500(l)	...	...	...	...	...	...	...
Missouri	...	...	...	...	...	...	...	...	...	...	5,000(l)
Montana	253(l)	...	...	...	...	...	...	...	17,045(l)	...	...
Nebraska	...	...	...	...	...	...	...	...	...	...	...
Nevada	...	...	...	...	...	...	...	...	...	...	...
New Hampshire	...	...	...	...	...	...	...	83,000(b,l)	7,325(l)	...	...
New Jersey	...	...	...	...	...	...	...	...	...	...	...
New Mexico	...	...	...	...	...	1,362(b)	...	...	...	2,000(b)	...
New York	6,200(b)	1,350(b)	...	...	...	...	...	...	...	...	...
North Carolina	...	...	...	...	...	...	...	...	...	...	...
North Dakota	...	...	...	...	...	1,343(l)	...	...	...	3,450(l)	...
Ohio	...	...	...	...	...	40,000(b)	...	...	305(l)	296,727(l) 1,315(l)	...
Oklahoma	...	7,000(l)	...	...	...	...	...	...	...	...	...
Oregon	...	...	...	...	...	...	...	18(l)	1,350(b)	9,062(b)	...
Pennsylvania	...	...	...	10,600(b)	...	...	...	...	...	...	...
Rhode Island	...	...	...	...	...	...	...	...	830(b)	734(b)	...
South Carolina	...	...	...	...	...	...	...	...	...	...	...
South Dakota	...	...	...	3,163(l)	...	...	...	...	...	...	...
Tennessee	...	...	...	...	...	...	...	...	...	40,000(l)	...
Texas	...	...	...	...	...	2,787(l)	...	...	11,057(l)	8,994(b,l)	...
Utah	...	1,308(l)	...	...	...	...	...	...	...	1,500(b)	...
Vermont	...	...	...	...	...	...	...	...	...	...	...
Virginia	...	...	...	125(l)	...	...	...	...	10,000(l)	...	...
Washington	...	9,300(l)	...	44(l)	...	...	...	...	3,700(l)	17,780(l)	...
West Virginia	...	...	...	...	...	...	...	...	700(l)	...	...
Wisconsin	...	...	...	...	...	...	626(b)	623(b)	8,096(b)	...	...
Wyoming	80(l)	474(l)	...	...	523(l)	...	...	...	3,888(l)	1,950(l)	...

Source: Information derived from survey of key state officials conducted by the Council of State Governments (1987) for the National Council on Public Works Improvement.

(b) bonds
(l) loans

AGRICULTURE AND RURAL DEVELOPMENT

By Judith C. Hackett

The farm crisis of the early 1980s caused many state leaders to focus attention on the needs of rural citizens. Until that time, state agriculture and farm programs were directly related to federal mandates, environmental and health responsibilities and marketing. Farm bankruptcies and the apparent inability of the U.S. Department of Agriculture and the Farm Credit System to resolve farmers' problems led both farmers and farm groups to turn their attention to state legislatures, governors and other state leaders.

Most state leaders realized that the factors which caused farm foreclosures, bank failures and small community bankruptcies were beyond their control. States, however, began to show an increasing interest in rural problems and a willingness to address the factors which they could control. During the late 1980s, agriculture and rural policy has become a growth area for state governments. Two goals tend to dominate the new programs: creating jobs in rural communities to ensure their survival; and encouraging economic development in agriculture and natural resource-based industries.

Agriculture and Rural Economic Problems

Rural stress has been a buzzword used to describe the conditions experienced by both the people and the economies in many states. With the exception of the Northeastern region of the country, unemployment is considerably higher in rural areas than in metropolitan areas. Rural employment growth is slower, and rural population is declining, due in part to downturns in several industries important to rural areas.

Rural Economies. Thirty years ago, agriculture was the dominant employer in rural America. In 1950, 15 percent of the population, 23 million people, lived on farms and one-third of the rural work force was directly engaged in

agriculture-related jobs. By the 1980s, less than 3 percent of the population lived on farms, and agriculture accounted for a much smaller proportion of rural income. Throughout the nation, manufacturing employment accounted for almost as many jobs as farm employment (see Table A).

In the South, mining (including oil and gas) and manufacturing are often as important as agriculture in rural counties. Most Midwestern states are farm-dependent, but manufacturing is a significant factor in many states outside of the great plains. The rural West is dominated by federal lands, and many states depend heavily on government jobs and retirement income. The Northeast is the most diversified (ungrouped) of the regions, but many rural counties are heavily dependent on manufacturing. Of the 240 rural counties with persistent low-income, only 20 are found outside of the southern region.

This increased diversity of the rural economy has been an important consideration as states have developed agriculture and rural programs. In the 1930s, when many of the nation's farm and rural policies were created, rural problems usually meant new agricultural programs. During the 1950s and into the 1960s, the focus turned to problems of poverty and high unemployment, and many of our regional and special focus group programs began in rural America.

Community development became an important aspect of rural development strategies during the 1960s and 1970s. Developed in part to assure equal access to rural residents, the regional planning and development commissions emphasized intergovernmental planning and growth strategies. The Economic Development Administration began and continues to

---

Judith C. Hackett is the director of the Center for Agriculture and Rural Development at The Council of State Governments.

fund many of these efforts, often in cooperation with other federal agencies and the states.

Economic development has become the dominant policy issue of the 1980s in state and local governments. The states, not the federal government, are in the forefront, and rural economic development has become a dominant theme in the states' approach to the economic difficulties which plague rural areas. In rural America, the reality of the global marketplace, the fluctuations of the dollar, and the growing service economy have hit home.

Rural Employment and Unemployment. While farming has declined in its importance as a source of income in rural areas, many rural people have continued to live on their farms. Instead of leaving rural areas, off-farm income has increased in its importance to many farm families, particularly medium sized and small farms. On the average, more than 50 percent of farm family income now comes from off-farm sources (see Table B).

Rural unemployment is now significantly higher than metropolitan area unemployment in most of the country. The average rural unemployment rate in 1986, the most recent data available, exceeds the metropolitan rate by 3.4 percent. Table C provides information on the total employment, unemployment rates, and changes from 1979 to 1986. States with the lowest rural unemployment rates (Rhode Island, Connecticut, Massachusetts, Delaware and New Hampshire) are primarily manufacturing-based, located in the Northeast and relatively small in size and urbanized. The states with the highest rural unemployment rates (Louisiana, West Virginia, Alaska, Arizona and Mississippi) are more diverse, located in the South and West, depend somewhat heavily on mining and are not urbanized (see Table D).

Rural Population. There has been a general population decline in rural areas since the turn of the century, which reversed itself during the 1970s. The 1980s first saw a slowed growth, and then a net population loss in many states' rural areas. If we ranked the states by the size of their rural population today, Texas would be the largest with 3 million. North Carolina, Ohio, Georgia, Illinois and Kentucky are next in line with rural populations of more than 2 million. Four of these top 6 states are located in the South and the remaining 2 are Midwestern. However, only North Carolina and Kentucky are truly rural states, with a large percentage of their population living in nonmetropolitan areas. Texas and Illinois might be classified (see Table

D) as urban since more than 70 percent of the population live in cities, and Ohio and Georgia are mixed.

Rural areas have actually lost population in 6 states during the 1980s: Illinois, Indiana, Iowa, Minnesota, Nebraska and West Virginia. In 5 other states, rural population is growing faster than in the metropolitan areas: California, Connecticut, Florida, Hawaii and Massachusetts. The rural population puts quite different demands on the states' leaders depending upon whether they are coping with the problems of growth or the problems of decline.

Leadership for State Agriculture and Rural Policy Development

State governments have been reluctant to create new agencies to address agriculture and rural development needs, and with good reason. The needs of farmers and rural communities are not different that than those of other citizens, they are merely harder to address because of remote locations. Some rural areas are trying to cope with growth, others with decline. Nevertheless, within the framework of existing federal and state programs, state leaders have been creative in their approach. In those cases where new programs and agencies are being created, careful thought and consideration come first.

Executive-Branch Action - State treasurers, lieutenant governors, attorneys general and commissioners of agriculture were among the first to establish special programs and services for farmers. The linked-deposit program, developed by the Ohio State Treasurer, and now also used for small business development purposes, has been created in many states. Linked deposit programs provide lower-cost financing by allowing banks with state deposits to pay below-market interest and give a corresponding lower interest to certain types of borrowers.

Disputes between farmers and lenders were the basis for another type of state program which evolved out of the farm crisis. Farmer-lender mediation programs, both voluntary and mandatory, developed with the advice and leadership of many state attorneys general. The purpose of these programs is to arrange third-party intervention where foreclosure is imminent to seek non-legal remedies such as refinancing and financial assistance.

More aggressive marketing of agricultural products has been the goal of departments of agriculture for many years. Some commissioners, directors and secretaries were visible as supporters of financial assistance programs and were instrumental in generating increased farm export activity and crop diversification. Hotlines were established, crisis services promoted, and these officials took a direct personal interest in promoting state farm products.

Most of the early state initiatives were the result of a executive branch agency official responding to the crisis needs of rural citizens and organizations. The absence of significant new agriculture or rural development action by federal officials and the elimination of Federal Revenue Sharing, which provided a significant proportion of intergovernmental aid to rural communities, led state leaders to reassess the situation. State officials took a careful look at what was happening in their rural areas and began developing longer-term responses. Many agree that the problems are not short-term, will not be resolved by farm programs or the federal government and may not lend themselves to national solutions.

Executive and Legislative Leadership - The New York Joint Legislative Commission on Rural Resources provides a good example of the evolution of state rural policy. Established in the mid-80s, it relied on an extensive base of facts about rural New York and suggestions from rural citizens before developing its strategic recommendations. As a result, the New York Office of Rural Affairs was established in 1987 as part of the Office of the Governor and serves as an advocate, ombudsman and facilitator for rural issues and problems.

In Illinois, the governor established a Task Force on Rural Affairs to identify problems and recommend solutions. Local community leaders and rural citizens held hearings and made recommendations resulting in a "Rural Fair Share" initiative, an Office of Rural Affairs, and an increase in interagency cooperation within the state. Growing out of a Task Force on Jobs, the North Carolina lieutenant governor recommended creation of a Rural Economic Development Center which was funded by the legislature. In Florida, both the Department of Commerce and the Department of Agriculture are undertaking increased efforts on behalf of rural communities, Minnesota has created a Rural Development Board and a number of vehicles for increased rural investment, California's Rural Renaissance increases resources for both infrastructure and community promotion, and the list is only just beginning.

State Agriculture and Rural Development Programs Today

State leaders view agriculture as an important and vital industry that provides citizens with high-quality, affordable, nutritious diets. They also view it as an industry in transition that is as worthy of assistance as the steel, automobile or textile industries. In fact, for most of this century government leaders have held agriculture in special regard because U.S. farmers feed both this nation and the world. Advances in the industry, such as mechanization, chemicals and biotechnology, promise even more changes during the coming years, changes which will have a tremendous impact on rural communities.

Economic studies of rural America have been conducted by the federal government, state agencies, colleges and universities, local development organizations and private consultants during the 1980s. Most studies recommended states consider both agriculture and non-agriculture approaches in crafting long-term solutions to the farm and rural crisis in their states. In a 1986 survey, conducted by the Center for Agriculture and Rural Development at The Council of State Governments, four basic approaches were identified: agriculture-related development, transition assistance, rural business assistance and rural community assistance.

In 1986, more than 500 state programs were identified in 34 categories. An update of this survey (see Table E) found over 1,000 programs in 39 categories. Three state agencies emerge as the principal actors in state agriculture and rural policy formation: agriculture, economic development and community affairs. Other executive branch agencies, such as mental health, education and labor are providing "transition assistance" to individuals and communities in distress.

Most states had previously provided programs in each of the areas listed, often with federal support, but now are directing attention to rural needs. They may target a certain share of resources to rural areas, provide information and outreach to distressed rural communities, coordinate with other agencies and increase the number of pilot projects, innovation and technology transfers to rural areas. While many of the programs listed in Table E are not new, state agencies now report them among their resources for rural economic development.

Most frequently listed are agricultural export assistance (30 states), marketing agricultural and rural products (38), farmer and agribusinesss assistance (45), infrastructure (39), business retention programs (43), small business assistance (45) and tourism (38). The largest grouping of state programs is in rural business assistance.

Trends

During the remainder of the 1980s, states will be the leading innovators in agriculture and rural development policy. Improvements in farm prices will begin to be felt in rural economies, but many people will not return to farming as their primary source of income. An increased emphasis will be placed on the importance of small business development in rural areas and utility companies and cooperatives will play an increased role in local economic development.

As state leaders increase the effectiveness of their rural economic development strategies, the number of programs may decline somewhat. State elected officials are likely to use their personal leadership skills and those of local communities, private foundations, and business and community organizations to create an environment for rural development. New direct state aid will be a part of some state strategies, but notably absent in others.

Table A
Nonmetropolitan Counties, by Type and State

State	Farm dependent	Manufacturing dependent	Mining dependent	Government dependent	Federal lands	Persistent low income	Retirement destination	Ungrouped	Total Nonmetropolitan Counties (a)
All states	695	655	204	321	266	240	484	356	2384
Alabama	6	36	1	4	0	18	4	3	48
Alaska	0	7	1	19	22	1	1	0	22
Arizona	0	0	3	6	9	0	10	1	13
Arkansas	28	24	0	2	7	13	34	5	65
California	8	3	0	9	15	0	13	1	27
Colorado	17	0	11	12	33	1	8	4	53
Connecticut	0	2	0	0	0	0	0	0	2
Delaware	0	1	0	1	0	0	2	0	2
Florida	13	6	0	11	3	6	28	13	36
Georgia	32	57	3	13	7	27	22	13	121
Hawaii	0	0	0	0	0	0	2	1	3
Idaho	16	0	2	5	31	0	9	3	43
Illinois	28	11	7	6	1	2	4	20	76
Indiana	13	15	3	3	0	0	5	7	62
Iowa	54	14	3	2	0	0	0	21	88
Kansas	40	7	1	4	0	0	5	40	97
Kentucky	34	24	23	8	2	33	14	11	101
Louisiana	6	11	5	6	0	9	4	11	45
Maine	0	7	0	3	0	0	5	0	13
Maryland	0	1	0	1	0	0	4	4	9
Massachusetts	0	1	0	0	0	0	3	0	4
Michigan	3	26	4	17	4	0	31	2	61
Minnesota	35	10	2	9	2	1	9	11	71
Mississippi	19	32	1	5	1	39	7	13	75
Missouri	36	17	3	8	0	8	33	19	98
Montana	24	3	8	21	21	0	3	4	54
Nebraska	63	5	1	2	0	0	1	19	88
Nevada	1	0	5	3	14	0	6	0	15
New Hampshire	0	3	0	0	0	0	2	2	7
New Jersey	...	...	...	...	...	...	...	...	...
New Mexico	6	1	6	13	13	3	8	4	31
New York	0	16	0	5	0	0	4	4	27
North Carolina	15	43	0	10	7	14	18	4	75
North Dakota	39	1	5	8	1	1	0	5	49
Ohio	1	40	6	1	0	1	2	6	52
Oklahoma	15	6	11	13	15	10	16	12	63
Oregon	5	11	0	4	1	0	8	2	28
Pennsylvania	0	21	3	1	0	0	2	8	34
Rhode Island	0	0	0	1	0	0	0	0	1
South Carolina	1	26	0	3	2	9	4	1	34
South Dakota	42	0	1	16	3	2	1	11	65
Tennessee	1	46	3	12	1	26	16	5	69
Texas	62	20	43	19	24	5	77	37	205
Utah	3	2	7	5	24	0	7	1	25

Table A (Continued)
Nonmetropolitan Counties, by Type and State

State	Farm dependent	Manufacturing dependent	Mining dependent	Government dependent	Federal lands	Persistent low income	Retirement destination	Ungrouped	Total Nonmetro- politan Counties (a)
Vermont	0	3	0	1	0	0	1	7	12
Virginia	3	30	5	8	3	5	23	10	68
Washington	9	9	0	5	8	0	8	1	28
West Virginia	0	5	19	10	2	6	4	10	45
Wisconsin	15	15	0	4	1	0	16	10	52
Wyoming	2	0	11	2	11	0	0	3	22

Source: U.S. Department of Agriculture, Economic Research Service based on data from the Department of Commerce, Bureau of the Census and Bureau of Economic Analysis.
Note: For explanation of the definition of county types see: Bender, Lloyd D., Bernal L. Green, Thomas F. Hady, John A. Kuehn, Marlys K. Nelson, Leon B. Perkinson, and Peggy J. Ross. *The Diverse Social and Economic Structure of Nonmetropolitan America.* RDRR-49. U.S. Department of Agriculture, Economic Research Service. September 1985.

Metropolitan or metro areas are areas so designated by the Office of Management and Budget (OMB) as of 1984; all other area are nonmetro or nonmetropolitan areas. In general, a metropolitan area is a county with a city of 50,000 or more people or a set of cities with a combined of over 50,000; counties surrounding the core standard metropolitan statistical area (SMSA) county are also designated as metropolitan if they are economically and socially integrated with the core county.

Key
...-not applicable.
(a) Details will not add to totals because the county classifications are not mutually exclusive, except Ungrouped.

Table B
Total net farm income (a), off-farm income and operator household income by farm size: 1986

Type of income	Annual sales of $250,000 or more	Annual sales of $40,000 to $249,000	Annual sales under $40,000	All farms
Net Farm Income (a) (in millions)	$26,867	$13,665	$223	$40,756
Off-farm Income (in millions)	1,671	6,702	36,336	44,708
Total operator household income (in millions)	28,538	20,367	36,559	85,464
Off-farm income as a percent of total operator household income	5.9	32.9	99.4	52.2

(a) Before inventory adjustment.

Table C

Selected employment and unemployment data for nonmetropolitan and metropolitan portions of States

State or other jurisdiction	Nonmetro employment in 1986		Percentage of employment in goods-producing industries: 1984		Percentage change in employment: 1979-1986		Unemployment rate: 1986 Actual		Change from 1979	
	Total	As a percent of state total	Nonmetro	Metro	Nonmetro	Metro	Nonmetro	Metro	Nonmetro	Metro
All states	23294	23.5	33.3	24.6	4	12.8	9	6.4	2.9	0.7
Alabama	588	38.1	43.2	24.8	5.3	12.3	11.4	9	3.7	2.1
Alaska	118	71.2	19.4	13.3	28.6	49.5	13.1	8.4	2.4	1
Arizona	257	23.5	21.9	25.3	14.8	40.3	12.7	5.6	5.1	1.3
Arkansas	556	60	39.8	25.5	2.7	9.9	10.1	7	3.3	1.6
California	491	4.6	29.1	24.9	12.8	18.3	10.9	6.5	0.2	0.5
Colorado	257	18.8	22.5	23.2	-1.5	18.9	9.9	6.9	4.5	2.3
Connecticut	133	9	39.2	30.5	21.7	12.4	4.4	3.7	-2.1	-1.3
Delaware	101	38.8	30.5	30.8	24.4	17.4	4.1	4.4	-4.8	-3.3
Florida	438	11.3	27.3	20.6	29.5	36.2	6.8	5.6	-0.2	-0.3
Georgia	932	39.9	41.1	21.1	8.9	28.9	7.3	5.2	2.1	0.2
Hawaii	114	29.1	18.2	8.1	36.7	13	6.4	4.4	-0.4	-1.6
Idaho	331	81.4	29.2	19.8	3.7	9.3	9.6	5.9	3.3	1.7
Illinois	820	16	31.2	25	-11.2	4.7	11	7.6	4.8	2.2
Indiana	790	32	41.2	30.8	4.4	3.8	7.5	6.4	0.6	0.2
Iowa	731	53.5	28.9	22.5	-6	2	7.1	6.8	3.2	2.4
Kansas	548	48.2	26.1	24.4	-4.6	8.5	6.1	4.9	3.1	1.2
Kentucky	743	48.9	33.6	26.2	-3.4	5.5	11.2	7.3	4.7	2.7
Louisiana	464	28.7	30.5	21.1	-0.7	9.9	16.8	11.7	8.8	5.6
Maine	308	66.4	33.1	25.3	15.8	13.7	6	4.5	-1.8	-1.9
Maryland	158	8	27.6	17.6	33.2	11.8	6.1	4.3	-3.3	-1.3
Massachusetts	128	4.7	16.8	27.2	30.3	7.1	3.8	3.8	-2.8	-1.7
Michigan	701	17.6	31.1	31.5	-1.8	1.3	11.5	8.2	2.4	0.7
Minnesota	628	32.1	28	25.1	-6.2	14.3	7.1	4.6	2	0.9
Mississippi	687	71.2	37.2	22.2	0.5	21	13.2	8.5	7.1	3.5
Missouri	720	33	28.3	24.7	5.2	10.3	7.2	5.6	2.6	1.1
Montana	283	80.3	19.9	12.4	5.9	7.2	8.2	7.8	3	3.1
Nebraska	388	52.5	26.1	17.3	-2.1	9.5	5.4	4.5	2.8	0.5
Nevada	88	23.1	20.6	10	44.9	31.6	6.3	5.9	1	0.9
New Hampshire	210	47.3	29.4	35.3	19.1	25.5	2.4	3.1	-0.7	0.1
New Jersey	0	0	NA	25.8	NA	11.6	NA	5	NA	-1.9
New Mexico	322	62	21.6	17.2	4.9	35.7	11.4	6.6	5	0.1
New York	705	9.5	29.4	20.5	2.9	6.4	7.4	6.1	0	-1
North Carolina	1236	46.5	43.5	32.8	7	18.8	6.5	4.5	1.1	0.2
North Dakota	182	62.6	21	11.7	-2.4	23.5	7.4	4.8	3.6	1.5
Ohio	936	19.7	38.7	29	-2.2	1.9	10.1	7.7	3.6	1.9
Oklahoma	562	44.4	29.1	23.2	10.1	19	9.6	7.4	5.9	4.1
Oregon	373	32.2	31.3	23	5.9	6.7	10.3	7.7	1.8	1.5
Pennsylvania	730	14.6	36.1	27.7	2.3	5.7	8.7	6.5	0.8	-0.2
Rhode Island	44	10.1	20.6	32.5	27.1	12	3.6	4.2	-2.6	-2.6
South Carolina	554	42.1	40.8	31	5.2	20.3	8.2	5.1	2.4	0.6
South Dakota	263	81.2	18.6	19.6	-0.2	9.1	4.8	4.1	1.1	0.8
Tennessee	676	35.2	46.6	25.8	7.9	11	11.1	6.5	3.6	1.6
Texas	1325	21.3	33.4	25.2	19.6	19.6	9.8	8.7	5.6	4.5

Table C (Continued)

Selected employment and unemployment data for nonmetropolitan and metropolitan portions of States

State or other jurisdiction	Nonmetro employment in 1986		Percentage of employment in goods-producing industries: 1984		Percentage change in employment: 1979-1986		Unemployment rate: 1986 Actual		Change from 1979	
	Total	As a percent of state total	Nonmetro	Metro	Nonmetro	Metro	Nonmetro	Metro	Nonmetro	Metro
Utah	146	25.1	31.9	22.1	8.3	26.2	7.7	5.5	3.1	1.3
Vermont	206	87.9	30.4	30.9	17.7	21.6	5.2	3.6	0	-0.4
Virginia	710	29.5	41.2	18.1	1.5	18.9	7.7	4.1	1.8	-0.2
Washington	331	18.3	30.2	22.3	0.2	13.1	11.1	7.6	2.1	1.4
West Virginia	394	54.5	29.4	25.2	-.9	-10	13.3	9.5	5.5	4.2
Wisconsin	691	31.1	35.2	30	-.2	1.3	8.2	6.5	3.1	2.2
Wyoming	197	90.7	25.6	27.3	9.2	-18.1	8.5	10.9	5.7	8.7
District of Columbia	0	0	...	4	...	-2.3	...	7.6	...	0.2

Sources: Bureau of Labor Statistics and the Bureau of Economic Analysis, U.S. Department of Commerce.
Note: Metropolitan or metro areas are areas so designated by the Office of Management and Budget (OMB) as of 1984; all other areas are nonmetro or nonmetropolitan areas. In general, a metropolitan area is a county with a city of 50,000 or more people or a set of cities with a combined population of over 50,000; counties surrounding the core standard metropolitan statistical area (SMSA) county are also designated as metropolitan if they are economically and socially integrated with the core county.

Table D
Classification of states: Rural and Urban Population (in thousands)

State	Rural/Small Town (1)	Urban/Metro (2)	Other (3)	Nonmetro Total 1986	Population % Change 1980-1986 Nonmetro	Population % Change 1980-1986 State Total	Population % Change 1970-1980 Nonmetro	Population % Change 1970-1980 State Total	# Counties Nonmetro	# Counties Metro
All states				56,625	4	6.4	14.4	11.4	2,383	714
Alabama			x	1,455	1.7	4.12	12.26	13.05	49	19
Alaska			x	298	31.3	33.8	29.07	32.81	22	1
Arizona		x		777	14.7	20.7	49.8	53.3	12	2
Arkansas	x			1,439	2.7	3.8	17.5	18.9	65	10
California		x	x	1,324	18.9	14	33.4	18.5	27	31
Colorado		x	x	602	6.9	13	28.7	30.8	53	10
Connecticut		x		259	4	2.6	9	2.5	2	6
Delaware			x	215	9.6	6.5	20.9	8.4	2	1
Florida		x		1,184	25	19.8	53.7	43.5	36	31
Georgia			x	2,182	5.9	11.7	15.7	19.1	121	38
Hawaii		x		246	21.5	10.1	45	25.3	3	1
Idaho	x			809	4.9	6.2	28.3	32.4	43	1
Illinois		x		2,033	-2.6	1.1	5.1	2.8	76	26
Indiana			x	1,760	-0.6	0.2	7.7	5.7	62	30
Iowa	x			1,629	-3.6	-2.2	1.2	3.1	88	11
Kansas	x			1,213	0.2	4.12	3.7	5.1	97	8
Kentucky	x			2,033	2.5	1.8	18.7	13.7	101	19
Louisiana			x	1,391	5.9	7	8.9	15.5	45	19
Maine	x			706	5.1	4.4	15	13.2	13	3
Maryland		x		316	6.5	5.8	16.3	7.5	9	15
Massachusetts		x		254	12	1.7	36.5	0.8	4	10
Michigan			x	1,810	1.6	-1.3	17.1	4.3	61	22
Minnesota			x	1,443	-0.9	3.37	6	7.1	71	16
Mississippi	x			1,837	1.8	4.1	9.2	13.7	75	7
Missouri			x	1,731	2.4	3	12.1	5.1	98	17
Montana	x			619	3.6	4.1	13.9	13.3	54	2
Nebraska	x			848	-1.6	1.8	3.2	5.7	88	5
Nevada		x		169	17.7	20.4	52.3	63.8	15	2
New Hampshire	x			397	7.8	11.5	21	24.8	7	3
New Jersey		x		0	NA	3.5	NA	2.7	0	21
New Mexico	x			882	12.1	13.6	24.6	28.1	30	2
New York		x		1,690	0.1	1.2	5.9	-3.8	27	35
North Carolina	x			2,847	6.3	7.6	14.9	15.7	75	25
North Dakota	x			426	1.9	4.1	-0.9	5.7	49	4
Ohio			x	2,277	0	-0.4	8.8	1.3	52	36
Oklahoma			x	1,370	5.3	9.3	15.5	18.2	63	14
Oregon			x	879	1.2	2.5	28.7	25.9	28	8
Pennsylvania				1,830	0.2	0.2	7.5	0.5	34	33
Rhode Island		x		85	4.2	2.9	-13.6	-0.3	1	4
South Carolina	x			1,343	6.9	8.1	15.6	20.5	34	12
South Dakota	x			585	0.7	2.5	1.8	3.7	65	1
Tennessee			x	1,674	3.5	4.6	18.7	16.9	69	26
Texas		x		3,209	9.8	17.2	17.7	27.1	205	49
Utah		x		383	15.3	14	40	37.9	25	4

Table D (Continued)
Classification of states: Rural and Urban Population (in thousands)

State	Rural/Small Town (1)	Urban/ Metro (2)	Other (3)	Nonmetro Total 1986	Population % Change 1980-1986		Population % Change 1970-1980		% Counties	
					Nonmetro	State Total	Nonmetro	State Total	Nonmetro	Metro
Vermont	x			411	5	5.7	14.4	15	12	2
Virginia			x	1,650	3	8.2	16.7	15	68	30
Washington			x	848	4.7	8	22.5	21.1	28	12
West Virginia	x			1,217	-1.2	-1.6	16.1	11.8	45	10
Wisconsin			x	1,601	2.6	1.7	11.6	6.5	53	19
Wyoming	x			436	9.7	8	41.5	41.3	22	1

a. **Rural:** 41 percent, or less, of the State's population (1980) residing in urban places within metropolitan areas as defined in 1980.
Urban: 70 percent, or more, of the State's population (1980) residing in urban places within metropolitan areas as defined in 1980.
Other: more than 41 percent and less than 70 percent of the State's population (1980) residing in urban places within metropolitan areas as defined in 1980.
Source: U.S. Department of Agriculture, Economic Research Service, Agriculture and Rural Economy Division based on data from the U.S. Department of Commerce, Bureau of the Census.
(1) **Rural:** 41% or less of population in metro areas
(2) **Urban:** 70% or more in metro areas
(3) **Other:** More than 41% but less than 70% of population in metro areas

Table E
STATE RURAL DEVELOPMENT PROGRAMS, By State: 1988

	I. Agriculture-Related Development	II. Transition Tools	III. Rural Business Assistance	IV. Rural Community Assistance
Alabama	A,C,F,G	H,J,K	M,N,O,P,R,T,U,V,W	Z,BB,CC,DD,EE,FF,GG
Alaska	A,C,D,E,F,G	J	M,N,O,R,S,T,U,W,X	Z,AA,CC,DD,EE,GG,II
Arizona	A		M,N,O,P,Q,R,S,T,U,X,Y	Z,AA,BB,CC,DD,EE,FF, GG,HH,II
Arkansas	A,B,F		P,T,U,V	CC,EE,GG
California	B,F	H,J	M,N,O,P,Q,S,T,R,U,V,W,X	Z,AA,BB,CC,EE,GG
Colorado	D		N,O,P,Q,T,U,V,X	
Connecticut	D,F			AA,DD,HH
Delaware			M,O,P,Q,T,U,V,W,X	AA,BB,CC,DD,GG
Florida	A,B,E,F	I,K	M	Z,BB,
Georgia	A,B,F,D	H,I,K	M,N,O,Q,S,TV	Z,BB,CC,DD,EE,FF,HH
Hawaii	A,B,C,D,E,F	H,I,J	P,V	Z,CC,GG,HH
Idaho	A,E,F,G	H,J,K	M,N,O,T,U,X	AA,CC,HH
Illinois	A,B,C,D,E,F	H,J,K	M,N,O,P,Q,R,S,T,U,V,W,X	Z,AA,CC,DD,EE,FF,HH, GG
Indiana	A,B,C,D,F	J,K	N,P,T,U,W	CC
Iowa	A,B,C,D,E,F,	H,I,J,K	M,N,O,P,Q,R,S,T,U,V	Z,AA,CC,DD,EE,FF,GG
Kansas		H,J,K	M,P,R,T,U,V,W	CC,GG
Kentucky	A,B,C,E	J,K	M,N,O,P,Q,S,T,U,V,W,X	Z,AA,BB,CC,EE,GG
Louisiana	A,B,C,D,E,F	H,J	M,N,P,Q,S,T,U,V,W,X	Z,AA,BB,CC,EE,GG
Maine	A,B,C,D,E,F	H,I,J,K	O,Q,R,S,T,U,V	EE,GG,HH
Maryland			T,U,V	Z,CC,EE,GG
Massachusetts			M,P,Q,T,U,V	AA,BB,CC,EE,HH
Michigan	A,B,C,D,E,F,	I,J,K	M,N,O,P,Q,R,S,T,U,V,W,X	Z,AA,BB,CC,EE,GG,HH
Minnesota	C,D,E,F	H,I,J	M,N,O,P,Q,R,T,U,V,W,Y	AA,CC,EE,GG,HH
Mississippi	A,E,F	H	P,Q,T,U,V,X,W	AA,CC,DD,GG,HH
Missouri	A,B,C,D,E,F	J,K,	M,P,Q,T,U,V,W	AA,CC,EE,
Montana	B,C,D,E,F,G	H,J,K,L	M,N,P,T,U,W	AA,BB,CC,DD,FF,GG,HH
Nebraska	A,B,C,D,E	J,K	M,N,O,P,Q,S,T,U,V,W,X	CC,DD,GG,HH
Nevada		H	M,N,O,P,R,S,T,U,V,W	Z,BB,CC,DD,EE,GG
New Hampshire	F		M,U,Q	DD,EE,GG,HH
New Jersey	A,B,C,F	I,J,K	P,Q,T,U,V,W	CC,GG,HH
New Mexico	A,B,D,E,F		M,N,P,R,T,U,W,X	Z,AA,CC,EE,GG
New York	D,F	H,I,J,K	M,N,O,P,T,U,V,W,X,Y	AA,BB,CC,DD,GG,HH
North Carolina	D	H	M,P,T,U,X	AA,CC,DD,HH
North Dakota	A,B,C,D,E,F	H,I,J,K	M,N,P,T,U,V,Y	Z,CC,DD,EE,GG,HH
Ohio	C,F	J	P,R,T,W	CC,DD,GG
Oklahoma	F	K	S,U,V,W	Z,AA,CC,DD,EE,GG
Oregon	A,B,D,E,F	H	M,N,P,Q,T,U,V,W	Z,CC,EE,GG
Pennsylvania	A	J	M,N,O,P,R,T,U,V,W,X	AA,CC,DD,EE,GG
Rhode Island	F		R,T,U	CC,DD,GG
South Carolina	C,F	H,J	M,N,P,U	EE,GG
South Dakota	C,F	H,J,K	O,Q,U,X	
Tennessee	A,B,C,D,E,F	H,I,J,K	N,P,R,T,U,V	Z,CC,DD,EE,GG
Texas	E	H,J	M,P,T,U	AA,CC
Utah	D,E,F	H,J,K	M,Q,S,T,U,X,Y	Z,AA,BB,EE,GG
Vermont	A,D,F	H	M,N,P,Q,T,U,V,X	AA,BB,CC,GG,HH
Virginia	A,B,C,D,E,F	H,J,K	M,N,P,Q,T,U,V,X	AA,DD,GG,HH
Washington	A,B,D,E,F	J	N,O,P,T,U,W	Z,AA,CC,DD,EE,GG,HH
West Virginia	A,B,E,F	H	M,O,P,S,T,U,W	BB,CC,DD,GG,HH
Wisconsin	A,B,D,E,F	H,I,J,K	N,O,P,Q,R,T,U,V,W,X	Z,DD,EE,GG
Wyoming	A,B,C,D,E,F	H,J,K	M,N,O,P,Q,S,T,U,W	Z,GG

Source: Information derived from survey of the states conducted by the Center for Agriculture and Rural Development, The Council of State Governments (1988).

I. Agriculture-Related Development
    A. Agriculture Export Development
    B. Attracting Value-added Business
    C. Beginning Farmer Programs
    D. Biotechnology & Technology Transfer
    E. Crop Diversification
    F. Marketing Ag/Rural Products
    G. Other

II. Transition Tools
    H. Ag & Rural Development Commissions, Agencies, Etc.
    I. Assessing Competitive Advantages
    J. Farmer & Agribusiness Financial Programs
    K. Farmer Retraining and Counseling
    L. Other

III. Rural Business Assistance
    M. Economic Development, Comprehensive
    N. Entrepreneurship, Business Incubators, Etc.
    O. Job Creation/Training
    P. Location of New Business/Industry
    Q. Marketing and Export
    R. Plant/Military Base Closing
    S. Procurement Assistance
    T. Retention and Expansion of Existing Business
    U. Small Business Assistance
    V. Rural Enterprise Zones
    W. Tax Incentives for Private Investments
    X. Technology Transfer
    Y. Other

IV. Rural Community Assistance
    Z. Culture and Arts
    AA. Financial
    BB. Housing
    CC. Infrastructure
    DD. Land Use
    EE. Parks and Recreation
    FF. Quality of Life
    GG. Tourism
    HH. Other
    II. Day Care Services

Table F
Number of Farms and Size of Farms, By States, June 1, 1985-87 (a)

State	Number of farms			Size of farms (1,000 acres)		
	1985	1986	1987 (b)	1985	1986	1987 (b)
All states	2,274,730	2,211,920	2,173,410	1,014,383	1,007,643	1,002,463
Alabama	54,000	51,000	49,000	11,500	11,000	11,000
Alaska	680	670	660	1,450	1,410	1,400
Arizona	8,500	8,600	8,400	37,500	37,200	37,000
Arkansas	53,000	50,000	49,000	16,000	15,700	15,400
California	79,000	79,000	77,000	32,900	32,800	32,600
Colorado	26,700	26,600	26,800	34,400	34,200	34,000
Connecticut	4,000	3,800	3,700	480	450	440
Delaware	3,500	3,200	3,100	650	640	630
Florida	39,500	39,000	39,000	13,000	13,000	13,000
Georgia	50,000	49,000	48,000	13,500	13,300	13,000
Hawaii	4,600	4,400	4,200	1,950	1,950	1,950
Idaho	24,600	24,000	23,000	14,500	14,200	13,800
Illinois	90,000	86,000	84,000	28,700	28,700	28,600
Indiana	80,000	77,000	72,000	16,400	16,400	16,200
Iowa	111,000	109,000	107,000	33,600	33,600	33,500
Kansas	72,000	70,000	70,000	48,000	47,900	47,900
Kentucky	100,000	99,000	99,000	14,500	14,500	14,500
Louisiana	36,000	36,000	36,000	10,100	10,000	9,700
Maine	7,800	7,800	7,800	1,520	1,520	1,520
Maryland	17,500	17,000	17,000	2,600	2,500	2,400
Massachusetts	6,000	6,000	6,000	680	680	680
Michigan	62,000	60,000	58,000	11,400	11,300	11,300
Minnesota	96,000	93,000	92,000	30,400	30,000	30,000
Mississippi	48,000	46,000	45,000	14,100	14,000	13,800
Missouri	115,000	115,000	114,000	30,800	30,700	30,600
Montana	23,800	23,600	23,300	61,000	60,900	60,800
Nebraska	59,000	57,000	56,000	47,200	47,200	47,200
Nevada	2,500	2,400	2,400	8,800	8,800	8,800
New Hampshire	3,400	3,200	3,200	540	520	520
New Jersey	8,700	8,200	7,600	940	900	850
New Mexico	13,800	13,600	13,500	45,000	44,600	44,600
New York	44,000	42,000	40,500	9,100	8,700	8,600
North Carolina	76,000	73,000	72,000	10,800	10,800	10,800
North Dakota	34,000	33,000	32,500	40,900	40,700	40,500
Ohio	89,000	88,000	84,000	15,800	15,800	15,600
Oklahoma	71,000	71,000	70,000	33,000	33,000	33,000
Oregon	37,000	37,000	37,000	18,000	17,900	17,900
Pennsylvania	58,000	56,500	56,500	8,700	8,500	8,500
Rhode Island	750	750	750	73	73	73
South Carolina	27,500	27,000	26,000	5,500	5,400	5,200
South Dakota	36,500	36,000	35,000	44,500	44,500	44,500
Tennessee	98,000	96,000	96,000	13,400	13,000	12,600
Texas	177,000	162,000	160,000	135,500	134,000	133,200
Utah	13,900	13,700	13,600	11,600	11,400	11,300
Vermont	7,000	7,100	7,200	1,600	1,600	1,600
Virginia	54,000	50,000	50,000	9,600	9,600	9,600
Washington	38,000	38,000	37,000	16,100	16,000	15,800
West Virginia	21,000	21,000	21,000	3,600	3,700	3,700
Wisconsin	83,000	82,000	80,000	17,700	17,600	17,500
Wyoming	9,000	8,800	8,700	34,800	34,800	34,800

Source: Agricultural Statistics Board, National Agricultural Statistics Service, United States Department of Agriculture.
(a) A farm is a place as of June 1 that sells or could sell $1,000 of Agricultural products during the year.
(b) Preliminary.

CHAPTER NINE

INTER-GOVERNMENTAL AFFAIRS

DEVELOPMENTS IN FEDERAL-STATE RELATIONS

By Norman Beckman

The nation's lawmakers face a year in which posturing for the 1988 elections and the ongoing struggle to control the budget deficit dominate the agenda. Congress also will have to sort out a complex set of unresolved federal-state issues that will significantly influence what role the states can play in such crucial areas as education, health care, welfare reform, environmental protection, energy and taxes.

The assessment of John Shannon, director of the Advisory Commission on Intergovernmental Relations, captures the current situation and the foreseeable future as well: "The changing fiscal fortunes of the national government now stand out as the single most important factor reshaping relations between Washington and the 50 state-local systems. It has transformed the expansive 'Great Society' federalism of the 1960s into the fairly austere and competitive fend-for-yourself federalism of the 1980s."

Budget-driven Federalism

The states and the federal government have essentially been operating on budgets that provide for inflation adjustments coupled with marginal program expansion. Despite discussion about reducing the federal deficit, the federal budget continues to rise, although at a slower pace. Federal spending increased 5.5 percent in fiscal 1988, with the president proposing an increase of 5.7 percent for fiscal 1989. State spending over the next two years will be slightly higher, however, states are operating with balanced budgets.

Other federal-state comparisons of recent federal budgets can be edifying. Robert Gleason reported in the Winter 1988 issue of *Intergovernmental Perspectives* that: "While in fiscal 1987 the federal government spent about $1.20 for every dollar of receipts, the 50 state-local systems had about $1.10 in receipts for every dollar spent. In the aggregate, state and local revenues exceeded expenditures by approximately $60 billion. Although these revenues cannot properly be considered surpluses (the vast majority went into public employee pension funds), the contrast is striking. At the same time that the federal government is obligating future interest payments, state and local governments are covering future obligations."

With the exception of welfare reform, the administration is proposing no major legislative changes in mandatory programs for 1988 or 1989. However, the administration is proposing funding increases for elementary and secondary education and for employment and training programs above 1988 levels and is also seeking more funding for select health block grants, justice assistance and AIDS programs.

The administration's 1989 budget calls for many program cuts motivated primarily by a desire for greater privatization and what they view as strengthened federalism. There are large reductions for mass transit programs. The penny gas tax for mass transit activities would continue to be used to fund mass transit capital spending, rural transit and operating subsidies to small cities, but general tax dollars would not be used. Operating subsidies for medium and large communities are slated for elimination.

Termination has also been proposed for Urban Development Action Grants, economic development assistance and Appalachian regional development grants. A phased termination of the sewage treatment construction and community services block grant is being recommended to allow grantees time to solicit other sources of federal, state, local and private funding.

However, significant programmatic reductions in poverty-related programs such as Medicaid, food stamps, housing and child nutrition that were proposed last year, were declared "off

---

Mr. Beckman is Director of the Washington office of The Council of State Governments.

limits" by a legislative-executive budget agreement on spending and taxes.

Nevertheless, the budget calls for savings in these programs through penalties on having too high an error rate and regulatory changes that will have an impact on state costs and benefits. However, a need exists for further deficit reductions. In 1990, the deficit will likely exceed $160 billion — $60 billion more than the Gramm-Rudman-Hollings target.

The functional composition of grant outlays has changed significantly over the years. The health function has increased from 3 percent of federal aid in 1960 to an estimated 29 percent in 1989. Transportation has declined from 43 percent in 1960 to an estimated 15 percent in 1989. During the same period, funding rates changed considerably for education, training and employment programs as well as social services programs which increased from 7 percent in 1960 to 18 percent in 1989.

The highest per capita aid in 1987 went to such areas as New York, New Jersey, Puerto Rico and the Virgin Islands. The lowest per capita aid in the same year went to the South and to the Plains states.

The 1987 highway reauthorization act, traditionally a classic formula grant program, may be the most precedent-setting legislative event of the past two years. Included in the act were 120 demonstration projects. The net effect of the act is to dictate priorities for certain specific roads and bridges, thereby superseding the discretion of the governors and state highway administrators.

Since 1978, when a "high water mark" was set for grant funding, federal grants have declined by approximately one-third, from 27 percent of state and local spending to an estimated 17.1 percent in 1988. If that decline continues over the next decade, federal grants will by 1998 amount to about 11 percent of state and local spending, the same level as during the mid-1950s.

Infrastructure and the Budget

After two years of study, the National Council on Public Works Improvement in February, 1988, issued its report to the president and Congress. In the report, entitled *Fragile Foundations: A Report on America's Public Works*, the council concluded that, "We have worn through the cushion built by past generations." The council issued a report card on eight categories of public works. It gave solid waste disposal systems a "C minus" because few states have moved toward more aggressive waste reduction, separation and recycling efforts. Although there may be a trend toward safer landfills, there has been little progress toward waste reduction. Public opposition to the siting of such facilities remains a major problem.

The poorest grade given by the council, a "D", was in the area of hazardous waste. Despite increased funding for site cleanup, only a fraction of the two tons of waste per capita produced in America each year is being treated safely.

In conclusion, the National Council recommended that annual spending on infrastructure be doubled, from $45 billion to $90 billion, by the end of the century.

One section of the council's report dealt with the federal-state partnership in meeting infrastructure needs. The president's 1989 budget reported that the federal share of state and local capital expenditures increased from 8.3 percent in 1955 to 23.9 percent in 1960. This increase was largely due to the initiation of federal trust fund financing for the interstate highway system. This share reached 36 percent in 1980, but had declined to 26.3 percent by 1987. The major capital investment programs are for highways, mass transit, community development block grants and sewage treatment systems. Grants for capital investment are estimated to be $24.8 billion in 1989, or 21 percent of total grants-in-aid. These patterns reflect a decline in capital spending by state and local governments as well as shifts in federal grants policy.

The National Public Works Council urged the president and Congress to recognize the importance of maintaining a continuing federal role in infrastructure finance. According to the council, intergovernmental aid will be needed to launch major projects of national interest and to help jurisdictions with limited fiscal capacity. However, some changes in the form of federal spending were recommended to accommodate shifting federal, state and local roles and relative fiscal capacities. The council concluded in its report that whatever form federal assistance takes, it should offer state and local governments:

• Stability over several years to aid long range planning,

• Flexibility in the use of funds through such mechanisms as block grants, and,

• Incentives for increased efficiency and improved maintenance.

In addition, the federal government should "exercise restraint in adopting legislation that would limit the revenue raising capacities of state and local governments," the report stated.

The council urged the president and Congress to pay close attention to the negative effects of tax reform on state infrastructure financing, and to remove unwarranted limitations on the power of state and local governments to finance public works. For example, the Tax Reform Act of 1986 drastically limits arbitrage earnings on borrowed funds and restricts the use of municipal bond proceeds for quasi-public projects by imposing ceilings on allowable issues. These and other provisions are expected to limit the growth of tax-exempt bonds and to increase the cost of state and local borrowing. The law also lengthens depreciation schedules and repeals investment tax credits, which will increase the cost of joint public-private development of certain public works. Overruling a 100 year precedent, on April 20, 1988, the U.S. Supreme Court in *South Carolina v. Baker* held that the Constitution does not protect state and local governments against federal taxation or the interest received by holders of their bonds. The combined provisions of the 1986 law and the South Carolina decision impede the financial plans of state and local governments, reduce their fiscal capacity and limit their ability to finance necessary improvements.

Environmental protection and improvement

Having authorized several major environmental laws in 1987 and 1988, Congress will continue to revise and initiate environmental legislation. Among the issues requiring legislative action are acid rain, groundwater contamination, outdoor air pollutants such as chlorofluorocarbons and lead, solid waste management and pesticide residues in foods.

On acid rain, accelerated research on its origin and effect is the only likely response proposed for the next two years. One reason for the lack of legislative action is the confrontation between coal-burning states and those most affected by acid rain. Consequently, the administration has adopted a position that a control program is not yet warranted. A second reason is the administration's commitment to a Clean Coal program.

The policy issues surrounding the groundwater debate include whether the nation's groundwater is being threatened by contamination and how to coordinate traditional state primacy over groundwater protection with a growing federal role. How to apply existing laws to the challenges posed by advances in biotechnology also is being examined. Other emerging issues are the public health problems associated with exposure to pollutants (such as radon) in homes or offices, rather than outdoor exposure.

Finally, there is an emerging recognition that fragmentation of pollution control programs adversely affects state administration. Fragmentation occurs when the same pollutant is treated separately under the Clean Water Act and the Safe Drinking Water Act, for example, signaling the need for more comprehensive approaches to pollution control.

Similarly, a reshuffling of the rural economy could continue for many years, prompting interest in a more comprehensive approach to farm policy and rural development. This covers such related policy areas as job retraining for farmers, revitalizing non-agricultural rural business and supplemental earnings programs for farm families.

Energy programs

The rebound of world oil prices has lessened pressure on Congress to help the domestic oil industry and the oil-producing states. However, rising oil imports will continue to provoke controversy as producers of domestic oil, gas, coal and some state governments debate the advisability of fees or limits on imports.

Controversy can also be expected over proposals to deregulate "old" natural gas supplies and to stimulate gas exploration. The effects of increasing oil prices and high-priced transport on U.S. coal demand will continue. Nuclear power presents issues including reconciling federal, state and local roles to counteract nuclear accidents and restoring confidence in the Department of Energy's nuclear waste disposal program.

The adequacy and quality of electricity supply can become a problem for Congress as utilities are increasingly reluctant to build large, new generating plants in the face of state regulatory policies, proposals for deregulation and environmentalist opposition.

Banking

Congress also is considering expanding the

securities powers of banks and permitting securities firms to engage in banking. In 1987, the Comprehensive Bank Equality Act placed a temporary moratorium on new state banking laws. Current leading federal proposals allow bank underwriting of state-local revenue bonds and retain the state role in authorizing real estate, insurance and other non-banking activities for state-chartered institutions. These bills threaten pre-emption of state legislation that prohibits affiliations between commercial and investment banking, regulates export of insurance products to other states, restricts insurance powers gained through reciprocal banking transactions or allows state-chartered subsidiaries of bank holding companies to exercise state-granted insurance powers.

Intergovernmental Regulatory Relief

The states also have to be concerned not only with federal appropriations, but with the ebb and flow of regulation of domestic activities. A Nov. 29, 1987 *Washington Post* article reports that business representatives are lobbying all three branches of the federal government "to pre-empt tough regulatory action at the state level." Corporate lobbyists are on Capitol Hill seeking full federal authority in such areas as "regulation of pesticides, rules for evacuating areas around nuclear power plants, product liability, minimum health insurance benefits, warning labels for tobacco products and corporate takeovers."

A case in point is a House bill that would substitute a federal standard for most state tort laws on product liability. This version of the long debated proposal has been advocated by manufacturers to stop trial lawyers from filing suits in states that have not enacted tort reform. Business groups claim their goal is liability insurance that is more affordable. They are eager to promote uniformity in product liability laws around the country - despite the fact that insurance companies have been paying out less than .30 cents for every $1 collected in premiums.

Another recent congressional initiative would require early notice to consumers about credit card interest rates and other fees. This would pre-empt the more stringent advance disclosure requirements of 11 states.

NGA on Federalism

The National Governors' Association adopted federalism as its priority for 1987-88. In a recent background paper, *Restoring the Balance: States Leadership for America's Future*, NGA succinctly stated the problems:

• The federal government assumes authority by mandating state and local programs or services without providing the required funding.

• The federal government denies state and local taxpayers the authority to control the use of their own tax dollars by requiring that a significant portion of state and local resources be used to match federal programs. (For example, Aid to Families with Dependent Children costs states $8.7 billion per year, Medicaid costs states $21.2 billion per year, EPA construction grants cost states $2.1 billion per year, and federally aided highway construction costs states $2.5 billion per year.)

• The federal government unnecessarily pre-empts lower level decisionmaking by the establishment of overly specialized programs.

• The federal government promotes inefficiency by denying lower levels of government the flexibility to organize and deliver services in a consistent and coordinated manner.

• The federal government denies local decisionmaking authority by pre-empting state and local actions where there is not sufficient justification for a single national policy. (Recent examples include federal pre-emption of state usury laws and limits on truck sizes and weights.)

Regulatory relief is an area where all the federalism partners claim to be seeking more flexibility and authority for state and local governments. In October, 1987, the president signed Executive Order 12612, "Federalism." This order is designed to restore a more balanced division of responsibilities between the federal government and the states and to ensure that the principles of federalism guide agencies in the formulation and implementation of policies.

NGA reported in July 1987, that the administration has taken action to implement more than half of the 80 proposals by the nation's governors as part of a special project to improve state management of federal assistance programs. Changes ranged from reducing costly, time-consuming record-keeping demands to modifying administrative requirements that made it difficult to serve people properly. For example, statutes have been changed and regulations will soon be issued to allow teenage girls assisted by the federal foster care program to receive Medicaid benefits for their children.

In response to comments from the National Association of State Budget Officers (NASBO), the U.S. Department of Health and Human Services has clarified that states may estimate third-party liability for "medically needy" Medicaid recipients. In May 1987, the U.S. Department of Agriculture issued regulations abolishing mandatory hearings on state plans for the Women, Infants and Children supplemental food program because the costs of the sparsely attended hearings considerably outweighed their public benefit.

An addendum to the president's 1989 budget reports a number of other reforms. In March 1987, the president directed all federal grant-making agencies to propose and simultaneously adopt a single, government-wide grants management rule.

In 1988, federal agencies will be meeting for the third consecutive year with state "Single Points of Contact," who are responsible for implementation of the Intergovernmental Review Process. The process, now in its fourth year, allows states to choose which federal programs they wish to review and requires that the federal agencies accommodate state concerns or explain why they cannot.

A state and federal task force continues to work on ways to improve the actual intergovernmental transfers of about $120 billion in federal assistance funds. Proposed legislation would require that states be charged interest on federal funds from the time they receive the funds to the time the intended recipients' checks clear the states' banks. Similarly, the federal government will pay interest when state funds are used for federal assistance payments.

Where Are We Going?

While the President may propose intergovernmental changes, it is Congress that must dispose. This has been especially true during the past few years. Congress can take much of the credit or blame for our current system of federalism, one that has been acquired through fits of absentmindedness, incrementalism and pragmatism.

Sandra S. Osbourn of the Congressional Research Service, writing in the January 1988, *CRS Review*, observes that: "The Congress seldom confronts issues of federalism directly. Although Members often dispute whether gov-

ernmental functions under debate are best performed by the states or by the national government, one does not often hear a voice characterized as a vote for or against federalism. Over the years [however], a number of proposals have been presented to focus congressional attention on the federalism factor in public policy. The intention has been to create mechanisms to ensure that the principles of federalism are given consideration along with other economic, social, political, or regional values."

Osbourn goes on to list some of the proposals:

• Mandate reimbursement — identification and reimbursement of costs incurred by state and local governments to carry out activities mandated by the federal government,

• Federalism convocation — periodic assemblies to assess the state of federalism and propose changes (which the Congress and the state legislatures would be required to consider),

• Federalism subcommittees — judiciary subcommittees on state and local government in each chamber, with joint jurisdiction over proposed legislation that affects state or local government practices or authority, and,

• Federalism assessments — analogous to environmental impact statements which would identify the likely impact of proposed legislation on federalism.

These proposals are intended to permit Congress to act as the guardian and shaper of our federal system. None of them, however, has been seriously debated in the halls of Congress.

A new administration and a new Congress will take office in January 1989. Whatever decisions are made by the nation's voters, no one can expect a return to major expansion of the federal role. As John Kincaid of ACIR has observed, "With a $2 trillion national debt and record trade deficit, the federal government can no longer ride to the rescue with a full complement of cavalry. Indeed, the states may have to rescue the national government occasionally, as they have to some extent in international trade."

On the one hand, according to some intergovernmental Cassandras, the trends toward reduced domestic appropriations and deregulation are increasing economic disparity among the states, reversing previous trends. The next few years are likely to bring a continuation of this unfortunate pattern, starting off with even larger projected federal budget deficits and an uncertain tax base caused by insecure economic conditions.

Perhaps the optimistic note offered by John Herbers in the October 1987, issue of *Governing* will prove to be more accurate: "The future seems likely to be one in which the federal government will build its programs around the innovations of the states and localities rather than returning to the pre-emption by Washington of state and local prerogatives that characterized the 1960s and 1970s."

Table 9.1
TOTAL FEDERAL AID TO STATES: FISCAL 1981-1986
(In thousands of dollars)

State or other jurisdiction	1986	1985	1984	1983	1982	1981
Total	$112,596,374	$105,478,200	$97,208,644	$92,711,726	$88,221,369	$94,806,164
Alabama............	1,758,540	1,719,040	1,532,194	1,469,539	1,429,024	1,493,313
Alaska.............	664,264	639,871	615,698	540,720	421,922	447,917
Arizona............	1,206,279	1,121,528	989,925	844,994	799,223	864,322
Arkansas	1,123,249	1,013,635	946,183	901,417	843,779	886,840
California..........	11,291,464	10,558,790	9,798,986	9,205,482	9,015,844	10,007,616
Colorado	1,220,384	1,165,999	1,176,127	1,058,269	966,730	1,021,503
Connecticut	1,501,285	1,377,388	1,221,429	1,190,471	1,120,139	1,180,030
Delaware	313,591	318,028	298,517	306,816	279,369	313,613
Florida	3,244,213	3,121,681	2,783,803	2,819,394	2,859,149	2,867,706
Georgia............	2,731,619	2,371,486	2,213,733	2,110,175	2,185,305	2,169,244
Hawaii	473,368	435,570	458,783	456,678	407,598	442,955
Idaho	434,913	444,926	413,181	375,421	349,847	361,130
Illinois............	5,009,911	4,688,411	4,303,812	4,191,166	4,102,545	4,610,352
Indiana............	2,000,307	1,825,318	1,759,904	1,610,777	1,558,397	1,728,750
Iowa	1,158,209	1,163,730	1,091,051	980,568	893,175	961,018
Kansas	883,894	855,971	804,770	762,936	706,359	773,800
Kentucky	1,784,168	1,763,550	1,589,665	1,488,891	1,424,407	1,433,417
Louisiana	2,038,882	1,785,154	1,776,119	1,709,614	1,591,449	1,729,516
Maine	672,328	659,419	590,372	575,000	526,788	535,999
Maryland	1,959,278	1,811,665	1,697,453	1,790,362	1,792,714	1,889,555
Massachusetts	3,081,662	2,842,210	2,634,160	2,897,635	2,745,416	2,888,996
Michigan	4,353,181	3,961,474	3,775,972	3,614,250	3,634,110	4,107,594
Minnesota	2,109,814	1,982,655	1,864,551	1,764,801	1,769,271	1,773,557
Mississippi	1,344,494	1,188,296	1,175,894	1,101,157	1,090,755	1,098,354
Missouri	1,982,447	1,935,316	1,774,670	1,674,905	1,651,796	1,662,812
Montana............	591,747	583,689	531,604	476,667	381,641	448,779
Nebraska	660,741	675,346	636,981	574,797	523,785	517,337
Nevada	418,308	387,267	340,350	356,360	346,200	350,592
New Hampshire	404,309	419,964	367,567	351,751	317,026	306,355
New Jersey	3,353,546	2,945,210	2,871,056	2,811,523	2,718,474	2,891,042
New Mexico........	856,588	891,071	862,668	675,756	727,234	715,855
New York	12,380,416	11,092,526	10,268,490	10,006,891	9,287,674	10,374,341
North Carolina	2,281,011	2,133,677	1,929,252	1,877,549	1,852,428	1,908,847
North Dakota	433,148	452,291	453,685	371,668	301,489	317,578
Ohio	4,763,920	4,158,358	4,044,258	3,641,767	3,611,567	3,725,226
Oklahoma	1,399,610	1,235,997	1,166,536	1,075,391	991,209	1,043,326
Oregon	1,339,996	1,449,139	1,246,130	1,162,916	1,167,622	1,174,601
Pennsylvania	5,717,963	4,963,560	4,667,346	4,817,080	4,629,305	4,886,585
Rhode Island	570,166	573,163	547,622	486,162	470,960	481,978
South Carolina	1,322,214	1,323,560	1,168,961	1,112,715	1,042,943	1,009,353
South Dakota	457,384	480,179	435,909	360,952	324,773	355,544
Tennessee	2,128,234	2,049,340	1,885,172	1,686,750	1,607,375	1,909,665
Texas..............	5,224,805	4,476,730	4,136,482	3,805,616	3,725,332	4,146,183
Utah	807,257	759,414	708,143	621,539	604,617	593,277
Vermont	334,006	336,386	331,008	312,181	270,662	279,382
Virginia...........	1,994,506	1,816,529	1,628,438	1,665,881	1,623,108	1,861,670
Washington	1,904,876	1,826,295	1,697,921	1,536,779	1,579,965	1,771,273
West Virginia	1,062,941	904,024	819,209	840,398	771,613	940,997
Wisconsin..........	2,309,880	2,111,744	2,063,878	1,903,748	1,894,379	2,298,782
Wyoming	471,237	503,437	556,326	425,629	348,521	320,876
Dist. of Col.	1,423,040	1,498,202	1,381,886	1,355,941	1,295,321	1,417,140
Puerto Rico	2,296,490	2,347,583	2,231,139	2,110,626	1,397,295	1,351,763
Virgin Islands	141,158	131,661	136,803	91,390	116,427	153,557
Other..............	346,486 (a)	314,330 (a)	341,672 (a)	347,784 (a)	270,008 (b)	277,515 (b)
Adjustments or undistributed to states...	858,675	1,856,417	465,200	406,081	-142,695	-273,164

Sources: Figures for 1979 through 1982 from U.S. Department of the Treasury, *Federal Aid to States, Fiscal Year 1982* (rev. ed.); figures for 1983 through 1986 from U.S. Department of Commerce, Bureau of the Census, *Federal Expenditures by State for Fiscal Year 1983; 1984; 1985; 1986.*

(a) Includes American Samoa, Guam, Northern Mariana Islands, and Trust Territory.
(b) Includes American Samoa, Guam, Northern Mariana Islands, Tokelau Islands, Trust Territory of the Pacific, and Saipan.

CHANGING STATE-LOCAL RELATIONSHIPS

By Joseph F. Zimmerman

The legal and other relationships between States and their political subdivisions continued to change during 1986 and 1987 as evidenced by statutory enactments and judicial rulings. In two States, major reports issued by state commissions addressed in broad terms the principal issues involving the two planes of government.

Connecticut Advisory Commission on Intergovernmental Relations released a 1987 report — *Home Rule in Connecticut* — that referred specifically to the State Supreme Court's decision in *Shelton v. Commission* [193 Conn. 506 at 521, 479 A.2d 208 at 216 (1984)]. The report maintained that "home rule legislation was enacted to enable municipalities to conduct their own business and control their own affairs to the fullest extent possible in their own way...," but added the Court's decisions have limited severely the ability of cities and towns to exercise "home rule" powers by charter or ordinance.

In May 1987, the New York State Legislative Commission on State-Local Relations issued a special report — *New York's State-Local Service Delivery System: Legal Framework and Services Provided* — stressing the need for "quality" information to assist the State in understanding "when, where, and how the legal structure needs to be adjusted and/or local initiative needs to be encouraged...."

LOCAL DISCRETIONARY AUTHORITY

The general trend in statutory enactments during 1986 and 1987 was to grant broader discretionary powers to general purpose local governments.

In Florida, new legislation (Chapter 87-287) authorizes the Division of State Fire Marshal to establish uniform fire safety standards and provides a conflict resolution method for local government building and fire code officials to use if they are unable to agree on the building code or fire code that is best. Although the offi-

cials must agree relative to the code providing the greatest degree of fire safety, no agreement can restrict the authority of the State Fire Marshal. The chapter also stipulates that local officials must review building plans to determine whether they comply with the applicable state minimum building code or fire code. The Division of the State Fire Marshal estimates that counties and municipalities will save approximately ten to fifteen million dollars annually by uncovering flaws in the construction plan review process.

Other new legislation (Chapter 87-233) clarifies procedures relative to municipal incorporation, creation of a dependent special district, amalgamation of municipalities or counties with special districts, and mergers of special districts. The previous wording of section 165.041 of the *Florida Statutes* was confusing and inconsistent. The 1987 law makes clear that a new municipality may be incorporated only by special act of the state legislature, and existing municipalities or special districts may merge with each other, and special districts may merge with each other by following a stipulated local procedure.

To assist local governments in coping with the problems of growth and escalating costs, the Florida Legislature enacted the "Local Government Infrastructure Commitment Act" (LOGIC Act) authorizing counties and municipalities to levy, subject to referendum, a one cent local option sales tax for a maximum period of fifteen years for infrastructure purposes.

Other changes in Florida are as follows: Chapter 87-259 authorizes counties to charge a maximum of fifty cents per line for recurring charges relative to the operation and maintenance of a "911" emergency telephone system. Previously, counties could charge a

---

Joseph F. Zimmerman is professor of Political Science, Graduate School of Public Affairs, State University of New York at Albany.

maximum of fifty cents per line for only start-up costs.

Chapter 87-88 authorizes counties and municipalities to enter into jurisdictional agreements with owners of private roads relative to the application of traffic laws on such roads.

Chapter 87-129 repeals the restriction — *Florida Statutes*, §162.05(2)(c) — upon the number of successive terms a member of a local government code enforcement board may serve. In addition, charter counties, by ordinance, may adopt an alternative code enforcement system under which code enforcement boards or county-designated special masters have the authority to hold hearings and assess fines against violators of county codes and ordinances.

Chapter 87-263 authorizes counties to include municipalities or a section of a municipality in a municipal service taxing unit. However, a municipality included in such a unit may remove itself from the unit by ordinance.

Chapter 87-190 removed the requirements in the *Florida Statutes* that all county records must be stored at the county seat by requiring that only official records — deeds, mortgages, and liens — be kept at the county seat.

Chapter 87-346 — *Florida Governmental Cooperation Act* — contains a mechanism for resolution of interlocal disputes which must be followed prior to the initiation of litigation. Notice of intent to file suit must be given to the potential defendant a minimum of 45 days prior to the filing of the suit, and the party receiving the notice must discuss the proposed litigation in an effort to resolve the dispute amicably.

Chapter 87-103 authorizes any municipality located within a county, defined in subsection 125.011(1) of *Florida Statutes*, to levy and collect a special assessment against a property benefited within a retail and/or wholesale business district and/or nationally recognized historic district through promotion, management, marketing, and similar services in the business districts of the municipality.

Other states have also recently made significant changes. The 1985 Wisconsin State Legislature enacted Act 29 — §59.025 and §29.026, *Wisconsin Statutes* — granting counties the authority to "exercise any organizational or administrative power, subject only to the constitution and any enactment of the Legislature which is of statewide concern and which uniformly affects every county," and directing that the grant of power "be liberally construed in favor of the rights, powers, and privileges of counties to exercise any organizational or administrative power."

The 1987 New Hampshire State Legislature enacted three major laws affecting cities and towns. Chapter 54 amends the *Revised Statutes Annotated* (§33.3-d) by allowing the governing body of a town, school district, or village district to issue refunding bonds with a public hearing required if the issue is in excess of $100,000. Chapter 329 authorizes the establishment and affirms the status of pooled risk management programs established for the benefit of substate units, and declares that pooled risk management is an essential governmental function not subject to regulation or taxation as an insurance activity by the State. Political subdivisions may join pooled risk management programs, by vote of their governing body, for any type of coverage. Chapter 79 requires the Departments of Transportation and Safety to hold regional conferences with local police departments, public works departments, and the general public for the purpose of discussions and recommendation to the two state agencies relative to highway markings, speed limits, traffic lights, and related safety matters.

A 1987 change in the New York Laws (Chapter 477) requires the State Department of Environmental Conservation, at the request of a municipality, to provide technical assistance relative to the development and implementation of solid waste management programs. A separate act (Chapter 490) authorizes the State Environmental Facilities Corporation to provide assistance to municipalities relative to the recovery, reduction, or recycling of industrial materials from the waste stream for disposal in municipal facilities. As of mid-1987, only two general purpose local governments in New York were granted authority by the State Department of Environmental Conservation to assume regulatory authority for the protection of freshwater wetlands within their boundaries under provisions of the State Freshwater Wetland Law.

FINANCE

The 1987 Minnesota Legislature enacted a law placing a stringent three percent levy limit on all cities effective with 1988 levies with each city's base defined as the payable 1987 levy plus 1987 local government aid, taconite aid, and wetlands/native prairie reimbursements. In payable year 1988 only, a city may appeal to the

Commissioner of Revenue for an adjustment in the base only if the city "can provide evidence satisfactory to the Commissioner that its levy for taxes payable in 1987 had been reduced because it had made expenditures from reserve funds, or for any other reason, or that it is necessary to levy additional amounts for taxes payable in 1988 which were not levied in 1987."

In Colorado, H.B. 1145 of 1987 allows municipalities with dormant police pension funds to use the funds for other pension or law enforcement purposes. Also, S.B. 100 clarifies the authority of counties to remove various refuse constituting a health hazard from private property and assessing costs to the property owners for the removal, while S.B. 23 authorizes counties to levy a tax on lodging up to two percent with the proceeds dedicated to local tourism marketing and promotion.

The 1987 Ohio Legislature enacted two laws granting local governments additional authority to raise revenue. H.B. 419 empowers general purpose local governments to raise road and bridge funds by enactment of additional permissive motor vehicle license taxes. Counties, municipalities, and townships may impose additional license fees. Counties, for example, may levy an additional ten dollars, in five dollar increments. The first increment must be enacted by April 1, 1989 and the second increment by April 1, 1991. H.B. 274, the "piggyback" sales tax law, authorizes the enactment of sales tax increase in one-fourth percent instead of one-half percent increments, and removes the requirement that the third one-half percent tax increase must be submitted to the voters for their action.

The 1987 Pennsylvania State Legislature enacted Act 47 — Financially Distresses Municipalities Act — appropriating $4.5 million in grants and no interest loans to severely distressed local governments, and providing planning and technical expertise to assist the units in avoiding bankruptcy. No funding received under the Act may be employed to retire municipal debt. The State Department of Community Affairs is charged with implementing an "early warning system" to assist in the identification of financial problems prior to a crisis occurring. To facilitate the process, the Department will post a "survey of financial condition form" to each municipal clerk or secretary annually by January 1st. The form must be completed and returned to the Department by March 15th.

Georgia House Bill of 1987 amended the Official Code of Georgia Annotated (§35-82-7) by allowing the deposit in Local Government Investment Pools of the proceeds of bonds issued by a political subdivision. Previously, such funds could not be invested in such pools.

LEGAL DECISIONS AND ADVISORY OPINIONS

In Johnson v. City of Fort Payne (20 ABR 1571), the Alabama Supreme Court held that the state constitution prohibits a local ordinance on a subject covered by a general law. The same Court, in Buskey v. Mobile County Board of Registrars (21 ABR 1276) ruled in 1986 that constitutional amendment 389 ratified all local acts enacted as "general acts of local application" prior to January 13, 1978, but added that such acts remain applicable to their respective counties and municipalities even if their population changes.

A decision of the Virginia Supreme Court in County Board v. Brown (229 Va. 341) made clear that the ulra vires rule remains in force in the Commonwealth relative to the powers of counties. The Court held that the legislative grant to municipal corporations of a general power to lease government property to others, when compared to a restrictive grant to counties to deal with their property, demonstrates a clear legislative intent to withhold from counties any power to lease not otherwise specifically granted.

In Pesticide Public Policy Foundation v. Village (no. 63297, June 1987), the Illinois Supreme Court ruled that a non-home rule village's pesticide regulation ordinance was invalid because the field of regulation was occupied by the State Pesticide Act of 1979 and the Structured Pest Control Act.

Also in 1987, the Georgia Supreme Court held in Wilson v. City of Snellville (352 S.E.2d 759) that the provision of notice of a rezoning action by publication as required by the City's zoning ordinance fulfilled the due process of law requirement.

The New York State Supreme Court, a general trial court, in October 1987 ruled that the Town of Colonie has the right to determine by means of its zoning ordinance where mines can be operated. The Guptil Holding Corporation had maintained that only the State Department of Environmental Conservation could decide where mines were permitted since the Corporation's mining activities predate the town's zoning ordinance and the Corporation's operations are a permitted non-conforming use.

On February 14, 1986, Attorney General Mary Sue Terry of Virginia issued an opinion that a county may not establish a voluntary transferable development rights program without the expressed approval of the General Assembly. On February 25, 1987, the Attorney General advised that a town or city may not adopt an ordinance limiting a group to one parade in the town or city annually because the ordinance "would be an impermissable prior restraint on constitutionally protected speech."

STATE MANDATES

Although a state mandate typically is defined as a legal requirement — constitutional provision, statutory provision or administrative regulation — requiring political subdivisions to undertake a specified activity and/or provide a service meeting minimum state standards, the Association of County Commissioners of Georgia identified a new type of state mandate — the "sneaky" mandate. Specifically, the Association refers to the failure of Georgia to pick-up state prisoners held in county jails, resulting in the overcrowding of county jails. In addition, the state pays the counties $10 per day for each state prisoner while the Department of Corrections estimates that it costs in excess of $25 daily to maintain each jail inmate. In effect, Georgia counties are subsidizing the state approximately $15 million annually. Moreover, the concerned counties are subject to constitutional challenges because of jail overcrowding. Fulton County paid more than $1.5 million in attorney fees over a two year period because of litigation alleging jail overcrowding.

A similar problem occurred in New York State in 1987 when the state failed to honor an agreement to admit patients directly from New York City operated hospitals to state psychiatric hospitals, resulting in overcrowding in the city's hospitals. The state admitted the problem and explained could not accept all city patients because of overcrowding in state operated facilities.

The 1987 Florida State Legislature enacted six state mandates imposing costs upon local governments. Chapter 87-92 increased the number of Medicaid-eligible clients and specifies that county health units must serve indigent clients. Chapter 87-363 requires Supervisors of Elections to provide voter registration information to any person request-ing it at no cost. Chapter 87-373 increases state retirees monthly benefits and will cost local governments an estimated $4.3 million in fiscal year 1988 and substantially more the following fiscal year when monthly benefits are increased by twice the amount of the fiscal 1988 increases. Chapter 87-95 changes the workload and the allowed charges for the child support depository required in each county clerk's office which must accept interstate child support orders, and file and issue various liens and deficiency statements. Chapter 87-408 mandates law enforcement officers and courts within 48 hours to notify the superintendent of schools when a school employee or student has been accused or convicted of engaging in felonious activities. The cost of this mandate is difficult to determine because the amount of time required by officials to carry out the mandate is indeterminate.

Also in Florida, Chapters 87-6 and 87-101, relating to the state sales and use tax, in effect prohibit local governments from acting as prime contractors for construction projects they undertake, resulting in the prime contractor, who must remit sales and use taxes to the State, passing the cost of the taxes on to local governments. Offsetting the increased local government cost is the expansion of the sales tax base which is estimated to increase local government revenues by approximately $53 million.

The 1987 New Hampshire State Legislature enacted Chapter 378 requiring cities and towns in "most but not necessarily all of the land areas in the district zoned permit residential uses" either (1) manufactured housing located on individual lots or (2) manufactured housing parks and subdivisions where manufactured housing can be placed on individually-owned lots or (3) both of the above. If a municipalities is not in compliance with the law by July 1, 1988, manufactured housing will be permitted where other housing is permitted.

Chapter 50 of the *New Hampshire Laws of 1987* requires cities and towns to file adopted capital improvement plans with the Office of State Planning. Previously, the units were required to submit plans for land use ordinances and regulations. Chapter 122 of the 1987 New Hampshire Laws authorizes the Legislative Budget Assistant to seek and use data and information from any source in preparing fiscal notes on bills. In the past, the assistant was limited to using data and information from state agencies and political subdivisions.

The 1984 New Hampshire Constitutional Convention proposed, and the voters ratified, a new article (28-a) of the state constitution stipulating that "the State shall not mandate or assign any new, expanded, or modified programs or responsibilities to any political subdivision in such a way as to necessitate additional local expenditure by the political subdivision unless such programs or responsibilities are fully funded by the State or unless such programs or responsibilities are approved for funding by a vote of the local legislative body of the political subdivision."

The provisions of the article were challenged by the leaders of the State Legislature, and the Superior Court in *Roy and Tucker v. Sununu and Gardner* (Merrimack County 85-E-145) decreed that "the Court find and rules that article 28-a was properly put before the public and validly adopted by the citizens..." The decision was not appealed to the New Hampshire Supreme Court.

In an advisory opinion issued in 1986, the New Hampshire Attorney General held that the Police Standards and Training Council may amend its regulations establishing minimum educational and training standards for police officers without triggering the constitutional requirement that the State reimburse municipalities for costs imposed. The Attorney General in 1986 also issued a ruling that the State Board of Education could revise its minimum standards for public elementary school approval without the state being required to reimburse school districts for mandated costs.

The South Carolina Advisory Commission on Intergovernmental Relations is conducting a comprehensive study of state mandates and has identified more than 500 statutory mandates and more than 100 administrative and judicial mandates. The commission also is conducting a study of intergovernmental agreements among local governments.

On December 23, 1986, the Task Force on County and Local Mandates, appointed by Wisconsin Governor-Elect Tommy Thompson, issued its report recommending enactment of "a clearly articulated statutory policy for the management of new and existing mandates, measured by a standard that includes the presumption that mandates must be funded." In addition, the Task Force recommended establishment of an Advisory Council on State and Local Relations, and a Joint Survey Committee on Local Mandates. Based upon the Task Force's recommendation, Senate Bill 1

was introduced in the 1987 State Legislature and provides that any proposed constitutional or statutory proposal that imposes a requirement or a limitation on substate units must be referred to a joint survey committee and no action can be taken on the proposal until the committee submits a written report on the fiscal effect of the proposal on Wisconsin and its municipalities.

In 1987, the New York Governor's Task Force on Mandate Reform issued a progress report containing three principal recommendations: The Secretary of State should be assigned responsibility for coordinating efforts to reform state mandates on local governments, a study should be made of the impact of State rules and regulations on local governments and a permanent mandate task force should be established.

Also in 1987, Governor Mario M. Cuomo of New York released a report, prepared by the State Division of the Budget, advocating repeal of the "Wicks" law requiring the State and its local governments to award separate contracts for the three major components of a construction project — electrical, plumbing, and heating, ventilation, and air conditioning — if the total cost is in excess of $50,000. The report estimated that the separate bids increase project costs by a minimum of 20 percent and taxpayers would save more than $300 million annually if the law were repealed. Although a repeal bill was introduced in the 1987 State Legislature, it failed to win approval.

On October 7, 1986, the National Conference of State Legislatures' Task Force on State-Local Relations published a report recommending "that States review their mandates placed on local governments...and consider relaxing or eliminating those requirements and in some cases assuming the cost of complying with them." Specifically, the Task Force recommended that mandates on personnel, environmental standards, service levels, and tax base exemptions should be subjected to the closest analysis. On the other hand, the Task Force stressed that local governments should finance state mandates establishing high ethical standards and requiring nondiscrimination and full disclosure of governmental affairs to the public.

SUMMARY

The actions of state legislatures during 1986 and 1987 revealed their ambivalence toward granting greater discretionary authority to their political subdivisions. While expressing concern about the impact of state mandates on local units, the state legislatures continue to impose mandates with the exception of New Hampshire where the constitutional reimbursement requirement has persuaded the General Court not to impose additional mandates upon local governments. Simultaneously, a number of state legislature broadened the grant of powers to some or all of their general purpose local governments. Available evidence suggests that the major trends of the past two years will continue in the foreseeable future.

STATE AID TO LOCAL GOVERNMENTS

By Vance Kane

State payments to federal and local governments increased to a new high, $132 billion in fiscal year 1986, compared to $108 billion in 1984. Of these amounts, $2 billion in 1986 and $1.7 billion in 1984 went to the federal government primarily to support the supplemental security income program which started in 1974 (see Table 9.2). As a percent of general expenditure, state intergovernmental payments remained constant at 35 percent for both fiscal years. For comparison, direct federal aid to state and local governments increased from $97 billion in 1984 to $113 billion in 1986, a 17 percent rise. State payments to local governments rose 22 percent from $107 billion in 1984 to $130 billion in 1986.

State Aid by Purpose

As shown below in Table A, education always has received the major share of state aid to local governments. In 1986, 62 percent or $82 billion of state aid went for education. Welfare support was second with $14 billion or 11 percent of the total. It should be noted that some states administer their welfare programs directly so no major welfare aid payments are made by these states to local governments.

General local government support received 10 percent of total 1986 payments. A large part of this aid is in the form of shared taxes with cities and counties. Most popular of these is some portion of a state imposed sales tax. States paid $6.5 billion to local governments for highways (just under 5 percent of all state aid) while "other purposes" increased to more than 10 percent or $13.9 billion. Much of this aid went for environmental improvements such as pollution control or waste disposal facilities.

Individual State Aid Payments

The average per capita amount of state aid was $549 in 1986 with 40 states falling between $300 and $750 in per capita payments. Two states spent more than $1,000 per capita in state aid payments — Alaska ($1,624) and Wyoming ($1,164). Both states contribute heavily to local education. Wyoming also shares its general sales tax, certain severance taxes and cigarette tax with its cities and counties. Hawaii has per capita aid payments of $28 and New Hampshire, $170; these are the only two states under $200 per capita in local government aid. As noted in Table B, education (except in Hawaii where the state government operates the local education system) receives the major share of state aid. These amounts reflect various foundation and equalization aid

Vance Kane is Assistant Division Chief for Programs, and was assisted by Sharon Meade, Social Science Analyst, both of the Governments Division, U.S. Bureau of the Census.

Table A
Percent Distribution of State Aid, Selected Years 1976-1986

Fiscal Year	Total	To Federal Government	General Local Government Support	To Local Governments, By Function			
				Education	Public Welfare	Highways	Other
1976	100.0	2.0	9.8	58.9	14.4	5.6	9.3
1978	100.0	2.2	10.1	59.6	12.8	5.7	9.6
1980	100.0	2.1	10.2	62.3	10.9	5.2	9.2
1982	100.0	1.8	10.2	61.5	12.1	5.1	9.3
1984	100.0	1.6	9.9	62.3	11.0	5.2	10.0
1986	100.0	1.6	10.1	62.1	10.8	4.9	10.5

programs, including federal dollars administered by the states.

Table B
State Per Capita Expenditure Distribution, 1986

Per Capita Amount	Number of States
Over $1,000	2
$750-1,000	3
$500-750	12
$400-500	18
$300-400	10
$200-300	3
Less than $200	2

Miscellaneous State Aid Programs

A growing source of state aid comes from lotteries. California, Iowa, Michigan, New Hampshire and New Jersey use all or part of their lottery revenue for education. State aid also reflects the geography of the state. For instance, California gives aid to its localities for coastal management and boating safety, while Maine gives grants for snowmobile trails.

Property tax relief aid for local governments is common. Indiana paid $478 million in 1986 property tax replacement and New Jersey, $11 billion. Often these property tax relief programs provide aid for senior citizens. Florida specifically provides reimbursement for property taxes lost through exemptions provided for senior citizens and the totally disabled.

A variety of cultural and recreational activities are supported in part by state aid to local governments. For instance, Kansas gives grants for art projects or events and historical preservation projects approved by the Kansas

Arts Commission. Kentucky and many of the rural states support local agricultural fairs. In an effort to compete for tourist dollars, states may subsidize local government promotion activities.

Type of Receiving Government

Tables 9.8 and 9.9 show which types of governments, by state, received state aid. In those states with independent school districts, these units received the largest percentage share of state aid. States where school activities are part of a city or county, such as Maryland, report education aid as revenue to cities or counties. Note Table 9.7 which shows $82 billion spent on education, while Table 9.9 shows school districts receiving $68 billion. The problem of locating receiving governments is also blurred by the $8 billion reported in the combined and unallocable column. These payments are not listed in sufficient detail to identify the actual recipient. It is safe to say (with the exception of Mississippi) that cities and counties received more funds than specifically indicated by Table 9.9. Any analysis of state aid to local governments should be conducted with considerable care and caution.

Note

1. Direct federal aid excludes all federal funds given to the state and later distributed to local governments. These funds, called "pass through" aid, are included in state intergovernmental aid under the U.S. Bureau of the Census' classification which was the basis used for compiling these data.

Table 9.2
SUMMARY OF STATE INTERGOVERNMENTAL PAYMENTS: 1942 to 1986
(In millions, except per capita)

	Total			To local governments					
			To federal govern- ments(a)	For general local gov- ernment support	For specified purposes				
Fiscal year	Amount	Per capita			Total	Education	Public welfare	Highways	All other
1942	$ 1,780	$ 13.37	...	$ 224	$ 1,546	$ 790	$ 390	$ 334	$ 32
1944	1,842	13.95	...	274	1,568	861	368	298	41
1946	2,092	15.05	...	357	1,735	953	376	339	67
1948	3,283	22.64	...	428	2,855	1,554	648	507	146
1950	4,217	28.11	...	482	3,735	2,054	792	610	279
1951	4,678	30.78	...	513	4,165	2,248	974	667	276
1952	5,044	32.55	...	549	4,497	2,525	976	728	268
1953	5,384	34.19	...	592	4,791	2,740	981	803	267
1954	5,679	35.42	...	600	5,078	2,934	1,004	871	269
1955	5,986	36.62	...	591	5,395	3,154	1,046	911	284
1956	6,538	39.28	...	631	5,907	3,541	1,069	984	313
1957	7,439	43.86	...	668	6,771	4,212	1,136	1,083	340
1958	8,089	46.76	...	687	7,402	4,598	1,247	1,167	390
1959	8,689	49.37	...	725	7,964	4,957	1,409	1,207	391
1960	9,443	52.75	...	806	8,637	5,461	1,483	1,247	446
1961	10,114	55.51	...	821	9,293	5,963	1,602	1,266	462
1962	10,906	58.94	...	844	10,062	6,474	1,777	1,326	485
1963	11,885	63.31	...	1,012	10,873	6,993	1,919	1,416	545
1964	12,968	68.06	...	1,053	11,915	7,664	2,104	1,524	623
1965	14,174	73.43	...	1,102	13,072	8,351	2,436	1,630	655
1966	16,928	86.79	...	1,361	15,567	10,177	2,882	1,725	783
1967	19,056	96.70	...	1,585	17,471	11,845	2,897	1,861	868
1968	21,950	110.27	...	1,993	19,956	13,321	3,527	2,029	1,079
1969	24,779	123.20	...	2,135	22,644	14,858	4,402	2,109	1,275
1970	28,892	142.73	...	2,958	25,934	17,085	5,003	2,439	1,407
1971	32,640	158.82	...	3,258	29,382	19,292	5,760	2,507	1,823
1972	36,759	177.16	...	3,752	33,007	21,195	6,944	2,633	2,235
1973	40,822	195.22	...	4,280	36,542	23,316	7,532	2,953	2,741
1974	45,941	218.07	$ 341	4,804	40,796	27,107	7,028	3,211	3,450
1975	51,978	244.71	975	5,129	45,874	31,110	7,127	3,225	4,412
1976	57,858	270.42	1,180	5,674	51,004	34,084	8,296	3,241	5,383
1977	62,460	288.65	1,386	6,373	54,701	36,964	8,756	3,631	5,350
1978	67,287	309.52	1,472	6,819	58,995	40,125	8,586	3,821	6,463
1979	75,975	346.18	1,493	8,224	66,258	46,206	8,667	4,149	7,236
1980	84,504	374.13	1,746	8,644	74,114	52,688	9,242	4,383	7,801
1981	93,180	412.47	1,873	9,570	81,735	57,257	11,009	4,751	8,718
1982	98,743	435.86	1,793	10,044	86,906	60,684	11,951	5,028	9,243
1983	100,887	437.09(r)	1,765	10,364	88,758	63,118	10,920	5,277	9,443
1984	108,373	460.11	1,722	10,745	95,906	67,485	11,923	5,687	10,811
1985	121,571	510.56	1,963	12,320	107,288	74,937	14,629	6,019	11,703
1986	131,966	548.83	2,106	13,384	116,477	81,929	16,298	6,470	11,779

Sources: U.S. Bureau of the Census, *State Payments to Local Governments (Census of Governments: 1982,* vol. 6, no. 3) and *State Government Finances.*

(a) Represents primarily state reimbursements for the supplemental security income program.
(r) Revised.

Table 9.3
STATE INTERGOVERNMENTAL EXPENDITURE, BY STATE:
1980 TO 1986

State	Amount (in thousands)				Per capita amounts				Percentage change in per capita amounts		
									1984 to 1986	1982 to 1984	1980 to 1982
	1986	1984	1982	1980	1986	1984	1982	1980			
All states	$131,966,258	$108,373,188	$98,742,976	$84,504,451	$ 548.83	$ 460.11	$ 435.86	$374.13	19.3	5.6	16.5
Alabama	1,563,108	1,310,399	1,136,158	1,036,721	385.67	328.42	291.77	266.51	17.4	12.6	9.5
Alaska	863,981	1,183,094	992,519	340,319	1,617.94	2,366.19	2,468.95	850.80	-31.6	-4.2	190.2
Arizona	1,913,685	1,547,438	1,192,237	1,040,614	576.93	506.86	438.64	382.86	13.8	15.6	14.6
Arkansas..........	988,755	789,131	667,184	624,261	416.84	335.94	291.86	273.20	24.1	15.1	6.8
California	24,929,013	19,125,775	17,625,121	15,360,365	923.95	746.46	744.68	648.97	23.8	0.2	14.7
Colorado..........	1,459,018	1,522,105	1,200,839	947,692	446.59	478.95	415.52	328.03	-6.8	15.3	26.7
Connecticut	1,147,052	967,483	760,415	671,287	359.69	306.75	244.66	215.99	17.3	25.4	13.3
Delaware..........	254,127	218,833	214,619	189,577	401.46	356.99	361.31	318.62	12.5	-1.2	13.4
Florida...........	5,198,824	3,561,701	3,512,218	2,925,889	445.30	324.50	360.38	300.40	37.2	-10.1	20.0
Georgia	2,604,968	1,947,978	1,781,763	1,613,179	426.76	333.73	326.15	295.24	27.9	2.3	10.5
Hawaii	30,034	25,231	27,875	35,530	28.28	24.28	28.89	36.82	16.5	-16.1	-27.5
Idaho	399,356	408,686	353,787	309,341	398.16	408.28	374.77	327.69	-2.5	8.9	14.4
Illinois	4,797,568	3,910,634	3,725,170	3,817,128	415.27	339.73	326.00	334.31	22.2	4.2	-2.5
Indiana	2,591,875	2,321,187	2,045,228	1,805,564	470.91	422.19	372.54	328.88	11.5	13.3	13.3
Iowa..............	1,457,094	1,321,682	1,262,391	1,148,360	511.08	454.19	433.22	394.22	12.5	4.8	9.9
Kansas	994,956	846,726.1	711,548	601,939	404.29	347.30	300.99	254.74	16.4	15.4	18.2
Kentucky..........	1,415,742	1,288,688	1,107,357	1,006,756	379.76	346.14	302.56	274.99	9.7	14.4	10.0
Louisiana	1,867,466	1,746,045	1,599,993	1,315,201	414.90	391.31	380.41	312.85	6.0	2.9	21.6
Maine	427,857	349,880	297,274	303,746	364.44	302.66	264.24	270.00	20.4	14.5	-2.1
Maryland	1,854,629	1,635,537	1,708,142	1,431,805	415.56	376.07	405.06	339.61	10.5	-7.2	19.3
Massachusetts......	3,325,747	2,617,378	2,315,564	2,116,477	570.26	451.43	403.62	368.92	26.3	11.8	9.4
Michigan..........	4,842,870	4,037,673	3,824,824	3,578,343	529.56	444.92	412.96	386.51	19.0	7.7	6.8
Minnesota	3,124,133	2,880,437	3,016,693	2,237,164	741.37	692.08	740.11	548.73	7.1	-6.5	34.9
Mississippi	1,237,181	1,065,912	948,128	856,350	471.31	410.28	376.09	339.69	14.9	9.1	10.7
Missouri	1,915,955	1,589,484	1,167,399	1,088,886	378.20	317.39	237.42	221.45	19.2	33.7	7.2
Montana	319,790	293,193	243,384	230,463	390.46	355.82	309.26	292.84	9.7	15.1	5.6
Nebraska..........	537,476	511,721	482,635	412,081	336.34	318.63	307.41	262.47	5.6	3.6	17.1
Nevada	590,225	487,427	456,728	265,956	612.90	535.05	570.91	332.86	14.6	-6.3	71.5
New Hampshire....	174,711	157,680	139,824	137,723	170.12	161.39	151.82	149.54	5.4	6.3	1.5
New Jersey	4,803,345	4,133,531	4,030,065	3,056,970	630.36	550.04	547.19	415.12	14.6	0.5	31.8
New Mexico	1,119,486	967,744	829,899	595,464	756.92	679.60	636.91	458.05	11.4	6.7	39.0
New York	15,182,153	12,262,857	11,849,950	10,252,802	854.27	691.45	674.90	583.97	23.5	2.5	15.6
North Carolina	3,402,507	2,722,596	2,440,069	2,028,170	537.44	441.62	414.84	345.28	21.7	6.5	20.1
North Dakota	399,352	412,386	355,610	216,844	588.15	601.15	544.58	332.07	-2.2	10.4	64.0
Ohio	5,536,665	4,779,871	3,561,699	3,249,696	514.94	444.56	329.85	300.98	15.8	34.8	9.6
Oklahoma	1,478,351	1,284,809	1,160,761	800,260	447.31	389.57	383.72	264.55	14.8	1.5	20.7
Oregon	1,105,928	993,012	1,014,603	879,899	409.91	371.36	385.34	334.18	10.4	-3.6	34.2
Pennsylvania	5,364,037	4,703,507	4,014,697	3,541,237	451.18	395.22	338.39	298.41	14.2	16.8	14.8
Rhode Island	347,862	275,000	235,816	217,255	356.78	285.86	249.01	229.41	24.8	14.8	25.9
South Carolina	1,429,440	1,095,298	1,024,500	781,643	423.16	331.91	328.16	250.61	27.5	1.1	12.5
South Dakota......	194,507	165,296	160,201	121,758	274.73	234.13	231.84	176.46	17.3	0.9	41.7
Tennessee	1,430,475	1,105,881	1,067,709	974,485	297.83	234.45	232.57	212.26	27.0	0.8	15.8
Texas	6,147,106	4,965,245	4,252,176	3,458,969	368.49	310.54	298.84	243.11	18.7	3.9	16.1
Utah..............	782,272	610,987	525,165	459,404	469.83	369.85	359.46	314.44	27.0	3.8	11.3
Vermont	158,962	135,974	110,722	110,786	293.83	256.55	216.68	216.80	14.5	18.4	8.8
Virginia	2,513,086	1,928,473	1,658,077	1,268,683	434.26	342.17	310.09	237.31	26.9	10.3	16.8
Washington	3,011,346	2,290,339	2,128,066	1,601,814	674.74	526.64	515.02	387.85	28.1	2.3	28.5
West Virginia	855,734	702,912	674,956	533,286	445.93	360.10	346.13	273.48	23.8	4.0	10.3
Wisconsin	3,286,305	2,638,645	2,761,315	2,643,133	686.79	553.64	586.76	561.77	24.1	-5.2	22.3
Wyoming	590,143	529,687	369,903	263,176	1,163.99	1,036.57	787.03	558.76	12.3	31.7	57.1

Source: U.S. Bureau of the Census, State Government Finances in 1986, and previous annual reports.
Note: Includes payments to the federal government primarily state reimbursements for the supplemental security income program.

Table 9.4
PER CAPITA STATE INTERGOVERNMENTAL EXPENDITURE, BY FUNCTION AND BY STATE: 1985

State	Total	General local govern-ment support	Education	Public welfare	Highways	Miscellaneous and unallocable
All states	$ 510.55	$ 51.74	$314.71	$ 61.44	$ 25.28	$ 57.39
Alabama..................	371.12	21.41	273.44	1.25	28.14	46.88
Alaska....................	3,014.84	280.63	66.00	0.00	360.33	1,132.43
Arizona..................	561.92	123.42	345.72	0.38	73.99	18.42
Arkansas	381.73	17.88	290.15	0.24	35.16	38.31
California................	841.36	60.39	444.51	223.63	29.24	83.59
Colorado	483.25	5.26	285.80	87.85	34.11	70.23
Connecticut	336.47	40.08	223.94	17.80	7.97	46.68
Delaware	383.85	0.00	341.77	0.73	8.65	32.70
Florida	458.51	69.81	292.59	0.17	15.95	79.99
Georgia..................	377.31	2.70	294.12	19.81	15.09	45.59
Hawaii	23.44	17.29	0.00	3.41	0.00	2.74
Idaho	388.74	24.83	301.59	0.03	45.34	16.95
Illinois...................	374.48	41.91	254.24	11.05	29.51	37.76
Indiana	450.05	90.70	273.29	39.18	37.17	9.70
Iowa	490.08	46.81	338.63	13.40	64.03	27.21
Kansas	376.88	22.17	306.77	0.90	27.52	19.52
Kentucky	348.12	0.00	287.55	0.00	11.84	48.73
Louisiana	354.33	40.96	280.90	0.01	6.82	25.63
Maine	323.11	31.66	255.40	12.22	11.75	12.07
Maryland	394.33	38.19	213.37	0.02	61.08	81.67
Massachuestts	511.69	119.23	245.15	19.15	11.03	117.13
Michigan	487.37	84.62	232.97	17.83	61.82	90.13
Minnesota	698.57	140.26	363.42	110.78	36.27	47.82
Mississippi	438.85	70.95	304.01	0.28	33.70	29.91
Missouri	338.35	0.77	279.85	1.75	21.45	34.53
Montana..................	372.83	30.77	277.39	9.27	17.34	38.05
Nebraska	340.78	50.79	178.98	2.82	50.40	57.79
Nevada	537.11	195.66	310.50	4.18	15.67	11.11
New Hampshire	165.22	38.19	65.13	27.07	12.91	21.92
New Jersey...............	585.48	134.85	310.83	92.79	6.46	40.55
New Mexico..............	749.95	182.67	528.73	0.00	9.13	29.41
New York	754.93	57.19	343.22	254.01	10.25	90.26
North Carolina	483.03	29.09	370.72	25.93	1.53	55.75
North Dakota	575.72	58.76	403.36	18.93	64.86	29.80
Ohio	475.90	41.91	295.12	54.47	41.94	42.47
Oklahoma	402.94	3.59	320.91	4.41	47.68	26.35
Oregon	409.52	61.13	252.69	0.86	51.20	43.64
Pennsylvania	419.01	7.18	259.27	51.50	19.96	81.11
Rhode Island	308.29	31.32	234.65	32.34	0.37	9.61
South Carolina	411.83	42.65	339.64	1.12	9.60	18.83
South Dakota	265.09	75.70	153.53	0.04	10.41	25.41
Tennessee	267.70	32.21	188.87	3.99	23.94	18.68
Texas....................	372.97	3.01	355.42	0.00	0.79	13.75
Utah.....................	443.03	2.64	367.89	2.10	19.02	51.38
Vermont	276.47	4.30	213.48	13.97	27.14	17.58
Virginia..................	379.08	4.15	266.99	32.79	15.84	59.30
Washington	553.90	14.36	435.43	8.14	31.86	64.11
West Virginia	412.74	5.52	395.22	0.00	0.00	12.00
Wisconsin.................	654.44	210.43	289.82	39.37	36.32	78.51
Wyoming	1,078.11	317.77	555.23	0.37	43.33	161.41

Source: U.S. Bureau of the Census, *State Government Finances in 1985.*
Note: Includes payments to the federal government, primarily state reimbursements for the supplemental security income program (under public welfare).

Table 9.5
PER CAPITA STATE INTERGOVERNMENTAL EXPENDITURE, BY FUNCTION AND BY STATE: 1986

State	Total	General local govern-ment support	Specified functions			
			Education	Public welfare	Highways	Miscellaneous and unallocable
All states	$ 548.83	$ 55.66	$340.73	$ 67.78	$ 26.91	$ 57.74
Alabama....................	385.67	22.37	287.08	1.25	33.88	41.08
Alaska.....................	1,617.94	284.04	838.96	0.00	142.17	352.77
Arizona....................	576.93	128.05	345.98	0.40	81.77	20.74
Arkansas	416.84	20.58	310.51	0.68	41.98	43.09
California..................	923.95	68.81	499.19	236.53	33.78	85.63
Colorado	446.59	9.24	291.97	84.13	35.54	25.72
Connecticut	359.69	47.79	243.48	19.18	7.92	41.32
Delaware	401.46	0.00	360.24	1.02	8.98	31.23
Florida	445.30	71.45	322.54	0.01	19.82	31.48
Georgia...................	426.76	2.64	341.90	22.45	8.64	51.14
Hawaii	28.28	17.11	0.00	3.49	0.00	7.68
Idaho	398.16	25.03	307.57	0.00	45.53	20.03
Illinois...................	415.27	41.85	282.92	10.76	30.96	48.78
Indiana...................	470.91	94.26	276.12	40.43	49.18	10.91
Iowa	511.08	45.65	352.87	13.30	69.13	30.13
Kansas	404.29	22.70	327.49	2.09	28.87	23.14
Kentucky	379.76	0.73	312.83	0.00	11.93	54.27
Louisiana	414.90	40.33	330.70	6.53	6.44	30.90
Maine	364.44	36.17	291.05	11.50	12.97	12.75
Maryland	415.56	34.99	226.69	0.02	61.81	92.04
Massachusetts	570.26	133.43	272.56	22.16	18.32	123.79
Michigan	529.56	92.14	256.95	19.24	65.01	96.23
Minnesota	741.37	141.97	388.72	111.14	45.91	53.63
Mississippi	471.31	69.91	339.12	1.64	30.77	29.86
Missouri	378.20	1.79	311.15	1.27	30.42	33.57
Montana..................	390.46	27.42	292.89	9.53	17.44	43.19
Nebraska	336.34	52.69	174.60	2.66	53.02	53.37
Nevada	612.90	210.49	371.39	4.65	15.51	10.85
New Hampshire	170.12	38.74	70.94	29.00	12.76	18.68
New Jersey................	630.36	139.19	347.31	93.74	3.75	46.36
New Mexico...............	756.92	185.24	530.80	0.00	8.48	32.40
New York	854.27	63.81	380.20	300.14	10.13	99.99
North Carolina	537.44	32.08	408.77	27.32	9.38	59.89
North Dakota	588.15	68.56	404.10	19.81	63.71	31.97
Ohio	514.94	58.46	317.90	57.12	38.44	43.02
Oklahoma	447.31	3.40	363.75	3.24	49.29	27.63
Oregon	409.91	49.16	257.78	0.86	58.23	43.88
Pennsylvania	451.18	7.55	273.19	58.48	18.33	93.62
Rhode Island	356.78	34.88	252.19	32.16	0.35	37.20
South Carolina	423.16	44.37	353.39	1.23	4.75	19.41
South. Dakota..............	274.73	65.21	175.40	0.05	8.27	25.80
Tennessee	297.83	33.75	204.79	4.40	35.68	19.21
Texas.....................	368.49	2.85	349.59	0.05	0.80	15.20
Utah	469.83	2.61	405.85	2.01	19.28	40.08
Vermont	293.83	5.99	231.66	15.10	29.18	11.90
Virginia...................	434.26	16.34	299.93	41.45	19.98	56.56
Washington	674.74	12.80	499.59	20.06	27.78	114.50
West Virginia	445.93	6.92	424.68	0.00	0.00	14.33
Wisconsin.................	686.79	219.44	282.45	44.20	39.50	101.21
Wyoming	1,163.99	316.19	625.42	0.43	42.71	179.24

Source: U.S. Bureau of the Census, *State Government Finances in 1986.*
Note: Includes payments to the federal government, primarily state reimbursements for the supplemental security income program (under public welfare).

Table 9.6
STATE INTERGOVERNMENTAL EXPENDITURE,
BY FUNCTION AND BY STATE: 1985
(In thousands of dollars)

State	Total	General local govern- ment support	Functions			
			Education	Public welfare	Highways	Miscellaneous and combined
All states	$121,571,151	$12,319,623	$74,936,970	$14,628,859	$6,019,069	$13,666,630
Alabama....................	1,492,642	86,131	1,099,757	5,024	113,182	188,548
Alaska.....................	1,573,744	146,491	648,033	0	188,094	591,126
Arizona....................	1,793,077	393,838	1,103,177	1,201	236,094	58,767
Arkansas	900,887	42,187	684,760	556	82,982	90,402
California.................	22,176,573	1,591,720 (a)	11,716,331 (b)	5,894,482 (c)	770,666	2,203,374
Colorado	1,562,837	16,996	924,280	284,119	110,308	227,134
Connecticut	1,066,940	127,079	710,124	56,458	25,266	148,013
Delaware	238,756	0	212,578	457	5,382	20,339
Florida	5,211,019	793,372	3,325,329	1,959	181,239	909,120
Georgia...................	2,254,410	16,117	1,757,368	118,367	90,170	272,388
Hawaii	24,637	18,173	0	3,581	0	2,883
Idaho	390,299	24,928	302,794	33	45,525	17,019
Illinois...................	4,320,715	483,586	2,933,463	127,460	340,487	435,719
Indiana	2,475,262	498,871	1,503,078	215,514	204,442	53357
Iowa	1,411,917	134,856	975,603	38,604	184,462	78,392
Kansas	923,348	54,324	751,575	2,217	67,415	47,817
Kentucky	1,297,089	0	1,071,411	0	44,102	181,576
Louisiana	1,589,533	183,752	1,260,124	66	30,615	114,976
Maine	376,750	36,920	297,800	14,253	13,705	14,072
Maryland	1,732,295	167,789	937,330	69	268,313	358,794
Massachusetts	2,977,536	693,804	1,426,516	111,422	64,205	681,589
Michigan	4,429,263	769,043	2,117,256	162,070	561,818	819,076
Minnesota	2,928,387	587,990	1,523,462	464,399	152,058	200,478
Mississippi	1,147,165	185,474	794,680	735	88,089	78,187
Missouri..................	1,703,603	3,890	1,409,049	8,803	107,978	173,883
Montana..................	307,582	25,389	228,849	7,649	14,307	31,388
Nebraska	546,944	81,516	287,268	4,521	80,887	92,752
Nevada	503,270	183,330	290,934	3,915	14,679	10,412
New Hampshire	165,050	38,148	65,065	27,043	12,900	21,894
New Jersey................	4,426,816	1,019,626	2,350,168	701,554	48,872	306,596
New Mexico...............	1,088,172	265,059	767,192	0	13,250	42,671
New York.................	13,396,972	1,014,822	6,090,778 (d)	4,507,722 (e)	181,864	1,601,786
North Carolina	3,024,220	182,156	2,321,047	162,373	9,564	349,080
North Dakota	394,367	40,252	276,303	12,969	44,430	20,413
Ohio	5,114,504	450,407	3,171,607	585,342	450,720	456,428
Oklahoma	1,332,122	11,868	1,060,930	14,581	157,638	87,105
Oregon	1,099,969	164,187	678,736	2,320	137,517	117,209
Pennsylvania	4,971,177	85,142	3,075,976	610,957	236,863	962,239
Rhode Island	298,113	30,282	226,906	31,276	360	9,289
South Carolina	1,373,468	142,225	1,132,700	3,730	32,013	62,800
South Dakota	187,686	53,598	108,699	28	7,370	17,991
Tennessee	1,276,127	153,559	900,340	19,022	114,142	89,064
Texas.....................	6,111,188	49,328	5,823,586 (f)	21	12,980	225,273
Utah	728,783	4,350	605,181	3,449	31,283	84,520
Vermont	147,911	2,303	114,213	7,473	14,519	9,403
Virginia...................	2,161,501	23,676	1,522,389	186,945	90,340	338,151
Washington	2,441,588	63,289	1,919,361	35,895	140,428	282,615
West Virginia	799,474	10,684	765,542	0	0	23,248
Wisconsin.................	3,125,629	1,005,031	1,384,157	188,038	173,448	374,955
Wyoming	549,834	162,065	283,165	187	22,098	82,319

Source: U.S. Bureau of the Census, *State Government Finances in 1985.*
Note: Totals may not add, due to rounding.
(a) Includes $1,132,782,000 shared motor vehicle license taxes.
(b) Includes $9,431,370,000 redistribution of federal funds to school districts and $1,122,773,000 community college grants.
(c) Includes $2,506,183,000 aid to local governments for families with dependent children and $1,354,877,000 reimbursement to federal government for supplemental security income program.

(d) Includes $5,693,164,000 general school support and $294,297,000 community college support.
(e) Includes $1,685,267,000 aid to local governments for families with dependent children, $888,531,000 vendor payments to New York City Hospital Corporation, and $451,743,000 for welfare medical assistance.
(f) Includes $5,349,601,000 available and school foundation funds distribution to school districts and $473,687,000 to community colleges.

Table 9.7
STATE INTERGOVERNMENTAL EXPENDITURE,
BY FUNCTION AND BY STATE: 1986
(In thousands of dollars)

State	Total	General local government support	Functions Education	Functions Public welfare	Functions Highways	Functions Miscellaneous and combined
All states	$131,966,258	$13,383,912	$81,929,467	$16,298,296	$6,470,049	$13,884,534
Alabama....................	1,563,108	90,672	1163544	5,069	137,306	166,517
Alaska.....................	863,981	151,679	448,004	0	75,920	188,378
Arizona....................	1,913,685	424,743	1,147,606	1,334	271,216	68,786
Arkansas	988,755	48,823	736,539 (b)	1,609	99,568	102,216
California..................	24,929,013	1,856,687 (a)	13,468,571 (b)	6,381,926 (e)	911,521	2,310,308
Colorado	1,459,018	30,181	953,853	274,869	116,094	84,021
Connecticut	1,147,052	152,403	776,444	61,156	25,265	131,784
Delaware	254,127	0	228,030	645	5,683	19,769
Florida	5,198,824	834,170	3,765,656	165	231,349	367,484
Georgia...................	2,604,968	16,117	2,086,963	137,010	52,721	312,157
Hawaii	30,034	18,173	0	3,710	0	8,151
Idaho	399,356	25,107	308,495	0	45,662	20,092
Illinois	4,797,568	483,537	3,268,546	124,297	357,640	563,548
Indiana	2,591,875	518,818	1,519,773	222,553	270,692	60,039
Iowa	1,457,094	130,134	1,006,029	37,928	197,090	85,913
Kansas	994,956	55,869	805,957	5,140	71,039	56,951
Kentucky	1,415,742	2,715	1,166,240	0	44,470	202,317
Louisiana	1,867,466	181,511	1,488,501	29,398	28,997	139,059
Maine	427,857	42,463	341,689	13,506	15,225	14,974
Maryland	1,854,629	156,167	1,011,724	80	275,876	410,782
Massachusetts	3,325,747	778,184	1,589,550	129,242	106,836	721,935
Michigan	4,842,870	842,657	2,349,810	175,909	594,489	880,005
Minnesota	3,124,133	598,257	1,638,062	468,336	193,472	226,006
Mississippi	1,237,181	183,522	890,203	4,301	80,768	78,387
Missouri	1,915,955	9,054	1,576,310	6,432	154,083	170,076
Montana..................	319,790	22,453	239,879	7,805	14,283	35,370
Nebraska	537,476	84,203	279,011	4,250	84,719	85,293
Nevada	590,225	202,705	357,653	4,482	14,939	10,446
New Hampshire	174,711	39,791	72,854	29,778	13,106	19,182
New Jersey	4,803,345	1,060,651	2,646,521	714,321	28,573	353,279
New Mexico...............	1,119,486	273,976	785,052	0	12,535	47,923
New York	15,182,153	1,134,029	6,756,946 (c)	5,334,172 (f)	180,041	1,776,965
North Carolina	3,402,507	203,093	2,587,914	172,942	59,371	379,187
North Dakota	399,352	46,554	274,382	13,452	43,257	21,707
Ohio	5,536,665	628,576	3,418,086	614,114	413,304	462,585
Oklahoma	1,478,351	11,224	1,202,203	10,698	162,907	91,319
Oregon	1,105,928	132,626	695,495	2,325	157,093	118,389
Pennsylvania	5,364,037	89,801	3,248,005	695,261	217,866	1,113,104
Rhode Island	347,862	34,007	245,881	31,360	340	36,274
South Carolina	1,429,440	149,882	1,193,768	4,168	16,041	65,581
South Dakota	194,507	46,169	124,186	32	5,853	18,267
Tennessee	1,430,475	162,092	983,624	21,115	171,379	92,265
Texas.....................	6,147,106	47,551	5,831,880 (d)	806	13,307	253,562
Utah	782,272	4,350	675,748	3,344	32,096	66,734
Vermont...................	158,962	3,240	125,330	8,168	15,784	6,440
Virginia...................	2,513,086	94,576	1,735,705	239,854	115,632	327,319
Washington	3,011,346	57,129	2,229,687	89,525	123,971	511,034
West Virginia	855,734	13,280	814,962	0	0	27,492
Wisconsin.................	3,286,305	1,050,003	1,351,509	211,493	189,014	484,286
Wyoming	590,143	160,308	317,087	216	21,656	90,876

Source: U.S. Bureau of the Census, *State Government Finances in 1986.*
Note: Totals may not add due to rounding.
(a) Includes $1,417,233,000 shared motor vehicle license taxes.
(b) Includes $10,979,278,000 redistribution of federal funds to school districts and $1,333,736,000 community college grants.
(c) Includes $6,532,624,000 general school support and $224,322,000 community college support.
(d) Includes $4,680,932,000 available and school foundation funds distribution to school districts and $458,536,000 to community colleges.

(e) Includes $3,807,428,000 aid to local governments for families with dependent children and $1,415,849,000 reimbursement to federal government for supplemental security income program.
(f) Includes $1,692,938,000 aid to local governments for families with dependent children, $732,996,000 vendor payments to New York City Hospital Corporation, and $703,025,000 for welfare medical assistance.

Table 9.8
STATE INTERGOVERNMENTAL EXPENDITURE,
BY TYPE OF RECEIVING GOVERNMENT AND BY STATE: 1985
(In thousands of dollars)

State	Total intergovern- mental expenditure	Federal	School districts	Counties	Municipali- ties	Townships and New England "towns"	Special districts	Combined and un- allocable
United States	$121,571,151 (a)	$1,963,468	$62,011,998	$27,218,762	$19,617,993	$1,345,789	$1,378,315	$8,034,826
Alabama.............	1,492,642	0	1,099,757	268,504	120,363	0	0	4,018
Alaska..............	1,573,744	2,081	0	517,283	921,943	0	0	132,437
Arizona.............	1,793,077	1,201	1,103,177	290,221	379,807	0	119	18,552
Arkansas	900,887	83	683,560	109,050	68,108	0	2,399	37,687
California...........	22,176,573	1,356,717	11,081,040	7,847,342	1,524,725	0	258,081	108,668
Colorado	1,562,837	1,300	924,247	424,832	189,549	0	12,960	9,949
Connecticut	1,066,940	15	11,505	0	522,477	403,379	1,198	128,366
Delaware	238,756	457	212,578	11,504	7,355	0	0	6,862
Florida	5,211,019	0	3,324,058	700,968	497,483	0	23,417	665,093
Georgia.............	2,254,410	71	1,757,368	405,674	61,416	0	5,244	24,637
Hawaii	24,637	3,581	0	10,454	9,279	0	0	1,323
Idaho	390,299	428	301,921	41,168	22,110	0	6,283	18,389
Illinois.............	4,320,715	672	2,933,463	425,460	625,070	65,229	210,534	60,287
Indiana	2,475,262	8,609	1,503,078	336,711	164,050	0	3,664	459,150 (b)
Iowa	1,411,917	15,161	975,603	214,737	148,622	0	530	57,264
Kansas	923,348	205	751,575	86,096	54,377	1,659	2,684	26,752
Kentucky	1,297,089	0	1,071,411	176,522	29,111	0	0	20,045
Louisiana	1,589,533	66	1,260,124	164,197	45,337	0	881	118,928
Maine	376,750	7,628	0	2,439	209	6,750	0	359,724 (c)
Maryland	1,732,295	69	0	1,038,765	539,663	0	0	153,798
Massachusetts	2,977,536	102,868	62,354	0	8,154	0	281,189	2,522,971 (d)
Michigan	4,429,263	63,945	2,117,256	1,242,491	606,488	138,016	62,655	198,412 (e)
Minnesota	2,928,387	0	1,523,230	857,339	463,360	21,392	14,966	48,100
Mississippi	1,147,165	35	794,005	165,567	185,731	0	0	1,827
Missouri	1,703,603	0	1,409,049	75,285	81,369	0	1,203	136,697
Montana............	307,582	871	228,849	56,774	20,938	0	0	150
Nebraska	546,944	1,441	287,268	66,182	74,374	0	15,361	102,318
Nevada	503,270	2,386	290,934	186,882	17,945	0	0	5,123
New Hampshire	165,050	0	13,729	29,996	33,207	32,659	393	55,066
New Jersey..........	4,426,816	25,041	1,697,806	958,621	587,263	22,924	1,856	1,133,305 (f)
New Mexico..........	1,088,172	0	767,192	23,923	296,124	0	168	765
New York	13,396,972	215,457	3,475,631	1,903,202	7,624,380	166,421	7,717	4,164
North Carolina	3,024,220	0	0	2,824,512	178,774	0	16,983	3,951
North Dakota	394,367	0	276,303	70,180	37,449	8,926	1,347	162
Ohio	5,114,504	0	3,098,124	1,249,863	173,622	33,953	7,096	551,846 (g)
Oklahoma	1,332,122	0	1,060,930	180,008	23,961	0	2,973	64,250
Oregon	1,099,969	0	678,736	248,146	84,279	0	11,219	77,589
Pennsylvania	4,971,177	46,808	3,075,976	999,744	334,110	121,087	318,462	74,990
Rhode Island	298,113	8,819	21,824	0	159,399	104,542	0	3,529
South Carolina	1,373,468	0	1,132,042	194,868	41,901	0	1,020	3,637
South Dakota	187,686	28	108,699	67,939	4,507	276	451	5,786
Tennessee	1,276,127	0	4,446	781,809	480,950	0	0	8,922
Texas...............	6,111,188	0	5,823,288	84,926	142,454	0	4,114	56,406
Utah	728,783	446	605,181	80,204	33,071	0	3,371	6,510
Vermont	147,911	7,473	114,213	0	2,286	18,460	223	5,256
Virginia.............	2,161,501	0	0	1,169,929	793,874	0	7,783	189,915
Washington	2,441,588	21,192	1,919,361	206,283	186,963	149	79,917	27,723
West Virginia	799,474	0	763,785	16,100	39	0	0	19,550
Wisconsin	3,125,629	68,162	1,384,157	329,943	849,789	199,967	0	293,611
Wyoming	549,834	152	283,165	76,119	160,178	0	9,854	20,366

Source: U.S. Bureau of the Census, *State Government Finances in 1985*.
Note: Totals may not add due to rounding.
(a) Includes $1,955,736,000 supplemental security income payments (additional transfers not separately identified by other States may not be included).
(b) Includes $457,841,000 property tax replacement distribution to local governments.

(c) Includes $296,404,000 for local schools.
(d) Includes $1,364,162,000 education subsidies. $539,340,000 assistance to cities and towns, and $146,903,000 lottery distribution.
(e) Includes $123,726,000 highway subsidies.
(f) Includes $1,018,970,000 property tax relief and shared revenues.
(g) Includes $438,216,000 tax relief payments.

Table 9.9
STATE INTERGOVERNMENTAL EXPENDITURE,
BY TYPE OF RECEIVING GOVERNMENT AND BY STATE: 1986
(In thousands of dollars)

State	Total intergovern-mental expenditure	Federal	School districts	Counties	Municipali-ties	Townships and New England "towns"	Special districts	Combined and un-allocable
United States	$131,966,258 (a)	$2,105,831	$67,966,662	$29,300,674	$21,249,653	$1,447,661	$1,423,262	$8,472,515
Alabama	1,563,108	0	1,163,544	289,548	106,012	0	0	4,004
Alaska	863,981	7,933	0	340,061	472,765	0	0	43,222
Arizona	1,913,685	1,334	1,147,606	348,656	411,484	0	0	4,605
Arkansas	988,755	731	735,171	126,253	80,314	0	3,186	43,100
California	24,929,013	1,419,184	12,778,014	8,590,210	1,803,048	0	215,136	123,421
Colorado	1,459,018	766	953,793	280,650	202,040	0	8,803	12,966
Connecticut	1,147,052	0	12,575	0	558,604	440,376	1,220	134,277
Delaware	254,127	645	228,030	9,247	7,871	0	0	8,334
Florida	5,198,824	0	3,763,959	789,157	493,636	0	14,169	137,903
Georgia	2,604,968	0	2,086,963	422,192	60,629	0	10,210	24,974
Hawaii	30,034	3,710	0	10,477	9,658	0	0	6,189
Idaho	399,356	286	308,037	42,027	23,433	0	7,108	18,465
Illinois	4,797,568	726	3,268,546	435,294	697,347	66,189	256,206	73,260
Indiana	2,591,875	12,723	1,519,773	347,924	219,569	0	4,547	487,339 (b)
Iowa	1,457,094	14,772	1,006,029	218,479	152,900	0	413	64,501
Kansas	994,956	142	805,957	90,324	53,680	1,719	2,768	40,366
Kentucky	1,415,742	0	1,165,887	184,137	26,154	0	23,430	16,134
Louisiana	1,867,466	2	1,488,501	168,486	45,010	0	613	164,854
Maine	427,857	7,575	0	3,172	610	5,986	0	410,514 (c)
Maryland	1,854,629	80	0	1,163,228	527,544	0	0	163,777
Massachusetts	3,325,747	116,444	70,376	0	6,778	0	314,846	2,817,303 (d)
Michigan	4,842,870	65,369	2,349,810	1,347,884	656,059	149,701	60,945	213,102 (e)
Minnesota	3,124,133	0	1,638,062	874,605	503,942	25,082	14,737	67,705
Mississippi	1,237,181	61	889,393	158,350	189,377	0	0	0
Missouri	1,915,955	7,222	1,576,310	77,922	118,852	0	2,678	132,971
Montana	319,790	820	238,787	56,217	22,389	0	0	1,577
Nebraska	537,476	1,343	279,011	64,402	69,318	0	11,149	112,253
Nevada	590,225	2,595	357,653	205,594	18,553	0	0	5,830
New Hampshire	174,711	0	14,832	31,838	25,703	39,200	408	62,730
New Jersey	4,803,345	28,084	1,982,693	953,056	616,158	27,428	1,739	1,194,187
New Mexico	1,119,486	0	785,052	25,675	307,882	0	224	653
New York	15,182,153	229,447	3,906,811	2,193,860	8,635,220	201,068	6,122	9,625
North Carolina	3,402,507	0	0	3,128,185	238,574	0	19,519	16,229
North Dakota	399,352	0	274,380	75,388	37,270	10,936	1,220	158
Ohio	5,536,665	0	3,347,441	1,263,462	162,022	32,108	6,389	725,243 (f)
Oklahoma	1,478,351	0	1,202,203	180,528	23,214	0	3,581	68,825
Oregon	1,105,928	0	695,495	275,838	78,966	0	7,149	48,480
Pennsylvania	5,364,037	67,751	3,248,005	1,134,702	381,580	110,264	315,110	106,625
Rhode Island	347,862	9,152	22,314	0	170,982	113,956	0	31,458
South Carolina	1,429,440	0	1,193,207	184,873	45,214	0	1,005	5,141
South Dakota	194,507	32	124,186	59,667	2,969	34	771	6,848
Tennessee	1,430,475	0	4,743	883,122	535,635	0	0	6,975
Texas	6,147,106	0	5,831,641	94,122	161,267	0	4,383	55,693
Utah	782,272	465	675,748	68,514	28,052	0	2,907	6,586
Vermont	158,962	8,168	125,330	0	2,113	20,146	167	3,038
Virginia	2,513,086	0	0	1,302,583	894,297	0	7,208	308,998
Washington	3,011,346	19,879	2,218,755	333,388	316,393	125	85,041	37,765
West Virginia	855,734	0	813,443	16,905	36	0	0	25,350
Wisconsin	3,286,305	78,215	1,351,509	368,120	890,106	203,343	0	395,012
Wyoming	590,143	175	317,087	82,352	158,424	0	8,155	23,950

Source: U.S. Bureau of the Census, *State Government Finances in 1986.*
Note: Totals may not add due to rounding.
(a) Includes $2,083,683,000 supplemental security income payments (additional transfers not separately identified by other States may not be included).
(b) Includes $478,409,000 property tax replacement distribution to local governments.

(c) Includes $339,562,000 for local schools.
(d) Includes $1,519,174,000 education subsidies, $597,309,000 assistance to cities and towns, and $174,097,000 lottery distribution.
(e) Includes $102,169,000 highway subsidies.
(f) Includes $616,462,000 tax relief payments.

Table 9.10
STATE INTERGOVERNMENTAL REVENUE
FROM FEDERAL AND LOCAL GOVERNMENTS: 1985
(In thousands of dollars)

State	Total intergovernmental revenue	From federal government					From local government				
		Total(a)	Education	Public welfare	Health & hospitals	Highways	Total(a)	Education	Public welfare	Health & hospitals	Highways
United States	$89,922,140	$84,469,204	$15,307,291	$38,664,238	$3,415,996	$12,701,561	$5,452,936	$395,146	$1,752,282	$709,421	$429,945
Alabama	1,545,381	1,514,688	370,614	522,352	57,286	84,861	30,693	6,843	125	6,499	8,546
Alaska	398,694	396,575	80,672	86,647	4,578	129,821	2,119	1,957	0	0	0
Arizona	775,858	695,007	221,348	126,678	33,311	237,066	80,851	2,647	63,073	3,670	7,122
Arkansas	818,143	813,780	156,584	384,974	40,617	110,587	4,363	836	0	0	2,142
California	11,429,201	11,221,196	1,903,442	5,192,883	260,016	1,123,743	208,005	31,632	647	33,876	66,489
Colorado	997,202	987,094	258,857	335,648	39,140	195,357	10,108	3,325	0	30	5,825
Connecticut	1,067,610	1,065,625	149,276	488,105	75,508	170,997	1,985	116	0	0	0
Delaware	238,731	235,512	58,270	61,227	12,365	45,325	3,219	2,226	0	0	0
Florida	2,408,396	2,361,618	584,812	840,116	201,000	366,355	46,778	3,487	1,039	25,469	1,413
Georgia	2,194,722	2,149,470	432,325	828,516	123,624	498,222	45,252	8,897	0	0	34,725
Hawaii	407,016	403,823	100,994	162,828	17,439	42,666	3,193	81	0	0	0
Idaho	368,402	353,083	53,586	111,312	18,118	80,046	15,319	1,017	2,682	8,756	1,227
Illinois	3,835,912	3,770,137	676,893	1,751,436	111,665	595,195	65,775	7,801	11,534	0	41,700
Indiana	1,636,226	1,616,794	305,771	709,483	88,829	264,847	19,432	2,856	0	200	8,028
Iowa	997,358	952,376	194,024	387,834	26,423	232,980	44,982	0	98	36,120	2,158
Kansas	738,994	725,208	149,036	250,763	35,986	189,111	13,786	1,847	0	0	11,939
Kentucky	1,460,369	1,450,784	245,115	618,857	62,305	248,574	9,585	3,743	0	0	568
Louisiana	1,585,052	1,572,808	324,244	721,368	91,477	237,584	12,244	1,483	86	8,143	0
Maine	568,508	564,417	84,113	257,949	12,024	68,980	4,091	14	0	0	2,999
Maryland	1,534,171	1,499,136	276,437	619,917	45,954	31,541	35,035	1,623	5,207	3,139	1,272
Massachusetts	2,391,623	2,185,979	322,220	1,253,109	62,760	138,115	205,644	2,908	0	2,539	0
Michigan	4,020,532	3,572,808	646,132	1,959,377	137,511	377,124	447,724	7,739	70,501	319,100	30,347
Minnesota	1,802,232	1,708,629	261,126	820,157	48,936	265,703	93,603	1,304	59,414	11,405	18,206
Mississippi	1,035,478	1,021,867	249,106	364,639	54,945	148,873	13,611	8,596	0	0	0
Missouri	1,500,690	1,478,738	271,080	659,330	62,612	286,596	21,952	3,993	0	220	11,480
Montana	433,770	421,623	54,862	114,015	18,151	128,715	12,147	334	10,965	0	510
Nebraska	554,325	524,963	80,732	192,286	20,829	143,188	29,362	1,851	15,972	1,975	8,926
Nevada	277,228	268,678	44,008	55,449	13,162	89,592	8,550	1,409	1,176	586	1,743
New Hampshire	334,418	307,475	50,081	123,869	15,944	62,432	26,943	1,720	18,993	268	3,875
New Jersey	2,794,368	2,670,693	356,666	1,208,096	94,966	513,216	123,675	13,448	14,046	64,866	6,520

STATE INTERGOVERNMENTAL REVENUE: 1985—Continued

State	Total intergovernmental revenue	From federal government					From local government				
		Total(a)	Education	Public welfare	Health & hospitals	Highways	Total(a)	Education	Public welfare	Health & hospitals	Highways
New Mexico	563,261	526,584	158,923	190,455	31,000	100,032	36,677	21,462	254	2,657	1,474
New York	12,081,750	9,160,574	1,025,846	6,263,051	248,736	520,509	2,921,176	61,120	1,360,808	4,091	0
North Carolina	2,039,201	1,933,027	448,852	739,594	88,138	365,475	106,174	6,510	89,151	795	3,612
North Dakota	363,635	341,083	57,628	112,446	10,612	98,587	22,552	1,252	8,837	35	11,039
Ohio	3,411,827	3,275,706	540,239	1,555,798	165,135	479,597	136,121	16,385	0	28,141	28,256
Oklahoma	964,834	942,074	193,794	431,860	42,167	128,194	22,760	4,279	754	1,232	11,468
Oregon	1,056,594	1,007,059	217,833	340,247	32,683	167,326	49,535	7,647	11,450	0	26,163
Pennsylvania	4,127,915	4,050,903	609,747	2,126,467	135,986	622,299	77,012	67,649	0	0	7,329
Rhode Island	478,263	456,029	63,551	225,852	18,404	64,735	22,234	541	0	0	0
South Carolina	1,083,303	1,057,989	236,461	430,581	58,642	146,528	25,314	10,759	171	5,655	844
South Dakota	313,821	306,313	50,111	97,568	20,315	88,986	7,508	0	1,874	2,819	0
Tennessee	1,648,068	1,611,640	311,171	599,975	90,955	282,280	36,428	6,500	1,349	11,955	13,074
Texas	3,858,259	3,846,622	981,479	1,458,862	201,683	676,536	11,637	9,440	0	0	2,184
Utah	756,122	735,943	165,077	199,905	36,958	200,438	20,179	9,071	1,770	469	0
Vermont	306,300	301,741	49,877	125,766	15,487	54,791	4,559	4,513	0	46	0
Virginia	1,630,212	1,536,460	355,044	622,227	77,982	258,208	93,752	9,092	0	37,217	22,172
Washington	1,914,123	1,774,686	375,899	602,869	147,182	369,257	139,437	28,572	0	87,439	2,486
West Virginia	748,838	744,020	139,495	239,425	38,294	198,719	4,818	1,337	0	0	0
Wisconsin	1,996,841	1,927,132	348,354	1,037,634	62,954	194,362	69,709	3,284	0	4	18,625
Wyoming	428,363	423,035	15,484	54,436	5,202	77,290	5,328	0	306	5	3,459

Source: U.S. Bureau of the Census, *State Government Finances in 1985.*
Note: Totals may not add due to rounding.
(a) Total includes revenue for other activities not shown separately in this table.

Table 9.11
STATE INTERGOVERNMENTAL REVENUE FROM FEDERAL AND LOCAL GOVERNMENTS: 1986
(In thousands of dollars)

State	Total intergovernmental revenue	From federal government					From local government				
		Total(a)	Education	Public welfare	Health & hospitals	Highways	Total(a)	Education	Public welfare	Health & hospitals	Highways
United States	$98,573,784	$92,666,253	$16,523,440	$41,801,896	$3,573,400	$13,854,777	$5,907,531	$379,564	$1,932,754	$813,885	$612,446
Alabama	1,549,087	1,520,193	395,544	489,781	55,063	301,701	28,894	6,853	49	7,288	4,880
Alaska	418,991	413,650	71,455	106,393	4,102	105,008	5,341	2,739	0	167	506
Arizona	806,831	733,331	238,661	132,056	35,043	205,252	73,500	2,953	60,195	2,940	3,899
Arkansas	931,920	926,972	162,454	425,200	39,191	159,078	4,948	916	0	0	3,261
California	12,411,304	12,090,006	2,145,349	5,477,467	265,574	1,122,551	321,298	37,280	344	28,655	171,410
Colorado	1,192,455	1,173,849	268,608	471,549	65,566	224,803	18,606	4,182	0	0	13,375
Connecticut	1,187,370	1,184,069	161,654	515,076	87,122	212,149	3,301	165	0	0	0
Delaware	280,580	277,903	65,130	67,136	16,160	48,146	2,677	2,314	772	0	0
Florida	2,709,768	2,612,283	669,883	931,321	194,161	431,813	97,485	591	772	73,863	3,430
Georgia	2,245,797	2,186,006	443,222	914,431	121,866	412,032	59,791	1,592	297	0	56,174
Hawaii	418,131	415,685	104,834	163,754	18,264	41,237	2,446	100	0	0	0
Idaho	403,513	385,623	57,674	111,745	18,454	98,969	17,890	1,338	3,583	10,745	479
Illinois	4,077,635	3,986,653	767,856	1,714,574	125,534	635,468	90,982	15,290	18,337	0	50,936
Indiana	1,832,384	1,808,547	357,883	802,798	87,441	259,937	23,837	2,348	0	194	11,689
Iowa	1,066,868	1,006,353	196,944	432,959	30,499	205,797	60,515	0	8,807	41,298	2,317
Kansas	807,100	794,482	161,715	260,292	42,416	200,192	12,618	2,080	0	0	10,538
Kentucky	1,537,151	1,525,082	267,657	655,540	60,372	273,129	12,069	4,184	0	8,667	280
Louisiana	1,768,820	1,752,156	353,108	757,127	91,253	264,539	16,664	1,617	0	0	0
Maine	610,973	608,288	88,147	305,371	20,135	74,269	2,685	442	0	0	947
Maryland	1,695,914	1,658,785	311,964	632,369	58,647	378,576	37,129	1,722	4,316	1,488	8,651
Massachusetts	2,526,385	2,376,733	353,823	1,294,867	66,035	160,699	149,652	2,594	0	2,603	0
Michigan	4,487,230	4,005,374	701,215	2,206,085	137,683	428,281	481,856	6,119	64,462	363,167	22,274
Minnesota	1,916,005	1,824,213	285,394	851,101	55,784	272,254	91,792	1,372	55,289	12,379	19,077
Mississippi	1,172,009	1,153,592	253,925	410,053	61,271	179,024	18,417	6,076	0	0	0
Missouri	1,550,109	1,541,151	239,076	661,761	65,200	326,009	8,958	912	2	232	5,044
Montana	468,100	455,421	49,868	141,413	16,184	130,506	12,679	437	11,788	0	309
Nebraska	590,242	561,408	86,707	217,164	24,839	128,339	28,834	2,023	12,869	2,172	10,800
Nevada	353,113	345,075	57,730	71,641	14,700	121,501	8,038	1,578	1,759	570	773
New Hampshire	359,857	327,616	49,248	126,143	14,970	66,180	32,241	1,194	22,158	137	3,465
New Jersey	3,066,194	2,906,405	371,439	1,316,027	95,225	428,823	159,789	17,256	17,453	65,402	48,970

STATE INTERGOVERNMENTAL REVENUE: 1986—Continued

State	Total intergovernmental revenue	From federal government					From local government				
		Total(a)	Education	Public welfare	Health & hospitals	Highways	Total(a)	Education	Public welfare	Health & hospitals	Highways
New Mexico........	630,638	600,101	184,970	196,719	32,745	115,111	30,537	13,648	350	3,320	1,389
New York.........	13,276,386	10,154,082	1,036,570	6,940,354	262,945	657,989	3,122,304	53,933	1,526,843	3,744	0
North Carolina....	2,141,705	2,017,531	438,248	822,839	89,863	316,413	124,174	5,391	94,950	843	3,843
North Dakota......	365,659	349,270	61,073	105,906	11,553	93,955	16,389	1,170	6,635	61	6,663
Ohio..............	3,926,726	3,787,963	596,381	1,835,548	170,266	532,245	138,763	16,068	0	24,627	33,364
Oklahoma.........	1,073,996	1,055,119	191,938	453,866	47,048	174,594	18,877	8,597	394	1,135	2,259
Oregon...........	1,099,486	1,062,500	223,100	372,800	27,120	168,450	36,986	7,673	12,753	0	13,885
Pennsylvania......	4,701,448	4,626,575	653,424	2,286,507	136,240	821,651	74,873	66,976	0	0	4,106
Rhode Island......	531,846	507,549	67,077	250,124	19,391	79,415	24,297	411	0	0	0
South Carolina....	1,210,191	1,179,669	256,638	497,443	66,262	144,493	30,522	11,632	4,461	6,381	327
South Dakota	349,743	343,257	54,214	103,730	25,524	95,442	6,486	230	649	2,669	0
Tennessee.........	1,852,921	1,812,191	328,882	729,678	83,435	341,393	40,730	5,391	911	12,872	18,426
Texas.............	4,558,617	4,546,954	1,089,834	1,493,564	210,646	959,884	11,663	8,966	0	668	1,724
Utah	835,226	810,931	184,382	236,442	51,000	197,274	24,295	11,733	2,328	738	0
Vermont..........	300,592	295,622	54,445	127,273	16,284	49,559	4,970	4,905	0	65	0
Virginia..........	2,052,707	1,948,917	444,385	660,026	87,855	379,909	103,790	2,681	0	38,687	38,643
Washington.......	1,771,313	1,624,651	370,281	539,022	130,212	321,436	146,662	28,481	0	95,052	4,448
West Virginia.....	891,472	885,693	151,947	296,925	29,049	225,223	5,779	1,305	0	0	0
Wisconsin.........	2,113,675	2,060,868	378,084	1,130,696	57,962	185,883	52,807	2,106	0	54	25,368
Wyoming..........	447,601	439,906	19,400	59,240	29,246	98,466	7,695	0	0	1,002	4,517

Source: U.S. Bureau of the Census, State Government Finances in 1986.
Note: Totals may not add due to rounding.
(a) Total includes revenue for other activities not shown separately in this table.

RECENT DEVELOPMENTS IN INTERSTATE COMPACTS AND AGREEMENTS

By Benjamin J. Jones and Duane Osborne

Interstate compacts are a constitutionally recognized legal device used to promote formal cooperation among states in dealing with common problems which overlap state borders. Compacts are authorized by the United States Constitution in Article 1, Section 10, which reads "No State Shall, Without the Consent of Congress, . . . enter into any Agreement or Compact with another State, or with a Foreign Power." From the beginning that phrase has implied that agreements between states which have congressional consent are legal. However, the Supreme Court held in *Virginia vs. Tennessee*, 148 U.S. 503 (1893), that only those agreements which affect the political balance within the federal system or which affect a power delegated to the national government must receive congressional consent. Throughout the years, Congress has granted the consent for states to enter into interstate compacts. The legal effect of the compact is a permanent agreement among the two or more participating states. The compact has not only the effect of a statute, but also the binding legal features of a contract. States who have validly entered into such an agreement may not withdraw without complying with withdrawal provisions contained in the agreement. Some compacts do not allow states to withdraw. The logic behind such force for these agreements may be seen by examining a common early form of compact, namely state boundary agreements. If party states could later withdraw from the agreement, its value as a binding, final settlement of a boundary question would be lost.

During the early years of our nation's history, the interstate compact was primarily used as a boundary settling device when disputes arose between two states. Between 1783 and 1920, only 36 compacts were adopted by the states, and by 1940 only 58. Today, the compact is more prevalent, with more than 170 interstate compacts currently in force in the U.S., covering such concerns as pest control; fire fighting; bridges, roads, subways and other transportation needs; environmental regulation; sharing of prison and other governmental facilities, and movement of juvenile and adult criminal offenders across state lines.

Recent Developments

The number of compacts developed was much less than during the last century. However, the number of states joining existing interstate compacts has continued at a relatively low, but significant level each year. Among the most recent developments involving interstate compacts was the appointment of a National Commission to Restructure the Interstate Compact for the Supervision of Parolees and Probationers and the creation of the Interstate Compact on Grain Marketing.

The Interstate Compact for the Supervision of Parolees and Probationers is the oldest compact in existence which has been entered into by all 50 states. The Compact derives its congressional consent from the Federal Crime Control Act of 1934 which stated: "An act granting the consent of Congress to any two or more states to enter into agreements or compacts for cooperative effort and mutual assistance in the prevention of crime and for other purposes."

The primary purpose of the compact is to ensure that parolees and probationers are allowed to cross state lines for their rehabilitation, when such movement is in the interest of society. The compact also insures that when such movement occurs the parolee or probationer will continue to receive supervision in the receiving state, with regular reports back to the state where the probation or parolee occurred.

Benjamin Jones is the director of the Center for Law and Justice at The Council of State Governments. Duane Osborne is a legal researcher with the Center.

The Parole and Probation Compact Administrator's Association (PPCAA) has been responsible for facilitating uniform transfer between the states. This responsibility has grown from governing a modest 12,077 parolees and probations in 1953 to 77,800 clients in 1985. In addition to the increased volume of activity, problems have arisen where states have decentralized their parole and probation activities, resulting in more than one administrator of the compact. In other cases, officials may be unaware of the compact's provisions and requirements and have inadvertently circumvented it. Changes in technology, such as automation of office functions, also have caused problems under the compact. Other problems are caused by new policies and programs, such as restitution and supervision fees, which require new approaches for an interstate context. Accordingly, the changes in parole and probation since 1934 have created a need to update and modernize the Interstate Compact for the Supervision of Parolees and Probationers. The lack of uniformity, acceptable interstate administration, poorly funded interstate operations, and outdated policies and procedures when combined with a 54-year old compact, illustrates the need for increased attention to the agreement.

In 1986, the Commission to Restructure the Interstate Compact for the Supervision of Parolees and Probationers was created through funding by the National Institute of Corrections. The commission identified eight major gaps in the interstate systems: 1) outdated client eligibility requirements which preclude acceptance of certain client groups from compact services (i.e. misdemeanants); 2) inefficient, inflexible and cumbersome operational procedures resulting in delays in all interstate processes (transfer, arrest/violation, and program delivery); 3) lack of authority in some states to arrest out-of-states violators; 4) inefficient interstate parole and probation violation processes; 5) lack of uniformity in administration of preliminary revocation hearings; 6) conflicting state policies in the areas of misdemeanant supervision, the administration of supervision fees and the supervision of certain difficult client groups (i.e. AIDS clients); 7) lack of knowledge within the criminal justice system of the compact and its authority over conflicting state statutes; and 8) deteriorated compact administration in some states.

In order to solve these problems the commission has employed a variety of methods. The commission's Task Force on Compact Office

Operational Standards is recommending minimum standards for compact offices. Additionally, the Enabling Legislation Task Force has recommended the drafting of national amendments to the compact, reciprocal legislation and in some instances, model state legislation to assist compact field service and paroling authority objectives. A final report by the Commission is expected in the fall of 1988.

Another recent development is the Interstate Compact on Agricultural Grain Marketing. The compact has been signed by five states, Nebraska, Iowa, Minnesota, New Mexico and Wyoming, to promote the use of new shipping and marketing techniques for grain products. Each of the five states has passed legislation within the last two years to officially join the compact. At least 10 more states will consider similar legislation in 1988. The compact is funded through state allocations and governed by a board with three appointees from each state. While eventually the compact may serve a number of important functions, current leaders plan to emphasize issues of grain quality, Midwestern transportation and alternative agricultural products.

A Midwestern grain marketing compact is not a new idea. In the late 1970s, such a compact was considered as a potential response to the damage done to the U.S. markets by the Soviet grain embargo. However, did not take effect until 1987 when it was ratified by the legal minimum of five states. Then, representatives from each state met for the first time on Sept. 28, 1987 in Omaha, Neb., and elected officers.

The governing commission has defined its mission to include: 1) Grain Marketing - the commission hopes to establish fairer dockage standards and stricter restrictions on mixing inferior grade grain with superior grade. 2) Transportation - Together states will work for shipping discounts and improvement of vital transportation lines. 3) Alternative Agricultural Products - The successful introduction of alternative agricultural products could result in a new market for low-grade grain. The commission is also investigating products such as ethanol, corn based road de-icer and biodegradable plastics.

The compact's steering committee has agreed in principle to a staggered payment for member states. After the first biennium, for which each state must appropriate $50,000, any state with more than $2 billion in crop value production will pay a full share. (The amount of that full share has yet to be determined.) Any state under $2 billion a year would pay a portion of a full share reflecting its crop value. Leaders hope that this "pro rata" funding system will entice other states to sign the compact, making it stronger and more efficient for the future.

THE COUNCIL OF STATE GOVERNMENTS

The Council of State Governments (CSG) is a non-partisan service organization whose goal is to foster excellence in all facets of state government. Founded on the premise that the states themselves are the best sources of insight, ideas and innovations, CSG provides a network for the dissemination of timely and useful information to state policymakers.

The activities of the Council are supported and directed by the states themselves. For over 50 years, CSG has served as a research arm and information broker for the states. The Council is the only national association that serves the executive, legislative and judicial branches of state government.

Through its national headquarters in Lexington, Kentucky, and regional offices in Atlanta, Chicago, New York and San Francisco, CSG works to synthesize the complex political, cultural, geographic and philosophical differences inherent in our federal system into cohesive and constructive regional and national approaches. With the approach of the 1990s, the responsibilities and challenges confronting the nation will dictate the role CSG will play in helping to improve decisionmaking at the state level.

Governing Structure

Each state has an equal voice in directing CSG activities through representation on the governing board and executive committee. The governing board includes all the nation's governors and two legislators from each state and the non-state territories. Also represented on the governing board are the national organizations of lieutenant governors, attorneys general, chief justices, secretaries of state, and state auditors, comptrollers and treasurers. The governing board meets annually to provide an opportunity for the diverse members of the CSG family to interact in sessions on current and emerging state issues.

An executive committee is selected from the approximately 175 members of the governing board to manage the day-to-day activities of the Council. State officials also serve on several standing committees that advise the executive committee.

CSG is funded in part through direct contributions by the states, U.S. territories and other non-state jurisdictions. In addition CSG administers federal and private foundation grants which support research and information-gathering projects on topics of interest to state officials. CSG also generates revenue from the sale of publications and by conducting workshops and conferences.

CSG's national headquarters is located in Lexington, Kentucky. The Council is organized around two central departments, the Department of State Services and the Department of Operations, which coordinate all program activities and report to the executive director. The headquarters office houses a policy analysis team, secretariat services, publications, direct inquiry services, data processing services and other national programs.

Also reporting to the executive director is the Intergovernmental Affairs Office located in Washington, D.C. This office monitors developments at the federal level and evaluates their impact on state legislation and policies. It also helps facilitate contact and cooperation among officials at the federal, state and local levels.

Department of State Services

CSG's research and policy analysis capabilities have been structured to emphasize the production of information on issues of growing concern to state executive, legislative and judicial decisionmakers. The Division of Policy Analysis Services produces in-depth analyses of major issues and offers a range of policy options for consideration by decisionmakers. The division is also responsible for CSG's ongoing efforts to highlight effective state programs, including an Innovations Transfer program and the compilation of an annual volume of *Suggested State Legislation*.

The gathering, evaluation and dissemination of timely and relevant information to state government practitioners is the function of the Division of Information Services. The division produces several high-impact periodicals covering important state issues and also operates the States Information Center (SIC) a personal, direct-access inquiry and referral service that fields nearly 10,000 questions each year from state officials. The SIC locates statistical and analytical information and identifies appropriate experts on specific topics. The SIC library maintains 20,000 documents, including CSG studies and an extensive collection of state legislative and agency reports. The information needs of state officials will be further served as CSG continues to develop its on-line, automated information database ISIS (Integrated State Information System).

Department of Operations

The Division of Secretariat Services provides administrative and informational support for the many national associations of state officials which are associated with the Council, and produces research and 50-state databases in the unit's program areas. Centers have been established for agriculture and rural development; management and administration; transportation; health and regulation; and environment and natural resources; and law and justice. The division is also responsible for Council-wide training programs, including the highly-acclaimed Toll Fellows conference, an annual, intensive week-long seminar for selected state officials from across the country, and the Council's annual State Summit meeting. A primary goal of these programs is to help state leaders become better decisionmakers.

Rounding out the departmental organization is the Division of Administrative Services which provides budgeting, personnel and other technical support for all units of the Council. Also under this division is the Publications unit which handles the production and marketing of the scores of publications, reports and other documents generated by the Council each year.

Regional Offices

CSG's regional structure distinguishes it among state service agencies. Offices in Atlanta, Chicago, New York and San Francisco serve regional conferences of state officials (Southern Legislative Conference, Midwestern Legislative Conference, Eastern Regional Conference and Western Legislative Conference, respectively, as well as the Southern Governors'

Association and the Midwestern Governors Association). Regions are the backbone of CSG, providing elected and appointed state officials the opportunity to address issues pertinent to specific areas of the country. Regional task forces and committees actively address their states' needs in agriculture and rural development, energy, environment and natural resources, fiscal affairs and other priority areas.

The issues and activities of each regional office are selected by a regional executive committee of state officials. Regional offices of CSG produce newsletters and substantive issue reports for officials in their region. In addition, annual conferences of regional organizations of state officials are staffed by CSG's regional offices.

Publications

CSG publishes a variety of materials about state government, including reference works, directories, periodicals, research reports, information briefs and newsletters. Major CSG publications are:

• *The Book of the States*, a biennial reference guide to all major aspects of state government. This volume contains quantitative and comparative data as well as essays written by experts in state operations.

• *State Elective Officials and the Legislatures, State Legislative Leadership, Committees and Staff, and State Administrative Officials Classified by Function*, supplemental directories that include names, addresses, and telephone numbers of state officials.

• *Suggested State Legislation*, an annual volume of draft legislation and legislative ideas selected by a committee of state officials.

• *State Government News*, CSG's monthly magazine on state developments, issues and innovations. It is distributed to over 14,000 subscribers, including all elected state officials, and features the Conference Calendar, a monthly listing of meetings involving CSG and its associated organizations.

• *The Journal of State Government*, a quarterly publication that provides a forum for the discussion of state issues from political, academic and practitioner viewpoints.

• *State Government Research Checklist*, a bimonthly inventory of state government reports and current information sources.

• *Backgrounder*, a series of brief, special issue reports covering current state actions and trends.

• Research and policy analysis reports, providing in-depth topical information on state programs and policies.

Affiliated and Cooperating Organizations

CSG is an umbrella organization that allows officials from the different branches of state government to come together on a regular basis and consider issues and challenges of mutual concern. CSG has a relationship with a wide range of state officials and their national associations. The more than 35 affiliated and cooperating organizations of CSG encompass nearly all state constitutional offices and many functional areas. Among the groups with which the Council enjoys formal ties are lieutenant governors, state treasurers, secretaries of state, general services officers, purchasing officials, surplus property administrators, personnel executives, archivists and records administrators, telecommunications directors, boating law administrators, emergency medical services directors and controlled substances administrators.

A list of CSG affiliated, cooperating and adjunct groups begins on page 471.

THE COUNCIL OF STATE GOVERNMENTS
OFFICES AND DIRECTORS

Headquarters Office

Carl W. Stenberg, Executive Director

Darrell D. Perry, Director
Operations

E. Norman Sims, Director
State Services

Iron Works Pike
P.O. Box 11910
Lexington, Kentucky 40578
(606)252-2291

Eastern Office
Alan V. Sokolow, Director
270 Broadway, Suite 513
New York, New York 10007
(212) 693-0400

Midwestern Office
Virginia Thrall, Director
641 East Butterfield Road, Suite 401
Lombard, Illinois 60148
(312) 810-0210

Southern Office
Charles J. Williams, Jr., Director
3384 Peachtree Road, N.E.
Atlanta, Georgia 30326
(404) 266-1271

Western Office
Daniel M. Sprague, Director
121 Second Street, 4th Floor
San Francisco, California 94105
(415) 974-6422

Washington Office
Norman Beckman, Director
Hall of the States
444 North Capitol Street
Washington, D.C. 20001
(202) 624-5460

THE COUNCIL OF STATE GOVERNMENTS

AFFILIATED ORGANIZATIONS

National Clearinghouse on Licensure Enforcement and Regulation
Conference of Chief Justices
Conference of State Court Administrators
National Association of Attorneys General
National Association of Secretaries of State
National Association of State Auditors, Comptrollers and Treasurers
National Association of State Personnel Executives
National Association of State Purchasing Officials
National Association of State Treasurers
National Conference of Lieutenant Governors
National Conference of State General Services Officers
National Conference of State Legislatures

COOPERATING ORGANIZATIONS

Adjutants General Association of the United States
American Probation and Parole Associations
Association of Juvenile Compact Administrators
Association of State Correctional Administrators
Association of State Dam Safety Officials
Association of State Floodplain Managers
Association of State and Interstate Water Pollution Control Administrators
Chief Officers of State Library Agencies
Coastal States Organization
Conference of State Sanitary Engineers
Council of State Administrators of Vocational Rehabilitation
Council on Governmental Ethics Laws
Interstate Conference on Water Problems
National Association of Extradition Officials
National Association of Regulatory Utility Commissioners
National Association of State Boating Law Administrators
National Association of State Departments of Agriculture
National Association of State Emergency Medical Services Directors
National Association of State Fleet Administrators
National Association of State Foresters
National Association for State Information Systems
National Association of State Juvenile Delinquency Program Administrators
National Association of State Land Reclamationists
National Association of State Mental Health Program Directors
National Association of State Telecommunications Directors
National Association of State Training and Development Directors
National Association of State Units on Aging
National Association of Tax Administrators
National Association of Unclaimed Property Administrators
National Conference of Commissioners on Uniform State Laws
National Conference of States on Building Codes and Standards
National Criminal Justice Association
National Emergency Management Association
National Reciprocal and Family Support Association
National State Printing Association
Ohio River Basin Commission
Parole and Probation Compact Administrators' Association

THE COUNCIL OF STATE GOVERNMENTS

ADJUNCT ORGANIZATIONS

National Association of Government Archives and Records Administrators
National Association of State Controlled Substances Authorities
North American Association of Wardens and Superintendents
Operation C.A.R.E.
State and Federal Directors of Correctional Education

RELATED COMMITTEES

Committee on Intergovernmental Affairs
Committee on Suggested State Legislation

THE COUNCIL OF STATE GOVERNMENTS
REGIONAL CONFERENCES 1987-88

EAST
Eastern Regional Conference
Representative Jane Maroney, Delaware, Chairperson

Eastern Association of Attorneys General
Attorney General Stephen E. Merrill, New Hampshire, Chairman

MIDWEST
Midwestern Governors' Conference
Governor Richard F. Celeste, Ohio, Chairman

Midwestern Legislative Conference
Senator Stanley J. Aronoff, Ohio, President Pro Tem

SOUTH
Southern Governors' Association
Governor Joe Frank Harris, Georgia, Chairman

Southern Legislative Conference
Representative Charles W. Capps, Jr., Mississippi, Chairman

Southern Environmental Resources Conferences
Thomas C. Andrews, Assistant Secretary
Department of Natural Resources, Maryland

WEST
Western Legislative Conference
Senator Bettye M. Fahrenkamp, Alaska, Chairperson

Conference of Western Attorneys General
Attorney General John K. Van de Kamp, California, Chairman

THE COUNCIL OF STATE GOVERNMENTS
OFFICERS AND EXECUTIVE COMMITTEE
1987-88

Chairman
Senate President Pro Tem Mary McClure, South Dakota
President
Governor James G. Martin, North Carolina
Vice Chairman
Speaker Thomas B. Murphy, Georgia
Vice President
Governor Terry Branstad, Iowa
Chairman-Elect
Senate President Arnold Christensen, Utah
President-Elect
Governor William A. O'Neill, Connecticut

Treasurer Edward T. Alter, Utah
Senate President Pro Tem Stanley J. Aronoff, Ohio
Governor Norman H. Bangerter, Utah
Representative Jane Barnes, Illinois
Governor Richard H. Bryan, Nevada
Representative Charles W. Capps, Jr., Mississippi
Speaker Pro Tem John H. Connors, Iowa
Representative Lee A. Daniels, Illinois
Secretary of State James H. Douglas, Vermont
Senator Ross O. Doyen, Kansas
Secretary of State Jim Edgar, Illinois
Senator Bettye Fahrenkamp, Alaska
Senator Hugh T. Farley, New York
Treasurer Joan Finney, Kansas
Treasurer Michael L. Fitzgerald, Iowa
Senator James I. Gibson, Nevada
Speaker Bob Griffin, Missouri
Chief Justice Gordon R. Hall, Utah
Assemblyman Kemp Hannon, New York
Representative Roy Hausauer, North Dakota
Auditor General Thomas W. Hayes, California
Senator John J. Marchi, New York
Representative Jane Maroney, Delaware
Lieutenant Governor Stephen A. McAlpine, Alaska
Attorney General Brian McKay, Nevada
Attorney General Stephen E. Merrill, New Hampshire
Representative John E. Miller, Arkansas
Comptroller Earle E. Morris, Jr., South Carolina
Deputy Director Bob Nebiker, Department of Health and Regulatory Boards, Virginia
Senate President Samuel B. Nunez, Jr., Louisiana
Senate President Pro Tem Carmen Orechio, New Jersey
Governor Robert D. Orr, Indiana
Senator Cary G. Peterson, Utah
Speaker A.L. Philpott, Virginia
Senator Mark G. Ricks, Idaho
Senate President Fred A. Risser, Wisconsin
Senate President Pro Tem David A. Roberti, California
Senate Deputy President Pro Tem Kenneth C. Royall, Jr., North Carolina
Lieutenant Governor George H. Ryan, Illinois

THE COUNCIL OF STATE GOVERNMENTS

Speaker Pro Tem Marion Shiflet, West Virginia
Speaker Irving J. Stolberg, Connecticut
Senate President Ted L. Strickland, Colorado
Senator George Stuart, Jr., Florida
Representative Donna P. Sytek, New Hampshire
Representative John J. Thomas, Indiana
Governor James R. Thompson, Illinois
Chief Justice C.C. Torbert, Jr., Alabama
Secretary of State Jim Waltermire, Montana
Representative W. Paul White, Massachusetts
Governor Wallace G. Wilkinson, Kentucky
Chief Deputy Director Elizabeth Yost, Department of General Services, California

CHAPTER TEN

STATE PAGES

Table 10.1
OFFICIAL NAMES OF STATES AND JURISDICTIONS, CAPITALS, ZIP CODES AND CENTRAL SWITCHBOARDS

State or other jurisdiction	Name of state capitol(a)	Capital	Zip code	Area code	Central switchboard
Alabama, State of	State Capitol	Montgomery	36130	205	261-2500
Alaska, State of	State Capitol	Juneau	99811	907	465-2111
Arizona, State of	State Capitol	Phoenix	85007	602	255-4900
Arkansas, State of	State Capitol	Little Rock	72201	501	371-3000
California, State of	State Capitol	Sacramento	95814	916	322-9900
Colorado, State of	State Capitol	Denver	80203	303	866-5000
Connecticut, State of	State Capitol	Hartford	06106	203	566-2211
Delaware, State of	Legislative Hall	Dover	19901	302	736-4000
Florida, State of	The Capitol	Tallahassee	32301	904	488-1234
Georgia, State of	State Capitol	Atlanta	30334	404	656-2000
Hawaii, State of	State Capitol	Honolulu	96813	808	548-2211
Idaho, State of	State Capitol	Boise	83720	208	334-2411
Illinois, State of	State House	Springfield	62706	217	782-2000
Indiana, State of	State House	Indianapolis	46204	317	232-3140
Iowa, State of	State Capitol	Des Moines	50319	515	281-5011
Kansas, State of	State House	Topeka	66612	913	296-0111
Kentucky, Commonwealth of	State Capitol	Frankfort	40601	502	564-2500
Louisiana, State of.....................	State Capitol	Baton Rouge	70804	504	342-6600
Maine, State of........................	State House	Augusta	04333	207	289-1110
Maryland, State of.....................	State House	Annapolis	21401	301	269-6200
Massachusetts, Commonwealth of	State House	Boston	02133	617	727-2121
Michigan, State of	State Capitol	Lansing	48909	517	373-1837
Minnesota, State of	State Capitol	St. Paul	55515	612	296-6013
Mississippi, State of	New Capitol	Jackson	39201	601	359-1000
Missouri, State of	State Capitol	Jefferson City	65101	314	751-2151
Montana, State of	State Capitol	Helena	59620	406	444-2511
Nebraska, State of	State Capitol	Lincoln	68509	402	471-2311
Nevada, State of.......................	Legislative Hall	Carson City	89710	702	885-5000
New Hampshire, State of	State House	Concord	03301	603	271-1110
New Jersey, State of	State House	Trenton	08625	609	292-2121
New Mexico, State of	State Capitol	Santa Fe	87503	505	827-4011
New York, State of	State Capitol	Albany	12224	518	474-2121
North Carolina, State of................	State Legislative Building	Raleigh	27611	919	733-1110
North Dakota, State of.................	State Capitol	Bismarck	58505	701	224-2000
Ohio, State of.........................	State House	Columbus	43215	614	466-2000
Oklahoma, State of	State Capitol	Oklahoma City	73105	405	521-2011
Oregon, State of	State Capitol	Salem	97310	503	378-3131
Pennsylvania, Commonwealth of	Main Capitol Building	Harrisburg	17120	717	787-2121
Rhode Island and Providence Plantations, State of	State House	Providence	02903	401	277-2000
South Carolina, State of................	State House	Columbia	29211	803	734-1000
South Dakota, State of	State Capitol	Pierre	57501	605	773-3011
Tennessee, State of	State Capitol	Nashville	37219	615	741-3011
Texas, State of	State Capitol	Austin	78711	512	463-4630
Utah, State of	State Capitol	Salt Lake City	84114	801	538-3000
Vermont, State of	State House	Montpelier	05602	802	828-1110
Virginia, Commonwealth of..............	State Capitol	Richmond	23219	804	786-0000
Washington, State of...................	Legislative Building	Olympia	98504	206	753-5000
West Virginia, State of	State Capitol	Charleston	25305	304	348-3456
Wisconsin, State of	State Capitol	Madison	53702	608	266-2211
Wyoming, State of.....................	State Capitol	Cheyenne	82002	307	777-7011
District of Columbia	District Building	Washington	20004	202	727-1000
American Samoa, Territory of............	Maota Fono	Pago Pago	96799	684	633-4116
Federated States of Micronesia	. . .	Kolonia	96941	. . .	NCS
Guam, Territory of	Congress Building	Agana	96910	671	472-8931
Marshall Islands	. . .	Majuro	96960	. . .	NCS
No. Mariana Is., Commonwealth of	Civic Center	Saipan	96950	. . .	NCS
Puerto Rico, Commonwealth of	The Capitol	San Juan	00904	809	721-6040
Republic of Belau	. . .	Koror	96940	. . .	NCS
Virgin Islands, Territory of	Capitol Building	Charlotte Amalie	00801	809	774-0880

NCS—No central switchboard.
(a) In some instances the name is not official.

Table 10.2
HISTORICAL DATA ON THE STATES

State or other jurisdiction	Source of state lands	Date organized as territory	Date admitted to Union	Chronological order of admission to Union
Alabama	Mississippi Territory, 1798(a)	March 3, 1817	Dec. 14, 1819	22
Alaska	Purchased from Russia, 1867	Aug. 24, 1912	Jan. 3, 1959	49
Arizona	Ceded by Mexico, 1848(b)	Feb. 24, 1863	Feb. 14, 1912	48
Arkansas	Louisiana Purchase, 1803	March 2, 1819	June 15, 1836	25
California	Ceded by Mexico, 1848	(c)	Sept. 9, 1850	31
Colorado	Louisiana Purchase, 1803(d)	Feb. 28, 1861	Aug. 1, 1876	38
Connecticut	Fundamental Orders, Jan. 14, 1638; Royal charter, April 23, 1662(e)	. . .	Jan. 9, 1788(f)	5
Delaware	Swedish charter, 1638; English charter, 1683(e)	. . .	Dec. 7, 1787(f)	1
Florida	Ceded by Spain, 1819	March 30, 1822	March 3, 1845	27
Georgia	Charter, 1732, from George II to Trustees for Establishing the Colony of Georgia(e)	. . .	Jan. 2, 1788(f)	4
Hawaii	Annexed, 1898	June 14, 1900	Aug. 21, 1959	50
Idaho	Treaty with Britain, 1846	March 4, 1863	July 3, 1890	43
Illinois	Northwest Territory, 1787	Feb. 3, 1809	Dec. 3, 1818	21
Indiana	Northwest Territory, 1787	May 7, 1800	Dec. 11, 1816	19
Iowa	Louisiana Purchase, 1803	June 12, 1838	Dec. 28, 1846	29
Kansas	Louisiana Purchase, 1803(d)	May 30, 1854	Jan. 29, 1861	34
Kentucky	Part of Virginia until admitted as state	(c)	June 1, 1792	15
Louisiana	Louisiana Purchase, 1803(g)	March 26, 1804	April 30, 1812	18
Maine	Part of Massachusetts until admitted as state	(c)	March 15, 1820	23
Maryland	Charter, 1632, from Charles I to Calvert(e)	. . .	April 28, 1788(f)	7
Massachusetts	Charter to Massachusetts Bay Company, 1629(e)	. . .	Feb. 6, 1788(f)	6
Michigan	Northwest Territory, 1787	Jan. 11, 1805	Jan. 26, 1837	26
Minnesota	Northwest Territory, 1787(h)	March 3, 1849	May 11, 1858	32
Mississippi	Mississippi Territory(i)	April 7, 1798	Dec. 10, 1817	20
Missouri	Louisiana Purchase, 1803	June 4, 1812	Aug. 10, 1821	24
Montana	Louisiana Purchase, 1803(j)	May 26, 1864	Nov. 8, 1889	41
Nebraska	Louisiana Purchase, 1803	May 30, 1854	March 1, 1867	37
Nevada	Ceded by Mexico, 1848	March 2, 1861	Oct. 31, 1864	36
New Hampshire	Grants from Council for New England, 1622 and 1629; made Royal province, 1679(e)	. . .	June 21, 1788(f)	9
New Jersey	Dutch settlement, 1618; English charter, 1664(e)	. . .	Dec. 18, 1787(f)	3
New Mexico	Ceded by Mexico, 1848(b)	Sept. 9, 1850	Jan. 6, 1912	47
New York	Dutch settlement, 1623; English control, 1664(e)	. . .	July 26, 1788(f)	11
North Carolina	Charter, 1663, from Charles II(e)	. . .	Nov. 21, 1789(f)	12
North Dakota	Louisiana Purchase, 1803(k)	March 2, 1861	Nov. 2, 1889	39
Ohio	Northwest Territory, 1787	May 7, 1800	March 1, 1803	17
Oklahoma	Louisiana Purchase, 1803	May 2, 1890	Nov. 16, 1907	46
Oregon	Settlement and treaty with Britain, 1846	Aug. 14, 1848	Feb. 14, 1859	33
Pennsylvania	Grant from Charles II to William Penn, 1681(e)	. . .	Dec. 12, 1787(f)	2
Rhode Island	Charter, 1663, from Charles II(e)	. . .	May 29, 1790(f)	13
South Carolina	Charter, 1663, from Charles II(e)	. . .	May 23, 1788(f)	8
South Dakota	Louisiana Purchase, 1803	March 2, 1861	Nov. 2, 1889	40
Tennessee	Part of North Carolina until land ceded to U.S. in 1789	June 8, 1790(l)	June 1, 1796	16
Texas	Republic of Texas, 1845	(c)	Dec. 29, 1845	28
Utah	Ceded by Mexico, 1848	Sept. 9, 1850	Jan. 4, 1896	45
Vermont	From lands of New Hampshire and New York	(c)	March 4, 1791	14
Virginia	Charter, 1609, from James I to London Company(e)	. . .	June 25, 1788(f)	10
Washington	Oregon Territory, 1848	March 2, 1853	Nov. 11, 1889	42
West Virginia	Part of Virginia until admitted as state	(c)	June 20, 1863	35
Wisconsin	Northwest Territory, 1787	April 20, 1836	May 29, 1848	30
Wyoming	Louisiana Purchase, 1803(d,j)	July 25, 1868	July 10, 1890	44
Dist. of Col.	Maryland(m)	. . .	. . .	. . .
American Samoa	------------------------------------Became a territory, 1900------------------------------------			
Federated States of Micronesia	. . .	May 10, 1979	. . .	. . .
Guam	Ceded by Spain, 1898	Aug. 1, 1950	. . .	. . .
Marshall Islands	. . .	May 1, 1979	. . .	. . .
No. Mariana Is.	. . .	March 24, 1976	. . .	. . .
Puerto Rico	Ceded by Spain, 1898	. . .	July 25, 1952(n)	. . .
Republic of Belau	. . .	Jan. 1, 1981	. . .	. . .
Virgin Islands	--------------------------------Purchased from Denmark, March 31, 1917--------------------------------			

HISTORICAL DATA—Continued

(a) By the Treaty of Paris, 1783, England gave up claim to the 13 original Colonies, and to all land within an area extending along the present Canadian border to the Lake of the Woods, down the Mississippi River to the 31st parallel, east to the Chattahoochie, down that river to the mouth of the Flint, east to the source of the St. Mary's, down that river to the ocean. The major part of Alabama was acquired by the Treaty of Paris, and the lower portion from Spain in 1813.

(b) Portion of land obtained by Gadsden Purchase, 1853.

(c) No territorial status before admission to Union.

(d) Portion of land ceded by Mexico, 1848.

(e) One of the original 13 Colonies.

(f) Date of ratification of U.S. Constitution.

(g) West Feliciana District (Baton Rouge) acquired from Spain, 1810; added to Louisiana, 1812.

(h) Portion of land obtained by Louisiana Purchase, 1803.

(i) See footnote (a). The lower portion of Mississippi also was acquired from Spain in 1813.

(j) Portion of land obtained from Oregon Territory, 1848.

(k) The northern portion of the Red River Valley was acquired by treaty with Great Britain in 1818.

(l) Date Southwest Territory (identical boundary as Tennessee's) was created.

(m) Area was originally 100 square miles, taken from Virginia and Maryland. Virginia's portion south of the Potomac was given back to that state in 1846. Site chosen in 1790, city incorporated 1802.

(n) On this date, Puerto Rico became a self-governing commonwealth by compact approved by the U.S. Congress and the voters of Puerto Rico as provided in U.S. Public Law 600 of 1950.

Table 10.3
STATE STATISTICS

State or other jurisdiction	Land area — In square miles	Land area — Rank in nation	Population — Size	Population — Rank in nation	Percentage change 1970 to 1980	Density per square mile	No. of representatives in Congress	Capital	Population	Rank in state	Largest city	Population
Alabama	50,708	29	4,053,000	22	13.1	78.7	7	Montgomery	184,963	3	Birmingham	279,813
Alaska	570,833	1	534,000	48	32.8	0.91	1	Juneau	21,778	3	Anchorage	226,516
Arizona	113,417	6	3,317,000	27	53.1	28.1	5	Phoenix	853,266	1	Phoenix	853,266
Arkansas	51,945	27	2,372,000	33	18.9	45.4	4	Little Rock	170,140	1	Little Rock	140,140
California	156,361	3	26,981,000	1	18.5	168.6	45	Sacramento	304,000	7	Los Angeles	3,096,721
Colorado	103,766	8	3,267,000	6	30.8	31.1	6	Denver	504,588	1	Denver	504,588
Connecticut	4,862	48	3,189,000	28	2.5	652.8	6	Hartford	136,000	2	Bridgeport	142,000
Delaware	1,982	49	633,000	47	8.4	313.8	1	Dover	23,512	3	Wilmington	70,195
Florida	54,136	22	11,675,000	5	43.5	210.0	19	Tallahassee	112,000	11	Jacksonville	577,971
Georgia	58,073	21	5,975,000	13	19.1	102.9	10	Atlanta	426,090	1	Atlanta	426,090
Hawaii	6,425	47	1,062,000	39	25.3	164.0	2	Honolulu(a)	805,266	1	Honolulu	805,266
Idaho	82,677	13	1,003,000	41	32.4	12.2	2	Boise	107,000	1	Boise	107,000
Illinois	55,748	24	11,553,000	5	2.8	206.9	22	Springfield	102,000	4	Chicago	2,992,472
Indiana	36,097	38	5,504,000	14	5.7	152.3	10	Indianapolis	710,280	1	Indianapolis	710,280
Iowa	55,941	25	2,851,000	29	3.1	51.6	6	Des Moines	190,832	1	Des Moines	190,832
Kansas	81,787	14	2,461,000	32	5.1	30.0	5	Topeka	119,000	3	Wichita	283,496
Kentucky	39,650	37	3,728,000	23	13.7	94.0	7	Frankfort	26,025	9	Louisville	289,843
Louisiana	44,930	31	4,501,000	18	15.4	99.7	8	Baton Rouge	368,571	2	New Orleans	559,101
Maine	30,920	39	1,174,000	38	13.2	37.6	2	Augusta	21,819	6	Portland	61,572
Maryland	9,891	42	4,463,000	19	7.5	444.0	8	Annapolis	31,910	5	Baltimore	763,570
Massachusetts	7,826	45	5,832,000	12	0.8	743.9	11	Boston	570,719	1	Boston	570,719
Michigan	56,817	23	9,145,000	8	4.3	160.0	18	Lansing	128,000	5	Detroit	1,088,973
Minnesota	79,289	12	4,214,000	21	7.1	52.9	8	St. Paul	265,903	2	Minneapolis	358,335
Mississippi	47,296	31	2,625,000	31	13.7	55.2	5	Jackson	208,810	1	Jackson	208,810
Missouri	68,995	19	5,066,000	15	5.1	72.9	9	Jefferson City	34,575	12	St. Louis	429,296
Montana	145,587	4	819,000	44	13.3	5.67	2	Helena	24,289	5	Billings	68,787
Nebraska	76,483	15	1,598,000	36	5.7	21.0	3	Lincoln	180,378	2	Omaha	332,237
Nevada	109,889	7	963,000	43	63.8	8.5	2	Carson City	34,597	1	Las Vegas	183,227
New Hampshire	9,027	44	1,027,000	40	24.8	110.6	2	Concord	30,706	3	Manchester	92,104
New Jersey	7,521	46	7,620,000	9	2.7	1,005.5	14	Trenton	92,124	5	Newark	314,387
New Mexico	121,412	5	1,479,000	37	28.1	11.9	3	Santa Fe	50,857	2	Albuquerque	330,575
New York	47,831	30	17,772,000	2	-3.7	371.8	34	Albany	101,727	6	New York	7,164,742
North Carolina	48,798	28	6,331,000	10	15.7	128.2	11	Raleigh	169,000	3	Charlotte	331,000
North Dakota	69,273	17	679,000	46	5.7	9.9	1	Bismarck	45,929	1	Fargo	62,576
Ohio	40,975	35	10,752,000	6	1.3	262.2	21	Columbus	566,114	2	Cleveland	573,822
Oklahoma	68,782	18	3,305,000	25	18.2	48.0	6	Oklahoma City	443,172	1	Oklahoma City	443,172
Oregon	96,184	10	2,688,000	30	25.9	27.9	5	Salem	89,233	3	Portland	365,861
Pennsylvania	44,966	33	11,889,000	4	-0.5	264.7	23	Harrisburg	53,264	10	Philadelphia	1,646,713
Rhode Island	1,049	50	975,000	42	-0.3	922.8	2	Providence	154,000	1	Providence	154,000
South Carolina	37,000	40	3,378,000	24	20.5	110.8	6	Columbia	101,208	1	Columbia	101,208
South Dakota	75,955	16	708,000	45	3.7	9.3	1	Pierre	11,973	9	Sioux Falls	81,343
Tennessee	41,155	34	4,803,000	16	16.9	115.2	9	Nashville	462,450	2	Memphis	648,399
Texas	262,134	2	16,682,000	3	27.1	62.5	27	Austin	397,001	6	Houston	1,705,697
Utah	82,073	12	1,665,000	35	37.9	20.0	3	Salt Lake City	164,844	1	Salt Lake City	164,844
Vermont	9,267	43	541,000	49	15.0	57.7	1	Montpelier	8,241	5	Burlington	37,712

STATE STATISTICS—Continued

State or other jurisdiction	Land area In square miles	Land area Rank in nation	Population Size	Population Rank in nation	Percentage change 1970 to 1980	Density per square mile	No. of representatives in Congress	Capital	Population	Rank in state	Largest city	Population
Virginia	39,780	36	5,787,000	13	14.9	143.4	10	Richmond	219,056	3	Norfolk	279,683
Washington	66,570	20	4,463,000	20	21.1	66.2	8	Olympia	27,447	15	Seattle	488,474
West Virginia	24,070	41	1,919,000	34	11.8	80.4	4	Charleston	63,968	1	Charleston	63,968
Wisconsin	54,464	26	4,785,000	17	6.5	87.7	9	Madison	170,745	2	Milwaukee	620,811
Wyoming	97,023	9	507,000	50	41.3	5.2	1	Cheyenne	47,283	2	Casper	51,016
Dist. of Columbia	67		626,000		-15.6	10,132.3	1(b)					
American Samoa	77		34,500		18.9	419.0		Pago Pago	3,075		Pago Pago	3,075
Federated States of Micronesia	271		73,160		....	572.0		Kolonia, Pohnpei	5,549		Moen, Truk	10,351
Guam	209		120,977		24.7	443.5	1(b)	Agana	896		Tamuning	13,580
Marshall Islands	192		12,177		34.9	91.1		Majuro	12,000		Majuro	12,000
No. Mariana Is	184		20,000		74.1	955.0		Saipan	16,532		Saipan	16,532
Puerto Rico	3,421		3,279,231		17.9	955.0	1(b)	San Juan	434,849		San Juan	434,849
Republic of Belau	192		12,177		8.1	63.4		Koror	6,222		Koror	6,222
Virgin Islands	132		107,500		54.6	814.47	1(b)	Charlotte Amalie, St. Thomas	11,842		Charlotte Amalie, St. Thomas	11,842

Key:
(a) Honolulu County.
(b) Delegate with committee voting privileges only.

Alabama

Nickname . . . . The Heart of Dixie
Motto . . . . *We Dare Defend Our Rights*
Flower . . . . Camellia
Gamebird . . . . Wild Turkey
Bird . . . . Yellowhammer
Tree . . . . Southern (Longleaf) Pine
Song . . . . *Alabama*
Dance . . . . Square Dance
Stone . . . . Marble
Mineral . . . . Hematite
Fish . . . . Tarpon
Nut . . . . Pecan
Fossil . . . . Species Basilosaurus Cetoides
Entered the Union . . . . December 14, 1819
Capital . . . . Montgomery

ELECTED EXECUTIVE BRANCH OFFICIALS

Governor . . . . Guy Hunt
Lieutenant Governor . . . . Jim Folsom Jr.
Secretary of State . . . . Glen Bowder
Attorney General . . . . Don Siegelman
Treasurer . . . . George Wallace Jr.
Auditor . . . . Jan Cook
Commr. of Agriculture
 & Industries . . . . Albert McDonald

SUPREME COURT

C. C. Torbert Jr., Chief Justice
Oscar W. Adams Jr.
Reneau P. Almon
Samuel A. Beatty
Gorman Houston
Richard L. Jones
Hugh Maddox
Janie L. Shores
Henry B. Steagall II

LEGISLATURE

President of the Senate Lt. Gov. Jim Folsom Jr.
President Pro Tem
 of the Senate . . . . Ryan deGraffenried Jr.
Secretary of the Senate . . . . McDowell Lee

Speaker of the House . . . . James S. Clark
Speaker Pro Tem
 of the House . . . . James N. Campbell
Clerk of the House . . . . John W. Pemberton

STATISTICS

Land Area (square miles) 50,708
 Rank in Nation 29th
Population 4,053,000
 Rank in Nation 22nd
 Density per square mile 78.7
Number of Representatives in Congress 7
Capital City . . . . Montgomery
 Population 184,963
 Rank in State 3rd
Largest City . . . . Birmingham
 Population 279,813
Number of Cities over 10,000 Population . . . 40

Alaska

Motto . . . . *North to the Future*
Flower . . . . Forget-me-not
Bird . . . . Willow Ptarmigan
Tree . . . . Sitka Spruce
Song . . . . *Alaska's Flag*
Sport . . . . Dog Mushing
Gem . . . . Jade
Mineral . . . . Gold
Marine Mammal . . . . Bowhead Whale
Fish . . . . King Salmon
Purchased from Russia by the
 United States . . . . March 30, 1867
Entered the Union . . . . January 3, 1959
Capital . . . . Juneau

ELECTED EXECUTIVE BRANCH OFFICIALS

Governor . . . . Steve Cowper
Lieutenant Governor . . . . Stephen McAlpine

SUPREME COURT

Jay A. Rabinowitz, Chief Justice
Edmond W. Burke
Allen Compton
Warren Matthews
Daniel Moore

LEGISLATURE

President of the Senate . . . . Jan Faiks
Secretary of the Senate . . . . Peggy Mulligan

Speaker of the House . . . . Ben Grussendorf
Chief Clerk of the House . . . . Irene Cashen

STATISTICS

Land Area (square miles) 570,833
 Rank in Nation 1st
Population 534,000
 Rank in Nation 48th
 Density per square mile 0.91
Number of Representatives in Congress 1
Capital City . . . . Juneau
 Population 21,778
 Rank in State 3rd
Largest City . . . . Anchorage
 Population 226,516
Number of Cities over 10,000 Population 3

Arizona

Nickname . . . . The Grand Canyon State
Motto . . . . *Ditat Deus* (God Enriches)
Flower . . . . Blossom of the Saguaro Cactus
Bird . . . . Cactus Wren
Tree . . . . Palo Verde
Song . . . . *Arizona March Song* and *Arizona*
Gemstone . . . . Turquoise
Official Neckwear . . . . Bola Tie
Entered the Union . . . . February 14, 1912
Capital . . . . Phoenix

ELECTED EXECUTIVE BRANCH OFFICIALS

Governor . . . . Rose Mofford
Secretary of State . . . . Karen Osborn
Attorney General . . . . Bob K. Corbin
Treasurer . . . . Ray Rottas
Supt. of Public Instruction . . . . C. Diane Bishop
Mine Inspector . . . . James H. McCutchan

SUPREME COURT

William A. Holohan, Chief Justice
Frank X. Gordon Jr., Vice Chief Justice
James Duke Cameron
Stanley G. Feldman
(Vacancy)

LEGISLATURE

President of the Senate . . . . . . Carl J. Kunasek
President Pro Tem of the Senate . . Jack Taylor
Secretary of the Senate . . . . . . Shirley Wheaton

Speaker of the House . . . . Joe Lane
Speaker Pro Tem
    of the House . . . . Bob Denny
Chief Clerk of the House . . . . Jane Richards

STATISTICS

Land Area (square miles) 113,417
    Rank in Nation 6th
Population 3,317,000
    Rank in Nation 27th
    Density per square mile 28.1
Number of Representatives in Congress 5
Capital City . . . . Phoenix
    Population 853,266
    Rank in State 1st
Largest City . . . . Phoenix
Number of Places over 10,000 Population . . . 17

Arkansas

Nickname . . . . The Land of Opportunity
Motto . . . . . . *Regnat Populus* (The People Rule)
Flower . . . . Apple Blossom
Bird . . . . Mockingbird
Tree . . . . Pine
Song . . . . *Arkansas*
Gem . . . . Diamond
Entered the Union . . . . June 15, 1836
Capital . . . . Little Rock

ELECTED EXECUTIVE BRANCH OFFICIALS

Governor . . . . Bill Clinton
Lieutenant Governor . . . . Winston Bryant
Secretary of State . . . . W.J. "Bill" McCuen
Attorney General . . . . Steve Clark
Treasurer . . . . Jimmie Lou Fisher
Auditor . . . . Julia Hughs Jones
Land Commr. . . . . Charlie Daniels

SUPREME COURT

Jack Holt, Jr., Chief Justice
Robert H. Dudley
Tom Glaze
Steele Hays
Darrell Hickman
David Newbern
John I. Purtle

GENERAL ASSEMBLY

President
    of the Senate . . . . . . Lt. Gov. Winston Bryant
President Pro Tem
    of the Senate . . . . Nick Wilson
Secretary of the Senate . . . . Hal Moody

Speaker of the House . . . . . Ernest Cunningham
Speaker Pro Tem
    of the House . . . . L. L. Bryan
Chief Clerk of the House . . . . Jo Kenshaw

STATISTICS

Land Area (square miles) 51,945
    Rank in Nation 27th
Population 2,372,000
    Rank in Nation 33rd
    Density per square mile 45.4
Number of Representatives in Congress 4
Capital City . . . . Little Rock
    Population 170,140
    Rank in State 1st
Largest City . . . . Little Rock
Number of Places over 10,000 Population . . . 29

California

Nickname.................The Golden State
Motto..............*Eureka* (I Have Found It)
Flower......................Golden Poppy
Bird...............California Valley Quail
Tree..................California Redwood
Reptile............California Desert Tortoise
Song.................*I Love You, California*
Stone......................Serpentine
Mineral.....................Native Gold
Animal.............California Grizzly Bear
Fish..............California Golden Trout
Insect.........California Dog-Face Butterfly
Marine Mammal......California Gray Whale
Fossil..................Saber-Toothed Cat
Gemstone.....................Benitoite
Entered the Union........September 9, 1850
Capital......................Sacramento

ELECTED EXECUTIVE BRANCH OFFICIALS

Governor...............George Deukmejian
Lieutenant Governor........Leo T. McCarthy
Secretary of State...........March Fong Eu
Attorney General.........John Van de Kamp
Treasurer...................Jesse M. Unruh
Controller....................Gray Davis
Supt. of Public Instruction........Bill Honig

SUPREME COURT

Allen E. Broussard, Acting Chief Justice
Malcolm M. Lucas
Stanley Mosk
Edward Panelli
(3 Vacancies)

LEGISLATURE

President
    of the Senate.....Lt. Gov. Leo T. McCarthy
President Pro Tem
    of the Senate.............David A. Roberti
Secretary of the Senate......Darryl R. White

Speaker
    of the Assembly.....Willie Lewis Brown Jr.
Speaker Pro Tem
    of the Assembly...............Mike Roos
Acting Chief Clerk
    of the Assembly...........R. Brian Kidney

STATISTICS

Land Area (square miles)...........156,361
    Rank in Nation.....................3rd
Population...................26,981,000
    Rank in Nation.......................1st
    Density per square mile..............168.6
Number of Representatives in Congress....45
Capital City....................Sacramento
    Population.......................304,000
    Rank in State.......................7th
Largest City.................Los Angeles
    Population.....................3,096,721
Number of Places over 10,000 Population..256

Colorado

Nickname.............The Centennial State
Motto.....................*Nil Sine Numine*
                (Nothing Without Providence)
Flower..........Rocky Mountain Columbine
Bird......................Lark Bunting
Tree.................Colorado Blue Spruce
Song...........*Where the Columbines Grow*
Stone......................Aquamarine
Animal......Rocky Mountain Bighorn Sheep
Entered the Union...........August 1, 1876
Capital.........................Denver

ELECTED EXECUTIVE BRANCH OFFICIALS

Governor......................Roy Romer
Lieutenant Governor........Michael Callihan
Secretary of State.............Natalie Meyer
Attorney General............Duane Woodard
Treasurer................Gail S. Schoettler

SUPREME COURT

Joseph R. Quinn, Chief Justice
William H. Erickson
Howard M. Kirshbaum
George E. Lohr
Mary J. Mullakey
Luis D. Rovira
Anthony Vollack

GENERAL ASSEMBLY

President of the Senate.....Ted L. Strickland
President Pro Tem
    of the Senate...........Harold McCormick
Secretary of the Senate.........Joan M. Albi

Speaker of the House.....Carl "Bev" Bledsoe
Chief Clerk of the House......Lee C. Bahrych

STATISTICS

Land Area (square miles)...........103,766
    Rank in Nation......................8th
Population...................3,267,000
    Rank in Nation......................26th
    Density per square mile...............31.1
Number of Representatives in Congress.....6
Capital City...................Denver
    Population.......................504,588
    Rank in State.......................1st
Largest City......................Denver
Number of Places over 10,000 Population...25

Connecticut

Nickname .... The Constitution State
Motto .... *Qui Transtulit Sustinet*
    (He Who Transplanted Still Sustains)
Animal .... Sperm Whale
Flower .... Mountain Laurel
Bird .... American Robin
Tree .... White Oak
Song .... *Yankee Doodle*
Mineral .... Garnet
Insect .... Praying Mantis
State Ship .... U.S.S. Nautilus
Entered the Union .... January 9, 1788
Capital .... Hartford

ELECTED EXECUTIVE BRANCH OFFICIALS

Governor .... William A. O'Neill
Lieutenant Governor .... Joseph J. Fauliso
Secretary of State .... Julia H. Tashjian
Attorney General .... Joseph Lieberman
Treasurer .... Francisco Borges
Comptroller .... J. Edward Caldwell

SUPREME COURT

Ellen Ash Peters, Chief Justice
Robert J. Callahan
Joseph F. Dannehy
Arthur H. Healey
Angelo G. Santaniello
David M. Shea

GENERAL ASSEMBLY

President
    of the Senate ..... Lt. Gov. Joseph J. Fauliso
President Pro Tem
    of the Senate .... John B. Larson
Clerk of the Senate .... Thomas Sheridan

Speaker of the House .... Irving J. Stolberg
Deputy Speaker
    of the House .... William J. Cibes Jr.
Clerk of the House .... Penn J. Ritter

STATISTICS

Land Area (square miles) 4,862
    Rank in Nation 48th
Population 3,189,000
    Rank in Nation 28th
    Density per square mile 652.8
Number of Representatives in Congress 6
Capital City .... Hartford
    Population 136,000
    Rank in State 2nd
Largest City .... Bridgeport
    Population 142,000
Number of Places over 10,000 Population ... 22

Delaware

Nickname .... The First State
Motto .... *Liberty and Independence*
Flower .... Peach Blossom
Bird .... Blue Hen Chicken
Insect .... Ladybug
Tree .... American Holly
Song .... *Our Delaware*
Mineral .... Stillimanite
Fish .... Weakfish
Entered the Union .... December 7, 1787
Capital .... Dover

ELECTED EXECUTIVE BRANCH OFFICIALS

Governor .... Michael N. Castle
Lieutenant Governor .... S.B. Woo
Attorney General .... Charles M. Oberly III
Treasurer .... Janet C. Rzewnicki
Auditor .... Dennis E. Greenhouse
Insurance Commr. .... David Levinson

SUPREME COURT

Andrew D. Christie, Chief Justice
Randy Holland
Henry R. Horsey
Andrew G.T. Moore II
Joseph Walsh

GENERAL ASSEMBLY

President of the Senate ..... Lt. Gov. S.B. Woo
President Pro Tem
    of the Senate .... Richard S. Cordrey
Secretary of the Senate ... Betty Jean Caniford

Speaker of the House .... Terry Spense
Chief Clerk of the House ...... JoAnn Hedrick

STATISTICS

Land Area (square miles) 1,982
    Rank in Nation 49th
Population 633,000
    Rank in Nation 47th
    Density per square mile 313.8
Number of Representatives in Congress 1
Capital City .... Dover
    Population 23,512
    Rank in State 3rd
Largest City .... Wilmington
    Population 70,195
Number of Places over 10,000 Population 3

Florida

Nickname	The Sunshine State
Motto	*In God We Trust*
Flower	Orange Blossom
Bird	Mockingbird
Tree	Sabal Palmetto Palm
Song	*Old Folks at Home*
Stone	Agatized Coral
Gem	Moonstone
Saltwater Mammal	Dolphin
Marine Mammal	Porpoise
Saltwater Fish	Atlantic Sailfish
Freshwater Fish	Florida Large Mouth Bass
Shell	Horse Conch
Animal	Florida Panther
Beverage	Orange Juice
Entered the Union	March 3, 1845
Capital	Tallahassee

ELECTED EXECUTIVE BRANCH OFFICIALS

Governor	Bob Martinez
Lieutenant Governor	Bobby Brantley
Secretary of State	Jim Smith
Attorney General	Robert A. Butterworth
Treasurer/Insurance Commr.	Bill Gunter
Comptroller	Gerald A. Lewis
Commr. of Education	Betty Castor
Commr. of Agriculture	Doyle Conner

SUPREME COURT

Parker Lee McDonald, Chief Justice
Rosemary Barkett
Raymond Ehrlich
Stephen Grimes
Gerald Kogan
Ben F. Overton
Leander J. Shaw Jr.

LEGISLATURE

President of the Senate	John W. Vogt
President Pro Tem of the Senate	John A. Hill
Secretary of the Senate	Joe Brown
Speaker of the House	Jon L. Mills
Speaker Pro Tem of the House	James C. Burke
Clerk of the House	John B. Phelps

STATISTICS

Land Area (square miles)	54,136
Rank in Nation	22nd
Population	11,675,000
Rank in Nation	5th
Density per square mile	210
Number of Representatives in Congress	19
Capital City	Tallahassee
Population	112,000
Rank in State	11th
Largest City	Jacksonville
Population	577,971
Number of Places over 10,000 Population	96

Georgia

Nickname	The Empire State of the South*
Motto	*Wisdom, Justice and Moderation*
Flower	Cherokee Rose
Bird	Brown Thrasher
Tree	Live Oak
Song	*Georgia on My Mind*
Fish	Largemouth Bass
Entered the Union	January 2, 1788
Capital	Atlanta

*Unofficial

ELECTED EXECUTIVE BRANCH OFFICIALS

Governor	Joe Frank Harris
Lieutenant Governor	Zell Miller
Secretary of State	Max Cleland
Attorney General	Michael J. Bowers
Comptroller General	Warren Evans
Superintendent of Schools	Werner Rogers
Commr. of Agriculture	Thomas T. Irvin
Commr. of Labor	Joe Tanner

SUPREME COURT

Thomas O. Marshall, Chief Justice
Richard Bell
Harold G. Clarke
Hardy Gregory Jr.
Willis B. Hunt
George T. Smith
Charles L. Weltner

GENERAL ASSEMBLY

President of the Senate	Lt. Gov. Zell B. Miller
President Pro Tem of the Senate	Joseph F. Kennedy
Secretary of the Senate	Hamilton McWhorter Jr.
Speaker of the House	Thomas B. Murphy
Speaker Pro Tem of the House	Jack Connell
Clerk of the House	Glenn W. Ellard

STATISTICS

Land Area (square miles)	58,073
Rank in Nation	21st
Population	5,975,000
Rank in Nation	11th
Density per square mile	102.9
Number of Representatives in Congress	10
Capital City	Atlanta
Population	426,090
Rank in State	1st
Largest City	Atlanta
Number of Places over 10,000 Population	39

Hawaii

Nickname . . . . The Aloha State
Motto . . . *Ua Mau Ke Ea O Ka Aina I Ka Pono*
(The Life of the Land Is Perpetuated
in Righteousness)
Flower . . . . Hibiscus
Bird . . . . Hawaiian Goose
Tree . . . . Candlenut
Fish . . . . Humuhumunukunukuapuaa
Song . . . . *Hawaii Ponoi*
Entered the Union . . . . August 21, 1959
Capital . . . . Honolulu

ELECTED EXECUTIVE BRANCH OFFICIALS

Governor . . . . John D. Waihee III
Lieutenant Governor . . . Benjamin J. Cayetano

SUPREME COURT

Herman T.F. Lum, Chief Justice
Yoshimi Hayashi
Edward Nakamura
Frank Padgett
James H. Wakatsuki

LEGISLATURE

President of the Senate . . . . Richard S.H. Wong
Vice President
of the Senate . . . . Patsy K. Young
Clerk of the Senate . . . . T. David Woo Jr.

Speaker of the House . . . . Daniel J. Kihano
Vice Speaker of the House . . . . Emilio S. Alcon
Clerk of the House . . . . Gerald I. Miyoshi

STATISTICS

Land Area (square miles) 6,425
  Rank in Nation 47th
Population 1,062,000
  Rank in Nation 39th
  Density per square mile 164
Number of Representatives in Congress 2
Capital City . . . . Honolulu
  Population (county & city) 805,266
  Rank in State 1st
Largest City . . . . Honolulu
Number of Places over 10,000 Population . . . 12

Idaho

Nickname . . . . The Gem State
Motto . . . . . *Esto Perpetua* (Let It Be Perpetual)
Flower . . . . Syringa
Bird . . . . Mountain Bluebird
Tree . . . . Western White Pine
Song . . . . *Here We Have Idaho*
Gemstone . . . . Idaho Star Garnet
Horse . . . . Appaloosa
Entered the Union . . . . July 3, 1890
Capital . . . . Boise

ELECTED EXECUTIVE BRANCH OFFICIALS

Governor . . . . Cecil Andrus
Lieutenant Governor . . . . C. L. Otter
Secretary of State . . . . Pete T. Cenarrusa
Attorney General . . . . Jim Jones
Treasurer . . . . Lydia J. Edwards
Auditor . . . . Joe R. Williams
Supt. of Public Instruction . . . . . Jerry L. Evans

SUPREME COURT

Allan G. Shepard, Chief Justice
Robert E. Bakes
Stephen Bistline
Robert C. Huntley Jr.
Byron Johnson

LEGISLATURE

President
of the Senate . . . . Lt. Gov. C. L. Otter
President Pro Tem
of the Senate . . . . James Risch
Secretary of the Senate . . . . Dorthea Baxter

Speaker of the House . . . . Tom Boyd
Chief Clerk of the House . . . . . . Phyllis Watson

STATISTICS

Land Area (square miles) 82,677
  Rank in Nation 13th
Population 1,003,000
  Rank in Nation 41st
  Density per square mile 12.2
Number of Representatives in Congress 2
Capital City . . . . Boise
  Population 107,000
  Rank in State 1st
Largest City . . . . Boise
Number of Places over 10,000 Population . . . 11

Illinois

Nickname.................The Prairie State
Motto....... *State Sovereignty-National Union*
Flower.....................Native Violet
Bird..........................Cardinal
Tree.........................White Oak
Song........................*Illinois*
Mineral.......................Fluorite
Animal..................White-tailed Deer
Insect...............Monarch Butterfly
Entered the Union.........December 3, 1818
Capital.......................Springfield

ELECTED EXECUTIVE BRANCH OFFICIALS

Governor...............James R. Thompson
Lieutenant Governor........George H. Ryan
Secretary of State.............James Edgar
Attorney General...........Neil F. Hartigan
Treasurer.................Jerry Cosentino
Comptroller..............Roland W. Burris

SUPREME COURT

William G. Clark, Chief Justice
Joseph H. Goldenhersh
Ben Miller
Thomas J. Moran
Howard C. Ryan
Seymour Simon
Daniel P. Ward

GENERAL ASSEMBLY

President of the Senate........Philip J. Rock
Secretary of the Senate.......Linda Hawker

Speaker of the House.....Michael J. Madigan
Chief Clerk of the House.....John F. O'Brien

STATISTICS

Land Area (square miles).............55,748
   Rank in Nation....................24th
Population....................11,553,000
   Rank in Nation.....................6th
   Density per square mile..............206.9
Number of Representatives in Congress....22
Capital City...................Springfield
   Population......................102,000
   Rank in State......................4th
Largest City....................Chicago
   Population....................2,992,472
Number of Places over 10,000 Population..177

Indiana

Nickname................The Hoosier State
Motto...............*Crossroads of America*
Flower.............................Peony
Bird..........................Cardinal
Tree......................Tulip Poplar
Song .. *On the Banks of the Wabash, Far Away*
Stone.......................Limestone
Entered the Union........December 11, 1816
Capital.....................Indianapolis

ELECTED EXECUTIVE BRANCH OFFICIALS

Governor....................Robert D. Orr
Lieutenant Governor..........John M. Mutz
Secretary of State...............Evan Bayh
Attorney General..........Linley E. Pearson
Treasurer...........Marjorie H. O'Laughlin
Auditor....................Ann G. DeVore
Supt. of Public Instruction.....H. Dean Evans

SUPREME COURT

Randall Shepard, Chief Justice
Roger O. DeBruler
Brent E. Dickson
Richard M. Givan
Alfred J. Pivarnik

GENERAL ASSEMBLY

President
  of the Senate........Lt. Gov. John M. Mutz
President Pro Tem
  of the Senate..............Robert Garton
Secretary of the Senate.......Carolyn Tinkle

Speaker of the House.....Paul S. Mannweiler
Speaker Pro Tem
  of the House.............Jeffrey K. Espich
Principal Clerk
  of the House......Sharon Cummins Thuma

STATISTICS

Land Area (square miles).............36,097
   Rank in Nation....................38th
Population.....................5,504,000
   Rank in Nation....................14th
   Density per square mile..............152.3
Number of Representatives in Congress....10
Capital City.................Indianapolis
   Population......................710,280
   Rank in State......................1st
Largest City.................Indianapolis
Number of Places over 10,000 Population...61

Iowa

Nickname .... The Hawkeye State
Motto .... *Our Liberties We Prize and*
Our Rights We Will Maintain
Flower .... Wild Rose
Bird .... Eastern Goldfinch
Tree .... Oak
Song .... *The Song of Iowa*
Stone .... Geode
Entered the Union .... December 28, 1846
Capital .... Des Moines

ELECTED EXECUTIVE BRANCH OFFICIALS

Governor .... Terry E. Branstad
Lieutenant Governor ..... Jo Ann Zimmerman
Secretary of State .... Elaine Baxter
Attorney General .... Thomas J. Miller
Treasurer .... Michael L. Fitzgerald
Auditor .... Richard D. Johnson
Secy. of Agriculture .... Dale Cochran

SUPREME COURT

W. Ward Reynoldson, Chief Justice
James H. Carter
K. David Harris
Jerry L. Larson
Louis A. Lavorato
A. A. McGiverin
Linda Newman
Louis W. Schultz
Charles R. Wolle

GENERAL ASSEMBLY

President
of the Senate ... Lt. Gov. Jo Ann Zimmerman
President Pro Tem
of the Senate .... George R. Kinley
Secretary of the Senate .... John F. Dwyer

Speaker of the House .... Don Avenson
Speaker Pro Tem of the House .. John Connors
Chief Clerk of the House ...... Joseph O'Hern

STATISTICS

Land Area (square miles) 55,941
Rank in Nation 25th
Population 2,851,000
Rank in Nation 29th
Density per square mile 51.6
Number of Representatives in Congress 6
Capital City .... Des Moines
Population 190,832
Rank in State 1st
Largest City .... Des Moines
Number of Places over 10,000 Population ... 29

Kansas

Nickname .... The Sunflower State
Motto .... *Ad Astra per Aspera*
(To the Stars through Difficulties)
Flower .... Native Sunflower
Bird .... Western Meadowlark
Tree .... Cottonwood
Song .... *Home on the Range*
Animal .... American Buffalo
Insect .... Honeybee
Entered the Union .... January 29, 1861
Capital .... Topeka

ELECTED EXECUTIVE BRANCH OFFICIALS

Governor .... Mike Hayden
Lieutenant Governor .... Jack D. Walker
Secretary of State .... Bill Graves
Attorney General .... Robert T. Stephan
Treasurer .... Joan Finney
Commr. of Insurance .... Fletcher Bell

SUPREME COURT

David Prager, Chief Justice
Donald L. Allegrucci
Harold S. Herd
Richard W. Holmes
Tyler C. Lockett
Kay McFarland
Robert H. Miller

LEGISLATURE

President
of the Senate .... Robert V. Talkington
Vice President
of the Senate .... Joseph C. Harder
Secretary of the Senate .... Lu Kenney

Speaker of the House .... James D. Braden
Speaker Pro Tem
of the House .... David Heinemenn
Chief Clerk of the House ...... Geneva Seward

STATISTICS

Land Area (square miles) 81,787
Rank in Nation 14th
Population 2,461,000
Rank in Nation 32nd
Density per square mile 30.0
Number of Representatives in Congress 5
Capital City .... Topeka
Population 119,000
Rank in State 3rd
Largest City .... Wichita
Population 283,496
Number of Places over 10,000 Population ... 34

Kentucky

Nickname .... The Bluegrass State
Motto ...... *United We Stand, Divided We Fall*
Flower .... Goldenrod
Bird .... Cardinal
Wild Animal .... Gray Squirrel
Tree .... Kentucky Coffee Tree
Song .... *My Old Kentucky Home*
Entered the Union .... June 1, 1792
Capital .... Frankfort

ELECTED EXECUTIVE BRANCH OFFICIALS

Governor .... Wallace Wilkinson
Lieutenant Governor .... Brereton C. Jones
Secretary of State .... Bremer Ehrler
Attorney General .... Fredric J. Cowan
Treasurer .... Robert Mead, CPA
Auditor of Public Accounts ...... Bob Babbage
Supt. of Public Instruction .... John Brock
Commr. of Agriculture .... Ward Burnette

SUPREME COURT

Robert F. Stephens, Chief Justice
William Gant
Joseph E. Lambert
Charles Leibson
James B. Stephenson
Roy Vance
Donald Wintersheimer

GENERAL ASSEMBLY

President
  of the Senate .... Lt. Gov. Brereton Jones
President Pro Tem
  of the Senate .... John A. Rose
Chief Clerk of the Senate ... Marjorie Wagoner

Speaker of the House ..... Donald J. Blandford
Speaker Pro Tem
  of the House .... Pete Worthington
Chief Clerk of the House ..... Evelyn Marston

STATISTICS

Land Area (square miles) 39,650
  Rank in Nation 37th
Population 3,728,000
  Rank in Nation 23rd
  Density per square mile............... 94.0
Number of Representatives in Congress 7
Capital City .... Frankfort
  Population 26,025
  Rank in State 9th
Largest City .... Louisville
  Population 289,843
Number of Places over 10,000 Population ... 30

Louisiana

Nickname .... The Pelican State
Motto .... *Union, Justice and Confidence*
Flower .... Magnolia
Bird .... Eastern Brown Pelican
Tree .... Bald Cypress
Song .... *Give Me Louisiana*
Fossil .... Petrified Palmwood
Gemstone .... Agate
Dog .... Catahoula Leopard
Reptile .... Alligator
Crustacean .... Crawfish
Insect .... Honeybee
Beverage .... Milk
Entered the Union .... April 30, 1812
Capital .... Baton Rouge

ELECTED EXECUTIVE BRANCH OFFICIALS

Governor .... Charles E. "Buddy" Roemer
Lieutenant Governor .... Paul Hardy
Secretary of State .... Walter McKeithen
Attorney General .... William J. Guste Jr.
Treasurer .... Mary L. Landriew
Supt. of Education .... Thomas G. Clausen
Commr. of Agriculture .... Bob Odom
Commr. of Insurance .... Douglas Green
Commr. of Elections .... Jerry M. Fowler

SUPREME COURT

John A. Dixon Jr., Chief Justice
Pascal F. Calogero Jr.
Luther F. Cole
James L. Dennis
Harry T. Lemmon
Walter F. Marcus Jr.
Jack Crozier Watson

LEGISLATURE

President of the Senate .... Allen Bares
President Pro Tem
  of the Senate .... Samuel Nenez
Secretary of the Senate .... Michael S. Baer III

Speaker of the House .... Jimmy Dimos
Speaker Pro Tem
  of the House .... Huntington B. Downer
Clerk of the House .... Alfred Speer

STATISTICS

Land Area (square miles) 44,930
  Rank in Nation 31st
Population 4,501,000
  Rank in Nation 18th
  Density per square mile............... 99.7
Number of Representatives in Congress 8
Capital City .... Baton Rouge
  Population 368,571
  Rank in State 2nd
Largest City .... New Orleans
  Population 559,101
Number of Places over 10,000 Population ... 34

Maine

Nickname . . . . The Pine Tree State
Motto . . . . *Dirigo* (I Direct)
Flower . . . . White Pine Cone and Tassel
Bird . . . . Chickadee
Tree . . . . Eastern White Pine
Song . . . . *State of Maine Song*
Mineral . . . . Tourmaline
Fish . . . . Landlocked Salmon
Insect . . . . Honeybee
Animal . . . . Moose
Entered the Union . . . . March 15, 1820
Capital . . . . Augusta

ELECTED EXECUTIVE BRANCH OFFICIALS
Governor . . . . John R. McKernan Jr.

SUPREME JUDICIAL COURT
Vincent L. McKusick, Chief Justice
Robert W. Clifford
Caroline D. Glassman
David A. Nichols
David G. Roberts
Louis Scolnik
Daniel E. Wathen

LEGISLATURE
President of the Senate . . . . Charles P. Pray
Secretary of the Senate . . . . Joy J. O'Brien

Speaker of the House . . . . John L. Martin
Clerk of the House . . . . Edwin H. Pert

STATISTICS
Land Area (square miles) 30,920
   Rank in Nation 39th
Population 1,174,000
   Rank in Nation 38th
   Density per square mile 37.6
Number of Representatives in Congress 2
Capital City . . . . Augusta
   Population 21,819
   Rank in State 6th
Largest City . . . . Portland
   Population 61,572
Number of Places over 10,000 Population . . . 12

Maryland

Nicknames . . . . The Old Line State and
Free State
Motto . . . . *Fatti Maschii, Parole Femine*
(Manly Deeds, Womanly Words)
Flower . . . . Black-eyed Susan
Bird . . . . Baltimore Oriole
Tree . . . . White Oak
Song . . . . *Maryland, My Maryland*
Dog . . . . Chesapeake Bay Retriever
Fish . . . . Striped Bass
Insect . . . . Baltimore Checkerspot Butterfly
Fossil . . . Ecphora Quadricostata (Extinct Snail)
Sport . . . . Jousting
Entered the Union . . . . April 28, 1788
Capital . . . . Annapolis

ELECTED EXECUTIVE BRANCH OFFICIALS
Governor . . . . William Donald Schaefer
Lieutenant Governor . . . . Melvin Steinberg
Attorney General . . . . J. Joseph Curran, Jr.
Comptroller of Treasury . . . . Louis L. Goldstein

COURT OF APPEALS
Robert C. Murphy, Chief Judge
William H. Adkins II
Harry A. Cole
James F. Couch Jr.
John C. Eldridge
John F. McAuliffe
Lawrence R. Rodowsky

GENERAL ASSEMBLY
President
   of the Senate . . . . Thomas V. Mike Miller Jr.
President Pro Tem
   of the Senate . . . . Frederick C. Malkus Jr.
Secretary of the Senate . . . . Oden Bowie

Speaker of the House . . R. Clayton Mitchell Jr.
Speaker Pro Tem
   of the House . . . . Donald B. Robertson
Chief Clerk of the House . . Jacqueline M. Spell

STATISTICS
Land Area (square miles) 9,891
   Rank in Nation 42nd
Population 4,463,000
   Rank in Nation 19th
   (tied with Washington)
   Density per square mile 444.0
Number of Representatives in Congress 8
Capital City . . . . Annapolis
   Population 31,910
   Rank in State 5th
Largest City . . . . Baltimore
   Population 763,570
Number of Places over 10,000 Population . . . 17

Massachusetts

Nickname . . . . The Bay State
Motto . . . . *Ense Petit Placidam Sub*
Libertate Quietem
(By the Sword We Seek Peace,
but Peace Only under Liberty)
Flower . . . . Mayflower
Bird . . . . Chickadee
Tree . . . . American Elm
Song . . . . *All Hail to Massachusetts*
Fish . . . . Cod
Insect . . . . Ladybug
Horse . . . . Morgan
Dog . . . . Boston Terrier
Beverage . . . . Cranberry Juice
Mineral . . . . Babingtonite
Entered the Union . . . . February 6, 1788
Capital City . . . . Boston

ELECTED EXECUTIVE BRANCH OFFICIALS

Governor . . . . Michael S. Dukakis
Lieutenant Governor . . . . Evelyn F. Murphy
Secretary of the
Commonwealth . . . . Michael J. Connolly
Attorney General . . . . James Shannon
Treasurer . . . . Robert Q. Crane
Auditor of the
Commonwealth . . . . A. Joseph DeNucci

SUPREME JUDICIAL COURT

Edward F. Hennessey, Chief Justice
Ruth I. Abrams
Paul J. Liacos
Neil L. Lynch
Joseph R. Nolan
Francis P. O'Connor
Herbert P. Wilkins

GENERAL COURT

President of the Senate . . . . William M. Bulger
Clerk of the Senate . . . . Edward B. O'Neill

Speaker of the House . . . . George Keverian
Clerk of the House . . . . Robert MacQueen

STATISTICS

Land Area (square miles) 7,826
Rank in Nation 45th
Population 5,832,000
Rank in Nation 12th
Density per square mile 743.9
Number of Representatives in Congress 11
Capital City . . . . Boston
Population 570,719
Rank in State 1st
Largest City . . . . Boston
Number of Places over 10,000 Population . . 149

Michigan

Nicknames . . . . The Wolverine State and
Great Lake State
Motto . . . . *Si Quaeris Peninsulam Amoenam*
Circumspice (If You Seek a Pleasant
Peninsula, Look About You)
Flower . . . . Apple Blossom
Bird . . . . Robin
Tree . . . . White Pine
Insect . . . . Dragonfly
Song . . . . *Michigan, My Michigan*
Stone . . . . Petoskey Stone
Gem . . . . Chlorastrolite
Fish . . . . Trout
Entered the Union . . . . January 26, 1837
Capital . . . . Lansing

ELECTED EXECUTIVE BRANCH OFFICIALS

Governor . . . . James Blanchard
Lieutenant Governor . . . . Martha Griffiths
Secretary of State . . . . Richard H. Austin
Attorney General . . . . Frank J. Kelley

SUPREME COURT

Dorothy Comstock Riley, Chief Justice
Dennis Wayne Archer
Patricia J. Boyle
James H. Brickley
Michael F. Cavanagh
Robert Griffin
Charles L. Levin

LEGISLATURE

President
of the Senate . . . . . . Lt. Gov. Martha Griffiths
President Pro Tem
of the Senate . . . . Nick Smith
Secretary of the Senate . . . . Willis H. Snow

Speaker of the House . . . . Gary M. Owen
Speaker Pro Tem
of the House . . . . Teola P. Hunter
Clerk of the House . . . . David H. Evans

STATISTICS

Land Area (square miles) 56,817
Rank in Nation 23rd
Population 9,145,000
Rank in Nation 8th
Density per square mile 160.0
Number of Representatives in Congress 18
Capital City . . . . Lansing
Population 128,000
Rank in State 5th
Largest City . . . . Detroit
Population 1,088,973
Number of Places over 10,000 Population . . . 88

Minnesota

Nickname . . . . The North Star State
Motto . . . . *L'Etoile du Nord*
(The Star of the North)
Flower . . . . Pink and White Lady's-Slipper
Bird . . . . Common Loon
Tree . . . . Red Pine
Song . . . . *Hail! Minnesota*
Gemstone . . . . Lake Superior Agate
Fish . . . . Walleye
Grain . . . . Wild Rice
Mushroom . . . . Morel
Beverage . . . . Milk
Entered the Union . . . . May 11, 1858
Capital . . . . St. Paul

ELECTED EXECUTIVE BRANCH OFFICIALS

Governor . . . . Rudy Perpich
Lieutenant Governor . . . . Marlene Johnson
Secretary of State . . . . . . Joan Anderson Growe
Attorney General . . . . Hubert H. Humphrey III
Treasurer . . . . M. A. McGrath
Auditor . . . . Arne Carlson

SUPREME COURT

Douglas K. Amdahl, Chief Justice
M. Jeanne Coyne
Glenn E. Kelley
Peter Popovich
John E. Simonett
Rosalie E. Wahl
Lawrence R. Yetka

LEGISLATURE

President of the Senate . . . . Jerome M. Hughes
Secretary of the Senate . . . Patrick E. Flahaven

Speaker of the House . . . . Robert Vanasek
Chief Clerk of the House . . Edward A. Burdick

STATISTICS

Land Area (square miles) 79,289
  Rank in Nation 12th
Population 4,214,000
  Rank in Nation 21st
  Density per square mile 52.9
Number of Representatives in Congress 8
Capital City . . . . St. Paul
  Population 265,903
  Rank in State 2nd
Largest City . . . . Minneapolis
  Population 358,335
Number of Places over 10,000 Population . . . 65

Mississippi

Nickname . . . . The Magnolia State
Motto . . . *Virtute et Armis* (By Valor and Arms)
Flower . . . . Magnolia
Bird . . . . Mockingbird
Water Mammal . . . . Bottlenosed Dolphin
Tree . . . . Magnolia
Song . . . . *Go, Mississippi*
Insect . . . . Honeybee
Fossil . . . . Prehistoric Whale
Beverage . . . . Milk
Entered the Union . . . . December 10, 1817
Capital . . . . Jackson

ELECTED EXECUTIVE BRANCH OFFICIALS

Governor . . . . Ray Mabus
Lieutenant Governor . . . . Brad Dye
Secretary of State . . . . Dick Molpus
Attorney General . . . . Mike Moore
Treasurer . . . . Marshall Bennett
Auditor of Public Accounts . . . . . Pete Johnson
Commr. of Agriculture
  and Commerce . . . . Jim Buck Ross
Commr. of Insurance . . . . George Dale

SUPREME COURT

Roy Noble Lee, Chief Justice
Reuben V. Anderson
Armis E. Hawkins
Ruble Griffin
Dan M. Lee
Lenore L. Prather
James Robertson
Michael Sullivan
Joseph S. Zuccaro

LEGISLATURE

President of the Senate . . . . . Lt. Gov. Brad Dye
President Pro Tem
  of the Senate . . . . Glen DeWeese
Secretary of the Senate . . . . . Charles H. Griffin

Speaker of the House . . . . Tim Ford
Clerk of the House . . . . . Charles J. Jackson Jr.

STATISTICS

Land Area (square miles) 47,296
  Rank in Nation 32nd
Population 2,625,000
  Rank in Nation 31st
  Density per square mile 55.2
Number of Representatives in Congress 5
Capital City . . . . Jackson
  Population 208,810
  Rank in State 1st
Largest City . . . . Jackson
Number of Places over 10,000 Population . . . 27

Missouri

Nickname . . . . The Show Me State
Motto . . . . *Salus Populi Suprema Lex Esto*
(The Welfare of the People Shall Be
the Supreme Law)
Flower . . . . Hawthorn
Bird . . . . Bluebird
Insect . . . . Honeybee
Tree . . . . Dogwood
Song . . . . *Missouri Waltz*
Stone . . . . Mozarkite
Mineral . . . . Galena
Entered the Union . . . . August 10, 1821
Capital . . . . Jefferson City

ELECTED EXECUTIVE BRANCH OFFICIALS

Governor . . . . John Ashcroft
Lieutenant Governor . . . . Harriett Woods
Secretary of State . . . . Roy Blunt
Attorney General . . . . William L. Webster
Treasurer . . . . Wendell Bailey
Auditor . . . . Margaret Kelly

SUPREME COURT

Andrew J. Higgins, Chief Justice
William H. Billings
Charles Blackmer
Robert T. Donnelly
Albert Rendlen
Edward Robertson Jr.
Warren D. Welliver

GENERAL ASSEMBLY

President
of the Senate . . . . Lt. Gov. Harriett Woods
President Pro Tem
of the Senate . . . . John E. Scott
Secretary of the Senate . . . . Terry Spieler

Speaker of the House . . . . Robert F. Griffin
Speaker Pro Tem
of the House . . . . Patrick J. Hickey
Chief Clerk of the House . . Douglas W. Burnett

STATISTICS

Land Area (square miles) 68,995
Rank in Nation 19th
Population 5,066,000
Rank in Nation 15th
Density per square mile 72.9
Number of Representatives in Congress 9
Capital City . . . . Jefferson City
Population 34,575
Rank in State 12th
Largest City . . . . St. Louis
Population 429,296
Number of Places over 10,000 Population . . . 51

Montana

Nickname . . . . The Treasure State
Motto . . . . *Oro y Plata* (Gold and Silver)
Flower . . . . Bitterroot
Animal . . . . Grizzly Bear
Bird . . . . Western Meadowlark
Tree . . . . Ponderosa Pine
Song . . . . *Montana*
State Ballad . . . . *Montana Melody*
Stones . . . . Sapphire and Agate
Fish . . . . Blackspotted Cutthroat Trout
Grass . . . . Bluebunch Wheatgrass
Entered the Union . . . . November 8, 1889
Capital . . . . Helena

ELECTED EXECUTIVE BRANCH OFFICIALS

Governor . . . . Ted Schwinden
Lieutenant Governor . . . . George Turman
Secretary of State . . . . (Vacant)
Attorney General . . . . Mike Greely
Auditor . . . . Andrea Bennett
Supt. of Public Instruction . . . . Ed Argenbright

SUPREME COURT

Jean Turnage, Chief Justice
L.C. Gulbrandson
John C. Harrison
William Hunt
R. C. McDonough
Frank B. Morrison
John C. Sheehy
Fred Weber

LEGISLATURE

President of the Senate . . . . Bill Norman
President Pro Tem
of the Senate . . . . George McCallum
Secretary of the Senate . . . . Bonnie Wallem

Speaker of the House . . . . Robert L. Marks
Chief Clerk of the House . . . . . . Bobbie Spilker

STATISTICS

Land Area (square miles) 145,587
Rank in Nation 4th
Population 819,000
Rank in Nation 44th
Density per square mile 5.67
Number of Representatives in Congress 2
Capital City . . . . Helena
Population 24,289
Rank in State 5th
Largest City . . . . Billings
Population 68,787
Number of Places over 10,000 Population 9

Nebraska

Nickname............The Cornhusker State
Motto...............*Equality Before the Law*
Flower........................Goldenrod
Bird.................Western Meadowlark
Mammal...............White-tailed Deer
Tree...................Western Cottonwood
Song.....................*Beautiful Nebraska*
Gemstone....................Blue Agate
Fossil.........................Mammoth
Grass...................Little Blue Stem
Insect........................Honeybee
Rock.......................Prairie Agate
Soil............Soils of the Holdrege Series
Entered the Union............March 1, 1867
Capital..........................Lincoln

ELECTED EXECUTIVE BRANCH OFFICIALS

Governor........................Kay Orr
Lieutenant Governor.......William E. Nichol
Secretary of State........Allen J. Beermann
Attorney General..............Robert Spire
Treasurer...................Frank Marsh
Auditor of Public Accounts..Ray A.C. Johnson

SUPREME COURT

William Hastings, Chief Justice
Leslie Boslaugh
D. Nick Caporale
Dale Fahrenbruch
John T. Grant
Thomas M. Shanahan
C. Thomas White

UNICAMERAL LEGISLATURE

President of the
    Legislature......Lt. Gov. William E. Nichol
Speaker of the Legislature.William E. Barrett
Chairman of Executive Board,
    Legislative Council........Bernice Labedz
Vice Chairman of Executive Board,
    Legislative Council.......Richard Peterson
Clerk of the Legislature..Patrick J. O'Donnell

STATISTICS

Land Area (square miles)............76,483
    Rank in Nation....................15th
Population....................1,598,000
    Rank in Nation....................36th
    Density per square mile...............21.0
Number of Representatives in Congress.....3
Capital City......................Lincoln
    Population....................180,378
    Rank in State....................2nd
Largest City......................Omaha
    Population....................332,237
Number of Places over 10,000 Population...12

Nevada

Nickname.................The Silver State
Motto...................*All for Our Country*
Flower........................Sagebrush
Bird..................Mountain Bluebird
Tree...................Single-leaf Pinon
Song.................*Home Means Nevada*
Animal..............Desert Bighorn Sheep
Metal...........................Silver
Grass...................Indian Rice Grass
Fossil.......................Ichthyosaur
Entered the Union..........October 31, 1864
Capital.......................Carson City

ELECTED EXECUTIVE BRANCH OFFICIALS

Governor.................Richard H. Bryan
Lieutenant Governor.........Robert J. Miller
Secretary of State......Frankie Sue Del Papa
Attorney General..............Brian McKay
Treasurer.....................Ken Santor
Controller.................Darrel R. Daines

SUPREME COURT

E. M. Gunderson, Chief Justice
John C. Mowbray
Charles E. Springer
Thomas L. Steffen
C. Clifton Young

LEGISLATURE

President
    of the Senate......Lt. Gov. Robert J. Miller
President Pro Tem
    of the Senate.........Lawrence E. Jacobsen
Secretary of the Senate.....Janice L. Thomas

Speaker of the Assembly...Joseph E. Dini, Jr.
Speaker Pro Tem
    of the Assembly.............Jim Schofield
Chief Clerk
    of the Assembly.......Mouryne B. Landing

STATISTICS

Land Area (square miles)............109,889
    Rank in Nation......................7th
Population......................963,000
    Rank in Nation....................43rd
    Density per square mile...............8.5
Number of Representatives in Congress.....2
Capital City.............Carson City
    Population....................34,597
    Rank in State......................5th
Largest City....................Las Vegas
    Population....................183,227
Number of Places over 10,000 Population....6

New Hampshire

Nickname . . . . The Granite State
Motto . . . . *Live Free or Die*
Flower . . . . Purple Lilac
Bird . . . . Purple Finch
Tree . . . . White Birch
Song . . . . *Old New Hampshire*
Insect . . . . Ladybug
Mineral . . . . Beryl
Rock . . . . Granite
Gem . . . . Smoky Quartz
Amphibian . . . . Spotted Newt
Entered the Union . . . . June 21, 1788
Capital . . . . Concord

ELECTED EXECUTIVE BRANCH OFFICIALS

Governor . . . . John H. Sununu

SUPREME COURT

David A. Brock, Chief Justice
William F. Batchelder
William R. Johnson
David H. Souter
W. Stephen Thayer II

GENERAL COURT

President of the Senate . William S. Bartlett Jr.
Vice President
  of the Senate . . . . Eleanor P. Podles
Clerk of the Senate . . . . Wilmont S. White

Speaker
  of the House . . . . . . W. Douglas Scamman Jr.
Clerk of the House . . . . Carl A. Peterson

STATISTICS

Land Area (square miles) 9,027
  Rank in Nation 44th
Population 1,027,000
  Rank in Nation 40th
  Density per square mile 110.6
Number of Representatives in Congress 2
Capital City . . . . Concord
  Population 30,706
  Rank in State 3rd
Largest City . . . . Manchester
  Population 92,104
Number of Places over 10,000 Population . . . 12

New Jersey

Nickname . . . . The Garden State
Motto . . . . *Liberty and Prosperity*
Flower . . . . Purple Violet
Bird . . . . Eastern Goldfinch
Tree . . . . Red Oak
Insect . . . . Honeybee
Animal . . . . Horse
Entered the Union . . . . December 18, 1787
Capital . . . . Trenton

ELECTED EXECUTIVE BRANCH OFFICIALS

Governor . . . . Thomas H. Kean

SUPREME COURT

Robert N. Wilentz, Chief Justice
Robert L. Clifford
Marie L. Garibaldi
Alan B. Handler
Daniel J. O'Hern
Stewart G. Pollock
Gary S. Stein

LEGISLATURE

President of the Senate . . . . John F. Russo
President Pro Tem
  of the Senate . . . . Carmen Orechio
Secretary of the Senate . . . . John McCarthy

Speaker of the Assembly . . . . . Chuck Hardwick
Speaker Pro Tem
  of the Assembly . . . . John A. Rocco
Clerk of the Assembly . . . . . Virginia E. Haines

STATISTICS

Land Area (square miles) 7,521
  Rank in Nation 46th
Population 7,620,000
  Rank in Nation 9th
  Density per square mile 1,005.5
Number of Representatives in Congress 14
Capital City . . . . Trenton
  Population 92,124
  Rank in State 5th
Largest City . . . . Newark
  Population 314,387
Number of Places over 10,000 Population . . 110

New Mexico

Nickname . . . . The Land of Enchantment
Motto . . . . . *Crescit Eundo* (It Grows As It Goes)
Flower . . . . Yucca
Bird . . . . Roadrunner
Tree . . . . Pinon
Songs . . . . *Asi es Nuevo Mexico* and
O, Fair New Mexico
Gem . . . . Turquoise
Fossil . . . . Ceolophysis
Animal . . . . Black Bear
Fish . . . . Cutthroat Trout
Vegetables . . . . Chile and Frijoles
Entered the Union . . . . January 6, 1912
Capital . . . . Santa Fe

ELECTED EXECUTIVE BRANCH OFFICIALS

Governor . . . . Garrey Carruthers
Lieutenant Governor . . . . Jack L. Stahl
Secretary of State . . . . . Rebecca D. Vigil-Giron
Attorney General . . . . Hal Stratton
Treasurer . . . . James B. Lewis
Auditor . . . . Harold H. Adams
Commissioner
of Public Lands . . . . . . William R. Humphries

SUPREME COURT

Tony Scarborough, Chief Justice
Richard E. Ransom
Dan Sosa Jr.
Harry E. Stowers Jr.
Mary Walters

LEGISLATURE

President
of the Senate . . . . Lt. Gov. Jack L. Stahl
President Pro Tem
of the Senate . . . . I. M. Smalley
Chief Clerk of the Senate . . . . Juanita M. Pino

Speaker of the House . . . . Raymond G. Sanchez
Chief Clerk of the House . . . . Steve Arias

STATISTICS

Land Area (square miles) 121,412
Rank in Nation 5th
Population 1,479,000
Rank in Nation 37th
Density per square mile 11.9
Number of Representatives in Congress 3
Capital City . . . . Santa Fe
Population 50,857
Rank in State 2nd
Largest City . . . . Albuquerque
Population 350,575
Number of Places over 10,000 Population . . . 13

New York

Nickname . . . . The Empire State
Motto . . . . *Excelsior* (Ever Upward)
Flower . . . . Rose
Bird . . . . Bluebird
Tree . . . . Sugar Maple
Song . . . . *I Love New York*
Fruit . . . . Apple
Gem . . . . Garnet
Animal . . . . Beaver
Fish . . . . Trout
Fossil . . . . Sea Scorpion
Beverage . . . . Milk
Entered the Union . . . . July 26, 1788
Capital . . . . Albany

ELECTED EXECUTIVE BRANCH OFFICIALS

Governor . . . . Mario M. Cuomo
Lieutenant Governor . . . . Stan Lundine
Attorney General . . . . Robert Abrams
Comptroller . . . . Edward V. Regan

COURT OF APPEALS

Sol Wachtler, Chief Judge
Fritz W. Alexander II
Joseph W. Bellacosa
Stewart F. Hancock Jr.
Judith S. Kaye
Bernard S. Meyer
Richard D. Simons
Vido J. Titone

LEGISLATURE

President of the Senate . . . . Stan Lundine
President Pro Tem
of the Senate . . . . Warren M. Anderson
Secretary of the Senate . . . . Stephen Sloan

Speaker of the Assembly . . . . Melvin H. Miller
Speaker Pro Tem
of the Assembly . . . . William F. Passannante
Clerk of the Assembly . . . . Francine Misasi

STATISTICS

Land Area (square miles) 47,831
Rank in Nation 30th
Population 17,772,000
Rank in Nation 2nd
Density per square mile 371.8
Number of Representatives in Congress 34
Capital City . . . . Albany
Population 101,727
Rank in State 6th
Largest City . . . . New York
Population 7,164,742
Number of Places over 10,000 Population . . . 86

North Carolina

Nicknames . . . . The Tar Heel State and
Old North State
Motto . . . . *Esse Quam Videri*
(To Be Rather Than to Seem)
Flower . . . . Dogwood
Bird . . . . Cardinal
Tree . . . . Pine
Song . . . . *The Old North State*
Mammal . . . . Gray Squirrel
Gem . . . . Emerald
Fish . . . . Channel Bass
Insect . . . . Honeybee
Reptile . . . . Eastern Box Turtle
Rock . . . . Granite
Entered the Union . . . . November 21, 1789
Capital . . . . Raleigh

ELECTED EXECUTIVE BRANCH OFFICIALS

Governor . . . . James G. Martin
Lieutenant Governor . . . . . Robert B. Jordan III
Secretary of State . . . . Thad Eure
Attorney General . . . . Lacy H. Thornburg
Treasurer . . . . Harlan E. Boyles
Auditor . . . . Edward Renfrow
Supt. of Public Instruction . . . A. Craig Phillips
Commr. of Agriculture . . . . . James A. Graham
Commr. of Labor . . . . John C. Brooks
Commr. of Insurance . . . . James E. Long

SUPREME COURT

James G. Exum, Chief Justice

Henry E. Frye	Burley B. Mitchell Jr.
Harry C. Martin	John Webb
Louis B. Moyer	Willis P. Whichard

GENERAL ASSEMBLY

President
of the Senate . . Lt. Gov. Robert B. Jordan III
President Pro Tem
of the Senate . . . . J.J. Harrington
Principal Clerk of the Senate . . . . . Sylvia Fink

Speaker of the House . . . . Liston B. Ramsey
Speaker Pro Tem
of the House . . . . John J. Hunt
Principal Clerk of the House . . . . Grace Collins

STATISTICS

Land Area (square miles) 48,798
Rank in Nation 28th
Population 6,331,000
Rank in Nation 10th
Density per square mile 128.2
Number of Representatives in Congress 11
Capital City . . . . Raleigh
Population 169,000
Rank in State 3rd
Largest City . . . . Charlotte
Population 331,000
Number of Places over 10,000 Population . . . 43

North Dakota

Nickname . . . . Peace Garden State
Motto . . . . *Liberty and Union, Now and*
Forever, One and Inseparable
Flower . . . . Wild Prairie Rose
Bird . . . . Western Meadowlark
Tree . . . . American Elm
Song . . . . *North Dakota Hymn*
March . . . . *Spirit of the Land*
Stone . . . . Teredo Petrified Wood
Fish . . . . Northern Pike
Grass . . . . Western Wheatgrass
Entered the Union . . . . November 2, 1889
Capital . . . . Bismarck

ELECTED EXECUTIVE BRANCH OFFICIALS

Governor . . . . George A. Sinner
Lieutenant Governor . . . . Ruth Meiers
Secretary of State . . . . Ben Meier
Attorney General . . . . Nicholas Spaeth
Treasurer . . . . Robert Hanson
Auditor . . . . Robert Peterson
Supt. of Public Instruction . . . Wayne Sanstead
Commr. of Agriculture . . . . Kent Jones
Commr. of Labor . . . . Orville Hagen
Commr. of Insurance . . . . Earl Pomeroy
Tax Commissioner . . . . Kent Conrad

SUPREME COURT

Ralph J. Erickstad, Chief Justice
H.F. Gierke
Beryl J. Levigne
Herbert L. Meschke
Gerald W. VandeWalle

LEGISLATIVE ASSEMBLY

President of the Senate . . Lt. Gov. Ruth Meiers
President Pro Tem
of the Senate . . . . Rolland W. Redlin
Secretary of the Senate . . . . Perry Grotberg

Speaker of the House . . . . Richard Kloubec
Chief Clerk of the House . . . . Roy Gilbreath

STATISTICS

Land Area (square miles) 69,273
Rank in Nation 17th
Population 679,000
Rank in Nation 46th
Density per square mile 9.9
Number of Representatives in Congress 1
Capital City . . . . Bismarck
Population 45,929
Rank in State 2nd
Largest City . . . . Fargo
Population 62,596
Number of Places over 10,000 Population 9

Ohio

Nickname . . . . The Buckeye State
Motto . . . . . . *With God, All Things Are Possible*
Flower . . . . Scarlet Carnation
Bird . . . . Cardinal
Tree . . . . Buckeye
Song . . . . *Beautiful Ohio*
Stone . . . . Ohio Flint
Insect . . . . Ladybug
Beverage . . . . Tomato Juice
Entered the Union . . . . March 1, 1803
Capital . . . . Columbus

ELECTED EXECUTIVE BRANCH OFFICIALS
Governor . . . . Richard F. Celeste
Lieutenant Governor . . . . Paul R. Leonard
Secretary of State . . . . Sherrod Brown
Attorney General . . . Anthony J. Celebrezze Jr.
Treasurer . . . . Mary Ellen Withrow
Auditor . . . . Thomas E. Ferguson

SUPREME COURT
Thomas Moyer, Chief Justice
Herbert Brown
Andrew Douglas
Robert E. Holmes
Ralph S. Locher
A. William Sweeney
Craig Wright

GENERAL ASSEMBLY
President of the Senate . . . . Paul E. Gillmor
President Pro Tem
  of the Senate . . . . Stanley Aronoff
Clerk of the Senate . . . . Martha Butler

Speaker of the House . . . . . . Vernal G. Riffe Jr.
Speaker Pro Tem
  of the House . . . . Barney Quilter
Legislative Clerk
  of the House . . . . William W. Pfeiffer
Executive Secretary
  of the House . . . . Aristotle Hutras

STATISTICS
Land Area (square miles) 40,975
  Rank in Nation 35th
Population 10,752,000
  Rank in Nation 7th
  Density per square mile 262.2
Number of Representatives in Congress . . . 21
Capital City . . . . Columbus
  Population 566,114
  Rank in State 2nd
Largest City . . . . Cleveland
  Population 573,822
Number of Places over 10,000 Population . . 150

Oklahoma

Nickname . . . . The Sooner State
Motto . . . . *Labor Omnia Vincit*
(Labor Conquers All Things)
Flower . . . . Mistletoe
Bird . . . . Scissor-tailed Flycatcher
Tree . . . . Redbud
Grass . . . . Indian Grass
Song . . . . *Oklahoma*
Waltz . . . . *Oklahoma Wind*
Poem . . . . "Howdy Folks"
Stone . . . . Barite Rose (Rose Rock)
Animal . . . . American Buffalo
Reptile . . . . Mountain Boomer Lizard
Fish . . . . White Bass
Colors . . . . Green and White
Entered the Union . . . . November 16, 1907
Capital . . . . Oklahoma City

ELECTED EXECUTIVE BRANCH OFFICIALS
Governor . . . . Henry Bellmon
Lieutenant Governor . . . . Robert S. Kerr III
Attorney General . . . . Robert Henry
Treasurer . . . . Ellis Edwards
Auditor and Inspector . . . . Clifton Scott
Supt. of Public Instruction . . . . . John M. Folks
Insurance Commr. . . . . Gerald Grimes

SUPREME COURT
John B. Doolin, Chief Justice
Rudolph Hargrave, Vice Chief Justice
Ralph B. Hodges   Robert D. Simms
Yvonne Kauger   Hardy Summers
Robrt E. Lavender   Alma Wilson
Marian P. Opala

COURT OF CRIMINAL APPEALS
Edgar Parks, Presiding Judge
Tom Brett   Hez J. Bussey

LEGISLATURE
President
  of the Senate . . . . Lt. Gov. Robert S. Kerr III
President Pro Tem
  of the Senate . . . . Rodger A. Randle
Secretary of the Senate . . . . Lee Slater

Speaker of the House . . . . Jim L. Barker
Speaker Pro Tem
  of the House . . . . Lonnie L. Abbott
Chief Clerk of the House/
  Administrator . . . . Larry Warden

STATISTICS
Land Area (square miles) 68,782
  Rank in Nation 18th
Population 3,305,000
  Rank in Nation 25th
  Density per square mile 48.0
Number of Representatives in Congress 6
Capital City . . . . Oklahoma City
  Population 443,172
  Rank in State 1st
Largest City . . . . Oklahoma City
Number of Places over 10,000 Population . . . 33

Oregon

Nickname	The Beaver State
Motto	*The Union*
Flower	Oregon Grape
Bird	Western Meadowlark
Tree	Douglas Fir
Song	*Oregon, My Oregon*
Dance	Square Dance
Poet Laureate	William E. Stafford
Stone	Thunderegg
Animal	Beaver
Fish	Chinook Salmon
Insect	Swallowtail Butterfly
Entered the Union	February 14, 1859
Capital	Salem

ELECTED EXECUTIVE BRANCH OFFICIALS

Governor	Neil Goldschmidt
Secretary of State	Barbara Roberts
Attorney General	Dave Frohnmayer
Treasurer	Bill Rutherford
Supt. of Public Instruction	Verne A. Duncan
Labor Commr.	Mary W. Roberts

SUPREME COURT

Edwin J. Peterson, Chief Justice
J.R. Campbell
Wallace P. Carson Jr.
W. Michael Gillette
Robert E. Jones
Berkeley Lent
Hans A. Linde

LEGISLATIVE ASSEMBLY

President of the Senate	John Kitzhaber
President Pro Tem of the Senate	William Frye
Secretary of the Senate	Maribel Cadmus
Speaker of the House	Vera Katz
Speaker Pro Tem of the House	Tom Mason
Chief Clerk of the House	Ramona Kenady

STATISTICS

Land Area (square miles)	96,184
Rank in Nation	10th
Population	2,698,000
Rank in Nation	30th
Density per square mile	27.9
Number of Representatives in Congress	5
Capital City	Salem
Population	89,233
Rank in State	3rd
Largest City	Portland
Population	365,861
Number of Places over 10,000 Population	29

Pennsylvania

Nickname	The Keystone State
Motto	*Virtue, Liberty and Independence*
Flower	Mountain Laurel
Game Bird	Ruffed Grouse
Tree	Hemlock
Dog	Great Dane
Animal	White-tailed Deer
Insect	Firefly
Fish	Brook Trout
Entered the Union	December 12, 1787
Capital	Harrisburg

ELECTED EXECUTIVE BRANCH OFFICIALS

Governor	Robert Casey
Lieutenant Governor	Mark Singel
Attorney General	Leroy S. Zimmerman
Treasurer	G. Davis Greene Jr.
Auditor General	Don Bailey

SUPREME COURT

Robert N.C. Nix Jr., Chief Justice
John P. Flaherty Jr.
William D. Hutchinson
Rolf Larsen
James T. McDermott
Nicholas P. Papadakos
Stephen A. Zappala

GENERAL ASSEMBLY

President of the Senate	Lt. Gov. Mark S. Singel
President Pro Tem of the Senate	Robert Jubelirer
Secretary of the Senate	Mark R. Corrigan
Speaker of the House	K. Leroy Irvis
Chief Clerk of the House	John J. Zubeck

STATISTICS

Land Area (square miles)	44,966
Rank in Nation	33rd
Population	11,889,000
Rank in Nation	4th
Density per square mile	264.7
Number of Representatives in Congress	23
Capital City	Harrisburg
Population	53,264
Rank in State	10th
Largest City	Philadelphia
Population	1,646,713
Number of Places over 10,000 Population	83

Rhode Island

Nicknames . . . . Little Rhody and
Ocean State
Motto . . . . *Hope*
Flower . . . . Violet
Bird . . . . Rhode Island Red
Tree . . . . Red Maple
Song . . . . *Rhode Island*
Rock . . . . Cumberlandite
Mineral . . . . Bowenite
Entered the Union . . . . May 29, 1790
Capital . . . . Providence

ELECTED EXECUTIVE BRANCH OFFICIALS

Governor . . . . Edward D. DiPrete
Lieutenant Governor . . . . Richard Licht
Secretary of State . . . . Kathleen Connell
Attorney General . . . . James E. O'Neil
General Treasurer . . . . Roger N. Begin

SUPREME COURT

Thomas F. Fay, Chief Justice
Thomas F. Kelleher
Florence K. Murray
Donald F. Shay
Joseph R. Weisberger

GENERAL ASSEMBLY

President
of the Senate . . . . Lt. Gov. Richard Licht
President Pro Tem
of the Senate . . . . William O'Neill
Secretary of the Senate . . . . . Kathleen Connell

Speaker of the House . . . . . . Matthew J. Smith
First Deputy Speaker
of the House . . . . Marion G. Donnelly
Reading Clerk
of the House . . . . Eugene J. McMahon

STATISTICS

Land Area (square miles) 1,049
Rank in Nation 50th
Population 975,000
Rank in Nation 42nd
Density per square mile 922.8
Number of Representatives in Congress 2
Capital City . . . . Providence
Population 154,000
Rank in State 1st
Largest City . . . . Providence
Number of Places over 10,000 Population . . . 27

South Carolina

Nickname . . . . The Palmetto State
Mottos . . . . *Animis Opibusque Parati*
(Prepared in Mind and Resources) and
Dum Spiro Spero (While I Breathe, I Hope)
Flower . . . . Carolina Jessamine
Bird . . . . Carolina Wren
Tree . . . . Palmetto
Song . . . . *South Carolina on My Mind*
Dance . . . . Shag
Stone . . . . Blue Granite
Dog . . . . Boykin Spaniel
Fruit . . . . Peach
Shell . . . . Lettered Olive
Beverage . . . . Milk
Entered the Union . . . . May 23, 1788
Capital . . . . Columbia

ELECTED EXECUTIVE BRANCH OFFICIALS

Governor . . . . Carroll A. Campbell Jr.
Lieutenant Governor . . . . Nick A. Theodore
Secretary of State . . . . John T. Campbell
Attorney General . . . . Travis Medlock
Treasurer . . . . Grady L. Patterson Jr.
Comptroller General . . . . . . Earle E. Morris Jr.
Supt. of Education . . . . Charlie G. Williams
Commr. of Agriculture . . . . D. Leslie Tindal
Adjutant General . . . . Eston Marchant

SUPREME COURT

Julius B. Ness, Chief Justice
A. Lee Chandler
Ernest A. Finney Jr.
George Tillman Gregory Jr.
David W. Harwell

GENERAL ASSEMBLY

President
of the Senate . . . . . Lt. Gov. Nick A. Theodore
President Pro Tem
of the Senate . . . . Rembert Dennis
Clerk of the Senate . . . . Frank B. Caggiano

Speaker of the House . . . . . . Robert J. Sheehan
Speaker Pro Tem
of the House . . . . John I. Rogers III
Clerk of the House . . . . Lois T. Shealy

STATISTICS

Land Area (square miles) 30,203
Rank in Nation 40th
Population 3,378,000
Rank in Nation 24th
Density per square mile 110.8
Number of Representatives in Congress 6
Capital City . . . . Columbia
Population 101,208
Rank in State 1st
Largest City . . . . Columbia
Number of Places over 10,000 Population . . . 28

South Dakota

Nickname................The Coyote State
The Sunshine State
Motto............*Under God the People Rule*
Flower....................Pasque Flower
Bird.................Ringnecked Pheasant
Tree....................Black Hills Spruce
Song...................*Hail, South Dakota*
Mineral.....................Rose Quartz
Gem.....................Fairburn Agate
Animal..........................Coyote
Fish..........................Walleye
Insect........................Honeybee
Grass............Western Wheat Grass
Entered the Union........November 2, 1889
Capital City.......................Pierre

ELECTED EXECUTIVE BRANCH OFFICIALS

Governor...............George S. Mickelson
Lieutenant Governor.......Walter D. Miller
Secretary of State...........Joyce Hazeltine
Attorney General.......Roger Tellinghuisen
Treasurer...................David L. Volk
Auditor.................Vernon L. Larson
Commr. of School
and Public Lands.......Timothy H. Amdahl

SUPREME COURT

George Wuest, Chief Justice
Frank E. Henderson
Robert A. Miller
Robert E. Morgan
Richard Sabers

LEGISLATURE

President of the
Senate..........Lt. Gov. Walter D. Miller
President Pro Tem
of the Senate............Mary A. McClure
Secretary of the Senate.........Fee Jacobsen

Speaker of the House......Debra R. Anderson
Speaker Pro Tem
of the House...................Royal J. Wood
Chief Clerk of the House.........Paul Inman

STATISTICS

Land Area (square miles)............75,955
Rank in Nation.....................16th
Population......................708,000
Rank in Nation.....................45th
Density per square mile.................9.3
Number of Representatives in Congress.....1
Capital City.......................Pierre
Population.......................11,973
Rank in State.......................9th
Largest City.................Sioux Falls
Population.......................81,343
Number of Places over 10,000 Population...10

Tennessee

Nickname..............The Volunteer State
Motto............*Agriculture and Commerce*
Flower.............................Iris
Bird.........................Mockingbird
Tree.....................Tulip Poplar
Wildflower................Passion Flower
Songs.......*When It's Iris Time in Tennessee;*
The Tennessee Waltz;
My Homeland, Tennessee;
My Tennessee; and *Rocky Top*
Stone.............................Agate
Animal.........................Raccoon
Insects.............Ladybug and Firefly
Gem................Tennessee Pearl
Rock.........................Limestone
Slogan........Tennessee—America at Its Best
Entered the Union.............June 1, 1796
Capital City....................Nashville

ELECTED EXECUTIVE BRANCH OFFICIALS

Governor...................Ned McWherter

SUPREME COURT

Ray L. Brock Jr., Chief Justice
Robert E. Cooper
Frank F. Drowota III
William H.D. Fones
William J. Harbison

GENERAL ASSEMBLY

Speaker
of the Senate......(Lt. Gov.) John S. Wilder
Speaker Pro Tem
of the Senate...............John N. Ford
Chief Clerk
of the Senate......Clyde W. McCullough Jr.

Speaker of the House............Ed Murray
Speaker Pro Tem
of the House..............Lois M. DeBerry
Chief Clerk of the House.....Bryant Millsaps

STATISTICS

Land Area (square miles).............41,155
Rank in Nation......................34th
Population....................4,803,000
Rank in Nation.....................16th
Density per square mile..............115.2
Number of Representatives in Congress.....9
Capital City....................Nashville
Population......................462,450
Rank in State.......................2nd
Largest City....................Memphis
Population......................648,399
Number of Places over 10,000 Population...37

Texas

Nickname . . . . The Lone Star State
Motto . . . . *Friendship*
Flower . . . . Bluebonnet
Bird . . . . Mockingbird
Tree . . . . Pecan
Song . . . . *Texas, Our Texas*
Stone . . . . Palmwood
Gem . . . . Topaz
Grass . . . . Sideoats Grama
Dish . . . . Chili
Entered the Union . . . . December 29, 1845
Capital . . . . Austin

ELECTED EXECUTIVE BRANCH OFFICIALS

Governor . . . . Bill Clements
Lieutenant Governor . . . . William P. Hobby
Attorney General . . . . Jim Mattox
Treasurer . . . . Ann W. Richards
Comptroller of Public Accounts . . . Bob Bullock
Commr. of Agriculture . . . . Jim Hightower
Commr. of General Land Office . . Garry Mauro

SUPREME COURT

John L. Hill Jr., Chief Justice

Robert M. Campbell	C.L. Ray
Raul A. Gonzalez	Ted Z. Robertson
Bill Kilgarlin	Franklin S. Spears
Oscar H. Mauzy	James P. Wallace

COURT OF CRIMINAL APPEALS

John F. Onion Jr., Presiding Judge

Charles F. Campbell Jr.	Michael J.
Sam Houston Clinton	McCormick
Thomas G. Davis	Charles Miller
Wilbur C. Davis	Marvin O. Teague
	Bill White

LEGISLATURE

President
  of the Senate . . . . . Lt. Gov. William P. Hobby
President Pro Tem
  of the Senate . . . . Carl Parker
Secretary of the Senate . . . . Betty King

Speaker of the House . . . . Gibson D. Lewis
Speaker Pro Tem
  of the House . . . . Hugo Berlanga
Chief Clerk of the House . . . . Betty Murray

STATISTICS

Land Area (square miles) 262,134
  Rank in Nation 2nd
Population 16,682,000
  Rank in Nation 3rd
  Density per square mile 62.5
Number of Representatives in Congress 27
Capital City . . . . Austin
  Population 397,001
  Rank in State 6th
Largest City . . . . Houston
  Population 1,705,697
Number of Places over 10,000 Population . . 151

Utah

Nickname . . . . The Beehive State
Motto . . . . *Industry*
Flower . . . . Sego Lily
Bird . . . . Seagull
Tree . . . . Blue Spruce
Song . . . . *Utah, We Love Thee*
Gem . . . . Topaz
Entered the Union . . . . January 4, 1896
Capital . . . . Salt Lake City

ELECTED EXECUTIVE BRANCH OFFICIALS

Governor . . . . Norman Bangerter
Lieutenant Governor . . . . W. Val Oveson
Attorney General . . . . David L. Wilkinson
Treasurer . . . . Edward T. Alter
Auditor . . . . Tom L. Allen

SUPREME COURT

Gordon R. Hall, Chief Justice
Christine M. Durham
Richard C. Howe
I. Daniel Stewart
Michael D. Zimmerman

LEGISLATURE

President of the Senate . . . . Arnold Christensen
Secretary of the Senate . . Sophia C. Buckmiller

Speaker of the House . . . . Glen E. Brown
Chief Clerk of the House . . . Carole E. Peterson

STATISTICS

Land Area (square miles) 82,073
  Rank in Nation 11th
Population 1,665,000
  Rank in Nation 35th
  Density per square mile 20.0
Number of Representatives in Congress 3
Capital City . . . . Salt Lake City
  Population 164,844
  Rank in State 1st
Largest City . . . . Salt Lake City
Number of Places over 10,000 Population . . . 22

Vermont

Nickname.........The Green Mountain State
Motto....................*Freedom and Unity*
Flower.......................Red Clover
Bird........................Hermit Thrush
Tree.......................Sugar Maple
Song......................*Hail, Vermont!*
Poet Laureate...............Robert Frost
Animal....................Morgan Horse
Insect........................Honeybee
Fish....................Brook Trout and
Walleye Pike
Soil................Tunbridge Soil Series
Beverage...........................Milk
Entered the Union...........March 4, 1791
Capital......................Montpelier

ELECTED EXECUTIVE BRANCH OFFICIALS

Governor...............Madeleine M. Kunin
Lieutenant Governor...........Howard Dean
Secretary of State.........James H. Douglas
Attorney General.........Jeffrey L. Amestoy
Treasurer................Emory A. Hebard
Auditor of Accounts......Alexander V. Acebo

SUPREME COURT

Frederic W. Allen, Chief Justice
Ernest W. Gibson III
Thomas L. Hayes
William C. Hill
Louis P. Peck

GENERAL ASSEMBLY

President of the Senate . Lt. Gov. Howard Dean
President Pro Tem
of the Senate..............Peter F. Welch
Secretary of the Senate.....Robert H. Gibson

Speaker of the House..........Ralph Wright
Clerk of the House..........Robert L. Picher

STATISTICS

Land Area (square miles)..............9,267
Rank in Nation.....................43rd
Population.......................541,000
Rank in Nation.....................49th
Density per square mile...............57.7
Number of Representatives in Congress.....1
Capital City...................Montpelier
Population.........................8,241
Rank in State.......................5th
Largest City...................Burlington
Population.......................37,712
Number of Places over 10,000 Population....3

Virginia

Nickname...............The Old Dominion
Motto.................*Sic Semper Tyrannis*
(Thus Always to Tyrants)
Flower...........................Dogwood
Bird..............................Cardinal
Tree.............................Dogwood
Song.........*Carry Me Back to Old Virginia*
Animal.........................Foxhound
Shell.............................Oyster
Beverage...........................Milk
Entered the Union............June 25, 1788
Capital.......................Richmond

ELECTED EXECUTIVE BRANCH OFFICIALS

Governor................Gerald Lee Baliles
Lieutenant Governor.......L. Douglas Wilder
Attorney General............Mary Sue Terry

SUPREME COURT

Harry Lee Carrico, Chief Justice
George M. Cochran
A. Christian Compton
Richard H. Poff
Charles S. Russell
Roscoe B. Stephenson Jr.
John Charles Thomas

GENERAL ASSEMBLY

President
of the Senate.... Lt. Gov. L. Douglas Wilder
President Pro Tem
of the Senate.....William F. Parkerson Jr.
Clerk of the Senate........Jay T. Shropshire

Speaker of the House...........A.L. Philpott
Clerk of the House....Joseph H. Holleman Jr.

STATISTICS

Land Area (square miles).............39,780
Rank in Nation.....................36th
Population.....................5,787,000
Rank in Nation.....................13th
Density per square mile.............143.4
Number of Representatives in Congress...10
Capital City...................Richmond
Population.....................219,056
Rank in State.......................3rd
Largest City.......................Norfolk
Population.....................279,683
Number of Places over 10,000 Population...33

Washington

Nickname . . . . The Evergreen State
Motto . . . . *Alki* (By and By)
Flower . . . . Western Rhododendron
Bird . . . . Willow Goldfinch
Tree . . . . Western Hemlock
Song . . . . *Washington, My Home*
Dance . . . . Square Dance
Gem . . . . Petrified Wood
Fish . . . . Steelhead Trout
Entered the Union . . . . November 11, 1889
Capital . . . . Olympia

ELECTED EXECUTIVE BRANCH OFFICIALS

Governor . . . . Booth Gardner
Lieutenant Governor . . . . John A. Cherberg
Secretary of State . . . . Ralph Munro
Attorney General . . . . . Kenneth O. Eikenberry
Treasurer . . . . Robert S. O'Brien
Auditor . . . . Robert V. Graham
Supt. of Public Instruction . . . . Frank Brouillet
Insurance Commr. . . . . . Richard G. Marquardt
Commr. of Public Lands . . . . Brian J. Boyle

SUPREME COURT

James M. Dolliver, Chief Justice

James A. Andersen	Barbara Durham
Robert F. Brachtenbach	William C. Goodloe
Keith Callow	Vernon R. Pearson
Fred H. Dore	Robert F. Utter

LEGISLATURE

President
of the Senate . . . . . Lt. Gov. John A. Cherberg
President Pro Tem
of the Senate . . . . A. L. Rasmussen
Secretary of the Senate . . . . Sid R. Snyder

Speaker of the House . . . . Joseph E. King
Speaker Pro Tem
of the House . . . . John L. O'Brien
Chief Clerk of the House . . . . . Alan Thompson

STATISTICS

Land Area (square miles) 66,570
Rank in Nation 20th
Population 4,463,000
Rank in Nation 20th
Density per square mile 66.2
Number of Representatives in Congress 8
Capital City . . . . Olympia
Population 27,447
Rank in State 15th
Largest City . . . . Seattle
Population 488,474
Number of Places over 10,000 Population . . . 36

West Virginia

Nickname . . . . The Mountain State
Motto . . . . *Montani Semper Liberi*
(Mountaineers Are Always Free)
Flower . . . . Big Rhododendron
Bird . . . . Cardinal
Tree . . . . Sugar Maple
Songs . . . *West Virginia, My Home Sweet Home;*
The West Virginia Hills; and
This Is My West Virginia
Animal . . . . Black Bear
Fish . . . . Brook Trout
Entered the Union . . . . June 20, 1863
Capital . . . . Charleston

ELECTED EXECUTIVE BRANCH OFFICIALS

Governor . . . . Arch A. Moore Jr.
Secretary of State . . . . Ken Hechler
Attorney General . . . . Charlie Brown
Treasurer . . . . A. James Manchin
Auditor . . . . Glen B. Gainer Jr.
Commr. of Agriculture . . . . Gus R. Douglass

SUPREME COURT OF APPEALS

Darrell V. McGraw Jr., Chief Justice
W.T. Brotherton Jr.
Thomas E. McHugh
Thomas B. Miller
Richard Neely

LEGISLATURE

President of the Senate . . . . . Dan R. Tonkovich
President Pro Tem
of the Senate . . . . Tony Whitlow
Clerk of the Senate . . . . Todd C. Willis

Speaker of the House . . . . Robert Chambers
Clerk of the House . . . . Donald L. Kopp

STATISTICS

Land Area (square miles) 24,070
Rank in Nation 41st
Population 1,919,000
Rank in Nation 34th
Density per square mile 80.4
Number of Representatives in Congress 4
Capital City . . . . Charleston
Population 63,968
Rank in State 1st
Largest City . . . . Charleston
Number of Places over 10,000 Population . . . 15

Wisconsin

Nickname .... The Badger State
Motto .... *Forward*
Flower .... Wood Violet
Bird .... Robin
Tree .... Sugar Maple
Song .... *On, Wisconsin!*
Rock .... Red Granite
Mineral .... Galena
Animal .... Badger
Wildlife Animal .... White-tailed Deer
Domestic Animal .... Dairy Cow
Fish .... Muskellunge
Symbol of Peace .... Mourning Dove
Insect .... Honeybee
Soil .... Antigo Silt Loam
Entered the Union .... May 29, 1848
Capital .... Madison

ELECTED EXECUTIVE BRANCH OFFICIALS

Governor .... Tommy G. Thompson
Lieutenant Governor .... Scott McCallum
Secretary of State .... Douglas La Follette
Attorney General .... Donald J. Hanaway
Treasurer .... Charles P. Smith
Supt. of Public Instruction ... Herbert J. Grover

SUPREME COURT

Nathan S. Heffernan, Chief Justice
Shirley S. Abrahamson
William A. Bablitch
William G. Callow
Louis J. Ceci
Roland B. Day
Donald W. Steinmetz

LEGISLATURE

President of the Senate .... Fred A. Risser
Chief Clerk
   of the Senate .... Donald J. Schneider

Speaker of the Assembly .... Thomas A. Loftus
Assembly Speaker
   Pro Tempore .... David E. Clarenbach
Chief Clerk of the Assembly ... Thomas Melvin

STATISTICS

Land Area (square miles) 54,464
   Rank in Nation 26th
Population 4,785,000
   Rank in Nation 17th
   Density per square mile 87.7
Number of Representatives in Congress 9
Capital City .... Madison
   Population 170,745
   Rank in State 2nd
Largest City .... Milwaukee
   Population 620,811
Number of Places over 10,000 Population ... 55

Wyoming

Nicknames .... The Equality State and
                        The Cowboy State
Motto .... *Equal Rights*
Flower .... Indian Paintbrush
Bird .... Meadowlark
Animal .... Bison
Tree .... Cottonwood
Song .... *Wyoming*
Stone .... Jade
Entered the Union .... July 10, 1890
Capital .... Cheyenne

ELECTED EXECUTIVE BRANCH OFFICIALS

Governor .... Mike Sullivan
Secretary of State .... Kathy Karpan
Treasurer .... Stan Smith
Auditor .... Jack Sidi
Supt. of Public Instruction ...... Lynn Simons

SUPREME COURT

C. Stuart Brown, Chief Justice
G. Joseph Cardine
Richard J. Macy
Richard V. Thomas
Walter C. Urbigkit Jr.

LEGISLATURE

President of the Senate .... John F. Turner
Vice President of the Senate .. Diemer D. True
Chief Clerk of the Senate .... Ed Wren Jr.

Speaker of the House .... Patrick Meenan
Speaker Pro Tem
   of the House .... Bill McIlvain
Chief Clerk of the House .. Herbert D. Pownall

STATISTICS

Land Area (square miles) 97,023
   Rank in Nation 9th
Population 507,000
   Rank in Nation 50th
   Density per square mile 5.2
Number of Representatives in Congress 1
Capital City .... Cheyenne
   Population 47,283
   Rank in State 2nd
Largest City .... Casper
   Population 51,016
Number of Places over 10,000 Population 8

District of Columbia

Motto.......*Justitia Omnibus* (Justice for All)
Flower...............American Beauty Rose
Bird........................Wood Thrush
Tree..........................Scarlet Oak
Became U.S. Capital.......December 1, 1800

ELECTED EXECUTIVE BRANCH OFFICIALS
Mayor..................Marion S. Barry Jr.

U.S. COURT OF APPEALS FOR THE DISTRICT OF COLUMBIA
Chief Judge...............Patricia M. Wald

DISTRICT OF COLUMBIA COURT OF APPEALS
Chief Judge...............William C. Pryor

U. S. DISTRICT COURT FOR THE DISTRICT OF COLUMBIA
Chief Judge.........Aubrey E. Robinson Jr.
U.S. Attorney...............Jay B. Stephens

THE SUPERIOR COURT OF THE DISTRICT OF COLUMBIA
Chief Judge.................Fred B. Ugast

COUNCIL OF THE DISTRICT OF COLUMBIA
Chairman..................David A. Clarke
Chairman Pro Tem........Nadine P. Winter

STATISTICS
Land Area (square miles)................67
Population.....................626,000
  Density per square mile.............9343.3
Delegate to Congress*.....................1

---

*Committee voting privileges only.

American Samoa

Motto...............*Samoa-Muamua le Atua*
                      (Samoa, God Is First)
Flower.....................Paogo (Ula-fala)
Plant..................................Ava
Song.....................*Amerika Samoa*
Became a Territory of the United States..1900
Capital........................Pago Pago

ELECTED EXECUTIVE BRANCH OFFICIALS
Governor.......................A.P. Lutali
Lieutenant
  Governor........Faleomavaega Eni Hunkin

HIGH COURT
Robert Gardner, Chief Justice
Charles V. Ala'ilima, District Court Judge
F. Michael Kruse, Pro-Tem District Court Judge
Thomas W. Murphy, Associate Justice

LEGISLATURE
President of the Senate..........Letuli Toloa
Vice-President
  of the Senate...........Utu Sinagege R.M.
Secretary of the Senate........Salilo K. Levi

Speaker of the House......Tuana'itau F. Tuia
Vice Speaker
  of the House...................(Vacancy)
Clerk of the House...............Wally Utu

STATISTICS
Land Area (square miles).................77
Population.........................34,500
  Density per square mile.............448.0
Capital City....................Pago Pago
  Population.......................3,075
Largest City....................Pago Pago
Number of Villages.....................76

Guam

Nickname . . . . Hub of the Pacific
Flower . . . . *Puti Tai Nobio* (Bougainvillea)
Bird . . . . *Toto* (Fruit Dove)
Tree . . . . *Ifit* (Intsiabijuga)
Song . . . . *Stand Ye Guamanians*
Stone . . . . Latte
Animal . . . . Iguana
Ceded to the United States
   by Spain . . . . December 10, 1898
Became a Territory . . . . August 1, 1950
Request to become a
   Commonwealth Plebiscite . . . November 1987
Capital . . . . Agana

ELECTED EXECUTIVE BRANCH OFFICIALS

Governor . . . . Joseph Ada
Lieutenant Governor . . . . Frank F. Blas

SUPERIOR COURT

Paul J. Abbate, Presiding Judge
Benjamin J.F. Cruz
Ramon V. Diaz
Joaquin V.E. Manibusan
Peter C. Siguenza Jr.
Janet Healy Weeks

LEGISLATURE

Speaker . . . . Franklin J. A. Quitugua
Vice Speaker . . . . Franklin J. Gutierrez
Legislative Secretary . . . . Pilar C. Lujan

STATISTICS

Land Area (square miles) 209
Population 102,977
   Density per square mile 572.0
Delegate to Congress* 1
Capital City . . . . Agana
   Population 896
Largest City . . . . Tamuning
   Population 13,580

*Committee voting privileges only.

Northern Mariana Islands

Tree . . . . Flame Tree
Flower . . . . Plumeria
Administered by the United States as a trusteeship
   for the United Nations . . . . July 18, 1947
Voters approved a
   proposed constitution . . . . June 1975
U.S. President signed covenant agreeing to
   Commonwealth status for the
   islands . . . . March 24, 1976
Became a self-governing Commonwealth
   . . . . January 9, 1978
Capital . . . . Saipan

ELECTED EXECUTIVE BRANCH OFFICIALS

Governor . . . . Pedro P. Tenorio
Lieutenant Governor . . . . Pedro A. Tenorio

COMMONWEALTH TRIAL COURT

Robert A. Hefner, Chief Judge
Herbert D. Soll

LEGISLATURE

President
   of the Senate . . . . Benjamin T. Manglona
Vice President
   of the Senate . . . . Jose P. Mafnas

Speaker
   of the House . . . . . Pedro R. DeLeon Guerrero
Vice Speaker
   of the House . . . . Benigno M. Sablan

STATISTICS

Land Area (square miles) 183.5
Population 20,000
   Density per square mile 91.1
Capital City . . . . Saipan
   Population 16,532
Largest City . . . . Saipan

Federated States of Micronesia

Administered by the United States as a trusteeship
for the United Nations . . . . July 18, 1947
Voters approved a
proposed constitution . . . . July 12, 1978
Effective date of constitution . . . . May 10, 1979
Capital . . . . Kolonia, Pohnpei

EXECUTIVE BRANCH
President . . . . John Haglelman
Speaker . . . . Jack Fritz

STATISTICS
Land Area (square miles) 271
   Kosrae District 42
   Pohnpei District 134
   Truk District 49
   Yap District 46
Population 73,160
   Kosrae District 6,000
   Pohnpei District 26,000
   Truk District 43,000
   Yap District 10,200
Capital City . . . . Kolonia, Pohnpei
   Population 5,549
Largest City . . . . Moen, Truk
   Population 10,351

Marshall Islands

Administered by the United States as a trusteeship
for the United Nations . . . . July 18, 1947
Voters approved a
proposed constitution . . . . March 1, 1979
Effective date of constitution . . . . . May 1, 1979
Capital . . . . Majuro

EXECUTIVE BRANCH
President . . . . Amata Kabua

STATISTICS
Land Area (square miles) 70
Population 35,000
   Density per square mile 443.5
Capital City . . . . Majuro
   Population 12,000
Largest City . . . . Majuro

Republic of Belau

Administered by the United States as a trusteeship
for the United Nations . . . . July 18, 1947
Voters approved a
proposed constitution . . . . July 9, 1980
Effective date of constitution . . January 1, 1981

EXECUTIVE BRANCH
President . . . . Lazarus Salil
Speaker . . . . Santos Oliking
Senate President . . . . Joshua Koshiba

STATISTICS
Land Area (square miles) 192
Population 12,177
   Density per square mile 63.4
Capital City . . . . Koror
   Population 6,222
Largest City . . . . Koror

Puerto Rico

Nickname . . . . Island of Enchantment
Motto . . . . *Joannes Est Nomen Ejus*
(John Is Thy Name)
Flower . . . . Maga
Bird . . . . Reinita
Tree . . . . Ceiba
Song . . . . *La Borinquena*
Animal . . . . Coqui
Became a territory of the United States
. . . . December 10, 1898
Became a self-governing Commonwealth
. . . . July 25, 1952
Capital . . . . San Juan

ELECTED EXECUTIVE BRANCH OFFICIALS

Governor . . . . Rafael Hernandez-Colon
Secretary of State . . . . Hector Luis Acevedo
Secretary of Justice . . . . Hector Rivera-Cruz

SUPREME COURT

Victor M. Pons Nunez, Chief Justice
Rafael Alonso
Federico Hernandez Denton
Antonio S. Negron Garcia
Peter Ortiz Gustafson
Francisco Rebollo Lopez
Miriam Naveira de Rodon

LEGISLATIVE ASSEMBLY

President
of the Senate . . . Miguel A. Hernandez Agosto
Vice President
of the Senate . . . . Sergio Pena Clos
Secretary
of the Senate . . . . Ramon Garcia Santiago

Speaker of the House . . . . Jose R. Jarabo
Vice President
of the House . . . . Samuel Ramirez
Secretary
of the House . . . . Elda Duran de Alvarez

STATISTICS

Land Area (square miles) 3,421
Population 3,279,231
Density per square mile 955
Delegate to Congress* 1
Capital City . . . . San Juan
Population 434,849
Largest City . . . . San Juan
Number of Places over 10,000 Population . . . 31

*Committee voting privileges only.

Virgin Islands

Nicknames . . . . St. John, St. Croix, and
St. Thomas
Flower . . . . Yellow Elder or Ginger Thomas
Bird . . . . Yellow Breast or Banana Quit
Song . . . . *Virgin Islands March*
Purchased from Denmark . . . . . March 31, 1917
Capital . . . . Charlotte Amalie, St. Thomas

ELECTED EXECUTIVE BRANCH OFFICIALS

Governor . . . . Alexander Farreley
Lieutenant Governor . . . . Derek M. Hodge

FEDERAL DISTRICT COURT

Almeric L. Christian, Chief Judge
David V. O'Brien

LEGISLATURE

President . . . . Ruby M. Rouss
Vice President . . . . Bingley G. Richardson
Legislative
Secretary . . . . Alicia Hansen

STATISTICS

Land Area (square miles) 132
St. Croix (square miles) 80
St. John (square miles) 20
St. Thomas (square miles) 32
Population 107,500
St. Croix 49,725
St. John 2,472
St. Thomas 44,372
Density per square mile 724.2
Delegate to Congress* 1
Capital City . . . . Charlotte Amalie, St. Thomas
Population 11,842

*Committee voting privileges only.

SUBJECT INDEX

(Page numbers in **boldface** indicate tables; a complete list of tables is on pages vi)

I

J

L

V

W

Z